WHO'S
WHO
IN
PROFESSIONAL
BASEBALL

WHO'S WHO
IN
PROFESSIONAL BASEBALL

Gene Karst
Martin J. Jones, Jr.

ARLINGTON HOUSE   New Rochelle, New York

Library of Congress Catalog Card Number 73-11870

MANUFACTURED IN THE UNITED STATES OF AMERICA

Library of Congress Cataloging in Publication Data

Karst, Gene, 1906–
   Who's who in professional baseball.

   1. Baseball--Biography. I. Jones, Martin J.,
1943–   joint author. II. Title.
GV865.A1K37   796.357'64'0922 [B]   73-11870
ISBN 0-87000-220-1

EDITOR'S NOTE

As every sports buff knows, the records of athletes and coaches are sometimes in dispute. Add to this the possibility of human error and you can see why the authors are asking every reader of this work to pass on any corrections he might discover.

Beyond that, can you think of any significant omissions? These will normally fall into the gray "matter of opinion" area. But if sentiment does build for including a particular athlete or official in a revised edition, the authors will want to.

If you have any suggestions or corrections, please write to the authors in care of Arlington House, New Rochelle, N. Y. 10801. Since this volume is likely to become one of the established sources, you will be making a significant contribution to sports research. Everyone who helps will be given a credit line in the revised, enlarged, updated edition we hope to bring out in the later 1970s.

FOREWORD

When I first knew Gene Karst he had formed no alliance, holy or otherwise, with Martin Jones to write this or any other book. He was doing public relations for the St. Louis Cardinals, a job that was uncommon in baseball then, if not unique. There were gregarious individuals who enjoyed wide popularity among the press, like Eddie Brannick, the traveling secretary of the New York Giants, and Bob Lewis, who held the same position with the Chicago Cubs, but not many clubs paid a man to make friends for the team.

In this respect the Cardinals were triply blessed. Although their owner, Sam Breadon, was known to hold a dollar in high esteem, he was also an enthusiastic host who loved Scotch whiskey and barbershop harmony. Clarence Lloyd, the road secretary, was a blithe spirit with friends everywhere. Those two kept the newspapermen entertained after dark and Gene kept them informed by day.

A search for bread took me away from St. Louis and years passed before I encountered Gene again, on a train between New York and Baltimore. He was the traveling secretary of the Montreal Royals in the International League. Naturally, I wondered how he had managed to work his way down from the world champion Cardinals to the Brooklyn Dodgers' farm system. He filled me in, and filled me with envy.

Some years earlier, he said, he had padded out his savings by selling his car and had set off around the world. He drifted as impulse dictated, pausing where he chose as long as he chose, traveling by tramp steamer or camelback or whatever.

7

After visiting most of the great cities of the globe, he selected San Francisco as the place where he preferred to live. He took a sublease on an apartment at the top of Telegraph Hill and landed a job with an advertising concern.

It is hard to imagine a pleasanter existence but for some the attraction of baseball is strong. He got in touch with Larry MacPhail or Branch Rickey—I forget which one was running the Dodgers at the time, but Gene had worked under both—and was assigned to the top farm club.

We have not met since that chance encounter on the train but in the meantime Gene has continued to go to and fro in the world and walk up and down in it, has begot children who begot children and has returned at last to his starting place—Missouri.

As this book shows, he has also returned to baseball. (It will be up to the reader, of course, to decide whether it is a case of the lover returning to his first love or the miscreant to the scene of his crime.) At any rate, although there have been many books with titles like *Who's Who in Baseball* or *The Baseball Encyclopedia* or *Baseball Register* or *Official Baseball Guide,* none but this will identify the infielder who blew a squeeze bunt foul, or tell about the electric clock in Clarence Lloyd's office, or report on Charley Barrett's speech to the Holy Name Dinner.

If tales like these were preserved and published as faithfully as the batting averages, perhaps baseball today wouldn't be worrying about professional football's inroads into its popularity.

RED SMITH

May 1973

PREFACE

How many men have played major league baseball? The number is well over 10,000. Add to these the thousands of club owners, league officials, umpires, employees and you have an idea of the potential scope of this book.

We can't include everyone; nor do we want to. Instead we have sketched superstars like Babe Ruth, Cy Young, Joe DiMaggio, Hank Aaron and Willie Mays; also the stars and journeymen players; we have included those who were great for a day, or a brief period, like Al Gionfriddo, Shucks Pruett, Eddie Gaedel. We also include men like Tom Greenwade, Doc Hyland, Charles Ebbets, George Magerkurth, whose names may mean nothing to younger fans. Yet they too, in a wide variety of ways, have helped make baseball our national game.

Record-breaking statistics about home runs, strikeouts, longevity, yes. But figures by themselves soon pall. We have tried to be selective in the mix of our sketches; to include only the most important or the unique records plus some unusual, colorful personality facets of the great and the not so great.

In some cases we have obtained our information directly from the person sketched, by interview, by firsthand observation or through question-naire. We have used our own notes and published articles, some of them dating back to the 1920s. We have dug into thousands of sources in our efforts to check the accuracy of birth dates, place names, death dates and statistics. We have gone to microfilm, magazine and newspaper files in old and new libraries.

In some cases it has been humanly impossible to know the truth. Baseball players (and some others) have been known to falsify their ages. In some past instances major league club officials have deliberately altered the ages of the men on their rosters. One in particular in the 1930s simply cut one year off the correct ages of *ALL* his players, in an effort to make fans believe he was fielding a younger team.

But an eagle-eyed editor has demanded that we check, double-check and triple-check almost everything in this book. We are not aware of any avoidable errors. However, we take full responsibility for any which may have crept in.

We are specially indebted to C. C. Johnson Spink, who publishes *The Sporting News*, *The Baseball Register*, the Official Baseball Guides, Daguerrotypes and numerous other books and booklets on baseball. Johnson and his dedicated staffers have given us frequent opportunity of cross-checking literally thousands of details that have contributed to the greater accuracy of this book.

We also are indebted to his father, the late J. G. Taylor Spink, who preceded Johnson as publisher of *The Sporting News*. Taylor, years ago, stimulated one of the authors to interview dozens of ball players for articles that later appeared in *The Sporting News*; he also generously allowed repeated consultation of his archives in the preparation of pamphlets and publications long before the present volume was dreamed of. So he too contributed to the accuracy of this book.

We also thank Dave Grote, publicity director of the National League, and both John Sheehan, past chief, and Thomas S. Monahan, current chief of publicity for the American League; and each of the publicity directors of the 24 major league teams. They have supplied us with Media Guides, Year Books and have promptly answered our queries.

Thanks also for the prompt assistance from Joe Reichler of the commissioner's office and from Clifford Kachline, historian for the Hall of Fame; and from numerous people who volunteered information.

We have confined ourselves in these sketches to men directly connected with major league baseball and those selected for the Hall of Fame. This has excluded a host of other colorful characters—the sports writers; radio and television sportscasters, unless they played in the majors; old-time Negro players who never appeared in major league box scores; and all the colorful personages who spent their lives in the minor leagues.

GENE KARST

MARTIN J. JONES, JR.

May 1973

10

AARON, HENRY LOUIS (Hank)   OF-1B-BR-TR. B. 2/5/34, Mobile,
Ala. 6', 180. Hank started 1973 season needing 41 homers to equal Babe
Ruth's record of 714 home runs (in 2503 major league games). Though
not modern Babe Ruth, Aaron still has had brilliant career, and certain
of Hall of Fame. Began 1973 with 10,896 times at bat, 1976 runs, 3391
hits, 572 doubles, 95 triples, 673 homers, 2037 RBI. Stole 238 bases.
Before long, only Ty Cobb with more at bats. Hank passed Stan Musial
in runs scored in 1972; only Cobb, Ruth, Mays still ahead of him. Five
men still ahead of him in total hits when 1973 started. Only Babe himself
has more RBI. Hit 700th homer 7/21/73.

Hank played sandlot ball while in his teens in Mobile, then got job
with team called "Black Bears." Offer of $200 monthly salary caused
him to sign with Indianapolis Clowns of Negro American League.
Shortstop at that time. In his first appearance, Clowns played doubleheader. Started five DPs that day; went 10 for 11 at bat. Boston Braves
scout Dewey Griggs was interested to tune of $350 per month. Braves
ended up paying management of Clowns $10,000, 6/12/52. Farmed
Hank to Eau Claire in Northern League. In 87 games, .336 average.
Jacksonville, South Atlantic League, 1953. Played second base, led
league in hitting with .362. Following season with Braves (who had
moved to Milwaukee). Outfielder. Hit .280 with 13 homers, 69 RBI in
122 games. Broke his right ankle 9/5/54. In 1955, hit .314, 27 homers,
with 106 RBI; 1956, won batting title with .328, led NL in hits and
doubles, got 26 homers. MVP 1957—.322, led NL in runs with 118,
homers with 44, RBI with 132. Another batting championship, 1959—
has more RBI. Hit 700 homer, 7/21/73; ended '73 with 713 HR.

11

.355, 123 RBI, 39 home runs. Ensuing years: eight more seasons above .300, three more years as RBI leader, two more home run crowns plus tie. Through 1972, seven seasons with 40 or more homers; 47 his peak, 1971. NL record for most consecutive seasons with 20 or more homers, 18. Most seasons with 300 or more total bases, 15. Averaged 150 games over 19-year stretch, despite broken ankle, bad knees, sore neck, other ailments.

Member of NL All-Star squads 18 consecutive times, 1955 to 1972, more than any other player. His first homer in All-Star competition, 1971, off Vida Blue. Another in 1972, before home folks in Atlanta, off Gaylord Perry (off whom he hit career home run number 600, 4/27/72).

In two World Series with Milwaukee, 1957, 58. Played 14 games, hit .364 with 20 hits in 55 times at bat, 2 doubles, 1 triple, 3 homers, 9 RBI; scored 8 runs.

Member of President's Council on Physical Fitness, Active in community and charitable enterprises. Representative from sports on list of ten best dressed men in America, 1971. Reportedly draws $200,000 salary, three-year contract signed before start of 1972 season.

ABERNATHY, TED WADE P-BR-TR. B. 3/6/33, Stanley, N.C. 6′4″, 210. Ted Abernathy belongs to the scarce breed of underhand pitchers; injury to arm while in high school forced him to convert from overhand pitching to sidearm. Another arm injury while with Washington Senators, 1957, caused him to go underhand completely. Also is specialist— relief man. Has been baseball gypsy. Kansas City Royals, for whom he toiled in 1972, was his sixteenth club in pro baseball.

Abernathy, at start of 1973, had record of just seven complete games among 681 appearances on mound in majors. Started 34 times, won 62 decisions, lost 69, and had an ERA of 3.47. In 1143 innings he had walked 591 men, struck out 765.

Abbie won the *Sporting News* Fireman of Year award in 1965 while with Chicago Cubs, and again in 1967 working for Cincinnati Reds. During 1965 set two NL records: one was most games pitched; other was most times appearing as relief pitcher, both of them 84. These marks, however, have since been broken. But he still shares NL record for games finished, 62, with Jim Konstanty of Phillies and Phil Regan of Cubs. Abbie did it in 1965.

Ted led NL in saves, 1965, with 31; again led loop in 1967 with 28. In 1971 had 23. His best ERA in majors was 1.27 with Reds, 1967.

List of his minor league clubs is long one, starting with Roanoke Rapids, N. C., 1952. Also pitched for Chattanooga, Louisville, Miami, Charlotte, Austin, Vancouver, Salt Lake City, and Jacksonville. In majors with Washington, 1955–57 and 1960; Cleveland, 1963–64; Chicago NL 1965–66 and 1969–70; Atlanta NL, 1966; Cincinnati, 1967–68;

St. Louis NL, 1970; Kansas City AL, 1971–72. Royals cut him loose Feb. 1973.

Ted is industrial representative for an oil company during off-season.

ADAIR, KENNETH JERRY (Jerry) Inf.-BR-TR. B. 12/17/36, Tulsa, Okla. 6'½", 183. Coach, Oakland AL, 1972–73. Spent most of major league career with Orioles after getting $40,000 bonus to sign, 1958. After attending Oklahoma State, Adair played 11 games with O's that season. Farmed to Amarillo, Texas League, 1959. Hit .309 in 146 games. Back to Orioles same season, for 12 contests. Spent most of 1960 with Miami, International League, hitting .266. Back with Orioles briefly same year, after which became regular with team. During 1966 season traded to Chicago AL. Following year traded to Boston AL in time for 1967 World Series. Big league career ended after 1968 season with Boston.

Jerry hit .256 in 1032 major league games and .125 in five Series games with Red Sox. Brilliant fielder. In 1964 set major league record for highest fielding average (.994) and fewest errors (5) by second baseman. Set major league record for consecutive errorless games by second baseman, 89; consecutive chances handled without an error, 485, from 7/22/64 through 5/6/65.

ADAMS, CHARLES BENJAMIN (Babe) P-BL-TR. B. 5/18/83, Tipton, Ind. D. 7/27/68, Silver Spring, Md. 5'11½", 180. Baseball records vary greatly as to when Charles Adams born. Some show he was born in 1882, others not till 1888. We can't say positively he was born in 1883, but much documentation for this date. Nevertheless, he probably got his moniker because he started pitching a blazing fast ball while still in his teens. After 12–3 record in his first full major league season, he captured three World Series victories for Pittsburgh Pirates in 1909. Babe's victims were Detroit Tigers, who had two fearsome sluggers—Ty Cobb and Wahoo Sam Crawford. Pirates took WS 4 games to 3.

Adams saw service with Parsons, Kans., team, Missouri Valley League, 1904–05. Brief tryout with St. Louis NL 1906. Denver, Western League, 1906–07. Pittsburgh NL 1907. Farmed to Louisville, American Association, 1908, he won 22, lost 12, meriting promotion to Pirates. He remained consistent winner with Pirates until 1916, when he had 2–9 record. Back to minors at St. Joseph and Hutchinson in Western League, 1917. Kansas City, American Association, 1918, where Adams proved he was not washed up. Returned to Pittsburgh. Continued with Pirates until 1926, reaching 17-victory level twice (1919, 20) during this span. Saw service in 1925 WS but pitched only one inning against Senators. Wound up with 482 NL games, 2995 innings, 194 wins, 140 losses. During most of life Adams considered Mount Moriah, Mo., home.

ADCOCK, JOSEPH WILBUR 1B-BR-TR. B. 10/30/27, Coushatta, La. 6'4", 232. Joe Adcock wrote his name in baseball history, summer 1954, when he went on batting spree at Ebbets Field, Brooklyn. Broke two major league records, tied two others, set one NL mark, equaled three others. Here's what happened: on 7/31/54 slapped four homers, double. Each homer off different Dodger pitcher. This created new major league records for total bases, 18; most extra bases, 13. Milwaukee won 15–7 over Dodgers. This only part of story. On 7/30/54 hit home run, double, single. Somewhere along line broke his bat and borrowed another, so heavy he could hardly lift it. Following his two-day spree, in second time at bat Adcock smashed double, 8/1/54. Next trip to plate Dodger pitcher Clem Labine hit him on left side of head. Adcock was wearing helmet, and it helped. Still carried off field.

Joe feasted on Brooklyn pitching that year. Tied one major league mark by hitting nine home runs on road against Dodgers. Two years later, 1956, Adcock tied another NL record by slamming 13 round-trippers against them in one season.

Adcock attended Louisiana State, 1944–47. Started pro career, Columbia, Sally League, 1947–48. Tulsa, Texas League, 1949. Cincinnati NL 1950–52. Milwaukee NL 1953–62. Cleveland AL 1963. Los Angeles AL 1964. California AL (formerly Los Angeles) 1965–66. Manager, Cleveland AL, 1967. Manager, Seattle, 1968.

That 1954 season was Joe's best year for batting average, .308. Hit 15 or more homers 11 seasons. Had 35 homers, 1961, and 38 in 1956. Best RBI production was 1961, with 108.

Adcock played 1959 major league games with 1832 hits in 6606 times at bat. Scored 823 runs. Had 295 doubles, 35 triples, 336 homers, 1122 RBI, .277 average. In World Series of 1957 and 1958, Adcock had .250 average, 7 for 28—no extra bases. Braves won in 1957, Yanks in 1958. In Adcock's solitary season (1967) as big league manager, his Indians finished eighth in 10-club AL, 75 wins, 87 losses.

AGEE, TOMMIE LEE OF-BR-TR. B. 8/9/42, Magnolia, Ala. 5'11", 195. Hit only .167 in 1969 World Series against heavily favored Baltimore but in third game was one-man show. N.Y. Mets and Orioles knotted, a game each. Put Mets in lead in first inning with home run off Jim Palmer. In fourth inning, with men on first and second, Elrod Hendricks of Baltimore hit terrific smash to left center, seemingly a triple. Tommie somehow grabbed ball backhanded at 396-foot sign for one of most magnificent catches in any WS. In seventh, Baltimore loaded bases. Paul Blair hit liner to right center, a certain base-clearing double or triple, it appeared. But Agee made headlong dive, came up with ball. Mets took that game, 5–0, and next two, to do in Birds.

Agee came from family of 11, which included nine sisters. Attended

Grambling College in Louisiana, where he won football scholarship; but played only baseball. Cleveland Indians give him $60,000 bonus, 1961. Played for Dubuque, Burlington, Jacksonville, Charleston, Portland and Indianapolis in minors and 31 games with Indians during years 1961–64. Traded to Chicago AL, played 10 games with White Sox, 1965. Made it big, 1966: 160 games, .273 average, 86 RBI, 22 homers. Led AL outfielders in DPs with seven. Named Rookie of the Year by both *Sporting News* and Baseball Writers Association. Chicago again 1967. Mets 1968–72. Traded to Houston after 1972 season, in which he dropped to .227. Tied NL record for grounding into three double plays in one game, 5/29/70.

Started 1973 season with over 1000 games; .258 lifetime average, 162 doubles, 24 triples, 119 homers, 940 hits, 520 runs, 411 RBI, 164 stolen bases. AL All-Star team, 1966,67.

AGUIRRE, HENRY JOHN (Hank) P-BR-TL. B. 1/31/32, Azusa, Calif. 6′4″, 205. Hank Aguirre started pitching professionally in 1951 with Duluth. Then with Bakersfield, Peoria, Reading, Indianapolis, Cleveland, San Diego, Charleston (W. Va.). Finally Detroit, more or less permanently, 1960. In 1962 led AL with 2.21 ERA; had 16–8 mark. Never again reached such heights. Left Detroit after 1967 season. Los Angeles NL 1968. Chicago NL 1969. Retired July 1970 with 72–72 record.

Became "Information and Services Coach" for Chicago, late 1971. Cub owner Phil Wrigley declared that Aguirre was to be Leo Durocher's liaison man with press and players. Leo's popularity at a new low then. Job lasted until Durocher was fired during All-Star break, 1972. Aguirre then returned to simple role as coach, under Whitey Lockman.

AKER, JACK DELANE (Chief) P-BR-TR. B. 7/13/40, Tulare, Calif. 6′2″, 203. Ancestors include Potawatami Indians. Outfielder, then pitcher. As minor league career progressed, Aker concentrated more and more on relief pitching. Since reaching majors, 1964, through 1972, never started ball game. Used in 359 AL games up to mid-May 1972, when sent to Chicago Cubs as part of deal which put Johnny Callison in Yankee uniform. In AL career Jack owned 3.20 ERA in 557 innings. Aker in 48 games after joining Cubs—6–6, saved 17, 2.96 ERA. This brought major league record to 41–38, 624 innings, 407 games, 3.17 ERA, as 1973 started.

Aker attended College of Sequoias before joining Grand Island, Nebr. State League, 1959. Lewiston, Northwest League, 1961; Albuquerque, 1962; Portland and Lewiston, 1963; Dallas, 1964; Vancouver, 1965; Kansas City AL 1964–67; Oakland AL 1968; Seattle AL 1969; New York AL 1969–72; Chicago NL 1972. During his AL days Aker won 35,

15

lost 32, but chalked up plenty of saves. Named Fireman of Year, 1966. With Yanks, 1969, had 8–4 record, 11 saves; 4–2 mark, 1970, 16 saves; 1971, allowed earned run in just 13 of his 41 appearances. His ERA marks stingy: 1.99 in 1966 with KC; 2.06 with Yankees in 1969, again in 1970; in 1971, 2.57.

Aker served as player representative for Yankees. When Jim Fregosi traded out of AL in winter of 1971–72, Jack became representative for all AL players until traded to Cubs.

ALDRIDGE, VICTOR EDDINGTON (Hoosier Schoolmaster) P-BR-TR. B. 10/25/94, Indian Springs, Ind. D. 4/17/73, Terre Haute, Ind. 5'9½", 175. Vic Aldridge rose to his greatest heights during 1925 while member of Pirates. During pennant drive captured eight straight victories, wound up with 15–7 mark, ERA of 3.63. Went on to win first two Pittsburgh victories in World Series against Senators. Ray Kremer won other two. Pirates world champs after trailing three games to one. Aldridge's first WS victory was 3–2, next one 6–3. Allowed eight hits in each game. Two years later, when Pirates faced Yankees in WS, Vic lost his only start, 6–2; Bombers flattened Pittsburgh in four straight. Aldridge's WS record: 4.91 ERA, 2–1, 25-2/3 IP; allowed 28 hits, walked 13, struck out 13.

Aldridge known as Hoosier Schoolmaster because he taught several years before entering pro ball, and part time afterwards. Minor league experience 1915–16, 1919–21: Indianapolis, Erie, Denver, Los Angeles (then in Pacific Coast League). Spent 1917 with Chicago Cubs. After brief spell with Cubs, 1918, joined U. S. Navy. To PCL, 1919. In 1922 had 16–15 record with Cubs, then 16–9, 15–12. Traded to Pirates late in 1924; came up with 15–7, 10–13, 15–10 seasons in succession. With N.Y. Giants, 1928—4–7. Then pitched briefly for Newark and Terre Haute. While with Indianapolis, 1916, pitched no-hitter. Came back with one day of rest and went into ninth inning without allowing hit or run. Went 19-1/3 innings without allowing hit or run; and in six consecutive games allowed total of 12 hits. After baseball Aldridge graduated from law school, passed bar, and for time served in Indiana State Senate.

Vic's major league totals: 97 wins, 80 losses (over 9-year period), 1600-2/3 innings; allowed 1671 hits, walked 512, struck out 526; ERA 3.76.

ALEXANDER, DAVID DALE (Moose) 1B-BR-TR. B. 4/26/03, Greenville, Tenn. 6'3", 210. Only two players have won major league batting titles while playing for two clubs in same season: Harry Walker in 1947, dividing his efforts between St. Louis NL and Philadelphia NL; Dale Alexander, who started 1932 with Detroit, then moved to Boston AL after 23 games with Tigers.

Alexander had three slugging seasons with Detroit, 1929–31. Hit .343 in 1929, in 155 games; in 1930, .326 in 154 contests; in 1931, .325 in 135 games. Tigers acquired Harry Davis, lefthanded first sacker, for 1932, to replace slower Alexander. Dale hitting only .250 when traded to Boston for Earl Webb 6/12/32. With Red Sox, Alexander hit .372; season average, .367, 124 games. Under rules adopted later, Alexander would not have qualified for batting title; 502 plate appearances needed. Dale at plate 454 times, including his walks and one occasion when he stopped pitched ball.

Dale started out with hometown club, Greenville, in Appalachian League, at age 20. Hit .251 in 83 games. One more year at Greenville, 1924: .331, 114 games. Two years at Charlotte. Two years at Toronto. Gaining fame as slugger. Last season at Toronto, 1928, batted .380 and slapped 31 homers, meriting his sale to Detroit, reportedly for $100,000. Hit 25 homers his first year with Detroit, but production never again reached that mark. In 1933, Dale dropped to .281 with Red Sox. Left major league scene. Big league totals: .331, 662 games, 811 hits, 164 doubles, 30 triples, 61 homers, 369 runs, 459 RBI, 20 stolen bases.

ALEXANDER, GROVER CLEVELAND (Old Pete) P-BR-TR. B. 2/26/87, St. Paul, Nebr. D. 11/4/50, St. Paul, Nebr. 6'1", 185. Best known for striking out Tony Lazzeri with bases loaded in decisive seventh game of 1926 World Series. Tony was slugging second baseman with Yankees and Alex was nearing end of his career. Cardinals led 3 to 2, seventh inning. Yanks loaded bases with two outs. Redbird pitcher Haines forced to leave game with bleeding hand caused by throwing knuckleballs. Alex had pitched and won sixth game of set, his second victory of Series; reputedly celebrated by heavy drinking afterwards. Nevertheless, Card mgr. Hornsby called him to relieve in crucial seventh contest. First pitch was strike. On next pitch Lazzeri lined terrific drive to left field stands, foul by only few feet. Next pitch, ball. Then threw curve. Lazzeri swung mightily—missed. Probably most famous strikeout since legendary "Casey at the Bat" struck out. Allowed no more Yankee base runners till he faced Babe Ruth, then at his peak, with two outs in ninth. Ruth walked but was out stealing. Thus Alex saved game and gave Cards their first world championship in modern times.

Alex famed for his control. Easy pitching motion, no windup. Won 28 games for Phillies his first major league season (1911). Won 31, 33, 30 games three consecutive years (1915–17) though Phillies won pennant only in 1915, finished second in 1916, second in 1917.

Holds NL record for complete games, 437; total shutouts, 90; all-time record for shutouts in one season, 16; pitched four consecutive shutouts 9/11; tied with Christy Mathewson for NL record of games won, 373. Hall of Fame 1938.

Alex suffered from epilepsy—and alcoholism. Wound up pro career at Dallas, 1930. Cardinals, recalling his contribution to their first pennant and world championship, offered him jobs from time to time but Alex spurned "charity" though he did accept small pension from team and from government for his military service in World War I.

Alex at Galesburg, Ill.-Mo. League, 1909, 15–8; Syracuse, N. Y. State League, 1910, 29–14; Phila. NL 1911–17; Chicago NL 1918–26; St. Louis NL 1926–29; Phila. NL 1930; Dallas, Texas League, 1930. Major league totals: 696 games, 5189 innings, 373–208 for .642, 2198 strikeouts, ERA 2.56. World Series record: Phila. NL 1915, 2 games, 17-2/3 innings, 1–1, ERA 1.53; St. Louis NL 1926, 3 games, 20-1/3 innings, 2–0, ERA 1.33; St. Louis NL 1928, 2 games, 0–1, ERA 19.80. WS totals: 7 games, 3–2 for .600, ERA 3.56.

After leaving pro baseball he joined House of David junketing baseball team which carried its own portable lighting system for night baseball, touring tank towns for most part. He and team played night exhibition game at Sportsman's Park, St. Louis, 9/22/32, and was honored by former teammates and fans. This was nearly three years before first major league night baseball game in Cincinnati, 5/35. Later Alex worked in flea circus on 42nd St., New York. Died 1950 at 63 in Nebr. birthplace.

ALLEN, ETHAN NATHAN   OF-BR-TR. B. 1/1/04, Cincinnati, Ohio. 6'1", 180. Ethan Allen spent thirteen years in majors and probably could have pursued later career as coach, manager or executive in game, but became head baseball coach at Yale over two decades. At University of Cincinnati studied physical education. Fine basketball player. B.S. degree 1926. Accepted Cincinnati offer of $8500 bonus; in 18 games that year, batting .308. Not power hitter. Allen generally close to or above .300 mark. Lifetime average: .300, 1281 games. Had 1325 hits in 4418 trips. Scored 623 runs. Had 255 doubles, 45 triples, 47 homers, 501 RBI. Remained with Reds until 5/27/30, when traded to N.Y. Giants. Spent 1933 with Cardinals; Philadelphia NL 1934—5/21/36; Chicago NL 1936. St. Louis AL 1937–38. Retired. Never played in minors.

Keen student during playing days. In off-season continued studies and received M.A. in physical education from Columbia U., 1932. During World War II served in Italy in Special Services sports program. Allen for time was motion-picture director in NL publicity department. Then collegiate coaching—highly successful. Authored several books on baseball techniques. Invented two scientific baseball games. Narrated series of instructional films on baseball after supervising photography. Recalls with satisfaction having been first player to hit ball over center field fence (very high wall) at Redland Field (later Crosley Field), Cincinnati.

ALLEN, JOHN THOMAS P-BR-TR. B. 9/30/05, Lenoir, N.C. D. 3/29/59, St. Petersburg, Fla. 6′, 190. Rugged competitor who actually got his start by doing favor to Paul Krichell, scout for N.Y. Yankees. Johnny, 1927, was hotel clerk in Sanford, N.C. Krichell's room steaming hot. Allen set up several fans in it. Scout told Allen he was in baseball, Johnny confided he was pitcher himself—in church league. Krichell impressed enough to watch Allen in action. Thus began his climb in Yankee organization. Five years later Allen burst on AL scene by winning 17 games, losing just 4, an .810 percentage, in his first year with Yankees. Between 1927 and 1932 Allen gained experience at Fayetteville, Greenville and Asheville, N.C.; Gadsden, Ala.; Jersey City, Toronto. Allen didn't fare very well in 1932 World Series. Started fourth and final game against Cubs, who jumped on him for five hits and four runs (three earned) in first inning. Allen retired before third out made, but Yanks went on to win 13–6, sweeping WS.

Allen won 50 games for Yankees over four-year period, losing 19. Traded to Cleveland for Monte Pearson and Steve Sundra. In five years with Indians Johnny won 67, lost 34. Took 20 his first year (1936), losing 10. Won 15 straight in 1937, losing but one, a heartbreaking 1–0 game to Jake Wade of Detroit, who set Indians down with one hit. His winning percentage, .938, set major league record, which stood until 1959 when Elroy Face had .947 record (18–1). Another winning streak of 12, 1938. Cleveland sold Allen to St. Louis AL 12/24/40. Was 2–5 for Browns. To Brooklyn on waivers 7/30/41—3–0 for Dodgers that year. Dodgers won pennant by 2-1/2 games. In WS against Yankees Allen relieved in three games; no runs in 3-2/3 innings. Had 10–6 record with 1942 Dodgers and 5–1 mark in 1943 before shifting to N.Y. Giants, 1–3. Retired after 1944 season, 4–7. Career: 142 victories, 75 defeats, 3.75 ERA. Had reputation for mean disposition on mound. Numerous run-ins with umpires. Opposing batsmen often accused him of doctoring ball.

ALLEN, RICHARD ANTHONY (Richie; Dick) Inf.-OF-BR-TR. B. 3/8/42, Wampum, Pa. 5′11″, 187. Controversial. Much traveled. But in 1972 seemed to have found safe haven in Chicago AL under management of Chuck Tanner (who grew up short distance from Dick's birthplace). Won MVP honors. Led league in HR with 37, in RBI with 113. Hit .308 in 148 games, stole 19 bases, scored 90 runs, hit 26 doubles, 5 triples. Allen had come to White Sox from L.A. Dodgers 12/2/71. Held out till 4/1/72.

Allen comes from family of eight. One brother, Ron, played for Omaha, 1972. Another brother, Hank, also with White Sox, 1973. Phillies signed Richie, 1960, for bonus estimated at $70,000. Sent to Elmira, played shortstop, 88 games, with .281 average. Shifted to second base at Twin Falls, 1961; hit .317 with 21 homers, 94 RBI. Williamsport, 1962, 20 homers, 109 RBI, .329 average. Arkansas, International League, 1963. First Negro to play there in pro ball. Rugged reception. Despite this, he managed to lead league in triples (12), homers (33), RBI (97); had .289 average. Same season his stormy career in Philadelphia began with 10 games. Played outfield for Arkansas, but in 1964 was used exclusively at third base in 162 games. Hit .318, but made 41 errors, tops for third sackers. Scored more runs than any other NL player, 125. Tied for league lead in triples, 13. Had 29 homers, 91 RBI. Led NL in total bases. His total number of games played tied major league record for most games, rookie season. Named NL Rookie of Year by Baseball Writers Association and *Sporting News*. Hit above .300 until 1967, playing third, short, outfield. Late in year went on disabled list after suffering severe cuts on right hand. Seriously damaged tendons and a nerve, handicapping his throwing in later seasons. During 1969 season, had trouble with fans, management; was fined $500 a day for 28 days, and suspended. Traded to St. Louis 10/7/69 in deal involving Tim McCarver and Curt Flood. Hit .279 for Redbirds, with 34 homers and 101 RBI. Cardinals dealt him to Los Angeles NL after 1970 season. Productive 1971 with Dodgers: 23 homers, 90 RBI, .295 average. Then to White Sox for 1972.

Entering 1973, NL totals: .298 average for his 1291 games; 1412 hits, including 236 doubles, 71 triples, 271 homers; 848 RBI. Stole 20 bases, 1967. NL homers averaged out at 29 per year over eight-year period. NL stats also include: fanning five times in one game, 6/28/64; leading NL in strikeouts, 1964, with 138; again in 1965, with 150. In 1968 he whiffed 161 times, but Donn Clendenon struck out 163 times. Allen's 201 hits his rookie season, 1964, tied major league record for rookie reaching 200 mark in his first qualifying season. In 1968 Richie walked five times during one contest, tying NL record. Same year had three homers in one game, 9/29/68. NL All-Star squads 1965–67, 70, 72–73.

ALLEY, LEONARD EUGENE (Gene) Inf.-BR-TR. B. 7/10/40, Richmond, Va. 6', 165. Various injuries have beset Gene Alley, who once seemed destined for superstardom. Steady, at times brilliant shortstop. Good base stealer. Excellent hit-and-run man. Twice on NL All-Star squad.

Alley signed with Pittsburgh organization 1/26/59. Farmed to Dubuque, Burlington, Grand Forks, Columbus (Ohio), Asheville before joining Pirates for 17 games, 1963. By 1965 was regular—153 games. His .299 mark, 1966, better than any other shortstop in majors. Helped Pirates make 215 double plays that year, one short of big league record. His .979 fielding average same year was highest ever by Pirate shortstop. During 1966, suffered beaning, above left eye, by Bob Shaw of Mets.

Nine stitches. Shoulder injury 1967. In 1971, left hand was hit by pitch from "iron mike" pitching machine, and broken. Later had knee problem, leading to operation for removal of cartilage.

Alley's second best season was 1967, when he hit .287. His major league totals till 1973: .257, 1119 games; 137 doubles, 42 triples, 53 homers among his 967 hits; 417 runs, 334 RBI. His 1971 WS performance was brief—two trips to plate, no hits.

ALLYN, JOHN W. Executive. B. 5/28/17, Chicago, Ill. John Allyn took over as president of Chicago White Sox, 1970, succeeding brother Arthur. John had been vice president of team. Graduate of Lafayette with A.B. in economics, 1939. Began financial career immediately after graduation. Specialist in internal brokerage operations such as company acquisitions and underwriting. Chairman of Artnell Company; chairman of board of investment firm F. I. DuPont, Glore, Forgan & Co.; director of motor supply company and publishing house; president and director of Home Theaters, Inc., of Little Rock, Ark.

Served as radar maintenance officer in U.S. Navy on USS *Nevada*, 1942–45. For two years, president of Chicago Mustangs, pro soccer team. Collects antique guns; has over 40 muzzle-loading guns. Lives in Winnetka, Ill.

ALMEIDA, RAFAEL D. Inf.-BR-TR. B. 7/30/87, Havana, Cuba. 5'9", 164. Believed to be first Cuban selected for major league tryout, 1911. Charles Bancroft, secretary of Cincinnati Reds, visited Cuba on vacation that year, saw Almeida play. Bancroft impressed. Returned home. Instructed Almeida to come to Cincinnati for tryout. Almeida wired back that he would comply only if he were able to bring his interpreter with all expenses paid. Club agreed. When pair performed for Clark Griffith, then Cincinnati manager, Griff liked interpreter better than Almeida. Interpreter was Armando Marsans, outfielder. Both signed contracts and played their first game in morning contest at Chicago, 7/4/11.

Almeida played mostly at third base for Reds. Got into 29 games that season, hit .313. Following year had .220 average in 16 games, and in 1913, .262 in 50 games. Lifetime average .270 in 95 games; 13 doubles, 6 triples, 3 homers, 7 stolen bases. His interpreter lasted eight years in majors, hitting .269 for his career with Cincinnati, St. Louis (Federal League), St. Louis AL, New York AL. With only minimal communication with Cuba, it is not known whether Almeida is stilll living. Marsans is dead.

ALOU, FELIPE ROJAS (Panque) OF-Inf.-BR-TR. B. 5/12/35, Haina, Dominican Republic. 6'1", 195. Eldest of three brothers who became major leaguers. All started out in Giants' organization and all briefly played for San Francisco at same time. All three went to bat in same inning 9/10/63, but none got ball out of infield. Couple of weeks later all three outfield positions manned by Alous: Matty left, Jesus center, Felipe right. Collectively, they had four hits that day—two singles for Jesus, double and triple for Felipe.

Alous' father's name was Rojas. In Spanish-speaking countries children usually bear last names of both parents. Alou was mother's surname. When Felipe came to U.S., Mike McCormick, who managed Lake Charles team in Evangeline League, began calling him Alou instead of Rojas. Easier to pronounce.

Felipe got $200 bonus for joining Giants. Played five games at Lake Charles, 1956, then transferred to Cocoa, Florida State League. Won batting championship, .380 in 119 games. Divided 1957 season between Minneapolis, American Association, and Springfield, Eastern League. Following year hit .319 in 55 games at Phoenix, Pacific Coast League, after which he was called up to Giants. In majors ever since. Batting average generally near .300. Best season with San Francisco was 1962— .316 in 154 games. Giants won pennant that year. In WS Felipe went 7 for 26, .269 average. Played all games, as Giants lost to Yanks in seven. After 1963 season, traded to Milwaukee. Braves moved to Atlanta after 1965. Best year with Braves was 1968: .317 average in 160 games. In 1970 Felipe with Oakland A's; played 154 games, hit .271. In 1971, played two games for Oakland, then to Yankees—.288 average in 133 games. Not an outstanding slugger, yet Alou hit 25 homers with Giants in 1962, 20 in 1963, 23 with Milwaukee in 1965, 31 with Atlanta in 1966. Entered 1973 with 1967 games behind him, over 2000 hits, 201 homers, 821 RBI, .289 average.

ALOU, JESUS MARIA ROJAS   OF-BR-TR. B. 3/24/43, Haina, Dominican Republic. 6'2'', 195. Youngest of Alou brothers. Like other two, got his start in Giants' organization, signing in 1959. Played at Hastings, Nebr., Artesia, N. Mex., Eugene, Oreg., El Paso and Tacoma before making San Francisco, 1963. That September all three brothers appeared in one game at Polo Grounds against N.Y. Mets. Jesus remained with Giants but following year Felipe was with Milwaukee; Matty traded to Pittsburgh after 1965 season.

Jesus came close to .300 mark twice while with Giants. When NL expanded after 1968 season, Montreal Expos drafted him from special expansion list, then traded him to Houston. In 1970, under management of Harry Walker, boosted his average to .306 in 117 games, first time beyond .300 mark in majors. Alou went 6 for 6 in one game, 7/10/64. Grounded into double play three times in second game 7/17/66, equaling NL record. Major league average .279 for 1039 games going

22

into 1973 season. His first hit in 1972 was No. 1000 of career. Had 145 doubles, 25 triples, 26 homers starting 1973.

ALOU, MATEO ROJAS (Matty) OF-1B-BL-TL. B. 12/22/38, Haina, Dominican Republic. 5'8", 160. Hittingest of Alou brothers—for average. Led NL in batting 1966 with .342 average for Pittsburgh. Brother Felipe has hit far more homers, while brother Jesus has hit just about as many as Matty in fewer games. Matty got break in 1972. Cardinals lost title hopes by midseason, dealt Matty (.314, 108 games) to Oakland A's. Aided A's flag drive: .281, 34 hits (several key blows), 16 RBI. In WS was stopped by Reds' pitchers—1 for 24, .042 average. Collected half share of WS spoils, $10,352.51. Shortly after Series, was traded to Yankees, joining brother Felipe for second time.

Matty hit .310 in 81 games for San Francisco, 1961, then tailed off until he landed under tutelage of Harry Walker in 1966, then manager of Pirates. Walker and Roberto Clemente changed his batting style. Used heavier bat, choked up more, waited for pitch. Improved his average 111 points over 1965, from .231 to .342. Continued his consistent hitting with .338, .332 and .331 next three years. Then after dropping to .297, was traded to St. Louis for 1971. Came back with .315 mark.

Matty played with Michigan City, 1957, then with St. Cloud, Springfield (Mass.) and Tacoma before joining S.F. Giants for four games, 1960. When he hit .145 for S.F., 1963, had another session at Tacoma. Back with Giants for 1964–65. Pittsburgh 1966–70. Cardinals 1971 till traded to Oakland late in 1972 season.

Matty appeared in 1962 WS with Giants; hit .333 in six games. Was on NL squad in All-Star games 1968, 69. Started 1973 season with Yankees with .310 lifetime average, 1485 major league games. Had 1611 hits, 211 doubles, 49 triples, 29 homers, 712 runs, 395 RBI. In 1969 Matty established major league record for most times at bat, 698; also led NL in hits with 231, in doubles with 41. When he won NL batting championship, 1966, brother Felipe was second, with .327—first time in major league history that brothers finished one-two in batting race.

ALSTON, WALTER EMMONS (Smokey) Manager. B. 12/1/11, Venice, Ohio. Walt Alston learned lesson early—produce, or else. Much to astonishment of New York sports writers, he became manager of Brooklyn, won in first major league game 4/15/54, from Pittsburgh, 7–4. Once before had played in major league ball game—one at bat, struck out. Back to minors.

Alston started out with modest one-year contract to pilot Dodgers. In 1973 was working on 20th one-year contract. Salary estimated to be over $70,000. Before reaching that salary, Alston had led Dodgers of Brooklyn and Los Angeles to six pennants, four world championships; had outlasted all who were piloting major league teams when he took over. Durocher only fellow piloting then who survived into 1973. But Leo idle from 1956 through 1965. Only two men managed same team longer than Alston—Connie Mack, 50 years, Philadelphia Athletics; John McGraw, 31 years, N.Y. Giants.

His father, farmer and later Ford Motor Co. worker, taught young Walt to play ball. And a lady history teacher helped coach him in baseball when in high school. Righthanded pitcher then. Went to Miami U. (Oxford, Ohio), majored in phys. ed., industrial arts. Became science, phys. ed. teacher between baseball seasons in his hometown, Darrtown, Ohio, where he still lives. But someone discovered Alston could hit long ball. Frank Rickey, brother of Branch, then general manager of Cardinals, heard about Alston's hitting ability. Signed him day after Walt got B.S. from Miami U., 1935. Contract was with Greenwood, Miss., Cardinal farm. Played third base. Following year to Cardinals for "cup of coffee"—Lon Warneke of Cubs promptly struck him out in only appearance in major league game. Back to minors—playing manager, Portsmouth, Ohio, 1940. Managed Cardinal farm team at Springfield, Ohio, and in 1944–45 piloted Trenton, N.J.

Alston managed Dodger farm, Nashau, N.H., 1946. One of his players was Roy Campanella. Business manager Buzzie Bavasi, later Alston's boss at L. A. Walt got into argument with Sal Yvars, player with Manchester, N.H., team. Fisticuffs. Shoulder hurt. Ended Walt's playing career. But not managing career. Piloted Dodger teams, St. Paul and Montreal, 1948 through 1953. Won three pennants, one Junior World Series. Charlie Dressen, having won pennant for Dodgers, 1952, 53, demanded long-term contract before he would sign for 1954. O'Malley, Dodger president, said no. Dressen soon learned pennant-winning manager not necessarily indispensable. Alston given job piloting Brooklyn. One-year contracts have worked out all right since. "I'd be lost without baseball," says Walt. "Only one of two things will get me to leave Dodgers. Either they'll fire me some day or my health will go bad."

Sports writers used to say each spring, "Alston must win pennant for Dodgers this year—or else." In 1958 Los Angeles finished seventh, 21 games behind league leader. Walt signed another one-year contract—led team to pennant, world championship, 1959. In 1964, Dodgers finished in sixth-place tie. But following year Walt led club to NL flag, another world championship. Since Alston manager of Dodgers, club has seven times passed two million in attendance, three times passing 2-1/2 million mark. Off-season, leads quiet life in Darrtown. Loves woodworking.

ALTROCK, NICHOLAS P-BL-TL. B. 9/15/76, Cincinnati, Ohio. D. 1/20/65, Wash., D.C. 5'10", 197. Nick Altrock was drawing card long after pitching days over. Became skillful coach—and clown, good one.

First teamed up with Herman (Germany) Schaefer and later with Al Schacht.

Altrock had three fine seasons with Chicago White Sox: 21–13 in 1904; 21–10 in 1905; helped "Hitless Wonders" with 20–13 mark in 1906 when Sox defeated powerful Cubs in first "city series" WS. Altrock was leadoff pitcher for White Sox, defeating famed Three Finger Brown 2–1. Cubs later beat Altrock, but Brown had to pitch shutout to win 1–0. Nick's ERA for this his only WS was 1.00 in 18 innings—11 hits, 2 walks, 5 strikeouts.

Never observed training rules very well, and this may have contributed to his relatively short career as pitcher. After his brilliant performance in 1906 his work fell off to 8–12 in 1907, 3–7 in 1908. During 1909, shifted to Washington, then dropped into American Association until recalled to Washington, 1912. That was when Altrock began mixing serious coaching job with amusing funny stuff with Schaefer. Altrock often mimicked umpire's movements; walked foul line as though it were tightrope; threw and caught baseballs in impossible positions; used baseballs like bowling balls; engaged in shadow boxing; plus dozens of other crowd-pleasing antics. After Schaefer left Senators, Nick teamed up with another natural, broken-down pitcher, Al Schacht. After time, Nick and Al didn't speak to each other. But their personal enmity did not affect their hilarious acts. Schacht went to Red Sox as coach, 1934. By now Altrock aging, but still coaching Senators. Was listed as coach years later, even though he no longer put on uniform.

Fielder Jones, White Sox manager, lauded Altrock as pitcher with fine curve, change of pace, remarkable control. Had deceptive move toward first base. Good fielder. With Los Angeles, Pacific Coast League, 1901, is said he deliberately walked seven batters, then picked them off first base. "It was only way I could get those sluggers out," said Nick. Nick's first major league pitching was done with Louisville NL 1898. Boston AL 1902–03. To White Sox during 1903. Major league totals: 84 wins, 75 losses. His ERA was in neighborhood of 2.67 though some early records inconsistent.

On last day of 1933 season, after Washington clinched pennant, Mgr. Joe Cronin used Altrock as pinch hitter for Johnny Kerr. He was 57 years and 16 days old—oldest man ever used in major league game up to that time. (Satchel Paige older when he pitched three innings for Kansas City AL in 1965.)

AMALFITANO, JOHN JOSEPH (Joey) Inf.-BR-TR. B. 1/23/34, San Pedro, Calif. 5'11", 175. As player, Joey Amalfitano played with N.Y. and San Francisco Giants, Chicago Cubs and Houston Astros. When playing days ended, during 1967 season, transferred to coaching lines with Cubs. Moved to Giants in same capacity after 1971 season.

Joey attended Loyola U., Los Angeles. Went directly to Giants from campus, 1954. Played nine games that year, 36 in 1955, then to minors for four years. After .308 average with Toronto in 1959, Giants drafted him; played over 100 games each in 1960 and 1961. Houston NL 1962. Back to San Francisco for 1963. Cubs 1964–67, as player. Took part in 643 major league games; lifetime average of .244.

AMES, LEON KESSLING (Red) P-BR-TR. B. 8/2/84, Warren, Ohio. D. 10/8/36, Warren, Ohio. 5'10½", 185. Red Ames had fancy debut in NL, 1903. Had started first pro season at Ilion, N.Y. State League, earlier that year; came to N.Y. Giants end of year. Pitched five-inning no-hitter against St. Louis, winning 5–0. Stayed with Giants until 1913, with most successful season 1905—22–8 record. Red had another no-hitter of sorts opening day, 1909, against Brooklyn. Pitched nine innings, no hits, no runs, but his club lost 3 to 0 in 13 innings. Traded to Cincinnati 5/22/13. Reds sold him to St. Louis NL 7/24/15. With Cards until 9/5/19. Then to Philadelphia NL on waivers. Kansas City, American Association, 1920–22. Playing manager, Daytona Beach, Florida State League, 1923. Major league totals: 533 games, 3195 innings, 183 wins,167 losses for .523 mark. ERA records not kept during earlier part of his career. In 1905, 1911, 1912 World Series with Giants. Pitched in four games, 0–1, ERA 2.45.

AMOROS, EDMUNDO ISASI (Sandy) OF-BL-TL. B. 1/30/32, Matanzas, Cuba. 5'7½", 170. Hero of 1955 World Series. N.Y. Yankees and Brooklyn Dodgers had battled through six games, each winning three. Now, 10/4/55, sixth inning of game at Yankee Stadium, Dodgers had 2–0 lead. Johnny Podres in trouble in last half when he walked Billy Martin. Gil McDougald bunted safely. With Yogi Berra at bat, Amoros playing toward left center for lefthanded batsman. Dangerous in clutch, Yogi sliced fly ball just inside left field foul line. Amoros raced at lightning speed. When ball seemed certain to fall safely, he grabbed with gloved hand. Instantly fired to Reese, Reese to Hodges, doubling McDougald off first. Both McDougald and Martin took off at top speed with crack of bat, convinced ball could not be caught. Had Amoros missed, Yankees would have tied game. Also Berra on second, or third, none out. Play saved game, Series for Brooklyn. Even Yankee fans had to applaud spectacular play. Later, *Sporting News* polled sports writers, sportscasters, asking them to name "outstanding sports thrill of year." Amoros' catch was it.

Amoros, with Dodgers until 1957. Spell with Montreal, International League. To Los Angeles with Dodgers for 1959–60. Wound up major league days with .149 mark in 65 games with Detroit Tigers, 1960.

Money, jobs ran out. Finally, in 1971, Amoros destitute, on relief, without prospects. Somehow sports writer discovered plight, wrote about it. New York's Mayor Lindsay read account, asked one of his assistants to track down Amoros. Couldn't find Sandy in phone book. Finally enlisted help of Jose Valdivielso, another Cuban and former teammate of Amoros. Jose knocked on Amoros' door after midnight. Sandy living in room in Bronx. Saw no reason to welcome anyone at that hour. "You've got a job," yelled Valdivielso, through door. "Get down to Parks Department early tomorrow morning." Sandy soon in custodial and managerial service of N.Y. Parks Department, with hopes of getting better job soon.

Amoros played at St. Paul, American Association, 1952, going to Dodgers same year. Spent 1953, part of 1954 at Montreal. Then part-time outfielder with Dodgers. Batting average in majors, .255 in 517 games. Hit only .161 in twelve Series games (1952,55,56). But most fans believe he earned keep with that fantastic catch.

ANDERSON, GEORGE LEE (Sparky) Mgr.-Inf.-BR-TR. B. 2/22/34, Bridgewater, S. Dak. 5'10", 170. When Sparky Anderson was named manager of Cincinnati Reds 10/9/69 some fans vaguely remembered he had played second base for Philadelphia NL, 1959. Others knew he was unostentatious coach for new expansion club, San Diego, 1969. But one year later Anderson piloted Reds into WS, earning respect of fans, baseball officials for his handling of "Big Red Machine." With Phillies, hit .218 in 152 games at second base. Then went back to minors. That 1959 season his only one in big leagues as player. Started in Dodger organization at Santa Barbara, 1953, then Pueblo, Fort Worth, Montreal, Los Angeles (Pacific Coast League) before Phils. Best year with stick, Montreal, 1956, .298. After Philadelphia, four years with Toronto as player; manager, 1964—finished fifth.

Bob Howsam, president and chief executive of Reds, but then G.M. of Cardinals, hired Sparky to manage their Rock Hill team in Western Carolinas League, 1965. In split season, team finished eighth in first half, first in second half, and won playoff. In 1966 he bossed St. Petersburg team in Florida State circuit, finishing second in first half, first in second half, but lost playoff. Repeated his St. Petersburg performance with Modesto, California League, 1967, losing playoff after finishing second, first in halves. Won pennant at Asheville, Southern Association, 1968. Then San Diego as coach. October 8, 1969, Sparky accepted offer from California Angels to become coach, but released when chance to manage Reds materialized immediately afterward, 10/9/69. After winning NL flag, 1970, Reds couldn't cope with Baltimore Orioles, lost WS four games to one. Following season was disappointing, team dropping down to fourth in Western Division. In 1972, Reds took NL flag, but lost World Series in seven to underdog Oakland A's.

ANDREWS, MICHAEL JAY 2B-BR-TR. B. 7/9/43, Los Angeles, Calif. 6'3", 195. Mike Andrews had four full seasons with Boston Red Sox before trade to Chicago White Sox 12/1/70 that brought Luis Aparicio to Beantown. Mike had fairly good season first year with Chuck Tanner's club, 1971, hitting .282 in 109 games, but dropped down to .220 in 148 contests in 1972. All of which brought his lifetime major league average down somewhat to .261 as he faced 1973. Mike had played 823 games in big time, with 66 homers, four triples, 130 doubles among his 767 hits. Scored 430 runs, drove in 306.

Andrews, outspoken fellow, was prep star in baseball, football, and basketball. Then was an All-American Junior College pass receiver at El Camino College in California before he took up pro baseball, 1962.

Played at Olean, New York–Pennsylvania League; Winston–Salem, Carolina League; Waterloo, Midwest League; Reading, Eastern loop, and Toronto, International League, before joining Red Sox for five games in 1966. During his time with Red Sox his best average was .293 in 1969, with 15 homers, 59 RBI. Following year his average dropped down to .253, partly because at one point he got just one hit in 62 trips to plate. However, he increased his homer production to 17 and his RBI to 65.

Andrews was member of American League All-Star squad, 1969. His WS experience came in 1967 when he hit .308, 4 for 13.

ANKENMAN, FRED NORMAN (Pat) Inf.-BR-TR. B. 12/23/12, Houston, Tex. 5'4", 125. Pat Ankenman never starred in major leagues. In fact, only played 15 games and hit .241. But one of smallest men, one of lightest ever to appear in big league uniform. Unusual experience: his father, Fred Ankenman, bought and sold his own son!

Pat attended Texas U. until summer 1934. Father president of Houston Buffs, Texas League farm club for St. Louis Cardinals. Nobody figured tiny shortstop could make grade in Texas League, then pretty fast circuit. So Pat grabbed chance to sign with another Cardinal farm team, Greensboro, Piedmont League. In less than week, Pat showed such skills in Piedmont League that Papa Ankenman decided he wanted son for his own club. Paid $2500 and one player, for him. Before 1936 over, Pat sold to Cardinals. Played one game in NL that year. Pat landed with Brooklyn Dodgers for 14 games during 1943,44 seasons. That was it for majors. Major league totals: 7 for 29 for .241; 2 runs, 1 double, 3 RBI.

ANSON, ADRIAN CONSTANTINE (Cap) 1B-BR-TR. B. 4/11/52, Marshalltown, Iowa. D. 4/14/22, Chicago, Ill. 6'1", 220. Cap Anson probably qualifies as first superstar of baseball. Piled up all kinds of hitting records. One of greatest first basemen of all time. Twice hit over .400. Player-manager, leading team to five pennants. Credited with starting custom of preseason spring training.

Anson started in 1870, playing at Marshalltown and Rockford, 1871. Next four years caught, played various infield positions for Athletics of Philadelphia in old National Association. Having demonstrated great ability to hit, joined Chicago White Stockings of National League in first season of its existence, 1876. Started out with .343 average. Hit over .300 for twenty seasons, still NL record. In 1879 took over White Stockings as manager, also hit .407. In 1880,81,82 piloted club to first place finish. In 1881 led league hitting again, missing .400 mark by one point. In 1885, another pennant winner. That winter Anson decided to do something about physical condition of his players. Many in habit of reporting for start of season hog-fat, out of shape. Cap ordered players to report almost two months before season started. Whisked them off to Hot Springs, Ark., to "boil out." Also demanded rigorous training sessions to get bodies in shape. Many squawks, but Cap's team won another pennant. Anson credited with setting fine personal example not only for his own team but for all other major leaguers of epoch. Noted for sobriety in era when many players drank excessively, behaved rowdily. Often enforced training rules with fists when players defied them.

Cap—players often referred to him as their captain, rather than manager—with Chicago NL through 1897. Briefly managed N.Y. Giants in 1898. Anson in two "world series," 1885 and 1886, against St. Louis Browns of American Association, then major league. Had .348 mark in 13 games. Lifetime average .339 in 2253 games. Had 3081 hits—first player in history to go over 3000 mark. His .421 average in 1887 fattened by fact walks counted as hits that year. However, his hitting needs no apology. Hall of Fame 1939.

ANTONELLI, JOHN AUGUST   P-BL-TL. B. 4/12/30, Rochester, N.Y. 6'1½", 185. Johnny Antonelli jumped from college campus to major leagues, receiving $65,000 bonus to do so. Fabulous sum in 1948. Became fine pitcher with N.Y. and San Francisco Giants. When hurling skills tapered off, Johnny went to minors for *first* time. Retired. Manager of Memphis (Dixie Association), then in 1973 moved to Tidewater of IL, both affiliates of N.Y. Mets.

Boston Braves paid Antonelli that bonus, 6/29/48. Pitched but four innings in NL that summer. Boston 1949–50,53 (1951–52, military service). Failed to live up to early expectations. After 12–12 mark, 1953, traded to Giants. Blossomed into 21-game winner 1954, losing 7. Tied for NL lead in winning percentage, .750. ERA of 2.29 topped senior circuit. Performance helped Giants win pennant. Dropped to 14–16, 1955. Won 20, lost 13, 1956. Best season after that was 1959, 19–10, when Giants in

S.F. In 1961 with Cleveland AL, Milwaukee NL—1–4 overall. Bowed out of majors.

One World Series, 1954: 3–1 victory over Cleveland. Also relieved final game. ERA 0.84 for Series, which Giants captured in four straight.

Major league performance: 126 wins, 110 losses, 3.34 ERA, 1162 strikeouts, 687 walks, 1992-1/3 innings. Pitched in 1954,56,59 All-Star games—4.26 ERA in 6-1/3 innings, credited with NL's 5–4 victory in 1959.

APARICIO, LUIS ERNESTO SS-BR-TR. B. 4/29/34, Maracaibo, Venezuela. 5'8", 162. Most durable shortstop in major league history. As 1973 season dawned had played in 2467 games—well above previous record, held by Luke Appling, 2218 games. Led AL shortstops in fielding eight straight years (1959–66).

Luis' father was fine shortstop in Venezuela, but not as big as Red Sox infielder, weighing just 145. Papa durable too—played until he was 41. Luis has son in his early teens who may follow in Aparicio tradition.

Luis led AL in stolen bases nine consecutive seasons, 1956–64. Four times he stole more than 50 bases; highest mark 57, in 1964, with Baltimore. With 493 stolen bases to his credit at start of 1973, he had more than any other AL player currently active.

Luis had two years in minors. Waterloo, III League, 1954; hit .282 in 94 games. Following year to Southern Association, Memphis; .273 in 150 games; led league in stolen bases with 48, in total putouts, assists for shortstops, and tied for lead in errors. In his first season in majors, 1956, with Chicago AL, Aparicio had similar record—hit .266, led AL in stolen bases (21), topped AL shortstops in putouts, assists, errors. Luis had seven fine seasons with Sox, then followed with five at Baltimore. Back to White Sox for three more years. In final year with Sox, 1970, hit better than ever before, .313 in 146 games. Then traded to Boston AL for 1971.

Brilliant fielding and fine base running resulted in Aparicio's being named to eight All-Star teams. Helped White Sox get into WS in 1959, Baltimore in 1966. Hit .308 in 1959 classic against Dodgers, .250 in 1966 WS, also against L.A., for .286 mark in 10 WS games. At beginning of 1973 season, Luis had been in 2467 big league games (total appearances), with .261 average, 83 homers.

APPLETON, PETER WILLIAM (Jake) P-BR-TR. B. 5/20/04, Terryville, Conn. 6', 180. Born Jablonowski, pitched under that name until 1934 when he legally changed it. Pete had only one year of minor league experience at Waterbury, Eastern League, 1926, when he got his chance with Cincinnati. Was 2–1 with Reds that season (1927); also pitched for Hartford, same year, for more seasoning. In 1928 with Reds and Columbus (American Association). At Columbus 1929, 18–12. Then started four-year stretch in majors, pitching for Cleveland, Boston, New York in AL, without distinguishing himself. Spent 1934 with Baltimore and Rochester in International League, then had 23-9 season at Montreal, same circuit, 1935. Back to majors, Washington, 1936; enjoyed best season of big league career, 14-9. With Senators through 1939. Chicago AL 1940-42. St. Louis AL 1942. Military service 1943-45. Browns again, 1945; later with Washington same season. Since then Appleton with Buffalo, N.Y.; Sherman-Denison, Tex.; Gladewater, Tex.; Augusta, Ga.; Erie, Pa.; Roanoke Rapids, N.C.; Charlotte, N.C.—as either pitcher or manager. Scouted for Washington Senators 1954-60, Minnesota Twins 1961-64. Managed Atlanta, Southern Association, part of 1964 season. Scout for Twins again, 1965-67. Major league record: 57-66, ERA 4.30, 1141 innings.

Graduate of Michigan, Appleton was pianist of rare ability. Makes home at Perth Amboy, N.J.

APPLING, LUCIUS BENJAMIN (Luke) SS-BR-TR. B. 4/2/07, High Point, N.C. 5'11", 200. Luke Appling, former coach for Chicago White Sox, and for 20 years player with same team, recently voted greatest White Sox player of all time. Batting champion of AL twice, 1936 with .388, 1943 with .328. Led AL in assists for shortstops seven seasons. Led AL in shortstop errors six times. Shares with Jo-Jo White unique distinction. Luke and Jo-Jo believed to be only coaches traded for each other. Happened in 1960 as aftermath of first major league managerial trade. Bill DeWitt, then bossing Detroit, traded Jimmie Dykes to Indians for Joe Gordon. Five days later only trade of coaches in history effected. Appling to Cleveland, White to Detroit.

After attending Oglethorpe College, Luke started pro career in fast circuit, Southern Association, 1930. Hit .326 in 104 games with Atlanta. Joined White Sox late that year, hitting .308, six games. Became regular 1931, but didn't get batting average above .300 until 1933—then kept above that mark next 15 of 16 years. In 1940, hit .348, but lost out to Joe DiMaggio.

Appling in military service 1944-45. Leaving Sox after 1950 season, he managed Memphis, Southern Association, 1951-53, winning pennant in 1953. Piloted Richmond, International League, 1954-55. Managed Memphis again, 1959. Coach, Detroit, 1960, until traded to Cleveland 8/8/60. With Indians through 1961. Managed Indianapolis to American Association pennant, 1962. Coach, Baltimore AL, 1963. Coach, Kansas City AL, 1964, until Alvin Dark was fired as manager late in 1967; Appling piloted club closing days of season. Scout, Oakland Athletics, 1968-69. Coach for White Sox 1971-72. His .388 batting average in 1936 stands as highest mark ever attained by AL shortstop. Holds several fielding records. Hall of Fame 1964.

ARLETT, RUSSELL LORIS (Buzz) OF-IB-BLR-TR. B. 1/3/99, Oakland, Calif. D. 5/16/64, Minneapolis, Minn. 6'3½", 225. If they had used designated hitters back in 1920s and 1930s Buzz Arlett probably would have spent many years in major leagues instead of just one. Buzz was with Philadelphia NL for 121 games, 1931, hit .313, had 18 homers, drove in 72 runs—but following season was back in minors.

Arlett, rightfully or wrongly, had reputation of being "loafer" on field. No question that he could hit for average and for distance, but his fielding was pretty atrocious, whether in outfield or at first base. Started out as pitcher with Oakland, Pacific Coast League, and won 22, lost 17 in 1919. Took 29 decisions, 1920, losing 17; then had 19–18 and 25–19 records. By this time club was beginning to utilize him as outfielder for his hitting ability. Also hurt his arm. Won four games, lost nine as hurler, but played total of 149 games and hit .330. After becoming outfielder always hit around .330 and up; usually stole at least 20 bases each year.

St. Louis Cardinals scouted him thoroughly in 1924, but didn't buy him because of his bad outfielding. Once was hit in head by fly ball while scout was watching. Verdict: he'd lose more games fielding than he'd win batting. In 1930 Brooklyn Dodgers were on his trail, but during big argument an umpire whacked him on head with his mask, so he was out of action three weeks. Dodgers bought Ike Boone instead.

After his one year with Phillies, Arlett was with Baltimore, International League, 1932. Hit 54 homers with .339 average. Slapped four homers in game on two separate occasions. Had .343 average with 39 homers in 1933. With Birmingham briefly in 1934, then moved to Minneapolis where he slugged 31 homers in 116 games and hit .319. It was .361 with 25 homers, 1935, and .316 with 15 homers, 1936. Shifted to Syracuse, played just four games in International League, then gave up game.

ARLIN, STEPHEN RALPH P-BR-TR. B. 9/25/45, Seattle, Wash. 6'3", 195. In dentistry you do the work before you send your bill. But Arlin, a dentist, collected a reported $108,000 bonus before he pitched one ball in pro baseball. Philadelphia NL paid Steve this sum, 1966, then gave up on him two years later, fearing dentistry would interfere with baseball development. San Diego Padres took him in expansion draft from Phillies. Finally stuck in majors late 1970. Then chalked up shutout over Atlanta, 2–0, 9/23/70. Lost more games, 19, than any other NL hurler, 1971, but could still be proud of his work. In 13 of 19 defeats, Padres scored two runs or fewer. Five of first 10 major league victories were shutouts. In 1972, Arlin pitched three more shutouts. San Diego and Phillies weakest hitting teams in NL, 1971. Padres weakest club in slugging percentage. Arlin's ERA 3.47. Struck out 156, walked 103 in 228 innings. In 1972, again lost more games than any other NL pitcher—21, with 10 wins, 3.60 ERA for 250 innings, 159 strikeouts, 122 walks. Developed outstanding move toward second; picked nine men off that bag in 1972.

Steve attended Ohio State and completed studies there June 1970. As undergraduate, had 13–2 record, 2.23 ERA in 1965; 11–1, 1.58 ERA, 1966. Ohio State was runner-up, 1965, and won college world series, 1966. Arlin named to all–Big Ten and first team All-America both years. Drafted by Detroit, but did not sign. Then drafted by Phillies, June 1966. Sent to Bakersfield 1966. Reading 1967. Tidewater and San Diego, Pacific Coast League, 1968. Columbus (Ohio) 1969. Brought up by Padres for four games same year—lost one. Salt Lake 1970, until recalled by Padres late in year. During earlier years in pro ball, Arlin continued his studies in dentistry, so 1971 was his first spring training with Padres. During off-season, Arlin practices dentistry. Plays some basketball in industrial league. Karate buff. Married, two children. Grandfather, Harold Arlin, credited with being first announcer to broadcast baseball game over air waves, Forbes Field, Pittsburgh, 1921, Pirates vs. Phillies.

ASHBURN, DON RICHIE OF-BL-TR. B. 3/19/27, Tilden, Nebr. 5'10'', 175. Philadelphia sports telecaster Richie Ashburn spent 15 years in major leagues as fine outfielder, good hitter, heads-up player. Twice led NL in hitting. Chalked up top statistics for circuit in several departments. Three times got more hits than any other NL player: 221 in 1951, 205 in 1953, 215 in 1958. Led league twice in triples; nine times in outfield putouts; three times in outfield assists. Once led, twice tied for lead in outfield double plays. Led NL in stolen bases, 32 in 1948. Hit safely in 23 consecutive games in 1948, NL record for first-year player. Played 731 consecutive games, 6/6/50 through close of 1954 season. Averaged 146 games for 15 seasons, which is about as durable as you can be.

Ashburn started out with Utica, Eastern League, 1945; hit .312 in 108 games. Military service 1946. Back at Utica, 1947; hit .362 in 137 games, winning promotion to Phillies. Besides his two batting titles (.338 in 1955, .350 in 1958) Richie hit .344 in 1951 and .330 in 1953. Not long-ball hitter, but seemed always on base. Four times he led NL in one-base hits, tying league record. Led NL in drawing walks three times, tied for lead once.

After dozen fine years in Philadelphia, traded to Chicago NL, 1/11/60. Two years in Chicago. With N.Y. Mets for 1962 season. Then television beckoned.

Major league totals: 2189 games, 8365 AB, 1322 runs, 2574 hits, 317 doubles, 109 triples, 29 homers, 586 RBI, .308 average, 234 stolen bases. World Series figures not comparable—.176 average in classic of 1950, when Whiz Kids were steamrollered by Yankees in four.

ASHFORD, EMMETT LITTLETON Umpire. B. 11/23/16, Los Angeles, Calif. 5'7", 190. Over 200 black players got their chances to make good in major leagues before Emmett Ashford, capable umpire, got his opportunity to make grade in big league. Emmett made most of it— without bitterness. At birthday party in his honor late in 1971 numerous whites and blacks joined to show affection, respect. "I wish all the bigots and militants could see the way it is," said Margaret, his wife. After retirement at 55 (mandatory age in AL), Ashford now public relations representative in baseball commissioner's office under Bowie Kuhn.

When Emmett broke into majors, 1966, some said he was too much a showboat. Despite perpetual hustling and dramatic gestures, soon won respect of players and managers.

At Jefferson High School, Los Angeles, Ashford was first Negro president of student body, and editor of school newspaper. Attended Chapman College, Orange, California. Entered U.S. Navy, 1944. Later in post office. Took leave of absence from this work to umpire in Southwest International League, 1951. Arizona-Texas League, 1952. Western International League, 1953. Began 12 years in Pacific Coast League, 1954. PCL umpire in chief 1963–65. Prior to joining AL staff, Ashford was umpiring winter ball in Dominican Republic, where Julian Javier one of big favorites. Emmett at one point called Javier out on three strikes. Javier lunged at him, gave him left to jaw. Ashford fought back until others separated the two. Javier was suspended, had to go on air to apologize because of Ashford's popularity. When Joe Cronin, AL president, heard details of incident, he was satisfied that Ashford could handle himself in tough situation and bought his contract.

Besides umpiring baseball, in earlier days Emmett officiated at high school basketball games, later at football and basketball games at UCLA and Southern Cal. Opera lover.

ASPROMONTE, KENNETH JOSEPH Mgr.-Inf.-BR-TR. B. 9/22/31, Brooklyn, N.Y. 6', 175. Manager, Cleveland Indians, 1972–73. Brother of Bob Aspromonte. Baseball has taken him to far corners of globe, literally. Played three years in Japan, with Taiyo Whales, 1964–66.

After leaving St. John's U., 1950, Ken joined Oneonta (N.Y.), Canadian-American League, but didn't linger long (18 games). Then Kinston (N.C.), Scranton, San Jose, Louisville, Roanoke, Birmingham between 1950 and 1955. Two years with San Francisco, Pacific Coast League, 1956–57, 140 games each year, winning batting title 1957 with .334. Red Sox brought him up for 24 games that year, but following spring was traveling again—traded to Washington, 5/1/58. Got into 98 games that year, hit only .219. All of 1959 with Senators, 70 games, .244

average. Then to Cleveland, 5/15/60. Hit .290 in 117 games for Indians. Divided 1961 between Cleveland and Los Angeles AL. Divided 1962 between Cleveland and Milwaukee NL. With Cubs 1963; sent to Salt Lake City later that year. At this point Aspromonte decided he wanted some security. Found it for three years in Japan. Skipped baseball 1967, but back with Cleveland organization 1968, managing Sarasota, Gulf Coast. Promoted to Reno, California League, 1969. Wichita, American Association, 1970–71. Then came chance to manage in majors.

AUSTIN, JAMES PHILIP (Pepper) 3B-BLR-TR. B. 12/8/79, Swansea, Wales. D. 4/6/65, Laguna Beach, Calif. 5'7½", 155. First of Branch Rickey's "Sunday managers." Rickey, field boss of St. Louis Browns, had promised his mother on entering pro ball that he would not go near ball park on Sabbath. So Austin, then Browns' third baseman, took charge once each week. (Later, when Rickey managed Cardinals, Barney Shotton was Sunday manager.)

Austin's father brought family to Cleveland when Jimmy eight. Became apprentice machinist but switched to baseball with Dayton, Central League, 1904–06. Next two seasons with Omaha, Western League. Then bought by New York AL, playing there 1909–10. St. Louis AL 1911–22, as player. After that, appeared in one game in each of four seasons, since fans loved his peppery play. Coached Browns from later days as player until end of 1932. Coach, Chicago AL, 1933–40. Served as interim manager of Browns for brief periods, 1913, 18, 23. Lifetime record: .246 average in 1580 major league games. Not power hitter. Stole 244 bases.

AUTRY, GENE Executive. B. 9/29/08, Tioga, Tex. Angel of Angels, California variety. If ball club doesn't make money for him it will be just about only enterprise old cowboy singer has invested in which hasn't. Autry is chairman of board of one of first AL expansion teams. Involved in countless revenue-producing deals. Oil wells, flying school, ranches, music publishing houses, movie theaters, company that produces films for television, hotel chain, crop-dusting service. Has endorsed scores of products from hair oil to cap pistols.

Railroad telegrapher at 18. Practiced guitar and singing between trains. Clicked with song he and pal wrote, "That Silver Haired Daddy of Mine." Has written many songs. Popularized "Rudolph the Red-Nosed Reindeer" and "Tumbling Tumbleweeds." Since 1930 has sold more records than anyone can count, perhaps 50 million. "Gene Autry's Melody Ranch" a favorite program in radio's heyday. His horse Champion probably better known than Man o' War or Bucephalus. Pilot, then flight officer, during World War II; ferried planes, cargo to India.

Angels finished eighth in first season, 1961. Surprised baseball world with third-place finish 1962. But team has not lived up to optimism engendered that year. Autry went along with Bill Rigney as manager until 1969, then selected Lefty Phillips and Del Rice to call signals. Fred Haney first general manager for Angels. Succeeded by Dick Walsh, later Harry Dalton. Haney remains as consultant. Team started out as Los Angeles Angels, playing games at Chavez Ravine, home of Dodgers. Moved to new stadium in Anaheim, 1965. Since known as California.

AVERILL, HOWARD EARL (Rock)   OF-BL-TR. B. 3/21/02, Snohomish, Wash. 5'9½'', 172. Back in 1928 $50,000 was fancy price to pay for ball player. But Earl Averill proved he was worth it to Cleveland Indians, who coughed up that sum and paid it to San Francisco, Pacific Coast League. Averill had three brilliant seasons with Seals: 1926, 188 games with .348 average; 1927, .324, 183 contests; 1928, .354 in 189 games. Plenty of extra bases, RBI. Made grade immediately with Cleveland. Played 152 games, hit .330 with 18 homers and 97 RBI. Continued slugging for rest of his AL career in Forest City. Best season for average, 1936, .378. In doubleheader, 9/17/30, slugged three homers in opener, one more in nightcap, plus single, double, triple. Began to slow down, 1939. To Detroit 6/14/39. Tigers dropped him after 1940 season. Boston NL 1941, eight games; retired after 78 games same season with Seattle, PCL. Major league totals: 318 average, 1669 games, 2020 hits in 6359 trips, 1224 runs, 401 doubles, 128 triples, 238 homers, 1165 RBI. WS appearances, three hitless times at bat in 1940 (Tigers lost to Reds in seven).

Earl's son, also Earl, catcher, played with Indians, White Sox, Cubs, Phillies, L.A. Angels, 1956–63.

AVILA, ROBERTO FRANCISCO GONZALEZ (Bobby)   Inf.-BR-TR. B. 6/7/26, Veracruz, Mexico. 5'10'', 175. Bobby Avila spent most of career with Cleveland. Climaxed it with AL batting title, 1954—.341, 143 games. Big name in Mexican baseball for many years as player, manager, executive.

Bobby had 56 games with Baltimore, International League, 1948, before making grade with Indians, 1949. Regular second baseman for Cleveland till 1958. Led AL second sackers in fielding, 1953. In 1952 had three unusual records for keystoners: set AL record for most assists in extra-inning game, 19; most chances in extra-inning contest, 19; equaled major league record for fewest chances in two consecutive games, one in 18 innings. Not power hitter, but had 80 round-trippers in 1300 major league games; 15 in 1954, best year. His 1296 hits also included 185 doubles, 35 triples. Scored 725 runs. Drove in 467. Stole 78 bases. Major league average, .281. Divided 1959 season among Baltimore AL, Boston AL, Milwaukee NL. One World Series, 1954, 2 for 15, .133 average.

AZCUE, JOSE JOAQUIN C-BR-TR. B. 8/18/39, Cienfuegos, Cuba. 6', 190. Joe Azcue sat out 1971 baseball season because of salary dispute with Dick Walsh, then general manager of California Angels. Had to earn living for wife, three children. Became laborer. Poured concrete, shoveled, cleaned up, eight hours every day, rain or shine. Returned to Angels, 1972, convinced that baseball hours and salary, even after being cut, better than laborer's.

Joe started pro ball in 1956. Douglas, Moultrie, Savannah, Ga.; Palatka, Fla.; Havana, Jersey City, Vancouver, Portland before Kansas City AL, 1962. Briefly with Cincinnati, 1960, 14 games. Kansas City sent him to Cleveland 5/25/63. Remained with Indians until sent during 1969 season to Boston AL, thence to Angels same year. Smart catcher. Backstop for two no-hitters: Sonny Siebert's, June 1966, against Washington; Clyde Wright's against Oakland A's, 7/3/70. Angel management gave Wright $500 bonus, ignored man who called game. Wright gave Joe $100 of bonus.

At time Azcue had salary dispute with Dick Walsh, he had been in 895 major league games, owned .252 batting average. In 1972, played three games with Angels, then sent to Milwaukee 7/28/72. Brewers used him in 11 games, released him 11/15/72. Hit .125 for season. Player-coach for Oklahoma City, 1973.

BAGBY, JAMES CHARLES JACOB, JR.   P-BR-TR. B. 9/8/16, Cleveland, Ohio. 6'2", 175. Son of old-time Cleveland pitcher who also became Cleveland pitcher. Young Jim won 97 major league games, lost 96, for .503 percentage. His father won 128, lost 88, for .593. Jim Jr. took part in 303 major league games, pitched 1666 1/3 innings, had 3.96 ERA (father's, 3.10). However, younger Bagby pitched with lively ball. Jim, like father, walked more men than he struck out—608 to 431. One WS, while with Boston AL, 1946: one earned run in three innings, 3.00 ERA; no decisions.

Young Bagby started out at Charlotte 1935. Rocky Mount 1936. Hazleton 1937. Next stop Boston AL, 15–11, rookie season, 1938. Broke even, 5–5, in 1939; optioned to Little Rock for part of same season. After 10–16 mark with Red Sox in 1940, traded to Cleveland. Best seasons at Cleveland, 1942 (17–9), 1943 (17–14). In 1946, back with Red Sox, 7–6. Like his father's, Jim Jr.'s final season in majors spent with Pirates. Had 5–4 record, 1947, with 4.67 ERA. During big league career, Bagby had 13 shutouts; his father 15.

BAGBY, JAMES CHARLES JACOB, SR. (Sarge) P-BLR-TR. B. 10/5/89, Barnett, Ga. D. 7/28/54, Marietta, Ga. 6', 170. Jim Bagby won 31 games in 1920 to help lead Cleveland to its first AL pennant. Many years later his son, Jim, Jr., pitched for Indians, but never approached dad's top year. Jim, Jr.'s best mark was 17–9 in 1942. Elder Bagby's 31 victories in 1920 not matched again until Lefty Grove took 31 decisions in 1931. In 1920 WS against Brooklyn, Jim 1–1, with 1.80 ERA. Started second game of classic, but lost to Burleigh Grimes 3–0. Touched for seven hits, two earned runs in six innings. Dodgers' other run scored on Bagby's error. Came back in fifth game to win 8–1, allowing 13 hits. Helped own cause with single and homer, driving in three markers. Also helped by Bill Wambsganss' famous unassisted triple play, ending incipient Brooklyn rally. In that historic game, Indian outfielder Elmer Smith hit first grand slam in WS history.

Bagby started out in 1910. Augusta, Ga., Hattiesburg, Montgomery, New Orleans through 1915, with brief spell at Cincinnati NL, 1912, 2–1. Made grade with Cleveland 1916, leaving Ohio metropolis after 1922 season. Final year with Pittsburgh, 1923. Had 23–13 record in 1917, then came up with 17–16 and 18–11 records before that 31–12 season. Dropped to 14–12, 1921; 4–5, 1922, before joining Pirates. Was 3–2 in final year in big time. Major league record: 128 victories, 88 defeats, 3.10 ERA, 1827 2/3 innings. Walked 458, fanned 450.

BAHNSEN, STANLEY RAYMOND P-BR-TR. B. 12/15/44, Council Bluffs, Iowa. 6'2", 188. Stan Bahnsen was traded to Chicago White Sox 12/2/71 in exchange for Rick McKinney, who went to Yankees. Won 21 games for manager Chuck Tanner in 1972. This was his best season since coming to majors. Victory total was four more than he gained in 1968 when he took Rookie of Year honors in voting by Baseball Writers Association of America. *Sporting News* named him AL Rookie Pitcher of Year. Bahnsen attributed some of his success to White Sox pitching coach Johnny Sain. Said Sain got him to throw his curve slower and to vary delivery of his slider so as to keep opposing hitters off balance.

Stan attended U. of Nebraska before joining New York Yankee organization, 1965. Received reported $30,000 bonus. Spent rest of 1965 at Columbus, Ga., in Southern Association—2–2. Was 10–7 at Toledo in 1966, and 1–1 with Yanks same season. Spent 1967 at Syracuse, 9–11. Rookie season with Yanks, 1968, resulted in 17–12 mark, 2.06 ERA; fanned 168, walked 68. Dropped to 9–16 in 1969. Then 14–11, 14–12 records before Yanks dealt him to Chicago. His 1972 record 21–16 accompanied by 3.61 ERA. Entered 1973 with 3.21 ERA for major league career consisting of 196 games, 41 complete; had 76–68 record, 691 strikeouts, 385 walks in 1238 innings.

While in International League Bahnsen pitched two seven-inning no-hitters. One of them, against Buffalo 7/9/67, was perfect game.

BAILEY, ROBERT SHERWOOD (Beetles) Inf.-OF-BR-TR. B. 10/13/42, Long Beach, Calif. 6', 185. Bob Bailey signed with Pittsburgh Pirates 6/16/61 for bonus reported to be $135,000, certainly one of largest ever paid an untried player. Son of Paul (Buck) Bailey, who was minor league infielder in 1939–40.

Bailey's best season probably was 1970 with Montreal Expos, when he hit .287, higher than before or since, slapped 28 homers, and drove in 84 runs. After completion of 1972 season he owned lifetime major league average of .252 for 1359 games. Had 1145 hits, good for 173 doubles, 35 triples, 126 homers, with 565 runs scored and 541 RBI.

Bob needed couple of seasons in minors after getting that big bonus. In high school never hit less than .450, but in first pro season his average was .220 in 75 games at Asheville, Sally League. But with that experience under his belt he moved up to Columbus, International League, and hit .299 for 153 games, with 28 homers, 108 RBI. That same season he also played 14 games with Pirates, then stuck in majors. Best season with Pittsburgh was 1964 when he hit .281 in 143 contests. Traded to L.A. Dodgers after 1966 season. Had two years under Walter Alston, but never got going with bat, hitting .227 in 221 games in those two seasons. Sold to Montreal NL 10/21/68. In 1971 had only 11 errors in 274 chances during 120 games played at third base. Also has played considerably at first base and in outfield.

Among his honors in minors were Player of Year and Rookie of Year in International League, 1962. *Sporting News* also named him Minor League Player of Year that same season. Led NL third basemen in double plays, 1963, with 38.

BAKER, DELMER DAVID (Del) C-BR-TR. B. 5/3/92, Sherwood, Oreg. 5′11½″, 176. Self-effacing Del Baker spent 50 years in baseball, 49 of them in uniform. Managed Detroit Tigers to AL pennant, world championship, 1940. One of Del's important moves as manager was selection of Floyd Giebell to pitch against Bob Feller 9/27/40. Rookie from Buffalo outpitched Feller and Cleveland Indians, clinched pennant for Tigers before 45,553 fans. Schoolboy Rowe had been expected to pitch. Ten minutes before game Del announced switch to Giebell. "Kid's hot," said Baker. Del did not want to manage Tigers, said so while coaching under Mickey Cochrane. However, when Mickey removed 8/6/38, front office persuaded him to take over. Fourth-place finish.

Del, as young man, was bookkeeper, catcher on side. Came from family of 11 children. Started pro ball at Helena, Mont., 1911–12. Lincoln, Nebr., 1913. Sold to Detroit for $5000. Spent 1914–16 with Tigers. San Francisco, Pacific Coast League, 1917. Military service 1918. Portland, PCL, 1919–21. Mobile 1922. Oakland, PCL, 1923–27. Ogden 1927–28. Fort Worth 1929. Playing manager, Beaumont (Detroit organization), 1930–32. Coach, Detroit, 1933 until he became manager. Manager through 1942. Coach, Cleveland, 1943–44. Coach, Boston AL, 1945–48. Manager, Sacramento, PCL, 1949. Manager, San Diego, PCL, 1950–51. Special assignments for Cleveland, 1952. Coach, Boston AL, 1953–60.

Baker great sign stealer as coach, but downplayed skills. Besides his pennant winner, had two fifth-place finishes, two fourths (one a tie). As major league player, took part in 172 games, hit .209—63 hits, with 9 doubles, 4 triples, no homers.

BAKER, JOHN FRANKLIN (Home Run) 3B-BL-TR. B. 3/13/86, Trappe, Md. D. 6/28/63, Trappe, Md. 5'11", 173. Frank Baker earned his nickname hard way. Was home run specialist in era when lively ball unknown. Pitchers doctored ball with foreign substances, making it rough on hitters. Spitball legal those days. Baker wielded 52-oz. bat, about 20 oz. heavier than those now generally used. Got nickname 1911 when he led AL in four-masters, nine. Slugged two more in World Series, helping Athletics beat Giants, four games to two.

Gained respect of opposing pitchers early. In first game as regular third baseman 4/24/09, first inning, A's put men on second and third with Danny Murphy due to hit. Red Sox intentionally walked Murphy, seasoned hitter, to get at Baker. Frank slapped first pitch over right field fence for bases-loaded homer. Baker hit only four homers that season but led league in triples with 19. In 1910 he managed only two circuit clouts but was top man in AL with 9, 10 and 12 in successive seasons. In 1914 his eight homers tied him for leadership with Wahoo Sam Crawford of Detroit.

In 1911 Series, Baker hit .375 and figured in a typewriter tiff between Christy Mathewson and Rube Marquard, Giant pitchers. In second game, banged homer off Marquard with one on base and A's took contest 3–1. In ghost-written newspaper column next day, Mathewson said Baker's homer due to Rube's carelessness. Column said Rube should have thrown Baker low curve ball, his weakness. Christy's turn came next day. After eight innings Giants 1–0 lead. With one out in ninth Mathewson fed Baker low curve ball. Bat met ball—Baker's second homer of Series, tying game. A's won game in 11th. Next morning Marquard, in *his* ghost-written column, wrote: "Just what happened, Matty? It couldn't be that you grew careless, or did you?"

Baker started as pitcher with semipro team at Ridgley, Md. His batting was so good he soon became third baseman. Scout for Baltimore, Eastern League, got him tryout but Jack Dunn, owner and manager, thought him too clumsy, releasing him after five games and .133 batting average, 1907. More semipro ball at Cambridge, Md., Reading, Tri-State League, 1908 with .299 average in 119 games. Bought by A's 8/28/08. Nine games that fall with .290, nine hits in 31 AB. With A's 1908–14. When refused sufficient raise for 1915, Baker spent season with semipros at Upland, Pa. Sold by A's to Yankees 2/15/16, for reported $35,000. With Yanks 1916–22 except 1920 when stayed home because of wife's illness and subsequent death.

Lifetime AL average .307. Hit .334, 1911; .347, next season; .336 1913. AL career total of 93 homers, 1,012 RBI. Left something to be desired as third baseman but led AL seven times in total putouts for hot corner; twice had most assists; led in fielding average three times. However, made 45 errors in each of two seasons, 42 in another. By contrast Brooks Robinson had 16 errors 1971 season.

Baker part of Connie Mack's famous $100,000 infield, along with Stuffy McInnis, Eddie Collins and Jack Barry—until Mack broke up team after A's lost 1914 Series to Boston Braves in four straight. In World Series 1910,11,13 batted .409, .375 and .450. In 1914 Series, average dropped to .250. With Yanks 1921, .250 in Series. Final Series 1922, also with Yanks, failed to hit in only time at bat as pinch hitter.

Leaving majors Baker played and managed Easton club, Eastern Shore League, 1924. Nonplaying manager 1925. President, Easton club, 1941. Had Jimmie Foxx on his 1924 team at Easton. Always farmer at heart, in later years Baker managed several he owned. Raised and trained hunting dogs, hunted for recreation. Hall of Fame 1955. "Never in all my dreams," he said, "did I dream that I would ever be in the Hall of Fame."

BAKER, JOHNNIE B., JR. (Dusty) OF-BR-TR. B. 6/15/49, Riverside, Calif. 6'2", 195. Pleasant surprise for Atlanta Braves, 1972, his first full year in majors. Young center fielder, 23, in running for NL batting championship until latter part of year. Finished third, .321, behind Billy Williams, .333, Ralph Garr, .325. Beautiful fielder as well; strong arm.

Signed with Braves 8/23/67 for modest bonus. Had attended American River Junior College in California after athletic career in high school. Baseball, halfback in football, forward in basketball, sprinter and broad jumper in track.

Nine games with Austin, Texas League, 1967. Six games with West Palm Beach, Florida State League, 1968; and 52 contests at Greenwood, Western Carolina League, where he hit .342. Brought up to Braves briefly that year, and in 1969,70,71, playing 51 games in all in NL, hit .226. But spent most of these summers at Shreveport, Texas League, and Richmond, International League. Twice hit better than .300 with Richmond. Then came 1972: .321 average, 17 homers, 76 RBI, 27 doubles, 2 triples, 62 runs. This brought major league record up to .305 average in 178 games, 67 runs scored, 84 RBI, 166 hits.

BALL, CORNELIUS (Neal) SS-2B-BR-TR. B. 4/22/81, Grand Haven, Mich. D. 10/15/57, Bridgeport, Conn. 5'7", 145. Neal Ball enjoyed one fabulous day in major leagues. True, he played in 496 games but was run-of-the-mill performer. Lifetime major league batting average of .251. Of his 404 hits, 56 were doubles, 17 triples, 4 home runs. Stole 92 bases.

In only three of his seven seasons in majors did he play in 100 games.

Yet 7/19/09 is written in gold for Mr. Ball. On that day, in second inning of first game of doubleheader, Ball was playing shortstop for Cleveland. No outs. Amby McConnell was batter for Boston Red Sox, Jake Stahl on first base, Heinie Wagner (years later manager for Red Sox) on second. McConnell hit sharp liner at Ball, who grabbed it, touched second base before Wagner could get back. Then tagged surprised Stahl coming into second. First recorded unassisted triple play in history of major leagues! To celebrate occasion, Ball came to bat in Cleveland half of same inning, smashed one of his four major league homers. (Several unassisted triple plays have been made since, notably famous triple killing made by Bill Wambsganss in 1920 World Series. But Ball had honor of doing it first.)

Ball with N.Y. AL, 1907–09; Cleveland, 1909–12; Boston AL, 1912–13. Appeared in 1912 WS with Red Sox, fanning his only chance as pinch batsman.

BALL, PHILIP DeCATESBY   Executive. B. 10/22/64, Keokuk, Iowa. D. 10/22/33, St. Louis, Mo. Tough, austere, frank individualistic baseball magnate. Helped promote old Federal League, then became outspoken owner of old St. Louis Browns. Stalwart friend of Ban Johnson. Antagonist of Branch Rickey. Fearless of Judge Landis, whom he fought in courts, baseball councils.

Son of engineer who built ice plants. Father wanted his middle name to honor Ap Catesby, famous Welshman. Mother balked at "Ap." Compromise, "De Catesby." Phil learned from father; used his skill to become millionaire. Baseball his first love. Promising catcher with Shreveport team until knife fight in barroom almost cost loss of left hand. Cowpuncher in Southwest. Worked on railroad. Earned $50 monthly, penny-pinched until he had $1000. Then bought into ice plant. Was on way to fortune. When idea for third major league blossomed, Ball, along with Harry Sinclair (later involved in Teapot Dome scandals), backed St. Louis entry in Federal League. When Federal League went under, Ball bought St. Louis Browns' franchise. Helped work out agreement allowing peaceful return of Federal League ball players AL, NL. One of his early acts was to remove Branch Rickey from field management of Browns. Rickey had contract, which was continued through 1917. Then Branch received offer from St. Louis Cardinals for $15,000 salary, about twice what he was making with Browns. Rickey claimed he had Ball's consent to accept Cardinal offer. Ball sought injunction for breach of contract, but eventually Rickey moved to Redbirds.

When "Black Sox" scandal hit baseball after 1919 WS, all major league magnates, except Ball, begged Judge Landis to become czar of game. Landis dictated own terms. All club presidents signed agreement—except Ball, who did permit his vice president, Bob Quinn, to sign, however. In early days of radio Ball fought to prevent broadcasts from major league parks. Nearly came to blows with Col. Ruppert, Yankee owner, in hassle that ultimately resulted in downfall of Ban Johnson.

Ball's dream, pennant for Browns, never realized while alive. Close, 1922, one game behind Yankees. In 1933, Ball signed Rogers Hornsby to manage Browns. Oddly, Branch Rickey, intermediary, worked out knotty details of contract—endless hours, days of negotiations. Rickey later confessed to never encountering more difficult job than getting those two rugged individualists together.

Aviation enthusiast. One of early businessmen to own his own plane.

BAMBERGER, GEORGE IRVIN P-BR-TR. B. 8/1/25, Staten Island, N.Y. 6', 190. Pitching coach, Baltimore Orioles, considered one of best in profession. In 1971 Oriole pitching staff boasted four 20-game winners, first time this was done since 1920 White Sox. Bamberger given credit for feat. Insisted that hurlers throw every day, run to keep legs in shape.

Bamberger took job of Baltimore pitching coach 1968. Dave McNally had elbow trouble—but finished with at least 20 victories, 1968,71. His first year with Baltimore, 1971, Pat Dobson had 20 victories, more than ever before during his career. Mike Cuellar joined Orioles, 1969; had 23–11, 24–8 and 20–9 records after George coached him. Never before had he come close to winning 20 in one season. Jim Palmer chalked up 16–4, 20–10 and 20–9 records in 1969,70,71 under Bamberger's tutelage. Most observers believe these things more than coincidence. George didn't pitch much in majors—a little over 14 innings, 1951–52 with N.Y. Giants, 1959 with Orioles. But playing career covered 18 years, 15 at Triple A level. Retired as player after 1963 season. In majors neither won nor lost decision. In minors won 213 games. Pitched no-hitter for Ottawa against Toronto, International League, 1951. Holds Pacific Coast League record for most innings pitched without walking batter, 68-2/3, set at Vancouver, where he played for seven years. Served as Orioles' minor league pitching instructor four years before taking present job with parent team. Suffered coronary ailment 1971; missed WS against Reds.

BANCROFT, DAVID JAMES (Beauty) SS-BRL-TR. B. 4/20/92, Sioux City, Iowa. D. 10/9/72, Superior, Wis. 5'9½", 160. Dave Bancroft played shortstop beautifully—especially during early 1920s when he was key man in N.Y. Giant infield along with Frankie Frisch, George Kelly and Heinie Groh. Missed .300 mark in 1920 by one point. Then gave Mgr. John McGraw .319, .321 and .304 averages next three seasons; club won pennant each year. Travis Jackson was coming along about this time and McGraw traded Bancroft to Boston NL. Managed Braves 1924–27, but had little material. Continued playing and hit above .300 twice while in Hub. After being released by Boston, Banny played two seasons with Brooklyn, 1928–29. Returned to Giants as coach, 1930, and took part in 10 games. Remained on coaching lines through 1932. Manager, Minneapolis, American Association, 1933. Piloted Sioux City, Western League, 1936; St. Cloud, Northern League, 1947.

Bancroft got his minor league experience starting 1909 with Duluth and Superior in Wisconsin-Minnesota League. Portland, Pacific Coast League, 1912–14. Then Philadelphia NL. Phils traded him to Giants 6/8/20. With four flag winners: Philadelphia, 1915; Giants, 1921–23. Hit .172 in 24 WS games. Major league totals: .279, 1913 games, 2004 hits, 320 doubles, 77 triples, 32 homers, 579 RBI, 145 stolen bases. Hall of Fame 1971.

BANDO, SALVATORE LEONARD (Sal) 3B-BR-TR. B. 2/13/44, Cleveland, Ohio. 6', 195. Sal Bando looks back to 1969, his second full season in majors, with special satisfaction: named captain of Oakland A's; only player in AL to play every inning of every game in season; named to AL All-Star squad; hit 31 homers, drove in 113 runs, hit .281, scored 106 runs. Had played in 162 games in his first full year with Oakland: 67 runs scored, 9 homers, 67 RBI, .251 average.

Bando attended Arizona State. Helped team to Western Athletic Conference championship, berth in college WS, 1964, with .347 batting average. Helped school repeat in 1965; this time Bando hit .480 in college WS and voted outstanding player. Then, for reported $30,000 bonus, signed with A's, then in Kansas City. En route to majors, Sal played at Burlington (Iowa), Mobile, Vancouver, 1965–67. Briefly with Kansas City 1966,67. Stayed with club 1968, A's first season in Oakland. Hitting dimmed, 1972, .236. Still played 152 games as A's Won flag. In WS: 7 for 26, .269 average, 1 RBI. Entered 1973 with .258 lifetime average, 842 games; 99 homers, 117 doubles, 17 triples, 759 hits, 417 runs, 433 RBI. Considered one of best defensive third basemen in majors, unusually fine arm. Again made AL All-Star team, 1972, 73.

BANKS, ERNEST Inf.-BR-TR. B. 1/31/31, Dallas, Tex. 6'1", 186. "Greatest Cub ever." That's what Chicago fans voted as proper designation for Ernie Banks. Quite an honor, considering other Cub luminaries throughout years—Hack Wilson, Phil Cavarretta, famed Tinker-Evers-Chance combination, Stan Hack, Gabby Hartnett, to name a few. Banks left active ranks after 1971 season to become full-time coach. Had been player-coach since 2/28/67. Age plus arthritic condition in left knee slowed Banks down late in career. Had compiled all kinds of Cub slugging and fielding records. Played more games than any other Cub, 2528; more at bats, 9421; more runs scored, 1305; more hits, 2583; more doubles, 407; more home runs, 512; more total bases, 4706; more RBI, 1636; more extra-base hits, 1009.

Ernie hit 12 grand slam homers during career; led NL in homers, 1958 and 1960; twice led NL shortstops in fielding. And more. MVP in NL, 1958, 59. Apart from performance on field, Banks popular, respected understanding of others.

Ernie was one of 11 children. Life wasn't easy. Father, who had played semipro ball, insisted Ernie go through high school. Ernie played end on high school football team. Also basketball. Good at broad jump in track. One day owner of Amarillo Colts, Negro team, spotted Banks playing softball. Signed him to play baseball with club which traveled through Texas, New Mexico, Kansas, Oklahoma. That was 1948. By 1950 Banks with Kansas City Monarchs, Negro American League—but only after finishing high school that year. Monarchs traveled up to 20,000 miles a year, according to Banks. Recompense uncertain—and modest. "Our biggest night was in Hastings, Nebr. We got $15 apiece." Spent most of 1951–52 in U. S. Army, including service in Europe. Rejoined Monarchs 1953. Cubs noted his diamond skills, paid Monarchs $15,000 for him. Joined Chicago 9/14/53, first black on Cubs.

On 9/30/53 Cardinal righthander Gerry Staley fed fast ball to rookie shortstop. Banks belted it into left field stands at Busch Stadium for his first major league home run. His 500th homer came 5/12/70, putting him in select company of Ruth, Ott, Mantle, Mays, Aaron, among others. Brilliant shortstop until 1961, when made shift to first base. Also played a bit at third base and outfield. Among his distinctions: in 1960 led league in double plays as shortstop—and later (1962) led NL in DPs as first sacker.

Ernie was wrist hitter. Did not make high averages—his best (for full season) was .313, 1958. Extra-base production consistently good. High mark for homers was 47, 1958. Five times had more than 40 homers; 13 times more than 20 homers. Improved his hitting early in career by cutting down weight of his bat. Had used 34-oz. stick. Got better results with 31-oz. bludgeon. Appeared in 13 All-Star games for NL.

BARBER, STEPHEN DAVID   P-BL-TL. B. 2/22/39, Takoma Park, Md. 6′, 198. Steve Barber's fast ball once clocked at close to 100 miles per hour, when winning pitcher for Baltimore Orioles. Injuries plagued him in recent years. Seemed to reach end of major league trail May 1972, when released by Atlanta Braves. But soon signed on with California Angels.

Barber owned 18–12 record with Orioles, 1961; 20–13 record two years later; 15–10, 1965; 10–5, 2.30 ERA in 1966, helping Orioles to pennant. However, Orioles defeated L.A. Dodgers four straight in WS without even using Barber. From that time on, downhill for Steve. After 4–9 with Baltimore, 1967, Yankees gambled on him. Trade came 7/5/67. Was 6–9 for Yanks, giving him 10–18 for season. Never pitched many innings after that.

Steve started out at Paris, Tex., Sooner State League, 1957. Then Aberdeen, S. Dak., Dublin, Ga., and Amarillo, Tex., before joining Baltimore, 1960. Good start as rookie, 10–7, 3.21 ERA. During stay with Orioles, pitched 8-2/3innings of no-hit loss to Detroit 4/30/67. Stu Miller pitched last out. Tied for AL lead in shutouts, eight, 1961. In 1960 tied for league lead in wild pitches, 10. In minors, led Alabama-Florida League in wild pitches, 30; tied for lead in wild pitches in Georgia-Florida League; led Sooner State League in hit batsmen, wild pitches with 20 each.

Barber pitched for Yankees and Syracuse 1968. Seattle AL 1969, Tacoma 1970. Chicago NL, Atlanta NL 1970. Richmond 1970. Back to Atlanta 1971, but pitched just 75 innings, 3–1. Early in 1972 pitched 16 innings, 5.63 ERA, before drawing unconditional release. Lifetime major league record as 1973 season began: 1895 innings, 403 games; struck out 1238, walked 906; 3.34 ERA. Two AL All-Star teams, 1963 and 1966. Injured in 1963, had to be replaced. Nor did he play in 1966 game.

BARLICK, ALBERT J. Umpire. B. 4/2/15, Springfield, Ill. 5'10½", 185. Bill Klem was right. Bill, in his 36th NL season when Al Barlick, 25, broke in, predicted Barlick would be top arbiter. Al didn't disappoint Klem. Retired after 1971 season. Now serves NL in liaison capacity, coaching young umpires, observing work of NL referees, scouting umps in Triple A leagues. NL career started 1940. Interrupted by two years in Coast Guard, 1944–45, and two more seasons, 1956–57, with enlarged heart condition. Also missed five days during 1960 over unexplained "misunderstanding" with NL officials. During first ten years never missed an inning because of ill health. In 1946 came close. Ran fever of 103 during night game but stayed on job. Next day fever gone.

Originally coal miner. During strike, took job as sandlot umpire at $1 per game. Went to Northeast Arkansas League, 1936, at $75 a month. Piedmont League same year. Eastern League 1938. International League 1939. Before end of 1940 season was taken by NL as youngest umpire in major league history. In first assignment worked on bases on day Johnny Vander Meer of Cincinnati defeated Phillies to clinch Rhinelanders' second straight pennant. Loud, clear calls of balls and strikes, with unambiguous arm gestures, soon attracted favorable attention from fans and players. Wrigley Field, crowd of 43,000. George Shuba of Brooklyn at bat with three-two count. Next pitch wild, got away from Bob Scheffing, Cub catcher. Barlick thought Shuba foul-tipped ball. Took new ball from pocket, handed to Scheffing as latter turned around to chase pitch. "He didn't foul that ball," yelled Scheffing. Barlick realized his mistake. Meanwhile Shuba reached second base during discussion. Barlick admitted he had made wrong call, also had deprived Scheffing of chance to retrieve ball and make play on Shuba. Made George return to first. When Dodgers protested, Barlock stopped argument, went to Brooklyn dugout, explained play to Mgr. Burt Shotton. Then had announcer explain to fans what had happened.

Once old Milwaukee Braves got on him as they passed umpires' room. Barlick taking shower. When badgering got rough, Barlick, naked, charged into Milwaukee clubhouse. Saw five Braves in shower. "Which one of you wants to take me on?" asked Barlick. "How about you, Mathews?" Eddie, 6'1", 185, all muscle. Cooler heads prevailed. No fisticuffs.

Barlick officiated Ewell Blackwell's no-hitter, 6/18/47, against Boston. Asked what player he would want if he were general manager of major league club, Barlick quickly said, "Roberto Clemente. He can do everything."

BARNARD, ERNEST SARGENT Executive. B. 7/17/74, West Columbia, W. Va. D. 3/37/31, Rochester, Minn. E. S. Barnard, president of American League about three and a half years, was ex-football coach, ex-sports editor. Raised in Westerville, Ohio, home of Otterbein College, which he attended. Graduated 1895. While undergraduate, organized that college's first football team, coached it. Team even defeated Ohio State. Later successfully coached U. S. Army and Ohio Medical University football teams. Secretary, Columbus Builders' Exchange. This organization on verge of disbanding but 18 months later Barnard had it flourishing. Quit to become sports editor, *Columbus Dispatch*. Teamed up with Robert (Bob) Quinn in helping organize National Association of Professional Baseball Leagues (minors). Quinn later executive with St. Louis Browns, Brooklyn Dodgers, Boston Red Sox. Barnard became secretary, Cleveland AL, 1903, then business manager, vice president, finally president. Elected president, AL, 11/2/27. Credited with much of success in adoption of major-minor league agreement. Also planned construction of Cleveland Stadium, seating 77,000 spectators.

BARNES, JESSE LAWRENCE P-BL-TR. B. 8/26/92, Guthrie, Okla. D. 9/9/61, Midway City, Calif. 6', 170. Jesse Barnes one of John McGraw's stalwart pitchers half century ago. In 1919 won 25 games for Giants, losing nine. Following year, 20–15; 1921, 15–9. Barnes topped that season with two World Series victories over Yankees. Younger brother Virgil also pitched for Giants. Jesse wound up major league career with 153–149 record; Virgil with 61–59.

Jesse pitched for Keokuk (Iowa), Central League, 1912; Davenport (Iowa), Three-Eye League, 1913–15, with brief tryout with Chicago NL. At end of 1915 season went up to Boston Braves, 4–0. Braves kept Barnes through 1917 season then traded to Giants. Was 6–1, 1918, before spending rest of year in military service. When mustered out, became one of McGraw's aces.

During 1921 WS against Yankees, Barnes relieved Fred Toney in third inning of third game. Pitched rest of way, allowing just one run. His first Series victory. In sixth contest, again relieved Toney, this time in first inning. Held Yanks to two runs rest of distance, struck out 10, captured second Series victory. Giants ultimately won Series five games to three. In 1922 Series Barnes was hurler in famous 3–3 tie game, stopped by "darkness." After 10 innings of play umpire Hildebrand stopped play, though many claimed sun still shining. Could have played at least half hour longer. Fans indignant, booed umpire and Judge Landis. Landis tried to mollify angry mob by giving receipts, about $120,000, to charity. Fans wanted to see battle to finish. Barnes had allowed eight hits, two earned runs. Bob Shawkey, Yankee pitcher, had allowed Giants same number of hits and three runs. But for an error by Giant shortstop Bancroft, Barnes would have had 3–2 victory in nine innings.

Jesse traded to Boston NL 6/7/23. Braves sent him to Brooklyn for 1926–27. Then retired. Wound up with lifetime ERA of 3.22 in majors in 2570 innings. Among his 153 victories were 26 shutouts and one no-hit game for Giants 5/7/22 against Phillies. His World Series totals: 26 innings, 2–0, 14 hits, 8 walks, 24 strikeouts.

Barnes with family on vacation trip; died in motel, heart attack.

BARNEY, REX EDWARD P-BR-TR. B. 12/19/24, Omaha, Nebr. 6'2½", 190. Rex Barney, at times, looked like combination of Walter Johnson, Dazzy Vance, Bob Feller. But Dodger fireballer had trouble finding strike zone. Unbelievably wild on many occasions. George Sisler, Chuck Dressen, Johnny Corriden, Clyde Sukeforth, Hugh Casey, Bobby Bragan, Branch Rickey, several others tried to teach him control. To no avail. Blazing fast ball went to waste. Had 35–31 major league record; 15 of those wins during 1948 season, when he also pitched no-hitter against New York Giants.

Rex had brief tryout with Detroit Tigers, then with Brooklyn, who signed, sent him to Durham, N.C., farm. Remembered there because one of his wild pitches crashed through backstop screen, hit, blackened eye of baseball writer in press box. That was 1943; was 4–6. Then briefly with Dodger farm in Montreal. Also nine games with Flatbush crew. Two years in military service. Then had 2–5, 5–2 records in 1946,47, before his good season. Wildness again set in, 1949. Dodgers even sent him to psychiatrist, in effort to help him throw strikes. No avail. Injury kept him idle half of 1949 season but had 9–8 mark; 2–1 in 1950. Farmed to Fort Worth, 1950. Walked 16 his first start—and quit pitching for season. Worked in brewery. Tried comeback, semipro circuit. Finally gave up. Became sportscaster for Mutual Broadcasting System and New York television station.

Record: 597-2/3 innings in NL, struck out 336, walked 410, ERA 4.34. Lost both his WS starts, one each 1947,49; walked 16, fanned 5, 9-1/3 innings.

BARR, JAMES LELAND (J.B.) P-BR-TR. B. 2/10/48, Los Angeles, Calif. 6′3″, 215. Jim Barr pitched equivalent of 1-1/2 games of perfect ball during 1972 season with San Francisco Giants. It happened this way: pitched shutout against Pittsburgh 8/23, retiring last 21 Pirates who faced him; another shutout against St. Louis Cardinals next time he pitched, 8/29, getting first 20 men to come to bat. This meant 41 men in order had been retired—equivalent of 27 for perfect game, plus 14 others. This set new major league record. Previous mark of 38 was held by Harvey Haddix, set in 1959.

Barr became starting pitcher, 1972. In 1971, spending part of year with Giants after being recalled from Phoenix, relieved in 17 contests, had 3.60 ERA. Jim has shown fine control. In that first part-season with Giants, walked five men, one intentionally, in 35 innings while fanning 16. Won one, lost one. In 1972 started 18 games, relieved in 26, completed eight contests. Victory percentage not impressive, 8–10, but had 2.87 ERA for 179 innings, saved two games.

Jim is graduate of U. of Southern California with degree in business administration. Fine fast ball enabled him to help his team win N.C.A.A. college world series, 1970. Joined Amarillo club in Texas League after that, won six, lost five. Started 1971 with Phoenix, Pacific Coast League. Had 6–3 record when called up by Giants.

Faced 1973 with brief overall record of nine major league wins, 11 defeats, with 2.99 ERA in 214 innings. Fanned 102, walked 46, nine of them intentional passes. Pitched eight complete games, finished 18 others, saved two, had two shutouts.

Barr is player representative for Giants. In off-season has been substitute junior college teacher and has done public relations work for Giants. Onetime wrestler in high school days, wears glasses, but uses contact lenses when he pitches.

BARRETT, CHARLES FRANCIS Scout. B. 6/14/71, St. Louis, Mo. D. 7/4/39, St. Louis, Mo. Charley Barrett never made majors as player but found niche in big time as scout. Scouted Pepper Martin, Art Fletcher, Jim Bottomley, Ray Blades, Charlie Grimm, Muddy Ruel, Bill Killefer,

Flint Rhem, Heinie Mueller, Don Gutteridge, many others. After death, *Baseball Guide* called him "probably best known scout in country" at that time. Charley started playing pro ball at Chattanooga. Had fling at Sedalia, Mo. Then Texas League, at Dallas, Houston, Galveston, winding up playing days 1907. While in Texas League, became acquainted with Branch Rickey, then catcher there.

Barrett took job in sporting goods section, department store, St. Louis. Followed local baseball. Through connections, arranged for Art Fletcher to get his start in Dallas. Fletcher eventually stellar shortstop with N.Y. Giants, coach of Yankees. Helped several other young players get pro jobs, all on personal basis, without pay. One day department store sent him to see Robert L. Hedges, president of Browns. After routine business, Hedges quizzed Barrett about ball players he had helped get pro jobs. Before leaving, Barrett agreed to scout for Browns. First player recommended to new employers was Bill Killefer. Bill spent parts of 1909,10 with Browns, but blossomed later with Philadelphia NL, Chicago Cubs.

Rickey with Browns, 1913. Barrett "Rickey man" from then on, except for one year as scout for Detroit AL. Barrett went with Rickey to Cardinals, contributed to pennant-winning teams of 1920s, 30s.

Barrett modest. Knew own shortcomings. Eighth grade education. Great storyteller, Irish sense of humor, but not public speaker. Father Dooley, St. Louis priest, sponsored sports dinner by Holy Name Society, organization dedicated to battling "taking the name of the Lord in vain." Leading sports figures in St. Louis attend. Barrett too, after extracting no-speech pledge from Fr. Dooley. "I've never made one in my life and I'm not going to start now," he declared. Branch Rickey, Jim Conzelman, Muddy Ruel, other well-known St. Louisians at head table. Barrett also. Each introduced, spoke briefly. Finally Fr. Dooley told audience: "Gentlemen, the next man I am going to introduce really needs no introduction. You all know him. But before I ask him to stand and take a bow, I will tell you that I have given him my word not to ask him to speak." Barrett blushed, quickly bobbed up, sat down. Jokesters in audience demanded speech. Uproar continued. Finally Fr. Dooley quieted group, said: "Charley, I am not going back on my word. I pledged you would not have to make a speech if you came. But you can see you are among friends. And I wonder if you wouldn't reconsider, and perhaps just tell us one of your funny stories, or maybe how you found your first ball player." Flattered but flustered, Barrett stood up, looked around, muttered, "Aw, I can't make no goddam speech." Sat down. Charley never again invited to Holy Name Society dinner.

BARROW, EDWARD GRANT Executive. B. 5/10/68, Springfield, Ill. D. 12/15/53, Port Chester, N. Y. Ed Barrow's selection for Hall of

Fame, 1953, came largely because of his outstanding role as business manager of Yankees. During his regime Yanks won 14 pennants, 10 Series. Other qualifications: found Hans Wagner, gave Fred Clarke his first chance in baseball, realized Babe Ruth's potential as hitter and switched him from pitching to outfield.

Mail clerk, later reporter then city editor of daily, Des Moines, Iowa. Became associated with Harry Stevens, baseball concessions man. Both backed Wheeling (W. Va.) team, Interstate League, 1894. Barrow manager, business manager. Acquired Paterson, N. J., club 12/95. Signed Hans (Honus) Wagner, later selling him to Pittsburgh. President, Atlantic League, 1897–99. Bought part interest in Toronto, 1900, becoming manager. Won pennant 1902. Manager, Detroit Tigers, 1903–04; Indianapolis, Montreal, 1905; Toronto, 1906. Out of baseball 1907–09. President, Eastern League, later renamed International, 1911–18. Manager, Boston Red Sox, 1918, winning pennant, and World Series, 4 games to 2 over Cubs. While Ruth had played some outfield and first base prior to Barrow's arrival in Boston, Barrow used Ruth as pitcher in 20 games, 1918, and 17 games, 1919. In latter season Babe took part in 130 contests, batted .322, hit record-breaking 29 HR. Ruth sold to Yankees 1/3/20.

Barrow managed Red Sox again, 1920. Business manager, Yankees, 1921–39. President, Yankees, 1939 until 1/45, when club was acquired by Dan Topping, Del Webb, Larry MacPhail. Chairman of board two years then retired.

Barrow forceful, straightforward character. Strict disciplinarian as manager, front office boss. Vital role developing Yankee farm system with George Weiss as assistant.

BARRY, JOHN JOSEPH (Jack) SS-BR-TR. B. 4/26/87, Meriden, Conn. D. 4/23/61, Shrewsbury, Mass. 5'8", 158. Jack Barry was shortstop in Connie Mack's famous $100,000 infield; helped him win four AL pennants, 1910–11, 13–14. That $100,000 figure, not Connie's investment, but, theoretically, market value of Eddie Collins, Stuffy McInnis, Home Run Baker and Barry at pre-World War I prices. Connie reportedly got $50,000 for sale of Collins to Chicago AL; Baker brought $25,000 from Yankees, according to reports; nobody seems to know what McInnis was sold for; and Red Sox seem to have paid $7500 for Barry, 7/5/15.

Barry, like Collins, was collegian—Holy Cross. Joined Philadelphia 1908. Played mostly second base that year, 40 games. Regular shortstop 1909. Kept job until transfer to Boston. Remained with Red Sox until big league stay ended, after 1919 season. In 1917, after Bill Carrigan (who'd led Red Sox to two straight pennants) retired from game, Barry became playing manager. Under his leadership, team finished second. Following year Jack in navy. Came back as player, under manager Ed Barrow, 1919; played 31 games, hung up spikes.

Barry no slugger—10 homers. Hit adequately for shortstop—.243, in 1222 games. Best mark .275, 1913. Fair at base stealing: 30 in 1911, career total of 153. WS play: .241 average, 25 games.

After big league career Barry returned to Holy Cross as baseball coach. Ten Eastern collegiate championships. In 1952, after Holy Cross won national collegiate championship, American Association of College Baseball Coaches named him Baseball Coach of Year. Coached Blondy Ryan, Gene Desautels, later major leaguers. Also worked with young players in amateur Blackstone Valley League; among proteges: Hank Greenberg, Bump Hadley, Wes Ferrell, Walt Dropo, Dick Hall.

BARTELL, RICHARD WILLIAM (Rowdy) SS-BR-TR. B. 11/22/07, Chicago, Ill. 5'9", 160. Dick Bartell is remembered as goat of 1940 WS. Also as peppery, aggressive shortstop who loved action. Strangely, went through 10-inning game, 7/3/35, without single fielding chance. Became goat of 1940 WS in seventh crucial contest between Detroit (his club) and Cincinnati. Buck Newsom, Paul Derringer in pitching duel. Tigers leading 1–0 until seventh inning, then McCormick doubled. Ripple hit long drive which hit right field screen. McCormick, fearing ball'd be caught, slow leaving second base area. When ball fell safely for two-bagger, Frank headed home. Right fielder Bruce Campbell fired ball to Bartell, relay man. Dick had back to plate, no way of knowing McCormick still some distance from plate. Noise of crowd drowned teammates' yells of "Home! Home!" Had Bartell thrown home immediately, most observers believe he would have caught McCormick. Frank's run tied score; Reds eventually got Ripple home with sacrifice bunt, outfield fly for 2–1 win and Series.

Dick's father semipro second baseman; once made unassisted triple play. Like father, Dick started as second baseman; soon shifted to short. Bridgeport, Eastern League, 1926—.280 in 148 games. When season over, Pittsburgh for one game. Joe Cronin trying to make good as Pirate shortstop in 1927, but management let him go, kept Bartell. Joe went to Kansas City, then in American Association, later making good with Washington. In 1928 Bartell hit .305 for Pirates in 72 games; .302 in 143 games, 1929; .320 in 129 games, 1930. Philadelphia NL 1931–34. New York NL 1935–38. Chicago NL 1939. Detroit AL 1940–41. New York NL 1941–43, 46 (military service 1944–45).

Hit above .300 seven times. Average of .284, 2016 games. His 2165 hits included 442 doubles, 71 triples, 79 homers. Scored 1130 runs, drove in 710. WS: 18 games, 20 hits in 68 AB, 6 doubles, 1 homer, .294 average. First two WS with Giants, 1936–37.

Once hit four doubles in one game, 4/25/33, equaling major league record. Two NL All-Star teams, 1933,37.

BASSLER, JOHN LANDIS C-BL-TR. B. 6/3/95, Mechanics' Grove, Pa. 5'9", 170. Johnny Bassler, old-time catcher for Detroit, later major league coach, slowest runner in AL during his playing days. But stole home one time. Late 1923, Tigers playing old St. Louis Browns. Bassler on third, teammate Bert Cole on first in eighth inning, two outs. After ball thrown to first base, Bassler suddenly started home. Brownie first sacker Dutch Schliebner seemed hypnotized, threw late. Bassler safe.

Lifetime major league average of .304, in 811 games. One homer. His 704 hits included 99 doubles, 16 triples. Scored 250 times, had 318 RBI.

Bassler played semipro ball in Pennsylvania, winter ball in California. After spell with Pensacola, Cotton States League, drafted by Cleveland on recommendation of Ivy Olson, old-time infielder. One game with Indians, 1913; farmed to Toledo same season. Cleveland 1914 until 6/10/15, when sold to Los Angeles, Pacific Coast League. Had been used sparingly by Indians. Came into his own at L.A., remaining there through 1920 season when he came up with .319 average in 147 games. Then to Tigers, catching over 100 games 1921 through 1925. Remained with club through 1927. During this period, four seasons over .300, peak being .346 in 1924. Back in PCL, Hollywood, 1928–35 (had averages of .365, .354, .357). Seattle, same league, hitting .354 in 111 games, 1936; .313 in 56 games, 1937. Coach, Cleveland, 1938–40. Coach, St. Louis AL, part of 1941, returning to PCL with Hollywood as coach through 1942. Retired from baseball some years, but returned to Seattle as coach briefly during 1949 season.

BATEMAN, JOHN ALVIN (Chick) C-BR-TR. B. 7/21/42, Killeen, Tex. 6'3", 200. John Bateman lost battle of bulge, 1970, when he reported to Montreal Expos overweight. Manager Gene Mauch fined him $800. Had to sweat off 35 pounds to get down to 195, weight Mauch felt was right for him. However, Bateman says he can gain or lose 10 pounds in day, so his avoirdupois fluctuates. Admits he has paid over $2000 in fines for this reason.

Bateman faced 1973 season having played 1017 NL games with Houston, Montreal, and Philadelphia. Owned .230 batting average with 81 homers, 375 RBI; his 765 safe hits also included 123 doubles, 18 triples. Scored 250 runs in majors.

During high school, football injury caused removal of one of his kidneys. Was handicapped in 1969 when his one remaining kidney was hurt. Bateman started at Modesto in California League, 1962; played some infield and outfield as well as catching; hit .280 in 121 games. Made jump from Class A baseball to Houston in majors, 1963, concentrated on catching and got into 128 games. Hit .210 but managed 10 homers and 59 RBI.

In 1964–65 divided his time between Astros and Oklahoma City, Pacific Coast League, then came back to Astros to stay, 1966. That time he had .279 average with 17 homers, 70 RBI. Dropped down to .190 in 1967, then came back with .249 in 1968. At this point Montreal Expos picked him in their expansion draft 10/14/68.

Bateman got into 139 games in both 1970 and 1971, had .237 and .242 averages. Started 1972 with Expos, but was traded to Phillies mid-June for Tim McCarver. Wound up year with .224 mark for 100 games, 3 homers, 20 RBI. Phils gave him unconditional release early 1973.

BAUER, HENRY ALBERT (Hank) OF-BR-TR. B. 7/31/22, East St. Louis, Ill. 6', 202. Hank Bauer holds all kinds of distinctions on and off baseball field. By 1973 still held impressive record of having hit safely in 17 consecutive WS games. Roberto Clemente approached this in 1971 WS when he notched 14 straight WS games. Also tied record, hitting four homers in 1958 WS. Played in nine WS; as manager led Baltimore Orioles to pennant, WS sweep over L.A. Dodgers, 1966. Twice managed clubs for Charles O. Finley—record of sorts! Saw action at Guadalcanal, Okinawa with U.S. Marines. Two Bronze Stars.

Bauer did some pitching before outfield. Began pro career 1941, Oshkosh, Wisconsin State League. Played 108 games, hit .262, pitched in 11 games, 2–1. Then World War II. In 1946, 109 games, Quincy, III League; hit .323. Kansas City, American Association, 1947–48, over .300 both years. Yankees late 1948. Then regular in outfield, 1949–59. During these 11 years, Yanks won nine pennants, seven championships. Bauer helped in all. Highest batting average, .320, 1950. Amassed his 17-game WS hitting streak during 1956,57,58 classics. Warren Spahn finally ended string, throwing two-hit shutout for Milwaukee Braves, fourth game, 10/5/58. His four homers came in same classic, helping Yanks vanquish Braves for championship. That WS Bauer's final as player. During winter was traded to Kansas City AL; deal brought Roger Maris to Yankees. Hank two years with Athletics. During latter season became manager, succeeding Joe Gordon 6/19/61. Finished ninth that year and next, after which Finley fired him. His Baltimore regime began 1964. Two third-place clubs, then came 1966 and championship. Sixth-place tie 1967. In 1968, Bauer had them in third, 10-1/2 games behind Detroit at All-Star break. Hank then dropped for Earl Weaver. Birds ultimately finished second. Hank rejoins Finley, to boss Oakland for 1969. Led team to second place in AL Western Division. But Finley fired him again, 9/10/69. Manager, Tidewater (Mets' affiliate), 1971,72.

Totals, as player: 1544 games, .277, 1424 hits in 5145 AB, 833 runs, 229 doubles, 57 triples, 164 homers, 703 RBI, 50 stolen bases. Nine WS:

53 games, .245, 46 hits in 188 trips, 21 runs, 2 doubles, 3 triples, 7 homers, 24 RBI. Three All-Star games, .286 average.

BAUMGARTNER, STANWOOD FULTON P-BL-TL. B. 12/14/94, Houston, Tex. D. 10/4/55, Philadelphia, Pa. 6', 175.Stan Baumgartner is better known as sports writer than as southpaw pitcher. Wrote sports 25 years for *Philadelphia Inquirer*. Knew many sports from youth. Attended Chicago U. In sophomore year was end on Mid-Western All-Star Football team—other end was Knute Rockne, later famed coach of Notre Dame.Played on U. of Chicago teams 1913–14 that won Big Ten titles in football, basketball, baseball. Chosen on All-Conference teams in each sport.

Baumgartner tried to make grade with Philadelphia NL 1914,15. Unsuccessful. Owned 15–12 mark with Providence, International League, 1916, then found independent ball more attractive than "organized" baseball. Philadelphia NL took him on, 1921. Won three, lost six. After two more seasons in minors 1922–23, Toronto and New Haven, Baumgartner joined Athletics. Most successful season in majors, 13–6, 1924. Was 6–3, 1925. Broke even in two decisions 1926. Lifetime major league record: 27–21, ERA 3.70.

Baumgartner had final fling with Portland, Pacific Coast League, 1926, after leaving Athletics. Then coaching, newspaper work. Coached baseball, football, basketball at Delaware U. before joining sports department of *Inquirer*. Authored *The Phillies* in collaboration with Fred Lieb.

BAVASI, EMIL J. (Buzzie) Executive. B. 12/12/15, New York, N.Y. President, director of San Diego Padres since NL expanded to 12 clubs. Successful vice president, general manager of Brooklyn and L.A. Dodgers for 17 years, during which Dodgers won eight pennants; tied for first twice, only to lose playoffs; had two runner-ups; one third placer; in four other years, Dodgers finished fourth, sixth, seventh, eighth.

Buzzie, like Ford Frick (1915 grad), attended DePauw. Graduated 1938. Friendship with Frick got him into baseball. Worked for Dodgers, then under Larry MacPhail, 1939. Following year began his minor league experience, Brooklyn organization: Americus, Ga., 1940, business manager; Valdosta, Ga., same role, 1941–42. From 1943 to 1946, machine gunner in U.S. Army infantry; discharged as staff sergeant. In 1947 with Walter Alston, Nashua, N.H.—Buzzie, general manager; Alston, field manager. Profitable contact for each. Nashua team second in New England League, 1947. Bavasi to Montreal, general manager, 1948–50. In final year there, Bavasi had Alston as field manager; club finished second, International League. Then vice president, manager of Dodgers, 1951–68. Alston came 1954. He and Bavasi together until

Buzzie moved to San Diego, 6/16/68. Padres, however, did not field team until 1969 season.

Buzzie voted minor league executive of year, Montreal, 1948. Major league executive of year, L.A., 1959.

BEARDEN, HENRY EUGENE (Gene) P-BL-TL. B. 9/5/20, Lexa, Ark. 6'3", 198. Another who flashed across major league scene, brilliantly though briefly. Sailor on USS *Quincy*; encountered surprise Japanese attack off Guadalcanal, 8/9/42. Gene hurt, fished out, patched up with aluminum plates in skull and knee.

Started in 1939 as minor leaguer. Joined Binghamton, 1945, after navy. Newark, 1945; Oakland, 1946–47. One game, Cleveland, 1947, then signed with Indians for $7500 for 1948. As Bearden picked up victories, Bill Veeck, Indians' front office boss, gave him an extra $2500 in June, another $2500 in August. Gene 20–7 for season. Pitched sixth shutout of year final Saturday, against Detroit. Indians tied Red Sox for AL lead, after last day. Playoff game, Fenway Park, Boston. Though southpaw, Bearden, Monday, 10/4/48, set Sox down with five hits. Mates pounded Galehouse, Kinder for 8–3 win and pennant. WS two days later, against Boston Braves. Bob Feller lost opener. Bob Lemon took second. Bearden pitched five-hit 2–0 shutout, third game, Friday, 10/8/48; got double, single, scored one run. Monday, Indians need victory to win Series. Bearden relieved tiring Bob Lemon in eighth inning, to save game. Bearden's ERA: 0.00, 10 2/3 innings. Allowed 6 hits, no runs, walked 1, struck out 4. Pocketed $6772.07 WS bonus. Following year Veeck upped Bearden's contract to $22,500 including bonuses, educational policies for Gene's children. But glory days over. Gene 8–8, 1949; 2.43 ERA of 1948 slumped to 5.10. To Washington during 1950. Detroit during 1951. St. Louis Browns 1952. Chicago White Sox 1953. Seattle, San Francisco, Sacramento, 1955–57. Retired. Hotel business, Niles, Ohio.

Pitched 788 1/3 innings in AL, 3.96 ERA, 45–38 record, 435 walks, 259 strikeouts.

BEAZLEY, JOHN ANDREW P-BR-Tr. B. 5/25/19, Nashville, Tenn. 6'1", 185. Johnny Beazley, now selling insurance, might have had brilliant baseball career but for three years in U.S. Air Corps, World War II. Cardinal hero of 1942 WS, 2–0, as Redbirds defeated Yankees four games to one. Bombers took first game, Mort Cooper victim. Johnny won next game, defeating Tiny Bonham. Cards won next two. Then Beazley wrapped it up with 4–2 victory, defeating veteran Red Ruffing.

During 1942 season, Johnny as rookie had won 21, lost 6, 2.13 ERA. Then into service, became captain. Pressed into service as pitcher in game for Army Relief Fund. Not in shape. Several major leaguers in opposing lineup. Johnny bore down, won game, but arm never same afterward.

Johnny did not pitch in high school. Somehow went to tryout camp in Nashville conducted by Charlie Dressen, manager of Cincinnati. In 1937 pitched for Leesburg (Fla.), Tallahassee and Lexington (Ky.); few wins. Greenville (S.C.) 1938, but was discouraged, returned home after 2–4 mark. Later that year joined Abbeville (La.). Montgomery, Columbus (Ga.), New Orleans, 1939–41. His 16–12 record at New Orleans occasioned promotion to Cardinals. Started, won one game for Redbirds, 1941—9 innings, 1 earned run. After war, with arm gone, Beazley 7–5 for Cardinals, 1946. With Boston NL, 1947–49, 2–1 over three-year stretch. Briefly with Dallas, Texas League, 1950, then retired 6/21/50. Major league record: 31 wins, 12 losses, ERA 3.01, 374 innings, walked 157, fanned 147. In WS, 1942, 46: 2–0, 2.37 ERA.

BECKERT, GLENN ALFRED (Bruno) 2B-BR-TR. B. 10/12/40, Pittsburgh, Pa. 6'1", 190. Had chance for NL batting title, 1971, until about one month before season's close. Dived for ball, suffered ruptured tendons in right thumb. Inactive rest of campaign. His .342 average bested by Joe Torre, St. Louis, and Ralph Garr, Atlanta. But Beckert's mark best of his career.

Glenn studied philosophy at Allegheny College. Captained baseball, basketball teams. Yankee tryout, but decided to finish college before signing pro contract. After A.B. degree, signed with Boston Red Sox for $8000 bonus. Beckert farmed to Waterloo (Iowa) 1962, Midwest League, .280 in 81 games. Then moved to Seattle, Pacific Coast League, then in Sox organization. Chicago Cubs had scouted him, drafted him 11/26/62, farmed him to Wenatchee, Wash., 1963. Salt Lake City 1964. Primarily shortstop those days. Cubs' promising young second baseman Ken Hubbs killed in light plane crash, 2/14/64. Chicago management made second sacker out of Beckert. Regular keystoner for Cubs, 1965, ever since. Until 1971 had not hit .300. Not power hitter. Rarely strikes out. Team man. Went into 1973 season with .286 lifetime major league average, 22 home runs. Highest total of homers, five, 1967. Fine fielder. Member of NL's 1969,70,71,72 All-Star squads. In 1968 Chicago sports writers voted him Chicago's Player of the Year.

Glenn's first flight as Cub was fateful. Met stewardess, also making her first flight in that capacity. Ten flights later, married.

BECKLEY, JACOB PETER (Old Eagle Eye) 1B-BL-TL. B. 8/4/67, Hannibal, Mo. D. 6/25/18, Kansas City, Mo. 6'1", 180. Beckley made Hall of Fame 1971. Perhaps should have been selected earlier as his longevity record for first basemen is something to behold. Played 2368 games there, major league record. Had 23,696 putouts at first base, another major league record, as are his 25,000 chances accepted at first base.

Beckley played with Pittsburgh, New York, Cincinnati, St. Louis NL clubs in period between 1888 and 1907. Playing manager, Kansas City, American Association, 1908–09. Managed Bartlesville Okla., Western Association, 1910. Umpired in Federal League, 1913. Lifetime major league totals showed 2373 games, 2930 hits in 9476 at bats and .309 average. Hit three home runs in one game, 9/26/97.

BELANGER, MARK HENRY SS-BR-TR. B. 6/8/44, Pittsfield, Mass. 6'2", 170. Fine fielder for Baltimore Orioles. Little power at plate. Made three errors in 1971 WS, but Orioles won both games in which they occurred. His .266 batting average for 1971 raised his lifetime major league average to .240 in 678 games. But in 1972, sagged to .186, dropping career mark to .233, 791 games.

Signed with Bluefield, W. Va. team, Baltimore affiliate, 6/19/62; hit .298, 47 games. Following year in military. Aberdeen (S. Dak.) 1964. Elmira (N.Y.) 1965, plus 11 games with Orioles. Farmed to Rochester, International League, 1966; hit .262, 139 contests, and considered outstanding shortstop in circuit. To Orioles for eight games that year. In 1967,69 contests, .174. Since then has played most of team's games, coming up with .208, .287, .218, .266 .186 averages, 1968–72. WS record: .200 average, 1969; .105, 1970; .238 in 1971.

BELINSKY, ROBERT (Bo) P-BL-TL. B. 12/7/36, New York, N.Y. 6'2", 187. Bo Belinsky pitched no-hit game 5/5/62 against Baltimore Orioles, won nine other games for Los Angeles AL during first season in majors. Had numerous opportunities afterward, but never again won 10 games in major league season. "Went Hollywood" before landing with Angels. Considerable publicity, gossip columns. Dated Mamie Van Doren, other movie queens.

Belinsky son of laborer. Reared in rough surroundings. Street brawls. Nicknamed Bo after Bobo Olsen, boxer. Did not play baseball in high school. Worked in overall factory. Sought money easier way. Tried pro baseball. Pitched for Brunswick, Ga.; Pensacola; Knoxville; Aberdeen, S. Dak.; Amarillo; Stockton, Calif.; Vancouver, B.C.; Little Rock. In years 1956–61, was 43–45. Most of 1960 in military service. L.A. Angels 1962, 10–11. Following year, 2–9, with a spell in Hawaii, Pacific Coast League. Returning to Angels, 1964, was 9–8. Suspended for time for breaking club rules. In 1965 Bo pitched for Philadelphia NL, 4–9 record. In 1966, 0–2 for Phils; 1967, 3–9 with Houston. In 1969 Pittsburgh tried him—0–3. Big league record: 28–51, 143 games.

BELL, DAVID GUS (Buddy) OF-3B-BR-TR. B. 8/27/51, Pittsburgh, Pa. 6'2", 190. Presence of Buddy Bell on Cleveland roster in 1972 enabled Cleveland Indians to trade Graig Nettles to New York Yankees. Bell, son of Gus Bell who played in majors generation ago, was outfielder for Indians in 1972, but before 1972 had been infielder. Played six games at third during 1972, must have convinced management he could do job in 1973. Buddy, tall, blond, with athletic build, is regarded as having potential to become superstar. Played 132 games in AL in 1972, hit .255 with 21 doubles, 1 triple, 9 homers among his 119 hits. Scored 49 runs, drove in 36, and stole 5 bases. One of his homers was grand slammer that helped defeat Baltimore Orioles. During August had streak of eight-for-eight.

Buddy attended Xavier and Miami universities in Ohio after starring in high school baseball and basketball. Had .410 batting average for three years of high school competition. First pro experience at Sarasota, Gulf Coast League, 1969; was that loop's All-Star second baseman although he hit just .229 in 51 games, with three home runs. Following season he was at Sumter, Western Carolina League. Raised his batting average to .265 in 121 games, with 12 homers, 75 RBI.

Next stop Wichita, American Association. His play there merited designation "Rookie of Year." Played mostly at third base, but had 11 games at second. In 129 contests batted .289 with 59 RBI. Eleven of his hits were homers, 23 doubles. Then came promotion to Indians and at least temporary conversion into an outfielder. All-Star team 1973.

BELL, DAVID RUSSELL (Gus) OF-BL-TR. B. 11/15/28, Louisville, Ky. 6'2", 196. Gus spent most of career driving in runs for Cincinnati Reds instead of Pittsburgh because of differences with Branch Rickey. Mahatma bossing Pirates' front office, 1951, when Gus chalked up 89 RBI. Following spring Bell held out for substantial raise. Finally, compromise, but no real meeting of minds. "Rickey took a dislike for me at start because I refused to be one of his hungry ball players," said Gus. Later Bell insisted his family travel with him, by train or driving their own car. Rickey objected, "Don't take your family, or you'll go back to minors." Bell ignored. Rickey sent him to Hollywood, Pacific Coast League. But Pirates needed outfielder. Bell recalled after about three weeks, played rest of 1952 season for them. Then traded to Cincinnati, 10/15/52. One scribe said, "Gus turned out to be too good a family man for Rickey." Gus raised his son, Buddy, to be pro ball player, now with Cleveland Indians.

Gus started out at Keokuk, Iowa, 1947; spent part of that year with Leesburg, Florida State League. In 1948 his .319 average with Keokuk led league. Albany, Eastern League, 1949, hitting .325. Hit .400 for Indianapolis, 38 games, during first six weeks of 1950 season; brought up to Pirates. Had .282 average, 111 games with Pittsburgh, 53 RBI. Then came 1951 campaign: 16 homers, 89 RBI, .278 average—and argument with Rickey. Nine years with Cincinnati, 1953–61. Twice hit .300 or better, came close most other times. Over 100 RBI four times. During final season with Reds hit 200th NL homer, 7/26/61. New York NL 1962, .149 average in 30 games; plus 79 games with Milwaukee Braves, 1962, hitting .285. Dropped out of majors after three games each year with Braves, 1963 and 1964.

Bell made NL All-Star squads 1953, 54, 56, 57, had .333 average, 2 for 6, 4 RBI. Homered in 1954 game. WS experience: three unsuccessful attempts at pinch hitting in 1961 with Cincinnati. Major league totals: 1741 games, 1823 hits, 311 doubles, 66 triples, 206 homers, 865 runs, 942 RBI, 30 stolen bases, .281 average.

BELL, HERMAN S.   P-BR-TR. B. 7/16/99, Louisville, Ky. D. 6/7/49, Glendale, Calif. 6′, 185. Herman Bell didn't win many games in majors but held one distinction—last NL pitcher to hurl and win two complete games in one day. Occurred 7/19/24, working for St. Louis Cardinals. Allowed one run each game. Bell had but one more win, eight losses. Two years later Emil Levsen pitched and won twin bill for Cleveland—last time in AL.

Bell pitched for Sioux Falls, Dakota League, 1922–23. Joined Cardinals 1924. Optioned to Milwaukee 1925, 18–19. In 1926 and 1927 was 7–9 with Cardinals. Then spent 1928–29 at Rochester, 21–8 and 11–5 records. Back with Cardinals 1929–30, 4–5 record for parts of two seasons. Rochester 1931, 16–11. N.Y. Giants drafted him, 1932. Three years with Polo Grounders, 18–12. Major league totals: 32 wins, 34 losses, 3.69 ERA. WS play: four innings, three games (1926, 1930 with Cardinals, 1933 Giants), ERA 4.50.

BENCH, JOHNNY LEE (Hands)   C-BR-TR. B. 12/7/47, Oklahoma City, Okla. 6′, 200. Some day Johnny Bench may paraphrase that famous classic *The Education of Henry Adams*, writing his own bestseller, *The Education of Johnny Bench*. Education of Johnny Bench in school of experience proceeded in 1971 season—and in 1972 WS. After fabulous year in 1970—winning MVP Award, clubbing 45 homers, driving in 148 runs and helping Cincinnati Reds to NL pennant, Bench learned he too could have an off-season; baseball fans who could cheer success, also could boo just about as loud. When Johnny's batting average sagged from .293 in 1970 down to .238 in 1971, with team dropping down to fifth place in six-club NL West, fickle fandom blamed Bench for most of problems. At one point Bench tipped his hat in resentment to booing fans; on other occasions berated them for their fickleness. Later repented, pledged more self-control in future. Bounced back in 1972: 40

homers, 125 RBI, and again helped Reds to NL flag.

Did it in most dramatic fashion in last time at bat during playoffs against Pittsburgh. Reds had their backs to wall in final game: ninth inning, with Pittsburgh leading 3–2. If Pirates took that one they'd go into WS. Bench, however, banged towering home run into right field stands, tying game. Cincinnati won shortly afterwards when Moose's wild pitch enabled George Foster to score winning run from third base.

Bench's education continued during WS, especially in third game. In eighth inning, when Reds had two men on base, Rollie Fingers of Oakland A;s ran count to three balls, two strikes. Out trotted Dick Williams, A's manager, for conference. When play resumed, Gene Tenace, catcher, pointed toward first base with his mitt, apparently signaling for fourth ball, an intentional pass. Fingers pitched. Tenace stepped back behind plate. Ball shot over strike zone while Bench stood there with bat on shoulder, apparently completely surprised. Almost 50,000 in stands—and millions on television—watched Johnny trudge back to bench, victimized by Williams' trickery.

Also learned value of settling contract arrangements more quickly than he did in 1971. Asked Reds for half-million dollars for three years, according to reports. Negotiations dragged out over couple of months. Finally signed for around $80,000 annual salary. Late for spring training; poor season followed. "I may have taken things for granted," said Johnny. In spring of 1972, however, signed his contract in two minutes.

Unnecessary to gild lily. Barring unforeseen misfortune, most observers undoubtedly go along with Ted Williams' estimate of talented young man. Johnny, before exhibition game against Washington Senators in Tampa, Fla., sought Ted's autograph on baseball. Ted wrote on ball, "To Johnny Bench, a sure Hall of Famer," followed by signature.

Bench started out with Tampa in Florida State League, 1965, after Reds acquired him as their No. 2 draft choice. Moved to Peninsula club of Carolina League, 1966, hit .294 in 98 games, with 22 homers, 68 RBI. Promoted to Buffalo, International League, during same season, 7/31/66, Johnny fractured right thumb in very first game and was out for rest of year.

Then had 98 games with Buffalo, 1967, 23 homers, 68 RBI; and 26 games with Reds, hitting just .163. In his first full season with Cincinnati, 1968, Bench walked off with NL Rookie of Year designation by both the *Sporting News* and Baseball Writers Association of America; set NL record for most games by rookie catcher, 154; but also led NL in passed balls with 18. His batting average was .275, 15 homers, 40 doubles, two triples, 82 RBI.

In 1969 Johnny raised his batting average to .293; upped his home runs to 26; his RBI to 90; scored 83 times; played in 148 games. Then came fabulous 1970 campaign. His 148 RBI were tops in majors, as was his total of 45 round trippers. Slapped 35 doubles, scored 97 times. Took part in 158 contests. No wonder the *Sporting News* named him Major League Player of Year. MVP in NL 1970, again in 1972.

No mention has been made so far of Johnny's brilliant catching. Not only does he possess great arm and do fine job as receiver, but is "take charge" guy, leader on field.

Johnny was named to NL squads for all All-Star games, 1968–73, hitting .417 (5 for 12) for five games, including one homer in 1969 contest. In 1970 WS Bench hit .211, 4 for 19, against Baltimore pitching. One of these hits was homer in second game. His 1972 WS performance showed .261, with 6 hits, 4 runs, scored in 23 times at bat. One of his blows was homer in sixth game. Overall WS record for both classics added up to .238.

Facing 1973, Bench had appeared in 782 NL games. His 781 hits were good for 142 doubles, 12 triples, 154 home runs. Had scored 421 times, driven in total of 512 markers. Stole 20 bases and owned .271 lifetime average. Hit 4 homers in 4 official at-bats 5/8,9/73.

Johnny has had own television show and has been popular making public appearances. Certainly seems on way to making Ted Williams good prophet about ultimate Hall of Fame designation. Johnny is youngest of Ted Bench's three sons. Ted wanted to be ball player but couldn't quite make it; vowed that he'd give sons every opportunity. Ted Jr. didn't seem to have tools. William looked like hitter but had appendicitis in senior year in high school; then married early and moved into other fields. When Johnny was seven, Dad knew he had something special. Johnny pitched and played third base, but became catcher because he wanted action every day. Valedictorian in his class in high school, fine athlete—and then he was on his way to superstardom in majors.

In December 1972, Johnny Bench undoubtedly reflected deeply on what he had learned on and off baseball diamond—about life, his life. A lesion in his right lung had been discovered. Would doctors find it benign or malignant? Two hours of surgery 12/11/72; tests revealed no malignancy. Within short time Johnny was out of hospital, one more chapter ended in *The Education of Johnny Bench*.

BENDER, CHARLES ALBERT (Chief) P-BR-TR. B. 5/5/84, Brainerd, Minn. D. 5/22/54, Philadelphia, Pa. 6'2", 185. Whether Chief Bender was full-blooded Chippewa Indian or not, fans used to yell at him, "Whoop! Whoop!" Unruffled. At times, returning to dugout, Bender would good-naturedly reply, "Foreigners! Foreigners!" Connie Mack once declared Bender greatest money pitcher of all time. "Given proper rest, Chief Bender did not once fail me in a dozen years," said Connie. Ten of 12 seasons with Athletics, won more than lost. In 1914, was 17–3; 1910, 23–5; 1913, 21–10. Lifetime record: 208–112. Losses piled up in solitary season (1915) Bender spent in Federal League, 4–16 for Baltimore Feds. Team bad, last, finishing 24 games behind *seventh-place* club! Pitched two no-hit games, one in majors, one in minors. His big league classic came 5/12/10 against Cleveland. Only one man reached base: Terry Turner, walk. Promptly picked off. In World Series, 1905—3–0 victory over N.Y. Giants in second game. Giants, however, took WS four to one. Bender on mound for final game, lost 2–0 to Christy Mathewson (Matty's third victory, all shutouts). ERA 1.06. In 1910, was 1–1 in classic against Chicago. ERA 1.93. Following season, Bender chalked up WS victories over Giants, 4–2 and 13–2, after losing opener, 2–1 (fanned 11, lost when reliable Eddie Collins fumbled grounder). A's took Series four to two. In 1913 WS Bender won two of A's four wins over Giants in five games. In 1914 George Stallings' miracle Boston Braves swept A's. Bender suffered defeat, charged with 6 runs, 5–1/3 innings. Complete WS totals: 10 games, 85 innings, 6–4, 64 hits, 23 earned runs, 59 strikeouts, 21 walks, 2.44 ERA.

Bender left Athletics after 1914 WS to join Baltimore Feds. When dispute between Federal League and American, National circuits settled, Chief member of Phillies, 1916, 1917. In 1918, while World War I in progress, Bender worked in shipyards. Richmond, Virginia League, 1919, playing manager, 29–2, .935 percentage tops. Following year shifted to New Haven, Eastern League, also managing. Took 25 victories against 12 defeats, for .676 tops. Dropped to 13–7, 1921, New Haven. Piloted Reading, International League, 1922, won 8, lost 13 pitching. Pitched for Baltimore, International League, 1923, 6–3 record. New Haven, 1924, 6–4 record. Chicago White Sox, 1925, coach under Mgr. Eddie Collins; pitched one inning, his final in majors. Back to managing in minors, 1927, Johnstown, Middle Atlantic League. Coached at U.S. Naval Academy, 1928. Coach, Giants, 1931. Manager, Wilmington (Del.), Inter-State League, 1940. Manager, Newport News, Virginia League, 1941. Scout, Philadelphia Athletics, 1945. Manager, Savannah, Sally League, 1946. Scout, Athletics, 1947–50. Coach, Athletics, 1951–53.

Bender well educated; attended Carlisle Indian School and Dickinson College, Carlisle, Pa. Standout billiard player. Skilled with shotgun; for some years toured country in off-season as representative of arms company. Hall of Fame 1953.

BENGOUGH, BERNARD OLIVER (Benny) C-BR-TR. B. 7/27/98, Niagara Falls, N.Y. D. 12/22/68, Philadelphia, Pa. 5'7'', 168. Benny's mother gave him push that started pro career as catcher. Benny making $5 a day as bullpen catcher for Buffalo, International League, 1918. Impatient, Mama finally called team's manager, wanted to know when her boy Benny was going to catch. Nonplussed, manager told Mama he'd catch Benny that day, and did so—and for five years more. Then moved up to Yankees. Took part in only 30 games 1923–24, but in 1925 became regular on same day Lou Gehrig replaced Wally Pipp at first base. Prematurely bald, Bengough kept secret from fans only until he chased first pop foul. Later as coach, got laughs by lifting cap, running hands through imaginary hair. As catcher, Bengough tried to distract opposing hitters with constant chatter. Benny left Yanks after 1930 season. Two years with St. Louis Browns. Went to minors as player-manager, winding up at Joplin Mo., Western Association, 1937. Returned to majors as coach for Browns, Senators, Braves, Phillies. Retired from field 1959. Joined public relations staff of Phillies. Popular public speaker.

Lifetime major league average .255 in 411 games. Hit .176 in two World Series, 1927–28, six games, with Yanks.

BENSON, VERNON ADAIR Inf.-OF-BL-TR. B. 9/19/24, Granite Quarry, N.C. 5'10", 160. Coach, Cardinals, Yankees, Reds. Former infielder, outfielder, playing for Philadelphia AL, St. Louis NL. With Athletics total of nine games, 1943 and 1946, military service interrupting. With Cardinals as infielder, 1951–53, 46 games. Major league average, .202, 55 games.

Vernon got his start as minor league manager, 1956, Cardinal organization at Winnipeg. Moved up through Winston-Salem, Tulsa, Portland. Joined Cardinals as coach, July 1961, when Johnny Keane became Redbird manager. Remained through 1964 season. Coach, Yankees, 1965. Special-assignment scout, N.Y. Mets, 1966, until July; joined Cincinnati Reds' coaching staff when Dave Bristol became manager. Cincinnati through 1969. Special instructor for younger players in Cardinal organization, 1970, until appointed coach, July 1970. Still lives in birthplace.

BENTLEY, JOHN NEEDLES (Jack) P-BL-TL. B. 3/8/95, Sandy Spring, Md. D. 10/24/69, Sandy Spring, Md. 6', 200. In early 1920s Jack Dunn had what was probably greatest minor league team in history. His Baltimore Orioles included Lefty Grove, Joe Boley, Max Bishop, Al Thomas, George Earnshaw, Johnny Ogden—and Jack Bentley. Chances are his Orioles, then in International League, could have finished high in either of majors. Baseball rules those years prevented major teams from drafting players from top minors. So Dunn kept his stars. Naturally Baltimore, while paying players well, did not pay as much as some could make in big leagues.

Jack Bentley, fine pitcher and great hitter, was ambitious to get into majors. Had record of 16–3, 1920; 12–1, 1921; and 13–2, 1922. Such a great hitter that he played first base when not pitching. In 1922, hit .350

in 153 games, second among players at bat 400 times or more. Dunn kept telling Bentley nobody in majors wanted his contract. Fed up, Jack seized chance to see for himself whether this was true. Went to Polo Grounds late in 1922, called on John McGraw, Giants' mentor. "I've been trying to buy you for three years," McGraw told him. McGraw made out check for $35,000, saying, "Take this back with you and see if Dunn will sell your contract to me for it." Bentley went back to Dunn, called bluff. Negotiations began to move. Dunn agreed to sell Bentley to Giants for $65,000 and three players. When McGraw couldn't deliver players specified, sent extra $7000. So Bentley in majors for $72,000.

Helped Giants win pennant in 1923 with pitching and batting. Had 13–8 mark. His name at top of list among hitters, .427 in 52 games as pitcher, pinch hitter. In World Series pitched quite well in one game, not so well in another, was charged with one defeat. However, his .600 batting average (3 for 5) was tops for both Giants and Yanks. Twice came through as pinch hitter.

His 16–5 record in 1924 helped Giants again win flag, McGraw's tenth. Had 1–2 record in Series; fated to be on mound when Walter Johnson won first WS game of long career. Jack lost second game of that Series, 4–3; allowed Washington just six hits. Winner in fifth game, 6 to 2. In seventh game, Bentley relief pitcher with score 3–3 in 12th inning. Twice in that round bad breaks. Bentley got Muddy Ruel of Senators to hit foul fly behind home plate. Catcher Hank Gowdy stumbled over own mask, missing fly. Given new life, Muddy doubled. Then Earl McNeely hit ordinary grounder to Freddy Lindstrom; took crazy bounce over third baseman's head, enabling Ruel to score winning run and giving Senators Series, four to three. Heartbreak for Bentley, but later said that if it had to happen, was glad Walter Johnson beneficiary.

While attending George School, 1913, Bentley pitched at picnic. Friend of Clark Griffith, manager of Washington, arranged tryout. Griffith signed him. In first start in majors, with no pro experience, pitched shutout over Philadelphia Athletics, 1–0. Did not blossom with Washington, despite early success. Loaned to Minneapolis, American Association, 1915, 16. U.S. Army, World War I. Then joined Baltimore.

Jack's major league pitching record 46–34; batting average .291, much of that as pinch hitter. Giants sent him to Philadelphia NL 1926. Played 56 games at first base, pitched some. Back with Giants 1927, then retired. Worked for national manufacturer as sales representative.

BENTON, JOHN C. (Rube) P-BL-TL. B. 6/27/90, Clinton, N.C. D. 12/12/37, Dothan, Ala. 5'11", 172. Benton's name conjures up controversy. Lefthanded pitcher seems to have had advance information that 1919 WS to be fixed. Testimony exists that Rube won $3200 betting on underdog Cincinnati. When Judge Landis barred eight of "Black Sox,"

Benton allowed to continue playing. After 1922 season, when Benton had successful season with St. Paul, American Association, Reds wanted to bring him back to majors. NL president John Heydler made it clear he would not be allowed to pitch in that circuit. AL prexy Ban Johnson felt same. Landis stepped in, declared Benton eligible to play in majors. Heydler repeated his statement. Conference, Landis and Heydler. Benton joined Reds.

Benton started in semipro league in Florida, 1909. Pitched for Macon, South Atlantic League, 1910, 11–5. By midseason Cincinnati paid $3500 for him. In 1911, optioned to Chattanooga, Southern Association, 18–13. Recalled 8/12/11, 3–3. Had 18–20 mark, 1912; 11–7 in 1913; 16–18 in 1914. By this time Benton notorious for wine and women. Disciplined several times. Once told manager sister sick. Manager wired Benton's family. All well, Benton on extended drunk. Fined $100. Next contract he signed contained clause limiting or banning consumption of alcohol, cigarettes, depending on judgment of manager. Benton pitched for three different clubs in 1915—Cincinnati, Pittsburgh, New York NL. Was 9–18 overall. John McGraw got three good seasons out of him: 16–8 in 1916; 15–9 following year; 17–11, 1919. In 1918, was 1–2; spent most of season in military service. In 1920, 9–16; 1921, 5–2. Left Giants. Unclear whether his "guilty knowledge" of 1919 WS fix was immediate cause, or McGraw wearied of him. Then came St. Paul, 1922, and hassle about his return to NL. After return, Benton 14–10 for Reds, 1923. Two losing seasons followed. Back to American Association, remaining with Minneapolis until 1934, when he joined semipro outfit. Benton's first major league game, 1910, was against Three Finger Brown of Cubs. Rube lost 1–0. Only WS appearance, 1917, with Giants. Pitched five-hit 2–0 win against White Sox, third game. Lost sixth and last game to Sox, despite allowing no earned runs; hurled five innings. Giants made three errors. Chicago won 4–2. Wound up with ERA of 0.00, 8 strikeouts, 1 walk. Lifetime major league record: 150 wins, 144 defeats.

BENTON, LAWRENCE JAMES (Larry) P-BR-TR. B. 11/20/97, Cincinnati, Ohio. D. 4/3/53, Amberley Village, Ohio. 5'11", 165. John McGraw, manager of N.Y. Giants, often traded away promising young ball players for men who could help him win pennants immediately. Years later frequently regained them. Among these: Heinie Groh, Eddie Roush, Larry Benton.

Benton impressed Giant scouts with work at Portsmouth, Virginia League, 1920–21: 13–10, his first pro season; 18–18, striking out 196, in 1921. Giants bought him, but sold to Memphis; 15–13 in 1922. Bought by Boston NL. Braves 1923–27: 5–9, 1923; 5–7, 1924; 14–7, 1925; 14–14, 1926. Boston second-division club all these years. McGraw wanted back. Got him in trade, 6/12/27 (Benton 4–2 at time). Larry posted 13–5 mark for McGraw and led NL pitchers with overall 17–7 mark. Giants finished third, only two games out of first. In 1928 Benton again led NL pitchers, 25–9. Giants second, again two games out. Downhill after that; 11–17 in 1929. During 1930 season, traded to Cincinnati. Reds farmed to Minneapolis for part of 1930, then brought him back for 1931–34. Boston NL 1935, last season in majors. Totals: 127 victories, 128 defeats, 4.03 ERA, 455 games; fanned 670, walked 691.

BERG, MORRIS (Moe) C-BR-TR. B. 3/2/02, New York, N.Y. D. 5/29/72, Belleville, N.J. 6'1'', 189. Moe Berg probably most erudite of all professional ball players. Other players spoke of him as "guy who could speak nine languages and couldn't hit a curve ball in any of them." Actually, statement not completely accurate. Moe spoke and read French, Spanish, Italian, but read only Latin, Greek, Provencal, Portuguese. Later learned enough Japanese to coach baseball in that country. A.B., Princeton, 1923. LL.B., Columbia, 1928. Passed New York bar exam, 1929. At Princeton, captain and shortstop of Tiger nine. Signed with Brooklyn Dodgers, 1923; hit .186, playing mostly shortstop. Minneapolis, Toledo, American Association, 1924. Reading, International League, 1925, .311 in 168 games. Chicago White Sox 1926, infielder still, .221 in 41 games. But in 1927 Sox manager Ray Schalk, catcher, broke thumb. Buck Crouse replaced him and foul tip promptly put him out of game. Next catcher was Harry McCurdy, who broke finger few days later. Berg volunteered to catch, did good job, catcher rest of career. Best overall season 1929: 107 games, hit .287. After that, fewer games a season. Left White Sox after 1930. Part of 1931 with Cleveland. Billy Evans, general manager of Indians, wanted to send him to Oakland, Pacific Coast League. Berg said he would not report. Evans gave him unconditional release. Berg grateful, told Evans he hoped some day to repay him for not insisting on sale to Oakland. Moe returned to New York, law practice. Following year with Washington, but free agent after Senators let him go in 1934. Cleveland needed catcher. Evans phoned Berg in New York, asking him to fill in at least temporarily. "How much do you want for signing?" asked Evans. "Nothing," replied Berg. "You gave me my release when you didn't have to. I haven't forgotten that." "What salary do you want?" asked Evans. "That's entirely up to you," said Moe. "You write in whatever figures you want and I'll play for that amount." Following year, 1935, Berg with Boston Red Sox, remaining until 1939. Lifetime major league average: .243, 663 games.

Moe with U.S. counterintelligence during World War II, mostly in Europe. After war, became highly competent attorney. Often appeared on network quiz shows, notably "Information Please."

BERGER, WALTER ANTONE OF-BR-TR. B. 10/10/05, Chicago,

ILL. 6'2", 198. Wally Berger enjoyed finest years with Boston Braves, 1930–37, when he hit flock of home runs, averaged over .300 in hitting. Later with New York NL 1937–38; Cincinnati 1938–40; finally Philadelphia NL 1940. Slugged 242 homers during major league career. Twenty times got pair of homers in one game. Seven grand slams.

Wally's first season in pro ball, 1927, Pocatello, Utah-Idaho League; won batting title—.385, 92 games—led in homers, 24. Los Angeles, Pacific Coast League, later that year—hit well over .300 that season and next two. Celebrated July 4, 1929, doubleheader against Portland, with 7 for 9, including 3 homers, 2 walks, 4 stolen bags, 9 runs. Braves 1930. As rookie hit .310 in 151 games, walloped 38 homers, drove in 119 runs. Only Hack Wilson, 56, and Chuck Klein, 40, ahead of him in NL homers. Led NL in homers 1935, with 34.

Berger played in two WS, 1937 with Giants, and 1939 with Reds. In 1937, failed in three attempts as pinch hitter. In 1939, hitless in fifteen trips, facing such Yankee pitchers as Ruffing, Pearson, Hadley, Murphy. Yanks swept. Major league totals: 1350 games, 5163 AB, 1550 hits, 299 doubles, 59 triples, 242 homers, 806 runs, 898 RBI, .300 average, 36 stolen bases.

BERRA, LAWRENCE PETER (Yogi)   C-BL-TR. B. 5/12/25, St. Louis, Mo. 5'8", 191.

Coach, N.Y. Mets, 1965–1972. Appointed manager of Mets 4/3/72, after death of Gil Hodges. Tried out with Cardinals 1942 but rejected $250 bonus offer; later signed with Yankees for $500. Farmed to Norfolk, Piedmont League, 1943. Navy service in Normandy landings and Mediterranean. Yankee farm club Newark, International League, 1946, till late in season, then seven games with Yankees batting .364. Hit homer in first major league game, another next day. With Yankees through 1963. Bench manager, Yanks, 1964. Stellar catcher. Occasionally filled in at first, third, outfield. Specially feared batsman with men in scoring position. Major league average .285 in 2120 games, 358 homers 1430 RBI. Five times in seven years had more than 100 RBI. Set major league record for most consecutive chances accepted by catcher without error, 950; for playing 148 consecutive games without error. Holds many other batting and fielding records including World Series high marks for most Series played, 14; most games, 75; most times as player on winning team, 10. With 16 pennant winners including one as Yankee skipper, one with Mets as coach.

Managed Yanks to pennant in first season as pilot, 1964. Fired after losing Series to Cardinals, managed by Johnny Keane who became his successor. Signed with Mets as player-coach, took part in four games, 1965, then gave up playing. MVP 1951, 54, 55. Hall of Fame 1972.

Married Carmen Short 1949. Three sons. Lives in northern New Jersey. Has been in bowling alley business, promoted soft drink. Widely hailed for "Berraisms." Best known was his brief speech when fans showered him with gifts on his "night," saying: "I want to thank all the baseball fans and everyone else who made this night necessary."

BERRY, CHARLES FRANCIS C-BR-TR. B. 10/18/02, Phillipsburg, N.J. D. 9/6/72, Evanston, Ill. 6', 210. There was Charlie Berry in old Union Association, 1884; had just one season in league then considered major. But son, also named Charlie, not only made good in big leagues as player, but was All-America football player. To cap career, was top-notcher as official in both baseball and football. Our Charlie Berry, who took part in AL games over 11-year period, attended Lafayette College, and left end on last All-America team selected by Walter Camp. B.S. degree, 1925. Joined Philadelphia AL when Connie Mack had such distinguished catchers as Mickey Cochrane, Cy Perkins, Jimmie Foxx. Charlie, catcher, did not tarry long. Shipped to Wichita, Portland, Dallas for 1926, 27. By 1928 back, Boston AL. In 1932 Red Sox traded him to Chicago AL. After 1933 season, with Mickey Cochrane gone to Detroit, Perkins about through, and Foxx playing first base, Berry finally landed regular job on Athletics. Remained with A's until 1938.

Berry neither drank nor smoked. Hard, clean player—asked no quarter, gave none. Blocked plate regardless of who was coming at him. Once the hulk coming from third base was Babe Ruth. Charlie stood ground. Babe failed to score—and out of lineup for two weeks.

Charlie says he never won debate with umpire. When playing days over, became one himself. Soon won respect of players. Knew rules, studied them every day. Known for fairness. Enjoyed similar respect on gridiron, when he capable linesman. One time officiating duties in baseball, football almost clashed. Had doubleheader at Comiskey Park in Chicago. Afterward dashed madly to Soldiers Field to officiate game between Cleveland Browns and College All-Stars. Barely made kickoff.

In 1946 World Series, Joe Cronin, Boston Red Sox mentor, charged out of dugout when Berry called obstruction play against Sox. Cardinal third baseman Whitey Kurowski singled. Joe Garagiola hit long drive which Dom DiMaggio lost in sun. As Kurowski passed third, Sox third sacker Mike Higgins gave him hip and Kurowski fell to ground. In course of play Garagiola out at third, trying to stretch hit into triple. When Berry ruled that Kurowski's run scored, Cronin asked Berry, "Are you sure you're right?" "I'm sure," replied Berry. End of argument. Had Berry called interference, ball would have been dead and Kurowski run would not have counted.

Another occasion Tony Cuccinello worked hidden ball trick on Lou Boudreau. Cuccinello so clever at this play, often fooled umpire as well as opposition. Tagged Boudreau two feet off bag. "Out," yelled Berry. Then, since he could not see ball, added, "if Cuccinello has the ball."

Berry retired after 1962 season. As player, took part in 709 games, hit .267 during major league career.

BEVENS, FLOYD CLIFFORD (Bill) P-BR-TR. B. 10/20/16, Hubbard, Oreg. 6'3", 210. Hero one minute, bum the next. This adage never more dramatically demonstrated than on 10/3/47, Ebbets Field. Bill Bevens pitching no-hitter in WS. Yanks leading Dodgers 2–1. Never a no-hitter in WS history. Sports writers, fans waiting to hail new hero. Bevens wild throughout game. Walks had led to Brooklyn's only run. Now, in ninth, Carl Furillo drew Bevens' ninth walk, after Lindell caught Edwards' long drive against left field wall and Jorgenson fouled out. Gionfriddo ran for Furillo; Pete Reiser pinch hit for Hugh Casey. With count two balls, one strike, Gionfriddo stole second. Now, with count three and one, Bucky Harris, Yankee manager, had Reiser walked intentionally, despite his representing possible winning run. Reiser had bad ankle, so Eddie Miksis ran for him. Veteran Cookie Lavagetto, pinch hitting for Eddie Stanky, swung at Bevens' first pitch, fast ball, and missed. Next pitch, another blazer, a bit high, toward outside. Lavagetto swung, hit ball toward right field corner, where he seldom hit. Right fielder Tommy Henrich, after hard run from right center, leaped, but ball six feet above outstretched glove. Runners scored, giving Brooklyn 3–2 win. Bedlam broke loose. Fans swarmed on field to congratulate Cookie for his double. Bevens, head down, ignored by mob, slowly walked to dugout. Never pitched another ball in major league competition after that WS. (Was 1956 before no-hitter in WS: 10/8/56, Don Larsen's perfect game against Dodgers.)

Bevens joined Yankees, 1944. Three winning seasons: 4–1 as rookie; 13–9 in 1945; 16–13, 1946. In 1947, 7–13, but Harris called on him to start fourth game of Series, with Yankees leading Dodgers two games to one. Despite Bevens' loss, Yanks went on to win WS four games to three. Mysterious ailment struck Bevens' arm before 1948 season. Back to minors. In 1951 won 20 games for Salem, Oreg., Western International League. Following spring, unsuccessful comeback with Cincinnati.

BICKFORD, VERNON EDGELL P-BR-TR. B. 8/17/20, Hellier, Ky. D. 5/6/60, Richmond, Va. 6', 180. Vern Bickford won 19, lost 14 for Boston Braves, 1950, his most successful season as big leaguer. One of victories was 7–0 no-hitter against Brooklyn Dodgers, 8/11/50. Led NL pitchers in games started, completed, and in total innings pitched that year, 312.

Bickford spent four years with Welch, W. Va., Mountain State League, 1939–42. Next three seasons in military service. In 1946 divided time between Hartford, Eastern League, and Jackson, Miss., Southeastern League. Though record in smaller minors never very sensational, he was brought up to Milwaukee, American Association, 1947. Following year made debut with Braves, 11–5. Had 16–11 mark, 1949. Then his big year. Was 11–9 in 1951, and 7–12 in Braves' final season in Boston. Was 2–5, 1953, for Milwaukee Braves. Final year in majors, Baltimore AL, 1954, 0–1. Bickford pitched 3-1/3 innings in 1948 WS for Braves; lost decision; 2.70 ERA. Major league totals: 66–57, 182 games, ERA 3.71.

BILKO, STEPHEN THOMAS 1B-BR-TR. B. 11/13/28, Nanticoke, Pa. 6'1", 250. Like many others, amiable Steve Bilko was great player in minors, but struggled to stay in majors as long as he did. Played 600 games, 10-year period: .249, 76 home runs, 279 RBI.

Steve hit .360 for Los Angeles Angels, Pacific Coast League, 1956; had 55 homers, 164 RBI. But best average in majors was .287 for 64 games in 1962, his last time in big time. Had .294 mark with St. Louis Cardinals back in 1949, but for only six games.

Steve started out at Allentown, Inter-State League, 1945. Later with Salisbury, Md., Winston-Salem, Lynchburg, Rochester, Columbus, with occasional brief periods with Cardinals. Traded to Chicago Cubs during 1954, then back to minors. Another chance in majors, 1958, with Reds, L.A. Dodgers. Minors 1959. Detroit Tigers gambled $25,000 on his contract for 1960. Hit .207, 78 games. Los Angeles AL 1961–62.

After leaving game, Bilko returned to birthplace. When last heard, was inspector of all incoming materials for Dana Perfume Co. Son Steve has played with Red Sox organization.

BILLINGHAM, JOHN EUGENE (Jack) P-BR-TR. B. 2/21/43, Winter Park, Fla. 6'4", 195. Oakland's Catfish Hunter, Blue Moon Odom, Vida Blue pitched great during 1972 WS, but Jack Billingham outpitched them all. Jack's record before WS anything but spectacular. During five years with Los Angeles, Houston, Cincinnati, won 44–44, with 3.45 ERA. But in 1972 fall classic, pitched like distant relative, Christy Mathewson. Cincinnati starter in third game of WS. Eight innings held A's to two bunt singles, one other infield hit. When he threw three balls to leadoff hitter in ninth, manager Sparky Anderson sent Clay Carroll to mound. Jack received credit for Reds' 1–0 victory. Relieved in fifth game, credited with save. In crucial seventh game, Jack again pitched magnificently. A's got one unearned run over first five innings when Tolan misjudged ball, then dropped it. Jack removed for pinch hitter after five-inning stint because Reds desperately needed runs in fifth inning. Billingham allowed no earned runs in 13-2/3 innings he pitched.

Jack started 1972 season losing first five decisions. Then came back, broke even with 12 wins, 12 losses. Club's most reliable pitcher latter part of year. Sinker ball pitcher led Cincinnati staff in innings pitched, 218, strikeouts, 137. Walked 64 men. Pitched 4-2/3 innings in one game of NL playoffs against Pittsburgh, allowing two earned runs, but Hall received credit for Cincinnati victory.

Jack started as pro back in 1961 at Orlando, Fla. Later pitched for St. Petersburg, Salisbury (N.C.), Santa Barbara, Spokane, Albuquerque.

Joined L.A. Dodgers, 1968: 50 games (all but one in relief), 3–0, 2.15 ERA.

Expansion Montreal selected him in intraleague draft, 10/14/68. Expos traded to Houston, 4/8/69. Three seasons with Astros. Mostly in relief, 1969—52 games. Starter, 1970. While at Houston, 29–32. Traded to Cincinnati 11/29/71. As 1973 dawned, career record of 788 innings, 217 games; 527 strikeouts, 254 walks; 302 earned runs, 3.45 ERA. His 1972 ERA with Reds, 3.18. NL All-Stars 1973.

BILLINGS, RICHARD ARLIN (Dick) C-BR-TR. B. 12/4/42, Detroit, Mich. 6'1", 190. Small war of words began between Whitey Herzog and Dick Billings shortly after Whitey became manager of Texas Rangers late 1972. Herzog said Dick wasn't his idea of first-string catcher in majors. Billings retorted that maybe Herzog had much to learn about communications if he wanted to become successful manager. Whitey had seen Billings play just three games when appointed pilot of Texas team.

Later Herzog was quoted as saying he liked Billings' versatility, his "bear-down" attitude, and fact he is hustler. "It's a credit to Dick Billings with the natural ability he has that he's made himself a big leaguer."

Dick graduated from Michigan State U. with degree in education. Played at Geneva, N.Y., 1965; later with Burlington, N.C.; York, Pa.; Buffalo and Savannah clubs, with couple of brief spells with Washington Senators. Was outfielder and third baseman for most part but management of Senators wanted him to try catching. Voluntarily went down to Denver, American Association, 1970 to learn backstopping. Hit .305 that season in 112 games, slapped 15 homers, drove in 67 runs.

Eleven games with Washington that year, then in 1971 caught 62 games but was used elsewhere in infield and outfield. Hit .246 in his first full season in majors; drove in 48 runs, had six homers. Then club was transferred to Texas. With Rangers, 1972, hit .254 in 133 games, 58 RBI, and credited with five home runs.

Ready for 1973 season, Billings had 299 major league games behind him, with .243 average. His 222 hits included 32 doubles, one triple, 13 homers, with 110 runs driven in. Had scored 82 times.

During off-seasons Billings has managed Zulia club in Venezuelan Winter League.

BISHOP, MAX FREDERICK 2B-BL-TR. B. 9/5/99, Waynesboro, Pa. D. 2/24/62, Waynesboro, Pa. 5'8½", 165. Fielding whiz, fine leadoff man with Philadelphia Athletics when they won last three AL pennants, 1929–31. As second baseman set an enviable record of 53 consecutive games without error, 1932. (Mark bettered by Jerry Adair, Baltimore Orioles, 1964–65: 89 games before miscue.) Bishop also set AL fielding records, 1926 and 1932: .987 mark in 1926, .988 in 1932. (Adair's .994 in 1964, is current major league record for second basemen.)

Max leadoff man throughout most of big league career. Had reputation of refusing to swing at any ball quarter inch outside strike zone. Usually high among leaders in drawing walks—his 128 led AL in 1929. Drew another 128 free passes, 1930, but Babe Ruth had 136 (many of them intentional—doubtful any of Bishop's were). Maxie played 129 games in 1929, 130 in 1930. In those two seasons, averaged almost one walk every game. Kept it up throughout career—1153 in 1338 games.

Bishop no slugger. Had 41 homers during career; high mark 1930: 10. Finished with 236 doubles, 35 triples. Batting average .271 (hit .316 in 1928). Stole 43 bases, scored 966 runs. In WS of 1929, 30, 31: .182, 18 games.

Max started career with Baltimore, International League, 1918; remained through 1923. His last season with old Orioles, hit .333, slapped 22 homers! Then sold to A's for reported $50,000.

BISSONETTE, ADELPHIA LOUIS (Del) 1B-BL-TL. B. 9/6/99, Winthrop, Me. D. 6/9/72, Augusta, Me. 5'11", 180. As player, Del Bissonette is remembered as first baseman for Brooklyn Dodgers, 1928–33. Later became major league coach, successful minor league manager. Also piloted Boston Braves about two months, 1945. Beset by unusual injuries, illnesses throughout career. Took them in stride until near 73rd birthday. Then apparently shot himself in stomach; died several days later. Shooting occurred in his apple orchard. Had been apple farmer in Winthrop during off-seasons when playing, coaching, managing; also after leaving baseball. Had .305 major league average in 604 games. His 699 hits included 117 doubles, 50 triples, 65 homers. Had 391 RBI.

Del started pro career in Eastern Canadian League, 1922. Later played at York (Pa.), Jersey City, Rochester; then hit .365 for Buffalo, 1927, with 167 RBI, 35 homers. This merited promotion to Brooklyn. Hit .320, 155 games, as rookie (1928); also 25 homers. Had .336 average, 1930. In 1932, severed Achilles tendon during spring training. Out entire year. Returned 1933, hit .246 in just 35 games; was through as big leaguer. Besides severing Achilles tendon, Del had arm surgery, mastoid operation, numerous sinus operations, during his career. Back in minors, played for Baltimore, Albany, Montreal. Then managed Des Moines in Western League; Glace Bay, Cape Breton Colliery League; Bradford, Pony League; Hartford, Eastern League. Won pennant at Hartford, and in 1945 coached Boston Braves. Manager of Braves, 7/31/46 until end of season: won 25, lost 36. Coach, Pittsburgh Pirates, 1947. Manager, Portland, New England League, 1948. Manager, Toronto, International League, 1949. Won at least four pennants as pilot.

Bissonette started as pitcher in boyhood. Hurled for New Hampshire

State College, Georgetown U. Aroused keen interest of several major league scouts. Arm injury dashed hopes of pitching in majors.

BITHORN, HIRAM GABRIEL P-BR-TR. B. 3/18/16, Santurce, P. R. D. 1/1/52, Ciudad Victoria, Mex. 6'1", 204. Hi Bithorn won 18, lost 12 for 1943 Cubs. Born of Danish and Spanish parents. Hot-tempered tavern owner, favorite in Caribbean. Died in mysterious circumstances in northern Mexico. Baseball stadium in Puerto Rico later named for him. Perhaps true story of death never be known. Allegedly en route to visit mother. Policeman reported he was trying to sell his car. When requested to show his documents permitting him to enter Mexico as tourist, and demonstrating ownership of car, Bithorn reportedly said he had none. Officer wanted to take him to police station, but Bithorn, according to cop, struck him, tried to get away. Policeman fired .45 into pitcher's stomach. Bithorn died few hours later. Another story circulated that Bithorn, before dying, said he was member of Communist cell, on important mission. Had $2000 on his person, so story that he wanted to sell expensive car for $350 seemed strange.

Bithorn came to mainland, 1936, to pitch for Norfolk in Piedmont League—16–9. Was 10–1 with same club, 1937; to Binghamton midseason, 7–8. Newark 1938. Oakland 1939. Hollywood 1940–41, winning 17 in last season before being drafted by Chicago NL. Had 9–14 record with Cubs, 1942, 3.68 ERA; 18–12, 2.60 ERA, 1943. Military 1944–45. Was 6–5 with Cubs, 1946, ERA 3.84. In 1947, pitched two innings for Chicago White Sox, then returned to Caribbean baseball.

Major league record: 34–31, 509 2/3 innings, 171 walks, 185 strikeouts, 105 games, 3.16 ERA.

BLACK, DONALD PAUL P-BR-TR. B. 7/20/16, Salix, Iowa. D. 4/21/59, Cuyahoga Falls, Ohio. 6', 185. Don Black not remembered as great pitcher in AL, although he did pitch 3–0 no-hitter 7/10/47 against Philadelphia Athletics. Career might have been different but for John Barleycorn. Broke into AL with Philadelphia, 1943—6–16, 4.20 ERA for tail-end club. Somewhat better 1944, 10–12, 4.07 ERA. In 1945: 5–11 and 5.17. Black, by now, repeatedly breaking training rules. Connie Mack suspended, later sent to Cleveland on waivers. Indians got one victory from him, two defeats, 1946, and sent to Milwaukee (American Association). There, in seven games, 0–5. That winter Bill Veeck, boss of Indians, got together with Black, induced him to join Alcoholics Anonymous. Was 10–12 for Indians, 1947, with 3.92 ERA, plus no-hitter. In 1948, pennant year, Don 2–2. While working game against Browns, 9/13/48, Black, at bat, fouled off pitch, then collapsed. Broken blood vessel in brain. Semicoma three weeks. Indians went on to win flag; Black collected full WS share, amounting to $6772. Operated on, 12/7/48, but playing days over. Veeck paid Black's bills, full salary for

1949 season. Additionally, Veeck staged benefit game for Black. Crowd of 76,772. Indians handed Don check for $40,000.

Black was sportscaster in postbaseball days. Later sold cars, insurance. Unemployed for time; Veeck again helped financially. Died watching old team on TV.

BLACK, JOSEPH P-BR-TR. B. 2/8/24, Plainfield, N.J. 6'2", 225. First black pitcher to win WS game. Started for Brooklyn 10/1/52 against Yankees in Ebbets Field. Held Bronx Bombers to six hits. Took decision 4–2. Subsequently charged with two defeats that Series but had 2.53 ERA, allowing six earned runs, 21-1/3 innings. Better than any other Dodger flinger in 4–3 Series loss.

Black compressed greatest achievments on ball field into that 1952 season and WS. During summer started two games, pitched one complete contest. Forte, relief man. Saved 15 games. Won 15, lost 4, as Dodgers finished 4-1/2 ahead of rival Giants.

Black 28 before his chance in majors. After 1952, unable to equal peak performance. In 1953, 6–3, 5 saves. One inning in WS that fall, allowing one run. Dodgers again bowed to Yankees. In 1954, pitched very little for Brooklyn. Transferred to Cincinnati during 1955, 5–2. In 1956, 3–2 with Reds. After brief spell with Washington Senators, 1957, called it quits. Major league record: 30–12, 25 saves, ERA 3.91.

Black attended Morgan State College on athletic scholarship. Schooling interrupted by military service. After World War II, signed with Baltimore Elite Giants of Negro National League and continued his education. Graduated, signed with Brooklyn organization, 1950. Spent 1951 with Montreal farm, International League, 7–9. Also in 1951, 4–3 with St. Paul, American Association, another Brooklyn affiliate. Then to Dodgers. After leaving baseball Black taught and coached in Plainfield, N.J. Later vice president of Greyhound Corp. Lives in Chicago.

BLACKBURNE, RUSSELL AUBREY (Lena) SS-BR-TR. B. 10/23/86, Clifton Heights, Pa. D. 2/29/68, Riverside, N.J. 5'11", 160. Lena Blackburne is remembered among baseball men principally because of three widely diverse factors. As shortstop for Chicago White Sox, got first hit ever made in Comiskey Park, 7/1/10. Some years later, as manager of White Sox, had blowhard, blustering young first baseman by name of Art (the Great) Shires. Though Shires outweighed manager by 30 or 40 pounds, Blackburne held his own in fistfight which was widely publicized. Lena's other claim to attention: believed to be the one who originated idea of rubbing mud on balls, to take off gloss.

Blackburne played sandlot ball around Philadelphia and made grade with Sox, 1910. Played 144 games with Chicago 1914 but hit only .222. In 1918 with Cincinnati. Boston and Philadelphia NL 1919. Coach, White Sox, 1927–28. Manager, White Sox, from July 1928 until end of

1929. Coach, St. Louis AL, 1930. Coach, Philadelphia AL, 1933–40 and 1942–47. Scout with A's until team was transferred to Kansas City, 1955. Then continued to scout in Philadelphia area. During minor league experience, helped Kansas City, American Association, win pennant and Junior World Series, 1923.

BLACKWELL, EWELL (Whip) P-BR-TR. B. 10/23/22, Fresno, Calif. 6'5", 190. Ewell Blackwell won 16 consecutive victories for Cincinnati Reds, 1947, team which finished in second division. Wound up year with 22–8 mark. Never again able to approach this effectiveness. Health problems caught up with him, though he pitched with Kansas City AL as late as 1955. Major league record 82–78. Had deceptive sidearm, cross-fire sinker pitch, particularly rough on righthanded hitters. "Buggy whip" delivery. Lanky frame.

Scout for Reds found him in San Dimas, Calif., 1939. Not quite 17 years old, junior in high school. Worked in lemon groves summers, pitching Sundays. When asked to explain his phenomenal control, explained he had fashioned triangular "control box" at home. Practiced every day for three years, pitching lemons, rocks, baseballs at homemade target. Reds nursed Blackwell along in minors. Reached International League with Syracuse, 1942, earning promotion to parent club with 15–10 record. Used in two games with Cincinnati, 1942, no decisions. Had 9–13 record, 1946, then banner season, 1947. Johnny Vander Meer wrote history by pitching two consecutive no-hit games, 6/11/38 against Boston NL and 6/15/38 against Brooklyn. Blackwell came close to equaling this. Shut out Braves with no hits 6/18/47. Next time he pitched, went into ninth without allowing safety. "Stinky" Stanky of Dodgers singled past shortstop to ruin Blackwell's chance. Jackie Robinson followed with line single to center. Then Blackwell got next three hitters, preserving shutout. Served in U.S. Army as mess sergeant, winding up in General Patton's Third Army; won two battle stars.

With Cincinnati until 1952, when transferred to Yankees. Had 1–0 record in first AL season, 2–0 mark with Yanks 1953. Tried comeback with Kansas City AL 1955, pitching in two games, losing one decision. Ewell's only World Series appearance, 1952. Yanks started him against Dodgers in fifth game. Gave up one run in first four innings, three in fifth. Lifted for pinch hitter in fifth. Sum: four hits, four runs; walked three, struck out four; ERA 7.20.

BLADES, FRANCIS RAYMOND (Ray) OF-BR-TR. B. 8/6/96, Mt. Vernon, Ill. 5'7½", 180. Primarily second baseman during early days in minor leagues. Reported to Cardinals late 1922. Clubs had holes in infield, outfield. Surprisingly, Branch Rickey, Redbird field manager, put Ray in left. On first fly, Blades started in, saw ball going deep, turned around, fell down, missed catch. Ball went for extra bases. Later fine outfielder; .301 major league average. Managed Cardinals, 1939, to second-place finish. In 1940 club got off to 15–24 start; Ray bounced, 6/8/40.

Blades started pro career in fast company, Memphis, Southern Association, 1920—.253, 140 games. Houston, Texas League (Cardinal farm then), 1921, 22. Hit .278 first season, .330 in second. Redbirds 1922, 37 games. Best season 1925: .342 in 122 contests. Divided 1929 between Houston, Rochester. Cardinals 1930–32, utility role. Playing manager, Columbus, American Association, 1933–34; full-time pilot, 1935. Managed Rochester, International League, 1935–38. Then tour as Cardinal boss. Managed New Orleans, 1941, last half of 1943. Coach, Cincinnati, 1942. Manager, St. Paul (AA), 1944–46. Coach, Brooklyn, 1947–48. Coach, Cardinals, 1951. Coach, scout, Chicago NL, 1953. Coach, Cubs, 1954–56.

Record: 767 major league games, 133 doubles, 51 triples, 50 homers, 726 hits, .301 average, 340 RBI, 467 runs. In WS, 1928,30,31, with Cardinals, mostly pinch hitter: 8 games, 1 for 12, .083.

BLAEHOLDER, GEORGE FRANKLIN P-BR-TR. B. 1/26/04, Orange, Calif. D. 12/29/47, Garden Grove, Calif. 5'11", 178. Credited by Bob Feller with originating slider, now considered important part of pitching assortment by most major league hurlers. Slider probably thrown by earlier pitchers but coaches used to discourage use, fearing it would ruin arm. At one point Jimmie Foxx considered Blaeholder most difficult pitcher for him to hit in AL—largely because of slider.

Blaeholder's major league record wasn't spectacular, 104–125. Pitched for St. Louis Browns 1927–35. Philadelphia AL part of 1935. Cleveland AL 1936. Only two of those teams ever got out of second division. ERA was 4.54 in 338 games. With Browns 1925; hurled two innings. Pitched for Terre Haute, Bloomington, Tulsa en route to regular job with Browns, starting pro career in 1923. Never got chance to pitch in WS.

BLAIR, PAUL L. D. (Motormouth) OF-BR-TR. B. 2/1/44, Cushing, Okla. 6', 171. Nicknamed Motormouth because he rarely stops chattering. Fine money player. With Baltimore Orioles parts of two seasons, all of seven others. At end of 1971: .264, 976 regular-season games in majors, 83 homers, 345 RBI; .270 in three playoff series; .278 in four WS, besides fabulous game-saving catches. His .233 average, 1972, seventh full year with O's, lowered career mark to .260 for 1118 games.

In 1966 Blair hit .277 in 133 games as Orioles won flag. Got only one hit in WS: 430-foot homer off Claude Osteen of L.A. Dodgers, giving Wally Bunker 1–0 victory in third game. In fourth game his dramatic leaping catch of Jim Lefebvre's drive deprived Dodger infielder of home run—preserving another 1–0 victory and giving Orioles sweep. Blair doubled hit quota in 1969 WS, both singles, .100 average. In 1970 WS he was leading hitter with .474 average.

His 9 for 19 in five games tied record for most safeties in WS of five games. In 1971 WS, 3 for 9, giving him .278 average for his four WS.

Paul's personal high in homers came in 1969, 26; in RBI, same year, 76. Suffered serious eye and facial injury May 1970 when struck by Ken Tatum pitch in game against California. Had three homers in one game, 4/29/70; grand slam 6/5/71.

Blair attended East Los Angeles Junior College. Signed with Mets' organization. Drafted by Orioles 11/26/62 after spending season at Santa Barbara, California League. Stockton 1963. Rochester, Elmira 1964; plus eight games at Baltimore. Played 119 games for Orioles 1965, 37 for Rochester. Then stuck with Orioles. AL All-Star squad 1969, 73.

BLASINGAME, WADE ALLEN (Blazer)   P-BL-TL. B. 11/22/43, Deming, N. Mex. 6'1", 190.

Reportedly received $100,000 in bonus money to cast his lot with Milwaukee Braves, 1961. Southpaw pitcher won 16, lost 10 with Braves, 1965, but otherwise unable to live up to prediction he would become star pitcher. In 1972, after many years of service in NL, was acquired by Yankees but did not help them in bid for AL division title in East. Pitched 17 innings, lost one decision, allowed eight earned runs and had 4.24 ERA.

Blazer went to Boise, Idaho; Austin, Tex.; and Denver for seasoning before his two games with Braves, 1963. In 1964 he combined 9–5 record at Milwaukee with 4–5 mark at Denver. Following season, his best, was able to put together aforementioned 16 victories with 3.76 ERA. Wild, however, with 116 walks allowed while he struck out 117.

In 1966 he divided his time between Atlanta Braves and Richmond; and in 1967 between Atlanta and Houston. Poor record with Astros, 1968–69 and was sent to Oklahoma City for part of 1970. Had 3–3 record with Astros, 1970, and 9–11 in 1971. Then in 1972 allowed eight earned runs in eight innings pitched for Houston before being sold to Yankees.

As 1973 dawned, Blasingame's major league record stood at 212 games, 864 innings pitched, 46 wins, 51 defeats, with 4.42 ERA. Walked 372 and fanned 512.

BLASS, STEPHEN ROBERT   P-BR-TR. B. 4/18/42, Canaan, Conn. 6', 170.

Failed in 1971 playoffs between Pittsburgh and San Francisco. Star pitcher in WS. With Pirates trailing Orioles two games to none, Mgr. Danny Murtaugh sent Steve to mound. Limited Orioles to three hits (one a homer by Frank Robinson), won 5–1. Another masterful performance in seventh and final game. Held Baltimore runless until eighth inning. By then Pirates had two. One Oriole scored in eighth. No more. Pirates champs. Blass' comeback not his first: 1971 season was comeback, 15–8, after mediocre 10–12 in 1970.

Steve signed with Pittsburgh organization 6/27/60. Early experience:

Kingsport, Tenn.; Dubuque, Iowa; Batavia, N.Y.; Asheville and Kinston, N.C.; Columbus, Ohio. Pirates 1964. First start: against Don Drysdale, Dodgers. Blass won. Record 5–8 that season. Then 13–11 with Columbus in 1965. Back with Pirates, 11–7 in 1966, 6–8 in 1967. Then two good seasons: 18–6 and 16–10. Rugged competitor. Fine control. Live fast ball. Slider. Change-up. Best ERA season 1968, 2.13. ERA for 1971, 2.85. Then came 19–8 season, 1972, with 2.48 ERA. Through 1972, major league mark of 258 games, 1505 innings, 3.24 ERA, 506 walks, 867 strikeouts. During 1972 playoff series against Cincinnati, won first game 5–1. Hurled 7-1/3 frames in crucial seventh, charged with two runs; loss absorbed by Guisti.

During 1971 playoffs Blass 0–1 against Giants. Started 2 games, allowed 14 hits, 9 earned runs, 7 innings, 2 walks, 11.57 ERA. But Murtaugh had confidence. It paid off. Two WS appearances: 2–0, 18 innings, 7 hits, 4 walks, 2 earned runs, 13 strikeouts, ERA 1.00.

BLATTNER, ROBERT GARNETT (Buddy) Inf.-BR-TR. B. 2/8/20, St. Louis, Mo. 6′1/2″, 180. One of numerous major leaguers who found place in sportscasting after playing days. Buddy had fine year at Sacramento, Pacific Coast League, 1941, hitting .294—including 17 home runs, 100 RBI—playing second base, and taking part in 176 games. This won promotion to St. Louis Cardinals but there only 19 games in 1942, batting .043. Military service kept him busy from then until 1945. After World War II, Blattner joined N.Y. Giants: 126 games 1946, mostly at second base, hitting .255; 55 games 1947, with .261 average; 8 games 1948. Shifted to Philadelphia NL for 1949: 64 games at second, short, third, with .247 average. Lifetime average .247 in 272 NL games.

Blattner worked into sportscasting after that. At one point shared microphone with Dizzy Dean. Later, voice of Los Angeles, then California Angels. Currently broadcasting for K.C. Royals. Enjoys respect of players, has great following among fans.

BLEFARY, CURTIS LEROY (Buff) OF-C-1B-BL-TR. B. 7/5/43, Brooklyn, N.Y. 6′1″, 200. Valuable because of versatility, pinch-hitting abilities. Yankees signed 1962, $40,000 bonus, after he attended Wagner and Towson State colleges. Yanks farmed to Greensboro where he played 1962–63; allowed to go to Baltimore AL on irrevocable waivers, 1963. Orioles farmed to Elmira, 1963; Rochester, 1964, where he hit .287, 31 homers, drove in 80 runs, scored 87, led International League in walks (102). With Orioles 1965–68; at least 130 games each year. His best average with Orioles was 1965, .260, Rookie of Year. Had 22 homers that year, 23 next, 22 in 1967. Outfield mostly, some first base, caught 40 games, 1968. Three homers in one game, 6/6/67. Houston 1969. Traded to Yankees for Joe Pepitone, 12/4/69. Though he hit .212 for N.Y., 1970, two of his pinch hits were homers, one in bottom of ninth with two men on against Boston, winning game 3–2. Divided 1971 between Yankees and Oakland. Again hit .212, but had another pinch hit four-master. Started 1972 with A's but in May sent to San Diego NL. Padres released him end of year. Agreed to minor league contract for 1973 with Atlanta Braves' organization at Richmond.

Blefary owned .237 lifetime major league average at start of 1973, in 974 games; 699 hits, 112 homers, 104 doubles, 20 triples, 382 RBI. In 1966 WS with Orioles he hit .077—1 for 13.

Claims Russian-Italian ancestry. Interested in working with mentally retarded children.

BLUE, VIDA, JR.   P-BLR-TL. B. 6/28/49, Mansfield, La. 6′, 192. Won 24 games, lost 8 for Oakland A's in 1971. Team won title in AL West but eliminated by Baltimore in playoffs. Blue 6–10 in 1972. Oakland again won AL West, vanquished Detroit in playoffs, went on to world championship victory over Cincinnati.

Blue sensation of 1971. Conservative estimates—drew perhaps 10,000 additional fans every time he pitched. Started 39 games. Owner Charles O. Finley balked at Blue's demands for fabulous contract in 1972. Blue requested $115,000, Finley offered $40,000. Word battle. Vida announced retirement. Became vice president, Dura Steel Products Co. Eventually compromise, said to be $63,000. Blue signed 5/2/72. Missed all of spring training. Never regained 1971 form. Pitched 24 complete games 1971; 5 in 1972—4 shutouts, though. Unhappy about not starting any of playoff games against Detroit. Used in relief, 5-1/3 scoreless innings. Saved crucial fifth game, 2–1. In WS, Blue again mostly relieved: final 2-1/3 innings in opener, holding Cincinnati scoreless, receiving save while A's won 3–2; 1/3 inning, third game; tagged for run in 1/3 inning, fourth contest. Started sixth game; touched for 4 hits, 3 runs; lifted in sixth. WS performance: ERA 4.15, 8-2/3 innings, 4 earned runs, 8 hits, walked 5, fanned 5, 1 wild pitch, 0–1 record.

Blue, as high school senior, led team to district championships in both baseball and football. Struck out 21 batters in seven-inning game; threw 35 touchdown passes as quarterback that year. Signed with Oakland for $40,000 bonus. First pro season at Burlington, Midwest League, 1968; 8–11, 2.49 ERA, but led in strikeouts with 231. Hurled seven-inning no-hitter. Much of 1969 at Birmingham: 10–3. Second straight year in All-Star game. Joined Oakland for twelve games same year: 1–1, ERA 6.21, 42 innings. One more season in minors, 1970, at Iowa: 12–3; led league in strikeouts, 165 in 133 innings; 2.17 ERA. To A's, six starts in September. In second appearance, threw one-hitter; two appearances later, pitched 6–0 no-hitter against Minnesota, 9/21/70. Then came dazzling season.

Blue drew salary of $15,000 for 1971. Finley gave Vida Cadillac, various credit cards, but did not tear up his contract. Blue 17–3 at All-Star break; starting pitcher for AL. Allowed three runs in three innings, but was winner as AL defeated NL, 6–4. Cooled off after that; finished 24–8. His 1.82 ERA best in AL. Led AL in shutouts. Struck out 301 but Mickey Lolich of Tigers fanned 308. Won Cy Young Award, MVP. Blue only fifth pitcher to win both honors (others: Don Newcombe, 1956; Koufax, 1963; Gibson and McLain, 1968). And youngest to win both. Also youngest major leaguer in modern times to pitch no-hitter when he did.

Blue's brief major league career through 1972: 544 innings, 82 games, 33–19, 148 earned runs, 166 walks, 471 strikeouts, 31 complete games, 2.45 ERA.

BLUEGE, OSWALD LOUIS (Ossie) 3B-BR-TR. B. 10/24/1900, Chicago, Ill. 5'10", 165. Ossie Bluege's connections with Griffith family go way back. Was secretary and controller for Cal Griffith's Minnesota Twins until retirement in 1972. Bluege began as player with Clark Griffith's Washington Senators in 1922. Managed Senators, 1943–47. Coached Senators in interim (1940–42) after quitting as active player. During regime as manager, led team to second-place finish, 1943; last in 1944; back to second, 1945; fourth in 1946; seventh, 1947. Moving out of manager's chair, Bluege filled various front office jobs for Senators, who later became Twins when transferred to Minnesota.

Began career with Peoria, Three-Eye League, 1920. Hit .286 that year, .293 following season, when Washington bought him for $3500. Played briefly with Washington, 1922; most of year at Minneapolis, American Association, hitting .293 in 44 games. In 1923 started long career with Senators, mostly at third base. Hit .272 in 1865 major league games. His 1751 hits included 276 doubles, 68 triples, 43 homers. Stole 140 bases, scored 883 runs, batted in 848. Took part in three WS with Senators, 1924,25,33: 17 games, .200 average.

Bluege's father wanted him to be accountant. Career as player and manager simply delayed process. Younger brother, Otto Bluege, played with Cincinnati Reds, 1932–33, as infielder.

BLYLEVEN, RIK AALBERT (Bert) P-BR-TR. B. 4/6/51, Zeist, Netherlands. 6'3", 200. Drives purple car with white racing stripe and pitches fireballs. One of Cal Griffith's best hopes for high finish for Minnesota Twins for years to come. Rookie of year among AL pitchers for 1970. Had hoped to pitch opening game of season for Twins in 1972, on day he would officially come of age, 4/6. But players' strike delayed start of season. Did pitch delayed opener; did not get credit for Minnesota victory. Won four subsequent decisions, giving him record of 10 straight wins (won 6 consecutive victories end 1971 season).

Blyleven grew up in California. Started career at Sarasota and Orlando, Fla., 1969, 7–2. Was 4–2 at Evansville, Ind., 1970; brought up to Twins in time for 10–9 mark, 3.18 ERA, rookie pitcher award. In 1971, plagued by poor batting support, was 16–15, 2.82 ERA. (In 15 defeats, Twins scored just 18 runs.) in 1972, 17–17, 2.73 ERA. To 1973: 729 innings, 2.86 ERA, 175 walks, 587 strikeouts, 43–41 record.

BODIE, FRANK STEPHAN (Ping) OF-BR-TR. B. 10/8/87, San Francisco, Calif. D. 12/17/61, San Francisco, Calif. 5'8", 195. Ping Bodie really was Francesco Stefano Pezzolo. Got his name, Bodie, from place where he is supposed to have lived for time. It's in California even if you can't find it on map. "Ping" came from sound of his 52-ounce bat stinging old dead ball used when he was young player.

Ping was one of earliest ball players of Italian ancestry; some claim his success inspired other Italians like DiMaggios, Tony Lazzeri, Crosetti, and others from Golden State to aspire to major leagues.

Ping no superstar, but colorful. Hit .181 as shortstop for Vallejo in California League, 1908; same season also played 36 games with San Francisco, Pacific Coast League, and hit .276. His .249 average for 157 games following year wasn't impressive; but somehow he hit 30 home runs in 1910, even with dead ball. His average was .263, and Chicago White Sox promptly drafted him. During four-year stay with Sox his best year was 1912 when he reached .294 with five homers. Had eight homers, 1913, but hit just .264. Back to San Francisco Seals for 1915–16; hit above .300 both years, then was back in majors with Philadelphia Athletics, 1917.

Bodie used to say, "Liberty Bell and I are only attractions in Philadelphia." Hit .291 in 148 games, slapped eight homers. Ping then spent next four seasons with New York Yankees. His best season with them was 1920, when he hit .295 in 129 games. Roomed with Babe Ruth. However, when quizzed about this, would insist, "That isn't true! I room with his suitcase!"

Bodie played 31 games with Yanks, 1921, then dropped back into minors. His final season was 1928 with San Francisco Missions of Pacific Coast League, when he hit .348. Worked as an electrician in California movie studios. Tried comeback with Oakland, PCL, 1931, but his days as player were behind him.

Ping had .275 average for his 1049 major league games. His 1011 hits included 169 doubles, 71 triples, and 44 home runs. Scored 393 runs, drove in 517, and stole 83 bases.

BONDS, BOBBY LEE (Bo Bo Junior) OF-BR-TR. B. 3/15/46, Riverside, Calif. 6'1", 198. Wasted no time letting NL know of presence with San Francisco, 1968. Hit .370 for Giant farm, Phoenix, Pacific Coast

League, 60 games. Giants called up. Broke into lineup 6/25/68, against rival L.A. Dodgers. Third trip to plate, bases full. Slapped grand slam. First time rookie had ever done this in first game, at least in this century. Good bet to become superstar. Has tools—fine throwing arm, good fielding ability, speed (possibly speediest in NL), hits with authority. After debut, hit eight more homers in 1968, then came up with 32,26,33,26 round-trippers next four seasons; total: 126 through 1972. Speed resulted in 45 stolen bases, 1969, more than any other Giant since move to San Francisco. Notable, since only five players, including Bonds, have hit at least 30 homers and stolen 30 bases same season. Had 90 RBI, tied for NL lead in runs scored with 120 in 1969. In 1970, raised thefts to 48, homers dropped to 26, with 78 RBI, .302 average, 134 runs, and in field 14 assists. Grounded into just six double plays, lowest in NL among players with 500 trips to plate. Often leadoff man, had .288 average in 1971, with 102 RBI, 33 homers, 26 steals. In 1972, hit .259, 26 homers, 80 RBI, 118 runs, 44 steals.

If Bobby could cut down strikeouts he would be even more formidable. In 1970, fanned 189 times, NL record. In 1971, reduced strikeouts to 137; same for 1972. Started 1973 season with .275 average, 704 games, 385 RBI, 179 stolen bases. NL All-Star 1973—2-run homer.

Bonds came from athletic family. Sister Rosie an Olympic sprinter; brother Robert pro football linebacker. Bobby starred in baseball, basketball, football, track in high school. Got his start at Lexington, in Western Carolina League, 1965; Fresno 1965–66; Waterbury 1967; Phoenix 1968.

BONHAM, ERNEST EDWARD (Tiny) P-BR-TR. B. 8/16/13, Ione, Calif. D. 9/15/49, Pittsburgh, Pa. 6'2", 215. Won 79 games, lost 50 for Yankees, 1940–46, not including fifth and final game of 1941 WS, 10/6/41. Set down Brooklyn Dodgers on four hits, giving Bombers 4–1 victory for Series. Won 24, lost 22 for Pittsburgh, 1947–49. Then cut down by illness, dying in September 1949.

Bonham's best year was 1942—21–5. In 1940, 41, 9–3 and 9–6. In his final year with Pirates was moving along at 7–4 pace with sixth-place club when he could not continue. Oddity 8/10/46: retired Red Sox on four pitches although they reached him for two safeties. Wally Moses singled to start inning. Pesky missed on his try to bunt, and Moses cut down at second. Two pitches. One out. On third pitch Pesky singled. Dom DiMaggio then hit into double play to retire side.

Bonham's first pro team was Akron, Middle Atlantic League, 1936—14–8. Later same year, 2–3 with Binghamton, N.Y.-Penn. League. Had 17–16 record at Oakland, Pacific Coast League, 1937; 8–2 record with Newark, International League, 1938. Kansas City (AA) part of 1938, all of 1939, part of 1940: 3–4, 10–9, 10–4. Then to Yankees; 9–3 record in rookie effort.

Major league career: 103–72, 231 games, 1551 innings, ERA 3.06. Lost one game each in WS of 1942, 43. WS totals: 4 games, 1–2, 28 innings, 7 earned runs, ERA 2.25.

BONURA, HENRY JOHN (Zeke) 1B-BR-TR. B. 9/20/08, New Orleans, La. 6′, 210. In 1937 piano-legged first baseman from New Orleans hit .345 for White Sox. Only Charlie Gehringer, Lou Gehrig, Joe DiMaggio had higher averages among AL regulars. According to story, Zeke wanted $500 raise for 1938; refused by management. Appealed to Jimmie Dykes, Sox manager, reminded, "But you were last in fielding." Jimmie, another time, declared, "This has got to be the worst first baseman who ever lived. He doesn't just let ground balls go by him. He doesn't wave at balls, he salutes them!" When Bonura, in 1936, had only seven errors in 1614 chances, Dykes said, "You can't miss what you can't get." Jimmie loved to tell how Bonura, after missing ground ball, would shout to pitcher, "Stay in there, kid!"

Zeke short for physique. Good hitter—lifetime major league average, .307. Played 917 games, had 1099 hits, 119 homers, 232 doubles, 29 triples. Somehow stole 19 bases, one a theft of home. Seems veteran coach Jim Austin working third base for White Sox against Yankees. Bonura reached third in 15th inning. Zeke whispered to Austin that he wanted to steal home. Austin said, "Don't you do it. It will cost me my job." But Bonura surprised everybody, including Yanks; won ball game.

Bonura, as youth, in baseball, football, basketball, track events. In 1925, set record for javelin throw, 213′, 10-1/2″, in meet at San Francisco. Turned down Notre Dame to play pro baseball. Started at New Orleans, 1929, .322, 131 games; boosted average to .352, same club, 1930. Divided 1931 between Indianapolis and New Orleans, with .375 average in 85 games that year with his hometown club. Batted .322 and .357 with Dallas, 1932–33. White Sox 1934–37. Lowest average with Sox, .295 in 1935. Washington 1938—.289. Hit .321 for N.Y. Giants, 1939, in 123 games. In 1940, divided time between Washington (79 games, .273) and Cubs (49 games, .264).

Zeke once known as "Banana King"; in banana business with father during playing days. Later turned to real estate.

BORBON, PEDRO P-BR-TR. B. 12/2/46, Valverde Mao, Dominican Republic. 6′2″, 185. Fast-baller, helped Cincinnati win NL flag 1972: 11 saves, 8 victories, all in relief. His first full season in NL. Spent 1969 with California Angels. Pitched 5-1/3 innings during 1972 playoffs; then in six of seven WS games. In playoffs, one earned run. But in WS, effective in most appearances, but charged with two Oakland runs in crucial seventh contest, and was loser, giving A's world championship.

Pedro started out in St. Louis Cardinal organization, farm at Cedar Rapids, Midwest League, 1966: 6–1. St. Petersburg 1967. Modesto, Calif., 1968. Drafted by Angels from Tulsa roster 12/2/68; one season in AL. Traded to Cincinnati 11/25/69; had 5–2 record at Indianapolis 1970, and 12–6 mark 1971. Spent part of 1970 with Reds, getting into 12 games. Rejoined Cincinnati during 1971, but pitched in only three games.

Major league record going into 1973: 99 games, 184 innings, 10–8 record, 86 earned runs, 78 strikeouts, 50 walks, 4.14 ERA.

BORDAGARAY, STANLEY GEORGE (Frenchy) OF-3B-BR-TR. B. 1/3/12, Coalinga, Calif. 5'7½", 175. Moustaches, sideburns were weird in 1930s. But fun-loving son of French parents enlivened NL scene not only with his facial adornment but with antics on—and off—field. Once accused of spitting in eye of umpire. Fined, suspended. Commenting on severity of penalties, was quoted, "Maybe I did wrong. But the penalty was a little more than I expectorated."

Frenchy, in 1937–38 with Cardinals, part of famed Mudcat Band with Pepper Martin et al. On diamond, never reached stardom. Busiest years with Brooklyn, 1935–36, again 1944–45—only years he played more than 100 games. Primarily outfielder, but played considerably at third base, reasonably well.

Frenchy started out on sandlots of Sacramento. Solid .300 hitter, Sacramento, Pacific Coast League, 1932–34. White Sox bought contract; played 29 games in AL, 1934, hit .322. Brooklyn 1935–36. St. Louis 1937–38. Cincinnati 1939. New York AL 1941. Brooklyn 1942–45. Major league totals: .283, 930 games. Two WS, only as pinch runner. Ran twice for Ernie Lombardi, Cincinnati, 1939 WS; once for Bill Dickey, Yankees, 1941 WS.

Past three decades operated glass and metal works, Ventura, Calif.

BOROWY, HENRY LUDWIG (Hank) P-BR-TR. B. 5/12/16, Bloomfield, N.J. 6', 175. Hank Borowy won 56 games, lost 30 for Yankees, helping them win two pennants. Sold to Chicago in waiver deal during 1945 NL pennant race. Was 11–2 for Cubs rest of season, helping them to flag.

Borowy joined Yanks, 1942: 15–4, 2.52 ERA. Followed with 14–9, 1943; won WS game from Cardinals in only start. In 1944, 17–12. Off to fine start in 1945 when Larry MacPhail, Yanks' general manager, sold him to Cubs for $100,000. All AL teams—most could have used 29-year-old strong-armed pitcher—waived chance at buying for waiver price. Without Borowy, Cubs could not have won NL pennant. MacPhail's bitter rival—and former boss—Branch Rickey, was top man with Brooklyn at time. Dodgers finished third in 1945. Borowy also beat

Cardinals three of four decisions after joining Cubs. Redbirds lost pennant to Cubs by three games. Borowy was 2–2 in 1945 WS against Detroit. Led off WS with shutout; defeated in fifth game; won sixth game in relief role; started seventh game but was driven to cover without retiring man, and charged with second loss.

After that Borowy had mediocre record: 1946–48 with Cubs; 1949–50 Philadelphia; 1950, Pittsburgh, Detroit; 1951 with Detroit. Major league totals: 108–82, 314 games, 1716 innings, 3.50 ERA. Had 94 complete games, 17 shutouts. Six WS games: 3–2, ERA 4.97.

BOSMAN, RICHARD ALLEN   P-BR-TR. B. 2/17/44, Kenosha, Wis.

6'3", 208. Bosman had 42–33 record over three-year span while Senators were still in Washington. Any pitcher who could have this winning percentage with Senators in their final days in nation's capital must have plenty of mound skills. Moving to Texas when franchise was shifted, Dick's record sagged a bit, 8–10. Rangers were still pretty futile their first season in Lone Star state. Traded to Cleveland 5/10/73.

Dick, in off-seasons, is in snowmobile business as an executive. In past has been drag racer who has traveled at speeds up to 187 mph.

Bosman attended U. of Wisconsin. Polished his pitching at Kingsport, Tenn., 1963, then went to Lexington, N.C.; York, Pa.; and had 2–6 record with Washington, 1966. Divided his time in 1967 between Hawaii and Washington. After 2–9 mark with Senators, 1968, came up with 14–5, 16–12, and 12–16 marks in successive seasons. Then came shift to Texas—won 8, lost 10 in 1972. In 1969 Dick's 2.19 ERA was most effective pitching in AL. In 1970 his 1.000 fielding mark for 51 chances was best in AL among moundsmen.

Dick belonged to Pittsburgh organization when he was at Kingsport. San Francisco Giants drafted him from Pirates' Columbus roster 12/2/63; later it was Washington that drafted him from Lexington, N.C., team 11/30/64.

Bosman had one game at Buffalo, 1969, but Senators kept string on him. He was ready for 1973 campaign owning overall major league record of 57 wins, 59 defeats in 197 games. Pitched 1063 innings, walked 286, struck out 559, and had 3.32 ERA.

BOSWELL, DAVID WILSON   P-BR-TR. B. 1/20/45, Baltimore, Md.

6'3", 195. One of several who have been punched by Billy Martin. Dave then pitcher for Minnesota Twins; Martin managing team. Martin gave Boswell going-over with fists, 1969. After battle, Dave 8–3; for season, 20–12, only time in major league career won 20. "Maybe Billy woke me up," said Dave. Later, commenting on fight, came out with remark which would have done credit to Yogi Berra: "Now it's just a forgotten memory."

Misfortunes plagued career. One year mononucleosis and pneumonia. Another time, arm trouble. Once hit in head by line drive. Spring 1969, severed two tendons in little finger of left hand cleaning fish. In 1970 following Twins' clinching of AL West title in Oakland, Boswell slugged by teammate Paul Ratliff. Dave holding glass; shattered. Needed 22 stitches.

Dave joined Minnesota, 1964: 2–0, with less than one season of minor league experience. Was 7–11 for Bismarck-Mandan, Northern League, that year; and 4–2 for Charlotte, Southern Association, same season. In 1965, 6–5 for Twins; then 12–5, 14–12, 10–13 before 20-victory season. In 1970, 3–7. Unconditional release 3/31/71 Signed with Detroit Tigers several days later. Brief reunion with Billy Martin, by now pilot of Tigers. Tigers released him 5/6/71 when he refused assignment to minors. Signed with Baltimore Orioles 5/28/71 after working out with club three weeks. Picked up his only AL victory of year by defeating his old club, Twins—first appearance day after he signed. Lost two decisions later, was optioned to Rochester 8/12/71. Was 3–0 in International League. Spring training Orioles, 1972; unconditional release. Major league record then: 68–56, ERA 3.52, 1065 innings, 205 games, 481 walks, 882 strikeouts. Fanned 204, 1967; 190, two years later. Pitched just 2-2/3 innings, 1965 WS; 3.38 ERA.

BOSWELL, KENNETH GEORGE 2B-BL-TR. B. 2/23/46, Austin, Tex. 6', 172. Ken Boswell went into 1973 holding NL record for consecutive games at second base without error, 85. Set this mark in 1970. Ken is same player who hit .422 in New York Mets' stretch drive to their first NL pennant, 1969; led club with five RBI in playoffs that fall to sew it up; then hit .333 in WS, although he got into just one game.

Boswell signed with Mets 6/15/65 but was farmed out to Auburn in New York–Pennsylvania League that season; to Williamsport, Eastern League, 1966; and to Jacksonville, International League, 1966–67. Had 11 games with Mets, 1967, then came back to stay, 1968. Best hitting mark with Mets prior to 1973 was .279 in 1969.

Ken isn't power hitter. Going into 1973 he had .255 mark, with 27 homers to his credit in 509 games in majors. His 455 hits also included 66 doubles, 13 triples. Had scored an even 200 runs, driven in 164.

Boswell attended Sam Houston State College in Texas as young man. Suffered broken finger on right hand, 1968, causing him to miss many games. In 1971 was out considerably with tendonitis of right shoulder. Slapped his first major league grand slam homer 8/7/71.

BOTTOMLEY, JAMES LEROY (Sunny Jim) 1B-BL-TL. B. 4/23/1900, Oglesby, Ill. D. 12/11/59, St. Louis, Mo. 6', 175. Smiling, swaggering, slugging Sunny Jim Bottomley garnered plenty of hitting honors during major league career. However, greatest thrill came in Brooklyn, 9/16/24, when Cardinals slaughtered Dodgers 17 to 3. Drove in 12 of those runs with two home runs, one double, three singles. One homer came with bases loaded. Wilbert Robinson, Brooklyn manager, held previous record for runs batted in during single game—11. So Robbie watched Bottomley not only wreck Dodger pitching staff but also erase own record from books.

Bottomley almost won NL batting title 1931; finished third although average seven-tenths of point behind leader! Teammate Chick Hafey won with .3489, Bill Terry next with .3486, and Bottomley .3482—closest batting race in NL ever. In 1928, tied Hack Wilson for NL lead in home runs, 31; led NL in triples, 20; in RBI, 136. All of which won him NL MVP Award, then carrying with it $1000 prize. In 1936, picked up fielding record, making eight unassisted double plays, major league record. Wore cap in jaunty angle, soon become Ladies' Day favorite—as well as popular with male fans.

Served as policeman in Nokomis, Ill., drove grocery truck, worked as blacksmith's helper in coal mine. Played semipro ball on Sundays, $7.50 per game. During 1919 Labor Day contest slugged two home runs, three triples. Scout Charlie Barrett of Cardinals got wind of this, signed him. Worked way up through Cardinal organization, making parent club 1922. That season hit .325 in 37 games. Average up to .371 in 1923, playing 134 games. From then on, terror of NL pitchers. After 1932 season, traded to Cincinnati, played three years. Back to St. Louis, this time Browns, 1936. Manager, Browns, 7/22/37 until end of season. Manager, Syracuse, International League, 1938, appearing in seven games. Scout, Chicago NL, 1957. Manager, Pulaski (Va.), Appalachian League, 1957. In later years lived on farm at Sullivan, Mo. Died in St. Louis parking lot, apparently of heart attack.

Bottomley's WS record spotty. Helped Cards defeat Yankees 1926, with .345 average and five RBI. Went 1 for 22 in 1930 Series against Athletics for .045 average. Hit .214 in 1928 Series, .160 in 1931 WS. Overall WS average .200, 24 games.

BOUDREAU, LOUIS SS-BR-TR. B. 7/17/17, Harvey, Ill. 5'11", 193. Father-in-law of Denny McLain. Sportscaster. Ex-manger. Stellar shortstop. MVP in AL, 1948. Lou's father, good semipro third baseman. Bought son full-sized infielder's glove when Lou quite young. Lou kept, used, repaired it until 1941, when it fell apart. By then, regular shortstop for Cleveland.

Boudreau attended U. of Illinois. Prepared to be basketball coach, phys. ed. teacher. Played baseball, basketball. A.B. 1939. Before that, lined up with Cleveland organization. Played 60 games with Cedar Rapids, III League, 1938—hit .290—one game with Indians, all as third baseman. Shortstop at Buffalo, International League, 1939; played 115 games, hit .331. Made grade at Cleveland same season; 53 games, hit .258. In 1940, 155 games, .295. Also led AL shortstops in fielding. Fixture in Cleveland until after 1950 season. During this time: led AL shortstops in fielding eight seasons; led AL in hitting 1944, with .327 mark (best average in 1948, .355, when Ted Williams led with .369).

While Lou with Indians twelve full seasons, his Cleveland career almost ended before his finest year, 1948. Roger Peckinpaugh managed Indians in 1941. Club tied for fourth. Peck became vice president of club, and manager's job open. Boudreau, 24 then, went to club president Alva Bradley and applied for job. Bradley appointed him playing manager, youngest in AL history. Finished fourth in 1942, third in 1943, three second-division teams, then fourth in 1947. Meanwhile, Bill Veeck had taken over Indians; wanted Al Lopez manager. During 1947 WS, Bill confided to Cleveland newsmen he was negotiating trade: Boudreau to St. Louis Browns for shortstop Vernon Stephens, two good pitchers (Kramer and Kinder), outfielder Paul Lehner. Bill DeWitt, boss of Browns, demanded more cash. Deal fell through. What had been whispered, now news copy. Indian fans on warpath. One newspaper printed ballot on page one, asked readers to vote. Of 100,000 responses, 90 percent insisted Lou stay as manager. Veeck acceded—gave Boudreau two-year contract as player-manager. Played inspired ball 1948. Veeck said, "Lou was determined to prove I was a jerk ... He did." When pennant race ended, Indians tied with Red Sox for lead. Playoff game in Boston. Led by Boudreau, who got four hits, including two home runs, Indians won 8–3, giving them first pennant since 1920. Indians then took on Boston Braves in WS, beat them four games to two. Contrite, Veeck burned Boudreau's old contract publicly, gave new one for two years at $75,000.

Boudreau's contract terminated at end of 1950 season; new owners had bought Indians. Hank Greenberg was general manager, released Lou unconditionally, hiring Al Lopez. Boudreau signed with Red Sox as player, hit .267 in 82 games. Nearly through as shortstop. Red Sox hired him as manager, 1952–54. Played four games, 1952, then managed from sidelines. Sox finished sixth once, fourth place twice under Lou. Manager, Kansas City AL, 1955–57. Expansion team could not rise above sixth during Lou's tenure. Final managerial chore, 1960. Phil Wrigley switched him from sportscasting Cub games to field manager, 5/5/60. Charlie Grimm, perennial Cub pilot, took Boudreau's place in front of microphone. Boudreau, Cubs finished seventh. Lou returned to sportscasting at end of year.

Boudreau hit .295, 1646 AL games. In 6030 AB, 1779 hits, 385 doubles, 66 triples, 68 homers. Scored 861 runs, drove in 789. One WS, 1948: .273, 6 games, 6 hits (4 doubles). Not fast in field, but fine fielder, smart. Led AL shortstops in double plays five seasons. Hall of Fame 1970.

BOUTON, JAMES ALAN   P-BR-TR. B. 3/8/39, Newark, N.J. 6', 170. N.Y. Yankees 1962–68, Seattle AL 1969, Houston NL 1969. Had two big seasons with Yankees: 1963, 21–7; 1964, 18–13. In 1963 Series against Los Angeles he pitched seven innings as starter against Drysdale, lost 1–0. Allowed 4 hits, walked 5, ERA 1.29. In 1964 Series against Cardinals, Bouton won third game 2–1, giving up 6 hits, 3 walks. Took decision in sixth contest, 8–3, though had to be relieved in ninth. Allowed 9 hits, 2 walks in 8-1/3 innings. Wound up Series that year with 2–0 record, 1.56 ERA.

Mostly relief pitcher in later years. Major league record, 57–54. Author of *Ball Four*, book allegedly telling tales about former teammates and opponents, meriting him widespread unpopularity among players, club officials and others. Is television sports announcer in New York area.

BOWA, LAWRENCE ROBERT (Larry)   SS-BLR-TR. B. 12/6/45, Sacramento, Calif. 5'10'', 160. Larry Bowa set some fielding records, 1971, playing shortstop for Philadelphia Phillies, but they did not last long. His .987 fielding average was major league record for shortstops playing as many games as he did. Equaled this mark again in 1972. However, Eddie Brinkman bettered record in 1972 with .990 average. Bowa made 11 errors in 1971, nine in 1972; but Brinkman set new mark, 1972, with just seven errors.

Larry played American Legion ball. Attended Sacramento City College. Drafted by Phillies 1966. Minor league experience, Spartanburg and San Diego, that year (San Diego then in Pacific Coast League). Bakersfield and Reading 1967. Reading 1968. Eugene 1969—led PCL in stolen bases, 48, hit .287, 135 games. Phillies 1970. Hit .250 in 145 games, with 34 RBI. In 1971 Bowa hit .249 in 159 games, with 25 RBI. Hit his first major league homer 1972. His 1972 average identical with his .250 career average for 456 big league games as 1973 began.

Larry works with youth groups in Philadelphia. Spent two weeks after 1971 campaign instructing youngsters 8 to 12 in baseball school in Florida. Also worked in Phillies' ticket office during winter; spoke at numerous affairs in Philadelphia area. Bowa's father Paul and uncle Frank both played minor league ball.

BOYER, CLETIS LEROY   3B-BR-TR. B. 2/8/37, Cassville, Mo. 6', 183. Exit from American baseball marked by plenty of verbiage, specially from Paul Richards, Bowie Kuhn and Boyer himself. Sixteen-year major league veteran wound up 1971 season as member of Hawaii club, Pacific Coast League. Then traded to Japan's Tayio Whales for John Werhas. First such trade ever. Last season in big leagues, with Atlanta, started routinely. After 134 games in 1970, Clete ready to play third base regularly again in 1971. But years had taken toll. When Clete hassled over enforcement of midnight curfew, Richards said, "For such a lousy player, Boyer does a lot of talking. I'll give him his release if he writes out a check for 60 days of pay."

Rules call for 60 days of severance pay when player is released. Boyer was willing to waive this. Eventually agreed to pay $10,000 for release, having effect of waiving severance pay. But deal nullified as violation of Basic Agreement between players and management. So Clete, paid $45,000 annually, received $15,000 check plus his pay up to time he left club. Left with blast: at Richards, Braves' vice president, suggesting he depart baseball; at Mgr. Luman Harris, calling him Richards' puppet, advising that Eddie Matthews, a coach, become manager. Another factor in case was fact two other major league clubs contacted Boyer after his release, then suddenly broke off talks. Reason, according to Boyer, was bulletin from Commissioner Kuhn's office, suggesting that he not be signed pending gambling investigation. Kuhn pointed out that investigation antedated Boyer's problems with Atlanta club. Kuhn, 6/10/71, announced $1000 fine for Clete's betting on college, pro football games, 1968–69. Boyer admitted bets in sums up to $150; insisted he had never bet on baseball game, had never placed bet with known bookie.

Boyer had .245 average for 30 games with Braves in 1971, and at Hawaii, hit .250 in 78 contests. Major league career: .242 average, 1725 games, 645 runs, drove in 654, 1396 hits, 200 doubles, 33 triples, 162 homers, 41 stolen bases.

Clete's batting never sensational, though did have his moments at plate. In 1962 WS, playing with Yankees, his seventh-inning homer in first game broke 2–2 tie, gave Whitey Ford his 10th WS victory. His highest average in majors was .272, 158 games, in 1962. In 1967, first year in Atlanta, hit 26 homers and had 96 RBI. During career, five grand slam homers. Third base play always strong point. Led NL third sackers in fielding 1967 and 1969. While in AL, though excellent, generally outshone by Brooks Robinson of Baltimore.

Boyer from baseball family. Brother Ken, now coach with Cardinals, had long major league career, mostly with Redbirds. Brother Cloyd is Yankees' minor league pitching instructor. Brothers Len and Ron also played minor league ball.

As bonus player, according to rules then in effect, Clete had to stay on major league roster from 1955 through 6/4/57, with Kansas City AL. During those years played 124 games; needed minor league experience. Traded to Yankees, who farmed him to Binghamton rest of 1957. Richmond 1958–59. Joined Yanks 1959 in time for 47 games. Then for seven full seasons was regular with Bombers, during which time club won five pennants. Transferred to Atlanta 1954, remaining with Braves until 1971 explosion.

In five WS with Yanks: 27 games, .233, 86 AB, 20 hits, 6 doubles, 1 triple, 2 homers, 11 RBI. His 65 assists tops third sackers; also in 4 double plays, tying record for WS third basemen.

BOYER, KENTON LLOYD 3B-BR-TR. B. 5/20/31, Liberty, Mo. 6'2", 208. Most talented of baseball-playing family. Brother Clete spent most of his major league career with Yankees. Ron played in Yankee organization. Cloyd was pitcher with Cardinals. Ken became batting coach for Redbirds, 1971, team he played with during most of career. Manager, Cards' Sarasota club, Gulf Coast Rookie League, 1973. Started out as pitcher with Lebanon, Pa., North Atlantic League, 1949, but .455 batting average, three homers in 16 games indicated he should play oftener than pitching allowed. Following year, .342, Hamilton, Ont., Pony League; made transition from pitching to third base, outfield. Then Omaha, Western League, batting .306, 151 games, 14 homers, 90 RBI. Military service 1952–53. Then Houston, Texas League, .319, 202 hits. Also put together hitting streak of 30 games that season. Major league career started 1955, St. Louis NL. Hit .264 his first season, 147 games. then marks over .300 in five of next six years. Soon recognized as outstanding fielder at third base; twice led league in fielding, set various records, including five years in which he led circuit in double plays by third sackers. In 1964, though average below .300 (.295), Ken won MVP Award; drove in 119 runs, tops in NL. Cardinals won flag. Then in WS hit two home runs, one with bases loaded (10/11/64). Came with Yankees leading 3–0. Final score, 4–3. (Al Downing victim of Boyer's smash.) Crucial seventh game: three runs, three hits, including two-bagger, second home run. Cards won, 7–5. Overall average, just .222, 6 for 27 trips. His only WS. Brother Clete played third base for Yankees, hit .208 in seven games. Clete made two errors, Ken one.

Cardinals traded Ken to N.Y. Mets after 1965 season. Mets sent him to White Sox during 1967. Chicago AL, Los Angeles NL, 1968. Played 25 games for Dodgers, 1969. Manager, Cardinals' farm team at Arkansas, Texas League, 1970. Then to parent club as coach.

Ken versatile. In 1957, most of year playing center field. Major league totals: 2034 games, 7455 AB, 1104 runs, 2134 hits, 318 doubles, 68 triples, 282 homers, 1141 RBI, .287 average, 105 stolen bases.

BRADLEY, THOMAS WILLIAM P-BR-TR. B. 3/16/47, Asheville, N.C. 6'3", 185. Tom Bradley won 15 games for Chicago White Sox in both 1971 and 1972, but was traded to San Francisco Giants in

November of latter year. Scholarly, bespectacled hurler, who owns degree in Latin from U. of Maryland, struck out more than 200 batters in each of his final two seasons with White Sox. But team needed center fielder and obtained Ken Henderson in exchange.

Bradley started out in organization of California Angels, 1969. Gained his minor league experience at Quad Cities, Midwest League, then at El Paso, San Jose, and Hawaii. With Angels briefly in 1969 but went back to minors, 1970. Won three, lost none in Texas League; had 11–1 mark at Hawaii; and 2–5 record back with California. Traded to White Sox 11/30/70. His performance was 15–15 with 2.96 ERA in 1971, and 15–14 in 1972 with 2.98 ERA.

Tom started out with Giants owning 3.17 overall ERA for his 105 major league games. Pitched 618 innings with 32 wins, 35 losses. Had 470 strikeouts against 172 bases on balls.

During off-season Bradley was member of White Sox advance ticket sales department. Continued in this job even after being traded to Giants.

BRAGAN, JAMES ALTON 2B-BR-TR. B. 3/12/29, Birmingham, Ala. 6′, 198. Quieter member of Bragan family. Brother of Bobby, who managed several major league teams and is remembered for altercations with umpires—until he became president of Texas League. Jimmy, coach with Montreal Expos, never made majors as ball player, but joined Cincinnati Reds as one of Dave Bristol's assistants, 1967. Coach, Montreal NL, 1970. Scout, Expos, 1973.

Jimmy Bragan, second baseman, played in old Brooklyn organization in days when Branch Rickey bossed Dodger system. Signed with Elmira, 1950. Later with Fort Worth, Newport News, Mobile, Columbia (S.C.), Nashville, Savannah, Monterrey Mex. Macon. In 1957, retired as player managed Bluefield club in Appalachian League and promptly won pennant. Scouted for Cincinnati Reds, 1958–66. During 1971 season was drafted for month and half as interim manager for Winnipeg (Expos' farm) when regular pilot, Clyde McCullough, suffered heart attack.

Bragan graduated from Mississippi State, 1951, B. S. education. Off-season, public relations man, freight solicitor for carloading company in Birmingham, Ala.

BRAGAN, ROBERT RANDALL C-BR-TR B. 10/30/17, Birmingham, Ala. 5′11″, 190. Former umpire-baiter par excellence. Ex-manager of Pittsburgh, Cleveland, Milwaukee, Atlanta, and several teams in minors. Now president, Texas League—and umpire-defender.

Bragan played shortstop regularly, 1940–41, Philadelphia NL; began conversion to catcher following year. Brooklyn Dodgers 1943–44, 47–48. Military service 1945–46. By 1949, playing manager at Fort Worth.

Never quite lived up to expectations as big league manager. In minors had first-place teams at Fort Worth and Hollywood; two second-placers, one third-placer, one fourth. In first seven seasons piloting, teams never finished out of first division. Bossed Pittsburgh, 1956 until 8/3/57: two seventh-place teams. Cleveland 1958; released 6/27 of that year, with Indians in sixth. Manager, Milwaukee Braves, 1963—65, part of 1966, with team in Atlanta. Had one sixth-place team, two in fifth. Had 52—59 record when Billy Hitchcock replaced him in 1966. Braves ultimately fifth in 10-club circuit. As player, Bragan began 1937, Panama City, Alabama-Florida League. Then two seasons at Pensacola, Southeastern League, before joining Phillies. Three years, Philadelphia. Then Flatbush 1943–48 (minus two years, military service). Between Cleveland and Milwaukee assignments as mentor, Bobby managed at Spokane, Pacific Coast League; coached L.A. Dodgers 1960; scout for Houston NL 1961; coach, Houston, 1962.

Bragan's bouts with umps now memorialized: bringing Coca-Cola onto field, offering to umpire; lying down on field to protest; sending up eight pinch hitters, one for another, in same time at bat, claiming that if umpires were making farce of game with their decisions, he would go along with them. Using same logic, once sent batboy to play third base. At times fired towels, catcher's masks, chest protectors, shin guards, caps, sweaters out of dugout. One night in Hollywood, after his team had lost argument over what time umpires should have called extra-inning game on previous evening because of curfew, Bragan collected all wristwatches in clubhouse. Sent coach Gordon Maltzberger with lineups to umpire at home plate. Maltzberger had six or eight watches on each arm, and carried alarm clock in one hand, lineup in the other.

Bragan's major league playing record: 597 games and .240 average. Off field, Bragan tireless worker in civic causes, church work, boys' organizations. Polite too. Once when managing Fort Worth for Brooklyn Dodgers, Branch Rickey sent him wire asking whether Carl Erskine, then under Bragan's wing, would help Dodgers' pennant run. Rickey, his desk laded with dozens of telegrams, other correspondence, received Bobby's economical reply of one word: "Yes." B.R. forgot what he had asked Bragan, again telegrammed Fort Worth: "Yes, what?" Replied Southern gentleman Bobby, "Yes, sir!"

BRANCA, RALPH THEODORE JOSEPH P-BR-TR. B. 1/6/26, Mount Vernon, N.Y. 6'3", 220. Winning pitcher, Brooklyn Dodgers, late 1940s. Better remembered as victim of Bobby Thomson's dramatic home run which gave rival N.Y. Giants pennant, final game of 1951 playoffs.

Branca attended New York U. 1943–45. Started pro career with Olean (Dodger farm), Pony League, 1943. Divided 1944 season between Dodgers and Montreal, International League; 1945 between St. Paul,

American Association, and Brooklyn. With Dodgers 1946, 3–1. Was 21–12, 1947; 2.67 ERA. Had 14–9 record, 1948, and 13–5 mark, 1949. Then seemed to lose something of his effectiveness.

Won one, lost one in 1947 WS; lost one, 1949 WS. In bullpen do-or-die third game of 1951 playoffs, Polo Grounds. First half of ninth inning Dodgers broke 1–1 tie, took 4–1 lead. Giants up. Newcombe was Brooklyn pitcher, arm began to tighten. Alvin Dark singled. So did Don Mueller, Dark taking third. Whitey Lockman then doubled, scoring Dark. Mueller twisted ankle going into third; carried off on stretcher. Hartung ran for him. First base open, one out. Would Dodgers walk Thomson (.293, 101 RBI during season), putting potential winning run on base? Mgr. Dressen called in Branca. First pitch fast ball, low inside corner, strike. Second pitch high and tight. Thomson swung. Ball sailed into left field seats, giving Giants ball game—and pennant.

Branca went to Detroit on waivers, 7/10/53. Shifted to Yankees during 1954 season, his last except for one game two innings for Dodgers in 1956. Major league totals: 322 games, 88–68, ERA 3.79, 1484 innings. WS play: 1–2, 6.35 ERA, 17 innings.

BRANDT, JOHN GEORGE, JR. (Flakey) OF-BR-TR. B. 4/28/34, Omaha, Nebr. 5′11″, 189. Jackie Brandt, having spent eleven years in majors as player, is back in minors striving to make it back to big leagues as manager or coach. Manager of Columbus Astros of Southern Association, 1972, after serving as boss of Sumter, Western Carolinas League, 1971. In 1973, became pilot of Alexandria, La., team in Texas League. Brandt was fine fielder. Considered best left fielder in NL, 1959, while with San Francisco Giants. Received Gold Glove Award.

Jackie attended Omaha University before joining Ardmore, 1953. Columbus, Sally League, 1954; Omaha, Western League, 1954. Rochester, International League, 1955. In 1956 made grade in majors, starting with St. Louis NL, then traded to N.Y. Giants. Hit .298 that year in 125 games. Following season and most of 1958, military service. When he came back, Giants were in San Francisco. After 1959 season, traded to Baltimore AL, where he remained until end of 1965. With Orioles, best season at bat was 1961—.297. Philadelphia NL, 1966. Philadelphia NL and Houston NL, 1967.

Lifetime major league record showed 1221 games, 3895 trips to plate, 1020 hits—including 175 doubles, 37 triples, 112 homers—540 runs scored, 485 RBI, .262 batting average. Brandt appeared in one All-Star game, 1961, for AL as pinch hitter, going hitless.

BRANNICK, EDWARD T. Executive. B. 7/22/93, New York, N.Y. "Secretary Emeritus," San Francisco Giants. Retired from active service with Giant organization spring 1971, after 65 years. Fall 1905 Eddie, 12, answered ad for boy to help work WS scoreboard in original Madison Square Garden. John T. Brush, president of Giants, selected Brannick, later gave office job. Eddie ran errands, acted as mail clerk, took care of ball bag—anything. Became assistant road secretary (though never west of Hoboken, N.J.). First trip, spring training, with Giants to Marlin, Tex., 1911. As train passing through Illinois, Eddie looked out window, saw farmland covered with stubble from last year's corn crop. "What is all of that out there?" he asked veteran newsman Sid Mercer, who replied, "Match sticks." "So that's where they all come from," said Eddie, impressed.

Became full-time road secretary, 1936. Later, secretary of club as well. Wore old-fashioned straw hat with bright band. Refrained from alcoholic beverages; drank uncounted gallons of coffee. Remained New Yorker till Giants' move to S.F. Wavered about leaving Gotham; finally went west with club. Golden jubilee dinner in his honor, Waldorf-Astoria, 8/28/55, while Giants still New Yorkers. Ever popular with all. Health began to fail in later years, leading to retirement.

BREADON, SAM Owner. B. 7/26/76, New York, N.Y. D. 5/10/49, St. Louis, Mo. President, St. Louis Cardinals, 1920–47. Breadon moved to St. Louis, 1902, to join friend in garage business. Eventually became local representative of Pierce-Arrow Company. After syndicate had acquired control of impoverished Cardinal franchise, Breadon bought $2000 worth of stock. As enthusiasm of others waned when there were no dividends, Sam picked up additional shares. Elected president 1920, but did not have control until he had 67% of stock in 1922. Eventually owned well over 80%.

About this time Cardinals initiated two moves destined to be copied by all other major league teams. One was Knothole Gang. Boys were invited to attend games free for purpose of stimulating new fans and keeping boys off streets. Second plan, farm system, more far-reaching and enabled financially pressed club in small population center to compete with richer teams in cities like New York, Chicago.

Knothole idea was brainchild of one of Cardinal stockholders, Jimmy Jones. Farm system was Branch Rickey's scheme, but eagerly embraced by Breadon. Starting with Fort Smith in Western Association and Syracuse, International League, Cardinal farms grew in number until about 30 clubs were included in system. For many years Cardinals bought no outstanding players from minor leagues or other major league teams. Scouted youngsters, placed them in their Class D or C leagues, advanced them as talents developed until ready for big league.

Among stars who came up this way were Jim Bottomley, Taylor Douthit, Chick Hafey, Ray Blades, Bill Hallahan, Dizzy and Paul Dean, Johnny Mize, Paul Derringer, Joe Medwick, Gus Mancuso. Stan Musial may have been most outstanding product of Cardinal farms.

Breadon went along with Rickey as his field manager until 1925 when he abruptly fired Rickey as pilot, retaining him as general manager. Rogers Hornsby was new manager, won pennant for Cardinals 1926, first full season at helm. Being direct, blunt man, Breadon wanted to discuss problem with Hornsby. Went to clubhouse. Before long equally blunt Hornsby disagreed with boss, told him to "get the hell out of my [Hornsby's] clubhouse."

White with anger, Breadon told Rickey "Hornsby must go." Rickey persuaded him to wait until end of season. Argument had developed over exhibition game Breadon had booked. Hornsby wanted Breadon to cancel, declaring club needed day's rest as pennant fight heated up. Breadon would not renege on contract. Despite word battle, Cards went on to capture first Cardinal flag in history, climaxed by win over Yankees in seven-game World Series. Breadon's enthusiasm for Hornsby had its limits. When Hornsby demanded three-year contract at $50,000 per annum, believing he had Breadon cornered because of fan adulation, Sam refused. When Rogers rejected offer, Breadon traded him to Giants for Frankie Frisch and Jimmy Ring, astonishing people of St. Louis.

Cards won flags again 1928, 30, 31 despite several managerial changes. Famous Gas House Gang developed 1934, with Dean brothers, Durocher, Medwick, Bill DeLancey, Pepper Martin helping bring another flag, World Series victory over Detroit.

Breadon and Rickey meanwhile were producing more young ball players than Cardinals needed. Sold dozens of men, either from minor league farm clubs or from Cardinal club, to other big league teams. At one point Rickey estimated Cardinals got between $2.5 million and $3 million for player sales.

More pennants 1942,43,44,46. During Breadon's presidency, team had taken nine pennants and won World Series six times. Sold Cardinals 1947 to former Postmaster General Bob Hannegan and associates when health went bad.

Breadon played leading role in selection of Ford Frick as NL president, 12/11/34. Branch Rickey reportedly was receptive to job but Breadon wanted him to stay in St. Louis as his productive general manager. Election of Frick forestalled any immediate Rickey move.

When Pasquel brothers began luring big league stars to Mexico with fabulous offers, Commissioner Happy Chandler was taking no action. Breadon flew to Mexico to confront Jorge Pasquel and to persuade him not to bother Cardinal players. Chandler demanded Breadon make report on his trip. Breadon refused. Chandler fined Breadon $5000 and suspended Cardinal club. NL club owners refused to support Chandler's action, penalties were canceled. Breadon said conference was something between him and Pasquel, nobody else's business.

During depression Breadon cut salaries of players, club officials and employees repeatedly. At one point, after stressing economies, Sam stopped in office of Clarence Lloyd, traveling secretary. While talking to Clarence, Sam noticed electric clock. "How much electricity does the clock use?" asked Breadon. Lloyd went over to clock, pulled plug and never again used it. Though Cardinals got well financially when team won 1934 pennant, Breadon never told Lloyd to start the electric clock.

BRECHEEN, HARRY DAVID (Cat) P-BL-TL. B. 10/14/14, Broken Bow, Okla. 5′10″, 168. Got nickname because of great fielding. Reminded people of cat springing on mouse when he pounced on ball hit near mound. Most of Cat's great pitching for St. Louis NL. Greatest heights in 1946 WS. Many years capable coach for Baltimore Al.

Early experience 1935–42: Galveston, Greenville, Miss.; Bartlesville, Okla.; Portsmouth, Va.; Houston; Columbus, Ohio. In 1939, Houston, 18–7; ended Texas League season with four consecutive shutouts, league record, and 38 straight scoreless innings. After 16–9, 16–6, 19–10 marks at Columbus, American Association, Brecheen joined Cardinals, 1943, to stay. Only once in 10 years with Redbirds did he fail to win more games than he lost. Six of those years had 14 victories or more; in 1948, 20–7. In 1945 his 15–4 mark topped NL pitchers in winning percentage, as did 1948 performance. After 1952 season with Cardinals, Brecheen switched to St. Louis Browns: 5–13; called it quits. Browns transferred to Baltimore, Cat became pitching coach.

Harry's first appearance in WS, 1943: 0–1. In 1944, defeated Browns in only WS game he pitched. In 1946, captured three games against Boston. First, four-hit shutout. Won sixth game, 4–1. Then relieved in crucial seventh game. Blanked Red Sox for two innings; credited with victory when Enos Slaughter made his famous dash home from first base on Harry Walker's hit to left center for winning run. Brecheen only lefthander to win three games in WS until Mickey Lolich did it, 1968.

Career: 133–92, 1905 innings, 618 earned runs, 901 strikeouts, 536 walks, ERA 2.92. In WS: 7 games, 32-2/3 innings, 4–1, ERA 0.83, 28 hits, 3 earned runs, 18 strikeouts, 12 walks.

BREITENSTEIN, THEODORE P. P-BL-TL. B. 6/1/69, St. Louis, Mo. D. 5/3/35, St. Louis, Mo. 5′9″, 167. Pitching end of famous "Pretzel Battery," along with Heinie Peitz, with St. Louis Browns, American Association, later with Cincinnati Reds. Wound up career losing more than he won, but some notable successes: three seasons as 20-game winner, two no-hitters. First no-hitter came in first start as major league hurler, 10/4/91, against Louisville. Used in relief after joining Browns. Had begun season with Grand Rapids. (St. Louis entered NL 1892.) After 1896 season sold to Cincinnati for $10,000, sensational amount of money for ball player then. Battery reunited when Peitz later went to Cincinnati. Pitched second no-hit game, 4/22/98, against Pittsburgh. Won 23 games his first year with Reds, 20 second season. In 1901, back with St. Louis NL. Had lost touch, went to minors. Played at St. Paul, Memphis, New Orleans. Retired from active play, 1911. Umpired then in Southern, Southwestern, Texas Leagues until retirement, 1921.

Old-time records differ, but won at least 160 major league games while losing 170. Never big man, but had remarkable speed and endurance.

BRESNAHAN, ROGER PHILLIP (Duke) C-BR-TR. B. 6/11/79, Toledo, Ohio. D. 12/4/44, Toledo, Ohio. Difference of opinion exists about when and where this Hall of Famer was born. Some "official" records say he came into world 6/14/80 at Tralee, Ireland. Others, just as "official," say it was the more prosaic Toledo almost one year earlier. No difference of opinion, however, about fact he invented shin guards for catchers. Inspiration came after watching cricket game. "If bowler needs something to keep from barking his shins, why not the catcher?" he reasoned. So he fashioned leg protectors in 1908. Undoubtedly would have made Hall of Fame even if hadn't invented shin guards. One sports writer described his play: "Watch him while he is catching. Watch him throw to bases. Absolute, unerring decision is his. Never a moment of hesitation, a second of doubt. He heaves that ball to second or to third or to first as the lightning chance may demand, with a sort of cold, infallible ferocity. And he possesses that alacrity of taking a chance, that audacity which differentiates soldiers of genius from the prudent plodder who, maneuvering beautifully, loses battles with skill and grace."

"Duke of Tralee" started out as pitcher with Washington NL, 1897. His first major league game 8/27/97, pitched 3-0 shutout over St. Louis NL, allowing six hits. Toledo, 1898; Minneapolis, 1899; Chicago NL, 1900. Bresnahan didn't do much these years, but when landed with Baltimore AL, 1901, was on way to greatness. Divided time between pitching and catching, but soon concentrated on receiver's job. Later played infield and outfield on occasion. Baltimore AL, 1902. New York NL, 1902-08, where he was Christy Mathewson's battery mate. Playing manager, St. Louis NL, 1909-12. Player, Chicago NL, 1913-14; player-manager, Cubs, 1915. Owner-manager, Toledo, American Association, 1916-23, playing during first three seasons there. Coach, Giants, 1925-28. Coach, Tigers, 1930-31. Hall of Fame 1945.

Major league records showed 1410 games, .279 batting average. In only World Series, 1905, hit .313, five games, helping Giants vanquish Philadelphia Athletics, four games to one. Bresnahan led off in batting order—as he did during much of career—because of his speed. Fine base runner, for catcher. Stole 34 bases, 1903; 25 bases, 1906; 19 in 1915.

BRESSLER, RAYMOND BLOOM (Rube) P-OF-BR-TL. B. 10/23/94, Coder, Pa. D. 11/7/66, Cincinnati, Ohio. 6′ 187. Rube Bressler's career filled with ups and downs. At age 19 broke into majors, was 10–3 with high-flying Philadelphia Athletics. Pitching staff included such greats as Eddie Plank, Chief Bender, Herb Pennock, Bob Shawkey, Bullet Joe Bush. Team romped to AL pennant—then lost four straight to miracle Boston Braves, 1914. Following season Bressler 4–17. For two years Rube couldn't win a single major league game, returned to minors, then managed 8–5 mark for Cincinnati Reds, 1918. In 1919, when Reds won flag and then took tainted World Series from White Sox, Rube contributed just two victories. Did not appear in Series. Next Bressler broke his ankle. Tried to pitch too soon afterward and unnatural motion, favoring leg, caused arm trouble. Finished as pitcher. But Rube didn't quit. Played some outfield in minors (New Haven, Eastern League, 1916; Newark, International League, 1917); not distinguished as hitter. Decided to concentrate on learning first base and outfield, as well as hitting. In 109 games, 1921, hit .307. In 1924, .347; following year, .248. In 1926 his .357 was tops in NL, but powers-that-be ruled that teammate Bubbles Hargrave was batting champion with .353 because Bressler went to bat only 297 times in 86 games. Bressler landed with Dodgers 1928, remaining there until Philadelphia NL had him for 27 games in 1932; then went to St. Louis NL for 10 games.

Bressler had 26–31 record as major league pitcher in seven seasons, ERA 3.40. As batsman, took part in 19 campaigns, hit .301 in 1305 games, 1170 hits in 3881 at bats. Drove in 586 runs. Extra-base hits—164 doubles, 87 triples, 32 homers. Scored 544 runs, stole 47 bases.

With Athletics, Bressler roomed with Chief Bender; with Dodgers, Dazzy Vance. In Cincinnati, roomie was Eppa Rixey.

BREWER, JAMES THOMAS P-BL-TL. B. 11/17/37, Merced, Calif. 6′1″, 190. Jim Brewer pitched only 78 innings in 1972, but had 1.27 ERA. In those 78 innings for L.A. Dodgers, 8 victories, 17 saves. Arm problems; stopped pitching mid-September. Postseason operation, removal of bone spur, left elbow. Before operation, signed 1973 contract calling for estimated $65,000. Brewer's won-lost record would hardly merit such salary. In 449 games as starter or reliever, before 1973 season, won 52, lost 51, with 669 strikeouts, 296 walks. Concentrated on being relief man, 1968, during five seasons since, won 36 games, saved 96, with ERAs of 2.49, 2.56, 3.13, 1.89 and 1.27—2.27 overall.

Brewer's tour of duty: Ponca City 1956–57; Burlington 1958–59; San Antonio 1959; Houston, American Association, 1960; Chicago NL 1960–61; Salt Lake City 1962; Chicago NL 1962–63; Los Angeles NL

1964 to present. Solitary complete game, 1964. Started two games 1965, none in 1966. Started 11 in 1967 but unable to complete any of them. Then moved to bullpen and hasn't started since. Brewer in WS 1965, 66: 3 innings, ERA 3.00.

BRIDGES, EVERETT LAMAR (Rocky) Inf.-BR-TR. B. 8/7/27, Refugio, Tex. 5'8½", 180. Struggled through 39 games at Santa Barbara in 1947; hit only .183. Following year, reported to Greenville, Sally League; teammates hooted when public address system boomed out, "Everett LaMar Bridges, shortstop." From then on, he was Rocky.

Montreal, International League, 1949–50 and briefly in 1952. Brooklyn 1951–52. Cincinnati 1953–57. Washington 1957–58. Detroit 1959–60. Cleveland 1960. St. Louis NL 1960. Los Angeles AL 1961. Bridges proved valuable infielder but never quite nailed down permanent job. Best season 1955: 95 games, .286.

Since playing days, Bridges has alternated between coaching Los Angeles and California Angels, and successfully managing minor league teams. Coach, Angels, 1962, 63, 68–71. Manager, San Jose, California League, 1964–66. Won league first-half title, 1965; second in both halves, 1966. In 1967, led El Paso, Texas League, to third place. Manager, Hawaii, Pacific Coast League, 1972–73—farm of San Diego NL.

Major league record: 919 games, 2272 AB, 245 runs, 562 hits, 80 doubles, 11 triples, 16 homers, 187 RBI, .247 average. All-Star game 1958.

BRIDGES, THOMAS JEFFERSON DAVIS P-BR-TR. B. 12/28/06, Gordonsville, Tenn. D. 4/19/68, Nashville, Tenn. 5'10¾", 165. Tommy Bridges came within one out of pitching perfect game 8/5/32. His second full year with Tigers, Tommy winning from Washington AL 13–0 until two out in ninth. Pinch hitter Dave Harris singled to spoil effort. Was consistent winner most of career with Detroit, 1930–46. Missed 1944 season, military service. Major league totals showed 194–138 mark, 3.57 ERA.

Opened pro career at Wheeling, Mid-Atlantic League, 1929, 10–3. Evansville, III League, 1930, 7–8, before joining Tigers same year, 3–2. In 1934, 35, 36, posted 66–32 mark, helping Tigers to pennants, 1934, 35.

World Series record: 1934, 1–1; 1935, 2–0; 1940, 1–0; 1945, 1-2/3 innings, no decision. Totals: 4–1, ERA 3.52.

Portland, Pacific Coast League, 1947–49, 33–25 over three-year span. One victory was no-hitter, 1947. San Francisco, Seattle, PCL, 1950, 11 games, no decisions. Coach-scout, Cincinnati, 1951. Scout, Detroit, 1958–60. Scout, Mets, 1963–68. Also salesman for Detroit tire company some years while scouting. Graduate of Tennessee.

BRIDWELL, ALBERT HENRY SS-BL-TR. B. 1/4/84, Friendship, Ohio. D. 1/24/69, Portsmouth, Ohio. 5'9", 170. Al Bridwell hit ball which sparked famous "bonehead" play by Fred Merkle, 9/23/08, Polo Grounds, New York. Score 1–1, two outs, last of ninth, Giants at bat, McCormick on third and Merkle on first. Bridwell cleanly singled into center. McCormick raced home. Crowd surged onto field, believing Giants had won. Merkle neared second base, but seems not to have tagged bag. Johnny Evers, Cub second baseman, shouted to his outfield colleague, Hofman, to throw ball. One version: Joe McGinnity of Giants scrambled onto field, got ball, threw into stands. Another version: Evers got original ball, tagged second, claimed forceout for third out, making McCormick's run meaningless. Crowd on field, confusion about what happened. Umpire in chief O'Day ruled tie game, too dark to continue play. When season ended, Cubs and Giants in tie. Disputed game replayed. Cubs won. Bridwell, later years, said he wished he had struck out since Merkle thereafter pilloried by fans, sports writers as bonehead. Facts were, this rule had been ignored in previous years.

Bridwell started with Columbus, American Association, 1903, signed by Bob Quinn, business manager of club. (Bob had long career with St. Louis AL, Boston AL, Brooklyn in front office. Father of John Quinn, ex-general manager of Phils.) Bridwell sold to Cincinnati before 1905 season. Boston NL 1906–07. New York NL 1908–11. Boston NL 1911–12. Chicago NL 1913. St. Louis, Federal League, 1914–15. Major league average of .255 in 1241 games; 2 homers; 136 stolen bases.

BRIGGS, JOHN EDWARD OF-1B-BL-TL. B. 3/10/44, Paterson, N.J. 6'1", 195. John Briggs came up with .467 slugging percentage with Milwaukee Brewers, 1971; higher than marks compiled by such clobberers as Harmon Killebrew, Boog Powell, Rico Petrocelli. Hit 21 homers, nine more than best total while with Philadelphia NL, eight years. Also .264 average, with 59 RBI. In 1972, hit .266; again 21 HR, with .455 slugging average. His power hitting more appreciated than his fielding abilities.

Briggs attended Seton Hall, selected for All-State teams in baseball, basketball and football. Also loves to bowl. Signed by Phillies. Bakersfield 1963—.297 in 120 games, 21 homers, 83 RBI, 94 runs. Phillies 1964. Remained until trade to Milwaukee AL, 4/22/71. Never quite lived up to expectations. Compiled .251 lifetime average in 695 NL games, with 52 homers, 209 RBI. Best mark with Phils was .282 in 81 games, 1966. Missed several weeks that season with back injury.

BRILES, NELSON KELLEY P-BR-TR. B. 8/5/43 Dorris, Calif. 5'11", 205. Versatile. Pitcher, Pittsburgh. Sometime singer, nightclubs; television sportscaster, off-season. Played football, basketball, baseball in high school. Averaged 40.5 yards a punt, senior year. Hobbies include music, dramatics, languages.

Briles' baseball career uneven. Started with Tulsa, American Association, 1964, after attending Chico State College and Santa Clara. Joined St. Louis NL 1965—3–3. Following year 4–15. But in 1967, 14–5. Helped Redbirds win pennant. Had been in bullpen when Bob Gibson broke his leg; given chance as starter. In 1968, 19–11; 15–13 in 1969. Pulled hamstring muscle in 1970, resulting in 6–7 record. Traded to Pittsburgh before 1971 season; spot starter, reliever, 8–4. Then sparkled in WS against Baltimore. In fifth game of set he blanked Orioles on two hits and put Pirates ahead, three games to two. Previous WS experience 1967–68. First WS start 1967, against Red Sox. Pitched 5–2 Cardinal victory in third game. Relieved in later game and had 1.64 ERA for classic. In 1968 WS, not so effective against Detroit: 5.56 ERA, $11^1/_3$ innings, 0–1. In his three WS: 31 innings, 9 runs, 13 strikeouts, 7 walks, ERA 2.61. As 1973 began, major league totals: 83–69, ERA 3.32.

BRINKMAN, EDWIN ALBERT SS-BR-TR. B. 12/8/41, Cincinnati, Ohio. 6', 171. Figured in what must have been Bob Short's most stupid trade. Eddie for several years had been recognized as fine fielding shortstop. Then came Ted Williams to manage Washington Senators. Brinkman, 1969–70, upped batting mark 70 or 80 points. Short, Washington owner, coveted Denny McLain, temperamental Tiger pitcher. To get McLain, Short, in Oct. 1970, gave away Brinkman, young third baseman Aurelio Rodriguez, pitchers Joe Coleman and Jim Hannan. Short also got three players; none tarried long in majors. McLain lost 22 games for hapless Senators. Rodriguez drew raves as hot corner guardian. Coleman won 20 for Tigers despite serious injury which sidelined three weeks. Brinkman spectacular afield. Set new fielding marks for shortstops in 1972—made only seven errors in 156 games, notched .990 fielding average, both topping existing marks. Went from 5/20 to 8/5, 72 games, without error, breaking John Kerr's major league record of 68 successive errorless games in 1947 with N.Y. Giants.

Eddie attended U. of Cincinnati. Received $65,000 bonus to sign with Washington, 1961. Farmed to Pensacola, Middlesboro (Ky.), Raleigh before sticking with Senators, 1962. Got into 54 AL games that year, hit .154. Next several years played most of team's games, but three times average under .200. Ted Williams, lured out of retirement, managed Senators, 1969. Brinkman, .188, .187 previous two seasons, raised mark to .266, with Ted's help. Hit .262 following season. Then came Short's brainstorm about McLain. In 1971 Eddie set AL record for most consecutive errorless games by shortstop in one season, 56. Led AL shortstops in double plays, 1963 and 1970; in putouts, assists, total chances, 1970.

Eddie dropped to .203 in 1972. Bespectacled shortstop's lifetime major league average at start of 1973 was .224. Best year for extra-base hits was 1964: 20 doubles, 3 triples, 8 homers; average just .224. Best average was .266, under Williams' influence. In minors, Eddie did manage .324 in 1962 with Raleigh, playing 58 games. In 1972 reached 1457 mark in total big league games. Has brother who has caught for White Sox.

BRISSIE, LELAND VICTOR, JR. (Lou) P-BL-TL. B. 6/5/24, Anderson, S.C. 6'4½", 210. Paratrooper corporal, World War II. In Italy with infantry, Lou led patrol of 12 men into battle zone. Shellfire. Lou only survivor. Both legs shredded; left leg all but torn off. Seven hours before being discovered. Patched up; 23 operations over two-year period. Braces for one leg, sort of artificial leg for other. Yet Lou made it to major leagues; won 14 games for Philadelphia Athletics, 1948; 16 in 1949. Later served seven years as national director of American Legion baseball program; coached and led teams of youngsters on foreign tours. When last heard of, selling insurance in Greenville, S.C.

Lou attended Presbyterian College two years. Signed with A's organization at 16. Then entered service. After operations on legs, determined to make it as ball player. In 1947, won 23 games for Savannah, lost 5, ERA 1.91. Won chance with Athletics. Lost only decision in majors that year. But in 1948 had 14–10 record, then 16–11, finally 7–19 mark in 1950. Traded to Cleveland during 1951 season, 4–5. Had 3–2 mark 1952. Retired after pitching 13 innings without decision, 1953. Brissie wound up with 44–48 mark, 4.07 ERA. As relief man: 29 saves, 2.67 ERA. All-Star team 1948, but not used.

Opening day 1948, Ted Williams drove terrific smash off Brissie's left shin. Ball bounded nearly to right field wall. Easy double, but Williams stopped at first, called for time, and came over to check Lou's condition. Brissie carried on. Another time, Lou entered game in fourth inning for Cleveland, Satchel Paige in for St. Louis. Score remained tied until 19th when Browns went ahead, 4–3. Then Rosen hit two-out, two-run homer and Brissie had 5–4 victory over future Hall of Famer.

BRISTOL, DAVID Manager. B. 6/23/33, Macon, Ga. Took over managment of Milwaukee Brewers 1970, after 3-1/2 years as Cincinnati pilot. Bristol guided expansion club to fourth-place tie in AL's Western Division, 1970; sixth, 1971. Replaced by Del Rice late May 1972, with Brewers in last place in their division. Coach, Montreal NL, 1973.

Bristol considered "low-key" guy, man of few words. Never played in majors. Started out in 1951 at Welch, W. Va. Then Ogden, Utah; Sunbury, Pa.; West Palm Beach, Fla.; Wausau, Wis. Began player-manager career, 1957, Hornell, N.Y., New York–Pennsylvania League. Continued at Geneva, N.Y.; Visalia, Calif.; Palatka, Fla.; Topeka, Kans. Following season, 1962, Bristol quit playing; managed Macon through 1963. Manager, San Diego, Pacific Coast League, 1964—65. Coach, Cincinnati Reds, 1966 until named manager, 7/13/66. After taking over, team was 39—38, seventh place. In 1967 Reds fourth. Fourth 1968. Third 1969. Replaced by Sparky Anderson. Had won 298 games, lost 265 in Cincinnati. Credited with developing such stars as Pete Rose, Tommy Helms, Lee May, Tony Perez.

Bristol in military service, 1954. As player, his best hitting seasons: 1957, Hornell, .332 in 85 games; 1958 at Geneva, .312 in 120 contests, 81 RBI. At Wausau, 1957, hit .333, but took part in only 21 games.

BROBERG, PETER SVEN P-BR-TR. 3/2/50, West Palm Beach, Fla. 6'3", 205. Pete Broberg got $150,000 contract from Washington Senators after leaving Dartmouth campus June 1971. Bought Tony Lupien, his college coach, car with part of bonus money and tried to keep it secret. Broberg dazzled major league scouts with his pitching for Dartmouth. His fast ball compares favorable with best in majors. In three years at Dartmouth, Broberg fanned 311 in 197 innings. In one game against Boston College, fanned 20 batsmen. Peter's father All-America basketball player at Dartmouth, later lost arm when shot down over Okinawa, World War II.

Pete reportedly received offer of $175,000 contract from Oakland A's when he finished high school, but wanted to go to college. When Washington made him No. 1 draft choice in secondary phase, June 1971, Pete accepted bonus, continued studies at Dartmouth off-season. Six days after signing, Mgr. Ted Williams sent him to mound 6/20/71. Broberg scared to death. Those who had seen him pitch in college said he was throwing harder than ever that day. Held Boston Red Sox in check, allowing four ground singles, struck out seven. Departed with one out in seventh inning with 3–0 lead, but Senators later lost game. First victory July 4. Went route against Cleveland, allowing six hits, winning 9–4. Ended first pro season: 5–9, 18 games, 125 innings, 104 hits, 53 walks, 48 earned runs, 89 strikeouts, 3.46 ERA. Also only Washington pitcher to slam homer in 1971 (9/19/71, off Rogelio Moret, Boston Red Sox). Transferred with team to Texas, Pete in 1972 was 5–12, with 4.30 ERA, for Texas Rangers.

BROCK, LOUIS CLARK OF-BL-TL. B. 6/18/39, El Dorado, Ark. 5'11", 165. Lou Brock, with 600 major league stolen bases to his credit by midseason 1973, broke Ty Cobb's record of eight years with 50 or more thefts. Stole 50th base 8/26/73 off Johnny Bench. In 1971 Brock set record for NL players since 1900 by pilfering more than 50 bases for seventh consecutive season. Cobb's eight years not consecutive.

Brock deal one of most successful trades Cardinals ever made. Lou with Cubs two full seasons, few headlines. Then, 6/15/64, Cardinals obtained in six-man deal—five others have since vanished from majors. Brock bargain from start. Had batted .251 with Cubs, 52 games, start of 1964 season; hit .348 for Cardinals, helped them win pennant. Also key in Redbird flags 1967, 68.

Lou attended Southern U., Baton Rouge, La. Received $30,000 bonus from Cubs, 1961, after third year in college on athletic scholarship. Impressive debut in pro ball: home run on first pitch, St. Cloud, Minn., Northern League. Went on to hit .361, 128 games, including 33 doubles, 6 triples, 14 homers, 82 RBI. Cubs called up, end of season—4 games, 1 for 11. Cubs 1962–63: .263 and .258, first two seasons as regular. Sensational base thief first full year with Cards: 63 steals. Then 74, 1966, tops. In 1971 Brock led majors in runs scored, 126; and fourth time in career reached 200-hit level. As 1973 started: 1681 major league games, 1088 runs, 2001 hits, 335 doubles, 105 triples, 125 homers, .293 average, 579 RBI. In 1968 Brock led NL in doubles, triples, stolen bases—not done since Honus Wagner did it, 1908. Brock's NL play exciting, even greater in WS. First Series, 1964, batted .300, 9 for 30—2 doubles, 1 homer, 5 RBI. Redbirds beat Yankees in seven. In 1967 WS: hit .414, 12 for 29—7 steals, 8 runs, 3 RBI, 2 doubles, plus triple, homer. Cards again won in seven. In 1968 Series, Detroit won seven. Not Lou's fault: again stole 7 bases, hit .464 (13 for 28), 6 runs, 3 doubles, 1 triple, 2 homers, 5 RBI. Brock's 14 WS steals overall, equaled Eddie Collins' mark. But Eddie's in 34 games; Lou's in 21 WS contests. No one has ever stolen seven bases in WS except Lou, who did it twice. And his six long hits in 1968 WS equaled mark set by several players, including Babe Ruth. His 13 hits, 1968, matched record set by Bobby Richardson in 1961.

Brock one of nine children. Spends considerable time with Lou Brock Boys Club, organization of about 1500 underprivileged youngsters in St. Louis. Lou made newscasts in 1969 when Small Business Administration admitted it had mistakenly guaranteed $135,000 loan to Brock for his business ventures. Brock insisted he had not asked for any special favors.

BRODIE, WALTER SCOTT (Steve) OF-BL-TR. B. 9/11/68, Warrenton, Va. D. 10/30/35, Baltimore, Md. 5'9½", 176. Carefree clown; also played outfield for dozen years in majors. Hit better than .300 for well over 1400 games, though accurate statistics impossible because of discrepancies in old records. Most of his career in NL, starting 1890 at Boston; also played for St. Louis, Baltimore, Pittsburgh and New York teams in NL, and spent 1901 with Baltimore AL Club.

Brodie could perform with ball and bat, even though considered No.

1 funny man of his era in baseball. Was with old Baltimore Orioles that won NL championships, 1894,95,96. Had batting averages around .350 mark two of those seasons.

Before reaching majors played semipro ball in Virginia; and with pro teams at Altoona, Pa.; Canton, Ohio; Wheeling, W. Va.; and Hamilton, Ont. After leaving majors, saw service at Binghamton, N.Y.; Providence, Newark, Roanoke; Portsmouth, Va.; Norfolk, Va.; and Wilmington, Del.

Coached baseball team at Rutgers College, 1912–14. Scouted for Brooklyn Federal League team, 1914, and then for several years coached U. S. Naval Academy baseball team at Annapolis. Member of Baltimore Park Board many years. Buried near graves of John McGraw and Wilbert Robinson, his colorful teammates in days with Orioles in 1890s.

BROSNAN, JAMES PATRICK P-BR-TR. B. 10/24/29, Cincinnati, Ohio. 6'4", 215. Mostly used as relief pitcher, winding up with 55–47 mark. Chicago NL 1954, 56–58, St. Louis NL 1958–59, Cincinnati NL 1959–63, Chicago AL 1963. Minor league experience: Springfield (Mass.), Fayetteville (N.C.), Macon, Nashville, Des Moines.

Kept diary during 1959 season, then wrote book, among first to "expose" inner secrets of ball players' intimate lives on and off field. Titled *The Long Season*, book attracted considerable attention. Brosnan has written additional book; also newspaper and magazine articles. Has worked for Chicago advertising agency in recent years.

BROUTHERS, DENNIS JOSEPH (Dan) 1B-BL-TL. B. 5/8/58, Sylvan Lake, N.Y. D. 8/3/32, East Orange, N.J. 6'2", 200. Dan Brouthers slugged his way into Hall of Fame, 1945. Led NL in hitting three times, tied once. Led American Association in hitting, 1891, when that circuit considered major league. Later led Eastern League in hitting, 1897, with .415 average.

Brouthers started with Troy, N. Y., then in NL, 1879. Moved to Buffalo NL 1881, remaining until 1885. Detroit NL, 1886–89. Boston, Players League, 1890. Boston AA 1891. Brooklyn NL 1892–93. Baltimore NL 1894–95. Louisville NL 1895. Philadelphia NL, 1896. Springfield, Eastern League, 1897–99; part of 1898 with Toronto, part of 1899 with Rochester, both Eastern League. Two final major league games with N.Y. Giants, 1904. When Brouthers was with Detroit, 1887, club won pennant; then won 8 of first 11 games of 15-game traveling WS from St. Louis Browns of American Association, managed by Charles Comiskey. "We slugged 'em to death," declared Brouthers.

Brouthers' credentials for Hall of Fame include .349 batting average for major league career, 1658 games, 1507 runs, 2349 hits,

446 doubles, 212 triples, 103 homers, 263 stolen bases. Dan scouted for Giants, 1907; later job at press gate, polo Grounds.

BROWN, JOE L. Executive. B. 9/1/18, New York, N. Y. Like many baseball players, Joe L. Brown served long apprenticeship in minor leagues before proving himself major leaguer. General manager, Pittsburgh Pirates, since 11/1/55, Brown started baseball career in Lubbock, Tex., as assistant to business manager of club, 1939. Became business manager next season, then moved to Pittsburgh Ice Hockey team during winter 1940–41 in same capacity. President, Waterloo, Iowa, baseball club, 1941.

World War II interrupted. Enlisted in U. S. Air Force. After three and half years emerged as captain. Back to baseball 1946–47, publicity chief for Hollywood Stars, Pacific Coast League. Then did publicity work for movie, *The Babe Ruth Story*. General manager, Zanesville, Ohio, baseball club, 1949. Then entered Pittsburgh organization, 1950. General manager, Waco, Tex., club, then same job at New Orleans till becoming president of latter team, 1952–54. During 1954 graduated to parent club, doing special administrative and scouting jobs. Succeeded Branch Rickey as Pirate general manager, 1955.

Brown's most successful seasons 1960, 1971. In former, Pirates won fantastic World Series victory over Yankees in seven games. In 1971, Pirates came from behind to defeat Baltimore Orioles in Series after Pittsburgh had lost first two games. Teams Brown responsible for have included, besides two pennant winners, one runner-up, three third-place clubs and two fourth-place teams. Pirates finished on top in NL Eastern Division, 1970, only to lose playoffs to Cincinnati.

Joe L. is son of old-time stage and movie comedian, Joe E. Brown. During high school days played football and baseball and was member of swim teams. Attended UCLA two years as journalism major. One year of varsity football. Has popular radio sports program, "Joe L. Brown Show," in Pittsburgh during baseball season. Received First Annual Humanitarian Award from *Pittsburgh Courier*, 1963.

BROWN, MORDECAI PETER (Three Finger) P-BLR-TR. B. 10/19/76, Nyesville, Ind. D. 2/14/48, Terre Haute, Ind. 5'10", 175. Two accidents turned Brown into pitcher who was able to win 208 games in majors. When quite young, Mordecai lost half of index finger on his right hand in corn shredder. In game between Coxville and Brazil, Indiana teams, Coxville pitcher failed to show up. Brown, third baseman, pressed into service as hurler, decided to stay with pitching.

In 1901 had 23–8 record for Terre Haute, III League, then went to Omaha, Western League, 27–15. St. Louis NL 1903. After 9–13 mark, traded to Cubs. Became famous. Won 15 games 1904, 18 in 1905, followed by six straight years of 20 wins or more. In 1908, record was 29–9; following season, 27–9. In 1912, dropped to 5–6. Traded to Cincinnati for 1913. With St. Louis and Brooklyn in Federal League, 1914; Chicago, Federal League, 1915; Chicago NL 1916. Back to minors 1917, with Columbus; called it quits after 1920 season with Terre Haute.

Brown managed St. Louis Feds, 1914; Terre Haute in 1919; Indianapolis, 9/19; Terre Haute again, 1920.

Brown's World Series performance with Cubs 1906,07,08,10: 5–4, 9 games, 57-2/3 innings, ERA 2.81. Took part in 411 major league games, had 208 wins and 111 losses for .652. ERA records not available for earlier part of his career.

Was fine fielder. Usually able to make opposing batsmen hit ball on ground. Besides descriptive moniker, was nicknamed "Miner" as he was reared in coal-mining area. Hall of Fame 1949.

BROWN, ROBERT WILLIAM (Golden Boy) 3B-BL-TR. B. 10/25/24, Seattle, Wash. 6'1", 180. Now heart specialist, Fort Worth, Texas. Called "Golden Boy" during playing days with Yankees because he got bonus in neighborhood of $50,000 for signing back in 1946 when that sum represented very fancy figure.

When Bobby was five, father gave him bat and started preparing him to be major leaguer. When in teens, decided to be doctor. Both careers blended together, though it took compromise on both sides. Sometimes studies made him late at spring training; in autumn, World Series play made him late for classes. Consequently it took quite a bit longer to get M.D., graduating from Tulane, 1950. Cardiology won out in end, Bobby retiring before his 30th birthday. Probably could have stayed in majors several years longer. By time Bobby was ready to sign a baseball contract, 15 of the 16 major league teams of that time reportedly interested. Story told that Horace Stoneham, president of N.Y. Giants, was interested. Bobby's father mentioned $60,000. Stoneham gasped. Father then said, "All right, Mr. Stoneham, how about double or nothing? If Bobby signs and makes good, you give us $120,000. If he doesn't make good, we get nothing." Apparently Stoneham wasn't that much of a gambler and Bobby signed with Yanks. Farmed out to Newark, 1946, Brown hit sturdy .341 in 148 games at shortstop. His 174 hits good enough to equal best hit production in International League that year. Recalled by Yanks at end of season, took part in seven games, 8 for 24 for .333. Hit .300 1947, did pretty well in World Series. Came through three times as pinch hitter, two of these being doubles, which set record for Series pinch batsmen. In another trip to plate as pinch hitter drew base on balls. Drove in three runs. Yanks won classic from Dodgers, four games to three.

Two years later Brown and Yankees again in Series. Bobby hit .500,

6 for 12, driving in five important runs as Yankees again defeated Dodgers, this time four games to one. Series average in 1950, .333, with Yanks sweeping Phillies. In 1951, when Yanks took Giants four games to two, Brown hit .357.

In midseason 1952 Brown entered army. Spent nine months in Korea, ten in Japan. Missed 1953 season, most of 1954. Rejoined Yanks for couple of months that year, then began practice of medicine. Had attended Stanford and UCLA before going to Tulane for his degree. Completed internship at Southern Pacific Hospital, San Francisco, 1952.

Lifetime records: 548 games, .279 batting average. World Series: 17 games, 18 hits in 41 times at bat, including 5 doubles, 3 triples, 9 runs scored, 9 RBI, for .439 Average.

BROWN, WILLIAM JAMES (Gates) Of-BL-TR. B. 5/2/39, Crestline, Ohio. 5'11", 225. Pinch hitter deluxe. First time as emergency batsman—also first at bat in big league—slapped homer, 6/19/63, fifth inning of night game. In 1971, set new AL record for total career pinch hits, 81—five more than Fothergill had, holder of old record. In creating new AL record, Brown's 1971 performance showed 9 pinch hits in 26 times at bat, .346 average. After player strike ended and 1972 season started, Gates had overall record of 356 appearances at plate as emergency batsman: 294 AB, 81 hits, .276 average, reaching base 131 times. Overall average in 1972 of .230. Pinch-hit average even lower.

Gates was renowned high school football halfback. But signed baseball contract with Detroit system, 1960. Played with Duluth-Superior, Durham, Knoxville, Denver, Syracuse before reaching Detroit during 1963 season. Picked up Carolina League batting championship, 1961—.324 average, 113 games. Played left field for time with Tigers but then became part-timer because of fielding limitations, plus knack of hitting in pinch. Best overall averages with Tigers: .370 in 1968, .338 in 1971. Hit .265 as pinch hitter in 1965; .325 in 1966; missed most of 1967 with dislocated wrist; .462 in 1968 (18 for 49). In 1968, two consecutive homers as pinch hitter, tied major league record. As 1972 dawned, had record of 11 pinch homers. Also one grand slam.

Brown's average in majors stood at .264 at start of 1973. Had 67 homers, 63 doubles, 18 triples among 463 hits in 806 games. Had scored 274 runs, driven in 252. One WS appearance, 1968: 0–1, pinch hitter.

BROWNING, LOUIS ROGERS (Pete) OF-BR-TR. B. 7/17/61, Louisville, Ky. D. 9/10/05, Louisville, Ky. 6'2", 200. Pete Browning loved to hit, cared little for fielding—training rules either. Led league in hitting three times; compiled .354 lifetime major league average. This mark, however, should be watered down somewhat, because his play included .471 average in 1887, when every walk counted as hit.

Browning colorful character. Had abscessed ear much of his career; deathly fear of being struck there by freak hop. Once, while playing on soggy field, refused to run through puddle and fined for missing fly ball. Called beer "German tea"; imbibed plenty, plus other liquids. Took pledge after .253 average, 1889—hit .391 following season.

Pete reportedly was first player to have his own bats made to order. Before 1884, players used whatever available. But Browning went to John Hillerich, in wood business in Louisville, had bat turned out to his own specifications. Gradually others followed. Louisville Slugger bat business evolved in firm, Hillerich & Bradsby.

Browning started off as champion. In his first year with Louisville, American Association (then major league), won batting title with .382. Took another title, 1885, with .367. Remained with Louisville until that .253 season, 1889. Till then, always well over .300. His .391 teetotaling season, 1890, with Players League (also major league). Divided 1891 between Pittsburgh and Cincinnati, NL; 1892 between Louisville and Cincinnati, NL. Louisville 1893. Divided 1894 between St. Louis and Brooklyn, NL.

Browning pretty poor fielder. In six of his seasons so many errors, unable to achieve .900 fielding average. Once, 68 errors, as infielder early in career. Chased to outfield—less chance to harm team. Most errors in outfield, 43, in 134 games, 1887. Hitting carried him. In 1180 games: 1719 safeties, 292 doubles, 89 triples, 46 homers. Career totals for stolen bases incomplete; stole 121 in 1887, and at least three other times, over 30.

BRUSH, JOHN TOMLINSON Executive. B. 6/15/45, Clintonville, N.Y. D. 11/26/12, St. Charles, Mo. Clothing merchant. Became important baseball leader. Moved into game with Indianapolis NL 1887, largely to publicize clothing business. Later president of Cincinnati. Bought N.Y. Giants for about $125,000, 1903. Despite bitter hostility toward AL at start of century, set up rules for World Series—used today with only minor alterations. Hatred of Ban Johnson, AL organizer, born when Ban newsman in Cincinnati, often criticized Brush. AL recognized as major league, 1901. In 1903 its champion team, Boston, met NL pacemakers, Pittsburgh Pirates, in first modern WS—team-to-team, not league arrangement. Giants won NL flag 1904, proudly spurned challenge of Red Sox. Brush said he saw no reason why dignity of NL pennant should be "cheapened and jeopardized" by series with best club of "minor league." Criticized by fans, sports writers, he reconsidered, came up with rules making it mandatory that pennant winners of each league meet in annual WS.

As club owner, Brush gave John McGraw, his field manager, carte blanche in dealing for players and running club on field. Once Brush signed player—on faith. Player turned out to be of stellar quality. Brush got into conversation with barber in Mount Clemens, Mich., where he had gone for his health. Barber sang praises of young Fred Merkle. Brush never saw him play, but told him to report to John McGraw. Merkle made good, played in majors 1907–26.

In 1911, wooden stands at Polo Grounds burned down. Giants used park of N.Y. AL club, then known as Highlanders, temporarily. Brush quickly negotiated new long-term lease with Mrs. Harriet Coogan, owner of park site, and began construction of new "mammoth structure." By middle of season, new Polo Grounds far enough along for Giants to play home games. Double-decked concrete, steel structure destined to be arena of countless epic battles. Disappeared after Mets moved to Shea Stadium.

One of Brush's moves was to poll fans about game time. Until 1912 Giants' games started 4 P.M. Critics said Brush kowtowing to Wall Street brokers by starting at that hour. When patrons voted for earlier start, time pushed back to 3 P.M.

When Brush president, Giants won four pennants. Poor health several years. After team captured flag, 1912, Brush sorely disappointed when team lost WS (4 games to 3) to Boston Red Sox. Many said this contributed to his death while on train to California for winter. Died passing through Missouri.

BRUTON, WILLIAM HARON OF-BL-TR. B. 12/22/29, Panola, Ala. 6′, 170. Bill Bruton, as member of Milwaukee Braves, led NL in stolen bases his first three seasons in majors, 1953–55: 26,34,25 respectively. Later suffered knee injuries, but still stole 207 bases in 1610 big league games. Missed 1957 WS because of knee operation, but in 1958 classic led both clubs in hitting with .412 average, one of hits homer.

Bill's speed apparent during first year in pro ball at Eau Claire. Led Northern League in steals, 66; hit .288 in 128 games. Spent 1951 with Denver. Then burned up American Association while with Milwaukee, 1952. Led that circuit in hits, 211; in runs scored, 130. Had 37 doubles, 7 triples, 5 homers, hit .325. Following year NL moved Boston franchise to Milwaukee. Bruton ready. Remained with Milwaukee NL until 12/3/60, when traded to Detroit. While with Braves twice led NL in triples. After move to Detroit, hit his greatest number of homers, 17, in 1961. Had 16 in 1962, with 74 RBI. Then tapered off, leaving majors after 1964 season.

Bill's best batting average in majors, .289, in 1959. Career average, .273. His 1651 hits included 241 doubles, 102 triples, 94 homers. Drove in 545 runs, scored 937.

BRYANT, RONALD RAYMOND P-BLR-TL. B. 11/12/47, Redlands, Calif. 6', 190. During latter part of 1972 baseball season Ron Bryant lugged around stuffed bear, three feet high, as mascot. Dressed it in small Giant uniform and put his own number on back. Whether there was any connection, doubled his victory total over 1971. San Francisco southpaw was 14–7, had 2.90 ERA, best season of his career in minors or majors.

Ron's being member of Giants something of afterthought. Scout Eddie Montague went to Davis, Calif., to take look-see at Bob Heise. Ron pitched no-hitter for his high school club, but lost. Montague gave him small bonus after he was selected in first free-agent draft, 1965.

From then until 1970, when Bryant came to Giants to stay, he had his apprenticeship at Twin Falls, Idaho; Decatur, Ill.; Fresno, Calif.; Amarillo and Phoenix, with couple of part seasons with parent club. Had 5–8 record, 1970, then 7–10 following year.

In 1972 Ron pitched 4 shutouts, won his 14 games despite bout with pneumonia during midseason. Went into 1973 with record of 30 major league wins, 28 losses, and ERA of 3.70. Pitched 508 innings, allowing 189 walks, striking out 284. Had taken part in 113 games but owned just 15 complete ones, with 6 shutouts.

Earns his bread with fine fast ball, good curve, and slider as well as pretty fair control.

BUCKNER, WILLIAM JOSEPH (BUCK) OF-1B-BL-TL. B. 12/14/49, Vallejo, Calif. 6'1'', 185. Ted Williams, spring 1970, saw Bill Buckner at plate, remarked: "There's a kid who has the swing to lead the league in batting." Bill hasn't led league yet, but in 1972 was among NL's top ten hitters, .319 average. Impatient, competitive. In 1971 fined $500 for starting towards Juan Marichal, after Giant pitcher hit him with ball. Bill, bat in hand, was prevented from getting close to Marichal by umpire Shag Crawford. Dodger pitcher had hit two Giants earlier; Marichal twice shaved L.A. pitcher before plunking Buckner. (Juan fined $50 for a warning about throwing at Dodgers, $100 for ignoring it.)

Bill didn't stick with Dodgers in 1970. Had .191 average for 28 games; most of season at Spokane, Pacific Coast League. There, .335 average, 111 games. Stuck with Dodgers 1971: .277 in 108 contests. As 1973 season started, Buckner had played 242 major league games, owned .289 batting average. His 234 hits did not manifest great power: 32 doubles, 5 triples, 10 homers. But always battles pitchers, seldom striking out.

Bill's first pro season was 1968 at Ogden, Utah. In 64 games he led Pioneer League in hitting with .344, in hits with 88, in triples with 8. Also led first basemen in fielding. Then, 1969, hit .307 at Albuquerque, Texas League, in 70 games, and .315 in 36 games at Spokane. One game with Dodgers that year. Then 1970.

During 1972–73 off-season Buckner attended Southern California School of Business Administration; filled engagements for Dodgers' speakers bureau.

BUFORD, DONALD ALVIN OF-BLR-TR. B. 2/2/37, Linden, Tex. 5'8", 160. Best leadoff man for Baltimore Orioles since they returned to AL, 1954. Small man, lots of dynamite: 17 homers, 1970; 19 in 1971. Strikeout-prone. Usually among leaders in getting on base. Walked 96 times, 1969; 109 in 1970; 89, 1971. But, tied AL record by fanning five times in one game; equaled another record by making it seven straight strikeouts in two games, 8/26, 28/71. Good base runner too—stole 51 bases in 1966, 34 in 1967 with Chicago White Sox. After becoming Oriole, with so much power behind him in batting order, he stole less—usually around 15 or 20 per season. After disappointing 1972, Don agreed to go to Japan with two-year contract with Fukuoka Lions, for reported total of $85,000 plus travel expenses, fringe benefits.

Don attended Los Angeles City College and Southern Cal on athletic scholarship. Starred on baseball, football squads. Compensated for size by trying harder, says Don. Had to be quicker, run faster, jump higher have better timing than bigger men. Member of NCAA championship baseball team, 1958. All-Pacific Coast football team same year. Pro career started, 1960, San Diego, Pacific Coast League, but most of season at Lincoln, Nebr. Charleston (S.C.) 1961. Savannah 1962. Indianapolis 1962–63. Chicago AL 1963–67. Baltimore 1968–72. Fine season last year in minors, Indianapolis. Led International League in runs with 114; hits, 206; doubles, 41; stolen bases, 42; batting, .336; assists, 311—as third baseman. Outfielder regularly only after joining Orioles.

By end of 1972 Buford had compiled .264 average in 1286 major league games, scoring 718 times (missed 100 mark by one, 1969–71). His 1203 hits included 157 doubles, 44 triples, 93 homers. Had 418 RBI. Helped Orioles win playoffs, 1969–71 with .357 average. In WS each of those autumns, came up with .207 mark. However, had one homer each of first two Series, two homers in WS of 1971, with seven RBI in WS play. In 1971 Buford started five regular-season games by hitting homers. Also made AL All-Star squad for first time that year.

Buford has spent some of his winters in Los Angeles working in Sears.

BULKELEY, MORGAN G. Executive. B. 12/26/37, East Haddam, Conn. D. 11/6/22, Hartford, Conn. First president NL, 1876. Politician, civic leader, businessman, banker. President of Aetna Life Ins. Co., 1879. Mayor of Hartford, 1880–88, giving salary to city's fund for poor. Elected governor, Connecticut, 1888, serving until 1893. Elected U.S.

senator, 1905.

Yale conferred Master of Arts 1889. Trinity College awarded LL.D. 1917. Elected to Hall of Fame 1937 for service to baseball apart from playing game.

BUNNING, JAMES PAUL DAVID   P-BR-TR. B. 10/23/31, Southgate, Ky. 6'3", 203. Few pitchers can approach record set by Jim Bunning. Those 224 major league victories represent goal worth shooting for. Additionally Jim won more than 100 games in each major league; pitched no-hitters in each league, one of them perfect game; took part in eight All-Star games; earned his way close to $100,000 level in salary; fathered nine children. Only participation in World Series missing. Maybe that will come as manager.

Bunning eventually got B.S. in economics at Xavier, Cincinnati, though had to skip couple of spring training trips to do so. Pitched at Richmond, Davenport, Williamsport, Buffalo, Little Rock and Charleston (W. Va.) from 1950 to 1956 before making good at Detroit with 5–1 output in 1956.

Following season Bunning pitched 267 innings, more than any other AL hurler; had 20–8 mark. Won 118 games, losing 87 for Tigers through 1963 season. Chalked up his AL no-hitter against Red Sox 7/20/58. Traded to Philadelphia NL 12/4/63. Won 19 games each of next three seasons; dropped down to mere 17 victories in 1967. At which point Jim went to Pittsburgh and had poorest mark of career, 4 wins, 14 losses. Broke even with Pirates, 9–9, in 1969 before going to L.A. Dodgers late that year. Took four decisions out of five after joining Alston's team.

Back with Phillies 1970, 10–15; 5–12 mark, 1971. Lifetime major league record 224–184. All-Star record for eight games showed 1–1, 16 IP, 6 hits, 2 earned runs for 1.13 ERA.

Bunning's perfect game came 6/21/64 against N.Y. Mets. First perfect game since Don Larsen's in 1956 World Series. Sandy Koufax pitched one in 1965 and Jim "Catfish" Hunter did it in 1968.

Leaving majors, Bunning signed to manage Phillies' farm team, Reading, Eastern League, for 1972. Manager, Eugene, Oreg., 1973, Philly farm in PCL. Off-Season, stockbroker in Cincinnati.

BURDETTE, SELVA LEWIS, JR. (Lew)   P-BR-TR. B. 11/22/26, Nitro, W. Va. 6'2", 201. After many years of brilliant pitching for Braves of Boston, Milwaukee, Lew Burdette returned to Braves for 1972 as coach. This time wandering Braves making their home in Atlanta.

Burdette probably would have been Yankee stalwart but for impatience of club management in 1951. Yanks wanted experienced hurler immediately. Braves had Johnny Sain. Burdette was promising youngster, but had not burned up any leagues anywhere. Package of Burdette plus $50,000 for Sain. Braves never regretted deal. Lew didn't really blossom until Braves moved to Milwaukee, 1953. Won 15, lost 5. Winning pitcher for rest of career with Braves, taking total of 179 games over 13-year span. Traded to Cardinals 6/15/63; 3–8 record for Redbirds that year. Divided 1964 between Cards and Chicago NL; 1965, Chicago and Phillies. California AL 1966–67; Seattle AL 1967. Scout, southeastern area, Central Scouting Bureau, 1968. Major league totals showed 203 wins, 144 losses in 626 games, ERA 3.66.

Burdette started with Norfolk, Piedmont League, 1947; Amsterdam, Canadian-American League, same season; Quincy, III League, 1948; Kansas City, American Association, 1949–50. Acquired by Yanks, farmed to San Francisco, Pacific Coast League, for 1951. After 14–12 record, recalled and traded to Braves.

Accused of using spitball through much of career. Used wide variety of pitches effectively. Hurled 1–0 no-hit victory over Phils 8/18/60. In 1957 Series against Yankees, Lew won three games, losing none, in spectacular fashion. Pitched two shutouts. Tied Series mark for most complete games pitched in seven-game Series, three. In fifth game, threw only 87 pitches—only two fly balls went to outfield. Pitched 24 straight scoreless innings; faced 101 batters and none crossed plate.

BURGESS, FORREST HARRILL (Smoky) C-BL-TR. B. 2/6/27, Caroleen, N.C. 5'8½", 200. Smoky Burgess played 1718 games in major league career, but isn't remembered for his catching. Was pinch hitter par excellence. After setting record for total pinch hits for career, with 115, carried on until upping to 145. As pinch batsman hit respectable .286. And conscientious. With Cincinnati, sent to pinch hit. Reds had total of 220 homers for year, just one shy of NL mark set in 1947 by N.Y. Giants. Birdie Tebbetts, Cincinnati manager, counseled, "A homer or nothing. We've got to equal that record." "Yes, sir," said Smoky. Without further ado, slammed ball out of park.

Smoky got his nickname from speed (or lack of it) on bases. Didn't use tobacco or alcohol. Strongest drink was milk.

Burgess was traveler from start. Began pro career in Pony League with Lockport (N.Y.), 1944. Subsequently with Portsmouth (Va.), Los Angeles, Macon, Fayetteville, Nashville, Springfield (Mass.) teams in various circuits. With Chicago NL briefly, 1949, but didn't stick with Cubs until 1951. Philadelphia NL 1952–55. Cincinnati 1955–58. Pittsburgh 1959–64. Chicago AL 1964–67. During career usually had healthy batting average, reaching .368 in 1954. Was behind plate when Harvey Haddix pitched 12 perfect innings for Pirates 5/26/59, only to lose in 13th. Wasn't proud of tying record for most passed balls in World Series—three. That was 1960 when Pirates conquered Yankees in seven games. Burgess hit .333 (6 for 18) in that Series, his only time in fall classic. One of his many red-letter days came 7/29/55 when he hit three homers in one game.

Smoky's major league totals: 1718 games, .295 average, 1318 hits, 4471 at bats. Among his hits were 230 doubles, 33 triples, 126 homers.

BURKE, MICHAEL   Executive. B. 6/8/18, Enfield, Conn. Perhaps no major league executive had as varied background as former president of N.Y. Yankees. Early years in Ireland. Graduated, Pennsylvania. Outstanding halfback; won award for football player with best scholastic record. Tryout with Philadelphia Eagles. Soon gave it up for job in insurance agency, marine cargo inspector. Commissioned ensign in U.S. Navy. Assigned to duty with Gen. Wild Bill Donovan's Office of Strategic Services. Spoke fluent French, good Italian. First clandestine mission: to subvert Italian fleet, get it to join Allied cause. In 1944 joined French resistance movement, dropping behind German lines in Vosges Mountains. Won Navy Cross for heroism, Silver Star for "conspicuous gallantry and intrepidity in action" during Italian campaign. After war, two years in Hollywood as screen writer. Warner Bros. film *Cloak and Dagger*, starring Gary Cooper, based on Burke's adventures. Three years as special intelligence advisor to U.S. high commissioner for Germany, John J. McCloy. General manager of Ringling Bros. Barnum & Bailey Circus. Joined Columbia Broadcasting System, 1956; president of CBS Europe, headquarters London. Returned to New York 1962, vice president in charge of developing new areas of business for CBS. CBS bought Yankees, 1964. Burke became president of ball club in autumn of 1966. Early 1973, CBS sold franchise to syndicate of 15, Burke among them, for reported $10 million. Burke then became chief operating officer for Madison Square Garden. Has been called "the executive hipster." Long hair. Mod clothes. Reportedly helped force resignation of General Eckert as baseball commissioner before Kuhn took over job.

BURKE, ROBERT JAMES   P-BL-TL. B. 1/23/07, Joliet, Ill. D. 2/8/71, Joliet, Ill. 6'1/2", 160. Bobby Burke won only 38 games in major leagues, but remained in big time over nine seasons. Pitched no-hitter against Boston Red Sox, 8/8/31. Won and lost (46) all his games for Washington Senators. Had 4.29 ERA for 254 games, 918-2/3 innings. Bobby seemed to lack stamina. In only four seasons did he pitch as many as 100 innings. Only twice won as many as eight games. Best performance 1931: 8–3. But Joe Cronin, manager of Senators part of time Burke with club, thought of him as stopper. "Whenever we'd lose two or three in row, I'd send Bobby in there and he'd frequently get us back on track," said Joe.

When 18, Burke won pitching job for Little Rock. Then Washington, 1927–35. Albany 1936. Philadelphia NL 1937, briefly. Then back to minors, finishing up with St. Paul, 1938. Though with Senators in 1933 when they won pennant, Bobby did not play. Had skills as commercial artist. In later years, operated fishing resort.

BURKETT, JESSE CAIL (Crab) OF-BL-TL. B. 2/12/70, Wheeling, W. Va. D. 5/27/53, Worcester, Mass. 5'8", 155. One of three players who hit .400 or better three times. Other two Ty Cobb, Rogers Hornsby. Lifetime average of .342 in 2,063 games over 16-year period, 1890–1905, places him high among best hitters in baseball.

Burkett started minor league career 1888, Scranton; Worcester, 1889. New York NL, 1890. Although batted .309 in 101 games that year, was back in minors 1891, Lincoln, Western Association. Hit .349 and moved same season to Cleveland NL. By second full season at Cleveland an established solid hitter, evidenced by .373 average. In 1895 hit .423, and following year .410, winning batting championships both years. Transferred to St. Louis Cardinals for 1899 when NL reorganized. Hit .402 but did not win batting title—that went to Ed Delahanty, who came up with .408. In 1901, however, his .382 mark was enough to top NL. Jess jumped to AL 1902 with St. Louis Browns. Hit .306 that year, his tenth consecutive season above .300. Dropped down after that. Left Browns for Boston AL 1905, last season in majors.

Burkett had over 200 hits six times, and once missed that mark by one. Good base runner, lifetime record of 392 steals. Scored over 100 runs nine seasons. In 1896 scored 159 times, not a record but total any player would be proud of.

From 1906 to 1913 was owner and manager of Worcester team, New England League, playing as well. Took batting championship there with .344 in 1906. Later managed at Lewiston and Lowell in New England. Coached for N.Y. Giants during 1920s. Hall of Fame 1946.

BURNETT, JOHN HENDERSON Inf.-BL-TR. B. 11/1/06, Bartow, Fla. D. 8/13/59, Tampa, Fla. 5'11", 175. Johnny Burnett wrote his name into record books 7/10/32, getting nine hits in one game. True, 18-inning game, but nobody has come close to equaling this record, regardless of number of innings. Cleveland Indian at time. Opponent was Philadelphia, at Cleveland. NL record in any game, nine or extra innings, is six, held by 10 players. Burnett at bat 11 times. Two of safeties were doubles.

Burnett attended Florida U. Signed with Cleveland shortly after graduation, 1927; appeared in 17 AL games. Terre Haute, III League, 1928, for experience; hit .326 in 133 games. His Cleveland record that year: 3 games, 5 for 10, .500 average. In 1929, 19 games with Indians; 72 with New Orleans, Southern Association, with .310 mark in Louisiana metropolis. Remained with Cleveland 1930–34. Then one season with St. Louis AL. Record: .284, 558 major league games; 521 hits, 94 doubles,

15 triples, 9 homers, 15 stolen bases, 288 runs, 163 RBI.

BURNS, GEORGE HENRY (Tioga) 1B-BR-TR. B. 1/31/93, Niles, Ohio. 6'1", 185. Fine hitting first baseman who won AL MVP 1926. Performed rarity with Red Sox—triple play unassisted, 9/14/23, against Cleveland. In second inning, George snared Frank Brower's liner, tagged Walter Lutzke, who had been on first base, then dashed to second and slid into bag before Riggs Stephenson could get back.

Burns started out in 1913, Burlington, Ottumwa, Sioux City, all in Iowa. One year in minors enough. Detroit's regular first baseman 1914, hitting .291 in 137 games. Tigers traded to Philadelphia AL after 1917 season. In 1920, Athletics sent him to Cleveland. Boston AL 1922–23. Back to Cleveland until released Sept. 1928. Signed with Yankees for rest of 1928. Yanks released during 1929 season; Burns caught on with Philadelphia AL in June. After that spent 1930–34 seasons in Pacific Coast League with San Francisco Missions, Los Angeles, Seattle, Portland.

Burns played 1,866 major league games, scored 901 runs, made 2,018 hits, .307 average. Extra-base hits: 444 doubles, 72 triples, 72 homers. Drove in 956 runs. Many red-letter days; one stands out. First game of twin bill 6/19/24, slammed six hits, including three doubles, one triple. In WS 1920, with Cleveland; 1929 as pinch hitter with Philadelphia AL: .250 average, 3 for 12, 3 RBI. In PCL, managed, played at Seattle, 1932–34; playing manager, Portland, 1934; bench manager, Portland, 1935.

BURNS, GEORGE JOSEPH OF-BR-TR. B. 11/24/89, St. Johnsville, N.Y. D. 8/15/66, Gloversville, N.Y. 5'7", 170. For dozen years both NL and AL had righthanded hitters named George Burns. American Leaguer was taller, 6'1", a bit heavier, and played first base. National Leaguer only 5'7", but very durable outfielder.

George Joseph Burns joined Giants 1911, after three seasons with Utica, N.Y. State League. Played 29 games in 1912. In 1913 began stretch of 11 seasons, playing at least 149 games in nine of them. Helped John McGraw's Giants to three pennants, 1913,17,21. Long time was used as leadoff man. When Giants had chance to get third baseman Heinie Groh from Cincinnati after 1921 season, Burns sent to Reds along with $100,000 cash for infielder. Burns had three years in Cincinnati. Final year in majors 1925, with Philadelphia NL. In 1927–28, playing manager for Williamsport, N.Y.-Pa. League; again at Hanover, Blue Ridge League, 1928; Springfield, Eastern League, 1929; San Antonio, Texas League, 1930. Coach, Giants, 1931.

Burns hit .287 in 1853 major league games, getting 2077 hits, 363 doubles, 108 triples and 41 homers. Scored 1188 runs, had 611 RBI, stole

383 bases. In WS play: 19 games, 19 for 74, .257 average, 7 runs, 6 doubles, 1 triple, 3 stolen bases, 5 RBI.

BUSBY, JAMES FRANKLIN   OF-BR-TR. B. 1/8/27, Kenedy, Tex. 6'1", 175. Jim Busby, coach for Atlanta NL, hit above .300 only once in his major league career of over 13 seasons. But could go and get them in outfield. Led AL in outfield putouts three years, in fielding another.

Divided time among Muskegon, Waterloo, Sacramento before becoming regular with Chicago White Sox, 1951. Had 18 games with Sox previous season, but in 1951 played 143 contests, hit .283. During 1952, shifted to Washington. Enjoyed best season at bat 1953: .312, 82 RBI. Traded him back to Chicago during 1955 campaign. Spent 1956 with Cleveland. During 1957, landed with Baltimore AL, staying through 1958. Boston AL 1959, part of 1960. Again Baltimore, 1960–61, with time out for 27 games with Miami, International League, in 1960. In 1962, 15 games with Houston NL, 23 with Oklahoma City, Pacific Coast League. Coach, Houston, 1962–67. Since, coach for Atlanta Braves.

Busby played 1352 major league games: .263 average, 1113 hits, 541 runs, 162 doubles, 35 triples, 48 homers, 438 RBI, 97 stolen bases.

BUSCH, AUGUST A., JR. (Gussie)   Executive. B. 3/28/99, St. Louis, Mo. Budweiser Stadium. That's what they were going to call Sportman's Park, St. Louis, when Anheuser-Busch, Inc., took over St. Louis Cardinals, 1953. But there were screams that commercialism in baseball was going too far. So the brewery changed name of ball park to Busch Stadium. By coincidence new president of Cardinals was August A. Busch, Jr. Brewery began big promotion for new beer called "Busch Bavarian" with emphasis on "Busch."

Gussie renovated old historic ball park where Hornsby, Sisler, Frisch, Pepper Martin, Dean brothers and many other immortals had performed. But it still left much to be desired for modern fans. So new park, this one called Busch Memorial Stadium, built near St. Louis river front. Project financed with private capital except for $60,000,000 in St. Louis city bonds to provide streets, street lights, other public utility improvements in area. New park, seating 50,126, opened for play 5/12/66.

Busch inherited Eddie Stanky as his manager. When no pennant appeared in St. Louis during next three seasons, Stanky was dropped in favor of Harry Walker. Then came Fred Hutchinson, Stan Hack, Solly Hemus, Johnny Keane. Still no pennant by time 1964 season well under way. Gussie became impatient, not only with his field manager but also with his general manager, Bing Devine. Result: Devine out 8/17/64. Keane reportedly was merely finishing out season, and would be replaced by Lippy Leo Durocher. But somehow, when season ended, Cardinals on top. Many of key players Devine had brought to Cards.

Redbirds then went on to win World Series from Yankees in seven games.

Presumably Busch would have to extricate himself from very embarrassing position of either firing man who had just won world championship for him, or offering him new contract. Keane, sensitive gentleman, respected by almost everyone, beat Busch to punch. Day after winning Series, announced his resignation from Cardinals. Promptly hired by Yankees, who had just dismissed Yogi Berra as their pilot. In this mixup Durocher lost out completely. Busch hired Red Schoendienst as new manager. Bob Howsam became general manager in place of Devine. Later Stan Musial replaced Howsam. Cards dropped to seventh, 1965. Moved up to sixth, 1966. Captured pennant, 1967, topping it off with World Series victory over Red Sox in seven games. By now Busch wanted Devine back as general manager. Bing came home, leaving N.Y. Mets. Musial, with restaurant and many outside business interests, became senior vice president of Cardinals. Busch-Devine-Schoendienst combination produced another flag, 1968. But this time Detroit won Series in seven games. No flags since.

Gussie, besides interest in baseball and beer, involved in variety of civic movements in St. Louis. Among numerous awards he has received was that of "Citizen No. One," from Press Club of Metropolitan St. Louis, 1967. Gave up presidency of Cardinals 3/28/73, became chairman of board and chief executive officer.

BUSH, GUY TERRELL (Mississippi Mudcat) P-BR-TR. B. 8/23/03, Aberdeen, Miss. 6′, 175. Stalwart of Cubs' pitching staff in late 1920s, early 1930s. Won 176 games during major league career, most for Cubs. Lost 136. ERA 3.84.

Guy impressed Chicago scout while pitching for Greenville, Miss., Cotton States League, 1923. Cubs promptly bought contract. But Bush disappeared, terrified over prospect of going to big city. Eventually found, persuaded to report to big league team. Divided 1924 between Cubs and Wichita Falls (Texas League). Was 9–3 with latter, 2–5 with Cubs. Cubs 1925 up and down; not surprising that Bush was 6–13. But Joe McCarthy took over as manager, 1926, and Guy was 13–9. Best seasons 1928 through 1934, winning at least 15 every year. Had 19–11 record, 1932; 20–12 following season. Pittsburgh acquired Bush for 1935—11–11. Released 7/20/36. Signed with Boston NL. Sold to St. Louis NL 2/2/38. Didn't tarry long. Los Angeles, Pacific Coast League, 1938—8–5. Retired. Comeback, Chattanooga, Southern Association, 1944—5–3. Final, brief session, Cincinnati Reds, 1945, pitching four innings.

Guy never pitched no-hitter in majors but did have two one-hit games 1931. In 1929, pitched Cubs' only WS victory over Philadelphia Athletics, 3–1 win over George Earnshaw. In 1932, after winning 19 during season, was starter in WS opener against Yankees. Disaster. Gehrig slammed one of Guy's pitches over fence for two-run homer. And in sixth inning, Yanks got five more runs. Bush had given four walks and single before being relieved. Bombers won 12–6. Followed with three more wins to sweep. Overall WS record: 1–1 16-2/3 innings, ERA 5.40.

BUSH, LESLIE AMBROSE (Bullet Joe) P-BR-TR. B. 11/27/92, Brainerd, Minn. 5′11″, 175. Over half century ago N.Y. Yankees needed help, Boston Red Sox needed money. Procession of stars left Hub for big city. Yankee reign began. Babe Ruth, Carl Mays, Red Ruffing, Wally Schang, Joe Dugan, Everett Scott, Herb Pennock were among them— and Bullet Joe Bush. Bush had helped Connie Mack win pennants in Philadelphia, 1913 and 1914, but hit peak 1922, after Boston sent him to N.Y. Captured 26 games, lost 7. His .788 percentage led AL pitchers— and aided in Miller Huggins' second straight pennant.

At age 19 Joe began pro career with 29–12 mark for Missoula, Union Association, 1912. Prompted $800 investment by Philadelphia AL to buy contract. Paid off quickly: 14–6 in 1913 plus five-hit victory over N.Y. Giants, only WS start that autumn. In 1914 Joe 16–12. Athletics won again, but like teammates, Bush victimized in WS Miracle Boston Braves, who swept A's. Lost third game 5–4; errors gave game to Boston. Connie Mack traded several stars after 1914 debacle, but Bush stayed. With weak hitting, poor fielding tyros behind him, Bush came up with 6–14, 15–22, 11–17 records. Traded to Red Sox, 12/20/17. After breakeven records his first years in Boston, was 16–9 in 1921. Then became Yankee. Had 19–15 mark, 1923, 17–16 in 1924. Traded to St. Louis AL in deal bringing Urban Shocker to Yanks. With Browns 1925. Washington and Pittsburgh 1926. Pittsburgh and N.Y. NL 1927. Philadelphia AL 1928.

Bush good hitter; often aided own cause. Frequently pinch hit. In 1924, 8 for 16 as pinch hitter. Hit .242, major league career. Besides WS performances with Athletics, Bush 0–1 in 1918 classic against Cubs; 0–2, 1922, against Giants; 1–1 against Giants, 1923.

Bush was 195–180 in majors. No-hitter 8/26/16 against Cleveland, for A's. Pitched, won ten 1–0 games during career; 35 shutouts in all.

BUSH, OWEN J. (Donie) SS-BLR-TR. B. 10/8/88, Indianapolis, Ind. D. 3/28/72, Indianapolis, Ind. 5′6″, 155. Donie Bush's playing career in majors began 1908, with Detroit. Managed Washington, Chicago in AL; Pittsburgh, Cincinnati in NL—nearly managed Yankees. Feisty little guy could only hit .250 in his 1945 major league games. But stole 403 bases— 53 in 1909. As pilot, perhaps outsmarted himself by ignoring Kiki Cuyler during 1927 WS. Argument during regular season; Bush benched brilliant player—and Pittsburgh lost to Yankees in four straight games.

Bush began at Sault Ste. Marie, 1905; later Saginaw, Dayton, South Bend, Indianapolis before joining Tigers and Ty Cobb, 1908. From 1909 to 1921, regular shortstop for Motor City team; to Washington late 1921 season on waivers. Clark Griffith named him manager of Senators 1923. Bush played his final ten games in majors that year, led club to fourth-place finish. Gave way to Bucky Harris before 1924 season began—Harris led Washington to its first AL flag. Next chance, manager of 1927 Pirates. Job ended late summer 1929—Jewell Ens succeeded him. Miller Huggins, mite manager of Yankees, died in September of that year. According to reports, coach Art Fletcher turned down chance to manage Yanks. Bush, meanwhile, gave verbal agreement to White Sox to manage that club. Shortly after, Yankees interested in Bush. But Donie stuck to word; piloted Sox 1930–31. No horses: team seventh in 1930, eighth in 1931. Final crack at major league managing, Cincinnati, 1933. Reds didn't have players either, finished in cellar. Bush also managed in American Association several years. Bossed Minneapolis when Ted Williams young player there. President and manager of Louisville for time. Then owned part of Indianapolis franchise until 1952. Continued association with Indianapolis afterward. Scouted for Boston Red Sox, and later for White Sox until his death.

Record: 1804 hits, 186 doubles, 74 triples, 9 homers, 1280 runs, 436 RBI.

BYRD, SAMUEL DEWEY OF-BR-TR. B. 10/15/06, Bremen, Ga. 5'10½", 175. They used to call him Babe Ruth's caddy—or Babe Ruth's legs. Sammy, outfielder for Yankees, frequently replaced Bambino late in game. If Yanks had comfortable lead, if Ruth weary, if Yanks needed pinch runner for Babe (especially later in his career), Byrd usually sent in. Sam in majors eight years, but probably better golfer than ball player. After baseball, became golf pro, won number of tournaments.

Byrd signed with Birmingham, Southern Association, 1926; quickly farmed to Jonesboro, Tri-State League—.348 in 59 games. Following year, .331 in 140 games at Knoxville, South Atlantic League. Yankees purchased, optioned to Albany, Eastern League, 1928; Byrd thrived, hitting .371 in 130 games. Then six-year stint with Yankees. Sold to Cincinnati 12/19/34. Two years with Reds. Then golf.

Sammy hit .274 in 744 major league games; 465 hits, 101 doubles, 10 triples, 38 homers, 220 RBI. Two most memorable games, 1932 and 1936. Playing left field for Yanks in 1932, Sam handled 11 putouts in game against White Sox. In 1936, Pirate Pitcher Cy Blanton had 3–0 lead over Cincinnati going into ninth inning, Crosley Field. Reds filled bases. Up came Sammy. Belted first pitch over left field wall for 4–3 Red victory.

BYRNE, THOMAS JOSEPH P-BL-TL. B. 12/31/19, Baltimore, Md. 6'1", 182. Champion wild man of AL, 1949–51; issued more free passes to first base than any other pitcher in circuit. Dangerous hitter for pitcher. Grand slam homer 9/18/51, toiling for St. Louis Browns, off Sid Hudson, Washington Senators, to win ball game. Another 5/16/53, pinch hitting for Vern Stephens, teammate on Chicago White Sox; defeated Yankees. (Stephens had thrice led AL in RBI, homers once.)

Tommy won 85 games in majors, lost 69. In 1362 innings, walked 1037, struck out 766. Good years mainly with N.Y. Yankees.

Attended Wake Forest—hit .593 in 1939, Southern Conference record, stood at least 30 years. Joined Yankee organization at Newark, 1940. Gradually improved, until 17–4 in 1942. Was 2–1 for Yankees, 1943. Military service until 1946. Rejoined Yanks, but farmed to Kansas City during 1947 season, chalking up 12–6 mark. Yanks 1948—8–5. Then followed 15–7, 15–9 records. Traded to Browns during 1951; remained through 1952. In 1953, Chicago AL and Washington, then sent to Charleston, American Association. Washed up, it seemed. Joe Becker, later Dodger, Cub coach, managing Charleston. Joe frankly told Byrne, "I've got troubles of my own. I've got a bad ball club. I don't have time to help you. Up to now you've been just a thrower. It's time you learned how to pitch." Byrne, 33, had been trying to get by on curve, fast ball. Now tried to learn slider, vary speeds of fast ball. Following season with Seattle, Pacific Coast League. During 1954 season, Yankees bought him. Was 3–2. Had 16–5 mark, 1955, with 3.15 ERA, probably best season ever. Was 7–3, 1956. Left majors after 4–6 mark with Yankees, 1957.

Byrne pitched briefly in WS 1949, 55, 56, 57. Most of hurling in 1955 Series. Won his first start against Brooklyn, 4–2. Defeated in decisive seventh game, though he allowed just one earned run. In 21-1/3 innings, four WS, was 1–1, with 2.53 ERA.

Graduated from Wake Forest with B.S. in mathematics, 1943, after pro career under way. After his retirement from game became part owner of Wake Forest Country Club. Served 10 years as chairman of Wake Forest's recreation committee.

BYRON, WILLIAM (Lord) Umpire. B. 9/8/72, D. 12/27/55, Ypsilanti, Mich. "Singing umpire" in NL, 1913–19. Once officiating when Casey Stengel of Brooklyn Dodgers, protested third-strike call. "To the clubhouse you must go, you must go, you must go. To the clubhouse you must go, my fair Casey!" sang Byron to tune of "London Bridge."

Other counsel, melodiously tendered: "Let me tell you something, son, before you get much older. You cannot hit the ball, my friend, with your bat upon your shoulder!"

Byron steamfitter by trade. Had ambitions as ball player. Signed with

Sherman, Texas State League, 1892. Couldn't hit weight. Said to have gone 24 games without hit. Stayed in lineup because of ability to get on base by stopping pitched balls. Back to steamfitting, ump on side. Umpired college game in Detroit, then signed as arbiter with Michigan State League, 1896. League folded. Steamfitting again, until league revived, 1900. With that circuit until 1904. Sally League 1905–07. Eastern League 1910. Southern Association 1911. International League 1912. NL 1913–19. Pacific Coast League 1920–24. Again back to steamfitting, semipro umpiring until almost 70.

Byron colorful. International League, one game Baltimore filled bases. Mgr. Jack Dunn coaching first base. Hitter lifted foul fly in first base area. First baseman, second baseman gave chase. Dunn yelled, "I got it, I got it." First baseman thought it was second baseman yelling, let ball drop. Byron called batsman out for interference. When Dunn protested vigorously, Byron replied, "Yes! Vocal interference!" Byron, 1917, involved in fracas with John McGraw, fabled Giant manager. After ball game, they met in runway leading from dugout, exchanged heated words. McGraw punched Byron. League president John K. Tener, on receiving Byron's report, fined McGraw $500, suspended 16 days.

CADORE, LEON JOSEPH P-BR-TR. B. 11/20/91, Chicago, Ill. D. 3/16/58, Spokane, Wash. 6'1", 190. Break-even pitcher most of career. Won 68 games, lost 72 in majors between 1915 and 1924. But is remembered because he pitched 26-inning game for Brooklyn against Joe Oeschger of Boston Braves, 5/1/20. Game ended in 1-1 tie because of darkness. Still stands as longest game in major league history.

In fifth inning Dodgers scored their run. Braves got theirs in sixth. That ended scoring for afternoon. Cadore, pitching next 20 consecutive scoreless innings, allowed 15 hits, 5 walks. Oeschger did even better, permitting no score over 21 innings in row, giving up only 9 hits, 4 walks.

Oddly enough, while neither side changed pitchers during marathon contest, each used two backstops. Then Dodgers, in their accustomed daffy manner, lost to Phillies next day in 13 innings. Back in Boston following day they played 19-inning game against Braves and lost 2-1. So, in 58 innings on three consecutive days, Brooklyn had no victories to show for all its work.

Cadore pitched for numerous minor league clubs before landing with Brooklyn, 1915. In 1923 shifted to Chicago AL and wound up big league career with Giants, 1924, taking part in just two games. Had lifetime ERA of 3.14 in 1257 innings. Pitched in one World Series, 1920, against Cleveland. Lasted two innings, charged with defeat, ERA 9.00.

CADY, FORREST LEROY (Hick) C-BR-TR. B. 1/26/86, Bishop Hill, Ill. D. 3/3/46, Cedar Rapids, Iowa. 6'2", 188. Hick Cady never was much of hitter. Once got up to .278, 1915, Boston AL. But early that year he had distinction of pinch hitting for Babe Ruth, pitcher those days. Evidently Mgr. Bill Carrigan yet unacquainted with Babe's bat potential. Cady pinch hit for Babe 4/24/15. By end of season, however, Ruth had .315 batting average, 4 homers; Cady .278, no homers.

Cady played at Kewanee (Ill.), Ottumwa (Iowa), Evansville and Newark before joining Red Sox, 1912. Got into 78 games both 1915 and 1916, but never more. With Red Sox through 1917. One game with Cleveland AL 1918. And 34 with Philadelphia NL 1919. Major league record: .240 in 355 games, 216 hits, 47 doubles, 11 triples, 1 homer. Homer came in final year, with Phillies.

CAIN, CULLEN Executive. B. 12/3/74, Warsaw, Mo. D. 11/26/58, Coral Gables, Fla. First publicity man for major league. Newspaper man in various parts of United States, from San Francisco to East Coast, after beginning as printer's devil at 15. Traveled with Presidents William Howard Taft and Woodrow Wilson on assignments. Ultimately became sports writer for *Philadelphia Ledger*, specializing in baseball.

NL created job of public relations man and chief of "service bureau" to help sports writers publicize circuit, 1922. Sent information and photos of NL players to newspapers; responded to special requests for information. Continued in post until 1933, when he retired and was succeeded by Ford C. Frick, later NL president and baseball commissioner.

Cain suffered serious eye injury when hit by baseball while watching spring practice one year at St. Petersburg. Blind during last 15 years of his life. After leaving baseball, editor and publisher for *St. Louis County Leader* briefly, then moved to Coral Gables. There he continued his interest in game and dictated weekly column for local newspaper.

CALLISON, JOHN WESLEY OF-BL-TR. B. 3/12/39, Qualls, Okla. 5'10", 178. Fine outfielder; strong, accurate throwing arm. Good left-handed power hitter. Became N.Y. Yankee 1/18/72 after 12 years in NL. Callison reportedly glad to leave Chicago Cubs. Leo Durocher unhappy with Johnny's .210 batting average in 1971. Callison seemed to think it would have been much higher if Durocher had played him oftener.

Callison's lifetime major league average at start of 1973 was .266 for 1841 games. This included 1733 hits, 317 doubles, 89 triples, 225 homers, 830 RBI. Also scored 916 times.

Defensive ability demonstrated 1969—three errors in 134 games. Holds major league record for most consecutive seasons leading league in assists, 1962 through 1965. NL All-Star squad 1962,64,65. Homered bottom of ninth, won 1964 All-Star game at Shea Stadium for NL. Other distinction: tied major league record for highest fielding percentage by outfielder, 100 or more games, 1968, no errors, so mark 1.000. Three homers in one game, 1964; again 1965.

Johnny started out at Bakersfield, 1957, with .340 average in 86 games. Divided his 1958 and 1959 seasons between Indianapolis and Chicago AL. Traded to Philadelphia NL 12/8/59 for Gene Freese. Phils, 1960 through 1969, when sent to Cubs. Reached .300 mark 1962. Hit over 20 homers four seasons, 1962–65, reaching 32 in 1965. Twice over 100 RBI, 1964–65.

CAMILLI, ADOLPH LOUIS (Dolph) 1B-BL-TL. B. 4/23/08, San Francisco, Calif. 5′10½″, 185. Delph Camilli best remembered for days in Brooklyn when Larry MacPhail, Leo Durocher, Dixie Walker, Pete Reiser, Pee Wee Reese, others in heyday. Slugging first baseman quit active playing 1945. Son Doug coocker for Boston Red Sox.

Dolph had fine season with Dodgers, 1941, leading NL in homers with 34, in RBI with 120, but didn't do so well in his only WS, batting just .167, 3 for 18, against Yankee pitching.

Eight years 1926–33 of minor league experience before Dolph reached majors. Played at Logan and Salt Lake in Utah-Idaho League; San Francisco and Sacramento, Pacific Coast League; finally, 1933, Chicago Cubs, in time for 16 games. Hit .224. June 1934, traded to Philadelphia NL. In 1937, .339 average in 131 games, led NL first sackers in fielding, and was coveted by Larry MacPhail. Cash outlay of $50,000, one player brought to Dodgers, 3/6/38. Usually drove in around 100 runs a season for Brooklyn. RBI production began to slip. On 7/31/43, traded to hated Giants. Shocked. Refused to report. Managed Oakland, Pacific Coast League, 1944; played 113 games, hit .289. Team tied for third. Started 1945 as Oakland pilot; resigned 6/12/45 to play with Boston Red Sox due to wartime shortage of players. Played 63 contests and hit .212; last appearance on active list. Managed Spokane, Western International League, late 1948 season. Coach, Sacramento, PCL, 1949. Manager, Dayton, Central League, 1950. Manager, Magic Valley (Idaho), Pioneer League, 1953. Coach, Sacramento, PCL, 1951,54–55. Scout, Yankees, 1960–67. Scout, California AL, 1969–71.

Dolph NL MVP 1941. Major league totals: 1490 games, 5353 AB, 1482 hits, 261 doubles, 86 triples, 239 homers, 950 RBI, .277 average, 936 runs. One record he'd rather forget: tied George Metkovich, Red Sox, by making three errors in one inning, 8/2/35. George turned trick 1945.

CAMILLI, DOUGLAS JOSEPH C-BR-TR. B. 9/22/36, Philadelphia, Pa. 5′11″, 190. Doug Camilli, Red Sox coach, another second-generation major leaguer. Father, Dolph, stellar first baseman for Brooklyn Dodgers in rollicking early 1940s. Three of Doug's brothers also played professional ball, but Doug was only one of brothers to reach big leagues.

Doug was born in Philadelphia while father still with Phillies. Attended Sacramento State College and Stanford. Played with Great Falls, Reno, Green Bay, Atlanta (Southern League), before joining L.A. Dodgers, 1960. Spent most of 1961 with Spokane and Omaha, then back with Dodgers 1962–64. Never made first string. Busiest season 1965, catching 59 games with Washington. After 1967, when he took part in 30 games, Camilli became coach for Senators for two seasons. With Red Sox as bullpen coach since 1970.

Major league totals: 321 games, 152 hits, 764 at bats, .199 average. Had 22 doubles, 4 triples, 18 homers. Scored 56 runs. One red-letter day in career, 6/4/64: caught Sandy Koufax's no-hit game against Phillies.

CAMPANELLA, ROY C-BR-TR. B. 11/19/21, Philadelphia, Pa. 5'9½", 205. Outstanding catcher for Brooklyn Dodgers 1948–57 until automobile accident 1/28/58 left him paralyzed. Driving home from his liquor store after midnight, car skidded on icy curve, turned over. Suffered broken neck and spinal cord almost severed. His own heavier car was being repaired and he had rented somewhat lighter car for interim.

Campanella among earliest Negroes to play in organized baseball. After Jackie Robinson signed with Dodger farm team Montreal, Int. League, to play 1946 season, John Wright and Don Newcombe signed contracts, then Campy. Earned about $5000 annually in Negro baseball but took cut to $185 monthly to sign with Dodger farm club at Nashua, N. H., New England League, 1946.

Played American Legion baseball. Signed with Baltimore Elite Giants, Negro team, for $60 monthly and winters played in Caribbean, averaging 200 games yearly. Made $1000 monthly with Monterrey, Mexico Returned to Elite Giants then joined Newark, Negro team. After 1945 season played against team of major league barnstormers managed by Charlie Dressen, then Dodger coach. Dressen set up appointment with Branch Rickey, leading to his signing with Nashua, where Buzzie Bavasi was general manager and Walter Alston first baseman and field manager. Bavasi now president of San Diego NL and Alston dean of major league managers with Dodgers. Hit .290. Moved to Montreal, 1947, hit .273 in 135 games. Though ready for majors in 1948 Rickey requested him to play at St. Paul, another Dodger farm, to break color line in American Association. Hit .325 there in 35 games then recalled to Brooklyn 6/30. Hit double and two singles in major league debut, next night triple, two singles, followed by two home runs and single with four RBI next day.

In 1949, first full season in majors, named to NL All-Star squad and caught most of game. Hit .287, 22 HR and 82 RBI, helping Dodgers win pennant. In that World Series picked two Yankee base runners off base, Tommy Henrich and Phil Rizzuto. In five World Series with Dodgers, 1949,52,53,55,56.

Major league average .276 in 1215 games, 242 HR, 856 RBI. Set major league record for most home runs hit by catcher, 41, 1953 which stood until Reds' Johnny Bench hit 45, 1970. Set major league record for most RBI by catcher, 142, 1953, also broken by Bench (148), 1970. Set NL record for consecutive years catching 100 or more games, 9. Holds several other batting and fielding marks. MVP 1951,53,55. (Stan Musial only other NL player to win MVP Award three times.) Hall of Fame 1969.

After Campanella's accident Walter O'Malley, president of Dodgers, then moved to Los Angeles, staged exhibition game against Yankees 5/7/59 in Coliseum, drawing baseball's largest crowd ever, 93,103, with 15,000 turned away. O'Malley gave Campanella $50,000 from gate receipts to help defray hospital and medical bills, also paid him his $50,000 salary for 1958.

Campy has had business connections with bank in addition to his liquor store. Began radio sports program, "Campy's Corner," 1958. Has lectured, specially to youth. Lives in Hartsdale, N.Y., with his third wife and her two children whom he adopted. Had five children by previous marriages.

But for accident, Campanella might have become first black manager in majors; smart catcher, had unusual leadership qualities, respected and well liked.

CAMPANERIS, DAGOBERTO BLANCO (Campy) SS-BR-TR. B. 3/9/42, Pueblo Nuevo, Matanzas, Cuba. 5'10", 160. Campy, in AL since 1964, selected for All-Star squad for third time, 1973. First honors in this respect in 1968, his first year after Oakland A's moved from Kansas City. Despite relatively modest batting average is still one of AL's most exciting players. Speed afoot enabled him to win AL stolen base honors 1965,66,67,68,70, with better than 50 SB four of those seasons. High water mark 62 in 1968. Repeatedly has stolen two bases in single game; known to make two bases on sacrifice bunts.

Campy has knack of being colorful. Versatility personified. Originally reported to A's as 140-pound catcher. Didn't impress too much, but determined to play pro ball somewhere and moved to infield where he made good after some minor league seasoning. Even pitched, but not like ordinary mortals. He pitched to lefthanded batters lefthanded; righthanded to righthanders. Pitching, however, confined to one game at Binghamton and three at Daytona Beach. In eight innings in minors allowed three earned runs. Demonstrated his versatility especially 9/8/65. In game against California Angels, played one inning at every position on diamond, first time this was done in majors in many years. Allowed one run in solitary appearance on mound in AL.

Campy played for Daytona Beach and Binghamton, 1962; Lewiston, Idaho, and Binghamton, 1963; Birmingham and Kansas City, 1964; remaining with K.C. until franchise was shifted to Bay Area. In 1964 Campaneris named to Southern Association All-Star team, and that same season named to major league rookie All-Star squad.

Started major league career with bang, 7/23/64. Facing Jim Kaat of Minnesota Twins, hit very first pitch for home run. Few innings later slapped another homer. This feat tied major league record of two homers in player's first game in big time. Led AL in hits in 1968 with 177, although he hit .276. But this average put him seventh among AL hitters. Has played more AL games than any other Oakland player. Second only to Luis Aparicio in career stolen bases among American Leaguers. Cousin of Jose Cardenal of Chicago Cubs.

Fiery Cuban proved to be thorn in side of Detroit Tigers during second game of AL playoffs, 1972. After A's won opener, 3–2, Campaneris socked three singles, stole second and third, scored two runs. When came to bat in seventh inning, Detroit pitcher, Lerrin LaGrow, threw pitch that hit Campy in ankle.

Campy went down, got up, then threw bat toward pitcher. LaGrow ducked, bat went over head toward second base. Almost instantly players from both clubs swarmed on field. Detroit manager Billy Martin, with long record of pugilistic endeavors, charged at Campaneris, but restrained by umpires John Rice and Larry Barnett.

When order restored, plate umpire Nestor Chylak had banished Campaneris and LaGrow from game. Oakland won game 5–0. Later, AL President Joe Cronin announced $500 fine for Campaneris and suspension from rest of AL playoffs. Suspension may have been academic, because injured Campy might not have been able to play adequate game for few days anyway.

Commissioner Bowie Kuhn, before start of WS, announced Campaneris would be able to play against Cincinnati, but would be suspended from first seven games of 1973 season. Cuban hit .179 against Reds, playing all seven games, getting five singles in 28 trips, drawing one walk, and scoring just one run.

Campaneris owned lifetime major league average of .261 going into 1973 season, with 1224 AL games behind him.

CAMPANIS, ALEXANDER SEBASTIAN Executive. B. 11/2/16, Cos, Greece. Al Campanis, vice president of player personnel and scouting for Los Angeles Dodgers, played seven games at second base for old Brooklyn Dodgers, 1943. Somehow managed to get two hits in 20 times at bat, but also walked four times and scored three runs; batting average,

.100. Smart enough to stay in Dodger organization ever since. Perhaps smartest move as scout and front office man was to sign Sandy Koufax for $14,000 bonus and salary of $6000 back in 1955. Interesting sidelight connected with Campanis' signing Koufax.

Sandy was ready to sign, but Dodgers didn't have room on their roster at time. Rules then required that bonus player stay on big league roster at least two years. After Campanis and Koufax had come to meeting of minds on terms, Branch Rickey, then Pittsburgh boss, reportedly offered Sandy $30,000 to sign with Pirates. Koufax kept his word with Campanis until Dodgers traded away Preacher Roe and Billy Cox. This made room for Sandy and he joined team. Campanis and Dodgers had to be patient, however. Koufax did not come through in grand style for six years.

Campanis, born in the Dodecanese Islands in Greece, came to U.S. at six and soon took to American sports. Majored in physical education at New York U.; lettered in baseball and football three years each. Captain of NYU's 1940 baseball team. Became physical ed instructor and coach for junior varsity football team at N.Y. City College.

Joined Reading, Interstate League, 1941; Knoxville, Southern Association, 1942; Montreal, International League, 1943. In U. S. Navy then till 1946. Managed in Brooklyn organization at Montreal; Nashua, N.H.; Lancaster, Pa.; Newport News, Va. Scout for Dodgers, 1950. In 1953–54 Al managed Cienfuegos club in Cuban Winter League, maintaining his connections with Dodgers. Became director of scouting late in 1957.

Al is author of book *How to Play Baseball* that has been translated into several languages. Speaks Spanish, French, and Greek in addition to English, and has conducted baseball clinics in Mexico, Japan, and Europe. Got Tommy Davis for $4000 bonus. Father of Jim Campanis, catcher, who had trials with Los Angeles NL, 1966–68. Papa traded son Jim to Kansas City AL 12/15/68 for two minor league players to be named later. Jim didn't quite make it with Royals and soon was in minors.

CAMPBELL, PAUL McLAUGHLIN 1B-BL-TL. B. 9/1/17, Paw Creek, N. C. 5'10", 185. Spectacular-fielding first baseman who eventually became traveling secretary for Cincinnati Reds. He never made it big in majors as player, but not because of lack of fielding ability. While with Montreal, International League, 1941, set all-time baseball record by starting 26 double plays from first base, breaking older major league mark of 18. Presumably Campbell's record still stands, as record books seem to have skipped this fascinating bit of information.

Campbell was property of Boston Red Sox and was with Montreal on option when he made his record. One game with Sox that year, then 26 with them in 1942 before joining air force. Served until well into 1946 season, then had 28 more games with Red Sox. Spent 1947 with Louisville, American Association, then had two years with Detroit. Hit .265 in 59 games, 1948, and .278 in 87 games following year.

While with Tigers 5/14/49 Paul tied major league record for first basemen by making two unassisted double plays in one game.

Paul started at Danville, Va., 1936, then played at Rocky Mount, N. C.; Little Rock, and Louisville before his spectacular season at Montreal. After his Detroit seasons was player-coach at Toledo, 1950–51; managed Williamsport, Eastern League, 1952; manager, Little Rock, 1953; manager, Hagerstown, Md., 1954, general manager, Wilson, N.C., 1956; general manager, Louisville, 1957; president, Louisville, 1958; area scouting supervisor for Cincinnati in Virginia and Carolinas, 1959–64. Then traveling secretary of Reds, 1965 to present.

Campbell's major league batting record .256 for 201 games, with 17 doubles, 5 triples, 4 doubles among 97 hits.

CANNON, ROBERT C. Legal Advisor. B. 6/10/17, Milwaukee, Wis. Circuit Judge Cannon is a vice president of Milwaukee Brewers, one of most dedicated devotees of baseball in Wisconsin. For six and one half years served as legal advisor for major league ball players' association, retiring 7/1/66. Received no pay for this. During time he served as players' counsel, many forward strides were made: players' pension benefits were improved, players received more meal money than ever before, and owners made numerous other concessions. In 1966 players' association offered him $50,000 salary and expenses to become full-time legal counsel. This was twice his salary as circuit judge. Cannon refused. One of reasons was that players wanted him to move to New York.

Cannon was son of Ray Cannon, who served as legal counsel for some of Chicago "Black Sox." Elder Cannon also tried to organize players' union but was unsuccessful. Younger Cannon attended Marquette U. Law School, and was hopeful of becoming pro ball player. Served on carrier Saratoga during World War II. Elected civil court judge at age 27. In 1953 elected circuit court judge; began another six-year term as circuit court judge 1/1/66.

Was enthusiastic worker in efforts to bring major league baseball to Milwaukee before Boston Braves moved there, and again when city obtained Seattle franchise.

CARBO, BERNARDO OF-BL-TR. B. 8/5/47, Detroit, Mich. 6', 185. Bernie Carbo hit .310 for Cincinnati Reds during 1970 season and helped them into WS that fall, driving in 63 runs in 125 games. Performance won him *The Sporting News* designation as NL Rookie of Year. Long salary dispute following spring seemed to get him untracked and average sagged to .219. Before 1972 campaign asked Reds to trade him; mid-

May they swapped him to St. Louis NL for Joe Hague. Did not bounce back with another season like 1970, but showed Cardinals enough to make them glad about their deal. Seems to be streak hitter. While had reputation of being bad fielder, work in outfield improved considerably in 1972. Has strong accurate arm.

Carbo was first player picked by Reds in baseball's first draft, 1965. Played at Tampa, Peninsula, Knoxville, Asheville, and Indianapolis before joining Reds, 1969, for four games. With Indianapolis hit .359 to lead American Association in hitting; slapped 21 homers, drove in 76 runs, tied for league lead in doubles with 37; MVP for league; batting champion of minors that season.

Bernie got into four games in WS, 1970, but was 0 for 8. Ready for 1973 season with overall major league average of .262 for 353 games, 33 homers to credit, 117 RBI, 131 runs scored, 52 doubles, 5 triples.

CARDENAL, JOSE DOMEC (Che) OF-BR-TR. B. 10/7/43, Matanzas, Cuba. 5'10", 160. Jose Cardenal denies he is problem to managers despite fact he landed with his sixth major league club in 1972 after brief sojourns in both AL and NL. Best season overall was 1970 with St. Louis Cardinals when he hit .293 in 148 games, with 10 homers and 74 RBI. In 1971, though he hit for lower average, his combined total of RBI with St. Louis and Milwaukee AL was 80, and he had 10 homers. Hit .291 with Chicago Cubs, 1972, including 17 homers, 70 RBI.

Cardenal signed with San Francisco Giants' organization, 1961, and broke into pro ball at El Paso that year with .355 average in 128 games. Also had eight games at Eugene, Oreg., club that season. Back to El Paso for 1963, and to Tacoma for 1964, with brief stays with Giants both years.

California AL, 1965–67; Cleveland, 1968–69; St. Louis, 1970–71 until 7/29/71 when traded to Milwaukee, AL. Brewers sent him to Cubs 12/3/71. By start of 1973 Jose had played in 1161 major league games and owned .264 average, including 176 doubles, 36 triples, 88 homers among his 1108 hits. Had 447 RBI.

CARDENAS, LEONARDO LAZARO SS-BR-TR. B. 12/17/38, Matanzas, Cuba. 5'10, 163. Another slick-fielding Latin American ball player. This one, however, combines much timely hitting with his fielding skills. In 1971, for example, besides setting AL record for best fielding average in history, .985, also drove in 75 runs for Minnesota Twins. At Cincinnati, 1966, had 20 homers and drove in 81 runs.

Cardenas was first acquisition made by Harry Dalton of California Angels after taking over general manager's job late in 1971.

Leo started at Tucson, Arizona-Texas League, 1956, hitting .316, driving in 78 runs, and led circuit in fielding average as well as putouts and assists for shortstop. Then had two good years at Savannah, Sally League. In 1959, while with Havana, International League, was dubbed "Mr. Automatic" because of fine fielding. In 1960 shifted to Jersey City in same league, then before year was out was taken to NL by Cincinnati for 48 games. Eight full seasons with Reds followed, including flag-winning campaign of 1961. In WS that year Leo a pinch hitter three times, hitting one double. Three fine seasons with Minnesota Twins, 1969,70,71, then traded to California. Twins received southpaw relief pitcher Dave LaRoche. Traded to Cleveland, April 1973.

Cardenas was named to four NL All-Star game squads, and to AL team, 1971. His 1973 season started with 1780 big league games played for .259 lifetime average, with 117 homers and 665 RBI.

Leo made only 11 errors at shortstop, 1971, as did Larry Bowa of Philadelphia NL same season. Bowa, however, handled more chances and had .987 average. But Cardenas' work broke previous AL record for fewest shortstop errors. Then Eddie Brinkman broke both records, 1972, making only seven miscues.

CAREW, RODNEY CLINE   2B-BL-TR. B. 10/1/45, Gatun, Panama. 6', 170. Rod Carew won second AL hitting title, 1972, with .318 average. Two things were notable: first-time batting champion won honors without single home run; and among his 170 hits were 15 bunt singles.

Won his first AL batting championship, 1969, with .332 average in 123 games. Boosted average to .366 in 1970, but didn't play enough games to qualify for title, which went to Alex Johnson with .329. Carew suffered serious knee injury 6/22/70 and played only 51 games.

In 1971, during early part of season, almost decided to retire after poor start. Was hitting at .215 pace in June, then got into groove with .359 clip for last 93 games. This gave him .307 for season.

Carew got his early experience at Melbourne and Orlando, Fla., and Wilson, N.C. during 1964–66. Then graduated to Minnesota Twins in 1967 and promptly made good with .292 average in 137 games. Named to AL All-Star squad, distinction he continued to merit each year since. Rod won the *Sporting News* Rookie of the Year nod, 1967, as well as similar vote by members of Baseball Writers Association of America.

Rod's average was .273 in 1968, then came his first bat title in 1969.

When Carew started 1973 season his lifetime average was .309 for 727 games; his 845 hits included 128 doubles, 32 triples, 23 homers, and 276 RBI. Had stolen 58 bases.

Rod felt his knee needed strengthening after 1971 season so he signed on to play winter ball at Aragua, Venezuela. In November, when club had 7–9 record, was asked to take over manager's job. Team was in fifth place in six-club league. Carew promptly led club to first-place tie at season's end, then went on to win playoffs. Carew himself led circuit in batting with .355.

Carew holds AL record for most times stealing home in one season, 1969, with seven. This equaled mark set 1946 by Pete Reiser of Brooklyn Dodgers.

CAREY, MAX GEORGE (Scoops) OF-BRL-TR. B. 1/11/90, Terre Haute, Ind. 5'11½", 170. Max Carey had long distinguished career in NL mostly with Pittsburgh. Remembered primarily as outstanding base runner. Stole 738 bases in all, modern NL record. In one season had 51 steals in 53 attempts. Six times stole more than 50 bases a season. But finest year was 1925 when stole only 46. Batted .343, helped Pittsburgh to pennant. Brilliant World Series against Washington, playing last two games with broken ribs. Had 11 for 24, including four doubles, for .458 average! Stole three bases. Four of hits came in crucial seventh game when hit three doubles, one single, all off Walter Johnson, scored three runs, drove in two others, pilfered one base. Pirates took game 9–7 and Series four games to three.

Carey compiled all sorts of records. Among them, major league mark for most years as leading base stealer, ten. NL record for most games in outfield, 2421, since surpassed by Willie Mays. Repeatedly led NL in outfield putouts and assists. Occasionally also led in errors.

Max attended Concordia College, Fort Wayne, Indiana, graduated 1909. Played at South Bend, Central League, that summer and next, landing with Pirates in time for two games, 1910. From 1911 until 1928 played well over 100 games each year with exception of 1919. In July 1926 released to Brooklyn on waivers. Played with Dodgers through 1929. Back with Pirates as coach, 1930. Manager, Dodgers, 1932–33. Manager, Miami, Florida East Coast League, 1940.

Carey played 2469 NL games, scored 1545 runs, had 2665 hits, 419 doubles, 159 triples, 69 homers, 797 RBI, .285 average. Hall of Fame 1961.

CARLETON, JAMES OTTO (Tex) P-BLR-TR. B. 8/19/06, Comanche, Tex. 6'1¾" 180. Tex Carleton won an even 100 games in NL, lost 76. One of his last victories came in 1940 for Brooklyn Dodgers, no-hitter against Cincinnati 4/30/40. Score was 3–0. Also happened to be Dodgers' ninth consecutive win. But Cincinnati won pennant that year, finishing 12 games ahead of Brooklyn.

Carleton's best years were those with Cardinals, 1932–34. After 10–13 record his first year in majors (1932), won 17, lost 11 in 1933; helped Gas House Gang to 1934 flag with 16–11 record. Traded to Chicago NL, had winning percentage during next four years with 16–8 mark for 1937. Did not play in 1939. In final year in majors, with Brooklyn Dodgers, won six, lost six. Dropped down to Montreal, International League, for 1941, winning four, losing same. Then back to Texas.

Tex started pro ball in East Texas League, 1925, playing with Texarkana and Marshall. With Austin, 1926; Houston, Texas League, 1927–28 and again in 1931. In 1929–30 pitched for Rochester, International League. Fated to work in shadow of Dizzy Dean at Houston, 1931. Won 20, lost seven and had 1.89 ERA. Dean, on same team, won 26, lost 10, and had 1.53 ERA. Both joined Cardinals, 1932. While Carleton was winning 43 games and losing 35 during next three seasons, Dizzy was taking 68 games against 40 losses. Dean again caught up with Carleton, 1938. Both pitched for Chicago NL. Carleton's record of 10–9 compared with Dean's 7–1 mark. Dizzy had ERA of 1.81, while Carleton had to be content with 5.42.

Tex pitched in 293 NL games, 1607-1/3 innings, had ERA of 3.91. Walked 561, struck out 808. Had 91 complete games and 16 shutouts. In WS, 1934,35,38, was charged with one loss, no victory, with 5.06 ERA.

CARLTON, STEVEN NORMAN P-BL-TL. B. 12/22/44, Miami, Fla. 6'5", 210. Steve Carlton became highest-paid pitcher in baseball when signed contract for 1973 reportedly calling for $167,000. Fancy recompense came after amazing season with Philadelphia Phillies, 1972, when won 27, lost 10 for one of most hopeless teams in majors. Texas Rangers were probably worse than Phils, but debatable. Rangers won 54 games without any Carlton. Phillies won only 32 games when Carlton not pitching victories for them. No wonder his selection for Cy Young Award in NL was unanimous. Steve not only pitched magnificently under adverse circumstances, but packed in crowds of fans—an estimated 10,000 more each time was advertised as starting hurler. Without Carlton, Phillies' 1972 attendance figures probably would have been disaster.

Carlton romped away with various honors. Struck out 310; led both majors in total victories and complete games. Started 41 games, completed 30 of them. Pitched 346 innings, had 1.98 ERA; walked 87. His strikeouts and ERA led NL. No other pitcher ever won 27 games for last-place club. No other pitcher with last-place team ever won Cy Young Award. Captured 46 percent of club's total victories. Won 22 of last 25 starts and finished with eight consecutive wins. Hurled eight shutouts.

One of satisfactions was fact his old club, Cardinals, got two runs off him all season; Steve beat them four times.

Carlton, after winning 44 games and losing 31 for St. Louis Cardinals over three-year period, asked for $50,000 contract for 1970, causing

Redbird owner Gussie Busch to say, "I don't care if he ever throws another damned ball for us." Eventually, through intervention of Dick Meyer, Cardinal vice president, impasse was overcome and compromise two-year contract signed reportedly giving Carlton $40,000 for 1970 and $50,000 for 1971. Steve had 10–19 record, 1970, but in 1971 doubled his victory total to 20, and cut losses to nine. Once again salary battle began, which ended in Carlton being traded to Philadelphia NL. Supposed to have signed for $75,000 for 1972 with Phils.

Carlton got $5000 to sign with Cardinal farm system originally. Won 10 and lost one with Rock Hill, S.C., team of Western Carolinas League, 1964, then moved up to Winnipeg and Tulsa, en route to parent club, which he made during 1966 season.

Carlton(9/15/69) struck out 19 members of N.Y. Mets to set new major league strikeout record but lost game 4–3 when Ron Swoboda hit pair of two-run homers. Fanned side four different innings that game and struck out at least one every inning. In 1970 Tom Seaver of Mets equaled Carlton's record of 19 strikeouts. Earlier Steve had pitched quite a game against Phillies. Fanned 16 (9/20/67) but lost game 3–1.

In 1967 Carlton started one WS game against Boston Red Sox, pitched six innings and was charged with loss, even though he did not allow an earned run. Third baseman Mike Shannon made an error, allowed one Boston runner to score, and Cardinals never tied it up, losing 3–1. In 1968 WS Carlton was ineffective in two games against Detroit. Had ERA of 2.70 for his 1967 and 1968 WS performances, with no win, one loss.

Carlton's strikeout totals were 210 in 1969, 193 in 1970, and 172 in 1971. His best ERA with Cardinals was 2.17 in 1969. Faced 1973 with record of 231 major league games; won 104, lost 72, including 24 shutouts. During career started 213 games; completed 96. Pitched 1611 innings, allowed 512 earned runs, 536 walks; fanned 1261 and had overall ERA of 2.86.

CARPENTER, ROBERT RULIPH MORGAN, JR. Executive. B. 8/31/15, Montchanin, Del. Chairman of board, Philadelphia NL. Only Horace Stoneham of S.F. Giants and P.K. Wrigley of Chicago Cubs are senior to Bob as NL chief executives, and Tom Yawkey in AL. Bob's father bought Phillies in 1944 after Judge Landis expelled previous club president, Bill Cox, for betting on own team. Paid about $400,000 for team. Carpenter family already owned Wilmington, Inter-State League. Bob took over presidency of Phils, 1944. After Herb Pennock, general manager, died 1/30/48, Bob assumed these duties for time. Then hired John J. Quinn as vice president and general manager.

As young man, Carpenter played football at Duke. Then joined public relations staff of E. I. du Pont de Nemours & Co. Army 1944–46. Phillies won pennant, 1950, under Carpenter regime, but lost WS to Yankees in four straight. In 1971 Phillies moved into new Philadelphia Veterans Stadium, 56,371 seating capacity. Midseason 1972, Carpenter appointed Jim Owens as general manager. At end of 1972 season, he became chairman of board; turned presidency over to son Ruly.

CARRIGAN, WILLIAM FRANCIS (Rough) C-BR-TR. B. 10/22/83, Lewiston, Me. D. 7/8/69, Lewiston, Me. 5'9", 175. Bill Carrigan really had three careers in baseball, all with Boston Red Sox. First was smart, rugged catcher, 1906–16; then was highly successful manager, 1913–16; finally, pilot of three tail-end teams, 1927–29. Took over management of Sox August 1913 and team finished fourth that year, second in 1914, first in 1915 and 1916. Red Sox won WS both autumns by 4–1 margin, Philadelphia NL the first victim, Brooklyn Dodgers the next.

Bill had plenty of money of his own and had married wealthy girl, so resigned at peak of his profession; entered banking and theatrical business. Was 33 years old at time. Interest in baseball continued, however, and Bob Quinn, then president of Red Sox (1927), persuaded Carrigan to come back and try to lead team out of doldrums. In those pre-Yawkey days, Quinn did not have money to buy good players, or farm system to develop them. So Red Sox stumbled into cellar, 1927, same as in two previous years. It was no different in 1928 and 1929, so Carrigan went back to more satisfying life in Maine.

Carrigan played both football and baseball at Holy Cross before lining up with Red Sox, 1906. Farmed to Toronto, 1907, returned following season and soon became capable receiver. Hit .296 one year and .289 another, but was not noted as batsman. Wound up with lifetime major league average of .257 in his 706 games. Did not distinguish himself in WS play, 1912, 15, 16. Had two hits in 12 trips for .167 average, appearing in just four games in three classics.

Credited with helping make Babe Ruth fine pitcher. Was manager when Babe arrived in majors, 1915. Ruth won 51 games, lost 18 for Carrigan. Babe often called Carrigan greatest manager of them all.

CARROLL, CLAY PALMER (Hawk) P-BR-TR. B. 5/2/41, Clanton, Ala. 6'1", 200. Clay Carroll, reliable reliefer for Cincinnati Reds, appeared in 20 of team's first 40 games in 1972, picking up where he left off in earlier seasons. Clay's early 1972 performance included three wins and nine saves. This brought his lifetime major league record of wins to 57 against 43 losses. Had started season with 3.14 ERA in 785 innings, 423 strikeouts against 259 walks.

Carroll proved valuable acquisition for Cincinnati from start after coming from Atlanta Braves 6/11/68. Where Carroll had lost oftener than winning while with Braves, he broke even with Reds in 1968, 7–7.

Then came up with 12–6, 9–4, and 10–4 records in subsequent campaigns.

In Reds' pennant-winning season, 1970, Carroll had 2.60 ERA and allowed no runs either in playoff games or in WS. Appeared in four games in WS and was pitcher of record when Cincinnati rallied to defeat Baltimore Orioles in.fourth contest, 6–5. This was only win of series for Rhinelanders. So Carroll had 1.000 winning percentage in WS and 0.00 ERA. Hard to improve on that. His work in 1971 was notable. During midsummer worked 15-1/3 innings and didn't allow single run in period between June 28 and July 31. Appeared in eight games against Mets during year, pitched 10 innings and didn't permit a score. His lifetime record against Mets was 8–2 at start of 1972 season; 8–3 against Astros; 5–1 vs. Expos.

One sports writer declared Carroll is rare combination of "guts, confidence and desire." Started career at Davenport, 1961, and gained his early experience at Boise, Denver, Austin. Joined Milwaukee Braves, 1964, shipped to Atlanta in International League for part of 1965, then returned to Braves, by that time making their home base in Atlanta. With Braves from then until June 1968, except for brief spell at Richmond, 1967.

Nickname comes from his hawklike nose.

CARTWRIGHT, ALEXANDER JOY, JR. (Father of Modern Baseball)
B. 4/17/20, New York, N.Y. D. 7/12/92, Honolulu, Hawaii. This gentleman, a surveyor, never played major league baseball as such. Member of Knickerbocker Club, New York City, Cartwright organized first recorded game, 6/19/46. Headed committee which decided such basic rules as 90-foot distance between bases, nine men on a side, entitling batter to make first base—if he could—if catcher let third strike get away from him.

In June 1846 Cartwright and other Manhattan young bloods journeyed to Hoboken, N.J., by ferry and played in place called Elysian Fields. Knickerbockers lost first game on record by either 23–1 or 21–1, depending on which history you read. On one occasion Cartwright reported to have umpired and fined member of N.Y. club six cents for swearing.

Before heading west in California gold rush of 1848, Cartwright also said to have eliminated earlier rule in baseball that runner could be retired by hitting him with ball. Eventually settled in Honolulu where spent last years. Hall of Fame 1938.

CARTY, RICARDO ADOLFO JACOBO (Rico) OF-BR-TR. B.
9/1/39, San Pedro de Macoris, Dominican Republic. 6'2", 190. Rico Carty's full name is long enough but it could well include one more

moniker—Vicissitudes. Has been beset by tuberculosis, shoulder separation, and other injuries on ball field. Off field, in August 1971, got involved with two men in civilian clothes who turned out to be policemen. Carty was beaten and arrested. Besides various bruises, one eye was damaged, possibly permanently. Mayor of Atlanta later suspended policemen and said it was "apparently an incident of blatant brutality."

Carty, however, was back playing for Braves, 1972, after having missed entire 1971 season because of knee injury. Then traded to Texas Rangers. In time with Braves before 1973, Rico had .3172 overall batting average in 829 games, with 137 doubles, 14 triples, 109 homers among 871 hits. This is highest lifetime batting average of any active player in majors—just fraction of point below that of Roberto Clemente, who had career mark of .3173 when he died.

When Rico led both majors in hitting, 1970, his .366 average was highest in big time since Ted Williams hit .388 in 1957.

Scout Ted McGrew signed Rico for Braves' organization 12/24/59. Carty got his minor league experience at Davenport, Eau Claire, Yakima, Toronto, and Austin during 1960–63. Two games with Milwaukee NL 1963, then he grabbed regular job with stellar .330 average in 133 games, 1964. Had 22 homers and 88 RBI. Although in his rookie year, was runner-up to Roberto Clemente for NL batting title; was second to Richie Allen in Rookie of Year balloting. Carty dropped out of .300 class in 1967, possibly due to onset of tuberculosis. Missed entire 1968 season because of this illness. But came back, 1969. Despite three shoulder separations that year, missing 58 games, hit cool .342 with 16 homers. Then came his banner season, 1970, winning batting championship. Had 31-game batting streak that year. On May 31 went four-for-four with three homers and six RBI.

Carty appeared in one playoff, 1969. After helping Braves to division title by slapping ball at .390 pace during closing weeks of season, hit .300 in games against N.Y. Mets. His one appearance in All-Star contest came as result of write-in campaign by fans, 1970. Received 552,382 votes, although his name did not appear on printed ballot.

Rico had unusual experience while in minors: hit two homers in one time at bat. This occurred while with Toronto. Slammed first pitch thrown him over left field wall. Umpire, however, ruled he had called time, so homer didn't count. Batting over, Carty homered again just to show it was no fluke.

CASANOVA, PAULINO ORTIZ C-BR-TR. B. 12/31/41, Colon, Matanzas, Cuba. 6′4″, 200. Paul Casanova doesn't hit much but is one of finest defensive catchers in baseball. Built his reputation with Washington Senators and led AL receivers in double plays, 1966,67,70. Keeps base runners honest with great throwing arm. On AL's All-Star game squad, 1967 but did not see action.

Paul attended Havana U. Played with Minot, N. Dak.; San Antonio; Geneva, N.Y.; Burlington, N. C.; York and Buffalo in minors, starting 1960. Had five games with Senators, 1965, and stuck with team, 1966, when he had his best season at plate with .254 average, including 13 homers, 44 RBI. In 1967 his average dropped to .248, his homers to nine, but he drove 53 runs across plate in 141 games. Atlanta Braves got him from Texas Rangers (née Senators) 12/2/71, to balance their catching staff and as insurance for 1971 rookie of year Earl Williams. Casanova, at time of his acquisition by NL club, was said to be able to catch tough knuckleballers like Phil Niekro of Braves.

Casanova brought with him an AL record of 686 games with batting average of .228. His 527 hits included 77 doubles, 12 triples, and 41 homers, with 216 RBI. Paul usually plays winter baseball for La Guaira of Venezuelan League. Hit .206 for Braves, 1972, in 49 games.

CASE, GEORGE WASHINGTON   OF-BR-TR. B. 11/11/15, Trenton, N.J. 6'1", 180.
Speedster who led AL in stolen bases six times in eight years, 1939, 40, 41, 42, 43, 46. In 1939 his total was 51; in 1943 it was 61. Case spent most of his big league career with Washington Senators after two years in minors. Started with Trenton, New York–Pennsylvania League, 1936. There he hit .271 in 62 games. Following year, his .338 average in 113 games won him tie with two other NYP players for batting championship. Went up to Washington later same season in time for 22 games. Hit above .300 in first two full seasons in AL, helped by his speed, but was able reach coveted .300 average only once later in career. His first time as leading AL base thief came in his second full year in majors.

After 1945 season Case moved to Cleveland for one year, then had final season back in Washington, playing just 36 games, his average dropping to .150. Had .282 lifetime average in 1226 AL games; stole total of 349 bases. George, after managing Oneonta in New York–Pennsylvania League in Yankee system, became special batting coach for Yanks' minor league teams, 1973.

CASEY, DANIEL MAURICE   P-BR-TL. B. 10/2/65, Binghamton, N.Y. D. 2/8/43, Washington, D. C.

> Oh! somewhere in this favored land the sun is shining bright;
> The band is playing somewhere, and somewhere hearts are light.
> And somewhere men are laughing, and somewhere children shout;
> But there is no joy in Mudville—mighty Casey has struck out.

No wonder Casey struck out. He was just a weak-hitting pitcher, usually batting around .160! Mighty slugger? What a joke!

Dan Casey is believed to have been the inspiration for Ernest L. Thayer's famous poem, "Casey at the Bat." Elocutionists and actors, notably DeWolf Hopper, have recited his poem thousands of times since the last part of the 19th century.

Thayer probably got his idea for "Casey at the Bat" in 1887 when Dan Casey was pitcher for Philadelphia NL team. Casey came up one day with bases loaded. Phillies needed runs. But Casey fanned ignominiously, ending incipient rally. Using poetic license, Thayer, sports writer, transformed puny-hitting pitcher into legendary slugger—and changed Philadelphia into Mudville.

Real Casey seems to have won between 96 and 100 games in NL, depending on whose records you believe. Lost either 90 or 92 decisions. Started with Wilmington, Union Association, then considered major league, 1884. With Detroit NL 1885; Phillies 1886–89. Syracuse, American Association, also major league then, 1890. Won 28 games for Phils 1887, either 24 or 25 in 1886. Rest of performance not noteworthy. Highwater mark as hitter in 1889—.221. Lifetime average, 202 major league games, .162.

Real Casey, Mighty Casey, struck out, not once, but many times!

CASEY, HUGH THOMAS P-BR-TR. B. 10/14/13, Buckhead, Ga. D. 7/3/51, Atlanta, Ga. 6'1", 207. Whenever great relief pitchers are mentioned, name of Hugh Casey is not forgotten. Casey achieved fame during swashbuckling 1940s with Brooklyn Dodgers. Pitching out of jams was specialty. Won 75 games, lost 42 in major league career.

Pitched well enough with Charlotte, Piedmont League, and Atlanta, Southern Association, 1932,33,34 to get trial with Cubs, 1935. Pitched 13 games, 26 innings without decision. Los Angeles, Pacific Coast League, 1936; Birmingham, Southern Association, 1937; Memphis, Southern Association, 1938. Minor league record to date not sensational.

Brooklyn, 1939, 15–10. In 1941 Casey began his tranformation into relief specialist, got heavy duty in bullpen from then on. Highlights of career came in 1941 and 1947 World Series, both against Yanks. Victimized in 1941 Series, fourth game. Yanks leading two games to one. Dodgers ahead 4–3 in fourth game, ninth inning, two out. Casey had entered game in fifth-inning jam, got dangerous Joe Gordon out and side retired with bases loaded. Now, in ninth, only one out stood between Dodgers and victory, which would even Series at two-all. Tommy Henrich strode to plate. Casey worked count to three balls, two strikes. Came in with low, breaking curve, inside to lefthanded batsman. Henrich swung and missed—a strikeout. But catcher Mickey Owen let ball get away from him, Henrich reaching first safely. Groans filled Ebbets Field. Soon they became wailing anguish when Joe DiMaggio singled, Keller doubled, Dickey walked and Gordon doubled. By this time score was 7–4 in favor of Yankees, who finished Series next day, four victories to one.

Casey missed service with Dodgers 1943–45, serving in U.S. Navy. Back with Brooklyn, 1946. Then came some personal revenge against Yanks in Series of 1947 though Dodgers lost classic, 4 games to 3. Casey's role in one game was overshadowed by other spectaculars in same contest. In fourth game Floyd Bevens of Yanks pitching no-hitter until top of ninth. Yanks led 2–1, Dodgers having got their run on two walks, sacrifice and infield out. In ninth Yanks loaded bases, one out. Dodger Mgr. Burt Shotton called fireman Casey to mound. Batsman— Tommy Henrich. Casey must have thought it wouldn't pay to strike Henrich out again, though Bruce Edwards was catching, not Mickey Owen. "Case" made one pitch, same type he had thrown Henrich six years earlier, low curve. Henrich swung, hit ball to Casey, who threw home for one out. Edwards fired to first for double play and Dodgers were out of inning. Still down by one run in last of ninth, Dodgers got two men on base with two out—still without hit. Up came pinch hitter Cookie Lavagetto, who blasted Dodgers' first and last hit of game, double off right field fence. Brooklyn chalked up 3–2 victory.

In that Series Casey won two of three games Brooklyn captured. Established record for relievers by taking part in six of seven games. Walked one, allowed five hits, two runs in 10 1/3 innings for 0.87 ERA.

With Dodgers through 1948. Divided 1949 between Pittsburgh and Yankees, winding up major league career with team which had been his bitter rival. Chalked up one AL victory to go along with his 74 in NL.

Back with Atlanta 1950, helped Crackers to pennant. That was all. Hard-drinking, hard-living Casey took himself out of picture 7/3/51, suicide.

CASH, DAVID, JR. 2B-BR-TR. B. 6/11/48, Utica, N. Y. 5'11", 168. Man who took second base job with Pittsburgh Pirates from Bill Mazeroski. Dave has been used largely as leadoff man because of his ability to get on base, and because of his speed. Not power hitter, but his .289 average in 123 games in 1971 nothing to be ashamed of. In previous two part seasons with Pirates, 1969 and 1970, hit .279 and .314 respectively. Had .282 mark in 1972, so, going into 1973, career average in majors was .290 for 304 games.

Cash, son of disabled Korean War veteran, was three-sport star in high school in Utica, N. Y. Set school mark for points scored in single basketball game; offered basketball scholarship by Syracuse. Pirates got him for their organization in selection of June 1966 in free-agent draft.

Dave was sent to Salem, Va., club that year, hit .266 in 58 games. Then moved to Gastonia for 1967, where he was all-star shortstop and batting champion of Western Carolinas League. Hit .335 and stole 23 bases. Back to Salem, 1968, with .277 mark in 124 games, then to Columbus, Ohio, club in AAA. Hit .291 and was called up to Pirates for 18 games. In 1970 his spell with Columbus resulted in .313 mark for 35 games, after which he was pressed into service with Pirates for 64 contests, alternating with Mazeroski at second base.

Cash hit just .125 in 1970 playoff series, but in 1971 playoffs he went 8 for 19, scoring 5 runs, for .421 mark. His 1971 WS record showed 4 hits in 30 AB for .133 mark. Played errorless ball in field.

CASH, NORMAN DALTON 1B-BL-TL. B. 11/10/34, Justiceburg, Tex. 5'11½", 190. Early in 1972 season Norm Cash passed 1000 RBI mark for his AL career. Slugging first baseman of Detroit Tigers had fairly typical day 4/28/72 with four runs batted in, two homers. Veteran also was then shooting for 1000 mark in runs scored. Had 978 when 1973 began. Lifetime average at time .273 for 1915 games.

Back in 1961 Cash led AL in hitting with .361. Several times since then so-called experts have counted him out, but in 1971 hit for better average than he ever had since 1961, with .283, and his 91 RBI also was best since 1961 when he had 132 runs driven in.

Norm's fielding won him top honors among AL first basemen 1964 and 1967. While Cash hasn't hit for high average since his banner year more than decade ago, his homer and RBI totals have been joy to Tiger managers. Prior to 1973, 11 times hit 20 or more homers, with his total reaching 41 in 1961. And had hit eight grand slammers. His career total of homers for Tigers has excelled that of Hank Greenberg. With 351 at start of 1973, was approaching total of teammate Al Kaline who had 376.

Cash attended San Angelo Junior College and got his B.S. degree from Sul Ross College; both institutions in Tex. Besides playing baseball in college, was good enough in football to be drafted by Chicago Bears as running halfback. Chose baseball, however, and signed with Chicago AL, 1955, as outfielder. Farmed to Waterloo that year and next; military service, 1957. Divided 1958 between Indianapolis and White Sox, then after playing 58 games with Sox in 1959 as first baseman, traded to Detroit.

From 1960 until 1971 played at least 121 games every year, with ups and downs, however. In 1965 voted Comeback King of AL in the *Sporting News* poll, on strength of .304 average, 23 homers, 58 RBI in 78 games after All-Star break, with 10 homers and 14-game hitting streak in September. Staged another comeback, 1968. Average stood at .195 July 27. Hit .333 rest of way, with 12 homers, 33 RBI in last 54 games. *Sporting News* poll again named him Comeback King of AL, 1971, when he bounced back after sagging to .259 in 1970.

Conversation piece in Detroit because of several of his prodigious drives out of Tiger Stadium. Four of them have cleared roof of right field stand, which soars 94 feet above ground. Mickey Mantle hit three over same roof, but no other players have come close to doing it four times.

First WS appearance, 1959, with White Sox, unsuccessful. Pinch hit four times without hit. But hit .385 in 1968 WS with Tigers. Ten hits, 26 AB, including one homer, five RBI. Member of AL All-Star squads 1961,66,71.

Norm should have paid his way into ball park 6/27/63. Tied major league records by having no putouts or assists at first base. Tied AL record by reaching first base safely six times in nine-inning game 8/30/60. Hit homer, single, walked three times, and was hit by pitched ball.

Cash has glib tongue, spouts repartee, makes speaking engagements as often as possible. Said to be eyeing some of that TV money available to ex-athletes like Joe Garagiola, Sandy Koufax, Don Drysdale, and others.

CATER, DANNY ANDERSON Inf.-OF-BR-TR. B. 2/25/40, Austin, Tex. 5'11", 198. Runner-up for AL batting championship in 1968 while playing with Oakland A's. His .290 average, in 147 games, second only to Carl Yastrzemski's .301. Played first base, second base and outfield; also third base for Yanks during 1970–71 seasons. Started out as shortstop at Johnson City, Tenn., 1958. Belonged to Philadelphia NL at time. In his second pro game in Appalachian League went five-for-six, with three homers and eight RBI.

Danny is line drive hitter. Best home run production in majors was 14 while with Chicago White Sox, 1965. Through 1972, in 1098 major league games, had .276 lifetime average with 1129 hits in 4095 trips; scored 444 runs, with 172 doubles, 29 triples, 60 homers, 473 RBI.

After his .345 average with Johnson City in 68 games in 1958, Cater got his minor league experience at Bakersfield, Williamsport, Buffalo and Arkansas. Phillies 1964. Chicago AL 1965–66. Kansas City AL 1966–67, then to Oakland along with franchise shift for 1968–69. Traded to New York AL 12/5/69. Exchanged for Sparky Lyle of Boston Red Sox just before opening of 1972 season. With Sox in 1972 Danny got into 92 games, hit .237, with eight homers.

CAVARRETTA, PHILIP JOSEPH 1B-OF-BL-TL. B. 7/19/16, Chicago, Ill. 5'11½", 175. Phil Cavarretta spent most of his playing career with Chicago Cubs; managed Cubs 2-1/2 seasons; captured NL batting title, 1945; and wound up with .293 lifetime major league batting average in 2030 games. Before saying farewell to Windy City, however, Phil played 77 games with White Sox, 1954–55, coming up with .309 AL average.

As manager of Cubs 7/21/51 until close of 1953, Cavarretta was no ball of fire. Cubs of 1951, piloted by Frankie Frisch before Phil was given job, finished last. Phil got them into fifth place, 1952, with .500 average. After club ended seventh in 1953, reins were turned over to Stanley Hack. Cavarretta continued managing in minor leagues. Bossed Buffalo, International League, 1956–58, playing 57 games his first year on job there. Managed Lancaster, Eastern League, 1960; coach, Detroit Tigers, 1961–63; scout for Tigers, 1964; manager, Salinas, California League, 1965; pilot for Reno, California League, 1966–67; manager, Waterbury, Eastern League, 1968. Mentor for Birmingham Oakland AL farm, Southern League, 1970–72. Batting coach, Mets' minor league teams, 1973.

Throughout most of career Cavarretta divided his time between first base and outfield. Started in 1934 with Peoria in Central League; moved up same season to Reading, New York–Pennsylvania League. With hitting averages above .300 in both circuits, he went all way to Cubs that first year and hit .381 in his first seven NL games. Besides year he won NL batting title, Cavarretta hit above .300 just three full seasons as regular. Not a real slugger, his highest homer total was 1950 when he banged ten. His best RBI total was 97 in 1945, year he won batting championship.

Phil's lifetime totals showed 990 runs scored, 1977 hits, 347 doubles, 99 triples, 95 homers, 920 RBI. In WS, 1935,38,45, 17 games, 63 AB, 9 runs, 20 hits, 3 doubles, 1 homer, 5 RBI and .317 average.

CEDEÑO, CESAR   OF-BR-TR. B. 2/25/51, Santo Domingo, Dominican Republic. 6'2", 191. Brilliant young outfielder began to blossom in earnest, 1972. Fourth-best hitter among regulars in majors, with .320 mark for 139 games. Hit 22 homers, drove in 82 runs, scored 103 times. Stole 55 bases, finishing behind Lou Brock and Joe Morgan.

Though Cesar Cedeño did not hit for high average with Houston Astros 1971, .264, led NL in doubles, hit 10 homers, stole 20 bases and drove in 81 runs in 161 games.

Got major league initiation, 1970, after brilliant record earlier same year at Oklahoma City. Leading American Association in almost every major department when called to Houston late in June. In 54 AA games was jogging along at .373 rate with 61 RBI. Joining Astros, hit consistently—110 hits in 90 games; stole 17 bases in 21 attempts; had .310 average. Houston organization signed Cedeño April 1967. Spent season at Covington, Ky., hit .374 in 36 games; then .256 at Cocoa, Fla., in 69 contests. In 1969, had .274 average at Peninsula club of Carolina League. Then caught fire at Oklahoma City, 1970, as indicated above.

Cedeño plays enthusiastically, seems well equipped in every department except possibly long-distance power: good arm, speed, fine fielding. After brilliant 1970 season, Cedeño got slow start, 1971, and was below .200 going into June. Hit .283 rest of year and got season mark up to .264. As he approached 1973 campaign major league average was .295 for 390 games when he reached ripe age of 22. His 450 hits included 100 doubles, 18 triples, 39 homers, 205 RBI. Career stolen bases 92. Member NL All-Star game squad 1972, 73.

CEPEDA, ORLANDO MANUEL (Cha-Cha)   1B-BR-TR. B. 9/17/37, Ponce, Puerto Rico 6'2", 205. Orlando Cepeda helped San Francisco Giants win one flag, St. Louis Cardinals two. His father was Babe Ruth of Puerto Rico and Orlando has followed in producing homers. Had 358 of them at end of 1972 season. Led NL with 46 homers, 1961.

Cepeda probably never reached his top potential because of knee problems. Right knee operated on in December 1964 and missed most of 1965 season. In 1971 injured left knee, had another operation in August. In 1972 his condition kept him down to 28 games with Atlanta Braves. Shifted to Oakland, appeared in only three games, and released at season's end. Signed with Boston Red Sox, 1973.

Orlando taken to Giants' minor league base in Florida when he was 17; got $500 for signing. Sent to Salem, Va., Appalachian League. Spoke almost no English, encountered discrimination, and didn't do too well. That was 1955. Shifted to Kokomo, Indiana, he belted ball at .393 pace in 92 games, good enough to lead league. Also hit 21 homers and drove in 91 runs. Spent 1956 at St. Cloud, Minn.; again led league in hitting, this time .355. Topped circuit in homers with 26; in RBI with 112; in hits and in total bases. Continued his solid stickwork 1957 with Minneapolis, American Association. This time .309, with 26 homers and 112 RBI. Jump to majors didn't bother Cepeda. In 1958 hit 25 homers and had .312 average, being named rookie of year. Had honor of hitting first home run ever hit in majors on West Coast, in opening game 4/15/58 against L.A. Dodgers. This of course was his first major league homer.

Cepeda's home run production varied from 24 to 27 in each of his first three years, then soared to 46 in 1961; varied from 31 to 35 his next three seasons. After his knee problems, 1965, plus fact Orlando usually held out for more money every spring, Giants traded him to Cardinals 5/8/66 for Ray Sadecki. Welcomed in St. Louis, Orlando had .303 mark in 123 Cardinal games, won Comeback of Year Award. Then, in 1967 became unanimous choice for NL's MVP by slapping ball at .325 pace, bopping 25 homers and leading league with 111 RBI. All helped Redbirds win pennant. In 1968 Cards won again, but Cepeda sagged down to .248. Another trade, this time for Joe Torre, and Orlando sent to Atlanta Braves. In 1970 Cepeda had fine season with .305 average, 34 homers and 111 RBI. This was his ninth year in big leagues hitting over .300, his fifth with over 100 RBI, his fifth with over 30 homers, and his sixth with over 30 doubles. Got his 2000th base hit 7/11/70.

As 1972 ended, Cepeda could look back on .298 lifetime average in 1949 major league games, 387 doubles, 27 triples, and 358 homers among his 2169 hits. Had 1261 RBI and 141 stolen bases. Fifteen times he hit two homers in one game; once hit three in single contest; twice hit homers as pinch hitter; and eight times hit homers with bases loaded.

Cepeda, at times, has irked his managers; at times has been irked by fans. Once he threw ball into stands in San Francisco and hit spectator.

CERV, ROBERT HENRY OF-BR-TR. B. 5/5/26, Weston, Nebr. 6', 225. Bob Cerv hit 38 home runs for Kansas City A's, 1958, drove in 104 runs and batted .305 on seventh-place ball club, despite fact he played 28 games out of 141, with his jaw wired. During that period Bob had to confine himself to soups, gruel, liquid diet. Couldn't talk, couldn't smile, but still was able to slug six homers and drive in 21 runs. Broken jaw came from collision 5/17/58 with Red Wilson, Detroit catcher. Left side of Cerv's face hit Wilson's shoulder.

Bob attended Nebraska, receiving B.S. in education, 1960. Joined Yankee organization and made grade at their Kansas City farm club immediately, hitting .304 in 94 games. Boosted his mark to .344 in 1951 in 109 games, with 28 homers, 108 RBI. And in 12 games with Yanks that same year, had .214 average. Also divided 1952–53 between Yankees and Kansas City, then had three full years with New Yorkers. Never got into more than 56 games a year, however. Joe DiMaggio, Gene Woodling, Hank Bauer and Mickey Mantle were his competition in outfield. Got his chance to play regularly after being sold to Kansas City AL 10/16/56. Hit .272 in 1957, then .305 and .285.

Once more Cerv shuttled from Kansas City to New York, 5/16/60, going to Yanks in trade for Andy Carey. Hit .252 that year. Divided 1961 between Yankees and L.A. Angels. Then, in 1962, played only 33 contests in his final big league season, 19 with Houston NL, 14 with Yanks.

Cerv's major league record showed .276 average for 829 games. Had 624 hits, 320 runs, 96 doubles, 26 triples, 105 homers with 374 RBI. Took part in 1955,56 WS, hitting .176 with three hits in 17 trips. One of those hits, however, was pinch-hit homer 10/2/55 off Roger Craig of Brooklyn Dodgers in fifth game of Series. Nobody on base. Member of 1958 All-Star squad for AL. Coaches and teaches at small college in Wahoo, Nebr. Father of 10 children.

CHADWICK, HENRY (Father of Box Score) B. 10/6/24, St. Thomas Exeter, England. D. 4/20/08, Brooklyn, N.Y. Pioneer baseball writer. Came to U.S. at age 13. Began newspaper work at 19. Reporter, *N.Y.*

Times, 1806. In 1858 joined staff of *N. Y. Clipper*, publication devoted to sports and amusements, starting his first baseball writing that year. Later worked for several N.Y. papers—*Herald, Sun, World, Evening Telegram* among others—as staffer or contributor. Editor of first weekly newspaper devoted exclusively to baseball, *Ball Players' Chronicle*, published 1867–69. Edited first fans' paper, *The Metropolitan*, 1882–84.

Author of *The Art of Pitching and Fielding*, 1889. Edited *Spalding Official Baseball Guide*, 1881–1908. Author of first rule book, 1858. Chairman of Rules Committee in first nationwide baseball organization, 1858–1870.

Hall of Fame 1938, for service to baseball apart from playing.

CHAMBLISS, CARROLL CHRISTOPHER (Chris) 1B-BL-TR. B. 12/26/48, Dayton, Ohio. 6'1", 200. Chris Chambliss took Ken Harrelson's job as first baseman for Cleveland Indians early in 1971, hit .275, and won distinction of being named AL Rookie of Year by Baseball Writers Association of America. In first part of 1972 season wasn't doing so well at plate, with .260 average in July. But after All-Star break got into gear and slapped ball at .311 pace for rest of season. Consequently wound up year with .292 mark for 121 games. In his first two seasons in AL had BA of .284 with 250 hits that included 47 doubles, six triples, 15 homers, with 92 RBI.

Chris played baseball for UCLA. Selected by Cleveland in free agent draft, 1970, and in first pro season at Wichita, American Association, captured that league's batting championship with .342 average. It is believed this was first time rookie ever walked off with hitting title in Triple A classification in minors. Named Rookie of Year. Started off 1971 again with Wichita, hit .286 for 13 games; called up to Cleveland and took over first base assignment for keeps. With his .275 average, had 9 homers, 4 triples, 20 doubles, with 48 RBI.

Chambliss, during winter of 1971–72, took up weight-lifting program to strengthen his legs. His fielding around first base improved greatly in 1972.

CHANCE, FRANK LEROY (Peerless Leader) 1B-BR-TR. B. 9/9/77, Fresno, Calif. D. 9/15/24, Los Angeles, Calif. 6'1", 195. First baseman in famed "Tinker to Evers to Chance" double-play combination which became legendary after Franklin P. Adams wrote about woes of N.Y. Giants trying to keep rallies going against Chicago Cubs. That was in days when Cubs won flags, 1906,07,08,10, with Chance as player-manager. Those were same years when Frank became the "Peerless Leader."

Hugh Fullerton, old-time sports expert, wrote that real beginning of Cubs' pennant-winning team occurred March 1898 when awkward, bowlegged player came from Pacific Coast for tryout as catcher. Bill Lange, great Chicago outfielder before turn of century, umpired amateur game in California and recommended him.

Veteran catchers did not welcome young competition. Made debut at Philadelphia, catching doubleheader. Thermometer close to 100. Clark Griffith and Nixey Callahan were pitchers. Start was not promising. That night Chance decided to return to California, enter business. Harold "Speed" Johnson, sports writer, talked him out of it. Chance played some outfield that year but continued as catcher with Cubs until 1902. Then threatened to quit baseball again when manager Frank Selee wanted to shift him to first base. Finally agreed, converting from mediocre catcher into one of game's greatest first basemen.

Smart, natural leader, "frank as his first name," according to one sports writer, Chance became manager of Cubs midseason 1905. Led team to third-place finish. Pennant winner following season (1906), but lost to Chicago AL in World Series upset, four games to two. One year later Cubs trimmed Detroit in Series, sweeping all four games. In 1908 Cubs captured another world championship, again beating Tigers, four games to one.

Pittsburgh nosed out Cubs, 1909, though Chance's team won 104 games. But Cubs back on top, 1910. This time 104 victories were more than enough to win. However, Cubs were crushed by powerful Philadelphia Athletics, four games to one. Team back to second 1911. Sagged to third, 1912. Chance released 9/28/12.

As player, Chance now about finished. Managed New York AL 1913–14, appearing in dozen games with old Highlanders, who finished seventh both years. Hung up spikes as player with major league average of .297 in 1232 games. 796 runs, 405 stolen bases. In World Series four times, .310 average in 20 games.

Chance out of game 1915. Owner, manager, Los Angeles, Pacific Coast League, 1916–17. Again retired from baseball but persuaded to manage Boston AL 1923. Didn't have players. Red Sox finished last. Due to manage White Sox 1924; poor health prevented. Baseball injuries, especially from being hit by pitched balls, reportedly hastened his death. Hall of Fame 1946.

CHANCE, WILMER DEAN   P-BR-TR. B. 6/1/41, Wooster, Ohio. 6'3", 204. Dean Chance was described by one sports writer as "mixture of arrogance and brazen innocence—a strange, paradoxical man." In 1966 Bob Rodgers, catcher for Los Angeles AL, said he was "dumbest pitcher I ever caught." But Chance was smart enough to get $30,000 bonus for signing with Baltimore Orioles and won 128 games in majors, losing 115, before his release by Detroit Tigers 10/6/71.

One reason Chance was cocky was fact he won 51 games pitching in high school, including 18 no-hitters. Lost only one contest all this time. Also starred in basketball and is said to have had offers from 30 colleges for athletic scholarships.

After signing with Orioles was farmed to Bluefield, Appalachian League, where he won 10, lost three, with 2.94 ERA in 1959. Then came AL expansion and new L.A. Angels drafted him off Baltimore roster. Optioned to Fox Cities, III League for 1960 and Dallas–Fort Worth, American Association, 1961. During those two years won 21, lost 21. Angels recalled him in time for five games, 1961, and he was charged with two losses. Won 14, lost 10, 1962, his first full season in majors. Next season, 13–18; then 20–9; 15–10; 12–17, and then Angels traded him to Minnesota AL. In first year with Twins, 1967, Dean again won 20 games, lost 14. Had 16–16 record, 1968, and after that pitched with less frequency. Cleveland Indians had him, 1970, let him go to N.Y. Mets 9/18/70. Pitched for Detroit, 1971.

Overall pitching record not terribly impressive. However, he did have his days—and nights. In 1964 won six 1–0 games to set major league record. And in 1968 he set new mark for inefficiency with bat—never before had major league pitcher struck out as many as 63 times! He did get five hits, however, and had batting average of .054.

In 1967, toiling for Twins, chalked up perfect game, 2–0 victory over Boston Red Sox 8/6/67. Less than three weeks later came up with 2–1 no-hitter win over Cleveland 8/25/67 in second game.

Led AL in shutouts, 1964, with 11, and same year received Cy Young Award. In 1964 also led AL in complete games, 15; and tied for lead in this respect, 1967, with 18.

Tried his hand on stage, with Bo Belinsky, during winter of 1964–65. Appeared for two weeks in *Damn Yankees.*

In his youth Chance was farm boy and many times declared he would return to raise hogs and cattle when his playing days ended.

Chance appeared in 406 major league games, allowed 697 earned runs in 2148 innings. Struck out 1534 and walked 739. That 128–115 mark added up to .527 winning percentage, with ERA of 2.92.

CHANDLER, ALBERT BENJAMIN (Happy) Executive. B. 7/14/98, Corydon, Ky. Ex-commissioner of baseball. Former U. S. senator and ex-governor of Kentucky. Though chairman of board of Daniel Boone Fried Chicken, Inc., better qualified as political ham. Sports columnist Red Smith called him "most relentlessly affable employee, most tireless handshaker, most indefatigable signer of autographs baseball has ever known. When he makes a speech, he recites poetry of the Edgar Guest stripe. When he makes a decision, his friends do not get worst of it."

Greatest claim to baseball fame was decision banning Leo Durocher from baseball for one year while another principal in case, Larry

MacPhail, then president of N.Y. Yankees, went scot free. Situation involved George Raft, gamblers, Lucky Luciano, charges of tampering, associating with characters inimical to baseball's best interests. Paradox in whole thing was fact that "Memphis" Engleberg, professional handicapper, and Connie Immerman, manager of Havana gambling casino, publicly appeared at exhibition game in box seats behind Yankee dugout. Evidence seemed to indicate they were guests of MacPhail, who sat just in front of gamblers. Chandler, some weeks before, had warned Durocher to stay away from unsavory characters, and Leo seemed to be trying to follow commissioner's instructions. Then, after hearing in which Chandler was prosecutor, judge, and jury, hazy, confusing sentence was handed down suspending Durocher for one year. Branch Rickey, then chief of Brooklyn organization, asked whether there was one standard for managers and another for club presidents. To this day, Happy never specifically explained how or why he reached decision. Was fact that MacPhail helped Chandler become commissioner reason why Larry got preferred treatment?

Selection of Chandler as commissioner got push from MacPhail. Judge Landis had died several months earlier. Major league meeting was called for April 1945. Dozen names were considered, among them Tom Dewey, Jim Farley, Ford Frick, J. Edgar Hoover, Postmaster General Bob Hannegan, and Chandler. Observers felt that low blows were dealt some of candidacies during meeting of magnates. In any case, MacPhail was one who lined up votes for Happy when most of others had been scuttled. Critics of Happy later thought there was favoritism when he refused to investigate MacPhail's "waiver" sale of Hank Borowy to Chicago Cubs. Some AL officials howled, but Chandler did nothing. One paradox came when newspapers published photograph of Chandler's wife and daughter at Churchill Downs day after Happy issued blast against baseball players and officials frequenting race tracks.

Chandler attended Transylvania College, where he received A.B. and LL.B. degrees; Harvard for time; then got LL.D. from Kentucky, 1924. In politics was lt. gov. of Kentucky 1931–35; governor, 1935–39, 55–59. Resigned from governorship 1939 to become U.S. senator.

Selected as commissioner of baseball, 1945, refused to resign from Senate for several months until magnates were willing to sign document pledging themselves "loyally to support commissioner" even when they believed him mistaken; and not to criticize him or each other. Lasted until 1951 as commissioner, then returned to his old love, Kentucky politics. Departure from baseball not lamented. One critic summed it this way: "He spouted platitudes, made snap judgments on subjects he wasn't familiar with."

At one point he was investigated by old Truman Committee. Sixty-foot swimming pool was constructed at his home, Versailles, Ky., 1942.

Chandler paid nothing for installation of pool. It was gift of Louisville contractor whose company had received four subcontracts from government on military projects, presumably as result of Chandler's influence in Washington. Chandler told committee pool "was gift built in name of friendship and accepted in same spirit."

CHANDLER, SPURGEON FERDINAND (Spud) P-BR-TR. B. 9/12/09, Commerce, Ga. 6', 180. Spud Chandler, graduate of Georgia, wasted no time in becoming winning pitcher. Eventually became MVP for AL, 1943, honor generally won by hitter.

Chandler started with Springfield, Eastern League, 1932, shortly after getting B.S. degree, and won his first game as pro, although he had to be taken out after six innings. Took three more victories, then league folded and he went to Binghamton, New York–Pennsylvania League. There he won six in row, for 10 straight. Lost 4–2 decision in 14 innings and then won two more. So he had 12–1 for year with both clubs. Chandler was back at Binghamton, 1933, with 10–8 record. Spent part of same year with Yankees' farm club at Newark, International League, with 1–4 record. Divided 1934 season among Newark and Syracuse, IL, and Minneapolis, American Association. In 1935 was with Oakland and Portland, Pacific Coast League, then back to Newark for 1936 and part of 1937. At that point, Chandler went to Yankees, his only major league team.

Spud's best seasons were 1938 with 14–5; 1941 with 10–4; 1942, 16–5 and 1943 with 20–4. In 1944 and 1945 he was with military much of time but came back with another fine season 1946, taking 20 decisions, losing eight. Then hung up his glove after 9–5 record in 1947.

Spud lost one decision in each of 1941 and 1942 WS but pitched creditably in both. Lost 1941 game by 3–2 score, but only two of Dodgers' runs were earned. But for Joe Gordon's error, Chandler might have gone on to ultimate victory. In 1942 WS lost game to Cardinals, allowing only one earned run. In 1943 WS Chandler again faced Cardinals, beat them twice. In one game he allowed just one earned run; in other shut Redbirds out.

When Chandler led AL pitchers in winning percentage with .833 in 1943 (20–4) he also led AL in effectiveness with ERA of 1.64. This was only fourth time in AL history both laurels won at once. Spud came back in 1947, his last year in majors, to lead AL second time in ERA, with 2.46.

In 211 major league games, Chandler won 109, lost 43 for .717 percentage. Pitched 1485 innings, allowed 1327 hits and fanned 614. Overall ERA 2.84. In 6 WS games: 2–2, 33-1/3 IP, 6 earned runs, 16 strikeouts, 9 walks, ERA 1.62.

CHAPMAN, RAYMOND JOHNSON SS-BR-TR. B. 1/15/91, Beaver Dam, Ky. D. 8/17/20, New York, N.Y. 5'10", 170. Ray Chapman died after being hit by pitched ball during 1920 pennant race but it took many years before protective helmets became standard part of equipment of professional ball players. Chapman considered to have good eye, but crowded plate. Carl Mays' (N.Y. Yankees) pitch must have sailed. In any event, according to Mays, instead of falling back, Chapman ducked and ball hit him. At first Mays thought ball had hit Chapman's bat, So fielded it and threw ball to first base. But Chapman's skull was fractured; removed to hospital and died next day. While many ball players have suffered serious injury on diamond, Chapman was only major leaguer to die almost immediately afterward.

Chapman a fine fielding shortstop, fast, good base runner, who hit .300 or better in four of his nine seasons in AL. Started in III League at Davenport, Iowa, 1910; also with Springfield, Ill., same league. Sold to Toledo, American Association, for 1911 and 1912. Before that year was up, Cleveland purchased his contract and he hit .312 for Indians in 31 games after reporting late in August. In 1917 hit .302; .300 in 1919 and .303 in 1920 before fatal injury. Ray led AL in walks in 1918 with 84. During six seasons stole over 20 bases a year, with high mark of 52 in 1917. Had 233 steals for his major league career.

Chapman took part in 1050 major league games with 3785 AB, 1053 hits, for a .278 lifetime average. He scored 671 runs, had 162 doubles, 80 triples, 18 homers and 364 RBI.

Was popular player, something of Beau Brummel, witty. Occasionally teamed up with teammate outfielder Jack Graney, doing impromptu comedy skits. Had been married one year when death came. Said to have planned to retire after 1920 season.

When Chapman died, Indians obtained Joe Sewell as replacement. Club went on to its first AL pennant and ultimate victory over Brooklyn Dodgers in WS that fall.

CHAPMAN, WILLIAM BENJAMIN (Ben) OF-BR-TR. B. 12/25/08, Nashville, Tenn. 5'11½", 190. AL leader in stolen bases 1931, 32, 33. Aggressive, rugged player, umpire battler. Controversial manager of Philadelphia NL when Jackie Robinson broke into majors.

Ben's father was minor league ball player 13 years; Ben became batboy for Birmingham Barons of Southern Association. Good enough high school player to get athletic scholarship to Purdue U. but stayed only two months. N.Y. Yankees signed him after scouts saw him playing semipro ball.

Shortstop at Asheville, 1928, playing 147 games and hitting .336 with 98 RBI. Third baseman at St. Paul, 1929, with .336 mark in 168 games, 137 RBI. New York, 1930 until 6/14/36. When he broke in with Yanks was considered fastest man in baseball. Joe McCarthy said to have let him steal on his own, without signs. Ran wild, 1931, stealing 61 sacks to lead AL for first time. Kept leadership following two seasons, but with only 38 and 27 respectively. Generally hit above .300 mark while with Yanks, and in timely fashion too. Twice went over 100 in RBI, missed it one season by two. Led AL in triples, 1934, with 13. Had 17 homers, 1931, but wasn't real fence-buster. However, did hit three homers in one game 7/9/32.

Apart from statistics, Chapman played hard, seriously. Once chased fan in stands at Yankee Stadium. On another occasion, when Detroit's catcher Birdie Tebbetts, chided him after strikeout, Ben slugged him, knocking him down. And once, after Umpire John Quinn called him out on close play, Chapman later fired ball at arbiter, apparently trying to hit him with it.

Traded to Washington, 1936, Senators sent him to Boston AL 6/10/37. Ben again led AL in base thefts that year with 35. Hit .340, 1938, his only full season with Red Sox. Cleveland, 1939–40; Chicago AL and Washington, 1941. Became manager at Richmond, Piedmont League, 1942, and had some ups and downs. Occasionally put himself into game as pitcher. Was 6–3, 1.71 ERA. Not bad for 33-year-old pitcher just starting out, in any league. But his temper got best of him. Allegedly struck an umpire, and was suspended from baseball one year. Back with Richmond, 1944, he divided his time between third base and pitching mound. Hit .303, won 13 games, lost 6, 2.21 ERA.

All of which led to return to majors, this time to Brooklyn Dodgers, reportedly for $25,000 and two players 8/1/44. Was 5–3 for Dodgers that year, with 3.40 ERA. Pinch hit occasionally when not pitching and wound up with .368 average for total of 20 games. In 1945 Ben 3–3 for Dodgers before traded to Philadelphia NL, late June. Phillies appointed him manager, post he held to 7/16/48. Phils finished last in 1945, fifth in 1946, seventh in 1947, and were on their way to sixth place in 1948.

It was during this period that Jackie Robinson broke color line with Dodgers. Chapman, southerner, was accused of racist attacks on Robinson. Ben admitted he and his club rode Robinson pretty hard; justified it by saying all players had to "take it," including rugged references to their ancestries, whether from Italy, Poland, Czechoslovakia, or anywhere else. Attitude toward blacks may have hastened his departure from managerial job in Philadelphia. Club owner Carpenter, on firing Chapman, said he was doing it for many reasons. News came about one hour before Ben was giving birthday party for his nine-year-old son. Chapman had invited Carpenter, other club officials. Little conversation among guests and host that afternoon.

Forthright character of Chapman reflected in another story told about him while with Yankees. In 1934, when Babe Ruth was definitely slowing down on base paths and in field, his teammates said nothing about his deteriorating play, that is, not to Ruth himself. Chapman, however, told Bambino, "If I were as old as you, and as rich as you are, I wouldn't risk my health by playing any more." Ruth took it.

Chapman had bowling alley in Birmingham and went into insurance business. Left them long enough to serve as coach for Cincinnati, 1952.

Ben played 1716 major league games, went to bat 6478 times, got 1958 hits. These included 407 doubles, 107 triples, 90 homers. Scored 1144 runs and had 977 RBI. Stole 287 bases and had .302 lifetime average. In pitching, 8–6, all with Dodgers. ERA 4.39 for 141-1/3 innings. Only WS 1932, hit .294 5 for 17.

CHASE, HAROLD HARRIS (Prince Hal)   1B-BR-TL. B. 2/13/83, Los Gatos, Calif. D. 5/18/47, Colusa, Calif. 6', 175. Concerning Hal Chase, one baseball historian flatly declares, "Until somebody worse can be found, he will serve as the archetype of all crooked ball players." Chase must have had marvelous ability as first baseman if we are to believe testimony of old-time players, managers, sports writers. In days when George Sisler was superstar with St. Louis Browns, it was always question, was he better first-sacker than Chase? So it has been with other fine fielders at same position ever since.

Unfortunately, Chase repeatedly involved with gamblers, accusations of fixing games; died without exoneration from most charges.

Played college ball at Santa Clara, Calif. After some semipro experience, landed with Los Angeles, Pacific Coast League, 1904. Hit .279 in 173 games. Reportedly played first base in manner never seen before, anywhere—quite far from bag. With his agility was able to get to bag when necessary. Covered wide area and cut off many balls which ordinarily had been getting through to right field for hits. Soon became artist in grabbing grounders and starting double plays, first to second to first.

N.Y. Highlanders (later Yankees) drafted Chase and he remained with club 1905–13. Fielding sensational from start, though hit only .249 in first season. Drew widespread attention 1906, when fine fielding accompanied by .323 batting average. One sports writer told of Chase's love of game. "He is buoyant, happy, smiling, and full of exuberance and unnecessary exertion." These were days when he became known as "Prince Hal."

In 1908 Chase accused of undermining Clark Griffith, then manager of Highlanders. Griffith was dropped, but Kid Elberfeld got job as pilot. Chase reportedly sulked, did not give his best, and finally, 8/15/08, jumped club to play outlaw ball in Stockton, Calif. Fined $200, was reinstated for 1909 season. George Stallings managed Highlanders that year and part of following season, but Chase named pilot finally during

1910 pennant race. In first full season as manager, 1911, led club to sixth place finish—same team which had come in second in 1910. Back in ranks as player only with Highlanders 1912 and part of 1913 when traded to White Sox. In June 1914 Chase, making $6000 a year, notified club in writing he was resigning from his contract with ten days' notice. Jumped to Federal League club at Buffalo, N.Y. Feds were trying to break into organized baseball monopoly as third major league. Hit .354 for Buffalo that season in 75 games after various court actions. Remained with Feds through 1915. When AL and NL worked out agreement with Federal League, which meant its demise, best players returned to majors for 1916. Chase landed with Cincinnati. With Reds through 1918. Final season in majors 1919 with Giants; hit .284.

Meanwhile, Chase had been acquiring unsavory reputation for game fixing, lying down on team at times, gambling and acting as agent for big gamblers. Deeply involved in Black Sox scandal, though never convicted, nor did Judge Landis officially bar him from baseball, as he did eight members of White Sox who were accused of throwing 1919 World Series to Reds. Probably smelly reputation and unstated blacklisting meant no more association with organized baseball. Chase now 36 years old, but probably could have played major league ball longer.

Lifetime average: .291, 1,917 major league games.

CHESBRO, JOHN DWIGHT (Happy Jack) P-BR-TR. B. 6/5/74, North Adams, Mass. D. 11/6/31, Conway, Mass. 5′9″, 180. Jack Chesbro almost won pennant for New York AL 1904 when he captured 41 Victories for highest total in major leagues in 20th century. Chesbro learned use of spitball that year. However, spitball probably his downfall; in crucial game against Boston, wild pitch gave opponents crucial game and Sox won pennant.

Jack served apprenticeship with Albany, Johnstown, Roanoke and Richmond clubs 1895–99, going to Pittsburgh 1899. Gradually improved record with Pirates, taking 21 victories 1901, 28 in 1902. That season his .824 pitching percentage (28–6) led NL. Jumped to N.Y. Highlanders in AL, winning 21, losing 15 in 1903. Then learned spitball from Elmer Stricklett and had record-breaking season. That year pitched 48 complete games, 455 innings, winning 41, losing 13.

When his victory total only 19 in 1905, was felt spitball had "ruined" arm. Won 24 in 1906, then dropped down to 10 wins in 1097, 14 in 1908. In 1909 with N.Y. AL and Boston AL, 0–4. Called it quits after that.

His 1902 record with Pirates and 1904 mark with Highlanders gave him distinction of being only pitcher to lead both NL and AL in percentage of wins for season. Hall of Fame 1946.

CHIOZZA, LOUIS PEO Inf.-OF-BL-TR. B. 5/11/10, Tallulah, La. D.

2/28/71, Memphis, Tenn. 6′, 172. Lou Chiozza strode to plate in old Crosley Field, Cincinnati, 5/24/35, wearing uniform of Philadelphia Phillies. And what made this one appearance of his worth remembering? He was first man ever to bat in night game in majors. His effort was routine—a harmless ground ball to shortstop, Billy Myers. But night baseball was launched. Spalding *Official Baseball Guide* for 1936 commented, "Cincinnati tried night ball as an experiment and it was fairly well attended, but only as a novelty. It was questioned whether it would be a success if it were played more generally."

Chiozza never star material, although he became Tallulah Bankhead's favorite because he was born in Tallulah, La. Lou played at Memphis; Vicksburg, Miss.; Monroe, La.; and Beckley, W. Va., before joining Phils, 1934. Traded to New York NL 12/8/36 and remained with Giants through 1939. Left majors with .277 lifetime average for 616 games. Played oftener at second base than anywhere else, but wouldn't be in this book except for historic time at bat back in 1935 under lights.

Two brothers, Dino and Joe, also played pro ball. Dino with Phils for two games 1935; Joe never rose above minors.

CHYLAK, NESTER   Umpire. B. 5/11/22, Olyphant, Pa. 6′, 195. Nester Chylak, AL umpire since 1954, remembers "good old days" but many aspects of those days were rather rugged for him. In Battle of Bulge during World War II, got pretty badly shot up and spent many months in veterans' hospital. After getting out, money didn't last long and he wound up broke. Ran into friend who offered him chance to umpire college game. "I got enough troubles," replied Chylak. "People hate umpires. Who wants to be an umpire?" But $25 fee looked like needed cash money, so Nester accepted. Must have done all right because soon there was offer to officiate in final six weeks of Pony League season, 1947. Moved to Canadian-American League, 1948; New England League, 1949; Eastern League, 1950–51; International League, 1952–53. Then came invitation to umpire in AL.

Chylak contrasts crummy hotels, sleeping in his car, driving late at night from one bush league town to another, with more luxurious life in major leagues. Also recalls with pleasure that he umpired Junior World Series, 1953, between Montreal and Kansas City; five major league All-Star games; 1969 AL playoffs; and WS of 1957,60,66,71. Chylak also points out he officiated in first night game in WS history, 1971.

Nester received "Umpire of Year Award" from Al Somers Umpire School in Daytona Beach, Fla., February 1972. Makes home in Dunmore, Pa.

CICOTTE, EDWARD V. (Knuckles)   P-BR-TR. B. 6/19/84, Detroit, Mich. D. 5/5/69, Detroit, Mich. 5′7″, 160. One of instigators of 1919

"Black Sox" plot to throw World Series to underdog Cincinnati. Barred from baseball for life, along with seven teammates.

Had tryout with Detroit 1905 but didn't stick. After minor league seasons at Augusta, South Atlantic League, 1905; Indianapolis, Des Moines, 1906; Lincoln, Neb., 1907, made grade with Boston AL, 1908. Sold to Chicago AL 7/10/12. Big season 1917, pitching most innings in AL, 346; winning most games, 28; best ERA, 1.58. In 1919 his 307 innings pitched led AL; so did his 29–7 mark for .806 pitching percentage. Had 1.82 ERA, but Walter Johnson's 1.49 ERA better.

White Sox won 1919 flag, were outstanding favorites to romp over Reds in Series. But Cicotte and seven companions succumbed to temptation of easy money from gamblers, and at least for time planned to throw Series to Cincinnati. In first game, Cicotte was supposed to hit first batsman to face him, as signal to gamblers that "fix" was on. Cicotte plugged Rath, Redleg second baseman, between shoulder blades. Knocked out of box in fourth inning. Reds took Series, five games to three. Cicotte had record of one win, two losses, 2.91 ERA.

Smelly Series resulted in investigation but Cicotte and six of "Black Sox" continued to play, 1920. Cicotte took 21 victories, lost 10 in final season in organized baseball. All eight suspended when AL had gathered enough testimony. Players indicted, but none would testify. Vital confessions and documents disappeared from court, so prosecution wound up without case. Jury said "not guilty" in 1921, but Judge Landis, baseball czar, blacklisted all of them for life.

In 1917 World Series Cicotte 1–1. Major league totals: 502 games, 3,208 innings, 210 won, 148 lost for .587 mark. ERA figures not complete.

CISCO, GALEN BERNARD P-BR-TR. B. 3/7/37, St. Mary's, Ohio.

5'11", 210. Former Rose Bowl football player now coach for Kansas City Royals. Pitched briefly for Boston Red Sox 1961,62,67. With N.Y. Mets 1962–65. Finally with Kansas City 1969. Major league record showed 192 games, 25 wins, 56 losses, 658 innings, 4.57 ERA.

Attended Ohio State. B.S. in education 1960. Was starting fullback three seasons. Helped Buckeyes to two Big Ten championships; national title 1957 when he captained team which defeated Oregon 10–7 in Rose Bowl, 1/1/58.

Played with Raleigh, Corning, Allentown, Waterloo, Minneapolis, Seattle teams en route to Red Sox for parts of 1961,62. After stint with Mets, pitched for Jacksonville, Toronto, Pittsfield, Louisville, Omaha, with brief stays at Boston and Kansas City. Busiest season in majors 1964: 192 innings, 6–19 record for tail-end club. Had 3.66 ERA that year. After 1970 season at Omaha, where he was 6–3, became pitching coach for Royals. Cisco tied major league record 9/21/62 when he struck out four pinch hitters.

CLARK, WILLIAM WATSON (Watty) P-BL-TL. B. 5/16/02, St. Joseph, La. D. 3/4/72, Clearwater, Fla. 6'1/2", 180. Watty Clark never saw a baseball until he left farm to go to Mississippi College, but had thrown good many rocks as country lad. Acquaintances persuaded him to go out for baseball team. Had natural curve, using left arm. Won 36 games, lost 4, and tied 2 in college. Then, after some semipro ball, got job with Peoria, 1924, was 4–2; went up to Cleveland same season. But was back in III League with Terre Haute for 1925 and 1926. Won 19 games, lost 9 latter season, meriting his sale to Brooklyn for $3,000.

Winning pitcher for Dodgers most of next seven years, with 20–12 mark in 1932. Spent parts of 1933 and 1934 with N.Y. Giants, then returned to Brooklyn, remaining until 1937 when he hurled only two games for Dodgers. Had 13–8 mark with team in 1935.

Watty took part in 357 major league games, won 111 and lost 97, with 1747-1/3 innings pitched. Unusually good control for lefthander; walked 383, fanned 643, pitched 14 shutouts.

CLARKE, FRED CLIFFORD OF-BL-TR. B. 10/3/72, Winterset, Iowa. D. 8/14/60, Winfield, Kans. 5'10, 165. Fred Clarke was one of great outfielders in earlier days of NL, hit .406 way back in 1897, won four pennants for Pittsburgh Pirates as playing manager. Credentials good for election to Hall of Fame, 1945.

Clarke played for four minor league teams 1892–94, then landed with Louisville NL in 1894. At that time NL was 12-club circuit. In 1895, first full season in NL, hit .354. In 1897 reached .406 in 129 games. When NL reduced to eight teams, Louisville and Pittsburgh clubs were consolidated, with Clarke playing manager. Team finished second 1900, first 1901,02,03. Another pennant 1909. After 1911, played only few games. Replaced as manager after 1915 season.

Had .315 major league average in 2204 games; stole 527 bases, 66 of them in 1898. As player, in two World Series (1903, 1909), 15 games, .245 average. As manager, lost first Series, 1903, to Boston Red Sox, five games to three; Won 1909 Series from Detroit Tigers, four games to three.

Clarke returned to Pirates 1925, toward latter part of season, serving as coach on club which won pennant and Series. Following year, had anomalous role of vice president—and assistant manager to Bill McKechnie. As VP, presumably outranked McKechnie. On bench, presumably Bill outranked Clarke. Dissension raked club. In 1927 both Clarke and McKechnie no longer with Pirates.

Later served as president, National Association of Leagues for Sandlot Clubs.

CLARKE, HORACE MEREDITH (Hoss) 2B-BLR-TR. B. 6/2/40. Fred-ericksted, St. Croix, Virgin Islands. 5'9", 179. Doesn't own fancy career batting average but set major league record when his first two home runs in big time were grand slammers. This becomes more notable when one examines his home run totals. Horace got six homers in 1966, but in 1969–70 had just four each season. In 1967 and 1972, hit three each year, and in 1968 and 1971 two each.

N.Y. Yankee second baseman also has reputation as spoiler. During 1970, three times in one month broke up bids for no-hit games in ninth inning. Joe Niekro, Sonny Siebert, and Jim Rooker were his victims.

Clarke has spent his entire pro career in Yankee organization. Signed by Yanks' Caribbean scout, Jose Seda, 1958; broke in at Kearney, Nebr. State League. Next stops were St. Petersburg, Fargo, Birmingham, Amarillo, Richmond, and Toledo, most of time playing shortstop. But with Bobby Richardson nearing retirement, New Yorkers needed second baseman. So Horace shifted to other side of bag. Then after hitting .301 in 89 games at Toledo, 1965, graduated to Yankees, getting into 51 games that season. Played 96 games for Yanks, 1966, but since then has been in almost all games as regular second sacker. Horace's best year with stick was 1969 when he hit .285.

Some critics have found fault with Clarke's ability to make pivot play at second, and consequently have downgraded his skill in making double play. But led AL keystoners in Twin Killings, 1972, with 104. Mean-while lifetime batting average was .256 as he reached 1058 games in 1972 with Yankees.

CLARKSON, JOHN GIBSON P-BR-TR. B. 7/1/61, Cambridge, Mass. D. 2/4/09, Cambridge, Mass. 5'10", 160. Back in days when pitchers really earned their living, John Clarkson pitched 485 complete games in majors. One year, 1885, won 53 games, lost 16. Two years later had to be content with 38 wins and 21 losses. And in 1889, won "only" 49 games, losing 19. During off-seasons, 1886 and 1888, took 35 wins one year, 33 other.

Clarkson pitched for Worcester NL 1882; Saginaw, Northwestern League, 1883–84. That season went up to Chicago NL, posting 10–3 mark for part of year. Then started his phenomenal pitching. Next eight seasons *lowest* victory total was 24.

To Boston NL after 1887 season, bringing $10,000 sales price. In 1892 after 8–6 record, developed arm trouble, released. Cleveland NL picked him up and he captured 17 wins, losing 10 rest of season. Dropped to 16–18 mark 1893. Retired after breaking even 1894, 8–8.

Lifetime totals in majors: 517 games, 327–176, .650 percentage, 4514 innings, ERA 2.81. Hall of Fame 1963.

CLEMENTE, ROBERTO WALKER   OF-BR-TR. B. 8/18/34, Carolina, Puerto Rico D. 12/31/72, San Juan, P.R. 5'11", 182. Death of Roberto Clemente came as rude shock to sports fans. Following disastrous earthquake in Managua, Nicaragua, Roberto headed committee gathering materials for relief of victims. He and four other persons were killed when their cargo plane crashed shortly after takeoff, headed for Nicaragua.

If Roberto Clemente had been playing in New York most of his career undoubtedly fans of the nation would be as conscious of his greatness as they were of Joe DiMaggio and Willie Mays. Instead, Roberto's big league career began and ended in Pittsburgh.

Clemente proved more durable than DiMaggio. Joe played 1736 major league games; Clemente took part in 2433 contests. While Jolting Joe outhit Roberto .325 to .317, Clemente had 51 more doubles, 47 more triples than DiMag. Joe, however, had more homers, 361, to Puerto Rican's 240. Willie Mays, on other hand, has played more games than Pittsburgh star, but Clemente had outhit him, .317 to .304, at time of Roberto's death.

Clemente's class brought national attention during 1971 WS when he hit safely in all seven games and helped mightily in Pirates' uphill victory over vaunted Baltimore Orioles. This was second time Roberto hit safely in all seven games of WS—did it first in 1960. Only other player to hit safely in all games of two WS was Hank Bauer. Roberto's WS hitting, 14 games, was .362. DiMaggio's was .271. Mays' WS record was .234.

Clemente, in 1972, was in his 18th year in Pittsburgh uniform. Missed much of season due to injuries and illness. But in 102 games, hit .312 and become member of exclusive 3,000-hit club.

Management of Los Angeles Dodgers probably moan quietly when they realize that Clemente could have been member of their team all those years. They had him—signed him to his first pro contract, for 1954 season with Montreal, then top farm club for Brooklyn in International League. Story goes that Al Campanis, now vice president for player personnel and scouting, wasn't sure what position Clemente played best. Roberto had played all over diamond, but when Campanis put him in outfield and watched him throw some 400 feet to home plate, his future was set. He was an outfielder.

Roberto played 87 games with Montreal that year, hit .257. So Dodgers left him on Montreal roster, gambling that some other player might be drafted. But Clyde Sukeforth, scouting for Pittsburgh, had seen enough of 20-year old speedster with great arm that he recommended Clemente as Pirates' draft choice. That one recommendation should have earned Clyde lifetime security and eternal gratitude from Pittsburgh organization.

Clemente won regular job in Pirate outfield, 1955 but hit only .255. But 1956 saw him blossom into .311 hitter, and few years later Roberto won NL batting title with .351, 1961. Again, in 1964 and 1965, finished at top of NL list with .339 and .329 respectively. "Slumped" to .317 in 1966, then came back with another batting championship, 1967, with .357.

As Clemente aged, he seemed to become more ageless—.345 average in 1969, followed by .352, and, in 1971, .341. Then came fabulous WS. Two hits in opening game, including double. Pair of safeties in second contest, with another two-bagger. Just one hit and one run scored, one RBI in third engagement, Pittsburgh's first victory. Three hits for Roberto in next game, and one in fifth game. In sixth game Clemente added two more safe blows, one a triple, other a homer. In crucial seventh game it was Clemente who put Blass in front with his second home run of classic. This was game Blass took by 2–1 score to give Pirates world championship. Not only did Clemente prove to be top batsman of WS, but his fielding was superb. His throwing was sensational; he allowed no liberties by Oriole base runners. Fans will never forget his basket catches, his ballet leaps, his shoestring plays.

One of Clemente's secrets was his physical conditioning. Was a keen student of anatomy through the years.

Roberto played for NL in all All-Star Games between 1960 and 1971 excepting 1968. Named to 1972 squad but was injured and did not play. Hit for .323 average. In 1960 WS he hit .310 with nine hits in 29 trips. In 1971 WS it was 12 hits in 29 AB for .414.

Among his many distinctions is fact he hit three triples in one game 9/8/58; led NL outfielders in double plays, 1961. NL MVP 1966.

After Clemente's death, was praised by many as "greatest ball player" they had ever seen. Also drew widespread praise as fine human being who died trying to help others. President Nixon promptly sent personal check for $1000 for fund to memorialize Roberto, "to be used for the relief of those he was trying to help." Fund soon grew. Pittsburgh ball club donated $100,000. Richard K. Mellon Foundation donated another $100,000. Private individuals and banks, business firms, also gave substantial amounts. It was planned to use money for relief of Nicaraguan earthquake victims and for baseball clinics in Puerto Rico. Clemente had devoted great deal of effort to such clinics while he lived, and planned to expand them for good of Puerto Rican youths.

In spring 1973, Baseball Writers Association of America held special election, overwhelmingly voted Clemente into Hall of Fame.

CLEMENTS, JOHN T. C-BL-TL. B. 6/24/64, Philadelphia, Pa. D. 5/23/41, Philadelphia, Pa. 5'8½", 204. If anyone tells you there haven't been any lefthanded catchers in major leagues, refer them to Jack

Clements, who caught in NL during 17 seasons, mostly with Philadelphia. Clements was described as "wide-shouldered grim-lipped man with stature of a growing oak." In 1884 divided his time between Philadelphia club of Union Association and Philadelphia NL team, then staying with NL team through 1897. Observers say he handled his catching job with finesse, without any sign of awkwardness. While with Phils was their mainstay and gate attraction. Pretty fine hitter too—batted .346 in 1894, .394 following year, and .359 in 1896. Played 1157 games in all, making 1226 hits good for 226 doubles, 60 triples, 77 homers. Scored 620 runs and had lifetime mark of .286.

Clements spent 1898 with St. Louis NL, 1899 with Cleveland NL, and 1900 with Boston NL. In more recent times Dale Long, lefthanded first baseman then with Chicago Cubs, caught in two major league games, 1958.

CLENDENON, DONN ALVIN 1B-BR-TR. B. 7/15/35, Neosho, Mo. 6'4", 205. Tower of strength to Pittsburgh Pirates many years but best remembered as star of 1969 WS while member of New York Mets. Hit three homers, record for five-game series. Hit .357, with five hits in 14 trips, drove in four runs. Designated MVP for that series.

With Pittsburgh seven years, 1962–68, hit 106 homers and drove in 488 runs.

Donn holds degrees in physical education and mathematics from Morehouse College in Atlanta; also attended Duquesne Law School. While at Morehouse was stellar athlete in baseball, football, and basketball. Good enough that Harlem Globetrotters and New York Knickerbockers offered him contracts. However, cast his fate with pro baseball.

Minor league experience started at Salem, Va., 1957. Also played at Jamestown, N.Y.; Grand Forks, N. Dak.; Wilson, N.C.; Idaho Falls, Idaho; Savannah, Ga.; Columbus, Ohio. Had nine games with Pirates, 1961, and 12 with Columbus, 1962. However, hit .302 for 80 games with Pittsburgh, also 1962. Following year got long-ball range with 15 homers; had 28 in 1966; twice had more than 95 RBI with Pirates. Montreal Expos selected him in expansion draft 10/14/68. Expos tried to trade him to Houston following January but he refused to report and stayed on Montreal roster. Expos then traded him to Mets 6/15/69. Had .248 average with 16 homers, 51 RBI, for season. Wasn't used in playoff games, but then came through with three homers in WS against Baltimore Orioles.

Clendenon had .288 average, 22 homers, 97 RBI, with Mets, 1970, but began to taper off. Released after 1971 season, signed with St. Louis Cardinals. Again handed his unconditional release August 1972. At time Donn had appeared in 1362 major league games, had .274 lifetime average; his 1273 hits included 159 homers, 192 doubles, 57 triples. Scored 594 runs and drove in 682.

CLEVELAND, REGINALD LESLIE (Grover) P-BR-TR. B. 5/23/48, Swift Current, Saskatchewan, Canada. 6'1", 195. Came from place some 100 miles west of Moose Jaw, in Canadian province north of Montana. He used to do lots of curling and hockey playing. Neither of these games, however, is suited for climate where he currently makes his home—St. Petersburg, Fla. Now he goes in for skin diving.

Reggie—that nickname "Grover" isn't very imaginative—was named Rookie Pitcher of Year 1971 by the *Sporting News*. Ticketed to be relief man, St. Louis Cardinal manager Red Schoendienst was impressed by his control and willingness to challenge opposing hitters. Matched against Juan Marichal three times, Cleveland defeated Giants' ace twice. Won five in row and finished season with 12–12 record for club that often was erratic. Won 15, lost 15 in 1972.

Cleveland's control in 1971 was evidenced by fact he issued only 41 walks which were not intentional, in 222 innings. Only Ferguson Jenkins, established star with Cubs, had better control among NL's top 15 pitchers in effectiveness.

Reggie was athlete of year in his high school, 1965. Set two Alberta provincial javelin records. Had pitched no-hitter earlier in Babe Ruth League competition. Started pro ball, 1966, at Eugene, Oreg.; stopped off in St. Petersburg; Lewiston, Idaho; Arkansas, and Tulsa en route to Cardinals, 1970, to stay. Had been with team briefly in 1969.

Won 53, lost 40 during minor league career. And went into 1973 season with overall NL record of 26–31, with 4.21 ERA. Had walked 132 in 483 IP.

CLINES, EUGENE ANTHONY OF-BR-TR. B. 10/6/46, San Pablo, Calif. 5'9", 168. Gene Clines seems to have everything young ball player needs to become superstar, except power. Fast, fine arm, and in first 235 games in majors hit .327. But among 203 hits there was only one home run. With Roberto Clemente gone from Pittsburgh outfield, temptation often is to play someone else who can hit long ball, even though he may not hit .327. Along with .327 average going into 1973, Clines had 29 doubles, 10 triples, had stolen 29 bases and driven in 44 runs, scored 108 times.

Clines joined Pittsburgh organization, 1966, in free-agent draft. Brought along from Salem, Va., to Raleigh; York, Pa.; and Waterbury. Joined Pirates during 1970 campaign, played 31 games and hit .405. In 1971 gave substantial help to Buccaneers in march toward NL flag, hitting .308 for season in 97 games. As pinch hitter that year, came through to tune of .368.

Originally Gene was pitcher in high school, twirled three no-hit games and won all kinds of honors for mound work and hitting. Also set record high jump mark of 6'7¾" in track.

While at Waterbury, 1970, led Eastern League in stolen bases with 32. While Gene, going into 1973, had only one homer to credit in NL seasonal play, he slapped one round-tripper against San Francisco Giants in third game of 1971 playoff series. Against Baltimore Orioles in WS, 1971, got just one hit in 11 trips, had .091 average.

CLONINGER, TONY LEE P-BR-TR. B. 8/13/40, Lincoln County, N.C. 6', 215. Tony Cloninger's finest seasons were 1964,65,66 with Braves. Won 19, lost 14 in first of these years, when Braves were still at Milwaukee. Had 24–11 record following campaign, and during first season of Braves' presence in Atlanta, had 14–11 record. His best ERA of his career came in 1965 when those 24 wins were helped by his 3.29 mark.

Cloninger's early years in professional ball were not very spectacular. Started at Eau Claire in Northern League, 1958, then moved to Midland. Tex., Sophomore League that same year. Won 9–2. But at Cedar Rapids, 1959, lost nine without single victory before moving to Boise. Saw service at Jacksonville, Austin, and Louisville before joining Milwaukee NL, 1961.

Had 7–2 record that year, and 8–3 following season. Was 9–11 in 1963 before he came up with the 19–14 record in 1964.

Cloninger was sent to Cincinnati Reds 6/11/68. Over three-season period with Cincinnati, won 23 but lost 30. Reds traded him to St. Louis Cardinals 3/24/72. Lost two, won none, then released midseason. At that time his lifetime record stood at 113 wins, 97 losses in 1768 innings pitched. His strikeouts exceeded his walks 1120 to 798. Lifetime ERA 4.07.

While Cloninger had only a .192 batting average in NL, he hit eleven homers and had driven in 67 runs during his career. He was particularly hot 7/3/66, day before firecracker day, when he set major league record for most RBI by pitcher, nine. Also tied major league record for most homers with bases loaded, two, that same day.

During his only WS, 1970, Cloninger 0–1. Pitched 7-1/3 innings and had 7.36 ERA.

COBB, ROBERT Executive. B. 2/8/99, Moberly, Mo. D. 3/21/70, Los Angeles, Calif. Bob Cobb, owner of Brown Derby restaurants in Los Angeles area in Hollywood's heyday, was one of early boosters for Chavez Ravine as site for major league park long before Brooklyn Dodgers moved to California. Cobb envisioned mammoth sports and playground area, including baseball and football fields, basketball arena, spacious areas where children could play under supervision, place that would attract young people for games where they could participate. It would not be center exclusively for spectator sports and parking lots.

Eventually Dodgers did invade Los Angeles and ball park was built at Chavez Ravine. But Cobb wasn't in picture until Angels, an expansion club, came into being some time later. Then Bob served on their Advisory Board.

Cobb got into baseball somewhat by accident. Pacific Coast League used to have two teams in San Francisco. Traditional club was the Seals. Second team was called "Missions." Missions were something of step-child in Golden Gate area, and eventually were put up for sale. Cobb was instrumental in raising money to purchase franchise and move it to Hollywood. Called Cecil B. DeMille, who agreed to put $5000 into pot. Bing Crosby, George Burns, Barbara Stanwyck, Robert Taylor, Bill Frawley, and Gail Patrick all put up money. Hollywood "Stars" ball club was born, playing games at Gilmore Stadium opposite Farmers' Market.

In order to move club into Los Angeles area, Hollywood club had to pay percentage of all home admissions to Los Angeles PCL club. So every time Hollywood Stars had capacity crowd at home, Phil Wrigley got his pound of flesh, since he owned Los Angeles.

Hollywood team did fairly well artistically, with Bobby Bragan as colorful manager for while; Babe Herman, Frank Kelleher, and other favorites attracted fans. In stands you could usually spot several well-known movie actors and actresses, as well as toothsome starlets anxious to make it big in Hollywood. Bob Cobb and his colleagues had fun—but through years, he personally lost half-million dollars on team, though he said he didn't regret it for one moment.

Born in Missouri, Cobb grew up in Montana; at 16 he went to California. Became barker on glass-bottom boats at Catalina; book-keeper in bank; one summer in Catalina sold bottled ocean water to midwestern farmers, postcards, and abalone shells—and netted $1500 for tourist season. Later got into real estate, wholesale grocery, and ultimately cafe business. Opened first Brown Derby restaurant, 1928.

Cobb was president of Hollywood ball club 1938 until Dodgers came and put him out of business. Not long after Branch Rickey moved into Pittsburgh organization, somebody recommended that Cobb seek tieup with Pirates. Cobb shuddered. Knew Rickey only by reputation and did not agree with Rickey approach to life—not attending ball games on Sunday, not drinking alcoholic beverages, etc.

"When I went to see him," Cobb revealed later. "I was looking for a pious old thief who would steal your watch if you took it out of your pocket. I thought he'd give me a temperance lecture and abhor my connection with Hollywood and my saloon business. But after I got to know him, I came away with the greatest respect in the world for him. I hope I'm doing business with him forever."

Cobb left session with working agreement with Pirates, which continued without disagreements until Hollywood team folded. Thus was born strange friendship between two men of tremendously different backgrounds, outlooks, and personal philosophies.

Cobb played an important part in getting AL franchise for Los Angeles area. Among colorful characters who played for Hollywood team were Dale Long, Lee Walls, Gus Zernial, Tony Lupien, Vince DiMaggio, Bill Cissell, as well as aforementioned Babe Herman and Bobby Bragan. Joe L. Brown was publicity chief for club before going to Pittsburgh. Fred Haney managed Hollywood before going up to pilot Pirates and, later, Braves.

Cobb was forward-looking promoter. Long before many major league teams gave much attention to racial problems in their areas, Cobb had black public relations man to represent Stars in Negro community and to advise him how Hollywood team could attract more blacks to PCL games. Also used to send "honorary player contracts" to newly born infants in area. About 2500 went out each season. Once gave away 1000 watermelons in promotion stunt—as well as more routine things like TV's, refrigerators, stoves, hams, turkeys. Sponsored baseball song contest and numerous other moves designed to get people interested in baseball. Worked hard, day and night—and enjoyed every minute.

COBB, TYRUS RAYMOND (Georgia Peach) OF-BL-TR. B. 12/18/86, Narrows, Ga. D. 7/17/61, Atlanta, Ga. 6'1", 175. Hundreds of young men have been endowed with far greater physical ability than Ty Cobb. But his name stands out today as one of greatest, if not greatest, ball player of all times—because he had desire to win, in infinite quantity.

Typical Cobb play occurred when Branch Rickey managing St. Louis Browns. Game went into eleventh inning tied, 1 to 1. First two Detroit batsmen out. Cobb next. Walked—and scored before another ball was pitched! Rickey described it:

"Ty took long lead off first base in deliberate effort to worry our pitcher. We tried to pick him off. He got back in time. Then with ball going back to pitcher, Cobb started for second. Pitcher threw ball into center field. Fielder recovered ball, fired it to third. Third baseman was waiting for Cobb. Cobb, coming into base like an express train, cleverly knocked ball from third baseman's hand. Ball rolled to grand stand and Cobb was off for plate, scoring winning run.

"We sputtered at this exhibition of greased lightning. Umpire came up to me and said, 'Give him credit, he made his own breaks.'"

Selfish, mean, egotistical, restless—these and similar adjectives applied to Cobb all his life. Probably hated—and admired—more than any player of his era. Hated by most opponents on field, even by some teammates. Yet his ferocious perseverance, accomplishments on diamond commanded at least grudging praise.

Cobb's .367 lifetime batting average in 3033 games stands well ahead of anyone's. Many records, among them: led AL in hitting nine consecutive seasons, major league mark; led AL in hitting twelve years, major league mark; made 4191 hits, major league record. Holds AL stolen base record for one season, 96. Stole 892 bases during major league career (modern major league record), leading AL six times. Led AL in total hits seven seasons and tied for lead once. Hit above .400 three times; led AL in runs scored five times; led AL in RBI four times.

Ty was son of school teacher. First tryout, Augusta, South Atlantic League, 1904. After 37 games and .237 batting average, released. Anniston, an independent league, 22 games, batting .370. In 1905, back at Augusta; this time made it—played 104 games, hit .326. Attracted Detroit scouts, others. Cobb to Tigers for reported $500, though some $750. Rough, unfriendly group at Detroit. Rookies not welcome. Had to fight for turn at batting practice. Determined to be best, not just good, in business. That season, 1905, hit only .240, 41 games. But next 23 seasons never hit less than .320!

To achieve greatness, Cobb practiced all aspects of game endless hours—bunting, place-hitting, catching fly balls, sliding. Developed fallaway slide, hook slide. Observed every aspect of play. Studied pitchers. Watched catchers. Learned psychological reactions of opposing players in critical situations.

Raised batting average from .320 in 1906 to .350 in 1907. Took batting championship for first time. Stole 49 bases that year, was on his way to superstardom. Helped Tigers to pennant, but team didn't fare well in World Series. After 3–3 tie in first game, powerful Cubs captured four straight. Cobb hit meek .200. In 1908 Series, same teams. Though Cobb got seven hits (.368 average), drove in four runs, Tigers took only one game. In 1909 Series, his last, Cobb's best was .231, as Tigers lost to Pirates in seven games. World Series play: 17 games, 17 hits in 65 times at bat, scored 7 runs, drove in 10, .262 average.

During AL seasons Cobb fabulous. Would steal second, third, home on successive pitches; go from first to third (sometimes home) on infield out. Philosophy: confuse opposition, get them to hurry their throws, throw poorly, or drop ball because of fear of his sharp spikes. Big hassle with Home Run Baker of Philadelphia Athletics at one point. Cobb accused of trying to cut Baker deliberately with spikes. Cobb gave no quarter in his play, expected none. One terrific brawl with umpire Billy Evans.

Cobb became manager of Tigers 1921. Finished sixth, first season at helm; third, 1922; second, 1923; third again, 1924; fourth, 1925; sixth,

1926, final year as pilot.

Mysteriously after 1926 season, Cobb and Tris Speaker, playing manager of Cleveland, were dropped by their clubs. Former pitcher Hubert "Dutch" Leonard made accusations against both men involving alleged betting and game fixing. Judge Landis, baseball commissioner, after investigating matter, gave both stars clean bill. Cobb then signed with Connie Mack, Philadelphia; salary and bonus arrangement gave him $70,000 for 1927. Speaker joined Senators. As player, Cobb took part in 134 games, hit .357, had 93 RBI, stole 22 bases. Not bad for old man of 40. Then, in 1928, Cobb was member of greatest big-name team ever assembled, excepting all-star aggregations. Tris Speaker came to A's from Washington. Among teammates that year—Al Simmons, Jimmie Foxx, Eddie Collins, Lefty Grove, Jimmie Dykes, Mickey Cochrane, Max Bishop, Joe Boley, Ralph Perkins, Howard Ehmke, Ed Rommel! Team won 98 games, finished second. Yankees took 101 games. In that final year Cobb played only 95 games, hit .323 as he approached 42nd birthday.

Ty could afford to quit. Friends in Detroit and in Georgia had advised him successfully about investments, specially with General Motors and Coca-Cola. Cobb never had to worry about money after that—but did. Oftentimes carried fantastic sums in cash on his person, fearing some unforeseen disaster when money might be needed instantly. Spent most of retirement years in California and Nevada. Restless, rarely relaxed. Went back to native Georgia. Before dying of cancer, endowed medical center at Royston, Ga., near birthplace. Also set up educational foundation.

MVP in AL 1911, winning Chalmers Award, new car by that name. Hall of Fame 1936.

COCHRANE, GORDON STANLEY (Mickey) C-BL-TR. B. 4/6/03, Bridgewater, Mass. D. 6/28/62, Lake Forest, Ill. 5'10½", 180. Protective helmet, now used routinely by professional baseball players, probably would have greatly prolonged playing and managing career of Mickey Cochrane. Mickey, fine catcher and batsman as well as zestful team leader, hitting at .306 pace May 1937. His Tigers battling Yankees. Had slugged homer in previous at bat. This time, with teammate on first base, Mickey giving pitcher, Irving "Bump" Hadley, battle. Count, three balls, one strike. Next pitch sailed up and in tight. Cochrane apparently lost it in his line of vision. Ball struck temple, he went down—unconscious. Carried off field. Unconscious 10 days. Skull fractured three places. Never played again. Just 34 at time; with his competetive spirit, might have gone on as top-notch player several more years. Continued as manager of Tigers until August 1938 but wasn't suited temperamentally to be bench manager.

Mickey one of finest players to come out of New England. Attended Boston University. Played at Saranac Lake, N.Y., 1923. From there to Dover, Del., Eastern Shore League. Preferred outfield, but made best of only opening on club—behind bat. Catching so-so, but hit .327 in 65 games, stole 14 bases. Contract sold to Portland, Pacific Coast League, $1500. PCL one notch below majors. Hit .333, 99 games. Though catching finesse lacking, Connie Mack, manager of Philadelphia AL, had him scouted. Portland put high price on Cochrane. Athletics got around that by buying controlling interest in team. Move probably cost A's more than $200,000, and Cochrane about only player of value they received. Mack later said Cochrane worth every penny of investment.

Mickey A's regular catcher immediately. Hit .331, 134 games, 1925. With intensive coaching from veteran Cy Perkins, catching improved greatly. Caught well over 100 games every year, 1925–35.

Great hitter, fine catcher, speedy base runner; fiery team leader as well. Contributions recognized 1928—MVP. Mack considered him greatest single factor in winning pennants for Athletics, 1929–31. Quite a compliment, since A's at that time included Al Simmons, Jimmie Foxx, Bob Grove and several other luminaries.

Mickey helped A's win World Series 1929,30, but stock market crash blamed for his work in 1931 World Series, when Pepper Martin of Cardinals ran wild. Cochrane hit extremely well during season—.349, 122 games. But in Series, Martin stole five bases and Mickey hit only .160 (4 for 25). Mickey reportedly worrying about his investments dwindling away as depression deepened. Cards took that Series in seven games.

Two years later Detroit bought Cochrane from A's for $100,000 and catcher John Pasek, and appointed him manager. Mickey fired up his new team and Tigers, 1934, won their first pennant since 1909. But once again ran into Cardinal buzz saw. By this time Dizzy and Paul Dean at peak. Dizzy won two games, Paul other two, as Cards won Series four games to three. Mickey held to .214, 6 for 28.

Second consecutive pennant 1935. This time world championship. Detroit took Cubs in seven games. Cochrane 7 for 24, .292.

Major league record: 1482 games, .320 average, 1652 hits in 5169 AB, 1041 runs, 333 doubles, 64 triples, 119 homers 832 RBI, 64 stolen bases.

Series record: .245 (27 for 110), 31 games, 17 runs, 4 doubles, 2 homers, 6 RBI.

After leaving Tigers as bench manager 8/6/38, Mickey served as coach and later general manager, Philadelphia AL, 1950. Scouted for Yankees 1955, Tigers 1960. Vice president, Detroit, 1961–62. At other times worked for trucking company, operated dude ranch in Wyoming. During World War II, served in U.S. Navy fitness program at Great Lakes Naval Training Station. Hall of Fame 1947.

COFFMAN, SAMUEL RICHARD (Dick) P-BR-TR. B. 12/18/06, Veto, Ala. D. 3/24/72, Athens, Ala. 6′2″, 195. Dick Coffman never won 10 games in any of his 15 seasons in AL, but man from Veto, Ala., vetoed Lefty Grove's chances of breaking AL record for consecutive victories, 1931.

Coffman and Browns weren't headed anywhere that year. Dick wound up with 9–13 mark, 3.89 ERA. Browns, as happened so many times before and after, were second division club without any chance to be contender, 35-1/2 games behind Philadelphia Athletics 8/23/31.

Sunday doubleheader at Sportsman's Park, St. Louis—first game pitchers were Grove vs. Coffman. Even though A's powerful slugger Al Simmons was out of lineup with infected toe, Grove seemed unbeatable, having piled up record of 16 straight wins. And it was Grove, not Coffman, who drew crowd of about 20,000 to see Lefty try to break record held by Walter Johnson and Joe Wood. Schoolboy Rowe later equaled this mark. In third inning Brownie outfielder Schulte singled. Then Oscar Melillo sent liner to left field, where Simmons normally played. His sub, Jimmy Moore, misjudged ball, raced in, then discovered that ball was dropping in spot he had just vacated. Ball rolled to fence and Schulte scored.

Athletics had plenty of fine hitters besides Simmons. After all, they waltzed to AL flag that year with 13-1/2-game lead. Mickey Cochrane, Jimmie Foxx, Bing Miller were certainly no pushovers at plate. But that solitary run was enough to give Browns victory. Coffman limited Athletics to three hits, one walk, and scored 1–0 victory over great (and then sizzling) Grove.

Coffman started career at Chattanooga, 1926, and pitched for Quincy, Ill.; Jersey City, and Birmingham in minors. Brief spell with Washington AL, 1927, then joined Browns, 1928. Traded to Washington 6/9/32. Milwaukee, American Association, 1933. St. Louis AL, 1933–35; New York NL, 1936–39. Boston NL 1940. Philadelphia NL 1945.

Dick was with Giants in WS 1936,37, pitched six innings, ERA 12.00. His major league totals: 72–95, ERA 4.65. In 1460-1/3 IP, walked 463, fanned 372.

COLAVITO, ROCCO DOMENICO (Rocky) OF-BR-TR. B. 8/10/33, New York, N.Y. 6′3″, 190. Most baseball fans in Detroit and Cleveland, where Rocky Colavito had his best years, remember him as slugging outfielder. Three times had over 40 homers a season. Led AL in RBI, 1965. Set some fancy fielding marks. But he owns 1.000 record as pitcher—1–0.

Rocky's hitting got him into $60,000 salary class at his peak. But his one victory as AL pitcher came in his final season in majors as member of Yankees, 8/25/68. By this time Colavito was earning about half what he had made few years earlier. Yankees had 28-inning doubleheader on Friday, single game Saturday. Then faced three doubleheaders in three days. Rocky had just joined Yanks and volunteered to help beleaguered pitching staff. In fourth inning of first game of that Sunday doubleheader, manager Houk sent Rocky to mound. Pitched 2-2/3 innings, walked two, allowed one hit, struck out one opponent, but allowed no runs. Yanks rallied and Colavito got credit for victory. When second game started, Rocky was in right field for Yanks—and scored winning run. Prior to that day, Rocky had pitched three innings for Cleveland in 1958. And though he walked three that day, allowed no runs. So his ERA was 0.00 for his two games.

Colavito made grade with Cleveland Indians, 1956, after apprenticeship in such places as Daytona Beach, Cedar Rapids, Spartanburg, Reading, Indianapolis, San Diego. Started pro career 1951. Soon became favorite in Cleveland, especially after slugging 41 homers, 1958, and 42 in 1959. Frank Lane, then boss at Cleveland, aroused ire of fans by trading Rocky to Detroit for Harvey Kuenn. Remained with Detroit through 1963. Kansas City AL, 1964. Back to Cleveland, 1965, enjoying good season with .287 average, 26 homers, 108 RBI to lead AL in this respect. Following year dropped to .238. Traded to Chicago AL during 1967 season. New York AL, 1968, and Los Angeles NL same season. Then took up mushroom farming at Temple, Pa.

Colavito had plenty of accomplishments. On 6/10/59 Indians were playing Orioles in Memorial Stadium, Baltimore. Orioles were in first place. Ball park not an easy one for home run hitters. Rocky blasted four that day, which tied AL record for most consecutive homers in one game and major league record for most homers in a single contest. Rocky tied another major league record in 1965 when he went through 1965 season without an error. Played 162 games. On 8/27/61 tied AL record for most homers in doubleheader, four, hitting one in first game and three in nightcap. Led AL in slugging percentage, 1958; total bases, 1959, 62; led outfielders in double plays, 1958, 60. Appeared in five All-Star games as member of AL squad, hit .250, 6 for 24 trips, .250 average. Hit three homers, one double and drove in eight runs in All-Star games.

Lifetime record in majors: 1841 games, 6503 AB, 1730 hits, 283 doubles, 21 triples, 374 homers, 1159 RBI, .266 average, 19 stolen bases. TV announcer for Cleveland Indians, 1972. Coach, Indians, 1973.

COLBERT, NATHAN, JR.   1B-BR-TR. B. 4/9/46, St. Louis, Mo. 6'2", 209. San Diego Padres acquired Colbert in expansion draft from Houston NL and he immediately captured regular first base assignment 1969. In first four seasons at San Diego propelled 127 homers, with 38 of them in 1970, another 38 in 1972. At same time struck out plenty often—123 times in 1969, 150 following year, and 119 in 1971. Fanned 127 times in 1972. However, his RBI totals were quite respectable, 66,86,84, and 111.

Colbert broke two records 8/1/72 at Atlanta. Five homers during doubleheader equaled 1954 performance of Stan Musial. Drove in 13 runs, new major league record for twin bill. Also hit two singles, giving him 22 total bases for doubleheader; Musial's 1954 mark was 21.

Colbert started out at Sarasota, Fla., 1964, after having been signed by St. Louis NL organization. Houston Astros drafted him 12/5/65 after he played that year with Cedar Rapids. Brief tryout with Astros, 1966, along with 120 games at Amarillo. Also played two games with Oklahoma City. In 1968 it was Oklahoma City and Houston; then came San Diego draft.

Nine times during career hit two or more homers in single game. Fourteen times during 1971 season his hits won games for Padres. Batted .436 against Mets' pitching staff that included Tom Seaver and some other pretty fair pitchers.

At start of 1973 Colbert had hit .254 in 641 NL games. Besides aforementioned 127 homers, had driven in 351 runs in majors.

During 1972–73 off-season Colbert did public relations work for *Sports Illustrated.* NL All-Star squads 1971–73.

COLEMAN, GERALD FRANCIS (Jerry) 2B-SS-BR-TR. B. 9/14/24, San Jose, Calif. 6', 165. Jerry Coleman played for six New York Yankee flag winners. In 1972 became play-by-play announcer for San Diego Padres; had been play-by-play announcer for Yanks, 1963–69. Also did air work for CBS television, as well as WS special assignments for CBS and NBC. Before joining Padres, announced sports for Los Angeles television station, including postgame shows for California Angels, UCLA sports, boxing, and golf.

Jerry signed with Yankee organization and spent his first year in pro ball at Wellsville in Pony League 1942. Hit .304. Then went into military service during World War II. Served again during Korean War. Flew total of 120 missions, receiving two Distinguished Flying Crosses, 13 Air Medals, and three navy citations. Holds rank of lieutenant colonel in Marine Corps.

Back from his first hitch in service Jerry briefly joined Kansas City, then farm club for Yankees, but spent most of 1946 at Binghamton. Back to K.C. for 1947; Newark, 1948; then with Yankees 1949–57. Missed most of 1952–53 serving in Korea. Best year for hitting was 1950 when he batted .287. Never distance hitter. Had total of 16 homers among his 558 major league hits; 77 doubles, 18 triples. Scored 267 runs, drove in 217 in 723 games.

In WS, 1949,50,51,55,56,57, hit .275 with 19 hits in 69 times at bat.

Scored six runs, drove in nine. Saved his best hitting for his final appearances in WS: hit .364 in series of 1957 against Milwaukee Braves. Then decided it was time to quit active play. Moved into Yankees' front office couple of years before entering radio-television field.

All-Star game of 1950. AL Rookie of Year, 1949.

COLEMAN, GORDON CALVIN 1B-BL-TR. B. 7/5/34, Rockville, Md. 6'2", 220. Gordy Coleman played 773 games in majors, all but six with Cincinnati Reds. His first six games were with Cleveland Indians, 1959. One of most popular players ever in Cincinnati. During major league career hit .273; had 98 homers, 102 doubles, 11 triples, with 282 runs scored, 387 RBI. Best homer-producing years were 1961 with 26; following year with 28. In latter season hit .287 in 150 games and helped tremendously in Reds' drive for NL flag. Had one homer in second game of WS, off Ralph Terry with one man on base, helping Cincinnati win only game of classic against New York Yankees that fall. WS average was .250, five hits in 20 trips.

Coleman attended Duke. Played at Reading, Pa., 1953, as first baseman, but was outfielder next couple of seasons at Spartanburg, S. C.; Keokuk, Iowa; and Indianapolis. Reconverted to first baseman 1956 at Mobile. Spent next two years in military service. Returning to Mobile, 1959, led league in hitting with .353; homers with 30; RBI with 110; total bases with 307; slugging percentage with .606. Selected as league's MVP; named to circuit's All-Star team and won "Minor League Achievement Award for 1959."

In six games with Cleveland that same year, had eight hits in 15 trips, for .533 average. In first time at bat in majors pinch hit for Minnie Minoso—and hit triple. Indians, however, traded him to Reds with Cal McLish and Billy Martin for Johnny Temple 12/15/59. Cleveland had Vic Power as first baseman at time.

Moving to Reds, Coleman had spectacular debut in NL, 1960. Banged Ernie Broglio's first pitch for home run; next time up singled. Couldn't last, however, and next time at bat, facing Bob Gibson, Gordy struck out. Coleman had 93 games at Seattle that same season, 1960; hit .324 in Pacific Coast League. Then back to Reds for rest of big league career, which lasted until 1967.

Best batting average with Reds was .302, 1965. In 1961 led NL first sackers in assists with 121. Did considerable effective pinch hitting for Cincinnati.

Coleman has been chief of Reds' speakers bureau recently.

COLEMAN, JOSEPH HOWARD P-BR-TR. B. 2/3/47, Boston Mass. 6'3", 195. Joe Coleman, pitcher for Washington, Detroit, is another second-generation ball player. His father, Joseph Patrick Coleman,

179

toiled from 1942 to 1955, mostly with Philadelphia Athletics, some later, with Baltimore AL, Detroit. And mostly for second-division clubs, often cellar-dwellers. Won 52, lost 76. Young Joe, before pitching in pros, received reported $75,000 bonus to sign with Washington organization. Papa may not have earned that much overall, certainly not much more than that. In 1965, not four months after leaving high school, he won first two starts in AL. Went distance beating Kansas City 6–1, Detroit 3–2. Between graduation and joining Senators, Joe hadn't done so well— 2–10 for Burlington, Carolina League. But Joe young, plenty of stuff. Following two years Joe mostly with York, Eastern League; lost oftener than he won. Brief spells with parent team. Completed and won only AL start, 1966, allowing just two runs. In 1967, was 8–9 for Senators. Then 12–16, 12–13, 8–12 records. To Detroit 10/9/70, along with Brinkman and Rodriguez in McLain deal. Coleman promptly won 20, lost 9 for Tigers. This despite skull practure when hit by line drive; out of action three weeks. In 1972 won 19, lost 14 during regular season, lowering ERA to 2.80, his best for any full season in AL. Capped season by pitching 3–0 win over Oakland A's, third game of AL playoffs. Struck out 14, playoff record. Exclusive of playoff performance, Coleman entered 1973 season with 82–73 record, 1417 innings, 503 walks, 1019 strikeouts—including 222 in 1972.

Coleman says father helped him tremendously in learning to pitch. Depends largely on fast ball, fork ball.

COLLINS, EDWARD TROWBRIDGE 2B-BL-TR. B. 5/2/87, Millerton, N.Y. D. 3/25/51, Boston, Mass. 5'9", 175. When baseball got around to having its first All-Star game in 1933, Eddie Collins was there as an AL coach. When baseball officially inaugurated its Hall of Fame in 1939, Eddie Collins was there as one of original list of immortals. Rightfully so. Collins, player, manager, executive, belonged with such greats as Walter Johnson, Babe Ruth, Tris Speaker, George Sisler, Ty Cobb, Honus Wagner.

Collins holds AL record for longevity as player, 25 years. Lifetime major league batting average of .333. Ten times stole 40 bases or more, yet led AL only three of those seasons; best year 1910—stole 81 bases. In 1912 pilfered six bases in one game, 9/11/12; repeated performance 9/22/12. Set record for World Series steals, 14, since equaled by Lou Brock.

Although he managed only two seasons 1925–26, he could have managed several major league clubs. Turned down chance to manage St. Louis Browns. Clark Griffith tried to get him to manage Senators before job went to Bucky Harris. Yankees wanted him. And believed that Connie Mack counted on his bossing Philadelphia Athletics after he (Connie) stepped down. But Tom Yawkey hired him as vice president and general manager of Boston Red Sox, 1933. Yawkey-Collins setup brought better times to Boston fans who had suffered through 11-year period when Sox finished in cellar nine times. But Yawkey's cash and Collins' savvy could bring only one pennant 1946 to New England while Eddie lived.

Eddie attended Columbia. Became 140-pound quarterback on football squad. Played baseball during summer for extra money. Connie Mack heard about him, signed him to Athletics' contract. For time, at Mack's behest, Collins used name "Sullivan" to keep his eligibility for college sports. Eddie played 20 games with A's during 1906 and 1907 seasons, and four games with Newark in Eastern League, 1907. But in 1908 was set with Athletics, appearing in 102 games as shortstop, second baseman, outfielder. Then became second baseman for rest of career. Good one too. Nine times led AL second sackers in fielding. Led in putouts and assists numerous times. In 1909 Collins had .346 average, stole 67 bases. Reached .365 in 1911. But high-water mark was .369 in 1920. Hit better than .300 in 19 of 25 seasons he played in AL. Tower of strength for Athletics during pennant-winning seasons of 1910,11,13,14. In first World Series Eddie hit .429, 9 for 21, including four doubles. In one game Johnny Kling, catcher for Chicago Cubs, called for three pitchouts while Collins on first base. Eddie stayed there. Then when Kling called for his pitcher to throw strike, Eddie stole second. Stole four bases that Series when A's defeated Cubs four games to one. Eddie hit .286 in 1911 Series but in 1913 classic batted .421 and stole three bases. Had another good Series with White Sox, 1917: hit .409, stole three bases.

Connie Mack broke up his ball club after team lost 1914 Series to Boston Braves in four games. Collins was sold to Chicago, reportedly for $50,000. Sox won in 1917, beat Giants in Series and won flag again in 1919. That was year of the "Black Sox" scandal. Gandil, Cicotte and others of the "Black Sox" knew better than to approach Collins to join them. Collins at time was serving as captain of team.

In 1920s playing managers were in style. Tris Speaker, Ty Cobb, Stanley Harris, George Sisler, Rogers Hornsby all became pilots while still playing regularly. So too Eddie Collins, bossing White Sox 1925–26. Sox finished last, 1924. Under Eddie's direction club finished fifth both years. Collins batted .346 his first year as playing manager, .344 second.

When White Sox released Collins after 1926 season, Eddie returned to Philadelphia as player and coach under Connie Mack. Club was on upswing and won three pennants, 1929–31. Eddie made his last appearance as player during 1930 season. Was member of that fabulous collection of stars who played under Connie Mack in 1928 not all at their peak: Ty Cobb, Tris Speaker, Eddie Collins; Jimmie Foxx, still improving; and Lefty Grove, George Earnshaw, Mickey Cochrane, Ed Rommel, Jimmie Dykes, Joe Hauser, Joe Boley, Max Bishop!

When Collins quit as player, had hung up enviable record: 2826 games, 9949 at bats, 3311 hits, 1818 runs, 437 doubles, 186 triples, 47 home runs, 1307 RBI, .333 average, 743 stolen bases. In Six World Series: 34 games, 128 AB, 20 runs, 42 hits, 7 doubles, 2 triples, 10 RBI, .328, 14 stolen bases.

Eddie was member of U.S. Marines during World War I. His son, Eddie, Jr., played in majors as member of Athletics, 1939,41,42.

In sixth and final game of 1917 Series, Collins hit ball to Heinie Zimmerman, third baseman for Giants. Zim made wild throw to first base for error and Collins reached second base. Right fielder Dave Robertson followed with another error, dropping easy fly ball. Next batsman hit to pitcher. Collins, thinking pitcher would try for second-to-first double play, was caught off third base. In strange rundown play, Giants left plate unguarded. Zimmerman wound up with ball and Collins eluded him. Zimmerman had no alternative but to try to catch Collins, whom he chased across plate with important run. Sox took game 4–2, and Series by same count. Though newsmen tried to make Zimmerman look ridiculous on play, Zimmerman rightly asked, "Who in hell was I going to throw the ball to, Umpire Bill Klem?"

COLLINS, JAMES ANTHONY (Rip) 1B-OF-BLR-TL. B. 3/30/05, Altoona, Pa. D. 4/16/70, Haven, N.Y. 5'9", 165. Whenever 1934 WS is mentioned, fans and experts alike refer to fact Dizzy and Paul Dean won all four games St. Louis Cardinals took from Detroit Tigers. But no pitcher can win without runs. Rip Collins, with healthy .367 average that series, helped provide Redbirds with runs needed to make Deans winners. Got 11 hits in seven games, scored four runs, drove in four others.

Versatile carefree refugee from Pennsylvania coal mines. Once when minor league scout refused to give him $5 to sign up, Rip continued mining coal. Eventually got tryout with York, New York-Pennsylvania League, 1923. Hit above .300 two seasons with Johnstown, Mid-Atlantic League. Next stops Savannah; Danville, Ill.; and Rochester, his .376 International League average in 1930 winning him advancement to Cardinals for 1931.

Rip seems to have been instigator of unforgettable prank in Bellevue-Stratford Hotel, Philadelphia, where Cardinals stayed. Observed ladders, paint buckets, white overalls, and other paraphernalia of painters in corner of service area of hotel. Rounded up Dizzy Dean, Heinie Schuble, Bill Delancey. Players donned overalls, took equipment into busy dining room and began painting walls and ceiling, splattering paint on patrons, shouting instructions to one another and promoting general chaos. Branch Rickey, general manager of Cards, happened to be in town. It took all his famed powers of persuasion and cajolery to prevent hotel management from evicting entire ball club instantly.

Rip also loved to sing. He, Dizzy Dean, Dazzy Vance, and Pepper Martin formed quartet that sang over 50,000-watt KMOX, 1933. Quite a slugger on ball field. Claimed title as "All-American Louse" because he broke up four different bids for no-hitters by getting only safe hit in each game. Admitted, however, "I felt like heel."

Ripper hit pinch-hit grand slam homer 9/19/36 off Curt Davis of Chicago Cubs. Following year was traded to Cubs, and during 1939 and 1940 was with Los Angeles, Pacific Coast League. Pittsburgh 1941. Playing manager, Albany, Eastern League, 1942–46. In 1944 his .396 average was highest in all minor leagues. Manager, San Diego, PCL, 1947–48 during which period called it quits as player. Later managed Hartford, Conn., and Middleboro, Mass., clubs and became scout for Cardinals, job he held at time of his death.

Together with baseball jobs, Collins spent several years as radio broadcaster; was with Wilson Sporting Goods Co. in sales and promotion work. In 1962 was one of 10 coaches who took turns bossing Chicago Cubs.

Rip hit .296 in his 1084 major league games, made 1121 hits, 205 of them doubles, 65 triples, 135 homers, with 659 RBI. His WS average for 13 games (1931,34,38) was .277, with five runs scored, four RBI.

COLLINS, JAMES JOSEPH (Jimmy) 3B-BR-TR. B. 1/16/73, Niagara Falls, N.Y. D. 3/6/43, Buffalo, N.Y. 5'7½", 160. Could Jimmy Collins have been equal of Brooks Robinson and Pie Traynor as third baseman? If you believe old-timers, he was. Jimmy's career spanned latter part of 19th century in NL, then spent eight years in AL, mostly with Boston. Successful manager, led Boston to world championship in first modern WS, 1903. Oldsters claimed that nobody could come in on grass to field bunts quite like Collins. Faced such experts as Wee Willie Keeler, Jesse Burkett, John McGraw, Hugh Jennings, Jack Doyle, and Billy Hamilton. And, they say, it was almost impossible to get ball past him.

Collins started out, 1893, with Buffalo, Eastern League, batting .286 in 76 games. Following year hit healthy .352 as outfielder, meriting promotion to majors. In 1895 was property of Boston NL, but was loaned to Louisville in same circuit for part of year. That was season he became third baseman. Concentrated on hot corner ever afterward.

In 1896, not only fielded brilliantly but batted .300. Followed with .346 in 1897 and .337 in 1898. After 1900 season jumped to AL, Boston club, and gained greatest fame with Red Sox, also known as Puritans. Playing manager, led club to second-place finish, 1901; third in 1902; and first in 1903. That fall, his club took on Pittsburgh Pirates and defeated NL champs five games to three; Collins hit .250, his only WS.

Led his club to another AL pennant, 1904, but there was no WS. In 1905 his team dropped to fourth. When club headed for basement, 1906, he was replaced by Chick Stahl. In 1907 started out as player-in-ranks with Red Sox but was traded to Philadelphia AL 6/7/07. Played rest of that year and next with A's. In 1909 playing manager, Minneapolis, and later managed Providence, Eastern League, 1910–11.

In 1899 Collins set NL record for most chances accepted, exclusive of errors, for third baseman, with 601. Lifetime major league totals: 1718 games, 6792 AB, 1057 runs, 1999 hits, 333 doubles, 117 triples, 62 homers, 188 SB and .294 average.

Hall of Fame 1945.

COMBS, EARLE BRYAN (Colonel) OF-BL-TR. B. 5/14/99, Pebworth, Ky. 6', 185. Teacher, farmer, ball player. Earl Combs received his teaching certificate from Eastern Tennessee State Teachers' College, 1919. Besides teaching, Combs acted as player-manager of local team. Went directly to Louisville, American Association, 1922; was immediate success. Played 130 games, batted .344. Following season boosted average to .380. When he came up with .368 in 1924, major league scouts knew he was for real. Yankees made best offer, reportedly $50,000.

As in Louisville, Combs was immediate success in New York. Reporting at end of 1924 season, hit .400 in 24 games. And in first full season with Yanks, hit .342. In 1927 led AL in times at bat, 648; in hits, 231; in triples, 23; in outfield putouts, 411—and hit.356. Continued his consistently fine play, interrupted only by fractured skull, 7/24/34, when crashed into wall in St. Louis. Still hit .319 that year in 63 games. When he dropped down to .282 in 89 games following season, Earle decided to retire from active play. Coached Yankees, 1935–44; Browns, 1947; Red Sox, 1948–52; Phillies, 1954.

Combs also sparkled in WS, 1926,27,28,32, with .350 average. In 16 games made 21 hits in 60 AB, scoring 17 runs. Smacked three doubles, one homer, drove in nine runs. Since retirement has spent most of time on farm.

COMISKEY, CHARLES ALBERT (Old Roman) 1B-BR-TR. B. 8/15/59, Chicago, Ill. D. 10/26/31, Eagle River, Wis. 6', 180. Elected to Hall of Fame 1939 for contributions to baseball as executive and his playing ability among those whose careers on field ended prior to 1900. Comiskey revolutionized first-base play. Became successful field manager before becoming club owner. One of pillars of AL, and founder of dynasty that owned Chicago White Sox until 3/10/59 when Bill Veeck acquired control.

Comiskey played pro ball at Dubuque, Iowa 1878–81 and then went to St. Louis Browns, American Association. Hit .245 his first season, in 78 games. Was not great hitter but soon began his innovations in field. First baseman had always been glued to bag in past. Comiskey edged out toward right field and moved farther away from foul line. Pitcher was instructed how and when to cover bag. In comparatively short time all first basemen followed Comiskey's lead. His next move was to shift whole infield as occasion demanded.

During 1883 season Comiskey, only 25, but full of ideas, became manager of team. In 1884, owner of ball club, Chris von der Ahe, was listed as manager, but Comiskey was manager again, 1885–89. Browns won pennants 1885–88. In 1889 his team finished second. At this point he shifted to Chicago, Player League, continuing as playing manager. That team finished fourth. Back to St. Louis, AA, 1891. Club finished in runner-up position. Then piloted Cincinnati NL 1892,93,94, finishing fifth, sixth and tenth those years. By this time Comiskey's playing days were drawing to close, though he played one season in Western League, minor circuit, 1895. Commy bought Sioux City franchise and transferred it to St. Paul. Was owner, manager, and player, 1895, but continued to run front office and field through 1899 without playing.

While in Cincinnati, Comiskey had become friendly with sports writer, Ban Johnson, who became president of Western League. In 1900 this became American League and Comiskey, working closely with Johnson, moved his St. Paul franchise to Chicago. Commy also managed team on field, 1900, winning pennant. In 1901 AL became recognized as major league. Comiskey then turned over field management to Clark Griffith and confined his efforts to front office.

Under Commy's ownership, White Sox won AL major league flags 1901, 1906, 1917, 1919. In 1906 and 1917, team won WS. Then came 1919 club, powerful aggregation. But several members of team conspired to throw games to Cincinnati, NL pennant winner. And in 1920 when facts came out in public, Judge Landis barred eight "Black Sox" for life, and team was wrecked. Second-division club from 1921 through 1935, after which Jimmie Dykes led club to third-place finish in 1936.

Comiskey figured in several controversies. Many blamed his parsimoniousness for willingness of 1919 players to listen to tempting offers from gamblers to throw games. And he was accused of callousness in his treatment of Dick Kerr. Kerr was one of honest group on 1919 team. Although Dick pitched and won two games in 1919 WS, Comiskey refused to meet Kerr's modest requests for raise. Kerr won 21 games in 1920 and 19 in 1921. Each year his salary was $4500. Had been offered $5000 to pitch for semipro team in Chicago, 1921. In 1922, when Kerr wanted more money, Comiskey remained unsympathetic. Kerr played independent ball, and was put on ineligible list by Judge Landis for playing in same games with "outlaws."

Comiskey's close friendship with Ban Johnson came to an end in 1918 when, in dispute over contract of pitcher Jack Quinn, AL president ruled in favor of Yankees. Hostility had numerous repercussions in later years in administration of AL affairs.

Commy was reported to have blocked effort by John McGraw to play Negro on Baltimore Orioles, AL, 1901, when Little Napoleon was managing that club. Charlie Grant, black bellboy from Cincinnati, was playing ball in Hot Springs, Ark., when McGraw saw him. McGraw tried to convert him into "Charlie Tokohoma, full-blooded Cherokee." But Comiskey had sufficient influence in AL circles so McGraw was never allowed to field team that included black.

Comiskey's lifetime major league record showed 1374 games, 5780 times at bat, 981 runs, 1559 hits, 199 doubles, 69 triples, 29 homers and 440 stolen bases for .270. In old WS play, under rules quite different from those in use in 20th century, Comiskey played in 38 games and batted .287.

CONCEPCION, DAVID ISMAEL   SS-BR-TR. B. 6/17/48, Aragua, Venezuela. 6'2", 155.

Luis Aparicio and Chico Carrasquel, also pretty fancy shortstops, came out of Venezuela—and so does Dave Concepcion, who plays with Cincinnati Reds. In 1970 and 1971 shared position with Woody Woodward, but latter retired before 1972 started. Then Dave had to share position with Darrel Chaney. Some observers felt Concepcion a bit too nonchalant in his first two seasons in NL. But he married during off-season, and in 1972 seemed more mature.

After attending Augustin Codazzi College, signed with Cincinnati system, 1968, and played at Tampa, Florida State League, that year. Next season at Asheville, Southern Association, hit .294 in 96 games. Then, transferred to Indianapolis, American Association, same year; hit .341 in 42 games.

During Cincinnati's pennant-winning season, 1970, as rookie, Concepcion hit .260 in 101 games and .333 in WS. Had three hits in nine trips, including one triple, with three RBI. In 1971 Dave got off to bad start; suffered torn ligaments in right thumb during spring training. Used largely as late-inning defensive replacement or pinch runner. Hit .205 in 130 games.

Concepcion's average for 1972 was .209 in 119 games. This gave lifetime major league mark of .222 for 350 games. During 1972 WS hit .308, with four hits in 13 trips, two runs scored, two RBI.

CONIGLIARO, ANTHONY RICHARD (Tony)   OF-BR-TR. B. 1/7/45, Revere, Mass. 6'3", 200.

Tony Conigliaro walked out of an eye doctor's office in Boston 2/24/72 and told world he was finished as professional baseball player. Thus ended dramatic story of former Little Leaguer who got $20,000 bonus, plus fringe benefits, to sign his first Red Sox contract; who led AL in home runs his second year in majors; who lived like swinger; who flirted with death and tragedy; who lived a miracle that evaporated.

In his fourth season with Boston AL, seemingly leading charmed life, Tony was felled by pitch thrown by Jack Hamilton in night game at Fenway Park (8/18/67). Hamilton, with California Angels, had been accused of throwing illegal spitball. Whatever pitch was, it sailed. Tony jerked back, his helmet falling to ground before ball hit left side of his head. Dislocated jaw; left cheekbone fractured; eye severely affected. Obviously was through for rest of season, and after brief period in spring training camp, 1968, it looked like he would never again play ball. Red Sox, who had paid all doctor bills, paid him in full for 1968 season. Then seemingly miraculously, after workouts in winter instructional league, Conigliaro found his eyesight had come back. So, was able to play 141 games in 1969 and 146 in 1970.

Tony's opening day in 1969 was of storybook variety. With all eyes focused upon him, struck out in his first time at bat. Then he walked. Later singled. And in 10th inning slammed home run off Richert of Baltimore Orioles to win ball game.

Seemingly, Conigliaro was just about as good ball player during 1969 and 1970 as he was before being injured: 20 homers in 1969, 36 in 1970; 82 RBI, then 116 in 1970.

But Red Sox club disappointed in 1970, and Tony C. was one of those to go. Traded to California Angels, Tony packed up and found quarters next door to Raquel Welch. Signed contract reportedly calling for $80,000 for 1971. But Tony never did get going for Angels; felt Mgr. Lefty Phillips and G.M. Dick Walsh didn't understand him. Hit just .222 in 74 games, with four homers and 15 RBI. Then, after emotional flareup following 20-inning loss to Oakland, announced he was retiring because of trouble with his eyes, as well as general dissatisfaction. Angels tried to cut him off payroll, but after months of hassle with Major League Players' Association, agreed Conigliaro should have been placed on disabled list. Consequently, club had to cough up about $30,000 to Tony for not playing rest of season. Tony talked about another comeback, took up karate to help get in condition—but eye examination early in 1972 quashed it.

Conigliaro started out as Little League player. Played American Legion Junior baseball. After signing with Red Sox was sent to Wellsville, New York–Pennsylvania League, 1963. Hit .363 in 83 games and grabbed regular spot in Boston outfield following year. Tony played 111 games and hit .290—and would have played more but for broken right arm that sidelined him several weeks. Following year hit 32 homers to lead AL, drove in 82 markers.

In 1966 Tony played 150 games, hit 28 homers, sent 93 runs across plate and owned .265 average. When felled by that fateful pitch in 1967 he was batting .287 with 20 homers and 67 RBI. Red Sox won pennant that year but of course Conigliaro did not participate. Had played in All-Star Game with AL squad before his injury.

Tony's lifetime major league totals follow: 855 games, 3164 AB, 456 runs, 842 hits, 138 doubles, 23 triples, 164 homers, 507 RBI, 19 SB and .266 average.

Younger brother, Billy, has been outfielder with Red Sox, Milwaukee Brewers and Oakland A's.

CONIGLIARO, WILLIAM MICHAEL OF-BR-TR. B. 8/15/47, Revere, Mass. 6', 190. Billy Conigliaro, former member of Red Sox, returned to Fenway Park for first time 5/29/72 and had his revenge for being traded by hitting two homers and triple, driving in four runs. George Scott, who was traded to Milwaukee AL in same deal, also drove in four runs against his old teammates. George had one homer and triple. Billy, glad to have left Boston, his hometown. Had been pretty unhappy ever since his older brother, Tony, was traded to California Angels 10/11/70. Rather vociferous in expressing his discontent to Red Sox management; also peeved over way Boston press handled various Conigliaro stories.

In 1964 Tony Conigliaro hit home run in his first time at bat as Red Sox rookie. Five years later younger brother Billy came along. But in his first trip to plate he struck out. Then he hit two consecutive homers. In final time at bat, struck out again. Next game Billy struck out his first two trips to plate, then he hit his third homer. Followed with single and double. You could say it had been colorful debut.

After Tony had made good with Red Sox, Billy may have had advantage of Conigliaro name. Tony's signing bonus reportedly was $20,000. But Billy is believed to have collected somewhere between $35,000 and $60,000 to sign. He had been an outstanding football player in high school, but turned down several college football scholarships to go with Boston organization, June 1965.

Billy, farmed out to Waterloo, Iowa, that summer, hit .272 in 70 games. Divided 1966 season between Pittsfield and Winston-Salem; Greenville, Western Carolina League, 1967; Pittsfield, 1968; and Louisville, 1969. There he hit International League pitching for .298 average with 13 homers, 81 RBI in 103 games. After that performance, was taken up to Boston for 32 games, hitting .288, with 4 homers, 7 RBI.

While still with Louisville, Billy blasted Dick Williams, then manager of Red Sox, for his handling of brother Tony. In 1970 Williams was gone, replaced by Eddie Kasko. Billy hit .271 in 114 games, with 18 homers, 58 RBI. Tony came up with .266 average, 36 homers, 116 RBI. Then Tony was traded to Angels, which touched off another series of popoffs by Billy. Billy wasn't too happy in 1971, when he hit .262 with 11 homers, 33 RBI in 101 contests. Was leading league in doubles with 23 at All-Star break, but played relatively little thereafter.

Billy took major league record of .269 in 247 games with him when traded to Milwaukee, together with Don Pavletich, Ken Brett, Jim Lonborg, George Scott, and Joe Lahoud, 10/11/71. At that time had 223 hits, with 48 doubles, six triples, 33 homers, and 98 RBI.

Of new surroundings, Billy said he was happy to be in Milwaukee. Admitted that at times he had been his own worst enemy and pledged would do everything he could "to restore the family name."

However, Billy left Brewers and $35,000 salary 6/25/72, saying wasn't happy. Returned to Nahant, Mass., to help Tony run their $700,000 golf club. Had .230 batting average for 52 games, including seven homers, when he quit. Later declared he'd never play for Brewers but did agree to play for Oakland A's for 1973.

CONLAN, JOHN BERTRAND (Jocko) Umpire. B. 12/06/02, Chicago, Ill. Jocko Conlan lasted just two seasons as major league outfielder with Chicago White Sox back in 1934 and 1935. Proved far more durable as NL umpire. Now is retired, bored because he misses baseball, especially banter with players and managers.

Got his nickname while playing at Rochester, International League, 1924,25,26 because he was great "jockey," constantly heckling opposing players. Love of snappy retort and repartee did not end when he took up umpiring as profession, 1936. Impatient with managers, coaches, and players who didn't know rules of game. No love for Leo Durocher; tells story about Durocher with relish. Leo was managing N.Y. Giants. Opposing team had righthanded batsman at plate. Durocher whistled to distant bullpen in Polo Grounds for righthanded pitcher to come in for Giants. "Guy went to mound, took his warmup pitches. Other team put in lefthanded pinch hitter. Leo jumped up and signaled to bullpen for lefthanded pitcher. I just stood there behind home plate laughing while this guy comes in from bullpen," continued Conlan. "Bullpen at Polo Grounds is located just outside Bridgeport, Conn. New Giant pitcher walks all that distance. When he reaches mound, I have pleasure of telling the 'Little genius of Coogan's Bluff' that relief pitcher has to throw to at least one batter, until he is safe or out. So lefthanded pitcher has to turn around and walk back. Leo has to send for the righthander who is on the way to showers now."

Conlan had plenty of verbal exercise with other players and managers, like Frankie Frisch, et al.

Conlan had three years at Wichita, Kans., Western League, 1920,22,23, then moved up to Rochester. Hit above .300 two of these seasons then had three .300-or-better years at Newark, also International

League. Spent 1930 at Toledo, American Association, and in 1931–32 played for Montreal, International League. (Out of game 1921 and 1933.)

Conlan's first umpiring job in New York–Pennsylvania League, 1936. After two years there, had three seasons in American Association, 1938–40. Graduated to NL in 1941. Umpired in WS and All-Star games.

CONLEY, DONALD EUGENE (Gene) P-BR-TR. B. 11/10/30, Muskogee, Okla. 6'8", 227. First man to play two major professional sports in same city, Boston. Gene was member of world champion Boston Celtics in National Basketball Association when traded from Philadelphia NL baseball club to Boston Red Sox. With Celtics 1958,59,60, later with N.Y. Knickerbockers.

Gene originally signed with Boston Braves, 1951, after his sophomore year at Washington State, where standout in baseball, basketball. Three years of preparation in minors; 1951 at Hartford, 20–9, with 2.16 ERA; 1952, with Milwaukee, American Association, 11–4 and 3.15 ERA; 1953 at Toledo, AA, 23–9 with 2.90 ERA. *Sporting News* named him Minor League Player of Year, 1951,53. During this period he was consistently striking out about three times as many hitters as he walked.

Conley's first days with Braves, 1952, were brief. Lost three games and had 7.82 ERA, and was shipped to Milwaukee for most of season. When ready to stick in majors, 1954, Braves had been moved to Wisconsin metropolis and he won 14, losing nine, with 2.97 ERA his first full year in big time. Remained with Braves through 1958 season but never quite lived up to expectations. Had 12–7 record 1959 with Phillies, 8–14 in 1960, then went to Red Sox. Came up with 11–14, 1961. Reached his peak number of wins, 15, in 1962, but lost 14 decisions. Then after 3–4 record in 1963 bowed out of majors.

Gene was tallest man in majors at time. Pitched just 1-2/3 innings in 1957 WS with Braves, allowing two earned runs, no decision. Played in three All-Star games on NL squad, 1954,55,59, with one win credited and one loss charged against him. But had 10.80 ERA for these contests.

Conley wound up with 91 wins, 96 losses in majors and an ERA of 3.82. Walked 511, fanned 888 in 1588-2/3 innings in 276 games.

CONNERY, ROBERT J. Executive. B. 3/20/80, St. Louis, Mo. D. 1/28/67, Dallas, Tex. Bob Connery bought Rogers Hornsby for St. Louis Cardinals for $700. Teamed with Paul Krichell in getting Lou Gehrig for Yankees for $1000. But was worried somewhat about price for Earl Combs—$50,000, plus veteran ball player, plus additional concessions. However, Combs came through and Yankees never regretted his purchase.

Bob one of earliest and best-known scouts in baseball back in days when horse and buggy was slowly but surely going out of style. Had been semipro first baseman in St. Louis but never made majors. Played in minors with Des Moines and other clubs starting in 1903. But one of those new-fangled horseless carriages involved him in an accident that ended his playing days. Managed at Hartford, Conn. through 1912, then became Cardinal scout.

Miller Huggins became manager of Redbirds, 1913, and became Connery's fast friend. Couple of years later Cardinals were trying to pick up few dollars in exhibition series. Bob was managing one squad while another group played elsewhere. Connery's team was playing Dennison club of Texas-Oklahoma League. Connery used top-flight pitchers Bill Doak, Red Ames, Slim Sallee, and Bob Harmon. Young choke hitter named Hornsby wasn't fazed by reputation of major leaguers, got hit or two in each game. Connery was impressed, and some time after series ended bought Rajah for seven C-notes.

Connery bought him decent spiked shoes and glove, changed his batting style from choke, and pitched to him morning after morning and repeatedly after ball games. Hornsby struck out great deal when he started but, with Connery's and Huggins' encouragement, began to get knack of hitting ball. Went on to win seven NL batting titles, hit over .400 three times, and wound up with lifetime batting average of .358, second only to Ty Cobb's .367.

When Miller Huggins left Cardinals to become manager of Yankees, Connery became Yankee chief scout. Had hand in getting Bob Meusel, Crosetti, Lazzeri, Koenig, Pipgras, and Lefty Gomez for New Yorkers. In 1923, after following Earl Combs, then with Louisville in American Association, Connery recommended his purchase. Bill Kneblekamp, president of Colonels, insisted not only on $50,000 cash, but Elmer Smith, and outfielder; also demanded that Yanks play exhibition game in Louisville with Babe Ruth guaranteed to be in lineup during spring of 1924. This netted Kneblekamp an additional $5000. But Combs came through as big leaguer, and once more Connery's judgment vindicated.

Left Yankees, 1925, to become owner of St. Paul team, American Association. Retired as owner 10 years later.

CONNOLLY, THOMAS HENRY Umpire. B. 12/31/70, Manchester, England. D. 4/28/61, Natick, Mass. Tommy Connolly never saw or played game of baseball until 15. Cricket only game he knew until family moved to America, 1884. But spent 60 years in umpiring profession, 53 in AL as umpire or chief of staff.

Tommy self-appointed batboy for Natick, Mass., baseball team, 1885. Asked to manage YMCA team, Natick, declined, saying he'd rather umpire. Tim Hurst, NL umpire, spotted Connolly, recommended him to New England League 1894. Four years later advanced to NL. Called plays through 1900. Connie Mack recommended him to Ban Johnson, organizer of new AL. Tommy hired.

Had distinction of umpiring first AL game ever played as major league. This was 4/24/01 in Chicago, as White Sox met Cleveland. Three other games that opening day rained out. Officiated at first games ever played at old Highlander (later Yankee) field in New York; Comiskey Park, Chicago; Shibe Park, Philadelphia; Fenway Park, Boston; Yankee Stadium, N.Y. Was AL umpire in first World Series of modern times, 1903. Later umpired seven other Series.

Connolly umpired alone in league games until 1907. Gave up work on field June 1931 to become chief of staff for AL arbiters. For many years was member of Rules Committee for organized baseball. Retired January 1954. Elected to Hall of Fame along with NL's Bill Klem, 1953; first umpires to gain this recognition.

CONNORS, KEVIN JOSEPH (Chuck) 1B-BL-TL. B. 4/10/21, Brooklyn, N.Y. 6'5½", 212. Most TV viewers who have seen Chuck Connors, especially in "Rifleman" series, probably know nothing about his early days as tyro first baseman with Brooklyn Dodgers, Chicago Cubs, and various minor league teams.

Chuck attended Seton Hall College where he played baseball and basketball. Later played pro basketball with Boston Celtics where his principal claim to fame is fact that he broke glass backboard at Boston Arena 11/5/46 during pregame warmup. Went in for shot at basket, hung up on hoop, and shattered glass backboard. This delayed start of game 45 minutes while management searched for replacement. Since that time Celtics are said always to have reserve backboard on hand in case of repetition.

Connors played for Newport, Ark.; Norfolk, Newport News, Mobile, and Montreal clubs in minors. One game with Brooklyn Dodgers as pinch hitter, 1949, but did not hit safely. Landed with Cubs, 1951, played 66 games but .239 average wasn't encouraging. Cubs sent him to their Los Angeles, Pacific Coast League, affiliate. Hit .321 in 98 games, 1951, and .259 in 113 games, 1952.

Recalls that once he came to bat with first base open. Los Angeles club had potential tying, winning runs on third and second respectively. Fred Haney, managing Hollywood Stars, ordered Connors intentionally walked, despite low batting average. Johnny Lindell, pitching for Stars, lobbed three wide ones. Everyone in park seemed relaxed but Chuck. On next pitch Connors reached across plate, lofted double into left field to win ball game. Haney fined Lindell $50 for getting ball anywhere within Chuck's reach.

But Connors realized his future in baseball had passed, so he drummed up chances to recite "Casey at the Bat," which led to job in movies. Got $500 for taking role of tough state trooper who bawled out Spencer Tracy while Katharine Hepburn listened, in *Pat and Mike*. But Chuck didn't click too well at start. Got job as door-to-door salesman for water softener. Became part-time sportscaster for TV. Then came big break when he got role in "Rifleman" series. Since that time, Connors has been in scores of movies and has appeared in thousands of television programs. But still remembers that in 1940 his salary at Newport, Ark., was $65 a month.

Chuck played 67 major league games, had overall average of .238. Among his 48 hits were 5 doubles, 1 triple, 2 homers.

COOKE, ALLEN LINDSEY (Dusty)   OF-BL-TR. B. 6/23/07, Swepsonville, N.C. 6'1", 205. Only club trainer who became major league manager.

Dusty Cooke, as young ball player, seemed destined for stardom, but injuries ruined his prospects of greatness. Had eight years in majors but never lived up to early expectations. Joined navy during World War II, 10/19/42; served in Okinawa Bay during Japanese air attack. When war was over Dusty was looking for work, any kind of work. Ben Chapman, then manager of Philadelphia NL, offered Dusty job of club trainer for 1946 season. Cooke, while in navy, had been given intensive training in conditioning young men in Pre-Flight School at Chapel Hill, N. C. Handled average of 360 men daily, including those suffering from everything from blisters to broken necks. So Dusty knew his way around rubbing table. Came day when Chapman was out as manager of Phils, 7/16/48. Cooke got tapped as temporary manager. Served as club pilot long enough to win six games, losing five. Then replaced by Eddie Sawyer, who in 1950, led team—Whiz Kids—to NL pennant.

Cooke had fine season at Durham, Piedmont League, 1927, his first in pro ball. Hit .319, stole 33 bases, slammed 15 homers in 116 games, scintillated as speedy outfielder, demonstrated fine arm. Yankees paid $15,000 to get him into their organization. Placed him with Asheville, South Atlantic League, 1928, where Cooke blasted ball at .362 clip in 146 games. Next stop was St. Paul, American Association, 1929. Dusty kept on with his brilliant work—hit .358 in 152 games, led American Association in homers with 33, in RBI with 148.

Landed with Yankees following year. Then misfortunes began. Dived for ball hit by Oscar Bluege of Washington Senators. Fell on his right shoulder, with resultant shoulder separation. Field had been slippery after rain that morning. His arm never regained its full power. Farmed out to Newark briefly, 1931.

In 1932, back with Yanks, when subbing for Earle Combs, Cooke, in his third game, suffered broken leg. There went considerable amount of his speed afoot. Yankees traded him to Boston AL before 1933 season.

Shifted to Cincinnati for 1938, after season with Minneapolis, 1937, when he hit .345 in 151 games. Best year in majors was 1935 when he hit .306 for Red Sox in 100 games. When he left big leagues had .280 average for 608 games. Rochester, 1939; Jersey City, 1940–41; Rochester, 1942. Then entered navy.

An unusual experience for Cooke: while with Cincinnati, hit ball in Sportsman's Park, St. Louis, and stopped at third base since ball hit girder supporting pavilion roof and rebounded onto field. Next day Cooke credited with homer. Bill McKechnie, managing Reds, protested to Bill Klem that ball should have been ruled homer. Klem ruled against Reds and Cardinals tied score in ninth inning, went on to win in overtime. But after ball game was over, Klem inspected park carefully and decided that Cooke's drive should have been ruled home run. This was so ordered and game was replayed at later date. But Cooke got his homer.

COONEY, JOHN WALTER   P-OF-BR-TL. B. 3/18/01, Cranston, R.I. 5'11'', 165. Only man who played in NL and AL, coached in both leagues, managed in both, and umpired in one. This is claim of Johnny Cooney, erstwhile southpaw pitcher who became fine righthanded-hitting outfielder. Came from baseball family. Father, James, played for Cap Anson with Chicago NL way back, 1890–92. Brother, Jimmy, with several major league teams, but mostly with St. Louis Cardinals and Chicago Cubs.

Cooney's record as pitcher wasn't sensational, but when any hurler could stop Rogers Hornsby in his fabulous .424 season, 1924, it is worthy of note. Was only pitcher who held Rajah hitless in three games. Cooney won 34, lost 44 during major league career, with ERA of 3.72. Walked 223 and struck out 224 in 795-1/3 innings, with 44 complete games.

Played semipro ball in New England as kid. His team manager took him to Boston for talk with Ed Barrow, then business manager for Red Sox. Barrow was ready to give Cooney $500 bonus and $300 per month contract. Called his secretary to make out check. "No checks," interjected semipro manager. "Cash or nothing!" Barrow was so shocked that anyone could question validity of his checks that he ran Cooney and semipro manager out of his office instantly. Johnny later signed with Boston Braves, getting $500 bonus and $400 a month. That was 1921. In eight games, 0–1. In 1922 it was most of year in New Haven, with four games with Braves, 1–2 record. Went 3–5, then 8–9, and, in 1925, 14–14. In 1926 was 3–3, and suffered arm injury. Paralysis and operation made it unlikely he'd ever play again. Wound up with his left arm three inches shorter than his right.

Cooney kept trying, with very little success, until 1930, when Braves let him go back to minors. Did some pitching in International League with Jersey City and Newark, and with Toledo and Indianapolis in American Association, but also was spending time at first base and in outfield. In his last season at Indianapolis, Cooney hit .371 as an outfielder, 1935. Casey Stengel, then managing Brooklyn, brought him back to majors for ten games that same season. Hit .310.

Played regularly with Dodgers 1936–37 chalking up .282 and .293 marks. Then player-coach for Braves five years. Hit .318 in 108 games, 1940, and .319 in 123 contests, 1941. Johnny then went back to Brooklyn as player in 37 games, 1943, but hit only .206. Following season he got three hits in four trips to plate, but was released; then signed with Yankees. In ten games his average was .125, and then it was back to minors with Toronto that same year. In 1945 he played 27 games for Kansas City, American Association, hitting .343 in final year as an active player.

Cooney wound up with 1172 games in majors. Had 3372 times at bat, 965 hits, 130 doubles, 26 triples, two homers, 408 runs scored, 219 RBI, 30 stolen bases for .286 average. Both of his homers were hit while with Braves. His first major league homer was hit 9/24/39; his second—and last—big league homer was hit very next day!

Johnny went back to Braves as coach, 1946, continuing in that capacity until he succeeded Billy Southworth as interim manager 8/16/49. Braves won 20, lost 25, and finished fourth under his direction. Back to coaching ranks, 1950, with Braves, through 1955 season. Moved with team from Boston to Milwaukee, 1953. Then coach for Chicago White Sox, 1957 through 1964. Sat out 1956 season at his home in Sarasota, Fla.

Cooney's managing White Sox came only when Al Lopez was away from club briefly. His umpiring experience in majors came while still with Braves. Regularly assigned umpires were traveling from Boston to New York and boat was delayed. Freddy Fitzsimmons, then with Giants, subbed as base umpire; Cooney worked behind plate.

Johnny believes that in all his 1172 games in majors he never struck out twice in any contest.

COOPER, ARLIE WILBUR P-BR-TL. B. 2/24/92, Bearsville, W. Va. D. 8/7/73, Van Nuys, Calif. 5'11½", 165. Wilbur Cooper won 202, lost 159 for Pittsburgh Pirates 1912–24. The 202 a Buccaneer record likely to stand for many years. Nearest candidate, Steve Blass, would have to win 120 more games, starting in 1972, to match old-time southpaw's achievement. Cooper's overall major league record: 216–178.

Cooper won 17 games for Marion, Ohio State League, 1911, his initial pro season; lost 11. One year with Columbus, American Association, 16–9. At end of that season Pirates paid $3,000 for him and he won three games immediately, going route in each of them, holding opposition to average of 1.67 per 9-inning game. Had 5–3 record, 1913; then in 1914, despite ERA of 2.12, trailed four other NL pitchers in effectiveness (Bill Doak, led pack with ERA of 1.72). Won 16, lost 15 that year. But led NL in 1916 with 1.87.

Wilbur won 17 in 1917, then two 19-game seasons, followed by three in which he won over 20. Losing record for 1923, 17–19, then 20–14 for 1924. Traded to Chicago Cubs that winter, Cooper had passed his peak. Spent little over one year with Windy City outfit and wound up his major league history losing four, winning none, with Detroit Tigers, 1926. Toledo, American Association, later in 1926; Oakland, Pacific Coast League, 1927–28; Shreveport, Texas League, 1929–30; San Antonio, Texas League, 1930. Managed in Pennsylvania State Association three years: McKeesport, 1935; Jeannette, 1936; Greensburg, 1937.

Cooper played in 517 games in majors, 3482 IP, 1119 earned runs, 1252 strikeouts, 853 walks with ERA of 2.89. No chance to pitch in WS, going to Cubs year before Pirates took 1925 NL flag and WS.

COOPER, MORTON CECIL P-BR-TR. B. 3/2/14, Atherton, Mo. D. 11/17/58, Little Rock, Ark. 6'2", 210. Extravagant claims were made that Mort Cooper was half of "greatest brother act in baseball." Brother Walker was about two years his junior. Coopers with Cardinals in 1940s. A couple of years Mort won more than 20 games while Walker was fine catcher and batting over .300. But we can't forget Waners, Ferrells, Meusels, Alous, Deans.

Mort Cooper, son of mail carrier who had been semipro ball player, started pro career 1933, pitching for three clubs in Western League: Des Moines, Muskogee, Springfield. Landed in Cardinal chain that year, then moved to Columbus, American Association; Asheville, Piedmont League; Houston, Texas League, en route to parent club. This took him to 1938 when landed with Cardinals without ever amassing much in way of record. Won 38, lost 28 during three seasons and part of another before reaching 22–7 mark in 1942. It was 21–8 in 1943, 22–7 in 1944. After his three 20-game seasons Mort had long, acrimonious debate over salary with Sam Breadon, Cardinal owner. Finally signed, but after winning two games, sold to Boston NL for cash. Was 7–4 for Braves that year. Had 13–11 mark 1946. Losing record 1947; to Giants, July, winning his final major league victory after that but losing five decisions. Skipped 1948. Comeback with Cubs 1949, but appeared in only one game, no decision.

Major league totals showed 128 wins, 75 losses, taking part in 297 games. Had two wins, three losses in World Series competition, 1942,43,44, with Cards. One of victories came under sad circumstances. This was only game Cardinals won from Yankees in 1943, second contest of classic. Brother Walker his catcher. Their father had died morning of game but they decided to play. "He would have wanted it that way," brothers said.

COOPER, WILLIAM WALKER C-BR-TR. B. 1/8/15, Atherton, Mo. 6'3", 205. There are some who believe Bill Dickey was outstanding catcher in AL and Gabby Hartnett best in NL. But Lon Warneke, former pitcher, later umpire, once declared that Walker Cooper greater than either. One argument favoring Warneke's conclusion was 1942 WS when St. Louis Cardinals, after losing first game to Yankees, swept next four games to win world championship. One key play came in final game. Ninth inning, Cards leading 4–2; Yankees got first two men on base, none out. Joe Gordon on second. Gerry Priddy missed bunt attempt and Cooper picked Gordon off second base, breaking back of N.Y. rally.

Cooper helped tremendously in Cardinal drive for NL pennant. Redbirds, after trailing Brooklyn 10 games in August, won 41 of last 48 games to grab pennant. Brother Mort Cooper, teaming up with Walker, won 22, lost 7. In WS Walker, besides catching in fine style, hit .286 and drove in four important runs. Incidentally, after singling in that final game in first half of ninth, he scored Cards' go-ahead run when Kurowski homered.

Another evidence of high value placed on Walker Cooper was willingness of N.Y. Giants to shell out $175,000 to buy him from St. Louis 1/5/46. Cooper was in U.S. Navy at time.

Began at Rogers, Ark., 1935; stopped off for experience in Springfield (Mo.) Sacramento, Mobile, Asheville, and Columbus (Ohio); then joined Cardinals in 1946. After his six years with Redbirds, spent three full seasons with Giants. Traded to Cincinnati 6/13/49, who in turn sent him to Boston NL 5/10/50. Remained with Braves three years in Hub and one in Milwaukee, 1953. Pittsburgh, 1954; Chicago NL, 1954–55; St. Louis NL, 1956–57.

Cooper's lifetime major league record showed 1473 games and .285 batting average. Hit an even .300 in WS of 1942,43,44 with Cardinals, playing in 16 games. In six All-Star games (1942,43,44 and 1946,47,48) hit .333, 5 for 15.

CORCORAN, LAWRENCE J. P-BR-TR. B. 8/10/59, Brooklyn, N.Y. D. 10/14/91, Newark, N. J. Larry Corcoran did it first—pitched three no-hitters. Back in early days of major leagues. Hurling for Chicago NL, turned trick against Boston, 8/19/80; Worcester, 9/20/82; and Providence, 6/27/84. Other pitchers who hurled three no-hitters came later: Cy Young, Bob Feller, Sandy Koufax. Sandy went on to twirl a fourth, that one his perfect game, 9/9/65.

With Chicago NL 1880–85. New York NL 1885–86. Washington NL

1886. Indianapolis NL 1887. Had 43–14 record 1880; 31–14 following year; 27–12, 1882; 34–20, 1883; and 35–23, 1884, last full year with Chicago. Thereafter seems to have been about through.

Lifetime major league record showed 177 wins, 89 losses, ERA 2.36. Pitched 2392-1/3 innings, fanned 1103, walked only 496. Larry played some infield and outfield when not busy on mound, but didn't hit too well—.223 in 326 games.

COURTNEY, CLINTON DAWSON (Scrap Iron) C-BL-TR. B. 3/16/27, Hall Summit, La. 5'8", 180. Clint Courtney was first major league catcher to wear glasses. Got his nickname, "Scrap Iron," because of his aggressive play; also called "Toy Bull Dog," but was quite capable of starting historic riot at old Busch Stadium in St. Louis while member of Browns. Outspoken in praise of his own abilities, which, after all, were somewhat limited. Satchel Paige called him "meanest man I ever met," while they were teammates on Browns. "Im glad I'm on his side," said Satch. "He's a great catcher. I'd like to see him hitting for me with winning run on third base and one out."

Courtney came up through minors in Yankee farm system. Started at Beaumont, Texas League, 1947 and saw service in Bisbee, Ariz.; Augusta, Ga.; Norfolk; Manchester; and Kansas City, then in American Association. Played one game for Yankees, 1951, but had no chance to oust Yogi Berra behind plate. So was traded to Browns 11/23/51. Played 119 games for St. Louis AL, 1952: hit .286, got reputation for rugged approach to game, won AL Rookie of Year honors. In game of 7/12/52, in Yankee Stadium, Clint slid into second base. Billy Martin made high, hard tag on him, after which Courtney rushed at Billy, who knocked off Clint's glasses. Another occasion Bob Cerv of Yanks, ex-football player from U. of Nebraska, banged into him at plate, adding fuel to fires of animosity. Riot broke out in St. Louis when Yankees played Browns 4/28/53. AL President Will Harridge later called Courtney instigator who "violated all rules of sportsmanship." McDougald of Yanks, earlier in game, had come into home plate standing up. Collided with Courtney even though play was not close, causing him to drop ball. Then, when Browns came to bat, Clint hit one of Allie Reynolds' pitches off right field screen. Tried to stretch hit into double, and slid high into shortstop Phil Rizzuto. At this point Yankee players rushed him. Reynolds reportedly was first man to strike Courtney. Free-for-all ensued, with Brown players getting into fray. Fans tossed pop bottles onto field to show their displeasure. Clint lost shoe in mixup. When peace finally was restored and Harridge conducted his investigation, Courtney was fined $250; Billy Hunter of Browns, $150; Billy Martin, $150; Joe Collins, Reynolds, and McDougald $100 each. Last four, of course, Yankees. One writer called Courtney "cussin', tobacco-chewing throwback to another era"—time of old Baltimore Orioles of 1890s.

Clint got nickname "Scrap Iron," during spring training, 1952. Players were standing around railroad station in Burbank, Calif. One word led to another with Buddy Blattner, sports announcer. Finally they decided to have race down railroad tracks in dark. Courtney was breezing along until he stumbled on ties or hit hole. He tumbled wildly, scraped hide off his arms, and cinders cut deep gashes in his legs. Though he was covered with tape and felt miserable, did not ask out of game next day. Courtney said it was a lot easier catching ball game than risking Mgr. Hornsby's wrath by telling him how he got his wounds.

Browns' franchise was transferred to Baltimore 10/29/53, so Clint played 1954 with Orioles. Traded to Chicago AL 12/6/54; traded to Washington 6/7/55. Traded back to Baltimore 4/3/60. Divided 1961 between Baltimore and Kansas City AL, playing 23 games in his final year in majors. Hit .309 for Senators and White Sox, 1955, and .300 for Senators, 1956. Overall major league record was .268 for 946 games, with 127 doubles, 17 triples, 38 homers among his 750 hits.

Clint was with Rochester; then Durham, Oklahoma City, and San Antonio, working for Houston Astros' organization. Coach for Astros, 1965; later was minor league instructor for Atlanta Braves; managed Shreveport Braves, 1970; manager, Savannah, in Braves' organization, 1972–73, Manager, Richmond, 6/15/73.

COVELESKI, HARRY FRANK (Giant Killer) P-BRL-TL. B. 4/23/86, Shamokin, Pa. D. 8/4/50, Shamokin, Pa. 6′, 180. Elder brother of Stan Coveleski, also major league pitcher. Harry got his nickname, "Giant Killer," late in 1908 season. After working in coal mines of Pennsylvania, scouts for Philadelphia NL signed him and he won one game for club, 1907, as relief pitcher. Following year was farmed out to Lancaster, Tri-State League, where he became known as brilliant strikeout pitcher. Recalled toward end of year, beat Giants three times in important five-game set and really knocked McGraw team out of pennant, though that was same year Merkle failed to touch second base. Many have focused loss of pennant on that. But had Giants been able to beat rookie southpaw instead of losing to him three times, Merkle's so-called boner would not have meant anything.

Following season, Giants harassed Covaleski at every meeting of two teams. Seems that Harry's fiancee eloped with drum major. Giants never let Coveleski forget it; organized sort of drum corps for use against him. Riding and noise is supposed to have rattled Coveleski sufficiently to ruin his effectiveness. Won six, lost 11 that year. In 1910 was with Cincinnati, then dropped back to minors. However, in 1913 Coveleski had 29–9 season at Chattanooga, and in 1914 he was back in majors, with Detroit. Won 22, lost 12. Had fine marks like 23–13 in 1915 and

21–10 in 1916, then tapered off, leaving majors after 1918 season.

Harry won 82 major league games, lost 54. His ERA seems to have been 2.39 but discrepancies in records might alter this figure slightly.

Family name originally was Kowalewski but was simplified somewhat when pitchers entered baseball.

COVELESKI, STANLEY ANTHONY P-BR-TR. B. 7/13/90, Shamokin, Pa. 5'9½", 178. Stanley and Harry Coveleski together won 36 games in AL, 1916, but they were not teammates like Dizzy and Paul Dean, brothers who pitched Cardinals to 1934 flag. Stanley was in first year with Cleveland while Harry was nearing end of career with Detroit. Stan lasted considerably longer than his elder brother and won 214 games while losing 141. Harry wound up with 82 big league victories and 54 defeats. Both of their winning percentages come out to .603, but Harry would have slight edge if you carried figures one more decimal point.

Besides Harry, Stan had two other ball-playing brothers: Frank, who pitched for an "outlaw" circuit, "Union League," 1907; John, who played third base and outfield in minors.

Stan's first pro experience was in 1908 with Shamokin, Atlantic League, then was in Tri-State League, 1909–12 with Lancaster, Pa., and Atlantic City. Had brief trial with Philadelphia AL, 1912, winning two, losing one, but went back to minors for more experience. Spokane, Northwestern League, 1913–14; Portland, Pacific Coast League, 1915. Then nine years with Cleveland, one of mainstays of Indian pitching staff.

Successful too—four consecutive 20-game winning seasons, 1918–21. After two seasons when he lost one more game than he won, 1923–24, Indians traded him to Washington. Proved he was not through by winning 20, losing five, with ERA of 2.84. Both of these marks were tops in AL. His help enabled Washington to win its second straight pennant.

In 1926 Stan took 14 games, lost 11, then dropped down to 2–1 in 1927. Final season was 1928 with N.Y. Yankees, winning five, losing one. Stan's lifetime ERA was 2.88 to go along with those 214 wins and 141 losses in majors.

Stan's performance in 1920 WS for Cleveland was outstanding. Won three games from Dodgers, allowed five hits each occasion, walked only two men, allowed just two runs and had one shutout. This meant an ERA of 0.67 for 27 innings pitched. In other WS, 1925, with Senators, Pittsburgh touched him for 16 hits, 7 runs (6 earned), in 14-1/3 IP, 2 losses. His overall WS record: 5 games, 41-1/3 IP, 3–2, ERA 1.74.

Stan was spitballer. Hall of Fame 1969.

COX, JOSEPH CASEY P-BR-TR. B. 7/3/41, Long Beach, Calif. 6'5", 215. Casey Cox, with Washington Senators several years, was first player from club to set up residence in Arlington, Tex., late in 1971 after franchise was transferred to Lone Star State. Sold tickets for club during winter. But before 1972 season was over Casey was member of New York Yankees. Yanks, however, gave unconditional release early in 1973 season.

Rangers got southpaw, Rich Hinton, six years younger than Cox, in exchange. Casey was ready for 1973 season with record of 39 wins, 42 losses in AL with 3.69 ERA. Had pitched 759 innings in 307 games, all but his last five with Senators and Rangers.

Cox attended Long Beach City and Los Angeles State colleges. Pro experience started at Rocky Mount, N.C., 1962, and included stops at Charleston, W. Va.; Burlington and Peninsula in Carolina League; Hawaii; York, Pa.; and Buffalo. With Washington, 1966, and parts of 1967–68, spending time in minors both seasons. Remained with Senators, 1969, won 12, lost 7, 2.77 ERA. Then had 8–12 and 5–7 records with Washington. His 1972 mark with Rangers and Yankees added up to 40 appearances, 3–6, 4.44 ERA.

COX, WILLIAM DROUGHT   Executive. B. 11/14/09, New York, N.Y.
Short-time owner of Philadelphia Phillies before Carpenter family took over. Judge Landis barred him from baseball for allegedly making small bets on his own team. In baseball—and out—all in 1943. In more recent years Cox has been known for his activities in promoting soccer on international scale. However, Cox has had many other interests from race horses to philately.

At 15 entered New York U., youngest in his class. Switched to Yale. Catcher on baseball team, took part in track, quit college after sophomore year. Went to work for Wall Street broker on fateful day, 10/29/29, of collossal stock market crash. However, Cox's perspicacity enabled him to exploit famous *N.Y. Sun* editorial, "Yes, Virginia, There Is a Santa Claus." Reportedly bought rights to it for $1000 and made $10,000 profit republishing it in book form.

Successful investments with lumber brokers. Linked this with philately by promoting issue of stamps depicting various trees. Headed syndicate that bought Philadelphia NL franchise during wartime for price believed to be $80,000. Hired Bucky Harris as manager. Club had finished last in 1942. Harris had team in fifth place, midseason 1943, just six games out of third place. Cox fired Harris, who was extremely popular with players.

Problems with Czar Landis too. When Judge found Cox owned race horse he ordered him to sell it. Cox did. Tom Dewey, then governor of N.Y. State, offered to make Cox state racing commissioner. Landis said acceptance would end Cox's connection with baseball. Cox stayed with Phils. Then came charges and countercharges about Cox betting sums of

$25 to $100 on own team. All-powerful Landis then barred Cox forever as ineligible to be connected with baseball. Cox sold interests, supposedly making small profit on deal.

Cox lost money in promotion of pro football in New York during 1940's; later promoted International Soccer League and for time was part owner of San Diego franchise. Promoted issuance of series of stamps by Nicaragua honoring outstanding soccer players from various nations; later did similar promotion of Olympic athletes on stamps issued by Dominican Republic. Has published various philatelic albums.

COX, WILLIAM RICHARD 3B-BR-TR. B. 8/29/19, Newport, Pa. 5'8½'', 150. Billy Cox was shortstop for Pittsburgh Pirates 1946–47 but made his name as brilliant-fielding third baseman for Brooklyn Dodgers after that. Helped Flatbush team into 1949,52, 53 WS, but "Bums" as they were called, lost each classic. One of Cox's distinctions is fact he went up to plate three times in one inning 5/21/52, equaling major league record.

Billy's pro career started at Harrisburg, Inter-State League, 1940. Hit .288 that first season, 120 games, but boosted his record to .363 to lead league following year. Starred in field as well, meriting his advance to Pittsburgh for ten games, 1941. Military service interrupted his career from 1942 through 1945, but he came back, 1946, to play in 121 games and bat respectable .290 for Pirates. Hit 15 homers with Pirates, 1947, taking advantage of "Greenberg Gardens." It will be recalled that Hank was with Pittsburgh that year, and left field fence was brought closer to plate so he could take advantage. This was Cox's best homer total for any season, though he did slap 10 of them in Ebbets Field, 1953. After 1947 season Cox, Preacher Roe, and Gene Mauch were traded to Brooklyn for Dixie Walker, Hal Gregg, and Vic Lombardi. Dodgers converted Cox into third sacker and he soon was recognized as one of finest in NL history. Billy's best hitting season in Brooklyn was 1953, when he had .291. He was with Baltimore AL, 1955, but hit just .211 in 53 games and dropped out of majors after that.

Lifetime batting average: .262 in 1058 games, with 66 homers, 351 RBI. In his three WS, played 15 games and hit .302, including one homer, five doubles, seven runs scored, and six RBI.

Billy now bartender in his birthplace, on Juniata River northwest of Harrisburg.

CRAIG, ROGER LEE P-BR-TR. B. 2/17/31, Durham, N. C. 6'4'', 192. Minor league pitching instructor for Los Angeles NL. Looks back to his days with Los Angeles Dodgers for his most successful seasons. Won 11, lost five in 1959, had 8–3 record, 1960. Then after 5–6 in 1961, New York Mets got him. Part of floundering expansion team of Casey Stengel.

Craig pitched first Met game in history, got off to ominous start. In first inning Bill White of Cardinals reached third base. Roger started his motion to plate; ball dropped out of his hand. Umpire ruled balk—and Mets were behind, 1–0. Cards eventually got 10 more runs.

Mets lost 119 more games that season and Craig's losses totaled 24. Somehow he must have been good to win 10. Following year he lost 22, but won only five times. Tied NL mark for consecutive losses, 18, during 1963 season. Reprieve came in 1964 when traded to St. Louis Cardinals, pennant winners that year. While Roger's record with Redbirds only so-so, 7–9, he did excellent relief work in two WS games, allowing no earned runs in five innings, and was credited with one of Cardinal victories over Yankees.

Attended North Carolina State College before starting his trek through minors. Newport News, 1950, then Valdosta, Elmira, Pueblo, Montreal before his 1955 debut with Brooklyn Dodgers. In 1958 and 1959 spent time with St. Paul and Spokane clubs, then back to Dodgers, now in Los Angeles. After St. Louis experience, Craig with Cincinnati, 1965; Philadelphia NL, 1966; also Seattle, Pacific Coast League, same season.

Roger's first appearance in WS came with Brooklyn, 1955. Won one decision over Yankees in fifth game, but had to be relieved in seventh. In 1956 he was charged with one loss, and again a loss in 1959 set with L.A. Overall WS performance: 2–2, ERA 6.58.

Major league totals: 74–98, ERA 3.82.

Craig managed Albuquerque to second place in Texas League's Western Division, 1968, then became pitching coach for San Diego Padres 1969–71.

CRAMER, ROGER MAXWELL (Doc) OF-BL-TR. B. 7/22/05, Beach Haven, N.J. 6'2", 185. Doc Cramer never planned on being doctor; expected to become carpenter. Spent lot of time with friend who was physician, and people began calling him Doc. Instead of becoming master carpenter, Cramer became skilled outfielder of major league quality.

Like so many others, however, Doc started as pitcher. Cy Perkins, old-time catcher for Philadelphia AL, was taking day off on orders from his manager, Connie Mack. Local folk in Cramer's home town persuaded him to umpire ball game. Cramer did pitching, and impressed Perkins. This led to his joining A's in spring of 1929.

Needed experience—but not much. Athletics farmed him out to Martinsburg. When they discovered how he could hit, Cramer wasn't used much on mound. Pitched 44 innings, 2–2. But played total of 104 games as infielder and pitcher—and led Blue Ridge League in hitting with cool .404. Back to A's that same year, for two games. Portland,

Pacific Coast League, most of 1930. Then remained in AL until close of 1948 season.

Twice went six-for-six, 6/20/32 and 7/13/35, equaling major league record. Hit for cycle—single, double, triple, and homer—6/10/34. While with Athletics hit .336, 1932, and .332 , 1935. Traded to Boston AL 1/4/36. To Washington 12/12/40. To Detroit 12/12/41. Unconditional release given him 11/11/48. Buffalo, International League, 1949; Seattle, 1950.

Cramer often used as leadoff man and was fine one. Not a power hitter. Made 37 homers during major league career but over four-year stretch in Boston, 1936–39, did not get single homer. In 1947, while with Detroit, Mgr. Steve O'Neill used Cramer great deal as pinch hitter. During early part of season he batted for Catcher Birdie Tebbetts six times, made four pinch hits. Then Tigers traded Tebbetts to Boston. Doc moaned disconsolately, "It's like tearing up my meal ticket. A game is not official until the announcement goes out, 'Cramer for Tebbetts.' What am I going to do now?" But Cramer went 9 for 33 as pinch hitter that season for .273, not bad for emergency batsman.

Doc left majors with lifetime record of 2239 games, 2705 hits, 1357 runs. Had 396 doubles, 109 triples, 37 homers, 842 RBI. His average was .296. In WS play, 1931, with Philadelphia and 1945 with Detroit: 9 games, .387, 12 for 31, 7 runs, 6 RBI.

Cramer acted as coach with Tigers, 1948, but appeared in four games as player that year. Also coached at Seattle, 1950, appearing twice as pinch hitter. Coach, Chicago AL, 1951–53.

CRANDALL, DELMAR WESLEY C-BR-TR. B. 3/5/30, Ontario, Calif. 6'1½", 202. Del Crandall, who spent most of major league career in Milwaukee as member of NL Braves, returned to his adopted home as manager of Brewers in AL late in May, 1972. Took over losing club from Dave Bristol.

Del caught 1479 major league games and appeared in several others as an outfielder and first baseman. Took part in 1573 contests in all, hit .254. His 1276 hits included 179 doubles, 18 triples, 179 homers. Eight times he was able to hit 15 homers or more, his highest number being 26 during 1955 season. Scored 585 runs, drove in 657. No great shakes as base thief; only 26 steals during 16 years in big time.

Crandall became pro in 1948 with Leavenworth, Western Association. Moved up to Milwaukee team of American Association for five games that same season. Spent several weeks at Evansville, III League, 1949, hitting .351 in 38 games. Then up to Braves, then still in Boston, appearing in 67 games and hitting .263 his first part season in majors.

Del spent 1951 and 1952 in military service. When he came back, club had moved to Milwaukee and there he remained through 1963 season.

During this period he became popular favorite as regular catcher, occasionally filling in at first base. In 1961 played just 15 games due to arm trouble.

San Francisco NL, 1964; Pittsburgh, 1955; Cleveland, 1966. In two WS with Braves, 1957,58, Crandall played 13 games, hit .227. Tied WS record for most double plays started by catcher in seven-game Series with two in 1957. Del was on NL All-Star squads 1955,59,60,62.

As minor league manager in Dodger organization, piloted Albuquerque in Texas League, 1969–70, winning flag in second season there. Shifted to Evansville, American Association, 1971; team finished fourth. Back in same assignment at start of 1972, his club was in second place when called up to manage Brewers.

Photography his hobby, Del is hoping to pose for pictures as successful major league manager.

CRAVATH, CLIFFORD CARLTON (Gavvy) OF-BR-TR. B. 3/23/81, San Diego, Calif. D. 5/23/63, Laguna Beach, Calif. 5'11", 185. Judge Gavvy Cravath, onetime home run king of NL, once fined fisherman two cents because he did not like detection methods of fish and game wardens. Culprit was convicted of illegally possessing abalone.

Cravath set home run record for major leagues for modern times with 24 in 1915. That was in dead-ball era, before Babe Ruth created new record, 29, in 1919.

Gavvy started pro career 1903 with Los Angeles, Pacific Coast League. After five years moved up to Boston AL for 1908 but hit only .256. Had 22 games with Chicago AL and Washington in 1909 before being shipped to Minneapolis that season. In his 1911 season there, hit 29 homers and merited another chance in big time. Spent next nine years with Philadelphia NL. In 1913 hit .341, slugged 19 home runs. Following year, his average dropped to .299 but still swatted 19 homers. Then came his 24-homer year, 1915. In all, led NL in homers five times—1913–15 and 1918, 19—and tied for lead in 1917.

In 1919 when Jack Coombs was released in midseason as manager of Phils, Cravath was asked to take over. Piloted Phils rest of year and through 1920. Team finished last both years. Spent 1921 season with Salt Lake, Pacific Coast League, and 1922 with Minnespolis. Then retired to California to sell real estate. Became justice of the peace and justice court judge, 1927.

Cravath had 1219 major league games, 3950 at bats, 575 runs, 1134 hits, 119 home runs, 89 stolen bases, lifetime batting average of .287. His only World Series came in 1915 when Phils lost to Red Sox in five games. Cravath got two hits in 16 trips, for .125 average.

CRAWFORD, SAMUEL EARL (Wahoo Sam)   OF-BL-TL. B. 4/18/80, Wahoo, Nebr. D. 6/15/68, Hollywood, Calif. 6', 190. Only player ever to lead both major leagues in home runs. Took NL title 1901, while with Cincinnati, hitting 16. Won AL title 1908, seven round-trippers, with Tigers. Ed Barrow, fine judge of playing talent, who converted Babe Ruth into slugging outfielder, once declared there never was better hitter than Crawford. Good fielder, strong, accurate arm.

Crawford as teenager was studying to be barber but traveled all over Nebraska with ball team, pitching, playing outfield. After game, players would pass hat for contributions. Landed job 1899 with Chatham, Ontario, Canadian League. Hit .370 in 43 games but club disbanded. Caught on with Grand Rapids, Western League, same season, hitting .333 for 60 games. Made grade with Cincinnati NL also same season, getting into 31 contests and batting .307.

After leading league in homers in 1901, had to be content to lead NL in triples, 1902. Then jumped to Detroit, leading AL in triples, 1903. Took lead in triples, AL, total of five different seasons. Potent factor in Detroit's pennant-winning seasons of 1907,08,09.

Crawford batted fourth in Detroit lineup, after Cobb. Told of play he and Cobb worked occasionally when conditions right. If Cobb should be on third base when Crawford walked, Ty would give him sign. Crawford would trot down toward first at leisurely pace. Then suddenly would start to run, tearing for second. If opponents tried to stop Crawford, Cobb would dash for plate. Sometimes, said Crawford, opponents would get one of base runners, but ofttimes neither.

Wahoo Sam continued with Detroit through 1917 season, winding up with 2505 major league games, 2964 hits in 9,579 times at bat for .309 average. Scored 1392 runs, made 455 doubles, 312 triples (major league record), 95 homers, stole 367 bases. Crawford's World Series batting not spectacular—.243, 17 games.

Spent 1918–21 with Los Angeles, Pacific Coast League. Umpired four years in same league before retiring to quiet life, puttering in his garden. Hall of Fame 1957.

CRAWFORD, WILLIE MURPHY   OF-BL-TL. B. 9/7/46, Los Angeles, Calif. 6'1", 200. As 1973 rolled around, Willie Crawford had not yet paid off fully on Los Angeles Dodgers' investment of $100,000 for his signature. Willie received this bonus when he left Fremont High School, 1964. This was same school that produced Brock Davis and Bobby Tolan. Crawford played football and baseball in high school, and was 9.6-second sprinter for 100-yard dash.

Crawford carried .252 career batting average into 1973 after 581 games with Dodgers. His 377 hits included 61 doubles, 21 triples, 40 homers. Scored 243 runs, had 162 RBI.

Willie was 17 when he signed. During next four summers he was at Santa Barbara, Albuquerque and Spokane, along with limited stays with Dodgers. In 1968, along with .295 average in 87 games at Spokane, Crawford played 61 contests with Dodgers and hit .251. Since then his best season was 1971 when he batted .281 in 114 games. Started that season hitting around .200, but changed his stance. Hit .421 as pinch hitter and finally began playing regularly; was able to hit .377 against left-handers with 20 hits in 53 trips. But in 1972 he dropped back to .251 in 96 games, one point below his lifetime big league mark.

Appeared in one WS, 1965, as pinch hitter. Got one single off Jim "Mudcat" Grant of Minnesota Twins but was unsuccessful in another attempt, so had average of .500.

CRITZ, HUGH MELVILLE 2B-BR-TR. B. 9/17/1900, Starkville, Miss. 5'8", 148. Hughie Critz, fine little second baseman for Cincinnati Reds and New York Giants in 1920's and 1930's, had superstitious habit. In those days ball players left their gloves on outfield grass when their team went to bat—all except pitchers and catchers. Once in great while batted ball might hit a glove and take fluke bounce. Occasionally player might step on glove and have his stride thrown off. So, some years ago ruling required players to remove all gloves from playing area.

Critz, in old days, would start every inning in field by going religiously to glove of rival second baseman and adjusting it, or moving it slightly, before he picked up his own glove. He constantly was picking up anything blown onto field—bits of paper, twine; or anything that might have worked its way out of skinned part of infield—pebbles, tiny bits of glass, or whatnot.

Critz was especially active removing real or imaginary objects from field if he made error on ground ball, which wasn't too often. This used to burn up Cincinnati groundkeeper, who had carefully manicured infield before every game. By implication, he felt Critz was blaming pebbles on infield for his errors. Once Critz muffed pop fly. Groundkeeper, on sidelines, yelled long string of profanity at Critz. "That's one error you can't blame on those imaginary pebbles, you————!"

Critz, however, was good fielder, regardless of pebbles. Holds NL record for most years with 500 or more assists, five, together with Bill Mazeroski of Pirates. As batsman, managed .322 his first season with Reds, 1924, in 102 games, but after that was able to reach .290 mark only twice. Finished major league career batting .268 in 1478 games. His 38 career homers were spread out so that he never hit more than six in any one season. Had 195 doubles, 95 triples, 97 stolen bases, and 531 RBI.

Hughie started with Chattanooga, 1920; Greenwood, Miss., 1921; Memphis, 1922; Minneapolis, 1923–24, being sold to Cincinnati for $30,000 and reporting for 102 games that same year, 1924. After sparkling in Cincinnati until 1930, N. Y. Giants acquired him in trade for Pitcher Larry Benton 5/21/30. After .187 hitting mark in 65 games, 1935, Critz said adieu to majors. His only WS was 1933 with Giants, with three hits in 22 at bats for .136 average.

CRONIN, JOSEPH EDWARD SS-BR-TR. B. 10/12/06, San Francisco, Calif. 6', 187. Joe Cronin's father, Jeremiah, born in Ireland, didn't have the luck of the Irish when he lost everything in the 1906 San Francisco earthquake and fire. But somewhere along the line, son Joseph came up with the luck his father lacked. Joe put hard work together with luck—and for most of his life has led charmed existence. Rejected in his first big league tryout with Pittsburgh; met lukewarm reception from Clark Griffith after Scout Joe Engel bought him from Kansas City; but he married Griffith's niece and went on to become outstanding player, successful manager. Ultimately became first player in history of AL to become its chief executive. Joe's most recent contract as AL president was due to expire 12/15/72 but club owners, late in 1971, voted to extend it another three years after 1972—and gave him additional title, chairman of board.

Joe gave early indications of athletic prowess while in grade school and high school. At 14 won junior tennis championship of San Francisco; played soccer, basketball, and baseball. Was offered athletic scholarship at St. Mary's College but turned it down because of need to work to help family. Worked in bank and became substitute instructor in public playgrounds. Worked with kids who later made grade in majors, including Frank Crosetti, Dario Lodigiani, and Eddie Joost.

Played Sunday baseball with semipros in Napa, Calif., attracting attention of Scout Joe Devine, who signed him for Pittsburgh organization. Sent to Johnstown, Middle Atlantic League, for 1925. There he hit .313 in 99 games. Played 38 games with Pirates, 1926, and hit .265. But spent most of season with New Haven, Eastern League, where he had .320 average for 66 games. In 1927 Joe was with Pittsburgh again, but played only 12 games and hit .227. Glenn Wright was Pirate shortstop that year, playing in 143 games, good hitter with power, so although Joe was eligible for WS play against Yankees, he did not get into game.

Following spring Pirates gave up on him, sold him to Kansas City, American Association. Joe fielded well but hit only .245 in 74 games. But something about skinny youngster appealed to Washington scout Engel, who surprised Kansas City management by offering to buy Cronin. Price of $7500 was pretty steep for young guy who couldn't hit .250. So

Washington President Clark Griffith was inclined to doubt wisdom of his scout's judgment. But Engel talked fast, told Griff to wait and see. Also told Griffith's niece, Mildred, working in Senators' front office, that in Cronin he had brought her a future husband. That was 1928. Griff didn't see much of hitter in fellow who batted .242 in 63 games rest of year. And while Cronin did marry Mildred ultimately, she later laughed and said it was no whirlwind courtship. They weren't married until 1934. Cronin, meanwhile, worked hard at becoming hitter, improving his fielding. So, in 1929 he got his average up to .283 in 145 games, and boosted it to .346 in 1930 with 14 home runs. Continued to hit above .300 and Griffith made him playing manager for 1933. All he did was lead Senators to pennant, batting .309 himself and driving in 118 runs. In WS that year he hit .318, but Senators went down to defeat at hands of Bill Terry's N.Y. Giants. After 1934 season when Senators dropped down to seventh place, Joe and Mildred got married. Meanwhile, Tom Yawkey, owner of Boston Red Sox, wanted Cronin as player and manager. Griffith wasn't anxious to sell his shortstop, manager, and now member of family. But Yawkey kept raising ante until he offered $250,000 cash, plus Lyn Lary. Furthermore, was ready to give Joe five-year contract at then-fancy salary of $50,000 annually. Griffith got Joe's consent to deal, and trade went through.

In Boston, Cronin was not able to get Red Sox into WS in his first eleven years as player-manager. Did very well as batsman, but during this period could come no closer to flag than second place four times. But in 1946 Red Sox finally made it—winning 104 games and beating out Detroit Tigers by 12 lengths. By this time Joe, who had broken his leg 4/19/45, was no longer playing. In 1946 WS Red Sox battled St. Louis Cardinals down to wire. Difference between victory and defeat was famous three-base sprint of Enos Slaughter of Cardinals in last half of eighth inning of seventh game. Cards won game and Series by identical scores, 4–3.

Red Sox finished fourth in 1947 standings, after which Tom Yawkey elevated Cronin to position of vice president, treasurer, and general manager, turning field management over to Joe McCarthy. AL tapped him for presidency of that circuit 1/31/59.

Joe had plenty of heroics during his playing career. The skinny youngster without power developed into a feared batsman, as 1423 RBI for his career total attest. From record of no homers in his first spells at Pittsburgh and Washington, Cronin hit 171 during lifetime, with high-water mark of 24 in 1940. And many of his later home runs were hit as pinch batsman.

He pulled that stunt twice in one day 6/17/43 during doubleheader against Philadelphia Athletics. That year he had three other pinch homers, for total of five; this set AL record for season.

It is noteworthy that Cronin, in 2124 major league games, hit .302. Had 2285 hits in 7577 AB, with 1233 runs scored. Hits included those 171 homers as well as 515 doubles, 117 three-baggers. MVP in AL, 1930. Hall of Fame 1956.

As AL president Joe has kept things on fairly even keel for most part. However, encountered considerable criticism when two umpires, Al Salerno and Bill Valentine, were fired as "incompetent" shortly after they led drive to organize AL umpires and seek better salaries and working conditions.

CROSBY, EDWARD CARLTON (Spider) Inf.-BL-TR. B. 5/26/49, Long Beach, Calif. 6'2", 180. Got his nickname because of his long legs. Uses contact lenses. Must be effective because he seldom strikes out. No great power, however.

Teammate of Bobby Grich in high school. Received much coaching and encouragement from father Crosby, who was all-round athlete at U. of Georgia. Attended Long Beach City College until he received modest bonus for signing with Cardinal organization.

Farmed to Lewiston, Northwest League, 1969. Hit .295 in 70 games. Then spent 78 games with Arkansas in Texas League, 1970, before joining Cardinals for 38 contests. Hit .253 and was sent down for further seasoning, this time to Tulsa, American Association. In 135 games there had .289 average, with 30 doubles, 5 triples, 4 homers.

Stuck with Cardinals, 1972, when Julian Javier was traded to Cincinnati. Crosby proved versatile infielder for St. Louis, 1972, filling in at second, third, short. Hit .217 in 101 games.

CROSBY, HARRY L. (Bing) Executive. B. 5/2/04, Tacoma, Wash. Vice president, Pittsburgh Pirates. Vocalist with Paul Whiteman's Orchestra at age 23. Originally derided as mere "crooner" in age of Rudy Vallee and Russ Columbo. Son of brewery bookkeeper, who loved baseball. Played semipro while working at Spokane Ideal Laundry.

Bing has finger in dozens of remunerative enterprises—oil wells, ranches, cattle, horses, race tracks, to name some. Sponsors golf tournament which annually attracts dazzling list of celebrities at Pebble Beach, Calif.

Has sold millions of popular platters, among them "White Christmas." Famed for several *Road* pictures—Singapore, Rio, Zanzibar, etc.—and *Going My Way* .

Unusually modest, almost retiring, for public figure in entertainment world.

CROSETTI, FRANK PETER JOSEPH (Crow) SS-BR-TR. B. 10/4/10, San Francisco, Calif. 5'10", 165. Frank Crosetti, who coached Minnesota

Twins 1970–71, must have waved home something like 16,000 base runners since he gave up active play for N. Y. Yankees. Began coaching as player-coach 1947; off active list as player after 1948. Remained as Yankee coach until close of 1968. Coached Seattle AL team, 1969.

Crow could have lived in lap of luxury without ever drawing salary in big leagues. Drew almost $150,000 in WS bonuses for first-place finishes alone. To this could be added several thousand dollars in bonuses when his teams finished "in the money" but not winning pennant. Not bad for fellow who was high school dropout after junior year. Early in career Crow became friendly with A. P. Giannini, fabulous financier and pioneer in far-flung Bank of America. Giannini told Frank to invest in real estate, apartments, business buildings. Now Crosetti probably could start bank of his own.

Crosetti, as kid, didn't have any baseballs. So he and pals would break nubs off corncobs and use them for ball. They's take a board, cut down one end to make a handle and used this for bat. Things did improve, however, and by age 17 Crow was playing for money in Butte, Mont. Later, attracted attention playing in winter league on sandlots of San Francisco. Signed with San Francisco Seals, Pacific Coast League, 1928. In exhibition game against Pittsburgh Pirates, youngster slapped homer off Joe Dawson with bases loaded. Frank hit only .248 that year in 96 games, but followed with .314, .334, and .343 averages, as well as showing PCL fans some fancy shortfielding. Yankees bought him for $75,000; made good immediately. Soon became recognized as outstanding shortstop but did play some at third and second.

Crow struck out good deal in majors and never hit .300, but was still dangerous man at plate. Once had dubious honor of striking out twice in one inning (9/9/32). Struck out oftener than any other player in AL, 1937,38. Went through 10-inning game without handling chance at shortstop, equaling major league record, 4/16/40. But generally covered lot of ground and set various fielding marks. Got opponents out using hidden ball trick; very adept at this. And when he couldn't hit pitcher, often had skill to get on base by getting hit by pitched ball.

Yankees won pennant eight times while Crosetti was player. Crow made his contribution each time, then followed up as Yankee coach in 15 more WS. Didn't always agree with umpires. In 1942 he protested play with such vehemence that after arbiter Bill Summers turned in his report, Crow was suspended for 30 days, into 1943 season.

Crosetti's major league totals add up to 1682 games, 6277 AB, 1006 runs, 1541 hits, 260 doubles, 65 triples, 98 homers, 649 RBI, 113 stolen bases, and an average of .245.

In 1938 WS Crosetti hit homer off fading Dizzy Dean, but his overall WS hitting averaged only .174 with 20 hits in 115 AB. Took part in 29 games, scored 16 runs, had 5 doubles, 1 triple, besides that four-master off Dean. Stole one base in WS play.

Makes his home in Stockton, Calif.

CROSLEY, POWEL, JR. Executive. B. 9/18/86, Cincinnati, Ohio. D. 3/28/61, Cincinnati, Ohio. 6'3". When radio began to be popular half century ago, Powel Crosley, Jr., like many of his contemporaries, was confronted with financial problems. Son, Powel III, nine years old, wanted radio. More and more families were getting crystal sets. Father and son went downtown in Cincinnati and priced some sets. Asking price of $135 was too much for Crosley budget, so father persuaded son to go along with idea they'd build their own—at cost of $20. Set worked—and before long Powel Crosley, Jr. took steps to become large manufacturer of radio receiving sets. Eventually his company manufactured refrigerators, other appliances. And, to stimulate sale of radios, Crosley felt there should be more broadcasting stations. Built WLW, Cincinnati, 500,000 watts, most powerful in country, and called it "The Nation's Station." Later also owned WSAI, Cincinnati. Crosley had been tinkerer and inventor from boyhood. During World War I, invented highly successful radiator cap for holding American flags on front of cars and sold thousands of them. Tried to market small car, but idea did not click then and had to give up idea that many years later became highly popular.

Crosley knew almost nothing about baseball when Larry MacPhail went to Cincinnati as general manager after club was taken over by bank after 1933 season. MacPhail needed far more working capital than bank was willing to risk, so he went to Crosley, who reacted favorably to MacPhail's salesmanship, put up necessary cash, and became owner and president of Reds. Under dynamic impetus supplied largely by MacPhail, club began improvement that led to NL pennants, 1939,40, although MacPhail and Crosley parted after 1936 season. During tieup with MacPhail, however, night baseball had been introduced to majors, 1935. Ball park, which had been called Redland Field, was renamed Crosley Field and continued in use until new stadium was built and opened, 1971.

Some years before his death Crosley sold his broadcasting facilities and appliance factories to Avco Corporation for $16 million. Set up Crosley Foundation, and when he died it was to administer ball club. Foundation sold Reds to Bill DeWitt, 1962.

CROWDER, ALVIN FLOYD (General) P-BL-TR. B. 1/11/99, Winston-Salem, N.C. D. 4/3/72, Winston-Salem, N.C. 5'10", 170. Alvin Crowder was no general but he was good enough pitcher to win 16 consecutive ball games in AL. Nickname came from those who remembered General Enoch Crowder who served in army during World War I.

Alvin toiled for Washington, St. Louis, and Detroit in AL, and won his 16 straight victories while working for Senators.

Crowder did serve in army, even though he never approached rank of general—almost three years, including 11 months in Siberia, then in Philippines. Signed with San Francisco, Pacific Coast League, 1922 but was released after one game. Got his real start following year in his home town, Winston-Salem, Piedmont League, winning 10, losing seven. Divided 1924 between Rochester and Waterbury; joined Birmingham, 1925. Won 17, lost 4, for Birmingham, 1926, and was sold to Washington. In his second season in majors, Senators traded Crowder to St. Louis and, given plenty of opportunity by Browns, in 1928 won 21 games while losing five. Had 17–15 record in 1929, and during 1930 season landed with Senators again. Had 18–16 record that year, and 18–11 in 1931. Crowder's long skein of victories started during 1932 season, when he grabbed 15 in row. Led AL pitchers in winning percentage, 26–13 for .667; also in innings pitched, with 327. Won eight games from Chicago AL that year, losing none.

As 1933 season started, Crowder added another win, 16th in row, before Boston Red Sox sent him down to defeat 4/17/33. While 16 consecutive victories is neither AL nor major league record, few have been so successful. Crowder had 10 straight wins in 1928, incidentally; that same season he struck out Ty Cobb three times in one game.

Pretty fair season for Crowder, 1933, his 24 victories against 15 defeats helping Joe Cronin win pennant for Senators. In 1934 season was traded to Detroit, had 9–11 record. In 1935 he won 16, lost 10. Thus in three years he was on three pennant winners with two clubs. Called it quits after 1936 season when he was still winning pitcher, 4–3.

Alvin pitched in 402 games for total of 2344-1/3 innings; won 167 big league games, lost 115. ERA of 4.12. In WS play he lost one game each in 1933 and 1934, but was victorious in his final WS game, 1935. Had 3.81 ERA in 26 WS innings.

CUCCINELLO, ANTHONY FRANCIS (Tony) Inf.-BR-TR. B. 11/8/07, Long Island City, N. Y. 5'7", 182. Tony Cuccinello got his start in Cardinal organization but never played with St. Louis NL. Signed with Syracuse, International League, 1926, when that team was Redbird farm. Four games at Syracuse; then Lawrence, Mass., for rest of that year and 1927. Danville, III League, 1928, until sold to Cincinnati, which optioned him out to Columbus, American Association, for 14 games. One full year at Columbus, 1929, with .358 batting average, 20 homers, and 111 RBI, after which he became regular with Reds. Hit .312 his first season in Rhineland, .315 his second.

Four years in Brooklyn; then was starting his fifth season with Boston NL when traded to N. Y. Giants 6/15/40. Giants sent him to their farm club at Jersey City to manage 1941 season and Tony continued to play. When chance came to return to majors was released from 1942 contract as pilot. Signed with Boston Braves 1942, released 7/19/43, and spent rest of that season, 1944, and 1945 with Chicago AL. Managed Tampa in Florida International League, 1947; coach, Indianapolis, AA, 1948; coach, Cincinnati, 1949–51; coach, Cleveland, 1952–56; coach, Chicago AL, 1957 until his retirement.

Tony played 1704 major league games, hit .280 for his career. His 1729 hits included 334 doubles, 46 triples and 94 homers. Batted in 884 markers, stole 42 bases, scored 730 runs.

Tony played most of his games at second base, but appeared at third in something over 450 games. Once made six hits in one game 8/13/31; another notable occasion was 8/25/36 when he hit two doubles in one inning. Brother of Al Cuccinello, who played infield with N.Y. Giants, 1935; uncle of Sam Mele, long-time AL outfielder and later manager, Minnesota Twins.

CUELLAR, MIGUEL ANGEL (Mike) P-BL-TL. B. 5/8/37, Santa Clara, Cuba. 5'11", 175. Baltimore's acquisition of Mike Cuellar 12/4/68 paid off just about as beautifully as any trade ever made in baseball. Mike had pitched extremely well in 1967 for Houston Astros, winning 16 games and losing 11 for team that finished ninth in 10-club league. But in 1968 he could not break even, winning eight, losing 11. And prior to that 1967 season with Astros, had bounced around National, International, Southern, Mexican Leagues, and American Association almost like ping-pong ball.

But with Orioles, Cuellar won 67 games, lost 28, with 2.97 ERA in 1969,70,71. In AL playoffs those three years Cuellar chalked up one victory and lost none, with ERA of 3.84. But in WS his performances added up to 3–2, with 3.00 ERA. The two losses occurred in 1971 WS vs. Pittsburgh.

Cuellar signed his first pro contract with Cincinnati, 1957, but spent that year and following with Havana, International League. Spent a few minutes with Redlegs, 1959, but went back to Havana until following year, when he joined Jersey City in same league. Divided 1961 between Jersey City and Indianapolis, AA, then spent 1962 with Monterrey, Mexican League. With Knoxville, Southern Association, and Jacksonville, International League, 1963,64,65 with brief spell with Cardinals thrown in. Joined Astros during 1965 campaign.

As 1973 season opened, Cuellar had record of 127 wins against 81 losses. Had strikeout record of 1246 against 515 walks given in 1905 IP. His ERA stood at 2.92.

Cuellar recalls with satisfaction his being co-winner of Cy Young Award with Denny McLain in 1969; that bases-loaded homer hit in first game of AL playoffs, 1970, against Minnesota; fact that he was only Oriole pitcher to defeat N. Y. Mets in 1969 WS; plus his winning fifth game of 1970 WS, which wrapped up Baltimore conquest of Cincinnati Reds.

CULLEN, TIMOTHY LEO Inf-BR-TR. B. 2/16/42, San Francisco, Calif. 6'1", 185. If Tim Cullen could hit—but, as 1972 season started, his major league average over five seasons and part of another was just .216. In 1970 tied existing major league record for highest fielding average for second baseman in at least 100 games, with .994. But Texas Rangers finally released him. Four games at Des Moines early in 1972 then moved to Oakland as one of many part-time second sackers. Change of climate must have agreed with him to some extent. Hit .261 in 72 games, 25 points better than had ever done with Washington Senators. This performance raised lifetime average to .220 for 700 AL games.

Tim got into couple of games during playoff series against Detroit, but was not used in 1972 WS.

Superb fielder attended Santa Clara in Calif., received B.S. degree in commerce. Played semipro ball in Canada, and once hit two grand slam homers in one inning while with Saskatoon, Sask., team in 1962.

Moved to Seattle club of Pacific Coast League, 1964, playing third base. In 78 games hit .254. Next two seasons in same league, with Hawaii; hit .221 first season and .295 next. Brought up to Washington for 18 games, 1966, had .235 mark.

Played 124 games with Senators following season, then was traded to Chicago White Sox 2/13/68. Landed back with Senators 8/2/68. Despite puny hitting, played more than 100 games each season for five years in AL prior to 1972. But in 1971 average had dropped to .191.

Cullen had 9 homers, 57 doubles, 9 triples, out of 387 hits. Voluntary retirement 1/24/73.

CULP, RAYMOND LEONARD, JR. P-BR-TR. B. 8/6/41, Elgin, Texas. 6', 202. Ray Culp won 51 games, lost 43, in NL before joining Boston Red Sox, 1968. With Sox his AL record stood 69 wins, 52 losses. Actually, Culp had only three seasons where defeats exceeded victories in his entire career.

Ray was stellar high school athlete in Austin, Tex., before signing with Philadelphia NL organization, 1959—baseball, football, track. His first experience was at Johnson City, Tenn., then Asheville, Des Moines, and Williamsport. In his first big league season with Phillies, 1963, won 14, lost 11. Had 14–10 record, 1965. Spent 1967 with Chicago Cubs, 8–11.

Traded to Red Sox, came up with three fine seasons, 16–6, 17–8, 17–14.

Sore arm, 1971, was important factor in his losing 16 games while winning only 14. When Red Sox released him at end of 1972 campaign, major league record showed 312 games pitched, 120 victories, 95 defeats, and ERA of 3.56. Strikeouts far exceeded walks, 1379 to 720. Pitched one inning on NL All-Star squad, 1963, and one for AL stars, 1969, allowing just one hit and no runs.

Signed with Pawtucket, IL, 1973; returned to Red Sox, June.

CUMMINGS, WILLIAM ARTHUR (Candy) P-BR-TR. B. 10/17/48, Ware, Mass. D. 5/16/24, Toledo, Ohio. 5′9″, 120. "It is generally conceded he invented curve ball now in common use everywhere," Said *Official Baseball Guide* about Cummings' induction into Hall of Fame, 1939.

Cummings reportedly used to throw clamshells along beach, watching them spin to left or right as they sped through air. Some time later, when as young man he took up baseball, wondered whether he could get ball to behave like clamshell. Will Irwin, writing for *Collier's* magazine in early years of 20th century, said Cummings, as member of "Stars of Brooklyn" team, 1867, finally got ball to behave curiously. Pitching against wind, his catcher nearly wrecked his bare right hand reaching for ball. Few days later, having told teammates about his accomplishment, Cummings tried again. This time wind was at his back. No curve. However, when "Stars of Brooklyn" were due to journey to Boston to meet powerful "Harvards of Cambridge," regular pitcher was sick. Cummings went along, subbed for sick teammate. Decided to try out his new pitch. Harvard players couldn't hit Cummings with any degree of success. After game they asked, "What were you pitching to us? It came at us and then it went away from us!" Cummings' use of "horizontal whip of wrist" not secret long. Soon curve ball in general use.

Cummings played with amateur teams in Fulton, N.Y., and Brooklyn before joining "Stars of Brooklyn." Later with New York Mutuals in National Association, Baltimore, Philadelphia, Hartford in same league. Was with "Live Oaks of Lynn, Mass.," Cincinnati and "Forest City of Cleveland" teams—all between 1866 and 1878. Records are incomplete, but seems to have won 34 games, lost 19 with Mutuals, 1872; had 34–11 mark with Hartford, 1875.

CUNNINGHAM, JOSEPH ROBERTS, JR. 1B-OF-BL-TL. B. 8/27/31, Saddle River Township, N.J. 6′1″, 188. Joe Cunningham hit .345 for St. Louis Cardinals, 1959, and many years later returned to Redbirds to work in special promotions and speakers' bureau. In 1973 became director of sales. As ball player, hit .291 in 1141 games, had 980 hits, including 177 doubles, 26 triples, 64 homers, with 525 runs scored, 436

RBI, and 16 stolen bases.

Joe once had unusual experience of pinch hitting and making two hits in same inning. This occurred 7/18/57, ninth inning. Tied major league record. Also pinch hit in second 1959 All-Star game, but was not successful. In his travels he never came up with pennant-winning team in majors.

Cunningham started out in 1949 with Johnson City club of Appalachian League; St. Joseph, Mo., 1950; Omaha and Winston-Salem, 1951; military service, 1952–53; Rochester, 1954–56, but also spent parts of 1954 and 1956 with Cardinals. Sticking with Cardinals, 1957, hit .318 in 122 games and followed up with his .312 and .345 seasons. In 1957, besides those two pinch hits in one inning, had three pinch home runs. One of these round trippers came in ninth inning with score tied and bases loaded. His pinch-hitting average that year was .433 with 13 hits in 30 trips.

Joe hit .280 and .286 with Cardinals, 1960–61, than moved to Chicago White Sox for 1962–64. After .286 average his first year in Windy City, his average dropped down. During 1964 joined Washington Senators, calling it quits after three games in nation's capital, 1966.

CUYLER, HAZEN SHIRLEY (Kiki) OF-BR-TR. B. 8/30/99, Harrisville, Mich. D. 2/11/50, Ann Arbor, Mich. 5'11", 185. Pittsburgh Pirates suffered very humiliating defeat in 1927 World Series, losing to Yankees in four straight. Donie Bush, Pirate manager, kept his stellar outfielder and fine hitter on bench throughout four games, never calling on Kiki Cuyler even as pinch hitter.

Kiki, who hit better than .350 four times in illustrious career, one of heroes of 1925 Series, was in perfect health, ready, willing, eager to get into game. Bush ignored him. We'll never know whether Cuyler's bat would have made difference.

Bush's pique against Cuyler started during regular season, 1927. Kiki accustomed to batting third in lineup. Bush wanted to place Cuyler second in lineup. Kiki objected. Ready to bat almost anywhere in lineup—except second. Perhaps superstition, or fear it might hurt his robust batting average, well over .300 as usual. Argument ensued. Donie benched Cuyler for rest of season. Pirates won pennant without Kiki's assistance in latter stages of flag race. But surely they could have used help against Yankee steamroller.

But for depression of 1920 you might never have heard of Cuyler. After finishing high school, got job as auto-top builder in Buick plant, Flint, Mich. Played with factory ball club. Drop in car sales caused employee layoffs. Cuyler able to get job with Bay City team of Michigan-Ontario League. Played 69 games, 1920, batted .258. Following season his .317 for 116 games, fine arm, flash base running attracted

Pittsburgh scout. Wound up year with Pirates, appearing in one game that year and one following season.

Farmed out, Kiki batted .309 at Charleston, South Atlantic League, 1922; .340 at Nashville, Southern Association, 1923. Also stole 68 bases, led latter league in outfield putouts and assists. Recalled by Pittsburgh at end of 1923. First full year at Pittsburgh, 1924, batted .354, pilfered 32 bases, slugged 27 doubles, 16 triples, 9 home runs, had 85 RBI.

In 1925 did even better, helping Pirates win pennant under Bill McKechnie. Played every game, batted .357, scored 144 runs, had 43 two-baggers, 26 triples, 17 homers, 102 RBI, 41 stolen bases. Led NL in runs scored and triples.

That autumn Cuyler delivered blow that gave Pirates World Series. Washington leading 7 to 6 in fateful seventh game. Last of eighth, Pirates filled bases against Walter Johnson. Up came Cuyler, made sign of cross, swung his bat and smashed double which drove in two runs to give Buccaneers Series.

After Cuyler's fracas with Donie Bush, traded to Cubs 11/28/27. Continued fine work with Chicago until 1935 when hitting fell off. Released 7/3/35, signed with Cincinnati two days later. In 1936 played 144 games and batted healthy .326. With Reds 1937, Brooklyn 1938. Managed Chattanooga, Southern Association, 1939, 1940, part of 1941, still playing part time. Manager, Atlanta, Southern Association, 1945–48. Coach, Cubs, 8/7/41 until end of 1943. Coach, Red Sox, 1949.

Ten hits in succession, 9/18, 19, 21/25, equaled NL record. Led NL in SB 1926, 28–30. Holds Pittsburgh record for runs scored in any season since 1900—144 in 1925; also holds all-time high for Pittsburgh for total bases—366 in 1925, better than Willie Stargell was able to accomplish in 1971 or Ralph Kiner at his peak.

Kiki's lifetime major league record showed 1879 games, .321 batting average, 2299 hits, 1305 runs, 1065 RBI. In World Series competition, 16 games, .281 average. Got his nickname early in career when teammates would yell for him to take fly ball, "Cuy, Cuy!" Newsmen soon translated it as "Kiki." Was avid hunter. Won several waltz trophies. Neither drank nor smoked. Hall of Fame 1968.

DAHLEN, WILLIAM FREDERICK (Bad Bill) SS-BR-TR. B. 1/5/71, Fort Plain, N.Y. D. 12/5/50, Brooklyn, N.Y. 5'8", 170. One of Walter Alston's predecessors as manager of Dodgers (1910–13); did some consistent hitting over one stretch, 1894, getting safeties in 70 of 71 consecutive ball games. Blanked completely, however, in his only WS, 1905, playing for N.Y. Giants.

Dahlen started in Cobleskill, N.Y. State League, 1890. Chicago NL, 1891–98; Brooklyn NL, 1899–1903; N.Y. NL, 1904–07; Boston NL, 1908–09; Mgr., Brooklyn NL, 1910–13, with one sixth-place, two seventh-place finishes.

Bill's hitting streak came with Chicago NL, then called Colts. In 42 games (6/20/94 to 8/6/94) slammed 74 hits, including 16 doubles, 7 triples, 4 homers. Failed to hit 8/7/94, then started new streak and hit safely in next 28 games.

Oddly, in the hitless game 8/7/94, his teammates made 20 hits off Cincinnati pitching. Bill Lange, just ahead in batting order, had five hits. Cap Anson, who followed, also had five hits. Dahlen had five chances to come through, but failed to reach base each time.

Holds NL record for most assists by shortstop, 7414; on two different occasions hit three triples in one game. WS record showed no hits in 15 times at bat, five games. His lifetime average was .275 in 2431 games. Stole 587 bases, twice reaching 60 thefts (1892 and 1896).

DAHLGREN, ELLSWORTH TENNEY (Babe) 1B-BR-TR. B. 6/15/12, San Francisco, Calif. 6', 190. Babe Dahlgren didn't have much work to do with Yankees, 1938, first part of 1939. In 29 games in 1938, eight of them at third base and six others at first base late in game, plus some pinch-hitting chores. Following season started with Dahlgren riding bench as usual. Day after day Lou Gehrig was adding to his iron-man streak of playing every day. This had been going on since 1925. Fourteen years later, Gehrig had put together unbelievable record of 2130 games. Then came day when Lou, realizing he was not helping team, benched himself. Page-one headlines all over U.S. told everyone that Gehrig was out of lineup—and Babe Dahlgren was playing first base for Yankees. News indeed. And Babe played position well enough that Yankees won their fourth consecutive AL pennant and WS. Didn't hit for much of an average—.235 in 144 games, but he drove in goodly total of 89 runs and swatted 15 homers. Not Gehrig-type record, but good enough.

Dahlgren signed with San Francisco Missions, Pacific Coast League, 1931, as soon as he graduated from high school. Farmed to Tucson. Then broke into Missions' lineup and set pretty nifty endurance record of his own—something over 600 consecutive games in PCL before going up to majors with Boston Red Sox, 1935. In his last season on Coast, hit .302, banged 20 homers and drove in 136 runs in 186 games. They used to play long season in PCL. Dahlgren got into 188 contests in 1932 and 189 following campaign.

Red Sox played Dahlgren in 149 games, 1936, hit .263 with nine homers, 63 RBI. Most of 1936 with Syracuse, International League, with .318 mark and 121 RBI, 16 home runs. Sixteen games with Sox that year, then landed with Newark, Yankee farm club, for 1937. Came up with .340 average, 18 homers, 86 RBI. One game with Bronx Bombers.

Utility role for Babe in 1938 with Yankees, aforementioned. After that 1939 season, Dahlgren again played first base for N.Y. in 1940—155 games with .264 average. Along came Johnny Sturm to play first, so Babe sold to Boston Braves 2/25/41. Forty-four games for Beantowners, then shifted to Chicago Cubs, with .267 average. Came up with respectable mark of 89 RBI, with 23 homers. Divided 1942 season among three clubs—Cubs, Brooklyn Dodgers, and St. Louis Browns. Philadelphia NL, 1943. Pittsburgh, 1944–45. Back to Browns for 1946.

Dahlgren wound up major league career with 1139 games played, .261 batting average with 1056 hits. Doubles, 174; triples, 37; homers, 82; RBI 569; runs scored, 470; stolen bases, 18. In WS of 1939, hit .214 in four games, all of which Yanks won from Cincinnati Reds. Babe had homer, double off Bucky Walters in second game, which American Leaguers won 4–0.

DAL CANTON, JOHN BRUCE   P-BR-TR. B. 6/15/42, California, Pa. 6'2", 205. Bruce Dal Canton won 20 games, lost eight, toiling for Pittsburgh Pirates but in first two seasons with Kansas City Royals was able to do little better than break even. Was 8–6 in 1971, and 6–6 in 1972. All of which brought overall major league record to 34 wins, 20 defeats, as 1973 started. By same time had appeared in 174 games, owned 3.49 ERA, with 263 strikeouts, 177 bases on balls, in 485 innings.

Bruce weighed about 250 pounds when Pirates first signed him, 1965. Slimmed down after that. Divided 1966 between Columbus, International League, and Asheville, Southern; part of 1967 with Macon, Southern Association, but also won two games, lost one with Pirates in eight appearances, with 1.88 ERA. Spent following summer at York, Pa., and Columbus, but also had seven games at Pittsburgh, winning one, losing one. His ERA again was quite low, 2.12, for 17 innings. Got into 57 games with Pirates 1969, pitched 86 innings, 8–2, 3.35 ERA. His mark in 1970 was 9–4, with 3.45 ERA for 41 games, 141 innings. Then came trade to Kansas City 12/2/70.

Attended California (Pa.) State College and West Virginia. Has bachelor's degree in education from latter, and during off-seasons has been substitute teacher doing graduate work. Doing thesis on arm ailments of pitchers. Shoulder irritation has limited effectiveness at times since joining Royals. Throws sinking fast ball, curve, knuckler, palm ball.

DALTON, HARRY Executive. B. 8/23/28, West Springfield, Mass. Harry Dalton got $47 weekly salary from Baltimore Orioles, 1953, as assistant to farm director. At end of 1971 signed five-year contract, reportedly at $60,000 annually with stock options, as executive vice president and general manager of California Angels. While at Baltimore, Orioles won pennants four times, WS twice. Dalton credited with much of success of Baltimore farm system that, in 1971, produced three pennant-winning teams in minors, two second-place clubs, and one fifth-placer. Farm system also had four league batting champions, three home run leaders and two who led leagues in RBI.

Dalton graduated from Amherst College, 1950; served 37 months as first lieutenant in air force; earned Bronze Star for his work as combat press officer in Korean War. Having been sports writer in Springfield, Mass., while attending high school and college, Dalton sought work connected with sports after returning to civilian life. Baltimore job was result.

When Lee MacPhail left Baltimore to go to Yankees, Dalton took over as vice president and player-personnel director, 1965.

Gene Autry, chairman of board of California Angels, first met Dalton during 1966 WS and was favorably impressed. This personal view plus fine record of Baltimore organization in producing steady flow of young players of quality led to his appointment to California job. Dalton began overhauling Angels immediately. Hired Del Rice as new manager, acquired Leo Cardenas and other players in effort to strengthen team.

DALTON, TALBOT PERCY (Jack) OF-BR-TR. B. 7/3/85, Henderson, Tenn. 5'10½", 187. Jack Dalton has probably been forgotten in Brooklyn and almost everywhere else. But when he joined Superbas—they became Dodgers many years later—he looked like superstar. All he did in debut was slam five consecutive hits off Christy Mathewson 6/21/10. That season Matty won 27 games for New York Giants, losing nine, with 1.89 ERA.

Dalton, however, found rest of pitchers in NL pretty difficult. Wound up season with .227 batting average for 77 games. Dropped from major league picture next three years; returned to Brooklyn, 1914, and hit .319 in 128 games. Next stop Buffalo, Federal League, 1915, where he hit .293 in 132 games. Last on big league scene, 1916, with Detroit Tigers; In eight games hit .182.

Played 345 games in big time, hit .286—and would be in complete oblivion but for spectacular debut against one of greatest pitchers of all time.

DANFORTH, DAVID CHARLES (Dauntless Dave) P-BL-TL. B. 3/7/90, Granger, Tex. D. 9/19/70, Baltimore, Md. 6', 175. Credited with originating "shine ball" in 1915 while pitching for Louisville, American Association. They used to put oil on infield to keep down dust; Danforth found that when he rubbed oil and dirt off ball on his trouser leg it became smooth and did some fancy "hopping" when pitched.

Danforth pitched for Chicago White Sox, 1916–19 then went to Columbus, 1919–21. When he returned to majors with St. Louis Browns, 1922, spitball had been limited to small number of practitioners and "doctoring" ball was forbidden. Opposing ball clubs immediately began badgering Danforth, accusing him of roughing up ball and tampering with it illegally. Batters repeatedly insisted that umpires inspect ball. On one occasion his pitch almost hit Wid Matthews of Philadelphia Athletics and Umpire George Moriarty threw Danforth out of game. Brownie players rushed to umpire in protest; Johnny Tobin took ball and tried to show arbiter there was nothing wrong with it. Players worked up petition to AL president, Ban Johnson, requesting that "persecution" be ended, but it was never sent since for unexplained reason Brownie manager, Lee Fohl, would not sign it. In another game umpire Billy Evans kept new balls in play throughout. Danforth used 58 new balls that day. Yankees won game 3–1.

Danforth attended Baylor two years. Got degree in dentistry from Maryland, 1915. But his pro baseball career started, 1911, with Philadelphia Athletics. Won four games, lost one, but shortly after 1912 season started, was sent to Baltimore, then in Eastern League. Won 12, lost 10. Had 16–14 record, 1913, and 12–15 mark, 1914, also with Baltimore, now in International League. Moved to Louisville part of 1914 and part of 1915, then was with Chicago White Sox into 1919 season. Best season with Sox 1917, 11–6. With Columbus 1919–21, winning 25 and losing 16 in his final season there. Joined Browns, 1922, 5–2, but also 6–4 for Tulsa, Western League. Had 16–14 mark, 1923, then 15–12, 7–9. By this time Dave was through as major leaguer. Pitched for Milwaukee, American Association; New Orleans, Dallas, Buffalo, Chattanooga, and Scranton before deciding to devote full time to dentistry in Baltimore.

Nickname "Dauntless Dave" pinned on him by Eddie Collins when both with Athletics. Appeared in one WS with White Sox, 1917—one inning, two runs, ERA 18.00.

DANNING, HARRY (The Horse) C-BR-TR. B. 9/6/11, Los Angeles, Calif. 6'1", 190. Got his nickname from Damon Runyon fictional character, Harry the Horse. Probably best-hitting catcher N.Y. Giants ever had in reasonably modern times. Son of native Russian who left old country in 1880s, going to Spain, Argentina, Mexico, and Central America before settling in U.S. Brother of Ike Danning, who caught in minors and was with St. Louis AL briefly, 1928.

Harry got into rug business and played independent ball before joining Bridgeport, Eastern League, 1931. Moved to Winston-Salem during 1932 season and to Buffalo, 1933, slugging ball well over .300 everywhere he went. Joined Giants late 1933 and remained with them through 1942. In 1938–40 seasons made .300 mark each year with 16 homers, 1939, his high-water mark in that department. Gus Mancuso was regular N.Y. catcher when Danning came up, but by 1937 Danning was in more games than Gus. Harry played in part of 1937 WS although he had broken hand, received from foul tip at end of regular season. Despite this handicap got double and two singles in fourth game.

Harry in military service 1943–45, developed arthritis in right knee. When mustered out coached Hollywood, Pacific Coast League, 1947. Worked in circulation department of N.Y. newspaper, then became successful insurance salesman in San Francisco.

In 890 major league games hit .285. His 847 hits included 162 doubles, 26 triples, 57 homers. Scored 363 times, drove in 397 runs. In WS play, five games, .214 batting average.

DARK, ALVIN RALPH Inf.-BR-TR. B. 1/7/22, Comanche, Okla. 5'11½", 175. Alvin Dark remains an enigma to some observers of baseball scene. Fine ball player, smart manager, yet there are paradoxes in his makeup, possibly inner conflicts in his personality. Dark managed San Francisco Giants to pennant in second year as pilot. Credited with welding disparate elements of club together, blacks, whites, Latin Americans, and creating fine esprit de corps. Yet two years later was out as manager—reportedly because of interview in which "Negro and Spanish-speaking players" were blamed for Giants' failure to win oftener.

Managed Kansas City AL two years, 1966–67; then took over Cleveland job, 1968. Seemed to be in solid. Not only ran club on field but took over many of front office functions formerly part of job of Gabe Paul, veteran and respected baseball man, president of Indians. Came up with five-year contract at $50,000 annually. Yet 7/29/71, with about 2-1/2 years to go on contract, Dark was released and began collecting pay for doing nothing.

Dark, according to Felipe Alou, has two rules of life: 1) he thinks out everything in advance; every word he utters, every action he takes, no matter how illogical it may seem at time, is result of deliberate plan; 2) he wants to win. Alou, who played for Dark in San Francisco, says that, in anger, Dark has violated his first rule at times, but never his second rule.

Dark starred at football at Louisiana State, then went into Marine Corps. When he emerged Boston Braves signed him, 1946, for $40,000 bonus. Played 15 games with them that year, hitting .231, then went to their Milwaukee farm, then in American Association. Hit .303 in 149 games, 1947, led league in doubles with 49 and also in runs scored, 121. Back to Braves, 1948, and for 13 years played regularly in majors at least 100 games per season. In his first full year with Boston, club won pennant, helped substantially by his .322 batting average and good work in 137 games, solving team's shortstop problems.

Braves dropped below .500 mark for 1949 and changes were in order. Dark and teammate Eddie Stanky landed with Giants in deal involving Sid Gordon and Buddy Kerr. Dark and Stanky provided Mgr. Leo Durocher with kind of keystone combination he wanted for 1950. Then came Giants' famed 1951 season. Dark starred at shortstop, led league in doubles with 41, hit .303 and Giants won pennant after trailing Dodgers 13-1/2 games at one point during August. Yankees downed Giants in WS, four games to two, but it wasn't Dark's fault—he hit .417, getting three doubles and homer among his 10 hits, scoring five runs and driving in four. Al continued to bat .300 next two seasons, but had .293 mark in 1954 when Giants won another flag and then swept Cleveland Indians in WS. Dark's average .412, 7 for 17. That was extent of Dark's WS play. Average for two WS with Giants and one with Braves came to .323 in 16 games.

Giants traded him to St. Louis NL 6/14/56. Cards in turn sent him to Chicago NL 5/20/58 getting Pitcher Jim Brosnan in return. After close of 1959 season Dark was on his way again, this time to Philadelphia NL for 1960 but moved to Milwaukee club 6/23/60. That year marked end of his playing career. Major league totals showed 1828 games, 2089 hits,

1064 runs scored. Had 358 doubles, 72 triples, 126 homers, and .289 batting average with 757 RBI.

Dark was traded to San Francisco NL 10/31/60 and appointed manager for following year, succeeding Bill Rigney and Tom Sheehan who had led Giants to fifth-place finish. One of Dark's first moves was to "integrate" black and Latin American members of team better by changing their lockers in clubhouse. Previously they had mostly been in one corner of room. Dark tried to break up cliques and have team play as unit. In his first year, Giants moved up to third place, and they won pennant following season. Lost bitterly fought WS to N.Y. Yankees when Ralph Terry took crucial seventh game by 1–0 score.

Giants finished third in 1963, fourth in 1964. This was about the time Dark gave long rambling interview to newsman. Reporter claimed Dark said blacks and Latino players on his team weren't as mentally alert as whites; furthermore, that they didn't have same pride in team's winning. Repercussions followed among players accused. Dark said his remarks had been distorted considerably, but at end of season he was out. It should be noted, Dark had no similar racial or ethnic problems managing Kansas City or Cleveland.

At Kansas City his club finished seventh in 10-club race, 1966, and tenth in 1967 when replaced by Luke Appling 8/20. In Cleveland Dark had tie for third place, 1968. In 1969 his team was on bottom in six-club Eastern Division of AL; in 1970 Indians were fifth; in 1971 they were again on bottom when he was released toward end of July. Between managerial jobs Dark coached Chicago Cubs, 1965.

Dark was known as conscientious churchgoer who took his religion seriously. Yet he had rule against "Christian testimony" or preaching of any sort while in uniform. His self-discipline failed him on at least two occasions. Once in Philadelphia, when Giants lost 1–0 game, his team outhit Phils 8–4 but left dozen men on base. Going to clubhouse, Dark picked up metal stool and threw it across room. Somehow, tip of his little finger got wedged in part of stool and went with flying stool. Club trainer recovered it and had it on display, preserved in alcohol.

Another time, when his club was losing its sixth straight game, Orlando Cepeda was called out on strikes by umpire Shag Crawford. Dark lost cool and purple prose flowed to such an extent that he was ejected. Next day a San Francisco newspaper quoted him as saying, "I should be ashamed of myself. That wasn't a Christian thing to do. It was Satan's work. The devil was in me. Never before have I so addressed any man—and with the Lord's help, I hope to have the strength never to do so again. Crawford is a fine man and a fine umpire. It was doubly wrong to say to him what I wouldn't willfully say to the worst of men. It's a long season and all of us are sinners. Faith is our salvation."

Alvin had definite ideas as manager. Told his pitchers to stop shagging flies in pregame workouts and take their turns in batting practice. Was convinced more batting practice might result in more hits during games they pitched. When his club won flag in San Francisco some called him "mad scientist" because of uncanny way some of his more unorthodox plays often succeeded. One of his maneuvers wasn't new among canny managers: when speedy Dodgers came to San Francisco they would usually find infield grass high and base paths watered down so as to discourage fast base running.

Dark, 50 years old in 1972, probably will be back in baseball. Was reported actively seeking connection with New Orleans people interested in bringing major league franchise to that city.

DARWIN, ARTHUR BOBBY LEE (Bob)   OF-BR-TR. B. 2/16/43, Los Angeles, Calif. 6'2", 200. Babe Ruth, Lefty O'Doul, and many other players were good-hitting pitchers before switching to regular outfield play. But Bob Darwin, who looked like Paul Bunyan in early games of 1972 with Minnesota Twins, was not good-hitting pitcher through all those years he was trying to make grade on mound.

Darwin grabbed headlines in Twins' opening day game against Oakland, 1972. With two men out in ninth inning, his tremendous homer into upper deck of Oakland stands, 460 feet from plate, tied score. Twins eventually lost game in overtime, but it wasn't Darwin's fault. Next day his homer beat A's. In third game he singled twice. In fourth contest had another homer, five RBI. When Bob made his first appearance in stadium at Bloomington, Minn., walloped another homer to start club on road to victory. In his first seven games, had hit in all of them, went 11 for 26, with four homers, eleven RBI. Amazing part about Darwin's performance was fact he was 29 years old, no youngster, when he started his heroics in AL. Although he is reported to have received $40,000 bonus as pitcher to sign with Los Angeles Angels, 1962, he never owned much of record as hurler. Bill Rigney was manager of Angels then, and was hardly impressed by Darwin's performance in one game. In three innings he walked four, allowed eight hits, six runs, four of them earned. In California League, same year, Bob won 11, lost six in class C circuit.

During next several years, Darwin pitched for Hawaii, Stockton, Elmira, and Spokane. Won four and lost none in part of season at Stockton, and had 10–6 record at Elmira one year, but rest of record was unimpressive. Still he got brief trial with Los Angeles Dodgers as pitcher, 1969. This came about in strange fashion. Dodger vice president Al Campanis was en route to airport. His car got involved in automobile accident. Darwin was member of tow-truck crew that came to Campanis' aid. Short time later Campanis spotted Bob's name on eligible list and picked him for Dodgers. Pitched four innings for Dodgers, 1969, allowed four hits, five walks, and four earned runs. Then landed with Spokane,

Pacific Coast League, where his pitching record was 6.49 ERA and all losses—six.

By this time, Darwin was pretty discouraged as pitcher. Had 42–50 record in minors. An operation on his elbow in 1966. After that his arm simply didn't have it. Demoted from PCL to Bakersfield for 1970, Darwin decided to try it as outfielder. Transition not easy; in 303 times at bat, struck out 127 times. Hit 23 homers and batted .297. But he never quit trying to improve. Went back to Spokane as outfielder, 1971, after hitting .488 in spring training with Dodgers. In 11 games with L.A., hit .250, with one homer. However, in 22 appearances at plate, walked twice, had five hits—and struck out nine times. His Spokane record was .293 in 91 games. After 1971 season Darwin moved into Mexican Pacific Coast League with Hermosillo. Had no great hopes of making it as regular in Dodger outfield. But when Dodgers, in October, traded him to Twins, he became so stimulated that he hit 10 homers in 12 games. "I kept on hitting long ball because I wanted to show I had power," he declared.

Darwin also said time in Mexico really helped. Could hit fast ball before going there, but was pushover for curves and any breaking ball. But, according to him, in Mexico they throw side-arm, underhand, come from any direction, and used spitball. That was when he learned to hit breaking stuff.

Darwin wound up 1972 season with .267 average for 145 games; 22 homers, 80 RBI. Led AL in strikeouts with 145.

DAUBERT, JACOB ELLSWORTH (Jake) 1B-BL-TL. B. 5/14/85, Llewellyn, Pa. D. 10/9/24, Cincinnati, Ohio. 5'10", 160. Won NL's MVP (Chalmers) 1913 and twice led league in batting (1913–14). Stalwart first baseman for Brooklyn Dodgers nine seasons (1910–18). Equally consistent first baseman for Cincinnati Reds (1919–24) until shortly before his death at age 39.

Jake had his minor league experience at Kane, Pa., 1907, later going to Marion, Ohio; Nashville, Toledo, and Memphis before joining Dodgers, 1910. Twice led NL first sackers in fielding and tied for leadership another year; twice led circuit in triples.

Daubert played 2014 major league games and amassed 2326 hits. Had 250 doubles, 165 triples and 56 homers, with 720 RBI for lifetime average of .303. In his earlier years usually stole in neighborhood of 25 bases each season and wound up with lifetime total of 251.

In 1916 WS Daubert hit just .176. In 1919 classic had .241 average. In 12 games, batted .217, with 10 hits in 46 AB, scored 5 runs, had 2 triples, 1 RBI, 1 stolen base.

DAUSS, GEORGE AUGUST (Hooks) P-BR-TR. B. 9/22/89, Indianapolis, Ind. D. 7/27/63, St. Louis, Mo. 5'10'', 160. George Dauss pitched beautifully for Detroit Tigers from 1912 to 1926, winning 221 games and losing just 183. In all that time Tigers did not win single pennant, so he never had chance to display his talents in WS. Those 220 wins made him Detroit's top winner. Among his victories were 21 shutouts, but Mickey Lolich and Denny McLain have beaten Dauss' record in this respect.

Dauss pitched for Duluth, Minnesota-Wisconsin League, 1909–10; St. Paul, American Association, 1911–12, going up to Tigers 8/29/12. Won one, lost one in AL that season, then began consistent pitching, 1913. Won 13, lost 12, but had 2.67 ERA. Next season won 18, then 23. Twice later passed 20 mark in wins, always had victories in double figures. Even in his final year with club, 1926, won 11, lost 7. Best ERA was 2.43 in 1917 when he was 17–14.

George took part in 538 games, pitched 3391 innings, allowing 3405 hits, 1244 earned runs, walked 1067 and struck out 1201. His lifetime AL ERA was 3.32.

DAVALILLO, VICTOR JOSE OF-1B-BL-TL. B. 7/31/39, Cabimas, Zulia, Venezuela. 5'7'', 154. Specialty: pinch hitting. In 1970 while playing for St. Louis NL, tied major league record by making 24 emergency safeties. Prior to that, Dave Philley, with 24 pinch hits for Baltimore, 1961, held record exclusively.

Vic started out as pitcher, but his ability at plate, plus speed in field, dictated that he be utilized more often than hurler. Began pro career at Visalia, Calif., 1958, and at various times called Palatka, Fla.; Topeka; Jersey City; Columbia, S.C.; and Jacksonville home base. Won 32 games, lost 27 as minor league pitcher. But in 1962 his .346 average in 150 games at Jacksonville topped International League in batting, as did marks of 200 hits, 296 total bases, 18 triples, and 24 stolen bases. With Cleveland following season, played 90 games, hit .292. In 1965 went up to .301 in 142 contests. California AL, 1968–69; St. Louis NL, 1969–70; Pittsburgh, 1971. In 1970, with Cardinals, Davalillo enjoyed highest major league average, .311 in 111 contests. In 1971, with world champion Pirates, hit .333 as pinch batsman but .285 overall in 99 games.

Among Vic's more noteworthy occasions was his first appearance in game for Cardinals, 1969. Belted three-run homer off Cincinnati's Gerry Arrigo. Pinch hit grand slam homer off Ron Taylor of N.Y. Mets 7/2/69. Played in 1965 All-Star game with AL. Got one hit in three trips to plate in 1971 WS. Good arm, fine fielding have won him many plaudits, including Gold Glove Award, 1964.

Vic's major league average as 1973 season got under way was .289 for 1209 games.

DAVIDSON, DONALD Executive. B. 5/27/25, Boston, Mass. Smallest of all major league executives, 4 feet tall. In other times would have been called midget, but Atlanta Braves' publicity release refers to him as "biggest small man" in majors, and assistant to president and traveling secretary.

Don is accommodating guy in extremely difficult job. Makes all arrangements for Braves' travel, hotel reservations, room lists, hands out meal money to players, handles countless other details. Let anyone try to keep 25 players, manager, scouts, and newsmen happy in pell-mell travel from one side of continent to other; it is next to impossible. Throw in a prima donna or two and one sorehead, and a traveling secretary who keeps his cool is something of a miracle. Has reputation for patience and efficiency.

When he was nine he tried to get autograph of Braves' players in front of dugout. One of players took him to clubhouse; he later was invited to become batboy. That was back when Casey Stengel was managing Boston NL team. Don finished high school, then majored in journalism at Boston U. Joined *Boston Post* as sports writer, 1943. Served as the shadow in "Me and My Shadow" routine for Skating Vanities. Three years later joined Braves as assistant in public relations department. Davidson's full-time employment with Braves began 1948 so has been with team longer than any other employee. In 1963 became traveling secretary and public relations director for team. Named assistant to president, December 1971. Often represents club president, Bill Bartholomay, at public functions.

Naturally Davidson followed Braves in line of duty from Boston to Milwaukee to Atlanta. Married, with three children.

DAVIS, BRYSHEAR BARNETT (Brock) OF-BL-TL. B. 10/19/43, Oakland, Calif. 5'10", 168. Brock Davis spent his career shuttling from majors to minors, starting 1963. No wonder he quit baseball couple of times. First time was 1968. Opened season with Dallas–Fort Worth, Texas League, then was shifted to Oklahoma City. In midseason went home to Los Angeles. Friends, however, persuaded him to go back, which he did after couple of weeks, anticipating scarcity of ball players due to major league expansion. Bus driver in off-season; at times figured he ought to keep bus job all year.

Got his nickname as Little Leaguer because teammate couldn't pronounce his correct moniker. Attended Los Angeles State College and signed with Houston NL organization. Brief stays with Astros, 1963,64,66. Served in minors with San Antonio, Amarillo, and Tacoma in addition to two teams he was with in 1968. Drafted by Chicago Cubs and played six games with Durocher team, 1970. In 1971 had 22 games at Tacoma, hitting .345, and 106 with Chicago. Leo installed him as regular center fielder. Burned up league for several weeks, hitting well over .300.

Then defensive miscue put him in manager's doghouse. Used sparingly thereafter, and finished first full year in majors with .256 average. Then traded to Milwaukee AL in deal that put Jose Cardenal in Cub uniform 12/4/71. At start of 1973 his career average stood at .260 for 242 major league games. Brewers then optioned to Evansville Ind. club in American Association.

DAVIS, CURTIS BENTON (Coonskin) P-BR-TR. B. 9/7/03, Greenfield, Mo. D. 10/13/65, Covina, Calif. 6'2", 185. Curt Davis won twelve games for Cardinals, 1938. That was five more than Dizzy Dean won that same season for Cubs. Fans compared records of these two pitchers because they figured in fantastic trade 4/16/38. Everybody knew Dizzy had bad arm. But Phil Wrigley was willing—no, anxious—to pay Cardinals $185,000 cash plus three players to get loudmouthed, brokendown hurler. Curt Davis was one of players Cardinals received. Others were outfielder Tuck Stainback and pitcher Clyde Shoun.

Davis won 22 games for Cardinals 1939, helped Brooklyn Dodgers win pennant 1941, with 13–7 record. When both pitchers hung up their uniforms as active players, Davis had 158 career victories—Dizzy Dean, 150.

Curt started pro career 1928 with Salt Lake City, posting 16–8 record. Spent next five years with San Francisco Seals, Pacific Coast League, twice winning 17 games and twice winning 20 or more. Drafted by Philadelphia NL, had 19–17 mark for seventh-place club, 1934. Another successful season 1935, 16–14. Moved to Cubs during 1936 season. Broke even in 26 decisions. In 1937, 10–5. Then came famous trade to Cardinals. Cards sent him to Brooklyn during 1940 season. In 1942, 15–6 for Dodgers. Retired after 1946 season with Brooklyn, went into real estate business. Lived in Azusa, Calif.

Lifetime major league record: 158 victories, 131 defeats, 3.42 ERA, 2325 innings, 24 shutouts. In World Series, 1941, lost one game, lasting less than six innings. Had 5.06 ERA.

DAVIS, HERMAN THOMAS, JR. (Tommy) OF-INF-BR-TR. B. 3/21/39, Brooklyn, N.Y. 6'2", 195. Tommy Davis twice led NL in hitting while member of Los Angeles Dodgers. Before joining Walter Alston's club already had won batting championships in Midwest League with Kokomo, Ind., and in Pacific Coast League with Spokane. Tommy left Dodgers 11/29/66 and since then has had variety of experiences. Reportedly helped Vida Blue as his roommate with Oakland A's, 1971. Released after hitting .324 in 79 games. Got small part as detective in movie, *Black Gunn*, after apparently being finished as major league ball player. Surprisingly turned up with Chicago Cubs 7/9/72, played first base twice in doubleheader against Cincinnati Reds. His single in first game drove in run; in second contest had two more hits, driving in two more markers, all of which contributed to Cubs' twin victories before largest crowd in Cincinnati history to that time, 52,116.

Tommy started, 1956, with Hornell club of Pony League. In 43 games hit .325, then came his successful year at Kokomo, where, in addition to winning bat title, led circuit in hits and runs scored. Had 17 homers and 104 RBI. Victoria, Texas League, and Montreal, International League, 1958, hitting above .300 with both organizations. Then came his PCL bat championship with Spokane, 1959. Also led league in games played, 153; in hits, 211; putouts as an outfielder, 414; but tied for lead in errors, 10. Davis joined Dodgers for one game, 1959, but played regularly in 1960,61, with averages better than .275. In 1962 his league-leading bat mark of .346 in 163 games was accompanied by 153 RBI, 230 hits, both of which also led NL. Had 27 homers that season. Following season .326 average gave him second consecutive NL batting championship. Dropped below .300 in 1964, and in 1965 broke his ankle early in season and played only 17 games. Came back with .313 in 1966 in 100 games. Then Dodgers sent him to N.Y. Mets. Tommy played 154 games for them, 1967, hit .302; then fell to .268 with Chicago White Sox, 1968. Seattle AL and Houston NL, 1969; 1970, Houston and Chicago NL, with several weeks at Oakland AL sandwiched between. Cubs released Davis unconditionally 12/22/70 after his NL average of .278 in 68 games. Following spring it was back to Oakland for Davis. Hit .324 in 79 games and again was injured during August. It looked like curtains when Tommy drew his release from Oaks in spring of 1972. But he was back with Cubs in July. Swapped to Baltimore following month.

When Tommy started 1973 his major league average showed .295 mark for 1508 games. His 1578 hits included 213 doubles, 30 triples, 126 homers, 631 runs scored, and 796 RBI. Had stolen 117 bases.

Davis owned .348 WS average for eight games with Dodgers, 1963 and 1966. Really starred in 1963 Series when L.A. defeated Yankees four straight. Got three hits and stole base in first game. Hit two triples and drove in run in second contest. Drove in Dodgers' only run in Don Drysdale's 1–0 victory in third game. Wound up with .400 average for Series.

Tommy's two triples in one WS game tied major league record; also was record for any four-game WS. On same day he got those two triples (10/3/63) Davis tied two other WS records by getting three putouts in one inning and six putouts as left fielder. Oddly enough, though Davis had two triples in one WS game, he went through 1967 season with no triples. This tied another major league record for fewest three-baggers in 150 or more games, one season.

Davis played both All-Star games, 1962 and 1963, on NL squad. Also proud of .481 pinch hitting average with Oakland, 1971. Had 15 clutch hits and 9 game-winning hits in 79 contests.

DAVIS, VIRGIL LAWRENCE (Spud) C-BR-TR. B. 12/20/04, Birmingham, Ala. 6'1", 220. Slugging catcher who hit .308 in his 1458 NL games over period 1928–45. Coach for Pittsburgh, 1941–43 and 1946; scout for Pirates 1947–49; coach, Chicago Cubs, 1950–53.

Although Davis hit .300 for Gas House Gang (St. Louis Cardinals) in 107 games, 1934, did not catch in WS that year; Mgr. Frankie Frisch preferred backstopping of 22-year old Bill Delancey. Spud, however, got into two WS games as pinch batsman and came through with two hits and drove in one run. Delancey, meanwhile, hit .172 in seven games of classic.

Davis started out with .356 average his first year in pro ball at Gulfport, Miss., 1926, in 27 games. Hit .308 at Reading, International League, 1927, then joined Cardinals, 1928. Cards traded him to Phillies with Homer Peel for Catcher Jimmie Wilson 5/11/28. Hit just .280 that year in 69 games, but for next five years hit well over .300, twice better than .340. During 1933 Frankie Frisch became manager of Cardinals and coolness developed between him and Jimmie Wilson, recognized as smart catcher and potential managerial candidate. Once again Davis was traded for Wilson, 11/15/33, infielder Delker also coming to Cards. Spud stayed with Redbirds through 1936. Cincinnati, 1937, then back to Philadelphia NL in deal that brought Bucky Walters to Rhineland 6/13/38. With Phils rest of that year and all of next, then played for Pittsburgh, 1940–41. During wartime shortage of younger men, Davis was returned to active list with Pirates for 1944–45.

Along with his lifetime average of .308 in NL, Davis scored 388 runs, made 1312 hits in 4255 AB, slapped 244 doubles, 22 triples, 77 homers. Had 647 RBI. Relatively rare accomplishment for backstops was unassisted double play 7/24/28.

DAVIS, WILLIAM HENRY (Comet) OF-BL-TL. B. 4/15/40, Mineral Springs, Ark. 6'2", 181. Willie Davis was named Minor League Player of Year by *Sporting News* because of his brilliant season at Spokane, 1960. Led Pacific Coast League in hitting, in hits, runs scored, triples and stolen bases. But nine years later, with Los Angeles Dodgers, had not lived up to promise. Talked about quitting baseball and becoming pro golfer. Joined Nichiren Shoshu, Buddhist sect, and now reads twice daily from religious scrolls. Stopped some of his wild swinging. Pulled himself together and for first time in his major league career hit above .300. Came back with .300 seasons again in 1970–71.

Willie is one of fastest men in game. Finally, in his 11th full season in NL, was named to All-Star squad, but was passed over in 1972 despite his 19 homers for year, with 79 RBI and .289 average. Had stolen 318 bases when he started 1973 season. Had 42 thefts, 1964, his best year in this respect. At same time had driven in 772 runs, his best season being 1970 when he had 93 RBI. His WS performance, 1963, 65, 66 with Dodgers, resulted in .167 average with nine hits in 54 times at bat. Set WS record by making three errors in one inning, fifth, during 10/6/66 game against Baltimore Orioles. In WS game of 10/11/65, tied record for most steals during one game, three.

Davis started out at Green Bay in III League, 1959, moving to Reno, California League, later that year. Copped league batting title with .365, then had his fine season at Spokane.

As 1973 dawned, Willie had lifetime major league average of .278 for 1800 games, with 292 doubles, 101 triples, 138 homers.

DAY, CHARLES FREDERICK (Boots)   OF-BL-TL. B. 8/31/47, Ilion, N.Y. 5'9", 165. Boots Day got batting average to .283 with Montreal Expos in 1971 but dropped back to .233 in 1972. Fine outfielder who can get ball with speed and dexterity, but lacking in long-distance power at plate. Manager Gene Mauch and coach Larry Doby have tried to persuade him to "hit where pitch is" and not try for homers. Had four home runs in 1971, none in 1972. Wears contact lenses.

Attended Mohawk Valley Community College, Utica, N.Y., after highly successful athletic record in high school. Was pitcher and first baseman in those days; 16–1 mark. Solitary game lost was due to own error—not his pitching.

Spent four years in St. Louis Cardinal chain, starting out, 1966, at Rock Hill in Western Carolina League. Made way up through St. Petersburg, Arkansas, and Tulsa, and played 11 games with Redbirds 1969. Cardinals swapped him to Chicago Cubs 12/4/69. Following season started with Cubs but traded to Montreal 5/11/70. Had .267 average for 52 NL games that year.

Day began 1973 season with .257 average for 318 major league games. His 226 hits included 4 homers, 21 doubles, 6 triples, with 102 runs scored, 68 RBI.

DAY, CLYDE HENRY (Pea Ridge)   P-BR-TR. B. 8/27/99, Pea Ridge, Ark. D. 3/21/34, Kansas City, Mo. 5'10", 175. One of baseball's unforgettable characters, even though only won total of five games in major league while losing seven. Ear-splitting hog caller who enlivened ball parks while pitching for St. Louis, Brooklyn and Cincinnati in NL and numerous minor league clubs. Astonished fans would suddenly hear unearthly yell emanating from dugout. Sound echoed through rafters of grand stands and aroused ire of opposing players.

Pea Ridge had other attributes. Used to win small bets by putting leather belt around his chest and buckling it tightly. Then, when money was put up that he couldn't break belt, would expand his chest. Usually something would give—belt buckle, rivets or leather itself. But one time, with $20 at stake in bet with Lefty O'Doul, belt, buckle, and rivets all held. Something had to give as Pea Ridge huffed and puffed, and something did give—he broke two of his ribs and lost bet!

According to Fresco Thompson, player then, later an executive with Brooklyn and L.A. Dodgers, Day kept listeners in stitches even when not hog-calling or chest-expanding. One day Judge Landis came to Clearwater, Fla., spring training camp of Dodgers. "Mr. Day, do you have any casualties?" asked jurist, then commissioner of baseball. "No, Judge," replied Pea Ridge, "but we have two Poles and a Swede in camp."

Rubber-lunged youngster got crack at major leagues after an exhibition game in Pittsburg, Kans., late in 1923. St. Louis Cardinals were barnstorming in area and Day pitched for locals. Although Cards had some fancy big league hitters in lineup, among them Rogers Hornsby, Day allowed Redbirds one solitary hit. Hornsby thought if Day could fool him, he'd be able to fool other major league hitters. Was with Cardinals, 1924–25; Cincinnati, 1926, and Brooklyn, 1931. With his major league experience, Pea Ridge also pitched in Fort Smith, Ark.; Muskogee, Okla.; Syracuse, Wichita, Omaha, and Kansas City in career that extended from 1922 to 1934. Became alcoholic in later years. As pitching skills faded, illusions of his own grandeur increased. Finally, after spell in hospital, tried to interest sports writers in helping him write book about his exploits. Then took his own life.

Pea Ridge 1–1 for Cardinals, 1924; 2–4 in 1925; 0–0 for Cincinnati, 1926; 2–2 for Dodgers, 1931. Had ERA of 5.30 in 122-1/3 innings pitching in majors.

DEAN, ALFRED LOVILL (Chubby) P-BL-TL. B. 8/24/16, Mount Airy, N.C. D. 12/21 /70, Riverside, N.J. 5′11″, 181. Chubby Dean went to Philadelphia Athletics from Duke U. after sophomore year. Never quite set world on fire, winning 16 and losing 26 while with A's, 1937–41. Traded to Cleveland during 1941 season, captured 17 decisions, lost 28, before entering military service, 1943. So overall major league record showed 30 wins, 46 defeats, with 5.08 ERA.

Dean was wild, walking 323 while in majors, striking out 195. After war rejoined Indians but was released. Sued them for $4450 which he said was due on $7000 contract. At time said was deducting $2500 earned in other employment. Also claimed that by being released when he was, missed getting pension by one day of service.

Pitched two games for Minneapolis, American Association, 1946; lost one decision, allowing nine runs in six innings pitched. Then dropped down to Class D League, Blue Ridge, where he won 12, lost seven; also played some outfield for Mount Airy N.C., and was at top of list as hitter with .419, though he went to bat just 124 times. Managed Mount Airy 1947. Later umpired in Tri-State League, 1955.

Chubby was pretty fair hitter and often was used as pinch batsman. In 1939, with Athletics, had .351 batting average, getting into 80 games, working on mound in 54 of them. His major league batting average came to .274 in 533 games, including 47 doubles, 7 triples, 3 homers among 287 hits.

DEAN, JAY HANNA (Dizzy) P-BR-TR. B. 1/16/11, Lucas, Ark. 6'3", 202. Dizzy Dean hasn't had too much limelight since early 1970 when Internal Revenue Service, working with local police in four cities, conducted raids designed to break gambling syndicate. Dean was searched in his hotel room in Las Vegas, but not arrested. Revenuers did arrest 10 persons, seized $172,000 in cash and over $450,000 in checks, plus gambling records. Dean named co-conspirator in indictment of 10 men by federal grand jury in Detroit, 2/24/70. Diz said he had made wagers for a friend and this was how he got involved.

In 1957, Dean quit CBS major league game-of-week squad, job which reportedly paid $62,500 a year. Was making his headquarters on five-acre grapefruit ranch in Phoenix. Now lives in Mississippi.

Dizzy flashed like comet across baseball firmament for five years with St. Louis Cardinals, then tapered off like dud firecracker. Averaged 24 wins a season, 1932–1936. Led NL in strikeouts four of those five years. Won 30 games 1934, then followed it up with two World Series victories. These, along with brother Paul's two wins, gave Cards world championship.

Might have compiled much better lifetime record but for misfortune during 1937 All-Star game. Earl Averill of Cleveland smashed liner which hit big toe on Dizzy's left foot. Diz continued to pitch, favoring injured toe, with resultant unnatural throwing motion. This ruined what had been great arm. Was never the same after that, although pitched with some degree of regularity until 1940 season.

Mystery clouds birthplace and birth date of Dean. In fact, Dizzy used to call himself Jerome Herman Dean. Has told so many conflicting stories about himself that there is genuine doubt about where and when he was born. Sometimes he said Oklahoma; sometimes Texas. Many baseball men believe Dean somewhat older than he ever admitted. Signed in 1930 by Cardinal scout Don Curtis. Diz was 17–8 that year for St. Joseph, Western League. Then went to fast-stepping Texas League where he was 8–2 for Cardinal farm at Houston. On last day of NL season that year, pitched Cards to three-hit victory over Pittsburgh, 3–1. Had made jump from completely unknown status to major league success in one year. Undoubtedly could have pitched winning ball with

Cardinals in 1931. But Redbirds were in comfortable position of having plenty of good pitching with fellows like Paul Derringer, Jesse Haines, Bill Hallahan, Burleigh Grimes. Romped to NL flag, winning 14 games more than second-place N.Y. Giants, then to victory in World Series. So Dean spent 1931 with Houston. Won 26, lost 10, fanned 303 batsmen in 304 innings, had 1.57 ERA.

Gifted but gabby Dizzy gave Branch Rickey and others in Cardinal organization plenty of headaches. Antics started at St. Joseph, where Oliver French was business manager for Cardinal farm team. Diz ran up bills in many places, blithely saying, "The Cardinals will pay it." Deep in debt to ball club by end of 1930 season. Rickey got him to live in Charleston, Mo., where French wintered, so Oliver could watchdog through winter. Trouble late in winter. Rumor had it that rival for affections of certain young lady was gunning for Diz. Oliver spirited Dizzy out of town, delivered him early to Cardinal training camp in Florida.

About 1930 radio had several embarrassing experiences when people ad-libbing used profanity and obscenity. Most radio stations instituted practice of demanding that everything be read from script—no ad-libbing by those being interviewed. When Dizzy was invited to Houston radio station, was given simple script to read over air. Diz hadn't gone beyond third grade in school. Prepared script was brief. Dizzy haltingly stumbled through couple of minutes in front of mike. Then read closing sentence; "Ladies and gentlemens, I have to leave now. I'm gonna pitch tonight. And I hope you'll all come to see me pitch and we have a, a capa, capa, capa-city crowd."

In 1934 Dean won 30 games despite fact he missed several pitching turns through own fault. In Sunday doubleheader both Dizzy and Paul were defeated before home crowd of 32,000. Unhappy about it all, Dizzy did not appear that night when Cardinals took train to Detroit for Monday exhibition game. Although Dizzy would not be expected to pitch in exhibition, Detroit fans at least wanted to see "great one" in flesh. So Dizzy was suspended. In argument that followed, Diz and Paul "went on strike." Diz tore up his uniform in anger. Claimed Paul was underpaid, at $3000 annual salary. Diz drawing $6500. While Deans suspended, Cards developed togetherness more than ever before. Pepper Martin volunteered to pitch—and did. When team began to win consistently, Dizzy and Paul decided to get back on bandwagon. When year was over, Diz had his 30 games, Paul 19, and each captured two games in 1934 Series conquest of Tigers. Dizzy probably never better than day he won seventh and crucial game 11–0. Dean did pitch more spectacularly, however. Fanned 17 Chicago Cubs 7/30/33.

By 1938 season Diz's future seemed pretty dim. Cubs decided they needed him, even though arm had gone bad. Would win *some* games and certainly help steam up fans' enthusiasm. To amazement of general manager Branch Rickey and owner Sam Breadon, Cub management indicated it would pay fancy price for Diz. Rickey warned Cubs that Dean's arm was not sound, but Cubs wanted him anyway. Cardinals then demanded—and got—$185,000, plus Curt Davis, Clyde Shoun and Tuck Stainback. Dizzy, using head more than arm, managed 7–1 mark for Cubs, helping them to pennant. Tried gallantly to cope with Yankees in Series. In second game was matched against Lefty Gomez. Kept Yanks in check until eighth inning, leading 3 to 2 most of way. But Yanks got two runs in eighth, and knocked Dizzy out in ninth. Yanks captured 1938 classic in four straight.

Dean did his last serious pitching for Cubs 1940. Same year tried to regain effectiveness by pitching for Tulsa, Texas League. Was 8–8. In 1941 pitched four innings for Cubs in spring; released as player and signed as coach 5/14/41. In July of that year quit Cubs to take broadcasting job in St. Louis. In 1947 left broadcasting booth long enough to pitch in final game of year for St. Louis Browns. Nothing at stake and Browns trying to boost the gate. Dizzy hurled four innings, allowed three hits, walked one, but nobody scored.

While with Cardinals, Diz married Pat Wash, who taught him more English. Still, when in broadcasting, made shrewd use of Ozarkian, hillbilly style, deliberately butchering king's English with such things as "the ketcher throwed the ball purty hard, but the runner slud into second base anyways." Made personal appearances in various parts of country. From local broadcasting went into network sportscasting. In recent years has spent most of time putting on weight and golfing. Reportedly makes substantial cash bets on own game, and wins much oftener than he loses.

When President Dwight D. Eisenhower found himself on same golf course with Diz, he asked, "For a man who plays golf so well, how can you permit yourself to get so overweight?" Dean, then around 300 pounds, replied, "I was on a diet for 25 years. Now that I'm makin' some money, I'm makin' sure I eat good to make up for the lean years."

Dean's major league totals showed 317 games pitched, 1966 innings, 150 victories, 83 defeats, .644 percentage. Allowed 1921 hits, 776 runs 663 of them earned, fanned 1,155 and walked 458 for ERA of 3.04. World Series: 5 games, 34-1/3 innings, 2 wins, 2 losses, 28 hits, 11 earned runs, 19 strikeouts, 6 walks, ERA 2.88.

Hall of Fame, 1953. Appearing at Cooperstown, Dean said: "I want to thank the good Lord for giving me a good right arm, a strong back and a weak mind."

DEAN, PAUL DEE (Daffy) P-BR-TR. B. 8/14/13, Lucas, Ark. 6', 175. It will be news to many baseball fans that in World Series of 1934 Paul Dean actually outpitched his more famous brother, Dizzy, when St.

Louis Cardinals vanquished Detroit Tigers. Compare: Dizzy won two games, lost one, had ERA of 1.73. Paul won two, lost none, had ERA of 1.00. Dizzy did strike out 17, compared with Paul's 11. Dizzy too made more noise, but Paul did effective, workmanlike job.

Nickname "Daffy" did not fit Paul. But for fact Dizzy boasted about everything so much, including "little" brother (Paul was three inches shorter), Paul would have been just another of the 10,000 or so who have played major league ball briefly.

Paul had brief tryout with Houston, Texas League, 1931, one season after Dizzy got his start with Houston and St. Joseph. Also with Columbus, American Association, for short time, 1931, and Springfield, Mo., same season. At Springfield, Western Association, Class C league, Paul was 11—3. Back to Columbus for 1932 and was 7—16 as club finished second. Came into his own following year with 22-7 record, helping Columbus win pennant and, later, Junior World Series. Then came 1934 season when Paul won 19, lost 11 for Cardinals. Threw only no-hitter in majors that year, 9/21/34, against Brooklyn. Had 3.44 ERA. Dizzy, meanwhile, was 30–7, with 2.65 ERA.

Paul again won 19 games in 1935, losing 12, reducing his ERA slightly to 3.37. Suffered arm injury after that and never again regained effectiveness. Had 5–5 record in 1936; 0–0, 1937; 3–1, 1938; 0–1, 1939; then Cardinals gave up on him. With New York NL 1940, 4–4. Five games with Giants, 1941, but no decisions. Dropped out of majors then until St. Louis Browns gave him last chance, 1943. Pitched in three games, just 13-1/3 innings, without winning or losing. Paul's major league totals showed 50 victories, 34 defeats in 787 innings, and ERA of 3.75. Took part in 159 games. Hurled 8 shutouts.

DELAHANTY, EDWARD JAMES (Big Ed) 1B-OF-BR-TR. B. 10/31/67, Cleveland, Ohio. D. 7/2/03, Fort Erie, Ont. 5'10", 170. Ed Delahanty held distinction of being only man to lead both NL and AL in hitting—NL, 1899, .408; AL, 1902, .376. One of five brothers, all of whom made major leagues. Seven times hit over .370. Wound up major league career with .346 average, 1825 games; 2593 hits, 7493 at bats. Scored 1596 runs, had 508 doubles, 182 triples, 98 homers, 478 stolen bases.

Big Ed was bad-ball hitter but this did not stop him from twice making six hits in game; ten hits in succession; four doubles, one game—and four home runs plus one single, one game (7/13/96).

Left home to join Mansfield, Ohio State League, 1887. At that time told his folks would make $3000 a year playing ball—made more. "They never thought I would, but I did," he said. Hit mere .355 that season. Upped to .408 with Wheeling, Tri State League, 1888, meriting immediate promotion to Philadelphia NL. Mainly second baseman that year.

Later outfield, first base. After two seasons at Philadelphia, jumped to Players' Brotherhood at Cleveland, then back to Philadelphia 1891 when Brotherhood disbanded. Continued with Philadelphia until after 1901 season when he jumped to Washington AL.

Ed enjoyed life, hated training rules, discipline. In 1903, when his club was in Detroit, manager suspended him. Left team in huff, took next train east. Tragic end never explained completely. One version was that he created such fracas on train that conductor put him off at International Bridge near Niagara Falls; that he started to walk across bridge and fell between railroad ties. Another version was that he fell from moving train to his death. In any case, his body was found week later at wharf. Hit .338 that final season in 43 games. Hall of Fame 1945.

DEMAREE, ALBERT WENTWORTH P-BL-TR. B. 9/8/84, Quincy, Ill. D. 5/2/62, Los Angeles, Calif. 6', 170. Al Demaree probably was better known as sports cartoonist than as pitcher; at one time syndicated in 200 newspapers. *The Sporting News* used his cartoons 30 years. Despite this, Demaree died penniless. Had been living on tiny old-age pension and social security. Shortly before his death was robbed of all his cash savings, $1100.

Demaree had three years with N.Y. Giants, 1912–14. Won 13, lost four, 1913. Two good seasons with Philadelphia NL, 14–11 in 1915, and 19–14 in 1916. With Chicago NL and Giants, 1917, remained with Giants through 1918; wound up with Boston NL, 1919. Al compiled 80–72 record in majors with 2.77 ERA. Had 14 shutouts. Pitched and won doubleheader for Phillies 9/20/16, against Pittsburgh.

Started his pro career in Cotton States League, 1908, with Columbus, Miss.; pitched for Newark, Savannah, Chattanooga, and Mobile before going to Giants. After leaving majors pitched and managed in Pacific Coast League.

Sold his first cartoon to *N.Y. Journal*, 1912, for $50. Retired from cartooning, 1952, saying "I was always lazy, hated work of any kind. When I played ball, I prayed for rain. Now I spend more for cigars than I do for rent."

DEMAREE, JOSEPH FRANKLIN (Frank) OF-BR-TR. B. 6/10/10, Winters, Calif. D. 8/30/58, Los Angeles, Calif. 5'11½", 185. Frank Demaree got his big chance to play regularly in majors when Kiki Cuyler broke his leg during spring training, 1933. Made most of it, and took part in 134 games, hitting .272, for Chicago Cubs. Cubs figured he could use a bit more experience, however, so he spent 1934 with Los Angeles, Pacific Coast League. A .383 average in 186 games meant his return to Windy City. Those 45 homers, 51 doubles and 173 RBI told pretty convincing story. Back with Cubs, 1935, Demaree played 107 contests, hit .325. Remained with Chicago through 1938. Had .350 average in 154 games, 1936. In 1939 and 1940 Frank was with N.Y. Giants, played regularly and hit above .300 both years. Sold to Boston NL 7/21/41. Average sagged to .216. In 1942 hit .225 in 64 games with Braves. Then spent 1943 with St. Louis Cardinals and shifted to St. Louis Browns for 1944, but took part in only 55 games over two-year period. That was all for Frank, winding up his major league career with .299 average in 1155 games. His 1241 hits included 190 doubles, 36 triples, 72 homers. Scored 578 times and drove in 591 runs. Stole 33 bases.

Demaree hit for .214 average in his 12 WS games with Cubs, 1932,35,38, and with Cardinals, 1943. Nine hits in 42 trips with one double, three homers, six RBI. One homer in 1932 Series, two in 1935 classic, but Cubs lost all three WS. Used only once in 1943 Series by Cards, who lost to Yanks.

As young man, Demaree played basketball, tennis as well as baseball; good at track. Semipro ball in Sacramento area, then lined up with Sacramento team, Pacific Coast League, 1930–32. In his last year at Sacramento hit .364 in 109 games, meriting his advancement to Cubs. Hit .250 in 23 games that same year, then filled in for Cuyler next season.

DERRINGER, PAUL (Duke) P-BR-TR. B. 10/17/06, Springfield, Ky. 6'4", 210. Branch Rickey was religious man who promised his mother he would never go to ball park on Sunday. Did not drink alcoholic beverages. Staunch member of Methodist Episcopal church. As rule, tried to live according to strict teachings learned at Sunday school in Lucasville, Ohio.

One day Paul Derringer left Rickey's second-floor office in Sportsman's Park, St. Louis. Rickey followed Paul out of office, cursing Derringer with vocabulary that would have shamed proverbial trooper. As Derringer descended stairs, air was blue with most violent profanity most witnesses had ever heard. Paul departed hurriedly. It is not recorded how soon after that Derringer was traded to Cincinnati. But his days as Cardinal righthander must have been numbered for causing "Deacon" to forget all his Sunday school maxims that day.

Jack Ryan, bizarre Cardinal scout, signed Derringer 1926. Paul was catcher in high school days. But one day his team's pitchers unmercifully battered. Coach, in desperation, told Derringer to doff mask and shin guards and see whether he could stop opposing club as pitcher. Exhibition was so good that Paul never went back to catching.

Two years at Cardinal farm club, Danville, III League, 1927–28. Danville won pennant first year, finished second in latter season. Two years at Rochester, International League: 17 victories first year, 23 next. Club won two pennants. Then, in 1931, competing with Dizzy Dean for place on Cardinal staff, Dean went back to Houston and Derringer stayed with Redbirds. Paul began as reliefer, but by Memorial Day had won place as starter. Captured 18 wins, losing 8, helping Cards to pennant. In World Series that year, Gabby Street defied tradition and started rookie Derringer, in first game. Paul lost, and lost again later in Series, but Cardinals defeated Philadelphia Athletics, four games to three.

Whole club slumped in 1932. Derringer 11–14. Then in 1933 Paul sent to Cincinnati in deal for Leo Durocher. Managed 22 victories in 1935 with second-division club and passable records next two seasons. Next three seasons 1938–40 won 21,25 and 20 victories for best years of career. In 1939 lost just seven decisions. Helped Redlegs to pennants, 1939–40. Dropped to 12 victories 1941, and 10 in 1942, after which was traded to Chicago Cubs. Best season with Wrigley Field team was 1945, his last in majors—16 wins, 11 losses.

Paul wasn't too successful in World Series, winding up with 2–4 mark and 3.42 ERA in 11 games, 53 innings. However, in 1940 was 2–1 as Cincinnati defeated Detroit Tigers four games to three. Paul pitched 5–2 victory in fourth game and was on mound in crucial seventh contest, taking 2–1 decision over Bobo Newsom.

Lifetime records as big leaguer showed 223 victories, 212 defeats in 579 games. Pitched 3646 innings, with 3.46 ERA.

Only Derringer can tell what he said to irk Rickey so. But guesses at time were that it had to do with hard-nosed salary negotiations on both sides.

DEVINE, VAUGHAN P. (Bing) Executive. B. 3/1/17, St. Louis, Mo. More than half century ago, Jimmy Jones, stockholder in St. Louis NL club, came up with idea of "Cardinal Knothole Gang." Idea was to make baseball fans out of teenage boys by letting them see Cardinal games free. Added appeal was that it would keep kids off streets and out of trouble.

In case of Bing Devine, idea produced not only fan but general manager for club many years later. Bing, as boy, sat in stands in St. Louis and dreamed of day he might mingle with his heroes. When not using his Knothole Gang privileges, Devine played baseball and basketball. As collegian, won letters at hometown Washington U. in both sports. While still in college, got job helping compile statistics in Cardinal office. Became assistant in public relations office, 1939. Two years later began administrative training in Cardinal farm system as business manager at Johnson City, Tenn., Appalachian League, 1941. Divided 1942 season between Fresno, Calif., and Decatur, Ill., clubs in Cardinal system. Then hitch with Navy Fleet Air Wing in Pacific, 1943–45.

Back from war, business manager of Columbus, Ga., Cardinal farm.

Team won two pennants, after which Devine was brought to St. Louis to become assistant to Fred Saigh, then president of Cardinals. Out to farms again, 1949, this time as general manager of one of top teams in Cardinal organization, Rochester. Remained there seven years.

In November 1955 Devine returned to Cardinals, this time as assistant to general manager Frank Lane, Two years later Lane moved out and Bing became G.M. Except for 1965–67 when he was with Mets, Devine has been Cardinal G.M. Took on additional title of executive vice president 3/28/73.

Under Devine's administration, trades brought Curt Flood, Lou Brock, Dick Groat, Bill White, Julian Javier, all of whom played key roles in Cardinals winning pennant and WS, 1964. Club owner, Gussie Busch, however, got impatient during 1964 season when team seemed to be floundering. Resulted in departure of Devine—and resignation of Johnny Keane, who managed Cardinals to pennant and WS victory over Yankees.

George Weiss, then president of Mets, hired Devine immediately as his assistant. Bing moved into president, G.M. slots when Weiss retired. Returned to Cardinals 12/5/67. Club, which had won pennant and WS that year, again took NL flag, 1968, but lost to Detroit in WS, four games to three.

DEWITT, WILLIAM ORVILLE   Executive. B. 8/3/02, St. Louis, Mo. Bill DeWitt has held about every conceivable job connected with a baseball club except those on field. Started out selling soda pop in ball park, then became office boy, and wound up owning ball club. Like Horatio Alger hero, got his start when Branch Rickey, then with St. Louis Browns, needed office boy. Rickey asked manager of ball park concessions to send up a bright youngster to be his office boy. DeWitt was 14-year-old kid recommended to Rickey. Rickey soon shifted to Cardinals and DeWitt went with him, doing office work after school and during summers. Eventually DeWitt took on full-time job and continued his education at night school. Attended St. Louis and Washington universities, 1925–31, studying law. Passed Missouri Bar examination, June 1931.

With Cardinals Bill had become club treasurer. When Pepper Martin and Dizzy Dean came into public eye, DeWitt became their business manager. Also promoted pro basketball on side. In 1936 organized group to purchase Browns and became vice president–general manager. In 1944 Browns won their only pennant in modern times. DeWitt was named Major League Executive of Year. Cardinals defeated his club in WS, four games to two.

Bill, with his brother, Charles, purchased total holdings of Browns 2/1/49. Bill became president-general manager. In 1951 sold his stock to

Bill Veeck but signed five-year contract to remain with club as vice president in advisory capacity and supervise farm clubs. In November 1953, Browns became Baltimore Orioles. DeWitt then worked for Baltimore club in St. Louis until 4/1/54 when he became assistant general manager of Yankees. Became "Baseball Coordinator" to administer $500,000 fund by major leagues to aid minor leagues 12/5/56.

Became president, Detroit Tigers, October 1959. During his term in Motor City cooked up deal with Frank Lane, then general manager at Cleveland, to trade managers, for first time in major league history. Jimmie Dykes went to Indians in exchange for Joe Gordon.

DeWitt shifted to Cincinnati, 11/2/60, becoming vice president and general manager. Then became president of Reds, October 1961, after death of Powel Crosley, Jr. Bought Cincinnati ball club 4/5/62; sold it 1/9/68. During DeWitt's first year in Cincinnati, club won NL flag, but lost WS to Yankees, four games to one.

DICKEY, WILLIAM MALCOLM C-BL-TR. B. 6/6/07, Bastrop, La.
6'1½", 185. Bill Dickey belonged to Yankees of push-button era. Took part in eight World Series, 1932,36–39,41–43. Did his part by catching efficiently, batting consistently, as his lifetime major league average of .313 and election to Hall of Fame 1954 attest. Now in business of selling securities in Little Rock, Ark.

Dickey might have been member of St. Louis Cardinals if Blake Harper, friend of Branch Rickey, hadn't gotten flat tire on his way to sign Bill. So Lena Blackburne, then connected with Little Rock club, Southern Association, got Dickey's name on dotted line, 1925. It took experience in Muskogee, Jackson (Miss.), Buffalo, Little Rock before Yankees, 1928. Yankee scout Johnny Nee wired Ed Barrow, then business manager of N. Y. club: "I will quit scouting if this boy does not make good."

Nee did not have to quit. In his first full season in majors, 1929, Dickey caught 127 games, hit cool .324. Not polished catcher at start, but through persistent effort, soon became recognized master. Hitting continued. Batted well over .300 in ten out of eleven years. Four times had over 100 RBI. Hit .362, 1936, and .351 in 1943. Compiled all sorts of records. Did not have passed ball for 125 games in 1931. Caught 100 or more games 13 consecutive seasons to set major league record. Hit three home runs in one game, 7/26/39. Made unassisted double play against St. Louis AL, 6/8/41. Made AL All-Star team seven times. World Series performance included .438 average in 1932 and .400 mark in 1938. Hit two homers in classic of 1939. Of eight Series in which he took part, Yanks won seven.

Bill had brief fling as manager of Yankees during Larry MacPhail era. In May 1946, Joe McCarthy and MacPhail came to parting of ways.

Dickey took over. By September, noble experiment ended. Bill left 9/12/46. Did not like job. Following year, however, managed Little Rock club, Southern Association. Club had disastrous 51–103 record. Dickey caught a little, hit .333 in eight games; then gave up active playing—and managing. Back with Yankees as coach, 1949–57. Scouted for Yanks 1959, and again coached team 1960, until July. Since that time, has concentrated on securities business.

Dickey played 1789 games in majors, scored 930 runs, had 6300 AB, 1969 hits, 343 doubles, 72 triples, 202 homers, .313 average. Drove in 1209 runs, stole 36 bases. In World Series play: 38 games, 37 hits in 145 trips, 19 runs, 1 double, 1 triple, 5 homers, .255 average.

Bill's younger brother, George (Skeets) Dickey, caught for Boston and Chicago AL teams six years, 1935-36, 41-42, 46-47, but never attained to older brother's stature.

DIERKER, LAWRENCE EDWARD   P-BR-TR. B. 9/22/46, Hollywood, Calif. 6'4", 210. Larry Dierker won 20 games, lost 13 for Houston Astros, 1969, first pitcher ever to win that many for that club. Joined Astros after pitching just 39 innings at Cocoa, Fla., in Rookie League. Made his big league debut 9/22/64, his 18th birthday.

Dierker had 0–1 record in three games that year. Followed with 7–8, 10–8 and 6–5 records. Won 12 and lost 15 in 1968. In his 20-game season, 1969, had ERA of 2.33 for club that finished fifth in six-club Western Division of NL. Had 16 wins, 12 losses in 1970, and though he had 10–1 record at one point in 1971 season, got arm trouble and wound up 12–6, with 2.71 ERA.

As 1973 season dawned Dierker had lifetime record of 236 games with 1625 IP, 98 wins, 76 losses, for team that has generally struggled to get up in NL races. Had 1080 strikeouts, compared to 437 bases on balls, and owned 3.17 ERA.

Lives in Houston.

DIETZ, RICHARD ALLEN   C-BR-TR. B. 9/18/41, Crawfordsville, Ind. 6'1", 185. Dick Dietz, who played 149 games for San Francisco Giants, 1970, hit .300, with 22 homers and 107 RBI, found himself out of job in spring of 1972. Giants decided to use Dave Rader and Fran Healy as their backstop staff. So Dietz went to Los Angeles Dodgers on day before season opened for waiver price. Didn't get much chance to work with Dodgers—22 games. Batting average for year: .161 in 27 contests. To Atlanta Braves just before 1973 season.

Dick banked some $90,000 in bonus money when he signed with San Francisco club, 1960, after spectacular prep school career in Greenville, S.C. En route to parent club, played for Artesia, N. Mex.; Fresno, El Paso, Eugene, Tacoma, and Phoenix. Got into 13 games with Giants,

1966, 56 following year, and 98 in 1968. Then came banner 1970 season when he had 36 doubles to go with aforementioned 22 homers and .300 batting average. Tapered off bit in 1971, but still banged 19 round-trippers, drove in 72 runs, with his .252 average.

Dick would rather forget he led NL catchers in passed balls in 1970 with 25. However, this did not prevent being named to NL All-Star Game squad that year. Got one hit, home run, in two trips to plate.

Dietz wound up 1972 season with lifetime average of .259 for 563 major league games. Had 63 homers to credit, 81 doubles, 5 triples, among 437 hits. Scored 204 times, drove in 277 runs.

DILLINGER, ROBERT BERNARD   3B-BR-TR. B. 9/17/18, Glendale, Calif. 5'11½", 170. Bob Dillinger led AL in stolen bases three times, 1947–49, with 34,28, and 20 thefts respectively. Played all of his major league career at third base excepting one game at short. But drew raves as center fielder, 1953, toward end of his career in minors.

Attended U. of Idaho two years on athletic scholarship. Football playing ended with broken collarbone, but took up pro baseball at Lincoln, Nebr., 1939. Later with Youngstown, Toledo, and San Antonio clubs before going into military service, 1943–45. St. Louis AL, 1946–49. Philadelphia AL and Pittsburgh, 1950; Pittsburgh and Chicago AL, 1951. Then to Sacramento, Pacific Coast League, 1952–55.

Major league career added up to 753 games, 888 hits, 123 doubles, 47 triples, 10 homers, and .306 average. Scored 401 runs, drove in 213, and stole 104 bases. Played for AL in 1949 All-Star game.

In minors, Dillinger's 67 stolen bases led Western League, 1939; and 67 more was enough to lead Mid-Atlantic League, 1940. In 1953 Bob led PCL in hitting with .366 and also in total hits. Not one of them was home run, only third time leading batsman had gone without homer in PCL.

DIMAGGIO, DOMINIC PAUL (Little Professor)   OF-BR-TR. B. 2/12/18, San Francisco, Calif. 5'9", 167. Multimillionaire brother of more famous Joe and less famous Vince. Made good money in baseball with Boston Red Sox but multiplied it in many businesses—textile-type manufacturing plants, sand and gravel company, incorporator of two banks, on board of directors of another, part owner of famed DiMaggio Restaurant in San Francisco. Wears thick-lensed glasses so they called him "Little Professor." Also allegedly looked like choir boy—but others called him "Jesse James without the horse" because he robbed so many hitters of doubles and triples in center field. Because brother Joe frequently dominated sports headlines Dom was never fully appreciated in most baseball circles. Great leadoff man, brilliant outfielder with fine arm, good hitter, though not known for long ball.

Dom made it completely on his own, without any coaching from his older brothers. As kid sold newspapers, worked in box factory in San Francisco. Pacific Coast League team ran joint tryout camp with Cincinnati Reds. Reds had first crack at any young phenoms, selected another player. Lefty O'Doul, manager of S.F. Seals, picked Dominic, possibly because he knew Vince and Joe had become great players. Dom jumped into S.F. lineup, 1937, and promptly hit .306 in 140 games. Came back with .307 following year, and .360 in his final year in PCL. Solid hitting that season also was reflected in his 48 doubles, 18 triples, and 14 homers with 82 RBI.

Fielding ability, especially his great arm, may be judged by fact he made 17 assists his first year in PCL, 29 his next year, and 27 in 1939. Joe Cronin bought him for Red Sox, price said to be around $75,000.

Dom had three years as regular in Boston outfield, then spent three years in navy. Back from wars, picked up where he left off, and had seven more stellar seasons. In 1949 hit safely in 31 consecutive games, setting record for any Red Sox player. In 1948 Dom set some AL fielding marks to shoot at. Made 503 putouts, best mark ever made in AL by outfielder. In 1972 Dom still held distinction of being only AL outfielder to make 500 putouts in one year. And his 516 chances accepted (excluding errors), 1948, still record in AL. By getting more than 400 putouts 1942, 47, 48, 49 Dominic equaled AL record. Co-holders are Sam Chapman of Philadelphia and Sam West of St. Louis.

Robbed brother Joe of numerous extra-base blows during Yankee-Red Sox encounters. Once Dom grabbed 460-foot smash off Joe's bat in Yankee Stadium. As they passed each other at end of inning, Joe remarked, "I should have pulled that one more."

In 1946 WS Dominic got seven hits in 27 times at bat for .259 average. Three of his hits were doubles. For time he figured to be hero of seventh game against Cardinals. In eighth inning Cards were leading by 3–1 score. Up came Dominic, who promptly doubled, driving in two runs and tying score. Dom, however, twisted right ankle and had to leave game. Culberson replaced him on base paths and later in center field. Then came famous run by Enos Slaughter, who scored all way from first base on Harry Walker's drive to left center, giving Cardinals ball game and WS. If DiMaggio had been in outfield at that time, many observers believe Slaughter never would have tried to score because of respect everyone had for Dom's great arm.

Dominic had eye infection during spring of 1953, and Mgr. Lou Boudreau used him sparingly. After being in just three games as pinch hitter, Dom decided to call quits and announced his voluntary retirement 5/12/53. Could have continued but did not want to ride bench. Guessing was that he disliked way Boudreau was running club. In public announcement of decision to quit, Dom praised owner Tom Yawkey and general manager Joe Cronin lavishly—but made no reference to manager.

Dom played 1399 AL games, went to bat 5640 times, scored 1046 runs; had 1680 hits, with 308 doubles, 57 triples, 87 homers, 618 RBI for .298 average. Stole 100 bases.

DIMAGGIO, JOSEPH PAUL (Yankee Clipper) OF-BR-TR. B. 11/25/14, Martinez, Calif. 6'2", 193. Born of humble immigrant parents, Joe was eighth child in family of nine children. Family had enough to eat, but no luxuries. Not long after Joe's birth, family moved to San Francisco where father earned living as fisherman. Youngster finished junior high school, but attended high school just one year. Tennis and baseball occupied his spare moments, but leisure limited by need to help family income with whatever jobs were available—crating oranges, picking crabmeat in cannery, for example.

Soon baseball meant money too—semipro variety. Once Joe hit two home runs, was rewarded with two baseballs and gift certificates, worth $15. This was 1931, depression deepening, and $15 hard to come by. Meanwhile, older brother, Vince, had become good enough ball player to make good as outfielder with Tucson, Arizona-Texas League, 1932; brought up to Pacific Coast League by San Francisco Seals end of season. Seals needed someone to play shortstop in final three games of year. Vince suggested brother Joe, shortstop in semipro games. Suggestion accepted; thus started fabulous pro career. Tripled, doubled, in nine trips to plate.

Following spring, after slow start, Joe converted into outfielder. Wasted no time proving ability. Though only 18, put together amazing streak hitting safely 61 consecutive games. His .340 batting average for season, plus 28 homers and league-leading 169 RBI, meant major league scouts were keenly interested. Seals fended off major league offers, believing DiMaggio's value would increase with another year's experience in PCL. It was increasing until Joe stepped out of taxi during 1934 season. Heard crack in knee, collapsed. Out of action for weeks with torn tendons. Seals' management had been dreaming of fancy sale price for DiMaggio, maybe $100,000, now scaled down sights, even though Joe batted .341, 101 games. Still depression, most major league clubs feeling financial pinch, and DiMaggio now big gamble at any price. Wealthy Yankees gambled $25,000, five minor league players. One of best bargains. Transaction provided that DiMaggio remain with San Francisco one more year before reporting to Yanks. That year, 1935, DiMaggio's .398 average in 172 games, plus leading PCL in RBI again, demonstrated recovery of knee, durability. Other major league club executives muttering about luck of the rich Yankees in getting prize prospect for relatively small cash outlay.

Joe got off to slow start with Yanks in 1936, due to diathermy burn. Still in 138 games, hit .323, led outfielders in assists. Pulled down long drives with graceful ease.

Some statistics about Joe's hitting: led AL in homers 1937, with 46. 1948, 39. Led AL in hitting 1939, 40—.381 and .352. Hit in 56 consecutive games. This eradicated old AL mark of 41 set by George Sisler; major league record of 44, set by Willie Keeler in 1897.

Streak started 5/15/41, ended 7/17/41 in Cleveland. Third baseman Ken Keltner made fine stops to get DiMaggio out in first two trips. In ninth inning it took great bare-handed stab by shortstop Lou Boudreau to cut off chance for hit. Lou, with lightning reflexes, rifled ball to first base, and streak was history. Of all records in major league annals, DiMaggio's probably has best chance of enduring—despite adage, "Records were made to be broken." After failing to hit in that game, Joe immediately started another string, hitting safely in 17 contests!

Joltin' Joe DiMaggio, as song called him, spent 1943–45 in military service. Had married Hollywood starlet, Dorothy Arnold, whom he met while taking small part in filming of *Manhattan Merry-Go-Round*, 1937. Son, Joe, Jr., aspired to be catcher in younger days. This marriage ended in divorce. Married Marilyn Monroe, 1954. Following year conflicts of their two careers caused rift, ultimately divorce. Joe, however, saw her occasionally until her death. Marilyn is said to have considered him true friend after separation.

After war, Joe's best full season was 1948. Led AL in homers (39), RBI (155) while batting .320 in 153 games. Had surmounted operation on left heel before 1947 season and another to take bone chips from right elbow before 1948 campaign. But developed bone spur on right heel. Another operation 11/48. Pain every time he tried to put weight on feet. Feared career ended. By 5/49 pain vanished. Began conditioning. Returned to Yankee lineup in Boston. Red Sox red hot, taking nine of their last 10 games. Crowd of 36,228 in stands. Joe singled first time up. Slammed homer next chance. In eighth inning, Sox threatening, slid hard into second to break up double play. And in ninth, after hard run caught Ted Williams' long fly ball for final out. Next game, Joe hit two more homers. Third game, still another homer. Yanks swept series. That was year Casey Stengel won his first pennant with Bombers—beating out Red Sox by one game. Though season abbreviated for Yankee Chipper, hit .346 in 76 games.

Joe played 139 games in 1950, hitting .301, but baseball began to be hard work. Legs, reflexes not responding as well as they had. Dropped to .263 in 1951, could appear in only 116 games. Personal pride dictated his own decision to quit. Club would have continued him as pinch hitter, part-time outfielder, drawing card at his $100,000 salary.

Helped Yankees to ten World Series, nine world championships. Played 51 Series games, had 199 at bats, 27 runs, 54 hits, 6 doubles, 8 homers, 30 RBI, .271 average. After making one error in his first series, 1936, fielded flawlessly.

Played on AL All-Star teams 11 times, batting .225. MVP three times—1939,41,47. Major league totals: 1736 games, 2214 hits, 6821 at bats, 1390 runs, 389 doubles, 131 triples, 361 homers, 1537 RBI, .325 average.

After retirement, DiMaggio out of baseball until Charlie Finley, owner of Oakland A's, lured him back into uniform 1968, title of vice president and coach. Though Oakland much closer to Fisherman's Wharf, San Francisco, just didn't seem right. Fans will forget that Oakland connection and remember him as Yankee Clipper, truly one of game's immortals. Election to Hall of Fame, 1955, merely verified what everybody knew. Joe belonged.

DIMAGGIO, VINCENT PAUL OF-BR-TR. B. 9/6/12, Martinez, Calif. 5'11½", 183. Vince DiMaggio was two years older than brother Joe, but Joe reached majors one season earlier. Vince was good enough to stick around majors ten years, but never came near equaling Joe. Nor was he as good a player as younger brother Dom. Vince set one record of which he is not particularly proud. Struck out 134 times in 1938. In fact, during career fanned 837 times. Four times had 100 strikeouts or more.

Elder DiMaggio played at Tucson, Arizona-Texas League, 1932, hitting .347 in 94 games. Brought up to San Francisco, Pacific Coast League, same year, played 59 games for Seals, hit .270. Following season started with Seals but was traded to Hollywood, same league. Remained with Hollywood through 1935. San Diego, PCL, 1936. Boston NL, 1937–38. Kansas City, American Association, 1939. Cincinnati 1939–40. Pittsburgh, 1940–44. Philadelphia NL, 1945–46. New York NL, 1946.

Vince's best season was 1940, hit .289 in 112 games. His major league record showed 1110 games, 3849 AB, 959 hits, 209 doubles, 24 triples, 125 homers, .249 average. Scored 491 runs, had 584 RBI, stole 79 bases.

DINNEEN, WILLIAM HENRY (Big Bill) P-BR-TR. B. 4/5/76, Syracuse, N. Y. D. 1/13/55, Syracuse, N. Y. 6'1", 190. Bill Dinneen best remembered as long-time AL umpire—and first man to win three games in "modern" WS (1903). Pitched for Toronto in 1890s before joining Washington NL, 1898. At that time had some idea of becoming outfielder, but could pitch much better than hit. Two mediocre seasons. Joined Boston NL for 1900–01. Boston AL 1902. Won 21 games but lost equal number. In 1903, 21–13.

That fall shut out Pittsburgh Pirates in second game of World Series 3–0; lost fourth game 5–4; won sixth game 6–3; another shutout in eighth game, 3–0. Red Sox won Series five games to three. Legendary Cy Young captured Boston's two other wins. Sox used just one other pitcher, Long Tom Hughes—pitched two innings. Dinneen's World Series totals: 29 hits in 35 innings, 4 complete games, 3–1 record, ERA 2.06. Struck out 28.

Bill 23–14 in 1904. So-so after that. Traded to St. Louis AL during 1907 after 0–4 mark. With Browns, 7–11 record. Following year, 14–7. Retired after 1909 season with Browns. Began long career as AL umpire 1910. Lifetime pitching record in majors: 171–178, 3.01 ERA, 391 games, 3475 innings. Allowed 2957 hits, walked 829, fanned 1127.

Only no-hit game came 9/27/05, pitching for Boston AL against White Sox. Had not appeared on mound during first 26 days of September.

In later years loved to play chef. Specialty, concoction called "Million Dollar Lemon Pie."

DOAK, WILLIAM LEOPOLD (Spittin' Bill) P-BR-TR. B. 1/28/91, Pittsburgh, Pa. D. 11/26/54, Bradenton, Fla. 6'1/2", 165. "Spittin' Bill" got his nickname from fact he was one of last major league pitchers to use spitball legally. In December 1920 major leagues banned spitter— excepting few pitchers (Doak included) in each league who depended largely on spitter. To have refused to let them throw it would have meant taking their livelihood from them. So they were permitted its use for rest of careers. As legal use of spitter was drawing to close, Spalding *Official Baseball Guide of 1935* commented:

> While no question has been raised as to effectiveness of this style of delivery, there is serious doubt whether it does not carry with it all elements of wild pitch in practically each delivery of ball to a bat. Pitcher may have ever so good control, but there will come dangerous slip which may incapacitate batsman.
>
> There is no doubt as to its unsanitary features, which make it almost repulsive. There might be traced to its use the carrying of disease, which is quite enough to condemn it, if there were no other objections to anointing ball freely with secretion of mouth.

Guide also referred to spitter as "only menace it [baseball] ever had to general health of its participants."

Doak pitched at Wheeling, Akron, Central League, 1910–12, getting brief tryout with Cincinnati 1912. With Akron, Inter-State League, 1913. Same season landed with Cardinals, 7/19/13. Start not auspicious, 2–8. But reached 19-victory level 1914, losing six; 20–12 mark 1920.

Cards traded him to Brooklyn during 1924 season; 11–5 for Dodgers that year. Following year moved to Florida, entered real estate business.

Two years stayed out of game, at one point spurning $15,000 contract from Dodgers and "sentimental appeals" from his teammates. Real estate boom slumped. Back with Brooklyn 1927, 11–8 record; 3–8, 1928. Retired for good after spending part of 1929 with Cardinals again, posting 1–2 mark. Final record in majors, 169–157 for 453 games.

Back in Florida Bill busied himself in Boys Club work and as midget baseball sponsor and coach. Operated confectionary shop in Bradenton for several years.

DOBSON, CHARLES THOMAS (Chuck) P-BR-TR. B. 1/10/44, Kansas City, Mo. 6'4", 200. Chuck Dobson was back on roster of Oakland A's in spring of 1973 after being sent to Birmingham, Southern Association, for 1972, following elbow operation. If Chuck could return to 1971 form, he would be winning pitcher again; captured 15 decisions that year with just five defeats.

Dobson starred in baseball, basketball, football in high school. Attended Kansas U. and won various collegiate honors, as well as pitched for U. S. Amateur All-Star team that toured Japan, Korea, Hawaii. Played in demonstration game at opening of Olympics, Tokyo, 1964. Signed by Whitey Herzog, then with Kansas City A's organization, for reported $25,000 bonus. Started with Birmingham, 1965; lost six decisions, but had 10–7 record same season with Lewiston, Northwest League. Up to Kansas City for 1966–67 with 4–6 and 10–10 records. Then moved to Oakland with franchise. Won 12, lost 14, 1968; had 15 wins, 13 defeats, following year. In 1970 led AL in shutouts with five, and in games started with 40. But was able to win just one more than he lost, with 16 victories, 15 defeats. Then came fine 1971 season—and elbow trouble.

Dobson ready for 1973 with record of 72–63; 3.65 ERA for 1099 innings in 187 games. Strikeouts exceeded his walks, 725 to 448.

DOBSON, PATRICK EDWARD P-BR-TR. B. 2/12/42, Depew, N.Y. 6'3", 190. One of Baltimore Orioles' four pitchers to win 20 games, 1971. Overall performance was best since he started pro career back in 1960 in Detroit organization. Pat had 12–9 record at Portland, Oreg., 1966, and 14–15 mark with San Diego Padres, 1970. but rest of his records in both minors and majors were not impressive. Won 16, lost 18 with Orioles, 1972, then traded to Atlanta Braves. To Yankees, June 1973.

In 1971 started in unspectacular fashion. In 13 starts through June 12, Dobson had won just three, losing four. Then he captured 12 straight. At one point pitched nine consecutive complete games. Amassed 17–4 mark in his last 21 decisions. Season 1971 was his personal high for wins, starts, complete games, shutouts, innings pitched, strikeouts. Led Oriole starters with 187 strikeouts; tied Mike Cuellar for club lead in shutouts with four.

Dobson got fancy bonus for signing with Detroit. After Durham, 1960, Tigers sent him to Knoxville, Duluth, Montgomery, Jamestown, Syracuse, Portland, and Toledo. With Detroit part of 1967, all of 1968–69. San Diego NL, 1970. Then traded to Orioles.

As 1973 campaign started, Dobson 61–61 in majors, ERA 3.08. WS performance in 1971 showed 6-2/3 innings pitched, 13 hits, four walks, and three earned runs for ERA of 4.05. Was not charged with loss nor did he win decision. Worked in 1968 WS while with Tigers, 4-2/3 innings, 5 hits, 2 earned runs, ERA 3.86, no decision.

Dobson toured Japan with Orioles after 1971 season and pitched no-hitter against Tokyo Giants, a first for any visiting American pitcher.

DOBY, LAWRENCE EUGENE (Larry)   OF-BL-TR. B. 12/13/24, Camden, S.C. 6'1", 180.

Jackie Robinson was first black player in NL; Larry Doby was pioneer in AL. While Jackie joined Brooklyn Dodgers just before opening day, 1947, Doby made debut 7/3/47 with Cleveland Indians. Currently is coach with Montreal Expos.

Bill Veeck, 1947 boss of Indians, paid $20,000 to Newark Eagles for Doby. Agreed to give Negro club $10,000 immediately, another $10,000 if Larry made good. Doby struck out in his first appearance as pinch hitter and had difficult time for rest of season, batting just .156 in 29 games as an infielder. Converted to an outfielder in 1948, he hit .301 in 121 games and helped Cleveland win AL pennant. Soon became recognized as fine fielder and long-ball hitter. Led AL in homers with 32 in 1952, and again in 1954 with same total. Five times batted in more than 100 runs per season. His 126 RBI led AL in 1954. Best hitting came in 1950, .326. Three homers in one game, 8/2/50. In 1956–57 Doby toiled for Chicago AL. Back with Cleveland, 1958. Divided 1959 season between Detroit and Chicago AL. Larry made AL All-Star team six consecutive summers, 1949–54 and batted .300 in these games. In WS play, 1948 and 1954, both with Cleveland, had .237 average in ten games. Fans remember that it was Doby's tremendous home run in fourth game of 1948 WS against Boston that helped Steve Gromek defeat Johnny Sain, 2–1 before 81,897 in attendance.

Doby struck out quite a bit—once whiffing five times in single game. His 121 strikeouts in 1953 set new AL record, since surpassed.

DOERR, ROBERT PERSHING   2B-BR-TR. B. 4/7/18, Los Angeles, Calif. 5'11", 185.

Consistently fine ball player for Boston Red Sox over period 1937–51. Named by *Sporting News* as MVP in AL, 1944. Repeatedly led AL second basemen in fielding, or tied for lead. Hit .409 in his only WS, 1946.

Bobby holds several creditable records even though two decades and more have passed since he played for Sox. Went from 6/24/48 to 9/19/48 without an error at second base, handling 414 chances, which is an AL record. Led AL second basemen in double plays, 1938,40,43,46,47, more than any other keystoner in league. Equaled modern major league record, 5/30/46, second game, and 6/3/46, first game, by accepting 28 chances, most by any AL second basemen in two consecutive games. Holds major league record for most double plays in doubleheader, eight, 6/25/50, mark that was later equaled by Bobby Knoop of Angels. Led AL second basemen in fielding, 1942,43,46,50, and tied for lead in 1940,48. In WS set new record for assists by second baseman in seven-game classic with 31, 1946.

Doerr started pro ball at Hollywood, Pacific Coast League, 1934, with .259 mark in 67 games. Following year boosted his hitting to .317 in 172 games, with 74 RBI. Had .342 season with San Diego, same league, 1936. Then began his long stay with Red Sox, interrupted only in 1945 by military service. Bobby hit above .300 only three times, but in most other seasons didn't miss it by many points. Consistently good with men on base as his RBI totals show; six times went above 100. Usually good for 15 to 20 homers, twice reaching 27 in a season.

Bobby played 1865 major league games, all with Boston. Got 2042 hits, 381 doubles, 89 triples, 223 homers, with 1247 RBI. Scored 1094 times and had major league career average of .288.

In his one WS went to bat 22 times, got nine hits, including double and homer, with three runs batted in. Scout for Sox, 1957–66, then coached for same team several years afterward.

DONLIN, MICHAEL JOSEPH (Turkey Mike) OF-BL-TL. B. 5/30/78, Erie, Pa. D. 9/24/33, Hollywood, Calif. 5'9", 170. Mike Donlin, besides being "personality kid" and fine ball player, was favorite of John McGraw, then manager of N.Y. Giants. Rightfully so—when Mike was on Giants, club never finished below second, won two pennants and only WS team played. Trouble was that Mike married stage star, Mabel Hite, went into vaudeville, and wound up in Hollywood making movies.

Donlin was handsome smiling "Irishman," good mixer, raconteur of great talent, singer, and held his liquor well. Many felt he could have been superstar had he taken baseball more seriously. As it was, he was fine outfielder, had great arm, and wound up with lifetime batting average of .334 in dead-ball era.

Mike was machinist in youth, southpaw pitcher in spare time. Took off from his native city, Erie, Pa., and headed for California where he played for Santa Cruz team, California League, 1899. He could hit—so he soon gave up pitching. Batted .402 at Santa Cruz in 29 games, and before year was up had made place for himself with St. Louis NL. Hit .330 and stole 20 bases that same season in 67 games, his first year in pro ball. Following year hit .327 in 77 contests.

Then jumped to Baltimore in new major, AL, where John McGraw was managing. Hit .341 in 122 games with Orioles. In 1902 McGraw had left Orioles to become manager of Giants. Donlin jumped again—this time to Cincinnati. Remained with Reds until July 1904 when Giants bought his contract. Back with McGraw, Giants went on to win NL flag. No WS that year, since John T. Brush, owner of Giants, spurned challenge of Boston AL. In 1905, however, Brush had changed his mind about postseason play with AL champions. Giants won pennant, took on Philadelphia A's and defeated them four games to one. Donlin had his best season that year, batting .356 in 150 games, with 33 stolen bases. Scored 124 runs to lead league in that department. Followed it with .316 average in WS. This led both clubs in hitting. Remember, Donlin was batting against three fine pitchers, Chief Bender, Eddie Plank, and Andy Coakley, whose combined ERA for series was 0.83.

In 1906 Donlin, newlywed, left Giants after 30 games. Came back for 155 games in 1908, batting .334, stealing 30 bases. In 1911 Donlin came back to Giants again briefly but was traded to Boston NL in August. Following year was with Pittsburgh for 77 games and .316 average. Then 36 games with Jersey City, International League, 1913, and back to Giants for final time, 1914. This time he quit majors after hitting just .161 in 35 games.

In 1917 managed Memphis club of Southern Association a while but didn't finish season. After that it was stage and pictures. Donlin left major league record of 1025 games, 3859 AB, 670 runs, 1287 hits for .334 average. Hit 174 doubles, 98 three-baggers, and 51 homers. Stole 210 bases. Among his feats was six-hit day 6/24/01, when he made two singles, two doubles, two triples against Detroit.

DOUBLEDAY, ABNER B. 6/26/19, Ballston Spa, N.Y. D. 1/26/93, Mendham, N.J. General Abner Doubleday, Civil War hero, allegedly invented baseball, laying out first diamond in cow pasture near Cooperstown, N.Y. Study by commission headed by A. G. Spalding in 1907 apparently based conclusions on testimony of one man, Abner Graves, boyhood pal of Doubleday. Findings were announced in *Official Baseball Guide* of 1908.

According to this version, baseball was American invention, starting in 1839. Many flaws. Many historians note Doubleday was attending classes at West Point when supposed to have been in Cooperstown. Also evidences of English origin of game. Seems to have evolved in slow process; crystallized pretty much in present form something over century ago. Yet Doubleday stands canonized by organized baseball, and Hall of Fame was built in town Abner may never have seen. Each year Hall of Fame becomes more entrenched in baseball's scheme of things. Major league clubs annually make pilgrimage there; each year new immortals are officially inducted.

In 1939 Hall of Fame came into being. *Official Baseball Guide* for 1940 declared: "Here it was that James Fenimore Cooper lived and conceived his still widely read novels, and where Abner Doubleday, later to take an important part in the Battle of Gettysburg, devised the scheme of baseball in 1839."

Ten thousand were on hand as Hans Wagner, Eddie Collins, Connie Mack, Cy Young, Babe Ruth, George Sisler, Larry Lajoie and others were officially proclaimed worthy of baseball's highest honors.

When Doubleday retired from army, did considerable writing about his career, specially Civil War, but wrote nothing about baseball. Lived until 1893, many years after professional baseball had come into existence.

DOUGLAS, PHILIPS BROOKS (Shufflin' Phil) P-BR-TR. B. 6/17/90, Cedartown, Ga. D. 8/1/52, Sequatchie Valley, Tenn. 6'3", 190. Phil Douglas could pitch, but life in major leagues was too much for him. Not high-salaried, but enough money to buy more liquor than he could handle. Then had misfortune to land on N.Y. Giants, managed by John McGraw, whose sharp tongue withered many players far better equipped with gray matter and character than Shufflin' Phil. Result: tragedy and banishment for life from organized baseball at age 32.

Phil pitched for various teams, Rome and Macon, Ga., Des Moines, San Francisco and Spokane before making majors with Cincinnati, 1914. Brief spell with Chicago AL prior to that. Bounced from Reds to Brooklyn to Cubs same season, 1915; back to minors, St. Paul, 1916. Cubs, 1916, winning 14, but losing 20. During 1919 season, despite so-so record, Giants obtained him from Chicago. Under McGraw for full season, 1920, took 14, lost 10, his best record in majors to that point. McGraw got 15 wins from him during 1921 season, against ten losses. Phil's World Series record that year good—two victories over Yankees, one loss. Helped make Giants champs.

In 1922 Cardinals giving Giants battle for pennant. In mid-August, Leslie Mann, reserve Cardinal outfielder, received a letter from Douglas. Seems that Douglas had been off on one of his periodic drunks. When returned to Giants, McGraw gave him another high-powered tongue lashing. Fed up, and possibly not yet sober, Douglas wrote note to Mann, which said in part: "I don't want to see this guy [McGraw] win the pennant. You know that I can pitch and I am afraid that if I stay I will win pennant for them. Talk this over with the boys, and if it is all right, send the goods to my house at night and I will go to the fishing camp." Mann, on advice of Branch Rickey, Cardinal manager, turned letter over to Judge Landis, who promptly expelled Douglas from baseball, barring him for life. Douglas, at time of expulsion, had won 11–4 mark, for peak performance of big league career. Giants, however, won flag without Douglas in final weeks of season.

Phil's major league totals: 93 wins, 93 losses in 299 games, 2.80 ERA. His WS work: 2–2, 2.00 ERA. One of those losses came during 1918 Series while with Cubs.

DOUTHIT, TAYLOR LEE (Ball Hawk) OF-BR-TR. B. 4/22/01, Little Rock, Ark. 5'11½", 175. Taylor Douthit studied agriculture at University of California, planned on going into canning business but became stellar major league outfielder. Wound up in insurance. Douthit was member of famed Cardinals of 1926 who won St. Louis' first pennant in modern times and then went on to world championship victory over Miller Huggins' New York Yankees. Fleet center fielder won moniker "Ball Hawk" because of fancy fielding. Helped Cards to more pennants, 1928 and 1930, then was ousted by younger Pepper Martin, of 1931 World Series fame.

Douthit was signed for Cardinal organization by history professor friend of Branch Rickey. Charles E. Chapman knew not only his academic studies but his ball players as well. Taylor agreed to terms before school was out, 1923, but got his B.S. degree. Had brief spell with Cardinals, but spent most of year at Fort Smith, Western Association, where he hit .305 in 94 games. Following year divided time between Cardinals (.277 in 53 games) and St. Joseph, Western League (.322 in 65 contests). In 1925 advanced to American Association. Hitting .372 in 92 games when recalled by parent club. Batted .274 that season in St. Louis. For next five years was Cardinal center fielder, three times batting above .300, and once missing it by only five points. Fine fielding helped many Cardinal pitchers. At age 30, began to lose trifle speed. Branch Rickey detected, feared he would become double-play hitter and begin to miss long drives in field which he had been gobbling up. Rickey also liked "hungry" players. Douthit had managed to get his salary up to $14,000 level despite depression, not bad income those days. But Pepper Martin had burned up International League in 1930, was "hungry" and played for Cardinals in 1931 for $4500.

Having spent entire career in Cardinal organization, Douthit didn't want to leave it. Nor did Cardinal manager Gabby Street want to take chance on Martin while he had proven Douthit on team. But Rickey, Street's boss, traded Douthit June 15 and Gabby had to play Martin. As trading deadline approached, Douthit was visibly worried. Then Rickey worked out scheme with Cincinnati to take Taylor. But Sidney Weil, Redleg president, did not okay deal until Sunday morning, too late for players involved to get to their new teams for that day's games. So it was agreed trade would not be effective until Monday, June 15, final day permitted for exchanges. Douthit got two hits in his last two trips to plate Saturday. Gabby Street was not informed that deal had been made, so Douthit played Sunday doubleheader for Cardinals. All Taylor did that day was lash out four hits in opener, including double, and drove in three runs. In second game he hit safely his first three trips, running his string to nine consecutive hits, with another two-bagger and three more RBI. Naturally he captured headlines in Monday morning's papers telling of Cards' double victory over Phillies. And probably rested easy, thinking he'd saved his job. But Monday morning Street was called into Rickey's office and told of trade. Bit later Douthit was summoned. There were tears in his eyes as he said goodbye to office workers.

Taylor's zest was gone with Redlegs. Played rest of that and next season in Rhineland, then was traded to Chicago Cubs during 1933. Cubs released him to Kansas City after 27 games. But didn't tarry there. California beckoned and has lived in Bay Area ever since.

Douthit's lifetime major league figures show 1074 games in 11, seasons, 4127 AB, 1201 hits, 220 doubles, 38 triples, 29 homers, .291 average, 665 runs, 396 RBI as leadoff man most of career, 67 stolen bases. World Series play: 13 games, 7 for 50, including 2 doubles, 1 homer, for .140.

DOWNING, ALPHONSO ERWIN P-BR-TL. B. 6/28/41, Trenton, N.J. 5'10, 182. Like Pat Dobson of Baltimore Orioles, after several years of mediocre records, Al Downing won 20 games in 1971 for first time in his career. Downing was pitcher of great promise back in 1963 and 1964 with Yankees. Had 13–5 record with 2.56 ERA then 13–8 mark with 3.47 ERA. In latter season led AL in strikeouts with 217—but also in bases on balls with 120. In 1967 won 14, lost 10 for Bombers, with 2.63 ERA, but something snapped in his left elbow during game he was pitching against Baltimore. For three years afterward he was just hanging on.

Al Campanis, Dodger vice president in charge of player personnel and scouting, however, must have received good reports from his sleuths. Downing, meanwhile, had been sent to Binghamton by Yanks for part of 1968 season, then to Oakland and Milwaukee. When Campanis and Frank Lane of Brewers started talking deals, Los Angeles offered Andy Kosco. Trade effected, but nobody danced in street over acquisition of southpaw who was 5–13 in 1970.

Downing took $2000 cut to $29,000 with Dodgers and quietly went to work. Mgr. Walt Alston reportedly planned on using Downing in relief, as "long man" to pitch middle innings of ball game if starter failed early. Al came through in very first chance, pitching 5-2/3 innings of scoreless ball as rescuer. Alston decided to try him as starter. Came through with 2–1 victory over St. Louis Cardinals. From then on Downing pitched regularly. Had six-game winning streak; also had nine victories in one stretch, with just two defeats—games in which Dodgers failed to score. Wound up 20–9, and 2.68 ERA. His five shutouts gave him tie for NL lead in this respect. Pitched 262 innings, struck out 136, and walked 84. In 1972, 9–9. As Downing faced 1973, had 106 major league victories and 88 defeats with 3.14 ERA.

Not proud of his WS record with Yankees, 1963,64. Went down to defeat once in each WS, and his ERA adds up to 7.11 in 12-2/3 innings. Downing did better in his one appearance in All-Star game. Pitching for AL, 1967, hurled two scoreless innings.

On basis of his 1971 work *Sporting News* selected him as Comeback Player of Year. National Baseball Congress named him their outstanding graduate of year.

Downing started with Binghamton, N.Y., 1961, and joined Yankee club same season. But had further seasoning at Richmond, 1962–63, then was with Yanks until 1968. After, had another spell at Binghamton; Oakland AL, 1970, until June, when he was sent to Milwaukee AL. Trade to Dodgers materialized February 1971.

DOYLE, JOHN JOSEPH (Dirty Jack) C-1B-BR-TR. B. 10/25/69, Killorglin, Ireland. D. 12/31/58, Holyoke, Mass. 5'9", 155. First pinch hitter in major league history was pugnacious Irishman who later managed New York NL. Made record books 6/7/92 when his boss, Pat Tebeau, of Cleveland Spiders ordered him to pinch hit against NL team then called Brooklyn "Ward's Wonders." Doyle was substitute catcher at time. Came through with single, sending teammate Jack O'Connor to third base. Later that season O'Connor appeared in another game as pinch batsman. So did Connie Mack that year. Cap Anson didn't do any pinch hitting until 1893. Before too long pinch hitters commonplace.

Doyle started out with Columbus, American Association, then major league, 1889. Besides Cleveland, Doyle played with Baltimore, New York, Chicago and Brooklyn, all of NL, and finally with New York AL, 1905. Eventually spent greater part of his time at first base, but played most positions except that of pitcher. Lifetime major league records: 1564 games, 1806 hits in 6039 times at bat for .299 average, 315 doubles, 64 triples, 25 homers, 971 runs, 924 RBI, 516 stolen bases.

DOYLE, LAWRENCE JOSEPH (Laughing Larry) 2B-BL-TR. B. 7/31/86, Caseyville, Ill. 5'10", 180. "It's great to be young and a Giant," said Laughing Larry Doyle, second baseman for N.Y. NL club back in 1911,12,13, when McGraw's team won three straight pennants. Doyle helped win those flags and enjoyed playing for McGraw, man whom many players respected, but hated.

Doyle played for Mattoon Ill. in Kitty League, 1906; Springfield, Ill League, 1907. There his .290 batting average and third base play attracted attention of Giants, who bought his contract 6/29/07 for $4500.

Larry was scared stiff as he approached metropolis. Train took him to New Jersey side of Hudson River. There he took wrong ferry, got completely lost in big city. Finally reached Polo Grounds, terrified at prospect of playing for famed McGraw, wondering how it would be to be teammate of immortal Christy Mathewson. Next day Doyle in lineup—as second baseman, position he had never played before. Thirty thousand fans crowded stands, watching Hooks Wiltse battle Three-Fingered Brown of Cubs in 1–1 game. Frank Chance of Cubs reached third base in late innings. Ball hit to Doyle. Instead of throwing to plate in effort to cut down Chance, Larry threw to first. Chance scored what proved to be winning run. Afterward McGraw raging mad. Following day as Doyle was getting into uniform in clubhouse, McGraw sent for him. Doyle figured he would be fired. With great trepidation approached Little Napoleon. Instead of berating Doyle, McGraw told him to forget all about yesterday's game. "I know you were playing strange position," said McGraw. "When you learn more about playing second you won't make those mistakes. The main thing is that you probably have learned, and you can hit!" Doyle had nicked Brown for single and double. Went out that day—and rest of time with club—and played his heart out for McGraw.

Hit .260 rookie year, 69 games, but raised average to .308, 104 games, 1908. Hit above .300 five times. His .320 average in 1915 won NL batting championship. Pretty fair base runner too, stealing 30 bases or more five different seasons. Doyle later declared 1911 Giants stole their way to championship. "Every time a man got to base, McGraw would be flashing a steal sign—at least that's the way it seemed," said Larry. Club set major league record of 347 stolen bases—Devore stole 61, Snodgrass 51, Merkle 49, Red Murray and Buck Herzog 48 each, and Doyle came in sixth in this competition with 38!

Larry traded to Cubs 8/28/16 but returned to Giants 1/8/18, remaining until end of 1920 season. Lifetime record showed 1765 games, .290 average over 14-season career. Stole 297 bases, drove in 793 runs. Chalmers Award (MVP) 1912.

In 1911 World Series Doyle hit .304, but Philadelphia Athletics took classic, four games to two. In fifth game Doyle on third in tenth inning with score tied, one out. Fred Merkle hit fly ball to outfield and Doyle came home after catch. Later plate umpire Bill Klem said if Athletics had tagged Doyle, he would have declared him out, as Larry did not touch plate. Larry hit .242 in 1912 Series, .150 in 1913 Series. World Series totals: .237 batting average, 19 games.

DRABOWSKY, MYRON WALTER (Moe) P-BR-TR. B. 7/21/35,

Ozanna, Poland. 6'2", 210. Most major league players were born in Western Hemisphere, but Moe Drabowsky is an exception. Unlikely he ever would have fared as well financially had he remained in his birthplace in Poland, overrun by Nazis few years after Moe was born, later by Russian Communists. Before he pitched single ball in pro baseball, socked away reported $50,000 bonus to sign with Chicago Cubs. That was back in 1956. While he hasn't made money like Sandy Koufax, Tom Seaver, or Denny McLain since he signed that bonus pact, has had major league salary close on to 20 years. Dropped into minors briefly during parts of four seasons, but not for long.

Drabowsky, starter in earlier years, has become relief specialist. Spent 1956–60 with Cubs, winning 32, losing 41. In his first sortie into minors, pitched five games for Houston, then in American Association, 1960, won them all and had ERA of 0.90. Divided 1961 between Milwaukee, NL, and Louisville, AA, and 1962 between Cincinnati and Kansas City, AL. In 1963 it was Kansas City and Portland, Pacific Coast League, and back to K.C., 1964–65. Another brief sojourn in minors, this time with Vancouver, PCL, 1965. Then Baltimore AL, 1966–68. Kansas City, 1969–70, and back to Baltimore midseason, 1970. St. Louis NL, 1971–72. Released in August; signed with Chicago White Sox. Released 10/6/72.

Sparkling moment of his career probably was performance in WS 10/5/66 when he was credited with beating Los Angeles Dodgers in first game of fall classic. That was WS that Orioles won in four straight. Hank Bauer, then manager of O's, declared that turning point of Series came in very first game when Moe entered game in relief, in third inning and slammed door shut on Dodger scoring. Dave McNally started for Orioles, who gave him four-run lead in first two innings. Allowed one run in second and loaded bases in third. With one out, in came Drabowsky. Moe got his first victim, Parker, on strikeout, but walked Gilliam to force run home. Run was charged against McNally. Then went rest of way, 6-2/3 innings, and allowed just one hit. fanned six men in row to match record set by Hod Eller of Cincinnati in WS game 10/6/19. Struck out total of 11 Dodgers, setting Series record for relievers. Naturally, 0.00 ERA for that Series.

Moe's great achievment climaxed season during which he won six games, lost none, saving seven other games. Pitched 96 innings, struck out 98 and walked just 29, chalking up ERA of 2.81.

Drabowsky got his ERA down to 1.61 with Orioles, 1967, and in following season it was still under two runs per game—1.92. After 552 major league games when curtain fell in 1972, Moe owned 3.73 ERA, with 88 victories, 105 defeats, but plenty of saves.

No wonder he got that bonus from Phil Wrigley. Was studying economics at Trinity College, Hartford, when he signed up. Graduated, 1957, and in off-season worked as Chicago stockbroker.

DRAGO, RICHARD ANTHONY   P-BR-TR. B. 6/25/45, Toledo, Ohio, 6'1", 191. Dick Drago won 17 games for Kansas City Royals, 1971, more than any other pitcher had done for AL team in Kansas City. Also had best record for most complete games by K.C. hurler to that time—15. Dick's ERA was 2.99 for 241 innings. While effectiveness in 1972 was practically same—3.01—he lost 17 and won only 12. Which may show that pitcher depends on how well rest of club supports his efforts in field and at bat.

Drago attended U. of Detroit, U. of Tampa; turned to pro ball, 1965. Divided that season between Daytona Beach, Fla., and Rocky Mount, N.C. In 1966 was back at Rocky Mount and pitched 5–0 no-hit victory over Greensboro in Carolina League 5/15. His teammate, Darrel Clark, also threw no-hitter in other game of doubleheader. Was 15–9, 1.79 ERA. Also led league in shutouts with seven. Dick spent most of following year at Montgomery, Southern Association; had 15–10 record, led circuit in strikeouts with 134. Joined Toledo for one game that year, then helped home city win International League championship, 1968, with 15–8 mark. Belonged to Detroit Tigers at this point. Recalled, Kansas City expansion club selected him in draft program 10/15/68. Came up with 11–13 and 9–15 marks in first two seasons with Royals.

So Drago faced 1973 with 49 major league victories against 56 defeats. Had worked in 145 games, 921 innings, during which time he allowed 344 earned runs, walked 234, and fanned 479. His ERA was 3.36. Pinpoint control.

DRESSEN, CHARLES WALTER   3B-BR-TR. B. 9/20/98, Decatur, Ill. D. 8/10/66, Detroit, Mich. 5'5", 146. Brash, loquacious, controversial player, coach, manager. Left school at 14, began pitching semipro ball at $7.50 per game. Moline, III League, 1919, .306 in 46 games; Peoria, same league, 1920–21, 138 games each year, batting .283 and .301 respectively. St. Paul, American Association, 1922–24 hitting .304 first two seasons and .347 in last. Cincinnati, 1925–31. Nashville, Southern Association, 1932–33. Got job of managing floundering Nashville team midseason 1932 by pledging club would win at least half of remaining games or he would forfeit salary for this period. Earned it by single game. Late 1933 bought by N.Y. Giants when Johnny Vergez injured. Played 16 games, batting .222.

Credited with helping get Giants out of jam in fourth World Series game against Washington. Senators filled bases in eleventh, one out. Giants leading 2–1. Cliff Bolton pinch hit for Senators. Manager Bill Terry conferred with pitcher (Carl Hubbell) and infielders. Unasked for advice, Dressen sprinted from bench to get into act. Told Terry Bolton was slow, infield should play deep for double play, that he (Dressen) had played against Bolton many times. Giants played back, double play ensued. Dressen never forgot his contribution to victory. Giants took Series four games to one.

Back to managing Nashville 1934. Larry MacPhail, then general manager, Cincinnati, secured his release to become manager of Reds midseason. Continued as Cincinnati manager until close of 1937. Nashville manager 1938. MacPhail, having left Cincinnati after 1936 season, now top man at Brooklyn. Leo Durocher moved in as manager and Dressen as one of coaches. When Branch Rickey succeeded MacPhail at Brooklyn at end of 1942, Dressen dismissed, reportedly because of his devotion to horse-race betting.

Contrite and needing job, Dressen rehired by Rickey at reduced salary, 7/43. With Dodgers until MacPhail, having taken over Yankees along with Dan Topping, Del Webb, hired Dressen as coach for 1947. Rickey considered this breach of contract since Dressen had agreed on two-year contract, 9/16/46, with Dodgers. Rickey had agreed to release him only if Dressen had chance to manage major league team. Ordinarily MacPhail's action would be considered "tampering" with another club's employee, since Rickey had not consented to MacPhail's conversations with Dressen. Rickey did not press point. Dressen coached Yanks 1947–48. Manager, Oakland, Pacific Coast League, 1949–50, finishing second in 1949, first in 1950. Meanwhile, Rickey had moved to Pirates. Dressen returned to Dodgers as manager, 1951. Dodgers 13-1/2 games in front in Aug.; Giants tied them. Pennant went to Giants when Bobby Thomson hit homer in playoff. Dodgers won flags, 1952,53, losing Series both years to Yanks. Dressen then sought two-year contract to continue managing Dodgers. Walter O'Malley, Brooklyn president, offered one-year agreement. Dressen refused. O'Malley named Walter Alston Dodger pilot. Dressen managed Oakland, PCL, 1955.

Manager, Senators, 1955–57. Coach, (Los Angeles) Dodgers, 1958–59, under Alston. Managed (Milwaukee) Braves to second place, 1960, third place, 1961. Manager, Toronto, International League, 1962. Manager, Tigers, 1963, until death in 1966.

DREYFUSS, BARNEY Executive. B. 2/23/65, Freiburg, Baden, Germany. D. 2/5/32, New York, N.Y. President, Pittsburgh Pirates, 1900–1932. One of pioneers of modern baseball. At age 17 came to U.S., got job in Paducah, Ky., as bookkeeper for distilling company. Developed keen interest in baseball; organized and operated Paducah baseball club. Later bought interest in Louisville team, American Association. In 1892 this circuit merged with NL to form 12-club league. Became secretary-treasurer of club, 1896. In winter of 1899 team was combined with Pittsburgh franchise and moved to Pennsylvania city. Among great players on club were Fred Clarke, Hans Wagner, Tommy Leach, Deacon

Phillippe, Dummy Hoy, and many others.

Dreyfuss owned half interest in club. One day, patron who had torn his coat on nail in ball park complained to secretary of team, Harry Pulliam. Pulliam told fan to have coat fixed and send bill to ball club. William W. Kerr, co-owner of Pirates, overheard convesation and blew his top. Said Pulliam should have consulted him before making any financial committment. Pulliam quit, although Barney sided with him. In argument that ensued, Kerr told Dreyfuss he could be sole owner if he came up with $70,000 cash for his stock. "I'll give you till Monday noon to raise the money," said Kerr. "I want hard cash, not cordwood or promises." The argument took place at noon Saturday. Banks were closed. Dreyfuss took night train to Louisville, spent Sunday talking to friends there. Back in Pittsburgh Monday morning, put $70,000 cash on Kerr's desk at 9 A.M., three hours before deadline, and became sole owner.

Pirates, under Dreyfuss' direction, won NL pennants 1901,02,03 after finishing second in 1900. Captured flag again in 1909, 1925, and 1927. In all, Barney had only six second-division teams and one tailender in his 32 years as club president.

Rivalry between NL and new AL was intense in early years of 20th century. However, in 1903, when Pirates won pennant, Dreyfuss proposed world series to Boston AL. Bitter opposition to such series from many NL sources. Red Sox, or Puritans, as they were often called, beat Pirates, five games to three. Dreyfuss, generous man, turned over all Pittsburgh's receipts to players, so losing players received more bonus than winners. In 1909 Dreyfuss opened new ball park, Forbes Field, one of first of steel and concrete construction. Pirates used park until 1971.

Dreyfuss became mortal enemy of Garry Herrmann, president of Cincinnati club and chairman of National Commission after dispute over contract of George Sisler. Herrmann sided with Ban Johnson on commission, awarding Sisler to St. Louis Browns, 1915. Dreyfuss' hostility to Herrmann eventually helped end National Commission's three-man government of major leagues and led to appointment of Judge Landis as baseball's czar.

For many years Dreyfuss was schedule maker, handling complicated job of making NL teams' home dates fit in with AL teams in two-club cities, so as to avoid conflicts.

DROPO, WALTER (Moose) 1B-BR-TR. B. 1/30/23, Moosup, Conn. 6'5", 225. Walt Dropo was traded to Detroit Tigers in June 1952, and following month he got red hot as batsman. Hit safely 12 consecutive times (7/14/52 and 7/15/52) over period of three games. This equaled major league record of Mike Higgins of Boston Red Sox, set in 1938. But in one way, Dropo's feat was more remarkable because he had no breathers during streak. Higgins actually went up to plate 14 times during his streak and drew two bases on balls. But Dropo just banged out hits every time. Dream of setting new mark fizzled when Lou Sleater of Washington Senators got him to foul out to catcher in his next time at bat. However, set AL record for most hits in three consecutive games, 13; and AL record for most hits in four consecutive games, 15—all in connection with his streak.

Dropo, born of Serbian parents who had emigrated from Europe, attended U. of Connecticut, captained baseball team. Good football player; end. Chicago Bears drafted, but he turned to baseball with Red Sox; Dodgers, Yankees, Phillies, Cubs also after him. Made his way up through Red Sox farm system, starting 1947 with Scranton. With Louisville, Birmingham, Sacramento, San Diego. In 1950 was voted Rookie of Year while with Sox, with .322 average, 34 homers and 144 RBI in 136 games. Never did quite as well afterward.

Red Sox sent him to Detroit (6/3/52); Chicago AL, 1955–58; Cincinnati, 1958–59; Baltimore AL, 1959–61. Wound up with .270 lifetime major league average in 1288 games; 1113 hits, with 168 doubles, 22 triples, 152 homers, and 704 RBI. Scored 478 times.

During World War II served with Seventh Army Engineers. After baseball career became partner in real estate investment firm, Marblehead, Mass. Turned down offers to be scout or coach for Baltimore Orioles, 1961.

DRYSDALE, DONALD SCOTT (Double D) P-BR-TR. B. 7/23/36, Van Nuys, Calif. 6'6", 208. Don Drysdale took up television work after many years of intimidating NL batsmen—and, in WS, AL hitters. In 1972 became part of Texas Rangers broadcast team, with Bill Mercer. Signed to air games of California Angels, starting 1973, with multiyear contract.

Big, blond, handsome, scowling Double D holds several records but one of most enviable is mark of 58 scoreless innings, pitching for Los Angeles Dodgers, 1968. At same time set another record of six consecutive shutouts.

Opponents used to say trick was to get Drysdale mad and he'd beat himself. But although Don got mad often, he won far more than he lost. And along way, numerous batsmen got hit by pitched balls or hit dust in hurry trying to avoid being hit. One of his pitches, 1962, broke hand of Jim Davenport of San Francisco Giants. Don, 1959, threatened publicly to sue NL for hiring umpires who said he threw bean balls. Nevertheless was fined and suspended for "brushback" pitches. Orlando Cepeda said trick was to hit him before he hit you. Once Drysdale so angry at momentary lack of success on mound that he slugged soft-drink cooler—and broke two bones in pitching hand. Another time, after being tagged for homer, threw next ball into stands. "It slipped," confided Don.

Don's father, Scott Drysdale, was minor league pitcher. Don was second baseman until his senior year in high school, then took up pitching. Several major league scouts were interested in him and two universities are supposed to have been ready to give him athletic scholarships. But $4000 bonus and $600-per-month contract lured him into Dodger organization. That was June 1954. Joined Bakersfield, California League; won eight, lost five. Following year went to Montreal, International League, one notch below majors. Had 11–11 record. Joined Dodgers in Brooklyn, 1956.

Though he broke even, 5–5 during season, and had so-so record in his first WS appearance that fall (two hits, one walk, two earned runs), Don was on way to 17–9 record in 1957. Then Dodgers deserted Ebbets Field for West Coast. After 12–13 mark, 1958, came back following season with 17 wins, 13 losses and led league in strikeouts with 242. Led league again in strikeouts, 1960, but his best year was 1962. That was when he was 25–9, workhorse of NL with 314 IP. Also led NL in strikeouts for third time. All of this won him Cy Young Award. Followed with 19–17, 18–16 and 23–12 marks in 1963–65. Meanwhile teammate Sandy Koufax had come up with four sterling seasons for Dodgers. Don and Sandy collaborated in their contract negotiations for 1966 season. Rumor said they were seeking $500,000 each for three-year span. For almost entire month of March they held out. Finally, 3/30/66, they signed one-year contracts. Supposition was they divided $225,000, with Sandy taking larger share of melon than Drysdale. Drysdale, however, never again approached his 1965 form. Finished his career with 13–16, 13–16, 14–12 and finally 5–4, after which he turned to television, with sports commentaries in Montreal, then moving to Texas Rangers for 1972.

Don earned certain distinctions: in both 1958 and 1965 hit seven homers, tying NL record; hit 154 opposing batsmen during career; pitched five shutouts in month of May, 1968.

In WS with Dodgers, 1959 and 1963 won one victory each classic. His 1963 win was shutout over Yankees. In 1965 WS was 1–1, while in 1966 he was 0–2. Overall: 7 WS games, 39-2/3 IP, 3–3, 36 hits, 13 earned runs, 36 strikeouts, 12 walks, 2.95 ERA.

His major league totals: 518 games, 3432 IP, 209 wins, 167 losses, 3084 hits, 1124 earned runs, 2486 strikeouts, 855 walks, 2.95 ERA.

DUFFY, HUGH OF-BR-TR. B. 11/26/66, River Point, R.I. D. 10/19/54, Allston, Mass. 5'7", 168. After Hugh Duffy batted .438 with Boston NL, 1894, got raise of $12.50 a month! This was highest major league batting average in all history for a regular. In this century Rogers Hornsby came closest with his .424 mark in 1924.

Duffy's first job was in mill at Jewett City, Conn; played ball Saturdays and Sundays, taking home salary of $30 per month. Next he made $50 monthly at Winsted, Conn. He was pitcher and shortstop those days. Got into pro ball in New England 1886, Hartford. By 1888 ready for Cap Anson's Chicago NL, hitting .282 as outfielder in 71 games. In 1891 was with Boston club of American Association, then a major league. Following season AA and NL consolidated, Duffy staying in Boston until close of 1900. Was consistently good hitter those years. Hit .378 in 1893; led league with .438 mark in 1894. That season he led league in hits with 236; in doubles with 50; in stolen bases with 49. His 18 home runs tied him for leadership in that department.

In 1901 Hugh became playing manager of Milwaukee, American Association. Playing manager 1902–03, Milwaukee, Western League; playing manager, Philadelphia NL, 1904–06. Owner and manager, Providence, Eastern League, 1907–09, winding up his playing career at this time. Managed Chicago AL, 1910–11; manager, Milwaukee, American Association, 1912; president-manager, Portland, New England League, 1913–16; scout, Boston NL, 1917–19; manager, Toronto, International League, 1920; manager, Boston AL, 1921–22; scout, Boston AL, 1924–54. Duffy also coached at Harvard College and Boston College for several years each.

Lifetime average in majors .330 in 1722 games; had 2307 hits, 597 stolen bases. Hall of Fame 1945.

DUGAN, JOSEPH ANTHONY (Jumping Joe) 3B-BR-TR. B. 5/12/97, Mahanoy City, Pa. 5'11", 160. Dugan went straight from campus of Holy Cross College to Philadelphia Athletics, 1917. That was period when Connie Mack was managing tail enders. Joe and other young players got plenty of chance to play. Dugan got into 43 games that year and hit .194, but Connie put him into 120 contests following season and he elevated his batting average one point! Still he had promise, and for rest of major league career came up with respectable batting marks.

Started out as shortstop, played some second base, but eventually became fine hot-corner guardian. After 1921 season Mack traded him to Boston AL. Dugan didn't tarry long with Red Sox. N.Y. Yankees needed third sacker, so Joe joined long parade of players who moved from Boston to big city, enabling Yankees to win their first AL pennants. Red Sox owner Frazee needed money—so Babe Ruth, Everett Scott, Red Ruffing, Carl Mays, Herb Pennock, and others moved to New York.

Dugan helped Yanks to five pennants, including their 1922, 23, 26, 27, 28 flags. WS record showed 25 games with 24 hits in 90 AB; scored 13 runs, and drove in 8; hit 4 doubles, 1 triple, 1 homer; .267 average. Yankees sent Dugan back to Boston, 1929, but this time it was Braves. Joe hit .304 in 60 games, his only season in NL. After eight games with Detroit, 1931, Dugan bowed out of major league picture for keeps. Owned .280 lifetime major league average in 1446 games.

During career, Joe left ball clubs several times without consent of management, acquiring nickname "Jumping Joe." Besides being fine fielder, had his share of superstitions. One of them was that he would never throw ball directly to pitcher unless it was for a putout. In infield practice, teammates sometimes turned their backs when warmup was over so he couldn't throw ball to shortstop or other infielder. On such occasions Joe would walk over and hand ball to pitcher, but never threw it to moundsman.

DUNCAN, DAVID EDWIN (Dunk) C-BR-TR. B. 9/26/45, Dallas, Tex. 6'2", 200. David Duncan was with Oakland A's 1968–72 but did not attract much attention until 1971 when he helped club win divisional AL title for West. His 19 homers in 1972 helped A's win AL flag, but Gene Tenace did most of catching during later stages of campaign. Dave hit .218 in 121 games; .200 in WS, with one hit in five trips. After salary dispute in spring 1973, traded to Cleveland just before season opened.

Dunk played high school baseball and football in San Diego with distinction; after graduation, 1963, spent rest of summer at Daytona in Florida State League. Hit .145 in 47 games. Had 25 games with Kansas City AL, 1964, but was able to hit just .170. Birmingham and Lewiston, 1965; Modesto, 1966; Kansas City and Birmingham, 1967; Vancouver, 1968, then called up to Oakland to stay. Duncan hit .191 in 82 games, 1968; .126 in 58 games, 1969. In 1970 finally got average up to .259 in 86 contests, and .253 in 1971, with 15 homers, 40 RBI in 103 games.

Duncan's promise as hitter indicated while at Modesto, 1966. Hit 46 home runs to lead California League, second greatest number in circuit's history.

Dave missed considerable time from baseball in 1970 and 1971 because of military obligations. Said to have received $65,000 bonus to sign with A's organization.

DUNCAN, LOUIS BAIRD (Pat) OF-BR-TR. B. 10/6/93, Coalton, Ohio. D. 7/17/60, Jackson, Ohio. 5'9", 180. Pat Duncan was first player to hit ball out of old Redland Field, Cincinnati. This was ball park later renamed Crosley Field, home of Reds before they moved to their modern Riverfront Stadium 6/30/70. Pat also holds distinction of having played three major league ball games on same day. Only three others played in all parts of this tripleheader, 10/2/20. This was only tripleheader since Brooklyn defeated Pittsburgh three times 9/1/1890.

Duncan was in his first full NL season, 1920, when he played three league games in one day. Pittsburgh had chance for thrd place finish on last day of season, with three games unplayed between Reds and Pirates.

Barney Dreyfuss, president of Pirates, tried to get consent of Pat Moran, Cincinnati manager, to play tripleheader. Moran refused, so Dreyfuss went to John Hydler, president of NL. Heydler ordered tripleheader to be played. Games started at noon at Forbes Field. Reds captured first game 12–4, Duncan getting two hits; went on and won second game by 7–3 score. This time Duncan got one safety. Cincinnati's two victories clinched third place for Reds, so third game of day really was anticlimactic. Pirates won it by 6–0, called for darkness after six innings. Duncan went hitless in third contest. Clyde Barnhart played in all three games for Pirates, as did Fred Nicholson. Maurice Rath played all three games for Reds, as did Duncan.

Duncan started his pro career, 1913, at Flint, Mich., later playing for Battle Creek, Grand Rapids, and Birmingham through 1919. Played three games in brief trial with Pittsburgh, 1915. Pat was jogging along with .317 average for Birmingham in 1919 when sold to Reds for $4500 on 8/20. Hit .244 for Cincinnati in 31 games during rest of season. Played all eight games of 1919 WS and hit .269 with 7 for 26. But drove in eight runs and scored three others.

Duncan didn't blast that first homer out of Cincinnati ball park until 6/2/21. Hit .308 that year, then came back with .328 and .327 averages in subsesquent seasons. After dropping to .270 in 1924, it was back to minors for Pat. Minneapolis, 1925–28, then was shifted to Rochester for tag end of 1928 season. Lifetime major league average .307 for 727 games, with 23 homers.

In his later years Duncan was building superintendent for Ohio Department of Highways in Jackson.

DUNLOP, HARRY ALEXANDER C-BL-TR. B. 9/6/33, Sacramento, Calif. 6'3", 200. You can't find Harry Dunlop's name in records of those who have played major league baseball. But Dunlop, in 1972, was only member of Kansas City Royals coaching staff who was with team at its inception, 1969. Dunlop began pro career in 1952 in Bristol, Tenn., and caught three no-hit no-run games that year. Besides spending couple of years in military service, Harry saw country. Played for Burlington, Iowa; Lincoln, Nebr.; New Orleans, Williamsport, Tucson, Stockton, and Quad Cities Davenport and Bettendorf in Iowa, and Moline and Rock Island in Illinois, Midwest League.

Dunlop's best season was at Tucson, Arizona-Mexico League, 1958, when he hit .349 in 112 games and led catchers in fielding average, putouts, and assists.

Dunlop also caught for team called Tri-Cities. Towns represented were Kennewick, Richland, and Pasco, Washington, in Northwest League.

Harry managed at Tucson, 1958, bringing club in second. Then managed again at Stockton, 1961–64; Quad Cities, 1965–66, after which he gave up playing. Managed San Jose team of California League, 1967. Coach for Seattle, Pacific Coast League, 1968, and coach for Kansas City Royals since that time. Coaches at first base and works especially with catchers.

Minor league management was done mostly in Baltimore and California Angel organizations. As pilot, minor league seasons were usually split. Came in first two different occasions and won playoffs twice.

DUNN, JACK, III Executive. B. 10/22/21 Baltimore, Md. The name Dunn has been associated with Baltimore baseball for over half century. Original Jack Dunn was owner and manager of Baltimore Orioles in International League in days when Lefty Grove, Jack Bentley, Dick Porter, George Earnshaw, Max Bishop, Joe Boley, and other future major leaguers graced team's roster. Dunn's Orioles won seven consecutive pennants, many observers felt team could have made good showing in big leagues with same personnel.

Second Jack Dunn died before his father and mother. When first Jack Dunn died, Mrs. Dunn continued connection with team, often traveling with club. So Jack Dunn III was practically born and raised member of Baltimore Oriole family. Acted as batboy; later became president, general manager, and part-time manager of, and player for, Centreville Orioles of Eastern Shore League, 1946. And for International League Orioles Jack III served at various times as owner, president, general manager and manager before AL transferred St. Louis franchise to Baltimore, 1953.

Since then has been traveling secretary, assistant to general manager, public relations director, play-by-play broadcaster, and administrative assistant to Lee MacPhail, then with Orioles. Jack was appointed to present position as vice president for business affairs, 1965. Supervises club's season-ticket sales, stadium operations, and concessions. Is third-largest stockholder in Orioles.

During World War II was fighter pilot in air corps. Graduate of Princeton.

DUREN, RINOLD GEORGE, JR. (Ryne) P-BR-TR. B. 2/22/29, Cazenovia, Wis. 6'2", 202. Ryne Duren wore very thick lenses in his glasses. Wild enough flamethrower to scare most batters. They said he couldn't see scoreboard; asked how he could control pitch to plate. It all added up to his being brilliant relief pitcher, especially 1958 and 1959 with Yankees.

Duren could trace his eye problems to 1945 when he lay in bed from March until September with rheumatic fever. Also acquired other problems—"Almost destroyed myself with drinking," he said later after working for rehabilitation of alcoholics with Norris Foundation outside of Milwaukee. Also worked as counselor for delinquent boys.

Ryne attended Illinois one year and joined Wausau team of Wisconsin State League, 1949. Was at Pine Bluff, Dayton, Anderson, Scranton, and San Antonio en route to majors, with his first trial with Baltimore AL, 1954. Pitched in one game, then back to Seattle, Pacific Coast League, San Antonio, and Vancouver through 1956. Fourteen games with Kansas City AL, 1957, losing three, winning none. Then traded to N. Y. Yankees, 6/15/57 and optioned to their Denver club for rest of season. There Ryne 13–2, with 3.16 ERA. With Yankees, 1958–61. In his first year in Gotham won six, lost four, saved 20 games in relief and came up with 2.01 ERA. In WS that fall, Duren relieved in three games, being charged with one defeat and gaining one decision. His ERA was 1.93. During series incurred wrath of Commissioner Ford Frick by making gesture to umpire indicating he thought arbiter was "choking up." Cost Duren $250 fine.

In 1959, Ryne 3–6 for Yanks, but saved 14, with 1.87 ERA. After that his work began to sag. In WS of 1960, worked four innings, had 2.25 ERA but no wins or losses. During 1961 moved to Los Angeles AL, remaining there through 1962. Philadelphia NL, 1963–64. Cincinnati, 1964 and finally six games with Philadelphia NL, 1965, finishing major league career with 27 victories, 44 defeats, and ERA of 3.83, taking part in 311 games. Started just 32, and completed only two, one of which was shutout. In 589-1/3 innings walked 392, fanned 630. In relief his record stood 22 won, 35 lost, with 57 saves.

One of highlights of early career was striking out 238 men in 198 innings while pitching for Pine Bluff in 1950. In 1960, when he made his first start in two years, he fanned first five Washington batters to face him, which equaled modern major league record at that time. It since has been broken by John Hiller, Ray Culp, and Bert Blyleven, each of whom fanned first six batsmen to face them.

DUROCHER, LEO ERNEST (Lippy) SS-BR-TR. B. 7/27/05, W. Springfield, Mass. 5'9", 175. Synonymous with controversy, noise, argument, shouting, rhubarbs, litigation, Durocher has been supreme egotist, brash loudmouth, natural ham, narcissistic monologist, hunch player, strategist. Has been strutting clothes horse, manicured, pedicured, perfumed; ruthless, sarcastic, bitter, amiable, affable, flirtatious, charming, dapper.

Durocher was "All American Out" as batsman. Weak switch hitter, brilliant shortstop, dangerous clutch man at plate, one of baseball's greatest managers—and one of its most disappointing. Branch Rickey, who played important part in salvaging Durocher, first as player with St. Louis Cardinals and later as manager in Brooklyn, declared: "Leo has

most fertile talent in world for making bad situation infinitely worse."
Run out of AL as far back as 1930; suspended from baseball for an
entire season, 1947; fined for tampering with coach on another ball club;
involved in civil suit and accused of breaking fan's jaw; repeatedly fired
by Larry MacPhail, only to continue working for him; led Brooklyn
Dodgers to one pennant and N.Y. Giants to two; his 1954 aggregation
won WS in four straight; but with Chicago Cubs won only nine more
games than he lost over period of seven seasons; said he "stepped aside"
just before 1972 All-Star game, although time in Chicago was running
out.

Durocher at 16 worked in tobacco fields for $6 a day, but even then
had fetish about clothes. Reportedly saved his salary till he could buy
$70 tailored suit. Eventually came to own 75 suits, 30 sport coats, 75
pairs of slacks, multiple monogramed shirts, 6 topcoats of different
weights, 30 alpaca sweaters, numerous tuxedos, dozens of bottles of
cologne, after-shave lotions, hair tonics, hair dyes, deodorants, neckties, scarves, whatnot. Used to change his underwear at least twice daily
(and maybe still does), as well as rest of outfit. Yet on ball field did not
hesitate to play dirty, literally and figuratively. Member of famed Gas
House Gang Cardinals of 1934—it was he who unwittingly gave that
club its unforgettable name. One day Frank Graham, sports writer, was
talking to Leo at Polo Grounds. Teammate Dizzy Dean came over, got
into conversation and bragged that Cards could win flag in any league,
including AL, which then was considered stronger of two majors. "Oh,
but they wouldn't let us play in AL," interjected Durocher. "They'd say
we were just a lot of gas-house players." Leo very definitely helped
Cardinals win that 1934 NL pennant and WS which followed, brilliant
fielding and timely hitting.

Durocher started out in pro baseball at Hartford in Eastern League,
1925. Played 151 games and hit only .220 but his fielding impressed N.Y.
Yankee scout enough that Leo was bought, and brought up to major
league club. Oddly enough, he was used once as pinch hitter—but did
not connect safely. Yankees farmed Leo out to Atlanta for 1926 season
and to St. Paul for 1927. Joined Yankees in spring training in St.
Petersburg, 1928. Walked into clubhouse where Babe Ruth, Lou Gehrig,
Bob Meusel, Tony Lazzeri, and Waite Hoyt ruled as superstars—but
Durocher acted as though he owned the place. Miller Huggins then was
"mite manager" of Yankees, and liked feisty youngster. Used him at
second base when Lazzeri was ill, and occasionally at shortstop in place
of Mark Koenig. Durocher had .270 average his first full year with
Yanks, and .246 in 1929, but no power. At that time those averages
weren't very impressive when player had to hit much closer to .300 if he
were to win regular job.

During this period, with Ruth at his peak, Leo incurred Babe's wrath, but Bambino's reputation didn't impress Durocher. Though his fielding abilities were recognized, practically nobody on ball club but Huggins could tolerate his popping off. Huggins died late in 1929 season and Durocher's exit from Yankees, as well as from AL, was inevitable.

Cincinnati Reds, then owned by Sidney Weil, bought Leo's contract on waivers. Reds were hopeless ball club at time. Attendance was poor; depression worsened situation immeasurably, and Weil was in process of losing his shirt. Kindly gentleman, with great deal of tolerance and human understanding, Sid befriended Durocher despite Leo's inept batting average, which in 1932 sagged to .217.

Cardinals, meanwhile, had lost their stellar shortstop, Charlie Gelbert, through hunting accident and desperately needed infield help. Branch Rickey, then general manager of Redbirds, engineered deal with Cincinnati that sent Paul Derringer to Reds 5/7/33, with Durocher one of players landing in St. Louis. Redbirds couldn't do much that season, but in final weeks of 1934 season, Durocher, with Rickey's personal help in many directions, remarried. Happy on field and off, Leo played brilliantly—hit .260, drove in plenty of timely runs in pinches, had 70 RBI, and was vital cog in Gas House Gang victory in pennant race. Played flawlessly in WS, hit .259, and Cardinals won championship from Detroit Tigers in seven. Durocher remained with Cardinals through 1937 season, but by this time playing manager Frankie Frisch had become fed up with Leo's personality; probably recognized that his presence on team represented threat to Frisch's job security. It was case of either/or—and Durocher was one to go.

Next stop Brooklyn. One season under Burleigh Grimes' management, then Leo got chance as pilot of Dodgers, 1939. Before spring training really started, Larry MacPhail, then top dog in Brooklyn, fired him by telephone. Leo, in Hot Springs, Ark., had won $750 at bingo in gambling house and had fight with caddy on golf course. But, like rest of MacPhail's firings, it didn't stick; Larry soon was on phone consulting Leo about players and plans for season.

Durocher led Dodgers to third-place finish, 1939, to runner-up spot following year, and in 1941, NL pennant. Grueling scramble for first place all year, with Durocher swiching pitchers and other players every 10 minutes, but keyed-up ball club won by 2-1/2 games over Cardinals. Dodgers clinched pennant 9/25/41 in Boston when Whit Wyatt shut out Braves. Ball clubs traveled by train those days. Brooklyn special left Boston soon after game, headed for Grand Central Station, Manhattan. Train was due to stop at 125th Street, en route downtown where Dodger fans crowded platform, and Durocher ordered train not to stop so as to hurry to destination. MacPhail, however, had hied himself to 125th Street, expected to board train there and share in triumphal arrival at Grand Central Station before thousands of cheering fans. When Dodger train sped past without so much as slowing down, MacPhail was furious. Larry missed all arrival hullabaloo at Grand Central. Durocher eventually reached hotel where MacPhail was staying; when he saw Larry, exuberant Leo yelled, "Mitt me! We're champs!" MacPhail glared at his manager, growled back at him, "You're through! You're fired!" It didn't stick, however, and Leo went on to manage Dodgers in Series, losing to Yankees, four games to one.

Brooklyn won 100 games, 1941, and 104 in 1942. But in latter season this was only good enough for second place. Cardinals won 106.

MacPhail left Dodgers after 1942 season, Rickey taking over. Durocher continued to pilot team through 1946, with two third-place clubs, one seventh-placer, and one runner-up. Then came Leo's suspension for year at hands of Commissioner Happy Chandler. Durocher had spent autumn living in home of George Raft. Rickey asked Chandler, through an intermediary, to warn Leo about his associations off field. Chandler met Leo on golf course. Leo promised to move out of Raft's house and to be good. Leo also had been involved in messy legal tangle connected with his marriage to Laraine Day, causing some Brooklyn fans to threaten boycott of club if Durocher wasn't fired. Then, in spring training 1947, charges and countercharges flew in Havana where Dodgers were conditioning. MacPhail, by then with Yankees, was irate at ghost-written column under Durocher byline appearing in *Brooklyn Eagle*. Article accused MacPhail of trying "to knock me and make life as hard as possible for me." Verbal hassle involved question as to whether two well-known gamblers were MacPhail's guests at ball game; whether there was one standard for managers and another one for club presidents; whether MacPhail had tried to hire Leo as manager of Yankees while still on Brooklyn payroll. Upshot of whole affair was Chandler's expulsion of Durocher for year. In his absence, Burt Shotton took over Dodgers and won pennant. Brooklyn club, however, paid Durocher in full for not managing team that season. But Rickey kept Leo dangling until 12/6/47 to announce he would again manage Dodgers in 1948. Leo, however, did not last long in 1948, that is, with Rickey. In one of most astonishing moves in all baseball history, Giants hired Durocher as their new manager 7/16/48. Horace Stoneham, president of Giants, finally decided to drop Mel Ott as his manager, and wanted Shotton as replacement. Rickey stepped in, sold Stoneham on scheme to make Durocher Giant manager—and Shotton came back to pilot's job in Brooklyn.

After learning to hate Durocher with passion through years, many Giant fans swore they'd never again go to Polo Grounds. Fans who did visit P.G., went to hoot and deride new pilot. Some carried signs like, "You got sawdust for brains!" "Go back to Brooklyn!" "Sorehead!"

As manager of Dodgers, Durocher had won 38 games from Giants, losing 18. As boss of Giants, his team won seven of first 10 games against Flatbush crew. Leo had two fifth-place teams with Giants, then finished third in 1950. In 1951, after trailing Dodgers 13-1/2 games at one point during August, Giants won 37 out of last 44 games to tie Brooklyn for first-place finish. Then came Bobby Thomson's home run in playoff game to give Durocher NL pennant. But Yankees won WS, four games to two. Another flag 1954; they entered WS as underdogs but swept Indians off their feet, winning four straight. This was Leo's only world championship as manager. One more year at helm; then, after third-place finish, retired from game to take job with NBC. Durocher came back to baseball, 1961, as coach for Los Angeles Dodgers. In 1966 Phil Wrigley brought Durocher to Chicago. Cubs finished tenth that year, but bounded up to third for 1967,68. Then had two second-place finishes in Eastern Division of NL. In 1971 club slipped to third, and in 1972 were in tie for third place, 10 games behind Pittsburgh, when axe fell.

Durocher's Chicago teams often looked like pennant winners, but they generally collapsed toward end of season. In later years several players seemed to have accumulated violent hatreds for former "Little Shepherd of Coogan's Bluff." Dissension was so bad late in 1971 that Wrigley, in effect, put Durocher on probation. When club did no better in 1972, probation came to end, although Leo continued to draw salary as "consultant" until hired by Houston. Astros won 14, lost 16 under Durocher during rest of season.

Ford Frick, ex-NL prexy, once fined Leo $100 and suspended him five days for "prolonged argument and conduct on field tending to incite riot." Another time, Leo called Umpire Majerkurth "cement head." Arbiter, chewing tobacco, allegedly splattered tobacco juice on Lippy's face as the two jawed at each other at close range, after which Leo reportedly sprayed saliva into umpire's face in retaliation.

Leo captained 1934 Cardinals. Missed military service during World War II because of punctured ear drum. Teetotaler because he didn't like taste of alcohol. Rugged card player, especially in gin rummy. Credited with being able to instill great self-confidence in some players—and to inspire violent hatred among others.

Leo seldom qualified as "nice guy," and when he did, it was only briefly. Quoted as declaring "nice guys finish last" to justify his own abrasive tactics. As player, took part in 1637 major league games, went to bat 5350 times, made 1320 hits for lifetime average of .247. Among his hits were 210 doubles, 56 triples, 24 homers. Stole 31 bases. In his two WS as player (1928 with Yankees, 1934 with Cardinals) got seven hits in 29 trips for .241 average. Member of three NL All-Star squads, 1936,38,40—2 for 6.

As manager of various major league clubs Durocher wound up 1972 with 1937 victories, 1629 defeats for .543 percentage. Won one WS, lost two. Manager of Year by *Sporting News*, 1939, 51, 54.

At age 65, in 1970, Leo began drawing baseball pension of almost $25,000 annually; will continue for rest of life. That beats $6 a day working in tobacco fields!

DURST, CEDRIC MONTGOMERY OF-BL-TL. B. 8/23/96, Austin, Tex. D. 2/16/71, San Diego, Calif. 5'11", 165. Cedric Durst hit .375 as center fielder for New York Yankees, 1928 WS, when Bombers smashed St. Louis Cardinals in four straight games. But this fine performance, as usual, was overshadowed by work of superstars, Babe Ruth and Lou Gehrig. That fall Ruth had three homers and .625 average for Series, while Columbia Lou had four round-trippers and .545 hitting record for set.

Durst, like Sammy Byrd and other ambitious young outfielders on Yankees of that era, was stymied by having to compete with Combs and Bob Meusel, as well as immortal Bambino. Cedric got to play center field during 1928 WS only because Combs had broken finger. Hit homer off Grover Alexander too. But it came only after Babe had hit his three homers in same game and Gehrig had belted one.

Cedric got his start in majors with St. Louis Browns, 1922–23 and 1926 after spells with Beaumont, Texas League, and Los Angeles, PCL. Yankees 1927–30. Boston AL 1930. That was his final year in majors and only time he was able to participate in 100 games, batting .243, just one point below his lifetime big league record for 481 contests.

Durst was at St. Paul, American Association, 1931–32; Hollywood, Pacific Coast League, 1933–35; San Diego, PCL, 1936–38; and managed San Diego, 1939–43. In 1944–45 was in military service; Quincy, Ill., Three-Eye League, 1946, as pilot; managed Rochester, International League, 1947–48; Omaha, Western League, 1949–50. In 1950 left baseball to become head of security at General Dynamics–Convair plant in San Diego.

DYER, EDWIN HAWLEY P-BL-TL. B. 10/11/1900, Morgan City, La. D. 4/20/64, Houston, Tex. 5'11½", 173. Eddie Dyer gave great promise of becoming stellar lefthanded pitcher when he made major league debut. Blanked Cubs in first start. Hurt arm, returned to minors. Became outfielder, then manager. Made name for himself when took over job as manager, St. Louis Cardinals, 1946. Club finished in tie with Brooklyn. Won two straight games in first playoff of major league history, qualifying for World Series. Cards took Series four games to three from Red Sox.

Series featured by fact Cards held Ted Williams to five singles and batting average of .200. Redbird lefthander Harry Brecheen won three games—and Enos Slaughter clinched payoff game with daring base running. With score tied in eighth Slaughter on first base with two outs. Harry Walker hit safely to left center. Slaughter never stopped sprinting, much to chagrin of Red Sox shortstop Pesky. His split-second delay in relaying ball enabled Slaughter to score deciding run of game and Series.

Dyer led team to three second place finishes after that, and Cards landed fifth, 1950. Following this, Dyer retired from baseball. Had business interests in Houston with former teammates Howie Pollet and Jeff Cross, in insurance, oil, real estate.

Eddie was captain of high school football team in Morgan City. Attended Rice University, class of 1924, but did not get diploma until 1936. Started pro career with Cardinal tryout, 1922; with Cardinals off and on till 1927, dividing time with teams in Cardinal organization. Managed at Springfield, Mo., Western Association, later Houston, Texas League; Columbus, American Association, before graduating to parent club.

Major league totals showed Dyer played in 129 games, won 15, lost 15 as pitcher; batted .223 as pitcher, pinch hitter, outfielder. Entire pro career with St. Louis NL organization.

Freshman coach of Rice football team, 1936, when completing few remaining hours needed for degree.

DYKES, JAMES JOSEPH   Inf.-BR-TR. B. 11/10/96, Philadelphia, Pa. 5'9", 192. Probably no other person connected with baseball ever enjoyed game more than Jimmie Dykes. Stories about and by Dykes are endless. For many years labored on tail-end Philadelphia Athletics, but finally did his share when A's won flags 1929–31. When playing career over, had numerous bizarre experiences as manager and coach before retiring to rocking chair—or golf course.

Dykes impressed Connie Mack back in 1917. Connie farmed to Gettysburg, Blue Ridge League. Jimmie hit .217, 79 games. Spent 1918 with A's: 59 games, hit .188. Following year had .184 average with A's, sent out for further seasoning. With Atlanta, Southern Association, hit .246 in 110 games. Back with Athletics 1920 to stay. Hit .256 in 142 games. Club finished last that year and again in 1921. Had second-division clubs next three years. During this discouraging period, Dykes never lost enthusiasm for winning. Foghorn voice from second or third base encouraged teammates. By 1925 Jimmie recognized as fine third baseman, good second baseman. Hit .312 in 1924. Helped Athletics finish second in 1925 with his .323 batting average.

By 1929 Connie Mack had rebuilt Athletics into pennant winner with men like Lefty Grove, Al Simmons, Jimmie Foxx. In World Series Chicago Cubs were victims. Jimmie helped cause along with .421 average

(8 for 19), four RBI. Another pennant 1930, then beat Cardinals in fall classic. Dykes hit .222. In 1931 Series, mark was .227 as Cards turned tables on A's. In those flag-winning seasons Dykes hit .327, .301, .273.

After 1932 season Dykes, Al Simmons and Mule Haas sold to White Sox for $150,000. Bargain for Sox. Was depression, and Mack needed money.

Dykes had four strong seasons 1933–36 with Sox as player, then tapered off 1937–39. In 1934 Jimmie made playing manager. Continued after his name no longer appeared in box score—until 5/25/46. Got mediocre team into fourth place three times, third place three times during his stay in Chicago.

Jimmie managed Hollywood, Pacific Coast League, after his release early 1946, and again 1947–48. Back to majors 1949 as coach under Connie Mack of A's. In 1951 became boss of Athletics until after 1953 campaign. Two second-division clubs, one fourth. Managed Baltimore Orioles AL 1954, finishing seventh with ex-Browns in their new surroundings. Switched leagues 1955, coaching Cincinnati until named manager 8/14/58. But Dykes 61 years old and Redlegs decided Jimmie was "too old" to manage their team. Back to coaching, 1959, with Pittsburgh. Didn't stay long, as Detroit management decided Jimmie was not too old. By 5/3/59 he was manager of Tigers. Finished fourth. In 1960 both Cleveland and Detroit headed nowhere. Bill DeWitt, then at Detroit, traded Dykes to Frank Lane at Cleveland for Indian manager, Joe Gordon. First time managers traded. Lots of headlines, plenty of laughs—but didn't help either team: Cleveland fourth, Gordon's new club sixth. Before 1961 season was over, Jimmie again traveling. Coach, Milwaukee Braves, 1962: Coach, Kansas City A's, 1963–64.

The antics of Jimmie Dykes are legion. At one point, when Cleveland was riddled with dissension under management of Oscar Vitt, Indians became known as the "Cry Babies." Jimmie, managing Chicago at time, was ready for them when they arrived at Comiskey Park. Had baby buggy in front of dugout, diapers strewn about. Sox players chorused "yoo-hoo," with Dykes, towel in band, wiping away imaginary tears.

Jimmie had great admiration for Babe Ruth. Tells story how Ruth, at peak of home run slugging ability, came to bat. Dykes playing deep third, respecting Babe's power. Score tied. Yanks had runner on third base. To surprise of everyone—especially Dykes—Ruth laid down perfect bunt, beat it out, runner scored, game over!

Dykes primarily third baseman and second baseman, but so versatile he played, one time or other, every position on diamond excepting catcher. Some fans claim he caught, but available records do not verify that he did it in league game. In 1927 he pitched two innings for Athletics, allowed two hits, one walk, one run—4.50 ERA. That was extent of his hurling though he often pitched batting practice.

Jimmie's major league totals: 2282 games, 8046 AB, 1108 runs, 2256 hits, 453 doubles, 90 triples, 109 homers, 1075 RBI, 70 stolen bases. Average: .280. Three World Series: 18 games, 17 hits in 59 trips, 6 runs, 4 doubles, 1 homer, .288 average, 11 RBI.

EARNSHAW, GEORGE LIVINGSTON (Moose) P-BR-TR. B. 2/15/1900 New York, N.Y. 6'4", 215. Won 127, lost 93. Might have had more spectacular record but for two factors. Did not have to pitch for living, thus did not sign minor league contract until he was 24. Then joined Jack Dunn's Baltimore Orioles, International League, 1924. Dunn reluctant to let stars go to majors. Rules then permitted him to hang onto players like Lefty Grove, Jack Bentley, Max Bishop, Joe Boley and others long after they could have made grade in big leagues. So Earnshaw pitched for Orioles until he was 28 before going to Philadelphia Athletics.

Earnshaw attended Swarthmore College, starred in basketball, football, baseball. Captain of court team 1922–23. Joined Orioles 1924, 7–0 in league just one notch below majors. Following year 29–11; 22–14 in 1926; then 17–18 mark. Several of Orioles had gone to majors by this time and Earnshaw was ready to quit unless sold. Clark Griffith reportedly had offered Dunn $100,000 for Earnshaw, but was turned down. Whether Dunn kept George too long to get top price is not known. But after 17–18 season, Earnshaw 3–5 in 1928. Finally sold him to Philadelphia AL—probably for much less than $100,000. George joined Athletics; 7–7 rest of 1928 season. In 1929, was 24–8, followed by 22–13, 21–7 marks next two years. These performances helped bring three consecutive pennants to Philadelphia, and WS victories 1929,30. Broke even in two decisions in 1929 WS. In 1930 Earnshaw vanquished Cardinals twice in WS, pitched 22 consecutive scoreless innings against them, and had ERA of 0.72. In 1931 WS, George pitched well against

Cardinals but 1–2, ERA 1.88. Pepper Martin too much. Moose 19–13 in 1932. Then tapered off. Chicago AL 1934. Divided 1935 between Chicago and Brooklyn; 1936 between Brooklyn and St. Louis NL. Then left majors. Coach, Philadelphia NL, 1949–50.

Earnshaw had 4.38 ERA for his 1,915-1/3 innings in 319 games. In WS play: 8 games, 4–3, 61-2/3 innings, 1.58 ERA.

EASTER, LUSCIOUS (Luke) 1B-BL-TR. B. 8/4/21, St. Louis, Mo. 6'4½", 250. Hit 93 major league home runs, all for Cleveland. Several prodigious. Late start: reached majors, 1949, age 28. Hit ball into upper grand stand in Cleveland, 6/23/50. Ball traveled 477 feet to right center; longest in Cleveland to that time. Hit off Joe Haynes, 3–0 count. Another in Polo Grounds, 1947, as member of Negro team, Homestead Grays. Hit 75 round-trippers that year. And in 1954, his best days past, hit a second homer over high 400-foot center field fence at Gilmore Field, Hollywood; first player to perform this trick. Played until 1965, when he hit 17 homers in 60 games for Rochester, hit for .302 average. Was 44 at time.

Calling Luke "Luscious" was "only mistake my mother ever made," according to affable Easter. Luke played with Cincinnati Crescents, 1946; Homestead Grays, 1947–48; Puerto Rican Winter League, 1948. Cleveland gave Grays $5000 for his contract. Easter played 80 games with San Diego, Pacific Coast League, 1949. Hit .363, 25 homers, 92 RBI, 80 games. With Indians that same season, hit .222 in 21 games; in 1950, batted .280, hit 28 homers, drove in 107 runs, scoring 96 himself; in 1951 .270 average, 27 homers, 103 RBI, 128 games. Suffered from two bad knees. In 1952, spent 14 games at Indianapolis, still drove in 97 runs for Cleveland with .263 average, 31 homers in 127 games. Hit .303 with Indians, 1953, 68 games, but homers down to 7, RBI to 31. Six games for Indians 1954. Returned to minors, playing with Ottawa, San Diego, Charleston W. Va., Buffalo, Rochester. In 1969 returned to Cleveland as coach.

Record: 491 major league games, .274 average, 472 hits, 93 homers, 54 doubles, 12 triples, 340 RBI, 256 runs. His lone stolen base came in 1952.

EBBETS, CHARLES H. Executive. B. 10/29/59, New York, N.Y. D. 4/18/25, New York, N.Y. When Charles Ebbets, early this century, declared, "Baseball is in its infancy," he was ridiculed far and wide. Ran Brooklyn club many years. Built Ebbets Field. As young man, was draftsman. Working for Brooklyn team, sold scorecards, took tickets, counted money, made decisions. Had helped draw plans for Niblo's Garden, an amusement park; Metropolitan Hotel; other New York buildings. In publishing business on small scale, producing novels, textbooks. Sold them door to door himself. Some baseball playing. Involved with politics. Member of Board of Aldermen; assemblyman in State Legislature. In fall of 1890 bought small amount of stock in Brooklyn club. Secretary of ball club, 1896. In 1898, elected president of team, though minor stockholder. Team then was playing its games in Manhattan. Insisted club should be brought back to Brooklyn.

In 1898 team had two managers, both of whom proved unsatisfactory to Ebbets. Finally, top hat, stiff collar, necktie and all, Ebbets took over as bench manager. Didn't do well either—38–68 during his tenure. Following season he turned job over to Ned Hanlon, went back to front office. During early 1900s Ebbets borrowed money to buy rest of team's stock. Club called Superbas those days. This was time arch rivalry with Giants started, continues to this day between S. F. and L. A. teams. While Superbas were struggling, Giants either winning or contending. Whenever Giants went to Brooklyn they swaggered, boasted of their superiority over lowly Superbas. Mgr. John McGraw of New Yorkers publicly insulted Ebbets, incited incidents that aroused resentment among Brooklyn fans. Superbas played in Washington Park. Ebbets' occasionally turned away cash customers because place overflowing. Bought property where he could build new, larger ball park. Difficulties delayed ground breaking for three years. At times lack of cash stalled construction. In August 1912, to carry load, went into partnership with McKeever brothers. Turned over 50 percent of club for $100,000. Two corporations set up. Ebbets president of ball club. Edward J. McKeever headed company which owned land and ball park stands. Opening day 4/5/13. Some 25,000 fans jammed new park. Flags. Dignitaries. Bands. And Dodgers (by now, Trolley Dodgers) vanquished hated Giants. Nap Rucker won ball game 3–2. No pennant till 1916, though. Then lost WS to Red Sox. Pennant meant money problems, holdouts. Zack Wheat and Hy Myers were vital to Dodgers. Both had had good year. Neither satisfied with new contracts. As 1917 spring training progressed Wheat home in Missouri. Ebbets refused to raise offer, refused to negotiate. Interested sports writer, however, sent Wheat telegram, "Report at once," signed Ebbets' name. Wheat thought this meant president finally acceding to request for healthy raise. Zack landed in training camp, confronted Ebbets, who told him it was forgery. Zack prepared to return home. Ebbets still adamant. Cooler heads persuaded antagonists to negotiate in locked room. Wheat signed.

Signing of Myers different. Hy wrote Ebbets more profitable farming than playing for Dodgers at figure offered. To make story credible, had few letterheads printed: "Myers' Stock Farm, Kensington, Ohio." Letterheads impressed Ebbets, who realized he needed fine center fielder, would have to raise him. Telegraphed Myers, saying he was coming to see him, negotiate contract. Myers, of course, had no prosperous stock farm; land never would have made him rich. Hurriedly went to neighbors, borrowed all cattle, horses and other livestock possible. On arrival, Ebbets saw animals in every direction. Myers got his raise. When Ebbets left, Hy returned all livestock to neighbors.

Dodgers won flag again, 1920, but lost to Cleveland. Spring 1925, beset by ill health, Ebbets died, 4/18/25. Estate valued at $1,275,811; owed $100,000.

ECKERT, WILLIAM DOLE Executive. B. 1/20/09, Freeport, Ill. D. 4/16/71, Freeport, Grand Bahama. Commissioner of baseball from 11/15/65 to 2/3/69. At time of selection was retired lieutenant general in U.S. Air Force. Was called "Unknown Soldier" in baseball circles because practically nobody in game had heard of him. Referred to as "General Who" by sports writers.

Eckert, known to intimates as "Spike," graduated from West Point, 1930. M.A., Harvard School of Business. Commander, 452d Bomb Group in Europe, World War II. Distinguished Flying Cross, Distinguished Service Medal, Legion of Merit with two oak-leaf clusters. Air force career mostly in logistics. Knowledge of baseball confined to what he remembered as first baseman in high school, in intramural program at West Point, and to casual interest as fan at World Series time. Signed seven-year contract as commissioner, seemingly because of executive ability. Shortcomings as commissioner soon apparent. Inept at speech-making, deficient in promotional ideas, lacking in give-and-take with sports writers, officials. Stepped out of baseball gracefully when magnates arranged cash settlement three years after they had given him job he had not sought. Was playing tennis when death called.

EDWARDS, HENRY PIERREPOINT Executive. B. 12/11/71, Dunkirk, N. Y. D. 8/1/48, Wilmette, Ill. First publicity man for AL. One of organizers of Baseball Writers Association of America, which he served for many years as secretary-treasurer. Son of U.S. congressman. Sports editor for *Cleveland Recorder*, 1898; editor of *American Sportsman*, weekly devoted to harness racing, briefly during 1901; sports editor, *Cleveland Plain Dealer*, 7/29/01 until 1928. Covered every WS from 1905 through 1927.

NL had hired Cullen Cain as publicity man in 1922; six years later AL created similar post and Edwards took job, keeping it until retirement 1/31/42.

EDWARDS, JOHN ALBAN C-BL-TR. B. 6/10/38, Columbus, Ohio. 6'4", 211. John Edwards, in 1972, had eighth season in which he caught at least 100 NL games. Also hit .268, highest average since batting .281 with Cincinnati Reds, 1964. Houston receiver, at start of 1973 season, had taken part in 1341 major league games, during which he hit for lifetime average of .242, with 75 homers, 487 RBI.

Edwards' backstopping, however, generally has attracted more attention than hitting ability. In 1970 set NL record for most consecutive errorless games by catcher, 138. In 1969 set major league records for most chances accepted by catcher during season, and most putouts. Four times has led NL catchers in fielding. Member, NL All-Star squads, 1963,64,65.

But in WS of 1961 it was Edwards who led Cincinnati Reds in hitting with .364, with two doubles, two singles in 11 trips, with two RBI. John also took part in 1968 WS while with St. Louis Cardinals. Pinch hit once without success.

John hit .305 as sophomore for Ohio State; signed with Cincinnati organization 11/23/58. Spent 1959 at Visalia, California League; 1960 at Nashville, Southern Association; part of 1961 at Indianapolis, American Association. Called up to Reds during 1961 season, in time to play 52 games. Though he hit only .186 for his first part season in NL he followed up with his .364 batting mark in WS that fall. Busiest season was 1963: 148 games; led league in most games caught, in fielding, most putouts, most assists, most total chances; tied for lead in double plays participated in. Furthermore he graduated same year from Ohio State with B.S. in ceramic Engineering.

Traded to Cardinals for 1968 season, then dealt to Houston 10/11/68. Has remained with Astros since.

EHMKE, HOWARD JONATHAN P-BR-TR. B. 4/24/94, Silver Creek, N.Y. D. 3/17/59, Philadelphia, Pa. 6'3", 190. Howard Ehmke saved his finest victory as major leaguer for his only WS. Never won another game after surprise conquest of Chicago 10/8/29. Struck out 13, setting WS record which stood until Carl Erskine of Dodgers fanned 14 Yankees in 1953. Cubs had sluggers in lineup—Rogers Hornsby, Hack Wilson, Riggs Stephenson and Kiki Cuyler, four of most dangerous hitters in NL history. Ehmke won 3–1; would have had shutout but for Dykes' wild throw on Cuyler's grounder. Kiki later scored. Connie Mack, manager of Philadelphia Athletics, had studied Cubs' lineup. Only one regular was lefthanded batsman, Charlie Grimm. Although Lefty Grove or George Earnshaw normally would have been selected as Athletics starter in opening game of WS, Connie figured Ehmke's sidearm delivery, with good curve and good control, might very well fool Chicago sluggers. Ehmke, during 1929 season, obviously nearing end of long pitching career. Had appeared in only 11 games, completed two of eight starts. One month before close of season, Mack quietly dispatched Ehmke to scout Cubs. Press box experts, fans—and A's catcher Mickey Cochrane—astonished at last-minute announcement of Ehmke. Had

Hornsby, Hack Wilson, Cuyler, Hartnett either breaking backs swinging, or watching tantalizing off-speed pitches float across plate for third strikes. Ehmke started fifth game of WS, but didn't get past fourth inning. However, opening gem had Cubs in tizzy, and Athletics captured championship, four games to one.

In 1930 Ehmke pitched in just three games; allowed 22 hits in 10 innings, walked 2, committed balk, wound up with ERA 11.70.

Howard pitched for Los Angeles, Pacific Coast League, starting 1914. Stays with Buffalo, Federal League, and Syracuse, New York State League, before landing with Detroit, 1916. Twice won 17 games for Tigers; in his six years in Motor City was 75–75. Transferred to Boston AL, 1923—won 20, lost 17. Had 19–17 mark in 1924, 9–20 following season. In 1926, divided time between Red Sox and Athletics, won 15, lost 14. In next four years with A's, won 28, lost 21. Wound up his career with 166 wins, 166 losses in 427 games; 3.75 ERA.

ELLIOTT, ROBERT IRVING 3B-BR-TR. B. 11/26/16, San Francisco, Calif. D. 5/4/66, San Diego, Calif. 6', 185. Bob Elliott came to majors as outfielder, played there first two years in majors, then took up third basing. Eventually led NL third basemen in fielding, 1947. Won MVP Award same season; hit .317, drove in 113 runs for Boston Braves.

Bob spent 1936–37 at Savannah, divided 1938 between Savannah and Knoxville. In 1939, Louisville, Toronto, Pittsburgh. Stayed with Pirates through 1946. Then five years with Boston NL. New York NL 1952. St. Louis and Chicago AL 1953. San Diego, Pacific Coast League, 1954. Manager, San Diego, 1955–57. Manager, Sacramento, PCL, 1959. Manager, Kansas City AL, 1960. Coach, Los Angeles AL, 1961.

As Kansas City pilot, team finished last. One WS, Braves, 1948: hit .333, 7 for 21; 2 homers; 5 RBI. 4 in fifth game when he got both his round-trippers (Braves won 11–5). Boston lost Series to Cleveland, four games to two.

Elliott's major league record: 1978 games, .289 average, 2061 hits in 7141 AB, 1064 runs, 383 doubles, 94 triples, 170 homers, 1195 RBI.

ELLIS, DOCK PHILLIP, JR. P-BLR-TR. B. 3/11/45, Los Angeles, Calif. 6'3", 200. Dock Ellis is paid to pitch, but is known to give free lectures. Like unsolicited advice to Pirate management during fall 1971. Accused front office of not treating players "first class." Despite management's inviting players' wives to make trip to San Francisco during playoffs. Mrs. Ellis was one who accepted. Dock wanted *suite* in Pirates' hotel in S.F. Finally wanted to know why son and friends of board chairman John Galbreath were traveling east on 98-passenger plane chartered by club. Queried, general manager Joe L. Brown refused to discuss charges—"We have other business to conduct." Like winning

WS from Baltimore Orioles, despite Ellis' loss of one game allowed 4 earned runs, 2-1/3 innings.

Ellis off to good start, 14–3, early in year; selected for All-Star squad. Before any announcement about NL starting pitcher, Dock predicted "they" wouldn't start "two soul brothers" (Vida Blue cinch to be AL starter). Ellis started against Blue; allowed four hits, four earned runs in three innings, charged with NL loss. Elbow problems bothered after All-Star break—5–6. Won one other decision: playoff, pitching five innings against San Francisco. Dock 15–7, 2.71 ERA, 1972—pitched four complete games. ERA best of his major league career, 3.17 prior to that time.

Ellis attended L.A. Harbor Junior College. Started pro career 1964, Batavia, N.Y. Later Kinston N.C., Asheville, Macon, Columbus, en route to Pittsburgh. Joined Pirates during 1968 season, 6–5; then 11–17, 13–10 before 1971. Good fast ball, curve, slider, change of pace. As 1973 season started: 64–48, 147 games (34 complete), 293 walks, 233 strike-outs. One no-hitter, 2–0 over San Diego Padres, 6/12/70. WS 1971: ERA 15.43. His 1971 All-Star game performance: ERA 12.00.

ENGEL, JOSEPH WILLIAM   P-BR-TR. B. 3/12/93, Washington, D.C. D. 6/12/69, Chattanooga, Tenn. 6'1½", 183. "Barnum of Bushes" stimulated more stories as minor league club owner than as major league pitcher. Joe was mediocre pitcher for Clark Griffith's Washington Senators, 1912–15, 17–22 record. Briefly with Cincinnati, 1917; Cleveland, 1919; Washington, 1920; added one more loss to his major league record.

Engel gained fame by signing small lefthanded girl pitcher to face Babe Ruth, Lou Gehrig, Tony Lazzeri in exhibition game, Chattanooga—before "women's lib" household word. Yankees proved gentlemen by striking out, rather than risk injuring the Southern belle.

Joe, many years, only scout Clark Griffith felt he could afford for Senators. Money often scarce. Sometimes long periods before Engel paid. In 1924, Washington won first AL pennant. Then WS. More cash. Griffith gave Engel the equivalent of one winning share of WS money plus additional $10,000. Engel had scouted Bucky Harris, Joe Judge, Goose Goslin, Ossie Bluege—all vital. Another Engel find—Joe Cronin, now AL president. Joe tried, failed with Pirates. Engel believed in young Irishman from San Francisco, pledged $7500 of Griffith's money to buy him. Griffith unhappy about investing this much in reject. Cronin became fine hitter, great shortstop, managed Senators to pennant 1933. Engel wrote Griffith's niece and secretary, about Cronin: "Tall and handsome, so be dolled up to meet him." Niece-secretary Millie Robertson now Mrs. Joe Cronin.

Engel performed vaudeville in Orpheum Circuit. Once led elephant down Pennsylvania Ave., Washington. Stage experience, imaginative mind inspired numerous publicity stunts when he became president of Chattanooga, Southern Association. Avenged General Custer by "scalping" Indians in teepees set up in ball park. Staged elephant hunts. Gave away house with car in garage. Sponsored bank nights. Deposited tub of coins on pitcher's mound—lucky fan given shovel, told to take what he could carry (usually not over $250)—some silver dollars, quarters, most nickels. One of these stunts helped set minor league attendance record by pulling 24,688 paid customers into 16,000-seat park. During depression fans staying away in vast numbers; Engel hung huge sign over box office: "This park is not quarantined!"

ENGLISH, ELWOOD GEORGE (Woody) SS-3B-BR-TR. B. 3/2/07, Granville, Ohio. 5'10", 155. Infielder for Cubs. Unspectacular, but consistent. Twice hit above .300, missed by point on another occasion. Helped Chicago to two pennants. Rounded out career with two seasons in Brooklyn. Played 1261 major league games, .286 average.

English started with Toledo, American Association, 1925; Hit .220, 131 games. Following year, same team, .301, 162 contests. Cubs paid $50,000 for his contract. In WS of 1929: .190 average, five games; .176 mark in 1932 Series. Teammates didn't fare much better, Cubs losing both WS. Traded to Brooklyn 12/5/36. Retired after 1938. Record, 12 years in majors: 1356 hits, 4746 AB, 236 doubles, 52 triples, 32 HR, 801 runs, 422 RBI, 57 SB.

ENNIS, DELMER OF-BR-TR. B. 6/8/25, Philadelphia, Pa. 6', 200. Del led NL in RBI once, 1950, with 126. During career usually near or over 100 RBI (seven times over). Most productive years with Philadelphia NL; one fine season with St. Louis Cardinals, 1957: .286, 105 RBI. Not best outfielder. Power at plate.

Del had one year with Trenton, Inter-State League, 1943. Military service, two seasons. Directly to majors, hit .313 in 141 games with Phillies, 1946; plus 17 homers, 30 doubles, 6 triples—all of which earned him designation as Rookie of Year by *Sporting News*. Over .300 mark twice more as NL regular. Averaged .284 for major league career, 1903 games. His 2063 hits included 358 doubles, 69 triples, 288 round-trippers. Scored 985 times, had 1284 RBI. Three homers 7/23/55. After final season in Philadelphia, 1956, with Cardinals 1957–58, then to Cincinnati, Chicago AL, 1959. Time was up.

While Ennis' 126 RBI, .311 batting average helped Whiz Kids to NL pennant, 1950, didn't do well in WS: 2 for 14, .143 average. Yankees flattened Phillies, four straight.

EPSTEIN, MICHAEL PETER 1D-BL-TL. B. 4/4/43, Bronx, N.Y. 6'4",
225. Mike Epstein, one of those players who seem always on edge of
greatness, though .249 average going into 1973 would belie this. Has
power—30 homers, Washington, 1969, with 85 RBI for team that
finished fourth in six-club AL Eastern Division. But still finds most
lefthanded pitchers difficult. Hit only .234 for Oakland, 1971, after
Senators traded to A's. In 1972 Mike hit .270 for Dick Williams' club,
with 26 homers. Went hitless in WS against Cincinnati, 16 official trips;
drew five walks, struck out three times. Then traded to Texas Rangers.
Took with him record of 117 major league homers, 336 RBI in 771
games.

Baltimore Orioles signed him for $50,000 bonus, 1964. Mike had
variety of athletic skills. Fullback, U. of California, Berkeley. U.S. Olympic baseball team, 1964. Farmed to Stockton, California League, 1965;
hit 30 homers, batted in 100 runs, hit .338 (tops in league). Then .309
season, Rochester, International League, leading circuit in homers with
29, in RBI with 102. Orioles called up for six games that year. In 1967,
wanted to send him to minors for more experience. Epstein balked.
Traded to Washington 5/29/67. Hit .226 that year, .234 following
season. Also played 11 games, Buffalo, 1968, with .400 average. Then
came his best major league season for average, .278 in 1969, with 30
homers. Dropped to .256, 20 homers, 1970. Flashes of great power. Tied
major league record by getting four consecutive homers in two games
6/15,16/71, two each contest. Three homers in one game, 5/16/69, plus
eight RBI. Led AL first basemen in double plays, 1971, with 123. Set AL
record for most putouts in extra-inning game by first basemen 6/12/67
with 32. Same day tied AL record by handling most chances, 34.

Epstein is ballistics expert. Makes own guns with lathe; has attracted
attention of experts by his innovations.

ERSKINE, CARL DANIEL P-BR-TR. B. 12/13/26, Anderson, Ind.
5'10", 165. Pitched two no-hitters for Brooklyn. Five times helped
Dodgers win NL flags. Won two WS victories, lost two. Retired after
compiling 122–78 record, all with Dodgers.

Carl, in U.S. Navy, attracted attention of Brooklyn organization
scouts. Signed for $3500 bonus while still in service. Commissioner
Happy Chandler nullified deal. Dodgers permitted to rebid; this time
Carl got $5000 bonus. Between 1946 and 1950, Danville (Ill.), Fort
Worth, Montreal, in Brooklyn farm system. Joined Dodgers for keeps
during 1950 season, but had helped win 1949 flag with 8–1 mark, mostly
in relief. In 1951, 16–12 record; then 14–6; in 1953, 20–6; following
season, 18–15. Began to taper off. Last two seasons, 1958,59, with
Dodgers in Los Angeles. Nearly perfect game 6/19/52: no hits, one

walk—pitcher, Ramsdell, Chicago Cubs. Another no-hitter, 5/12/56, against rival Giants. One of his WS victories was record-breaker; in 3–2 win over Yankees, 10/2/53, he struck out 14 men—one more than Howard Ehmke had fanned in opener of 1929 WS. Sandy Koufax improved on Erskine's record in 1963, then Bob Gibson of St. Louis Cardinals set current mark of 17 in his classic against Detroit Tigers, 10/2/68.

Erskine pitched in 335 major league games: 1,718-2/3 innings, 981 strikeouts, 646 walks, ERA 4.00, 14 shutouts. WS mark: 2–2, 11 games, ERA 5.83.

Carl lives in birthplace, where he's partner in insurance brokerage.

ESSEGIAN, CHARLES ABRAHAM, JR. (Chuck) OF-BR-TR. B. 8/9/31, Boston, Mass. 5'11", 200. Chuck Essegian played 404 major league games for seven different clubs, hit .255. But Los Angeles fans especially remember him for pinch hitting, 1959 WS. Hit two pinch homers, something no other player ever done. And Dodgers, second year in L.A., won world championship. White Sox defeated Dodgers in first game, 11–0; were ahead 2–1 in seventh inning of second game when Walter Alston sent Chuck in to bat for Podres. Homered, tied score. Dodgers eventually won 4–3. Took next two games. Lost fifth. Captured sixth, decisively, 9–3. Essegian's second pinch homer, ninth inning of final game, decoration only. Batted for Duke Snider. In all, 2 for 3, walked once, .667.

Chuck graduated from Stanford, 1954, with A.B. Started minor league career, 1953, Sacramento. played with eight other clubs. Major league experience: Philadelphia NL 1958. St. Louis and L.A. NL 1959. L.A. 1960. Baltimore AL 1961. Kansas City AL 1961. Cleveland 1961–62. Kansas City AL 1963.

ETCHEBARREN, ANDREW AUGUSTE C-BR-TR. B. 6/20/43, La Puente, Calif. 6'1", 197. French-Basque descent. Early in 1972 seemed to have taken over principal catching duties for Baltimore Orioles. Had been with club six full seasons, parts of two others, but had only .235 batting average, 535 games. Mostly had been used when southpaw pitcher toiling for opposition.

Andy got $85,000 for signing with Baltimore, 1961. Orioles farmed to Aberdeen S. Dak., Elmira, Lynchburg, Rochester before finally keeping him on Baltimore roster in 1966. With Orioles briefly 1962, 1965. In first full year with Orioles, 11 homers, 50 RBI, but hit just .221. Used regularly late in 1971 when Ellie Hendricks ill; went 30 for 87, raised batting average 44 points, .270 for year, his highest in majors. Good catcher. Excellent on pop fouls, grabbing pitches out of dirt.

Named to AL All-Star squads 1966,67, but not used either year. WS

1966,69,70,71: 9 games, 2 for 27, .074 average. Financial interest in business, Hacienda Heights, Calif.

ETTEN, NICHOLAS RAYMOND 1B-BL-TL. B. 9/19/13, Chicago, Ill. 6'2", 200. Nick Etten didn't quite reach 1000-game mark; hit .277, 89 homers in 937 games. However, former first baseman for Philadelphia AL and NL, Yankees had unusual experience in 1943. Went 17 games without single—7/30 to 8/15 inclusive. Was either home run, double or nothing. Playing for Yankees at time. Got two hits 7/29, both singles. Then unique streak: 5 homers, 9 doubles, no triples, 16 RBI.

Etten started out in Mississippi Valley League, Davenport, Iowa, 1933: .357, 114 games, 14 homers, 90 RBI. Next, Little Rock, .291. Divided 1935 between Birmingham and Elmira. Then two seasons at Savannah, South Atlantic League, above .300 both years. Hit .370 for Jacksonville, same league, in 144 games, 1938; gained promotion to Philadelphia AL. Hit .259 and .252 for Athletics in parts of 1938 and 1939. Then .299 for Baltimore, International League. One more year with old Orioles, 1940: .321 average in 160 games, 24 homers, 128 RBI. Hit .311 in 151 games with Phils, 1941, first full year in majors; 14 homers, 79 RBI. Dropped to .264 in 1942, 8 homers, 67 RBI. Yankees 1943–46. Best season there 1944: 22 homers led AL, as did 93 RBI; hit .293 in 154 contests. Phillies final season in majors, 1947. Hit .244, 14 games.

His 921 major league hits included 167 doubles, 25 triples, 89 homers. Scored 426 runs, drove in 480, stole 22 bases.

EVANS, WILLIAM G. (Billy) Umpire. B. 2/10/84, Chicago, Ill. D. 1/23/56, Miami, Fla. Versatile: umpire, sports writer, baseball front office man, football executive—capable in all. Hall of Fame 1973. Set out to become lawyer. Entered Cornell, 1901. Father died two years later, had to stop education. Cub reporter for *Youngstown* (Ohio) *Vindicator*, then sports editor two years later, $18 weekly. When regular umpire for Ohio-Pennsylvania League game failed to show up, two managers okayed Evans instead, at $15 fee. Continued umpiring as sideline for two years. Ban Johnson, AL prexy, hired him, 1906. Billy continued on staff till 1927. Then general manager, Cleveland Indians. As AL arbiter, outstanding in field. Officiated WS 1909,12,15,17,19,23. In 1906 umpires often worked alone. One of their chores was to announce batteries. Billy in league less than week, umping Athletics–Red Sox game. Connie Mack, manager of A's, told him battery would be Rube Waddell and Ossie Schreck. For Boston, Cy Young and Lou Criger. Two of greatest pitchers of all times, rival hurlers. "I was awed by their reputations," said Evans. "A friend of mine . . . said that when I announced batteries, my lips moved, but no sound came from my throat. I suppose you can say I choked up." Once fought Ty Cobb under

Washington stands, over a call. Was umpiring in St. Louis, hit by pop bottle, thrown by 18-year-old. For weeks Evans between life and death. Many wanted Evans to prosecute boy. Billy asked police to release him to mother's custody with reprimand.

Though umpire, Evans continued sports writing. For years, only person active in sports who wrote under his own name. By 1920 over 100 newspapers using his syndicated articles. Became sports editor for Scripps-Howard's Newspaper Enterprise Association. Wrote for *Collier's* magazine.

Billy took over seventh-place team in Cleveland. During eight years as general manager, club became first-division team. Paid $45,000 for Earl Averill, $40,000 for Dick Porter. Signed Wes Ferrell, Oral Hildebrand and Bob Feller as well as Tom Henrich. Farm director for Boston Red Sox six years; replaced by Herb Pennock. Took over Cleveland Rams football team for one season.

President, Southern Association. Recalled his umpiring days in AL when Ban Johnson demanded special report on any game lasting over two hours, gave $300 bonus to umpire who officiated in shortest ball games over season. Evans insisted umpires speed up games in SA—cut average game's time by half hour. League had been drawing 700,000; went over two-million mark 1944–46.

Joined Tigers as general manager, December 1946, remaining until 7/28/51 when replaced by Charlie Gehringer. Gave $70,000 bonus to sign catcher Frank House, put through $125,000 deal bringing Jerry Priddy to Tigers. Detroit finished runner-up twice during Evans' regime, 1947 and 1950.

EVERS, JOHN JOSEPH (Trojan)   2B-BL-TR. B. 7/21/81, Troy, N.Y. D. 3/28/47, Albany, N.Y. 5'9'', 140. Johnny Evers probably owed his election to Hall of Fame, 1946, to poem rather than to skill as ball player. Played second base for Chicago Cubs who won pennant 1906,07,08. One day Franklin P. Adams, columnist for old *New York Evening Mail*, penned eight-line lament about plight of Cubs' victims. Started with words, "These are the saddest of possible words,/Tinker to Evers to Chance." Referred to double plays made by Chicago team against N.Y. Giants. Poem caught public fancy, and today plenty of fans think this was greatest of double-play combinations. Actually, many double-play combinations have far excelled old Chicago trio. Over four-year period (1906–09), Tinker-Evers (or Evers-Tinker)-Chance combo accounted for only 54 double plays. Many good keystoners, better than Evers, probably never will make Hall of Fame. Many hitters have had far better averages, done everything better at plate without getting voted into Hall. However, Evers smart, aggressive, driving player. Played game hard. Often referred to as "Crab." For years never spoke to his shortstop, Tinker.

Started pro career with hometown club in N.Y. State League, dividing time between short and second. After hitting .285 that year, 1902, in 84 games, went up to Cubs same season in time for 26 games. Batted .225. Thereafter, average usually around .250–.270, though he reached .300 in 1908, and .341 in 1912. Expert at drag bunts, fast enough to beat out infield rollers for hits.

When Evers reached NL many thought him too light for wear and tear of long pennant races. Scrappy fighter, however, played ten seasons with over 120 games each. Sparked famous play which threw 1908 NL race into tie. Spotted fact that Fred Merkle had not touched second base and called for ball. Famous "boner" resulted in replay to decide pennant, which Cubs won from Giants.

Evers continued with Cubs through 1913 season. Managed club that year, after which drew his release. Signed with Boston NL. Member of famous "miracle team" which rose from cellar in July to world championship in October, winning pennant, then taking Series from powerful Philadelphia Athletics in four games. Boston NL until 7/12/17 when sent to Philadelphia NL. Days as regular ended, 1917, hitting .214.

Coach, N.Y. Giants, 1920. Manager, Chicago NL, 1921. Coach, Chicago AL, 1922–23. Manager, Chicago AL, 1924. Assistant manager, Boston NL, 1929–32. Scout, Boston NL, 1933–34. Manager, Albany, International League, 1935. Vice president, general manager, Albany, Eastern League, 1939.

WS performances showed .150 batting average, 1906; .350 each in 1907, 1908; .438 in 1914; overall record .316 in 20 games. Major league average .270 in 1776 games.

Chalmers Award as most valuable NL player, 1914.

EWING, WILLIAM (Buck)   C-BR-TR. B. 10/17/59, Hoaglands, Ohio. D. 10/20/06 Cincinnati, Ohio. 5'10", 188. How Buck Ewing would compare with Bill Dickey, Mickey Cochrane, Johnny Bench, other famed receivers is hard to say. But old-timers used to claim he was greatest catcher ever. Their testimony plus .311 batting average for 1280 major league games in eighties and nineties earned him election to Hall of Fame, 1939. Versatile, playing many games at all other positions on diamond, including few as pitcher. Players had to be versatile then, since player limit was much lower.

Ewing started with Mohawk Browns in Cincinnati before joining Troy (N.Y.) team, then in NL, 1881. In 1883 became charter member of New York NL, continuing through 1889. Six times during this period hit above .300. Became star, favorite. Spent 1890 season as player-manager with N.Y. team in Players (Brotherhood) League, then back to Giants for 1891–92. Cleveland NL 1893–94. Player-manager, Cincinnati NL, 1895–97. Manager, Cincinnati, 1898–99. Manager, Giants, 1900. As pilot, modest success. In eight-club Players League 1890, finished third.

In 12-club league had two third-place teams, one fourth, one sixth and one eighth. In 1900, when NL became eight-club league, Buck's Giants lost 41 games, won 21; he was replaced. Team ultimately finished last. Clubs he managed won 489 games, lost 395.

Ewing was good base thief, six times going over 30 mark in NL Home run total modest; led NL in 1883 with 10.

FABER, URBAN CHARLES (Red) P-BLR-TR. B. 9/6/88, Cascade, Iowa. 6'1", 195. Red Faber spent 20 years with Chicago White Sox; had four 20-game seasons; won three games of 1917 World Series against New York. Toiled in such quiet, workmanlike manner that one "rock" he pulled still spoken about.

In second game of 1917 Series, fifth inning, Sox at bat. Buck Weaver hit grounder to Giant shortstop Art Fletcher. Art bobbled ball, Weaver safe at first. Schalk retired on grounder to Zimmerman at third base, Weaver taking second. Faber then singled to right. When right fielder Dave Robertson threw to plate, Weaver stopped at third but Faber able to go to second. On next pitch Red "stole" third. Much to his astonishment, looked up and saw teammate Weaver serenely standing on bag. "Where do you think you're going?" asked Weaver. "Back to the mound to pitch," replied embarrassed Faber.

Won his game too, 7 to 2, plus two other victories. Lost one contest. Sox took Giants, four games to two.

Faber bounced around minors 1908–13, graduating to White Sox after two 20-game seasons with Des Moines, Western League. Stayed with Chicago for rest of playing career which ended at close of 1933. Finished with 254–212 mark with club which spent many years in second division. Incapacitated by injury, did not pitch in 1919 World Series when "Black Sox" allowed Cincinnati to win. Lifetime ERA 3.15. World Series record: 3–1, 27 innings, ERA 2.33. Coached White Sox 1946–48. Hall of Fame 1964.

FACE, ELROY LEON (Roy) P-BRL-TR. B. 2/20/28, Stephentown, N.Y. 5'7½", 158. When baseball men speak of relief pitchers they usually get around to mentioning Firpo Marberry, Johnny Murphy—and Roy Face. Roy pitched only six complete games in his major league career—but won 100 games and saved 189 others. Lost 93 decisions.

One season Face compiled fabulous record—18–1—setting major league record for highest winning percentage, .947. Chief Bender, Joe Wood, Walter Johnson, Bob Grove, Whitey Ford, Freddy Fitzsimmons, and others had better-than-.800 winning percentages, but only Face went above .900 mark among regulars.

Face started with Bradford in Pony League, 1949 and 1950, with 14–2 mark first season; 18–5 in next. Spent 1951 with Pueblo, Western League, winning 23, losing nine. Then 14–11 season at Fort Worth, Texas League. Had 6–8 record with Pirates, 1953, then farmed to New Orleans, Southern Association, 1954. Won 12, lost 11. Then back to Pittsburgh until during 1968 season. Won his complete games in his first two seasons with Pirates and never again hurled entire contest. His last game as starting pitcher came in 1957. But he got plenty of work thereafter in relief roles. In September 1956 Pirates used him in nine consecutive games as fireman. In this stretch he pitched 14-2/3 innings, allowed 14 hits and three earned runs, walked two, fanned nine; won three games and lost one.

Set various records with his relief pitching—and equaled one other mark for pitchers, making unassisted double play, 4/21/64. In his 18–1 season, 1959, had ERA of 2.71. Best ERA came 1962, 1.88.

Face completed his career with Detroit, 1968. Major league totals showed 3.45 ERA in 804 games. Pitched 1315-2/3 innings, allowed 1285 hits, walked 347, struck out 843. In WS play, 1960, pitched 10-1/3 innings in four games, neither won nor lost decision, had 5.23 ERA. Pitched in four All-Star Games without decisions.

FAIN, FERRIS ROY (Burrhead) 1B-BL-TL. B. 3/29/22, San Antonio, Tex. 5'11", 174. Ferris Fain repeatedly made more errors playing first base than any other player in AL and Pacific Coast League, but still led AL in hitting twice while toiling for old Philadelphia Athletics. Burrhead led PCL in errors by first basemen four times, and might have done it oftener but for three years in military service. Joining Athletics, 1947, had to be content sharing distinction of most errors with Mickey Vernon. Each had 19. But in 1948–50 and 1952 Fain muffed oftener than any other AL first sacker.

Fain handled everything that came in his direction and four times he also led AL first basemen in assists; tied major league record by completing six double plays at first base in one game 9/1/47; set high mark for taking part in most double plays, 194, in 1949; led first basemen in twin killings, 1949–50. Ferris also holds AL record for most assists by first baseman in extra-inning game, seven, 6/9/49. That contest went 12 rounds.

Fain joined San Francisco, Pacific Coast League, 1939, in time to play 12 games, and, but for his military service, remained with Seals until 1946. That year he led PCL in runs scored (117), in RBI (112), hit .301, and was drafted by Athletics. His batting titles came in 1951 with .344 in 117 games; and in 1952 with .327 in 145 contests. Athletics traded him to Chicago AL for 1953 and his average sagged to .256. Back to .302 in 1954. In 1955 divided his time between Cleveland and Detroit, hit .260 and dropped out of majors.

Fain played 1151 major league games, hit .290. His 1139 hits included 213 doubles, 30 triples, 48 homers. Scored 595 runs, had 570 RBI. Stole 46 bases. Never in WS. Three All-Star games, 1950,51,52; hit .429, 3 for 7, including triple.

FAIRLY, RONALD RAY 1B-OF-BL-TL. B. 7/12/38, Macon, Ga. 5'10'', 175. Ron Fairly was long-time favorite with L.A. Dodgers before moving to Montreal Expos 6/11/69. Timely hitter—known as "Mr. Clutch" on Dodgers. Put together .300 batting average for four WS while with Walter Alston's club, 1959,63,65,66; and in 1965 classic equaled all-time record by hitting safely in all seven games against Minnesota Twins. With Expos has done consistent work. In 1972 had .278 mark with 17 homers, 68 RBI. Brilliant fielder at first base, expert at first-second-first double play. NL All-Star team 1973.

Ron got reported $60,000 bonus to sign with Dodgers in 1958. Attended Southern Cal. Played with Des Moines and St. Paul that year as well as appearing in 15 games with Dodgers. Spent all of following season with Los Angeles club, but went back to minors at Spokane for most of 1960. Returned to Dodgers, 1961, hit .322 for them that season, his best in majors. After 30 games in 1969 he was sent to Montreal, hitting .219 up to that point. Promptly hit .289 for Expos, raising his overall season mark to .274. Hit .288 in 1970.

Fairly went into 1973 season with 1781 games behind him in majors; lifetime mark of .265 with 1433 hits for 2166 total bases; 238 doubles, 147 homers, 27 triples; 689 runs, 780 RBI. Got one triple in 1972, none in 1963,66,67,70,71. During 1965 WS when he hit .379, Ron had two homers and three doubles among his 11 hits, in 29 times at bat. Scored seven runs, drove in six.

FALK, BIBB AUGUST (Jockey) OF-BL-TL. B. 1/27/99, Austin, Tex. 6', 180. Bibb Falk, who hit .314 during 12-year AL career with Chicago White Sox and Cleveland Indians, received 476 cigars when he retired as baseball coach at U. of Texas, 1967—one for each victory his team had won.

Falk, as student at U. of Texas, pitched for collegiate team, 1918–20 and never lost game. But could hit and play outfield better than he could pitch—at least as far as being major league prospect. Joined White Sox, 1920, played seven games. Copped regular job, 1921, hit .285 in 152 games, with 82 RBI in first full season. Boosted his mark to .298 following year, then hit .307. Had .352 mark, 1924 and .345, 1926; five seasons, better than .300 for White Sox. Had 99 RBI in both 1924–25, and 108, 1926. Traded to Cleveland 2/28/28, Bibb had three seasons with Indians batting above .300.

In 1354 major league games amassed 1463 hits, scored 656 runs; had 300 doubles, 59 triples, 69 homers, and 785 RBI. Then became playing manager for Toledo, American Association, hitting .321 in 79 games, his only year in minor leagues. Club finished fourth.

Returned to Cleveland, 1933, as coach. Scout, Red Sox, 1934–39. Joined U. of Texas coaching staff, 1940; put in 25 seasons, interrupted only by air force during World War II.

FANNING, WILLIAM JAMES (Jim) C-BR-TR. B. 9/14/27, Chicago, Ill. 5′11″, 180. Montreal's general manager didn't make much of splash as major league catcher, but is credited with helping improve Expos through shrewd trading ability. Played 64 games, all with Chicago NL, 1954–57, hit .170 in major league lifetime. Grew up in northwest Iowa. Attended Buena Vista College, Storm Lake, Iowa, getting bachelor's degree there; master's degree in physical education from Illinois.

Spent eight years in Cubs' organization. Managing career began 1958, Tulsa, Texas League. Managed Dallas, American Association, 1959. In 1960, Dallas–Fort Worth. Joined Milwaukee organization 1961, manager at Eau Claire, Wisconsin. In 1962 continued as manager but also was general manager. Scout, Braves, 1963–64; then became assistant general manager of Braves. Served as director of Baseball Scouting Bureau, 1968, then took over general manager's job for Expos eight months later. Now makes home in Montreal where he can ski in spare time.

FARRELL, MAJOR KERBY (Kerby) 1B-BL-TL. B. 9/3/13, Leap-wood, Tenn. 5′11″, 172. Kerby Farrell had one year as manager of Cleveland Indians, 1957, when he succeeded Al Lopez. Team finished sixth, half game behind Baltimore Orioles, and Farrell gave way to Bobby Bragan in turn. As first baseman he had played 85 games for old Boston Braves, 1943, and hit .268; later showed up as member of Chicago White Sox, 1945; hit .258 in 103 contests. So his overall major league average shows .262 for 188 games.

Farrell, however, has had long, frequently successful career in minors. After attending Freed-Hardeman College in Tennessee two years, where he played basketball, Farrell had pro baseball experience at Jackson, Miss.; Beckley, W. Va.; Tyler, Tex.; Memphis, Tenn.; Greenville, Miss.; Scranton, Pa.; and Canton, Ohio, during 1932–41. Player-manager, Erie, Pa., 1941–42. Moved to Boston Braves for 1943. Indianapolis 1944. Chicago AL 1945. Little Rock 1946. Playing manager at Spartanburg, S.C.; later at Cedar Rapids, Iowa; Reading, Pa. Manager, Indianapolis, 1955–56. Then came his stint at Cleveland as pilot of Indians. Won 76 games, lost 77 that year. Later managed at Miami, Buffalo, Salinas Calif., Lynchburg Va. In 1973 became manager of Tacoma club for Minnesota Twins organization.

In 1956, while with Indianapolis in American Association, Farrell's club won Junior WS from Rochester team of International League in four straight; in 1961 his International League Buffalo club again won Junior WS in four straight, this time against American Association entry from Louisville.

FAUST, CHARLES VICTOR (Victory)   P. B. 10/9/80, Marion, Kans. D. 6/18/15, Fort Steilacoom, Wash. Charlie Faust qualified as true "baseball nut." Had illusions that he was potentially great pitcher. Actually pitched in two NL games; wound up in an insane asylum. But John McGraw, manager of N.Y. Giants, later wrote, "I give him full credit for winning a pennant for me—NL pennant of 1911." Strange incident began when town's practical joker faked telegram from Giants asking Faust to report to team in St. Louis. Charlie somehow borrowed enough money to get there by train. Buttonholed McGraw in hotel lobby, told surprised manager he was reporting for duty. Giants had been doing badly, so McGraw decided to go along with joke in order to give team laugh. Faust reported at ball park and Giants put him through staged workout. Hitters deliberately missed his "curves" and "fast balls." He practiced sliding into bases in awkward fashion and gave them plenty of laughs. Sat on bench—and Giants swept series with Cardinals.

Giants moved into Chicago—without Faust—and lost series. Team continued to stumble, and after bad road trip who should appear but Faust, who beat his way on freight trains to rejoin club. Giants won next two games. Whenever Faust was around Giants won; when absent they lost. Finally, McGraw and players figured he was really good-luck piece and paid him to stay with club rest of season. Giants wrapped up pennant with 7-1/2-game lead; when nothing at stake Faust went into two different games. Pitched two innings, allowed two hits and two runs; officially had ERA of 4.50. Somehow, Faust got lost during WS. Philadelphia Athletics defeated Giants, four games to two.

Declared insane in 1914, Faust died 1915.

FEENEY, CHARLES STONEHAM (Chub)   Executive. B. 8/31/21,

Orange, N.J. Nephew of Horace Stoneham, president of San Francisco Giants; grandnephew of Charles Stoneham who for many years was president of N.Y. Giants before son Horace took over. Almost became baseball commissioner early in 1969. Succeeded Warren Giles as NL president December of same year, when latter retired. Chub was vice president of Giants when selected to take over top league job. Had spent 24 years with Giants in N.Y. and S.F. doing about everything connected with front office.

Feeney attended Dartmouth and Fordham Law School before admission to N.Y. Bar Association. Three years in navy.

Reportedly gets $60,000 annually in present job. While league president is only one of countless intangibles determining popularity of baseball, Feeney was happy about NL attendance in first two years of his regime. Drew over 16 million in 1970; over 17 million, 1971. AL meanwhile drew 12 million, 1970, and dropped down some 200,000 in 1971.

Feeney opposes interleague play; also opposes fusing AL and NL offices into one headquarters with commissioner's office.

FELLER, ROBERT WILLIAM ANDREW　P-BR-TR. B. 11/3/18, Van Meter, Iowa. 6', 185. Rapid Robert they called him. Once his pitching was timed by a split-second device that found he could throw ball at 98.6 miles an hour. But there were big league athletes who believed he threw even faster. Probably did too, on days like when he fanned eight men in three innings of an exhibition game against Gas House Gang Cardinals when he was 17. Or perhaps he was faster on day he pitched his first no-hitter, 4/16/40, against Chicago AL. Or time he struck out 18 men against Detroit, 10/2/38. Feller led AL in strikeouts seven times and set his top figure of 348 whiffs in 1946 after being out of major league competition 1942–44 and much of 1945. By that time Bob was an extremely clever pitcher, fooling batsmen not only with good fast ball but by other canny serves.

Statisticians argued about whether Feller's 1946 strikeout record was tops for all times. Some claimed Rube Waddell, in 1904, struck out 349 hitters, while others said he fanned only 343. Question became slightly academic some years later when Sandy Koufax, 1965, set unquestionable record of 382.

Feller did all his big league pitching for Cleveland Indians. Judge Landis liberated scores of other ball players, making them free agents because, in his judgment, magnates manipulated their contracts in violation of rules. Tommy Henrich and Pete Reiser were two who were set free by Landis. After Feller had fanned those eight Cardinals in exhibition game in 1936, Des Moines club of Western League protested it had attempted to sign Feller in summer of 1935. Claim was made that

Cleveland had Bobby "covered up" in violation of Major-Minor League Agreement and Rules. Landis, however, found loophole of sorts, allowed Feller to remain with Indians, although Judge awarded $7500 to Des Moines club. No doubt there had been inducements for Bobby and his father because, during hearings before Czar Landis, both "zealously sought" validation of Cleveland contract.

Had Feller been declared free agent, Yankees and other wealthy clubs stood ready to offer him probably greatest bonus ever paid baseball player up to that time.

Feller followed up his exhibition against Cardinals in 1936 by winning five, losing three for Indians in 1936. Next year it was 9–7. Then he got rolling with 17–11 mark in 1938, leading AL in strikeouts for first time with 240. Followed with 24–9; 27–11; and 25–13 records before going into military service. In those three 20-game seasons Bobby led league in strikeouts; in innings pitched; also led league in ERA, 1940, with 2.62.

Bobby's numerous records are listed in statistical books. Here it is enough to note he holds AL record of pitching three no-hitters. Twelve times during career he hurled one-hitters. And besides the time he fanned 18 in one game, he also had games where he struck out 17 and 16. His record of having allowed 208 bases on balls, 1938, set major league mark.

Overall, Bobby pitched in 570 major league games with 3828 IP; won 266 and lost 162 for .621 percentage. Allowed 3271 hits, 1384 earned runs, and fanned 2581. Walked 1764. ERA was 3.25. Hall of Fame 1962.

Feller's WS performance in 1948, his only chance, not memorable. In two games against Boston Braves, charged with two losses. Pitched 14-1/3 innings, allowed 10 hits and 8 runs (all earned), fanned 7, walked 5, ERA 5.02.

Five All-Star games: 12-1/3 innings, 1 run, 5 hits, 4 walks, 13 strikeouts, 1–0 record.

Bobby won eight battle stars while in navy. On his return to civilian life, had slider in his catalogue of pitches. This helped him to his spectacular 1946 season. Immediately after major league races were over and WS finished, Bobby promoted all-star barnstorming plane trip. His team won 29 out of 35 games; Feller pitched in all but one contest. He and his players earned juicy sums to supplement their regular salaries, which had not yet reached anything like present-day levels. Bobby, however, earned better than $80,000 annually with his peak contract with Indians.

Feller owed at least part of his success to tip from Ben Chapman, former AL outfielder, later manager of Philadelphia NL. When Bobby broke into AL, Chapman watched him pitch. Told Feller, "I can steal second base on you any time you pitch." "I don't believe it," said Feller. Next time Chapman was on base he stole second with ease. Chastened,

Bob asked older player, "What am I doing wrong?" Ben told Feller to change his stance on rubber, that every time Bob was going to throw to first base, runner could see light under his right heel. When runner couldn't see light, he knew Bob was pitching to batsman. Feller got big mirror, practiced three days on end. From then on Chapman couldn't steal—or any others—with regularity.

FERGUSON, TOM Executive. B. 7/2/30, Brookline, Mass. Another Horatio Alger story, from batboy to vice president in little over 20 years. Tommy Ferguson, now vice president of Milwaukee Brewers, got job as clubhouse boy with Boston Braves, 1945. Moved out on field as batboy 1946 and continued in that capacity through 1951. In 1948 Braves won NL pennant, giving Tommy his biggest thrill yet. Climax came following year, 1949, when he was presented NL championship ring along with Boston players.

Then into army, 1952, serving in honor guard at Fort Meyer, Va., before heading for Korea, where he saw action with 45th Infantry. Discharged 2/5/54 with rank of staff sergeant. Braves meanwhile had moved to Milwaukee. Ferguson rejoined organization as manager of visiting clubhouse soon after leaving army. In 1960 Braves made him equipment manager. Fred Haney managed Braves, 1956–59. And when Fred moved into picture with new AL franchise in Los Angeles, Ferguson left Braves, 1961, to become traveling secretary of Angels. Left Angels to take similar post with new Seattle AL club, 1969. Seattle franchise lasted just one season before being transferred to Milwaukee. Tommy became traveling secretary of Brewers 4/1/70. In October 1971, became officer and vice president of Brewers. Tommy is married, has two children. Winters in Santa Ana, Calif.

FERRELL, RICHARD BENJAMIN (Rick) C-BR-TR. B. 10/12/06, Durham, N.C. 5'11", 170. Elder of two brothers who formed Ferrell battery for Boston Red Sox and Washington Senators almost five years. Rick almost went with St. Louis Cardinal organization as youth; signed with Detroit system, but was liberated by great emancipator, Judge Landis; as result picked up $25,000 bonus to sign with St. Louis Browns.

Besides brother Wes, Rick had still younger brother, Ewell, who was headed for pro baseball career when fatally shot back in early 1930s. Two other Ferrell brothers, George and Marvin, who played in minor leagues but didn't reach majors.

Rick always wanted to be catcher. Saved his pennies until he had $1.50 and was able to buy second-hand mitt. Ferrell tribe won championship of Guilford County, N.C., 1921, playing against Glenwood. Wes pitched, Rick caught; George was in outfield; Marvin coached from sidelines; Ewell acted as batboy. Ferrells triumphed 2–1.

Rick attended Guilford College, starting 1922. Three years later, Cardinals tempted him with $1000 bonus. Caught exhibition game with Redbird farm club, Syracuse, International League, without signing. However, Rick decided to wait another year before starting his pro career. Then it was with Detroit organization, his bonus $1500. Tigers assigned Ferrell to Kinston, N.C., in Virginia League. Played 64 games, hit .265, then was moved to Columbus in American Association for five games same season. Played with Columbus again in 1927 and 1928, getting into more than 100 games each year, hitting .333 in 1928. By this time Ferrell was recognized as one of finest catching prospects around. When Judge Landis investigated handling of Rick's contract, white-haired jurist decided to make Ferrell free agent. This opened way to spirited bidding for his signature. Although there was depression and money had far greater value than today, Browns offered him $12,500 contract and $25,000 bonus, to top various bidders.

Rick was with Browns 1929 until 5/11/33 when traded to Red Sox. Following year Brother Wes also landed with Red Sox, giving them their chance to perform as Ferrell battery. Both members of battery were dealt to Washington 6/10/37, and they remained together until Wes was released in August of following year. Rick, however, stayed with Washington until 5/15/41, when he returned to St. Louis AL. Stayed with Browns three seasons, then had three more years with Senators.

Rick never had power like his brother Wes. In fact, his major league homer total came to 28 in 6028 times at bat, contrasted to Wes's total of 38 homers in 1176 trips to plate. However, Rick was fine catcher and hit above .300 five times in majors. Had 324 doubles, 45 triples, scored 687 runs, and drove in 734. His lifetime average was .281 in 1884 games.

FERRELL, WESLEY CHEEK P-BR-TR. B. 2/2/08, Greensboro, N.C. 6′2″, 195. Wes Ferrell, now vice president of Detroit Tigers, holds several enviable records as pitcher and hitter. Signed with Cleveland Indians, 1927, pitched one inning and spent most of 1928 season at Terre Haute, III League, 20–8. Back to Cleveland that year; pitched well (2.25 ERA) but lost two games. Then Wes hit his stride. Won over 20 games in each of his first four full seasons in majors. No other pitcher ever has done this in either league. Reached 25–13 mark in 1930. Traded to Boston AL 5/25/34, joined his brother Rick, catcher, who was already member of Red Sox. Formed brother battery 1934–36, then 6/10/37 both were traded to Washington, remaining on same team until 8/12/38 when Wes was given his unconditional release.

Wes had banner season with Boston, 1935—25–14. Led AL in innings pitched, had 3.52 ERA. Came back following year to win 20, losing 15, again workhorse of league. And in 1937, toiling for Boston and Washington, led AL in innings pitched for third year in succession, although his victory total dropped to 14–19.

After his release by Senators in 1938, Wes caught on with Yankees for rest of 1938 and 1939. Brooklyn 1940. Boston NL 1941. Then dropped into minors as manager at Leaksville, N.C.; Lynchburg, Va.; Marion, N.C.; and Tampa, Fla., doing a little pitching as well. Continued as manager in Greensboro, N.C. through 1949. Coach, Detroit Tigers, 1950–53. Scout, Tigers, 1954–58. General manager, Tigers, 1960–61. Then vice president of Tigers. During foregoing period took time out to manage teams at Rock Hill and Shelby, N.C., briefly.

As hitting pitcher, Wes stands very high on list; lifetime average of .280 puts him close to such fine batsmen as George Uhle and Red Lucas, who had lifetime marks of .294 and .281 respectively.

Besides hitting for average, Ferrell had power, as his 38 homers will attest. This is better lifetime mark than any other pitcher in majors. One season, 1931, Ferrell hit nine homers. Four years later had great season. Pinch hit for Lefty Grove in ninth inning in game against Detroit Tigers 7/21/35; two men were on base. Wes homered off Tommy Bridges, giving Red Sox 7–6 victory. Next day Ferrell pitched—won his own game with ninth-inning four-master off Dick Coffman of Browns, by 2–1 score. One week later Buck Newsom, then with Senators, was his victim. Ferrell slammed two home runs and captured decision, 6–4. In all, Ferrell had 52 hits that year, equaling record set by George Uhle of Indians. Wes hit .347 for season. His 32 RBI set new record for runs driven in by pitcher in one season. Red Ruffing came close to Ferrell's homer mark, with 37 during his lifetime. But Ruffing went to plate more than 300 times more than did Ferrell. Ruffing, however, drove in more runs during career than Ferrell. Red had 266, against 208 for Wes.

Incidentally, Ferrell, at 40, besides managing Marion team in Western Carolina League, pitched, played infield and outfield, in total of 104 games, hit .425, and won batting championship of circuit. That was 1948.

In AL, Ferrell hit two homers in one game on five separate occasions. Also hurled no-hitter while with Indians, blanking St. Louis Browns, 9–0, 4/29/31.

Wes pitched in 374 major league games, 2623 innings, won 193, lost 128, .601 percentage. Allowed 2845 hits, 1177 earned runs, and walked 1040, with 985 strikeouts. His ERA was 4.04. As batsman his totals came to 548 big league appearances, 329 hits in 1176 AB, 175 runs scored. Had 57 doubles, 12 triples, 38 homers, and .280 average.

FERRISS, DAVID MEADOW (Boo) P-BL-TR. B. 12/5/21, Shaw, Miss. 6'2", 208. Boo Ferriss was one of those brilliant rookies, in 1945, who burst into AL with 21 victories for Boston Red Sox. Came back following year with 25–6 record to lead league in winning percentage with .806. Then never again won as many games in majors as he did in his rookie year! Had 12–11 mark in 1947, 7–3 in 1948, then gave up after brief trials in 1949–50.

Boo had 2.96 ERA as rookie with Sox, and 3.25 ERA in 1946, winding up his career with 3.64 in 880 innings as big leaguer. Overall record, 65–30.

Ferriss had WS shutout to his credit, having blanked St. Louis Cardinals 4–0 in third game of Series 10/9/46, allowing six hits. Boo tried to win seventh and crucial game of set. Started against Murry Dickson but removed in fifth inning when Cardinals took 3–1 lead. Redbirds eventually won 4–3, and WS by same. Ferriss had ERA of 2.02 for WS, with one victory, no defeat; loss of final game charged against his teammate Bob Klinger.

FETZER, JOHN EARL Executive. B. 3/25/01, Decatur, Ind. John Fetzer has been sole owner of Detroit Tigers since 1962. Prior to that, had been key figure in syndicate that bought franchise from W. O. Briggs estate for $5-1/2 million, 1956.

Fetzer is radio and television tycoon. In 1914 became interested in wireless telegraphy through relative who was railroad train dispatcher. After entering Purdue, 1921, began building broadcasting units. Left college to do engineering work in radio, but later earned bachelor's degree at Andrews U., Michigan; did graduate work at Michigan, extension work at Wisconsin.

During 1920s constructed radio stations in various places, including Chicago and Indianapolis. Pioneered in fostering development of directional antenna, innovation that paved way to license 3000 stations.

Radio chain grew and eventually got into television, with nine stations in Midwest. Later expanded holdings into film production, background music franchises, oil production, Arizona land development, mining, and manufacturing.

While an executive, Fetzer has kept his hand in as working broadcaster. Has interviewed Tito of Yugoslavia, de Gaulle, Shah of Iran, Adenauer, and others. During Hungarian revolt against Soviet domination (1956), interviewed numerous Hungarians on tape for broadcasts in U.S. Also has served as radio advisor and supervisor for U.S. government in various assignments.

In baseball, Fetzer was member of committee that selected Joe Cronin as president of AL. In battles in connection with major league expansion, Fetzer was tireless behind-scenes negotiator and peacemaker. In 1960 became two-thirds owner and president of Tigers. Club finished second in 1961, then dropped down for several years. Finally had another runner-up, 1967, and won AL pennant and WS, 1968.

Fetzer at times has been impatient with baseball organization, but is pleased that there is "complete trust" in game. "A handshake seals a deal in baseball—and that's good," he says.

FINGERS, ROLAND GLEN (Rollie) P-BR-TR. B. 8/25/46, Steuben-ville, Ohio 6'4", 195. Rollie Fingers was one of reasons Oakland was able to win its first AL pennant and follow it with world championship, 1972. Enjoyed best season of his career from almost any standpoint. Reliever in 11 games where he was credited with Oakland victory. Saved 21 other games. Had 2.51 ERA; pitched extremely well in AL playoffs and WS. Captured decision in first game against Detroit in AL championship series, relieved in two others; and in classic against Cincinnati appeared in six of seven games; won one, lost one; saved two games, and had 1.74 ERA.

When 1973 season started, although Rollie had appeared in 219 AL box scores during his career, apart from playoffs and 1972 WS, he had pitched just four complete games, one each in 1969,70, and two in 1971. In 508 innings owned 3.31 ERA; had 28 victories, 31 defeats; 351 strikeouts, 152 walks. AL All-Star squad 1973.

Fingers is son of George Fingers who once played in St. Louis Cardinal organization but never made majors. Rollie attended Chaffey Junior College in California, but made name for himself in American Legion ball. Pitched Upland American Legion Post No. 73 to national championship, 1964. Signed with Kansas City AL, 1965, before A's moved to Oakland. Got minor league experience starting with Leesburg, Fla., that year; then pitched for Modesto, Calif., and Birmingham before joining A's during 1968 season for one game. In his first full season with A's, 1969, Rollie was used in 60 games, started eight. Won six, lost seven, saved dozen others. In 1970 he appeared in 45 games, 7–9. Started 19 games, finished one. In 1971 saved 17 games, was 4–6. At one point pitched 30 consecutive scoreless innings.

Fingers' work in 1971 playoff games against Baltimore was not up to his usual standard. Pitching just 2-1/3 innings, allowing two earned runs, ERA 7.71. Rollie's 1972 WS performance included 11 strikeouts, 4 walks, 10-1/3 innings.

Pitches with wired jaw. Was pitching in opening game for Birming-ham, Southern Association, 1967, when hit by line drive that fractured his cheekbone as well as jaw.

FINLEY, CHARLES O. Executive. B. 2/22/18, Birmingham, Ala. Reached pinnacle of baseball success 1972, when his Oakland A's de-feated Cincinnati in seventh game of WS for world championship, Contro-versial, unpredictable, indefatigable insurance tycoon, who started as la-borer in steel mills of Gary, Ind., finally won top prize in game he loved since childhood. Among his honors, *Sporting News* designation as 1972 Sports' Man of Year. Baseball is probably sport closest to Finley's heart, but also owns California Golden Seals of National Hockey League, Memphis Tams of American Basketball Association, and various farm clubs. Besides large insurance brokerage, based in Chicago, also owns fertilizer company.

Sought big-league franchise for seven years before finally buying 52 percent of Kansas City club 12/19/60 for slightly less than $2 million. Bought remaining 48 percent few weeks later. Baseball experience has been marked by almost constant bickerings with other officials, press, and, sometimes, players. Numerous arguments with civic leaders in Kansas City that culminated in his moving club to Oakland 10/18/67. Finley claimed press "did everything possible to break me physically, mentally, morally and financially."

Repeatedly shifted field managers and front office employees; in recent years has served as own general manager. At one point said he had to do it from economic standpoint. Promoted various bizarre stunts on ball field, including use of mule as team's mascot. Dressed his team in yellow and green uniforms with white shoes, revolutionary move in conservative sport, although Larry MacPhail had Cincinnati Reds use red pants back in 1930s. Later, other major league clubs have followed Finley's lead with more colorful haberdashery.

Finley got cool reception moving team into Oakland. Spent $500,000 in promotion during 1970–71, and for first time since he owned team A's got into AL playoffs, only to be eliminated by Baltimore Orioles. Said to have spent $7 million, including cost of franchise, to get A's into current position. One of attractions of Bay Area was fact Finley received contract for radio and television that nets him $1.1 million annually. Replying to queries about whether he might move his team to another city, Finley said there was no basis for story (Dec. 1971). Reportedly signed 20-year contract with people of Oakland requiring him to keep A's there at least until 1987.

During first four years in Oakland, Finley enjoyed modest success, especially in 1971 when attendance reached 914,933, increase of more than 136,000 over 1970. This might be traced in large part to sensational pitching of Vida Blue. In 1972 Oakland attendance reached 921,323 exclusive of playoffs and WS games.

Finley as young man played first base in semipro baseball in Indiana. Owns 280-acre farm at La Porte, Ind.

FISHER, EDDIE GENE P-BR-TR. B. 7/16/36, Shreveport, La. 6'2", 200. Busiest relief pitcher in AL history. Gained this honor in 1972, passing Hoyt Wilhelm who had been fireman in 570 AL games.

Once appeared in 82 games while pitching for Chicago AL 1965. In 1971 had one stretch of nine games, 21 innings, without yielding run.

Fisher started at Corpus Christi, 1958; Phoenix, 1959, and to San

Francisco NL same season; with Tacoma and San Francisco, 1960 and 1961. Then four full seasons with White Sox. In his busy 1965 season was 15–7, had 2.40 ERA, meriting selection by *Sporting News* as Fireman of Year. Sox sent him to Baltimore during 1966. With Orioles 1967; Cleveland, 1968; California Angels after that until late 1972 season, then waived to Chicago White Sox.

Fisher finished 1972 season with ERA of 3.30, having pitched 1423 innings in 658 games. His strikeouts were well above his base-on-balls total—754 to 399.

Eddie received his B.S. degree in education from Oklahoma.

FISK, CARLTON ERNEST (Pudge) C-BR-TR. B. 12/26/47, Bellows Falls, Vt. 6'2", 205. Carlton Fisk needled couple of his teammates on Boston Red Sox during summer, 1972. Team responded by snapping out of doldrums and almost won Eastern Division title in AL. Fisk's barbs were misinterpreted, he said later, but did not deny making remarks about attitude of two players in particular, Carl Yastrzemski and Reggie Smith. Newsman quoted young catcher as saying pair were not lending inspiration to team; added that perhaps security of big salaries removed something from their desire on field. When Fisk spoke out, Red Sox were playing about .500 ball, headed nowhere in particular. After that, Sox perked up, helped make horse race in AL East, moved ahead of N. Y. Yankees and Baltimore Orioles, losing out to Detroit by half-game.

Fisk, rookie, proved himself take-charge guy. Handled pitchers well, called plays for infielders, hustled at all times, tried to keep Sox on their toes. Apart from his field generalship, youngster not only did fine backstop job but hit .293, with 22 homers, 61 RBI, to say nothing of 28 doubles, 9 triples. Pleasant surprise all around. Rated best catcher in International League, 1971, he hadn't done much hitting in minors. Manager Eddie Kasko, before 1972 season, frankly said Fisk would have to prove he could hit major league pitching if he were to be seriously considered for regular spot. In spring training, two more experienced catchers, Josephson and Montgomery, were his competition. Josephson seemingly won job because he looked like best hitter of trio. But he was hurt in second game of season. Montgomery got next call to duty. But when Cleveland Indians stole several bases on him, Pudge went into lineup.

Once he got chance, was No. 1 catcher for rest of year without question. Instead of being dubious hitter, proved himself best on Red Sox. Outhit all his teammates for average, and in homers, triples.

Earl Weaver of Orioles, who managed AL All-Star squad, 1972, recognized Fisk's abilities early. Named him for team. Carlton made hit and scored run. He was only rookie on AL team.

Fisk, 1972, was talk of New England. Vermont had claims on him because he was born there; New Hampshire claimed him because he grew up there. But whole area became proud of young man who, among other things, hit more home runs than any other catcher in history of Red Sox.

Pudge was chubby as child, but was fine athlete by high school days; standout in baseball, basketball, soccer. Fine arm, good speed, as well as hitting power. Jack Burns, former AL first baseman, was scout who signed Fisk. His older brother, Calvin, also catcher, played for while in Baltimore organization. Signed, 1967, Pudge spent that year in military service. Hit .338 at Waterloo, Midwest League, 1968; 1969 dropped off to .243 in 97 games at Pittsfield, Eastern League, and to .229 in 93 games at Pawtucket, Eastern League. His mark at Louisville, 1971, was .263 for 94 contests.

Had brief spells with Red Sox, 1969 and 1971, so his AL career totals, entering 1973, were 149 hits in 147 games; 81 runs scored, 30 doubles, 10 triples, 24 homers, with 67 RBI. Overall average .292.

Unanimous choice as AL Rookie of Year, 1972.

FITZSIMMONS, FREDERICK LANDIS   P-BR-TR. B. 7/28/01, Mishawaka, Ind. 5'11", 205.

Chunky pitcher with corkscrew windup. They called him "Fat Freddie," but he was brilliant pitcher for Giants of John McGraw and Bill Terry, later stalwart with Brooklyn Dodgers under Leo Durocher. Manager of Philadelphia NL, 1943–45.

Fitzsimmons toiled for 6-1/2 years before reaching majors—three seasons with Muskegon, Central League, 1920–22; and then with Indianapolis, American Association, 1922–25. Had 14–6 record his last season with Indianapolis; moved to Giants 8/8/25 and continued his winning ways with six victories, three defeats. During next nine seasons with N.Y. won at least 14 games every year but one. Had 20–9 mark, 1928, and his 19–7 record in 1930 led NL in winning percentage. Freddie's victory total dropped down to four in 1935 when he suffered arm injury. In 1937 Fitz had won two and lost two for Giants when he was traded to Brooklyn for Tom Baker, pitcher.

This had to be one of worst deals Giants ever made. Baker won exactly one game for Giants and dropped out of sight. Fitzsimmons, landing with Bill Terry's hated rivals, Dodgers, came back to win 47 games for Flatbush, losing 32. In 1940 Freddie 16–2, .889 winning percentage that stands next to Roy Face's record .947 in 1959 among NL pitching records.

Fitzsimmons' pitching style was unique. Complicated windup included instant when he turned his body to face second base before releasing ball to batsman. Undoubtedly contributed much to his pitches confusing hitter.

Fred didn't fare well in 1933 and 1936 WS with Giants, 0–3. Allowed

11 earned runs in 18-2/3 IP. In 1941 WS was on his way to shutout when disaster struck. Pitching against Yankees, Fitz blanked Bombers on four hits for seven innings. Last man up in seventh was his pitching opponent, Marius Russo. Russo hit savage drive that caromed off Freddie's left leg high into air. Pee Wee Reese caught ball before it hit ground, for putout, but Fitzsimmons went down and had to be helped from field. Yanks then won game by scoring twice in eighth off Hugh Casey, to win 2–1. Overall WS performance resulted in 3.86 ERA for four games and 25-2/3 innings.

As major league pitcher, Fitzsimmons compiled 217–146 record in 513 games with 3225 IP. Allowed 3335 hits, 1257 earned runs, walked 846, and fanned 870. His ERA was 3.51.

Freddie got chance to become manager of Phillies at end of July 1943, and gave up active pitching at that point. Inherited sixth-place club but would up seventh. His 1944 and 1945 teams landed in basement though he did not last through latter season, being replaced by Ben Chapman June 30.

Fitzsimmons was coach as well as part-time pitcher in his final year and half in Brooklyn. After his managerial experience at Philadelphia, returned to coaching with Boston Braves, 1948; coached N.Y. Giants 1949–55, with brief time out as interim manager of Minneapolis, American Association, during 1953; manager, Binghamton, Eastern League, 1956; coach, Chicago NL 1957–59; Kansas City Athletics, 1960; coach Salt Lake City, Pacific Coast League, 1961; coach, Chicago NL, 1966.

FLACK, MAX JOHN OF-BL-TL. B. 2/5/91, Belleville, Ill. 5'7", 148 Memorial Day 1922. Max Flack and his teammates, Chicago Cubs, played St. Louis Cardinals morning game at Wrigley Field. Max lived in house three blocks from ball park. After luncheon at home he walked back, entered Cubs' clubhouse, ready to suit up for afternoon game. Bill Killefer, then manager of Bruins, told him, "Maxie, boy, you're in the wrong clubhouse!" "And I was," said Flack later. "They had traded me to Cardinals for Cliff Heathcote. So he played for the Cubs that afternoon and I was in right field for Cardinals. There wasn't much to radio those days; and of course there hadn't been time to have it published in a newspaper. So fans were astonished when they saw us in different uniforms."

Max played briefly at Burlington, Iowa, 1911 and was with Peoria, III League, 1912–13. One of few players who, when lying about their age, made themselves one year older. Told Peoria management he was 23 when he signed, 1912. Actually he was 22. Anyway, hit .352 and was sold to Milwaukee, American Association late in 1913. But played 1914–15 with Chicago Whales of Federal League. When league folded, landed with Cubs.

While never power hitter, was good leadoff man; twice hit better than .300 for Cubs. Remained with Cardinals through 1925 season. With Syracuse, 1926; then quit. Spent 22 years with custodial services of East St. Louis, Ill., public school system before retiring.

Lifetime average .278 for 1411 major league games. Hit .263 in six games of 1918 WS with Cubs.

FLAGSTEAD, IRA JAMES (Pete) OF-BR-TR. B. 9/22/93, Montague, Mich. D. 3/13/40, Olympia, Wash. 5'9", 165. Detroit fans of an older generation remember Ira Flagstead trying to break into outfield that often included Ty Cobb, Bob Veach, Harry Heilmann, Heinie Manush, and others. Ira, however, only hit above .300 five times during career and had just 40 home runs in 1217 major league games. Tigers sent him to Boston Red Sox during 1923 season. Later played briefly with Washington Senators and Pittsburgh Pirates.

Flagstead played third base and outfield at Tacoma, Northwestern League, 1917; hit .381 in 70 games. Tigers invested $850 for him and he reported for four games that year. Spent most of 1918 in military service, but still played 49 games with Chattanooga, again hitting at .381 pace. In first full season at Detroit, 1919, Ira hit cool .331 in 97 games. Didn't ever get that high later in career. Best home run production was eight, in 1923. After five full seasons and parts of two others with Boston AL, divided 1929 season with Red Sox, Senators, and Pirates. Played 44 games with Pittsburgh, 1930, then left major leagues.

Flagstead retired with major league batting average of .290. His 1200 hits included 261 doubles, 49 triples, plus earlier-mentioned 40 homers. Stole 71 bases, scored 643 runs, drove in 450.

FLETCHER, ARTHUR SS-BR-TR. B. 1/5/85, Collinsville, Ill. D. 2/6/50, Los Angeles, Calif. 5'10½", 170. Art Fletcher, like Casey Stengel, Miller Huggins, Johnny Mize, and several others, spent their best days as players in NL, but still are remembered for their achievements with N. Y. Yankees. Fletcher's great days as shortstop were those with John McGraw's rugged old N. Y. Giants, but his last 19 years in baseball were with Yankees as coach. Could have been named manager of Yanks, but big league pilots rarely last in one job very many years. Fletcher preferred fewer headaches and more security acting as assistant to Miller Huggins, Joe McCarthy, and others at Yankee helm.

Charlie Barrett, old-time Cardinal scout, got Fletcher his first job in pro ball at Dallas, Texas League, 1907. After hitting .273 in 147 games there, 1908, he was ready for Giants, remaining with McGraw's team until 1920. In that time helped Giants to four pennants; became known as aggressive, even pugnacious, competitor. Best season at bat was 1911 when he hit .319. His overall major league average was .277 in 1529 games. Had 33 homers over 13-season career, with 238 doubles, 76 triples. Scored 684 times, drove in 675 runs, and stole 159 bases. Traded to Phillies during 1920 season. Sat out 1921, and came back to game, 1922, for final season as player, hitting .280 in 110 games. Managed Phils, 1923–26 but had two cellar teams and never got club higher than tie for sixth place. Front office simply did not give him material to work with. Headaches were such that he swore off managing when he joined Yankees as coach, 1927. In 1929, when Huggins died, Art did boss team for final weeks of season, but purely on interim basis. Reportedly was offered job for 1930 but firmly refused. Is said to have turned down several other offers to manage major league teams.

Remained Yankee coach through 1945. During this time Yankees won 10 pennants and nine WS. So though Fletcher did not draw manager's salary, was well rewarded with WS bonuses.

His four seasons as WS player came with Giants, 1911,12,13,17. Giants, however, lost all four WS. Fletcher had .191 average for 25 WS games, getting 18 hits in 94 trips, three of them doubles. Scored five runs, drove in eight, and stole twice.

FLETCHER, ELBURT PRESTON   1B-BL-TL. B. 3/18/16, Dorchester, Mass. 6', 180. Elbie Fletcher played 1415 NL games and had career average of .271, but never achieved status of superstar. From 1937 to 1946 played almost all his club's games, averaging better than 147 games per season. Then Hank Greenberg crossed his path. Though Elbie had been good enough to play 148 games with Pittsburgh, 1946, Hank came to club and, with his reputation and homers, Fletcher dropped back to second-string status. In 1947 Greenberg played 125 games, Fletcher 69. Greenberg hit .249—Fletcher .242. But Hank hit 25 homers, Fletcher, one. Though Elbie never played for Cleveland, his contract belonged to Indians in 1948. During that season Hank, having drawn his release from Pittsburgh, joined Bill Veeck in Cleveland as vice president and part owner. This prompted Fletcher to remark: "First he takes my job in Pittsburgh. And now he owns me!" Did not play in majors in 1948 but came back for one final season with Boston Braves, 1949, hitting .261 in 122 contests.

Elbie played with Harrisburg, Wilkes-Barre, and Buffalo, 1934–36, and had brief spells with Braves two of those seasons. In 1937 stuck with Boston as regular first baseman. Braves traded him to Pittsburgh in June 1939; remained with Pirates through 1947 except for service in navy, 1944–45. Best hitting average was .290 in 1939. Had 104 RBI in 1940.

Fletcher hit .305 for Minneapolis, 1948. Had 19 games at Jersey City, 1949, besides those 122 games with Braves. During his big league career Elbie had 1323 hits, 228 doubles, 58 triples, 79 homers, and stole 32 bases. After retiring from baseball became recreation director in Melrose, Mass.

FLICK, ELMER HARRISON OF-BL-TR. B. 1/11/76, Bedford, Ohio. D. 1/9/71, Bedford, Ohio. 5'8½", 160. AL batting champion, 1905, with .306 average. This was lowest average to lead either AL or NL until 1968, when Carl Yastrzemski led AL with .301. Flick was named to Hall of Fame, 1963. Had lifetime average of .315 in majors, playing 1480 games. His 1764 hits included 268 doubles, 170 triples, 46 homers. Scored 948 runs and stole 342 bases. In 1904 and 1906 was able to tie for AL leadership in stolen bases with 42 and 39 respectively. By leading AL in triples, 1905,06,07, earned mark that is shared with Sam Crawford and Zoilo Versalles. In one game hit three triples, 7/6/02, which was and remains something unusual.

Flick started out at Youngstown, Inter-State League, 1896, with .438 average in 31 games. Following year, playing for Dayton, same league, hit .386 in 126 contests. Then began big league career with Philadelphia NL with .318 average, 133 games. Boosted his mark to .344 his second year in majors. In third season reached his peak, statistically: hit .378 and banged 11 homers; stole 37 bases too. Sold to Cleveland 5/16/02 and remained with Indians through 1910 season. Wound up career with two seasons in Toledo, American Association.

Flick almost figured in trade that would have changed AL baseball history. In 1907 Hugh Jennings, manager of Detroit, got fed up with Ty Cobb, then 20. Reportedly offered Ty to Indians for Flick but deal did not materialize. Cobb went on to win batting championship that year and 11 more times, eventually taking Jennings' job as pilot. Flick was almost washed up, 1907 being his last good year in majors.

FLOOD, CURTIS CHARLES OF-BR-TR. B. 1/18/38, Houston, Tex. 5'9", 160. Curt Flood spent 12 highly successful years with St. Louis Cardinals, was recognized as outstanding center fielder, batted close to .300, and eventually was drawing $90,000 annual salary. After 1969 season Cardinals traded him to Philadelphia NL. "When Cardinals traded me . . . it violated logic and integrity of my existence," said Flood. "I was not a consignment of goods. I was a man, rightful proprietor of my own person and talents." Although Flood had voluntarily signed numerous contracts agreeing to club's right to assign him to another team, now decided he would not report to Phillies. Filed suit 1/16/70 in federal court charging baseball with violation of antitrust laws; asked court for injunction that would prevent baseball from invoking "reserve clause" binding him to report to Phils. If granted, Flood indicated he would seek $75,000 damages already suffered; if denied, indicated he planned to seek nearly $3 million in damages. Lost his bid for temporary injunction 3/4/70. In his legal efforts to become free agent and have courts throw out reserve clause, Flood had support of Major League Baseball Players Association. His attorney was Arthur Goldberg, former justice of U. S. Supreme Court.

Meanwhile, Phillies had offered Flood $100,000 contract for 1970, which Curt turned down, apparently in hopes of winning his legal maneuvers. Took off for Copenhagen, Denmark. Legal battle continued, and in Washington owner Bob Short of Senators decided he wanted Flood to play center field for that club in 1971.

Obtained permission from Phillies to contact Flood and reached him in Denmark; offered to pay round-trip expenses for trip to New York. When the two met, Short offered $110,000 contract for 1971 with stipulation Washington would not trade him to another team without his consent; would pay him full salary if Senators released him before season ended; and would release him unconditionally if no agrement could be reached on 1972 contract. Flood's legal advice was that he could play for Senators without prejudicing his court case against baseball. Curt reported to Senators for 1971 season but jumped club after 13 games in AL, during which batted .200 with just seven singles in 35 AB. Scored four runs, batted in two, and was thrown out in his only attempt to steal base. Not much of a record for man drawing $110,000 for year. Flood disappeared. Reportedly went to Europe, and eventually was doing sportscast in English in Madrid, Spain. Short was left holding bag because, in addition to substantial sum paid Flood, Washington also had paid Philadelphia club for assignment of Curt's contract.

Flood's legal case finally reached Supreme Court. Ruling handed down, mid-1972, upheld reserve clause and indicated that if anything was to be done about it legally, Congress, and not courts, should lay down conditions. Majority opinion delivered by Justice Harry A. Blackmun, however, referred to reserve clause as "aberration." But Curt was still "property" and not free agent, as far as baseball was concerned.

These aspects of Flood's career tended to obscure fact he had come far from humble surroundings in Oakland, Calif., where he grew up. As kid he helped Frank Robinson, Vada Pinson, and other teammates win American Legion Junior baseball championship. Played in winter league in California.

Frank Robinson had signed with Cincinnati organization and had progressed to parent club by 1956. Flood, two years younger, signed with Reds' organization for 1956 and was sent to High Point-Thomasville club in Carolina League, class B. Played 154 games, led league in hitting with .340, scored 133 runs, batted in 128, and slugged 29 homers. Took part in five games with Cincinnati that year, but had only one time at bat. Farmed out to Savannah, Sally League, Class A, for 1957. Hit .299 and led league in scoring runs with 98. Another brief spell with Reds that same season: three games, three times at bat. His first major league hit was home run off Moe Drabowsky of Chicago Cubs. That winter, Cincinnati traded Flood to Cardinals and for next dozen years he had center field job sewed up. Redbirds sent him to their Omaha, American Association, farm briefly in 1958. Flood hit .340 there in 15 games and then it was back to St. Louis and regular job. Played 121 games for Cards 1958 and 121 in 1959, but thereafter never took part in less than 130 games a year.

Flood's major league totals came to 1759 games over 15 seasons: 6357 AB, 851 runs, 1861 hits for 2475 TB, with 271 doubles, 44 triples, 85 homers, and 636 RBI. Stole 88 bases and had lifetime average of .293.

In WS play with Cardinals Flood took part in 1964, 67, 68 classics, each of which ran seven games. In 86 AB had 19 hits and scored 11 runs. Made two doubles and one triple and drove in eight runs for .221 average. Cards won two of these three WS with Flood's help.

While with St. Louis Flood had developed skill as portrait painter and had art studio in suburban Clayton. When he began suit against baseball's reserve clause, also published book entitled *The Way It Is*, story of mixed-up young man through years in and out of baseball, with sour, negative viewpoint about most people mentioned in it.

FOLI, TIMOTHY JOHN (Crazy Horse)   SS-BR-TR. B. 12/8/50, Culver City, Calif. 6', 179. Intense, explosive, high-strung infielder. Gene Mauch, manager of Montreal Expos, says he wouldn't trade combination of Tim's glove, arm, and instinct for playing shortstop for anyone else in baseball. Mauch says that Foli's temper reflects "constant search for perfection." Sometimes his words and actions have been directed at umpires; fined three times for this during 1972. Other occasions he has exchanged punches with teammates. One such occasion came during spring training, 1972, while still member of N.Y. Mets. Opponent was Joe Pignatano, coach. Dispute arose over free tickets left at gate for exhibition game. No real damage to either participant. During 1971 season, small battle between Tim and Ed Kranepool of Mets. Foli was playing third base. During infield warmups Tim made some bad throws to first base. Kranepool refused to throw any more practice grounders to third base. Later, in dugout, Foli demanded explanation why he wasn't getting his grounders. Two-punch shoving match ensued.

Foli got bonus estimated at $75,000 to sign with Mets, 1968. Had been captain of his high school baseball, basketball, football teams. Planned on entering Southern Cal, but in end took Mets' offer. Farmed to Marion, Appalachian League; Memphis, Texas League; Visalia, California League; and Tidewater, International League. Five games with Mets, 1970. Played 97 games for them, 1971, at second, short, and third base. Hit .231. Traded to Montreal in spring of 1972, Mauch had Foli concentrate on shortstop. Into 1973 Tim carried .237 career average in NL for 251 games. Had 199 hits, 24 doubles, 4 triples, 2 homers, 60 RBI, 77 runs scored. Stole 16 bases. Wears spectacles. Claims he is becoming more tactful with umpires. Wants to become nightclub singer.

FONSECA, LEWIS ALBERT 2B-1B-BR-TR. B. 1/29/1900, Oakland, Calif. 5'10½", 175. Like Casey Stengel, Lew Fonseca was educated for profession of dentistry but got sidetracked by baseball. Seriously considered singing for living, but that too fell by wayside. Led AL in hitting with .369 average, 1929, while with Cleveland. Managed Chicago White Sox, 1932 until 5/8/34.

Lew went to spring training camp with San Francisco, Pacific Coast League, 1920, but jumped into independent ball when Seals wanted to farm him out. However, Cincinnati so impressed by his play with semipros that it bought his contract. So Fonseca joined Reds, 1921, without ever having played minor league ball. Reds used him at first, second, and in outfield. Hit .276 in 82 games, then in 1922 boosted his mark to .361 in 81 contests, concentrating on second base. Batting sagged next couple of years and 1925 found him with Philadelphia NL. Hit .319 in 126 games. Phillies wanted to cut his salary for 1926 and Fonseca balked, so they sold him to Newark, International League. Fonseca slammed ball at .381 pace in 148 games, had 126 RBI and 21 homers, and was sold to Cleveland 9/4/26 for reported $50,000. Back in majors, Lew continued as dangerous batsman with .311, then .327, warming up for hefty .369 for AL title in 1929. Dropped to .279 following year, then Indians traded him to White Sox for Willie Kamm 5/17/31. Hit .312 that year in 147 games. Lew played little in 1932 and 1933 while bossing White Sox, after being injured. For record, Lew pitched one inning for Sox, 1932. Allowed no hits, walks, or runs.

Fonseca pioneered use of motion pictures in baseball. In 1939 became director of AL motion picture promotion, and later took over job for both majors. Currently hitting consultant for Reds and Cubs. Lew's lifetime major league record was .316 in 937 games; 1075 hits, 203 doubles, 50 triples, 31 homers, 518 runs scored, 485 RBI, and 64 stolen bases.

FORD, EDWARD CHARLES (Whitey) P-BL-TL. B. 10/21/28, New York, N.Y. 5'10", 181. Whitey Ford was always regarded by his fellow players as just about finest model of pro pitcher. Name of game was always "win ball game." When Whitey, after suffering circulatory blockage in left shoulder, found he couldn't win oftener than he lost, he retired from game, became customer's man in brokerage house. Until almost end of career Ford never had losing season, regardless of league, regardless of where club finished in standings. Few, if any, pitchers could

314

equal this record over period of two decades.

Whitey grew up in tenement district of midtown Manhattan. Played first base and pitched on high school team. Two months after graduation appeared in tryout for Yankee organization, with 40 others. Nobody paid much attention to him. Later, in well-pitched game, began to arouse interest of Yanks, Red Sox, and Dodgers. Bidding for his services didn't get very far before Dodgers and Red Sox bowed out of picture. Yanks signed him for $7000 bonus. That was 1946. Fresco Thompson, then top man for Brooklyn, soon saw his mistake in not offering more to get Ford. "By midseason 1947 I knew Whitey would have been bargain at $50,000," said Fresco.

Yanks sent Whitey to Butler, Mid-Atlantic League; won 13, lost four. In 1948 it was 16–8 for Norfolk, Piedmont League; then 16–5, 1949, at Binghamton, Eastern League. Next stop, Kansas City, American Association. After twelve games there, 1950, Whitey had won nine, lost three. Yanks realized young left-hander was ready for majors. Called up during season, Whitey took nine victories with just one defeat. Pummeled in first major league appearance. Relieved in game against Red Sox. Gave up seven hits, walked six, and had five runs scored against him in five innings. After that inauspicious beginning Whitey said, "I'm not worried"; won his next six straight. During final weeks of season Mgr. Casey Stengel sent Ford in to pitch crucial game against Detroit. Tigers had half-game lead over Yanks when game started. At game's end young rookie had 8–1 victory, Yankees were in first place. Captured pennant.

In WS that year southpaw pitched fourth game against Philadelphia NL. Had shutout within grasp until Woodling's error with two outs in ninth enabled Phils to score two runs. But victory was his by 5–2 score, allowing no earned runs. Ford was not yet 22 at time.

Whitey entered army 1951 and spent two years at Fort Monmouth, N.J., with Signal Corps. At one point had brush with death; fell 15 feet from telephone pole. Then was transferred to desk job as radar operator. Back with Yanks, 1953, and resumed winning ways with 18–6 season. Whitey's two outstanding seasons were 1961 and 1963. Cy Young Award 1961.

Had record of 25–4, with ERA of 3.21, in 1961. Won "only" 17 games, 1962, with eight losses. Came back following year with 24–7 record and 2.74 ERA. During this period Ford's "poorer" seasons were the kind any pitcher would be proud of: 18 victories in 1955; 19 in 1956; 16–10 in 1959; 17–6 in 1964. In 1961 Ford had 18–2 record into July, with 14 consecutive wins.

In WS play, Whitey took part in 11 classics, 22 games, 146 IP, 10 wins, 8 losses with 2.71 ERA. In three different Series, 1955,60,61, won two games each time, losing none. Holds various WS records: most series played by pitcher, 11; most games pitched, total Series, 22; most games started, 22; most opening games started, 8; most games lost, total Series, 8; most innings pitched, total Series, 146; most walks, total Series, 34; most strikeouts, total Series, 94.

In WS of 1960 Ford pitched two shutouts against Pittsburgh Pirates. Following year, against Cincinnati, Whitey hurled another shutout in opening game, allowing Reds just two singles. Returned to mound in fourth game and was on way to another shutout when swollen foot forced him to leave game after five innings. Had been hit by batted ball. This record broke long-standing record set by pitcher Babe Ruth in days before he became home run slugger. Ruth had gone 29-2/3 innings in WS without allowing run. Ford's new mark was 32 scoreless innings. In 1962 WS Ford ran record up to 33-2/3 innings before Willie Mays scored for San Francisco Giants.

Ford pitched in six All-Star games for AL. In 12 innings, 13 runs, 0–2.

In 1966 Whitey's left shoulder began troubling him and it showed in his record. For first time in his life did not win as many games as he lost. Had two wins, five losses for year. Underwent operation. Following year, 1967, Whitey tested arm until Memorial Day. Hurled in seven games, won two, lost four. Rather than struggle along with mediocrity, walked off mound one night in Detroit. When teammates got to clubhouse he was gone, as were his clothes. Packed and went home, retired at age 38. Scout and minor league coach rest of 1967; pitching, coach with Yanks, 1968.

Lifetime major league record 498 games, 3171 IP, won 236, lost 106, for .690 percentage. Allowed 2766 hits, 1107 runs, 967 earned runs. Struck out 1956 men, allowed 1086 walks. ERA overall was 2.74.

Whitey was involved in famous Copacabana incident 5/16/57. He and five other Yankees, Mantle, Berra, Bauer, Kucks, and Billy Martin were celebrating Billy's birthday at nightclub. Patron of club claimed Bauer beat him. Each Yank was fined $1000 by Yankees.

On mound Ford was rugged competitor, cocksure, intense, arrogant, challenging opposition every moment. Off field was smooth, self-confident, polished gentleman. Summing up pitching philosophy, Ford said a man needed "arm, heart, head." He had them all in generous portions.

FORD, RUSSELL WILLIAM P-BR-TR. B. 4/25/83, Brandon, Manitoba. D. 1/24/60, Rockingham, N.C. 5'11", 175. Russ Ford won 26 games, lost six for New York Highlanders, as they were known in 1910. But his principal claim to fame is fact he is credited with perfecting emery ball, which later was outlawed. In any case he could and did make ball do strange tricks after really roughing up surface. Ford, however, did not last long as successful pitcher. Had 21–11 record for New Yorkers, 1911, then lost more than he won following two years. Jumped to Federal League for 1914, 20–6 for Buffalo club. Then after 5–9 for same team, 1915, dropped out of major league scene.

During his banner season, 1910, Ford got into amusing situation while pitching against Philadelphia Athletics in N.Y. Sizzling hot afternoon. It was pitching duel against Jack Coombs. Both hurlers, between innings, sat on bench and were fanned by teammates. In fifth inning it was Coombs' turn to bat, two men on base, one out.

Connie Mack, manager of Athletics, decided Coombs should do pitching, let others in lineup do hitting. So he ordered Jack to go to plate and strike out, to conserve his energies for mound. Ford, however, had orders to walk Coombs purposely, hoping such strategy would help to wear him down. Coombs won battle; struck at three balls several feet wide of plate. But returned to bench, protesting to Connie Mack, "That second one was near enough for me to have stepped in and killed it." Mack's scheme won, as Ford lost decision, with heat helping exhaust him.

Ford played in III League and Southern Association before joining Highlanders. Won his first seven AL starts before suffering defeat. His major league totals, including two seasons in Federal League, showed 98 wins, 71 losses, with 2.59 ERA. In 1487-1/3 innings walked 376, struck out 710, 14 shutouts.

FORSTER, TERRY JAY   P-BL-TL. B. 1/14/52, Sioux Falls, S. Dak. 6'3", 200. Brilliant young southpaw with Chicago White Sox who won six and saved 29 other games for his team, 1972—at ripe old age of 20. Besides this and 2.25 ERA for 100 innings, Terry exhibited great control for pitcher was as much stuff. Walked 44 men, compared to his 104 strikeouts. And nobody tagged him for home run during his 62 trips to mound.

Forster did pretty well in first season with White Sox, 1971. Won two, lost three, saved one game, and had 3.96 ERA. In first appearance at Yankee Stadium he was sent to mound with bases loaded, none out. Terry retired next three batters on four pitches.

Young man attended Grossmont College, El Cajon, Calif. His pitching in high school so sensational that all major league clubs after him. White Sox, however, got him as their No. 2 draft pick, 1970, and sent him to Appleton, Wis., in Midwest League—6–1, 1.33 ERA. Ten games, 54 innings, constituted entire minor league experience before joining Sox.

So Forster went into 1973 with eight victories, eight defeats, and 30 saves in 150 innings over 107 games in majors. Walked 67, struck out 152, with an ERA of 2.82. Started three games, 1971, none in 1972, but had no complete games to credit.

FOSSE, RAYMOND EARL (Mule) C-BR-TR. B. 4/4/47, Marion, Ill. 6'2", 210. Ray Fosse has been mentioned as one of best young catchers in major leagues, with Johnny Bench of Cincinnati Reds. Fosse hasn't hit as often or as hard as Bench, nor has he made money Bench has been able to rake in. But he's working hard and seems to be improving with experience. After four full seasons with Cleveland, was traded to Oakland, 3/24/73.

During early stages of 1972 season Fosse, for first time since All-Star game of 7/14/70, was again completely sound. On that occasion there was jolting collision at home plate. With score tied 4–4 in 12th inning, two out, Pete Rose, Grabarkewitz, and Hickman singled. Rose approached plate; Fosse tried to block plate. Pete came in like tank—and scored. Left shoulder muscle-and-ligament damage kept Fosse shelved for more than month. Other wounds, on left wrist and right hand, came 6/20/71 when he challenged Bill Deheny, pitching for Detroit. Deheny's pitch hit Fosse. Ray scurried to mound. Deheny defended himself with kick in general direction of Indians' catcher. Fosse was cut on right hand, requiring five stitches; strained tendon in left wrist. Only after 1972 season started was Fosse able to swing bat and use both hands completely naturally.

Ray attended Southern Illinois U. Played baseball, football, basketball, and was Cleveland's first selection in June 1965 free-agent draft. Farmed to Reading, Pa.; Reno, and Portland, 1965–68, with couple of brief stints with parent club. In 1969 stayed with Indians but got into just 37 games. Hit .172. Then came on strong, 1970, with 120 games and .307 average. This performance got him AL All-Star selection and "Indians' Man of Year" award from Cleveland sports writers. Also had 23-game batting streak, 1970, best in AL that year. Hit 18 homers, 1970, but in 1971 his average dropped to .274 and home run production fell to 12. Selected for 1971 All-Star squad but did not play.

Fosse, at start of 1973, had appeared in 432 major league games and had overall .264 average. One of his distinctions, which he would rather forget, is that in 1970 was tied for AL high total of passed balls for year with 17. Is real estate agent in off-season.

FOTHERGILL, ROBERT ROY (Fats) OF-BR-TR. B. 8/16/97, Massillon, Ohio. D. 3/20/38, Detroit, Mich. 5'10½", 230. Bob Fothergill looked like professional football player and was one for several off-seasons until he decided game might endanger his baseball activities. Especially active with bat, and throughout his 14 years in baseball missed .300 mark only three times—then not by much.

Powerful fellow played semipro ball before joining Bloomington, III League, 1920. Slugged .332 that first year, in 136 games. Then hit .338 with Rochester, International League, 143 games, 1921. In 1922 had .322

mark with Detroit Tigers for 42 games and .383 with Rochester in 101 contests. Continued his consistent hitting for Detroit until traded to Chicago AL during 1930 season. Meanwhile, three great years with .353, .367, and .359 in 1925,26,27.

Dropped down to .317 following year but came back with .350 in 1929. Below .300 mark 1930,31,32 with White Sox, then had .344 mark in 28 games with Boston AL, 1933. Wound up with lifetime average of .326 in 1072 games. His 1064 major league hits included 225 doubles, 52 triples, 36 homers. Scored 453 times and had 582 RBI.

FOURNIER, JACQUES FRANK (Jack) 1B-BL-TR. B. 9/28/92, Au Sable, Mich. 6', 195. Jack Fournier led NL in home runs, 1924, with 27, while with Brooklyn Dodgers. Hit three homers in successive times at bat 7/3/26. Also slugged for Chicago White Sox, St. Louis Cardinals, and Boston Braves.

Fournier started as catcher in 1908 at Aberdeen, Idaho; later played at Seattle, Portland, Sacramento, Moose Jaw, and Montreal en route to majors. Thirty-five games with Chicago AL, 1912, hitting just .192, but stayed with White Sox, 1913–17. Hit .311 in 1914 and .322 following year. Two seasons with Los Angeles, Pacific Coast League, 1917–18. Briefly with N.Y. Yankees, 1918; hit .350 in 27 games but went back to Los Angeles for 1919. St. Louis Cardinals had him 1920–22, then Brooklyn Dodgers, 1923–26; Boston NL, 1927, and Newark, International League, 1928.

Fournier was .343 hitter with Cardinals, 1921, and .350 batsman with Dodgers in 1925. His major league totals came to 1530 games with .313 average, including 1631 hits, 252 doubles, 113 triples, 136 homers. Scored 821 runs and drove in 859.

After his active days were over Fournier managed Johnstown, Middle Atlantic League, 1937; Toledo, American Association, 1943; coach for UCLA, 1934–35; scout, St. Louis AL, 1938–42, 1944–47; scout, Chicago NL, 1950–57; scout, Detroit, 1960; scout, Cincinnati, 1961–62.

FOWLER, JOHN ARTHUR (Art) P-BR-TR. B. 7/3/22, Converse, S.C. 5'11", 180. Pitching coach for Detroit Tigers whose pro career goes back to 1944. While not outstanding pitcher himself, Fowler absorbed much knowledge on art of trying to fool opposing batsmen, and uses it, along with human understanding, in efforts to coax wins from Tiger staff. Though Art doesn't claim credit, it is possible his presence on Detroit coaching staff may have had something to do with Mickey Lolich winning 25 games in 1971.

Fowler signed up for pro ball with Bristol in Appalachian League as youngster—and has seen most of U.S. since then. In minors pitched for Danville, Va.; Jersey City, Minneapolis, Jacksonville, Atlanta, Milwaukee, Spokane, St. Paul, Seattle, Omaha, and Denver. Major league experience started at Cincinnati, 1954–57. Part of 1959 with Los Angeles Dodgers. Los Angeles AL 1961–64. In majors won 54 games, lost 51; highest victory count in 1954 while with Reds. Had 12–10 mark that year. Overall effectiveness in big leagues showed 4.02 ERA.

Art's last pitching at Denver, 1970. Had coached Minnesota Twins, 1969, then became pitching coach for Detroit, 1971.

FOX, CHARLES FRANCIS (Irish)   Manager. B. 10/7/21, New York, N.Y. Charlie Fox began dreaming about day he would be with New York Giants while still small kid in Bronx. Dream was realized briefly— long enough for Charlie to compile .429 average in 1942 in three games. As tyro catcher, came to bat seven times, got three hits, scored one run, drove in another.

Fox couldn't make grade as player, but finally reached Giants to stay almost three decades later, as manager. By this time they had been transplanted to San Francisco. Faithfully, Fox has never been employed by any other ball club but Giants. His elevation to job once held by John McGraw came in this manner: Charlie was managing Phoenix, Pacific Coast League, in Giants' organization, 5/23/70. Sitting in hotel room, Portland, Oreg., listening to Giants playing wild game against San Diego Padres on radio. Rosy Ryan, trouble shooter for Horace Stoneham, president of Giants, walked into room. Fox suspected trouble, thought Ryan was going to ask him to send couple of pitchers to parent club since Giants' staff was in real difficulty. Ryan didn't say why he was there until game was over. San Diego finally captured contest, 17–16. Fox turned radio off. Then Ryan spoke, told Fox: "When that game ended, you became manager of Giants. Horace sent me to tell you personally."

After 1971 season, first full season at helm, poll of 24 major league skippers by *Sporting News* resulted in his selection as outstanding pilot in big leagues for 1971. After leading club to third-place finish, 1970, Giants won Western Division, 1971. Lost to Pittsburgh in playoffs. Won admiration of fellow managers for bringing team home at top of division, despite fact club frittered away 10-1/2-game lead due to injuries, batting slumps. Pilots recognized that slumping, skidding team is awfully hard to stop on its downward path.

Charlie needed persistence and courage to reach majors. When he began to show promise as American Legion player in New York, Yankee scout Paul Krichell tried to sign him. Fox's father, dyed-in-wool Giant fan, frankly told Krichell Yankees didn't have chance. If son was to play ball professionally, it would be with Giants. Bill Terry got his signature on dotted line. Youngster was farmed to Bristol, Appalachian League; did well enough to get brief tryout in September of that year. With

World War II on, Fox entered navy; spent about three years in service, some of it on ships making dangerous run to Murmansk in frigid northernmost Russia. Returned to Giants' organization, 1946, at Manchester, New England League. "We had lot of wild guys on club, just out of service," says Fox. "There were so many problems that manager got nervous breakdown. So they put me in charge late that year." Fox led team to third-place finish. Guess who beat him out in race for second? None other than Walter Alston, piloting Nashua for Dodgers. One wonders if they ever dreamed they'd be bitter rivals bossing major league teams in California many years later?

Fox managed Bristol, St. Cloud, Sunbury, Tacoma, and Phoenix for Giants through years that followed, along with seven years of scouting. Coached Giants 1965–68. Calm, patient fellow, gets along well with players. Good Irish tenor.

FOX, JACOB NELSON (Nellie) 2B-BL-TR. B. 12/25/27, St. Thomas, Pa. 5'9", 160.

Nellie Fox likes Christmas. Born on Christmas. Had first date with girl he later married, on Christmas. Married her on Christmas two years later. Daughter, Bonnie, born on Christmas.

According to his father, Nellie played first game of baseball at age nine. Used as pinch hitter, promptly lashed single over second base. After father encouraged Fox to play baseball, parents tried to keep him in high school when pro baseball beckoned. That was 1944. Philadelphia Athletics had their wartime spring training camp at Frederick, Md., about 50 miles from Fox residence. Nellie, 16, pleaded with parents to let him go for tryout.

Elder Fox finally consented, thinking son would be willing to come back to high school after he saw how big leaguers played. Then Nellie might be so impressed that he'd see difference between high school players and those in AL. But it didn't work that way. Connie Mack, manager of A's, was impressed with kid, told father that Nellie deserved chance in minors. So Nellie stayed in Athletics' camp most of spring. A's sent him to Lancaster, Interstate League. Hit .325, 24 games, playing first base and outfield. After hurting ankle, was transferred to Jamestown, N.Y., Pony League. Sixteen-year-old kid hit .304 there as outfielder in 56 games. Back at Lancaster, 1945, led league in times at bat, runs, hits, triples, and took honors as second baseman. Led circuit in fielding, putouts, assists. Drafted, spent 1946 in Korea. Lancaster again, 1947, in time for 55 games, with brief spell with Athletics. Most of 1948 at Lincoln Nebr., Western League, hit .311, led circuit in hits, 179, also in putouts, assists. Back to Philadelphia at end of season, and in 1949 stuck with A's all year. Hit .255, 88 games.

Traded to White Sox, 10/19/49. With Sox through 1963. During Chicago years became fine second baseman, pesky, dangerous batsman.

Al Lopez, his manager with Sox much of time, declared, "Fox hustled his way to stardom."

Nellie didn't have power, but hit .300 or better six times, close to mark four other seasons. Led AL in total hits three times, tied for first another. Repeatedly chalked up best fielding average among keystoners, most putouts and most assists. Led major league in singles seven consecutive years, 1954–60: Went 98 games in 1958 without striking out—setting major league record. Went twelve years with fewest strikeouts, another big league mark. Created major league record for consecutive games at second base, 798, from 8/7/55 through 9/3/60. Topped AL in being hit by pitcher, 17 times in 1955. Led AL keystoners in DPs five times, tying record held by Bobby Doerr, formerly of Red Sox. MVP 1959. Many lesser awards.

Fox left White Sox after 1963 season. Traded to Houston Astros for 1964, hit .265, 133 games. Player-coach, Astros, 1965, appearing in 21 games. Coach, Astros, 1967. When Ted Williams became manager, Washington Senators, 1969, Fox became one of coaches. Team transferred to Dallas–Fort Worth after 1971 season. Fox coached Rangers through 1972 season.

In 1959, White Sox won AL pennant. Lost Series to Los Angeles NL. Fox turned in .375 average, 9 for 24, six games. Fielded flawlessly.

Major league totals: 2367 games, 9232 AB, 1279 R, 2663 H, 355 doubles, 112 triples, 35 homers, 790 RBI, 76 stolen bases. Lifetime fielding mark in majors, .984.

FOXX, JAMES EMORY (Beast) Inf.-BR-TR. B. 10/22/07, Sudlersville, Md. D. 7/21/67, Miami, Fla. 5'11", 185. Frank "Home Run" Baker got his nickname a half century ago when he led AL in home runs four consecutive times, 1911–14, with high mark of 12 HR in 1913. Many years later his influence was felt when his protege Jimmie Foxx slugged scores of homers, including 58 one season (1932), just two short of fabled Babe Ruth record.

Foxx led AL in HR 1932,33,39 and tied Hank Greenberg for lead, 1935. His major league totals showed 534 home runs in 2317 games and a batting average of .325. Soon became feared batsman after entering AL. During 1929–40 never hit fewer than 33 homers a season and five times surpassed 40 HR mark. Repeatedly slugged well over 100 runs across plate, and in 1938 led AL with 175 RBI.

Baker managed Easton, Md., club, Eastern Shore League, 1924 and his 16-year-old protege batted .296, including 11 homers in 76 games. Caught, played third and outfield. Baker then sent Foxx to his old friend and mentor, Connie Mack, manager of Philadelphia Athletics. Mack remarked, "Now I'll be charged with robbing the cradle."

Foxx farmed out to Providence, International League, 1925. Youngster hit .327 in 41 games; bounced back to A's same season. Batted .667—6 for 9—appearing as pinch hitter and catcher. Was 17 years old. Shifted to first base early in career but played considerable third base and some outfield, as well as catching. In final major league season, 1945, pitched some for Philadelphia NL, winning one game, losing none. Athletics 1925–35. Traded to Boston AL 12/10/35 with John A. Marcum for Rhodes, Savino and reported $150,000 cash. Boston AL 1936–42. Chicago NL 1942,44. Phila. NL 1945. MVP 1932,33,38. Hall of Fame 1951.

His 30 or more home runs 1929–40 is major league record. Tied major league record with most home runs, consecutive times at bat, four, 1933. Hit three home runs in game twice, 1932, 1933. Hit four home runs in doubleheader, 1933. Hit 500th homer of career 9/24/40. World Series record, 1929,30,31: .344 average in 18 games, four home runs.

Foxx, farm boy, won many honors as schoolboy sprinter and high jumper. Original box scores carried his name simply as Fox. One day sports writer glimpsed "Foxx" on Jimmie's suitcase. Queried about additional "x" he explained, "Search me. But that's how my grandpappy spelled it, so I reckon it belongs there."

Nickname "Beast" originated because of his powerful physique and prodigious home runs he pummeled. Also nicknamed "Double-X."

FRANKS, HERMAN LOUIS C-BL-TR. B. 1/4/15, Price, Utah. 5'11", 200. Herman Franks, as manager of San Francisco Giants, won 367 games, lost 280; but, like almost all managers, time came when his contract was not renewed—or, in blunter terms, he was fired. All those victories got Giants nothing but second-place finishes. So Clyde King succeeded Herman after 1968 season. Franks' first season at helm, 1965, was most productive of victories—95. Each year Giants sagged a trifle—93 in 1966; then 91 wins, and finally 88.

Herman was good minor league catcher but never quite made it as big league regular. Maximum catching in majors was in 1941 when he was backstop in 54 games. His lifetime batting average in big leagues was .199 in 188 games; his 80 hits included 18 doubles, 2 triples, 3 homers. One WS game, 1941, with Dodgers: 0–1.

Franks attended U. of Utah. Played at Hollywood, Pacific Coast League, 1932, then started travels to Omaha, Jacksonville, Houston, Sacramento; Columbus (Ohio), Montreal, St. Paul in minors, with brief spell in St. Louis NL, 1939. Between 1940 and 1946 had tours with Brooklyn Dodgers, mixed with three years in service and some shuttling to Montreal, then Dodgers' top farm club. Spent part of 1947 and 1948 with Philadelphia AL, and was with N. Y. Giants for one game, 1949. Then coached Giants 1949–55; scout for same club, 1957; coach, S. F. Giants, 1958; scout, Giants, 1959–60; coach, Giants, 1964, then manager for four seasons.

During various gaps in baseball career, Franks was making hatful of money investing in supermarkets and other successful ventures. After leaving Giants as manager, Herman joined Chicago Cubs briefly as coach for part of one season.

FRAZEE, HARRY H. Executive. B. 6/29/80, Peoria, Ill. D. 6/3/29, New York, N.Y. Red Sox president 1917–23, remembered particularly because of dealings with N. Y. Yankees. Boston AL club won 1918 AL pennant with Ed Barrow as manager; followed up with WS victory over Chicago Cubs. Carl Mays, Babe Ruth, Sam Jones, and Joe Bush were pitchers for this world-championship club. Wally Schang was catcher and Everett Scott was shortstop. Within few years all of these players—and others—had been sent to N. Y. Yankees, enabling Yanks to start long succession of pennant winners and contending clubs. Behind it was Frazee's penchant for backing Broadway shows. Constantly short of money because most of them didn't pan out, Frazee turned to Yankees for financial help. Yankees loaned him $300,000 and took mortgage on Fenway Park.

Frazee liquidated loan by sending stellar players to Gotham. Ruth represented $125,000 investment; Mays $40,000. Besides those already mentioned, Red Sox sent Waite Hoyt, Elmer J. Smith, Jumping Joe Dugan, Herb Pennock, and George Pipgras to Yankees. How important these players were to Yankees may be seen by looking at WS rosters for 1920s and 1930s. No wonder they said Frazee converted Red Sox into "Dead Sox." Yankees even took Sox manager—Ed Barrow—and made him their highly successful business manager. No indication how Boston team was recompensed for this maneuver. Sox, however, after winning flag in 1918, were sixth in 1919 and remained either in second division or in AL basement for years to come.

Frazee played important role in dethronement of Ban Johnson as powerful president of AL. Friction started when Carl Mays, with Sox, walked off field in game in Chicago, 1919, saying he'd never pitch another game for Boston club. Johnson suspended Mays, but Frazee sold pitcher to Yanks. Court battle ensued, Johnson losing case. Deal stood, and Johnson began to lose control. Ultimately was out completely.

Frazee died in Park Avenue apartment in New York with Mayor Jimmy Walker at bedside.

FREDERICK, JOHN HENRY OF-BL-TL. B. 1/26/01, Denver, Colo. 5'11", 165. Johnny Frederick dates back to days of Uncle Wilbert Robinson, colorful manager of old Brooklyn Dodgers. No great outfielder, but better than Babe Herman. Averaged .308 for his 805 major league games; but inscribed his name in record books because of pinch hitting in 1932. Slapped six homers as emergency batsman, mark that still stands after four decades. Joe Cronin was AL player coming closest, with five pinch homers in 1943, playing and managing at Boston.

Frederick played with Regina in Western Canada League, 1921. Semipro ball, 1922. Salt Lake, Pacific Coast League, 1923,24,25. A teammate in Utah metropolis was Lefty O'Doul, and later both were members of Dodgers at same time. Frederick spent 1926–27 at Hollywood, PCL; then moved to Memphis in Southern Association where he hit .359 and won promotion to Brooklyn. Hit .328 his first year in NL, 1929, in 148 games; followed with .334. Played with Dodgers through 1934. His 954 major league hits included 200 doubles, 35 triples, 85 homers. Scored 498 times and drove in 377. During his time with Dodgers, besides making that record of six pinch homers in one season, had an overall pinch-hitting average of .307 with 19 hits in 62 times at bat. Eight hits were home runs.

FREEHAN, WILLIAM ASHLEY C-BR-TR. B. 11/29/41, Detroit, Mich. 6'3", 208. Slugging catcher—and author whose book *Behind the Mask* recorded some of events of 1969 season when Detroit Tigers finished in second place in AL. Club had been world champions in 1968. Freehan's opus may have contributed to firing of Mgr. Mayo Smith and trading of Denny McLain. Book, in diary form, told how McLain flouted rules rest of players had to observe. McLain had won 31 and lost six in 1968; in 1969, according to Freehan, Denny repeatedly failed to show up for pregame workouts, clubhouse meetings.

Freehan reportedly received $100,000 bonus for signing with Detroit, 1961. Had attended Michigan, graduating with B.S. in history. Farmed out to Duluth-Superior, Northern League, for 30 games, where he hit .343. Shifted to Knoxville, Sally League, same season, batting .289 in 47 games. Also had four games with parent team, going 4 for 10, for .400 average.

In 1962 Freehan spent summer at Denver, American Association. Took part in 113 games and batted .283. Joined Tigers in 1963 and has remained with Detroit since then. Took part in 100 games, 1963, hit .243. following season raised his average to .300 in 144 games; had 18 homers and 80 RBI. Dropped to .234 in 1965, with 10 homers, 43 RBI. That year he won recognition as best-fielding catcher in AL, getting Gold Glove Award. Also tied major league record for most putouts in game for catcher, 19, 6/15/65. Led AL catchers in total putouts for season, 865.

Bill hit .234 again in 1966 in 136 contests; .282 in 1967 in 155 games, with homer output of 20. In 1968 his record showed .263 average with 25 homers, 84 RBI, helping Detroit to pennant. Didn't hit so well in WS, 2 for 24 trips, .083 average. But played all seven games and drove in two runs as Tigers defeated Cardinals.

In 1969 Freehan had .262 mark in 143 games; in 1970 it was .241 in 117 games; and .277 in 148 contests in 1971. Had 21 homers in 1971, with 71 RBI. In 1972, 10 homers with .262 average, 111 games. AL All-Star teams 1965–73.

Freehan has been bothered by injuries from time to time. Once it was broken nose; another time a pinched nerve that deprived him of all feeling in his left leg for two months during 1969 season. Also is subject to back trouble because of malformation of vertebra. Freehan often played in spite of these ailments. Lives in Birmingham, Mich.

FREEMAN, JOHN F. (Buck) OF-1B-BL-TL. B. 10/30/71, Catasauqua, Pa. D. 6/25/49, Wilkes-Barre, Pa. 5'9", 150. Home run king of NL, 1899, with 25, playing with Washington. This came within two of mark set by Ned Williamson in 1884 with Chicago NL club. But Freeman's 25 round-trippers was best any major leaguer could come up with until Babe Ruth hit 29 with 1919 Red Sox. Gavvy Cravath came close to Freeman's mark in 1915, hitting 24 for Phillies. Freeman led AL in homers in 1903 with 13, becoming first man to lead both NL and AL in circuit smashes. Freeman was member of Red Sox.

Buck played with Washington, American Association, 1891; Washington NL, 1898–99; Boston NL, 1900; then Boston AL, 1901 into 1907. Besides his two home run crowns, led AL in three-baggers, 19, in 1904; had 25 with Washington NL, 1899. Statistics vary as to exactly how many major league games Freeman played. But it is certain he was in more than 1100 contests, and hit about .294. Had over 1200 big league hits, with 199 doubles, 131 triples, 82 homers. Scored close to 600 runs.

Freeman was making $225 monthly when he led NL in homers, 1899. Highest pay he reached was $3500 annually while toiling for Red Sox.

FREGOSI, JAMES LOUIS Inf.-BR-TR. B. 4/4/42, San Francisco, Calif. 6'2", 195. Six-time AL All-Star shortstop who became 46th man to play third base for N.Y. Mets as season opened, 1972. Jim was mentioned as managerial possibility for California Angels before his trade to Mets. But when Harry Dalton moved into Anaheim picture, one of his early moves was to trade Fregosi. Possibly an alleged resemblance to Joe Namath and certain off-beat remarks and actions attributed to Fregosi may have influenced Dalton's decision. Fregosi, Alex Johnson, and Tony Conigliaro were three well-known members of 1971 Angels who left team after disappointing season. Jim stirred up considerable controversy after being traded. Said Angels were supposed to win divisional title but wound up blaming everybody else when things went wrong. This was resented by former teammates. In new league, playing new position, Fregosi got off to good start with Mets but hardly earned salary, reported to be at $90,000 level. Played 101 games, hit .232, and his weight rose close to 220 before season ended.

Jim joined Mets after 1429 AL games with .268 career average. Had 1408 hits, with 219 doubles, 70 triples, 115 homers. Had scored 691 times and driven in 546 runs, with 71 stolen bases. Went through 1970 season, however, without stealing even once, which equaled major league record for players taking part in 150 or more games.

Fregosi originally lined up with Boston Red Sox organization after attending Menlo College in California, 1960. Played that year with Alpine, Tex., team in Sophomore League. Then was selected by newly-formed Angel club in expansion draft, off Red Sox roster 12/14/60. Angels farmed him out to Dallas–Fort Worth, American Association, for 1961–62, but gave him brief stay with parent team 1961 and brought him in for 58 games in 1962.

Jim hit .291 that year for Angels and nailed down shortstop berth for years to come. By 1964 was hitting 18 homers with 72 RBI, and gained his first recognition as member of AL's All-Star squad. Continued as fine player through 1970, when he had his best season. In 158 games had .278 average, with 22 homers, 82 RBI, 33 doubles, five triples. Beset by problems, 1971. Had two-week siege of flu during spring training, sore arm, pulled side muscle. Underwent surgery for nerve tumor between big and second toes of right foot 7/14/71, then had infection. Managed Ponce club in Puerto Rican Winter League after 1969 campaign, leading his club to pennant.

Jim had several notable records during his AL career: led shortstops in double plays with 125 in 1966 and tied for lead with 92 in 1968; was first Angel to hit for cycle, 1964, and repeated performance 5/20/68; equaled AL record by starting five double plays 5/1/66. In 1969 was voted "Greatest Angel Ever."

FRENCH, LAWRENCE HERBERT (Larry)   P-BRL-TL. B. 11/1/08, Visalia, Calif. 6'1", 194. Larry French was fine pitcher in NL 1929–42 but saved his best year in baseball for last. His 15–4 performance for 1942 Brooklyn Dodgers led NL in winning percentage; and it was his personal high percentage, .789, although it was ninth time he had won 15 or more games in majors.

Not only was 1942 record dazzling, but Larry said farewell to baseball in brilliant performance 9/23/42. Pitched 6–0 shutout over Philadelphia NL, allowing only one hit; faced just 28 batsmen.

French then went into navy—and came out 27 years later as captain. Now retired, living in San Diego.

Larry had brief experience, 1926, with Ogden, Utah-Idaho League; spent rest of 1926 and 1927–28 with Portland, Pacific Coast League, earning his promotion to Pittsburgh NL, 1929. After 7–5 record that year, got into double figures as winner, 1930 and stayed with Pirates until 11/22/34. Best years with Pirates, 1932 (18–16) and 1933 (18–13). Had 17–10 record his first year in Chicago, 18–9 in 1936, and 16–10 in 1937. Also won 15 while losing eight in 1939.

Brooklyn picked him up at bargain waiver price 8/20/41 after he had won five and lost 14. Took part in six games with Dodgers in 1941, but neither won nor lost. Then came his final year in majors when he hung up his 40th shutout in his last appearance in pro baseball. Missed pitching 200 complete games, by one. Wound up with 197 major league wins, 171 losses. Had ERA of 3.44 for 3152 innings pitched. Struck out 1187 and walked 819.

Lost two games in 1935 WS with Cubs. No decision in his WS of 1938, also with Cubs. Pitched just one inning for Dodgers in WS of 1941. WS totals came to 15 innings, no wins, two losses, and ERA of 3.00 in seven games. Walked three, fanned ten, allowed five earned runs, 16 hits.

FRICK, FORD CHRISTOPHER   Executive. B. 12/19/94, Wawaka, Ind. Retired commissioner of baseball, former NL president. Frick, after high school, spent year in business college. Worked for company making engines for windmills. Enrolled at DePauw U., graduated 1915. Taught English in Colorado. Began newspaper career with *Colorado Springs Gazette*. Did rehabilitation work for U.S. Army, 1918. Back to sports writing, in Colorado Springs with *Telegraph*. Friend sent sample of his writing to Arthur Brisbane, then righthand man to William Randolph Hearst, newspaper tycoon. Job with *N.Y. Evening American* resulted, 1922, covering Giants. Followed Brisbane to *N.Y. Evening Journal*, 1923, covering Yankees. Ghosted articles with Babe Ruth byline. Did radio work, news and sports. Announcer on André Kostelanetz program for time. Became head of NL "service bureau," doing league publicity. Elected president NL 11/9/34. When term started several NL clubs in financial straits. Frick helped bring new money to teams. Credited with idea for Hall of Fame which was started at Cooperstown, N.Y., 1939.

When Jackie Robinson broke color line in NL 1946, were reports of possible strike by players opposed to entry of blacks. Most serious was that forming among Cardinals. Frick warned them, "If you strike, you're through—I don't care if it wrecks league for ten years." No strike materialized.

Frick continued as NL president until 10/8/51 when became commissioner of baseball. Though term as commissioner involved threat of third major league, "Continental League," shifting of Brooklyn and New York NL franchises out of metropolis and other drastic moves, including expansion, Frick apparently gave little leadership. Some sports writers accused him of being tool of club owners, with motto, "Speak softly and carry no stick at all." Continued as commissioner until retirement 1965.

Lives in Bronxville, N.Y. Hall of Fame 1969.

FRIEND, ROBERT BARTMESS P-BR-TR. B. 11/24/30, Lafayette, Ind. 6', 190. Bob Friend was first pitcher in majors ever to lead league in earned-run effectiveness while hurling for last-place team, 1955. In his first seven seasons in NL, 1951–57, his team, Pittsburgh Pirates, finished last four times and no higher than seventh other three years. In 16 years in big leagues, Friend was with one pennant winner, one runner up, and one third-placer. In his final year, divided his time between Mets, who finished ninth—and Yankees, who ended up tenth. Despite calibre of clubs, Bob won 197 games, lost 230. Wonder what his record could have been with team like Yankees of Mickey Mantle–Whitey Ford–Casey Stengel era?

Friend had just one year in minors, 1950. Broke in with Waco, Big State League; won 12, lost nine with 3.08 ERA. Finished season with Indianapolis, American Association, with two wins, four losses, then moved up to Pirates. Couldn't get over .500 until 1955, when won 14, lost nine for cellar club and had his league-leading 2.84 ERA. In 1958, when Pittsburgh climbed up to second place in Danny Murtaugh's first full season as skipper, Bob won 22 games, lost 14 and had 3.68 ERA. Then came 8–19 mark in 1959. Pittsburgh won flag, 1960, ably assisted by Friend's 18–12 mark and ERA of 3.00.

Pirates of 1961 dropped down to sixth—and Friend's record sagged to 14–19. Came back with 18–14 mark, 1962. In his final effort in majors, 1966, Friend won one game with tenth-place Yankees, lost four; then when released to Mets 6/15/66, won five games, lost eight for ninth-place team.

Friend took part in 602 major league games, pitched 3612 innings, allowed 1438 earned runs, fanned 1734, walked 894, and had 3.58 ERA. In WS play was quite ineffective in that hectic classic (1960) that Pirates ultimately won from Yankees: 6 innings, 2 losses, 9 earned runs, 7 strikeouts, 3 walks, ERA 13.50.

FRISCH, FRANK FRANCIS (Fordham Flash) Inf.-BRL-TR. B. 9/9/98, New York, N.Y. D. 3/12/73, Wilmington, Del. 5'10", 185. Dame Fortune seems to have decreed eventful, well-rounded life for Frankie Frisch from birth. Son of a well-to-do lace linen manufacturer, attended Fordham University. Caught for Fordham Prep, but played shortstop for varsity squad. Became captain of baseball, football and basketball teams. Considered great halfback in World War I period. Walter Camp placed him on second All-American team, 1917. As collegian who batted cross-handed then, Frisch showed baseball potential. In exhibition game against Baltimore Orioles, International League, slammed five hits, including two doubles and triple. Graduated with A.B., 1919. Signed with N.Y. Giants immediately, in time to play 54 games. Hit only .226, but stole 15 bases. Won regular job when McGraw played him at second during crucial series of three straight doubleheaders against Cincinnati. First Redleg batter, Rath, smashed hot grounder toward rookie keystoner. Ball bounced off Frankie's chest but he pursued it, grabbed it and nailed Rath at first.

Immediately won headlines with spectacular fielding, timely hitting from both sides of plate, flashy base running. Often lost cap diving for grounders, chasing pop flies, running bases, especially with head-first slides. Soon recognized as one of most colorful, dashing players in majors. Spent 1920 at third base but thereafter was primarily second baseman.

Giants won NL flag 1921–24 with Frisch sparkling. During 1922–23 teamed up with George Kelly, 1B; Dave Bancroft, SS; Heinie Groh, 3B; to form brilliant infield.

World Series performances for Giants dazzling. In first game, 1921, Carl Mays, Yankee submarine hurler, allowed Giants five hits. Frisch had four for four. Went on to hit .300, .471, .400, .333 in successive Series, only player to hit .300 or better four classics in row.

Manager John McGraw nagged Frisch as team captain when club sagged 1926. Frankie, fed up, jumped team in St. Louis. When he returned to Giants, hit important home run which knocked Cincinnati out of race for NL flag. Despite .314 in 135 games, 23 stolen bases, his days as Giant were numbered.

Meanwhile, Cardinals took advantage, winning pennant under Rogers Hornsby. Went on to Series victory over Yankees. Joy was unbounded in Midwest; Cards' first pennant. Hornsby became hero of fans who relished flag victory until 12/20/26 when owner Sam Breadon traded his manager and second baseman to Giants for Frisch and pitcher Jimmy Ring. Disgruntled Card fans promised to stay away from ball park or if they went, it would be to boo Breadon. So Frisch's welcome as Hornsby's successor as player only, was frigid. Cards played St. Louis Browns in spring series, 1927. In first inning with bases loaded, Frankie allowed double-play ball to slither between his legs. Hostile crowd roared, "We want Hornsby!" In eighth inning, Frisch slammed home run which made up for error and won game.

Frisch won countless games for Cards that year; he "made 'em like it" in St. Louis. Fabulous season at bat, in field and on bases. Set major league record for most chances accepted by second baseman, 1037; most assists at second, 641; led NL keystoners with .979 fielding average. Banged 208 hits, including 31 doubles, 11 triples, 10 homers, 78 RBI. Also stole 48 bases, batted .337.

Cardinals missed pennant by 1-1/2 games but not Frisch's fault. By end of 1927 Breadon felt vindicated. Frisch new Card hero. Helped

Cards win flags 1928,30,31, with .300, .346 and .311 averages

In 1931 Series, Redbirds vanquished powerful Athletics—Series in which Pepper Martin ran wild. Cards slowed down in 1932 and 1933; Breadon dropped Gabby Street as manager, placing Frisch in charge 7/24/33. Before long, Cards became known as Gas House Gang—with Dizzy Dean, Joe Medwick, Leo Durocher, Paul Dean, Rip Collins and Pepper Martin in their prime. Frisch still pretty fair second baseman— but Branch Rickey, general manager of Cardinals, believed he was slowing down in field and on bases. In fact, during spring training, 1934, Rickey, watching Frankie in Florida exhibition games, expressed view privately that club couldn't win with Frisch as second baseman. Rickey seriously considered flying to St. Louis to convince Breadon to trade Frisch, even though Frisch was playing manager. Rickey probably realized it would be fruitless mission since Frank had saved Breadon's hide, having played such consistently fine ball after Hornsby trade. Frisch stayed. Cards captured flag, beating out Bill Terry's Giants on last day of season, then tackled AL champions, Detroit Tigers, headed by Mickey Cochrane.

Each team took three games. In crucial seventh contest, score read 0–0 in third inning with men on second and third, none out. Cochrane ordered Jack Rothrock walked intentionally, filling bases. Frisch proved this to be costly mistake, as he belted two-bagger to right field corner, sending three runs home. Cards went on to score seven times before inning ended. Ultimately defeated Tigers, 11 to 0, Dizzy Dean pitching shutout. That was Series when Dizzy won two decisions and brother Paul other two. Also same Series when Detroit fans pelted Joe Medwick with so many ripe fruits, vegetables and other missiles that Judge Landis removed him from game.

Frankie managed Cardinals till 9/10/38; Pittsburgh, 1940–46; Cubs, 6/10/49 until 7/21/51. Only pennant winner as pilot came in first full season at helm, 1934. Wound up as player in 1937, with 2311 NL games, 2880 hits, 1532 runs, 466 doubles, 138 triples, 105 home runs, 1242 RBI and lifetime batting average of .316. His steals totaled 419. Four World Series with Giants and four with Cardinals: 50 games, 16 runs, 58 hits, 10 RBI, 9 stolen bases, .294 average. MVP 1931.

Frisch took part in first All-Star game, 1933. While Babe Ruth hit first homer of contest, Frisch hit first round-tripper ever made by NL player few innings later. No fluke; homered again 1934 All-Star game. Great "money player" again showed his mettle with four hits, four runs in seven times at bat in the two contests, for .571 average.

Frankie did considerable radio and television sportscasting in Boston and New York sandwiched in with his managerial jobs. In later years picked up nickname "Dutchman." Lived in New Rochelle, N.Y., many years but later moved to Quonochontaug, R.I. Was avid ski enthusiast, ice skater, horticulturist and lover of symphonic music, good books. Hall of Fame 1947.

FRISELLA, DANIEL VINCENT P-BL-TR. B. 3/4/46, San Francisco, Calif. 6', 195. Fork-ball reliever who is married to Pam Marshall, who was defensive back on all-girls pro football team. Pitched for New York Mets three full seasons, parts of three others. Once he shaved before game and Hank Aaron hit home run off him. Solved this problem by not shaving any more before games—and becoming teammate of Hank's. Mets traded him to Atlanta Braves after 1972 season. At that time he had taken part in 148 games in NL, won 24, lost 26, with an ERA of 3.08. Started 16 games prior to 1973, but never completed any of them. Busiest season was 1971 when he got into 53 contests. Began his Atlanta playing with 354 major league innings behind him; had walked 137, struck out 296.

Dan attended Washington State and College of San Mateo, in California. Milwaukee Braves put him on their draft list, 1966, but he refused to sign, remaining in college. While at Washington State, was 10–0, had 1.42 ERA as he led team to third-place finish in college WS. Started pro career, 1966, and during first two seasons pitched for Auburn in N.Y.-Pa. League; Durham, Carolina League; and Jacksonville, International. Also had 14 games with Mets, 1967 without distinguishing himself. Divided 1968 season between Mets and Jacksonville. In 1969 with Pompano Beach, Florida State League; also with Mets and Tidewater, International League. In 1970 had 7–3 record with Tidewater. In June of that year got his break. Was called up to Mets to be two-week replacement for Nolan Ryan who had been called to military duty. Pitched so well that he stuck rest of season. Chalked up 8–3 record with 3.00 ERA in 30 appearances in NL. Then came busy 1971 season: 8–5, 12 saves, finished 42 games, ERA 1.98. Struck out 93, walked 30.

FRYMAN, WOODROW THOMPSON (Woodie) P-BR-TL. B. 4/15/40, Ewing, Ky. 6'2", 205. Woody Fryman, despite arthritic elbow, proved valuable addition to Detroit pitching staff, 1972, after winning just four games, losing 10 for Philadelphia Phillies earlier same season. Woody found things lot more to his liking in Motor City than in City of Brotherly Love. Tiger infielders, especially Brinkman and Rodriguez, help any pitcher tremendously. Also, in AL Fryman doesn't have to pitch on artificial turf nearly as often as he did in NL. Used in relief same night he reported to Detroit; pitched couple of shutout innings. After hurling total of eight runless innings in relief, Woody was Tiger starter against N.Y. Yankees in their stadium. It was first time he had seen Bronx ball park. Pitched his first AL shutout. Although Woody 10–3 for Tigers to help them into AL playoff series, was charged with two of 'Tigers' three losses to Oakland. Started second game of set, but was driven to cover in fifth inning, A's winning by 5–0 score. Woody pitched masterfully in crucial fifth game. A's scored one run on double steal, and got their other marker on Gene Tenace's single later in game. Fryman lost that one 2–1.

Fryman's elbow causes him pain whenever he pitches. Gets some relief afterward by soaking arm in ice water.

Woody might not have followed baseball as career if U. S. government had not reduced subsidy on growing tobacco. Owns 40 acres in Kentucky; raises tobacco, corn, and Black Angus cattle. Started at Batavia, N.Y.-Pa. League, 1965, and spent part of same season at Columbus, International League. With Pittsburgh, 1966–67; had 12–9 and 3–8 marks with Pirates. Traded to Philadelphia Phillies, 12/15/67, remaining with them until his midsummer sale to Detroit, 1972.

Although Fryman had 2.78 ERA with Phillies, 1968, was able to win only 12 games while losing 14. It was 12–15 following year, then 8–6 and 10–7.

Fryman's major league totals as he entered 1973 were as follows: games pitched, 237; innings, 1248; 71 victories, 72 defeats; 504 earned runs allowed, with 403 bases on balls, 822 strikeouts; 47 complete games. Overall ERA 3.63. In 1972 his ERA with Phillies was 4.35, but with Tigers he enjoyed best effectiveness record of his career—2.05. Member NL All-Star squad 1968, but not used.

FUCHS, EMIL E. (Judge) Executive. B. 4/17/78, Hamburg, Germany. D. 12/5/61, Boston, Mass. Judge Fuchs lost more than million dollars as owner of Boston Braves but died with no regrets. Brought great baseball names to Boston but, unfortunately, most of them were well past their prime when he acquired them. Without any pro baseball experience as player, managed hapless team for few weeks and was ridiculed for trying. Although Fuchs brought Babe Ruth, Rogers Hornsby, George Sisler, Casey Stengel, and Christy Mathewson to Boston baseball scene, Braves never finished above seventh while he was connected with club. Among big names, only Hornsby was still superstar while connected with Braves.

Fuchs was graduate of New York U. Law School. Became "Judge" as magistrate, N.Y. City, 1915–18; later attorney for N. Y. Giants for a time. Friend of John McGraw. Owned Braves 1923–35. Paid $550,000 for club and was in debt $300,000 when it was sold during depression. But Fuchs resumed law practice in Brookline, Mass., and paid off all debts.

Mathewson was president of Braves at start of Fuchs' ownership, but died, 1925, and Judge took top spot. Paid Hornsby $40,000 salary, 1928. Rogers managed club most of season, then was sold to Chicago NL. In 1929, Fuchs took over management himself. Players paid little attention to Fuchs on bench. Assistant manager Johnny Evers gave what effective direction there was on field, but confusion reigned. Evers was running team completely before season's end. Club finished last, 10 games behind seventh-placers.

Ruth's return to Boston also proved fiasco. Babe was almost finished as player. In role of vice president and assistant manager (Bill McKechnie had been taken on as pilot), Ruth flouted anything resembling training rules, was law unto himself. Hit six home runs, three in one game at Pittsburgh 5/25/35, but fly balls dropped all around him in outfield and his batting average was .181 after 28 games. So noble experiment came to ignominious end before midsummer.

In Hornsby's one season at Boston, led NL with .387 average. George Sisler, while past his prime, hit .340 same year, 1928. Rabbit Maranville, one of heroes of 1914 Miracle Braves, returned to team, 1929, had pretty fair season with .284 average in 146 games. Stengel, as outfielder, hit .280 for Fuchs' team, 1924. But big names were not enough. Judge paid dearly for his experience in baseball.

FUENTES, RIGOBERTO (Tito) 2B-BLR-TR. B. 1/4/44 Havana, Cuba. 5'11", 175. Tito Fuentes wears regular baseball spiked shoe on his left foot; uses rubber-cleat shoe on right foot. Says this gives him better traction.

Besides his nickname, which often inspires Candlestick Park fans to chant "Tito! Tito!" when they want him to hit safely, he is variously called "Cuban Cat," "Hot Dog," "Parakeet," and "Channel 32," because of his constant chatter and irrepressible energy that attract attention whenever he is on field. Has been accused of showboating, but it seems to be his nature.

Fuentes first joined San Francisco Giants 1965, played 133 games for them in each of 1966 and 1967 seasons but went back to Phoenix for 1968 and part of 1969. Returned to Giants for 67 games, 1969, hit .295, and then established himself as regular second baseman. Had seen considerable service at short and third base. Hit .267 in 1970 and .273 in 1971. In 1972 his average was .264.

Tito's first pro club was Lakeland, Florida State League, 1962, but also played at Salem, Va.; Decatur, Ill.; El Paso, and Tacoma before his first spell with Giants. Got his first major league homer 5/7/66 and slapped eight more that year, his best season ever with respect to round trippers. Had seven in 1972. Suffered broken leg and torn ligaments sliding into second base 5/9/68 while at Phoenix and was out for rest of season.

His major league record going into 1973 showed .260 average for 786 games. Owned 28 homers, 112 doubles, 26 triples; scored 306 runs, drove in 221.

FURILLO, CARL ANTHONY (Skoonj) OF-BR-TR. 3/8/22, Stony Creek Mills, Pa. 6', 190. Carl Furillo led NL in hitting, 1953, and helped Brooklyn Dodgers win club's fourth pennant. Had great throwing arm. Always played well over 100 games a season until last two of 15 years in majors. But career ended in big hassle with Los Angeles Dodgers. Released, 1960, Carl sued club. Won $21,000 against team for dropping him without pay following injury. Now makes living as construction worker in New York City.

Furillo played at Pocomoke City, Md., Eastern Shore League, 1940; hit .319 in 71 games and before year was up had been promoted to Reading, Inter-State League. Hit .313 there in 1941, meriting advancement to Montreal, then Brooklyn's International League affiliate. Carl had .281 average there in 129 games. At this point they called him "Little Flower" because of name's similarity to Fiorello LaGuardia's. But Carl no fragile blossom. Once his hand was spiked in first game of doubleheader; needed seven stitches. But he played second game and came up with two hits. Three years in military separated his Montreal experience from his Brooklyn debut, 1946. Started with .284 average. With one exception, hit better than that until his very last season in majors when he appeared in only eight games. Six times drove in better than 90 runs per season, twice going above 100 mark in RBI. When he won bat title, 1953, hit .344 in 132 games.

Furillo wound up with 1806 major league games and .299 lifetime average.. Drove 1910 hits in 6378 trips, had 324 doubles, 56 triples, and 192 homers. Drove in 1058 runs, stole 48 times. In WS play in seven sets, hit .266 in 40 games. Nine doubles among his 34 hits, also two homers. Scored 13 times, had 13 RBI.

GAEDEL, EDDIE Pinch Hitter-BR-TL. B. 6/8/25, Chicago, Ill. D. 6/18/61, Chicago, Ill. 3'7", 65. Everlasting fame came to this midget 7/19/51 during St. Louis Browns' observance of Golden Anniversary of AL. At Sportsman's Park doubleheader was played on Sunday afternoon against Detroit Tigers. Between games giant birthday cake was wheeled out to home plate. Out of cake popped unknown midget, 3'7", with his number, "1/8," on back of his Brownie uniform. Fans didn't know what was happening until after Tigers had taken their half of first inning at bat. With last half of inning ready to start, Eddie Gaedel, walked up to plate umpire Ed Hurley and told him he was batting for Frank Saucier. Hurley was prepared to argue, but up stepped Mgr. Zack Taylor. Zack showed umpire Gaedel's signed contract and copy of notification club president Bill Veeck had mailed to AL president's office night before. Bob Cain, Detroit pitcher, couldn't get ball into Gaedel's tiny strike zone, walked him on four pitches. Midget trotted down to first base, then gave way to pinch runner.

Browns were tailenders that year and hardly anybody paid any attention to them. Only showmanship of Bill Veeck and die-hard fans kept team from playing in complete privacy. Nevertheless, that day 18,369 people paid their way into ball park for lack of anything better to do.

Next day Browns were in headlines all over country. Reaction from conservative Will Harridge, AL president, was quick. Stiff telegram on Veeck's desk Monday morning advising him never again would any such stunt be permitted. But Veeck and faithful fans had already had their

337

fun, and midget's story would be told and retold thousands of times through years.

Veeck paid $100 to Gaedel for his solitary appearance in AL game. But Eddie garnered enough renown to get bookings for rest of his short life. Some years later, after Browns went off to Baltimore to be miraculously, if slowly, transformed into powerful Orioles, Gaedel again appeared in major league ball park.

Veeck, out of baseball for time, had come back as majordomo of Chicago White Sox. Out of skies dropped helicopter behind second base. Out jumped Gaedel and three other midgets, dressed in "Martian" costumes. Little men "captured" Luis Aparicio and Nellie Fox. More laughs for fans present—but nothing midget did ever got attention given his solitary appearance as bona fide AL pinch hitter.

GALAN, AUGUST JOHN (Augie) OF-BLR-TR. B. 5/25/12, Berkeley, Calif. 6', 175. Augie Galan spent 16 years in major lagues and hit .287 in 1742 games despite painful elbow injury that dated to when he was 11 years old. Almost constant pain certainly handicapped his performance. One can only speculate how much better ball player he might have been if shattered elbow had been cared for at time of injury.

Augie deliberately concealed injury from his parents, fearing their reaction. And for many years in majors Galan was successful in hiding his painful handicap from managers and teammates. Only during World War II, when Augie was examined physically for draft, did his secret become public.

Galan desperately wanted to become big league ball player. When still a boy, playing, fell on right arm on concrete. Elbow was badly shattered, but Augie never told parents. Arm should have been put in cast but, despite pain, Augie never went to doctor.

After playing on Oakland sandlots Augie played at Globe, Arizona-Texas League, 1931, later was with Tucson club. Played shortstop for most part, 1932–33, with San Francisco, Pacific Coast League; 183 games first season and 189 the next. Hit .291 and .356. It was amazing Galan could play infield at all with that right arm as bad as it was. Despite shortcomings in throwing, Chicago Cubs bought him, played him at second base, 1934. Hit .260 in 66 games, then was shifted to outfield. Augie later confessed that much of time had no feeling in arm, which accounted for some of inaccurate throws. Hit .314 for Cubs, 1935, in 154 games, led NL in stolen bases with 22. Led league in thefts again, 1937, with 23. Hit .304 for Cubs, playing most of team's games, 1939. Galan's hitting fell off in 1940 and 1941, and Chicago wanted to send him to Los Angeles, PCL. Augie was positive he could help big league team, got permission to talk to Larry MacPhail, then general manager of Brooklyn. Convinced MacPhail he would be able to help Dodgers.

MacPhail paid Cubs $2500 and got Galan. One of best bargains MacPhail ever made; Galan had more than five good years with Dodgers, helped them win 1941 pennant, and hit above .300 for Brooklyn three times. In 1943,44,45 played 139, 151, and 152 games respectively.

Galan had other injuries besides that bad arm. In 1937 collision on field lossened cartilage of left knee. Another injury following season—same knee. And in 1940 crashed into concrete wall pursuing foul fly. That shattered same knee.

Augie, meanwhile, suffered excruciating pain in right arm. So much so that, after being switch hitter during earlier years in majors, took to hitting lefthanded exclusively, which seemed to minimize pain when he swung bat.

After 1946 season at Brooklyn, Galan with Cincinnati 1947–48; New York NL 1949 and Philadelphia AL later same year. Coach, Oakland, PCL, 1950–51; and manager 1952–53. Coach, Philadelphia AL, 1954.

In his youth Augie worked in his father's cleaning and dying plant and was proud of his ability to iron fancy dress shirts. As his baseball career tapered off, owned meat markets in Bay Area of California.

Augie played 1742 major league games, got 1706 hits, including 336 doubles, 74 triples, 100 homers. Scored 1004 times, had 830 RBI, and overall average of .287. Stole 123 bases. In WS (1935,38 with Cubs; 1941 with Brooklyn), played 10 games, 4 for 29, .138 average, with 1 double, 2 runs, 2 RBI.

GALBREATH, JOHN W. Executive. B. 8/9/97, Derby, Ohio. Chairman of board, Pittsburgh Pirates. Millionaire sportsman. Financier with far-flung business interests. With Bing Crosby, Tom Johnson and Frank McKinney, he bought Pirates, 1946. Two years later, took over McKinney's interest.

Son of farmer, Galbreath's early occupations included grinding, bottling and selling horseradish. Photographer. Bicycle repair man. Printer's devil. Waiter. Saxophone player. Worked way through Ohio U. Some success in real estate but lost almost everything during depression. Made comeback selling property for banks. Built skyscrapers, promoted other construction projects. Owner of two Kentucky Derby winners—Chateaugay, 1963, and Proud Clarion, 1967. Only man to win two derbies, two WS—Pirates took all in 1960, 1971.

GALLAGHER, ALAN MITCHELL EDWARD GEORGE PATRICK HENRY (Al) 3B-BR-TR. B. 10/19/45, San Francisco, Calif. 6′, 180. If possible to field a team composed of San Francisco native sons you could start with Joe Cronin, Dom DiMaggio, Tony Lazzeri. Then you could add Lefty O'Doul, Harry Heilmann, Willie Kamm, George Kelly, all outstanding players of yesteryear. Of present crop you'd want to consider Al Gallagher, third baseman of California Angels, before that with San Francisco Giants. Al got all those names because parents had waited many years before son arrived. Decided to give him all names they might have given to an entire family.

Al good athlete at Santa Clara and Arizona State universities. Spent 1965–69 gaining experience at Tacoma, Springfield (Mass.), Fresno, Amarillo, Phoenix. At Fresno, 1966, hit .316, 120 games; had 78 RBI; led California League in triples, putouts, assists. In Amarillo, 1968, pitched and won one game, allowing just one run in nine innings, but concentrated on hot corner. Giants 1970, 109 games, .266, 4 homers. In 1971, .277, 136 games, 5 homers, 57 RBI. In 1972, played 82 games, hit .223, two homers. Traded to Angels early 1973 season. Developed popular following during off-seasons as member of Giants' speakers bureau.

GALLAGHER, JAMES T. Executive. B. 6/9/09, Lorain, Ohio Jim Gallagher attended Notre Dame before joining sports staff of *Chicago Evening American*, 1928. Five years later became baseball writer; from time to time known to be critical of way Chicago Cubs ran things. About 1940, Phil Wrigley, owner of Cubs, listened patiently to Gallagher's opinions about what should be done. At end of conversation Wrigley offered him job. Became general manager. Took title of vice president, 1944. Later, title of vice president was dropped and he was business manager until 1956. Wrigley may have had in mind precedent set by father, William Wrigley, Jr., who also hired critical newspaper man, Bill Veeck, Sr., to run Cubs many years earlier. While Gallagher was with Cubs they won pennant, 1945, but have not been successful since then.

Jim's big jobs with Cubs were modernization and mechanization of concessions, million-dollar rehabilitation of Wrigley Field.

Gallagher was out of baseball, 1957; spent that time as partner of Bill Veeck, Jr., in public relations firm. Spring 1958, Jim joined Philadelphia Phillies in their farm club setup. Resigned as director of scouting for Phils late in 1961. Following year joined Ford Frick's staff in office of baseball commissioner. Holds title of director of amateur and college baseball. For many years has served as chairman of baseball rules committee.

GALVIN, JAMES F. (Pud) P-BR-TR. B. 12/25/56, St. Louis, Mo. D. 3/7/02, Pittsburgh, Pa. 5'8", 190. One of pitching workhorses of 19th century. Won 37 games, lost 27 in 1879 with Buffalo NL. And in 1883–84 won 46 games each season with same club. Hall of Fame 1965.

Despite all this exercise, Galvin reportedly went all way to 300 pounds before his pitching career ended, 1894. Major league totals showed 685 games pitched, 5959 IP, 361 wins, 309 losses. Fanned 1786 batsmen, walked only 744. Hurled 639 complete games, had 57 shutouts.

Galvin spent 1875 with St. Louis in National Association. Was with St. Louis Red Stockings, 1876; Allegheny, International Association, 1877; Buffalo, same league, 1878. Then followed seven years with Buffalo, NL; two seasons with Allegheny, American Association; Pittsburgh NL 1887–1892; released and signed with St. Louis NL June 1892. Buffalo, Eastern League, 1894.

Besides the two years when he won 46 games each season, Galvin had several other big years. Ten times he had 20 or more victories. Pitched no-hit games for Buffalo, against Worcester NL 8/20/80 and against Detroit NL 8/4/84. Galvin served briefly as manager of Buffalo in 1885.

GANDIL, CHARLES ARNOLD (Chick) 1B-BR-TR. B. 1/19/88, St. Paul, Minn. D. 12/13/70, Calistoga, Calif. 6'2", 195. "I feel that we got what we had coming." These were words of Chick Gandil, one of ringleaders of "Black Sox" scandal, not long before died. Referred to Judge Landis' expulsion of eight members of Chicago AL team who threw, or conspired to throw, or seriously discussed throwing 1919 WS to Cincinnati. Confusion still exists as to exactly what happened. Conflicting testimony. Missing documents. Confessions disappearing from court records. Legal acquittal. But Kenesaw Mountain Landis barred all eight from organized baseball for life.

Many considered 1919 White Sox one of greatest teams in baseball history. Great with physical ability, not with cohesion, morale or team spirit. One of "Black Sox", Shoeless Joe Jackson, undoubtedly one of finest hitters of all times. Another, third baseman Buck Weaver, judged just about tops as hot corner guardian, possibly including Pie Traynor and Brooks Robinson. Eddie Cicotte, stellar pitcher who won 210 games and lost 148 in ill-starred career. Claude Williams, 81–45 in majors, reportedly considerably better hurler than Cicotte. Others involved in plot were Oscar Felsch, center fielder; Swede Risberg, shortstop; Fred McMullin, utility infielder.

Gandil ran away from home at 17. Rode freight train to Amarillo, Texas, to play semipro ball. Also played in Mexico near Arizona border. Did some heavyweight fighting, $150 per bout. Toiled part time in copper mines as boilermaker.

Shreveport, Texas League, 1908, hitting .269, 116 games. Drafted by St. Louis AL but released to Shreveport, Texas League. Refused to report. Transferred to Sacramento, Pacific Coast League, for 1909. Played 206 games, hit .282. Following year with Chicago AL, 77 games,

.193 average. Montreal, Eastern League, 1911, .304 average, 138 games. Hit .309, 1912, with same club for 29 games, then to Washington AL, hitting .305, 117 contests.

Regular first baseman for Senators through 1915. Cleveland 1916. Sold to Chicago AL 2/25/17. There hit .273, .271, .290 in these three seasons (1917–19). In 1917 Sox won pennant and World Series. Gandil hit .261, drove in five runs, more than any of his teammates, as Sox downed Giants, four games to two.

Sox sixth place 1918. Came back to win 1919 under freshman manager Kid Gleason. Meanwhile, dissension was order of day. Many players hated pinchpenny tactics of owner Charles Comiskey. No esprit de corps. Cicotte, who won 28 games in 1917, was earning $6000. Joe Jackson making only slightly more. Gandil had been drawing $4500 for three years. Eddie Collins, with $14,000 salary, only one in big money, probably because had been paid fairly well before being traded to Chicago.

Gandil and others on team freely mixed with gamblers and shady characters. Unclear whether plot to throw games in World Series was original idea of Gandil and Cicotte, or whether gamblers approached them first. In any case, scheme developed that seven or eight players would get $10,000 each to see that Series went to Cincinnati, underdogs in betting. To underpaid stars, very tempting. Unclear whether some of players changed their mind about deal, whether they were double-crossed by gamblers or whether they double-crossed gamblers. *New York Times* called conspiracy "one of the most amazing and tangled tales of graft and bribery, and interlocking double-crossing."

In any event, several questionable plays developed during Series, including some by Gandil. White Sox, picked by experts to win with ease, lost, taking just three out of eight games. Cicotte supposed to have received $10,000 at one point. Gandil reported to have received $20,000 but divided it equally among Williams, Jackson, Risberg, Felsch. Gandil later insisted he never got penny for himself.

Gandil, 1920, asked for $2000 raise, not expecting to get it. Comiskey promptly refused. Gandil stayed on West Coast, played semipro ball at Bakersfield, Calif., twice weekly for $75 a game. Seven other plotters returned to Sox. Stink from Series so bad that investigations started early. Finally, September 1920, case went to grand jury. All eight indicted. Meanwhile, suspected players suspended. When Judge Kenesaw Landis came into new job as czar of baseball few weeks later, he suspended all eight for life. In 1921 certain confessions and other documents turned up missing, and jury gave "not guilty" verdict since there was no evidence. Each of "Black Sox" had refused to testify. But Landis' edict stood. None ever took part in anything connected with organized baseball thereafter.

Gandil quit with .276 lifetime batting average in 1146 games. Died in obscurity after spending number of years in Oakland, Calif., as plumber.

GARAGIOLA, JOSEPH HENRY C-BL-TR. B. 2/12/26, St. Louis, Mo. 6' 190. October 10, 1946, may have been climax of Joe Garagiola's major league career. Had three singles, one double, three RBI World Series game for Cardinals against Red Sox. Cards won that day. Also took Series, four games to three.

Today most think of Joe as TV, radio personality. Joe kids about his shortcomings as pro. He'll never make Hall of Fame on his hitting record—.257 in 676 big league games. Did hit .316 in that 1946 Series, with 6 for 19. Joe might have been better ball player but for shoulder separation, 1950.

Garagiola from neighborhood that produced Yogi Berra, his boyhood friend. Both had tryout with Cardinals. Garagiola, with hair those days, looked more the athlete than Yogi. Cards gave him $500 to sign, but offered Berra just $250. Indignant Berra walked out, later getting his $500 from Yankees.

Garagiola was just 15 when Cardinals grabbed him. At that age there was risk another ball club would take too great an interest in him. After all, he was minor, and sometimes contracts made by minors do not stand up, even though parents also have signed them. In any case Joe was shipped to Springfield, Mo., Cards' farm club. Was groundkeeper, batting practice catcher and general helper—for $60 a month. Following season, 1942, played on Springfield club, dividing time between catching and outfield. Hit .254 in 67 games.

Made big jump to Columbus, American Association, 1943, caught in 81 games, hit .293. Military service 1944–46. When he came out, joined Cardinals, played 74 games, hit .237. Following year, 1947, hit .257. After 24 games and .107 average, back to Columbus for most of 1948, despite 1946 World Series performance. Hit .356 there in 65 games, returning to St. Louis for 1949,50 seasons. Traded to Pittsburgh 6/15/51. In 118 games with Pirates 1952, most he ever played in one campaign. Hit .273. Again traded 6/4/53, to Chicago NL. Cubs sent him to Giants 9/8/54 on waivers. In five games, after which Garagiola through as major leaguer.

Following year began broadcasting for Cardinals over radio and TV. This led to his joining NBC team for "Game of Week." Also broadcast World Series for NBC. Two years did play-by-play for Yankees. After varied other assignments for NBC, was many years on "Today Show." Also on "Monitor," "Sale of the Century," various sports programs. Author of *Baseball Is a Funny Game*, 1960.

GARCIA, EDWARD MIGUEL (Mike) P-BR-TR. B. 11/17/23, San

Gabriel, Calif. 6'1", 198 Nicknamed "Bear" because of his bearlike build. Bear of a pitcher for Cleveland Indians, especially over four-year period 1951–54 when he captured 79 victories, lost 41. His ERA of 2.64, when he won 19 and lost eight, 1954, led AL pitchers in effectiveness. Had 20–13 mark, 1951, followed by 22–11 and 18–9.

Mike started at Appleton, Wisconsin State League, 1942, then had three years in military service. At Bakersfield, California League, 1946, won 22, lost nine, leading league in strikeouts and effectiveness. Had 2.56 ERA. At Wilkes-Barre, Eastern League, 1947, had 17–10 record. Briefly with Cleveland, 1948 but spent most of year with Oklahoma City, Texas League, with 19–16 mark. In his first full season in majors, Mike 14–5 for Indians, 1949. Then, after breaking even in 22 decisions, 1950, began his highly successful four-year span. Mike dropped below break-even marks next two seasons, then had 12–8 season, 1957. Sore arm, 1958, and was in just six games. Moved to Chicago AL for 1960 and Washington AL for 1961, but his effectiveness never returned and he was through as big leaguer.

Garcia won 142 games in AL, all for Indians. Lost 97, all but one while with Cleveland. Finished with ERA of 3.27 in 2174-2/3 IP. Struck out 1117 and walked 719 in his 428 major league games, 111 of which were complete.

Mike's only WS appearance, 1954, with Cleveland, was not stellar: in five innings allowed six hits, walked four, struck out four, permitted three earned runs, charged with one loss; ERA 5.40.

GARDELLA, DANIEL LOUIS (Tarzan) OF-BL-TL. B. 2/26/20, Bronx, N.Y. 5'8", 170. When Danny Gardella's suit against organized baseball reached U.S. Supreme Court in late 1940s, consternation among baseball magnates reached such a pitch that they paid him $60,000 to drop his case. Danny might have held out for more—he was suing for $300,000. But at time, ex-New York Giant outfielder was supporting himself, wife and child by working as orderly in New York hospital. Had Gardella won his case in Supreme Court, organized baseball would have been thrown into chaos, since fate of reserve clause hung in balance. Gardella claimed reserve clause violated Sherman and Clayton anti-trust laws; further, that his suspension under terms of reserve clause deprived him of his livelihood, destroyed his ability as major league player. In 1946, Danny, like many other major leaguers, defied baseball's reserve clause and jumped to Mexican "outlaw" baseball headed by Pasquel brothers. Commissioner Happy Chandler suspended jumpers for five years. Jumpers included Mickey Owen, Sal Maglie, Fred Martin, Max Lanier; 18 in all. Before long most of jumpers became disillusioned with playing conditions in Mexico; some claimed Pasquel brothers welched on their promises. So most jumpers wanted back in organized baseball.

With five-year suspension preventing their return, some entered suit against organized baseball. Then, with Mexican threat removed, several players returned to fold, with Chandler giving general amnesty June 1949. Lanier and Martin reportedly received $5000 cash apiece to drop their case against baseball. Presumably Gardella received similar offer. But he continued his legal battle, getting his case as far as top level in American legal system. That was when organized baseball upped its offer to $60,000, which Gardella accepted in October 1949. Gossip had it that each of 16 major league teams put $5000 into kitty to settle Gardella suit out of court. This was denied. Danny, however, some years later, said he netted just $29,000 from settlement. Rest went to his lawyer. In any case, baseball's reserve clause had no more serious threats until Flood suit and agitation by Major League Baseball Players Association, headed by Marvin Miller, in 1970s. When Gardella case settled, Giants agreed to give him his unconditional release. St. Louis Cardinals gave him contract for $5000 to play for them in 1950. This reportedly was $1000 more than his contract with Giants for 1945 season. After all this litigation settled, Gardella appeared in just one major league game—for Cardinals as pinch hitter; unsuccessful. Then they sent him to their Houston farm club in Texas League 4/26/50. Danny didn't click in minors and was hitting .211 against Texas League pitching. Cardinals gave unconditional release 6/20/50. Received 30 days' severance pay on release and headed back to New York.

Gardella's legal fight against baseball brought him far more notoriety than his abilities as ball player warranted. Could hit fairly well, but atrocious outfielder. Played 121 games for Giants in 1945. Slapped 18 homers, drove in 71 runs, with .272 average. In 1944 had played 47 games with Giants with 6 homers, 14 RBI. When he quit majors, had lifetime average of .267 for 169 games, with 24 homers, 12 doubles, 3 triples among his 145 hits; scored 74 runs, drove in 85, stole 2 bases.

Danny's muscles showed so much that he acquired nicknames "Tarzan" and "Little Atlas." Worked as athletic teacher and body builder in Manhattan gymnasium. Player in minors, 1939, at Beckley, W. Va. Later played at Newport, Ark., Fulton, Ky., Shelby, N.C., Wilson, N.C., and Jersey City. While with Arkansas team Gardella decided to go fishing one morning. Came to railroad bridge about 100 feet long. Half way across he heard train coming. Instead of hurrying to other end of bridge, Danny decided to hang onto iron bar below bridge and let train pass over him. Train wasn't fast passenger train, which could have crossed bridge in few seconds, but slow freight. Danny had to hang on for dear life several minutes. When freight train finally got past, Gardella scrambled back on top of structure. Arms were practically paralyzed. Couldn't play important ball game that afternoon. That ended his brief stay in Newport. Manager told him to get moving. Next stop was Fulton.

Another stunt of Gardella's took place in Buffalo, N.Y. Danny, with Jersey Giants, had Nap Reyes as roommate. While Reyes was taking shower, Gardella penned farewell suicide note on mirror in bedroom. When Reyes came out of shower, read note and found window open, he assumed that Danny had jumped.

Reyes then left room to tell his teammates about apparent tragedy. Gardella then crawled back from ledge outside window, went down to lobby and jokingly greeted mourning teammates.

GARR, RALPH ALLEN (Road Runner) OF-BL-TR. B. 12/12/45, Ruston, La. 5'11", 185. June 18, 1967, should be red-letter day in history of Atlanta Braves. That day Scout Mel Didier signed Ralph Garr, who in 1971 proved himself one of finest young players in majors. Finished with second-highest batting average in majors, .343. Then, to prove it was no fluke, hit .325 in 1972, again second-best average in big leagues. Speedy colorful "Road Runner" stole 30 bases in his first full season in NL, then pilfered 25 in 1972. Broke into NL in 1968; played just 11 games with Braves that year, but his first stolen base in majors was theft of home.

Garr seems synonymous with spectacular. As second baseman for Grambling College in Louisiana, 1967, won batting championship in National Association of Intercollegiate Athletics with .568 average. Played 58 games with Austin, Texas League, that summer, hitting .274. Following year had .293 mark with Shreveport, Texas League, leading circuit with 35 stolen bases in 127 games. Eleven games with Braves that same season.

In 1969–70 Garr spent most of both seasons at Richmond, International League. Led league in hitting both years, with .329, then .386; also led that loop in stolen bases both years with 63 in 1969 and 39 in 1970. Also with Braves briefly both years. Then came his sensational first full season in NL, when he led circuit in sacrifice bunts; had four hits in single game seven times; made three hits in game 19 times. Played winter ball in Dominican Republic during off-seasons. In 1970–71 broke Dominican League record by hitting .457. Garr missed being named to NL All-Star squads, 1971–72. But in 1971 led all write-in candidates for spot.

When 1973 season started Ralph's major league totals showed 358 games with .328 average. Scored 215 times, made 434 hits, with 50 doubles, six triples, 21 homers, 107 RBI. Owned 62 stolen bases in NL.

GARVER, NED FRANKLIN P-BR-TR. B. 12/25/25, Ney, Ohio. 5'10", 190. Ned Garver was only pitcher in history of majors to win 20 games for club that lost 100 games during same season, 1951 St. Louis Browns. In 14 years in AL never pitched for first-division club; in 11 of those years his team ended sixth or lower. Still won 129 games, losing 157. One can only speculate what record he could have had if just a few of teams had finished in contending position.

Browns finished sixth when Garver as rookie was 7–11, 1948. Then Browns followed with two seventh-place clubs. In 1951 his record was 20–12, with 3.73 ERA, although his teammates finished eighth with 102 losses, 52 victories.

Then in August 1952, when Browns were en route to slightly higher finish—seventh—Garver was traded to Detroit Tigers, who finished last. However, Tigers managed to rise to sixth, 1953, and had three fifth-place finishes. Garver then found himself with Kansas City AL, 1957,58,59, for three seventh-place windups. Kansas City was eighth in 1960; then fates sent Garver to Los Angeles AL, another eighth-placer. His only consolation in final season was that there were 10 clubs in AL, 1961, first year of expansion.

Garver started out at Newark, Ohio, 1944, 21–8. Then pitched for Elmira and Toledo, 1945; San Antonio, 1946–47, before joining Browns. Ned's best ERA in AL was 2.82 while pitching for Tigers, 1954, when he won 14, lost 11. In 1950 he tied for most complete games pitched in AL, and led in this respect, 1951.

Finished with 2477-1/3 IP in majors, ERA of 3.73, 881 strikeouts and 881 walks, with total of 18 shutouts. Now personnel and industrial relations director for food company in his native town, Ney.

GARVEY, STEVE PATRICK 3B-BR-TR. B. 12/22/48, Tampa, Fla. 5′10″, 190. Steve Garvey, in minors, displayed power that caused Manager Walter Alston to hang onto him when Los Angeles Dodgers made numerous personnel changes during off-season, 1972–73. At Albuquerque, in 1969, drove in 85 runs in 83 games; at Spokane, 1970, drove in 87 runs in 95 contests. While used mostly at third base with Dodgers, may see plenty of service at first base or in outfield, depending on how other teammates fare in field and at bat.

Garvey attended Michigan State, jumped into pro ball at Ogden, Utah, in Pioneer League, 1968, hit .338 with 20 homers, 59 RBI. At Albuquerque following summer average was .373, with 14 home runs; also played three games with Dodgers that year. Spent most of 1970 with Spokane, Pacific Coast League, where he clipped ball at .319 pace. Started year with Los Angeles, but sent down after going 23 times with just two hits. Returning from Spokane, finished 1970 with Dodgers, hitting .370 down stretch. However, NL average for year was only .269.

In 1971 out of action with injured left hand and had to have surgery. Played 81 games and hit .227, with seven homers. In 1972 hit .269 in 96 games, with nine homers, 30 RBI; so went into 1973 with .254 average for 214 major league games.

GASTON, CLARENCE EDWIN (Cito) OF-BR-TR. B. 3/17/44, San Antonio, Tex. 6'4", 210. Clarence Gaston missed numerous games in 1972 due to torn ligaments in right ankle. Injury came as he was hit in left arm by pitch by Billy Champion; tried to avoid being hit. This and other injuries plagued him but he looks back with pleasure on performance as pinch hitter 6/14/72 in Chicago. Hit grand-slam home run off Ferguson Jenkins. Had seven homers for year; seventh one enabled San Diego Padres to beat Don Gullett of Cincinnati Reds by 1–0 score.

Gaston originally signed with Milwaukee Braves; got his first pro experience at Binghamton in New York–Pennsylvania League, 1964. Wore uniforms of Greenville, S. C.; West Palm Beach, Fla.; Batavia, N. Y.; Austin, Tex.; Shreveport, La.; and Richmond, Va. Joined Atlanta Braves, 1967 in time for nine games. Spent following summer in minors, but was recalled by Braves and landed with Padres in expansion draft 10/14/68. Best season with Padres was 1970 when he hit .318 in 146 games. Dropped to .228 following year, then came back with .269 mark in 1972; all of which meant that at start of 1973 season owned .263 batting average for 536 major league games; 55 of 499 hits were homers; also had 64 doubles, 26 triples; scored 200 runs, drove in 227.

GEHRIG, HENRY LOUIS (Iron Horse) 1B-BL-TL. B. 6/19/03, New York, N.Y. D. 6/2/41, Riverdale, N.Y. 6'1", 212. If competition for young ball players had been keener half century ago Lou Gehrig probably would have been member of Cubs or Giants instead of spending his entire major league career with Yankees. Gehrig, age 16, slugged home run over right field fence at Chicago's Wrigley Field during intercity competition between High School of Commerce (Lou's School), New York, playing against Lane Tech of Chicago. Fans amazed but apparently no major league scouts heard of feat.

A year later, 1921, unimpressive workout with Giants in Polo Grounds. Entered Columbia University. Needed money for education. Got job with Hartford, Eastern League, playing under assumed name, Lewis. Hit .261, 12 games; one double, two triples, no homers. Enough pro ball for while. Lou suspended from freshman sports but in 1922 played fullback on Columbia's grid squad. In 1923, pitcher and first baseman on Columbia's baseball club.

Paul Krichell, Yankee scout, stumbled onto Gehrig. When one appointment was canceled, scout decided to journey to New Brunswick, N.J., to see Rutgers and Columbia play. Arranged for Gehrig to work out with Yankees. Slugging impressive. Yanks gave him $1500 bonus to sign. Optioned to Hartford. Hit .304, 59 games, slugging 24 homers. Recalled in September. Late that month, their first baseman, Wally Pipp, broke couple of ribs. Gehrig subbed for him in nine games, pinch hit in four others. Hit .423, one home run. Manager Huggins wanted to use him in World Series against Giants; McGraw would not consent to waiving rule against use of men not on squad September 1.

Yanks again optioned Gehrig to Hartford, 1924. Burned up Eastern League—.369 average in 134 games, with 40 doubles, 13 triples, 40 home runs. Also ten games with Yanks, going 6 for 12.

On 6/1/25, when Pipp complained of headache, Gehrig went to first base for Yanks. Date marked start of most amazing endurance record in baseball history. Never missed another league game until after he had played on 4/30/39! Almost fourteen years, 2130 consecutive games! In July 1934 suffered attack of lumbago, but hobbled out to bat as leadoff man (usually batted cleanup). Singled, then retired for pinch runner, keeping record intact.

Led AL in homers twice, tied with Ruth another season. Led AL in RBI four times, tied for lead another year. Despite averages above .370 three times, did not lead AL any of those years. His .363, however, led pack in 1934. His 184 RBI, 1931, set AL record. Holds major league record for most grand slams, 23. Hit four home runs consecutively 6/3/32, first time in history of AL. Did not win top headlines on sports pages—that day Giant manager John McGraw resigned.

Gehrig destined to play on same team with, and to be overshadowed in many respects by, Babe Ruth. Gehrig wound up career with 493 homers; Ruth, 714. Ruth finished with .342 lifetime average, two better than Gehrig. Babe flamboyant, colorful performer; Gehrig steady, workmanlike, effective technician. Ruth dramatically flouted almost all known training rules. Lou observed regulations and caused no trouble. Despite regular habits, Lou never reached 38th birthday; cut down by amyotrophic lateral sclerosis.

Gehrig MVP 1927, 31, 34, 36. World Series debut 1926 against Cardinals. Hit .348 in seven games; two doubles. Following year Yanks swept Pittsburgh in four. Gehrig hit .308, two doubles, two triples, no homers. In 1928, four homers, one double, one single in eleven times at bat, nine RBI, as Bombers again swept Series; Cardinals their victims. Lou's average .545. Another sweep, Cubs, 1932. Gehrig merely hit .529, three homers, double, eight RBI. In Series of 1936, 37, 38—.292, .294, .286 marks, only one homer.

Gehrig's AL career totals: 2164 games, 8001 AB, 1888 runs, 2721 hits, 535 doubles, 162 triples, 493 homers, 1991 RBI and .340 average. World Series totals: 34 games in 7 Series, 119 times at bat, 30 runs, 43 hits, 8 doubles, 3 triples, 10 homers, 35 RBI, .361 average. Series fielding almost perfect, one error in 322 chances, for .997 average. His AL fielding mark for career, .991.

Lou basically quiet, almost self-effacing man, but capable of standing up for what he thought right. During 1932 Series Lou, captain of Yanks, took issue with veteran NL umpire Bill Klem over strike call. "Get back there, you big lout, take care of your job and I'll take care of mine," bellowed Klem. Then in fourth and final game of Series, Klem umpiring on bases. Gehrig came to bat. Klem had stationed himself on first base side of second. Lou waved to Klem several times to move to other side of bag or elsewhere. Klem never budged. Gehrig smashed drive straight at Klem. Bill had to jump quickly to keep legs from being cut from under him. Short time later Gehrig and Klem exchanged remarks. Eventually Gehrig complained to Judge Landis that Klem had insulted him. Landis discussed matter with Klem, but no further repercussions.

Hollywood came up with movie about Gehrig, *The Pride of the Yankees*. One place showed Gehrig as love-sick young man. Opposing batsman hit ball to Gehrig while Lou gazing into grandstand, making eyes at his fiancée. Ball went through Gehrig's legs for error. Impossible! On field Gehrig all business; never would have allowed distraction in stands to hurt his play.

Not long after Gehrig removed himself from Yankee lineup, 1939, trip to Mayo Clinic, Rochester, Minn., indicated his ailment was incurable. Spent rest of season on Yankee bench, then when could no longer walk, served as city parole commissioner for Mayor LaGuardia. Yanks had "day" for Gehrig 7/4/39, Yankee Stadium, before 61,808. Gehrig told fans he believed himself "luckiest guy in world" to have played for Yankees.

That same year Gehrig voted into Hall of Fame. In 1941, after Gehrig's death, Yankees retired his uniform, No. 4, and set up monument to him in center field. Twelve years later, New York City unveiled plaque in his honor at his birthplace, 309 East 94 Street.

GEHRINGER, CHARLES LEONARD   2B-BL-TR. B. 5/11/03, Fowlerville, Mich. 5′11½″ 185. Gehringer did job so well, effortlessly, that they called him "Mechanical Man." Repeatedly led AL second basemen in putouts, assists, fielding average. Hitting consistently good, .321 major league average. Hit .321 in 20 World Series games, .500 in six All-Star games. In stretch of 14 seasons hit better than .300 in 13 of them—missing magic mark by only two points one year. Led AL in hitting 1937, .371. MVP same season.

Major league totals: 2323 games, 1773 runs, 2839 hits, 574 doubles, 146 triples, 184 homers, 1427 RBI.

Fowlerville roughly 30 miles from Detroit. Gehringer as high school student revered Tiger players of that era. Sluggers included Bob Veach, Harry Heilmann, Cobb. Ty was manager. Friend of Veach saw Gehringer play. Veach arranged for tryout. Cobb so impressed he immediately went to front office, even though in uniform, requesting Gehringer be given contract. Farmed to London, Michigan-Ontario League, 1924;

.292 in 112 games. Five games with Detroit same season batting .545 with six hits in eleven trips. Toronto, International League, 1925; .325 in 155 games. Eight games with Tigers same season, .167 average. Regular 1926, hitting .277, starting string of 16 seasons taking part in over 100 games. Raised average to .317, 1927. From then on, respected hitter until 1941 when average dropped to .220 in 127 games. Hit .267 in 45 games 1942, when became coach. Entered U. S. Navy after 1942 season. Served in physical fitness program near San Francisco, rising to rank of lieutenant commander at end of war. Back in Detroit, devoted full time to sales agency supplying auto manufacturers with upholstery buttons, other items used in car interiors.

W. O. Briggs, Tiger owner, persuaded Gehringer to become general manager, and vice president 8/10/51. Resigned as general manager 10/53. Continued as vice president until 1959. Started Fred Hutchinson on career as manager, 1952.

Gehringer says Ty Cobb coached him great deal. Highlights of career included homer off Dizzy Dean, fifth game 1934 World Series, giving Tigers Series lead in 3–1 victory, though Cards later won Series four games to three. Helped Tigers win 1935 Series from Cubs. On "day" when 500 Fowlerville fans honored Gehringer, facing George Pipgras, Yankee pitcher, slugged homer on first trip to plate. Got three more hits same game then stole home. (Fans gave him righthanded golf clubs though he played lefthanded. Learned to play righthanded, generally shooting in 70s.) Often stole third, claiming it easiest base to steal. Hall of Fame 1949.

Continues business dating back to playing days, supplying auto factories with wide variety of accessories, with office in Birmingham, Mich., ten miles from downtown Detroit.

GELBERT, CHARLES MAGNUS OTT   SS-BR-TR. B. 1/26/06, Scranton, Pa. D. 1/13/67, Easton, Pa. 5'11", 172. Gelbert's major league career short, blasted by hunting accident 11/32. But for this, probably would have been one of game's great shortstops. Instead, became outstanding college baseball coach.

Parents gave him name, Magnus Ott Gelbert. He decided to use father's name, Charles, since elder Gelbert had been All-American football player at Pennsylvania. Cardinal scout Charles Kelchner signed him for St. Louis farm club, Syracuse, International League, 1926. Played six games there, 1926–27. Optioned to Topeka, Western Association, 1927, .286 in 45 games. Rochester, International League, 1928, .340 in 164 games.

Regular Cardinal shortstop 1929; averaged .281 for four seasons, with high-water mark .304, 1930. Played errorless ball 1930 World Series, leading Redbird attack with .353. In 1931 Series set record for best fielding average in seven-game Series, accepting 42 chances without an error. Hit .261 for Series. Lifetime batting average .267 in 876 major league games.

After accident, which tore away muscles and part of calf of leg, Gelbert could not play for two years. Previously fast on feet, now slowed down tremendously. Utility infield roles with Cards 1935–36, Reds 1937, Tigers 1937, Señators 1939–40, Red Sox 1940. Coach, Montreal, International League, briefly. Became baseball coach, Lafayette College, Pennsylvania, 1945, also assistant football coach, assistant basketball coach. Over 21-year stretch his Lafayette teams took seven postseason tournaments, five titles in District II, NCAA, winning over 300 victories those years. Battled, eventually won right, to have college coach go to coaching lines on diamond.

GENTILE, JAMES EDWARD (Diamond Jim) 1B-BL-TL. B. 6/3/34, San Francisco, Calif. 6'4", 215. Jim Gentile hit 179 home runs during his major league career, mark pretty far down from Babe Ruth's record 714. But Jim hit two grand slam homers in two consecutive innings 5/9/61, something Babe never did. Gentile was first major leaguer to hit grand slam four-masters in two consecutive times at bat. Since then Jim Northrup equaled this feat 6/24/68. In 1961, also equaled major league record for most homers with bases loaded during one season, five. Generally remembered for slugging, he led AL first basemen in double plays, 1962, and in fielding average, 1963.

Jim started pro ball, 1952, at Santa Barbara, and changed uniforms repeatedly en route to majors; Pueblo, Mobile, Fort Worth, Montreal, Spokane, St. Paul all had Gentile briefly. So did Dodgers, first at Brooklyn, then at Los Angeles. But he didn't make grade until 1960, when he played 138 games for Baltimore Orioles, hit .292, drove in 98 runs, and slammed 21 homers. Following year he blasted 46 round-trippers and drove in 141 runs, with .302 average. From then on pitchers evidently kept him partially in check, as his average hovered around .250 mark rest of his career. Homer production fell to 33,24,28,17, then 9.

Gentile had four years at Baltimore, one at Kansas City AL, 1964. Traded to Houston NL 6/4/65. Divided 1966 between Houston and Cleveland and then bowed out with .260 major league average in 936 games. Had 549 RBI. Struck out quite often, four times going over 100 mark during season, and finished with 663 whiffs. His 759 hits included 113 doubles, six triples, and aforementioned 179 homers. Scored 434 times. Never got into WS, but took part in four All-Star games as AL first baseman—two singles in 11 trips for .182 average.

GENTRY, GARY EDWARD P-BR-TR. B. 10/6/46, Phoenix, Ariz. 6', 183. Gentry hasn't lived up to early scouting reports that he was potentially "another Tom Seaver." But won several important games for N.Y. Mets. One of these was contest that clinched divisional title for 1969 "miracle" Mets. Also won one of Mets' four victories in WS that fall, defeating powerful Baltimore Orioles. Traded to Atlanta Braves 11/1/72 after 7–10 record for Mets in 1972.

As youth, Gentry was football end, basketball star, and sensational pitcher. Captured 16 straight games for Arizona State, including two tournament games in college WS, taken by his team, 1967. Struck out 229 men in 174 innings, one of best strikeout records ever in collegiate history.

Gary has had to control fiery temper, though this has been difficult. Repeatedly has thrown glove in anger when things went wrong for him. Also has demonstrated ire when an outfielder misjudged fly ball. Teammates said he had to learn to "grow up." Late Mgr. Gil Hodges used to tell him to channel his fury into next pitch. There are signs that Gentry is doing this.

Gentry spent 1967 at Williamsport and 1968 at Jacksonville. Stuck with Mets, 1969; had 13–12 record with 3.42 ERA. In 1970 it was 9–9, with 3.69 ERA, and in 1971, 12–11, with 3.24.

Thus Gentry started 1973 season having played in 131 games, 121 of which he started. Completed just 22 of them, with 41–42 record. In 789 innings owned 3.56 ERA, with 563 strikeouts against 324 walks allowed.

In that WS game, 1969, Gentry hurled shutout ball until seventh inning. When he loaded bases with walks, Ryan replaced him, with two outs. Mets won ball game 5–0.

GERBER, WALTER H. (Spooks) SS-BR-TR. B. 8/18/91, Columbus, Ohio. D. 6/19/51, Columbus, Ohio. 5'10", 152. Wally Gerber tried for Honus Wagner's shortstop job at Pittsburgh when veteran star was beginning to slow down, but didn't quite make it. That was in 1914–15. But he came back to majors, 1917, with St. Louis Browns and became dependable regular with them for about decade.

Gerber averaged .256 for his 1521 major league games, but during most of his time with Browns was in .270–.280 range; could be depended upon for timely hits, although he often batted eighth in lineup. One of his blows was called "$18,000 hit," because it came in crucial game late in 1925 season against Detroit Tigers. It meant difference between third-place money for Brownies and no bonus at all for finishing fourth. It gave Browns one-game margin. By time money was divided up among his teammates, Gerber collected just few hundred dollars, but in those days that wasn't "hay."

Wally started out in Ohio State League at Marion, home town of President Warren Harding, 1910. Later played for Akron and Columbus, reaching Pirates 1914. Back to Columbus, 1916–17, then to Browns, for whom he toiled until early 1928. Traded to Boston Red Sox, and dropped out of majors after 1929 season. In four consecutive games in 1923, Gerber handled 48 chances at shortstop without error. This set record for majors to that time. For a while Gerber was considered best shortstop in AL. Played for St. Paul, American Association, 1929. Later umpired in Mid-Atlantic League, 1936–37. Then back to Columbus, where he served as men's supervisor in City Recreation Department. Ill health forced him to retire from this work, 1949.

GIBBS, JERRY DEAN (Jake) C-BL-TR. B. 11/7/38, Grenada, Miss. 6′, 180. Jake Gibbs left Yankees after 1971 season to become head baseball coach and chief football recruiter for alma mater, Mississippi. Still has distinction of having received more money—over $100,000—to sign than any other Yankee got as bonus.

Jake signed up 5/26/61 after becoming All-American infielder and All-American quarterback at Ole Miss. But Yankees wanted him to catch. Actually took part in only one game in majors as third baseman. Rest of time was catcher, considered by many one of finest reserve backstops in league. Catching didn't come easy. Gibbs swears that when he first tried it in spring of 1962 it cost him four broken fingers and broken arm.

Gibbs farmed out to Richmond 1961, 62, 63, 64, to Toledo 1965. Four of those years had brief stays with Yankees. Finally stayed with Yanks, 1965–71. Caught 121 games 1968, 99 in 1967. Used sparingly other seasons.

Jake missed playing in World Series. Was all set to, 1964, when he returned to big city after summer in Richmond. Broke finger in 13th inning, last game of season. Gibbs looks on 1970 season as one of his best. Hit .301 in 49 games; got eight homers in only 153 at bats. Had two homers in one game, 8/11/70, and seven times knocked in runs which gave Yankees victory.

Major league totals: 538 games, 382 hits in 1,639 at bats, .233 average, 157 runs, 53 doubles, 8 triples, 25 homers, 145 RBI.

GIBSON, GEORGE (Moon) C-BR-TR. B. 7/22/80, London, Ontario. D. 1/25/67, London, Ontario. 5′11½″, 190. George Gibson has distinction of being only Canadian ever to manage big league teams. Two cracks at managing Pirates: 1920 to mid-1922, 1932–34. Also managed Cubs briefly, 1925.

Gibby started out in Hudson River League, 1903, with Kingston team. After 32 games and .322 average, advanced to Buffalo, Eastern League (later named International), same season. Montreal, Eastern League, 1904, part of 1905, moving up to Pittsburgh for 44 games later in year. Soon regular catcher, staying with Pirates until 8/5/16. With

Giants thereafter until 1918, when played his last four games in majors. Major league totals: 1213 games over 14 seasons, .236 batting average.

Gibson behind plate for all games in 1909 World Series which Pittsburgh won from Detroit, four games to three. Battery mate for Babe Adams, who won three of those games. Gibson hit .240, scoring two runs, batting in two, stealing two bases.

As manager, led Pirates to fourth place, 1920, second place, 1921. That was year his club blew big lead after Labor Day, losing out to Giants. During 1922 season replaced by Bill McKechnie. Team finished third. Gibson coaching Cubs 1925 when club came up with one of its many noble experiments, naming Walter ("Rabbit") Maranville to managership midseason, replacing Bill Killefer. Maranville, veteran playboy shortstop, had about two hilarious, wild, inebriated months as pilot before being fired. Gibson tried to pick up pieces rest of season. Cubs finished last. Back with Pirates 1932, Gibson's team came in second. Again runner-up, 1933. In 1934 club faltered, Gibson replaced by Pie Traynor. Pittsburgh finished fifth.

GIBSON, ROBERT (Hoot) P-BR-TR. B. 11/9/35, Omaha, Nebr. 6'1", 195. Winningest pitcher in history of St. Louis Cardinals. Jesse Haines, Hall of Famer, won 210 games for Redbirds, record that stood until Gibson surpassed it, 6/21/72. Walter Johnson only major league hurler to fan more hitters during career.

Bob won two Cy Young Awards. Set various WS records, including 17 strikeouts in one game. Hit numerous home runs, including two in WS. But was approaching his 36th birthday before pitching first no-hit game 8/14/71. Besides his many records, Gibson has surmounted such difficulties as chronic trouble with left knee, arthritis in right elbow, two broken ankles, and disabling torn thigh muscle. Was fine enough basketball player to make grade for several months with Harlem Globetrotters during younger years. Acted as sports commentator in NL playoffs. Owns radio station in Omaha. Commands $150,000 contract from Cardinals.

Bob started out modestly, receiving $4000 to sign with Cardinal system, 1957, after attending Creighton. Four years later was winning pitcher in majors; has kept it up ever since. During his apprenticeship, pitched for Omaha; Columbus (Ga.), Rochester, with couple of spells with parent club. Won 13, lost 12 in his first full year with Redbirds, 1961. In each of next five seasons improved his victory total each year, having 21–12 in 1966. In 1964 Gibson won nine out of his last eleven starts and had 19–12 record. Cardinals won pennant on last day of season, then took on Yankees in WS. Bob started second game of set, but was defeated by Mel Stottlemyre. Gibson allowed four runs, struck out nine, six of them in first three innings.

In fifth game, Gibson had Yankees 2–0 in ninth inning. An error by Cardinal shortstop Dick Groat put Mickey Mantle on base. Pepitone then smashed vicious drive that hit Gibson and bounded away. Catlike, with amazing speed, Gibby pounced on rolling ball and, despite intense pain, fired to first base in time to retire Pepitone by eyelash. This saved game for Cardinals since Tom Tresh followed with homer that tied game and sent it into overtime. Redbirds won in 10th on McCarver's homer. This was first of seven consecutive WS victories for Gibson, which stands as all-time record. Gibson also won rubber game of that WS and chalked up total of 31 strikeouts during classic.

In 1967 Bob suffered broken leg in midseason when hit by line drive and was on disabled list until end of August. Had 13–7 record that year. Then followed up with dazzling WS effort against Boston Red Sox. Won opener by 2–1 score, striking out 10. Blanked Sox 6–0 in fourth game, with six strikeouts. Won seventh and decisive game 7–2, with 10 Boston players whiffing. His victories in three games tied several existing records. ERA for set was 1.00. In 1968 Gibson set NL record for lowest ERA for any pitcher hurling at least 200 innings: just 1.12 earned runs per nine-inning game. Was 22–9. Won first of his two Cy Young Awards. Helped Cardinals win another pennant. In WS drew Detroit's Denny McLain as his opponent in opening game. It was Gibson all way; Bob won 4–0, set new WS strikeout record with 17. This broke mark of Sandy Koufax, set in 1963. Gibby came back for 10–1 victory in fourth game, thus winning his seventh consecutive WS decision. Also hit homer, his second in WS. Thus became first pitcher in history with two WS round-trippers to his credit. Bob lost final game 4–1, giving Detroit Series four games to three. By this time Gibson had 7–2 record WS, 81 innings, 17 earned runs, 92 strikeouts, 17 walks, ERA 1.89. Those 35 strikeouts Bob chalked up in 1968 WS were new high-water mark. His overall total of 92 strikeouts was second only to mark set by Whitey Ford with 94. Took Ford 22 games to make his mark; Gibson nine! In three WS Gibson started nine games, completed eight. Five times he struck out 10 or more batsmen, more than any other pitcher.

On NL All-Star squads 1962,65,66,67,68,69,70,72. In 1966 did not play because of injury.

Bob's ability to fan opposing batsmen can be seen by total of 2786 strikeouts to his credit at start of 1973 season. This was accomplished in 3341 innings. At same time had allowed 1113 walks and owned 2.79 ERA. In 1972 was still adding to his big total of career shutouts, and passed 50 mark of Three Finger Brown. Still far away from Grover Cleveland Alexander's 90 and Christy Mathewson's 83, however.

Among Bob's other distinctions are following: MVP in NL, 1968; set major league record for most years with 200 or more strikeouts, eight; tied major league record of four strikeouts in one inning; tied NL record for striking out first five batsmen to face him in one game.

In 1972 Gibson lost his first five decisions. Ran into couple of games where rain washed out starting efforts after few innings had been played. Finally got on track. When he eventually won game putting him ahead of Jess Haines' mark, contributed homer to cause—his 19th career homer; had five in 1972, for 22 total in majors. While Bob's record is good in this department, he is still quite a distance behind Wes Ferrell, who had 38 career homers. Gibby posted 19 victories, 11 defeats in 1972, bringing career record to 225 wins, 141 losses.

GIEBELL, FLOYD KARL P-BL-TR. B. 12/10/14, Pennsboro, W. Va. 6'2", 175. King for a Day. TV writers might have called it so if they had written dramatic fiction telling story of Floyd Giebell's performance 9/27/40. With 45,553 fans on hand in Cleveland stadium, unknown pitcher vanquished mighty Bob Feller and clinched pennant for Detroit Tigers.

Giebell had been with Tigers briefly during 1939 season, winning one game, losing one in relief. Then during 1940 had spent most of year at Buffalo without distinguishing himself. Won 15, lost 17 for that International League team, with 3.73 ERA. Giebell had been called up to Tigers late, so late he was ineligible to take part in WS if Detroit won. Had won 13–2 victory over Philadelphia Athletics 9/14/40, but Chubby Dean was loser and the A's were cellar dwellers that year.

When pitchers were announced for crucial game with Indians, experts figured Tigers were saving their ace, Schoolboy Rowe, and "sacrificing" rookie. Nobody expected man from Buffalo to outpitch great Bob Feller, who was having one of his greatest seasons ever. All Bob did in 1940 was win 27 ball games, lead league in effectiveness with ERA of 2.61, lead in strikeouts and in total innings pitched. More than anyone, Feller was principal reason why Indians were still in battle for AL pennant right down to wire. But it was Giebell's day. Allowed six hits—but effectively kept Indians away from plate. With one out in fourth inning, Feller walked Charlie Gehringer. Bob fanned Hank Greenberg but Rudy York sent drive down left field line. Ben Chapman, in left for Cleveland, tried to reach ball; instead it fell into stands. Detroit had two runs. That was all Giebell needed.

Floyd stifled Indians with men on base. Walked to dugout after ninth inning, having clinched pennant for Tigers. Did he dream he would never again win ball game in major leagues?

That was his fate. In 1941 Floyd appeared in 17 games, mostly in relief. Pitched 34-1/3 innings but wasn't effective, as his 6.03 ERA shows. Neither won nor lost. Then back to minors and to oblivion.

Giebell began career, 1938, at Evansville in III League, 18–6, 1.98 ERA. Spent 1939 bouncing from Beaumont to Toledo to Detroit. Won one game, lost one, for Tigers that year. Then shuffled off to Buffalo for 1940. Going to Buffalo again in 1941, Giebell won five games and lost one. In 1942 his mark was 8–6, and in 1943, 12–17. Then Giebell entered armed forces, remaining out of game till after war. Pitched briefly for Syracuse and Dallas, then retired 1949.

Giebell's lifetime record: 3–1, ERA 3.99, 28 games (started 4, finished 2), 67-2/3 innings; walked 42, struck out 30, allowed 78 hits.

GILES, WARREN CRANDALL   Executive. B. 5/28/96, Tiskilwa, Ill. Warren Giles, president emeritus of NL, started out in general contracting business after hitch in U. S. Army in which served as first lieutenant in infantry, World War I. Got involved with Moline, Ill., club, III League; elected president of team, November 1919. First thing Giles did was trade Charlie Dressen, saucy young infielder destined to go far, as manager. Years later Giles found himself general manager at Cincinnati—and Dressen was field manager he inherited. Giles again got rid of Dressen.

In Giles' second year as head of Moline club, team won pennant. He moved to St. Joseph, Mo., Western League, 1923–25, where path crossed that of Branch Rickey, then Cardinal general manager. Rickey hired him to become president of Cards' International League farm at Syracuse, 1926–27. Cardinal farm system beginning to flower about this time. Franchise shifted from Syracuse to Rochester. With Bill Southworth as manager most of time, Rochester team won four consecutive International League pennants.

Giles undoubtedly helped win those flags. Persistently moaned to Rickey about sad state of playing roster at Rochester. Cardinals had to supply players for Houston farm team in Texas League and later Columbus farm in American Association, as well as Giles' club. But Giles on telephone almost every day pleading with Rickey for slugging outfielders, strong-armed pitchers, infielders, catchers. Other Cardinal organization men not so insistent, and none of them compiled record like Giles' four flags in row. In his nine years at Rochester, Giles' team won four pennants, finished second three times, fifth once, seventh once—two Junior World Series titles.

Chance to move to Cincinnati, late 1936, when Larry MacPhail and Powel Crosley, then president of Reds, came to parting of ways. Giles became general manager, Cincinnati. Before 1937 season was ended, Dressen was no longer manager of Reds. Bill McKechnie, who had managed Rochester team briefly in 1929, hired for 1938. After fourth-place finish that year, Giles-McKechnie combination brought two pennants to Cincinnati, 1939,40. Reds suffered humiliation of losing four straight in World Series to Yankees, 1939, but captured 1940 Series from Detroit, four games to three. Under Giles' administration, Reds thereafter finished among also-rans.

When Ford Frick moved into job as baseball commissioner, Giles elected president of NL, 10/8/51. Retired after 1969 season. During that time NL captured ten World Series, lost eight. In annual All-Star games, NL won 17, losing only four.

Among problems Giles wrestled with during his term was major league expansion. NL went from eight teams to ten, then to twelve-team setup with eastern and western divisions. Giles' son, Bill, is executive vice president, Philadelphia NL.

GILES, WILLIAM YALE Executive. B. 9/7/34, Rochester, N.Y. Executive vice president, Philadelphia NL. Supervises overall business and stadium operations, as well as overseeing public and community relations. Son of former president of NL. Made nation's sports pages while operating scoreboard in Houston Astrodome. On one occasion, fans disagreed with ruling by umpire John Kibler. Baseball commissioner Bowie Kuhn in audience. Young Giles flashed question on giant electric scoreboard: "Who is most unpopular man in stadium tonight? A) Bowie Kuhn; B) Pete Rozelle; C) Frankenstein's Monster; D) XXXX XXXXXX." By no coincidence, number of X's equaled number of letters in umpire's name. Kuhn later reprimanded Bill for "ridiculing umpire and making fun of commissioner's office." On another occasion, after same umpire had ejected Houston player from game, scoreboard spelled out, "Kibler did it again." Bill's father, still NL prexy, got his son on long-distance phone. "Who put that message on scoreboard," asked elder Giles. "Whoever it was," replied Bill, "I'll tell him not to do it again." Next day scoreboard message read: "I shall not write messages about umpires—fifty times!"

Bill irked Leo Durocher, among others. Cub manager had gone to mound to remove one of his pitchers in distress. Scoreboard showed player in full uniform, drowning in shower stall. Durocher called stunt "bush" and tore clubhouse phone out by roots. Young Giles retorted that scoreboard is like Durocher—loud and colorful.

Bill graduated from Denison College, Granville, Ohio, 1956, with A.B. in economics. His thesis was 134-page document, *The Economic Aspects of Professional Baseball*. On way to majors, Bill was business manager at Morristown, Tenn., where Cincinnati Reds had Class D team. League folded in three days. Later served as business manager, Nashville, Southern Association, and spent three years in air force as navigator. Became press agent and road secretary for Houston NL, 1962, remaining there until present connection developed with Phillies, 1969.

GILLIAM, JAMES WILLIAM (Junior) Inf.-OF-BRL-TR. B. 10/17/28, 5'11", 175. Only member of Dodger squad who has been wearing

Dodger uniform longer than manager Walter Alston, Junior, one of early black players to make good in majors, joined Brooklyn team 1953. Began fine playing career by taking over second base job. When season was over was voted Rookie of Year then moved into World Series like veteran. Got eight hits off Yankee pitching, including three doubles, two homers. This, however, was just first of seven World Series for Gilliam.

Gilliam didn't waste any time in low minors. Started out with Montreal, International League, 1951, one notch below majors. Hit .287 in 152 games, led league in runs scored, 117; drove in 73, hit 7 homers, stole 15 bases. Following year again led league in run scoring with 111, hit .301, had 112 RBI, 9 homers, 18 stolen bases.

With Dodgers in Brooklyn and Los Angeles, Gilliam, year in and year out, played consistently fine game anywhere on diamond. Played all positions excepting shortstop and battery. Good eye at plate. Drew 100 walks first season in majors, several times walked more than 90 times.

Gilliam was player-coach 1965–66. Has coached since then. Major league totals: 1956 games, 7119 at bats, 1889 hits, .265 average. 304 doubles, 71 triples, 65 homers, 1163 runs, 558 RBI, 203 stolen bases.

In World Series play—39 games, 31 hits in 147 times at bat for .211 average, 15 runs, 12 RBI, 4 stolen bases.

GIONFRIDDO, ALBERT FRANCIS OF-BL-TL. B. 3/8/22, Dysart, Pa. 5'6½", 155. Made one of most sensational catches ever seen anywhere— and in tense atmosphere of WS, before 74,065 witnesses; robbed Hall of Famer Joe DiMaggio of an extra-base hit, and kept powerful Yankees from victory in sixth game of autumn classic 10/5/47. Unforgettable heroics. Fans, sports writers called catch amazing, impossible, unbelievable. With Dodgers enjoying three-run lead, Brooklyn manager Burt Shotton sent Al Gionfriddo to left field as defensive measure in sixth inning. Then in Yankee half of inning Shotton's strategy paid off immediately. Clark batted for Newsom and flied out. Stirnweiss walked. Henrich fouled out to Edwards. Berra singled. With two men on base DiMaggio represented tying run at plate. Jolting Joe slammed first pitch into left field, seemingly miles away from any Dodger outfielder. But Gionfriddo took off with fierce burst of speed, headed in general direction of ball. Then, in desperation, at last instant, leaped high into air, grabbed ball just inside bull pen fence of Yankee Stadium. By this time DiMaggio, near second base, stopped, shook his head, unbelieving. Kicked dirt with his spikes, trotted off to center field, muttering to himself. Catch took place 415 feet from home plate, and would have been home run under ordinary circumstances. Catch is remembered, but Al's contribution to Dodger victory that afternoon also included stolen base in first half of sixth; played important part in Brooklyn rally that gave NL club four runs and put it ahead of Yankees.

That catch off DiMaggio's bat was Gionfriddo's only chance in left field. And when Al trotted off field after game, his name never again appeared in big league box score. That fall, despite his WS performance, Gionfriddo was sent to minors. Gone, but not forgotten.

Gionfriddo's NL career was brief—228 games. His time with Brooklyn was briefer—part of one season, 1947. Al started pro ball at Oil City, Pa., 1941, hitting .334. Following year with same club boosted his average to .348. Military service, 1943. Then had .330 year at Albany, 1944, and went up to Pittsburgh in time for four games that same season. Played 122 games for Pirates, 1945 and hit .284. Dropped to .255 in 64 games, 1946. His 1947 average was .175 for 38 games with Pirates and Dodgers. All this added up to .266 major league average for his career.

Al spent four seasons with Montreal, Brooklyn farm in International League, 1948–51. Dropped down to Fort Worth, Texas League, for 1952. In 1953 managed Drummondville, Quebec, club of Provincial League, also playing. Moved to Newport News that same season as player, then played for Visalia in California League, 1954–56, after which he retired from game.

Gionfriddo scouted for San Francisco Giants, 1960–61. Became insurance agent in Visalia and spent considerable time coaching youngsters, working with Little League and Babe Ruth baseball. More recently owned, operated restaurant, "Al's Dugout," in Goleta, Calif, suburb of Santa Barbara.

GIUSTI, DAVID JOHN, JR.   P-BR-TR. B. 11/27/39, Seneca Falls, N.Y. 5′11″, 203. Roberto Clemente, Sanguillen, Stargell, Robertson, and rest of 1971 Pittsburgh Pirates were vital to success of club. But where would team have finished without Dave Giusti and baffling palm ball? Veteran relief pitcher saved 30 games during season; then, in playoffs saved three wins over San Francisco Giants. Then saved fourth game of WS against Baltimore Orioles.

His ERA for 1971 was creditable 2.93, but in playoffs and WS it couldn't have been improved upon. It was 0.00: 5 IP in playoffs, 5-1/3 in WS. Forged ahead in 1972 with 7–4 mark, 22 saves, 1.92 ERA.

Dave played Little League, Pony League and American Legion baseball and attended Syracuse U., studying physical education. Captain of 1961 team that finished third in College WS. Started his pro career with Jacksonville, Fla., club, 1961, but didn't get his Master's degree until 1967. Briefly with Houston, Texas League, 1961, then Houston, NL, 1962. Oklahoma City, 1962–64, returning to Houston NL 1964. Best season there was 1966 with 15–14 record. St. Louis NL 1969. Pittsburgh since then.

Danny Murtaugh made him into relief pitcher—started only one game in first three years with Pirates. But saved 27 games, 1970, with 3.06 ERA.

Giusti's highlight as starting pitcher came, 1966, when he twirled one-hitter against Giants, facing just 28 men. As 1973 season started, Giusti had pitched in 376 NL games, 35 of them complete. Win total was not impressive, 71–73, but ERA was getting better with age, 3.71.

Natural leader, fine competitor, serves as Pirates' player representative.

GLADDING, FRED EARL (Bear) P-BL-TR. B. 6/28/36, Flat Rock, Mich. 6'1", 225. Fred Gladding pitched in 100 ball games for Houston Astros, 1971–72. During this period was touched just once for home run: by Billy Buckner of Los Angeles Dodgers during 1972.

Fred saved dozen ball games for Astros, 1971, 14 in 1972. As 1973 got under way, Gladding, whose major league career started 1961 with Detroit Tigers, owned 2.94 ERA for his 434 games in big time.

Tigers signed him in 1956 for $4000 bonus; although had several brief trials with them in meantime, did not stick until 1965. Minor league experience in Valdosta, Ga.; Charleston, W. Va.; Birmingham, Augusta, Knoxville, Denver, Syracuse. Though with Detroit only part of 1964, Was 7–4 with them. In first full season was 6–2, with 2.83 ERA. In 1966, 5–0. In 1967, another standout season for effectiveness: had 1.99 ERA with six wins, four losses. Had surgery for bone chips in elbow, 1967.

Gladding traded to Houston NL 11/22/67 as part of deal for Eddie Mathews. Busy reliever since then; in 1970 got into 63 ball games.

GLEASON, WILLIAM J. (Kid) 2B-BL-TR. B. 10/26/66, Camden, N.J. D. 1/2/33, Philadelphia, Pa. 5'7", 158. Kid Gleason had misfortune to manage one of greatest baseball teams—White Sox of 1919. After winning AL pennant, lost World Series to weaker Cincinnati. Eventually truth leaked out that eight members of Sox had schemed to lose Series and collect payoffs from gamblers who bet on underdogs. So White Sox of 1919 now remembered as "Black Sox"—at least eight of them are. Gleason had players like "Shoeless" Joe Jackson. Some claim he was greatest hitter who ever lived—regardless of Ruth, Cobb and anyone else. Had terrific pitchers Eddie Cicotte and Claude Williams; Buck Weaver, fine hot corner guardian; Eddie Collins, brilliant second baseman and fine hitter, who was not involved with fix.

Kid managed White Sox again, 1920–23. His 1920 club finished second, as disclosure of crookedness did not wreck team until late that year. But in 1921, bereft of most of his stars who had been banned forever by Judge Landis, White Sox finished seventh. Fifth place 1922, but in 1923 sagged again to seventh.

Gleason never same after 1919 experience. And after 1923, never managed again. Coach, Philadelphia NL, at time of death.

Gleason one of rough-and-ready types whose pro career started back in 1888 with Phils. St. Louis NL 1892–94. Baltimore NL 1894–95. New York NL 1896–1900. Detroit AL 1901–02. Philadelphia NL 1903–08. Played briefly with Chicago AL 1912. Lifetime major league average over 22 seasons, 1966 games, .261. Stole 328 bases.

Got nickname "Kid" early in career. Small, wore cap cocked to one side. Combative, but mellowed in later years and was very helpful to younger players.

GOLDSMITH, FRED ERNEST   P-BR-TR.   B. 5/15/52, New Haven, Conn. D. 3/28/39, Berkley, Mich. 6'1", 195. Fred Goldsmith claimed he invented curve ball. But many say honor belongs to William "Candy" Cummings, who was named to Hall of Fame, 1939. *Sporting News*, bible of baseball world, in 1939 referred to Goldsmith and Cummings as "co-originators" of curve. *Brooklyn Eagle* 8/17/1870 described Goldsmith's exhibition of curve ball on previous day. Account was written by Henry Chadwick, generally recognized as first real baseball writer. Chadwick wrote that Goldsmith's ball "twisted" and "proved to countless spectators that a sphere could cheat natural laws." Poles were set up 45 feet apart, with another one half way between, all in direct line. Goldsmith took his position on left side of chalkline. Plan was to have ball cross chalkline, "circle center pole" and return to same side from which it was thrown before reaching last pole. This was accomplished six or eight times, according to *Eagle*, adding, "What had been an optical illusion now is an established fact."

Goldsmith played semipro ball at Bridgeport, Conn., 1875, and started 1876 at New Haven. During May of that year received fabulous salary of $300 monthly to pitch for Tecumsehs of London, Ontario. Springfield, Mass., 1879 until August, then joined Troy NL club. Chicago NL, 1880–84; Baltimore, American Association, 1884.

Fred had 116 major league victories against 67 defeats during his career. Played considerable time in outfield when not pitching.

GOMEZ, PEDRO (Preston)   Coach-manager.   B. 4/20/23, Central Preston, Oriente, Cuba. 5'11", 185. Like many managers, coaches in recent years, Preston Gomez, former boss of San Diego Padres, played in major leagues very briefly—eight games with Washington Senators, 1944. After that, bounced around minor leagues until 1957 when he began managing. Coach, L.A. Dodgers, 1965-68. When appointed pilot of San Diego Padres 8/29/68, Walter Alston, dean of NL bosses, said of him, "Best coach I ever had." Taking over expansion club, trying to build from scratch, Gomez finished sixth in NL West each of first three years. When Padres got off to miserable start in 1972, Gomez replaced in mid-May by Don Zimmer.

Gomez attended Belen College in Cuba. After his tryout with Senators, journeyed to Buffalo, Vicksburg, New London, Florence (S.C.), Saginaw, Three Rivers, Toledo, Charleston (W. Va.), Havana, Yakima as player. Began managing 1957 at Fresnillo, Mexico; then Mexico City, Havana, Spokane, Richmond. In 1959, piloting Havana, International League, won Junior WS, defeating Minneapolis, American Association. Signed on as coach for Houston Astros, 1973.

GOMEZ, VERNON LOUIS (Lefty) P-BL-TL. B. 11/26/09, Rodeo, Calif. 6'2", 178. Lefty Gomez pitched six WS victories without ever losing decision; won 189 major league games while dropping just 102. Twice led AL in winning percentage, and twice in ERA. And three times led AL in strikeouts. But when he gets up to talk, generally doesn't brag about accomplishments on pitching mound. Instead complains about nonrecognition of his talents as batsman.

Back in All-Star game of 1934, Carl Hubbell struck out Babe Ruth, Gehrig, Foxx, Simmons, and Cronin in succession. Bill Dickey broke string of strikeouts by singling. Then Gomez struck out. Lefty is still perturbed all these years later that hardly anybody recalls he too was a victim of Hubbell's screwball—just like all those other AL sluggers.

Lefty wasn't much of hitter, though he did get 21 safeties in 1937. That was his high-water mark. Claims he had bet with Babe Ruth about his hitting. If Lefty got 10 hits during year, Ruth was to pay him $500. If he didn't get 10 hits, Lefty would have to give Babe $50. Says that on opening day, 1934, he got four hits, really throwing scare into Ruth. "Then I went into a 42-game hitting slump," Gomez tells his audiences. Makes a good story—but Lefty actually made 13 hits in 1934, and we still wonder whether he collected from Babe. Gomez' lifetime batting record shows he made 133 hits in 904 AB, for .147 average.

People who hear Gomez today think of him as humorist. He is that, but his main claim to fame is that he could fire fast ball across plate with sizzling speed despite slim physique. In fact, when Yankees bought him for $35,000, they expected pitcher with much more weight than he actually was carrying at time. Gomez weighed 146 when he first reported to Yanks, but major league meals plus maturing body got weight up to 178 eventually.

Gomez, mixture of Spanish and Irish ancestry, pitched for Salt Lake in Utah-Idaho League, 1928, winning 12, losing 14. Following year he had 18–11 record with San Francisco, then in Pacific Coast League. Also led circuit in effectiveness with 3.44 ERA. Sold to Yankees, Lefty won two, lost five; was farmed out to St. Paul, American Association part of same year, 1930, 8–4. That was all seasoning needed. Was 21–9, with 2.63 ERA, his first full season in majors, 1931. Had 24–7 record following year, then 16–10, 26–5. In 1937 Lefty won 21, dropping 11. His last year as good winner was 1941 when he won 15, lost 5. In all, Lefty hurled 2503 innings in 368 games. Those 189 victories against 102 defeats gave him .649 percentage. Fanned 1468, walked 1095, and had 3.34 ERA. Hall of Fame 1972.

Lefty came to end of line in majors during 1943 season. Yankees sold him to Boston NL in January, but Braves released him 5/19/43 and he signed with Washington. Pitched four innings for Senators, allowed four hits and three earned runs, then called it quits. In his first two seasons as manager of Binghamton, Eastern League, 1946 and 1947, pitched part of one game each year. In final year as Binghamton pilot, 1948, did not pitch.

Gomez's WS performances sparkled. His first game, 1932, against Chicago Cubs, allowed one earned run. In 1936 set he won two decisions from Giants, but he didn't have to struggle. Bombers got 18 runs for him in first game he pitched, and 13 in next. Won two games from Giants in 1937 series, this time giving up one run in one game, and two in another. In 1938 while he won his sixth WS victory, allowed three earned runs. So in seven WS games, had allowed 51 hits, 16 earned runs, fanned 31, and walked 15 for 2.86 ERA.

Lefty is exaggerating when he says he made Joe DiMaggio famous. "They didn't know he could go back on a ball until he played behind me."

Tony Lazzeri had reputation of being highly intelligent ball player. Once when Gomez was pitching and man was on first base, batsman hit to Lefty. Crosetti was covering second base on play. Tony, many yards from bag, was in no position to make any play. But Lefty threw ball to him instead of to Crosetti. Lazzeri demanded an explanation. "You're supposed to be the smartest guy on this ball club," said Lefty. "I wanted to see what you'd do with the ball under these circumstances."

GONZALEZ, MIGUEL ANGEL CORDERO (Mike) C-BR-TR. B. 9/24/92, Havana, Cuba. 6'1", 165. One of earliest Cuban players to make good in majors. Despite years in U.S., spoke colorful broken English. Originated "Good field, no hit" description of weak hitting but fine fielding players. One game with Boston NL 1912. Returned to NL 1914 at Cincinnati. St. Louis NL 1915–18. N.Y. NL 1919–21. St. Louis NL 1924–25. Chicago NL 1925–29. St. Louis NL 1931–32. On occasion played first base and outfield.

Cardinal coach several years in Gas House Gang era. Interim manager for Cardinals during 1938 and 1940 seasons. Probably would have been named regular Cardinal manager had his English been better.

Managed Cuban teams in winter baseball. Lifetime batting average .254 in 1042 NL games. Lives in Cuba.

GOODMAN, IVAL RICHARD   OF-BL-TR. B. 7/23/08, Northview, Mo. 5'11", 165. Ival Goodman "grew up" in Cardinal chain but when was ready to play in majors was sold to Cincinnati. Reported to Reds in spring of 1935 when Powel Crosley was president; Charlie Dressen, manager; and Larry MacPhail, general manager. Remained with Reds through 1942, helping club win two pennants and one WS. Spent 1943 and 1944 with Chicago Cubs.

Goodman hit 30 homers in 1938; had 92 RBI that year, with .292 average. Best season for average was 1939 when Reds won their first pennant since 1919. Hit .323. Led NL in triples 1935, with 18, and again following year with 14. When career ended, Ival had played in 1107 major league games. Got 1104 hits, with 188 doubles, 85 triples, 95 homers, and had 525 RBI. Overall average was .281. Stole 49 bases.

Ival spent first three years in pro baseball in Western Association with three different teams—Shawnee, Fort Smith and Bartlesville, 1930–32. Columbus, Ohio, American Association, 1932; Rochester, International League and Houston, Texas League, 1933. Then after full year with Rochester , 1934, where hit .331 in 140 games, was dealt to Cincinnati.

Goodman's WS record showed .333 average, 1939, when N.Y. Yankees vanquished Reds four straight. In 1940 Ival batted .276 and had five RBI, helping team to 4–3 victory in games over Detroit Tigers. So two WS marks added up to .295 average, with 13 hits in 44 trips, including 3 doubles, 6 RBI, 1 stolen base.

After leaving majors Ival managed Portsmouth, Va., 1945, and led them to first pennant in 30 years. Later managed Dayton, Ohio, and Davenport, Iowa. Then sold chemicals for 25 years before retiring. Blood clot caused right leg to be amputated. Honored at 1972 WS by throwing out first ball for sixth game from box of Commissioner Bowie Kuhn.

GOODMAN, WILLIAM DALE   Inf.-OF-BL-TR. B. 3/22/26, Concord, N.C. 5'11½", 160. AL batting champion, 1950, with .354 average in 110 games for Boston. Played 1623 major league games, but managers never seemed to know where to play him since his hitting was better than his fielding. Had 624 games as second baseman, 406 as first sacker and 330 at third. Also played 111 contests in outfield. His .992 average in 1949, however, was good enough to lead AL first basemen in fielding.

Billy began pro ball, 1944, at Atlanta; hit .336 in 137 games. Spent following year in military, then back to Atlanta with .389 average in 86 games. Up to Red Sox for 1947 but spent most of season at Louisville where his .340 was well up among American Association batsmen. In 1948 Billy was Red Sox regular first baseman; hit .310 in his first full year in majors. Then .298, after which won AL batting crown. Continued above or close to .300 mark rest of his time in Boston, which ended 6/14/57 with trade to Baltimore AL. Orioles sent him to Chicago AL for 1958 and he remained with White Sox until his unconditional release 5/9/62. Signed with Houston NL shortly afterward and played 82 games with Astros that season.

Playing manager, Durham, Carolina League, 1963–64, with .354 and .325 averages as part-time performer. Managed Houston farm team at Cocoa, Fla., 1965. Scout, Red Sox, 1966. Instructor, Kansas City AL farm organization, 1967. Coach, Atlanta Braves, 1968.

Goodman was not power hitter; never got more than four homers during any major league season and wound up with 19, averaging little more than one a year. His overall major league average, however, was .300. Had 299 doubles among his 1691 hits, 44 triples, 591 RBI, 807 runs scored. In his only WS, 1959, played five games as third baseman, got 3 for 13, had .231 average.

GORBOUS, GLEN EDWARD OF-BL-TR. B. 7/8/30, Drumheller, Alberta. 6'2", 175. Glen Gorbous isn't remembered by many people even though he did play 115 major league games, and not too long ago. Outfielder with Cincinnati Reds, 1955, and Philadelphia Phillies, 1955–57. Lifetime average .238. Not much of hitter, and not much speed afoot. But OH, how he could throw! *Sporting News* reports that he made longest throw ever recorded for baseball—445 feet, 10 inches. Was accomplished 8/1/57 at Omaha, Nebr. Gorbous had six-step running start before he let go of ball. This exceeded record held for many years by Sheldon LeJeune, who threw ball 426 feet, 9-1/2 inches at Redland Field, Cincinnati, 10/9/10. On that occasion LeJeune had four trials. On his third attempt, about 15 feet better than his two previous trials, Sheldon reached 401 feet, 4-1/2 inches. Then came his record, which stood until Gorbous came along.

Gorbous had 6 games with Cincinnati in 1955, 91 with Phillies. Hit .244 that year. Following season in 15 games batted .182. Went to bat just twice in 1957, one hit. His 66 hits in majors included 13 doubles, 1 triple, 4 homers, 29 RBI. No stolen bases.

GORDON, JOSEPH LOWELL (Flash) 2B-BR-TR. B. 2/18/15, Los Angeles, Calif. 5'10", 175. Joe Gordon helped five Yankee teams win AL championships and four WS victories; helped Cleveland to pennant and world championship, 1948. But as manager of AL teams was not so successful.

Gordon and Jimmie Dykes were in famous first trade of major league managers in 1960. Joe had bossed Cleveland Indians 1958–59. Then Frank Lane swapped him to Detroit 8/3/60, receiving Jimmie Dykes in his place.

Joe attended U. of Oregon, then joined Oakland, Pacific Coast League, 1936, as shortstop. Hit even .300 in 143 games. Second baseman at Newark, International League, 1937, with .280 mark in 151 contests, with 89 RBI. Timeliness of his hitting was indicated following season, his first with Yanks. Though he hit just .255, drove in 97 runs. While not real power hitter, drove out 20 or more homers per season seven times in AL, reaching 30 one year with Yanks and 32 one year with Indians. On four occasions was able to mark up better than 100 RBI, while his lifetime major league average came to .268 in 1566 games.

Gordon remained with Yankees 1938–46, excepting 1944–45 while he was doing military service. Then traded to Cleveland for Allie Reynolds 10/19/46. Deal worked out well for both clubs. In 1946 Gordon hit .210 for Yankees; then .272 in first year under Lou Boudreau, 1947. In 1948 helped Indians to flag—144 games, .280, 32 homers, 124 RBI. Joe bowed out of Cleveland picture as player after 1950. Playing manager, Sacramento, Pacific Coast League, two years.

Scout, Detroit, 1953–55. Started 1956 as Detroit coach; became manager San Francisco, PCL, 7/9/56, through 1957. Manager, Cleveland, 6/27/58 until August 1960 when traded for Dykes. Piloted Tigers rest of season, then quit. Signed as manager of Kansas City Athletics 10/5/60. Out of that job 6/6/61. Scout and batting instructor Los Angeles AL, 1962–68. Manager, Kansas City Royals, 1969.

Gordon won AL's MVP award 1942, .322 in 147 games, drove in 103 runs, slammed 18 homers. In his first WS, 1938, batted .400 against Chicago NL pitching—one of years when Yanks swept opposition. Hit .500 in 1941 Series against Dodgers. Overall WS average was .243 in 29 games, with 25 hits in 103 AB, 12 runs, 5 doubles, 1 triple, 4 homers, 16 RBI.

As field leader, Gordon's best year was 1959 when his Cleveland club finished second, five games behind Chicago White Sox.

GORMAN, THOMAS DAVID Umpire. B. 3/16/19, New York, N.Y. 6'3", 210. Tom Gorman didn't last long as ball player but has been NL umpire since 1952. Tom was southpaw pitcher as young man, 15–9 in his first pro season at Blytheville, Northeast Arkansas League, 1938. Following season he had 7–8 record with Clinton, in III League, and went up to N. Y. Giants. Pitched five innings but neither won nor lost. Back to Clinton 1940. After breaking even, 11–11, Tom went into military service.

After World War II umpired in New England League, 1947–48; moved to International League, 7/24/48, remaining in that circuit until he began his big league career in NL.

Tom was an all-round athlete in high school. Held many basketball records that stood for quarter of century—until Lew Alcindor came along. He was officiating at basketball game when offered chance to become baseball umpire in New England League.

In first game he worked where Don Newcombe was pitching and Campanella was catching for Nashua (N.H.) club. Thought job was easy. Three days later changed his mind when, after calling man out at plate, fans mobbed him and he was lucky to escape in one piece.

Gorman was behind plate in 1968 WS game when Bob Gibson of Cardinals struck out 17 men to defeat Denny McLain of Detroit Tigers. Says that established players do not give him trouble; most difficult ones are fringe players.

Most embarrassing thing for umpire occurs when he calls play one way and fellow umpire calls it another way, says Tom. This occurred once in 1953 game between Cardinals and Chicago Cubs. With runners on base, ball was hit to Kiner. He made shoestring catch and threw to second base to double runner off bag. Tom's umpiring colleague Al Dixon ruled that Kiner had trapped ball. Eddie Stanky, then managing Cardinals, came storming onto field. "I called it a catch," Gorman told Stanky. "I don't know what you're going to do, but I'm calling it a double play, and that's the way it was." Gorman justified his call, saying umpire nearest play is supposed to call it, and he was closer than Dixon was.

In 1970 Gorman received Bill Slocum Award for "long and distinguished service to baseball." Award is given by N.Y. Baseball Writers Association of America. Others so honored include Babe Ruth, Judge Landis, Branch Rickey, John McGraw. Gorman was fourth umpire to get it, others having been Bill Klem, Larry Goetz, Jocko Conlan.

GOSLIN, LEON ALLEN (Goose)   OF-BL-TR. B. 10/16/1900, Salem, N.J. D. 5/15/71, Bridgeton, N.J. 5'11", 180. Goose Goslin once hit into four double plays in four consecutive times at bat (4/28/34). But he offset this and his 585 major league strikeouts by such feats as leading AL in hitting (1928); hitting three homers in one game three different times; setting WS record for most consecutive hits in one series, six, in 1924; and retiring with .316 big league average in 2287 games. So he earned his election to Hall of Fame, 1968.

Goslin spent most of major league career with Washington—and helped Senators win their only three AL pennants in history. Also managed to get into two WS with Detroit Tigers.

Goose pitched well enough around New Jersey to impress Bill McGowan, later an AL umpire. Bill recommended him to Columbia club of Sally League, 1920. In pro ball it soon became evident he could hit with best of them—but his pitching was not so hot. Soon concentrated on outfielding and batted .317 in 90 games. Following year pummeled ball to tune of .390 in 142 games, leading league. Also led circuit in hits (214), runs (124), and RBI (131). So, at age 21, before close of AL season, Clark Griffith bought him for Senators. Played 14 games and hit .260. But in 1922 he was off and running in AL, with his first of eleven seasons with average of .300 or better. Mark in first full year was .324 in 101 games. In 1924 it was .344 in 154 contests, and led AL in RBI with 129. Eleven times he had at least 100 RBI in majors. Climbed to .354 average in 1926, and then peaked at .379 in 1928, year he led AL in batting. Washington traded Goose to St. Louis Browns 6/14/30; after 1932 season another deal put him back in Senator uniform—in time for his third year with pennant winner, under management of Joe Cronin.

Goslin got another break after being with 1933 Senators. They traded him to Detroit, where Mickey Cochrane led Tigers to two straight flags, 1934 and 1935. Spent two more years with Detroit, and, after batting .238 in 79 games, 1937, drew unconditional release. Clark Griffith had spot for him in 1938, his third tour with Senators. Goose didn't do much for his old friend, hitting just .158 in 38 games. Following season it was back to minors for Goose, back to his native New Jersey. Played and managed at Trenton, Inter-State League; hit .324 in 99 games and team won 51 games, lost 51, to finish second in four-club circuit. Following year Trenton finished third; league had expanded to eight clubs. But Goose dropped down to .250 in 49 games, and in 1941 Goose stayed on sidelines as player, led his club to fourth-place finish in eight-club league. Then back to fishing.

In WS play, Goslin's best average came in 1924 games against N.Y. Giants. Eleven hits in 32 trips, with three homers and a double, seven RBI, and .344 average. That was year he set record for six consecutive safe hits in games of October 6,7, and 8. But with this hitting he struck out seven times in that WS. Against Pirates in 1925 WS Goose again slugged three homers and one double, drove in six runs. One of his hits fooled Pittsburgh infield, however. In third game, came up with two men on base and laid down perfect bunt, filling bases. Senators later sewed up contest 4–3. That year Goose hit .308 for classic. Later WS performances not quite as newsworthy, although he had quite an experience in 1934 games against St. Louis Cardinals—and afterward. Goose and other members of Tigers rode Umpire Bill Klem pretty hard. Knowing that vet arbiter hated nickname "Catfish," they used that and other epithets to agitate him. It happened Tigers were staying in same hotel as Klem. Next day they boarded same elevator. It was jammed. Somewhat contrite about sharp words of day before, Goslin extended hand and said, "Mr. Klem, I am sorry about what happened yesterday." Those were Goose's last words in encounter. Klem proceeded to bawl him out in front of crowd. Elevator stopped to let him out, but Bill put foot in door and continued his blasts. Many of fans present at time either wrote

Judge Landis or told him about episode. Landis slapped $200 fine on Klem. Goslin later said, "Never talk back to an umpire—and never try to apologize—in a crowded elevator.

Goose made 2735 hits in major league career. There were 500 doubles, 173 triples, and 248 homers, with 1609 RBI and 1483 runs scored. His 18 WS games included. 129 times at bat, 16 runs, 37 hits, 5 doubles, 7 homers, 19 RBI, .287 average.

GOWDY, HARRY MORGAN (Hank) C-BR-TR. B. 8/24/89, Columbus, Ohio. D. 8/1/66, Columbus, Ohio. 6'2½", 192.

Hank Gowdy wrote his name in history books three times. In between, put together fine record as catcher, coach, gentleman and onetime manager of Cincinnati Reds. First attracted attention in 1914 World Series when he batted .545, record for many years. Had helped Braves miracle team win NL pennant after being in cellar mid-July. That season Mgr. George Stallings surprised sports world smashing Philadelphia Athletics four straight.

Gowdy's next claim to fame: first major leaguer to enlist in U. S. Armed Forces (6/2/17) during World War I, serving in Rainbow Division at Chateau-Thierry, St. Mihiel and in Argonne, among bloodiest battles of war.

Hank's third brush with history was unintentional. Came in crucial seventh game of 1924 Series, quirk of fate which probably cost Giants world championship. Muddy Ruel, at bat in 12th inning for Senators, hit foul fly behind plate. Gowdy, catching for Giants, flipped off mask, started pursuit. His eyes skyward, Hank didn't see that mask had bounced directly in his path. Foot got tangled with mask, causing him to lose that split second needed to catch otherwise easy foul ball. Given another life, Ruel doubled. Scored moments later when Earl McNeely's grounder toward third hit pebble and bounced over Lindstrom's head for base hit, giving Senators game and world championship.

Gowdy started as first baseman at Lancaster, Ohio State League, 1908, batting .228 in 98 games. Next year in 95 games, batted .263. With Dallas, Texas League, 1910, hit .312. Less than dozen games with Giants, 1910–11, then traded to Boston NL with SS Al Bridwell for 3B Buck Herzog (7/22/11). Became catcher early in Boston career. Optioned to Buffalo, International League, 1913, hit .317 in 104 games. Took regular catching job with Braves 1914, played 128 games, batted .243, had three homers. Came Series with A's who were overwhelming favorites. John McGraw, famed manager of Giants, said Braves would be lucky to win one game. Overconfident A's had just won fourth pennant in five seasons. In first game Gowdy drove in first Boston run with double, then scored. Next time he tripled and scored. With one on base in eighth, singled runner to third. Gowdy stole second, helping teammate to score on other end of double theft. In third game Hank doubled twice and hit homer. With score tied in tenth, A's pushed two more runs across plate. Trailing by two, Hank slammed his homer in bottom half of same inning. Braves then tied score with walk, single and sacrifice fly. It was 4–4 until bottom of 12th. Hank ripped his second two-bagger to left. Leslie Mann came in to run for him. Gowdy trotted off field amid deafening roar of applause. Pinch batsman was purposely passed. Moran bunted. Pitcher Joe Bush threw ball past third into left field. Mann dashed home with winning run. In fourth game Gowdy hitless in two trips, but caught brilliantly. Broke up A's rally by throwing out base runner after strikeout, for double play. In four games had six hits, including homer, triple, three doubles. Walked five times. Vital contribution toward Braves' spectacular victory, including his backstop work for pitchers Dick Rudolph, George Tyler and Bill James.

Gowdy returned to Giants midseason 1923; back with Braves 1929–30. Lifetime NL batting average .270 in 1044 games. Coach for Braves, then for Reds. Managed Cincinnati briefly 1946, succeeding Bill McKechnie. Spent later years in retirement at Columbus.

GRABARKEWITZ, BILLY CORDELL Inf.-BR-TR. B. 1/18/46, Lockhart, Tex. 5'10", 170. Billy Grabarkewitz made NL All-Star squad, 1970, after overcoming serious injuries, may be All-Star again if can avoid further physical troubles. Son of Irish mother and Polish father, Billy hit 17 homers and drove in 84 runs with Los Angeles Dodgers, 1970; hit .289 and played in 156 games. But 1971 almost total loss due to shoulder injury in spring: no homers, six RBI, .225 batting average in 44 games. More injuries in 1972—in just 53 games hit .167. After season traded to California Angels, then to Phillies.

Billy attended St. Mary's U. in San Antonio, and Southwest Texas State College before going into pro ball, 1966, with Tri-City club of Northwest League. Santa Barbara, 1967; Albuquerque, 1968. There encountered first serious injury. Crashed into Hal King at plate; broke right ankle in three places, ripped ligaments. Needed six casts during next couple of months and wound up with right leg one inch shorter than left. Undaunted, Grabby used to run up and down steps of grandstand to strengthen leg. Injury ended good season. Hit .308 and stole 31 bases in 85 games, scored 76 runs that year. In 1969, 34 games with Dodgers, with .092 batting average; 51 games at Spokane, with .264. Then came fine performance with Dodgers. Despite difficulty many fans had with his name, won All-Star selection as write-in candidate. Many simply wrote "Billy G." instead of trying to spell it further. Got one hit in three trips to plate in 1970 All-Star game.

Billy had tonsils removed after 1971 season, and operation on right shoulder in November. Competetive spirit was manifest at time of tonsilectomy. Billy was busy in off-season as member of Dodgers' speakers bureau. Entering hospital, but after checking in asked for evening out—so he could deliver speech.

GRANEY, JOHN GLADSTONE (Jack) OF-BL-TL. B. 6/10/86, St. Thomas, Ontario. 5'9", 180. First batsman to face pitcher Babe Ruth in AL, 1914. First player in majors to go to bat wearing number on his uniform 6/26/16. First former player to become play-by-play radio announcer, 1931.

Graney started out as lefthanded pitcher at Fulton, N.Y., 1906. Had brief trial with Chicago Cubs, 1907, but spent season at Rochester, Eastern League, and Wilkes-Barre, Pa., New York State League. Acquired by Cleveland, 1908, loaned to Columbus, American Association, but returned to Forest City club. Graney liked to tell his experience with old-time star Larry Lajoie, then managing Indians. "I was pitching batting practice. Lajoie came up. I thought that if I could make him look bad at the plate I'd have plenty to write home about. So I tried to throw the ball past him. I wound up, and my first pitch hit him, kerplunk, on the top of his head, knocking him out. That night Lajoie called me to his room. 'Kid, you've got lots of stuff,' he said. 'But wild men belong out west. I'm going to send you as far west as I can. Here's ticket to Portland, Oreg.'"

Graney spent rest of that season in Pacific Coast League, and following year began transition to outfield. Played 137 games at Portland, 1909, mostly in outfield, batting .252. Following season made grade as regular outfielder with Cleveland, taking part in 116 games but hitting just .236. Never made .300 as hitter but was fine outfielder, smart base runner, and regular most of career that ended after 1922 season. Took part in 1402 games in majors with .250 batting average. His big league pitching was confined to 3-1/3 IP in 1908 with ERA of 5.40.

When chance came to become radio sports announcer, Graney made most of it. Was considered careful reporter with sincere, vital voice. Gave details of complicated plays. Used good grammar, spoke complete sentences, in contrast to some announcers. Announced Cleveland AL games 1931–54.

Number that Graney wore on uniform, 1916, was sewn on sleeve. Football began use of numbers on players and for some years fans and newsmen had suggested their use on baseball players' uniforms. However, Graney's and other Cleveland numbers were small, hardly visible from stands. Numbering of ball players' uniforms did not become rule until 1929.

GRANGER, WAYNE ALLAN P-BR-TR. B. 3/15/44, Springfield, Mass. 6'2", 165. Since he arrived in majors late May 1968, Wayne Granger has been tireless relief pitcher. Over five-season period appeared in 324 games, far more than any other big league hurler in same period. Set major league record for most appearances by pitcher, 1969, with 90. In 1971 led NL with 70 appearances. In 1970 enjoyed brilliant season, saving 35 ball games while leading NL for second straight season in "fireman points"—victories plus saves. This added up to 41, tying major league record held by Ron Perranoski and Dick Radatz. Granger won *Sporting News'* Fireman of Year Award, 1969–70.

St. Louis Cardinals got Granger into pro ball, 1965, signing him for reported bonus of $20,000. Got minor league experience in Cardinal farms at Tulsa, Raleigh, and Arkansas before reporting to Redbirds few weeks after 1968 season started. Won four, lost two and had four saves, with 2.25 ERA. Nevertheless, was traded, along with Bob Tolan, to Cincinnati 10/11/68 for Vada Pinson. Bing Devine, Cardinal general manager, regained him after 1972 season in deal with Minnesota. Cards traded to Yankees, 8/7/73.

When Granger returned to Cardinals had pitched 464 innings and had ERA of 2.87, with 229 strikeouts, 135 bases on balls. Besides 96 saves, had won 30 games, losing 25. Granger's WS experience included two innings in classic of 1968, allowing no runs. But in 1970 set with Cincinnati, Baltimore Orioles jumped on him for five runs in 1-1/3 innings' which gave him ERA of 33.75, and 13.50 ERA for both classics. Despite foregoing seasonal records, Reds traded Granger to Minnesota Twins for Pitcher Tom Hall, 12/4/71. Cincinnati wanted lefthanded reliever; Twins wanted righthander.

GRANT, EDWARD LESLIE (Harvard Eddie) 3B-BL-TR. B. 5/21/83, Franklin, Mass. D. 10/5/18, Argonne Forest, France. 5'11½", 168. First major league baseball player killed in World War I. Thoughtful, serious-minded young man, thrifty, abstemious, conscious of his sense of duty. Enlisted as soon as U.S. entered war, joined first body of American soldiers sent overseas. Became captain of infantry battalion attached to 77th Division. Was leading unit after all superior officers in his group had been killed or wounded. Rallied troops and moved through forest for four days in effort to rescue "lost battalion" near Verdun. Killed by shell.

Grant graduated from Harvard, had trial with Cleveland AL, 1905, and came back 1907 to make grade with Philadelphia NL, 1907, remaining there until end of 1910 season; Cincinnati, 1911–13; N.Y. Giants, 1913–15; captain of Giants. Fine defensive fielder, but hit just .249 in 987 major league games during career. Practiced law, New York City, 1915, until he enlisted.

GRANT, JAMES TIMOTHY (Mudcat) P-BR-TR. B. 8/13/35, Lacoochee, Fla. 6', 185. Singing pitcher who came to end of line in majors,

1972. Had tryout with Cleveland Indians, but wasn't kept. So Mudcat's major league record shows 571 games, 2441 innings pitched, 145 victories, 119 defeats, with an ERA of 3.63. Walked 849 men, struck out 1267. Joined TV broadcasting team for Indians, 1973.

Popular Grant in later years was successful relief pitcher for Oakland and Pittsburgh. Was 21–7 for Minnesota, 1965; led AL in shutouts that same season, with six; named AL Pitcher of Year by *Sporting News*. Member of AL All-Star squads, 1963,65.

Grant started pro ball, 1954, at Fargo-Moorhead in Northern League; Next stops Keokuk, Iowa, and Reading, Pa.; 18–7 for San Diego, Pacific Coast League, 1957, then graduated to Cleveland where remained until 1964. At Cleveland, Mudcat was strong moundsman, but did not have sensational record; however, had 15–9 mark in 1961. Then Indians needed cash, and Minnesota Twins reportedly gave $75,000 plus two players for Mudcat, 6/15/64. Following season Grant's presence on Twins' pitching staff enabled team to win AL flag. Mudcat followed with two WS victories against one defeat. L.A. Dodgers, however, took world championship. Then two seasons with 13–13 and 5–6 records with Twins, and Grant was traded to Los Angeles, spending one season with Dodgers, 1968.

Montreal and St. Louis 1969. Oakland and Pittsburgh 1970. Pittsburgh, then back to Oakland 1971. In first tour with A's, Grant 6–2, saved 24; sold to Pittsburgh, September of that year, won two big games in relief over New York Mets in final week of season, helping Pirates win NL Eastern Division title. In 1971 won five, lost three, saved seven, then unexpectedly sold back to Oakland 8/10. Chalked up one victory, saved three others; released at end of year.

GRANTHAM, GEORGE FARLEY (Boots) Inf.-BL-TR. B. 5/20/1900, Galena, Kans. D. 3/16/54, Kingman, Ariz. 5'10", 155. Pittsburgh Pirates got George Grantham from Chicago Cubs 10/27/24 in trade involving Charlie Grimm, Rabbit Maranville, and Wilbur Cooper, who went to Windy City. Pitcher Vic Aldridge and first baseman Al Niehaus landed with Pirates along with Grantham. While Grantham was not known as classy fielder, in his seven years with Pirates, never playing in less than 110 games, never hit less than .305. In 1929 hit 12 homers and had 90 RBI; following year had 18 round-trippers and 99 RBI. Grantham was fast enough to steal 43 bases with Cubs, 1923; but, as second baseman, while he led NL in putouts and assists, also made 55 errors, tops for NL keystoners. In 1924 his 44 errors again topped league. So, despite .316 batting average, he was traded. Pirates shifted him to first base. Thereafter, played either first or second, depending on personnel situation.

George started at Tacoma 1920. Tacoma and Portland 1921. Omaha

1922. Chicago NL 1922–24. Pittsburgh 1925–31. Cincinnati 1932–33. New York NL 1934; Nashville 1934. Seattle 1935. Lifetime major league record: 1444 games, .302 average, 1508 hits, 292 doubles, 93 triples, 105 homers, 712 RBI, 132 stolen bases. In two WS with Pirates, 1925–27, eight games, .231 average.

GRAY, PETER J. OF-BL-TL. B. 3/6/17, Nanticoke, Pa. 6′1″, 170. One-armed outfielder who played 77 games for St. Louis Browns, 1945. Probably most handicapped man who ever played in majors. Chance came at peak of World War II player shortage when callow kids and ancient veterans manned major league rosters. Gray, born Peter Wyshner, lost arm as young boy. Reached through spokes of farmer's truck for baseball just as driver put truck in motion. Right arm was badly mangled and had to be amputated near shoulder. Pete, however, loved game, developed skill in catching ball with gloved left hand, quickly slipping glove under right-arm stump, and throwing baseball to infield. At plate was able to anchor base of bat against body and hit ball, powered by strong left arm.

Pete's burning desire to play enabled him to make grade with strong semipro team, Brooklyn's famed Bushwicks. In 1942 joined Three Rivers club in Canadian-American League. Hit .381 in 42 games, no homers, 13 RBI. Moved up to Memphis for 1943 and hit .289 in 126 contests. This time he drove in 42 runs but had no homers.

In 1944 Gray blossomed into MVP of Southern Association. Again with Memphis club, played 129 games, batted .333, and stole 68 bases. This time hit 5 homers, 9 triples, 21 doubles, and drove in 60 runs. His 68 base thefts tied mark set by Kiki Cuyler in 1923 for relatively modern times in Southern circuit.

Then came Gray's chance in majors. Pete was leadoff man for Browns. Didn't set world afire at plate, batting .218 in 77 games. His 51 hits included six doubles, two triples. Drove in 13 runs and stole five bases. At that, Gray hit just three points less than Billy Goodman did in 1944—and Goodman, in 1950, was to lead AL in hitting.

Gray's best day with Browns came 5/20/45. Reached base five times in doubleheader against Yankees, with four hits and one walk. Drove in two runs, scored twice, and handled nine chances afield. Browns won both ends of twin bill before crowd of 20,507 that cheered Pete at every opportunity. And while wartime competition in majors was down, Browns finished third in AL, just six games out of first place—with one-armed outfielder playing half their games.

With peace in 1946, Gray was back in minors. Hit .250 for Toledo; out of baseball, 1947. Elmira, 1948, with .290 average; and finally Dallas, 1949, hitting .214.

When last heard of, Gray was back in Nanticoke avoiding publicity.

Neighbors say he still plays fine brand of golf—using that good left arm.

GRAY, SAMUEL DAVID P-BR-TR. B. 10/15/97, Van Alstyne, Tex. D. 4/16/53, McKinney, Tex. 5'10", 175. Sam Gray won 111 games in AL and one of victories started in most unpromising way. Pitching for Philadelphia Athletics against St. Louis Browns, 1926, first 15 offerings were balls. This meant that there were three men on base, none out, and call of three balls, no strikes, on hitter. Mgr. Connie Mack stuck with him, however. Sam's next pitch was strike. Then batsman swung at next pitch and triple play resulted. Gray allowed only two hits that game and won it by 3–1 score!

Gray pitched for Athletics 1924–27, winning 44 and losing 33. Best season in Philly was 1925 when he had 16–8 record. Then was traded to Browns for Bing Miller. Sam had two good years for Browns. Won 20, lost 12, 1928, helping team to one of its best finishes ever, third place. Had 18–15 record, 1929, when Browns ended up fourth. After that Gray's performance sagged with team. Browns were second-division club during rest of Gray's stay, and when he hung up glove after 1933 season, his major league record showed 111 wins and 115 defeats with 4.20 ERA.

Sam pitched in 379 games, total of 1943-1/3 innings. Had 101 complete games, walked 639, and fanned 730. Fifteen games were shutouts.

Before making grade in majors Gray pitched for Sherman and Paris in Texas-Oklahoma League, starting 1921; Buffalo, International League, and Fort Worth and Beaumont in Texas League. Briefly with Detroit Tigers, 1921, but was turned back.

GREEN, RICHARD LARRY 2B-BR-TR. B. 4/21/41, Sioux City, Iowa. 5'10", 180. Dick Green, brilliant-fielding second baseman for Oakland A's, was lost to club for most of season, 1972, because of herniated disc. Surgery used 5/18 to remove source of trouble. Back in game late in campaign, Green played in all seven games of WS; four singles, two doubles in 18 trips, for .333 average. Greenie does not have impressive batting average—.240 for 1055 AL games, but pulls ball well and managed to get 15 homers in 1965, and 12 in both 1969 and 1971.

Led AL second basemen in fielding with .986 average in 1970. Usually right up there in ground-covering ability—putouts and assists—as well as in double plays.

Green first attracted attention of pro baseball scouts playing American Legion and semipro ball in S. Dak. Also starred in basketball, football, and track. Attended Black Hills State College. Entered A's organization, then in Kansas City, 1960.

En route to majors, played for Sanford, Fla.; Lewiston, Idaho;

Albuquerque; Portland, Oreg. Joined Kansas City AL for 13 games 1963. In lineup for well over 100 games each season excepting 1968 and 1972. Went to Oakland with A's after close of 1967 season.

Dick and father operate lucrative moving business, Rapid City, S. Dak.

GREENBERG, HENRY BENJAMIN (Hank) 1B-OF-BR-TR. B. 1/1/11, New York, N.Y. 6'3½", 215 Hank Greenberg hit 311 home runs and batted in 1224 markers for Detroit Tigers, but his highest salary came from Pittsburgh Pirates, for whom he played one season after he passed his peak. Hank was first National League player to earn $100,000—eleven years before Stan Musial reached that figure. Now, many years after his playing days and his front office experiences with Chicago and Cleveland AL clubs, Hank is millionaire, thanks in part to wise investments in stocks.

Greenberg's departure from Detroit still remains strange story. Back from military service 7/1/45, Hank helped Tigers to pennant with 13 homers, 60 RBI, and .311 batting average. In WS that year, hit .304, drove in seven runs with two singles, three doubles, two homers. His salary was $55,000. However, his contract called for Detroit club to pay him cash bonus of $20,000 if he was released, if he retired, or if his contract was assigned to another team.

Despite Greenberg's fine record in 1946, all American League clubs waived on him; could have claimed him for $10,000 waiver price. It is probable that Hank's age, plus his expensive contract, played factor in other AL teams not claiming him. Baseball clubs were not accustomed to many $55,000 contracts in 1946.

So Pittsburgh bought Greenberg for an estimated $35,000. Greenberg then demanded and got his $20,000 cash bonus from Detroit. Pirates first offered Hank same salary he received in Detroit. Hank then said he would retire from game. Pittsburgh club kept raising ante until Hank finally signed contract for $100,000 plus choice of any yearling horse from stock of John Galbreath, one of Pirate owners. Galbreath's horses, incidentally, twice have won Kentucky Derby. His yearlings were valued anywhere from $10,000 to $20,000 at the time.

It is believed Greenberg had wanted to move into Detroit front office as general manager, but Billy Evans, former umpire, had been appointed. Rather than keep disappointed player on club, Detroit sold him to Pirates. Greenberg spent one season in Pittsburgh, batted .249 in 125 games, hit 25 homers, and announced retirement as player.

Hank, as big awkward kid, was turned down by John McGraw of N.Y. Giants. Yankees offered $7500 to sign, but Lou Gehrig was their first baseman at time, and it looked like he would last forever. So Greenberg rejected offer, feeling he would do better elsewhere. Senators offered $12,000. But Greenberg enrolled at New York U., 1929, with athletic scholarship; following spring decided to play ball professionally immediately, and signed with Tiger organization for $9,000 bonus. Farmed out to Hartford, Eastern League, for 17 games, 1930; and to Raleigh, Piedmont League, for 122 contests same season, hitting .314. Also had one game with Tigers. Hit .318 at Evansville, III League, 1931, and had three games at Beaumont, Texas League. Then in 1932 led Texas League in homers, with 39, hit .290. In 1933 Greenberg made grade in Detroit, hit .301. During his first eight full years in AL hit above .300 each season. His best mark for full year was .340 in 1940. Hit .348 in 1936, but played only 12 games due to broken arm.

Hank led AL in homers three times and tied once for lead. His 58 round-trippers in 1938 came close to Babe Ruth's record of 60 homers— but Hammering Hank couldn't quite reach coveted goal. Greenberg also led AL in RBI four seasons. MVP 1935 and 1940.

Hank was at Cleveland with Bill Veeck as farm director, and later became general manager of Indians. He was with Veeck again in Chicago, with White Sox. Both of these teams won AL pennants, Indians in 1954 and Sox in 1959.

Hank set major league record, 1938, for most times hitting two or more homers in one game, eleven for season. In WS his best average was .357 in 1940; his lowest .167 in 1935. Overall, hit .318 in 23 WS games, with seven doubles, two triples, and five homers among his 27 hits. Drove in 22 runs.

His overall major league average was .313 in 1394 games. Had 1628 hits in 5193 AB; scored 1051 runs; had 379 doubles, 71 triples, 331 homers, 1276 RBI. Hall of Fame 1956.

GREENWADE, THOMAS Scout. B. 8/21/04, Willard, Mo. Baseball people know that Tom Greenwade, Yankee scout, signed Mickey Mantle to his first contract for $1,100 bonus and $140 per month. But few know that he was man who scouted Jackie Robinson for Brooklyn Dodgers; and that it was on basis of his reports that Branch Rickey decided that Robinson must be fine major league prospect. Tom secretly followed Jackie, then playing for Kansas City Monarchs, for 50 days. Rickey undoubtedly had other opinions from various people who saw Robinson play—but Greenwade was only Dodger scout to see him play before he signed. Apparently Branch thought it might hurt Greenwade's chances of signing other white youngsters if they knew he had given favorable reports on first black major leaguer. So other members of Brooklyn organization received credit for scouting Robinson. Tom scouted plenty of other fine major leaguers since he took up profession in 1941. Besides Mantle and Robinson, they include Gil Hodges, Carl Erskine, George Kell, Cal McLish, Elston Howard, Ralph Terry, Hank Bauer, Tom

Sturdivant, Bill Virdon, Jerry Lumpe, Rex Barney, Vic Power, Bon Swift—and possibly his greatest find since Mantle and Robinson, Bobby Murcer.

Greenwade was minor league pitcher with hopes of becoming major leaguer until he hurt arm picking up house jack. Played at Fort Smith, 1923; later at Joplin; Bartlesville; Palestine, Tex.; Casper, Wyo.; Blackwell, Okla.; Enid, Okla.; Denver, and St. Paul. Managed farm clubs for St. Louis Browns three seasons at Joplin; Independence, Kan.; and Paragould, Ark. After winning flag there, 1940, Bill DeWitt, top man with Browns, made him scout. Brooklyn Dodgers gave him better pay— $4000 annually—to scout 17 states for them, starting 1946; signed by Branch Rickey, Jr., then boss of Dodgers' farm organization. After World War II, when Larry MacPhail went to Yankees, he offered Tom almost twice what he was making at Brooklyn. If Tom never signed another player than Mickey Mantle, he more than earned all that Yankees have paid him through years. Tom, however, confesses he did not realize Mantle's potential for becoming great ball player he was. Also reveals Jackie Robinson was not first black player Rickey thought about signing. Branch sent Tom to Mexico to scout Cuban Negro shortstop, Sylvio Garcia, in 1944; Tom's report said Garcia couldn't make it in majors. On that same trip, however, Tom saw Roy Campanella in action, and tipped Dodgers off on him as future possibility. Others later scouted Campanella and he was signed—after Robinson got contract with Montreal farm club of Dodgers.

Tom is "semiretired" officially, in accord with rules that covered all CBS employees, including those working for Yankees while CBS owned team. Receives annuity and got profit-sharing bonus on retirement at age 65. Besides his baseball activities, Tom is chairman of board of prosperous bank in home town, Willard, Mo.; bank is on property just few yards from actual place he was born. Additionally he and son operate 379-acre farm nearby with 100 head of cattle.

Although "semiretired," Tom says he is as busy as ever tracking down future prospects. During summer of 1972 scouted from Anchorage, Alaska, on one end, to Puerto Rico and Dominican Republic on other— on special assignments.

Tom, with Cherokee Indian blood in his veins, is relative of pitcher Ben Tincup who was with Philadelphia Phillies several decades ago.

GRICH, ROBERT Inf.-BR-TR. B. 1/15/49, Muskegon, Mich. 6'2", 180.When Baltimore Orioles' veteran players faltered early in 1972 season, Bobby Grich was one of youngsters who kept club afloat. "I'd hate to think where we'd be without Grich, Crowley, and Baylor," said Mgr. Earl Weaver at one point. Critics were predicting Bobby was on way to become another Brooks Robinson. Grich hit .278 in 133 games, with 12 homers, 50 RBI, 13 stolen bases. Played all infield positions, but mostly second base. Made 1972 All-Star game with AL squad.

Baltimore scout Al Kubski, one of men in Oriole organization who followed Grich as young prospect in Long Beach, Calif., was probably first to compare him to Robinson. In report to headquarters, Kubski declared Grich had more speed than Brooks and had a little better arm. "Most important, in high school, Bobby showed Brooks Robinson instincts," wrote the scout.

Drafted, Orioles signed Grich for $40,000 bonus 6/29/67. Spent rest of summer at Bluefield, Appalachian League; following season at Stockton, California League; 1969 with Dallas–Fort Worth, Texas League, with .310 average in 121 games. In 1970 was leading league at .383 clip with Rochester, International League, in 63 games, when recalled by Orioles. With Orioles, however, hit just .211 for 30 games. Sent back to Rochester, spring of 1971, with instructions to concentrate on hitting with power. Up to then Grich had slapped just 22 homers in four years in pro ball. Grich proceeded to follow instructions; banged 32 homers, 26 doubles, nine triples, and drove in 83 runs. But at no great sacrifice to his batting average—hit very respectable .336. His 32 homers and 299 total bases led International League. His overall play won him recognition as top fielding shortstop in minors. *Sporting News* named him "Minor League Player of Year," 1971. Honors of this type were not new to Bobby. His year in Texas League won him MVP Award, 1969. Orioles recalled Grich after he hit five homers in postseason play with Rochester, 1971. In first game with Orioles after recall, banged three hits. Later slapped first major league homer off Stan Bahnsen, then of Yankees. Nine hits in 30 trips, for .300 average.

Bobby attended UCLA. During off-season, 1971–72, he and wife attended Fresno State College.

GRIFFITH, CALVIN ROBERTSON Executive. B. 12/1/11, Montreal, Quebec. Clark Griffith, founder of Griffith dynasty, acquired seven children and major league baseball club about same time, 1920. Ball club took care of him and family for many years. After he died 10/27/55, ball club continued to take good care of family.

Calvin Griffith, president of Minnesota Twins, was one of seven children who lost their father, 1920. He was brother of Mrs. Clark Griffith. Elder Griffith adopted some of children officially, including Calvin. Rest of family was taken in, however. Two of girls married baseball players. One of them, Thelma Haynes is vice president and assistant treasurer of Twins. Mildred married Joe Cronin, former ball player, major league manager, and now president of American League. One of boys taken in—Sherry Robertson—became major league outfielder. Two others are vice presidents of Twins. Calvin's son, Clark, is also vice president. And Tom Cronin, son of AL president, assistant director of public relations for Twins.

Elder Clark Griffith was crafty pitcher of 1890s and early 1900s. Was one of comparatively few ball players who invested his money in ball club. Managed Washington Senators and acquired controlling interest of team, 1920. By time Senators blossomed into world champions, 1924, Cal Griffith was their batboy. Cal took time out from baseball to attend Staunton Military Academy and George Washington U. Played both baseball and basketball in prep school and college.

In 1935 Cal became secretary of Chattanooga team, Southern Association. President and field manager, July 1937. While at Chattanooga Cal did everything from catching games to manicuring infield, counting gate receipts, sweeping out clubhouse. In 1942 Cal returned to Washington in charge of concessions at ball park. Soon he was involved in all other aspects of club. When Clark Griffith died, 1955, he was ready to administer club as president—with help of rest of family. Senators finished seventh during Calvin's first season as president. Then came three last-place finishes. Griffith family were making living, but weren't getting rich in Washington area. Out in Northwest was virgin area around Minneapolis and St. Paul, anxious and ready for major league franchise. Day of decision came, 10/26/60, and old Senators became Minnesota Twins. A newly formed expansion team took over name "Senators" and represented nation's capital. But Griffith's club, now showing signs of coming to life on ball field, was reborn.

Twins came in seventh in ten-club league, 1961; following year were second. Finally, 1965, Twins took AL flag, only to lose WS to Los Angeles Dodgers in seven games. Second-place finish, 1966. When AL was split into two divisions, 1969, Twins won in west but lost to Baltimore in playoff. Same thing happened again 1970. Twins wound up fifth in Western Division of AL, 1971.

GRIFFITH, CLARK CALVIN (Old Fox) P-BR-TR. B. 11/20/69, Stringtown (Vernon County), Mo. D. 10/27/55, Washington, D.C. 5'8", 175. Clark Griffith and wife were childless but when her brother died, Griffiths took the seven children to raise. One of them, Calvin, is now president of Minnesota Twins. Another is wife of Joe Cronin, president of AL. Another married Joe Haynes, Washington pitcher, later an official of Twins. One was Sherrard Robertson who played outfield with Senators. Two other nephews, William and James Robertson, managed ball club's concessions.

Griff, however, had plenty of laurels of his own. Small in stature, became known as Old Fox during pitching days. Kept nickname as manager, later as club owner, through crafty baseball strategy, skill in judging players, perspicacity in competing with millionaire clubs while he had to run his team on shoestring. President Harry Truman went to Washington ball park one night in August 1948 to help pay tribute to Griff. Declared he was "shining example of what this country can produce." Born in log cabin, incidentally.

Griffith pitched in Bloomington, Ill., Milwaukee, Tacoma and Oakland, as well as with St. Louis and Boston when these cities were in old American Association. Started these travels 1888. Landed with Chicago NL 1893, remaining until close of 1900 season. During this stretch had six years with over 20 victories.

Jumped to Chicago AL as playing manager 1901, first year it was recognized as major league. Has 24–7 mark, for best pitching percentage in circuit. Sox won pennant. One more year with Sox, then at request of AL president Ban Johnson, moved to New York to manage old Highlanders, later renamed Yankees. Little talent to work with but brought team home in second place twice. By this time was tapering off as active pitcher.

Griffith managed Cincinnati 1909–11, then bought 10% interest in Washington, becoming pilot there. One of first moves was to persuade President William Howard Taft to throw out first ball at start of 1912 season. Became custom for American President to dignify all baseball by this act almost every spring.

With Senators, Griff's principal assets were Walter Johnson and his own sagacity. In 1919, with a Philadelphia grain dealer who put up $400,000, got control of Washington club. Became president 1920; turned over field management to others, 1921. In 1924 appointed Stanley Harris, young second baseman, as manager. Harris led team to pennant and World Series victory that year. In 1925 repeated, but lost Series.

Few years later named Joe Cronin, his stellar shortstop, as playing manager, 1933. Led Senators to pennant in first year as pilot, but lost Series to Giants. Washington seventh 1934. Cronin married Griffith's niece, Mildred Robertson, 9/27/34. Following month Griff sold new "son-in-law" to Boston for $250,000 and Lyn Lary.

During pitching days Griffith drew admiration from many sides. "No brainier pitcher ever lived," said veteran sports writer Hugh Fullerton. Once fooled Al Selbach, pretty fair hitter, with men on second and third. Taunted, nagged, delayed pitching. Selbach's team needed one run to tie. "You big stiff, you couldn't hit this one with hard board," yelled Griff. Proceeded to throw wild ones, tempting overanxious batsman to swing at bad balls. After working count to three and two, Griff smiled at exasperated Selbach, called out, "Here, hit this, you big bloat!" With that, deliberately tossed ball underhanded toward plate, so slowly that Selbach in eagerness to hit, fell on hands and knees before ball reached plate, striking out.

Griffith allegedly nicked ball with sharp spikes, rubbed sand on it and used other deceptions then legal. Spent 67 years in professional ball. Hall of Fame 1946.

GRIMES, BURLEIGH ARLAND (Old Stubblebeard) P-BR-TR. B. 8/18/93, Emerald, Wis. 5'10", 195.

Rugged competitor, one of "old school" players who "would break a leg" to win ball game. Pitched for numerous major league clubs, winning 270 decisions in big time, earning niche in Hall of Fame 1964. One of last spitball pitchers.

Pitched—and won—deciding game of 1931 WS for St. Louis Cardinals despite ailing appendix, although had to be relieved with two out in ninth. Burleigh 17–9 that year, helping Redbirds to NL pennant. During final weeks of season, appendix became inflamed. Refused to have operation. Ice packs applied to affected area when he pitched. Hurled two-hitter in third game of WS against powerful Philadelphia Athletics, winning by 5–2 score. When Series tied three-all, Grimes again went to mound for Cardinals. Blanked A's for eight innings. As game progressed, appendix began acting up. Took more and more time between pitches, obviously working with great pain. Ice packs used between innings. In ninth, allowed two runs. Finally, with one out to go and tying runs on base, left game. Bill Hallahan pitched to final batsman, and Cards were world champs.

Grimes' pro career dates back to 1912 when he started in Minnesota-Wisconsin League at Eau Claire. Ottumwa, Iowa, Central Association, 1913; Chattanooga, Southern Association, 1913–14; Birmingham, same league, 1914. Richmond, Virginia League, 1914, with 23–13 record; two more seasons at Birmingham, with 17–13 and 20–11 marks.

Pittsburgh, 1916–17. Two wins, three losses, his first part season with Pirates. Lost 13 straight games in 1917 when Pittsburgh finished last in NL with 103 defeats, 51 wins. Grimes' record was three and 16.

Following year Grimes landed with Brooklyn Dodgers where he played for nine years. Was 19–9 his first year in Flatbush. In 1920 his 23 victories helped Dodgers capture their first NL flag. Lost 11 games, leading league in winning percentage, .676. Had ERA of 2.22. Pitched second game of WS against Cleveland, hurling 3–0 shutout, but lost his next two starts. Indian outfielder Elmer Smith hit one of Grimes' pitches in fifth game for first WS homer ever made with bases loaded. Five victories were needed to win WS in 1920. With games standing four to two in favor of Cleveland, Burleigh again started for Brooklyn. Stan Coveleski outpitched him and Indians won final contest by 3–0 score.

Grimes followed with 22–13 mark in 1921, 17–14 in 1922, 21–18 in 1923, and 22–13 in 1924. Won twelve games in 1925 and again in 1926. But lost 19 in 1925, and 13 in 1926. Traded to N.Y. Giants, Burleigh won 19 and lost eight in 1927. Another trade landed him with Pittsburgh for 1928. There he won 25, losing 14. In 1929 had another good year with

Pirates, taking 17, losing seven.

Burleigh was shifted again, this time to Boston NL, but didn't tarry long. With Braves and St. Louis Cardinals, 1930, had 16 wins, 11 losses, helping Cards to flag. That autumn he lost two decisions to Athletics in WS. Homers by Mickey Cochrane and Al Simmons helped to defeat him in one contest; homer by Jimmie Foxx in another game.

After 1931 WS, Grimes moved to Chicago NL, back to St. Louis, to Pittsburgh again, and wound up his major league career with Yankees, 1934. His final pitching was done for Bloomington, III League, 1935, where 10–5.

Grimes' final WS effort was in 1932, with Cubs, when they were demolished by Yankee steamroller, four straight.

Burleigh managed Bloomington, 1935; Louisville, American Association, 1936; Brooklyn Dodgers, 1937–38; Montreal, International League, 1939; Grand Rapids, Michigan State League, 1940, until suspended 7/7/40 for one year; Toronto, International League, 1942–44; Rochester, International League, 1945–46; scout, New York Yankees, 1947–52; Manager, Toronto, 1952–53; coach, Kansas City AL, 1955; scout, Kansas City, 1956–57; scout, Baltimore AL, in 1960s.

Grimes' lifetime major league record showed 615 games, 4178 IP, 270–212 for .560 percentage, 3.52 ERA. His WS totals came to nine games, 56-2/3 IP, 3–4, with 4.05 ERA.

GRIMM, CHARLES JOHN (Jolly Cholly) 1B-BL-TL. B. 8/28/99, St. Louis, Mo. 5'11½", 173. "Jolly Cholly" Grimm, in recent years honorary vice president of Chicago Cubs, believed in having fun in baseball. Along with enjoying game, however, Grimm was fine first baseman, pretty fair hitter, and managed Cubs to three pennants; called "baseball's only lefthanded banjo player." Personable, good speaker, practically an institution in Chicago's Wrigley Field; and had several unforgettable years in Milwaukee, with plenty of gemütlichkeit—with American Association team there, later with Milwaukee Braves.

Grimm, while still in teens, had brief tryout with Philadelphia AL, 1916, and with St. Louis NL, 1918. Early minor league experience included 1917 at Durham, and couple of seasons at Little Rock, 1918–19; joined Pittsburgh for 14 games, 1919. Remained with Pirates until after 1924 season, during which period became known as brilliant-fielding first sacker. Hit .345 in 1923, drove in 99 runs, for finest season at bat.

Cholly had developed reputation of being something of playboy, but was solid performer for Cubs, hitting above .300 several times. In 1932 became manager in August when Rogers Hornsby was fired. Club was in second place at time. Nine days later Cubs were in first. Won flag by four-game margin but lost WS to N. Y. Yankees who made it four-game sweep. In 1935 Grimm led Cubs to another pennant but again went down to defeat in WS, this time at hands of Detroit. In 1938, after Cholly had retired as player, Cubs switched managers 7/20/38 and Gabby Hartnett took team on to NL flag. But Grimm was far from through as Cub manager. His second tour of duty began 5/17/44 and continued until 6/10/49. He led team to 1945 pennant, and once again big prize eluded him. Detroit took WS four games to three. Cholly's final term bossing Cubs on field came in 1960 and following year until 5/4/61.

Grimm coached Cubs part of 1941, resigning to go to Milwaukee with Bill Veeck. Cholly became part owner and manager of AA Brewers. Teamed up with Veeck, who played "jazzbo"; Rudie Schaffer, bull fiddle; and Mickey Heath, washboard drums, to produce something alleged to be music. Cholly played banjo. All this during dull games when Brewers were likely to be trailing. Stayed at Milwaukee as pilot through 1943. Came close to winning AA pennant, 1942, At one point, as his birthday approached (1943) press asked him what he wanted as gift. "I'll take a lefthanded pitcher," he replied. Veeck staged birthday celebration on field, gave him $1000 war bond—and mammoth "birthday cake." When celebration was at end, out of birthday cake stepped Julio Acosta, southpaw pitcher, who had been secretly purchased from Norfolk team. Acosta pitched that day, fanned 17—but lost game in 13th inning. However, Julio won next three starts, saved several games in relief, and helped Brewers capture pennant.

Grimm managed Dallas, Texas League, 1950, then went back to Milwaukee, AA, 1951, until named boss of Boston Braves 5/31/52. Braves moved to Milwaukee, 1953, Grimm returning to scene of his AA triumphs and remaining pilot until 6/17/56. Vice president, Cubs, 1957 59, then came final chapter as Cub field manager.

Cholly managed 12 first-division teams in majors and three second-division clubs in full seasons he was at helm.

His shift from field management in 1961 was innovation. Lou Boudreau had been doing microphone work, sportscasting. Cholly and Lou traded jobs, Grimm going back to broadcasting, which he had done between field jobs.

Grimm's 2166 major league games resulted in .291 lifetime average. Made 2299 hits in 7917 trips; scored 908 runs; made 394 doubles, 108 triples, 79 homers; drove in 1083 markers. His WS play, 1929 and 1932, added up to .364 average with 12 hits in 9 games; 33 AB, 4 runs, 2 doubles, 1 homer, 5 RBI.

GRIMSLEY, ROSS ALBERT, III (Crazy Eyes) P-BL-TL. B. 1/7/50, Topeka, Kans. 6'3", 195. Ross Grimsley has plenty of self-confidence, especially after pitching Cincinnati Reds to victory in crucial fifth game of 1972 playoffs against Pittsburgh, then winning two of three decisions in WS against Oakland. Ross 10–7 for Reds, 1971; so was pretty unhappy when sent to Indianapolis in spring of 1972. Reds called him back, however, in May and he was 14–8 rest of campaign.

Grimsley is son of pitcher who had brief stay with Chicago White Sox back in 1951. Papa Grimsley, also southpaw, pitched 14 innings in AL that year, but neither won nor lost decision. Had 3.86 ERA.

Ross attended Jackson State Community College in Tennessee. Pitched his American Legion team to national championship, 1968. Started pro ball 1969 at Sioux Falls, Northern League, winning nine, losing four. Then up to Indianapolis for 1970, with 11–8 record. Unhappy about being sent to Indianapolis, 1971, but won six, lost none, while there. When Manager Sparky Anderson did not use him in early games of 1972 playoffs, Grimsley again grumbled. But when chips were down and he was sent to mound, came through, allowing Pirates just two hits. Anderson started Grimsley in second game of WS. Ross pitched five innings, allowed two runs and six hits, then was removed for pinch hitter. He was charged with loss of game that went to A's by 2–1 score. In fifth game of set, Ross was used 2/3 of an inning in relief, and was credited with Reds' win. Came back in sixth game, also in relief. Threw one inning and was credited with another victory when Cincinnati rallied.

Grimsley also appeared briefly in seventh game, striking out only man he faced. His performance in WS added up to seven innings pitched, two earned runs allowed, with an ERA of 2.57 to go along with two wins, one loss. Walked three, struck out two.

Grimsley's brief "lifetime" record in NL showed an ERA of 3.28 as 1973 season got under way. Had pitched 359 innings, winning 24, losing 15; fanned 146, walked 93; 10 complete games.

Sparky Anderson, after his brilliant victory over Pittsburgh in pennant-clincher, 1972, predicted that Grimsley might well become "another Steve Carlton." Nickname "Crazy Eyes" bestowed upon him by teammates because of unusual blue color of his eyes.

GRISSOM, MARVIN EDWARD P-BR-TR B. 3/31/18, Los Molinos, Calif. 6'3", 230. Marv Grissom did most of his major league pitching in NL but was AL coach 1961–71, most of it on teams managed by Bill Rigney. Brother of eccentric lefthander Lee Grissom, who pitched with Cincinnati, Brooklyn, and Philadelphia NL, 1934–42. Uncle of Jim Davis, who was with Chicago, New York and St. Louis in NL 1954–57.

Grissom had his first spell with N.Y. Giants, 1946, but didn't spend full season in big time until 1949, with Detroit. Had bounced around, starting 1941 in San Bernardino, making way stops in Jersey City, Minneapolis, Sacramento en route. Spent 1950 with Toledo and 1951 with Seattle. After winning 20 games, losing 11 in Pacific Coast League that season, moved up to Chicago White Sox for 1952. Boston AL 1953. New York NL 1953–57, then moved to San Francisco when Giants went to Coast. Best season with Giants 10–7 in 1954. Spent 1959 with St. Louis NL. Coach, Los Angeles and California Angels, 1961–66. Coach, Chicago AL, 1967–68. Coach, Angels, 1969. Coach, Minnesota Twins, 1970–71.

Won 47 games, lost 45 in major league in 356 games, with ERA 3.42. Took part in one WS game, 1954: three innings, one hit, three walks, no runs, ERA 0.00.

GROAT, RICHARD MORROW   SS-BR-TR. B. 11/4/30, Swissvale, Pa.

6′, 170. Dick Groat was All-American basketball star at Duke. More lasting fame came in baseball with Pittsburgh Pirates and St. Louis Cardinals. Game, smart player, leader on field.

Dick was bargain at $25,000 bonus Branch Rickey gave him to join Pirates, June 1952, after he received his A.B. degree. At Duke, Groat scored 1783 points on basketball court in 77 games, averaging 23.2 per game. In 1951 scored 831 points, then national collegiate record. Unanimous choice as All-American in junior and senior years. Considered deft, clever, agile court player; impossible to figure what next move would be. Also All-American shortstop in collegiate circles in junior and senior years.

Groat played 95 games for Pirates, fresh from campus, and hit .284. In off-season played some pro basketball with Fort Wayne Pistons, NBA, but Rickey requested him to give up game. Spent 1953–54 in army.

Back with Pirates, 1955. In 1957 got average up to .315 and hit .300, 1958. Following season average was down to .275 and Joe L. Brown, who succeeded Branch Rickey as Pirate general manager, wanted to cut Dick's salary 25%. Talked Brown into giving smaller cut but pledged he'd make Joe want to give it all back in 1960.

Groat did that exactly. Got off to great start, hit .350 during early part of season. Late in year Lew Burdette hit his left wrist with pitched ball, fracturing a bone. After period of idleness, Groat's average was still tops in NL batting race. Dick's stellar play had helped Pirates sew up first NL pennant since 1927, so final three games of season really meant nothing. But Groat was able to play.

By remaining idle, could have clinched bat title. Instead, despite weakened wrist, took part in final three games and won batting championship with .325 mark.

Dick did not distinguish himself at bat during Pirates' WS victory over Yankees that fall, hitting just .214, with six hits in 28 trips. In field, handled all except two chances cleanly. Neither error affected outcome of game.

MVP in NL that year; first Pirate to win it in 30 years.

Branch Rickey, meanwhile, had joined Cardinals as player consultant. His admiration for Groat probably led Redbirds to acquire him in trade 11/19/62. Dick hit .319 for Cardinals in 1963, 158 games, and helped them to pennant, 1964, with .292 average in 161 contests. Though Groat was spark plug for Redbirds throughout season and in WS, again he did not do well at bat in fall classic. Got five hits in 26 chances for .192 average. Made two errors, but Cards won both those games—as well as two others—taking Yankees in tow four games to three. One more season in St. Louis, then moved to Philadelphia NL for 1966. In 1967 played only 10 games for Phillies then shifted to San Francisco NL for 34 more. Time had taken its toll: Dick had lost most of his hair, and slowed down physically. Turned to a Pennsylvania steel company for job as public relations man.

Dick had much to look back upon. Led NL shortstops in making double plays five years, which tied major league record. Made six hits (three singles, three doubles) 5/13/60. Won Lou Gehrig Memorial Award, 1960 (given by Phi Delta Theta fraternity, to which Gehrig belonged at Columbia U.).

Groat's major league totals showed 1929 games with .286 average. Made 2138 hits in 7484 trips. Had 352 doubles, 67 triples, 39 homers. Scored 829 times, had 707 RBI, and 14 SB. In WS play hitting averaged .204 in 14 games.

GROH, HENRY KNIGHT (Heinie) 3B-BR-TR. B. 9/18/89, Rochester, N.Y. D. 8/22/68, Cincinnati, Ohio. 5'7" 157. One day in 1912 N.Y. Giants having rough day and John McGraw, Giants' manager, was riding plate umpire Bill Klem throughout game. Late in game McGraw sent rookie Henry Groh in to pinch hit. Groh was small, youthful-looking. Fan with foghorn voice boomed out at Klem, "McGraw's sending the batboy in, to show you up!" Klem asked Groh, "Young man, are you under contract with the New York club?" "I am," replied Groh, who promptly singled in his first major league appearance.

Heinie got plenty of hits for Giants before he was through—and good many for Cincinnati. Heinie was famed for his "bottle bat." Early in career McGraw recommended Heinie use heavier bat. Did so, but handle was too thick. Whittled it down until it was comfortable to grip. Used this type of bat rest of days as player. Looked like milk bottle with long neck. Heinie held it high over his shoulders in horizontal position until pitch was made.

Groh started at Oshkosh in 1908 as shortstop. Next stop Decatur, Ill., then Buffalo, before landing with Giants in 1912. Subbed that year, getting into 27 games. Traded to Cincinnati 5/22/13, immediately became regular. Soon recognized as fine third baseman and good hitter, never hitting less than .280 and four times going over .300 in years at

Cincinnati. McGraw wanted him back and got him for 1922 season, giving Reds George Burns, Mike Gonzalez and $100,000 for infielder he had traded away nine years earlier. Helped Giants win flags, 1922–24. In 1922 Series hit .474, while Babe Ruth, with Yanks, hit .118 in same Series. Used "474" for license plate after that.

Groh wound up major league career with Pittsburgh, 1927. Managed Charlotte team after that in South Atlantic League. Later part-time cashier at River Downs Race Track, Cincinnati.

Had major league average of .292 in 1676 games. Batted .264 in 21 World Series games (Cincinnati, 1919; Giants 1922–24; Pittsburgh, 1927).

GROOM, ROBERT P-BR-TR. B. 9/12/84, Belleville, Ill. D. 2/19/48, Belleville, Ill. 6'2", 175. Bob Groom pitched no-hit victory for St. Louis Browns, 5/6/17, vs. Chicago White Sox. Interesting angle: 11 no-hit innings that day—nine in his own no-hitter, also two in first game of doubleheader that afternoon. Oddly, it was second no-hitter for Browns in two days. Ernie Koob allowed no safeties in winning 1–0 decision, 5/5/17. Then came Brownie 8–4 victory in first game of twin bill next day, Groom working last two rounds. Groom's 3–0 no-hitter followed. Another distinction: first year in majors, 1909, Bob lost 26 games for Washington Senators, won seven. Only one other AL pitcher lost as many, John Townsend (5–26), also with Senators, in 1904.

Groom pitched for Fort Scott and Springfield, Mo.; Portland, Oreg., before sold to Senators for $1750. Salary, $333.33, monthly, as rookie. Was 24–13 for Washington, 1912. Offered salary cut, 1914, so joined St. Louis Federal League team—13–21. Was 12–11 in 1915. Back to Browns—14–9, 8–19 marks next two seasons. Cleveland, 1918, 2–2. Major league record: 122–151, 3.10 ERA, 367 games. President and operator of two coal companies; coached boys' baseball teams in hometown area.

GROTE, DAVID J. Executive. B. 7/3/20, Cincinnati, Ohio. In his third decade as NL director of public relations. Staunch defender of all that is wonderful and attractive about baseball, as "the national game" competes with such upstart sports as pro football, pro basketball for love and devotion of America's millions.

Dave attended Xavier U., Cincinnati; joined navy, 1942. Served at Anzio and Salerno in Mediterranean; China-Burma-India theater; England, and at Normandy landings in France. Shot at, but escaped. Mustered out November 1945. Continued studies at Xavier, doing part-time publicity work for university for one year, after which it became full-time job. Became publicity chief for Cincinnati Reds, March 1948, under Warren C. Giles, then general manager of team. Giles became president of NL at end of 1951. Shortly thereafter Grote was named to present position.

Giles moved NL offices to Cincinnati from New York. There was some agitation that Grote should work in New York, close to nation's big newspapers, radio and television networks. But Grote insisted he could do job from Cincinnati, and after year's trial period did such excellent work servicing media that office continued in Ohio city. However, when Giles retired and Chub Feeney became NL prexy, Grote somewhat reluctantly moved to San Francisco, where NL headquarters are.

Annually publishes *NL Green Book*, packed with information about present players and heroic deeds of past in senior circuit. Grote is widower with three children.

GROTE, GERALD WAYNE (Jerry) C-BR-TR. B. 10–6–42, San Antonio, Tex. 5'11", 190. Jerry Grote took over catching job for New York Mets, 1966, and for six seasons played in well over 100 games every year. Then, in 1972 season, Grote didn't do any more catching. There was no explanation except that Duffy Dyer was "swinging hot bat." Dyer's average for 1972 was .231 for 94 games; Grote had .210 mark for 64 games. During September, however, reason for Grote's sidelining was revealed—bone chips in his right elbow required surgery. So Jerry faced 1973 something of question mark as to his throwing arm. Lifetime record at time showed .240 average for 895 games. His 661 hits included 103 doubles, 10 triples, 26 homers, with 240 RBI, and 232 runs scored.

Grote saw more action as pitcher during his high school days in San Antonio. Also excelled in track as mile runner. Attended Trinity U. in Texas. Started out with San Antonio in Texas League, 1963, AA classification, and made good immediately. Hit .268 in 121 games, with 14 homers. Three games with Houston NL that same year, then played 100 games for Astros, 1964. Hit just .181 and was sent back to minors at Oklahoma City, Pacific Coast League. That year, hit .265 in 118 games, with 11 homers.

Mets bought him from Astros 10/19/65 and he became their regular catcher following year. Set NL record for most innings caught in one game, 24; made no error in that game, also NL record, as was fact he had no passed ball. Set other records also, and was named to NL All-Star squad, 1968. In his one WS, 1969, with "Miracle Mets," Grote hit .211 in five games; fielded flawlessly.

GROVE, ROBERT MOSES (Lefty) P-BL-TL B. 3/6/1900, Lonaconing, Md. 6'3", 204. Lefty Grove's record of 300 AL victories might have been much higher if Jack Dunn, owner and manager of Baltimore International League club hadn't been such a keen judge of ball players.

Dunn, who put together long string of pennant-winning teams, outbid N. Y. Giants, Boston Braves, Brooklyn Dodgers, all of whom were interested in stringbean southpaw then pitching for Martinsburg team of Blue Ridge League, 1920. Fireballer had attracted attention by striking out 60 batsmen in 59 innings. With Orioles of that day, Grove showed class immediately by winning 12, losing two that same season. Following year, 25–10. In another era, Grove could have been drafted by major league team. But International League refused to go along with draft agreement for several years. So Baltimore kept Grove, just as it kept Jack Bentley, Joe Boley, Max Bishop, and other players who might easily have made grade in majors much sooner.

After winning 27 games in both 1923 and 1924 and leading league in strikeouts for fourth time, Dunn finally agreed to let Grove go up—for price, $100,600. Connie Mack of Philadelphia Athletics was ready to meet hundred-grand tag, but Dunn suggested investment of $600 would set cost higher than that paid by Yankees for Babe Ruth and get well over $600 of publicity for A's and their new pitcher.

Grove was wild as rookie. Led AL in walks that first season, 1925, and only 10–12 mark. But led league in strikeouts. This was first of seven consecutive years leading AL in strikeouts. Though won-lost record in 1926 was 13–13, Lefty led pitchers with 2.51 ERA. Then in 1927 got right combination with first of seven consecutive 20-game winning seasons. Won 24 in 1928; 28–5 in 1930; 31–4, 1931; won 25 in 1932, 24 in 1933.

Lefty was mean, tough loser. Couldn't seem to understand how teammates might make an error, misjudge fly ball or fail to hit when he was on mound. In 1931, slight change in luck might have given Grove record of 34 victories and one defeat. Rookie shortstop booted double-play ball in one game and Grove lost 2–1. Mule Haas misplayed line drive on another occasion, resulting in defeat. And 8/23/31, with 16 straight victories under his belt, Grove was matched against Dick Coffman of St. Louis Browns. Browns were second-division club headed nowhere. But Coffman pitched terrific game, shutting out A's. Goose Goslin scored only run of game. Got blooper single. Up came Jack Burns, not fearsome hitter. Drove what appeared to be easy liner to left, but Jimmy Moore, subbing for Al Simmons, misjudged ball. When it got past him and rolled to fence, Goslin scored. Grove practically wrecked visitors clubhouse after that game.

Lefty's pitching had tremendous part in Athletics' three straight flags, 1929–31. Was 2–1 in WS of 1930 against Cardinals; same record for 1931 WS. After 1933 season Connie Mack began peddling his stars once again. Grove, Rube Walberg, and Max Bishop went to Boston Red Sox for $125,000 and two undistinguished players. Didn't do so well that first year in Boston, breaking even, 8–8. But got back in groove, 1935, with 20–12 record. Won 17 games each of next two seasons, then had 14–4 for

1938, 15–4 for 1939. By this time old zing was beginning to fade. Grove stayed on to win seven in 1940 and seven in 1941. Final victory was number 300 of major league career.

Grove retired to Maryland mountains after that, later moving to Norwalk, Ohio, after his wife died.

Many will argue that Grove's fast ball moved faster than that of Bob Feller and other noted hardballers. Compiled his brilliant pitching record at time when AL had as many as 20 or 25 men batting over .300, not counting those who played less than 100 games. Besides that 31–4 mark and 16 straight victories in 1931, Grove had 14 consecutive wins, 1928. Nine times Grove led AL in effectiveness, his lowest being 2.06 in that grand 1931 season.

When Grove was finished, had 300 major league victories against 140 defeats. Pitched in 616 games, 3940 IP, allowing 3849 hits, 1339 earned runs. Fanned 2266 and walked 1187. Winning percentage was .682, and ERA 3.06. In WS play, pitched in eight games. 51-1/3 IP, 4–2, 46 hits, 10 earned runs, 6 walks, 36 strikeouts, 1.75 ERA.

MVP 1931. When elected to Hall of Fame, 1947, was pointed out none of other immortals in shrine had as good winning percentage as Grove's .682.

Lefty pitched in three All-Star games, 1933,36,38 for AL. Hurled eight innings, allowed 10 hits, four runs; walked two and struck out eight; 0–1.

GULLETT, DONALD EDWARD P-BR-TL. B. 1/5/51, Lynn, Ky. 6′, 190. At 19, Don Gullett won five NL games, lost two. At 20 he led NL pitchers in winning percentage with 16–6, three of victories shutouts. At 21 Don didn't do so well, 9–10. But he remains one of outstanding young southpaws in majors, likely to have great future.

When Don joined Reds in 1970 and threw his fast ball, Cincinnati outfielder Pete Rose declared pitch was rapid enough "to sail through car wash without getting wet." Reds used him in relief first season in majors, but he added slider to collection of pitches, 1971, and became starter. Gullett is quiet shy type, studious, eager to improve. Cool. Never cooler than on 8/18/71. His opponent that night was Bob Gibson of St. Louis Cardinals; last previous appearance Gibson had thrown first no-hitter of career. This didn't bother Don—with 28,228 paid witnesses, blanked Cards 5–0 for 14th win of year. Gullett almost had no-hitter himself in winning 13th game; Chicago Cubs got one hit and it didn't come until eighth round.

Gullett's only minor league pitching was for Sioux Falls, 1969, in Northern League—7–2.

Don appeared twice in 1970 WS in relief, pitching 3-2/3 innings without allowing run. In 1972 NL playoffs against Pittsburgh, was starting pitcher in crucial fifth game. Pitched until fourth inning and charged with Pirates' three runs. But Reds rallied in ninth to win game and pennant. Then Don pitched fourth game of WS against Oakland. Red-hot Gene Tenace hit one of pitches into stands for homer, only run scored off Gullett in seven innings. Don was not charged with defeat, which went to Clay Carroll.

Going into 1973 Gullett had appeared in 110 NL games; pitched 431 innings and had 3.01 ERA. Owned 30 victories against 18 defeats. Six games were complete ones, three shutouts. Walked 151 men, struck out 279.

GUTIERREZ, CESAR DARIO (Cocoa) Inf.-BR-TR. B. 1/26/43, Coro, Venezuela. 5'9", 155. Cocoa Gutierrez got seven hits in 1971—his entire season's total with Detroit Tigers. But 6/21/70 Gutierrez got seven consecutive hits in ONE game. This set major league record. Tigers got Eddie Brinkman from Washington Senators during 1970–71 off-season, and Gutierrez rode bench most of 1971.

Cocoa was signed originally by Pittsburgh, 1960, but released. Then played at Johnson City, Tenn.; Hobbs, N. Mex.; Lexington, KY.; Fresno, and Phoenix, with couple of brief spells with San Francisco Giants 1967 and 1969. Detroit bought him from Phoenix 9/2/69. In 1970 Cocoa played 135 games for Tigers, hit .243. But he got into just 38 games as utility man, 1971, batting .189.

Cesar dropped out of majors with .235 lifetime mark in 223 games. His best hitting in minors was done at Fresno, 1966, when he hit .338 in 114 games. Gutierrez usually plays most of wintertime in Caribbean.

GUTTERIDGE, DONALD JOSEPH 3B-BR-TR. B. 6/19/12, Pittsburg, Kans. 5'10", 175. Back in 1932–33 St. Louis Cardinals had so many young ball players that Branch Rickey, then general manager, stocked entire Nebraska State League with players, with privilege of selecting best performers for Redbird organization. Don Gutteridge, later manager of Chicago White Sox, was one of youngsters Cards took from Class D circuit at Lincoln. Don led league in hitting, 1933, with .360 average. Moved to Houston, Texas League, 1934, and Columbus, American Association, 1935 and 1936, then to Cardinals before end of 1936 season. Remained with Cards through 1940. Spent 1941 with Sacramento, Pacific Coast League, then with St. Louis AL, 1942–45. Playing manager for Toledo, AA, 1946. Boston AL brought him back to majors late 1946, and for 1947. Pittsburgh NL, 1948 for four games; Indianapolis AA, 1948–50. Manager, Indianapolis, 1951; manager, Colorado Springs, Western League, 1952–53; manager, Memphis, Southern Association, 1954; coach, Chicago AL, 1955–66; manager, Indianapolis, 1967; scout, Kansas City AL, 1968, as Royals were preparing for their expansion entry for 1969. In July 1968, Al Lopez returned to White Sox as manager and hired Gutteridge as coach. When Al retired 5/4/69 because of poor health, Don became Sox manager and piloted team through 1970. Scout for Yankees since 1971.

Gutteridge had fifth-place team in AL West, 1969, and sixth-placer, 1970.

Don's fielding average of .978 for Cardinals, 1937, is best mark ever achieved by St. Louis NL third sacker. But, playing second base for Browns, 6/30/44, Don equaled major league record by taking part in five double plays. This has since been beaten by Bob Knoop, in first game of 5/1/66, playing for California Angels.

Gutteridge hit .256 for lifetime major league average in 1151 games. In WS—1944 with Browns; 1946, Red Sox—hit .192 in nine games.

HAAS, BERTHOLD JOHN Inf.-OF-BR-TR. B. 2/8/14, Naperville, Ill. 5'11", 180. Bert Haas played most of his major league games with Cincinnati, but also saw service with Brooklyn, Philadelphia NL, New York NL, Chicago AL. Hit .264 in 723 games 1937–51. But did something we believe never happened on baseball diamond before or since. Year was 1940. Scene, Jersey City. Bert playing third base for Montreal Royals, International League, then Brooklyn farm. Joe Becker, former Cleveland Indian and later major league coach with Cubs, was catching for Royals. Bert Niehoff manager for Jersey Giants, farm team for N. Y. Giants. Wayne Ambler was Jersey base runner on third base. Woody Jensen, former Pirate outfielder, was batsman for Jersey City. Chuck Solodare, later NL umpire, was calling balls and strikes. With pitch, Ambler was headed for plate. Jensen laid down perfect squeeze bunt which took Montreal infield by surprise. No chance to get Ambler at home, nor any of catching Jensen at first. Only hope for Royals was that ball would roll foul. Ball twisted down foul line, gradually losing speed until it seemed about to stop in fair territory. But no! Inches away from ball was Bert Haas, stretched on stomach, blowing ball for all he was worth. Standing few feet away, Becker yelling, "Blow, Bert, blow!" Haas blew, and blew, and blew ball foul. Umpire Solodare yelled "foul ball" with his dramatic arm gesture. Jensen, who had passed first base, ordered back to bat over; Ambler, at dugout, returned to third base. Strangely, no protest, not even peep, from Jersey club. Next day International League president Frank Shaughnessy issued bulletin saying in effect: You can't blow ball foul any more in this league.

HACK, STANLEY CAMFIELD 3B-BL-TR. B. 12/6/09, Sacramento, Calif. 6', 175. Popular third baseman with Chicago Cubs, 1932–47, but not very successful manager of same team, 1954–56. Team finished seventh, sixth, and eighth under Stan's direction. As player wound up with .301 lifetime average, .348 mark in four WS and .400 in four All-Star games. Led NL third sackers in fielding twice, in putouts five times, and twice in assists.

Stan made grade with hometown team, Sacramento, Pacific Coast League, 1931, playing 164 games and batting .352. Moved up to Cubs for 1932, but found NL pitching somewhat difficult—hit .236 in 72 contests. Spent 1933 with Albany, International League, hitting .299 in 137 games. Back with Cubs that same season, had .350 mark in 20 games. Then took over hot corner as regular for rest of playing career, with an occasional game at first base in emergencies.

In 1938 games made 2193 hits with 363 doubles, 81 triples, 57 homers. Stole 165 bases, leading NL in thefts, 1936, with 16; and tying for leadership following year with 17. Scored 1239 runs and drove in 642.

In 1938 WS Stan hit .471, with 8 for 17. In 1945 WS his mark was .367. With his other two WS (1932,35), played 18 games, had 24 hits in 69 AB, with 5 doubles, 1 triple, 5 RBI.

Hack managed Des Moines, Western League, 1948–49; Springfield, International League, 1950; Los Angeles, Pacific Coast League, 1951–53; Cubs, 1954–56; infield and batting coach for St. Louis Cardinals, 1957–58; interim manager of Cardinals, 1958, winning three and losing seven games. Manager, Denver, American Association, 1959. Manager, Salt Lake, PCL, 1965. Manager, Dallas–Fort Worth, Texas League, 1966, until 5/28.

HADDIX, HARVEY (Kitten) P-BL-TL. B. 9/18/25 Medway, Ohio. 5'9", 155. Harvey Haddix. Red Sox pitching coach, 1971, recalls two World Series victories over Yankees in 1960 classic. Also remembers day when he pitched 12 perfect innings, 5/26/59—and lost ball game in 13th.

Haddix got nickname because teammates thought he resembled another fine lefthanded pitcher, Harry Brecheen, whom everybody called "The Cat." Like Brecheen, Haddix was Cardinal farm product. Started out 1947, Winston-Salem; won 19 Carolina League games, lost five. Columbus, American Association, 1948–49, so-so. In 1950 led AA pitchers with 18–6 mark, 2.70 ERA. Military service 1951, most of 1952. But was ready for Cardinals. Had 20–9 record 1953. Following year 18–13. Those his best seasons. Traded to Philadelphia 5/11/56. Phils kept him that year and next. Sent to Cincinnati for 1958. Pittsburgh 1959–63. Baltimore AL 1964–65.

This wound up his playing career. Pitched in 453 games, won 136, lost

113, 2235 innings, 3.63 ERA. Pitching coach, N.Y. Mets, 1966–67; Cincinnati, 1969. In 1968,70, minor league pitching coach, Pirates. Joined Red Sox coaching staff 1971.

Haddix had been nursing head cold when called upon to pitch against Milwaukee in what proved to be fabulous performance. Thought he would be lucky to last five innings. Yet, inning after inning ... Nine innings passed. Not a Brave had reached base. Pirates couldn't score. Tenth, eleventh, twelfth—Haddix perfect. Still scoreboard 0–0. Thirteenth started sadly. After retiring 36 Braves in order Felix Mantilla grounded to third baseman Don Hoak. In his eagerness, Don threw poorly to first base for error. There went perfect game. Bad throw also changed complexion of game. Next man sacrificed Mantilla to second. With dangerous Hank Aaron coming up and first base open, intentional walk was in order. This brought up Joe Adcock, also dangerous. Still, percentages favored pitcher and there was chance for double play, specially with righthanded batsman and play at any base. But Adcock gave ball ride for first hit of game, Mantilla came home with winning run. Joe's drive actually should have been homer, as it hit over fence. But Aaron had seen frantic leap by Bill Virdon, Pittsburgh outfielder, and thought ball had dropped onto field. Instead, it had gone over fence. But Aaron, after touching second base, headed straight for dugout. And Adcock was deprived of homer, for technically "passing" previous base runner.

In 1960 World Series, hectic set won by Pirates, Haddix started fifth game and won (5–2) over Yankees, though relieved in seventh inning. In crucial seventh contest, Haddix went to mound in ninth with Pirates leading by one run. But there were two men on base. Haddix allowed single by Mantle, which tied score. Held New Yorkers after that. Then came Bill Mazeroski's famous homer, giving Pirates world championship and Haddix his second Series victory.

HADLEY, IRVING DARIUS (Bump) P-BR-TR. B. 7/5/04, Lynn, Mass. D. 2/15/63, Lynn, Mass. 5'11", 190. Bump Hadley got his nickname long before he suffered his bumps in AL. It was hung on him when member of Boy Scout troop, stuck with him during high school football days.

Among bumps Hadley experienced was debut in majors. Pitching in one game for Washington, he emerged with ERA of 12.00, and immediately departed for Birmingham, Southern Association. That was 1926. Some years later Bump encountered 13-game losing streak. Managed to break it by pitching shutout for St. Louis AL against Philadelphia Athletics. It was struggle, however, as Hadley walked 12 men during game. Browns were sixth-place team that year (1932). Hadley 13–20 for St. Louis, 1–1 for White Sox early part of season, so record for 1932 was 14–21.

Hadley attended Mercersburg Academy after high school in Lynn. Quit in sophomore year to join Washington. After his 14–7 mark at Birmingham, Hadley returned to Senators for 1927. Had 14–6 record that year. Jogged along in Washington until 1932 season which he started with White Sox, then moved to Browns 4/27/32. Back with Washington for 1935 season. Then traded to Yankees. After years with mediocre or poor teams, Bump finally had good club behind him, and his record showed it. Took 14 decisions for Yankees, 1936, losing just four. Followed up by pitching and winning World Series game, against Giants.

In 1937 Hadley was 11–8. Was wild, ineffective in only World Series appearance, again against Giants, who got him out of game in second inning. Had 12–6 mark for 1939 Yanks after 9–8 season in 1938. Yanks won flag again in 1939. Hadley won third game of that World Series (against Reds), relieving Lefty Gomez in second inning and pitching rest of way. After 1940 season (3–5 mark), Hadley divided 1941 between Philadelphia AL and Giants. Had 4–6 mark with A's, 1–0 for Giants.

Major league totals: 161 victories, 165 defeats, 4.25 ERA. Pitched 2945 innings, allowed 2980 hits, walked 1442, struck out 1318. In World Series competition, 2–1, 4.15 ERA.

Wildness plagued Hadley. Regrettably one of his pitches felled Mickey Cochrane, 1937, fracturing skull in three places. Cochrane never played again.

After leaving majors, Hadley became one of pioneer television sportscasters in Boston area. Made home in Swampscott on Boston's North Shore, until heart attack, 1963.

HAFEY, CHARLES JAMES (Chick) OF-BR-TR. B. 2/12/03, Berkeley, Calif. D. 7/2/73, Calistoga, Calif. 6'1", 185. In parlance of Cardinal organization 40 years ago, Chick Hafey was "coconut snatcher." Branch Rickey, then GM of Cards, loved to relax tension of endless skull sessions with minor league managers, coaches, and scouts in organization with occasional story, legend, homily, or joke. After working with kids in tryout camps all morning, 20 or 30 of Rickey's minions, having taken notes on each young man in camp, would gather in large room to try to separate major league prospects from those who would never make it. Oftentimes such sessions went as many as 10 or 12 hours straight. Sandwiches, coffee would be brought in; work would continue, sometimes until 1 or 2 A. M. Rickey invented one favorite story about monkeys in jungle. According to him, monkeys set up system for gathering coconuts for group. Some monkeys always climbed to top of tree to pick coconuts. They would drop coconuts to other monkeys on ground, who would snatch fruit from air, passing it on to other monks who carried the nuts to monkeys' village. One day, according to Branch, one of coconut snatchers fell ill and another monkey substituted for him. Sub proved far more adept than one he replaced, so when first monkey returned he had to take up job of carrying nuts to village. New snatcher was real whiz grabbing fruit, regardless of how bad coconut pickers aimed them. So Rickey occasionally asked, when young ball player had looked bad at one position, "is he a coconut snatcher?" This meant, if he couldn't field ground ball, could he make it as out-fielder? Or, if he wasn't so hot as pitching prospect, could he run, could he hit, could he throw?

Hafey was one of Rickey's "coconut snatchers." Came to camp in Bradenton, Fla. Claimed he was pitcher. But after failing to impress on mound, slammed ball country mile during batting practice. Two more long drives dented fence in center field. Running to first base after last drive was part of camp routine; Rickey watched Hafey fly.

Later, just before time for practice game, Coach Joe Sugden came over to Rickey, saying, "Branch, you've got a boy wrong here. Hafey is pitcher, and you have him in your lineup as outfielder." "He was pitcher," whispered Rickey confidentially. "He's an outfielder now." What an outfielder! Hall of Fame 1971.

After that session in Bradenton, 1923, Hafey went to Cardinal farm at Fort Smith, Western Association, where he played 141 games, hit .284, banged 42 doubles, 14 triples, and 16 home runs. He was 19 at time. Houston got him next year. Slugged .360; slammed 20 triples to lead Texas League in that respect. Cardinals had him for 24 games that season but decided to farm him out one more time. Started 1925 with Syracuse, International League, but stayed only 21 games, batting .286. Back to St. Louis, played 93 games in NL and hit .302. Dropped back to .271 in 1926, but for next six years never got below .329. In 1931 captured NL batting title with .349. That was closest battle ever for hitting championship. Hafey's mark came out to .3489; Bill Terry was next with .3486 and Jim Bottomley .3482.

In 1929 Hafey had sinus trouble that affected his eyes; began wearing glasses. Prior to that time very few players had used glasses (excepting sunglasses) on field. Didn't seem to bother his hitting. However, Cardinal front office was bothered by his demands for more money. After he held out long time in spring of 1932, owner Breadon and Rickey traded him to Cincinnati. Reportedly received $50,000 cash and two players.

Illness held down Hafey's playing in 1932 to 83 games, but he batted .344. Shoulder injury kept him out of all but 15 games, 1935. Retired from game after that, but returned to Reds for 1937. After hitting .261 in 89 games that year, stayed in California where he had ranch.

Chick's major league totals: 1283 games, 4625 AB, 777 runs scored, 1466 hits, 341 doubles, 67 triples, 164 homers, 833 RBI, .317 average. In WS play, four years with Cardinals: 23 games, 88 AB, 5 runs, 18 hits including 7 doubles, 2 RBI; average .205.

HAGUE, JOE CLARENCE, JR. 1B-OF-BL-TL. B. 4/25/44, Huntington, W. Va. 6', 195. Outspoken player with apparently fine potential whom St. Louis Cardinals traded to Cincinnati early 1972 for Bernie Carbo. Hague, in two full seasons and three part seasons with Redbirds, hit 36 homers, but generally didn't get share of other base hits. Got in front of too many pitches, so many long drives were simply foul balls down right field line. Then too, Joe often said what was on his mind, which did not help team spirit. Nor was it considered favorable to getting more fans to pass through turnstiles. Once criticized Richie Allen and Jose Cardenal while they were with Cardinals, and his comments were published in Peoria, Ill., and picked up elsewhere. But when Redbirds traded him to Cincinnati, Hague blamed Cardinal president, Gussie Busch, for low standing of ball club, noting that Busch had traded away Steve Carlton and Jerry Reuss.

Hague was stellar football player in high school and won athletic scholarship at Texas. Quit after freshman year but regained athletic scholarship as baseball player. Topped Texas team in batting, 1965, and signed with Cardinal organization, 1966. Spent that summer at Cedar Rapids, Midwest League, hitting .251 for 119 games. Debut in pro ball rather impressive: hit grand slam homer in first trip to plate, and got eight more homers before season's close. Arkansas, Texas League, 1967, with .271 average, 27 homers, 95 RBI, in 140 contests. Following year, .293 average with Tulsa, Pacific Coast League. This time 23 homers, 99 RBI, and his 274 total bases led circuit. Seven games with Cardinals. In 1969, 84 games at Tulsa with .332 mark, 16 homers. And 40 games with Cardinals, batting .170, with two homers, eight RBI. Then in his first full season with Redbirds, batted .271 in 139 games, 14 homers, 68 RBI. Dropped down to .226 with 16 homers, 1971. This put his major league average at .242 for 315 games.

In 1972 Joe had three homers while with St. Louis before trade to Rhineland. Promptly slapped four round-trippers with Reds, but tapered off after strong start. Had .243 mark for season, in 96 games. No hits in three trips during 1972 WS.

One grand slammer while still with Cardinals 9/24/71. Came in 10th inning against Montreal Expos. Mgr. Gene Mauch, in effort to keep Hague from hitting ball through infield, used five infielders. Joe hit ball over their heads for home run, winning game.

HAHN, FRANK GEORGE (Noodles) P-BL-TL. B. 4/29/79, Nashville, Tenn. D. 2/6/60, Candler, N.C. 5'9", 160. Got nickname because as youth he sold mother's homemade noodle soup. Remembered in Cincinnati especially because he holds club records for most games started, 42;

most complete games pitched, 41. Achieved these 1901.

Started out in Mobile as pitcher, 1895. Made grade with Cincinnati, 1899; 23–8 record. Had 16–21 mark, 1900. Then 22–19, 23–12, 22–12 and 15–18 records following years. Hurt arm. Was 8–5 in 1905–06, spending latter season with New York AL. No-hitter 7/12/1900, 4–0, against Philadelphia. Major league totals: 130 wins, 94 losses.

After leaving major leagues, became veterinarian with U.S. government meat inspection service. Until retirement, after 30 years, had locker at Cincinnati ball park, pitching batting practice for Reds during home stands.

HAINES, JESSE JOSEPH (Pop) P-BR-TR. B. 7/22/93, Clayton, Ohio. 6', 180. Jesse Haines won his selection to Hall of Fame, 1970, for 210–158 record for St. Louis Cardinals, 1920–37. Won three World Series victories, lost one; boasted .444 batting average in World Series competition, including one home run.

Jesse had strong right arm, burning fast ball. But this wasn't enough to make fine pitcher until he learned two things—how to control his temper, how to throw knuckle ball. These, plus fast ball, enabled Cardinals to collect dividends on $10,000 investment for his contract— small fortune 50 years ago, especially for Redbirds and Branch Rickey. Rickey and host of small stockholders trying to run ball club on shoestring. Virtually no money in treasury. Rickey went out on limb, persuading directors to buy Haines from Kansas City for $10,000 cash. Money had to be borrowed from bank. Note endorsed by at least dozen persons before Rickey could get greenbacks.

Fortunately for Rickey, Haines proved to be workhorse. In second season with club, 1921, 18–12 for team that finished third. When Cardinals won their first pennant ever, Haines had 13–4 mark. That was 1926 when Grover Cleveland Alexander came to Haines' rescue in seventh game of World Series, fanned Tony Lazzeri with bases loaded, then held Yankees rest of way. Cards thereby took Series.

But Haines had pitched shutout against Bombers in third game of Series. Allowed just five hits and helped his own cause with home run. Then Haines was Mgr. Hornsby's starter in seventh and final game. Pitching carefully against Ruth, Bob Meusel, Gehrig, Lazzeri, cohorts, Jesse had made frequent use of knuckle ball. So much so that in seventh inning his knuckles were bleeding. Was losing effectiveness. Cards ahead 3 to 2, but Yanks managed to load bases with two outs. When Hornsby saw Jesse's hand, Alexander was called in.

Haines lost one decision to Yanks in 1928 Series. Came back to win four-hitter in 1930 Series against Athletics. Though 12–3 in 1931 season, missed World Series because of illness.

Jesse bowed out as active player after 1937. Spent 1938 as coach with

Brooklyn Dodgers. Had pitched in 555 major league games, 3207 innings, 210 wins, 158 losses, ERA 3.64. World Series: 6 games, 32-1/3 innings, 3–1 mark; 1.67 ERA.

HALL, TOM EDWARD (Blade) P-BL-TL. B. 11/23/47, Thomasville, N.C. 6′,155. Cincinnati Reds regarded Tom Hall highly enough to give away Wayne Granger, outstanding relief pitcher, to get him from Minnesota Twins 12/4/71. Strikeout is word when talking about Hall, skinny southpaw. In 1971 fanned 137 batters in 130 innings; struck out 184 in 155 innings previous year. In 1970 barely fell short of qualifying as AL's most effective pitcher. Had he pitched another seven innings, his ERA of 2.55 would have been considered tops in circuit.

Hall attended Riverside City College in California before signing with Minnesota organization, 1966, at Sarasota. Later pitched for Orlando, Wisconsin Rapids, Charlotte, and Denver, with brief spell with Twins in 1968. Remained with Twins, 1969, posting 8–7 record with 3.52 ERA. Had 92 strikeouts, allowed 50 walks in 141 innings. Despite 4–7 record in 1971 and 3.32 ERA, Sparky Anderson, manager of Reds, declared he believed Hall to be "one of best lefthanded relief pitchers in baseball."

Hall's AL record showed an overall total of 456 innings pitched, 431 strikeouts, 186 bases on balls, and an ERA of 3.00. Pitching rating system developed by George Sisler and son, George, Jr., ranked Hall as most "efficient" pitcher in 1970, ahead of such stars as Tom Seaver, Sam McDowell, Fergie Jenkins, and others who have gained more publicity.

In 1972 Tom justified Sparky's confidence. In 47 games, won 10, lost one, saved eight others; pitched one shutout, had 2.61 ERA in 124 innings. Followed this with four relief appearances in WS—allowed no runs, struck out seven in 8-1/3 innings.

HALLAHAN, WILLIAM ANTHONY (Wild Bill) P-BR-TL. B. 8/4/02, Binghamton, N.Y. 5′10½″, 180. To Bill Hallahan wildness was at once an asset and liability. His sizzling fast ball terrified opposing batters— Bill didn't always get pitch in strike zone. Wild pitches, walks hurt his effectiveness, but seemed to do best work in clutch.

Hallahan's best season was 1931; 19–9 for Cardinals, helping team romp to NL pennant. Brilliant World Series performance followed. Baffled powerful Philadelphia Athletics who then had Al Simmons, Jimmie Foxx, Mickey Cochrane, Bing Miller, other sluggers in lineup. Allowed just one run in 18-1/3 innings, pitched one shutout, got two decisions, saved final and crucial seventh game. Had ERA of 0.49 for that Series. Bill's finest game, however, may have been one he pitched in old Ebbets Field, Brooklyn, 9/30. Cards, Cubs, Giants, Dodgers battling to wire for NL flag. Hallahan due to start for Redbirds in crucial contest—against Dazzy Vance. But night before, somehow slammed taxi door on right hand. Although not his pitching hand, this did not lessen pain. All night long "Doc" Weaver, Cardinal trainer, worked on Hallahan, massaging arm, packing hand with ice. Next afternoon Bill took to mound with two fingers in splint, sticking outside glove on right hand. Duel of fast-ballers watched by 30,000. Hallahan retired 20 Dodgers in order until his own error allowed base runner. Had no-hitter until eighth inning. Score 0–0 inning after inning. In fifth inning Cards almost scored. Sparky Adams, on third, "stole home," apparently sliding safely across plate. But Vance's pitch was wild, hit Chick Hafey, and Adams had to return to third where he died. In Cardinal half of tenth, Redbirds finally got run. Andy High's double, followed by sacrifice and Douthit's single, made score 1–0. In last of 10th Glenn Wright doubled. Bissonette walked. Hendrick sacrificed runners along. Hallahan then walked Jake Flowers intentionally, to fill bases. Al Lopez hit to Sparky Adams, shortstop. Adams juggled ball momentarily, recovered in time to start double play. Hallahan had 1–0 victory over Vance.

Hallahan played semipro ball after finishing high school. Signed with Cardinal organization, joining club in 1924 training camp. Weighed 135 at time, but had dazzling speed. Spent four years in minors, with couple of hitches in St. Louis. Won 19, lost 11 at Syracuse, International League, 1927; 23–12 record, Houston, Texas League, 1928, with 244 strikeouts. Back with Cardinals to stay, 1929. Posted 15–9 mark to help Cards win flag, 1930; 19–9 in 1931. Had 12–7, 1932; 16–13, 1933. Next winning season was 1935—15–8. Traded to Cincinnati during 1936 season. Redleg 1937. Left majors following 1938 with Philadelphia NL.

Major league record: 102 wins, 94 losses, 1740 innings, ERA 4.03. World Series record—3 wins, 1 loss, 1 save, 1.36 ERA, 39-2/3 innings.

HALLER, THOMAS FRANK   C-BL-TR. B. 6/23/37, Lockport, Ill. 6'4", 210.

Veteran NL catcher who moved into AL, 1972, where his brother Bill had umpired since 1963. Spent season with Detroit, then shifted back to NL with Philadelphia. However, Haller then announced retirement from game.

Tom probably has had more take-home pay than Bill. Tom got bonus reportedly as high as $54,000 to sign with San Francisco Giants, 1958, and also got WS money with that team, 1962. Tom was phys. ed. major at Illinois, receiving B.S. degree.

Served apprenticeship at Phoenix; Springfield, Mass.; Tacoma, before sticking with Giants, 1962. With Giants through 1967. Los Angeles NL 1968–71. Traded to Tigers 12/2/71. In AL, Haller went 0 for 9 before he got hit. Then hit homer, his first safety in circuit. Had .207 mark in 59 games, 1972, then sold to Phillies.

Tom then had lifetime record of .257 for 1294 games. Had 134 homers among his 1011 hits, with 153 doubles and 31 triples. Had 504 RBI. His highest BA was 1970, when he hit .286 in 112 games.

In 1968 set NL record for double plays by catchers, with 23. In 1962 WS with Giants, Haller hit Whitey Ford for two-run homer in fourth game of Series and had .286 average for four games. Giants, however, lost WS to Yankees, four games to three. Tom was member of three NL All-Star squads, 1966,67,68.

HALLER, WILLIAM EDWARD (Fox) Umpire. B. 2/28/35, Joliet, Ill. 6′4″, 205. Brother acts in baseball are not too unusual. DiMaggios, Waners, Meusels, Alous, many others. But 1972 started an AL brother act different from others—Bill Haller umpiring game where brother Tom was catching for Detroit Tigers. Both Hallers are long-time pros, but it was first time in majors their names had been in same box score.

Bill and Tom, however, had been together in same games while both toiled in Pacific Coast League, 1960–61. Bill, two years older than Tom, attended Joliet Junior College before becoming umpire in Georgia-Florida League, 1958; N.Y.-Pa. League, 1959; Northwest League, 1960; Pacific Coast League 8/5/60 to 9/10/61, then AL rest of season. International League, 1962. AL since then. First WS umpiring, 1968. Worked All-Star games 1963, 1970.

Bill did not officiate many games while Tom was catching. But Earl Weaver, manager Baltimore Orioles, complained to AL prexy, Joe Cronin. Weaver said he was not saying Bill would be dishonest, but perhaps would "lean one way or another" subconsciously when brother was catching.

Cronin did shift Bill from working in at least one series where Tom might be catching. All of which got Cronin severely criticized in some quarters. Leonard Koppett, writing in *Sporting News*, declared Cronin's action cast doubt on umpire's integrity because of family realtionship. Then asked how Joe Cronin, "of all people," could do this, since wife is member of Griffith family, owners of Minnesota Twins. Also pointed out "father-son" relationship between Cronin and Tom Yawkey, owner of Boston Red Sox. Might have pointed out also that Joe's own son works for Twins. Question became academic when Tom was sold to Phillies at end of 1972 season.

HAMILTON, WILLIAM ROBERT (Billy) OF-BL-TR. B. 2/16/66, Newark, N.J. D. 12/16/40, Worcester, Mass. 5′6″, 165. Hall of Famer who still holds NL record for stolen bases with 115 pilfered during 1891 season. Modern record, of course, belongs to Maury Wills, who reached 104 in 1962. Billy Hamilton also passed century mark in steals in 1890, with 102; came close with 99 in 1894,95 in 1895. Stole 117 bases in old American Association, 1889, then considered major league. Add all his major league steals together and you get 937. Throw in fact he won NL batting championship, 1891, with .338, and had lifetime major league mark of .344, and you see he rightly should be in Hall of Fame.

Hamilton started out at Worcester, New England League, 1888. Kansas City, AA, 1888–89; Philadelphia NL, 1890–95; Boston NL, 1896–1901; Haverhill, New England League, 1902–08, with exception of 1905 when he was with Harrisburg in Tri-State League. Lynn, New England League, 1909–10.

Billy had marks of .395, .399, .393 in NL in 1893,94,95. Also won three New England League batting championships.

Played 1578 big league games. His 2157 hits included 225 doubles, 94 triples, 37 homers. Managed throughout his New England League and Tri-State League years. Piloted Fall River, New England League, 1913, and Springfield, Eastern League, 1914. Part owner and manager, Worcester, Eastern League, 1916. Scout, Boston AL, 1911–12. Hall of Fame 1961.

HANDS, WILLIAM ALFRED, JR. P-BR-TR. B. 5/6/40, Hackensack, N.J. 6'2", 195. Bill Hands, chess player and pitcher, won 92 NL games, lost 88 before reporting to Minnesota Twins, 1973. Traded from Chicago Cubs in deal involving Dave LaRoche, 11/30/71. Hands had couple of losing seasons when he first joined Cubs, 1966–67, then came up with three fine years, 16–10, 20–14, 18–15. Was 12–18 in 1971, 11–8 in 1972. Steady workman. In four of his years with Cubs, pitched more than 240 innings each; had 300 innings during his 20-victory season, 2.49 ERA.

Hands started pro baseball, 1959, Hastings, Nebr. Pitched for Fresno; Eugene, Oreg.; Springfield, Mass.; Tacoma. Joined San Francisco Giants, 1965, four games; traded to Chicago along with Randy Hundley for Lindy McDaniel and Don Landrum, 12/2/65. Busy during his winters. Attended Ohio Wesleyan and Fairleigh Dickinson, latter near home, Parsippany, N.J. Has worked for engineering and petroleum company.

Owned 3.23 ERA, 280 major league appearances, when he joined Twins; 1570 innings, 395 walks, 905 strikeouts.

HANEY, FRED GIRARD (Pudge) 3B-BR-TR. B. 4/25/98, Albuquerque, N. Mex. 5'6", 170. Fred Haney went further as manager and broadcaster than as ball player though he did reasonably well with Detroit back in days of Ty Cobb. Fred was infielder with Portland, Pacific Coast League, 1918; Los Angeles, PCL, 1919–20; Omaha, Western League, 1920–21. Joining Tigers, Haney got in tune with sluggers Cobb, Veach, Heilmann et al., batted .352 in 81 games, 1922. Boston AL, 1926; during 1927, to Chicago NL. After bowing out of majors, had brief comeback with Cardinals, 1929. Major league totals showed 622 games, 1977 trips, 544 hits, .275 average, 66 doubles, 21 triples, 8 homers, 338 runs, 50 stolen bases.

Haney took up managing in minors. Until June 1956, insists he had never been with any solid pennant contender. That was when he joined Milwaukee Braves and brought club home in second place. Won 1957 NL flag; followed it up with World Series victory over Yankees in set which went seven-game limit.

Fred tells about one managing experience in American Association, 1935. Was bossing Toledo. Club owner was automobile dealer. Haney says he thinks car salesmen were doubling as scouts, "offering any prospective buyer a premium in the form of a Toledo contract for any male relative who had ever played catch or bean bag." His Mud Hens finished seventh that year.

Haney's first big league management was with St. Louis Browns, 1939. Team finished last. Sixth in 1940. Also sixth 1941, though during season Haney had been replaced by Luke Sewell. Then turned to radio, broadcasting Hollywood and Los Angeles games in Pacific Coast League. Hired as Hollywood manager, 1949. Club was closely linked with Pittsburgh Pirates by working agreement; this led to his selection to manage Buccaneers 1953. Club finished last 1954,55. Then joined Milwaukee as coach under manager Charlie Grimm. Reluctant to become pilot when Grimm dropped, but Charlie insisted he should take job.

After his World Series victory, 1957, Haney's club first again 1958, but lost autumn classic to Yankees, four games to three. In 1959 Braves finished in first-place tie with Dodgers. Lost playoff. At this point Haney quit managing. When AL expanded, 1961, Haney became general manager of Los Angeles Angels, who later transferred to Anaheim and became California Angels. Haney eventually gave up this job to Dick Walsh. Since then has been "consultant" for team.

HANLON, EDWARD HUGH (Ned)   OF-BL-TL. B. 8/22/57, Montville, Conn. D. 4/14/37, Richmond, Va. 5'9½", 170. Ned Hanlon didn't look part of "choke-'em-Charlie" ball player. Those who knew him said he resembled more an undistinguished clerk or bookworm. And while not remembered as great player, his fame as manager persists. Piloted old Baltimore Orioles of 1890s, winning NL flags 1894, 95, 96. Then won pennants at Brooklyn NL 1899,1900.

Typical of Hanlon, however, was play pulled to get on base. Pitch was near him, lefthanded hitter. Hanlon dropped to ground, writhing, screaming, apparently in pain. Jumped up and started to first base. Umpire Tim Hurst yelled for him to get back, that ball had not hit him but had tipped bat. At this point Hanlon showed Hurst red spot on his arm, claiming ball had hit him there. Awarded first base. Years later Ned confided that while rolling on ground he pinched own arm to make it appear he had been hit.

Hanlon had fast team, including such men as Willie Keeler and John McGraw; quick-witted fellows too, ready to use anything to win. This included use of mirrors to reflect sunlight in opposing players' eyes as they were about to make play. Home diamond was set up so Orioles could take greatest advantage: oppenents claimed third-base foul line was built up so Oriole bunts would stay fair, in case ball had any inclination to roll foul; first base was said to be "downhill," helping Baltimore speedsters. Grass was allowed to grow long in outfield, with extra baseballs strategically hidden. If opponents hit one too far, Oriole fielders could sneak one of planted balls into play instead. Ground in front of plate was hardened almost like concrete. Oriole players practiced and perfected art of hitting ball downward on hard spot. Ball would bounce high into air, with infielders or pitcher helpless to make play until it came down. This was famous "Baltimore chop." Depending on who was pitching for opposition, mound would be watered, and, it was claimed, spots were sprinkled with powdered soap to make it slippery. Opposing hurler might try to make play on batted ball, and have his leg slip from under him.

As player, Hanlon started out 1880 with Cleveland NL. Detroit NL, 1881–88; Pittsburgh NL, 1889; Pittsburgh, Players League, 1890; Pittsburgh NL, 1891; Baltimore NL, 1892. Old records vary, but Hanlon hit somewhere around .260 and several times stole more than 50 bases in one season.

Managed Pittsburgh teams part of 1889 all of 1890 and into 1891; managed Baltimore part of 1891 and through 1898; Brooklyn, 1899–1905; Cincinnati, 1906–07. Hanlon won five pennants and had three second-place teams as pilot. President of Baltimore club, Eastern League, 1908–09. Later connected with Baltimore, Federal League, 1914.

Besides tricks mentioned earlier, Hanlon's Orioles were credited with perfecting use of bunt and "hit and run" play, which of course was perfectly legal though some opponents claimed it was unfairly deceptive. On more illegal side, Hanlon's players were adept at blocking base runners, grabbing their belts, tripping them. Often got away without penalty being called; there was only one umpire in those days and he couldn't watch everything on diamond simultaneously.

HANNEGAN, ROBERT E. Executive. B. 6/30/03, St. Louis, Mo. D. 10/6/49, St. Louis, Mo. Bob Hannegan, more than anyone else, was responsible for putting Harry Truman in Presidency of U.S. Bob, long before he ever heard of Truman, loved baseball. Sold peanuts in bleachers of St. Louis ball park so could see Cardinals play. Joined Knothole Gang so could see games when not selling peanuts. Took part in 10-mile runs twice, allegedly because long-distance runners wound up inside ball park before annual Tuberculosis Society benefit game. Day came when Hannegan bought Cardinals. Then, little over one year later, sold interest in club at million-dollar profit.

Hannegan played baseball, basketball, football as youth. Graduated from St. Louis U. 1926, took up practice of law. Accumulated $200,000 from law, and investments in tea and coffee company, beverage firm, finance company, trucking outfit, movie theaters, real estate.

So could afford to take job as collector, Internal Revenue, $6500 a year, 1942. Late following year moved to Washington, D.C., as commissioner of Internal Revenue. In January 1944 became chairman of Democratic National Committee at $20,000 annual salary. Pulled strings that resulted in Truman becoming Democratic candidate for vice presidency; Truman became President 4/12/45 on death of Franklin Roosevelt. Following month Truman appointed Hannegan Postmaster General at preinflation salary of $15,000.

Hannegan, with Fred Saigh, bought Cardinals late in 1947 and resigned job as Postmaster General. Theoretically Cardinals cost $4,060,000, but banks put up cash; Hannegan supplied most of security. Hannegan became president of Redbirds, but little over year later, on physician's advice, he sold out to Saigh. Died about eight months later.

HANSEN, RONALD LAVERN Inf.-BR-TR. B. 4/5/38, Oxford, Nebr. 6'3", 200. Ron Hansen, who made an unassisted triple play, 1968, apparently came to end of his major league career, 1972. Played just 16 games for Kansas City AL and hit .133. So he left big time with .234 average for his 1384 games. Had 1007 hits good for 156 doubles, 17 triples, 106 homers. Scored 446 runs and drove in 501.

Ron was designated AL Rookie of Year, 1960, by both *Sporting News* and Baseball Writers Association of America. With Baltimore Orioles that year, played 153 games, led AL shortstops in putouts with 325, had .964 fielding average and hit .255 with 22 homers and 86 RBI.

Hansen set major league record for most chances accepted by shortstop during doubleheader, 28, 8/29/65. Twin bill went total of 23 innings. Also tied an AL record for most chances accepted during an extra inning game, with 18 putouts and assists in first game that same day 8/29/65. Unassisted triple killing came while he was with Washington Senators 7/30/68 during night contest. Joe Azcue, then with Cleveland, was hitter. Indians had men on first and second. Hansen caught Azcue's liner, stepped on second to double runner off that bag, then tagged runner headed from first to second. It was first unassisted triple play in majors since 1927. Also led AL shortstops in double plays in 1961, 1964 and 1967.

Started pro ball at Stockton, Calif., 1956. Played with Vancouver,

B.C.; Knoxville, Tenn., with brief trials with Orioles, 1958–59 Stuck with them, 1960, remaining four full seasons. Chicago AL 1963–67. With Washington first part of 1968 then traded back to White Sox 8/2/68; remained with Sox through 1969, then spent two years with Yankees. In 1970 hit two pinch-hit homers for New Yorkers. Released after 1971 season and signed with Kansas City as free agent. Then dropped by Royals after 16 games. Suffered from ruptured spinal disc, 1966, later had two spinal operations.

HARDER, MELVIN LE ROY (Chief)   P-BR-TR. B. 10/15/09, Beemer, Nebr. 6'1", 210. Mel Harder pitched his entire major league career for Cleveland Indians, but as coach moved from Cleveland to N.Y. Mets to Chicago Cubs to Cincinnati Reds. Won 223 AL games, lost 186. WS play eluded him as he pitched his last games with Indians, 1947. Following year they won pennant. Had one distinction, however: was Cleveland pitcher day they opened Municipal Stadium. Crowd of 82,000 was on hand; lost to Lefty Grove by 1–0 score. Mel started pro career, 1927, with Omaha, Western League. Though he won four and lost seven, Indians bought him, farmed him out to Dubuque, Mississippi Valley League, same season. Won 13, lost six, but league folded. Then spent all 1928 with Cleveland with 0–2 mark. In 1929 more seasoning with New Orleans, Southern Association, 7–2 in games; 1–0 with Indians. In 1930 back to Cleveland to stay. By 1932 won 15 games, repeated this in 1933. Then had 20–12 performance, 1934, and 22–11 in 1935. Best record after that was 17–10 in 1938.

During major league career Mel took part in 582 games, pitched 3426 innings and had 3.80 ERA. Pitched 24 shutouts, six of them in 1934, when this gave him tie for AL leadership that year.

Coach for Indians 1949–63; Mets, 1964; Cubs, 1965–66; Reds, 1967–68.

HARGRAVE, EUGENE FRANKLIN (Bubbles)   C-BR-TR. B. 7/15/92, New Haven, Ind. D. 2/23/69, Cincinnati, Ohio 5'10½", 168. Batting champion, NL, 1926, with .353 average, although, under rules adopted later, would not have qualified because had only 326 official trips to plate. Drew 25 bases on balls that year. Later majors adopted uniform system requiring player appear at least 502 times at plate to qualify for title.

Hargrave spent his most productive years with Cincinnati Reds. Started 1911 with Terre Haute, Central League. Late in 1913, after hitting .309 in 126 games, Bubbles went to Chicago NL for three games. Spent two seasons with Cubs but didn't get into many games. Then 1916–17 with Kansas City, American Association. Divided 1918 between Memphis, Southern Association and St. Paul, AA. Then after .335 year with Saints in 1920, on top of .303 average in 1919, Cincinnati bought his contract for $10,000.

In eight years with Reds his lowest average was .289. Back to St. Paul for 1929, this time as playing manager. Hargrave promptly led AA in batting with .369 average. Spent 1930 with N.Y. Yankees; Minneapolis, AA, 1931; Buffalo, International League, 1932. Out of the game, 1933, then managed Cedar Rapids, Western League, 1934.

Bubbles had younger brother, Pinky, also major league catcher, mostly in AL. Bubbles played 852 big league games; hit .310. His 786 hits included 155 doubles, 58 triples, 29 homers, with 375 RBI.

HARPER, TOMMY OF-BR-TR. B. 10/14/40, Oak Grove, La. 5'9", 160. When Tommy Harper stole 73 bases in 1969 for Seattle it was greatest number in AL history since Ty Cobb pilfered 96 in 1915. Speedy outfielder for Boston Red Sox had lifetime total of 296 when 1973 season started, giving him third place among active American Leaguers. Only Luis Aparicio and Bert Campaneris are ahead of him. Harper, however, stole 124 of those bases in NL before being traded from Cincinnati to Cleveland 11/21/67.

Tommy attended Santa Rosa Junior College in California and signed up with Cincinnati organization, 1960, going to Topeka for 79 games, hitting .254. Back at Topeka, 1961, hit .324. Hit 15 homers, drew 136 walks, scored 131 runs, had 11 triples, 27 doubles. Led league in walks, runs, and triples—and won MVP for III League. Following spring, with just one full season and part of another in professional ball, Harper was Cincinnati's starting third baseman. Youngster pressed too hard, hit just .174, and after six games Mgr. Freddy Hutchinson decided he needed bit more seasoning in high-class league.

Sent to San Diego, Pacific Coast League, Tommy led that circuit in runs scored, with 120; in walks, with 105; hit 26 homers, stole 22 bases, drove in 84 runs. His batting average of .333 in 144 games gave him runner-up position. With Cincinnati, 1963–67, playing infield and outfield. When he left NL, owned .255 batting average. In 1965 led NL in runs scored with 126 and had 18 homers. Cleveland, 1968, but after .217 record for 130 games, was put on Indians' list of players available for expansion draft. Seattle Pilots selected him 10/15/68; in 1969 had his fabulous record as base stealer, though he hit just .235. Seattle franchise transferred to Milwaukee for 1970. With Brewers, Tommy stepped up his performance. Hit .296 in 154 contests, slapped 31 homers for highest total of his career, drove in 82 runs, scored 104. In 1971 average dropped down to .258, with 14 homers in 152 games. Tommy hit .254 for Red Sox in 1972; 144 games, 14 homers.

When multiple deal between Brewers and Red Sox was discussed after 1971 season, Boston owner Tom Yawkey insisted Harper be included or there would be no trade. Harper has been exciting player for Red Sox, perhaps best base runner they have had since Tris Speaker was with club in 1915. At All-Star break in midseason was right up there with teammates Reggie Smith, Petrocelli, and Cater in home runs and RBI. Did not steal bases like he did in Seattle, but came up with such plays as going from first to third on sacrifice bunt.

Tommy was member of 1970 AL All-Stars, being used as pinch runner. Holds distinction of being one of few players in major league history to hit 30 home runs and steal 30 bases same season, 1970, when he had 31 round trippers, 38 thefts.

HARRELSON, DERREL MCKINLEY (Bud) SS-BLR-TR. B. 6/6/44, Niles, Calif. 5'11", 150. Some of signs in Shea Stadium refer to Mets' slender shortstop as "Twiggy." Weight has varied, often in relation to length of ball games; on hot muggy days, from 158 down to 146. Regardless of weight, is highly regarded as outstanding fielder and was so voted by poll of NL managers and coaches, 1971. Besides sensational shortstopping, Harrelson, during off-season, sings country and western songs in small nightclubs around New York—and hopes to make entertaining his career after baseball days end.

Bud's family used to live in dust bowl during depression days; left Oklahoma for San Joaquin Valley, Calif. Pa Harrelson got job in San Francisco Bay area during World War II and then came Bud. Bud attended San Francisco State College and signed up with Mets' organization, 1963, lured by bonus of slightly over $10,000. That year and following season Harrelson played at Salinas, California League. Spent most of 1965 with Buffalo, International League, but had 19 games with Mets. With Jacksonville, 1966, for 117 games, then back to Mets for 33 contests. With Mets ever since.

Knee injury while at Jacksonville resulted in surgery 9/24/68 for removal of cartilage. During 1968–69 Bud stole total of five bases—but in 1970–71 pilfered 51. Never hit much for distance or for high average. Had seven homers in minors. First homer in majors, 8/17/67, was inside-park variety. Next one came 4/17/70; that one went over fence. Then, 5/1/72, "Mister Muscles," as he is called, slapped home run number three, line drive over left field wall in Candlestick Park, San Francisco. His third big league homer came in his major league game number 749.

Harrelson's best year for average was 1967, when he hit .254; lifetime average is hovering around .237 mark. In his only WS, 1969, Bud got three hits in 17 trips, for .176 average. Played in 1970,71 All-Star games as member of NL squad. During 1970 season, Harrelson tied then-existing major league record for most errorless games at shortstop, 54.

HARRELSON, KENNETH SMITH (Hawk) 1B-OF-BR-TR. B. 9/4/41,

Woodruff, S.C. 6'2", 190. Ken Harrelson retired from baseball at 29 during early part of 1971 season to take up professional golf. Before autumn, dropped out of Professional Golfers' Association qualifying tournament when made 24 over par. Has been deliberately "flake" since high school days. Colorful antics, long hair, sartorial splendor, controversies. Nose broken three times, once in baseball, once in football, once in fight. Hence nickname "Hawk." Other major leaguers have last names on backs of their uniforms, Ken had "Hawk" on his. Awhile had TV show, "Hawk's Nest." Admits being "best all-round schoolboy athlete in Savannah." Football, baseball, basketball, arm wrestling, pool, auto racing, fighting, blackjack. Poor grades. Graduated from high school 1959. Several major league clubs interested in him. Picked Kansas City AL offer of $27,000 bonus payable over three-year period. Farmed to Olean, N.Y.-Penn. League—.192, 43 games. Following season A's farmed him to Sanford, Florida State League. Led league in hitting until midseason when felled by German measles; average sagged to .227. Hit .301 in 135 games at Visalia, California League, 1961. In 1962, Binghamton, Eastern League, hit .272., set homer and RBI records for circuit: 38 round-trippers, 138 RBI. To Portland, Pacific Coast League, 1963, for 41 games, batting .300; Kansas City midseason, .230, 79 engagements. Back to minors, Dallas, PCL, 1964, 18 home runs but .232 average; again to Kansas City, in time for 49 games in 1964. Following year Kansas City, all season. Led team with 23 HR and 66 RBI but hit only .238. Traded to Washington 6/66. Says Mgr. Gil Hodges and he had instant personality clash but Hodges made him into good-fielding first baseman. Hit .237. Traded to Kansas City 6/9/67. Ruckus on ball club—charges, countercharges among players and owner Charlie Finley. Manager Alvin Dark fired. Harrelson told newspapers Finley's actions bad for baseball. Finley demanded retraction. Hawk refused, given unconditional release. Financial break for Harrelson. Had been earning $12,500 with Kansas City. Had $20,000 debts. Soon other major league teams were bidding for signature. Red Sox gave him $73,000 bonus plus $25,000 contract. Later salary boosted to $50,000. Outlay didn't help Red Sox much. Hawk played 23 games late that year, batted .200. Club won flag. Lost to Cardinals in WS, four games to three. Harrelson .077, 1 for 13, 1 RBI.

Red Sox fourth 1968. Harrelson hit .275, 150 games. Early in 1969 Sox not too happy with big investment in Hawk—batting only .217, first 10 games. Traded to Cleveland. Shocked, Harrelson announced retirement from baseball. Two days later, lured by Cleveland cash, agreed to report. Hit .221, 30 home runs (27 with Indians). Broken leg early 1970; out for season. Then came bad start 1971, retirement.

Investments in golf course, sandwich shop, movie company, travel agency, other enterprises.

HARRIS, CHALMER LUMAN (Lum) P-BR-TR. B. 1/17/15, Birmingham, Ala. 6'1", 180. Lum Harris might be called Paul Richards' alter ego. Has been associated with Paul during most of baseball career. Harris-Richards friendship and mutual confidence blossomed in 1938–40 when they were battery mates at Atlanta, Southern Association. Richards was manager in AL from 1951 to 1961, first at Chicago, then at Baltimore, and Harris was always his pitching coach. When Richards left Orioles 8/31/61 Lum took over for rest of season as manager.

Richards became general manager of Houston Astros, September, 1961; Harris then became coach for Astros, 1962–64, moving into managerial spot at Houston 9/9/64. After one full season at helm, Harris scouted for Houston, 1966; piloted Richmond, International League, 1967; managed Atlanta Braves from 1968 to 8/7/72. Richards, of course, had become vice president of Atlanta club, in charge of baseball operations.

As player, Harris pitched for Charlotte and Atlanta, 1937. In 1938–40 won total of 42 games while dropping 23 decisions. Then advanced to Philadelphia AL. Never won more than 11 games in any AL season. In 1943, 7–21. Spent 1945 in military service. Divided 1947 between Washington AL and Louisville and Minneapolis, American Association; 1948, Minneapolis, then Jersey City and Buffalo, International League. Buffalo 1949. Baltimore, International League, 1950.

Harris' complete major league record: 819 IP, 151 games, 35–63, ERA 4.16. As manager, took over third-place club final month of 1961 for Baltimore, winning 17, losing 10, finishing third. In his two years at Houston, club finished ninth. Captured first place in solitary season bossing Richmond. At Atlanta, had fifth-place team, 1968; first in Western Division, 1969, but lost play-offs to N.Y. Mets; fifth in Western Division, 1970; third in 1971.

Winter of 1961 managed San Juan club in Puerto Rican League, taking pennant.

HARRIS, JOSEPH (Moon) 1B-OF-BR-TR. B. 5/20/91, Coulters, Pa. D. 12/10/59, Pittsburgh, Pa. 5'9", 175. Joe Harris played on two cellar teams and one seventh-place club before he got break. Hapless Red Sox of those days traded him to pennant-winning Washington 5/1/25. Helped Senators to second flag in two years, hitting .324 after transfer. Had great World Series, but despite fine hitting, Pirates won in seven games. Harris had 11 hits for .440 average, scored five runs, drove in six, hit three homers.

"Moon" got another break, landing with Pirates in time for their 1927 pennant. Hit .326 for season, but got only three hits, 15 trips, in Series, which Yanks took in four-game sweep.

Played at McKeesport, Bay City, Chattanooga in period from 1912 to

1916, getting brief tryout with Yankees, 1914. Cleveland 1917 and 1919 (1918, military service, World War I). Skipped 1920,21 to play "outlaw" ball, thus missing Cleveland's pennant winner in 1920. Then Boston AL 1922–24, start of 1925. Washington 1925–26. Pittsburgh 1927–28, moving to Brooklyn 6/8/28. Back to minors, spending next three years at Sacramento, Toronto, Buffalo.

Lifetime major league record: .317, 970 games. World Series totals: 11 games, 14 hits in 40 trips, 2 doubles, 3 homers, 7 RBI, .350 average.

Harris raised fruit trees and kept hunting dogs, living on farm in later years of his life.

HARRIS, STANLEY RAYMOND (Bucky) Mgr.-2B-BR-TR. B. 11/8/96, Port Jervis, N.Y. 5'10" 156. Stanley "Bucky" Harris, "Boy Manager" of 1924 Washington Senators, got first baseball job at Pittston, Eastern Pennsylvania League, 1915; continued in organized baseball until retired recently as scout for Senators. Besides winning pennant in first season at helm, 1924, had more than quarter of century managing in AL plus brief spell in NL as pilot. Playing manager, 1924, his team vanquished Giants in World Series, won flag next season but lost to Pittsburgh. Years later, 1947, took another AL pennant with Yankees as bench manager, went on to win WS from Brooklyn four games to three.

After Pittston, Detroit took Harris's contract for 1916 but sent him to Scranton, N.Y. State League, then Muskegon, Central League, same year. Norfolk, Virginia League, and Reading, N.Y. State League, 1917. Buffalo, International League, 1918–19 then to Washington at end of season. Regular second baseman 1920, batting even .300. Not power hitter but good in clutches.

While making name as fine second baseman Bucky also playing pro basketball during winters until Clark Griffith, Washington owner, put clause in his contract forbidding it. One year the clause wasn't there, possibly by mistake. Harris went back to basketball to make extra dough, not advertising fact. Late December 1923 came up with shiner on eye. Attended New Year's Eve dance at old Wardmann Park Hotel, Washington, and ran into club secretary. Story of shiner got to Griffith. Owner called him in, persuaded him to leave for Florida immediately. Asked whether he'd be willing to shift to third base as Griff hoped to make deal with White Sox to secure Eddie Collins who would play second and manage Senators. Deal never materialized. Some weeks later Harris astonished when Griff offered him manager's job. Bucky jumped at it. Sports writers unimpressed. Not one accompanied Senators on first road trip. But before summer was too far along, entire nation seemed rooting for Senators to overcome Yankees, who had taken AL flags 1921, 22, 23. When Series started it was 27-year-old tactician matching wits with veteran manager John McGraw of Giants. McGraw's tenth pennant. As player, Harris hit .333 in series. In sixth game, with Giants ahead, three games to two, Harris drove in both Washington runs in 2–1 victory, bringing up seventh game.

Meanwhile, Bill Terry, Giants' lefthanded hitting first baseman, had been thorn in Senators' side throughout Series. McGraw platooning him, sending George Kelly to first when southpaw toiled for opposition. Harris had Curly Ogden, RHP, warm up for crucial seventh game. But secretly, beneath stands, had George Mogridge, LHP, also warming up. McGraw put Terry in lineup. Fans and sports writers moaned at selection of Ogden as Washington hurler. Ogden struck out first Giant batsman, started for dugout in accord with plan. Harris called him to come back to mound. Walked next hitter, at which Bucky went to original plan, sending for Mogridge. McGraw kept Terry in lineup against southpaw but Bill went hitless in two trips. Finally McGraw took Terry out. Then Harris countered with RHP Fred Marberry. Seesaw game stood 3–3 after eight innings. Harris had driven in all Washington runs with homer and single. Got one other hit. Veteran Walter Johnson pitched final four innings, gaining his first Series victory. This came when Ruel doubled, rode home on McNeely's fluke hit which bounced over third baseman Lindstrom's head. If Terry had stayed in game, maybe outcome might have been different. Had hit .429 for Series.

Bucky's 1925 flag winners lost seven-game Series to Pirates. Piloted Senators till end of 1928 season when traded to Detroit for Jack Warner. Managed Detroit five years, almost entirely as bench manager. Piloted Boston AL 1934. Back to Washington for eight seasons, after which piloted Philadelphia NL briefly, resigning 7/43. When Larry MacPhail took over Yankees, 1947, Bucky got job. Yanks won flag by 10 games, went on to victory over Brooklyn in Series. Following season piloted Yanks into third place. Another term with Senators, 1950–54. Back to Detroit as manager, 1955–56. Thereafter Harris confined self to scouting and advisory capacity. After Bob Short took over Washington club as owner, appointing Ted Williams manager, Harris continued to draw pay as team advisor for one year. Though Harris watched all home games from press box, never once did new owner and manager ask for advice. Had Short done so he might have avoided some of disastrous trades he made, such as deal for Denny McLain.

Bucky rates high place among gentlemen who have played baseball professionally. Associated with Senators, (baseball and other,) so long and often he married daughter of U.S. Senator Sutherland, 1926.

HART, JAMES RAY OF-3B-BR-TR. B. 10/30/41, Hookerton, N.C. 5'11", 185. Injuries beset Jim Ray Hart in latter stages of his career, which, in majors, has been mostly with San Francisco Giants. Was solid hitter both for distance and average. At start of 1973 season owned .282 lifetime batting average, with 157 home runs in 996 NL games, and 525 RBI. Some of Hart's miseries began in his second major league game, 7/7/63. Bob Gibson of Cardinals threw pitched ball so hard it broke shoulder blade. Little more than one month later, four days after returning to action after shoulder healed, Giants again played Cardinals. This time Curt Simmons was Redbird pitcher—and Hart was beaned. After 1969 season Jim needed surgery on his shoulder; had throwing problems, 1971; then in infield practice 9/19/72 injured left knee, more surgery resulting.

Hart began pro ball, 1960, at Salem, Va.; later played at Quincy, Ill.; Fresno; Springfield, Mass.; Tacoma, before reporting to Giants during unfortunate 1963 season when he got into just seven NL games. But following year established himself with fine record—.286 average, 31 homers, 81 RBI. Followed with .299 and .285 marks in next two seasons; 23 homers, 96 RBI in 1965; 33 round-trippers, 93 RBI in 1966.

Jim went .289 in 1967: 29 homers, 99 RBI; and .258 with 23 homers, 78 RBI in 1968. Since then Hart has played less than 100 games per season. Also has done some shuttling to Phoenix, Giants' farm club in Pacific Coast League, 1969,71,72.

N.Y. Yankees acquired Hart early in 1973 season, mainly to be designated hitter.

HARTNETT, CHARLES LEO (Gabby) C-BR-TR B. 12/20/1900, Woonsocket, R.I. D. 12/20/72, Park Ridge, Ill. 6'1", 218. Gabby Hartnett, "Old Tomato Face," hit 236 home runs during career as great NL slugger, catcher, and manager. But one was greatest of all—it won pennant for Cubs 9/28/38. Shadows were falling at Wrigley Field, Chicago; score tied with Pittsburgh; Pirates held half-game lead. With two outs and two strikes on him, Gabby swung hard. Ball soared into left field seats and game was over. If Gabby had not hit homer, umpires would have called game because of darkness. Blow not only gave Cubs pennant, but climaxed Hartnett's brief career as Chicago manager. Had been named boss of Cubs little over two months before. Story would have had more dramatic ending had Cubs been able to take WS, but that was one of series when Yankees swept all four games.

Hartnett was eldest of 14 children. Worked in Worcester, Mass., factory, but by age 20 found he could get paid for playing ball. Signed with Worcester, Eastern League, 1921; played 100 games, hit .264, and was sold to Cubs for $2500.

Grover Cleveland Alexander was with Cubs those days and soon indicated he liked to pitch to husky New Englander. Later Hartnett said Alex was greatest he ever caught, throwing at three different speeds. Alex also threw pretty fair screwball, according to Gabby.

In second year as Cub, Hartnett got into 85 games, 31 at first base. Cubs had fine catcher in Bob O'Farrell, so it wasn't easy to oust man of this caliber from first-string job. But by 1924 Hartnett's hitting and aggressive leadership had grown to such extent that he caught 105 games, O'Farrell 57. So in 1925 Cubs traded O'Farrell to Cardinals, where he enjoyed some great years. Gabby caught over 100 games 12 years, eight of them in succession. Those eight years in row came after 1929, when it looked like Hartnett might never catch again. Intense spirit got best of Gabby early in spring training. Fired ball to second base like bullet. Something snapped in arm. Caught in only one league game that year; used occasionally as pinch hitter.

After winning pennant, 1938, Cubs dropped to fourth in 1939, fifth in 1940. Released 11/13/40 and signed with N.Y. Giants as player-coach for 1941. Manager, Indianapolis, 1942. Manager, Jersey City, 1943. Manager, Buffalo, 1946. Coach, Kansas City AL, 1965; scout, member of Kansas City public relations staff, 1966.

Hartnett's highest batting average was .354 in 1937; hit .344 in 1935. But in 1930 had banner season with .339 average in 141 games, including 37 homers and 122 RBI. NL MVP 1935. Hall of Fame 1955.

Lifetime major league statistics: 1990 games, 6432 AB, 867 runs, 1912 hits, including 396 doubles, 64 triples, 236 homers, for .297 average. Drove in 1179 runs, stole 28 bases. In WS 1929,32,35,38: 16 games, 13 for 54, 2 doubles, 1 triple, 2 homers, for .241 average, 3 RBI. Five All-Star games.

HARTSFIELD, ROY THOMAS (Mousey) 2B-BR-TR. B. 10/25/25, Chattahoochee, Ga. 5'9", 165. Roy Hartsfield joined Atlanta Braves as coach, 1973, after four years as coach for Los Angeles Dodgers. Hartsfield had relatively brief period as major league ball player with old Boston Braves, but gained considerable reputation as instructor of young ball players. Managed in minors from 1958 through 1968. Got nickname because he succeeded "Mousey" Markland at second base with Dallas and Milwaukee.

Hartsfield played for Boston NL, 1950–52. Put in 265 games, with total of 30 doubles, 7 triples, 13 homers, among his 266 hits. Had .273 average, with 59 RBI. Before joining Braves as player, was in minors at Atlanta, Charleston, S.C.; Dallas, and Milwaukee during period 1943–49, with two years out for military duty. Back to minors, 1952; played with Milwaukee, Baltimore, Montreal, Fort Worth, St. Paul, and Los Angeles (then in Pacific Coast League). Player-manager at Des Moines, 1958; manager, Odessa, Tex., 1959; at Panama City, Fla., 1960; Greenville, S.C., 1961–62; St. Petersburg, 1963–64; Albuquerque, 1965; Spokane, 1966–68. Several of Hartsfield's clubs finished first in division races or split-season contests.

During off-season Roy works in photo and reproduction lab at Georgia Tech while filming football, basketball games.

HARTUNG, CLINTON CLARENCE (Floppy) P-OF-BR-TR. B. 8/10/22, Hondo, Tex. 6'4", 225. Some called him "Superman"; others named him "Baseball's Paul Bunyan." Possibly, in a setting other than New York, he might have lived up to advance billing. But in 1947 Giants had finished in NL second division seven of eight previous years. Competition for postwar dollar in Gotham was keen in baseball world with Brooklyn Dodgers doing well and Yankees grabbing publicity with Larry MacPhail at helm. Giants probably oversold Clint Hartung. Youngster got plenty of space on sports pages, radio, budding TV reports. But he would have had to be another Ty Cobb and Babe Ruth rolled into one to live up to advance billing.

Hartung played in low minors before going into air force. In Honolulu, with aviators, pitched and won 25 games, lost none, averaged 15 strikeouts a game. Between times played outfield, hit .567 in 67 games, making 30 home runs. No wonder they called him "Hondo Hurricane."

While he was property of Minneapolis, American Association, did not play there, 1946. Sold to Giants for $25,000 and four players, largely on basis of Honolulu record.

Though he occasionally hit ball tremendous distance in Giants' spring training camp, was pretty terrible as fielder; great arm, either in outfield throws or from pitching mound. After season opened and his future was doubtful, relieved in NL game 5/9/47, pitched six shutout innings, fanned five. Eventually realized that if he had any future, probably as pitcher. Blazing fast ball helped, but he couldn't master curve. Was 9–7 1947; had so-so record three more seasons. Then gave up pitching, hoping to make grade as pinch hitter and outfielder. Finally out of NL after 1952 season with major league record of 29–29, 5.02 ERA. As hitter, batted .238 in 196 big league games.

After that Hartung played briefly in minors—then drifted back to Texas oil fields at Sinton, near Corpus Christi.

HATTON, GRADY EDGEBERT, JR. 3B-BL-TR. B. 10/7/22, Beaumont, Tex. 5'8½", 172. Grady Hatton went into executive side of game, then returned to field. After serving as vice president Houston Astros, became coach under Leo Durocher, 1973.

Grady spent most of playing days with Cincinnati Reds. Began in 1946; hit .271 in 116 games. Gained momentary notice that same year when Johnny Sain of Boston Braves almost had perfect game. Hatton's pop fly fell safely among three of Sain's teammates in left field. Grady was only man to reach base against stellar righthander.

Hatton remained with Reds until 1954, when he also played with Chicago and Boston AL. In 1955 with Boston all year, then, 1956 went from Red Sox to Baltimore AL and St. Louis NL. After an absence of three years from major league scene, Hatton joined Chicago Cubs, 1960, for 28 games. In 1960, with 11 years of big league experience behind him, Grady hit .342 in 38 times at bat—first time he went above .300 mark during career. Lifetime average was .254 for 1312 games. After managing at Oklahoma City, Grady managed Houston Astros 1966–67 and until was replaced by Harry Walker 6/18/68. Astros finished eighth, then ninth, and were on way to 10th place under Hatton's leadership. Then vice president until returned to uniform in 1973.

HAUSER, JOSEPH JOHN   1B-BL-TL. B. 1/12/99, Milwaukee, Wis. 5'10½, 175. Joe Hauser, in 1924, seemed destined to be consistent home run hitter in major leagues. Hit 27 round-trippers and drove in 115 runs in third season in AL, and batted .288. But following spring was trotting to position at first base in exhibition game. Suddenly he fell to ground on his face with broken kneecap, and was out for entire season. Though he remained in AL 1926, 1928, and 1929, was never same again. Instead he set home run records in minor leagues: 399 in league games, including 67 at Baltimore, International League, 1930; and three years later, 69, at Minneapolis, American Association. This record stood until Joe Bauma hit 72 with Roswell, N. Mex., in Longhorn League, 1954.

Hauser played for Providence, Eastern League, 1918–19; then had two years at Milwaukee before landing with Philadelphia Athletics, 1922. Hit .323 that first year, in 111 AL games, and .307 in 146 contests, 1923. Dropped down to .288 in 1924.

Joe's last season in majors was 1929 with Cleveland. Had been in and out of lineup with injury, and that final season played 37 games, hit .250. His AL totals showed 629 games, 580 hits in 2044 AB, 103 doubles, 29 triples, 79 homers, and 356 RBI, for lifetime average of .284.

After his minor league homer records Hauser managed Union City club in Kitty League for Brooklyn Dodger organization.

HAYNES, JOSEPH WALTON   P-BR-TR. B. 9/21/17, Lincolnton, Ga. D. 1/6/67, Hopkins, Minn. 6'2½", 190. Joe Haynes never quite lived up to Clark Griffith's expectations as pitcher but did all right as son-in-law and coach. After Clark died, Haynes became vice president of club, first in Washington and then in Minnesota when Cal Griffith moved team there.

Haynes had 11–11 record at Jacksonville, South Atlantic League, 1937, his first professional engagement. Moved up to Chattanooga, Southern League, same year with 0–0 mark. In 1938 reported to Washington club for spring training but was sent back to minors because of bone infection in left arm. Needed operation. With Charlotte, Piedmont League, that year managed 18 wins and lost nine.

Joe 8–12 with Senators, 1939, and after 3–6 record in 1940 Washington traded him to White Sox. Pitched only eight games for White Sox, 1941; neither won nor lost decision. However, that autumn married Thelma R. Griffith, Clark Griffith's niece and adopted daughter. Remained with White Sox through 1948 season. Best year in Chicago was 1947 when he captured 14 wins and dropped six, with ERA of 2.42. Haynes was back with Washington 1949–52, winning 10 games, losing 21 in four-year stretch. Coach for Senators, 1953–55. After death of Clark Griffith, October 1955, Haynes became vice president of Senators; executive vice president, 1959. Club moved to Minnesota in 1961 and he remained in same capacity there until his death. Thelma is now vice president and assistant treasurer of Twins.

Haynes lifetime major league record showed 380 games pitched, 76 victories, 82 defeats with ERA of 4.01.

HEALY, FRANCIS XAVIER C-BR-TR. B. 9/6/46, Holyoke, Mass. 6'5", 210. Fran Healy is better informed about San Francisco's Symphony Orchestra than any other baseball player. As part of studies toward B.S. in history, presented 50-page paper orally before classmates in autumn of 1971 after doing considerable basic research and interviewing members of musical group. Healy got his degree at American International U., Springfield, Mass., in addition to catching for San Francisco Giants. Fran is taller than most catchers, having reached 6'5" before he stopped growing.

Comes from baseball family. His father, Bernard, was outfielder in Cardinal organization, 1937–38. His uncle, also Francis Healy, caught for N.Y. Giants and later for St. Louis Cardinals, 1931–34 but had only 42 major league games. Current Healy took part in more games than that in 1971 with S.F. Giants, getting into 47 contests and batting .280. Had two homers, and both won games for Giants.

Healy dropped to .152 in 45 games, 1972; at end of season had lifetime average of .223 for his 98 games, having had four hits in 10 trips with Kansas City AL, 1969.

Healy signed with Cleveland Indians, 1965, and was farmed out to Dubuque, Pawtucket, and Waterbury, 1965–68. In expansion draft was selected by new Kansas City Royals after 1968 season; spent most of 1969 with Omaha, where he hit .282 in 64 games. Six games with Royals that year, then back to Omaha for 82 contests in 1970, with .294 mark. Sold to Giants 10/19/70. Traded to Royals spring 1973. Besides hoping for fine major league career, is considering studying law off-seasons.

HEARN, JAMES TOLBERT P-BR-TR. B. 4/11/21, Atlanta, Ga. 6'3", 205. Jim Hearn made his way to majors with St. Louis Cardinals, 1947. Three years later Cards gave up on him as big league pitcher, allowed to go to New York Giants for waiver price, 7/10/50. Modest investment paid off immediately, Jim 11–3 rest of that season. ERA of 2.49 was tops among NL pitchers. In 1951 his 17 victories vital in Giants' historic drive to tie Dodgers for NL flag. Playoff against Brooklyn decided by Bobby Thomson's famous homer. Hearn pitched one of Giants' two victories in WS that fall against New York Yankees, had 1.04 ERA. Came back with another winning season, 1952, 14–7. After that, downhill.

Hearn played with Columbus, Ga., Sally League, 1942, before entering military service. After war, with Columbus, Ohio, Cardinal farm in American Association, 1946. Was 12–7 with Cardinals, 1947; 8–6 in 1948; 1–3 with Redbirds and 8–3 with Rochester, 1949. Back with Cardinals 1950; 0–1 before going to Giants. Remained with Giants through 1956 season. Then three years with Phillies. Big league career: 109 victories, 89 defeats, 3.81 ERA, 1703-2/3 innings. Walks nearly equaled strikeouts—665 bases on balls, 669 whiffs. Had 10 shutouts.

HEATHCOTE, CLIFTON EARL OF-BL-TL. B. 1/24/98, Glen Rock, Pa. D. 1/19/39, York, Pa. 5'10½'', 160. Cliff Heathcote, cruelly ribbed as "Rubber Head," sat in visitors' club house at Wrigley Field, Chicago, Memorial Day 1922, and wept. Branch Rickey, then manager of St. Louis Cardinals, broke news to him he had been traded to Cubs for Max Flack, another outfielder.

Both Heathcote and Flack had played in their original lineups in morning game. That afternoon each of them played in different uniforms, much to surprise of fans. There was little radio in those days, no TV, and newspapers had not had time to convey news of trade to public. It is believed this was first time major league players ever swapped sides between morning and afternoon games.

Cliff, one of fastest men in baseball at time, had come to Cardinals after attending Penn State, 1918. Flack, older than Heathcote, took trade philosophically. Pleased he would be playing for team so close to home, just across river from St. Louis in Illinois.

Heathcote was farmed out to Houston, Texas League, 1918, briefly. Hit just .181 in 20 games and was brought back to Cardinals where he did better—.259 in 88 contests that same season.

Cliff's best year with Cardinals was 1920 when he got up to .284, but dropped down to .244 following season. Got nickname "Rubber Head" from fans after game at old Sportsman's Park against N. Y. Giants. Playing center field, with Emil "Irish" Meusel at bat, Meusel hit tremendous drive to deep center. Heathcote dashed back to get under ball, turned around to make catch. Dazzling sun got directly in his eyes. Put up his hands to shield his face and ball landed squarely on top of his head. Heathcote sagged to knees, then went down. Left fielder came over and recovered ball, but Meusel landed at third with triple. St. Louis fans never forgot incident and rode Heathcote years afterward whenever he played for Cubs.

Heathcote had several good seasons with Cubs, and got his average up to .309 in 1924, and .313 in 1929. Not much power, but dazzling speed enabled him to beat out many infield rollers. With Cincinnati, 1931; divided 1932 between Cincinnati and Philadelphia NL, then left majors with .275 batting average for 1415 games. Among his 1222 hits were 206 doubles, 55 triples, and 42 homers, many of them inside-park variety. Scored 643 runs and drove in 448.

His only appearance in WS was in 1929 with Cubs as pinch batsman. Failed to hit in one time at bat.

HEBNER, RICHARD JOSEPH 3B-BL-TR. B. 11/26/47, Boston, Mass. 6'1", 194. Frustrated hockey player on verge of stardom as third baseman. In 1966 turned down bonus contract with Boston Bruins; entered pro baseball with Pittsburgh organization. Still wondering whether he could have made it big in pro hockey. In wintertime still works out with hockey clubs whenever possible. Wears several false teeth because of hockey—three natural teeth knocked out by puck. However, in another game scored five goals, like hitting three homers in baseball game. Aggressive skater in school days, good scorer. Says people of town where he grew up, Norwood, Mass., outside Boston, still think of him as hockey player, not baseball player.

Hebner joined Pirates late in 1968 after seasons at Salem, Va.; Raleigh, and Columbus, Ohio. At Salem, 1966, had .359 average in 26 games; .336 at Raleigh, and .276 in Columbus. In first full year with Pittsburgh, Richie hit .301 in 129 games, then .290 in 1970, and .271 in 1971. In 1972 hit even .300 in 124 games.

Richie has done well in clutches. In 1970 NL playoffs got four hits in six trips, including two doubles, although Cincinnati Reds vanquished Pirates. In 1971 playoffs hit key homer with two men on base in fourth game, enabling Pittsburgh to tie score 5–5 against San Francisco Giants. Pirates went on to win game and NL flag by 9–5 score.

Hebner missed number of games in recent years because of military obligations, virus, and fact Mgr. Danny Murtaugh often platooned him with Jose Pagan, righthanded hitter. Hebner hit 17 homers, 1971, drove in 67 runs in 112 games, and hoped Bill Virdon, Murtaugh's successor, would use him on daily basis, against southpaws as well as righthanded pitching. Richie had .291 major league average in 487 games when 1973 season started. His only WS play, 1971, showed two hits in 12 trips, for .167 average; one of hits was homer off Jim Palmer in second game.

HEGAN, JAMES EDWARD C-BR-TR. B. 8/3/20, Lynn, Mass. 6'2". 195. Father of Mike Hegan, Oakland first baseman. Fine catcher but never any great shakes as hitter. After long career with Cleveland, during which he caught three no-hitters, Jim has become fixture as coach for N.

Y. Yankees. Tenure as coach dates to 7/31/60, before Ralph Houk became manager of Yanks for first time.

Hegan led AL catchers in fielding besides catching those three no-hitters. Also chalked up several other interesting records: led AL catchers in double plays, 1948, and tied for lead 1947 and 1955; made unassisted double play 6/21/49. In late 1940s and early 1950s handled one of greatest pitching staffs ever assembled—Bob Feller, Bob Lemon, Mike Garcia, Early Wynn. Wynn, now Hall of Famer, declares Hegan was finest receiver he ever pitched to. No-hitters Hegan caught were thrown by Don Black, Bob Feller, Bob Lemon.

Jim started in 1938 with Springfield, Mass., team and learned catching at Wilkes-Barre, Oklahoma City, and Baltimore before making grade at Cleveland, 1942. Spent next three seasons in military service. Back with Indians 1946 through 1957. Detroit, 1958; Philadelphia NL, 1958 and 1959; San Francisco NL, 1959; Chicago NL until 7/30/60, when unconditionally released. Signed as Yankee coach next day.

Jim's highest average as major league regular was .249 in 1947. Best home run production came 1948 and 1950—14 each year. Played 1666 big league games, hit .228, including 1087 hits; 187 doubles, 46 triples, 92 homers, with 525 RBI. Scored 550 runs. In WS play hit .188 in 10 games; hit .250 in two All-Star contests.

HEGAN, JAMES MICHAEL (Mike) 1B-BL-TL. B. 7/21/42, Cleveland, Ohio 6'1", 190. Mike Hegan is fine glove man at first base, but not too hot with the bat. Played some outfield in recent years. Son of Jim Hegan, coach for N. Y. Yankees, Mike got something like $50,000 to sign with Yankee organization, 1961. Had attended three colleges—Holy Cross John Carroll, Calvin Coolidge (Boston).

Mike had five games with Yankees, 1964, but most of time between 1962 and '67 was spent in minors—Fort Lauderdale; Idaho Falls; Columbus, Ga.; Toledo. Thirteen games with Yanks in 1966 and 68 with them in 1967. Also served in military at this time. Syracuse, 1968; Seattle, AL, 1969; Milwaukee AL, 1970–71. Sold to Oakland AL 6/14/71. Hit .329 when A's won pennant in 1972, but was at bat only 79 times in 98 games. Back with Yankees, August 1973.

Hegan's best year in majors, playing more or less regularly, was 1969 at Seattle. Batted .292 in 95 games, many of them in outfield. Overall major league average as 1973 dawned was .245 for 538 games, with 25 homers, 44 doubles, and 12 triples among his 284 hits. Had one hit in five AB's in 1972 WS.

Hegan led AL first basemen in assists, 1970. His competition at first base often has been rough—Mickey Mantle in his declining years with Yankees; Don Mincher at Seattle; first Mike Epstein, then Gene Tenace at Oakland. All of them better hitters, but none could field with him.

Off-season, has been sportscaster in Milwaukee.

HEILMANN, HARRY EDWIN (Slug) OF-BR-TR. B. 8/3/94, San Francisco, Calif. D. 7/9/51, Detroit, Mich. 6'1", 200. Line-drive hitter, probably among top five right-handed batsmen of all times. Four times batting champion AL. Possessed lifetime average of .342 when he hung up uniform, right up with all-time leaders. Battled alcohol and won. Became fine broadcaster. Finally lost to cancer. Rhythm governed Heilmann's batting average 1917–30. During that period was down in even years, up in odd years, without exception. Won AL batting titles: 1921 with .394; 1923 with .403; 1925 with .393; and 1927 with .398. In years between, his "down beat," Heilmann hit for averages like .356 in 1922; .346 in 1924; and .367 for 1926.

Heilmann hit .305 with Portland, Northwestern League, 1913, his first year in pro ball. Went up to Detroit for 1914, batting .225. Tigers sent him to San Francisco for further seasoning, 1915. There, at age 21, batted .364 in 98 games as first baseman. Back with Detroit, 1916, hit .282, appearing in 136 games. Went over .300 mark in majors for first time, 1919, then stayed up until his last season when played only 15 games. Not great home run hitter because drives were usually "clothes-line" variety. They dented many fences. In 10-year period 1921–30, Heilmann averaged better than 41 doubles every year. If had put more loft on ball, probably would have been right up there among home run leaders, even though most ball parks favored lefthanded batsmen.

As player Heilmann enjoyed life—and liquor. Used to tell how once, under influence, drove small Austin car right down flight of stairs into basement speakeasy and up to bar itself. Recalled one occasion when he arrived at ball park plastered, still in tuxedo from night before. Ty Cobb, managing Tigers then, called him drunken bum and insisted that he play. Despite fogginess, slammed triple on first trip to plate, collapsed as he slid into third base. Cobb later followed with vitriolic tongue-lashing, but later asked Harry, "How in hell am I going to fine a .400 hitter?" Hit .344 in his final season at Detroit. Though he was 35, it was surprising waivers could be obtained on slugger of his caliber in AL. However, Heilmann landed in NL with Cincinnati. Hit .333 in 142 games in only full season in other league. Arthritis kept Heilmann from playing, 1931. In 1932 played just 15 games and coached Redlegs; that ended playing career.

Began broadcasting, 1940, in Detroit. Worked hard at new job, became very capable sportscaster.

Heilmann's figures show 2146 major league games, 7787 AB, 1291 runs, 2660 hits, 542 doubles, 151 triples, 183 homers, 1549 RBI, and .342 average. Never had chance to play in WS. Hall of Fame 1952.

HELMS, THOMAS VANN   2B-BR-TR. B. 5/5/41, Charlotte, N.C. 5'10, 175. Tommy Helms, stellar second baseman for Cincinnati Reds several years, including their pennant-winning club of 1970, got news 11/29/71 that he and Lee May had been traded to Houston Astros. Texas fans were pleased to get man who had just led keystoners with .990 fielding average, nine errors in 150 games. In 1972 Tommy played 139 games for Astros, hit .259.

Helms signed with Cincinnati organization, 1959, spent that year and next at Palatka, Fla., with 56 games, .252 average his rookie season, and .292 for 137 games as sophomore player. Topeka 1961. Macon, 1962, hitting .340 in 139 contests. Spent next three seasons at San Diego, Pacific Coast League, batting well over .300 in 1964 and 1965. Played two games with Reds, 1964, and 21 in 1965. Then made good with .284 average in 138 games, 1966.

Helms went into 1973 with lifetime average of .267 in 990 games. His 992 hits included 165 doubles, 17 triples, 23 homers, with 334 RBI. Stole 27 bases. In 1970 WS appearance average was .222 for five games, with four hits, all singles.

In off-season Tommy has vending-machine business in Charlotte.

HEMOND, ROLAND A. Executive. B. 10/26/29, Central Falls, R.I. *Sporting News* named Roland Hemond Executive of Year after close of highly successful 1972 season for Chicago White Sox. Hemond is director of player personnel. Joined Sox 9/14/70 when they were one of worst clubs in majors. With dynamo Hemond at helm, numerous deals were made, many of them highly profitable for White Sox. Not only did team rise to contender status in AL, but fan interest multiplied. In 1970 Sox won 56, lost 106; lost money at gate with 495,000 attendance. Following year club record was 79–83, with attendance almost doubled. In 1972 White Sox finished 20 games above .500, with 87 victories, 67 defeats; attendance zoomed to 1,186,000. Day after Hemond joined White Sox, tried to snag Dick Allen, then still property of St. Louis Cardinals. Wasn't successful, but did get him little over one year later from L.A. Dodgers. Where Allen was hot potato in Philadelphia, unwelcome in St. Louis, and didn't fit into Walter Alston's scheme of things in Los Angeles, Dick became MVP for White Sox with finest year of career. Another deal that turned out extremely well for Hemond and Sox was one that brought Stan Bahnsen from New York Yankees. Steve won 21, lost 16—first time he had more than 17 victories in any season.

Hemond doesn't claim credit for all of White Sox success. Pays tribute to manager Chuck Tanner who, in his words, "has done the best job of managing I've ever seen"; also has praise for owner, front office staff, coaches, and scouts, as well as personnel in White Sox minor league system.

Roland went from school into Coast Guard for four years. In 1951 lined up job with Hartford, Conn., club where he did about everything from sweeping stands, answering phones, cleaning wash rooms, to working on public address system. Went from there to front office of Boston Braves as temporary assistant. Two years later became assistant farm director of Braves when club transferred to Milwaukee.

When AL expanded, Fred Haney, general manager of Los Angeles Angels, hired Roland as farm and scouting director, 1960. During this period Hemond and his scouts lined up many prospects who since reached majors, including Andy Messersmith, Jim McGlothlin, Marty Pattin, Aurelio Rodriguez, Paul Schaal, Dave Marshall, and Rick Reichardt. Hemond's next move was to Chicago late in 1970.

Besides acquiring plenty of experience, Roland also acquired wife from family that has produced numerous baseball executives. She is daughter of John Quinn, who retired during 1972 as vice president and general manager of Phillies. John held similar position with Braves when he became Hemond's father-in-law.

HEMSLEY, RALSTON BURDETT (Rollie) C-BR-TR. B. 6/24/07, Syracuse, Ohio. D. 7/31/72, Washington, D.C. 5'10'', 170. Rollie Hemsley, colorful character in major leagues for almost two decades, told this story about himself. "I was with Browns and Rogers Hornsby was manager. He was against cards, beer, everything. So I decided to have some fun. On way to train one night as we were leaving Chicago, I bought knitting set. I got corner seat in smoker and pretended to knit. I wasn't doing too bad, either. When Hornsby came around and saw me, he fined me $150. I'll bet I'm only ball player who ever got fined for knitting." Hemsley might have added he probably had bit of alcohol under his belt before he bought knitting set.

Despite carefree approach to life and nerves relaxed by multiple alcoholic infusions over years, Hemsley fine catcher, speedy base runner, pretty fair hitter. Six times batted over .270, wound up with lifetime average of .262 in 1593 games. Hit safely 1321 times, with 257 doubles, 72 triples, 31 homers. Scored 562 times and had 555 RBI. After about dozen years in majors Hemsley joined Alcoholics Anonymous and continued to have fun as big league ball player.

Rollie had three seasons with Frederick club of Blue Ridge League, 1925–27, before joining Pittsburgh, 1928. Pirates sent him to Chicago NL during 1931 season. With Cubs through 1932. Cincinnati 1933. St. Louis Browns 1933–37. Cleveland 1938–41. During spring of 1939, Oscar Vitt, then manager of Indians, sent him home for being drunk on train. This wasn't Rollie's first offense, but was his last. Went into hospital for four days, took no drugs, but joined A.A., and was reformed man. Divided 1942 between Cincinnati Reds, and Yankees; with Yanks through 1943–44. Philadelphia NL 1946–47. During parts of 1947 and 1948 Hemsley was with Seattle, Pacific Coast League; Nashville, 1949, where he managed team to first place in Southern Association; bossed Columbus, American Association, 1950, to third-place finish; piloted Texas City into sixth place, 1951; Toledo-Charleston, American Association, 1952, winding up eighth. Out of baseball, 1953. Coach, Philadelphia AL, 1954. Scout, Kansas City AL, 1955. Later was with Washington AL, 1961, as coach.

With just one major league pennant winner, Chicago Cubs, 1932. In WS three games; went hitless in three trips, striking out each time.

HEMUS, SOLOMON JOSEPH Inf.-BL-TR. B. 4/17/24, Phoenix, Ariz. 5'9", 175. Solly Hemus, like most ball players in twilight of careers, was traded to another club that hoped to get few more years of useful service from veteran. But unlike most ball players, Hemus wrote letter to president of ball club that traded him away. Solly assured Gussie Busch, head of St. Louis Cardinals, he deeply appreciated treatment he had received in St. Louis; it was genuine pleasure to have been with Redbirds. Busch was pleased with letter he received after trade of 5/14/56 sent Hemus to Philadelphia NL. And when Busch needed manager for 1959, Hemus got job. Solly had not managed ball club before, had not been coach, but that letter got him chance to boss big league team.

Hemus led Cardinals to seventh-place finish, 1959. Got them into third spot, 1960, but in 1961, when team sagged, Solly was fired after 33 victories, 41 defeats. Club wound up season in fifth place, with Johnny Keane replacing Hemus. Critics felt Hemus' continual feuding with umpires, off-the-cuff decisions, plus somewhat brusque handling of aging Stan Musial paved way for dismissal. Also had problems with Jim Brosnan, then with Cardinals. As result, Brosnan was traded to Cincinnati and later helped (10–4, 16 saves) Reds capture 1961 NL pennant.

As player, Hemus never quite qualified as star, though hit .304 in 1954 with Cardinals in 124 games. Hit 15 homers in 1952, 14 in 1953. His career batting average for 961 games was .273. His 736 hits included 137 doubles, 41 triples, 51 homers. Scored 459 times, drove in 263 runs, stole 21 bases. Rather adept at stopping pitched balls: led NL in this respect with 20 in 1952, 12 in 1953, and tied for lead with eight in 1958.

Solly started pro career at Pocatello, Idaho, in Pioneer League, 1946. Lost close race for batting championship: Hemus had .3630 average; Charles Henson, .3631. Next three seasons at Houston, Texas League, climaxed by .328 average in 109 games, resulting in advancement to Cardinals. Twenty games with St. Louis, 1949, with .333 average. Eleven games with Cardinals, 1950, with .133 mark. Spent most of that season with Columbus, Ohio, in American Association. Hit .297 in 84 games. Returned to Cardinals, 1951, remaining with them until trade to Philadelphia, 1956. Phillies traded him back to Cardinals 9/29/58, after which he became Redbird pilot.

HENDERSON, KENNETH JOSEPH OF-BLR-TR. B. 6/15/46, Carroll, Iowa. 6'2", 180. Polished outfielder with strong accurate arm. Highly successful base runner who at one point had record of 38 steals in 44·attempts. Was overshadowed by teammates on San Francisco Giants: McCovey, Mays, Bonds, Marichal. But highly regarded by insiders despite lack of flamboyance.

Ken received sizeable bonus from Giants, 1964, after being athletic star in high school in San Diego. Divided that season among Fresno, Twin Falls, and Tacoma clubs. Spent 1965 with S.F., but played comparatively little and hit just .192. Though in 63 games, went to bat only 73 times.

Hit .272 at Phoenix, 1966, in 133 games, and .310 for Giants in 11 contests. In 1967 again divided time between S.F. and Phoenix and same was true 1968. Since 1969 has remained with Giants. In 1970 got average up to .294 in 148 games, including 17 homers, 88 RBI. Broken thumb handicapped him in 1971, but still managed .264 average with 15 homers, 65 RBI, and 18 stolen bases in 141 contests. In 1972 had .257 mark with 18 homers, 51 RBI, and 14 thefts in 130 games.

Henderson traded to Chicago White Sox following winter. Started AL career with major league record of .256 for 674 games; 551 hits included 101 doubles, 17 triples, 61 homers; with 270 RBI.

HENDRICKS, ELROD JEROME (Ellie) C-BL-TR. B. 12/22/40, St. Thomas, Virgin Islands. 6'1", 175. Virgin Islander, like Horace Clarke of N.Y. Yankees—and born same year. Reached peak during 1970 WS, when he hit .364. Homer in fifth inning of opener vs. Cincinnati gave Baltimore Orioles vital run in 4–3 victory. In second game his double with score tied gave Orioles go-ahead counters for 6–5 win over Reds. Two more hits and one RBI in fourth contest, but Baltimore lost that one, then came back to take fifth and crucial game. Hendricks figured in disputed play in opener, catching for Orioles. Bernie Carbo of Reds tried to come home from third on teammate Ty Cline's high bounder in front of plate. Mixup involved collision of Ellie, Carbo, and umpire Burkhart, who called Carbo out. Reds protested Carbo was never tagged. Instant replay films and other photos showed Hendricks tagged Carbo with his mitt—while holding ball in bare right hand some distance away. But decision stood. Carbo's run would have given Reds a fourth run, but final score was Baltimore 4, Cincinnati 3.

Took Ellie long time to get to majors after first pro game at McCook, Nebraska State League, 1959. Service in Wellsville, N.Y.; Winnipeg; El Paso; Jalisco, Mexico; and Seattle, then in Pacific Coast League. Belonged to California Angel organization at Seattle, but was drafted by Baltimore 11/28/67. Earl Weaver, who became Oriole manager, 1968, had been his boss in Puerto Rico while Ellie played winter ball. Played

79 games for Baltimore, 1968, but hit just .202. Then got his average to .240–.250 range for next three seasons, playing over 100 games each year. Hendricks has been bothered by shoulder pains and weakness in right hand. Guessing has been that possibly these ailments date to when he was playing in Santurce, P.R. Willie Montanez was batting, Ellie catching; Willie's follow-through with bat struck Hendricks at base of neck for painful injury.

In three WS with Orioles, 1969,70,71, had .250 average with 10 hits in 40 trips, 5 runs scored, 5 RBI, 2 doubles, 1 homer.

Chicago Cubs got Ellie in waiver deal 8/18/72. However, he returned to Baltimore roster after season's close. Lifetime big league average at time was .228 for 441 games, with 42 homers.

HENRICH, THOMAS DAVID OF-BL-TL. B. 2/20/13 Massillon, Ohio. 6′, 180. Tommy Henrich played all his major league career with N.Y. Yankees, after starting in Cleveland organization. Reason? Cy Slapnicka, general manager of Indians, tried to "cover up" young prospect, thereby preventing his chance to go to major league club. This was decision of Judge Landis, then baseball's czar. Facts are that Henrich was scouted by full-time employee of Cleveland club, but signed to contract with Zanesville team of Middle Atlantic League. Shuttled among that club; Monessen, Pennsylvania State Association; New Orleans in Southern; and Milwaukee, American Association, over three-year period, 1934–36. Landis ruled that Cleveland club controlled all these movements, violating rules. Henrich had shown great promise those three years and was in Milwaukee training camp when Landis decreed he would be free agent 4/14/37. Had hit above .325 each year, and in 1936, with N.O. Pelicans, .346 in 157 games. Ruling barred Indians from bidding for his contract and Yankees got signature for $25,000 bonus. Went to Newark, Yankee farm, for seven games, then was recalled on basis of .440 batting average. In 67 games for Bombers, 1937, hit .320. In 1940, when Indians lost AL pennant by one game, Henrich, who hit .307 for Yankees that year, undoubtedly would have meant difference between losing flag and winning had Cleveland been able to keep him.

Joe DiMaggio thought Henrich smartest player in majors. In 1941 WS Tommy was at bat in ninth inning when Mickey Owen lost third strike in Brooklyn and, given reprieve with two out, Yankees went on to 7–4 victory. In 1949 Henrich hit homer that clinched another Yankee flag; won pitching duel between Newcombe of Dodgers and Allie Reynolds, 1–0, by slamming four-bagger in ninth inning, first game of WS.

After 1950 season Henrich called it quits with major league record of 1284 games and .282 batting average. Went to bat 4603 times with 1297 hits. Had 269 doubles, 73 triples, 183 homers, and 901 runs. Batted 795 tallies across plate. In four WS, 1938,41,47,49, batted .262 in 21 games. In four All-Star appearances, record was .111.

HERMAN, FLOYD CAVES (Babe) OF-1B-BL-TL. B. 6/26/03, Buffalo, N.Y. 6'4", 190. Babe Herman will always be remembered as man who "tripled into double play." Happened 8/15/26, in "Daffiness Days" of old Brooklyn Dodgers when Wilbert Robinson managed Flatbush team. Setting: One out. Three men on base for Brooklyn: Fewster on first, Vance on second, Deberry on third. Mogridge pitching for Boston. Herman hit vicious line drive off right field wall, DeBerry scoring immediately. Ball bounced back, all way to second baseman. Herman rounded first, headed for second. Second baseman threw to shortstop in effort to make play on Herman, who was sliding into bag. Somebody yelled to throw ball to plate. "I thought Fewster was trying to score," said Herman. "I never dreamed it was Vance." Herman started for third. But it was Vance, who had been afraid liner might be caught. When ball thrown to plate, Vance went back to third. When Herman got there, Vance was there and so was Fewster—all three on one base! Babe also had reputation of getting hit on head by fly ball, playing Brooklyn outfield. Herman, however, stoutly denies it ever occurred. Gangling fielder, not graceful, but certainly not worst outfielder who played in majors.

Herman's family took him to California at age of two. First pro job at Edmonton, Western Canadian League, 1921, 107 games, .330 average. Had been called "Lefty" everywhere but Edmonton feminine fan with loud voice persistently yelled "Tiny" or "Babe" when lanky 18-year-old went to bat. "Babe" stuck as nickname.

Reading, International League, 1922, for eight games; Omaha, Western League, 1922, for 92 contests, batting .416. Next three years played at Atlanta, Memphis, San Antonio, Little Rock and Seattle, hitting ball well over .300 wherever he was. Brooklyn, NL, 1926–31. Hit .340, 1928; .381, 1929; .393, 1930. Even .393 average didn't give him batting title— that was year Bill Terry hit .401. Dodgers traded Herman to Cincinnati, along with Ernie Lombardi and Walter Gilbert, for Joe Stripp, Tony Cuccinello and Clyde Sukeforth, 3/14/32. After one season with Reds, traded to Cubs 11/30/32. Traded to Pittsburgh 11/22/34. Sold to Cincinnati 6/21/35. Sent to Detroit 4/1/37, on waivers. After 17 games with Tigers, 1937, returned to minors, first to Toledo, American Association, 1937; Jersey City, International League, 1938, then Hollywood, Pacific Coast League, 1939–44. With wartime player shortage, Herman back at Brooklyn 1945, playing 37 games, batting .265 at age 42.

Major league totals showed 1552 games, .324 average, 181 home runs, 997 RBI. Among notable accomplishments were three homers in one game, 7/20/33; hit first home run ever made by major league player under lights, 7/10/35, in Cincinnati.

Scouted for Pittsburgh 1946–50; coach, Pirates, 1951. Coach, Seattle, 1952. Scout, Yankees, 1953–54. Scout, Phillies, 1955–59. Scout, Mets, 1961. Scout, Yankees, 1962–63. Scout, San Francisco NL, 1964.

HERMAN, WILLIAM JENNINGS BRYAN 2B-BR-TR. B. 7/7/09, New Albany, Ind. 5'11", 195. Casey Stengel called Billy Herman one of smartest players in NL. Carl Hubbell, an established star when Herman joined Chicago Cubs, 1931, had this to say: "In his first couple of years Billy couldn't get hit off me. Then he set out to figure me out. From that time on, I could hardly ever get him out."

Brilliant player, but not so successful as major league manager. Managed Pittsburgh, 1947 and club finished in tie for seventh place. Must be said, however, Billy didn't have many major league players that season. Later piloted Boston Red Sox, 1965–66; team wound up ninth both years. Following season Dick Williams made some changes and Boston won pennant. In minors, Herman steered Minneapolis, American Association, to fourth place, 1948, and Bradenton, an Oakland farm, to pennant in Gulf Coast Rookie League, 1958, with 5-1/2 games to spare.

Herman was born on farm; father was southpaw pitcher. While Billy had chores to do like milking cows, gathering and selling eggs, elder Herman allowed son time to play ball. At 18 pitched Sunday school team to championship and won trip to Pittsburgh to see first two games of 1927 WS. Signed by Louisville, AA, 1928; had five hits in 15 trips but spent most of season at Vicksburg, Cotton States League, where average was .332 for 106 games. Divided 1929 season between Dayton, Central League, batting .329 in 138 games, and Louisville, .323 in 24 contests. Two more .300-hitting seasons in Louisville. Was batting .350 in 1931 after 118 games when Cubs bought him to succeed Hornsby, who was beginning to slip. Continued fine hitting with .327 in 25 games same season.

Billy soon began to demonstrate smart play, covering second base area "like blanket." Generally hit above .300, reaching .341 in 1935. Led NL keystoners in fielding three times. Consistently led or was among leaders in putouts and assists—and four times led second basemen in errors committed. After helping Cubs to pennants, 1932,35,38, was sold to Brooklyn, 5/6/41 and gave Dodgers what they needed to win 1941 NL pennant. It was reported that Jimmy Wilson, then managing Cubs, thought Herman might be threat to his job, hence traded him to Brooklyn. Billy had three good years in Flatbush, then spent 1944–45 in military service. Back with Dodgers, 1946; traded to Boston NL 6/15/46. Then came year as manager at Pittsburgh; played just 15 games. Also played 10 games piloting Minneapolis, 1948. Out of baseball one season, then 71 games with Oakland, Pacific Coast League, hitting .307 in final playing days.

Billy's record of 16 putouts at second base in doubleheader 6/28/33 is major league record.

His major league totals showed 1922 games played, 7707 AB, 1163 runs, 2345 hits, 486 doubles, 82 triples, and 47 homers. Batted in 839 runs. Had .304 lifetime average. In WS play, 18 games, 16 hits in 66 AB for .242 mark, with seven RBI. Hit .433 in 10 All-Star games.

Besides managerial assignments, Herman was coach for Dodgers, 1952–57; Milwaukee NL, 1958–59; Red Sox, 1960–64; California Angels, 1967. Had one other job as manager, at Richmond, Piedmont League, 1951.

HERRMANN, AUGUST (Garry) Executive. B. 5/3/59, Cincinnati, Ohio D. 4/25/31, Cincinnati, Ohio. Garry Herrmann, for many years president of Cincinnati Reds and chairman of old National Commission that ruled major league baseball, 1903–20, got his name while working as a young printer. Another printer was nicknamed Bismarck in honor of Prussian chancellor, so Herrmann's fellow workers nicknamed him Garibaldi for famed Italian statesman. Soon was shortened to Garry.

Gregarious fellow who spoke with gutteral Teutonic accent; happiest when talking baseball among friends in beer-garden atmosphere. Exerted plenty of power in baseball structure though skipped as many meetings as possible, setting up court in Waldorf or other hostelry for all who savored food and potables. Somehow, in later years, managed to have plenty of draught beer despite Volstead Act.

Although president of a NL club, was held in such high regard by Ban Johnson, then president of AL, that Ban agreed to setup of three for National Commission. One was Johnson, second was president of NL, with Garry serving as third commissioner and chairman. Though system worked pretty well for many years, was discarded after disclosure of 1919 WS scandal when White Sox offered to throw games and enable gamblers to win sure-thing bets. Then Judge Kenesaw Mountain Landis became sole commissioner of baseball with virtaully unlimited powers.

Hermann also was important man in Cincinnati politics. Took over presidency of Reds, 1903, remaining in that capacity until 1927. Not rich, but had $12,000 expense account and used it for beer and food. Often took large groups of friends to New York, St. Louis, or other cities where ball club was playing, picking up tab.

Garry, who helped make modern WS reality, had only one club in WS, 1919 Reds, which won tainted world title from White Sox. In depression days, Garry, whose term as club president ended in 1927, became deaf and knew hard times. Club voted him $10,000 annual pension, but this fell by wayside before his final days. Baseball voted him $500 monthly pension until he died.

HERZOG, DORREL NORMAN ELVERT (Whitey) OF-BL-TL. B.

11/9/31, New Athens, Ill. 5'11", 187. When Whitey Herzog succeeded Ted Williams as manager of Texas Rangers, 11/2/72, he declared they were "one of the worst major league teams I've ever seen. . . . They were worse than the old Mets." Whitey had served as director of player development for N.Y. Mets, for whom he never played. His big league career extended from 1956 through 1963: 634 games, hit .257, 414 hits, 60 two-baggers, 20 triples, 25 home runs, 213 runs, drove in 241, stole 13 bases.

Whitey's pro career began at McAlester, Okla., 1949. Then to Norfolk, Joplin, Beaumont, Quincy (Ill.), Kansas City, Denver, Miami, in minors. Two years in military service. First major league chance at Washington, 1956; played 117 games, hit .245. Senators sent him to Miami, part of 1957, then sold him to Kansas City AL, 5/14/58. Illness 1959–60, missing much of both seasons. Traded to Baltimore AL, 1/24/61. Played 113 games, hit .291. Traded to Detroit, 11/25/62. In his final year in AL 1963 played 52 games, hit .151. Scout, Kansas City AL, 1964. Coach, Kansas City, 1965. Coach, Mets, 1966. Then moved into job as director of player development for Mets.

HEYDLER, JOHN ARNOLD Executive. B. 7/10/69, Lafargeville, N.Y. D. 4/18/56, San Diego, Calif. John Heydler began as printer's apprentice in Rochester, N.Y.; moved to Washington, D. C. to work in Bureau of Printing and Engraving. Played baseball on amateur teams, gaining some local attention as sports lover. Attended NL game between Washington and Pittsburgh, May 1895, after work. When regular umpire failed to show. Heydler was asked to take place. Did job that impressed N.E. Young, then president of NL; became assistant umpire. Resigned, 1898, and took fling at sports writing. In 1903 Harry Pulliam, then NL president, asked Heydler to help compile statistics, offering job as private secretary. Became secretary-treasurer, NL, 1907. Pulliam died 1909 and Heydler served temporarily as president. Former umpire Thomas Lynch and John K. Tener were next NL presidents, with Heydler continuing in secretary-treasurer job. Became president NL, 1918. Continued until 12/14/34, when resigned account ill health. Continued as chairman of board NL until death.

Once, while still in Bureau of Printing and Engraving, errand took him to White House. Met President Grover Cleveland; conversation turned to baseball. Heydler wound up reciting "Casey at the Bat."

Heydler's term as NL chief executive marked by desire not to "make waves." Was criticized for "pussyfooting" in investigation of Hal Chase, accused of betting on games and attempting to get game thrown. Heydler gave Chase clean bill of health, 1919, and Chase played one more year in majors, with N.Y. Giants. Then, after

Chase's apparent involvement in "Black Sox" scandal later that year, Chase left organized ball and never played again.

HICKMAN, JAMES LUCIUS OF-BR-TR. B. 5/10/37, Henning, Tenn. 6'4", 205. Jim Hickman rose to greatest heights, 1970, when he hit .315 in 149 games for Chicago Cubs, with 32 homers, 115 RBI. Also had 33 doubles, four triples. This in contrast to his lifetime performance in majors that shows most of time over past decade he hit in neighborhood of .250. Had 17 homers, 64 RBI in 1972, with .272 average.

Jim first came to majors in 1962 with Casey Stengel's N.Y. Mets. Played there five years before going to Los Angeles Dodgers for 1967. Cubs acquired contract 4/23/68 and sent him to Spokane and Tacoma in Pacific Coast League for 27 games, then brought him up for 75 games same year. Has remained with Cubs since then.

Hickman attended Memphis State and U. of Mississippi. Signed by St. Louis Cardinal organization, 1956. Minor league experience gained at Albany, Ga.; Winston-Salem; Billings, Mont.; Tulsa; Dallas–Fort Worth; Rochester; Portland, Oreg. When NL expanded, newly formed Mets drafted Hickman from Cardinals 8/10/61. Hit 60 homers for Mets in five years, but best batting average was .257 in 1964. With Cubs, had 21 homers, 1970; 32 following year; 19 in 1971.

Hickman was member of NL All-Star squad, 1970, drove in game's winning run. That same year he earned *Sporting News* designation as Comeback Player of Year. Jim also voted Tennessee Pro Athlete of Year by home state.

Jim hit three homers in one game 9/3/65. Tied major league record for most assists for outfielder in one inning, two, 5/4/70. Has suffered from ulcers since 1967. Owns 60-acre farm outside Henning, Tenn.

HIGBE, WALTER KIRBY P-BR-TR. B. 4/8/15, Columbia, S.C. 5'11", 188. Some ball players parlay major league experience and contacts into lucrative and successful careers. Others leave organized baseball with little more than memories. Kirby Higbe, who helped pitch Brooklyn Dodgers to pennant in 1941, has had rough time since leaving NL. Long periods of unemployment, plus time in jail for writing checks that bounced.

Kirby was 22–9 for Durocher's team, 1941. Had next three successful seasons with Dodgers, 16–11, 13–10, and 17–8, then in 1947 was traded because didn't want to play on same ball club with Jackie Robinson, a black. Won two decisions for Dodgers in 1947 before he went to Pittsburgh 5/3/47. But days of glory were past.

Higbe finished seventh grade in school, later began pitching in American Legion ball. Signed with Pittsburgh organization, 1932, for $500 bonus and $300 a month at Tulsa, Texas League. Though had strong right arm, was terribly wild and did not make grade. Played semipro ball briefly, then in 1933 landed with Muskogee, Western League. Spent next few years with Atlanta and Birmingham Southern League; Portsmouth and Columbia in Piedmont League; Moline, III League; with brief spells in NL with Chicago. Higbe finally made grade with Cubs, 1939, but went to Philadelphia NL in deal for Claude Passeau 5/29/39. Had 12–15 record for first full year in majors. In 1940, record was 14 wins, 19 losses. Performance attracted attention because Phillies were cellar club both 1939 and 1940.

Larry MacPhail, Brooklyn general manager, engineered trade for Higbe 11/11/40 and Kirby had first of four fine seasons for Dodgers. In WS, 1941, started fourth game of classic against Yankees but was driven to cover in fourth inning. Pitched 3-2/3 innings, allowed six hits, walked two, gave up three earned runs for ERA of 7.36.

In 1947, with Pirates, had 11–17 mark; 8–7 in 1948. In 1949, after losing two games, winning none, Pirates traded him to N.Y. Giants 6/6/49. Durocher was managing Giants then; hoped Kirby would perform as he had for Leo in Brooklyn. But though was credited with two wins, no losses, with Giants, his ERA wasn't too good—5.08 for year. In 1950 Higbe 0–3; in July was sent to Minneapolis, American Association. Released at end of season, Higbe went to Atlanta, Montgomery, Rock Hill (Carolina League), and finally Forest City, Western Carolina League, 1953. Kirby then took job with post office, later worked for chemical company, and was unemployed when he wrote checks that bounced. Spent 40 days in jail. Later ran afoul of law by smuggling sleeping pills into jail; given three-year suspended sentence, put on probation for three years. Began receiving baseball pension of $209.93 when he reached age 50 in 1965.

Higbe's major league totals: 418 games, 1952-1/3 IP, 118 victories, 101 defeats, ERA 3.69.

HIGGINS, MICHAEL FRANKLIN (Pinky) 3B-BR-TR. B. 5/27/09, Red Oak, Tex. D. 3/21/69, Dallas, Tex. 6'1", 190. Pinky Higgins played all but a few of 1802 major league games at third base for Philadelphia, Boston, and Detroit clubs in AL; for several years was manager of Red Sox, later executive vice president and general manager of same team. Unfortunately, his last days were spent in jail; died two days after being paroled. Had served two months on four-year sentence for vehicular homicide. Supposedly had been under influence of liquor when fatal accident occurred, resulting in jail term.

Higgins was fine third baseman, good hitter but not slugger. His top homer production was 23, in 1935, while with Athletics. Hit 141 round trippers during career in majors, 374 doubles, 50 triples. Scored 930 runs after getting 1941 hits. Had 1075 RBI, and .292 lifetime average.

Pinky had tryout with Athletics after graduating from U. of Texas, 1930; played 14 games and was farmed to Dallas and San Antonio, Texas League, 1931. Hit .284 in 131 games. Then one season at Portland, Pacific Coast League. In 189 games there hit .326. Became regular third baseman of Athletics, 1933, and held job until 12/9/36, when traded to Boston for Bill Werber. Two years in Boston, then six full seasons with Detroit. Traded to Boston early 1946, last season in majors as player. Mike hit .208 in WS that year in seven games. His earlier WS was with Tigers, 1940 when he had .333 average, including three doubles, triple, and homer in his eight safeties. Batted in six runs that classic. Overall WS average was .271 in 14 contests.

Higgins' record as manager included two third-place clubs, two fourth-placers, and rest were second-division finishes. Piloted Red Sox 1955–59, being replaced by Bill Jurges midseason. Bill started 1960 as Boston mentor, but Higgins called back to manage club in midyear, and continued in post until end of 1962. Then in Boston front office for three years.

Pinky had several red-letter days. During 1938 season set major league record by hitting safely twelve times in succession. This mark equaled by Walt Dropo in 1952. Higgins had one three-homer day 6/27/35. However, Pinky had miserable day 5/2/38: committed four miscues. This tied major league record for third basemen.

HIGH, ANDREW AIRD 3B-BL-TR. B. 11/21/97, Ava, Ill. 5'6", 175
Small in stature, but pesky hitter who repeatedly got base hits when they really counted toward winning ball games. Brother of Hugh High who played with Detroit and New York AL; and of Charlie High who was briefly with Philadelphia AL. Andy hit .328 for Brooklyn Dodgers 1924, in 144 games, and helped St. Louis Cardinals to three pennants, 1928,30,31, although didn't make .300 mark with Redbirds. Sample of his peskiness: 8/30/30, when Cardinals battled Chicago Cubs in 20-inning game, Andy's hit scored Taylor Douthit to give Cardinals victory. Then, in September of same season, Cardinals went into Brooklyn and knocked off Dodgers in three straight games. In first contest, 9/16/30, Dazzy Vance and Bill Hallahan battled 10 innings without score until High's double gave Redbirds 1–0 victory over Dazzler. Next day, Andy's hit off Adolfo Luque gave Cardinals 5–3 victory.

Andy started as outfielder with Memphis, Southern Association, 1919; shifted to third base with same team, 1920–21. Brooklyn, 1922–25, until shifted to Boston NL 7/25/25. St. Louis NL, 1928–31; Cincinnati, 1932–33; Philadelphia NL, 1934. High had spell with Columbus, American Association, 1933; besides stint with Phillies in 1934, also managed Syracuse team, International League. Later managed Hazleton, N.Y.-Pa. League, and scouted for Brooklyn. Trailed Pee Wee Reese for month and urged Larry MacPhail to borrow $75,000 to buy his contract from Boston Red Sox organization. Pee Wee was youngster with Louisville at time. Andy served in military 1917–19 during World War I, and was in Seabees 1943–45 during World War II.

Played 1314 major league games, got 1250 hits, including 195 doubles, 65 triples, 44 homers. Scored 618 runs, drove in 482. Stole 33 bases and wound up with .284 average. As pinch batsman, apart from timely hitting as regular, Andy had respectable average of .292, with 42 hits in 144 ABs. WS play: 9 games, 34 AB, 10 hits, including 2 doubles, .294 average, 5 runs, 1 RBI.

HILL, JESSE TERRILL OF-BR-TR. B. 1/20/07, Yates, Mo. This is fellow who hit into one of those once-in-a-lifetime double plays. Probably never occurred before, probably never will happen again. Playing for Yankees 7/26/35, went to bat against Washington pitcher Ed Linke. Man on second. Slammed drive straight at Linke, who automatically threw up both hands in self-protection. Too late. Ball struck Linke in head, bounded high into area in direction of third base. Alert Senator catcher Redmond scrambled down foul line, caught ball before it hit ground. Fired it to Red Kress, covering second, before base runner could return. Double play. Meanwhile Linke on ground. Carried off field on stretcher, but apparently no permanent damage.

Hill had promising career in front of him but did not set majors afire. Graduated from Southern Cal 1930, joined Hollywood club, Pacific Coast League. First pro game, first time at bat, slammed first pitch over fence for home run. Hit .356 that year, fresh out of college, with 18 home runs in 115 games. All of which caused Yankees to buy him. Farmed him out to St. Paul, American Association, and Newark, International League. After 1934 average of .349 in 154 games at Newark, won graduation to AL.

Hit .293 in 107 games for Yanks, 1935; .305 in 85 games for Washington, 1936. Was .217 batsman in 33 games with Senators, 1937, then hit .293 in 70 games same season with Philadelphia Athletics. Lifetime average .289 in 295 games.

HILLER, CHARLES JOSEPH (Chuck) 2B-BL-TR. B. 10/1/35, Johnsburg, Ill. 5'11", 170. Chuck Hiller's moment of glory came during 1962 WS between S.F. Giants and N.Y. Yankees. In fourth game, with score tied, Hiller came to bat in seventh inning with bases loaded. Facing Marshall Bridges, lefthander, Chuck, lefthanded batsman, lined ball into right field stands. First time in WS history NL player hit grand slammer. Giants won game 7–3, but lost Series four games to three.

Chuck had eight seasons in majors, hit .243 in 704 games. His 516 hits included 76 doubles, 9 triples, 20 homers. Scored 253 times, drove in 152, stole 14 bases.

Career in pro ball started 1957 at Cocoa, Fla., and continued at Minot, N. Dak.; Eugene, Oreg.; Rio Grande Valley, Tex.; and Tacoma, Wash. Part season with Giants, 1961, remaining with San Francisco until sale to N.Y. Mets 5/12/65. During 1967 traded to Philadelphia NL; had 11 games with Pittsburgh, 1968, then dropped out of majors. Coach, Texas Rangers, 1973. Only WS, 1962: .269 average, 3 doubles, 3 singles, homer, 26 AB, 4 runs, 5 RBI. Best season at bat as regular was 1966 when had .280 mark for Mets.

HILLER, JOHN FREDERICK   P-BR-TL. B. 4/8/43, Scarborough, Ont. 6′, 170. Courageous southpaw who came back strong in midsummer 1972 after missing season and half because of heart attack. Pitcher, whose 9–6 mark helped Detroit win 1968 pennant, suffered myocardial infraction 1/11/71. Missed all of 1971 but religiously obeyed doctor and returned to Tigers July 1972. Completed season with 2.05 ERA for 44 innings, 1–2 record, 3 saves. Tipped scales at 215 before heart attack. Tough diet took off nearly 50 pounds. Also lost seven feet of lower intestines. Physician Louis Zako told Michigan Heart Association: "It takes discipline, hard work and single-minded determination to win ball games. That same mental attitude is critical in recovering from a heart attack. I would have to call John Hiller a hero. You have to have the will to win. Without that even the best medical advice won't help."

Hiller was signed off Toronto suburban sandlots without bonus. Learned his trade at Jamestown (N.Y.), Duluth, Knoxville, Montgomery, Syracuse, Toledo, from 1963 to 1967, with couple of "cups of coffee" at Detroit. First full year with Tigers was 1968—2.39 ERA accompanied 9–6 record. Fared less well in World Series against St. Louis: three earned runs in two innings for 13.50 ERA. Was 4–4 in 1969, 6–6 in 1970.

During latter stages of 1972 pennant race manager Billy Martin called on Hiller to protect one-run leave over Baltimore. Man on base with dangerous Boog Powell hitting. Struck Boog out on four pitches, then got Paul Blair on forceout to end game. John pitched 3-1/3 innings in three games in 1972 playoff series against Oakland: allowed no runs and was credited with victory. As 1973 began, overall major league record was: 25–23, 203 games, 2.82 ERA, 179 walks, 347 strikeouts.

HINES, PAUL A.   OF-BR-TR. B. 3/1/52, Washington, D.C. D. 7/10/35, Hyattsville, Md. 5′9 ½″, 173. Older record books credited Hines with being only outfielder ever to make triple play unassisted (5/8/78), playing with Providence against Boston in old NL. However, one claiming to be eyewitness said Hines made 35-yard run to catch ball behind short, kept running and tagged base runner near third, then threw to second baseman to catch other base runner. Triple play, but not unassisted.

Hines member of Chicago NL in year league organized, 1876. Hit .330 in 64 games. Chicago 1877. Providence 1878–85. Washington NL 1886–87. Indianapolis NL 1888–89. Pittsburgh and Boston NL 1890. Washington, American Association (then major league), 1891.

During his era Hines ranked seventh among best hitters in majors. Went six for six 7/26/79. Lifetime record: 1456 games, .304 batting average.

HITCHCOCK, WILLIAM CLYDE Inf.-BR-TR. B. 7/31/16, Inverness, Ala. 6'1½", 185.

Currently president of Southern League after varied career as player, scout, coach, manager. Played 703 major league games, hit .243. His 547 hits included 67 doubles, 22 triples, five homers. Stole 15 times.

Billy attended Auburn, left with B.S. in business administration. Kansas City, American Association, 1939–41. Detroit, 1942–46, though missed 1943–45 seasons due to military service. Traded to Washington 5/16/46. St. Louis AL 1947. Boston AL 1948–49. Philadelphia AL 1950–52. Detroit 1953. Buffalo, International League, 1954, with 25 games as player; also managed club. Coach, Detroit, 1955–60. Manager, Vancouver, Pacific Coast League, 1961. Manager, Baltimore AL, 1962–63. Field coordinator, Baltimore, 1964. Scout, Milwaukee Braves, 1965. Coach, Atlanta Braves, 1966; manager, 1967. Scout, Montreal NL, 1968. Then moved into present post.

Billy led Orioles to seventh-place finish, 1962; to fourth, 1963. His Braves, 1967, were seventh.

HOAG, MYRIL OLIVER OF-BR-TR. B. 3/9/08, Davis, Calif. D. 7/28/71, High Springs, Fla. 5'11, 180.

Myril Hoag had smallest feet in major leagues when he played from 1931 to 1945. Wore size-four shoe on right foot, four-and-a-half on left. Yankees bought him for $75,000 after he hit .337 for Sacramento, Pacific Coast League, 1930. Never quite lived up to expectations for Yankees, but did hit .301 in both 1936 and 1937. Played only 45 games, 1936. Collided with Joe DiMaggio chasing fly ball, suffered severe head injuries requiring brain surgery; but was able to play in 106 games following season.

Hoag started with Sacramento, 1927; farmed to Twin Falls, Utah-Idaho League, same year. Didn't play professionally, 1928. Back with Sacramento for 1929–30. Played 90 games for Yanks in 1931–32. With Yanks' farm team, Newark, International League, 1933. Back with Yankees, 1934–38. St. Louis AL 1939–41. Chicago AL 1941–44; Cleveland AL 1944–45.

Lifetime records showed major league average of .271 in 1020 games over 13-year span. Hit safely 854 times, with 141 doubles, 33 triples, 28 homers. Scored 384 runs, had 401 RBI, 59 stolen bases. Noted for strong arm; Yankees seriously considered trying to convert him into pitcher.

Later did pitch in one game for Browns, in two for Cleveland: total of four innings, allowing three hits and one walk, but no runs.

Hoag managed in smaller leagues with fairly good success, playing occasionally; bossed teams in Palatka, Gainesville, and St. Petersburg in Florida, and Rome, Ga.

Not WS star, Hoag did well in autumn classics, 1932, 37, 38, with 8 for 25, .320 average, including home run in 1937 Series that Yanks took from N.Y. Giants.

HOAK, DONALD ALBERT (Tiger) 3B-BR-TR. B. 2/5/28, Roulette, Pa. D. 10/9/69, Pittsburgh, Pa. 6'1", 180. Don Hoak was one of most aggressive, competetive ball players who ever strode diamond. Volatile temperament, low boiling point, ready to go to almost any lengths to win ball game, including personal injury. Often played when hurt and in great pain. Probably learned this rugged approach to life while in marines. At age 16 got into corps, lying about his age; battle experience at Saipan in Pacific. Could be cruel, hateful, vulgar in baiting opposition. Never hesitated to badger own teammates if thought they weren't bearing down hard enough. Once tried to help one of teammates and got slugged by Charlie Neal of Dodgers. But getting slugged wasn't new to Don. Tried to become pro boxer but decided on baseball after being cut up and nose broken couple of times. Suffered other bone breaks too. Wore crew cut, with auburn hair. Dent in his nose from breaks.

They still talk about play he made while in minors. Playing third base, figured squeeze play was on; dashed toward plate with pitch. Onlookers shuddered at what would have happened had batsman swung and hit ball in his direction. But Hoak grabbed bunted ball, tagged base runner coming in from third, then threw to first base for unique double play, probably never duplicated. This while playing for Montreal in International League.

Hoak no superstar. Hit .265 in his 1263 major league games. Got 1144 hits, 214 doubles, 44 triples, 89 homers, 64 stolen bases. Ignominiously equaled record set by pitcher Carl Weilman in 1913: fanned six times during extra-inning game 5/2/56.

Hoak started at Valdosta, Ga., 1947. Made his way to NL, 1954, after apprenticeship in Nashua, N.H.; Greenville, S.C.; Fort Worth, St. Paul, and Montreal. Joined Brooklyn Dodgers, hit .245 in 1954. Two seasons with Brooklyn, then one with Chicago Cubs. Good season at Cincinnati, 1957, playing 149 games, hitting .293, with 19 homers, 89 RBI. Dropped down to .261 following year, then moved to Pittsburgh where he hit .294 in 155 contests, 1959. Had .282 average, 1960, and .298 in 1961, then tapered off. Spent 1963 and part of 1964 with Philadelphia NL.

Got into two WS, one with Brooklyn, 1955, with one hit in three trips. Played seven games in 1960 WS with Pittsburgh. Hit .217: 5 for 23. Overall WS average .231 for 10 games. NL All-Star game 1957.

HODGES, GILBERT RAY 1B-BR-TR. B. 4/4/24 Princeton, Ind. D. 1/2/72, West Palm Beach, Fla. 6'2", 200. Gil Hodges rode to triumph in autumn of 1969: managed N.Y. Mets to NL flag and then surprised almost everyone when his club romped to victory in WS over mighty Baltimore Orioles in just five games. Gil had learned how to manipulate players in way to make them most effective against opposition, how to win. But long before that WS victory day, 10/16/69, Hodges had learned how to lose—and not quit.

At start of playing days Gil had some discouraging times. In first big league game, with Brooklyn Dodgers, 1943, Hodges had two trips to plate—and struck out twice. Playing third base, made two errors in five chances. Four years later, after spell in marines and trip to minors, Gil hit just .156 in 28 games—but did not give up.

Years passed. Gil, having shifted to catching, was asked to take up first-basing. Did it beautifully, mastered position, and helped Dodgers to pennants. Then came WS of 1952. After four years of fine clutch hitting and driving in over 100 runs, and having hit as many as 40 homers in one season, Hodges was bust as hitter in fall classic of 1952. Batted .000 in 21 fruitless trips to plate! But came back with several more fine seasons as well as four excellent WS.

Hodges finished his playing days in spring of 1963 when Washington Senators obtained services as manager 5/22/63. Inherited floundering ball club at that point; but though Senators won just 40 games that year, he improved them steadily in years that followed: 70 victories in 1965, then 71, and 76. Owners of Mets wanted popular Gil to manage their club. Took over team in spring of 1968. Mets had finished ninth previous year—and Gil couldn't do much in first season at helm. Another ninth-placer. Then came heart attack 9/24/68. Odds seemed to be against Gil surviving. Doubtful if he could manage, even if he did improve. Again Hodges did not quit—and in 1969 fans all over country cheered as Mets won 38 of last 49 games. Mets trailed division-leading Chicago Cubs by 9-1/2 games 8/13/69. After winning Eastern Division, knocked off Atlanta in playoffs to clinch NL pennant. Then came astonishing WS victory.

Hodges' team dropped down couple of notches in 1970 and 1971.

Gil's playing career started in Midwest where he attended Rennselaer, Ind., college, St. Joseph's. Hoped to become college coach. In 1943 signed with Dodgers. Later, between seasons, attended Oakland City College, Indiana, 1947–48. In marines, Hodges served at Pearl Harbor, Tinian, Okinawa. Back to civilian life after becoming sergeant.

Gil achieved distinction as graceful first baseman—often compared to ballet dancer. Led league in fielding three times, also three times in putouts, and in assists for first sackers. In hitting department, while batted over .300 just twice, slammed 370 homers, 295 doubles, and 48 triples during major league career. Seven times had over 100 RBI , and came quite close another time. His lifetime average was .273—and his fielding .992.

Hodges had just one season in minors, 1946 at Newport News, Piedmont League. With Brooklyn until close of 1957, then went to Los Angels with Dodgers until close of 1961. As new expansion club, Mets selected him in draft from Dodgers, paying $75,000 for contract. Played 1962 and start of 1963 before heading for Washington as manager.

Among Gil's notable achievements were four homers in single game, 8/31/50, tying major league record. Still holds NL record for most homers with bases loaded, 14. Was four times NL leader among first basemen in making twin killings. Hodges in seven WS, 39 games in all. Despite miserable showing at plate in 1952, batted .267 overall, with 35 for 131, including 5 homers, 2 doubles, 1 triple, 21 RBI.

HOERNER, JOSEPH WALTER P-BR-TL. B. 11/12/36, Dubuque, Iowa 6'1", 200. Joe Hoerner started 1973 season one of best relief pitchers in majors, with 33 victories, 25 defeats, 72 saves. At same time his ERA stood at 2.45 for 434 innings pitched in 347 games. Reliever from start of big league career—never started ball game, consequently had zero complete games to credit. Control one of his strong points, as evidenced by figures of bases on balls allowed and strikeouts. Had 323 strikeouts to credit at start of 1973, contrasted with just 122 walks allowed.

Tied NL record for most consecutive strikeouts in game by relief pitcher: six, 6/1/68. Member NL All-Star team, 1970, but did not play. Hoerner started his baseball travels in 1957 at Duluth-Superior in Northern League; since then has pitched for Davenport, Iowa; Charleston, S.C.; Lincoln, Neb.; Oklahoma City, Savannah, San Antonio, and for San Diego when still in Pacific Coast League. With Houston Astros briefly, 1963–64, then joined St. Louis Cardinals 1966. Started off with 1.54 ERA, five victories, one defeat, as rookie in 76 innings spaced out over 57 games. Another good record, 1968, eight wins, two losses with 1.47 ERA. Cardinals traded him to Philadelphia NL 10/7/69 in big deal that involved Curt Flood and Richie (Dick) Allen. Was 9–4 for Phils, 1970. Atlanta Braves acquired him in trade 6/15/72. Hoerner got into 1967 WS as member of Cardinals but emerged with 40.50 ERA—allowed three earned runs in 2/3 inning. Did somewhat better in WS of 1968, permitting two earned runs in 4-2/3 innings. Overall WS ERA is 8.44; 0–1.

Joe is co-owner of Cardinal Travel Agency in St. Louis with Dal Maxvill.

HOFFBERGER, JEROLD C. Executive. B. 4/17/19, Baltimore, Md. Chairman of board, Baltimore Orioles, since October 1965. President of

National Brewing Company since 1947. Brewery holds controlling interest in ball club. In first six years as chairman of board for Orioles, team won four pennants, two WS. Man of many interests. Businesses. Power in Democratic party. When new to baseball did not hesitate to take leadership; was one of those who took initiative in firing General Eckert as baseball commissioner. Said he was lovely man, but ineffectual in job.

Hoffberger was instrumental in helping bring major league baseball back to Baltimore, 1953, when St. Louis Browns' franchise was transferred there. In younger days played lacrosse, football, hockey; attended U. of Virginia. Served in armed forces in Africa, Italy, France during World War II. Mustered out as captain. Joined brewery owned by family. It was 150th in rank, 1946. Twenty years later, largely through Hoffberger's drive and promotion, had moved up to 14th in field.

Besides leadership in baseball and interest in selling beer, Hoffberger has served as director in other businesses; has investments in trucking, warehousing, real estate, mortgage banking. Partner in syndicate that owned Kaui King, winner of Kentucky Derby and Preakness, 1966. Has often consulted Bill Veeck, former owner of Cleveland, St. Louis AL, and Chicago AL franchises, and espouses some of Veeck's somewhat less than conservative views on how baseball should be run.

HOFHEINZ, ROY Executive. B. 4/10/12, Beaumont, Tex. Wheeler-dealer, politician, sportsman; son of man who drove laundry truck. Lawyer at 19; member of Texas legislature at 22; began first of four terms as county judge at 24. At 40, began first of two terms as mayor of Houston. In eight-year period immediately after World War II made himself multimillionaire. Left judgeship deeply in debt. Made fortune in radio, television, real estate, slag, oil, and in law practice. In 1960 Houston effort to get major league franchise seemed stalled. Hofheinz believed air-conditioned, domed stadium would prove so attractive NL could not turn it down. When whole concept was unveiled at NL meeting in December 1960, magnates voted to accept Houston in league, franchise to operate starting 1962. Judge and oil man, R. E. "Bob" Smith, underwrote costs. Temporary 32,000-seat stadium was built and two bond issues were approved by voters to build Astrodome. Grand opening 4/9/65, with President Lyndon B. Johnson among those present.

Hofheinz reported to have invested close to $10 million in baseball venture. Besides baseball, Astrodome has offered football, basketball, bull fights, boxing, polo, boat shows, concerts, Billy Graham's crusades, circus, soccer, motorcycle races, midget auto races. Astrohall houses conventions, livestock shows, rodeos. Astroworld, nearby, is amusement park and recreation center.

Hofheinz has been called brash, dreamer, crude, suave, profane, shy, flamboyant, dynamic, charming. Senior chairman of board of Houston NL club, "considered unusual, even in Texas."

HOGAN, JAMES FRANCIS (Shanty) C-BR-TR. B. 3/21/06, Somerville, Mass. D. 4/7/67, Boston, Mass. 6'1", 240. Shanty Hogan's appetite and losing battle to keep his weight under control are sure to be remembered whenever his name is mentioned to fans who can recall four decades of baseball. Hogan fairly good catcher—caught for John McGraw for more than four years. Slow on bases, held his own at plate, batting .300 or better in four of five years with Giants. Wound up major league career with .295 average, 989 games.

Outfielder when Boston NL signed him for 1925. Played nine games for Braves at age of 19, hitting .286. Braves optioned him to Albany-Worcester club, Eastern League; hit .296 for rest of year. Four games with Braves 1926, and 97 with Lynn (Mass.), New England League, hitting .368. By this time had switched to catching. Then back to Boston for 1927, remaining in majors until 1937.

When John McGraw decided to ship Rogers Hornsby away from Giants, Hogan one of two players received in return. Other was Jimmy Welsh, outfielder. Hogan played 131 games for Giants, 1928, hitting solid .333. Dropped to .300 following season, but hit .339 in 1930. In 1931 his mark was .301. Bill Terry took over Giants early in 1932. By end of season Terry decided to trade Hogan and replace him with Gus Mancuso, obtained from Cardinals. Hogan went back to Boston NL, remaining through 1935. Spent 1936–37 with Senators, playing only 40 games for them. Had powerful vocal chords, used generously while behind plate; often could be heard by fans in center field bleachers.

HOLLAND, JOHN DAVID Executive. B. 2/18/10, Wichita, Kans. John Holland has been vice president of Chicago NL since 1956; On board of directors since 1963. Had 19 years of experience as minor league executive, during which teams he was connected with finished in first division 13 times. Even better record after joining Cubs organization: eight first-division teams in minors in 11 years.

Holland practically grew up in ball park as father was widely known Jack Holland, owner of Oklahoma City franchise, Western League. John had ambitions to be ball player; began as catcher with father's team, 1929. Father farmed him out to Sherman, Tex., team in Lone Star League, then called him back as reserve backstop. But after watching him at bat, said, "Son, I don't think you'll ever be hitter. From now on you're business manager."

Secretary, Oklahoma City, 1933–35, after serving apprenticeship as concession and park manager. Father died, 1936, and John succeeded to presidency. Continued until 1942, then went into aircraft plant until 1945. Joined Chicago NL organization, 1946, as head of Visalia club, ·California League, after selling interest in Oklahoma City team. General manager, Des Moines, Western League, 1948. Became president of Los Angeles, Pacific Coast League, 1/6/55, and continued there until promoted to Cubs' major league front office.

It took Holland and rest of Cubs' organization some years to get club into contender class, but team rose from tenth (1966) to third (1967) and Bruins have been battling for NL lead generally into final weeks of season since then.

HOLLINGSWORTH, ALBERT WAYNE (Boots) P-BL-TL. B. 2/25/08, St. Louis, Mo. 6'1", 185. Al Hollingsworth won 70 major league games, lost 104. But during most of career as pitcher toiled for mediocre or poor clubs; except in 1944 when St. Louis Browns won AL pennant. Many years later, when Oakland A's became world champions, 1972, Al was given considerable credit for careful scouting of Cincinnati Reds. Reportedly, Hollingsworth's notes on individual Cincinnati players were items Oakland manager Dick Williams carried to mound in many conferences with players during Series. It is believed Al's advice about Johnny Bench stimulated Williams' decision to walk him intentionally during seventh game; Bench represented potential winning run. "Don't let Bench beat you with his bat if at all possible," said Hollingsworth before WS started. Numerous other tips by Al are believed to have helped tremendously in Oakland WS victory.

Hollingsworth's scouting reports helped defeat team with which he made big league debut in 1935. Al started in municipal leagues in St. Louis. Often played first base in minors before concentrating on pitching. Had trials with Wayncsboro, Pa.; Nashville, Canton, Cedar Rapids, and Bloomington, Ill.; then with Rock Island, Ill., team of III League where his 15–8 record in 1933 attracted attention. Won 11, lost six for Toronto, International League, 1934, then went to Cincinnati, 1935. Managed to win nine games each of 1936 and 1937 seasons, but lost more often. Reds traded him to Philadelphia NL 6/13/38, with Virgil Davis and $55,000 for Bucky Walters. Hollingsworth had 7–18 mark that year. Divided 1939 between Phils and Brooklyn—two wins, 11 losses. Briefly with Washington, 1940, being credited with one victory, no defeats. With St. Louis AL, 1942 until early in 1946 season. Best seasons of his career were 1942 with 10–6, and 1945 with 12–9. Finished in majors with Chicago AL, 1946.

Al's big league record showed ERA of 3.99 for 1520-1/3 innings pitched in 315 games. Like many lefthanders, had trouble with control. His WS performance with Browns in their city Series against St. Louis Cardinals, 1944, showed four innings pitched, allowing one earned run

447

for ERA of 2.25. Neither won nor lost.

After active playing days, Hollingsworth coached and scouted for various teams. Coach for St. Louis Cardinals, 1957–58, and has been Oakland scout in recent years.

HOLLOMAN, ALVA LEE (Bobo) P-BR-TR. B. 3/27/24, Thomaston, Ga. 6'2", 211. Bobo Holloman pitched exactly one complete game in major leagues—and that was no-hitter. Accomplished feat 5/7/53 for St. Louis Browns, club that finished in AL cellar that year. Strangely enough, Holloman couldn't last till end of season with tail-end ball club that needed pitchers desperately. After all major league clubs passed up chance to get him for waiver price—or less—Bobo was sold outright to Toronto, International League, 7/23/53.

Holloman's day of glory witnessed by 2473 fans. Legend has it that Bill Veeck, then bossing Browns, so elated over surprise performance he told all patrons present they could come back to another home game anytime simply by presenting rain checks for that historic date. Facts are, however, he made offer to reward Brownie fans for enduring that cold, rainy day, and made it halfway through game. Marty Marion was managing Browns that year. Actually sent Holloman to mound in desperation. Bobo was 16–7 for Syracuse previous season. All spring Holloman pestered Marion to let him start ball game. Marion was not impressed by Holloman's workouts, figured his only chance to stick with ball club would possibly be as reliefer. Time for roster cutdown was approaching, 6/15/53. Then came fateful day. Jim Dyck of Browns took double away from Gus Zernial of Philadelphia AL. Billy Hunter made fabulous play on Joe Astroth's liner. And other Brownie fielders sparkled in robbing Athletics of "certain" hits. Bobo walked five men, one reached base on error—but it was no-hit game. Browns won 6–0.

Bobo started career at Moultrie, Ga., 1946, and pitched for Macon, Nashville, Shreveport, Albany, Augusta, Syracuse before joining Browns. In 1950 had trial with Chicago Cubs, then managed by Frankie Frisch. Always confident of own abilities, Bobo gained notoriety by calling Frisch "meathead" for not pitching him and for sending him back to minors. Frankie not impressed with Holloman's "stuff."

Holloman credited with two other victories that season and seven losses. Major league totals: 65–1/3 innings, ERA 5.23, 69 hits, walked 50, struck out 25. His day of glory was last no-hitter ever pitched by Brownie hurler. Club moved to Baltimore following year, transformed into Orioles. Bobo moved from Toronto to Columbus (Ohio) to Chattanooga to St. Petersburg to Augusta in lower minors. By mid-August 1954, had pitched last game in pro ball—about 15 months after historic no-hitter.

HOLMES, THOMAS FRANCIS OF-BL-TL. B. 3/29/18, Brooklyn, N.Y. 5'10", 180. Product of N.Y. Yankee farm system; sold to Boston

NL after 1941 season because wasn't power hitter. Yet Tommy, 1945, led NL in homers, in slugging percentage, in doubles, and almost won batting title. Missed that by three points to Phil Cavarretta, who batted .355.

Capping this highly successful season, which won him MVP for NL in selection made by *Sporting News*, Holmes had fewest strikeouts among regulars. This was first time in modern major league history that home run king also led in fewest number of strikeouts.

Holmes started with Norfolk, Piedmont League, 1937, and hit .320, slugging 25 homers, 31 doubles, 8 triples, and batting in 11 runs that year. Led Eastern League in hitting with .368 at Binghamton, 1938. Seven games with Kansas City, American Association, 1939, then shifted to Newark, International League farm for Yankees. There had three seasons batting above .300 and was sold to Boston.

With Braves in Beantown until close of 1950 season. Player-manager, Hartford, Eastern League, 1951 until 6/19, when returned to Braves as playing manager. Succeeded Billy Southworth. Club finished fourth. In 1952 Braves sagged, and Tommy was let out 6/1/52, making way for Charlie Grimm; team ultimately wound up in seventh place, its last year in Boston. Signed with Dodgers as player 6/17/52.

Holmes played 31 games with Brooklyn, 1952, but hit only .111. Managed Toledo, American Association, 1953 until May 14, when he was released. Scout for Brooklyn rest of year.

Player-manager, Elmira, Eastern League, 1954. Later managed Fort Worth, Texas League; Portland, Pacific Coast League; and Montreal, International League. Became scout for Los Angeles Dodgers, 1958.

In Holmes' banner season with Boston, 1945, set modern NL record for hitting in 37 consecutive games; led league in hits with 224; in doubles with 47; in homers with 28. Drove in 117 runs and batted .352. Career tally for 1320 major league games: 1507 hits, 698 runs, 292 doubles, 47 triples, 88 homers, .302 average. WS record for 1948, Boston, and 1952, Brooklyn: 9 games, 27 AB, .185 average, 1 RBI.

HOLTZMAN, KENNETH DALE P-BR-TL. B. 11/3/45, St. Louis, Mo. 6'2", 175. Ken Holtzman graduated from U. of Illinois, received $75,000 bonus for signing with Chicago NL organization, 1965. After pitching 12 games in minors that year, joined Cubs in time to pitch four innings, allowing one earned run. With Cubs, southpaw pitched two no-hit games, had perfect 9–0 record in season abbreviated by military duty, and won 74 games, lost 69, before was traded to Oakland 11/29/71. In 1972 won 19, lost 11, with 2.51 ERA. Pitched 12-2/3 innings during 1972 WS— credited with one victory and had 2.13 ERA. AL All-Star 1972, 73.

Oakland trade sparked by Holtzman's blast during ball game at Wrigley Field September 1971. After being touched for home run,

Holtzman returned to bench, moaned: "I hate this ball park. It stinks. I don't ever want to pitch here again or anywhere else for the Cubs." Cub manager, Durocher, did not use Holtzman in remaining games of season and Ken wound up final year in Chicago with 9–15 mark, 4.48 ERA—and $56,000 salary. Pitched first no-hitter 8/19/69 at Wrigley Field against Atlanta; second no-hitter took place in Cincinnati 6/3/71 against Reds. Another feather in cap—struck out first five batsmen faced in game against Mets 9/5/70.

Holtzman's minor league experience in 1965 was 27 innings pitched for Treasure Valley, Idaho, in Pioneer League. Won four games, lost none. Then went to Wenatchee, Washington, team in Northwestern League; won four, lost three in 59 innings. ERA at Treasure Valley was 1.00; at Wenatchee 2.44. Was 11–16 in first full year with Cubs, 1966; in 1967 military duty kept him away from club for all but six weeks of season. But in those six weeks was 9–0, 2.52 ERA. In 1968 his work not as effective: 11–14, 3.35 ERA. Then two years straight won 17 games each. Lost 13 in 1969; 11 in 1970.

Holtzman strung together 33 shutout innings during 1969. As 1973 began, Holtzman had major league record of 1042 strikeouts against 494 walks, and ERA of 3.40 overall. Had 93 victories, 80 defeats.

HOOPER, HARRY BARTHOLOMEW OF-BL-TR. B. 8/24/87, Bell's Station (Santa Clara County), Calif. 5'10", 168. Harry Hooper, often mentioned in earlier days of AL as one of that circuit's greatest outfielders, was voted into Hall of Fame 1971 by Veterans' Committee. Member of Boston Red Sox world championship teams of 1912,15,16,18. Postmaster at Capitola, Calif., quarter of century.

Hooper, who played 17 years in big league, took up baseball originally as sideline. Planned on being engineer. Received degree in civil engineering at St. Mary's College of California, 1907. Took up ball playing for Sacramento, California State League, that summer because manager promised to get him job as surveyor after baseball season. Made $85 a month playing ball, $75 a month surveying. So he continued arrangement through 1908 season. Batted .344 in 77 games. Red Sox took him 1909. Soon won regular job. From 1910 through 1925 played over 100 games a season, nine of those years at least 140 contests each. Major league totals: 2308 games, 8784 at bats, 1429 runs, 2466 hits, 389 doubles, 160 triples, 75 homers, 813 RBI, .281 average.

Hooper teammate of Tris Speaker through 1915 season. Often has been mentioned with "Spoke" and Ty Cobb as being among finest gardeners of that era. In four World Series Hooper had averages of .290, .350, .333, .200, for overall mark of .293. Played 24 games, getting 27 hits in 92 trips, scoring 13 times, with 3 doubles, 2 triples, 2 homers. Hooper traded to White Sox after 1920 season. Spent five years with Sox.

Released after club owner Charles Comiskey wanted to carve his 1926 contract almost in half, even though Hooper had played 127 games in 1925.

Hooper called it quits for good after hitting .284 in 78 games for Missions team, Pacific Coast League, 1926. Entered real estate business. Coached Princeton nine for two years. Then back to California where they made him postmaster. Never did utilize that civil-engineering degree.

HOOTON, BURT CARLTON P-BR-TR. B. 2/7/50, Greenville, Tex. 6'1", 210. "This is only beginning," Mgr. Leo Durocher declared after Burt Hooton, rookie, pitched no-hitter for Chicago Cubs in second game of 1972 season. It was first no-hitter for any NL rookie in 60 years. And though most fans around country had never heard of him, this was third NL victory against no defeats. Fresh from U. of Texas and 12 games in Pacific Coast League, late in 1971 won two games, lost none. Hooton throws "the thang," which is knuckle curve. Where ordinary knuckler floats, Hooton throws "thang" with motion used for fast ball. It reaches plate faster than any curve—acts strangely, sometimes shooting down, sometimes in, sometimes out. Has been called "dry spitball." Burt has thrown "thang" since was 14. Besides "thang," Hooton throws fast ball most pitchers would be proud of.

Cubs drafted him June 1971 on basis of collegiate record of 35 wins against three losses, with 1.14 ERA in 291 innings. Three times All-American. Represented U.S. in World Amateur Baseball Tournament in South America in autumn 1970. Pitched no-hitter against Cuban team that ultimately won tournament. But no-hitters fairly routine for Hooton: pitched four in high school, two more in college, besides one against Cubans. Philadelphia Phillies were his victims in first start of 1972. After reporting to Cubs, 1971, watched new teammates for nine days, then drew starting assignment against St. Louis Cardinals. First pro hitter he faced was toughie, Lou Brock; Hooton struck him out. Pitched 3-1/3 innings that day, with no decision. Then farmed out to Tacoma, PCL; was 7–4 with 1.68 ERA. Struck out 135 in 102 innings, allowing just 19 walks. One of victories, against Eugene, Ore., struck out 19 batters. This tied PCL record that had stood since 1905. Back with Cubs in September, started against Mets in second game of doubleheader 9/15/71. Threw three-hitter and struck out 15! This tied all-time Cub record. Mets didn't get first hit until two men were out in seventh inning. Won by 3–2 score. Six days later again faced Mets: this time even stingier with hits, allowing only two. Shut them out and took game by 3–0 score. So wound up 1971 with NL record of two wins, no losses in 21 innings, with 22 strikeouts, 10 bases on balls, and 2.14 ERA.

During 1972 Cubs' ace, Ferguson Jenkins, had 20 victories—but

Hooton had lower ERA! Fergie's mark was 3.21; Burt's 2.81.

HOPE, LESLIE TOWNES (Bob)   Executive. B. 5/29/03, Eltham, Kent, England. Best known to everyone as film star, television and radio comedian, but also part owner of Cleveland Indians. Bob has been on board of directors many years. At one point, during reorganization of Pittsburgh Pirates, Bob expected to have modest financial interest in that team too, but it was ruled he could not own stock in two major league clubs, even though in different leagues.

Bob brought to Cleveland from England when four. Family not prosperous; as boy, sold newspapers; used then-soprano voice to sing for fare on streetcars. Got tired of being called "Hopeless" and adopted "Bob." Tried boxing; gave dance lessons; became hoofer, blackface comedian. First big stage part in *Ballyhoo of 1932*. Played in *Roberta*, which established him before footlights; later in *Ziegfeld Follies*. Film career started 1938, in *Road to Zanzibar*, first of successes with "Road" movies. Tried to enlist during World War II but told could serve country best by entertaining troops. Traveled to all parts of world entertaining military. During more recent years led troupe of entertainers and sports stars to military bases in Korea, Vietnam, and elsewhere.

Golfer and quipster. Friendly rival Bing Crosby so far has enjoyed more success as part owner of ball club than has Hope. Bing has piece of Pittsburgh Pirates.

HORLEN, JOEL EDWARD (Joe)   P-BR-TR. B. 8/14/37, San Antonio, Tex. 6', 170. Joe Horlen found himself out of job during player strike in spring 1972. But when autumn rolled around collected $20,705.01 WS check as member of Oakland A's, world champions. Then given release at end of 1972. Joe was player representative for Chicago White Sox during 1971 and spring of 1972 until handed his release. There was speculation this might have influenced Sox in decision not to retain him after having been Chicago AL property since 1959. After signing with Oakland he became A's player rep. Horlen, after 1972 season, expressed view White Sox might very well have won AL pennant had they retained him. With A's, pitched in 32 games, won three, lost four as spot starter and long reliever. In five of his starts Oakland scored total of just two runs. As middle relief man, often kept A's in ball games they later won, with another pitcher getting credit for victory or save. Wound up with 3.00 ERA, compared to 3.11 ERA for career with White Sox.

Joe attended Oklahoma State on baseball scholarship. Pitched team to National Collegiate Athletic Association championship and recommended to White Sox by Scout Ted Lyons. Sox gave him an estimated $50,000 bonus to sign. Pitched for Lincoln, Ill.; Charleston, S.C.; Indianapolis; San Diego, then in Pacific Coast League, during apprenticeship. First appeared in AL game, 1961, and had 113–113 record when released. Best season was 1967 when won 19 games, lost seven, and had 2.06 ERA, which led AL in effectiveness. In 1964 won 13, lost 9, with 1.88 ERA. Dean Chance of Los Angeles was AL leader that year with 1.65.

Horlen faced 1973 having been in 361 major league games. In 2003 innings had struck out 1065, walked 554; won 116, lost 117. Pitched no-hitter against Detroit 9/10/67, winning by 6–0. AL All-Star squad 1967.

HORNSBY, ROGERS (Rajah) Inf.-BR-TR. B. 4/27/96, Winters, Tex. D. 1/5/63, Chicago, Ill. Considered by many the greatest righthanded hitter of all time. Hit above .400 three times. Holds modern record for highest average, .424 in 1924. Checkered managerial career started 6/1/25 when he succeeded Branch Rickey as pilot of St. Louis Cardinals. Won pennant and World Series 1926, first Cardinal flag of 20th century. Lionized by fans, Hornsby demanded three-year contract at $50,000 annually. Owner Sam Breadon offered one-year contract at this figure or three years at $40,000. Impasse followed. Breadon grabbed phone, traded Hornsby to Giants. Received Frank Frisch, stellar infielder who had been suspended during 1926 season over differences with manager, John McGraw. Pitcher Jimmy Ring also went to Cards. St. Louis fans stunned at trade of their hero. Many protested, trying to get cancellation of deal. Others swore to boycott team forever, but trade stood—with one big problem. When Hornsby became Card manager he had bought Rickey's stock at $45 a share. After team won pennant and WS Hornsby reportedly felt stock now worth $120 a share. With over 1000 shares involved considerable money involved. Breadon refused to pay over $45 a share. Hornsby wouldn't budge. Judge Landis, baseball czar, said Hornsby could not play for one team while remaining stockholder in another. Since NL owners considered Hornsby drawing card every-where, they each put up $5000 to meet Hornsby's price, Breadon sticking to his refusal to pay over $45 a share. And Rogers was able to play for Giants. Tactless, outspoken Rajah soon wore out welcome with McGraw who apparently thought Hornsby would undermine him. After one season Hornsby traded to Boston Braves for two players never in stellar class. Became manager of Braves 5/23/28 and piloted club rest of season when again traded, this time to Cubs in exchange for five players and $200,000. Became Cubs manager 9/23/30 and continued till 8/2/32 when unconditionally released. By this time Hornsby was finished as regular. Though he had made big money in era of low taxes, Rajah was broke and owed considerable because of gambling losses. Somewhat contrite and needing job, returned to Cardinals as substitute infielder and pinch hitter. Redbirds hoped he would help gate and mollify some fans still angry over his firing in 1926. Hornsby hit .325 but was slow in field. As 1933 season progressed, Cards were not drawing because of depression plus mediocre team. Chance to unload Hornsby and his fairly good salary gracefully came when St. Louis Browns signed him as manager 7/27/33. Lasted there as pilot till 7/20/37. Managed Browns again briefly in 1952 under Bill Veeck. Later managed Cincinnati Reds that same season and most of 1953.

Hornsby's bluntness, peppered with colorful profanity, alienated many. Was just as likely to tell off his boss as he was a rookie ball player. His only pennant winner as manager came his first full season at helm—1926. Didn't smoke or drink, loved ice cream; refused to go to movies and read very little, believing these things hurt his batting eye. Married three times, divorced twice and had two sons, one of whom played minor league ball briefly.

Hornsby began career in Texas-Oklahoma League, 1914; with Cardinals 1915–26; Giants 1927; Braves 1928; Cubs 1929–32; Cardinals 1933; Browns 1933–37. Coached Baltimore, International League, 1938. Managed Baltimore 1939. Later managed Oklahoma City, Fort Worth, Beaumont, Seattle. Coach, Cubs, 1958–59. Scout, Mets, 1961. Coach, Mets, 1962.

Won NL batting title seven times, six in succession, 1920–25. Lifetime major league batting average .358, second only to Ty Cobb's .367. Had 2930 hits, 541 doubles, 168 triples, 302 HR, 1579 RBI; scored 1579 runs. MVP 1925, 1929. Hall of Fame 1942.

HORTON, WILLIE WATTISON (Boozie) OF-BR-TR. B. 10/18/42, Arno, Va. 5'10½", 209. Willie Horton signed by Detroit organization when 18, in August 1961. But Tiger scouts had eye on him from time was 16 and hit homer into right field pavilion at Tiger Stadium. Had sensational career in high school and on Detroit sandlots before turning pro. Bonus estimated at $50,000 sweetened things for Willie. Farmed out to Duluth-Superior in Northern League, 1962; Syracuse and Knoxville, 1963, with brief spell with Tigers, 15 games. Gave an indication of hitting ability by swatting .326, including homer, triple, two doubles among 14 hits. Back to Syracuse for 135 games, 1964, however; same season with Tigers, hit just .163 in 25 games but managed to get second major league home run. Stuck with Tigers, 1965, and remained with team since then.

In first full season in AL, Willie hit .273 in 143 games, slapped 29 homers, and drove in 104 runs. In May that year had sensational week: hit .600, with six homers, five doubles, 16 RBI in seven games. Following year continued cannonading with 27 homers, 100 RBI with .262 average. Missed 43 games, 1967, with Achilles tendon injuries but still had 19 homers, 67 RBI. Operation after season. Came back with 36 homers in 143 games, 1968, with .285 mark and 85 RBI. Following season, hamstring muscle bothered him, missed 18 games, but still drove in 91 runs, slapped 28 round-trippers including three grand slams. In 1970 torn ligaments in left ankle kept him out of last 66 games, but still owned .305 mark and 17 homers. Three homers came in one game; also hit grand slam No. 5.

Willie had .289 average in 1971, hit 22 for circuit, had 72 RBI. On last day of season Mgr. Billy Martin took Horton from lineup for not running hard on infield ground ball. Willie threatened to quit Tigers but reconsidered. Willie's hitting dropped off in 1972 to .231, with 11 homers. So he faced 1973 owning .271 lifetime mark for 1058 major league games; 191 homers among his 1014 hits, with 154 doubles, 26 triples; 495 runs scored, 638 RBI.

Horton was member of AL All-Star squads in 1965, 68, 70, 73; went two for two in 1970 game at Cincinnati. In WS play, 1968, hit .304 against St. Louis Cardinals, including double, triple and homer among seven hits. Scored six times, drove in three runs.

Willie's nickname has nothing to do with alcoholic refreshment. Parents called him Boozie when learning to walk because unsteady afoot.

HOUK, RALPH GEORGE C-BR-TR. B. 8/9/19, Lawrence, Kans. 5'11", 190. Ralph Houk, Yankee manager, had 1.000 batting average in 1947 World Series. Got single in only appearance, as pinch hitter. Five years later, his Series batting average was .000—no hit in one chance as pinch batsman. Had 1.000 record as manager of Yankees for three years—three AL pennants, 1961–63. Elevated to general manager's job. Next time he managed Yankees, 1966, they finished last—tenth! As player, Houk never played more than a few games a season with Yanks. If Yogi Berra and Elston Howard had not been on club, might have been different. So Houk spent much time in bullpen, occasionally warming up pitchers. Between warmups Ralph wasn't snoozing. Studied game in progress, storing information.

Ralph born on farm near Lawrence, Kans. Four uncles played semipro ball, so he started baseball early. At 15 his solid 170 pounds helped him as catcher to block plate effectively. Also starred as football player. Finishing high school, had several college offers of athletic scholarships. Turned them down to sign with Yankee organization. Got $200 bonus and $75-a-month contract at Neosho Mo., 1939. Joplin, Binghamton, Augusta, Beaumont, Kansas City 1940–49; spells with Yanks interspersed. During this period, service with U.S. Army. Second lieutenant, European sector. In one rugged engagement two of his superior officers killed. Houk put in command, extricated his group from Germans who had surrounded them. Once got bullet through his helmet—missed his head. Left service as major, with Silver Star, Bronze Star, Purple Heart. Spent 1950–54 as reserve catcher with Yanks, doubling as coach 1953–54. Went to Denver, American Association, as manager for three seasons. Finished in tie for third, then had two second-place clubs. His 1957 team took Shaughnessy playoffs, then captured Little World Series. Back to Yanks as coach, 1958–60; manager, 1961–63. During Houk's time in front office, team sagged from its first-place finish, 1964 to sixth in 1965. Following year team started badly under Johnny Keane; Houk returned to field management of club in May. Finished tenth. Ninth in 1967. Two fifth-place finishes. Then second place, 1970. In 1971, fourth. Houk designated AL Manager of the Year, 1961; again, 1970.

As player, Houk in 91 games, had 158 times at bat, 43 hits, 20 RBI, .272 average. Never hit major league homer—had only four in minors.

HOWARD, ELSTON GENE C-BR-TR. B. 2/23/29, St. Louis, Mo. 6'2", 210. After 14 years as outstanding player, Ellie Howard became first black coach in AL, with Yankees, 1969. MVP 1963. Nine times, AL All-Star team.

Howard started as outfielder but Yankees needed catcher. Began pro career at Muskegon Mich., Central League, 1950, hitting .283, 54 games. Military service 1951–52. Had .286 season at Kansas City, American Association, 1953, in 139 games. Following year at Toronto, International League, hit .330, won MVP. Then 12 full seasons with Yankees. Played over 100 games in each of 10 of those seasons, mostly behind bat, occasionally outfield, first base. Hit .348 in 1961. Led catchers in fielding averages three times. Yanks sent Howard to Boston Red Sox during 1967, in time for him to help that club win flag. This was his tenth World Series. Best was 1960 Series—.462. World Series totals: 54 games, 42 hits, 171 at bats, .246 average, 7 doubles, 1 triple, 5 homers, 19 RBI.

Howard had distinction of swatting home run first time at bat in World Series, 9/28/55; In 1960 Series against Pirates, hit homer as pinch hitter, 10/5; made two hits in one inning 10/6. In six All-Star games Howard fielded perfectly but got no hits in nine trips to plate. Lifetime totals in majors: 1605 games, 5363 at bats, 619 runs, 1471 hits, 218 doubles, 50 triples, 167 homers, 762 RBI, .274 batting average, 9 stolen bases.

After 1968 season with Red Sox, Howard returned to Yankees as coach following year.

HOWARD, FRANK OLIVER (Hondo) OF-1B-BR-TR. B. 8/8/36, Columbus, Ohio. 6'7", 285. Columnist Jim Murray called him "Gulliver in Baseball Suit. Also called "The Horse" and "The Monster." One sports writer said his strike zone is so big it should be subdivided. While some record books say he weighs 250 pounds, Frank would be emaciated at that weight. Whether it's his altitude or beef plus suet, it adds up to tremendous power. All over majors, fans talk about his long-distance clouts. Nobody hits ball farther. In 1968 Howard had hottest home run streak in baseball history. Clouted 10 homers in 20 at bats, spread over six games. Climaxed that display of power against Mickey Lolich at Detroit; Blast hit atop left field roof at Tiger Stadium, bounded out of park. Was only player to reach upper deck in dead center field in Washington, doing this twice. Hit 237 homers while with Senators over seven-year period. In four of those seasons, 1967–70, hit 172 home runs, average of 43 per year. One of most dramatic round-trippers came in last game Senators played in nation's capital. Drove ball out of park in sixth inning off Yankees' Mike Kekich. Standing ovation lasted for minutes and Hondo had to be persuaded to take two curtain calls. Later this game was forfeited to Yankees because fans swarmed all over field scrounging for souvenirs. But Howard's homer and all other personal performances counted—except there was no winning or losing pitcher. Came 1972. Senators had been transformed into Texas Rangers; at home debut in Arlington stadium, between Dallas and Fort Worth, Frank stole show. First time at bat in first inning, smacked Texas-sized 400-foot home run blast to dead center field. Rangers ultimately won ball game from California, and Howard was off and running in new surroundings. This was homer No. 361 of major league career.

But Howard did not prosper as season progressed. Toward end of campaign was sold to Detroit for $30,000. Tigers hoped he would supply punch to put them over top in fight for AL flag. Frank got just eight hits in 14 games; one of hits, homer, won ball game from Baltimore. Overall average for entire season was .244 for 109 games, with 10 round-trippers for year. Despite poor season in 1971, reportedly was playing on $120,000 contract in 1972. At end of year, was obvious was being overpaid. Lifetime average at time was .274 for 1810 major league games. Had 1716 hits in 6261 official trips to plate. Scored 838 runs, drove in 1090. Extra-base hits included 236 doubles, 34 triples, 370 homers. Homer production for career was good, but still far behind fellows like Hank Aaron, Willie Mays, and other players still active at time.

Detroit management and Howard laid cards on table at end of season. Frank agreed to contract for 1973 estimated to be about $60,000; necessary to get Commissioner Kuhn's approval for such drastic cut. But Howard wanted to stay with Tigers—and must have known couldn't get job anywhere for previous salary.

Frank should have bank accounts and investments salted away. Got $108,000 bonus to sign with Los Angeles Dodgers back in 1958. Had attended Ohio State. Dodgers farmed him to Green Bay, III League. Typical season for Frank: led league in homers with 37; in RBI with 119; in runs scored, with 104; led league in total bases—and strikeouts. Batting average, .333. Had couple of brief visits with Dodgers, but spent

457

most of 1959 with Victoria, Texas League, and parts of 1959–60 with Spokane, Pacific Coast League. Howard also played 117 games for Dodgers, 1960, getting 23 homers and batting .268. When he hit ball, it traveled. But strikeouts were numerous and fielding wasn't entirely satisfactory. Hit .296 in 1962, with 31 homers and 119 RBI, but after average sagged to .226 in 1964, Walter Alston consented to trade his power for pitching—specially Claude Osteen.

Twice led AL in homers while with Washington, and once in RBI. Became gate attraction because of dramatic blows—and almost equally dramatic strikeouts. Record books list his many statistical achievments. Among them are AL marks for most homers, one week; most homers, five consecutive games; most homers, six consecutive games; most consecutive years, 100 or more strikeouts; etc. Also has led AL in hitting into double plays—and receiving most walks.

Howard played in one WS, 1963, with Dodgers; hit one homer, one double, one single in 10 trips to plate, for .300 average. In All-Star games, on AL squad 1968–71, his average was .167, one hit in six trips—homer.

HOWSAM, ROBERT LEE Executive. B. 2/28/18, Denver, Colo. Named president and chief executive of Cincinnati 3/12/73. Had been executive vice president, general manager of Reds since 1967. Team finished seventh previous season, but came in fourth in 1967 and 1968. Third in NL's Western Division, 1969, then first, winning NL playoff, but losing WS to Baltimore Orioles, 1970. In 1971 club dropped back to fourth. In 1970 Reds drew 1,803,568 fans; in 1971, 1,501,122 customers. In 1972 figure was 1,611,459. All these marks were higher than ever before in history of Cincinnati baseball. Bob inherited Dave Bristol as field manager in 1967. Bristol had taken over club 7/13/66; he continued as Redleg manager through 1969, when Howsam appointed Sparky Anderson as pilot. "Who he?" many fans asked. But Anderson led club to victory in Western Division of NL, then eliminated Pittsburgh, winner in Eastern Division, to capture pennant in first year as big league manager.

Howsam was Navy test pilot during World War II, then administrative assistant to Colorado's Senator Edwin Johnson. From there moved into reorganized Western League, and in 1948 became general manager of Denver Bears in that circuit. Bears drew 463,000 one year and set 10-year minor league attendance record. Howsam 12 years with Bears. Involved with Branch Rickey in promotion of Continental League, which resulted in expansion of AL and NL.

In August 1964 became general manager of St. Louis Cardinals. Team won pennant that year but Howsam couldn't claim any credit as had been on job only few weeks. Cardinals then had couple of second-division teams before Howsam made move to Rhineland. In Cincinnati Howsam immediately beefed up organization and doubled scouting department. Traded away favorites like Leo Cardenas and Vada Pinson. During off-season 1971–72, daringly traded away Lee May, Tommy Helms, in effort to revive club that had disappointing year in 1971. Men Reds got—Joe Morgan, Menke, Geronimo, and Billingham—all played vital roles in winning 1972 NL pennant.

HOY, WILLIAM ELLSWORTH (Dummy) OF-BL-TR. B. 5/23/62, Houcktown, Ohio. D. 12/15/61, Cincinnati, Ohio. 5'5", 155. Dummy Hoy overcame deafness, carved fine career in major leagues. Was born with hearing, speaking abilities but lost these faculties as child when he suffered from "brain fever." Handicaps did not prevent him from graduating with highest honors and as valedictorian of his class, School for Deaf, Columbus, Ohio, 1879.

Hoy with Oskosh, Northwestern League, 1886–87, then up to Washington NL. That season he hit .274, 136 games; led league in stolen bases, 82. Washington again, 1889; Buffalo, Players League, 1890; St. Louis, American Association, 1891; Washington NL, 1892–93; Cincinnati NL, 1894–97; Louisville NL, 1898–99; Chicago AL, 1900–01; Cincinnati NL, 1902; Los Angeles, Pacific Coast League, 1903.

Dummy contrived system of signals to communicate with teammates during game. Also credited with working out system with umpires. As batsman, couldn't hear call of balls, strikes. Asked ump to raise right arm to signify strike. Idea soon became standard and persists until today. Hoy often made brilliant plays in field. Fans developed method of communicating their appreciation to him. After great play by Hoy, crowd would arise en masse, wildly wave hats and arms. Merited applause aplenty with 605 stolen bases during time in majors. Often able to nip runners trying for extra bases. In one game, 6/19/89, threw three runners out at home plate.

Dummy wound up major league career with 1784 games, 2057 hits in 7053 times at bat, 1419 runs, 236 doubles, 118 triples, 41 homers, .292 average. Died at age 99, highly respected by all who had seen him play, or who knew him in later years.

HOYT, WAITE CHARLES (Brooklyn Schoolboy) P-BR-TR. B. 9/9/99, Brooklyn, N.Y. 6', 180. Waite Hoyt, after brilliant pitching career, was one of earliest big leaguers to make shift to microphone, 1939. After couple of years in Brooklyn doing commentary before and after game, moved to Cincinnati where did play-by-play for 25 years before retiring. Couldn't stay away, however. Back sportscasting, 1972. Red Barber, famed sportscaster for Cincinnati, Brooklyn, Yankees, and voice on numerous WS and football broadcasts, declared Hoyt was "best of all former athletes who went to microphone, highly intelligent, industrious, great story teller."

Hoyt got schoolboy nickname when pro ball player at age 16 with Mount Carmel, Pennsylvania State League, 1916. By 1918 had brief tryout—and turndown—with N.Y. Giants. Three years later came back to haunt John McGraw in 1921 WS as member of N.Y. Yankees. Won two games, lost one, that Series.

Waite bounced around to Hartford, Lynn, Memphis, Montreal, Nashville, and Newark teams as well as Giants before landing with Boston Red Sox, 1919. Nothing sensational about record with these clubs, or with Sox in 1919 or 1920. But was evident that with bit more maturity "Schoolboy" would become fine pitcher. Red Sox traded Hoyt to Yankees 12/15/20. Under Miller Huggins' guidance, Hoyt came through with 19 victories, 13 defeats in 1921, helping club win its first AL flag. Then in WS pitched two-hit shutout in second game, winning 3 to 0. Came back in fifth contest with 3–1 victory. Despite this, when final game came around, Yankees trailed four games to three. (Five victories needed to clinch WS that year.) Hoyt went to mound in effort to even series. Lost 1–0 heartbreaker when solitary Giant run scored on Roger Peckinpaugh's error. Hoyt allowed no earned runs in 27 innings pitched that series, but Giants walked off with championship. Hoyt won 19 games again in 1922, 17 in 1923, with Yankees finishing on top both years. Helped them to more pennants, 1926,27,28, with 16, 22, and 23 wins those years. Hoyt's overall WS performance was 12 games, 83-2/3 IP, 6–4 record, 81 hits, 28 runs (only 17 earned); fanned 49, allowed 22 walks, ERA 1.83.

Days as Yankee came to end 5/30/30 when traded to Detroit. In June 1931 released on waivers to Philadelphia Athletics. Brooklyn and New York NL 1932. Pittsburgh 1933–37. Brooklyn 1937–38. Enjoyed successful season, 1934, with Pirates, 15–6.

Hoyt's major league record: 675 games, 3762 IP, 237 victories, 182 defeats, 4037 hits, 1780 runs, 1500 earned runs; fanned 1206, walked 1003, ERA 3.59. Hall of Fame 1969.

HUBBARD, ROBERT CAL (Cal) Umpire. B. 10/31/1900, Keytesville, Mo. 6'2½", 265. A-B-C's helped make Cal Hubbard fine umpire and, in later years, excellent supervisor of AL arbiters. Ability, bulk, coolness— Cal had them. Looked part of pro football player, which he was for many years. Good one too.

Attended Centenary College two years; A.B., Geneva College, 1927. Pro football, N.Y. Giants, 1927–28; Green Bay Packers, 1929–33. Line coach, Texas A. & M., 1934. Player, Giants, 1935. Head football coach, Geneva College, 1941–42.

Cal's umpiring began 1928, Piedmont League. Southeastern League

1928–29. Piedmont League and South Atlantic Association 1930. Piedmont and International leagues 1931. Western Association 1932. International League 1932–35. AL 1936. Ultimately succeeded Tommy Connolly as supervisor of umpires. Officiated in four WS, three All-Star games. Retired 1968. Lives at Milan, Mo.

HUBBELL, CARL OWEN (King Carl) P-BR-TL. B. 6/22/03, Carthage, Mo. 6'1", 175. Through years, lefthanded pitchers almost synonymous with wildness. But Carl Hubbell, southpaw, never accused of being typical of his breed. Only thing eccentric about Carl was way his screwball acted as it danced past opposing batsmen. Throughout career Hubbell quiet, almost self-effacing gentleman. One of game's finest hurlers from late 1920s until 1943 when he quit to become field director, N.Y. (later San Francisco) Giants.

Among Hubbell's spectacular deeds was performance in 1934 All-Star Game, played in Polo Grounds, New York (7/10/34). Gehringer led off for AL with single to center. Heinie Manush walked. Not very imposing start. Up came Babe Ruth. Hubbell wasted fast ball, then threw three straight screwballs. Ruth watched third strike go by. Then it was Gehrig, about as tough as Ruth. Four pitches later he sat down, also by strikeout route. Jimmie Foxx next. One pitch missed plate but three screwballs didn't—and Double-X went down swinging. Twelve pitches had fanned three of game's most feared batsmen.

No fluke. Hubbell fanned Al Simmons and Joe Cronin at start of second inning. Bill Dickey broke spell with single. Lefty Gomez third strikeout victim of inning. Hubbell doesn't brag about fanning Gomez—one of game's worst hitters. But the others? Fabulous performance, never quite equaled in baseball annals.

King Carl did a few other things any pitcher would be proud of. Set NL record in 1933 by hurling 46 consecutive innings without allowing run. That year he chalked up 10 shutouts. No-hitter 5/8/29 against Pittsburgh. Even more spectacular performance against Cardinals 7/2/33, pitching all 18 innings, finally winning 1–0—didn't walk man! Won 24 Consecutive NL games 1936–37, major league record. Other jewels: five consecutive 20-game winning seasons, 1933–37; led NL in total victories three times, with high-water mark, 26 wins, 1936; topped NL pitchers in winning percentage, 1936,37; best ERA in NL 1933,34,36, including 1.66 mark in 1933 when also led league in total innings pitched, 309.

World Series record also commendable—4–2, ERA 1.79 (1933,36,37).

Lifetime: 253–154, .622 percentage, 535 games, 3591 innings, 3461 hits, 1188 earned runs, fanned 1677, walked only 725, ERA 2.98. MVP 1933,36. Hall of Fame 1947.

Hubbell grew up in Oklahoma on pecan farm. Signed with Cushing team, Oklahoma State League, 1923. League folded 1924. Same season pitched briefly with Ardmore, Western Association, 1–0; Oklahoma City, Western League, 1–0. In 1925, 17–13 for latter club, after which Detroit Tigers gave him tryout. Farmed to Toronto, International League, 1926, 7–7; to Decatur, III League, for much of 1927, 14–7.

During spring tryouts with Tigers Hubbell had experimented with screwball. In 1926 Ty Cobb, still managing Tigers, and coach George McBride advised Carl not to throw it. They—and many others—believed screwball an unnatural pitch, would ruin arm. Cited example of Hub Pruett, lefthander with St. Louis Browns few years previously. Pruett, as youngster, had fabulous record of striking out Babe Ruth several times with his screwball. But his arm gave out shortly and his career, promising at start, was painfully brief.

In 1928 Hubbell was sold outright to Beaumont, Texas League. Despite earlier advice, Hubbell began throwing screwball in earnest. Won 12, lost 9. Detroit scouts began having doubts about club's decision to let Hubbell get out of their farm system. But baseball laws prevented their buying him back until other major league teams had crack at him. Billy Evans, former umpire, then general manager for Cleveland. Later recalled that Detroit offered to arrange Hubbell's sale to Cleveland if Indians would give Joe Shaute in return. Evans turned down deal, fearing Cleveland fans would scream if traded away man who once had won 20 games in majors for an unknown. "I knew Shaute never would be great," said Evans. "But he was still pretty fair pitcher." Evans—and many others—wondered what "might have been" if Hubbell had gone to Cleveland. Perhaps dozen scouts turned in good reports on Hubbell in 1928—but Giants' cash offer of $30,000 or so was firm, and Carl joined John McGraw's team immediately. That year 10–6—and was on his way to magnificent career.

HUDLIN, GEORGE WILLIS (Ace) P-BR-TR. B. 5/23/06, Wagoner, Okla. 6′, 190. Willis Hudlin, after spending most of major league career pitching for Cleveland Indians, maintained connection with baseball as scout for Chicago White Sox in Little Rock, Ark. Won four letters in high school for football, baseball, and track and could have had any of four college athletic scholarships. Instead, joined Waco club, Texas League, 1926; won 16 games, losing 11. All of which brought promotion to Cleveland before year was up. After 1–3 record with Indians, 1926, took 18 games in 1927 while dropping 12. From then until 1940 toiled for Cleveland. Most of those years Indians weren't going anywhere, winning no pennants. His best years were aforementioned 1927; 1929 with 17–15 record; 1934 with 15–10; and 1935 with 15–11. Military service, 1942–44.

Hudlin bounced around during 1940. After winning two games, losing one, at start of season, subsequently went to St. Louis and Washington in AL, and New York NL, winding up with three wins and five losses for year. Then had final session, with St. Louis Browns, 1944. Finished with 158 major league wins, 156 losses, and ERA of 4.41. Hudlin coached with Detroit Tigers, 1957–59, and eventually turned to scouting.

HUDSON, SIDNEY CHARLES P-BR-TR. B. 1/3/17, Coalfield, Tenn. 6'4", 190. Sid Hudson won 104 games, lost 152, during major league career, but it must be pointed out that only three times in twelve seasons was he toiling for club that finished as high as fourth. Half of clubs was with finished seventh—and one was in last place.

Hudson had two winning seasons at Sanford, Fla., 1938 and 1939, with 11–7 record one year, 24–4 mark the next. Graduated to Washington Senators, 1940, winning 17, losing 16, for seventh-place team. In 1941 mark was 13–14; in 1942, 10–17, each time Senators missing basement by one notch. Spent 1943–45 in military service. After return best season was 1950, 14 wins, 14 losses. Traded to Boston AL 6/10/52. That year Washington finished fifth, but Red Sox were sixth. Wound up active pitching after 1954 season with Sox. ERA for career 4.28.

Sid scouted for Boston AL 1955–60, then became coach for Senators 1961–71, taking time out in 1965–66 to act as minor league pitching instructor for Washington. Senators transformed into Texas Rangers during winter of 1971–72, Hudson remaining with team as coach through 1972 season.

HUGGINS, MILLER JAMES 2B-BRL-TR. B. 3/27/79, Cincinnati, Ohio. D. 9/25/29, New York, N.Y. 5'4", 146. Miller Huggins was so small that in later years they called him "Mite Manager." Could have used another adjective, "mighty." He was pilot who led Yankees to their first series of pennants, world championships. Yanks won 1921–23, 26–28 under Hug's direction. Captured World Series 1923 from Giants after losing to same club, 1921,22; lost 1926 World Series to Cardinals; took 1927 Series from Pirates, sweeping all four games; and did same to Cards in 1928.

Practically everyone connected with Yankee club those days was head taller and close to 100 pounds heavier than Huggins, especially Babe Ruth. Swashbuckling Bambino, setting home run records all over place, broke just about every training rule. Crisis came in 1925 when Huggins got fed up. Yankees were flirting with cellar, instead of pennant, due in part to Ruth's poor work. Babe had not hit homer that season until June 11. Batting average sagged, so did his fielding. Explosion came in St. Louis in August. Ruth, drawing $52,000 salary, then fantastic sum before inflation and high taxes, wasn't even hitting .250. Ruth was staying out night after night, taking other Yankee players with him. Babe hadn't come back to club's hotel three nights in row, missed batting practice. Stumbled into ball park late, umkempt. Hug waiting for him in clubhouse. Ruth mumbled regrets at being late because of "personal business." Huggins told clubhouse boy to call all Yankee players in, off field. When all had gathered, Mite Manager read riot act to entire club. Announced he was fining Ruth $5000 and suspending him indefinitely, sending him back to New York. Reason given was "general infractions of training and disciplinary rules." Until that time no club had ever fined one of its own players more than $500. Babe shouted epithets and threats at Huggins. Huggins stuck to his guns. "You go to Ruppert [club owner]," said Hug. "Tell him I am giving you raw deal. Show him your .246 batting average!" Ed Barrow, Yankee general manager, supported Huggins' move to limit. So did owner. Though Ruth blustered, talked about barnstorming on his own, eventually he apologized, rejoined club, and for some years to come was great ball player. Fine stuck, however.

Huggins started out in pro ball at Mansfield, Ohio, 1899, got to St. Paul for 1901,02,03 seasons, hitting above .300 each year. Joined Cincinnati 1904, remaining until 1909. With Cardinals 1910–16. Playing manager, Cards, 1913–1916, bench manager, 1917. Then to Yanks for rest of life. During playing days, Huggins got few extra-base hits, but was excellent leadoff man. Hit .265 in 1573 major league contests. As manager, resembled youngster telling older brothers what to do. Well liked by players and fans, respected everywhere. Original profession law, but gave it up for baseball.

HULBERT, WILLIAM AMBROSE Executive. B. 10/23/32, Burlington Flats, N.Y. D. 4/10/82, Chicago, Ill. Second president of NL, serving from 1877 to 1882. First professional baseball club formed in Cincinnati, 1869. During next several years loose National Association formed, but gambling became closely involved with game. So much so that every error, every failure to hit caused someone to say it was due to player's crookedness.

Hulbert, Chicago businessman and fan, bought stock in Chicago team, and soon was elected president of club. He and Al Spalding, fine pitcher with Boston club, feared budding game would be ruined by gamblers unless something was done to clean up sport. Spalding later founded famed sporting-goods company. Hulbert persuaded Spalding to come to Chicago club and bring several teammates. Hulbert also enlisted support of representatives of St. Louis, Cincinnati, and Louisville teams for "new look" in baseball. Then decided to take on eastern clubs, some of which had pirated players from western rivals. Managed to get eastern team representatives into New York hotel room. With dramatic flourish, when all had assembled, Hulbert strode to door, locked it, put key in pocket. "Don't be alarmed," said Chicagoan; "we don't want any intrusion from outside." Then added: "There is some business that has to be finished. No one will leave this room until I have explained everything." Hulbert then sold visitors on reorganization into new league. Reached into pocket, took out draft for NL constitution and professional player contract. Convinced listeners game must be cleaned up, and adopted following objectives:

1. To encourage, foster, and elevate game of baseball.
2. To enact and enforce proper rules for exhibition and conduct of game.
3. To make baseball playing respectable and honorable.

NL thus formed, with membership consisting of Chicago, Boston, New York, Philadelphia, Hartford, St. Louis, Cincinnati, and Louisville. Seventy-game schedule drawn up. Admission 50 cents, but reduced to 10 cents after third inning. Morgan G. Bulkeley, distinguished citizen of Hartford who later became mayor, eventually governor of Connecticut and U.S. senator, was chosen first president of NL. Bulkeley provided "front" for new circuit, but Hulbert was power behind throne. After one year in office, Bulkeley resigned due to pressure of other affairs and Hulbert became president. Late in 1876 New York and Philadelphia clubs had refused to make last scheduled western trip, fearing financial losses. When Hulbert took over, his first move shocked easterners who thought league could not prosper without them. Hulbert expelled them both, and NL operated with only six clubs, 1877–78. During 1877 season four Louisville players were found to have had dealings with gamblers involving alleged throwing of games. Hulbert banished them for life.

HUNDLEY, CECIL RANDOLPH (Randy) C-BR-TR. B. 6/1/42, Martinsville, Va. 6', 175. Catching is rugged business but Randy Hundley appeared in 612 games during first four seasons with Chicago Cubs. Averaged 153 games a year. Then iron man ran into miseries, 1970–71; but for his ailments, Cubs might very well have finished on top in their division in NL.

Hundley is one of those big-bonus boys who made good—but not for team that paid him reported $110,000 to sign. Randy got that fancy check from San Francisco Giants, 1960. Bounced around minors six years with couple of "cups of coffee" at Candlestick Park, then was allowed to go to Cubs in trade 12/2/65. Randy got experience at Salem (Va.), Fresno, El Paso, Tacoma, Atlanta, then in International League. Wasted no time making good for Cubs. In first season, 1966, set NL record for games caught by rookie, 149, which since has been broken. Set major league record for catcher in rookie season hitting most homers, 19. During next three seasons took part in 152, 160, and 151 games respectively. The 160 games in 1968 set major league record for receiver. Skipped just two games in 162-game season, and 147 of games Randy caught were complete ones. Then came 1970. Chipped bone in left hand 3/26/70, and out of action until mid-April. Played one week—damaged cartilage in left knee—surgery one month later. Back on active list in July and got into 73 games. In 1971 Hundley sprained right knee severely during spring training. Got into nine games but more surgery in June kept him out for rest of year. Also developed gall bladder and stomach trouble, lost 30 pounds. In 1972 played 114 games, hit .218. Went into 1973 season praying his injuries and illnesses were all behind.

In four good seasons Hundley never hit above .267, but always had at least 60 RBI. After rookie season when he hit 19 homers, had 14, 7, 18 in next three years. Lifetime major league average as he went into 1973 season was .242. Principal value to Cubs has been brilliant catching and field generalship. Leo Durocher, then manager of Chicago team, claimed loss of Hundley for extended periods in 1971 cost club some 12 victories.

HUNT, RONALD KENNETH (Zeke)   2B-BR-TR. B. 2/23/41, St. Louis, Mo. 5'11", 170. In 1971 Ron Hunt got hit by pitched ball 50 times, breaking long-standing record of Hugh Jennings, hit 49 times while with Baltimore Orioles, 1896. Stopped 26 more pitches in 1972, breaking major league record set by Minnie Minoso who was hit 192 times. Hunt had 203 when 1973 season began. When not getting hit by opposing pitchers, Hunt is stellar keystone man for Montreal Expos. Hit .279 in 1971, but when you added up his hits, walks, and being hit 50 times, his "reached-base" average was .403. Only once did Hunt ground into double play, 1971. This was best record for any major league player taking part in most of club's games. No wonder Montreal sports writers named him Expos' MVP for season.

Hunt started with McCook in Nebraska State League, 1959, then had two years at Cedar Rapids, III League, before joining New York Mets, 1963. While he hit .303 in 127 games in 1964, generally average has been below .300 mark. Makes no claims to be slugger. Once was quoted as saying only way he can hit 400-foot homers is when there are ideal conditions. "That means calm air, 1000-mph. wind blowing toward fence, and good swing. Otherwise I need a driver and a No. 3 wood to hit that far." Ron spent one season, 1967, with Los Angeles Dodgers, then shifted to San Francisco Giants for 1968–70. Landed with Montreal, 1971.

Hunt crowds plate. Said to have created some sort of record in spring training, 1971. Teammates twice hit him with baseballs in batting practice and three times was hit by pitching machines. Sometimes getting hit isn't fun. Once stopped pitch by Tom Seaver that put him in hospital. Another time Steve Arlin of San Diego hit him in jaw with pitch, twice. Usually is hit above waist on side or on left arm. After being hit by Milt Pappas of Cubs for 50th-time-hit during 1971, Milt complained Hunt could have avoided pitch. Later Ron said, "I don't know why Pappas made such a stink. After all, I put him in record book." Prior to 1971 Hunt had stopped pitched balls maximum 25 or 26 times per year.

Hunt claims he is part Cherokee. He and wife adopted Indian baby girl who is Apache and Navajo. Named her Suncere, which means Morning Star. Hunt has 170-acre farm with cattle and horses near town where he operates liquor store with father-in-law, Wentzville, Mo.

HUNTER, GORDON WILLIAM (Billy) SS-BR-TR. B. 6/4/28, Punxsutawney, Pa. 5'11, 190. Billy Hunter parlayed mediocre record as player into steady job as third base coach for Baltimore Orioles since 1964. Good fielding shortstop; never much of hitter, even in minors. Best year in bushes 1952, .285, Fort Worth, Texas League. This gave him chance with hapless St. Louis AL, tail-enders in 1953. Browns' franchise transferred to Baltimore following year. Billy went with it. Played 125 games with Orioles, 1954; hit .243, his highest major league mark playing regularly. New York AL 1955–56. As reserve infielder hit .280, 1956, 39 contests. Then two years at Kansas City AL, one at Cleveland. Major league record: .219 in 630 games.

Hunter attended Indiana State College Pa. Played at Three Rivers, Que.; Nashua, N.H.; Newport News; Pueblo, 1948–50, before going to Fort Worth. MVP, Texas League, 1952. After leaving majors, managed Bluefield to consecutive Appalachian (rookie) League pennants, 1962–63. Then joined Orioles as coach. Appeared in 1953 All-Star game.

HUNTER, JAMES AUGUSTUS (Catfish) P-BR-TR. B. 4/8/46, Hertford, N.C. 6', 195. Catfish Hunter pitched five no-hit games, including one perfect game, while high school boy. Signed with Kansas City AL organization for $75,000 bonus and eventually pitched one of those extremely rare perfect games in major leagues 5/8/68 against Minnesota. This was only 11th time feat has been accomplished in major league history.

Hunter got nickname from his parents. Ran away from home as boy; when he came back, had two catfish with him. In high school was so outstanding as athlete in baseball, football, and track that A's were willing to risk good-sized bonus to get him. But, for time in 1964, when A's had him on roster at Daytona Beach, Florida State League, brilliant future was endangered by hunting accident. Needed operation to remove shotgun pellets. Then in 1965, without ever having pitched in minors, made grade at Kansas City. Won eight, lost eight, pitching 133 innings with 4.26 ERA. Evidence of skill reflected in walks vs. strikeouts: fanned 82, gave just 46 bases on balls.

In 1967 got his ERA down to 2.80, but Kansas City team didn't give much support either in field or at bat, and he was not able to break even in 30 dicisions, winning 13, losing 17. Following year, when team moved to Oakland, Hunter broke even with 13–13. In 1970 improved to 18–14, and in 1971 raised win total to 21, with 11 defeats. Did still better, 1972, with another 21-victory season against seven defeats, with lowest ERA of career, 2.04.

Hunter, starting in 1966, struck out over 100 batsmen every season. Highest mark prior to 1973 was 196 in 1967. Started 1973 campaign with 115 wins, 96 losses, and 3.20 ERA. By this time had 1253 major league strikeouts against 572 bases on balls in 1882 innings. Hunter pitched brilliantly in 1972 AL playoffs and WS. Hurled 15-1/3 innings against Detroit; neither won nor lost, but had ERA of 1.17. Credited with two victories over Cincinnati in WS; 16 innings, 5 earned runs, 11 strikeouts, 6 walks, 2.81 ERA. AL All-Star teams 1966–70, 72–73.

Jim helps own cause as hitter. Hit .350 in 1971. Good fielder too— didn't make single error, 1971, in 274 innings pitched.

HUTCHINSON, FREDERICK CHARLES (Big Bear) P-BL-TR. B. 8/12/19, Seattle, Wash. D. 11/12/64, Bradenton, Fla. 6'2", 200. Detroit Tigers scouted Fred Hutchinson while he was still in high school. Fred's father insisted that young man was worth $5000 bonus for signing with Detroit. When Tigers would not meet price, Hutch signed with Seattle, Pacific Coast League. Shortly after observing his nineteenth birthday (1938), had chalked up 25–7 record. Led league in percentage of victories, .781, also tops in ERA—2.48. Hutchinson's value soared. Team which refused to pay $5000 bonus now gave Seattle $50,000 and four players to get him.

Divided 1939 season between Tigers (3–6) and Toledo, American Association (9–9). Part of 1940 with Tigers, 3–7; part with Buffalo, International League, 7–3. Most of 1941 with Buffalo, 26–7, 2.44 ERA. Demonstrated hitting ability with .392 average, 58 hits in 148 trips, being used as pinch batsman 36 games. Recalled to Detroit 1941; appeared in two games as pinch hitter without success. Career interrupted by service in U.S. Navy, 1942–45. Back with Tigers 1946, 14–11; 1947, 18–10; 1948, 13–11; 1949, 15–7; 1950, 17–8; 1951, 10–10; 1952, 2–1; 1953, no decisions.

Hutch replaced Red Rolfe as manager of Tigers 7/5/52, inheriting last place club. Finished sixth, 1953; fifth, 1954. Wanted more than one-year contract for 1955, resigned when Detroit refused. Managed Seattle 1955, winning PCL pennant. Manager, St. Louis NL, 1956, finished fourth; second in 1957. Voted NL Manager of the Year, 1957, by the *Sporting News* and United Press. Continued as Cardinal manager until 9/17/58 when replaced by Stan Hack.

Piloted Seattle 1959, until accepted management, Cincinnati, 7/8/59. Manager of Reds through 1964. Pennant 1961. Lost World Series

Yankees, four games to one.

Cut down by cancer, took leave of absence during part of 1964 season. Resigned 10/19/64, shortly before death. Pitching record in majors 95–71. Hit .263, 354 games.

HYLAND, DR. ROBERT F. (Surgeon General of Baseball) B. 3/6/86, Grand Rapids, Mich. D. 12/14/50, St. Louis, Mo. Among baseball players Dr. Hyland treated were Ty Cobb, Rogers Hornsby, Lou Gehrig, Frankie Frisch, Herb Pennock, Billy Southworth, Bill Killefer. Once after examining Cobb, Hyland told friends that Ty, from hips down, all spike wounds and strawberries. "There is a game guy," he said.

Hyland hoped to become pro ball player but medicine won. Graduate of St. Louis University Medical School, 1911. Club physician for Cardinals, Browns; medical supervisor of St. Louis Public Service Co.; later, chief surgeon of St. John's Hospital, St. Louis. Credited with prolonging playing careers of several major leaguers. Earl Combs crashed into bleacher wall in St. Louis, 7/24/34, fracturing skull, suffering other injuries. Yankee outfielder's shoulder rebuilt; many said Hyland saved Earl's life. Treated Mel Ott once when skulled by Cardinal pitcher. Operated on Mort Cooper, whose arm went dead after 1941 season. Cooper returned, won over 20 games each of next three seasons. Cardinals made conditional deal to sell Johnny Mize to Cincinnati while young player. Reds would have paid $55,000 for his contract, but Mize had calcium formations in both groins, was returned to Redbirds. Dr. Hyland performed successful operation on Johnny, who went on to brilliant years with Cardinals, Giants, Yankees. Tony Lazzeri returned to Yankee lineup after receiving Hyland treatment in St. Louis.

Dr. Hyland had wide circle of friends. Did much charitable work, quietly. Ever popular among newsmen. In 1959 St. Louis chapter of Baseball Writers' Association originated Dr. Robert F. Hyland Award for Meritorious Service to Sports. Award has gone to persons like Ernie Banks, Archie Moore, Willie Mays, Hank Aaron. The 1972 awards were to Sandy Koufax, Warren Giles, Danny Murtaugh, Leo Ward (traveling secretary, Cardinals, 35 years; retired after 1972 season).

Son, Robert F. Hyland, Jr., has been general manager of KMOX, 50,000-watt radio station in St. Louis which devoted special attention to sports.

IRVIN, MONFORD MERRILL (Monte) OF-BR-TR. B. 2/25/19, Columbia, Ala. 6'1", 195. Monte Irvin was 30 years old before he reached major leagues but still was able to compile .293 lifetime average for 764 games in big time. Like many other black players, Monte might have had much longer and more impressive career but for racial bar when he was youngster.

Football, basketball, and track star in high school days in New Jersey. One of best javelin throwers, good with shot put. Attended Chester College, had two years at Lincoln U. Led Negro National League in hitting with .422 average, 1941. Served in army during World War II. Returned to Negro National League, also played in Caribbean and Mexico. Joined Jersey City, International League farm club of New York Giants, 1949, hit .373 in 63 games. Also played 36 games with Giants, with .224 mark. Reached .299 in 1950 with Giants, and had .510 mark for 18 contests at Jersey City. Remained with Giants 1951–55, batting well over .300 three of those seasons. Missed much of 1952 season, however, after breaking ankle in exhibition game in Denver during April. Monte was also with Minneapolis, American Association, 1955; hit .352 in 75 games and was drafted by Chicago Cubs. Hit .271 in 111 games with Cubs, 1956, last season in majors. Monte's 731 major league hits included 97 doubles, 31 triples, 99 homers, 366 runs scored, 443 RBI.

Irvin scouted for New York Mets, 1967–68. Later joined staff of baseball commissioner Bowie Kuhn, doing special work in public relations. Selected to Hall of Fame, 1973, by special committee, in recognition of his brilliant play in Negro leagues before admission of blacks into organized baseball.

IRWIN, ARTHUR ALBERT (Doc) SS-BL-TR. B. 2/14/58, Toronto, Ontario. D. 7/16/21, Atlantic Ocean. 5'8½", 158. This is fellow credited with using glove in baseball for first time, playing shortstop for Providence club of NL, 1883. No great hitter, as lifetime average of some .240–.250 indicates. Played for Worcester, Mass., then in NL, 1880–82; then Providence, 1883–85; Philadelphia NL, 1886–89; Washington NL, 1889; Boston, Players League, 1890; Boston, American Association, 1891; Philadelphia NL, 1894.

Acted as player-manager at Washington, 1889; Boston, 1891, and Philadelphia, 1894. Also was nonplaying manager at Washington, 1892; Philadelphia, 1895; New York NL, 1896; Washington NL, 1898–99. Apparently played at least 1000 games in old majors but, like his other records, it is difficult to determine facts with complete accuracy.

JACKSON, JOSEPH JEFFERSON (Shoeless Joe) OF-BL-TR. B. 7/16/88, Brandon Mills, S.C. D. 12/5/51, Greenville, S.C. 6'1", 175. Tragic fate for man many have described as greater hitter who ever lived. One of few major leaguers to bat better than .400. Had lifetime average of .356 in big time. But banned from baseball forever because of participation in "Black Sox" scandal of 1919 WS.

Joe was illiterate mill hand in cotton factory who loved baseball and often played game without shoes, giving rise to nickname. Won batting title in Carolina Association, 1908, hitting .346 for home-town team, Greenville. Good enough to get trial with Philadelphia Athletics same season, but went just three for 23 in five games, and was back at Savannah, South Atlantic League, 1909. Won bat title with .358. Five more games at Philadelphia that year, this time getting three hits in 17 trips. Athletics sent him to New Orleans for 1910. Once again finished at top of list, gaining Southern Association batting championship with .354 average. Athletics traded title to Jackson to Cleveland during 1910 season, and once again Jackson was in AL by end of year. This time he gave evidence of future ability by batting lusty .387 in 20 games.

Playing first full year in majors, 1911, Jackson came up with .408 average in 147 games. Ordinarily would have meant batting title—but Ty Cobb came up with .420, and Joe had to be content with runner-up position. Missed .400 mark following season by five points. After .373 in 1913 and .338 in 1914, Jackson dropped to .331 in 1915, after which was traded to Chicago White Sox 8/20/15. Hit .265 for remaining 46 games and had .308 mark for season. Up to .341 in 1916, .301 in 1917, and .354

in 1918. In year "Black Sox" scandal developed, Jackson jogged along at .351 and was hitting .382 in 1920 when exposure of 1919 scandal ended career late in September.

Joe's fancy average in final season still did not get him an AL bat title. George Sisler took honors with .407 and Tris Speaker hit .388. When curtain rang down, Jackson had played 1330 major league games. His 1772 hits included 307 doubles, 168 triples, 54 homers. Scored 873 runs, drove in 822 and stole 202 bases. In WS play, 1917 and 1919, both with White Sox, hit .304 first classic and .375 in tainted series. In fact, had 12 hits, including three doubles and home run in 1919 WS. Overall figure for both series was .345 in 14 games, with eight RBI.

Oddly, Jackson never made five hits in any major league game; nor did he ever get two homers in any contest. Highest home run total was 12 in final season. Many of his hits were blasted with bat with top part black; he called it "Black Betsy."

In confession about 1919 WS, given late in 1920 season, Jackson reportedly said had received $5000, but had been promised $20,000 by gamblers. Said had moved slowly to retrieve balls hit in his direction during 1919 series; and had made throws that would deliberately fall short. When Jackson left court after his confession, newsmen reported that unknown ragged boy who was baseball fan approached and said, "Say it ain't so, Joe!" But Jackson did not deny confession at that time. Later, however, his confession, along with those of Cicotte and Williams, were stolen from court records. In 1922 Jackson and Happy Felsch brought damage suits against Charles Comiskey, White Sox owner, charging "conspiracy against them by the defendant and other unknown persons." In another suit Jackson asked for $19,000 allegedly due him for back pay under contract. Joe reportedly had been making slightly more than $6000 annually when gamblers tempted him to throw games in 1919 WS. Despite charges and countercharges, denials and different versions of what actually happened, Judge Landis, newly appointed commissioner of baseball, barred Jackson from organized ball for life, with seven other members of 1919 White Sox. In later years Jackson ran liquor store in South Carolina.

JACKSON, LAWRENCE CURTIS (Larry) P-BR-TR. B. 6/2/31, Nampa, Idaho, 6'2", 198. Larry Jackson won 194 NL games, pitched in four All-Star games (1957, 58, 60, 63), never got chance in WS. With St. Louis Cardinals, 1956–62; Chicago Cubs, 1963–66; Philadelphia Phillies, 1966–68.

Outstanding high school and college athlete. In high school once pitched doubleheader, had no-hitters in both. Football at Boise Junior College; A.B. at U. of Idaho. Signed by Cardinal scout Ollie Vanek. First year in pro ball, 1951, at Pocatello, 3–11. But got rolling at Fresno,

1952. Pitched 300 innings, was 28–4, struck out 351 men, had 2.85 ERA. Led California League: innings pitched, winning percentage, strikeouts. Cardinals moved him to Houston, Omaha, Rochester farms in 1953–54. Brought to St. Louis, 1955. First two seasons in majors: 11–16. In 1957, 15–9. Then 13–13, 14–13, 18–13, 14–11, 16–11 successively. Traded to Chicago Cubs, 10/17/62. Big winner in his second season, 1964, with 24–11, 3.14 ERA. Record sagged after that. Traded to Phillies, 4/21/66. Continued in majors through 1968. Quit with 194–183 record, 3.40 ERA, 558 games, 3262-2/3 innings. Walked 824, struck out 1709, pitched 37 shutouts, started 429 games, completed 149.

Has worked as sports writer in Boise.

JACKSON, REGINALD MARTINEZ (Reggie) OF-BL-TL. B. 5/18/46, Wyncote, Pa. 6′, 195.

Reggie Jackson is one of numerous ball players who have clashed with Charles O. Finley, owner of Oakland A's. But both seemed chummy when Oakland won AL pennant and followed it with WS victory over Cincinnati Reds, 1972. Jackson's 25 homers and 75 RBI, as well as fine play in center field, helped wrap up flag, but he was on sidelines during autumn classic, due to pulled hamstring muscle suffered stealing home in fifth game of playoff series against Detroit. A's won top baseball honors, 1972, even though neither Jackson nor Vida Blue, were performing at peak. Reggie's best season was second full year in majors, 1969, when he slapped 47 homers, drove in 118 runs, hit .275.

Then came disastrous holdout session spring of 1970. Reggie wanted $60,000 salary, a 300-percent raise. Finley offered $40,000. For six weeks Jackson and Finley couldn't get together. Ultimate compromise gave Reggie approximately $47,000. But Jackson's home run output was cut in half, RBI nearly so, and batting average sagged 38 points to lowly .237.

Jackson is highly emotional, self-confident young man with tools to become superstar. Good enough that A's reportedly gave him $95,000 bonus to sign with their organization, 1966—and, it is alleged, Finley later turned down million-dollar offer for contract. Reggie attended Arizona State U. There he played baseball, football, basketball. On gridiron was flanker and defensive back; on diamond, All-American outfielder. Fourteen months after signing he was in major leagues to stay.

Got minor league experience 1966–67 with Lewiston, Northwest League; Modesto, California League; and Birmingham, Southern Association. Joined A's during last season in Kansas City, 1967, played 35 games. Took part in 154 games during first full season, at Oakland. Had respectable number of homers, 29; 74 RBI and .250 average. Then came fine season and acrimonious holdout.

Through years, Jackson has been noted for great power. While still in college was first collegian ever to hit ball out of Phoenix Municipal Stadium, distance estimated at 480 ft. Fans are still talking about homer he hit in Detroit during 1971 All-Star Game, stupendous clout that hit transformer on top of roof in right center. Tape-measure homers also have been hit in Kansas City, Minnesota, Boston, and in Yankee Stadium, New York. Offsetting undoubted ability to propel baseball into distant horizon, Jackson has consistently led AL in strikeouts. Tends to do much wild swinging in impatience to get four-masters. For example, in 1968 fanned 171 times.

Reggie faced 1973 season having played 775 AL games with 700 hits to credit for .258 lifetime average. With 395 singles, 128 doubles, 20 triples, 157 homers, had driven in 419 runs and scored 434 times. Base thefts were 79. Named to AL All-Star squads, 1969, 71–73.

When Jackson received bonus money from A's, Charlie Finley helped invest much of it. Off-seasons, besides playing some ball in Caribbean, Jackson has had prosperous real estate business in Tempe, Ariz.

JACKSON, ROLAND THOMAS (Sonny) SS-OF-BL-TR. B. 7/9/44, Washington, D.C. 5'9", 155. Sonny Jackson divided his time in 1972 between Atlanta Braves and Richmond club of International League, but at start of 1973 was hoping for better luck with regard to injuries. Career to then had been checkered with series of mishaps including pulled hamstring muscles and other ailments, as well as 1970 collision with Dick Dietz.

Jackson faced 1973 with .254 lifetime average in 814 major league games, including 721 hits. Seven of blows were homers, four of them inside-park variety in Houston's Astrodome.

Sonny signed with Astros 6/18/62, turning down scholarship to become first black football player at U. of Maryland. Got minor league experience at Modesto, California League; San Antonio, Texas loop; and Oklahoma City in Pacific Coast League. Brief spells with Astros, 1963,64,65, then took over as Houston's regular shortstop, 1966; played 150 games and hit .292, with 49 stolen bases. His thefts set record for NL rookies; also led league in sacrifice hits; helped his cause with five hits in game of 9/16/66. Hitting fell off after that; Houston traded him to Atlanta 10/8/67 in deal involving Denis Menke. After playing shortstop most of time when not injured, through 1970, Braves converted him into center fielder for 1971. In 149 games that year hit .258. His 1972 mark with Braves was .238 for 60 games; .215 for 20 contests with Richmond.

JACKSON, TRAVIS CALVIN SS-BR-TR. B. 11/2/03, Waldo, Ark. 5'10½", 160. Stellar shortstop for New York Giants in days when John McGraw and Bill Terry, managed team. Spent last two years playing third base. Took part in four WS. Played 1656 major league games and had lifetime average of .291. Plagued by knee problems dating to undergraduate days at Ouachita Baptist College in Arkansas.

Travis played less than two seasons in minors with Little Rock, Southern Association, 1921–22, before being sold to Giants. Played three games for McGraw, 1922; in 1923 was used in 60 games at short, 31 at third base, one at second. Hit .275 and displayed enough talent that Giants traded away veteran shortstop Dave Bancroft to become manager of Boston Braves. Jackson made good in fine style, 1924: played 151 games, hit healthy .302; Giants again won NL flag, fourth in row. Travis continued fine play for new York through 1936, except for 1932 and 1933 when injuries kept him on sidelines about 100 games each season. Hit above .300 four seasons, with highest mark .339 in 1930.

Amassed 135 homers during career, reaching 21 in 1929. Good clutch hitter, as RBI totals indicate: 929 for career, five times driving in 80 or more runs. High RBI mark came 1934 with 101. Also slapped 291 doubles, 86 triples among 1768 hits, scored 833 runs, and stole 71 bases.

Jackson, in four WS, 1923,24,33,36, played 19 games, had 10 hits in 67 at bats for .149 average. Leaving Giants after 1936 season, Travis came back as coach 1939–40 and 1947–48 for same team.

JACOBSON, WILLIAM CHESTER (Baby Doll) OF-BR-TR. B. 8/16/90, Cable, Ill. 6'2½", 210. In days when St. Louis Browns had genuine hopes of winning AL pennant they boasted one of greatest hitting outfields ever assembled on one team. For five years all regulars hit .300 or better. String was broken in 1924 when two still hit .300, but one missed mark by one point. In 1921, lowest average among three was .347 for Johnny Tobin; Baby Doll Jacobson and Ken Williams both hit .352. Good fielders too. Jacobson, in center, got nickname because was such a dreamboat, ranging far and wide to pull down long drives. Ken Williams, in left, had one of greatest throwing arms ever seen in AL. And Tobin was skilled specialist with drag bunt. With these three stalwarts in outfield, George Sisler at first base, Urban Shocker on mound, and other fine dependable players elsewhere, Browns came within one game of winning flag in 1922. But they had to wait until wartime, 1944, to capture their solitary AL pennant.

Jacobson started at Rock Island, 1909, and played in Mobile, Chattanooga, and Little Rock before making grade with Browns, 1917. Had brief spell with Detroit Tigers and Browns, 1915, but hit only .211 in 180 trips to plate. Spent 1918 in military service, then in 1919 began his contribution to Brownie cause with .323. Followed with .355, .352, .317 and .309. In 1924, when Tobin dropped out of .300 circle, Jake hit .318, followed with .341. In 1926 Tobin had been sent to Washington, and Jacobson soon was on way. Involved in three-cornered deal 6/15/26 and landed with Boston Red Sox. For first time since military service

Jacobson missed .300 mark—by one point. In 1927 Baby Doll was gypsy, playing for Red Sox, Cleveland, and Philadelphia Athletics. Then dropped into minors with Baltimore, Chattanooga, Indianapolis, and Toledo, all in 1928. Gave up active play after hitting .304 with Quincy in III League, 1929, in 130 games.

Jacobson hit three triples in one game 9/9/22. In 1924 season set AL records for putouts and chances accepted in outfield, but these have been surpassed since then. Never got crack at WS. Wound up with 1472 major league games, 1714 hits, 787 runs, 328 doubles, 94 triples, 84 homers, and 821 RBI for lifetime .311.

JAMES, WILLIAM LAWRENCE (Seattle Bill) P-BR-TR. B. 3/12/92, Placer County, Calif. D. 3/10/71, Oroville, Calif. 6'3'', 196. Bill James won 26 games, lost seven, for .788 winning percentage to lead NL pitchers, 1914. Was one of famous trio of hurlers, including Rudolph and Tyler, whose combined efforts brought Miracle Braves to pennant in Boston after club in cellar July 4. James won two of Braves' four straight WS victories over powerful Philadelphia Athletics that fall. Wonderful while it lasted—but James' entire major league career record showed only 11 other victories.

James joined Braves in 1913, won six, lost ten, with 2.79 ERA. Then came fabulous seas╌   der Mgr. George Stallings: Bill pitched 332-1/3 innings with E╌   ╌ 1.90, and pitched four shutouts. In second game of WS shut out White Elephants, 1–0 on two hits. Relieved in next game, which went 12 innings; held Athletics hitless and scoreless in last two frames, Braves winning in their half of 12th by 5–4 score. Bill didn't get into final game, since Dick Rudolph, winner of opening contest, won it by 3–1 count.

When 1915 came around, James about through. Won only five games, lost four. Dropped out of majors, and though he tried comeback with Braves in 1919, pitched only 5-1/3 innings and called it quits. Big league record showed 37 victories, 21 defeats; 541-2/3 innings pitched, 199 walks, 253 strikeouts, and ERA of 2.28.

JANSEN, LAWRENCE JOSEPH (Larry) P-BR-TR. B. 7/16/20, Verboort, Oreg. 6'2'', 201. Larry Jansen, in 1973, was serving second season as pitching coach for Chicago Cubs and 13th full year in NL advising younger hurlers. Spent 11 of these years as coach for San Francisco Giants, helping several pitchers, notably Juan Marichal and Gaylord Perry, enjoy considerable success.

Jansen was pitcher in NL nine seasons and won 122 games, lost 89, with an ERA of 3.58 for 1767 innings. Most of big league career was with New York Giants, for whom he toiled 1947–54 inclusive. Larry began at Salt Lake City, Pioneer League, 1940, with 20 victories, seven defeats.

With San Francisco Seals, Pacific Coast League, 1941–42; dropped out of pro ball for two years, returning to Seals in 1945 for seven games. Won 30, lost six, in 1946, earning promotion to Giants. Jumped into majors with 21-victory season (five losses) for best winning percentage in NL. Followed with 18–12, 15–16, and 19–13. Won 23 games, lost 11, in 1951, then dropped back to 11–11, 11–16, and 2–2, finishing 1954 as coach. Pitched for Seattle, PCL, 1955–56, and returned to majors with Cincinnati for part of 1956, winning two, losing three.

Playing coach, Seattle, PCL, 1957. Then three years as playing coach for Portland. Coach, Giants, 1961–71.

Jansen lost two decisions in 1951 WS, with ERA of 6.30 in 10 innings. Did not win. In 1950 pitched five scoreless innings for NL in All-Star game. During major league career Jansen walked 410 men, struck out 842, hurled 17 shutouts.

JARVIS, ROBERT PATRICK (Pat)   P-BR-TR. B. 3/18/41, Carlyle, Ill.

5'10", 180. Life is never dull for Pat Jarvis. Used to ride bucking broncos in rodeos and once was kicked in face by bull. Had to have corrective surgery. During time of players strike in spring of 1972, got out of bed at 6 A.M., drove car through Doraville, Ga., suburb of Atlanta, with horn blaring, warning residents to evacuate area. Gas fire had followed explosion, and homes were in danger. Pat's act undoubtedly saved many injuries, perhaps lives. When not pitching, Ja. ends great deal of time at two rehabilitation centers for boys. One is for boys on parole; other is for those on probation. Jarvis and directors of centers offer counseling to boys, guide them, help them find jobs. Recreational facilities are included in centers.

Pat's 11 victories for Atlanta Braves in 1972 brought major league career record to total of 83 wins. Eight 1972 victories were in relief. Also saved two other games. Lost seven decisions, so entered 1973 with 72 defeats. Pitched in 221 big league games, 1244 innings, striking out 736, walking 364. His 4.09 ERA in 1972 did not lower lifetime effectiveness mark, which had been 3.55. But perhaps fact Braves shortened fences had something to do with it. Traded to Montreal Expos just before spring training 1973.

Jarvis was track and baseball star at Murray State College, Kentucky. Signed with Detroit Tigers' farm system, 1960. Pitched for Morristown in Appalachian League; Jamestown, New York–Pennsylvania League; Montgomery, Alabama-Florida League; Austin, Texas League; Atlanta and Richmond, International League. While pitching for Duluth-Superior, Northern League, 1963, teamed with Denny McLain to chalk up total of 342 strikeouts for that club. Pat had most of them—185, which led league; McLain had 157. Years later, 1972, Pat and Denny again were teammates.

Jarvis acquired by Braves 10/14/63 but didn't stick with NL team until 1966 when won his first six decisions. Had 15–10 record 1967 then 16–12, and 13–11. Broke even, 16–16 in 1970, had 6–14 mark in 1971. Most effective seasons, from earned-run standpoint, were 1966 with 2.32 and 1968 with 2.60.

JAVIER, MANUEL JULIAN (Hoolie) 2B-BR-TR. B. 8/9/36, San Francisco de Macoris, Dominican Republic. 6'1", 179. Julian Javier, who lost second-base job with St. Louis Cardinals to Ted Sizemore, complained about riding bench so much during spring of 1972. Cardinals traded him to Cincinnati Reds where had more inactivity than ever. But had consolation of playing for pennant-winning team, with $15,000 check as loser's share of WS. Short time later Reds handed him unconditional release.

Javier one of finest fielders at second base during 1960s. No power hitter; managed 14 homers one season, 12 another. In 1964 played 155 games, hit .241 but drove in 65 runs, helping Cardinals win first pennant in 18 years. Hip injury at end of regular season prevented him from playing more than one game in WS that fall. But in 1967, when Cards won again, Julian hit .281 for year, drove in 64 markers, had 14 homers. And in WS hit healthy .360. Hit three-run homer off Jim Lonborg and made two of finest defensive plays of Series. No slouch in 1968 WS either: hit .333 with three RBI. But in Cincinnati WS, 1972, went hitless in two official trips. Overall WS average was .333, with 18 hits in 54 trips.

Julian started pro ball at Brunswick, Ga., 1956; played at Jamestown, N.Y.; Douglas, Ariz.; Lincoln, Nebr.; and Columbus Ohio, while gaining minor league experience. Joined Cardinals during 1960 season. Played in at least 110 games 10 of 12 years with St. Louis. Leg ailment kept him down to 113 games, 1961, otherwise would have been member of NL All-Star squad. Broken finger kept him out of much of 1965 season. Presence of Ted Sizemore meant was used only in 90 games, 1971. Member of NL All-Star squad, 1963, 68. When Reds gave him release, Javier had appeared in 1622 NL games; his 1469 hits included 216 doubles, 55 triples, 78 homers. Scored 722 runs, drove in 506, stole 135 bases. Lifetime major league average .257.

JENKINS, FERGUSON ARTHUR P-BR-TR. B. 12/13/43, Chatham, Ontario. 6'5", 205. Ferguson Jenkins, whose 20-victory season in 1972 was sixth consecutive year he reached this number, didn't want to be starting pitcher when joined Chicago Cubs. Fergie had been relief man for Philadelphia NL. Shift from fireman's job to starter has paid off artistically and financially. Won coveted Cy Young Award, 1971; then signed two-year contract for salary estimated at $125,000, taking him through 1973 season.

Fergie frankly says that Joe Becker, former Cub pitching coach now retired, was vital factor in transformation. "He told me was going to help me make million dollars. Listed four things I had to do: (1) work hard, (2) concentrate, (3) make batter hit my pitch, and (4) be ready to go out and pitch every fourth day." Becker got Jenkins to reduce big windup. Got him to study movies of own pitching, enabling him to correct mistakes. Result has been highly successful for both Jenkins and team. As Fergie went into 1973 campaign, owned 135 NL victories against 93 defeats. Despite fact pitches home games in relatively small Wrigley Field, had 3.03 ERA for 2031 innings pitched in majors. Worked in 304 games, struck out 1650 men, and walked amazingly low total of 432 batters. Rarely needs help of relief man. Usually pitches complete games. A factor, besides mound skill, is power at plate—for this reason isn't pulled out for pinch hitter as often as other pitchers when club is trailing. At end of 1972 season Fergie had 13 home runs to credit. Six of them came in banner 1971 season.

Fergie one of limited number of Canadians in majors. In earlier days, standout hockey and basketball player. Turned down several offers from pro hockey teams to follow baseball as career. Started with Miami, Florida State League, 1962, winning seven of nine decisions. Later played with Buffalo, Chattanooga, and Arkansas clubs before joining Phillies, 1965. Two wins, one loss in first part-season in NL. Following spring Cubs got him in trade 4/21/66; that year had six wins, eight losses. Then began skein of 20-victory seasons: 20–13, 20–15, 21–15, 22–16. In 1971, when he captured Cy Young Award, reached 24 wins against 13 losses; led league in innings pitched, with 325.

With bit of luck Jenkins might have had better won-lost record. In 1968 tied major league record for being starting pitcher in five 1–0 losses; also was starting pitcher in nine games when Cubs were shut out.

Fergie led NL in complete games in 1967 with 20; in 1970 with 24; in 1971 with 30. Member of NL's All-Star squads, 1967,71,72.

JENNINGS, HUGH AMBROSE (Ee-Yah) SS-BR-TR. B. 4/2/70, Pittston, Pa. D. 2/1/28, Scranton, Pa. 5′8½″, 165. Member of fabled Baltimore Orioles of 1890s when was teammate of John McGraw, Willie Keeler et al; lawyer; coach for New York Giants; manager of Detroit Tigers when Ty Cobb was in prime. Hall of Fame 1945.

Colorful Jennings got nickname from sound effects he originated while coaching on sidelines. Started out "That's the way," then abbreviated to "way-uh," and eventually to "ee-yah." Hughie would jump up, give his yell repeatedly in effort to stir up team and fans in stands to get rally started.

Ty Cobb had come to Detroit Tigers in 1905. Within short time had plenty of enemies, not only on opposing clubs but on own team. So when

Jennings became manager of Tigers, tried unsuccessfully to trade Tyrus. When no trade materialized, Jennings made best of things, gave Cobb plenty of leeway. And Tigers, who had finished sixth in 1906, won AL pennant in 1907. Then led them to pennants again in 1908 and 1909. Jennings freely confessed later that like many others, he thoroughly hated Cobb. But, he admitted, "There is nothing I can teach Cobb. He can be greatest player of all time if allowed to go own way." Ty went own way, won flock of batting and base-stealing championships.

Jennings' approach to managing was summed up in resolution never to rebuke player in anger. Instead, preferred to wait until cooler atmosphere prevailed, and then talk quietly with player about mistakes that occurred. Reportedly Jennings never fined any player while manager of Tigers. "If you have to fine player it's time to get rid of him," reasoned Hughie. This approach diametrically opposed to that used by friend John McGraw. Despite differing philosophies, Jennings and McGraw, teammates with old "Choke-em Charlie" Orioles, remained close friends until death separated them.

Jennings started at Allentown, Pa., 1890, advanced to Louisville, American Association, 1891 and to Louisville's NL club, 1892. Before long had brilliant reputation as shortstop and good hitter, though not for distance. Joined Baltimore Orioles, NL, in 1893. They won pennant 1894, 95, 96. In 1899 moved to Brooklyn, NL, played with flag winner that year and next. Captain, Philadelphia NL, 1901–02. Briefly with Brooklyn, 1903; then to Baltimore, then in Eastern League, as playing manager. Continued in this role until moved to Detroit as manager, 1907. Hugh played total of seven games while with Detroit, but could not be considered playing manager.

Ban Johnson, president of AL, was hostile to Jennings' entry into AL because of hatred of old Baltimore Orioles. But Hughie managed Tigers to three pennant winners, two second-place finishes; had 10 first-division teams out of 14 he bossed.

Jennings' Tigers did not win any of three WS, falling prey to Chicago Cubs twice and Pittsburgh Pirates once. After seventh-place finish in 1920, Tigers, apparently impressed by fact Tris Speaker, as playing manager, had led Cleveland to pennant and WS, appointed Ty Cobb as playing pilot at Detroit. Hughie then moved to N.Y. Giants with old friend John McGraw, as coach and assistant manager, 1921–25. Bad health caught him after that, spinal meningitis bringing death early in 1928.

Jennings played 1264 major league games, hit .314. Slammed only 19 homers among 1520 hits, but scored 989 runs and had 227 doubles, 88 triples. Stole 373 bases, thrice getting as many as 60 in single season. Helped lifetime average by hitting .386 in 1895, .398 in 1896, and .353 in 1897. Led NL shortstops in fielding three times during Baltimore days.

JETHROE, SAMUEL (Jet) OF-BLR-TR. B. 1/20/22, East St. Louis, Ill. 6'1, 178. First black to wear Boston uniform in majors, 1950. NL Rookie of Year same season: led NL in stolen bases with 35; hit .273 in 141 games. Started slowly that year, then dazzled fans with hitting, fielding, base running. Injured leg stealing his third base during one game against N.Y. Giants. Came back in 1951 with .280 average and again led NL in steals with 35. Tapered off following year, with .232, but still had 28 steals.

Jethroe had good power also—18 homers in each of first two seasons, and 13 in last one with Braves. After 1952 dropped out of majors. Came back briefly—was in two games with Pittsburgh Pirates, 1954, before final exit. Played 442 major league games, got 460 hits, including 80 doubles, 25 triples, 49 homers. Scored 280 runs, drove in 181, and stole 98 bases. Lifetime average .261.

Before joining Braves, Jethroe had two seasons at Montreal, International League, then Brooklyn Dodger farm. Hit well over .300 both years there, and in 1949 pilfered 89 bases.

"Rookie of Year" designation started 1947 with Jackie Robinson. In 1949 was Don Newcombe. So when Jethroe won it in 1950, marked third time in four years black player won honor. And Willie Mays, Joe Black, and Junior Gilliam won this honor in succeeding years.

JOHN, THOMAS EDWARD P-BR-TL. B. 5/22/43, Terre Haute, Ind. 6'3", 185. Tommy John faced 1973 something of question mark after off-season operation on throwing arm for removal of bone chips. Had just finished first season in NL after seven years with Chicago White Sox and parts of two others with Cleveland Indians. Dodger southpaw by this time had won 95 games, lost 96 in majors. Pitched in 297 contests, total of 1793 innings, with 541 walks charged against him; struck out 1079.

Tommy's 2.89 ERA for 1972 was slightly better than 3.00 ERA he had prior to 1972. In first year with Los Angeles John won 11, lost five. Could easily have compiled better record with bit of luck. In his five defeats allowed only 11 earned runs. And several times pitched extremely well, only to leave game before decision was reached; Dodgers simply didn't get many runs for him. John came to Dodgers in deal for Dick Allen 12/2/71.

Tommy attended Indiana State College after starring in high school basketball. He received 35 offers of college basketball scholarships but only one baseball scholarship, and that from U. of Illinois.

Started pro ball, 1961, at Dubuque, Midwest League. Pitched for Charleston, Eastern League; Jacksonville, International League; and Portland, Pacific Coast League, into 1964, with part-season stints with Cleveland, 1963–64. Joined White Sox 1/20/65 and won 14, lost seven in first full season in majors. Had 10–5 season, 1968, but other years with

483

Chicago team were not outstanding. 1968 season cut short after battle with Dick McAuliffe of Detroit Tigers, suffering severe shoulder injury; on disabled list from 8/22/68 until end of season. Notched 1.98 ERA that year.

Tommy's strong pitch is sinker ball; used fork ball in youth, but told to forget it. Is excellent golfer.

JOHNSON, ALEXANDER OF-BR-TR. B. 12/7/42, Helena, Ark. 6', 205. Cleveland Indians obtained Alex Johnson from California Angels after 1971 season. While no repetition of bizarre occurrences that took place in Anaheim, Indians hardly got their money's worth. Alex drew $55,000 salary, same as had received from Angels, but former batting leader of AL hit just .239 in 108 games in 1972. Cleveland traded Johnson to Texas Rangers, March 1973.

When Johnson won bat title in 1970 was fined several times. During spring of 1971 Alex stood in shadow of light tower during exhibition game, played in lackadaisical manner, and was benched. Failed to run out grounders. After season started, played brilliantly at times but other occasions jogged instead of running at full speed. Fined 29 times and total of $3750 taken away in penalties. Finally was suspended. Another aspect of case involved gun taken to clubhouse by teammate Chico Ruiz. Johnson said that Ruiz threatened him. Ruiz reportedly told Alex that while "white guys" on Angels disliked him, "I'm as black as you are, and I hate you! I hate you so much I could kill you!"

Eventually Johnson contacted Players Association; after considerable testimony from various sources, including psychiatrists, arbitration panel ruled that Angels had to give Johnson $29,970 in salary held up because of his suspension; fines were not remitted; and psychiatrists hired by both sides agreed that Johnson "was and is unable to perform because of a mental condition." Panel said Alex should have been placed on disabled list rather than being suspended.

Johnson traded to Indians 10/5/71; next day manager Lefty Phillips of Angels was fired; two weeks later general manager Dick Walsh fired, although still had four years to go on seven-year contract.

Alex started first season in pro ball, 1962, at Miami and led Florida State League in hitting with .313. Hit .329 in Pioneer League at Magic Valley, 1963, this time copping home-run honors with 35, and RBI leadership, with 128. Then hit .316 for Arkansas, Pacific Coast League, in 90 games, and had .303 average for Philadelphia NL in 43 contests same season. Put in full season with Phils, 1965; hit .294. Traded to St. Louis NL 10/27/65. In 25 games with Cards, 1966, hit just .186, but had .355 average when farmed out to Tulsa for 80 games that same year. After .223 average with Cardinals, 1967, again traded, this time to Cincinnati. In two seasons there, playing most of Reds' games, hit .312

and .315. Then another trade, this one to California Angels 11/25/69.

Johnson has not been home-run specialist. Hit 17 one year with Cincinnati; had 14 with Angels in year he won batting championship. Drove in 88 runs last year with Reds and 86 first season with California.

Alex made 1970 All-Star squad and went hitless in one trip as pinch hitter for AL.

Going into 1973 season: 863 major league games behind him; 868 hits, good for 119 doubles, 24 triples, 58 homers; scored 372 times, drove in 354, and had lifetime average of .292.

JOHNSON, BYRON BANCROFT (Ban)   Executive. B. 1/8/64, Norwalk, Ohio D. 3/28/31, St. Louis, Mo. First president of AL. Dominating personality in baseball during first quarter of 20th century. Vital force in changing game from rowdy pastime into recreation appealing to whole family. Sturdy catcher at Marietta College in youth. Sports writer in Cincinnati, where became close friend of Charlie Comiskey, then manager of Reds. When Comiskey dismissed, 1894, Johnson and Commy revived Western League. Comiskey took over St. Paul club, later moved to Chicago; Ban became president of circuit. Name changed to AL, and before 1901 season declared itself major league. NL did not recognize upstart and AL clubs raided older organization for many of best players. Warfare ended in 1903 and interleague rivalry thereafter conducted under rules both circuits negotiated. Johnson insisted on respect for umpires, end to use of profanity on field; banned sale of liquor in parks; demanded upgrading of all aspects of game. Meanwhile, AL became firmly established, with players like Ty Cobb, Tris Speaker, Walter Johnson, Joe Jackson, Babe Ruth, George Sisler, and many others sparkling in junior circuit. While Johnson presided over AL, it won 14 WS, lost 10, and many observers believed it stronger organization than NL.

Ban with NL president and Garry Herrmann, president of Cincinnati Reds, formed National Commission that ruled major league baseball until after "Black Sox" scandal. Johnson usually dominated decisions of commission, even though there were two NL members. Example of ability to push commission to his viewpoint was Sisler case: Pittsburgh Pirates claimed George Sisler belonged to them; Johnson's presentation in complicated case resulted in Sisler going to St. Louis Browns.

Johnson's downfall as dominating figure in baseball started when he doggedly conducted investigations of skullduggery connected with 1919 WS. Comiskey's White Sox lost that classic to Cincinnati Reds. Rift started when Commy found it difficult to believe many of his players had sold out to gamblers. Johnson insisted on full exposure, which came late in 1920 season. Whole mess not only ended lifelong friendship of Comiskey and Johnson, but led to election of Judge Landis as czar of all baseball, which Ban opposed. Landis demanded and got dictatorial powers. Then, after 1926 season, when Cobb-Speaker case developed (see sketch on Hubert "Dutch" Leonard), breach between Johnson and Landis widened. Sometime later, AL executives, fearing Landis' wrath, stripped Johnson of remaining powers. His bad health complicated matters and, disillusioned by all that had happened, resigned 10/17/27. Hall of Fame 1937.

JOHNSON, DAVID ALLEN 2B-BR-TR. B. 1/30/43, Orlando, Fla. 6'1", 185. Dave Johnson had three brilliant seasons with Baltimore Orioles, 1969–71, helping them to AL pennants each of those years, but in 1972 his hitting fell off. Orioles felt Bobby Grich was ready to take over position full time, so Johnson was traded to Atlanta Braves. Still considered just about best second baseman in majors in making double play; in 1972 led AL keystoners in fielding among those appearing in at least 100 games.

Johnson went into NL at start of 1973 with .259 major league average for 995 games. His 904 hits included 66 homers, 16 triples, 186 doubles; had scored 382 times, driven in 391 runs. During his three banner years Dave hit .280, .281 and .282, then dropped to .221 in final season at Baltimore. Overall WS average was .192 for 21 games, but in 1970 classic it was .313 against Cincinnati Reds, including two homers.

Dave spent two years at Texas A. and M. before signing with Oriole organization, 1962. Also attended Trinity U. in Texas and Johns Hopkins U. in Maryland. Holds college degree in math and is licensed pilot. Got minor league experience at Stockton in California League; Elmira in Eastern; and at Rochester, International league. Led AL second basemen in double-plays, 1971, with 103. Cited by *Sporting News* and other organizations for brilliant fielding abilities. Member of AL All-Star squads, 1968, 69, 70; NL 1973.

JOHNSON, DERON ROGER Inf.-OF-BR-TR. B. 7/17/38, San Diego, Calif. 6'2", 209. If Deron Johnson is sound, still has potential for several good years in majors. Hard to forget his two tremendous seasons, one with Cincinnati Reds, 1965, when he led majors with 130 RBI, hitting 32 homers; and 1971 with Philadelphia NL when he slapped 34 round-trippers and drove in 95 runs for last-place club in Eastern Division.

Johnson suffered from peroneal palsy in left leg during most of 1972 season; played 96 games, hit .213, with nine homers, 31 RBI. Suffered broken hand bones in 1963, again in 1968. Carried .251 lifetime average for 1346 major league games into 1973, with 201 doubles, 27 triples, 193 homers among 1127 hits. Scored 541 runs, drove in 719. Stole nine bases. Oakland A's acquired him 5/2/73 in trade with Phils.

Johnson spectacular high school athlete in baseball, football, basketball. Five teammates made it in pro football. Deron got offers from colleges in all parts of country but spurned them to sign with New York Yankee organization. Bill DeWitt, then assistant general manager there, was instrumental in his signing. Deron went to Kearny, Nebr., 1956, later played with Binghamton and Richmond. With Yanks briefly, 1960–61, then traded to Kansas City AL 6/14/61. In 96 games that year hit .209. Military service in 1962 after 17 games. Spent 1963 with San Diego, Pacific Coast League. Had .277 average, led league in homers with 33. Bill DeWitt by then was president of Cincinnati Reds; bought Johnson, who had .273 average with 21 homers, 79 RBI, 1964; then had .287 average in his fine 1965 season. Average dropped to .257, with 24 homers, 81 RBI, 1966. Hit .224 following year, then traded to Atlanta. After one mediocre season there went to Phillies for cash 12/3/68. Seventeen homers for Phils, 1969, then 27 in 1970 and 34, 1971.

Johnson is president of construction firm in San Diego and beef-cattle breeder on 40-acre ranch.

JOHNSON, ROBERT DALE   P-BL-TR. B. 4/25/43, Aurora, Ill. 6'4", 220. Bob Johnson loved motorcycles until one almost cost him his leg and baseball career. That was in 1967 while pitching for Williamsport in Eastern League. Skidded on three feet of gravel: left leg mangled, ankle broken. Two doctors recommended amputation, but another doctor saved it. Ten weeks later was in uniform again. But while still in hospital swore off motorcycles until playing career was over.

Johnson originally signed by New York Mets' organization. Started at Auburn, New York-Pennsylvania League, 1964; later played for Williamsport, Jacksonville, Tidewater, and Memphis en route to Mets, with 1968 interruption for military service. Got into two games with Mets, 1969, then traded to Kansas City AL for 1970. Won eight, lost 13 for 10th-place team but struck out 206 batters in 214 innings; had 3.07 ERA and walked 82 with his live fast ball and sharp curve. Pittsburgh got him 12/2/70 in deal that involved Fred Patek. Inconsistent during 1971 season, but pitched brilliantly in duel with Juan Marichal of San Francisco Giants in playoffs. Won third game of that set by 2–1 score, although Nelson Briles had been scheduled to pitch. Johnson sent in as 11th-hour replacement and did nobly. Wasn't able to do so well in WS. Started second game against Baltimore Orioles and driven to cover in fourth inning, charged with four runs; Pirates lost 11–3. Bob's ERA for WS was 9.00 for five innings he worked; was responsible for one defeat.

In 1972 Johnson's work somewhat disappointing. Managed to complete only one game, won four, lost four, and had 2.95 ERA. However, saved three games in relief. His effectiveness ratio also was best of his career. Going into 1973, had pitched in 104 games, total of 507 innings; won 21, lost 27; struck out 387 while walking 184. Owned 18 complete games.

Johnson credits Whitey Herzog, then with Mets organization, for encouraging him to stay in game. In 1969 was ready to quit, figuring should have been in majors by then. Whitey told him to keep trying—and he did.

JOHNSON, ROBERT LEE (Cherokee) OF-BR-TR. B. 11/26/06, Pryor, Okla, 6', 180. Bob Johnson, Cherokee Indian, brother of Roy Johnson, another major leaguer of 1930s, was born in Oklahoma but grew up in Pacific Northwest. Played 1863 games in AL, rapped 288 homers, just missed .300 lifetime average by four points. Brother Roy also hit .296 for his overall major league average. Bob played most of his career for Connie Mack and Philadelphia Athletics. Started out in Western League with Wichita and Pueblo, 1929; joined Portland, PCL, same year. Three full seasons with Portland—solid hitter with power. Athletics 1933, after Mule Haas and Al Simmons traded. Johnson soon a regular. In 142 games hit .290, lofted 21 homers. Following year, 34 round-trippers, .307 average. In 10 seasons with Philadelphia: 30 or more homers three times, 20 or more nine times. Best season for average was 1939: .338. Spent 1943 with Washington Senators, next two years with Boston Red Sox. Seventeen homers with Sox in 1944, .324 average; .280 with 12 homers in 1945. Retired. Besides 288 career homers, Bob had 1283 RBI, scored 1239, had 396 doubles, 95 triples.

Johnson, 6/12/38, drove in eight runs against St. Louis Browns, all his team scored. Athletics won 8–3. This is AL record for most RBI for man responsible for all his club's markers.

JOHNSON, ROY CLEVELAND OF-BL-TR. B. 2/23/04, Pryor, Okla. 5'9", 175. Bet you never knew Cherokee Indian managed Chicago Cubs—for one day, in 1944. Jimmie Wilson, veteran catcher, started season as manager. Team won opening game when Hank Wyse blanked Cincinnati Reds and Bucky Walters, 3–0. Then disaster: 10 consecutive defeats. Wilson tendered resignation. Roy Johnson, coach, took charge for one day—Cubs lost. Next day, 5/17/44, Charlie Grimm took over. Cubs lost two more, for 13 straight defeats, before slide stopped. Johnson, however, coached in majors for 15 years, 1935–39 and again 1944–53, all with Cubs. As player, Roy spent most of his career in AL. San Francisco, PCL, 1926–28, except for 112 games at Idaho Falls, Utah-Idaho League. Hit .360 average in his final season in PCL, with 22 homers, 142 runs, 29 stolen bases. Detroit Tigers bought contract for cash and players. In first year with Bengals Johnson hit .314 in 148 games, had 10 homers, 67 RBI, 20 stolen bases. Traded to Boston AL 6/12/32, with Dale Alexander, for Earl Webb. To New York AL after 1935 season. Divided 1937 between Yankees and Boston Braves. Eight games with Braves, 1938; retired as major league player.

Wound up with .296 lifetime average for 1153 games in big leagues; 58 homers, 83 triples, 275 doubles among 1292 hits; scored 717 runs, drove in 556, stole 135 bases. Best record for single season steals was 1931 when he pilfered 33 for Tigers.

Got into two games in 1936 WS while with Yankees as pinch runner and pinch hitter. In one time at bat was struck out by Hal Schumacher of New York Giants.

JOHNSON, WALTER PERRY (Barney) P-BR-TR. B. 11/6/87, Humboldt, Kans. D. 12/10/46, Washington, D.C. 6'1", 200. Comparisons, when they involve players from different eras, must remain inconclusive. But in spite of testimony about Bob Feller, Sandy Koufax, Lefty Grove, and other fireballers, it is probable Walter Johnson was fastest pitcher who ever lived. Grantland Rice, famed sports writer, once wrote of dilemma of hitters facing Johnson: "How do they know what Johnson's got? Nobody's seen it yet!" And Ring Lardner summed it up in story about rookie who insisted, "He's got a gun concealed about his person. They can't tell me he throws them balls with his arm." In early days of century, when railroad trains represented pinnacle of speed, they called Walter "Big Train." But his fast ball traveled faster than speediest railroad trains of time. Bob Feller's fireball once was timed at 98.6 miles per hour. Johnson was modest, never boastful, scrupulously honest; in 1941, Washington sports writer Shirley Povich pushed him into answering whether he or Feller could pitch faster. Johnson admitted that in his prime he threw faster than Feller.

Much of Johnson's career spent with ball club that floundered in second division. If had been with team that could have given runs to work with, perhaps he, and not Cy Young, would have record for most major league victories. As it was, Walter won 416 games, lost 279. Young won 511. Johnson won 38 games during career when Senators gave just one run to work with. And lost 26 other games when he allowed opposition just one run, and Senators were not able to score at all. Pitched 113 shutouts. And, during career, lost total of 65 games when Washington shut out.

Record books full of Johnson's achievements. Some are: twelve times won 20 games or more during one season. Won 36 ball games, lost seven in 1913. Won 32, lost 12 in 1912. Due in large measure to Johnson's efforts, Washington finished in second place both seasons. He fanned 3508 hitters during career, far more than Cy Young; and well ahead of Bob Gibson, second in majors. Pitched most games in AL history, 802; more complete games in modern times than any other major leaguer, 531. In 5924 innings allowed 1902 runs. Difficult to say with certainty how many of these runs were earned, since such records were not kept during first several years he was in AL. But diligent research seems to indicate had an overall career ERA of 2.17. Led AL at least four times in ERA. In that 36-victory season, 1913, it was 1.14. In 1918 it was 1.27, and following year 1.49. In Senators' first pennant-winning season, 1924, Walter again led circuit in effectiveness with 2.72. Twelve times Johnson led AL pitchers in strikeouts; maximum in one season was 313 in 1910. Tied AL mark for consecutive victories with 16 straight wins in 1912. Made an enviable mark in 1908: facing New York AL team, Johnson pitched three games in four days—and shut Highlanders out in all three!

Oddly, Johnson, who did not drink or smoke, landed with Washington club through efforts of traveling liquor salesman. Salesman repeatedly wrote Joe Cantillon, then manager of Senators, about young pitcher he had seen in Weiser, Idaho. Cantillon sent injured catcher Cliff Blankenship to bushes to sign an outfielder named Clyde Milan. Blankenship got Milan all right, but also saw Johnson lose 12-inning game 1–0 through errors, and corraled him for Senators, for $350 month salary. Walter won five games, lost nine in 1907, broke even in 1908 with 14–14, and won 13, lost 25 for 1909 Senators who finished in cellar. For next seven years Walter never won less than 25 games, then had to be content with two seasons in which he won 23 games each. Seemed to taper off in 1920, with eight victories against 10 defeats, then came back with six consecutive seasons in which always won at least 15 games. In this latter period also had two 20-game seasons—1924 and 1925.

Johnson's 23–7 mark in 1924, for winning percentage of .767, was best in AL and helped Bucky Harris win first Washington pennant in AL. In WS that fall, veteran fireballer lost opening game in 12 innings by 4–3 score; also fifth game, 6–2, though three of N.Y. Giants' runs were unearned. But Walter came through in crucial seventh engagement. Pitched shutout ball in final four rounds of 12-inning struggle and emerged victorious when Earl McNeely singled home winning run to give Senators world championship. Following fall fates reversed things. Johnson defeated Pittsburgh in his first two starts, allowing just one run in opener and shutting Pirates out in fourth game. But when Series went down to wire, Johnson lost crucial seventh game by 9–7 score. So his WS records showed three wins, three losses, with ERA of 2.16. Had 35 strikeouts, walked 15. In 50 innings allowed 56 hits and just 12 earned runs. With all his great speed, Johnson had good control. Walked 1353 during career, compared to those 3508 strikeouts. Lived in fear one of pitches might injure opposing batsman. Fortunately this did not occur.

Stories about Johnson's exploits are endless. Once was pitching against Detroit; Tigers filled bases on two errors and walk. Johnson proceeded to strike out three great lefthanded hitters—Ty Cobb, Sam Crawford, and Bobby Veach—on nine pitches.

Once Johnson struck out four men in one inning, one of batsmen reaching first when third strike got away from catcher. Pitched opening game of 1910 season when President William Howard Taft was in attendance. This was first of "presidential openers" that became tradition while Washington had AL ball club. Walter won that game, allowing Philadelphia Athletics only one wind-blown two-bagger, taking game by 3–0 score. Johnson pitched 14 opening-day games in all—and usually won them. Each time added baseball autographed by President to his collection.

His only no-hitter came 7/1/20, but had numerous one-hitters. Once pitched 56 scoreless innings, 1913, which is AL record. Against Yankees, 5/11/19, pitched 0–0 tie game in which allowed just two hits. Johnson received MVP (Chalmers) Award for 1913, and AL league award for MVP in 1924. Hall of Fame 1936.

While Johnson was fabulous pitcher, did not find niche as manager. Piloted Washington Senators 1929–32 after one season (1928) as boss of Newark club in International League. Johnson's Senators were fifth-placer in 1929; then second-, third-, and third-placers. Cleveland Indians took him on in 1933 in June. Club finished fourth; third in 1934, and was replaced in August 1935 with Indians on way to third place. Thus managerial record not bad, but it was felt someone else might have gotten more out of material he had to work with.

Johnson's only minor league appearance took place in season at Newark. Pitched in one game, walked hitter, then retired. After managerial experiences, Walter had one season as play-by-play radio announcer in Washington; raised pure-bred cattle on farm near nation's capital; made unsuccessful race for election to U.S. Congress from Maryland; died of brain tumor at age 59.

JOLLEY, SMEAD POWELL OF-BL-TR. B. 1/14/02, Wesson, Ark. 6'3½", 210. Smead Jolley allegedly was an outfielder but there was no doubt that he was hitter. Didn't last too long as major leaguer, 473 games, but they still talk about his attempts at fielding, and how he convinced baseball men he wasn't catcher either.

While playing with Boston Red Sox, Smead, in left field, had considerable trouble trying to catch fly balls near fence, where there was an incline. Seemed to trip and fall climbing "hill." Finally, they got him out mornings and hit fungoes to him enough so he actually improved.

One day Joe Cronin, then with Washington Senators, hit long fly to left during game. Looked like it could be caught if Jolley could run up hill. Smead climbed incline all right, turned around at fence, and discovered had overrun ball. Started down incline, but fell on face and ball hit him on head. On bench, rubbing head, Jolley berated his teammates. "Fine bunch, you guys. For ten days you teach me how to go up hill, but none of you have brains enough to teach me how to come down!"

Jolley hit .305 for his big league career; would have had much longer major league sojourn but for his fielding. He demonstrated plenty of hitting in Pacific Coast League. Started at Shreveport, Texas League, 1922; also played for Greenville, Miss.; Texarkana and Corsicana, before joining San Francisco, PCL, 1925. In 38 games that year hit hot .447. Then had .346 and .397 seasons playing regularly, and batted .404 in 1928, 191 games. When he came back with .387 for 200 games in 1929, Chicago White Sox decided perhaps powerful hitting might offset punk fielding. Smead hit all right—.313 in 152 games for White Sox, 1930. Used in 54 games, 1931, hit .300; then Lew Fonseca, pilot of Sox, tried to convert him into catcher. Appeared in five AL games behind plate, but that was all. White Sox traded him to Boston 4/29/32. Played 149 games that season, hit .312 with 18 homers, 106 RBI. Following season took part in 118 games, hit .282, and dropped out of majors. Back in PCL, 1934, continued hitting, this time for Hollywood, with .360 average for 171 games.

Jolley had 521 hits in majors, with 111 doubles, 21 triples, 46 homers. Scored 188 runs, drove in 313, with that .305 lifetime average.

JONES, CLEON JOSEPH OF-BR-TL. B. 8/4/42, Plateau, Ala. 6', 198. Jones grew up in Mobile where Hank Aaron, Satchel Paige, Willie McCovey, Billy Williams, Tommy Agee also blossomed. Cleon was natural left-hander, but as boy, playing stick ball, life got complicated if ball hit too far to right field. Porch on first base side—teammates didn't want to lose ball. So Jones became righthanded hitter, though they let him continue throwing lefthanded.

Cleon's finest season came in 1969, year of "Miracle Mets." That year hit .340 in 137 games, including 12 homers and 75 RBI. Didn't perform too well in WS: .158 average, three hits in 19 trips.

In high school teamed up with Tommy Agee. In football set state record of 26 touchdowns in one season; was 9.7 dash man on track squad; pitcher, first baseman, and outfielder on baseball team that lost one game in three years; accepted football scholarship at Alabama A. & M. and had 17 TD's in two seasons. Signed with Mets' organization after sophomore year. Divided 1963 with 14 games at Auburn, N.Y.-Pa. League; 49 at Raleigh, Carolina circuit; and six with Mets. Spent most of 1964-65 with Buffalo, joining Mets for 30 games, 1965. Played regularly with Mets since then. Had .297 mark with 14 homers, 55 RBI, in 1968. In 1970, handicapped by hamstring and groin-muscle pulls, hit .277 but had 10 homers, 63 RBI. Came back to .319 in 136 games, 1971, with 14 homers, 69 RBI. Then sagged to .245 in 1972, five homers, 52 RBI.

Jones, at start of 1973, had appeared in 964 games in majors; 958 hits included 145 doubles, 32 triples, 69 homers. Scored 451 runs, drove in

111, and had 87 base thefts, with an overall average of .284.

Cleon was member of 1969 NL All-Star game squad, got two hits in four trips. Led NL in grounding into double plays, 1970, with 26. Wife, Angela, is cousin of Chicago Cub star Billy Williams.

JONES, DAVID JEFFERSON (Kangaroo) OF-BL-TR. B. 6/30/80, Cambria, Wis. 5'10", 165. Lawyer, pharmacist, outfielder, first man to face Walter Johnson when great Washington pitcher made AL debut. Member of Detroit Tiger pennant winners 1907,08,09. Jumped three separate times, once to Milwaukee AL, then to Chicago NL, finally to Pittsburgh, Federal League. Played 1085 big league games, hit .270.

Davy attended Dixon College in Illinois on athletic scholarship for ability in baseball and track. Law graduate. After collegiate team played exhibition game against Rockford club of III League, signed with that team for $85 monthly, 1901; hit .384 that summer, and was sold to Chicago Cubs. AL just going for major league status then and offered Jones better salary than Cubs, so he jumped first time. Played 14 games, didn't hit much—.173—but impressed with speed and potential. Milwaukee franchise shifted to St. Louis for 1902. Davy started season with Browns, making $2400 for year. After 15 games, Chicago Cubs offered him $3600 contract with $500 cash bonus, so Jones again jumped. Hit .305 for Cubs in 64 contests, but after .282 and .244 seasons in subsequent years found himself back in minors with Minneapolis, American Association. A .346 performance there resulted in sale to Detroit for 1906, where continued through 1912. Best average with Tigers was .294 in last year there. Chicago AL 1913. Then final jump, to Pittsburgh, Federal League, 1914, bowing out after 14 games in 1915.

Jones, while still playing baseball, helped brother who had drug store. After retiring from game studied pharmacy himself, passed examinations, and stayed in drug business 35 years before retiring. At one point Jones brothers had five stores in Detroit.

When Davy took up pro baseball his romance with young lady ended. Girl's father broke it up; insisted all ball players were rowdies. Davy later married, had 52 happy years before becoming widower. Some time later met girl he had gone with originally. She was widow, so they married more than half century after first dates.

Jones did not hit for power; usually was leadoff man. His 1020 hits in majors included 98 doubles, 40 triples, nine homers. Stole 207 bases. In WS play had .265 mark for 15 games, 13 hits in 49 trips.

JONES, FIELDER ALLISON OF-BL-TR. B. 8/13/74, Shinglehouse, Pa. D. 3/13/34, Portland, Oreg. Fielder Jones was outfielder—and playing manager of Chicago White Sox "Hitless Wonders" of 1906 who, as underdogs, won world championship from highly favored Chicago

Cubs. Jones bossed Sox 1904–08; managed St. Louis Federal League team 1914–15; St. Louis Browns 1916–18.

Jones attended Alfred College, became civil engineer, but with financial recession limiting job chances, turned to pro baseball. In 1891 in Oregon State League; later played nearer home at Corning and Binghamton, N.Y., and Springfield, Mass. Went to Brooklyn NL 1896 through 1900; Chicago AL 1901–08. Fielder hit well in earlier years in majors, going above .300 six times in first seven seasons. Good base thief also, stealing 48 in 1897, 38 in 1901, and generally pilfering at least 20 each year. In 1904, hitting dropped off to .243 when he succeeded Jimmy Callahan as manager of White Sox. Team won 67, lost 47, finished third under his leadership. In 1905 club was second, three games behind Philadelphia Athletics. Then came year of "Hitless Wonders." Sox hit .228 as team, lowest average of any club in AL. Jones led Sox in homers that year—with *two*. Cubs were heavy favorites to smash Sox in WS. But Jones had pitching and fielding. Big Ed Walsh won two games, Nick Altrock and Doc White one each. When it was all over, White Sox had world championship four games to two. Sox finished third both 1907 and 1908, after which Jones stayed in Northwest in lumber business, since owner Comiskey did not raise salary enough to make it financially interesting. But though Jones made plenty in lumber, call of diamond got him few years later. Joined St. Louis Feds late in 1914 as manager, and club finished last. Following year led team into second place. When Federal League folded, Jones took over management of St. Louis AL. Team finished fifth, then seventh; was breaking even in 1918 when he quit. Turned in resignation when Browns blew 5–1 lead in ninth inning, losing to Washington Senators 6–5.

Jones played 1780 major league games and had lifetime average of .287.

JONES, JAMES DALTON   Inf.-BL-TR. B. 12/10/43, McComb, Miss. 6'2", 185. Dalton Jones got about $60,000 of Tom Yawkey's money in 1961 as bonus when he signed with Boston Red Sox. Had been stellar baseball and basketball star in prep school and attended LSU. At 17 turned pro, was tabbed in "can't miss" category. Never quite lived up to expectations. Best hitting mark was .289 in 89 games in 1967 with Sox. However, in WS that fall he was Boston's second-best hitter, with .389 average—7 for 18.

Jones played at Alpine, Tex., York, Pa., and Seattle in minors before graduating to Fenway Park, 1964. Remained with Red Sox until 12/13/69 when he was traded to Detroit for Tom Matchick. Tigers kept him until early 1972 when he was sent to Texas Rangers. Hit .152 in 79 games and couldn't win spot on Rangers' 1973 roster. Had lifetime major league average of .235 for 907 games over nine-year period. Among his

548 hits were 41 homers, 91 doubles, 19 triples. Scored 268 runs, drove in 237.

Dalton never played more than 118 games in any single season in majors. Did well at times in pinch-hitting roles. In 1970 had .379 mark as emergency batsman. During 1967 WS against Cardinals, tied record for most double plays started by third baseman, two, 10/4/67.

JONES, SAMUEL (Toothpick) P-BR-TR. B. 12/14/25, Stewartsville, Ohio. D. 11/5/71, Morgantown, W. Va. 6'4", 205. Also called Sad Sam (there was another Sam Jones who pitched in AL from 1914 through 1935 with that nickname). But this Sam Jones really had mournful appearance. Had plenty of reason to be sad—knew real poverty as youth, and died of cancer at age 45 after long illness. Got nickname "Toothpick" because liked to pitch—or cogitate—with toothpick in mouth.

Sam pitched one full-length no-hitter for Chicago Cubs 5/12/55, with Pittsburgh as victim. Held Cardinals hitless 9/26/59, pitching for San Francisco Giants, but game called account of rain after two men out in eighth inning.

Sam started pitching in Negro leagues and said to have learned to pitch curve from Satchel Paige. Spent 1950 with Wilkes-Barre; 1951 with San Diego; then in Pacific Coast League. Cleveland, 1951–52; Indianapolis, 1952–54. Two seasons with Chicago Cubs, 1955–56. Won 14 but lost 20 his first season in NL; also led circuit in strikeouts with 198 and in walks with 185. Following season, with 9–14 record, again topped NL in whiffs with 176 and walks with 115. With St. Louis 1957–58, chalking up 12–9 and 14–13 records. In latter season once more led NL in strikeouts (225) and in walks (107). San Francisco NL 1959–61. Enjoyed best year in 1958, with 21 victories, 15 defeats, with 2.82 ERA. This was lowest earned run average in NL. However, once again Sam led league in giving free tickets to first base with 109. After 18–14 record, 1960, dropped down to 8–8 with Giants. Detroit AL, 1962 (2–4); St. Louis NL, 1963 (2–0), and finally Baltimore AL, 1964 (0–0). In minors, pitched and coached at Columbus, Ohio, 1967.

Jones had control problems throughout career, as total of 822 walks indicates. However, struck out 1376 men in 1643-1/3 innings. Won 102 games, lost 101 in majors, had overall ERA of 3.59, with 17 shutouts.

When Sam pitched no-hitter against Pirates, wildness almost caused removal from game before completing it. Walked first three men to face him in ninth inning. Mgr. Stan Hack was ready to take him out, but catcher Clyde McCullough persuaded him to let Jones continue since Cubs had 4–0 lead. Sam then proceeded to strike out Dick Groat, Roberto Clemente, and Frank Thomas, all dangerous hitters.

JONES, SAMUEL POND (Sad Sam) P-BR-TR. B. 7/26/92, Wood-field, Ohio. D. 7/6/66, Barnesville, Ohio. 6', 170. Sam Jones and Cy Young—two pitchers who worked 22 consecutive seasons in majors. No other twirlers have actually equaled their record. Record books say Early Wynn pitched 23 years in AL, but one of those seasons, 1945, he was in military service. Herb Pennock and Red Ruffing are listed with 22 consecutive seasons in majors, but both careers were interrupted by military service.

Sam believed he owed nickname "Sad Sam" to Bill McGeehan, New York sports writer, who referred to him as "Sad Sam, Sorrowful Sage from Woodsfield." Jones said he may have looked sorrowful because he wore cap down low over eyes. Nevertheless, name stuck.

Jones pitched for six AL clubs; helped Boston Red Sox to one pennant, N.Y. Yankees to three. Won 229 games in majors, dropping 217 decisions, with 3.84 ERA in 3884 innings. Walked 1396, fanned 1263.

Sam started at Zanesville, Inter-State League, 1913. Portsmouth, Ohio State League, 1914, then with Cleveland club of American Association same season, and finally with Cleveland Indians before year was out. In 1915 Sam won four, lost nine, then included in big trade that transferred Tris Speaker to Cleveland from Boston. Jones didn't win game for Red Sox next two years. This was no reflection on abilities—Sox were loaded with pitching talent. Won pennant, 1916, with Babe Ruth, Dutch Leonard, Carl Mays, and Ernie Shore, each of them winning at least 15, with Babe taking 23 mound victories. In 1917 Ruth won 24, Mays 22, Leonard 16, Shore 13.

Following year, when Ruth was used more in outfield and less on mound, Jones got chance and came through with 16 wins, five losses, to lead AL with .762 percentage. Had 2.25 ERA. From then on Sam recognized as established pitcher.

Twenty-three wins against 16 defeats in 1921 must have made N.Y. Yankees envious. With Red Sox in debt to Yankees, Jones, Bullet Joe Bush, and Shortstop Everett Scott were used to reduce obligation.

Sam broke even, 13–13, in first season with Yanks, 1922; came up with 21–8 record, 1923. Then dropped out of big-winner class. With Browns in St. Louis, 1927, won eight, lost 14. But came back with 17–7 at Washington, 1928. Had one more good season with Senators in 1930 with 15–7 record.

With Chicago White Sox, 1932–35, but best days behind him. Dropped out of game until 1940, then was coach for Toronto, International League, and did a little pitching; 12 innings, won one, lost one.

Sam pitched no-hit game 9/4/23 for Yankees against Philadelphia, climaxing fine 21–8 season. In 1923 WS allowed just one earned run in 10 innings but lost when Casey Stengel, then playing with N.Y. Giants, smacked fast ball into right-field seats at Yankee Stadium. Charged with that defeat and one loss in 1918 series with Red Sox, but still came through with ERA of 2.04 for 22 innings of WS competition. Did not win any in WS.

JOOST, EDWIN DAVID SS-BR-TR. B. 6/5/16, San Francisco, Calif. 6', 175. Many baseball fans remember Eddie Joost as shortstop who spent most of his career as member of Cincinnati Reds and Philadelphia Athletics. Others recall that he was third and last manager of White Elephants, as they used to be called. Connie Mack, of course, bossed team almost forever. Then came Jimmie Dykes—finally Joost, in A's last season in Philadelphia, 1954. Eddie didn't have much to work with. Ball club was broke. Before 1955 rolled around, was sold and moved to Kansas City. Athletics won 51, somehow, lost 103 and finished in basement, three games behind Baltimore Orioles who were in their first year after being transformed from hapless St. Louis Browns. As player, however, Joost was fine fielder. Wasn't much of hitter in early days. After joining Athletics, seemed to find his power, actually hit 134 major league homers in 1574 games. Overall average was .239 over 17-year span.

Joost played with Omaha, San Francisco Missions, Syracuse and Kansas City when it was in American Association. Minor league experience from 1933 to 1938, plus couple of brief spells with Cincinnati. Followed up with four full seasons with Reds, then traded to Boston Braves 12/4/42. Stayed out of baseball during 1944 season. Broken toe and broken wrist plagued him in 1945, played only 35 games for Braves that year. Dropped down to Rochester in International League for 1946, then returned to majors with Athletics for six seasons as player, one as player-manager. Eddie then put in one final year in majors as member of Boston Red Sox, 1955.

Joost's best home run record for any season was six, in 1942 with Reds, until he joined Athletics. Then he hit 109 in next six seasons—average of more than 18 each campaign. Eddie set various records at shortstop, some since excelled.

JOSS, ADRIAN (Addie) P-BR-TR. B. 4/12/80, Juneau, Wis. D. 4/14/11, Toledo, Ohio. 6'3", 185. Addie Joss one of rare pitchers who hurled perfect ball game—27 men up, 27 down. Fourth man in history of organized ball to turn trick. Working for Cleveland, defeated Ed Walsh of Chicago White Sox by 1–0 score, 10/2/08. Mowed down Sox so methodically they never came close to safe hit. In ninth inning, two out, Cleveland third baseman, Bill Bradley, fielded grounder and threw dangerously high to first base. But George Stovall, first sacker, stretched high enough to grab ball and curtains came down on White Sox. Ed Walsh pitched pretty fair game himself that day—allowed four hits, one run, and struck out 15. That was year Big Ed won 40—yes, 40—games, lost 15.

Joss threw what was described as "jump" ball. An expert observer said ball did not depend on spin; could have been called "false rise." Reported that Joss got this effect throwing overhand, aiming ball at level of batter's knees. "Ball, coming downward with great speed, packs air below it. Just when the ball begins to lose speed, the elastic air cushion, for fraction of a second, has equal power with the attraction of gravitation. The air cushion carries ball horizontally a few feet, until further loss of motion brings it to the ground." See?

Addie one of first collegians to become major leaguer. Pitched for U. of Wisconsin; then Toledo, Inter-State League, 1900. Toledo was in Western Association following year, then Joss went up to Cleveland. Remained with Forest City team 1902–10.

Joss won 17 his first year up, then 18. Four 20-victory seasons, 1905–08, winning more games than lost every year until last one when had 5–5 record. In 1907, mark was 27–11. Never got crack at WS. Major league career totals showed 160 wins, 97 losses. Career ERA 1.88. Started 261 games, finished 235 of them! Struck out 926, walked 370. Besides that perfect game, pitched another no-hitter, this one 4/20/10 against Chicago.

Joss died early, at age 31, just as 1911 season about to open. Cleveland club due to play in Detroit day of funeral but players, fearing refusal on part of management, simply stayed in Cleveland for services. Game rescheduled later. Benefit game set up for Addie's widow; total receipts, nearly $13,000, went to her.

JUDGE, JOSEPH IGNATIUS 1B-BL-TL. B. 5/25/94, Brooklyn, N.Y. D. 3/11/63, Washington, D.C. 5'8½", 160. Senator from Brooklyn went to Washington, 1915, and stayed there almost all rest of life. One of most popular ball players ever to perform in nation's capital, Joe Judge captured affections of Washington fans, captained team four years, and wound up as coach of Georgetown U. baseball squad. Though smaller than most first basemen, Joe performed in fine style; led league in fielding five times and tied for lead once. Compiled .297 batting average in 2170 major league games. No great slugger, but consistent batsman who went over .300 mark nine times as regular. His 2350 hits included 433 doubles, 159 triples, 71 homers. Top production of homers for any season was 10, which he reached in 1922 and again in 1930. Scored 1184 runs, drove in 1044, stole 213 cushions.

Judge got windfall 6/28/30 as his days as regular in Washington were approaching end. Clark Griffith staged "day" in his honor. Obtained agreement in advance from Frank Navin, owner of Detroit Tigers, to settle for 9,000 admissions that day. Anything over would go into cash tribute to Senators' aging first baseman. Washington fans turned out in unexpected numbers—well over 18,000. And Joe received check for $10,500 real money then as his share of receipts, as well as another $400 purse contributed by admiring fans in Alexandria, Va.

Joe helped Senators win flags in 1924,25, but he was released unconditionally by Senators 1/27/33 before Senators took third pennant. Caught on with Brooklyn Dodgers, but drew release in July. Spent rest of that season and part of 1934 with Boston Red Sox, then called it quits as active player.

In 1924 WS he hit .385. Judge had .286 average for 14 games in WS, 1924,25, with one homer off Vic Aldridge in second game against Pittsburgh in latter classic.

JUDNICH, WALTER FRANKLIN OF-BL-TL. B. 1/24/17, San Francisco, Calif. D. 7/12/71, Glendale, Calif. 6'1", 205. Walter Judnich was ball player "raised" in New York Yankee farm system, but got sidetracked to St. Louis Browns. Off to fine start with Browns, 1940–42, hitting above .300 twice and having .284 average in other season, playing regularly. Browns' investment was reportedly $12,000 paid to Yankee organization.

After three seasons in majors Judnich joined air force, serving three years. Back with Browns, 1946, hit .262 and .258; after which was traded to Cleveland Indians 11/20/47, in time to be with his only pennant-winning club. In 79 games hit .257, but made only one hit in 13 trips in WS for .077 average. Following year was with Pittsburgh Pirates for ten games, then went to minors, playing with San Francisco, Seattle, and Portland, all in Pacific Coast League. Retired, 1956.

On way up, Walter was with Akron, 1935; Norfolk, 1936; Oakland, PCL, 1937; Kansas City, American Association, 1938; Newark, International League, 1939. In majors, Judnich played 790 games, hit .281. Hit 24 homers his first year with Browns, and in next four seasons always had at least 14 to his credit. Overall total 90, with 420 RBI, 424 runs scored, 150 doubles, 29 triples, 782 safe hits for career. Started as first baseman, but preferred outfield. Twice led AL outfielders in fielding.

KAAT, JAMES LEE (Kitty) P-BL-TL. B. 11/7/38, Zeeland, Mich. 6'4",
207. Jim Kaat and Minnesota Twins were hoping for comeback in 1973.
Jim, who had 10–2 record when he broke left hand sliding, 7/2/72, was
enjoying one of best seasons of career when misfortune struck. His ERA
of 2.07 lowest in his entire time in baseball, back to 1957 when started
with Superior club in Nebraska State League. Besides Winning 179
games during major league career, Kaat in 1973 was working to improve
strikeout total of 1758. In 455 AL games had pitched 2831 innings,
walked 690. Losses totaled 147. Prior to 1972, best ERA mark was 1966
with 2.74 when he won 25, lost 13. Kaat also cat out there fielding his
position. For 11th consecutive season, AL managers and coaches voted
him "gold glove" award as best fielding pitcher in loop.

Kaat used to overpower opposition when was young. Started pro
career after attending Hope College in Michigan. In second season in
minors, 1958, won 16, lost nine for Missoula in Pioneer League. Led that
circuit in effectiveness with 2.99 mark. Spent 1959 at Chattanooga until
called up by Washington Senators. Charged with two losses. Also
divided 1960 season between Washington and Charleston, West Va.,
dropping five of six decisions with Senators. Washington franchise
shifted to Minnesota, 1961, and Kaat with Twins ever since. Among
better seasons there have been 1962, with 18–14; 1964, with 17–11; and
1965, with 18–11. After 25-victory season in 1966, Kaat had 16–13 mark
following year. In next three seasons won 14 each campaign, losing fewer
than he won. Dropped under .500 mark in 1971 when he lost 14, won 13.

Jim was member of AL All-Star squads in 1962–66. Pitched in one

WS, 1965. won one, lost two. Victory was against Sandy Koufax by 5–1 score. In 14-1/3 innings had 3.77 ERA.

Jim's distinctions include having been named AL "Pitcher of Year" by *Sporting News*, 1966. Led AL pitchers in hitting batsmen with 11 in 1961 and 18 in 1962; tied for league lead in wild pitches with 10 in 1961, led with 13 in 1962. In game he won from Dodgers in 1965 WS, Jim set WS record by making five putouts, most ever made by hurler in nine-inning contest during autumn classic.

Besides unfortunate broken bone in left hand in 1972, Kaat injured arm in final outing, 1967. After 1969 season, had operation to remove calcium deposit from left thigh that threatened to end pitching days. But came back afterwards.

KALINE, ALBERT WILLIAM OF-1B-BR-TR. B. 12/19/34, Baltimore, Md. 6'1", 185. Al Kaline signed first $100,000 contract 12/20/71, one day after 37th birthday. Didn't play too often during 1972 season, due to pulled muscle in left leg. But saved his heroics for end of season, when had an 11-game hitting streak and helped mightily in Detroit's first-place finish in AL East. He drove home deciding run in crucial game against Boston Red Sox, wrapping up honors. This was 22nd hit in 44 times at bat. Did his best in playoffs against Oakland. First game went into eleventh inning, tied at one all. Al's homer put Tigers ahead, but in last half Oakland scored twice to win. A's got winning run home when Kaline's fine throw to third base somehow skipped past Rodriguez. Al hit safely in first four games of playoffs, but was hitless in fifth when Oakland captured AL pennant by 2–1 score.

Kaline has been tower of power to Tigers ever since they paid $35,000 bonus to sign, 1953. Played just 30 games that summer, hit .250. But from 1954 through 1972 always played at least 100 games, and in 15 seasons played at least 130 contests every year. Never played in minors. This despite several serious injuries: broken cheek bone, 1959; broken collar bone, 1962; rib injury, 1965; foot malformation, resulting in operation, 1965; broken finger, 1967; broken right arm, 1968. Al won AL batting championship with .340 mark, 1955, second full season in majors. Youngest man ever to win it, age 20. Hit above .300 eight times, going into 1973 season. Lifetime average dropped to even .300 when hit below that mark four seasons, 1968–71, but .313 average in 1972 raised career record to .301 in 2596 games. As of start of 1973, Al had 2782 hits, scored 1511 runs; had 457 doubles, 73 triples, 376 homers, with 1474 RBI.

Kaline played in just one WS, 1968. Helped Tigers win in seven games with .379 average, including two doubles, two homers, eight RBI. In 15 All-Star games hit .382, including two homers among 13 hits. Named to 1964 and 1967 AL squads but replaced due to injury.

Al hit three homers in one game 4/17/55. Good fielder—led AL in 1966; tied for lead, 1971, when had no errors in 133 games.

KAMM, WILLIAM EDWARD   3B-BR-TR. B. 2/2/1900, San Francisco, Calif. 5'10½", 170. Willie Kamm was always on shy, retiring side. Despite this, was brilliant third baseman, consistent hitter, as .281 lifetime average would indicate. In days when $100,000 represented pretty fabulous sum, 1922, White Sox paid San Francisco that sum for his contract—and never regretted it. Willie hit .342 for San Francisco, Pacific Coast League, that season, his fourth with club. In June that year Kamm had charley horse, so bad that Seals left him at home when team went on road. Willie, with time on his hands, was wandering around downtown when he heard newsboy yelling, "Willie Kamm sold to White Sox for hundred thousand dollars! Read all about it!"

Kamm, amazed, went over to buy paper. Newsboy recognized him, started yelling to everyone in earshot, "There he is! It's Willie Kamm!" On ball field Willie accustomed to attention of crowds, but this was different. Panicked, started running as hard as he could, despite charley horse. Ran until he found refuge in movie house and its darkness. Stayed in theater until could go out on street without being recognized among crowds.

Willie made good in Chicago from start, hitting .292 in 149 games, 1923. Seals had kept him entire 1922 season as part of sale agreement. Remained with Sox until 5/17/31, when traded to Cleveland for another Californian, Lew Fonseca. Despite fact Kamm had never given White Sox any trouble and had often led AL in fielding as well as being pretty fair man at plate, club officials did not have decency to tell him personally he had been traded. Heard it first as unconfirmed rumor, then read it in newspapers; this after more than eight years with club. Charlie Comiskey, club president, tried to rectify situation next day by writing letter in which he wished Willie good luck. Also commended him for "splendid manner in which you conducted yourself off the field," as well as fine efforts while in uniform. Kamm remained with Indians into 1935, then headed back to Golden Gate. During big league career played 1692 games, made 1643 hits, with 347 doubles, 85 triples, 29 homers. Scored 802 runs and drove in 826. Swiped 126 bases. Best hitting year in majors was 1928 with .308; drove in 84 runs.

As youth Willie worked in grocery store, jewelry shop, and factory. Brief trial with Sacramento, Pacific Coast League, 1918, but was released. Joined San Francisco Seals following year and made good from start.

KARST, GENE   Executive. B. 6/25/06, St. Louis, Mo. First publicity man for any major league club. Former newspaper reporter and fan presented idea to Branch Rickey, then general manager of St. Louis Cardinals, 1931. Believed sports editors, and radio stations would welcome reliable well-prepared material if presented to them in usable form. Initiated regular releases to news media from the ball club in area from which Cardinals could draw fans—up to some 300 miles from St. Louis. Also supplied pictures to newspapers, mats to smaller publications. Arranged for hundreds of radio interviews with ball players and officials. Wrote and directed radio dramatizations of players' lives. Got bushels of free publicity, free time on air for Cardinals, whose only cash investment was Karst's modest salary. Gene started miniature newspaper with tidbits of information about Cardinals and visiting players. Published once or twice weekly during baseball season and distributed to fans in stands—often 50,000 copies handed out free.

Karst traveled through Missouri; Illinois; and parts of Indiana, Kentucky, Tennessee making personal contact with newspaper editors and sportscasters. Whipped up so much interest that Sam Breadon, not noted for squandering dough, gave Gene $50 bonus after 45,715 crowded into old Sportsman's Park to see Sunday doubleheader against Chicago Cubs. That attendance record stood as long as ball park stood—name later changed to Busch Stadium, but not until new Busch Memorial Stadium built and opened, 1966, was record broken.

After four years with Cardinals, Karst spent two years in similar post with Cincinnati Reds during which time publicized first night games in history of major leagues. Later wandered around world and had three years as traveling secretary of Montreal Royals, International League, and one season as publicity director of Hollywood Stars, Pacific Coast League.

Gene also spent 27 years with U.S. Department of State and U.S. Information Agency, with periods as press attache for American embassies in Buenos Aires, Manila, Asuncion, San Salvador; two years as deputy public affairs officer at U.S. Embassy, Rio de Janeiro. Had three years as chief of Latin American Division of Voice of America, supervising short wave broadcasts in Spanish and Portuguese.

Free-lance writer on baseball and other subjects, frequent contributor to *Sporting News,* old *Baseball Magazine, Christian Science Monitor, Baltimore Sun, Liberty,* other publications.

KASKO, EDWARD MICHAEL Inf.-BR-TR. B. 6/27/31, Linden, N.J. 6', 185. Eddie Kasko managed Boston Red Sox to third-place finishes in AL East, 1970–71, then took team into second spot, 1972, missing Eastern Division title by half game. Signed two-year contract to manage

Sox 1973 74, reportedly for $65,000 annually. Whatever he is paid, probably earns it; has to deal with highly critical sports writers, and Red Sox who seem constantly whining, complaining, or bickering. Once, when Rico Petrocelli asserted that Kasko showed favoritism, owner Tom Yawkey said, "Nothing surprises me in this business anymore. It does disappoint me though."

Kasko took up managing, 1967, after playing 1077 major league games. During career got 935 hits, scored 411 runs for .263 average. Had 146 doubles, 13 triples, 22 homers, 261 RBI. Started in 1949 with Baltimore, International League, directly from high school. Saw service at Suffolk, Va.; Schenectady, N. Y.; Richmond, Va.; and Rochester, N. Y.; landing with St. Louis Cardinals, 1957. Also put in couple of years in army as combat engineer. Two seasons with Cardinals, then with Cincinnati 1959–63; Houston NL, 1964–65; Boston AL, 1966. Best season in majors was 1960 with Reds when hit .292 in 126 contests. Played five WS games with Cincinnati, 1961; hit .318 with seven singles in 22 trips. Appeared in second All-Star game of 1961, getting one hit in one trip for National Leaguers. As manager, 1967, his Toronto club was sixth in International League; 1968, Louisville, American Association, sixth; then led club into second place, 1969, after which was promoted to Red Sox.

Sports Illustrated once characterized him as "quiet scholarly man with fondness for pistachio nuts."

KAUFF, BENJAMIN MICHAEL (Benny) OF-BL-TL. B. 1/5/90, Middleport, Ohio. D. 11/17/61, Columbus, Ohio. They called him "Ty Cobb of Federal League." Seems to have hit somewhere between .365 and .370 to lead that circuit in 1914 while playing with Indianapolis; was top batter in same league, 1915, with average in .340's playing for Brooklyn Feds. Statistics for this would-be third major league were kept haphazardly, so can't say exactly what Benny Kauff's career "major league" average was if Federal League figures are included. Probably around .310 for some 860 games.

Kauff could run fast and talk fast. Ex-coal miner became flashy dresser, sported big diamonds, liked to show off lots of folding money he carried with him. Once jumped to Federal League, later persuaded by John McGraw to jump to New York Giants. Wound up being barred from baseball for life by Judge Landis.

Benny played semipro ball around Ohio before joining Parkersburg club of Virginia Valley League, 1910. Following year was with New York AL club briefly, then Bridgeport, Connecticut League; Rochester, Eastern circuit; Brockton, New England League; and Hartford, Connecticut League. After 1913 season was sold to Indianapolis club of American Association but jumped to Indianapolis Feds.

Kauff had been with Brooklyn Feds when McGraw persuaded him to join Giants during 1915 season. NL President John K. Tener refused to allow him to play in NL at this time because negotiations were progressing between majors and Federal League; agreement had been made there would be no more raids. When Giants tried to play him in their lineup, game was delayed an hour until Kauff was removed. McGraw later paid Brooklyn Feds $35,000 for him and he played with Giants 1916–20.

Kauff had two or three pretty fair seasons with Giants but never threatened Ty Cobb's laurels. Had .264 average, 1916, playing 154 games and stealing 40 bases. Following year hit .308 in 153 games, pilfered 30 sacks, scored 89 runs. Then had .315 average for 67 games, 1918; dropped down to .270s for 1919 and 1920. Had .343 for 79 games with Toronto, also in 1920.

Benny hit two homers in 1917 WS against Chicago White Sox. Both came in fourth game when Ferdie Schupp beat Urban Faber and Dave Danforth by 5–0 score. Kauff, however, hit just .160 in his only WS, 4 for 25.

Benny was involved with an auto-theft ring; though he was acquitted in court, Czar Landis barred him from baseball because of "association with thieves."

KAUFFMAN, EWING   Executive. B. 9/21/16, Garden City, Mo. Ewing Kauffman, owner of Kansas City AL, began multi-million-dollar pharmaceutical business in basement. But when he took over Royals few years ago, did not have to start in basement, even though they were brand-new expansion team. In first season in AL, 1949 Royals finished ahead of Chicago White Sox and Seattle Pilots in Western Division. Also finished with better won-and-lost record than Cleveland Indians in Eastern Division. Royals also did quite well for expansion club in 1971. Came home second in division with 85–76 record. Cedric Tallis, executive vice president and general manager, was named by *Sporting News* as Executive of Year in baseball.

Kauffman took over Royals 1/11/68 and immediately started to build organization of executives, scouts, players, managers, coaches for system that would give Kansas City contending team. In 1969 Kauffman came up with idea of baseball academy to develop young men into baseball players even though they might not have played before. Idea was to select youths with good bodies, keen minds, and physical potential. Then coaches would try to channel these abilities into pitching, batting, fielding, base-running skills. Academy opened 8/10/70 after 126 tryout camps and look at 7682 would-be students. Royals Academy now is $1.5-million complex at Sarasota, Fla.; operates throughout year. Early results have been extremely promising. Kauffman is looking forward to one or more graduates of academy making grade with Kansas City club.

Kauffman attended Kansas City Junior College. Entered navy, 1942. After discharge at end of World War II, went to work for pharmaceutical firm. Two years later started own operation, Marion Laboratories, Inc., now one of top drug companies in country—and Kauffman is multimillionaire. Now has keen interest in Kansas City civic affairs. Was one of strong supporters for building Harry S. Truman Sports Complex, home of Royals starting with 1973 season.

KEANE, JOHN JOSEPH Manager. B. 11/3/11, St. Louis, Mo. D. 1/6/67, Houston, Tex. 5'10½'', 165. Johnny Keane, journeyman bush league shortstop, spent entire career to 1964 in St. Louis Cardinal organization: became minor league manager, then Cardinal coach, eventually Cardinal manager. Piloted ball club to runner-up position, and finally to NL pennant. Capped this with victory in WS—and very next day resigned. Few managers have left ball club that just won world championship, none with such dramatic suddenness. Rogers Hornsby was traded away from Cardinals in December 1926 after winning WS in October. Danny Murtaugh retired after winning 1971 fall classic, for reasons of health, but his departure was expected. Keane, however, left Cardinals as matter of principle; reason was Gussie Busch, president of Redbirds. Johnny took over management of Cardinals 7/6/61 when club was in sixth place. Got them up to fifth that year but ended up sixth in 1962. In 1963 Cardinals were second. In 1964 Redbirds were jogging along, apparently headed nowhere all summer long. When Philadelphia Phillies collapsed, Cardinals put on drive, climaxed by winning NL pennant on last day of season. Busch, however, had been very unhappy through summer months; decided to clean house, starting in front office. Bing Devine, general manager, was fired 8/17/64, and it was noised about that Keane would simply finish out contract and be dropped as soon as season was over. Rumors, apparently based on solid information, said Busch was going to hire Leo Durocher for 1965, replacing Keane.

After winning pennant and WS for Busch, first since Busch became club president, Keane quit. By coincidence, Yogi Berra, Yankee manager, pilot of losing club in WS, was dismissed very same day.

Johnny got in car Saturday morning and started driving home to Houston; drove over 850 miles so as to be near phone. He was out of job, voluntarily, but wanted to stay in game he loved. Late Sunday night Ralph Houk, general manager of Yankees, arrived in Houston. Talk with Keane followed—and on Tuesday Keane was in New York for news conference where his appointment as Yankee manager was announced.

Somehow, Keane's quiet personality never quite clicked in New York. After such colorful characters as Casey Stengel and Yogi Berra, Johnny did not capture imagination of press, radio, and television people. Ball club sagged; Mickey Mantle and Roger Maris both dropped off in home run production. Yankees wound up sixth in 10-club race. And in 1966 they were worse. After winning just four of their first 20 games, Keane was released and Houk once again took over manager's job. Thus ended managerial career of Johnny Keane.

Johnny's peregrinations in Cardinal organization started 1930 at Waynesboro in Blue Ridge League, later taking him to Springfield, Mo.; Columbus, Ohio.; Houston, Elmira, Rochester, Mobile, New Iberia; Albany, Ga.; and Omaha. Gave up playing, 1948, but had started managing as early as 1938. Built fine reputation as intelligent manager, good at teaching fundamentals to young players. After four years as manager at Omaha, Keane became Cardinal coach, 1959, keeping that job until named pilot. Never played major league game.

KEEFE, TIMOTHY JOHN　P-BR-TR. B. 3/27/60, Cambridge, Mass. D. 4/23/33, Cambridge, Mass. 5'10½", 185. Tim Keefe named to Hall of Fame 1964. Must have been great pitcher to win 343 major league games back before turn of century. Nineteen of those victories came consecutively in 1888, while he was toiling for New York NL. This record stood until Rube Marquard came along in 1912 and equaled it.

Keefe performed another feat that has not been equaled. While working for Metropolitans of American Association, 7/4/83, Tim pitched morning game against Columbus, allowed just one hit and won it 9–1; that afternoon came back with two-hitter, winning 3–0.

Keefe pitched for Utica, New Bedford, and Albany in old National Association, 1879–80, then moved to Troy, NL, 1880–82, winning 42, losing 59 over three seasons; with Metropolitans, 1883, won 41, lost 27; had 37–17 record following year. New York NL, 1885, leading off with 32–13 mark; then 42–20, 35–19 and 35–11; dropped down to 28 wins in 1889, 13 defeats.

With New York, Players League, 1890, won 17, lost 11. Had off season, 1891, with New York and Philadelphia NL, winning five, losing 11. Then came back with 19–16 in 1892, and 10–7 in final year in majors. Umpired in NL, 1894–95.

Tim got some of effectiveness from change-of-pace pitch. Pioneered in use of "slow ball." During major league career, pitched 5052 innings, 599 games, winning 343, losing 224. Struck out twice as many as he walked—2542 to 1225. Had 40 shutouts and 555 complete games. In WS play, 1884,88,89, won four games, lost three.

KEELER, WILLIAM HENRY (Wee Willie)　OF-BL-TL. B. 3/13/72, Brooklyn, N.Y. D. 1/1/23, Brooklyn, N.Y. 5'4½", 140. "Hit 'em where they ain't!" That was how Wee Willie Keeler expressed philosophy of hitting. And how he could hit! Only one man in majors ever hit for higher average than Keeler's .432 in 1897. Hugh Duffy did better—in 1894 with Boston NL, hitting .438. Willie really was "wee" for ball player—just 4-1/2 inches more than five feet. But this didn't keep him from hitting for lifetime average of .345; thirteen times in succession hit above .300 as regular for Baltimore Orioles, Brooklyn NL, and New York AL, 1894–1906. That .432 average gave one batting championship, and following year he won second bat title even though he dropped down to .379.

Keeler, with John McGraw, Hugh Jennings, and other legendary names, was with fabulous old Orioles of 1890s. He and McGraw are supposed to have invented, or at least perfected, hit-and-run play. Both were left-handed batsmen. At first opposing clubs could not believe it was intentional when these players would consistently hit ball to opposite field. So, often, when an Oriole would start for second base with pitch, shortstop would head for bag to cover. McGraw, Keeler, and other temmates would hit ball through spot vacated by shortstop. Then when opposing team expected ball to be hit through shortstop, second baseman would cover. Keeler and McGraw were adept enough bat handlers to slap ball through second baseman's normal position. And, if by chance, hitter missed ball, frequently Oriole had stolen base. This "inside baseball," along with many other tricks, made Orioles 1894–96 NL flag winners. Keeler not only hit exceptionally well during this period (.368, .395 and .392) but stole 30 bases in 1894, 57 following season, and 73 in 1896.

Keeler used lightest bat ever seen in majors. Had keen eye and rarely struck out. While old-time statistics are not completely reliable, it has been reported that Willie once went through entire season without striking out. He could bunt, and frequently did so successfully even when infielders crowded in. On those ocasions, with excellent bat control, Keeler would push ball past first baseman or third sacker. Also master of "Baltimore chop"; would hit ball down so that it bounced high into air. Opposing fielders stood helpless, waiting for ball to come down as Keeler streaked safely to first base.

Willie started as pitcher but shifted to third base when he signed with Binghamton, 1892. Led Eastern League in hitting with .373 average. Went up to New York NL that same season; played 13 games. Following year had 29 games with New York and Brooklyn, but also had 15 with Binghamton. Baltimore career started 1894. In 1899 accompanied Mgr. Ned Hanlon and several other Orioles in shift to Brooklyn. After close of 1902 season jumped to AL with Highlanders or Hilltoppers, as forebears of Yankees were called. After 13th consecutive season above .300, Keeler dropped off to .234 in 1907, then had .263 and .264 marks, 1908–09. Spent 1910 with New York Giants as pinch hitter, but went to bat only 10 times. Got three hits. Gave up active play after 39 games with Toronto in 1911. Coach, Brooklyn Federal League club, 1914; scout, Boston NL, 1915.

Keeler set consecutive 44-game hitting streak in 1897 that stood as major league record until Joe DiMaggio broke it with 56-game performance in 1941. Willie also set another record that stood for years—his 243 hits in one season, 1897. George Sisler holds present big league mark, 257, set in 1920.

Fans never ceased to marvel at Keeler's batting skill. So small that, according to one story, an umpire is supposed to have told manager to "'get that batboy off field; we're ready to play game!" Manager replied, "Heck no! He's no batboy! He's our best hitter."

Keeler's lifetime major league record follows: 2124 games, 8564 times at bat, 1720 runs, 2955 hits, 234 doubles, 155 triples, 32 home runs, and 519 stolen bases, for .345 average.

Willie reportedly could have become manager of New York AL club late in career but declined as he doubted own ability to discipline players. Hall of Fame 1939.

KEKICH, MICHAEL DENNIS   P-BR-TL. B. 4/2/45, San Diego, Calif. 6'1", 206. Mike Kekich has reputation of being relaxed, free spirit, ready to discourse on astrology, skiing, motorcycle riding, photography, philosophy, and pitching. On mound hasn't yet reached potential believes he will reach. As of spring 1973, Mike had won 32 major league games, but lost 10 more than he won. Pitched 674 innings in 150 NL and AL games, allowing 321 walks and striking out 393. Eight of games were complete.

Kekich spent his earlier years in Los Angeles Dodger organization. Began pro career, 1964, shuttling between Santa Barbara, St. Petersburg, Spokane. Spent 1965 with Dodgers but pitched only 10 innings and was charged with one loss. Divided 1966 between Albuquerque and Santa Barbara and did same in 1967. Back with Dodgers, 1968, but was able to capture only two games while losing 10. Traded to New York Yankees 12/4/68. Came up with 4–6, 6–3, and 10–9 records in first three years with New Yorkers. Then lost 13, winning 10, 1972. His ERA generally has been above 4.00 throughout his career. Has live fast ball, baffling change of pace, plenty of self-confidence, but has difficulty in late innings. While with Dodgers, twice went into seventh inning without allowing hit. However, isn't finishing many games—just two in 1972, for example. Sent to Cleveland, June 1973.

KELL, GEORGE CLYDE   3B-BR-TR. B. 8/23/22, Swifton, Ark. 5'10", 170. AL batting champion of 1949 who parlayed baseball skills into post-playing career as Detroit sportscaster and Tiger scout. Kell started major league career with Philadelphia Athletics, 1943, but had greatest seasons with Detroit, both as hitter and fine third baseman. Seven times led AL hot-corner guardians in fielding.

George started at Newport in Northeast Arkansas League, 1940–41. Moved to Lancaster, Pa., Inter-State League, for 1942 and 1943. In latter season not only led that circuit in hitting, but .396 mark for 138 games was highest anywhere in organized baseball. Besides that healthy swat mark, George led league in hits, with 220; in runs, with 120; in triples, with 23; and in putouts, assists, and fielding at third base. Athletics brought him up for one game that year, and in 1944 nailed down regular job at third base. Hit .268 in 139 games. Athletics traded Kell to Detroit for Barney McCosky 5/18/46. George hit .322, first of eight consecutive years above .300. His .343 took batting title, 1949; but did quite well in 1950 with .340, leading AL in hits with 218; in doubles with 56, and for first time went above 100 in RBI. Also won fielding laurels at third base for third time. Tigers sent him to Boston AL 6/3/52. Red Sox dealt him to Chicago AL 5/23/54, with Grady Hatton and $100,000 as bait. Traded to Baltimore AL 5/21/56 and called it quits as active player after 1957 season.

Kell suffered two serious injuries in 1948, both in games against Yankees. Vic Raschi broke his wrist with pitched ball, and some weeks later Joe DiMaggio's line drive fractured his lower jaw, putting him out for season. That year missed 57 of club's games.

Kell can look back on 1795 major league games and .306 average. Hit safely 2054 times, with 385 doubles, 50 triples, 78 homers. Scored 881 runs, drove in 870. Became Tiger scout, 1966, and in summer is TV sports announcer for Tiger games.

KELLER, CHARLES ERNEST (King Kong) OF-BL-TR. B. 9/12/16, Middletown, Md. 5'11", 190. Charlie Keller helped New York Yankees win four pennants and three WS. And how he hit in first two WS: three homers, one double, one triple, two singles, with .438 average in first one, 1939; two doubles, five singles, and .389 mark in 1941 classic. Career extended over 13-year period. Quit with .286 major league average for 1170 games during which hit safely 1085 times, scored 725 runs, and drove in 760. Had 189 homers, 72 triples, 166 doubles among his base hits, exclusive of those in World Series play.

Keller's salary never went above $27,500 in baseball, but with WS bonuses and his savings bought himself 100 acres in Maryland near Frederick and has been operating horse farm. Specializes in harness horses and frequently gives foals names like Gay Yankee, Yankee Slugger, Fresh Yankee. Calls place Yankeeland Farm, but seldom sees baseball these days, unless on television.

Charlie doesn't particularly like moniker "King Kong" given because of his brute strength. Retiring fellow, holds degree in agricultural

511

economics from U. of Maryland. Didn't need much minor league seasoning, going direct to Newark club, International League farm team of Yankees, 1937, one notch below majors. Promptly hit .353 in 145 games; 13 homers, 88 RBI, 120 runs scored. Boosted average to .365 for 150 contests following campaign, tossing in 22 homers, 129 RBI, and 149 runs scored. No wonder Keller full-fledged Yankee in 1939. Started off with .334 for 111 games; 11 homers, 83 RBI. That proved to be best average of big league career, but he raised homer total to 30 or more three times; and three times drove in more than 100 runs. After fine rookie season, 1939, Charlie was batting king in WS, helping Yanks whitewash Cincinnati in four straight games. It was he who banged into Ernie Lombardi, stunning him in 10th inning. Ernie lay prostrate as Yanks scored their third run of inning, won game and Series.

Keller's .389 average in 1941 WS was at expense of Brooklyn pitchers. In 1942,43 WS Charlie hit .200 and .222 respectively. Overall WS record was .306 for 19 games, with 18 runs scored, 18 RBI, 5 homers, 2 triples, 3 doubles among 22 hits.

Charlie spent 1944–45 in merchant marine. Suffered back injury, 1947; broken hand, 1948. With Detroit Tigers 1950–51, and played final two games in majors with Yankees, 1952.

His younger brother, Hal, was catcher with Washington Senators briefly, 1949,50,52, later became their farm director. Continued in same position when Senators changed to Texas Rangers.

KELLEY, JOSEPH JAMES OF-BR-TR. B. 12/9/71, Cambridge, Mass. D. 8/14/43, Baltimore, Md. 5'11", 190. Left fielder for Baltimore Orioles in glory days of 1890s when Ned Hanlon was manager; team included John McGraw, Hugh Jennings, Willie Keeler, Wilbert Robinson, Dan Brouthers. One of Kelley's more notable exploits was slapping out nine hits in nine trips to plate during doubleheader, 9/3/94. Coach, manager, scout; played 1829 major league games in all and quit with .321 lifetime average. Hall of Fame 1971.

Kelley was with Lowell, New England League, 1891; Boston and Pittsburgh briefly same year. Omaha, Western League, 1892; then with Pittsburgh and Baltimore same season. Remained with Orioles through 1898. Then Hanlon took Baltimore franchise and most of Orioles with him to Brooklyn. Left Brooklyn to join Baltimore AL club, 1902; played 60 games and then jumped to Cincinnati, 7/16/02. Stayed with Reds through 1906. Toronto, Eastern League, 1907. Boston NL 1908. Toronto 1909–10. Retired as player. Served as playing manager at Cincinnati part of 1902, all of 1903–05; playing manager, Boston NL, 1908; playing manager, Toronto, 1907, 09–10. Manager, Toronto, 1911–14. Scout, New York AL, 1915–16. Coach, Brooklyn, 1926. Best record as manager in majors was 1904 when Cincinnati finished third in NL with 88–65 record.

In six full seasons at Baltimore Kelley's lowest average was 311. Four times .370 or better—.390 in 1897, .391 in 1894. After turn of century still hit for fine averages, though he did not approach his record with Orioles. Wound up with .321 mark, with 2245 hits good for 353 doubles, 189 triples, 66 homers. Stole 458 bases; scored 1425 runs, drove in close to 1200 (last figure cannot be verified; such records not systematically kept in his era).

KELLY, GEORGE LANGE (High Pockets) 1B-OF-BR-TR. B. 9/10/95, San Francisco, Calif. 6'4", 200. George Kelly, first baseman for John McGraw's four pennant winners in 1920s, had one of greatest arms of era. Also could hit long ball—and played fine game in field regardless of position. Set NL record 6/14/24 by driving in all eight runs N.Y. Giants scored as they beat Cincinnati by 8-4 score. This record still stands as highest number of runs when one player was responsible for all his club's markers. Kelly also is remembered for brilliant throw in 1921 WS that ended crucial eighth game, Giants winning 1-0. Winner needed five victories to capture world championship that year. Giants had four wins, Yankees three, 10/13/21. Giants scored one run in first inning and kept lead going into last half of ninth. Then with one out and Aaron Ward on first base, Frank "Home Run" Baker came to bat. Veteran third baseman hit sizzling grounder that Johnny Rawlings, Giants' second sacker, was barely able to stop in sensational play. Rawlings threw to Kelly at first, to get Baker. Meanwhile Ward, having had good jump, set sail for third in surprise play, but Kelly was alert and fired perfect throw to Frankie Frisch, playing third. In very close play, Frisch tagged Ward as he slid in, and WS was over.

Kelly was one of earliest players in modern baseball to hit three homers in one game. Starting with 1900, Walter Henline and Cy Williams had done it in 1922 and 1923 respectively. Ken Williams of St. Louis Browns was only man in AL who had done it when George had first three-homer game 9/17/23. Then repeated performance 6/14/24.

George led NL in homers, 1921, with 23, which was goodly number in those days for everyone except Babe Ruth. Had 21 in 1924, and 20 in 1925. Hall of Fame 1973.

Kelly, nephew of Chicago NL star Bill Lange of 1890s, started at Victoria, B.C., 1914. Following season Giants bought him 8/20/15 for reported $1200. Reported that same year for 17 games but hit only .158. Remained with Giants until 7/25/17 but didn't play much. Pittsburgh had him briefly, then was sent to Rochester for 32 games. Military service 1918. Back to Rochester, 1919, for 103 games, hitting .356, then reported to Giants that season and hit .290 in 32 contests. Kelly was regular first baseman thereafter until Bill Terry appeared on scene in New York. Had six consecutive seasons batting well over .300 and drove in plenty of runs. Led NL with 94 RBI in 1920 and 136 in 1924. When

Terry came along, McGraw wanted both men in lineup as much as possible. So Kelly, being more versatile, shifted to outfield for many games and played second base in 145 games during career. Even appeared at third base twice and pitched five scoreless innings for Giants in 1917. Traded from Giants to Cincinnati before 1927 season, remained with Reds into 1930, then was shifted to Chicago Cubs. Played his last season with Brooklyn Dodgers, 1932. Took part in 1622 games; made 1778 hits, good for 337 doubles, 76 triples, 148 homers. Scored 819 runs, drove in 1020, and stole 65 bases. Lifetime major league average .297.

In four successive WS, 1921–24, Kelly played 26 games, had 25 hits in 101 at bats, including two doubles—and a home run off Walter Johnson in opening game of 1924 series. WS average was .248. After retirement as active player, Kelly coached Cincinnati 1935–37 and 1947–48; coached Boston NL 1938–43 when Casey Stengel managed Braves.

KELLY, MICHAEL JOSEPH (King) C-OF-Inf.-BR-TR. B. 12/31/57, Troy, N. Y. D. 11/8/94, Boston, Mass. 5'10", 180. King Kelly played baseball when it was brand new as professional sport. Imaginative, quick thinker, studied rules then in existence and tried to take every advantage of them. Started career, 1878, with Cincinnati, just two years after formation of NL. As Kelly found ways to circumvent rules, league found it necessary to amend them. But it must have been fun when many plays now prohibited were allowed. For example: Once, while with Chicago White Stockings, "Silver" Flint was catching game against Detroit. Kelly, also with Chicago, was on bench. Detroit filled bases, and it looked like certain defeat for White Stockings if Detroit got one more hit. Batter hit high foul, out of reach of first baseman and catcher. While ball was still in air, Kelly shouted at top of voice, "Flint, you're out of game!" Then Kelly calmly caught ball himself and proceeded to take over catching duties. Naturally there was argument when Umpire Gaffney refused to recognize switch of players while ball was in air. Kelly got rule book, argued vociferously but in vain. However, rules were revised.

Versatile fellow could do just about everything on diamond; played every position, including pitcher. Most of time, however, was spent either catching or in outfield. Slugged ball for .313 lifetime average. As base runner had more than five years in succession when he pilfered at least 40 bases. Best year in this respect was 1887 when he stole 84. That same year had .394 batting average—somewhat inflated by fact that was season bases on balls were counted as hits. Nevertheless, in 1886 had batted .388 to lead NL hitters. In eight seasons as major league regular batted over .300.

Kelly did things with flair—including his base running. Fans loved to see him go into base; it was their cheering him that originated famous yell, "Slide, Kelly, slide!" Got good money for those days, spent much of it for clothes. Old-timers used to tell how handsome, carefree idol used to ride to ball park in style, at times using ornate carriage pulled by two white horses. Admiring fans, at least on some occasions, surrounded their hero, unhitched horses, and themselves pulled carriage to park. Some claimed Kelly best-dressed man in world.

Kelly was with Cincinnati 1878–79. Chicago NL 1880–86. Boston NL 1887–89. Boston, Players League, 1890. Cincinnati, American Association, part of 1891, as playing manager; later same season with Boston, AA. Boston NL 1891–92. New York NL 1893. Manager, Allentown, Pennsylvania State League, 1894; later same season with Yonkers, Eastern League.

Lifetime totals showed 1434 games, 1853 hits, 351 doubles, 109 triples, 65 homers, with 1359 runs scored. Hall of Fame 1945.

KENNEDY, JOHN EDWARD (J.K.) Inf.-BR-TR. B. 5/29/41, Chicago, Ill. 6', 185. John Kennedy hit home run in first time at bat in major league as member of Washington Senators 9/5/62. In 1970, in first time at bat with Boston Red Sox, hit home run; it was inside-park variety and he had to scamper to make it. John, however, hasn't made his salary in majors as slugger. After 779 games at close of 1972 season, he owned .229 batting average with total of 30 homers.

Kennedy's claim to recognition rests upon ability to fill in at any infield position and do fine job as substitute. Qualifies as one of most valuable utility men in game. Has had to be ready to travel, however. Temporary addresses as pro ball player since 1961 have included Pensacola, Raleigh, Washington; York, Pa.; Hawaii, Los Angeles, New York (Yankees), Syracuse; Columbus, Ohio; Seattle (AL Pilots), Milwaukee (AL Brewers), and Portland, Oreg. Joined Red Sox after sale by Portland 6/26/70. Tarried with Dodgers long enough to get into WS of 1965,66 and had .167 average with one hit in six at bats. Before becoming professional, Kennedy was three-year standout athlete in football, basketball, and baseball at Harper High School in Chicago. During off-season has worked for Red Sox in ticket sales.

KENNEDY, ROBERT DANIEL OF-BR-TR. B. 8/18/20, Chicago, Ill. 6'2", 193. Bob Kennedy, early in 1973, took charge of all St. Louis Cardinals' player personnel. Bought airplane so could have his own schedules for hurried trips around country to make personal observations of current and potential members of St. Louis team. Played in majors from 1939 to 1957; who also managed Chicago Cubs, Oakland A's.

Bob started pro experience, 1937, with Dallas, Texas League, and with Vicksburg, Miss., in Cotton States circuit. Longview, East Texas loop,

1938; Shreveport, Texas League, 1939. Reported to Chicago White Sox for three games that same season. Was third baseman then, later shifting to outfield with just occasional fling at hot corner. Remained with White Sox until 6/3/48, but skipped 1943–45 for service with marines. With Cleveland 1948–54. Baltimore AL 1954–55. Chicago AL 1955–56. Detroit 1956. Chicago AL 1957. Brooklyn 1957. As major leaguer Kennedy played 1483 games; hit .254, with 63 homers among 1176 hits. Scored 514 runs, drove in same number; also had 196 doubles, 41 triples. Three games in 1948 WS with Cleveland: two trips to plate, one hit, struck out.

Bob was coach for Indians, 1958–60; managed Chicago Cubs, 1963–64, and first part of 1965; scouted for Cubs, 1965; coach for Atlanta Braves, 1967; managed Oakland AL 1968. Before being given direction of all Cardinal player personnel, Kennedy was director of player development. As major league manager, Bob's teams won 264 games, lost 278. Also managed in minors.

KERR, RICHARD HENRY (Dickey) P-BL-TL. B. 7/3/93, St. Louis, Mo. D. 5/4/63, Houston, Tex. 5'7", 155. Dickey Kerr pitched and won two games for Chicago White Sox in 1919 WS despite fact that eight teammates later were barred from baseball forever for trying to throw Series to Cincinnati Reds. Kerr, with Eddie Collins, Ray Schalk, and others had nothing to do with gamblers. He shut out Reds on three hits in third game of WS after Sox had lost first two. Pitched and won sixth game of set, 5–4. Reds took Series, five games to three. After that performance, Kerr won 21 games for Sox, 1920. Then came revelation of crookedness; eight White Sox expelled, and team tumbled to seventh, 1921. Despite lowly finish of team, Kerr captured 19 games, lost 17, pitching 308-2/3 innings.

Dickey was reportedly making $6500 salary and thought it time for raise. Other versions had it Kerr was making only $4500. Owner Comiskey refused to consider any raise, even few hundred dollars. So, for self-respect, Kerr turned to semipro ball for three years and was suspended. Unsuccessful comeback 1925: 12 games, losing one, winning none. His complete major league record showed 53 wins, 34 defeats, with ERA of 3.84.

Sports writers insisted on referring to him as Dickie, but Kerr himself declared it should be Dickey.

Comiskey's treatment of Kerr often criticized. Chicago fans, tried to show appreciation in 1921 by presenting a 52-piece set of silverware, which Kerrs treasured.

Dickey played important role in career of Stan Musial. Years after 1919 WS, Kerr was managing Daytona Beach club in Florida State League. Stan young pitcher-outfielder on team, making $100-per-month salary and wife expecting first child. Kerrs insisted Musials move in with them, gesture Stan never forgot. Many years later, after Musial was in big money, he showed deep appreciation by buying home for Kerrs in Houston, where they were living. Dickey had job then, 1958. Not destitute, neither in position to own home. House Musial gave probably in $15,000–$20,000 range at time. Musial tried to keep gift secret, but news leaked out in Houston.

After Kerr left major leagues, 1925, pitched for San Francisco, Pacific Coast League, 1926. Coach at Rice Institute, 1928. Out of baseball 1929–37, except for brief spell as instructor at baseball school in Jackson, Miss. Managed team at Wausau, Wis., 1937; Daytona Beach, 1940. Piloted Hutchinson, Kans., team in Chicago Cub organization, 1946. Worked for cotton company during many of these years; later worked for electrical firm. After his death, Houston fans raised $3000 for statue of him, placed in Astrodome.

By sterling pitching in 1919 WS, Kerr is believed to have cost "sure-thing" gamblers some $125–$150,000. In his first start during Series, the three hits allowed were scratch hits; retired 19 men on infield outs; only four flies went to outfield; only six balls were hit outside infield. His WS performance showed 2–0, 1.42 ERA, 19 innings.

KESSINGER, DONALD EULON SS-BLR-TR. B. 7/17/42, Forrest City, Ark. 6'1", 175. Don Kessinger took over shortstop job, 1965, for Chicago Cubs and when 1973 started, management of club was still happy with his work. Smooth, graceful fielder who knows opposing hitters, covers his position effectively. Don's skills recognized in many quarters; five years, 1968–72, was starting shortstop for NL in All-Star games.

Kessinger's .274 batting average in 1972 equaled highest previous posted average in 1966. Don is no slugger; at start of 1973 season had 10 homers, 51 triples, and 133 doubles among 1167 major league hits. Overall average was .255, with 557 runs scored, 300 RBI. Played in 1181 games.

Don all-conference baseball and basketball player at U. of Mississippi before accepting $25,000 bonus to line up with Cubs. Received B.S. in business administration. Brief apprenticeship in minors was of 77 games at Fort Worth, 1964, and 44 games with Dallas–Fort Worth, 1965. Cubs had him in four games, 1964, and played him in 106 games following season. For next seven years played in at least 145 games each season.

Kessinger set major league record for shortstops by playing 54 straight errorless games in 1969; this has since been surpassed. Led NL short-stops in fielding; also scored 109 runs. Has chalked up various honors for starting double plays. In 1971 had six-for-six on one occasion, first time any Cub had gone six-for-six since Frank Demaree did it in 1937.

Don, teetotaler, nonsmoker, keeps in fine physical condition; active member of Fellowship of Christian Athletes.

KILKENNY, MICHAEL DAVID (Killer) P-BR-TL. B. 4/11/45, Bradford, Ontario. 6'3", 165. He knows his name is Mike Kilkenny but don't be surprised if he forgets his address—at least his summer address. Mike spent three summers with Detroit Tigers, which in no way prepared him for what happened in 1972. Got into one game with Billy Martin's club, then was on way. Before season was over had been with Oakland A's, San Diego Padres and Cleveland Indians. No player has ever been with more than four major league clubs in one season, so Mike tied record. Managed to win four games in AL, lose one, save another. Was not credited with victory or charged with loss in five appearances in NL.

Mike hasn't put together any sensational record yet: going into 1973 season, had appeared in 134 major league games, won 23, lost 18, and had 4.36 ERA in 407 innings. But his winter occupation is somewhat offbeat for ball player; invested his savings in modest string of harness racing horses and hopes to make them profitable.

Kilkenny signed with Detroit organization off sandlots of Toronto, 1964. Got experience that year and next at Cocoa, Lakeland, and Daytona Beach, all in Florida, then pitched for Montgomery, Southern Association, 1966–68; also pitched for Toledo, 1968, before joining Tigers, 1969. Posted 8–6 mark that year, with 3.38 ERA. Then had 7–6 record, but allowed 5.16 earned runs per nine-inning game. ERA in 1971 was also above five runs per game, but he garnered four victories and lost five. Then came his traveling year—preceded by journey to Vietnam, sponsored by USO. Specializes in breaking-ball deliveries.

KILLEBREW, HARMON CLAYTON 3B-1B-BR-TR. B. 6/29/36, Payette, Idaho. 5'11", 214. Not many have hit 500 major league home runs, but Harmon Killebrew joined select circle 8/10/71. By end of 1972 had boosted career total to 541. No. 500 came off southpaw Mike Cuellar. Harmon nearing close of illustrious playing career that began in 1954 when U.S. Senator Herman Welker of Idaho kept telling Clark Griffith, then president of Washington Senators, about slugging youngster from his home state. Griff finally sent Ossie Bluege to Idaho and signed him. Joined team in Chicago before 18th birthday.

Cal Griffith, president of Minnesota Twins, who transferred old Washington franchise to Northwest, has indicated he may consider Killerbrew for manager of Twins after playing days over. Believes pilot's job is full time assignment, without trying to get into game himself.

Killebrew appeared in nine games with Washington, 1954, hit .308, but in 1955 it was evident he needed polishing. In 38 contests hit an even .200, although did smack four homers. First one came 6/24/55 off Billy Hoeft. Divided 1956 between Washington and Charlotte and did same in 1957. Shuttled among Washington, Charlotte, and Indianapolis, 1958; finally stuck with Senators following season. By this time was ready to display fairly consistent slugging ability. When he got hold of ball it traveled—42 homers that year, with .242 batting average. His 132 hits showed just 20 doubles and two triples, but he drove in 105 runs. His 42 homers tied for league leadership. Was first of eight seasons when he exceeded 40-mark in four-baggers. In 1960 Harm got average up to .276 but homer total dropped to 31, RBI to 80. Then came franchise shift to Minnesota. Killebrew's best hitting average came in first season with renamed Twins, .288. Slapped 46 homers, drove in 122 runs. In 1962 hit 48 homers; in 1963, 45; and following season, 49, making him home run king three straight years. Tied for lead, 1967, with 44, then won another long-ball trophy, 1969, with 49. This time drove in more runs than ever before, 140. MVP honors for AL.

Harmon shifted from one position to another quite often. Seems to be more at home at first or third, but has seen considerable service in outfield. Problem has been tendency to strike out—led AL in this respect, 1962, with 142. Struck out more than 100 times in each of seven seasons. However, has drawn flock of walks, great many of them intentional. Repeatedly has hit two or more homers in one game. On 9/21/63 hit four homers in doubleheader; three in one game, one in other.

Killebrew, with 541 career homers, now stands next to Babe Ruth as most prolific home run hitter in AL. During 1972 passed Mickey Mantle, Jimmy Foxx, and Ted Williams. Hank Aaron and Willie Mays in NL are still ahead of Harmon. Man from Idaho holds several other slugging records. Played on just one WS team, 1965 Twins; hit .286. Member of 11 AL All-Star squads.

Lifetime record before 1973 started showed 2138 big league games; 1890 hits, 1201 runs, 1454 RBI, and .261 average. Had 261 doubles, 23 triples among extra-base hits. Was leading AL in homers with bases loaded—11 in all.

KILLEFER, WILLIAM LAVIER, JR. (Reindeer) C-BR-TR. B. 10/10/88, Bloomingdale, Mich. D. 7/2/60, Elsmere, Del. 5'10½", 200. Bill Killefer first gained fame as battery mate of Grover Cleveland Alexander when Alex starred for Philadelphia Phillies. When both were sent to Chicago Cubs 12/11/17 for two players and $55,000 cash, was most sensational baseball news in years. Alexander-Killefer combination helped Phillies to their 1915 pennant. And after being traded to Cubs, they won pennant immediately, 1918, although Alex won only two ball games before joining army. Bill was fine catcher, no great hitter although reached .286 in 103 games, 1919, and .323 in 45 contests, 1921. Major league average was .238 for 1035 games. In the two WS, hit .111.

Killefer used to be called "Paw Paw Bill," since he attended school in Paw Paw, just 10 miles from birth place. Later attended college in

Watertown, Wis., and Austin, Tex. Started pro career in Southern Michigan League at Jackson, 1907. Following year was with Austin, Texas League, and briefly with San Francisco, Pacific Coast League. In 1909 had 119 games with Houston, Texas League, going up to St. Louis Browns 9/2/09. Had .124 average in 74 games, 1910, and landed with Buffalo, Eastern League, for 1911. By 8/12/11 had shown enough to be bought by Phillies, reporting in time for six games.

Bill slowed down in later years as base runner, giving birth to nickname "Reindeer." Nevertheless, managed to steal 39 bases during big league career. Cubs named Killefer as manager during 1921 season. With fine catcher like Bob O'Farrell on team, Bill gave up active catching after becoming pilot. Cubs were seventh-place team, 1921. Bill got them over .500 mark in 1922 and finished fifth. Rose to fourth in 1923 but dropped back to fifth, 1924. Disaster struck in 1925—team won 33 games, lost 42 at start of season. Killefer was replaced, first by Rabbit Maranville, later by George Gibson. Cubs finished last. Joined St. Louis Cardinals as coach, 1926, as playing-manager Rogers Hornsby's right-hand man. When Hornsby was fired that winter after leading team to NL pennant and world championship, Sam Breadon, Cardinal owner, offered job to Bill. Loyal to Hornsby, Bill refused and signed with St. Louis Browns as coach, 1927–29. Managed Browns 1930–33. Had two sixth-place teams and one that finished fifth. With Browns on way to last place during 1933 season, Killefer was dropped. His successor? Rogers Hornsby.

Coached Brooklyn Dodgers, 1939, and Phillies, 1942, and scouted on various occasions for other teams.

KINDER, ELLIS RAYMOND (Kinny) P-BR-TR. B. 7/26/14, Atkins, Ark. D. 10/16/68, Jackson, Tenn. 6'1", 195. One of foremost relief pitchers of his era. Saved 14 games in 1951 while pitching for Boston Red Sox; had 11–2 mark. In 1953 set AL record with 69 appearances on mound, which since has been broken. That year Kinder saved 27 games, had 10 victories, six defeats, and ERA of 1.85.

Wasn't always old, but in later years his nicknames included "Old Folks" and "Old Granddad." Career record, after 484 major league games, showed 102 victories, 71 defeats, with 3.43 ERA. Pitched 1479-2/3 innings, gave 539 walks, fanned 749, with 10 shutouts. Six shutouts came before he was specializing in relief, in one season, 1949. That was banner year, with 23 wins, six defeats, leading AL pitchers in winning percentage with .793.

Kinder started in Kitty League, 1938, at Jackson, Tenn. Didn't reach majors until 1945, after spell at Binghamton and couple of seasons at Memphis. While he belonged to St. Louis Browns, 1945, didn't get into any games until 1946 because of military duty. Two unspectacular seasons with Browns, then traded to Boston AL 11/18/47. Won 10, lost seven with Red Sox, 1948, then had big year. Took 14, lost 12, 1950, and began to be used mostly in relief.

Ellis underwent open-heart surgery at age 54 and seemed to be on road to recovery before relapse.

KINER, RALPH McPHERRAN OF-BR-TR. B. 10/27/22, Santa Rita, N. Mex. 6'2", 195. "Singles hitters ride jalopies; home run hitters ride in Cadillacs." Thus spake Ralph Kiner, who seldom hit .300 but often hit homers—in fact, Ralph either led or tied for leadership in each of first seven years in NL. Hit 369 of them in majors; got salary up to fancy $90,000 mark in days when that figure still astronomical.

Kiner had one NL home run championship under his belt when Hank Greenberg joined Pittsburgh Pirates, 1947. Hank became Kiner's roommate and Ralph was biggest beneficiary of arrangement. Greenberg was veteran, Kiner had played just one season in majors. Hank shared many hitting secrets with personable young man.

Pittsburgh management also helped by deciding to bring left-field fence closer to home plate, thereby creating famous "Greenberg Gardens." But Kiner benefitted most. Where he had hit 23 homers in 1946, his 1947 total soared way up to 51. Greenberg hit 25.

Management benefited also—fans flocked to Forbes Field to see Kiner, Greenberg et al. in action, even though Pirates finished last in standings. Kiner tied with Johnny Mize for home run leadership, 1947. In 1948 same two were tied again, this time with 40 apiece. Next three seasons Kiner was undisputed leader with 54, 47, and 42 respectively. In 1952 his record 37 round-trippers were tied by Hank Sauer of Chicago Cubs. By this time Branch Rickey had become general manager of Pirates. Club was in last place with no immediate prospect of moving up in league standings. So Rickey unloaded Kiner and his big contract on Chicago Cubs. In so doing, three other players, including Joe Garagiola, went to Chicago while Pirates received six players—AND estimated $100,000 cash. Deal was consummated 6/4/53.

That year Kiner proved could hit goodly number of homers even without Greenberg Gardens in home park; slapped 35. But in 1954 production slipped to 22. That fall Cubs traded him to Cleveland, and Kiner, in solitary AL season, hit 18 homers.

Ralph, as high school boy, got habit of hitting home runs. Had ten in 24 games. At age 18 made good in pretty fast Eastern League, hitting .279 for Albany in 1941. Eleven homers that season. But his 14 round trippers in 1942 led Eastern League. Played 43 games for Toronto next season before going into military service. When Kiner reported to Pirates in spring of 1946, plan was to farm him out one more year. But Frankie Frisch, then bossing Pirates, used him in exhibition game against

Chicago White Sox in Pasadena, Calif. Facing Bill Dietrich, experienced and capable pitcher, Kiner whaled two balls out of park, and Frisch revised plans to farm Kiner out. During first few weeks of 1946 campaign Ralph didn't hit worth much. But finally got started and, though average was only .247, got those 23 homers for league leadership.

Record books tell about numerous home run standards set by Kiner. Among them are these: hit 12 grand slams; hit two or more homers in 34 games; three times had three homers in one game; five homers in two consecutive games (accomplished twice); four homers in doubleheader; eight homers in four consecutive games.

Kiner's major league performance sums up like this: 1472 games, 5205 AB, 971 R, 1451 H, 216 doubles, 39 triples, 369 homers, 1015 RBI, 22 SB, lifetime average .279. Led NL in RBI, 1949, with 127.

Kiner turned to radio and television sportscasting after leaving active play. One of voices of New York Mets. Also served as special batting coach in Florida Instructional League, 1971.

KIRBY, CLAYTON LAWS, JR. P-BR-TR. B. 6/25/48, Washington, D.C. 6'3", 195.

Clay Kirby went into 1973 season with 3.52 ERA for his 143 games in majors; had 44 wins and 63 losses, but with bit of luck could have turned record around. For example, during 1970 season he pitched eight hitless innings for San Diego Padres—but was taken out for pinch hitter because you can't win no-hitter without sufficient runs. And in 1972, when his mark was 12–14, Padres were shut out in five of losses; in three others they scored just one run each outing.

Kirby started out with St. Louis Cardinal organization, 1966, at Sarasota. Then with St. Petersburg, Modesto, Arkansas and Tulsa through 1968. Back on Cardinal roster that fall, Clay was selected by Padres in expansion draft 10/14/68 and has been hard worker for San Diego since then. Was 7–20 in 1969; then had 10–16 and 15–13 records. In 1972 pitched 239 innings, fanned 175, allowed 116 walks.

Clay attended Old Dominion College in Virginia, and Benjamin Franklin University in Washington, D.C. In his spare time likes to build miniature racing cars.

KISON, BRUCE EUGENE P-BR-TR. B. 2/18/50, Pasco, Wash. 6'4", 178.

Bruce Kison, then 21-year old pitcher, was one of Pittsburgh heroes of 1971 WS. Not only did he pitch extremely well, but his youth, his wedding in evening after seventh game, all captured attention of fans. Bruce had set wedding for 7 P. M. Sunday in Pittsburgh. Problem was fact Pirates were playing crucial game in Baltimore that afternoon— several hundred miles away. Kison made it, with assist from Bob Prince, Pirates' veteran broadcaster. Prince had helicopter waiting outside Baltimore stadium. Pirates sewed up game and world championship.

Wild, enthusiastic celebration ensued in Pittsburgh clubhouse, but Bruce changed clothes, tore himself away, and was whisked to Friendship Airport where he boarded plane for destination. Married on time.

Pirates needed assists from youngster to get into WS and also to win world championship. Bruce didn't even figure in Pittsburgh plans in early 1971. Started season at Charleston, in International League. Won 10, lost one. When Bob Moose was called for military duty, Kison joined Pirates July 3. Pitched so effectively he stayed with club permanently. Won six, lost five. Then in playoff games against San Francisco Giants, Bruce was called on in fourth contest. Relieved in third inning, went 4-2/3 rounds without allowing run, and credited with vital win. First appearance in WS came in second game. Walked only two men he faced, and was removed. But Danny Murtaugh gave another chance in fourth game. This time pitched 6-1/3 innings of masterful ball in relief, allowed one hit, no runs. Did not walk anybody, struck out three, but did plunk three Orioles in ribs with sidearm pitches. This set WS record. Pittsburgh won game 4–3.

Kison, one year before he starred in WS, played hooky from classes in history and physical education at Central Washington State College to watch 1970 series between Orioles and Cincinnati Reds. Bruce signed with Pirate organization June 1968; pitched for Bradenton in Gulf Coast League that summer; Geneva, N.Y.-Pa. League, 1969; then in 1970 for Salem, Carolina League, and Waterbury, Eastern League. Led circuit in hit batsmen with 21.

Kison's work with Pirates in 1972 was not sensational: 9–7, 3.26 ERA, walked 69, fanned 102. Six of games were complete. Suffered Sore arm in spring of 1973; optioned to Pirate farm at Charleston, W. Va. to work back into shape.

Overall NL record as he went into 1973 showed 50 games pitched, 247 innings, with 15 wins, 12 defeats; 91 earned runs allowed, with 162 strikeouts, 105 bases on balls; eight complete games. Career ERA, 3.32. WS record showed 0.00 ERA for 6-1/3 innings, one victory, no defeat. Bruce is philatelist and numismatist.

KLEIN, CHARLES HERBERT (Chuck) OF-BL-TR. B. 10/7/05, Indianapolis, Ind. D. 3/28/58, Indianapolis, Ind. 6', 185. Chuck Klein took full advantage of old Baker Bowl, called "bandbox park" because of short fences. Playing for Philadelphia Phillies, 1928–33, led NL in several hitting departments, won *Sporting News* unofficial MVP designation 1931,32. In this period Klein led NL in homers with 43 in 1929, first full year in majors; scored 158 runs in 1930, mark that still stands as NL record; also led league in doubles with 59 that same year. In 1931 again led NL in homers with 31, in RBI with 121, and tied for leadership in runs scored with 121. In 1932 had to be content with tie for homer honors with 38, but led NL in hits with 226 and in runs scored with 152. Then, in following season, Chuck led league in hitting with .368, in hits with 223, in doubles with 44, in homers with 28, and in RBI with 120.

For some years other NL clubs had coveted Klein, especially Chicago Cubs. As early as 1930, William Wrigley, Jr., president of Cubs, offered Phillies $100,000 cash for Klein's contract but offer was spurned. Phillies meanwhile had floundered in second division all these years, except 1932 when they managed to reach fourth place. Depression was on and club treasury was bare, so Klein went to Chicago for $65,000 and three players. Good season in 1934 with Cubs, but nothing like great years in Philadelphia. Swatted .301 in 115 games, and blasted just 20 homers, with 80 RBI. In second season with Cubs Klein's record was about same, his average dropping to .293. And 5/21/36 he was back with Phillies in trade that brought Curt Davis to Chicago. Phillies again received cash in transaction—$50,000. Hit .306 that year and .325 in 1937, but never again reached .300 mark. Unconditionally released 6/7/39 and signed with Pittsburgh. Released by Pirates, Chuck returned to Phils once again 3/26/40. Hit .218 in 116 games that year, and .123 in 1941. Player coach for Phillies, 1942–44, then had one season only coaching Phils.

Klein got pro start at Evansville, III League, 1927, hitting .327 in 14 games. Was hitting .331 for Fort Wayne in Central League, 1928, after 88 games when summoned to Philadelphia. Played 64 games with Phils that year and found NL pitching easier—hit .360. Chuck's subsequent marks with Phils were .356, .386, .337, and .348 before winning NL batting title with .368 in 1933. Played in almost all his club's games during these glory years.

Established or tied plenty of slugging records during five full seasons while with Phillies. Hit four home runs in 10-inning game 7/10/36. Twice chalked up 26-game hitting streaks during 1930. Led NL in stolen bases, 1932, with 20. In outfield had ups and downs: made 23 errors in 1936 to lead NL in this respect; on two other occasions tied for lead in making errors. But in 1930 set modern big league record for outfielders by making 44 assists.

Klein had six grand slams during career that lasted through 1753 major league games. Had 2076 hits, with 398 doubles, 74 triples, 300 homers. Scored 1168 times, drove in 1201 runs. Lifetime average of .320, with 79 stolen bases. Only WS, 1935, with Cubs. Hit .333, 4 for 12. In fifth game of set had homer and single, with two RBI, enabling Bill Lee to defeat Schoolboy Rowe by 3–1 score. Tigers, however, won Series, four games to two.

KLEM, WILLIAM JOSEPH (Old Arbitrator) Umpire. B. 2/22/74, Rochester, N.Y. D. 9/1/51, Miami, Fla. 5'7½", 157. Bill Klem believed he was as close to being an infallible umpire as any human could be. Not so strangely, many close critics of baseball shared this view. Undoubtedly he was one of, if not the, best of all time. Once, in an interview, Klem responded to question, "Did you ever make a mistake?" with reply, "No, I never made a mistake." When he said this, he pointed to his heart, indicating he had never deliberately called one wrong.

Bill knew all rules, backward and forward. Enjoyed respect and confidence of managers, players, everyone connected with game. However, John McGraw, manager of N.Y. Giants, carried on feud with Klem for long time. McGraw often tried to intimidate opponents and umpires, but got nowhere with Klem, who called them as he saw them. In 1928, when McGraw had been particularly abusive in impugning Klem's ability, Bill resigned from NL staff, fearing NL president John Heydler was going to kowtow to McGraw. Klem, however, was vindicated after some weeks and returned to game before next season opened.

Klem was famous for drawing line in dirt with his spiked shoe. Told arguing players, managers, and coaches if they stepped past line, they were out of game. Often, after drawing line, Klem would move away, putting considerable distance between self and frustrated dissenter.

Bill could dish out expletives on occasion, as Goose Goslin once found out after WS game. But generally, if he really wanted to set down someone who questioned his rulings, about worst thing he would say was, "Sir, you are an applehead!" On other hand, it would be brave person who would ever call Klem by most hated nickname, "Catfish," at least at close distance.

Klem wanted to be ball player; was first baseman and catcher, but arm trouble kept him out of pro ball. Was steel worker at Berwick, Pa., playing some semipro ball on side when pressed into service as umpire. Did first umpiring in pro ball in Connecticut State League, late in 1902. New York State League, 1903; American Association, 1904. Harry Pulliam, then NL president, got Klem to umpire postseason series between Pittsburgh and Cleveland, and following year, 1905, Klem began long NL career. Was plate umpire exclusively 16 years. At start, was just one umpire, but when league began using two, Klem was such fine ball-and-strike umpire that continued to call them behind plate. Continued umpiring until retirement, 1941, then held job of chief of NL umpiring staff until death. Umpired in 18 WS, more than any other arbiter. Was one of umps who officiated in games played around world when Giants and White Sox made famous tour, 1913–14.

Klem crusaded for better treatment, better dressing rooms for umpires, contending they were important part of game. Initiated NL practice that plate umpire stand slightly to side of catcher so as to better judge balls and strikes.

Once came from retirement to umpire exhibition game between Yankees and Brooklyn Dodgers; was congratulated warmly on performance. Klem laughed, "You know I'm blind in one eye and have cataracts on other. But I wanted to show these young punks that umpiring is not just matter of eyesight, but of instinct."

Klem had special protege late in career—Al Barlick, who became fine umpire. Bill, with Tommy Connolly of AL, selected for Hall of Fame by Committee on Veterans, 1953—first umpires to gain honor.

KLING, JOHN GRADWOHL (Noisy) C-BR-TR. B. 11/13/75, Kansas City, Mo. D. 1/31/47, Kansas City, Mo. 5'9½", 160. Johnny Kling was one of great catchers during early part of this century. Gained fame with Chicago Cubs, though managed Boston Braves, 1912. In 1233 major league games hit .271, but twice had marks above .300. Once was in 1906, when Cubs won pennant, only to lose WS to "Hitless Wonders" White Sox. Other time was in 1912, when bossing Braves and club finished in NL cellar.

Oldtimers said Kling was "born knowing baseball." Started as pitcher for team in Kansas City known as "Schmeltzers." Though only 18 years of age, 1893, was manager, pitcher, and first baseman in spare moments. In 1895 went to Rockford, Ill., club but was quickly released. Back to Schmeltzers. Briefly with Houston, Tex., club, then signed with St. Joseph, Mo. There was discovered by Ted Sullivan, scout for Cubs. Remained with Chicago from 1900 through part of 1911, except for 1909 when held out for entire season.

In this period Cubs won NL flags, 1906,07,08,10, Kling doing most of catching. While Johnny was fine catcher with great arm, he holds record for allowing most passed balls in WS play—five. But also holds another WS record, with several other receivers: made four assists in one game 10/9/07 as Cubs defeated Detroit Tigers, 3–1. Kling led NL catchers in fielding average, 1902–05.

During 1911 season Kling was shifted to Boston NL; became manager following year. Club won 52 games, lost 101, finishing six games out of seventh place. Johnny's final season in majors was 1913, with Cincinnati. In four WS, Kling played 21 games, hit just .185.

Kling successful business man after playing days. Ran billiard hall, had two Kansas City hotels and dairy farm. Bought Kansas City club, American Association, 1934; sold it to Yankees, 1937.

KLUSZEWSKI, THEODORE BERNARD (Klu) 1B-BL-TL. B. 9/10/24, Argo, Ill. 6'2", 250. Ted Kluszewski might never have entered professional baseball but for Cincinnati groundkeeper, Lennie Schwab, seeing him use rake and hoe. That was in 1945 when ball clubs had spring training in north, due to wartime travel restrictions. Schwab needed strong backs to help get playing field in shape at Bloomington, Indiana. Klu, then student at Indiana U.; was one of those who showed up. This

lcd directly to signing with Cincinnati organization. Up to time he signed with Reds, Kluszewski had concentrated on football and softball. Used to catch softball with left hand, throwing hand. So when he tried to catch ball in mitt on right hand, he had plenty of problems. But he could hit. Led Sally League in first season, with .352 average at Columbia, S.C., 1946. Drove in 87 runs in 90 games. Nine games with Reds, 1947, and 115 with Memphis. Another bat title, this time .377 to top Southern Association. Had 68 RBI, but only 7 homers; 9 triples, 32 doubles.

Took plenty of hard work, study, concentration for Klu to improve first-basing; and though had great power, learned to use it to maximum only after exhaustive study of movies taken while batting. Paid off, however. After first full season with Reds, 1948, Klu hit above .300 seven times; hit 25 homers, 1950; 40 in 1953; 49 in 1954; and 47 in 1955. Led NL in homers, 1954. Five seasons with more than 100 RBI; his 141 led league, 1954. In fielding, led NL first sackers five consecutive seasons 1951–55.

Hit three homers in one game, 7/1/56. Klu had 35 homers, 1956, but suffered from slipped disc that affected his power from then on. Six homers in 1957 in 69 games. Then traded to Pittsburgh for 1958. After 60 games with Pirates, 1959, traded to Chicago White Sox 8/25. Klu helped Sox win AL pennant with .297 average in 31 games, then starred in his only WS. Drove in 10 runs, setting record for six-game Series. Hit three homers, had .391 batting average, but despite this, White Sox lost to Los Angeles Dodgers. One more season with Chicago AL, 1960, then selected in expansion draft by Los Angeles AL, 12/14/60. Played 107 games for Angels, 1961, then gave up game for his restaurant in Cincinnati and baseball school at Bainbridge, Ohio, 100 miles from Cincinnati.

Ted became Cincinnati minor league hitting instructor, 1969, coach for Reds, 1970.

Klu played in All-Star games of 1953–56 and hit .500, with seven hits in 14 trips. Lifetime major league record shows 1718 games, 1766 hits, with 290 doubles, 29 triples, 279 home runs. Hit .270 in AL games and .301 in NL, giving overall mark of .298. Scored 848 times in big leagues, drove in 1028 runs.

KNOOP, ROBERT FRANK   2B-BR-TR. B. 10/18/38, Sioux City, Iowa. 6'1", 180. Brilliant fielder, especially at second base, where led AL in fielding average, 1966. Led three times in assists; tied or set various records for double plays. Also led AL keystoners in errors, four times. At end of 1972 season had played in 1153 major league games with Angels of Los Angeles and California; with Chicago White Sox and 1971–72 with Kansas City Royals. Utility role with K.C. No great slugger, as .236 batting average shows, but had 56 homers.

Knoop spent 1956–63 gaining experience at Leesburg, Fla.; Lawton, Okla.; Cedar Rapids, Iowa; Austin, Louisville, Toronto, Hawaii, Vancouver, and San Diego while that city was still in Pacific Coast League. Played 162 games with Los Angeles Angels, 1964; moved with club to Anaheim following year when name changed to California Angels. Traded to Chicago AL 5/14/69; sold to Kansas City AL 3/24/71. Bobby was in Milwaukee Braves' organization at Hawaii when Angels drafted him. Best season with bat in majors was 1969 when hit .283 with 67 RBI. But best year for driving runs across was 1966 when he sent home 72 markers but hit only .232. *Sporting News* named Knoop as its second baseman on All-Star fielding teams, 1966–68.

KNOWLES, DAROLD DUANE P-BL-TL. B. 12/9/41, Brunswick, Mo. 6', 190. Darold Knowles knocked self out of AL playoffs and 1972 WS by falling down late in season, fracturing left thumb. Was running to first base after hitting fly ball to outfield. But by this time had made fine contribution to Oakland A's drive to AL pennant. Saved 11 games as fireman, won five others in relief, suffered only one defeat. Chalked up 1.36 ERA for season, pitching 66 innings in 54 ball games.

Knowles attended U. of Missouri and signed with Baltimore Orioles' organization. Started at Aberdeen, S. D., 1961; promptly led Northern League in strikeouts with 183 while winning 11, losing five. With Elmira, Charlotte, and Stockton, 1962, most of year with last team. There captured twelve games, lost seven, and led California League in effectiveness with 2.29 ERA. At Elmira again, 1963, had 16–7 record. Rochester, 1964–65, winning 17, losing 13 over two-year span. Five games with Orioles, 1965, being charged with one defeat.

Orioles traded him to Philadelphia NL 12/6/65. Had 6–5 mark in 1966, then moved to Washington Senators in deal 11/30/66, remaining until 5/8/71. Best performance there was 1969 when won nine, lost two. Despite 2.04 ERA in 1970, Knowles could win only two while losing 14 for club that finished in ninth place.

Knowles went to Oakland A's early in 1971 in same deal that made Mike Epstein an ex-Senator; Charlie Finley sent big chunk of cash to swing transfer. Darold got off to bad start but pitched well second half of season. In last 32 appearances allowed eight runs; had ERA of 1.85; won five, lost none; saved five others. Made 13 consecutive appearances on mound without allowing a run; permitted just one homer in those last 32 appearances.

Major league statistics as he went into 1973 season showed 400 games, 36 wins, 36 losses; 606 innings pitched, with 178 earned runs; struck out 444 men and walked 268. Overall ERA 2.64. AL All-Star game squad 1969; pitched 2/3 inning without allowing run.

KOENECKE, LEONARD GEORGE OF-BL-TR B. 1/18/06, Baraboo,

Wis. D. 9/17/35 Toronto, Ontario. 5'11", 180. Len Koenecke represented $75,000 investment for N.Y. Giants in 1932. Brief career ended tragically after he played just 265 major league games. Len was railroad fireman before becoming pro ball player. Played for Escanaba, Mich.; Springfield, Ill.; Moline, Ill.; Quincy, Ill.; Jersey City, Indianapolis, Buffalo en route to majors.

In 42 games with Giants, 1932, hit .255 and was optioned out. Came back to NL with Dodgers, 1934, and had .320 mark for 123 games. Was moving along at .283 pace in 1935 in 100 games, but repeatedly incurred wrath of Mgr. Casey Stengel for breaking training rules. Stengel finally told him he was through with Dodgers, and he took commercial plane for Chicago. On plane he and companions began drinking heavily, talking loudly, argued with and shoved stewardess, and finally, when plane landed in Detroit, was put off. Koenecke then hired private small plane to take him to Buffalo, where had played previously. Drunk, he tried to take over controls of plane while in air. Plane started to plunge, rocked in air, and copilot grabbed nearest weapon to subdue him, fire extinguisher. Hit Koenecke in head, but he continued to struggle. Finally pilot grabbed fire extinguisher and clubbed him again. Toronto was nearest airport; when plane landed Koenecke was dead.

Major league record showed 265 games played, with .297 average. Had 274 hits, good for 49 doubles, 9 triples, 22 homers. Scored 155 runs, drove in 114, stole 11 bases.

KOENIG, MARK ANTONY   SS-BLR-TR. B. 7/19/02, San Francisco, Calif. 6', 180. Mark Koenig is remembered most often as member of New York Yankees in days when they were known as "Bombers." Member of same club as Babe Ruth, Lou Gehrig, Bob Meusel, Bill Dickey, other legendary players. Mark, however, is also remembered as being with Yankees' opposition in WS of 1932, when Yanks rode Chicago Cubs unmercifully because of their treatment of Koenig. Mark had been waived out of majors and sent to Pacific Coast League 4/24/32. In August of that year Cubs were battling Pittsburgh for NL flag. Woody English had started season at shortstop but was shifted to third base and Billy Jurges took over position. But club decided veteran Koenig could help down stretch. So Koenig was bought from San Francisco Missions, 8/5/32. Played most of remaining games. Hit .353 in 33 contests. Charlie Grimm had just taken over management of club from Rogers Hornsby. Cubs put on sensational drive to sew up pennant. Chicago players, in voting division of WS spoils, gave Koenig partial share of $2122.30. Yanks, headed by Babe Ruth, accused Cubs of being cheapskates in their treatment of man who helped tremendously in their winning pennant. Without Koenig, Cubs might never have got into WS. Constant jockeying certainly didn't help Cubs, but they probably didn't have much chance anyway against sizzling bats of Yanks who captured Series in four straight games.

Koenig played at Moose Jaw in Western Canada League, 1921, later with Jamestown (N. Dak.), Des Moines, and St. Paul. Yankees paid reported·$50,000 in cash and players for Mark during 1925 season. Took over regular shortstop job almost immediately. Traded to Detroit 5/30/30. Remained with Tigers through 1931; with Missions, PCL, for 89 games, 1932, until he went to Cubs. Cincinnati 1934. New York NL 1935–36.

Had .279 lifetime average for 1162 major league games. Hit .237 for his 20 WS games with Yanks, 1926–28; with Cubs, 1932; with Giants, 1936.

KONETCHY, EDWARD JOSEPH 1B-BR-TR. B. 9/3/85, La Crosse, Wis. D. 5/27/47, Fort Worth, Tex. 6'2½", 195. Ed Konetchy spent on entire day in room in old Planters Hotel, St. Louis, arguing with Roger Bresnahan about 1909 contract. Ed was Cardinal first baseman; Roger was Cardinal manager. No lawyers, no agents, no charges and counter-charges in press. When day ended, player and manager emerged, apparently satisfied. Waiters and chamber maids found so many empty beer bottles on bargaining table they wondered how Konetchy found space on it to sign contract.

Konetchy had a distinction in St. Louis. Was one of handful of players ever able to hit ball out of old Robison Field, park Cardinals used before move to old Sportsman's Park, which antedated present Busch Memorial Stadium. Also one of players who lasted all through famous 26-inning game in 1920. With Brooklyn Dodgers at time.

Ed played 2083 major league games, including 152 with Pittsburgh team in Federal League, 1915. Compiled .281 batting average with 2148 hits, 971 runs, 992 RBI. Extra-base blows included 344 doubles, 181 triples, 74 homers. Also stole 255 bases.

Ed started pro ball with home-town club, La Crosse, Wisconsin State League, 1905, and went to Cardinals during 1907 season. Became their regular first baseman immediately. By 1909 was hitting .286 with 80 RBI. Went over .300 first time in 1910, and later had three more .300 seasons. Best year for home run production was 11, in final season in majors, 1921. With Cardinals through 1913 campaign. Pittsburgh NL 1914. Pittsburgh, Federal League, 1915. Boston NL 1916–18. Brooklyn 1919–21. Philadelphia NL 1921. Played in Texas League after that, hitting flock of homers there. Managed Fort Worth club, 1925, winning pennant. Managed La Crosse team, 1940.

During World War II worked as· foreman in Fort Worth Convair plant. Died in sleep, age 61.

KONSTANTY, CASIMER JAMES (Jim) P-BR-TR. B. 3/3/17, Strykersville, N.Y. 6'1½", 195. Jim Konstanty, B.S. in physical education from Syracuse U., made science of relief pitching; did so well Philadelphia won NL pennant, 1950; he was MVP. That year took part in 74 league games and three WS contests. Won 16 games, lost seven, saved 22 others. Played vital role in 38 of Phillies' 91 victories. Had ERA of 2.66. Taking part in 74 games set new major league record for pitchers, up to that time; finishing 62 games also was new high. Former has been excelled; record for finishing most games has been equaled. That 1950 season was Konstanty's peak performance. Over 11 seasons in majors, won 66, lost 48, saved 74 games in relief. Pitched just 14 complete games. Had lifetime ERA of 3.46.

Jim, son of Polish immigrant, once lived largely on cabbage and potatoes. Attended college on half-scholarship. Lettered in baseball, basketball, football, soccer. Helped make ends meet by wiping dishes in girls' dorm. In summer worked as meat mixer in food plant. Pro career started, 1941, with Springfield, Eastern League. Three seasons with Syracuse, then brought up to Cincinnati Reds during 1944 campaign. Following season was in navy. Briefly with Boston NL, 1946, then joined Toronto. During all this period Konstanty did not have impressive record; no fast ball to speak of; curve wasn't much; did have slider and "change-up" or palm ball. Was about to give up baseball, but Eddie Sawyer, manager at Toronto, seeing ability to stand up late in game, urged him to persist. Sawyer moved to Phillies as manager, and during 1948 season Konstanty also joined same team, won one game, saved two others, and had 0.93 ERA for 9-2/3 innings. In 1949 won nine, lost five, saved seven. Then came banner season, 1950.

Jim's best season after that was 1953 when had 14 victories, 10 defeats, with five saves. Phils let him go to Yankees during 1954 season. Following year was 7–2, with 11 saves. Last year in majors divided between Yankees and St. Louis Cardinals.

After not starting single game during 1950 NL season, Sawyer started Konstanty in first game of WS against Yankees. Pitched brilliantly, but Phillies couldn't get any runs for him off Raschi, who held them to two singles. Yanks managed to get one run on double by Bob Brown, followed by two outfield flies, and took contest 1–0. Jim relieved in two later games. Yanks swept Series. Konstanty's WS ERA was 2.40 for 15 innings.

KOOSMAN, JERRY MARTIN P-BR-TL. B. 12/23/43, Appleton, Minn. 6'2", 208. Jerry Koosman's first two full seasons with New York Mets were brilliant. In 1968 had 19 victories, lost 12, with ERA of 2.08. *Sporting News* named him NL Rookie Pitcher of Year. Came back with 17–9 mark in 1969, year of "Miracle Mets." ERA that time was 2.28. Followed up with fine work in WS against Baltimore Orioles. In second game of classic pitched six hitless innings. Allowed one run in seventh on two hits. Mets led Orioles by 2–1 score in ninth. After two men were out, Jerry walked two men, and Manager Gil Hodges sent Ron Taylor to mound to get third and final out. In fifth game of set, Koosman needed no help; set down Orioles by 5–3 score, giving Mets world championship. Jerry's record was two WS victories, no defeats, with ERA of 2.04. Walked four, struck out nine. Had 12–7 record following season, then ran into arm trouble, 1971, and won six, lost 11. Jerry had most problems as starter in both 1971 and 1972. Latter season, as reliever, went to mound seven times, pitched 12-2/3 innings without allowing run, giving up just five hits. Walked three, struck out 11. Record for year, however, was 11 wins, 12 losses; four complete games, one shutout, and one save. At start of 1973 Koosman had ERA of 2.88 for 166 major league games.

Some of Jerry's early arm trouble started 4/29/69 when arm went dead. However, it came back strong and that was year he won 17.

Koosman came to attention of Mets through Shea Stadium usher, 1964. Jerry was in Texas and teammate wrote to father, usher for Mets. Pitched for Greenville in Western Carolina League and Williamsport, Eastern League, 1965; Auburn, N.Y.-Pa. League, 1966; Jacksonville, International League, and Mets, 1967. Then stuck with Mets. Pitched two innings of scoreless ball in All-Star games of 1968,69 for NL.

KOUFAX, SANFORD (Sandy) P-BR-TL. B. 12/30/35, Brooklyn, N. Y. 6'2", 198. Sandy Koufax wanted to be architect but instead became fabulous pitcher and landed in Hall of Fame, 1972. Didn't like baseball, preferred basketball, but became very capable baseball telecaster. One of weakest hitters in majors, but hit grand-slam homer for Los Angeles Dodgers, 1963. Modest, retiring fellow despite four no-hit games and numerous strikeout records. After that grand slammer, Sandy said, "When I got to second base I didn't know whether to continue or to stop and apologize to the pitcher!"

Sandy's basketball play in high school got him athletic scholarship at U. of Cincinnati. Since had played some baseball in Brooklyn, was persuaded to try for pitching staff in college. Did so well, Brooklyn Dodger scout gave $14,000 bonus plus $6000 salary to sign up. Dodgers also invested plenty of patience. Koufax could throw hard, but pitching involves technique besides getting ball over or near plate. Sandy had to learn all about pitching in majors, since never played in minors. Won just two games first year with Dodgers, 1955, and two more in second season. Record was 5–4 in third season, then club moved to Los Angeles. Broke even, 11–11, first year in L.A., then had 8–6 mark in 1959. Following season Sandy won eight—but lost 13.

During much of this period Koufax was trying to throw ball past hitters, but at cost in overall effectiveness. In first six years in majors, won 36, lost 40. However, in 1961 Sandy began to show results of experience. Won 18 games, lost 13, and improved effectiveness. Led league in strikeouts with 269 in 256 innings, and kept his control—walked just 96 men. In 1962 record was 14–7, and led NL pitchers in effectiveness with ERA of 2.54. Following season was 25–5, led NL in strikeouts with 306 and in effectiveness with ERA of 1.88. In 1964, 19–5; then 26–8. Finally, in 1966, 27–9. In final five years in majors Sandy led NL in effectiveness each season, saving best effort for last, ERA of 1.73. And in last two seasons led NL in innings pitched, and also in strikeouts.

Koufax's earning power had increased to point where he was reportedly making $135,000 annual salary. Chalked up no-hitters, 1962,63,64, then hurled best one, 9/9/65: perfect game against Chicago Cubs. Led NL in shutouts with seven in 1964, 11 in 1965, and tied for lead with five in 1966. Member of NL All-Star squads 1963,64,65,66. Winner of Cy Young Award, 1963,65,66. Most Valuable Player 1963. All these honors achieved with pain and difficulty. Sandy developed circulatory problems in pitching hand, 1962. Later, problem diagnosed as traumatic arthritis of left elbow. Often would have to keep arm packed in ice for half-hour after game. Doctors told him if he continued pitching might lose use of arm for life. So Sandy was finished before he was 31.

Koufax was with four Dodger pennant winners. Lost 1–0 decision to Chicago White Sox in 1959 WS and had 1.00 ERA for classic. In 1963 started first game against Yankees by striking out first five batters he faced. Struck out 10 more before game ended, and won by 5–2 score. Also captured final game by 2–1 score, giving Dodgers world title; merely struck out eight that time.

In 1965 Sandy lost first start against Minnesota Twins, but took next two starts by 7–0 and 2–0 scores; ERA for that series was 0.38. Lost his final WS game in 1966 when Baltimore Orioles ran roughshod over Dodgers, taking four straight. Koufax started second game and was loser by 6–0 score to Jim Palmer. Allowed just one earned run, however, in six innings pitched. Overall, Koufax took part in eight WS games, pitched 57 innings, won four, lost three, allowed 36 hits, six earned runs, fanned 61, walked 11, and had ERA of 0.95.

Major league totals came to 397 games pitched, 2325 innings, 1754 hits, 713 earned runs, 2396 strikeouts, 817 walks for 2.76 ERA. Won 165 games, lost 87.

In addition to above, Sandy had two games in which struck out 18 batters each—8/31/59 against San Francisco and 4/24/62 against Chicago Cubs. Set major league record for most games in which fanned 10 or more batsmen—97 times. Holds record for most strikeouts in two consecutive games: before first 18-strikeout game in 1959 had fanned 13 in previous appearance on mound.

Koufax signed 10-year contract with NBC-TV, 1966, but voluntarily severed connection with network before 1973 baseball season. Declared he never was comfortable being on television.

At 36, Sandy was youngest player yet chosen for Hall of Fame.

KRANEPOOL, EDWARD EMIL 1B-OF-BL-TL. B. 11/8/44, New York, N. Y. 6'3", 210. Steady Eddie Kranepool wasn't with New York Mets when they made NL debut in spring of 1962, but joined club later that year, played three games. So, in 1973 season, was only man on club who had been with Mets in all 12 years of their existence. Eddie left club briefly in 1970, seriously thought of retiring when was sent to Tidewater club of International League. But reconsidered, gave best in 47 games, and was back in big city 8/14.

Kranepool is generally quiet fellow, poised, handsome. When graduated from James Monroe High School in Bronx, June 1962, Mets dangled $80,000 bonus in front of him. That was Tuesday. Signed Wednesday. Had been captain of basketball team, and expected to be an outfielder. High school coach used to put water pail on its side at home plate. Gave Eddie nickel for every time throw from outfield went into bucket.

Mets sent him to Syracuse, Knoxville, and Auburn, N. Y., before calling him up to parent club late that same year. Farmed out to Buffalo for parts of 1963 and 1964, he played 86 games with Mets in 1963 and 119 in 1964. After that was with New York club five full seasons. In 1970 it looked like curtains for him, but during spell with Tidewater he hit .310. Hit just .170 for Mets in 43 games that year. In 1971 Eddie got into 122 contests, hit .280; slapped more homers than ever before, 14; drove in more runs than any previous season, 58. Then, in 1972, Kranepool hit .269 in 122 games. This brought major league totals to .252 for 1174 games, with 84 homers, 387 RBI; also had 145 doubles, 21 triples among 927 hits; scored 357 runs.

When Eddie got that big bonus, took first plane ride to join team in Los Angeles; soon bought first car; then moved mother from cramped Bronx apartment to comfortable home in White Plains, N.Y.

KRAUSSE, LEWIS BERNARD, JR. (Lew) P-BR-TR. B. 4/25/43, Media, Pa. 6', 186. Lew Krausse had spectacular record as high school athlete at Chester, Pa., starring in baseball, football, and basketball. Good enough that Charles O. Finley, top man for Kansas City AL at time, 1961, forked out $125,000 bonus to get signature on dotted line. Few days later, was sent to mound against Los Angeles Angels. After learning was to start big league game without ever having thrown ball in pro baseball, Lew never slept wink, nor did he eat. Youngster faced Albie Pearson, Angels' leadoff man, no bigger than last hitter he had faced in high school. First pitch was strike. Then proceeded to retire first nine men to face him. Kept Angels in check rest of way, winning three-hit shutout. In ninth inning Ted Kluszewski came up as pinch hitter. Dangerous man, especially on fast balls. After two strikes, catcher called for fast one. Ted went down swinging.

Including debut, won 64 AL games, lost 88, as of start of 1973. Had 2–5 record with Kansas City, 1961, then farmed out to Binghamton, Portland, Dallas, Vancouver. Briefly with Kansas City, 1964–65, then remained with team 1966, with 14–9 mark. That was best season for games won. Allowed 2.98 earned runs per nine-inning game. Spent 1968–69 with Oakland (Kansas City franchise was moved there). Milwaukee AL 1970–71. Boston AL 1972. Major league record, going into 1973: 291 games, 1216 innings pitched, 64 victories, 88 defeats; 693 strikeouts, 460 bases on balls; ERA of 4.00.

Lew's father pitched for Philadelphia Athletics 1931–32; was 5–1.

KREMER, REMY PETER (Wiz)   P-BR-TR. B. 3/23/93, Oakland, Calif. D. 2/8/65, Pinole, Calif. 6'1", 190. Wiz Kremer, who helped Pittsburgh Pirates win 1925 flag and then took two WS victories that fall, might have had much longer major league career but for two misfortunes. In 1915 had tryout with N.Y. Giants during spring training. Came up with inflammatory rheumatism in Marlin, Tex., and spent next two months on crutches. Back to West Coast, Kremer made good with Oakland club of Pacific Coast League within few years, but Oaks put fancy price on contract, which big league clubs refused to meet.

PCL in those years, like American Association and International League, refused to let players be subject to major league draft. Won 15 games for Oaks, 1919; 16 in 1921; 20 in 1922, and 25 in 1923. During this time undoubtedly could have helped several major league clubs. But only after 25–16 record in 1923 did big league team meet Oakland's price tag.

Kremer, skilled pitcher as rookie, won 18, lost ten for Pittsburgh in 1924. In 1925 mark was 17–8, helping Pirates to flag. In WS lost third game to Washington, 4–3; came back in sixth game and won it, 3–2; then, in seventh and final contest, was relief pitcher. Hurled last four innings and received credit for victory when Pirates came from behind to win, 9–7, defeating Walter Johnson. So 2–1, with 3.00 ERA that Series.

Wiz won 20, lost six in 1926 and led NL pitchers in winning percentage with .769. Also led NL hurlers in effectiveness with ERA of 2.61. Following year took 19 victories, dropped eight,; again was stingiest twirler in earned runs with 2.47. Continued fine pitching—15–13, 18–10, and 20–12 records in next three seasons. Lost touch after that: 11 wins in 1931 against 15 losses; 4–3 mark in 1932, and after working seven games in 1933, released unconditionally in July. Had ERA of 10.35 for 20 innings that season, though was credited with one victory and not charged with defeat.

Kremer's final major league totals were 143 wins, 85 defeats, with 3.76 ERA. Pitched in 308 games, 134 of them complete. In 1954 2/3 innings walked 483 and struck out 516. Had 14 shutouts. Besides fine work in 1925 WS, Kremer pitched five innings in 1927 classic against Yankees; was Pirates' starting pitcher in opening game. Yankees got two earned runs, three unearned markers off him. But even one of "earned runs" was tainted since Lou Gehrig hit pop fly that went for triple when Paul Waner tried for shoestring catch and missed. Kremer's overall WS record: 2–2, 3.12 ERA.

KUBEK, ANTHONY CHRISTOPHER (Tony) SS-OF-BL-TR. B. 10/12/36, Milwaukee, Wis. 6'3, 193. Tony Kubek, Curt Gowdy's partner on NBC "Game of Week" telecast, spent nine years with Yankees. Though called "color man," his comments and interviews are devoted mainly to baseball fundamentals; can discuss fine points of game many good fans overlook or never dreamed of. Doesn't try to be abrasive or humorous, but natural, objective. Though pro in most aspects of job, like other baseball announcers, has failed to learn pronunciation of Latin American players' names—while millions who know Spanish cringe in horror. Turned to broadcasting when bad back forced retirement from game after 1965 season.

Had three years of minor league experience with Owensboro; Quincy, Ill.; and Denver. Reported to Yankees, 1957, hit .297 in 127 games. *Sporting News* named him AL Rookie of Year.

Tony got two hits in second game of WS, 1957, in Yankee Stadium. Saved fireworks for opening game in Milwaukee, his birthplace. In debut before home folks, but in uniform of opposition, hit two home runs, got three hits, drove in four runs, paced Yanks to 12–3 victory. Braves, however, won Series 4–3. Tony hit .286 for classic.

Kubek played 1092 major league games, hit .266. Best year for average (.314) was 1962, but played only 45 games due to military duty. His 1109 career safeties included 178 doubles, 30 triples, 57 homers. Scored 522 runs, drove in 373; stole 29 bases. In six WS, Kubek played 37 games, had 35 hits in 146 trips. Had two doubles and those two homers, with 16 runs scored, 10 RBI. Overall WS average .240.

KUENN, HARVEY EDWARD Inf.-OF-BR-TR. B. 12/4/30, West Allis, Wis. 6'2", 200. If Harvey Kuenn makes Hall of Fame, election may have been delayed because was placed on active playing roster of Milwaukee Brewers late in 1971. Rules provide five years must elapse between man's retirement from active play and placement on ballot for possible selection for Cooperstown honors. Kuenn retired in 1966, but in September, 1971, general manager Frank Lane of Brewers put him on active roster in order to increase his ultimate retirement benefits. At age 65, Kuenn should be eligible for $765 monthly instead of $760, as result of being activated late in 1971. Kuenn, however, did not play. Took up role as coach in 1972 for Brewers. Before going on active playing list, 1971, had been hired as special batting instructor.

Kuenn will be successful if pupils emulate him. Owns .303 lifetime batting average for 1833 games. Batting champion for AL, 1959, with .353 mark for Detroit Tigers. Hit better than .300 in eight full major league seasons. Made 2092 hits, with 356 doubles, 56 triples, 87 homers. Scored 951 runs, drove in 671.

Harvey attended U. of Wisconsin and played sandlot ball in and around Milwaukee. Signed with Detroit, 1952, and had just 63 games of seasoning that year with Davenport, III League. Hit .340 and moved up to parent club that same year. Managed .325 average for 19 contests.

Those 19 games were not enough to disqualify for AL Rookie of Year honors, 1953, which he won by getting .308 average in 155 games. Led AL in hits with 209. Laughed at so-called sophomore jinx by having almost identical record, 1954—.306, with 201 hits in 155 games. Consistency was amazing, following year again batting .306. Then was even better, with .332 in 1956.

Up to this time Kuenn had been shortstop. Began playing other positions, and in 1958 was used exclusively in outfield. Thereafter was primarily outfielder but also appeared at all infield positions.

Although had won AL batting title, 1959, before next season started was wearing uniform of Cleveland Indians, traded for Rocky Colavito. One season with Indians, and then to San Francisco NL. Four full seasons with Giants, then traded to Chicago Cubs 5/29/65. Next transfer to Philadelphia NL 4/23/66, and after 89 games that year retired from play. Member of AL All-Star squads eight consecutive seasons, 1953–60. In his only WS, 1962, with San Francisco, hit .083, 1 for 12.

KUHN, BOWIE KENT Executive. B. 10/28/26, Takoma Park, Md. 6'5", 230. Baseball commissioner, elected February 1969. First given one-year contract at $100,000 annually, then, following August, given seven-year contract. Bass-voiced, big fellow whose oversize physique impresses some—but not particularly Charles O. Finley, among club owners, or Marvin Miller, director of Players' Association.

Reportedly descendant of Jim Bowie, credited inventor bowie knife. Attended Franklin and Marshall College, then Princeton U. where received A. B. degree, 1947; law degree from U. of Virginia, 1950. With various job opportunities open, Kuhn decided for law firm Willkie, Farr and Gallagher in New York, partly because one of clients was NL and Bowie liked baseball.

Starting about 1950, Kuhn played active role in baseball legislation. Then when General William Eckert was eased out of commissioner's job, club owners found difficulty in selecting successor. John McHale had considerable support for job but withdrew name to remain with Montreal Expos. When deadlock between Charles (Chub) Feeney and Mike Burke ensued, Kuhn's name came up as compromise candidate.

Since taking office Kuhn has made occasional headlines. One of first times was ruling in case of trade between Montreal and Houston clubs of NL involving Donn Clendenon. Latter refused to go to Houston. Bowie ruled he could remain on Montreal roster, but that other compensation would have to be made to Astros. Judge Hofheinz, president of Houston, publicly criticized Kuhn. Commissioner demanded and got public apology from Hofheinz.

Kuhn involved in Ken Harrelson deal between Boston Red Sox and Cleveland Indians. When Ken threatened to retire, Bowie intervened, persuaded him to report to Indians. Kuhn worked hard but unsuccessfully to prevent players' strike in spring of 1972; criticized by Marvin Miller, although same Miller in early 1969 had praised Kuhn for "constructive role" in negotiation of new contract between players and owners that upped pension benefits.

Finley, president of Oakland A's, has been credited with sponsoring idea of having WS games played during week at nighttime so TV audience could be greatly augmented. Kuhn also has been credited for this innovation. However, after Kuhn entered salary dispute between Finley and Vida Blue in spring of 1972, Oakland owner criticized commissioner, and Bowie slapped $500 fine on him. Kuhn later fined Finley for circumventing rules when latter gave new contracts to some Oakland players for their work in AL playoffs and WS.

Kuhn loves classical music, opera; plays it in office during working hours. Also devotee of golf, gardening, chess, and football on TV.

LABINE, CLEMENT WALTER P-BR-TR. B. 8/6/26, Lincoln, R.I. 6'1/2", 195. Anybody who could stop Stan Musial from hitting safely 49 times in row should be included in this book. However, same person, now general manager of textile factory in Rhode Island that specializes in sports jackets, reports he never could get Hank Aaron out. Rhode Islander in question is Clem Labine, winner of 70 games for Brooklyn and Los Angeles Dodgers, as well as two WS decisions.

Perhaps Clem's finest hour came during 1956 WS. Eight times previously had been used in WS games in relief, with record of one victory, two defeats, and two saves. Then was called upon as starter in sixth game against New York Yankees. Dodgers had to win to stay in Series, as Yanks already had three games to Brooklyn two. Labine hooked up in pitching duel with Bob Turley. After nine innings neither man had allowed score. Clem then blanked Yankees in 10th. In last half of that frame, walk, sacrifice, and Jackie Robinson's single gave Dodgers 1–0 victory and brought them even with Yanks in Series. Unfortunately for Flatbush crew, Yankees won next day and took another world championship. Having pitched two innings earlier in series in relief, Labine had ERA of 0.00 for Series. Overall record in five WS shows two wins, two losses with ERA of 3.16. All his appearances were in relief except the 10-inning shutout over Yanks. Besides 1956 WS, Clem got into classics of 1953 and 1955 with Brooklyn; 1959 with Los Angeles NL, and 1960 with Pittsburgh.

Labine started out, 1944, with Newport News, Piedmont League, then spent two years in military service. After World War II, saw service with Greenville in South Atlantic League, Asheville, Pueblo, and St. Paul. On Brooklyn roster for first time, 1950, but had more trips to minors before staying with Dodgers for first full season, 1953. Won greatest number of games in any season in 1955, 13. Saved 11 others and lost five. Had ERA of 3.25.

Gypsy in 1960, serving with Dodgers, Detroit, Pittsburgh. Put in full season with Pirates, 1961, then landed with N.Y. Mets, 1962. After three games drew release.

Career totals show 77 wins, 56 losses, with ERA of 3.63. Saved 96 games in relief. Since was used primarily as relief hurler, threw only seven complete games in majors besides that 10-inning WS shutout over Yankees. Walked 396 men, fanned 551 in 1079-2/3 innings.

LAJOIE, NAPOLEON (Larry) 2B-BR-TR. B. 9/5/75, Woonsocket, R.I. D. 2/7/59, Daytona Beach, Fla. 6'1", 195. When Hall of Fame was started, Ty Cobb, Babe Ruth, Christy Mathewson, Honus Wagner, and Walter Johnson were first immortals selected to grace its edifice, 1936. One year later, Larry Lajoie entered select group of those so honored. Argument could be made he should have been among very first chosen. Lajoie hit for higher batting average in 1901 than Cobb, Ruth, George Sisler, Ted Williams, or any other American Leaguer ever did—.422. Compiled .339 lifetime average in 2475 major league games. Member of 3000-hit club—with plenty to spare; he had 3251. Won five major and minor league batting titles; six times led league in fielding at second base.

Statistics, however, do not tell whole story. Eyewitnesses, most of them now gone, have said Lajoie played second base with rare grace and unbelievable skill. Among more recent keystoners, Charlie Gehringer came closest in smoothness, according to those who saw both men play. Larry's principal rival in AL was Ty Cobb, man of completely different temperament and background. Lajoie generally was considered on lethargic side, quiet, retiring. Fiery Cobb was cantankerous, constantly irritating, belligerent, full of nervous energy as caged tiger. Lajoie won three AL batting championships before Cobb came into league, in 1901,03,04. Ty also outhit Larry over whole career, .367 to .339. But Cobb's best effort in any one season was .420, two points less than Lajoie's peak.

Born of French-Canadian parents, Lajoie worked in cotton mills of New England, drove hack for livery stable, and played baseball in spare time. Was driving hack at $7.50 a week when manager of Fall River club, who had heard about "Frenchy," offered him $100 a month to play. Contract was scribbled on back of envelope. Lajoie signed quickly, reported for duty, and hit .429 to lead New England League. Played outfield, took part in 80 games. Then comes strange part of story. Scout for Philadelphia NL took fancy to another Fall River outfielder, Phil Geier, and offered Fall River club $1500 for him. For unexplained reason, manager of Fall River offered to throw in Lajoie's contract— possibly because needed cash and didn't want Philly scout to change mind. Both outfielders went to Philadelphia that same season, 1896; rest is history. Any claim to fame by Geier is his link with Lajoie. Geier hit .232 with Phils that year in 17 games while Larry played 39 games and hit .328. Geier hung on few years in majors and dropped out of sight after 342 games and .252 batting average. Lajoie went on to Cooperstown after long illustrious career. In first full season in NL, as first baseman and outfielder, Lajoie hit .363 in 126 games, led league in homers with 10. Up to .380 in 1899; .422 in 1901, his first with Philadelphia Athletics. That year he also led AL in runs, hits, doubles, homers (13), putouts at second base, and in fielding. His next AL batting titles were won with .355 in 1903 and .381 in 1904. In 1910–12 came up with .384, .365, .368 respectively.

Dropped to minors in 1917; was pushing age 42 when he added an International League batting championship to trophies—.380 in 151 games.

They didn't play Sunday ball in Cleveland in early part of 20th century. So Larry has odd record of striking out only six times in 1902— but turned this trick in five different cities! Cleveland club played some regularly scheduled AL games in Dayton and Canton, Ohio. Larry struck out once in Dayton, once in Canton, twice at Detroit, once at Boston, and just once in Cleveland.

Larry had plenty of red letter days. One came 10/9/10 when had seven singles, one double in eight at bats during doubleheader. Hit four home runs in two consecutive games 8/9/01. That eight-for-eight performance, however, did not smell right. In those days Chalmers automobile company offered one of fancy cars as prize for player winning batting championship. Cobb by this time had acquired enemies everywhere because of his rugged individualistic play. Lajoie, on other hand, was popular among teammates and men on opposing clubs. Practically all players were rooting for Larry to win automobile instead of Cobb. Ty, enjoying fairly comfortable lead over Larry as end of season approached, sat out last two games, protecting his margin. Larry, in that final twin bill, played in St. Louis, bunted safely six times that afternoon! Each time, Red Corriden, rookie third baseman, played back, apparently on orders from manager, Jack O'Connor. Ban Johnson, then czar of AL, dug into matter. Upshot was that O'Connor was fired, never to return to AL. And Harry Howell, pitcher for St. Louis Browns, who apparently had some special interest in batting race, also was out— seemingly on orders from Johnson. Cobb won title by fraction of point,

.3848 to .3841. Chalmers people decided to give both players automobiles.

Lajoie's departure from NL came after close of 1900 season when he was drawing $2400 annually, salary limit imposed by league. Jumped to Philadelphia Athletics. After .422 season with A's, 1901, court injunction barred him from playing in 1902. Connie Mack, manager of Athletics, then let him go to Cleveland, away from jurisdiction of Pa. courts. For time, whenever Cleveland club was due to perform in Philadelphia, Larry had few days off. Dispute ended with NL recognition of AL.

Playing manager, Cleveland, 1905 until midseason 1909. During this period, and even after Larry returned to ranks as player only, team was known as "Naps," since he was kingpin of club. Led team to second place in 1908, losing to Detroit Tigers by half-game. Playing manager at Toronto, 1917, and for Indianapolis, American Association, 1918, after which retired. Salesman for rubber company, then took it easy in Florida until his death.

Though Lajoie hit for high average, ball was dead, and 13 was his high water mark in homers, 1901, when this figure led AL. Altogether had 82 round-trippers, 162 triples, 650 doubles, and scored 1503 runs. Drove in many teammates, though this statistic was not kept officially when he performed on diamond. Stole 396 bases, never dropping below 10 in any full year in majors.

LANDIS, KENESAW MOUNTAIN Executive. B. 11/20/66, Millville, Ohio. D. 11/25/44, Chicago, Ill. Czar of baseball, 1920 until death. Judge Landis, aided by Babe Ruth, "return to normalcy" after World War I, and other factors, "saved baseball" after "Black Sox" scandal. Most Americans believed in Landis' integrity, felt kept game clean and honest. Blacklisted several ball players for wrongdoing. Fined club owners for breaking rules. Freed numerous players, acting as modern emancipator. Grabbed headlines without press conferences.

Landis, appointed U.S. district judge by President Teddy Roosevelt, 1905, first attracted nationwide attention by fining Standard Oil Company $29,240,000 in freight-rebate case. But fine didn't stick—U.S. Supreme Court got appeal, and Standard Oil paid nothing.

Few years later "outlaw" Federal League charged NL and AL with conspiracy, monopoly, and violation of antitrust laws. Landis, baseball fan, took case under advisement, kept it under advisement so long it became academic—Federal League collapsed, made peace with majors. Landis never rendered judgment.

When "Black Sox" revelations became public, 1920, gloom bordering on panic prevailed in baseball circles. Club owners sought Landis, urged him to restore confidence of American people. Landis dictated terms of contract that gave sweeping power over just about everything in baseball. If he alone decided something or someone was "detrimental to baseball," there would be no court of appeal. New czar then barred eight players from Chicago White Sox "forever." Though there probably were degrees of guilt in men involved, Landis treated all eight in identical fashion. Nevertheless, was great variation in approach to several other cases of admitted or alleged dishonesty. Men like Rube Benton, Jean Dubuc, Hal Chase, and Charles Comiskey, who seemingly had "guilty knowledge" of 1919 dealings with gamblers, were left untouched.

After 1921 WS, Babe Ruth, Bob Meusel, and Bill Piercy of Yankees went on barnstorming trip in violation of then rule. Landis suspended players until May 20, 1922, fined them their WS shares. Once more Judge grabbed headlines, slapping down most famous player in game. But, once again, fines didn't stick, though suspensions did.

Landis barred N.Y. Giants' rookie Jimmy O'Connell and coach Cozy Dolan, for involvement in bribe offer to Philadelphia Phillies to throw ball game to New Yorkers. Another member of Giants, Phil Douglas, also was evicted from baseball when he offered to "go fishing" so St. Louis Cardinals might take advantage of situation.

Saintly Connie Mack even got fined $500 for illegal transfer of player's contract. But Landis' hand came down most heavily on St. Louis Cardinals and Detroit Tigers. Landis freed scores of young players in both farm systems, gaining reputation as "Great Emancipator." Yet, in somewhat similar situation, allowed Cleveland club to keep Bobby Feller, even though he ruled Indians were guilty of breaking regulations; ordered them to pay Des Moines club of Western League $7500 damages.

Another widely criticized decision of Landis came during 1934 WS. St. Louis Cardinals and Detroit Tigers were in seventh and final game of autumn classic. With Dizzy Dean pitching in top form, Cardinals were romping over Tigers to tune of 7–0 when sixth inning rolled around. Joe Medwick of Cardinals went into third base on close play, colliding with Detroit third baseman, Marvin Owen. Medwick accused Owen of roughing him up, while Owen felt Cardinal outfielder slid into bag unnecessarily, banging into him. Argument ensued, but umpires did not see reason to eject either player. Cardinals chalked up two more runs that same inning, making score 9–0. When Medwick returned to post in left field, frustration of bleacher bugs was so intense they showered Joe with fruits, vegetables, debris of all kinds. Long delay followed, while umpires and players appealed to fans to stop, since play could not continue in circumstances. When all appeals were unavailing, Landis called brief conference at his box seat, then ordered Medwick off field. Only then did bleacher fans stop rain of refuse. Cardinal manager Frankie Frisch and Medwick protested vainly. Landis was roundly criticized for bowing to violence of Detroit fans; others felt if Medwick were ejected, Owen also should have been put out. Landis later indicated had ordered Medwick off field "for his own safety." Some observers felt if Detroit management could not properly police fans, game should have been forfeited to Cardinals. In any case, with Dizzy in rare form, Tigers had no chance of winning. Final score St. Louis 11, Detroit 0.

Any time magnates showed sign of revolt against Landis' decisions, Judge would offer to tear up contract and resign. This brought them all into line. Famous for soft fedora hat, inscrutable frown as he sat in box seats at ball games, resting chin on hands, never smiling, never talking for publication. Before he died, Judge requested there be no funeral ceremonies of any kind, no viewing of remains. Hall of Fame 1944, less than month after his death.

LANE, FRANK C. (Frantic Frankie) Executive. B. 2/1/96, Cincinnati, Ohio. Often described as "man in motion—perpetual motion." General manager for various teams, among them Cleveland Indians, St. Louis Cardinals, and Chicago White Sox; connected with Baltimore Orioles, Kansas City A's, and Milwaukee Brewers; former president of American Association; worked for Cincinnati and New York Yankee organizations; has jolted hundreds of players with his trades. First major league executive to enlist in armed services after Pearl Harbor; hired and fired numerous times; involved in arguments by dozens; has been paid for not working, during which time gravitated toward Acapulco, Mexico.

Frank had been president of semipro baseball league in Ohio and had officiated in football and basketball games when Larry MacPhail arrived in Cincinnati, 1934, to take over general management of Reds. Lane had played 50 games for Marion, Ohio, ball club in 1913, when that team had Warren G. Harding as one of its backers. So MacPhail put Lane on his payroll as "business manager." Lane later became business manager of Reds' Durham club in Piedmont League, then became an assistant to Warren C. Giles, who had succeeded MacPhail at Cincinnati.

During World War II Lane was commander in navy. After leaving service gravitated to Larry MacPhail, who had become one of owners of New York Yankees. Frankie bossed front office for Kansas City farm team, was in charge of Yankee minor league clubs in western part of country. Next stop was presidency of American Association for couple of years. Then seven years with White Sox as general manager.

In October 1955 Gussie Busch hired him as general manager of Cardinals. After 1957 season it was on to Cleveland in similar job. While there made his mark by trading managers—Jimmie Dykes to Cleveland in exchange for Joe Gordon, who had been managing Indians and would now manage Detroit Tigers. Unprecedented in majors to trade managers. But the trade that sent Rocky Colavito to Detroit in exchange for

Harvey Kuenn really aroused ire of Cleveland fans; Lane hanged in effigy for that. Frankie's stay in Cleveland wasn't too long either.

Charles O. Finley hired Lane to be business manager of Kansas City A's, 1961. Lane lasted just eight months. He got something like $113,000 in court settlement of long-term contract when he left. Before long Lane caught on with Baltimore Orioles as a sort of "superscout." Then became vice president and director of baseball operations for Milwaukee AL club after it moved franchise to Wisconsin from Seattle. Finally, at end of 1972 season, Lane was shifted again to job as sort of "superscout" for Brewers, turing over title as "director of baseball operations" to Jim Wilson, but still retaining title as vice president.

LANGE, WILLIAM ALEXANDER (Little Eva) OF-BR-TR. B. 6/6/71, San Francisco, Calif. D. 7/23/50, San Francisco, Calif. 6'3", 215. If Clark Griffith and Connie Mack had lived longer, Bill Lange might very well be in Hall of Fame. Never heard of him? Well, Bill was one of finest outfielders who ever lived, possibly greatest, according to plenty of competent testimony. Played for Chicago NL before turn of present century. Had seven fine seasons in majors, batting well over .300 in six of them, and .288 in first year up. Stole 399 bases, averaging 57 for his seven years. Since rules covering entry of black players into Hall of Fame have been adjusted in recent years, case could be made to consider adjusting regulation requiring that other players have at least 10 major league seasons before meeting Hall standards.

Griffith and Mack probably would have attested to Lange's credentials if they had thought Hall of Fame rules would become somewhat flexible. Not long before he died, Griffith, president of Washington Senators and teammate of Lange in 1890s, declared, "Bill Lange was greatest outfielder I ever saw." Honus Wagner, Connie Mack, and other contemporaries sang praises. Frank Chance said, "Bill Lange's equal as center fielder never lived. Lange could field as good as Tris Speaker, run bases as good as Cobb, and only once failed to hit .300." Chance said that Lange, righthanded batsman, usually hit to right field, and opposing team shifted infield and outfield accordingly. But despite this, said Chance, "they couldn't stop him from getting his hits."

Lange's base-stealing record compares favorably with any of Cobb's best seven consecutive seasons. From 1906 to 1912 inclusive, Ty's first full seven years, Georgia Peach stole 396 bases compared to Lange's 399 thefts over seven-year major league career. Ty, in seven years from 1910 to 1916 inclusive, stole 460 bases, average of slightly over 65 per season. Better than Lange's average of 57, but Bill's mark is still pretty impressive.

Honus Wagner told about first time he tried to put ball on Lange. Honus was playing shortstop when Bill essayed steal. "Pulled prettiest hook-slide you ever saw," said Wagner, "and there I was, standing sort of foolish-like, with ball, nowhere near him."

Lange played for keeps. Was big indestructible fellow who asked no quarter, gave none. "I was never out until I was called out," said Lange late in life. "In those days when there was only one umpire we could get away with more than players could when two or more umpires were officiating. If there was a play at second base on me, the single umpire would run over to call the decision. After calling me safe, he'd turn and walk away, in direction of pitcher's box. "The instant the umpire turned his head, I would sometimes knock ball out of hands of shortstop or second baseman. The umpire wouldn't see it. As soon as ball was rolling on ground, I'd set sail for third base, and many times I made it."

W. A. (Bill) Phelon, one-time Cincinnati sports writer whose opinions were widely respected, said at height of Cobb's career: "Despite all the praise they lavish on the Georgian today, I cannot see where gigantic Lange was inferior. . . . Lange had no foul strikes to handicap him, but in his day, a caught foul tip was an immediate out. Then too, he faced great pitchers, who during at least part of his career, worked from shorter distance, and there were no 'sacrifice flies' in score to help his average. I distinctly remember many of Cobb's tricks as exact duplicates of Lange's tricks, forgotten when Bill left game, and revived long afterward by Georgian."

Lange was blithe spirit until day he died. In 1895 Bill missed train in Boston; Mgr. Cap Anson fined him $100. Two days later missed another train, this time being able to get to ball park in Washington just before game time. Because he missed practice, Anson fined him another $100 but put him in center field. Game went 11 innings, Chicago scoring one run in top half of inning. With one man on base and Kip Selbach at bat in Washington half of 11th, Selbach drove terrific blow far over Lange's head toward fence. Looked like certain home run. Lange sprinted desperately away from plate. At last instant he leaped, stuck up both hands, turned somersault, and crashed into fence. Boards splintered. Out of wreckage came lange, holding ball in his hand. Limping back to bench, Bill said to Anson: "Fines go, Cap?" "Nope," replied Anson. Hugh S. Fullerton, another old-time baseball scribe, an eyewitness, declared Lange's catch was "greatest running catch ever made."

Bill started as catcher, played semipro ball, then in 1892 joined Seattle team. In midseason graduated to Oakland club of California League, ancestor of Pacific Coast League. Joined Chicago NL 1893 and was utility man until midseason. Jimmy Ryan, regular center fielder, was hurt in railroad accident; from that day Bill had regular job in center field until retired.

In 1896 Chicago fans voted him most popular player in Windy City. Polled 26,000—nearest competitor had only 4700. Late in 1890s Lange met young lady destined to become his wife. Desire to spend most of time at home with bride, plus offer of an excellent setup in real estate business prompted Bill to retire from active play. Said farewell at end of 1899 season and later turned down repeated offers of more pay to play major league ball again.

Back in beloved San Francisco, Bill became popular man about town, once being considered best-dressed man in Bay Area. Society-minded management of swank St. Francis Hotel offered him suite free at his disposal at all times. Lange attracted attention not only as famous ex-ball player, but as smooth dancer of current steps such as tango, bunny-hug, and others. Was uncle of George Lange Kelly, strong-armed first baseman for N.Y. Giants in 1920s, who later played with Cincinnati Reds and then coached for Reds when Charlie Dressen managed there.

Lange played 808 major league games, hit .336. Had 1055 hits with 133 doubles, 79 triples, 41 homers. Scored 690 runs, drove in 579.

LANIER, HAROLD CLIFTON Inf.-BLR-TR. B. 7/4/42, Denton, N.C. 6'2", 186. Hal Lanier, son of former major league pitcher Max Lanier, used to don New York Giants' uniform when 10 years old and take mild workouts. Few years later, after displaying fine pitching and hitting ability, as well as basketball skills, as high school athlete, big league scouts and representatives of 15 colleges besieged him and his father with offers. Father was out of baseball at time, wanted to renew his connections. So, when Hal, minor, and Max, father, signed contract, Laniers banked $50,000 bonus money and Max got three-year contract as scout for Giants. That was 1961, after Giants had moved to San Francisco.

Hal got minor league experience at Quincy, Ill.; Fresno, Calif.; Springfield, Mass.; Tacoma, Wash. Joined Giants during 1964 season. But when he became pro, was shifted to infield. Came to majors as second baseman but later moved to shortstop as Giants' regular there for five seasons. When Chris Speier came along in 1971, Lanier had to be content with utility role.

Originally righthanded hitter, Lanier became switch hitter 1968. Best average in majors was .274 for 98 games in 1964, year he joined Giants. Traded to New York Yankees 2/2/72 and played 60 games, hitting .214. All of which brought Hal's lifetime major league record to .228 for 1161 games. His 825 hits included eight homers, 20 triples, 108 doubles.

Hal wears small necklace and medal on which is marked "epilepsy." Has had three seizures since entering pro ball. Medication usually keeps it in check. However, Hal reports each seizure came while taking showers after switching from hot to cold water. Has received considerable publicity because of this; wishes to convince others that epilepsy can be kept under control; and that those who have it may take part in strenuous athletics.

LANIER, HUBERT MAX P-BR-TL. B. 8/18/15, Denton, N.C. 5'11",
180. Max Lanier originally was righthanded thrower. At age eight, broke
right arm and began to use left; went on to become major league
southpaw who won total of 108 games, lost 82; also captured two WS
decisions while losing one. Career was interrupted by suspension
1946–49 because he jumped to Mexican baseball, then considered
"outlaw." In 1944 Lanier was working on $10,500 salary for St. Louis
Cardinals. Won 17 games, lost 12, had 2.65 ERA. Followed with victory
over St. Louis Browns in WS that clinched world championship for
Cards. Sam Breadon, Cardinal owner, offered Lanier same salary for
1945. After some wrangling, Max finally got $500 raise. Went into
military service shortly after having 2–2 record, 1945. Returned to club,
1946, and won first six starts, with 1.93 ERA. Then Pasquel brothers
offered him large bonus and five-year contract at $30,000 per year. Max
went to Mexico. About year and half later Pasquel reneged on pledges
to Lanier, but Max found doors of organized baseball closed to him, to
Mickey Owen, and to other American players who had accepted
Mexican offers. Max played some semipro ball. He and Fred Martin,
another jumper, sued organized baseball for $2-1/2 million. Case finally
settled out of court and Lanier returned to baseball, suspension lifted,
1949.

Lanier, standout athlete as youth, turned down athletic scholarship at
Duke U. to sign with Cardinal organization. Then refused to go to low
minors after tryout; played semipro ball couple of summers. Finally
reported to Cardinal farm club at Columbus, Ohio, 1937, one notch
below majors. Was 10–4. Had 3–1 record there in 1938 when Cards
decided he could help them, but Max lost three decisions and was back
at Columbus, 1939, for most of year. However, had 2–1 mark with
Redbirds in St. Louis that same season. During next four seasons Lanier
won 47 and lost 29 for Cardinals. Then came fine 1944 campaign. After
supension was lifted, Max won 27, lost 22 for St. Louis, 1949–51. Before
1952 season, was traded to New York Giants. Divided 1953 between
Giants and St. Louis Browns, but in last two seasons in majors won
seven, lost 13. Later coached and scouted in minors, then got three-year
contract to scout for San Francisco Giants as part of agreement when
son Hal signed with them, 1961. Max suffered heart attack June 1968.
Major league record: 3.01 ERA for 1618-1/3 innings in 327 games;
walked 611, fanned 821, pitched 21 shutouts. In WS play, 1942,43,44
with Cardinals: 2–1, 1.71 ERA. NL All-Star squad 1943,44; saw no
action.

LARSEN, DONALD JAMES P-BR-TR. B. 8/7/29, Michigan City, Ind.

6'4", 230. Don Larsen's main claim to fame when he toed rubber for fifth game of 1956 WS was fact he had lost 21 games in one season for Baltimore Orioles while winning just three. In season just ended, Larsen had won 11, lost five, with 3.25 ERA. So no one expected what Don did 10/8/56 to Brooklyn Dodgers—pitched a perfect game for first time in history of WS. Such games are rare enough during regular season; last time before was 4/30/22, more than 34 years earlier, by Charlie Robertson of Chicago White Sox.

In 1955 WS, one year before, Yanks used Larsen against Dodgers with disastrous results. Started fourth game and was driven to cover in fifth inning with five runs charged against him. Brooklyn won by 8–5 score.

Late in 1956 season Larsen developed no-windup delivery that seemed to improve effectiveness greatly, so Casey Stengel decided to start him in second game of WS. Don was so wild gave four bases on balls and one hit, causing removal in second inning. Despite this, Stengel gave another chance in fifth contest. Larsen reversed himself so completely that Dodgers never seriously threatened to have base runner. Only one Brooklyn batsman, Pee Wee Reese, got as many as three balls. And nearest Dodgers came to safe hit was drive by Sandy Amoros in fifth inning that curved foul at last moment. Struck out seven, seven were retired on infield grounders, nine on fly balls to outfield, and one on liner to infielder. Crowd of 64,519 in Yankee Stadium witnessed what may have been greatest WS performance ever.

Larsen had checkered career. Jimmie Dykes had been his manager at Baltimore. So when Don, during spring training, 1956, not only broke curfew but smashed car into tree at 5:30 A. M., Dykes said, "Only thing Larsen fears is sleep." Stengel told reporters, "Man was either out too late or up too early."

Larsen pitched from 1947 through 1952 in minors before landing with St. Louis Browns. Travels took him to Aberdeen, S. Dak.; Springfield, Ill.; Globe and Miami, Ariz.; and Wichita Falls, Tex. After one disappointing season with Browns (7–12), franchise was transferred to Baltimore, where Don's record was worse—3–21. Trade put him on Yankee roster after that, but Yanks put him on their farm at Denver. Working under Ralph Houk, then manager for Colorado team, Larsen won nine games, lost one, and merited promotion to Yanks that same season. Did very well, winning nine, losing just two games for parent club.

After pitching perfect WS game, Don had 10–4 record, 1957; 9–6 following year, then 6–7 for 1959. Travels began after that, to Kansas City AL, Chicago AL, Houston and San Francisco, NL, Chicago NL, and second brief term with Baltimore. During this period best performance was with White Sox, for whom won seven and lost two in 1961.

Major league career ended with 81–91 won and lost record; pitched 1548 innings, had 3.78 ERA. Walked 725, struck out 849. Had 44 complete games and 11 shutouts.

Apart from WS appearances mentioned earlier, Larsen won one game, lost one in 1957 Series, both in relief role. Following autumn, Don credited with one victory as starter though removed after seven shutout innings because of elbow injury. And, in 1962, while working for San Francisco Giants, received credit for win over his old mates, Yankees, even though he pitched just 1/3 inning that day, 10/8/62, in relief.

His WS efforts in five classics: 4–2, ERA 2.75; 10 games, 36 innings, 19 walks, 24 strikeouts.

Besides records set in or connected with his perfect WS game, Larsen can look back on some other unusual achievments. Set major league record for consecutive hits by pitcher, seven, in 1953. Good enough hitter to be used as pinch batsman fairly frequently, with 12 hits in 66 times at bat. Pummeled 14 homers in majors, four of them in 1958, when batted .306. Lifetime major league average .242.

LARY, FRANK STRONG (Mule) P-BR-TR. B. 4/10/31, Northport, Ala. 5'11'', 180. Frank Lary won 128 major league games, most of them for Detroit Tigers. Lost 116 decisions, had career ERA of 3.49 for 2162-1/3 innings pitched. Seemingly at his best whenever he pitched against Yankees. Beat them seven times in 1958. At one point, 26–9 against New Yorkers.

Lary twice went over 20-win mark for Tigers, 1956 and again in 1961. Mean competitor on mound: could throw knuckler, fast ball, curve, sinker, slider—some claimed also threw spit ball. Off field was good-humored, folksy, guitar-playing jokester. Loved to mimic others, especially Casey Stengel.

Grew up on farm, son of Mitt Lary, semipro pitcher. In high school played football; once punted 80 yards. Attended U. of Alabama, but did not play football. Spent 1950 with Thomasville in Georgia-Florida League, and Jamestown, Pony circuit. Military service, 1951–52, then two seasons at Buffalo, joining Tigers for three games in 1954. Had 14–15 record in 1955; then won 21, lost 13, next season. In 1959 had 17–10 record, and 23–9 mark in 1961, after which suffered sore arm from time to time. Tapered off, dropped by Detroit during 1964, and had brief spells that same season with Milwaukee NL and New York NL. Divided 1965 between New York NL and Chicago AL, then left majors. AL All-Star squads 1960,61.

LARY, LYNFORD HOBART (Broadway) SS-BR-TR. B. 1/28/06, Armona, Calif. D. 1/9/73, Downey, Calif. 6', 165. Lyn Lary isn't remembered for slugging ability, but hit home run in first game he played in Yankee Stadium. Hit another homer 7/14/31, day he married Mary Lawlor, musical comedy star. Also boasted he smacked grand slam against Chicago White Sox. But Lyn cost Lou Gehrig AL home run championship, 1931, something he didn't boast about. Lyn was on base when Lou drove ball into stands. Somehow Lary got idea ball was caught while he had back to play, running between second and third. Passed third base and went directly to dugout. Gehrig meanwhile, trotted around bags, tagged first, second, third—and home plate. But Gehrig was called out "for passing another base runner." This was correct ruling by umpire, but it kept him from winding up with 47 homers. Babe Ruth hit 46, so they ended in tie.

Lary was bought by Yankees with Jimmy Reese for reported $125,000. Reese was second baseman, Lary shortstop for Oakland Acorns of Pacific Coast League. Lary reported to Yanks for 1929 season, Reese in 1930. Lyn had four stellar seasons in PCL, hitting .314 in last year in minors before going to big league. Hit .309 in 80 games with Yanks, 1929. Played 117 games in 1930 with .289 average, and 155 in 1931, with .280 mark. After that played less often, with Frank Crosetti taking over most of shortstop duties. Traded to Boston AL 5/15/34. At end of that season, figured in famous Joe Cronin deal where Tom Yawkey paid Washington Senators $250,000 for man who ultimately became president of American League. Lary went to Washington in exchange. Senators passed him along to St. Louis Browns 6/29/35. Browns sent him to Cleveland 1/17/37. Then to Brooklyn 5/3/39 and to St. Louis NL 7/14/39. With Browns again, 1940. Left majors after that; played with Milwaukee, American Association; Knoxville, and Buffalo and finally retired, 1942.

Lyn led AL in stolen bases with 37 in 1936. In his last five full years in AL played at least 130 games every season despite fact he was with five different teams in this period. Wound up with .269 average for 1302 major league games, including 38 homers. Had 247 doubles, 56 triples among 1239 hits, with 805 runs scored, 526 RBI and 162 stolen bases.

LATHAM, WALTER ARLINGTON (Arlie) 3B-BR-TR. B. 3/15/59, West Lebanon, N.H. D. 11/29/52, Garden City, N.Y. 5'8", 152. Arlie Latham enjoyed baseball to fullest, but at times his antics were costly. Bubbling with zest for life, Arlie seemed always to be in motion, chattering, tumbling, doing somersaults while running bases, cavorting capriciously forever. One of pranks cost his ball club victory in important game; but not pennant, as some storytellers would have it. In 1889 Brooklyn and St. Louis teams fighting for American Association pennant. St. Louis took early lead, 4–2; in eighth inning got so dark St. Louis players clamored for umpire to call game. Brooklyn team, behind, protested play should continue. Latham got batboy to bring him dozen candles. Arlie lined them up in front of St. Louis dugout, lit them. Crowd roared. Umpire came over, blew candles out, ordered game to go on. Latham relit candles. Again ump blew them out; warned that further attempts to embarrass him would result in forfeiture of game. Arlie proceeded to pull stunt third time. Umpire had final say: game forfeited to Brooklyn 9–0, despite fact St. Louis had been ahead 4–2. Brooklyn finished season with two-game lead over St. Louis—not one game, as after-dinner speakers would have it.

Another of Latham's pranks hurt his playing, may have shortened career. Got into throwing contest, trying to see who could fire ball farthest. Arlie won $100 bet—but tore muscle in arm. Never fully recovered.

Latham was with Buffalo NL 1880. St. Louis AA 1883–89. Chicago, Players League, 1890. Cincinnati NL 1890–95. St. Louis NL 1896. Voluntarily retired 1897–98. Washington NL 1899. New York NL 1909.

Managed at St. Louis, 1896, very briefly, losing both games he bossed. By this time was through as player, to all intents. As sideline, had brief stage career. In 1889 was invited to make world tour with baseball players going abroad but declined because of stage commitments. Song written for him entitled "The Freshest Man on Earth."

Played something over 1600 major league games, hitting in vicinity of .265. Spent later days as press-box attendant at Polo Grounds, New York.

LAVAGETTO, HARRY ARTHUR (Cookie) 3B-BR-TR. B. 12/1/14, Oakland, Calif. 5'11", 170. Cookie Lavagetto played more than 1000 major league games but mention name in Brooklyn and everybody remembers day he pinch hit and made double at Ebbets Field. They won't remember date—10/3/47. They probably have forgotten opposing pitcher—Floyd Bevens of N. Y. Yankees. But Cookie was hero that day. His double didn't win WS for Dodgers—they lost that one, four games to three. But Cookie's hit was enough to keep Flatbush fans talking about it for rest of lives. Bevens was on way to first no-hit game in WS history; needed just one more out in ninth inning. Yanks had won two games to Dodgers' one. Bombers were leading by 2–1 score. Only Brooklyn run had scored as result of two walks, sacrifice, and infield out. Gloom filled followers of "Dem Bums." They had two men on base as result of walks, but one more putout would give Yanks three to one lead in games. Manager Burt Shotton sent Cookie in to hit for Eddie Stanky. There wasn't much difference in their batting averages, but Cookie could hit longer ball. Strategy proved sagacious—Cookie picked on Bevens' second offering, drove it against right field wall for two bases. Both runners scored, and instead of defeat, game suddenly was transformed into glorious victory over hated Yankees from Bronx.

Besides playing 1043 games in majors, mostly at third base, Lavagetto also managed Washington Senators most of 1957, and all of 1958–60. Unfortunately for Cookie, Senators finished in cellar first three years at helm, but rose to fifth place, 1960. Then Cookie was replaced by Mickey Vernon.

Lavagetto got nickname and first chance in pro ball from "Cookie" DeVincenzi, then owner of Oakland Oaks in Pacific Coast League, 1933. Players started calling him "Cookie's boy," then dropped last part. One season with .312 batting average and 100 RBI in 152 games convinced Pittsburgh Pirates Lavagetto ought to be in majors. Cookie was second baseman then. Didn't hit much, just .220 in 1934, but following season upped mark to .290, and began playing some third base. One more season with Pittsburgh, then traded to Brooklyn, where began concentrating as hot-corner guardian. With Dodgers until end of 1947 WS except for four years in military service, 1942–45. Became dangerous hitter with Brooklyn, four times going to 70 or more RBI in one season. Hit .300 in 1939 with 87 RBI. After his famous two-bagger, Cookie had four more times at bat during 1947 WS but got no more hits. Then back to Oakland, PCL, for 1948–50.

Cookie once made six hits in six consecutive times at bat 9/23/39. Full career record showed .269 average with 945 hits, including 183 two-baggers, 37 triples, 40 homers. Scored 487 runs, drove in 486. In WS play, 1941,47, just two hits in 17 trips, for .118 average, but one of those hits made history. NL All-Star squads 1940,41.

Lavagetto returned to Brooklyn as coach, 1951–53; coach for Oakland, 1954; coach for Washington, 1955, until named manager 5/7/57. Cookie's boss as coach at Brooklyn, Oakland, and Washington was Chuck Dressen, whom he succeeded as manager in Washington.

LAW, VERNON SANDERS (Deacon) P-BR-TR. B. 3/12/30, Meridian, Idaho. 6'3", 200. Vernon Law, ordained elder of Church of Jesus Christ of Latter-Day Saints, received Cy Young Award, 1960, as outstanding major league pitcher. Won 20, lost nine, with 3.08 ERA, helping Pittsburgh Pirates to win NL flag. Followed with two WS victories over Yankees. Next four years rocky for Vern. But won 17, lost nine in 1965 and had 2.16 ERA. This performance got him *Sporting News* designation Comeback Player of Year.

Law started out, 1948, at Santa Rosa in Far Western League; next stop Davenport, 1949 and New Orleans, 1950. Won six, lost four in Southern Association, then moved up same season to 7-9 record with Pirates. Spent 1952–53 in military service but had in-and-out record until 1958 when won 14, lost 12. Improved on this in 1959, taking 18 games against nine losses, and getting ERA down to 2.98. Then came his Cy Young season. Sore arm afflicted Law in 1961; was able to win just three games, losing four; pitched just 59 innings. Had 10–7 record, 1962, then went on voluntary retired list for time. For brief period tried out arm with Kinston team in Carolina League. Won two games easily and went back on Pittsburgh roster for 4–5 record, 1963. In 1964 it was 12–13. After fine comeback in 1965, had 12–8 season in 1966. Then called it quits as active pitcher with 2–6 record in 1967. In 1968 was pitching coach for Pirates.

Won 162 major league games, lost 147, with 3.77 ERA; walked 597 and fanned 1092 in 2672 innings. Took part in 483 games, 119 complete, with 28 shutouts. In that wacky 1960 WS, Law was winner in first game, though needing help from Roy Face in eighth inning. Captured decision in fourth game also, again needing Face's help, this time in seventh. Starting crucial seventh game, was driven to cover in sixth inning, but Pirates rallied to win contest 10–9 and Series, when Bill Mazeroski hit famous home run. Vern had two wins, no losses, and 3.44 ERA in 18-1/3 innings of WS pitching. Also has All-Star game victory to credit. In 1960 pitched in both games and credited with victory in second one. Allowed no runs in 2-2/3 innings altogether.

LAZZERI, ANTHONY MICHAEL (Push-'em-Up Tony)   2B-BR-TR. B.

12/6/03, San Francisco, Calif. D. 8/6/46, San Francisco, Calif. 5'11", 170. Tony Lazzeri's strikeout in 1926 WS with bases loaded is just about as famous as that of Mighty Casey, who fanned and caused all that sorrow in Mudville. Countless others have swung in vain in crucial situations, but Lazzeri's strikeout has become one of baseball's legends. As in so many legends, storytellers have tried to improve on truth. Tony did *not* strike out for last out in ninth inning of final game of Series. Instead, strikeout came in *seventh* inning and left three Yankees on base and St. Louis Cardinals leading by 3–2 score. Grover Cleveland Alexander was hero of occasion; had just relieved Jesse Haines on mound. Yet slight twist of fate and hero-villain roles would have been reversed. Just before Lazzeri swung in vain, he hit tremendous drive over left-field wall into stands, foul by few feet. A shift of wind, an infinitesimal change in Tony's swing—and Yankees would have had four runs.

Tony was rookie that year. But even after strikeout, Yankees had two more innings before going down to defeat. Fans often wonder what might have happened if Babe Ruth had not tried to steal second base with two men out in ninth inning. Bob Meusel, dangerous hitter, was at bat; Lou Gehrig was on deck. Plenty of ball games have been won and lost with two men out in ninth inning.

Lazzeri was taciturn man who suffered from epilepsy. It is believed this caused him to fall and suffer fatal injury while still relatively young. Tony also considered one of smartest ball players of time. Lefty Gomez, teammate, knew this to be true. Once fielded ball near pitcher's mound;

realized he had no chance to get man at first base, so threw to Lazzeri. Tony was at his normal position near right-field grass. Dumbfounded, Tony asked Gomez why. "Well," said Lefty, "I've always heard how smart you are. I wanted to see what you would do with the ball in a situation like this!"

Lazzeri came to Yankees with record as slugger in Pacific Coast League. Though native of San Francisco, Tony got start with Salt Lake City team, then in PCL, 1922. Father was riveter in boiler factory and Tony worked there for while. But ball playing beat factory work, so he stuck to baseball although batted just .192 in first season in Utah in 45 games, 1922. It was Peoria and Salt Lake, 1923; Lincoln and Salt Lake following season. Finally, in 1925, Tony stuck with PCL club all season and made it big. In 197 games, hit safely 252 times; scored 202 runs; hit 60 home runs; drove in 222; stole 39 bases; came up with .355 average, 512 total bases. Paul Waner, however, took PCL batting championship that year with .401. Small wonder Yankees happy to invest $55,000 in cash, and ball players valued at another $20,000, to get Lazzeri. Investment paid off immediately. Tony played 155 games for Yanks, 1926, hit .275, had 18 homers, and drove in 114 markers. Then had five seasons above .300 in next six years. During career with Bombers had seven seasons with more than 100 RBI; ran bases well; fielded position well, and was always threat with long ball.

Among Tony's more stellar achievments were following: hit two home runs with bases loaded in one game 5/24/36 and drove in three more markers for total of 11 RBI in one game. Had record of five homers in two consecutive games, six homers in three straight games, and seven round-trippers in four consecutive contests in same batting spree late in May 1936. Day he hit two grand slammers, Yankees nosed out Philadelphia Athletics 25–2.

Tony played most of games at second base in majors, though in 1927 and 1929 played great deal at shortstop. Had some third-basing too, especially in 1930 and 1931. Yankees gave him unconditional release 10/15/37, and he signed with Chicago Cubs for 1938. Played 54 games, batted .267, and drew release at end of year. Fourteen games with Brooklyn Dodgers, 1939, and 13 with N. Y. Giants, then headed for Pacific Coast.

Tony's major league career totals: 1739 games, 6297 AB, 986 runs, 1840 hits, 334 doubles, 115 triples, 178 homers, 1191 RBI, 148 SB, average .292. Six WS with Yankees, one with Cubs. Hit .262 with 28 hits, 16 runs scored, 19 RBI. Four homers, two in 1932, and one each in 1936 and 1937.

LEACH, THOMAS WILLIAM 3B-OF-BR-TR. B. 11/4/77, French Creek, N.Y. D. 9/29/69, Haines City, Fla. 5'6½", 150. Home-run king of NL back in 1902, with six, all inside-park variety. Wouldn't qualify as slugger, since had only 61 homers in 2130 games over period from 1898 to 1918. Spent his palmy days with Pittsburgh Pirates, first as third baseman, later as outfielder. Speedy base runner, did lot of bunting, got his average up to .303 one season, 1907. Had .269 career average with 1352 runs scored, 277 doubles, 170 triples. Stole 364 bases. High mark was 43 in that banner year, 1907.

Leach grew up in Cleveland in same neighborhood as Delahantys who made grade in major leagues. Tommy was printer's devil, then at 18 joined Hanover club in Cumberland Valley League, semipro outfit, 1896. Also played at Petersburg and Hampton, Va.; Youngstown, Ohio; and Auburn, N.Y., joining Louisville NL team late in 1898. One more season at Louisville, then whole club was merged with Pittsburgh Pirates and transferred to Pennsylvania city. Remained with Pittsburgh until June 1912.

Tommy played in first modern WS, 1903, against Boston AL. Hit .273, 9 for 33, with four triples. Also stole two bases. Took part in 1909 WS against Detroit, this time hitting .320 with eight hits in 25 trips; four doubles, one stolen base, scored eight runs.

Leach moved to Chicago NL 1912, remaining through 1914 season. Cincinnati, 1915. Playing manager, Rochester, 1916; Kansas City, 1917; Chattanooga, 1918. Also had 30 games with Pirates that year, but was back in minors, 1919, with Shreveport; playing manager at Tampa, Florida State League, 1920–22, and bossed same team from sidelines, 1923 and 1927. Manager, Lakeland, 1924; manager, St. Petersburg, 1928. Scout for Boston Braves 1935–36.

Teammate of Honus Wagner, Fred Clarke, other legendary figures.

LEE, LERON   OF-BL-TR. B. 3/4/48, Bakersfield, Calif. 6', 197. When Leron Lee hit an even .300 for San Diego Padres, 1972, it marked just second time member of that expansion club had reached .300 mark. First one was Clarence Gaston, who had .318 for Padres in 1970. Although lefthanded batsman, Lee hit better against southpaws in 1972 than he did against righthanders: .327 against lefthanders, .295 against righthanders.

Lee was brilliant athlete in high school. Played fullback and halfback on his prep school team in Sacramento. In one game, carried ball three times: ran 75 yards first time, 54 second time, 63 third time. Each run produced touchdown. About two dozen major universities tried to line him up for athletic acholarships. But Lee, first draft choice of St. Louis Cardinals, 1966. Signed for estimated $50,000 of Owner Gussie Busch's money. Cardinals farmed him out to Modesto, Arkansas, and Tulsa, for three seasons, brought him up to parent club for seven games, 1969. In his only full season with Cardinals played 121 games, hit .227. Was hitting .179 for 25 games in 1971 when traded to Padres 6/11/71. Got into 79 games with San Diego that season, hit .273 rest of way. Then seemed to find himself in 1972, despite injuries which confined him to but 101 games. Had 47 RBI, hit 12 homers, 23 doubles, 7 triples, scored 50 runs. Broke up Tom Seaver's bid for no-hitter with one out in ninth inning during game on July 4. Also displayed big improvement in his fielding.

Lee went into 1973 with .267 overall major league batting average for 333 games. Owned 23 homers among his 251 hits, with 58 doubles, 10 triples. Scored 113 runs, had 93 RBI.

LEFEBVRE, JAMES KENNETH (Frenchy) Inf.-BLR-TR. B. 1/7/43, Inglewood, Calif. 6′, 185. Jim Lefebvre, released by Los Angeles Dodgers after 1972 season, reportedly signed three-year contract with Lotte Orions of Japan for something over $100,000. Versatile fellow had eight seasons in majors, won NL Rookie of Year Award from Baseball Writers Association of America, 1965. Played second base then, had 12 homers, 69 RBI in 157 games. After that season Mgr. Walter Alston shifted him around great deal, mostly in infield, but also used him as outfielder and frequently as pinch hitter. Switch hitter with power. Had 24 homers in 1966, sophomore year with Dodgers. Able bunter.

Jim's best season for average was that same year when he batted .274 in 152 games. When he left majors had .251 major league career average for 922 games; His 756 hits included 126 doubles, 18 triples, 74 homers. Scored 313 runs, drove in 404. In two WS, 1965,66, batted .273 in seven games. Member 1966 NL All-Star squad.

Jim devoted great deal of time to young people, giving talks at schools and elsewhere, especially in combating drug abuse. Organization was known as "Athletes for Youth."

Prior to coming to Dodgers, Lefebvre spent 1962 at Reno in California League; 1963 at Salem, Northwestern League; and following season at Spokane, Pacific Coast League. Military service 1964. One record he would rather forget: tied modern NL record for most errors in one inning by third baseman 4/25/67; muffed three times.

LEMASTER, DENVER CLAYTON (Denny) P-BR-TL. B. 2/25/39, Corona, Calif. 6′2″, 185. It took some $60,000 in bonus money to get Denny Lemaster to sign pro contract with Milwaukee Braves, 1958. Didn't make major league club, however, until 1962 season. In interim he learned about pro pitching at Eau Claire, Wis.; Jacksonville, Austin, and Louisville. In 1964 Denny had 17 victories against 11 defeats, but since then his records have not been so impressive. Remained with Braves when they moved to Atlanta, 1966, then traded to Houston NL 10/8/67. Never could get started with Astros. After four seasons in which lost oftener than he won, Astros sold him to Montreal Expos 10/14/71. Converted into relief pitcher, 1970. Disappointing season with Montreal, 1972, although credited with two wins, no losses. In 13 games pitched 17 innings, but had 7.65 ERA.

While Lemaster was serving final season with Braves, was named to NL All-Star squad but couldn't pitch because of back ailment. Lemaster finished 1972 with major league mark of 90 wins, 105 defeats, 3.58 ERA. Walked 600, struck out 1305 in 1788 innings.

LEMON, JAMES ROBERT   OF-BR-TR. B. 3/23/28, Covington, Va. 6'4", 205. Dwight Eisenhower, then President, watched baseball game at Griffith Stadium, Washington, 8/31/56, with 15,325 other customers. Wasn't surprised when Mickey Mantle slammed 47th homer. But Mantle not big news that night; Jim Lemon stole show. Jim rapped Whitey Ford for homers in second, fourth, and sixth innings—in succession. Jim only second man to hit three homers in one game in Griffith Stadium. Other was Joe DiMaggio, but his not in succession.

Lemon, besides playing dozen years in majors, managed Washington Senators, 1968. Did not have much in way of playing talent to work with and club finished last in 10-club circuit. Jim gave way to Ted Williams when new owner, Bob Short, took over ball club in 1969.

Lemon started at Pittsfield, Mass., 1948, and saw service in Bloomingdale, N.Y.; Harrisburg, and Oklahoma City before joining Cleveland, 1950. Played 12 games, then spent much of next three seasons in military service. Got out in time for 16 games in 1953 with Indians and 93 with Indianapolis. Washington bought him, 1954, used him in 37 games, and then farmed him out to Charlotte, 1954, and Chattanooga, 1955. Back with Senators, 1955; won regular job with them, 1956, hitting .271. Swatted 27 homers, drove in 96 runs, scored 77 times, and tied for AL lead in triples with 11. Raised average to .284 in 1957 but homer total dropped off to 17. Had 26 homers, 1958, and 33 following season; raised total to 38 in 1960. Had 100 RBI in each of 1959 and 1960 seasons. Senators became Minnesota Twins, 1961, and Lemon's work began to taper off. In 1963 saw service with Twins, Chicago White Sox, and Philadelphia Phillies. Lemon's first managerial experience came in 1964 with Senators' farm club at York, Pa., Eastern League. Coach for Minnesota Twins, 1965–67.

Jim's major league totals showed 1010 games, 901 hits, 120 two-baggers, 35 triples, 164 home runs, 446 runs scored, another 529 driven in. Stole 13 bases and had .262 average. While managing Senators, team won 65, lost 96, finishing 1-1/2 games behind ninth-place Chicago White Sox.

Bad knee plagued Lemon during much of career; operated on to correct it. Afterward shoulder trouble caused retirement as active player.

LEMON, ROBERT GRANVILLE (Lem) P-BL-TR. B. 9/22/20, San Bernardino, Calif. 6', 180. Conversation with newspaper man probably cost Bob Lemon job as manager of Kansas City Royals at end of 1972 season. John Hall, in column in *Los Angeles Times* late in July, quoted Lemon as saying he was glad he was just couple of years away from retirement; that as soon as he could, would leave baseball, retire to some remote island. Anyone familiar with pressures of baseball season, especially for major league manager, can understand how Bob felt. In any case, K.C. owner, Ewing Kauffman, read column and began thinking about future of Royals—and decided he wanted younger man to boss team. When dismissal came, Lemon said newsman had not quoted him properly. Bob said he had mentioned wanting to lead quiet life ultimately, but he had not set time for retirement: "Anybody in their right mind knows I'm in no position to retire." In Bob's three seasons at helm in Kansas City, team finished fourth, 1970; in second-place tie, 1971; and fourth, 1972.

Lemon, during playing days, was outstanding pitcher with Cleveland Indians. One of four pitchers in AL history to win 20 games seven times. Won 207 major league games, lost 128, even though got late start and was nearly 26 before pitching in majors. Delay because he started as infielder, had three years in navy, and didn't turn to pitching as full-time job until after he joined Indians in 1946. In brief spells with Cleveland, 1941–42, tried to make grade as third baseman.

Bob started pro career at Springfield, Mass., 1938, and saw service at Oswego, N.Y.; New Orleans; Wilkes-Barre; and Baltimore, then in International League, before U.S. entry into World War II. During this period was used on mound only twice; earned pay as infielder and outfielder in minors.

Could hit well, but not enough to make grade as infielder. With a strong right arm, shift to mound was in order. Had 4–5 record, 1946; became winner, 1947, with 11–5 mark. For next nine years was stalwart pitcher, with victories ranging from 23 to 17, and always finishing well above .500 percentage. Led AL in total innings pitched four times. Averaged better than 20 wins in this period, with losses less than 12. In 1957 dropped down to six wins, 11 losses, and during 1958 season went back to minors, winning only two games that year for San Diego, Pacific Coast League. Scout for Cleveland, 1959; coach for Cleveland, early 1960; coach for Philadelphia NL, 1961. Manager, Hawaii, PCL, 1964; manager, Seattle, PCL, 1965–66; coach, California Angels, 1967–68; manager, Vancouver, PCL, 1969; coach, Kansas City AL, 1970, until appointment as manager, 6/9/70. In 1948 Bob pitched 10 shutouts; one was no-hitter against Detroit Tigers 6/30. In 1953 set major league record for pitcher by taking part in 15 double plays. Named to AL All-

Star squads seven times, 1948–54. Helped Indians win two pennants, 1948 and 1954. In WS of 1948 won two games, lost none, had 1.65 ERA. Not so effective in 1954 classic, losing two decisions. Overall WS record showed two wins, two losses, with ERA of 3.94 for 29-2/3 innings pitched.

Sporting News honored him as Minor League Manager of Year, 1966, after his Seattle club finished first in PCL Western Division, then won playoffs from Tulsa, champion of Eastern Division.

Lemon pitched 2849 innings in AL, allowed 1024 earned runs, with 1277 strikeouts, 1251 walks, and ERA of 3.23. As hitter, had .232 overall average; his 274 hits included 54 doubles, nine triples, 37 homers. In 1949 had seven home runs.

LEONARD, HUBERT BENJAMIN (Dutch)   P-BL-TL. B. 7/26/92, Lorain Co., Ohio. D. 7/11/52, Fresno, Calif. 5'10½", 185. Dutch Leonard, old lefthanded pitcher, is remembered now not so much for anything he did while pitching, as for involvement with names of Ty Cobb and Tris Speaker. Dutch with Boston Red Sox, later with Detroit Tigers between 1913 and 1925. Ty Cobb and Tris Speaker, veteran AL stars who were still fine players, had both been serving as team managers through 1926 season. Then both announced their retirement from baseball. This was sensational news, but it wasn't whole story. Eventually, Judge Landis, czar of baseball, gave out further details. Dutch Leonard had just accused Cobb and Speaker of betting on game back in 1919. Contest in question was played 9/25/19 between Tigers and Cleveland Indians. Cleveland had clinched second place in AL, but had no chance to win pennant, already sewed up by Chicago. There was question whether Tigers or N.Y. Yankees would finish third in AL standings. Third-place finish, of course, meant few hundred dollars in bonus money for each player. According to Leonard, it was arranged for Detroit to win game in question and bets were placed; bettors won $420 when Tigers were victorious by 9–5 score. Efforts to place larger bets had failed. Ban Johnson, president of AL, conducted early investigation into affair and apparently planned to let Cobb and Speaker resign without public announcements since Leonard himself refused to face men he was accusing. Then Johnson turned matter over to Landis, who issued public announcement on background of two resignations. Cobb and Speaker both protested innocence. Cobb called it "frame-up." Speaker said he knew nothing of any wagers or any fix. Hugh Jennings, who had been manager of Tigers in 1919, issued statement saying he knew nothing whatever of affair, and would have gone limit "to oust guilty parties." Landis, 1/27/27, exonerated Cobb and Speaker. Cobb signed with Philadelphia Athletics and Speaker with Washington. "Spoke" signed with Athletics, 1928, so two immortals wound up on same club, playing under another legendary figure, Connie Mack. Leonard reportedly was angry at Cobb for having released him to Vernon club of Pacific Coast League after 1925 season. Pitcher also is said to have been peeved at Speaker because Cleveland club did not claim him when waivers were asked.

Leonard had brief trials with Philadelphia AL and Boston AL, 1911–12, spent brief period at Worcester in New England League, 1912, and won 22, lost nine with Denver that same season. Then moved up to Red Sox for 1913, started with 14–16 record; came back with 19–5, 14–7, and 18–12 marks in next three seasons. Couple of so-so seasons, then traded to Tigers after 1918 season. Didn't do much with Tigers until 1925, when 11–4. Despite this, Leonard, then 33, sent to PCL.

Dutch pitched and won two WS games for Red Sox, one in 1915, other in 1916. Allowed one earned run in each game. Sox won both Series. Leonard's lifetime record showed 139 victories, 112 defeats. In 1914 his ERA of 1.01 made him all-time most effective hurler in major leagues. His career ERA was 2.77.

LEONARD, WALTER FENNER (Buck) 1B-BL-TL. B. 9/8/07, Rocky Mount, N.C. 5'11", 185. One of great black players who never played in majors but now in Hall of Fame; selected, 1972, by special committee. Slugger, called by some "black Lou Gehrig." Brilliant first baseman. Roy Campanella said he handled himself like Gil Hodges. Leonard had belated chance to play in majors. Offer from St. Louis Browns when Bill Veeck was there. But Buck was 45 by then, turned it down. Said knew he couldn't play every day, didn't want to make fool of self. Now in real estate work after retiring from job as assistant probation officer. Like most black ball players before Jackie Robinson joined Brooklyn Dodgers, 1947, Leonard played under poor, difficult conditions. For most part no statistics were kept.

Buck left school at 14, worked at various jobs, played baseball for Portsmouth, Va., "Firefighters,"; later Baltimore Stars and Brooklyn Royal Giants. Hooked up with Homestead, Pa., "Grays," 1934. Most of playing after that was with Grays. Received $125 per month starting with Grays; $500 monthly, plus 75 cents daily for food, in 1941; best year financially, 1948, when made $10,000, but had to play all year long, summer and winter. Summers barnstorming all over U.S., winters in Caribbean countries and Mexico.

Usually hit above .300, and above .400 in 1947. Often teamed up with Josh Gibson, another great black hitter who also landed in Hall of Fame. Monte Irvin, who works in baseball commissioner Kuhn's office, says Gibson could hit ball farther, but Leonard hit it just as often. When Leonard was 40 he could still hit; belted 42 home runs and batted about .390 in 80 games.

LEPPERT, DONALD GEORGE C-BR-TR. B. 10/19/31, Indianapolis, Ind. 6'2", 215. Don Leppert's major league career as player wasn't long, but he did accomplish certain deeds of note. For example, in his first time at bat in big time smacked home run, 6/18/61. Another red-letter occasion 4/11/63: three consecutive homers, unique for Robert Kennedy Stadium in District of Columbia.

Leppert, in 1973, was going into his sixth season as coach for Pittsburgh Pirates. Handles coaching of catchers and first base.

Don attended Wabash College in Indiana. Originally signed with Milwaukee Braves, 1955. Played at Evansville (Ind.), and Corpus Christi that year. Wichita 1956. Austin 1957–58–59. Dallas 1959. Dallas–Fort Worth 1960. Columbus (Ohio) 1961. Pittsburgh 1961–62. Washington 1963–64. Hawaii 1965. Columbus (Ohio) 1966—player-coach, his last year in active player ranks. Quit with .229 average for 190 major league games. His 122 hits in big time included 15 homers, 22 doubles, 2 triples, 46 runs, 59 RBI. AL All-Star team 1963, but did not play. In 1967, managed Gastonia club, Western Carolina League. Finished second. Following year joined Pirate coaching staff. Operates insurance business, Greenwood, Ind., off-seasons.

LEVSEN, EMIL HENRY (Dutch) P-BR-TR. B. 4/29/98, Wyoming, Iowa. D. 3/12/72, Minneapolis, Minn. 6', 186. Last pitcher to hurl—and win—double header in major leagues. Working for Cleveland 8/28/26 against Boston Red Sox, won first game by 6–1 score, allowing only four hits. Teammates Joe Sewell and Jack Burns ribbed him about how easy victory had been. Banter continued until Levsen went to Mgr. Tris Speaker and asked if could pitch second half of twin bill. "Spoke" agreed. Repeated performance—allowed four hits in nightcap and again just one run. Cleveland took game by 5–1 count. Levsen took 14 other victories that season, winding up with 16–13 mark, his best year in game. Did those 18 innings in one day shorten career? Following spring Dutch came up with arm trouble. That year 3–7. And in 1928, after 0–3, was sold to New Orleans, Southern Association; then retired after brief spell in minors.

Dutch started out at Cedar Rapids, Iowa, 1923—19–4. That got him trial with Cleveland, pitching 4-1/3 innings. Terre Haute, 1924, 14–8. Another brief spell with Indians, 1–1, same season. Farmed out to Rochester, 1925, 14–9 mark; then joined Indians, 1–2. Then came best season, 1926.

Levsen won 21, lost 26 in majors and had 4.17 ERA for 404 innings.

LINDBLAD, PAUL AARON P-BL-TL. B. 8/9/41, Chanute, Kans. 6'1", 195. When Washington fans couldn't wait for one more out to ravage their baseball stadium for souvenirs of last big league game in nation's capital, they also stole a victory from Paul Lindblad. Score was tied when Paul entered game in seventh inning. Senators scored two runs in last half of eighth, putting them ahead of N.Y. Yankees, 7–5. Then with two out in ninth, fans began digging up home plate, stealing bases, walking off with pieces of turf, lights from scoreboard, and various other bits and pieces. This was 9/30/71. Lindblad still did creditable work for Senators that year. Won seven, lost four, and had eight saves for hapless team. His ERA was 2.79. In 1972, with Senators transformed into Texas Rangers, Paul's won-lost record not impressive, but rest of statistics were excellent. Won five, lost eight for punk ball club; but saved nine other games, quite an achievment for team Whitey Herzog declared had to be one of worst clubs he had ever seen. Lindblad could hope for better things in 1973, since he would belong to World Champion Oakland A's. This was homecoming for Paul, who spent five full seasons with A's, first while they were in Kansas City, and later when they moved to Oakland.

Paul attended Chanute Junior College and graduated; also attended Kansas U. Excelled in track sports: won state prep javelin title and was runner up twice in National Junior College championships. Started pro career at Burlington, Iowa, 1963; won 10, lost two, had 1.58 ERA. Had 11–8 mark 1964 at Birmingham, and 12–11 at Vancouver, 1965. Joined Kansas City that same year and posted 0–1 record. A's finished 10th that year. They were seventh in 1966, 10th again in 1967. Two fourth-place finishes, and Paul landed with an 11th-place club, Washington, when traded 5/8/71. In 1972 Texas Rangers finished bad last in AL West.

Lindblad had 2.41 ERA, 1968. In 1970 it was 2.70, and in 1971, 2.79. Then had 2.61 mark in 1972, despite disouraging fielding support from his teammates. Paul faced 1973 with record of 43 wins, 42 losses. Pitched in 374 major league games. In 641 innings had walked 207, struck out 417.

Off-season, salesman for toy manufacturer.

LINDELL, JOHN HARLAN   P-OF-BR-TR. B. 8/30/16, Greeley, Colo. 6'4½", 238. Johnny Lindell had some brilliant pitching records in minor leagues, but in majors, as hurler, was quite another story. Won eight games, lost 18, with 4.47 ERA. However was good enough hitter to play in majors as outfielder; hit .273 for 854 games; had .324 mark in three WS with New York Yankees, 1943,47,49.

Lindell won 15 letters in high school, playing baseball, football, basketball, and taking part in track events. Offered scholarship for football and track activities at U. of Southern California; attended for few months, but then signed with Yankee organization. First stop Joplin, Western Association, where won 17 games, lost eight, in 1936. Then to Binghamton, N.Y.; Newark, Oakland, and Kansas City, all farm clubs for Yankees. Had 18–7 record at Kansas City, 1940, and 23–4 at

Newark, 1941, leading International League in winning percentage with .852 and in ERA with 2.05. Joined Yanks for one game, 1941, remained with them until during 1950 season. However, said Johnny, "I wasn't Joe McCarthy's type of pitcher." Had knuckleball, curve, but fast ball wasn't really fast enough to fool many major league hitters. But McCarthy could and did use Johnny as outfielder, with a few games at first base. Hit even .300 in 149 games in 1944; .283 in 41 games, 1945; and .317 in 88 games, 1948. Best year for homers was 1944 when he slapped 18; also led AL in triples that season with 16. In 1947 WS average was .500, with nine hits in 18 trips against Brooklyn Dodger pitching. Three hits were doubles and one a triple; scored three times, had seven RBI.

After seven games with Yanks in 1950, Johnny found himself with St. Louis Cardinals, who didn't keep him long. Sold to Hollywood, Pacific Coast League, reported to Fred Haney, then manager there. "Welcome to our pitching staff," said Haney as he greeted Lindell. "I beg your pardon," said Johnny. "I'm an outfielder." "You're the same Lindell who pitched for Yankees, aren't you?" "I am also the same Lindell who played outfield with Yankees. Now if you'll show me where right field is in this ball park, I'll suit up!" "Pitch or no pay," said Haney. "No pitch, no pay?" "Inescapable," replied Fred. "Well, you might say I'm a pitcher with eight years of rest." Lindell pitched. Batted cleanup. Pinch hit. Had 12–9 record, 1951; 24–9 in 1952; also had 14 games in outfield. Waltzed off with MVP Award for PCL. Then back to majors with Pittsburgh, then Philadelphia NL, 1953. Won six, lost 17. With Phils, 1954, briefly, then became sports director for Seven Up Youth Foundation in California until 1961. Then joined Los Angeles and California Angels organization in speakers bureau, later moving into group sales. Remained with Angels until late 1972.

LINZY, FRANK ALFRED   P-BR-TR. B. 9/15/40, Fort Gibson, Okla. 6'1", 195. Sinker-ball specialist, another of those guys who are concentrating on relief pitching. Started one game in 1963 with San Francisco Giants, but didn't finish it. When 1973 began, had record of pitching in 452 games, 451 of them in relief. During this period won 57, lost 49, and had 2.79 ERA.

Linzy had bizarre debut in NL, 1963. Struck out first two men to face him in majors, but eight of next 11 men he faced got to base.

Frank attended Oklahoma State and Northwestern State, also in Oklahoma. Billy McLean was impressed with him as athlete, wrote report to home office after seeing him play semipro ball: "I've just signed something, but I don't know what it is, outfielder or pitcher. The one thing I'm sure about is that it's a big league prospect at either position." No bonus involved. First stop Salem, Va., in Appalachian League, 1960; then Quincy, Ill.; Springfield, Mass.; and Tacoma. Stuck with Giants,

1965, won nine, lost three, had 1.43 ERA in 57 games. *Sporting News* named him NL Rookie Pitcher of Year. Came up with 1.50 ERA in 96 innings with Giants, 1967, although broke even in 14 decisions. Two years later won 14, lost nine, but saved 11 other games. In 1970 appeared in 67 games, 20 with Giants, and 47 with St. Louis Cardinals after trade 5/19/70. Following year got off to good start with five saves and one victory by May 10. Collided with first baseman Bob Burda during June, suffered multiple fractures around left eye, necessitating surgery. Still got into 50 ball games and had 2.14 ERA; four victories, three defeats, six saves. Cardinals traded him to Milwaukee AL 3/26/72. Some said that with his type of pitching, artificial turf in NL worked against him. With Brewers had 12 saves, two wins, two losses, appearing in 47 games.

LIPON, JOHN JOSEPH (Skids) SS-BR-TR. B. 11/10/22, Martins Ferry, Ohio. 6', 175. Johnny Lipon had brief period as manager of Cleveland Indians, 1971, after dismissal of Alvin Dark. Then gave way to Ken Aspromonte after close of season. Manager Toledo, American Association affiliate of Detroit Tigers, 1972–73. Resigned 7/23/73.

Lipon's major league playing days were mostly with Tigers. Started at Muskegon, Michigan State League, 1941; then with Beaumont, Texas League, 1942; also 34 games with Tigers that season. Skipped next three seasons because was in navy. Fourteen games with Detroit, 1946, then spent 1947 with Dallas, Texas League. Back with Tigers, 1948, until traded to Boston Red Sox 7/3/52. Sox kept him until late following season, when was sent to St. Louis AL on waivers. Had one game with Cincinnati, 1954, last appearance as player in majors.

Johnny wasn't power hitter but in two seasons as regular hit .290 or better for Tigers. Five seasons in majors playing at least 100 games. Wound up with .259 lifetime major league average for 758 games.

After leaving Reds, Johnny was with Havana, International League, 1954–55; Columbus, Ohio, in same circuit, 1956; playing coach for Columbus, 1957–58, playing manager at Selma, Alabama-Florida League, 1959; also played five games while managing Mobile in Southern Association, 1960; manager, Lakeland, Florida State League, 1960; bossed Toronto, International League, 1961; Charleston, Eastern League, 1962–63, and Portland, Pacific Coast League, 1964–67. Captured three pennants during this period. Voted "Manager of Year" in Eastern League, 1963, and again in 1967 in Pacific Coast League. Designated "Oregon's Man of Year in Sports," 1964, while with Portland. Became Cleveland coach 1969, continuing until elevation to manager's job 7/30/71.

LOBERT, JOHN BERNARD (Hans) 3B-BR-TR. B. 10/18/81, Wilmington, Del. D. 9/14/68, Philadelphia, Pa. 5'9", 180. Certainly one of more colorful old timers, even though name probably means nothing to 99 percent of present-day baseball fans. Played 1310 major league games, stole 316 bases—also ran foot races against horses, automobiles, motorcycles. First of these races was at Oxnard, Calif. Exhibition game was scheduled—and somebody, having heard of Lobert's speed afoot, dreamed up idea of racing horse against a man. Plan was for Lobert to touch all bases while horse's course was just outside bases so as not to trample on Hans. Veteran umpire Bill Klem was to judge race. Lobert was ahead of horse by five feet at first base; 10 feet ahead at second. Then horse began crowding into Lobert's path and Hans had to dodge to avoid being knocked down. On home stretch between third base and plate, horse overtook Hans and Klem ruled horse winner.

Other strange race took place in Havana, Cuba. Entries were Lobert, two horses, two automobiles, two motorcycles, and one professional runner. Cars and motorcycles had to cover seven-eighths of mile; horses two furlongs; Lobert and professional runner, 535 yards. Prize was $500. Lobert's wife was in stands at time and is said to have bet sizable chunk of money on husband. Hans won race—and reportedly got more cash winnings than he earned all that year as ball player.

Hans grew up in Williamsport, Pa.; developed love for baseball at early age. Later recalled getting baseball uniform as boy and using Christmas money to buy spiked shoes. Although snowing at time, put on uniform and shoes, ran outside to get feel of new spikes. Joined semipro club in Pittsburgh, which led to tryout with Pirates. Old Honus Wagner befriended youngster, called him "Hans Number Two." Wagner also known as Hans as well as Honus. That was in 1903. Lobert attracted attention of John McGraw, then manager of N.Y. Giants, that year. Later Lobert and McGraw became good friends, and Hans played for McGraw, coached for Giants, and managed one of their minor league teams. Batting against Joe McGinnity of Giants, Lobert had not been able to hit safely. In eighth inning, McGinnity soon got two strikes on Hans. Lobert then bunted safely down first base line, beat it out. Between innings McGraw, coaching at third base, asked him, "Young man, who ever taught you to bunt with two strikes?" "Nobody," replied Lobert. "I just like to bunt, and nobody was looking for a busher to do that."

Lobert was farmed out to Des Moines for 1904; then with Johnstown, an "outlaw" club, 1905. That fall Chicago Cubs brought him back to majors, but in 1906 traded him to Cincinnati where he remained until 1910. Philadelphia NL, 1911–14, then to New York Giants three seasons.

Coached West Point baseball team 1918–25. Douglas MacArthur was head of Academy four of those years. Back to Giants as coach four years, then managed Bridgeport team, farm club for Giants, 1929–31. Managed Jersey City club. Coach, Philadelphia NL, 1934–41. Manager,

Phillies, 1942. Coach, Cincinnati Reds, 1943–44. Scout, Giants, first in New York, then San Francisco, until 1967. Hans served briefly as interim manager of Phillies, 1938, after dismissal of Jimmy Wilson. In his only year in charge of team, 1942, club, which had been in cellar before his taking over, again finished last.

Lobert hit for .281 average in NL. Reached .300 mark four times but was never considered slugger, although in 1911 had nine home runs, goodly total in those days. Had 32 round-trippers during career, 159 doubles, 82 triples. Scored 640 runs, drove in 488. Four times went as high as 40 or more steals during one season.

In field day at Cincinnati 10/10/10, in baseball uniform, circled bases in 13-4/5 seconds and beat out bunt to first base in 3-2/5 seconds.

Lobert made world tour with New York Giants and Chicago White Sox during winter of 1913–14, visiting Japan, China, Australia, Egypt, England, and other countries. In 1924 served as secretary to John McGraw when Giants and White Sox made European tour.

LOCKER, ROBERT AUTRY P-BLR-TR. B. 3/15/38, Hull, Iowa. 6'3", 195. Bob Locker won six games, lost just one, and saved 10 others for Oakland A's in 1972 but in 1973 found himself with another club in another league, traded to Chicago Cubs. After Oakland won WS against Cincinnati, Charles Finley and Dick Williams did not stand pat. Veteran reliever was dealt for Bill North.

Chicago general manager, John Holland, and field manager, Whitey Lockman, may have been intrigued that Locker, pitching 78 innings in regular AL season, 1972, allowed only one home-run ball. In 1971 allowed only two homers in 72 rounds twirled. Bob, however, could hardly expect to escape with so few homers in Wrigley Field, smaller ball park than Oakland's.

Locker graduated from Iowa State U. with degree in geology. Played baseball there and signed by Bill Kimball of Chicago White Sox, 1960. Spent that summer and next with Lincoln, Ill., team in III League and at Idaho Falls, Pioneer League. Two years in military service, then posted 16–9 record with Indianapolis, Pacific Coast League. Next four full seasons with White Sox. Traded to Seattle Pilots, then in AL, 6/8/69 for Pitcher Gary Bell. That franchise shifted to Milwaukee for 1970. Locker was sold to Oakland 6/15/70.

Bob, working in 491 games in majors prior to start of 1973 season, had 2.69 ERA for 739 innings. With fair fast ball and sinker, was able to demonstrate good control, allowing 199 bases on balls while striking out 487 batsmen. Appeared in just 1/3 inning in 1972 WS, allowed one hit, and was taken out in another of Williams' scores of strategy shifts.

LOCKMAN, CARROLL WALTER (Whitey) OF-1B-BL-TR. B.

7/25/26, Lowell, N.C. 6'1", 182. Whitey Lockman at age 18 broke into lineup of N.Y. Giants, banged home run in first time at bat 7/5/45, and hit .341 in 32 games. It was 1948, however, before was able to play regularly. Entered army in August 1945, spent 1946 in service. Rejoined Giants in spring 1947. Trying to break up double play in exhibition game, suffered dislocated right ankle and broken fibula above ankle. Didn't play again until September when pinch hit on two occasions. Whitey was outfielder at time and continued in field until 1951. Owner of Giants, Horace Stoneham, felt Lockman couldn't play first base. Mgr. Leo Durocher believed team would be stronger if he could. After repeated discussions, Stoneham finally told Leo to try him at first base, adding, "if it doesn't work, it's your neck."

Lockman was put at first base late in May— and Giants won pennant. From then on, though Whitey did play some outfield and second base, he saw most service at first base. Traded to St. Louis NL 6/14/56. Traded back to Giants 2/26/57. Giants moved to San Francisco, 1958. Traded to Baltimore AL 2/14/59. To Cincinnati 6/23/59. Unconditionally released by Reds 7/1/60.

Lockman's major league career added up to 1666 games played and .279 batting average. Hit 114 homers, 49 triples, 222 doubles. Hits totaled 1658; scored 836 runs and drove in 563. Best home-run production was 18 in 1948. In 1952 led NL first basemen in double plays. Hit .186 in 10 WS games, 1951,54 with Giants, including one homer. Played in 1952 All-Star game.

Lockman was coach for Giants, 1961–64; managed Dallas–Fort Worth in Texas League, 1965, bringing club home second in Eastern Division. Coach, Chicago Cubs, 1966. Managed Tacoma, Pacific Coast League, 1967–70, in Cub organization. Became super scout, 1971, and early in 1972 appointed assistant to vice president and director of player development. Became full vice president, and at All-Star break, 1972, took over management of Cubs from Leo Durocher. Later signed for 1973 season.

Looking back on playing career, Lockman recalls one particularly important game—playoff game for NL pennant, 1951. Whitey's double in ninth inning knocked Don Newcombe out of box. Dressen, Dodger manager, then sent Ralph Branca to mound. Thomson's homer followed, giving Giants flag.

LOGAN, JOHN, JR. (Yachta) SS-BR-TR. B. 3/23/27, Endicott, N.Y. 5'11", 175. Johnny Logan joined television team of Milwaukee Brewers, 1973—same fellow whose "Loganisms" have brought chuckles to many. Same fellow who played many years with Boston, Milwaukee Braves and wound up major league career with Pittsburgh Pirates, 1963, with lifetime mark of .268 for 1503 games. One suspects that some Loganisms now may be contrived, though many of them were original. Such as time was invited to visit on yacht of Braves' club owner, Lou Perini. Speaking to wife of owner, Johnny told her, "Mrs. Perini, you sure have a very homely boat here." Once, asked what he intended to do during winter, Johnny replied, "I'll probably go into public relationship." When Norm Larker of Dodgers banged into him at second base during final playoff game for 1959 pennant, someone asked whether he'd get even with Larker. "Well," replied Logan, "an elephant never forgets, not that I'm an elephant." Also surprised listeners with introduction of then baseball commissioner thus, "my great and good friend, Frick Ford." Also has referred to Stan Musial as "one of baseball's great immorals."

Logan was competetive, aggressive ball player whose list of fisticuff opponents is long—Vern Bickford, Jim Greengrass, Johnny Temple, Vic Power, Don Drysdale, Hal Jeffcoat, and Clint (Scrap Iron) Courtney. Logan had strong hands; started milking cows at age eight, claims was pro milker by age 11. Claims milking developed finger and arm muscles. Attended Harpur College one year. Pro career began, 1947, at Evansville, Ind., and continued in minors at Dallas, Pawtucket, and Milwaukee, then in American Association. Had 62 games with Boston NL, 1951, and 117 in 1952. However, first full season in majors was following year when Braves moved franchise to Milwaukee. Best year at bat was 1955 when had .297 average for 154 games. Regular shortstop for Braves until 1961, then traded to Pittsburgh, remaining with Pirates through 1963. Later played in Japan for one year. After retiring from game became Milwaukee sports announcer.

While rookie with Braves, trying to make good, played exhibition game against New York Yankees. Before contest began, asked Frank Crosetti, long-time shortstop for Yanks, to study his play and to tell what he (Logan) was doing wrong. Three weeks later Johnny received long letter from "Crow." Page after page of tips on how to play position, which Johnny says helped him tremendously.

Logan wasn't long-distance hitter but in six seasons hit 10 or more homers, with 15 his high water mark in 1956. Had 93 during major league career; 41 triples, 216 doubles among 1407 safe hits. Scored 651 runs, drove in 547. In 14 WS games with Milwaukee Braves, 1957,58, Johnny hit .154 with eight hits in 52 trips, including one homer. NL All-Star squads 1955, 57, 58, with one hit in four trips.

Nickname "Yachta" is Ukranian for John.

LOLICH, MICHAEL STEPHEN (Mickey) P-BLR-TL. B. 9/12/40, Portland, Oreg. 6', 210. Mickey Lolich won 25 games for Detroit Tigers, 1971; pitched 376 innings, more than any other AL pitcher in almost six decades. He, and many others, believed his performance should have won Cy Young Award—but it went to Vida Blue. Started 45 games, finished 29. All of which got him $80,000 contract, according to best guesses. Nevertheless, some believe winning three WS games in 1968 against St. Louis Cardinals represented his greatest deed. At time was toiling in shadow of Denny McLain, who won 31 games that season. Denny won one game, lost two in WS. Lolich started and won second game of WS after McLain had failed in opener. Denny failed in fourth game, but Mickey won fifth contest. McLain finally notched 13–1 victory in sixth contest. Then Lolich handcuffed Cardinals in final, crucial seventh game. Shut them out for eight innings and allowed solitary run in ninth after Tigers had safe four-run lead. His ERA for WS was 1.67 for 27 innings pitched. Lolich, in some respects, was improving in 1972. While he won three less decisions than in previous season, lowered ERA from 2.92 in 1971 to 2.50 in 1972. Pitched 327 innings. Struck out 250, while walking 74. Best strikeout record, however, was in 1971—308.

Mickey became southpaw because of childhood accident. During period 1959–63 gained minor league experience at Knoxville, Durham, Denver, Portland, and Syracuse. Joined Tigers during 1963 season, won five, lost nine. Came up with 18–9 record, 1964, first full year in majors. After that never failed to win at least 14 games. Had 17–9 mark in 1968, 19–11 in 1969. Then went from losingest hurler in AL, 1970, to top winner: 14–19 record followed by 25–14 mark in 1971.

Member of AL All-Star squads, 1969,71,72. Mickey's first home run ever was hit in first at bat during 1968 WS off Nelson Briles, then with Cardinals.

Mickey's overall major league record at start of 1973: 393 games, 2505 innings, 163 victories, 121 defeats; ERA 3.29, 793 walks, 2124 strikeouts, 32 shutouts.

LOLLAR, JOHN SHERMAN (Sherm) C-BR-TR. B. 8/23/24, Durham, Ark. 6'1", 205. Sherm Lollar performed creditably behind bat through 1752 major league games, but is especially proud of his catching while with Chicago White Sox. In 1954 nobody stole base while he was catching from May 11 for rest of season. In that period threw out 18 would-be base stealers. Only four men had stolen on him during first weeks of season.

Lollar worked in same zinc mine where Mutt Mantle, father of Mickey, worked in 1943. That was season he signed with Baltimore Orioles, then in International League. Bonus? "It never occurred to me to ask for one," said Sherm later. Played 12 games for Birds that year, but was their regular catcher next three seasons until went to Cleveland late in 1946. Traded to Yankees, who put him on their Newark farm team for 1947. With Yanks 11 games that year, then spent 1948 with New Yorkers, getting into just 22 contests. By this time Yankees decided

Yogi Berra would stick to catching, and Lollar went to St. Louis Browns 12/13/48. Three seasons with Browns, then with Chicago White Sox, 1952–63; coach, Baltimore AL, 1964–66. In 1973 manager of Tuscon club of PCL.

Sherm led AL catchers in fielding four seasons while with White Sox, 1953,56,60,61; led catchers in double plays three times—but also led in grounding into double plays, 1959. Best season at bat, for average, 1956, with .293; but hit 20 homers, 1958, and 22 in 1959. Lifetime major league average .264; his 1415 hits included 244 doubles, 14 triples, 155 home runs; scored 623 runs, drove in 808.

Once caught six fouls in one game, tying major league record. At one point in 1955 hit seven homers in 10 days. AL All-Star Game squad, 1956,59,60. In WS play with Yanks, 1947, and White Sox, 1959, hit .308 in eight games; eight hits in 26 trips, with two doubles, one homer; six runs scored, six RBI.

LOMBARDI, ERNESTO NATALI (Schnozz) C-BR-TR. B. 4/6/08, Oakland, Calif. 6'3", 230. If slow-moving big Lom had possessed speed of average major leaguer undoubtedly would have hit closer to .400 than lifetime average of .306 compiled over 17 seasons in big time. When Lombardi came to bat, opposing infielders moved at least 10 or 15 feet back from normal positions onto grass. Ernie generally pulled ball too, so whole infield moved toward left-field foul line. Once or twice during career, opposing third baseman played so far back that Lombardi bunted—and beat it out. Seemed incredible, but there are eyewitnesses. Not surprising, however, that Lom set NL record for grounding into double plays with 30 in 1938. Holds record for grounding into most double plays four different seasons, 1933,34,38,44.

They called him Schnozz because of big proboscis. Big, good-natured guy who seldom had much to say. Used interlocking grip when batting, like some golfers. When he met ball solidly, opposing pitcher and infielders took lives in their hands if they tried to stop liners. Prayed for grounders instead of those cannon balls.

Legend has it that Lombardi allowed N.Y. Yankees to win 1939 WS from Cincinnati Reds. Fact is Yanks had flattened Reds in first three games of Series. Somehow Reds managed to keep Bombers from winning fourth game in nine innings. But in 10th, combination of walk, sacrifice, two errors and single by Joe DiMaggio put Yankees two runs ahead. This was point when King Kong Keller, going into plate hard to score second run, banged into Lombardi.

Ernie apparently was dazed by collision and was slow in recovering ball, so that DiMaggio also scored. But game was lost anyway, and unfair to accuse Lombardi of "snoozing," as many newsmen did.

Lombardi got trial with hometown club, Oakland, Pacific Coast

League, 1927, but went to Ogden, Utah, where he tore cover off ball at .398 rate for 50 games. Back with Oakland, 1928–30, hit .377, .366, and .370 in succession—playing regularly too. Sold to Brooklyn Dodgers for 1931, where batted .297 as rookie in 73 contests. Traded to Cincinnati before 1932 season and had best years there. Lom caught such pitching stalwarts as Eppa Rixey, Paul Derringer, Bucky Walters, and Johnny Vander Meer. In 1935 hit .343, then had couple of years batting only .333 and .334. Came back in 1938 to lead NL with .342, dropped to .287 in 1939, and went back to .319 in 1940.

After .264 season in 1941, Reds sold him to Boston NL. Lom promptly won another batting title with .330 average. Then moved to N.Y. Giants for five seasons, batting above .300 twice in this span. Given unconditional release late in 1947, Schnozz lined up first with Oakland, then with Sacramento in Pacific Coast League, 1948. This was last season as active player.

Lombardi, despite slowness afoot, was solid asset to team. Won NL MVP, 1938. Lifetime major league record showed 1853 games with 1792 hits. These included 277 doubles, 27 triples, 190 home runs. Scored 601 runs and drove in 990. Eight stolen bases for his career. In 1939,40 WS Lombardi didn't sparkle at bat—4 for 17, .235 average. Ankle injury during 1940 Series, used as catcher in only one game.

Owns major league record for most two-baggers in one game, four, 5/8/35.

LONBORG, JAMES REYNOLD   P-BR-TR. B. 4/16/42, Santa Maria, Calif. 6'5", 210. Road back from ski accident in December, 1967, has been slow, painful for Jim Lonborg. Won 14 games, lost 12, for Milwaukee Brewers, 1972, and had 2.89 ERA. In 1967 Jim won 22 games, lost nine, for Boston Red Sox, helping them win AL pennant. Followed it with two WS wins over St. Louis Cardinals, one defeat. Won Cy Young Award for AL; on top of world at age 25. Then came badly broken leg while skiing. Lonborg struggled through 6–10 record, 1968, and 7–11, 1969. In 1970 Red Sox sent him to Louisville farm club briefly, and repeated process in 1971. In 1970–71 Jim won five, lost three, in Louisville; won 14, lost eight, with Red Sox. Then came trade to Milwaukee 10/11/71.

Lonborg graduated from Stanford U. with A.B. in biology, then signed with Red Sox, 1963. Spent 1964 at Winston-Salem (6–2); and at Seattle, Pacific Coast League (5–7); then joined Boston AL, 1965. Came up with 9–17 record as rookie, followed by 10–10, 1966.

After skiing accident, Lonborg was beset by arm trouble and injuries. Broke toe, 1969, when foul ball hit it. For four years served as player representative for Red Sox; after trade to Milwaukee, elected by Brewers to serve in same capacity.

Lonborg faced 1973 season with record of 82 wins, 77 losses in majors. His ERA was 3.75. Member of 1967 All-Star AL team, but did not get into contest. His WS performance, 1967: 2–1, 2.63 ERA.

LONG, RICHARD DALE 1B-OF-BL-TL. B. 2/6/26, Springfield, Mo. 6'4", 220. Dale Long got his name into record books because of couple of home runs sprees and because he, lefthanded thrower, caught two games in majors, only man in modern times to try this. Ordinarily Dale was first baseman, though used occasionally as outfielder in minors, and briefly as pitcher. While with Pittsburgh Pirates, Long, May 1956, set major league record which even Babe Ruth never achieved: eight home runs in eight consecutive games. Some off good pitchers too— Warren Spahn (Hall of Famer), Carl Erskine, Lindy McDaniel. Dale also equaled major league record for consecutive home runs by pinch hitter in 1959 while with Chicago Cubs. Hit two homers in two trips as substitute batter. It was Bob Scheffing who defied modern tradition by using Long as catcher. Bob managed Cubs in 1958.

Long played 1013 major league games, hit .267, with 132 homers among his 805 hits. Had 135 doubles, 33 triples, scored 384 times, drove in 467. St. Louis Browns and Pittsburgh 1951. Pittsburgh 1955–57. Chicago NL 1957–59. New York AL and San Francisco NL 1960. Washington 1961–62. New York AL 1962–63. Two WS, with Yankees, 1960, 62; used mostly as pinch hitter—.250 average, two for eight.

Started out at Milwaukee, then in American Association, 1944. With about dozen clubs in various sections of country, climaxed by one year (1952) in New Orleans when he hit 33 homers, and two with Hollywood, where he had 35 homers one season, 23 next. His best season for homer production in majors was 1956 when he hit 27 for Pirates.

LOPAT, EDMUND WALTER P-BL-TL. B. 6/21/18, New York, N.Y. 5'10", 195. One of many who have managed AL clubs in Kansas City, Ed is prouder of pitching ability than managerial record. Won 166 games in AL career, losing 112, greatest years being with New York Yankees. Managed K.C. into eighth place, 1963, in 10-club circuit. Started 1964 in same job, but gave way to Mel McGaha during season. Team finished 12th.

Eddie's real name was Lopatynski. Seven years minor league experience before he made it to majors with Chicago White Sox, 1944. Progress slowed by nervous disposition and tendency to throw temper tantrums when things went wrong during ball game. Once had 3–2 lead going into last inning; second baseman made error. Lopat so angered threw wild pitch over catcher's head, then walked next four batsmen forcing home run that beat him. Finally, with doctor's help, learned to stop worrying.

Was told, "When you are ready to blow your top, count your blessings, not your troubles." Wife told him he could earn living elsewhere if didn't make grade in baseball. After embracing new philosophy, began to study pitching zealously. Buttonholed other pitchers and coaches, learned to throw screwballs, knuckleballs, sliders. Battled fatigue by leaving dugout between innings, sitting in camp chair, concentrating thoughts on matters far removed from ball game in progress. System worked. In 1943 won 19 games, lost 10 at Little Rock. Led Southern Association in innings pitched and in effectiveness. Then four years with White Sox. Had 16–13 record, 1947, then traded to Yankees 2/24/48. Won 109 games for Yanks in next seven years, losing just 51. Had records like 17–11, 18–8, 21–9. In 1953, besides leading AL in winning percentage with 16–4 for .800, led in effectiveness with ERA of 2.43.

Lopat at times had to fight jitters even after becoming highly successful pitcher in majors. One time was pitching 0–0 ball game in eighth inning. Two men out, two men on base. Felt stomach start to churn; called Yogi Berra out to mound. While Yankee Stadium crowd thought they were scheming what to throw slugger Gus Zernial, dangerous hitter, Lopat asked Yogi, "What's the penalty for bigamy?" "I dunno," said Berra. "Two mothers-in-law," replied Eddie. Yogi trotted back behind plate. Lopat struck out Zernial, Yankees won ball game an inning or two later by 2–0. Had 12–4 mark in 1954, then began to lose touch. Sent to Baltimore Orioles 7/30/55, finished that year with 7–12 record and was handed unconditional release 10/10/55. Pitched for Richmond, International League, 1956, winning 11, losing six.

On way up to majors, played first base for Greensburg, Pennsylvania State League, 1937. Then pitched for Jeanerette in Evangeline League; Kilgore, East Texas circuit; Shreveport, Longview, Salina, Oklahoma City, and Little Rock.

Helped Yankees to WS, 1949, 50, 51, 52, 53; won four games, lost one with 2.60 ERA for 52 innings. Pitched in 1951 All-Star game for AL and was charged with loss. Career major league record showed ERA of 3.21 for 2439 innings, with 859 strikeouts, 645 walks allowed.

Pitcher-manager for Richmond, 1956, then managed same club, 1957–58. Returned to Yankees as coach, 1960.

Known as "junk man," pitcher who threw "garbage" at opposing hitters. While offerings rarely had much speed, was able to fool hostile sluggers with wide variety of deliveries.

LOPEZ, ALFONSO RAMON C-BR-TR. B. 8/20/08, Tampa, Fla. 5'11", 180. Living refutation of Durocher axiom, "Nice guys finish last." After long career as brilliant NL catcher, put together distinguished record as AL manager. Did not win many pennants as pilot, but still had amazing skill handling teams with limited talent. Led Cleveland Indians to 1954 flag, and Chicago White Sox to 1959 pennant. In 15 full seasons as manager had 12 years when team was either first or second in AL. Even in minors Lopez was successful manager. In 1948, first year at helm, won American Association pennant in Indianapolis, then came up with two runner-up clubs.

If Bill Veeck had been able to swing it, Lopez would have managed Cleveland in 1948, without minor league experience as pilot. Lou Boudreau, playing manager for Indians, did not please Veeck as field boss. With this in mind, Veeck traded Gene Woodling to Pittsburgh for Lopez, still an active player, 12/7/46. Bill wanted Lopez on Cleveland payroll for time when he could conveniently drop Boudreau.

Lopez played 61 games for Indians, 1947. Then during WS that fall, Veeck cooked up trade with St. Louis Browns. Plan was for Boudreau, two outfielders, and $100,000 cash to land in St. Louis, while Vern Stephens, then hard-hitting shortstop, two pitchers, and an outfielder would come to Indians. Veeck had Lopez sitting in hotel lobby, waiting for completion of deal. Then press conference was to be called, introducing Al as new Cleveland manager. However, Bill DeWitt, then boss at St. Louis, demanded that Veeck raise ante by $90,000. This was to cover difference Browns would pay Boudreau if they were to pay him same salary he was getting in Cleveland, over three-year period. Story of impending deal leaked to newspapers and Cleveland fans howled bloody murder. So Veeck retained Boudreau. Lou and Indians won pennant, 1948, while Lopez was manager at Indianapolis. Indians dropped to third in 1949, to fourth in 1950. Then Hank Greenberg, general manager of Cleveland, acting on behalf of new club owners (Veeck had sold out), handed Boudreau unconditional release. Lopez was Lou's replacement for 1951, remaining on job until close of 1956 season. Al then moved to White Sox, managed that team through 1965. By that time Al had health problems and decided to leave manager's job in younger hands—Eddie Stanky's. When White Sox came up with hatful of problems in 1968, Lopez was persuaded to take over reins again. Team won 33 games, lost 48, under Al's management in last half of season, but finished ninth in 10-club circuit. In 1969 White Sox were fifth-place team in six-club Western Division of AL, and Lopez had hired Don Gutteridge as coach. Al's health once again caused him to step aside, which he did 5/4/69. Gutteridge thus handled Sox through most of 1969.

When Indians won pennant for Lopez, 1954, club took 111 victories against 43 defeats, with margin of eight games over N.Y. Yankees. Early Wynn, Mike Garcia, and Bob Lemon all had great years on pitching mound. Bob Feller won 13 and lost only three. Bobby Avila won AL batting championship. Larry Doby won top spot in AL for homers and RBI's. Team went into WS as heavy favorite. However, N.Y. Giants, under Leo Durocher, flattened Indians in four straight.

When Lopez led White Sox to AL pennant, 1959, observers said he did it with mirrors and black magic. Bill Veeck had taken over Sox and frankly did not believe they could win pennant because of lack of power. Lopez, however, insisted Sox could win. Veeck later wrote, "A typical White Sox rally consisted of two bloopers, an error, a passed ball, a couple of bases on balls, and, as a final crusher, a hit batsman. Never did a team make less use of lively ball. We won 35 games by one run, and it seemed as if we won most of them in ninth inning or extra innings." "Go-go" White Sox surprised everyone in first game of 1959 WS by defeating Los Angeles Dodgers 11–0. But Dodgers caught up, and took Series four games to two.

In his book *Veeck—As in Wreck*, Bill declared, "If Al Lopez has a weakness as a manager—and I said if—it is that he is too decent. . . . Al was completely relaxed. In that cool, calm way of his he squeezed every possible drop of talent out of his team. When I think of that season (1959), I think of a squibbling hit and everybody running."

As player, Al started in Ybor City, Spanish-speaking area in Tampa. Signed with Tampa club of Florida State League, 1925, and moved to Jacksonville for 1927, Macon for 1928. Brooklyn Dodgers had him for three games in 1928, but he needed one more year of seasoning. This he got in 1929 at Atlanta, Southern Association, where played 143 games and hit .327 with 85 RBI. For next six years was stalwart with Dodgers, taking part in at least 110 games every season. While not power hitter, hit above .300 twice for Dodgers. Maximum home run production was eight in 1936. Traded to Boston Braves 12/12/35 and to Pittsburgh Pirates 6/14/40. Remained with Pittsburgh until traded to Cleveland for Gene Woodling. Took with him .261 lifetime NL average for 1889 games. At Cleveland, 1947, hit .262 in 61 games. In last year as active player, 1948, when he also managed Indianapolis, hit .268 in 43 contests. Al wound up with major league totals of 1950 games, 1547 hits, with 206 doubles, 42 triples, 52 homers. Had .261 average overall, with 613 runs scored, 652 RBI.

Lopez holds major league record for most games caught during career, 1918; NL record for most games caught, 1861; tied major league mark for fewest passed balls by catcher working in 100 or more games— none in 1941; tied Gabby Hartnett for NL record of most years catching at least 100 games, 12. Also caught at least 100 games eight consecutive seasons, NL mark since broken by Roy Campanella, who turned trick nine straight years.

LOWE, ROBERT LINCOLN (Link) 2B-BR-TR. B. 7/10/68, Pittsburgh, Pa. D. 12/8/51, Detroit, Mich. 5'10", 150. Before they invented night baseball and twi-night doubleheaders, major league teams often played morning and afternoon games on holidays such as Memorial Day, Fourth of July, Labor Day. Management got two admissions and players had breather between games. On one such occasion, 5/30/94, Link Lowe, infielder with Boston NL, used time between games to consume shore dinner at North Boston Railroad Station. Partook of generous quantities of clams, lobster, and fish; then went back to ball park. Slammed home run in third inning. Teammates got batting fever, and Lowe, up for second time in same round, slapped another homer. Later in game spanked two more round-trippers. Four home runs in one game during spree! Fans were so pleased they showered Link with coins and some folding money and he went home richer by $160. Being superstitious, Lowe went back to same restaurant next day and ordered same menu. But it didn't work; this time went hitless. While hit 13 more homers that season, never again was he able to duplicate feat of four in one game. In fact, has been done very infrequently in all years since then. In relatively modern times Rocky Colavito, Lou Gehrig, Joe Adcock, Gil Hodges, Chuck Klein, Pat Seerey, and Willie Mays have accomplished it once each.

Lowe was with Boston NL 1890 through 1901. Played mostly at second base but took whirl at other infield and outfield positions. Chicago NL 1902–03. Pittsburgh 1904. Detroit AL 1904–07. Played 1820 major league games, had 1929 hits, scored 1131 runs; 230 doubles, 85 triples, 70 homers, 984 RBI, 302 stolen bases, for .273 average.

Lowe managed Detroit Tigers part of 1904 season after Ed Barrow left club. Team won 30, lost 44, wound up in seventh place. As player didn't help team much that year—batted just .208 in 140 games. Best season was year he got all those homers—batted .346 in 133 games.

LOWREY, HARRY LEE (Peanuts) OF-Inf.-BR-TR. B. 8/27/18, Los Angeles, Calif. 5'8½", 170. "Peanuts" has been around. But got nickname before had been around very long. According to *Sporting News*, an uncle looked at him shortly after birth and remarked, "Why he's no bigger than peanut!"

Lowry has been with various minor league clubs as player; and with several major league teams as player and coach. Played just about every position but pitcher during career that began in 1937 at Moline, Ill. Saw service at Ponca City, Okla.; St. Joseph, Mo.; Los Angeles, Seattle, and Milwaukee while those cities were in minors; Buffalo, New Orleans, and Austin. In NL was with Chicago, 1942–49; Cincinnati, 1949–50; St. Louis NL, 1950–54; Philadelphia NL, 1955.

Managed at New Orleans, 1957; Austin, 1958; and Idaho Falls, 1960. Coached Phillies, 6/1/60 through 1966; San Francisco NL, 1967–68; Montreal NL, 1969; Chicago NL, 1970–71; and California AL, 1972.

During long major league service, interrupted by one season in military, 1944, Peanuts played total of 1401 games and hit .273. No great shakes as long ball hitter: 37 homers, 186 doubles, 45 triples. Scored 564 runs, drove in 479. NL All-Star squad 1946; Went 1 for 2, .500 average. In 1945 WS while with Cubs, seven games, 9 for 29, .310 average; scored four runs.

LUCAS, CHARLES FRED (Red) P-BL-TR. B. 4/28/02, Columbia, Tenn. 5'9", 185. Red Lucas won 157 NL games as pitcher despite toiling many years for second-division or cellar-dwelling clubs at Cincinnati. Won many other games, however, as capable pinch hitter. Records say that Red, during 16 major league seasons, made 114 pinch hits. Good enough batsman that Boston Braves played him at second base briefly during 1924 and 1925 seasons.

Red started pro ball with Nashville and Rome, Ga., in 1920; Nashville and also Jackson, Greenwood, Mississippi State League, 1921; Won 20 games, lost 18 with Nashville, 1922. N.Y. Giants took look at him, 1923 but sent him to San Antonio where won 18 and lost nine that same season. Lucas next came up with Boston Braves, 1924, won one, lost four as pitcher, and played two games at second base. Six more games at second base in 1925 with Braves, who then shipped him to Seattle. Lucas went back to pitching at Seattle; won nine, lost five, and in 1926 was back in majors, this time with Cincinnati. Remained with Reds through 1933 season. Came up with four winning seasons, starting with 8–5 in 1926, then 18–11, 13–9, and 19–12. Reds finished fifth in both 1927 and 1928, and seventh in 1929. In next four years Cincinnati had three cellar clubs and one seventh-placer, and Lucas won more than he lost only in 1931, with 14–13 record. Pittsburgh rescued him from depths, 1934. Red came up with 10–9, 8–6, and 15–4 records in first three seasons with Pirates. Won eight, lost 10 in 1937, then bowed out of majors after 6–3 record in 1938.

Red's major league totals: 157 wins, 135 losses, 3.72 ERA; 396 NL games, started 301, completed 204. In 2542 innings walked 455 and fanned 602. Had batting average of .281. After leaving majors, pitched, coached, and pinch-hit for while with Montreal, then Brooklyn farm club in International League.

LUCCHESI, FRANK JOSEPH Manager. B. 4/24/26, San Francisco, Calif. 5'8", 180. Frank Lucchesi, who managed Philadelphia Phillies 1970–71 and part of 1972, moved into Cleveland Indians' organization as pilot of Oklahoma City club, 1973. Frank led Phils to fifth-place finish first year with club, landing in bottom spot, sixth, in Eastern Division of NL, 1971. Hapless team again was headed nowhere in particular, 1972, so once more managerial change was made, 7/10/72. Paul Owens took over.

Lucchesi never got far as minor league player after starting with Portland, Pacific Coast League, 1945. Served at Salem, Oreg.; Victoria,

B.C.; Bisbee, Ariz.; Ventura, Calif.; and Twin Falls, Idaho, as outfielder. Then became player-manager at Medford, Oreg.; Thomasville, Ga.; Pine Bluff, Ark.; Pocatello, Idaho; Salt Lake City; High Point, N.C.

After quitting as player, 1957, continued to manage from sidelines at High Point; Williamsport, Pa.; Little Rock, Ark.; San Diego in Pacific Coast League; Reading, Pa.; and Eugene, Oreg. When he came to Phillies as pilot, had 19 years' experience as minor league manager, 14 with Phillies' organization. Also managed briefly in St. Louis Browns' system and that of Baltimore Orioles. Received Manager of Year awards five different seasons in minors.

LUDERUS, FREDERICK WILLIAM   1B-BL-TR. B. 9/12/86, Milwaukee, Wis. D. 1/4/61, Milwaukee, Wis. 5'11", 185. Captain and first baseman for first Philadelphia NL pennant winner, 1915. First member of Phillies to hit two home runs over fence in one game. Played most of dozen seasons with Phils but started with Chicago Cubs, 1909. Hit .277 in 1346 major league games, with 84 homers to credit. Had 16 round trippers in 1911, 18 in 1913, goodly numbers those days.

Started in minors at Sault Ste. Marie, Northern League, 1905. Then three years with Winnipeg, Copper League and Northern League; Freeport, Ill., 1909; then 11 games with Cubs that same season. Cubs sent him to Phils during 1910 season and he remained there until played 16 games for them in 1920. During this period hit better than .300 twice, with best season 1915 when Phils captured pennant. Hit .438 in WS that fall, but Boston Red Sox still took classic four games to one. His seven hits included two doubles, one homer; drove in six runs.

Luderus was modest fellow: admitted had been struck out by many pitchers like Grover Alexander, Christy Mathewson, and others. But was proud of fact he never was taken out for pinch hitter. After leaving majors, played and managed in minors until 1928; was with Toledo, Kansas City, Oklahoma City, Shreveport, and Omaha. In 1958 was selected for Wisconsin's Hall of Fame.

LUM, MICHAEL KEN-WAI   OF-BL-TL. B. 10/27/45, Honolulu, Hawaii. 6', 180. First Hawaiian to represent islands in majors since they achieved statehood. Mike, however, now is Texas rancher in off-seasons. After high school days in Honolulu, chose to sign with Atlanta Braves rather than accept baseball scholarship to Brigham Young U. in Utah; however, did attend there for one semester.

Mike was with Waycross in Georgia-Florida League, 1963; Binghamton, N.Y.-Pa. circuit, 1964; Yakima, Wash., in Northwest League, 1965; Austin, Texas League, 1966; and Richmond, International League, 1967. Joined Braves that year for nine games and, starting in 1968, played at least 120 games each season for next five years. Best hitting average was

.268 in 1969 and again in 1971. Career average for 643 games, as he started 1973, was .249; his 383 hits were good for 558 total bases, with 60 doubles, 8 triples, 33 homers.

Lum's red-letter day has to be 7/3/70 when slapped three homers in three consecutive trips to plate against San Diego Padres, driving in five runs. Also remembers time he got four hits in one game 10/2/69 against Cincinnati Reds.

LUQUE, ADOLFO P-BR-TR. B. 8/4/90, Havana, Cuba. D. 7/3/57, Havana, Cuba. 5'10'', 172. Dolf Luque was one of earliest Latin American players to make good in majors for long period of time. Pitched in NL in 20 seasons, mostly with Cincinnati Reds, but later did valuable work for Brooklyn Dodgers and N.Y. Giants. Chalked up 194 major league wins against 179 defeats. In 550 games pitched 3221 innings and had 3.24 ERA. Walked 918 and fanned 1130.

Luque came to U.S. to pitch for Long Branch in New York-New Jersey League, 1913. Won 22, lost five, and was drafted by Boston NL. Briefly with Braves, 1914–15, but spent most of 1914 with Jersey City and 1915 with Toronto. Braves gave up on him and released him to Louisville, where pitched 1916–18. Won 26 games, lost 14 over this span, then was bought by Cincinnati. Won six and lost three for Reds, 1918, and remained with team through 1929. Hard luck pitcher, 1921 and 1922, with 17–19 record, then 13–23. But turned tables, 1923, with 27–8, which led NL with .771 percentage. Also topped circuit in effectiveness with 1.93 ERA. Traded to Brooklyn 2/10/30. Had 14–8 and 7–6 records in two seasons with Dodgers, then drew unconditional release. Signed with Giants—used almost entirely as reliefer with considerable success. Still had good curve, cagey on mound, and mean. Pitched five scoreless innings in first WS appearance, 1919, with Reds, and 4-1/3 more in 1933 with Giants, so had WS ERA of 0.00. Won fifth game of classic that year, in relief, clinching N.Y. victory over Washington Senators, four games to one.

Luque was coach for Giants, 1935–37 and 1941–45; later managed Havana club in Florida International League, 1951; and Mexicali, Nuevo Laredo, and Merida teams in Mexico.

LYLE, ALBERT WALTER (Sparky) P-BL-TL. B. 7/22/44, Reynolds-ville, Pa. 6'1'', 180. Southpaw flake was his reputation in Boston. But while he continued eccentricities in N.Y. Yankee uniform, 1972, also showed self to be brilliant relief pitcher. Saved 35 games and won nine others while toiling in relief. Lost five games; had ERA of 1.92. Yankees obtained him in trade for Danny Cater after had put in 4-1/2 seasons with Red Sox. Originally property of Baltimore Orioles; Red Sox drafted him off Orioles' farm team at Rochester, end of 1964 season. Baltimore organization signed him after struck out 31 in 17-inning sandlot game.

Lyle spent 1964 with Bluefield and Fox Cities; 1965 with Winston-Salem; then to Pittsfield for 1966. Spent part of 1967 with Toronto, then promoted to Red Sox. During minor league apprenticeship Lyle did not come up with any fancy statistics but intrigued baseball men with potential. Nor was his 1967 performance with Red Sox notable. In 1968 had 6–1 mark, and 8–3 in 1969, used exclusively in relief. Things were tough, 1970: won one, lost seven, and 3.90 ERA was least impressive of his career. But came back, 1971 with 6–4 mark, 16 saves. Complained, however, that did not pitch often enough.

Some critics believe Lyle profited in 1972 from more spacious premises of Yankee Stadium, compared to Fenway Park. He worked in 59 games, 108 innings, and brought total saves for his career to 98. Had 31 victories to credit against 22 defeats as 1973 rolled around, with 350 career strikeouts, 162 walks allowed, in 439 innings.

One reason for his reputation as "flake" was seating himself squarely on top of cake once in Boston clubhouse. Ken Harrelson earlier had pushed another cake into Sparky's face. In 1972, while with Yankees, volunteered to caress reportedly wild tiger for publicity stunt for animal preserve. Result: front-page cover picture in *Sporting News*, and national circulation. Sparky is photography fan himself, owning much expensive equipment. Also owns Russian wolfhound. Red Sox once fined him $500 for reporting to training camp considerably overweight, but later refunded the money.

In minors Lyle pitched just seven complete games. In majors, as of spring of 1973, had never started single game—used exclusively in relief.

LYONS, THEODORE AMAR (Ted) P-BLR-TR. B. 12/28/1900, Lake Charles, La. 5'11", 200. High school second baseman and basketball player who made it into Hall of Fame as pitcher. Did it hard way, since he pitched for Chicago White Sox who finished in second division 16 times in 21 years Lyons toiled for them. Won 260 games, lost 230.

Ted managed Sox part of 1946, all of 1947 and 1948 seasons. Record as pilot wasn't good: 185 wins against 245 losses. However, didn't have much to work with, and teams finished fifth, sixth, and finally last in AL.

Lyons played semipro ball in Louisiana as youth, but that did not affect amateur status when enrolled at Baylor U. Team needed pitching and Ted was pressed into service on mound. Pitching good enough to attract several scouts, but didn't sign until Ray Schalk, White Sox catcher, warmed him up in visit to Baylor campus. That was 1923. Ted went direct from college to big leagues, in fact winning two games and losing one in AL that very summer. Ted in AL six years, with second-division club, before had losing season. Won 12, lost 11 in 1924, first full year. Then came up with 21–11; 18–16, 22–14, and 15–14 seasons before finished lower than .500. Won 14, lost 20 for 1929 Sox, who finished seventh. Ups and downs for next several seasons, along with rest of teammates. Managed 15–8 record in 1935, but thereafter was never able to pass 14 victories in any season. Military service 1943–45. When he rejoined Sox, 1946, pitched in just five games, winning one, losing four. Named manager of Sox 5/25/46, replacing Jimmie Dykes. In 1949 joined Detroit Tigers as coach, through 1953; coach, Brooklyn, 1954; returned to White Sox, 1955, as scout and continued this role many years.

Ted had no-hitter against Boston AL 8/21/26; almost had another, 9/19/25, against Washington, but Bob Veach singled with two men out in ninth. He was only man to reach first, depriving Lyons of perfect game. White Sox won contest, incidentally, by 17–0 score. Lyons never got chance to pitch in WS. Major league record for 594 games showed 4162 innings pitched, allowing 1696 earned runs for 3.67 ERA. Walked 1121 men and struck out 1073. Best ERA came in last full season as pitcher, 1942, when 14–6 winning mark was accompanied by 2.10 ERA, leading AL pitchers in effectiveness.

Lyons was fairly good hitter for pitcher. In 1930 hit .311. Lifetime average was .233, with 364 hits, 49 doubles, nine triples, five homers, with 149 RB I. Tied major league record 7/28/35 with two doubles in one inning. Hall of Fame honors came in 1955.

McAULIFFE, RICHARD JOHN (Muggs) 2B-SS-BL-TR. B. 11/29/39, Hartford, Conn. 5'11", 175. Dick McAuliffe, aggressive infielder for Detroit Tigers, was never more rugged than in two plays during 1972 AL playoff series against Oakland. In both cases Dick was base runner. Got away with football-tackle tactics. Many observers felt umpires should have declared penalties for interference; but he got away with it. At plate Dick has been described as bulldog. During 1972 restrained desire to emulate power hitters: hit only eight homers, but raised average to .240 after it sagged to .208 in 1971.

McAuliffe has had to struggle to become regular in majors. Signed with Tigers at age 17, out of high school. Detroit press-radio-television guide frankly admits he was ragged fielder as second baseman. But he stayed in there, made grade as shortstop for Tigers, later shifting to second base. AL All-Star squads 1965,66, shortstop; 1967, second baseman.

Dick played with Erie, Augusta, Valdosta, Knoxville, and Denver between 1957 and 1961. Eight games with Tigers, 1960, but had .884 fielding average with five errors at shortstop. Eighty games with Tigers, 1961, then became regular, although moved around from short to third to second. Concentrated primarily on shortstop 1963–66; since then used mostly at second base. Unorthodox stance at plate, but hit 24 homers, 1964, and 23 in 1966 when had best average, .274. In 1970 average dropped to .234 with 12 homers, and in 1971 to .208 with 18 round-trippers. Then McAuliffe decided had better concentrate on average, rather than compete with Norm Cash and other sluggers on club.

As 1973 approached, Dick had played 1550 AL games, making 1377 hits. These included 200 doubles, 69 triples, 180 homers. Scored 817 runs, drove in 625, and owned career average of .248.

McAuliffe had enviable record, 1968. Tied major league record for those appearing in at least 150 games—did not ground into any double plays. In one WS, 1968, Dick hit .222. One of hits was home run off Washburn of St. Louis Cardinals. Dick's average in three All-Star games was identical with WS mark, .222.

McCARTHY, JOSEPH VINCENT (Marse Joe) 2B-BR-TR. B. 4/21/87, Philadelphia, Pa. 5'8½", 195. Joe McCarthy had been bouncing around minor leagues since 1907 when New York Yankees made deal for him, 1915. But deal was canceled and Joe decided to join Brooklyn club of Federal League, an outlaw organization that considered itself major league. Then that league blew up before McCarthy could join Brooklyn Feds, so Joe never played big league ball. McCarthy finally made Yankees, 1931, as manager, and when he did, he valued this association. Again and again reminded his players, "You are a Yankee now!" Demanded they conduct themselves with dignity on and off field—dress neatly, wear neckties, jackets. McCarthy could be proud of his Yankees. Good ball players—won eight AL pennants and seven WS for him. Jimmie Dykes accused him of being "push button manager." But Joe had to boss such varied personalities as Babe Ruth, Lou Gehrig, Tony Lazzeri, Lefty Gomez, Johnny Allen, Jake Powell, Joe DiMaggio, and Joe Gordon. Some of those fellows—and others—could test manager's psychological skill at times.

Joe must have shown leadership abilities fairly young. At 26 was playing manager at Wilkes-Barre in New York State League. That was only year he hit above .300 in any league. Went to Buffalo, International League, as player after that, then had six years at Louisville in American Association as player. During fourth year at Kentucky metropolis was named playing manager, continuing this role through 1921; then was bench manager at Louisville through 1925.

That was season Chicago Cubs tried to make manager of Rabbit Maranville, with disastrous results. So they turned to experienced minor league pilot. Cubs had finished last in 1925, so McCarthy sent several players on their way, including Grover Cleveland Alexander who was ignoring prohibition law. He added Riggs Stephenson and some others, and brought club home in fourth place. Another fourth-placer, 1927, then third-place finish, 1928. In 1929 Cubs won NL flag with 10-1/2-game lead. One of McCarthy's most dismal experiences followed in 1929 WS against Philadelphia Athletics. Leading by 8–0 score in fourth game, Connie Mack's crew blasted 10 runs across in seventh inning and snatched victory. Next day Cubs went down to defeat, losing Series four games to one. McCarthy had team in contention, 1930, but Cubs dropped him just before season's close, and following year Joe's long stay with Yankees began. McCarthy had to be content with second place in 1931, but won first AL pennant, 1932. Followed up with winners in 1936, 37, 38, 39, 41, 42, 43, and each fall Yankees won WS, except 1942. In 1932, 1938, and 1939 Yanks swept series in four straight games. It was rare satisfaction for Joe to win sweeps in 1932 and 1938 especially, since they were against Chicago Cubs, team that had let him go in 1930. Other WS sweep came in 1939 versus Cincinnati Reds.

Larry MacPhail could try patience of saint. And while Joe McCarthy probably has no claims to canonization, when MacPhail became president of Yankees, 1945, handwriting was on wall. It was only question of time until MacPhail would second-guess or needle manager. McCarthy's health was not best, and combination led to his departure 5/24/46. McCarthy left Yanks with record of eight pennant winners, four runners-up, two third-placers and one fourth-placer in 15 full seasons. Then, in 1948 McCarthy came out of retirement to lead Boston Red Sox to runner-up position both that year and next. Left Sox for permanent retirement 6/23/50. Hall of Fame 1957.

McCARTHY, THOMAS FRANCIS MICHAEL OF-BR-TR. B. 7/24/64, Boston, Mass. D. 8/5/22, Boston, Mass. 5'6", 145. Small but skilled outfielder who made Hall of Fame, 1946, although had lifetime batting average several points short of .300. With Hugh Duffy, was part of "Heavenly Twins" famed in baseball legend. This pair, while playing for Boston NL in 19th century, baffled opposing hitters in outfield. McCarthy perfected trapped fly ball. If base runners stood on base, Tommy would let ball hit ground and get forceout, and at times double play. If base runners ran, McCarthy would usually catch fly ball and then double runner off base. Sure-handed fielder. He and Duffy had hit-and-run play they saved for special occasions. Tommy was brilliant base runner; stole 93 bases for St. Louis club of American Association, 1888; led in thefts with 83 in 1890. Had grand total of 506 thefts during major league career.

Tommy played for Boston, Union Association, 1884. Boston NL 1885. Philadelphia NL 1886–87. St. Louis AA 1888–91. Boston NL 1892–95. Brooklyn NL 1896.

While not power hitter, McCarthy hit .351 in 1890 while with St. Louis AA; had two seasons above .340 with Boston, 1893, 94; made close to 1500 hits; slapped 43 homers, most probably inside-park variety. Overall major league average .294 for 1258 games.

McCARVER, JAMES TIMOTHY (Tim) C-OF-BL-TR. B. 10/16/41, Memphis, Tenn. 6'1", 200. Phil Gagliano and Tim McCarver were teammates while at Christian Brothers High School in Memphis. Tim also attended Memphis State U.; was in great demand for athletic scholarships and by professional ball clubs. Signed with St. Louis Cardinals, 1959, for reported $75,000 bonus, causing Gagliano to wisecrack, "We were gold dust twins. Tim got the gold. I got the dust."

McCarver served apprenticeship at Keokuk, Rochester, Memphis, Charleston, and Atlanta in minors before sticking full season with Cardinals, 1963. Hit .289 with 51 RBI that year in 127 games. Played oftener, 1964, but hitting was just about same until autumn, when was red hot in WS against Yankees. Led regulars of both teams with .478 average, 11 hits in 23 trips. Also provided Redbirds with winning runs in fifth game by slamming home run with two men on base in 10th inning. Had one double, one triple, drove in five runs altogether, scored four times. All this, with his team winning world championship one day before 23rd birthday.

Tim's best average with Cardinals was .295, with 14 homers, 69 RBI in 1967. But management wasn't entirely satisfied with his catching, and obtained Joe Torre who did backstop work and played first base. Then Ted Simmons came along as fine young prospect, and Cardinals traded McCarver to Philadelphia 10/7/69 in same deal that ended Curt Flood's career in St. Louis. Two full seasons with Phils, then during 1972 traded to Montreal. Gene Mauch, manager of Expos, used Tim in outfield, at third base, and behind plate. McCarver's 1972 average sagged to .246 in process. Traded back to Cardinals 11/6/72. Began 1973 with lifetime major league average of .273. Played 1277 games; his 1193 safeties included 182 two-basers, 45 triples, and 82 round-trippers. Scored 450 runs, drove in 487.

Besides stardom in 1964 WS, Tim played in fall classics of 1967,68. Overall record: .311 for 21 games, 23 hits good for 2 doubles, 3 triples, 2 homers, with 11 RBI. All-Star games of 1966, 67; made 3 for 3.

Tim had plenty of passed balls in 1963—tied for NL lead with 16; led in this regard, 1965, with 18. During off-season, operates restaurant he owns in Memphis.

McCORMICK, FRANK ANDREW (Buck)   1B-BR-TR. B. 6/9/13, New York, N. Y. 6'4", 205. Frank McCormick was "bucket hitter" but became one of best inside-ball hitters in majors. Bucket hitting probably reason did not impress Philadelphia Athletics and Washington Senators after brief tryout with each. Then managed to get workout with N. Y Giants. Frank had job in New York art store. During morning, he accidentally dropped Early American cream pitcher and sugar bowl valued at $625. As he got down on floor to pick up pieces, boss said he was through, fired. Then young man headed for Polo Grounds and baseball workout. Giants didn't give an answer immediately. Ironically, few days later, he received letter from Giants saying that if he had job, had better keep it—would never be able to hit because was bucket hitter. McCormick didn't have job, didn't want one, and kept trying to impress somebody in baseball.

After Cincinnati Reds gave him workout, was sent to their Beckley, West Va., club, 1934, where he slapped ball at .347 pace in 120 games. And in 12 games with Reds, hit NL pitching for .313. Needed further seasoning, however, and got it at Toronto, Fort Worth, Nashville, Decatur, Durham, and Syracuse, finally sticking with Reds as regular, 1938. Hit .327 that season, with five homers, 106 RBI. Got homer range following year, with 18; hit .332 and drove in 128 markers. Then hit .309, with 19 homers, 127 RBI. About this time McCormick suffered back injury that became chronic. Dropped below .300 couple of seasons, then went above it two more years. Hit 20 homers, 1944, but Cincinnati fans began to boo him unmercifully and he was accused of not giving best. Sold to Phillies for 1946 season; moved to Boston Braves during 1947 and played final major league campaign for Boston, 1948. Manager, Quebec, 1949, playing 13 games; manager, Lima, Ohio, 1950, getting into 10 games.

Frank did some scouting and was coach for Cincinnati, 1956–57. When he called quits, had played in 1534 big league games, had .299 average. His 1711 hits included 334 two-baggers, 26 triples, and 128 homers. Scored 722 runs, drove in 954. His 128 RBI, 1939, led NL; so did his 209 hits. This was first full season in majors. MVP 1940. In two WS with Cincinnati, 1939,40, hit .279. Played for NL squad in All-Star games of 1938, 39, 40, 41.

McCOVEY, WILLIE LEE (Stretch)   1B-OF-BL-TL. B. 1/10/38, Mobile, Ala. 6'4", 230. Even when handicapped by injuries, Willie McCovey is just about most feared and respected batsman in major leagues. At plate, is home run threat to extent he is given intentional walks more often in clutch situations than any other batsman. Willie has had more than share of injuries. In 1971, for example, an ailing left knee required surgery. Early in 1972 suffered spiral fracture of right arm in collision with Johnny Jeter of San Diego Padres. Wore cast and was out of action six weeks. When he returned, in first game poled home run off Steve Blass of Pittsburgh. Then more misfortune—was hit by pitched ball from delivery of John Strohmayer of Montreal Expos. Ball hit McCovey in right arm, in exact spot where he was still wearing pin in arm as result of surgery.

McCovey played in 81 games, 1972, lowest total for full season since joining Giants. Hit .213, far below normal performance. Hoping for better times, McCovey faced 1973 season with lifetime average of .279.

for 1712 major league games. His 1547 hits included 237 doubles, 40 triples, 384 home runs; scored 933 runs, drove in 1090. Seven times Willie's home run totals have been better than 30 for season. In 1963 reached 44, tie for league leadership. Won home run honors, 1968, with 36, and following season with 45, his high-water mark.

Willie played at Sandersville, Georgia State League, 1955; Danville, Carolina League, 1956; Dallas, Texas League, 1957; Phoenix, Pacific Coast League, 1958, and 95 games, 1959. Was bouncing along with .372 average, leading league in homers with 29, and tied for lead in RBI with 92. Joined Giants, faced Robin Roberts in first game. Clicked off four for four—two were three-baggers. NL pitchers have been terrified ever since. Hit .354 in 52 games that year, 13 home runs, and was voted Rookie of Year. Didn't prove consistent, 1960. Hit .238, with 13 homers, in 101 games. Giants farmed him to Tacoma, PCL, for 17 games, then he came back to stay, 1961. Best hitting average since then was .295 in 1966. Willie drove in more than 100 runs in four NL seasons, twice leading league, 1968,69. MVP 1969.

Willie has friendly smiling disposition, regarded as team leader with Giants. Six times on NL All-Star game squads. In only WS, 1962, had to be content with .200 average, three hits in 15 trips. One of hits was tremendous home run off Ralph Terry in second game, at Candlestick Park. Giants won 2–0, but lost WS to Yankees, four games to three.

McCRAW, TOMMY LEE 1B-OF-BL-TL. B. 11/21/40, Malvern, Ark. 6', 185. Tommy McCraw hasn't hit for very high average in AL during first 1245 games extending to end of 1972 season. However, had 64 home runs, some coming at crucial moments. For example, after joining Washington Senators was sent to plate as pinch hitter for first appearance with club in 10th inning of game 4/9/71. Drove homer to give Denny McLain 5–4 victory over New York Yankees. Hit two more pinch homers for Senators that season.

McCraw also smacked three homers in one game while playing for Chicago White Sox 5/24/67. Going into 1973, owned .240 lifetime big league mark, with 341 RBI, 414 runs scored; 126 doubles, 41 triples.

Tommy attended Santa Monica City College in California. Began pro career at Clinton, Iowa, 1960, then moved to Idaho Falls and Indianapolis before graduating to Chicago White Sox during 1963. Counting 1972 season, Tommy played in well over 100 games in AL every year since then, with exception of 1969. Best season at bat was 1964, when he hit .261. Remained with White Sox until 3/29/71, when traded to Senators. One season in nation's capital; hit just .213 and was traded to Cleveland during spring of 1972. In 129 games with Indians and hit .258. Traded to California Angels on eve of 1973 season.

Tommy led AL first basemen in double plays, 1968, with 103. But also tied major league record for most errors in one inning, three, 5/3/68.

McDANIEL, LYNDALL DALE (Lindy)   P-BR-TR. B. 12/13/35, Hollis, Okla. 6'3", 196. Lindy McDaniel, who got reported $50,000 bonus for signing with St. Louis Cardinals in 1955, has been one of best relief specialists in majors. Twice won *Sporting News* designation as Fireman of Year, 1960, 63. Before 1973 season: won 102 games in relief, saved 160; pitched last complete game in majors in 1960; took part in 862 games. In 1795 innings won 123 decisions, lost 108 with 693 earned runs and an ERA of 3.47. Walked 526 men, struck out 1181.

McDaniel was starter with Cardinals but along about fourth season in pro ball switched to relief specialist. Began pitching as sidearmer, shifted to three-quarters, finally became overhand hurler. Specializes in fork ball. Most productive season as starter was 1957 with Cardinals. Pitched 10 complete games, 15–9 mark. Following year effectiveness was off and was sent to minors. Pitched in six games for Omaha, American Association, 4–1, and returned to St. Louis. Traded to Chicago NL 10/17/62, to San Francisco Giants 12/2/65, to Yankees 7/12/68, in deal for pitcher Bill Monbouquette. In 1968 McDaniel set NL pitchers' record by having been in 225 games without having made an error. In 1968 also tied an AL record by retiring 32 consecutive batsmen who faced him. Brother Von McDaniel had brief period with Cardinals as pitcher; another brother, Kerry Don McDaniel, pitched in Cardinals' minor league organization.

McDOUGALD, GILBERT JAMES   Inf.-BR-TR. B. 5/19/28, San Francisco, Calif. 6'1", 180. Gil McDougald was known as Yankee "glue man." Could play capably at second, short, or third base. Religious, family man, good team player. When he broke in, had somewhat off-beat batting stance with feet spread widely apart, left foot pointed toward pitching mound. Held bat high, well back of him, with heavy part of bludgeon dropping loosely. Hit .306 in 131 games as rookie with New York AL. Curve-ball pitchers caused Gil to alter stance after that. Was able to pass .300 mark only once after opening season with Yanks. Wound up career with .276 average for 1336 games. Had 1291 major league hits good for 187 doubles, 51 triples, 112 homers.

McDougald substantially helped Yankees into eight WS. In his first classic, 1951, after Baseball Writers Association of America named him AL Rookie of Year, Gil was first rookie to hit grand slammer. Turned trick in fifth game, as Yankees won 13–1. Had three other RBI that Series and hit .261. Overall WS record was .237 for 53 games, including seven homers. Drove in 24 markers, scored 23 in WS play. His work in

1958 WS was particularly notable. After .250 average during regular season, Gil fielded brilliantly, hit .321 in WS, including two homers. Played for AL in All-Star games 1952,57,58,59.

From 1948 to 1950 McDougald played for Twin Falls, Idaho; Victoria, B.C.; and Beaumont, Tex. Drove in six runs in one inning 5/3/51, which equaled major league record. In 1952, however, made four errors in WS as third baseman, which tied record.

McDOWELL, SAMUEL EDWARD THOMAS (Sudden Sam) P-BL-TL. B. 9/21/42, Pittsburgh, Pa. 6'5", 220. Cleveland Indians, 11/29/71, pulled one of most masterful trades of recent years when they exchanged Sam McDowell for Gaylord Perry and shortstop Frank Duffy. Sudden Sam is four years younger than Perry. Had led AL in strikeouts five times. But his 1971 record was 13–17 with an ERA of 3.39 compared to Gaylord's 16–12 mark and 2.76 ERA. Giants wanted "lefthander who can strike somebody out," in words of Mgr. Charley Fox. One year later Fox, Stoneham and Company had second thoughts about deal. McDowell pitched in 28 games for San Francisco, 1972, but finished with four complete games and 10–8 mark, 4.34 ERA. Perry was 24–16, had 1.92 ERA, won Cy Young Award. Indians' desire to trade McDowell was partially stimulated by his salary disputes, 1971. Although Sam won 17, lost 11 in 1965, and had 20–12 mark, 1970, rest of career had been mediocre. Wanted something near $100,000 for 1971. Alvin Dark, combination field manager and general manager at time, worked out deal involving bonuses based on performance on field. Reportedly signed for $72,000 base pay. Depending on innings pitched, games won, McDowell might have received as much as $90,000. Commissioner Bowie Kuhn outlawed deal because of rule forbidding bonus contracts, fined Cleveland club $5000. McDowell then left club, claiming should become free agent, and was suspended. After couple of days Sam returned to Indians; reportedly signed satisfactory contract for 1971. Not long after season ended, Indians worked out trade with Giants.

Sam, as high school athlete in Pittsburgh, was standout in basketball, football, swimming, tennis, and track as well as baseball. Pitched his team to Pennsylvania state championship, 1960, with no-hitter and blasted home run in final game. Cleveland Indians obtained signature by giving estimated $75,000 bonus. Served at Lakeland, Fla.; Salt Lake City, Jacksonville, and Portland before finally sticking with Indians during 1964 season, when won 11, lost six.

While in AL, McDowell set record for most strikeouts in two consecutive nine-inning games, 30; and record for most strikeouts in three straight games, 40, in 1968. Tied major league record by twirling two one-hit games in succession, 1966; twice led AL in wild pitches and tied for lead one other season. Pitched in four All-Star games for AL;

named to two other squads but replaced due to injury.

Going into 1973 McDowell had played in 364 big league contests; won 132, lost 117; pitched 101 complete games in 2273 innings; allowed 1158 bases on balls, struck out 2281. Lifetime ERA stood at 3.09.

MacFAYDEN, DANIEL KNOWLES (Deacon) P-BR-TR. B. 6/10/05, North Truro, Mass. D. 8/26/72, Brunswick, Me. 5'11", 172. Mild-mannered, soft-spoken, bespectacled pitcher who won 133 games in majors and lost 159. When Danny did lose temper once, was so out of character veteran baseball men still talk about it. Legendary Bill Klem was umpiring behind plate; Danny on mound for Pittsburgh. After count went to three balls, two strikes, umpire called next pitch "ball four." MacFayden rushed to plate, took off glasses, and handed them to Klem shouting, "You need these worse than I do!" Naturally Danny was ordered off field forthwith, but before departing argued that banishment was too severe. Klem then allegedly declared was putting MacFayden out of game not because of offering him his glasses but because Danny had been shouting so loud he could be heard in stands. As MacFayden departed he explained to any who were listening, "I was shouting in case Klem's hearing was as bad as his eyesight!"

Danny went to majors direct from semipro ball, 1926. Made good with Boston Red Sox, then tail-end ball club. In 1931 Danny's 16 victories against 12 defeats helped team climb to sixth place after succession of cellar finishes. Traded to Yankees 6/5/32, was less than sensational in New York. With Cincinnati Reds and Boston Braves, 1935, remaining with Boston through 1939. Had two good seasons with Braves, 17–13 in 1936 and 14–9 in 1938. Pittsburgh 1940. Washington 1941. Boston NL 1943.

MacFayden had ERA of 3.96 for 2706 innings pitched in majors. Liked to recall time he blanked Yankees 5–0 in 1930. Struck out Ruth, Gehrig, and Lazzeri with bases full. From 1946 until 1970, when he retired, MacFayden was baseball coach at Bowdoin College in Maine. At times also served as hockey coach.

McGILLICUDDY, CORNELIUS (Connie Mack) C-BR-TR. B. 12/22/62, East Brookfield, Mass. D. 2/8/56, Germantown, Pa. 6'1", 150. "Tall Tactician." Patriarch. Institution in City of Brotherly Love. Managed Philadelphia Athletics half century. Won nine AL pennants, captured five WS while losing three. Built powerful baseball clubs with scant expenditure of cash. Free spender to rebuild Athletics after years of wallowing in second division. Iconoclast who twice destroyed teams he had carefully built up. Most baseball people, including many rough customers among players, gave him respectful title of "Mr. Mack." Some would have canonized him. Some saw him as tightwad, skinflint. Former in vast majority. Not surprising he was elected to Hall of Fame, 1937, for service apart from playing game. Philadelphia gave him Bok Award, 1930, for having rendered greatest service to city during preceding year. This carried not only honors, scroll, and medal, but also cash gift of $10,000. Prior to that time, recipients of Bok Award had always been men of achievment in learned professions or scholarly vocations.

Mack was born while Civil War still raged in this country, son of Irish immigrants. Quit grade school after six years; worked in cotton mill, shoe factory, but found time to play baseball on side. Started in 1884 as pro with Meriden and Hartford clubs in Connecticut, and briefly with Newark before joining Washington NL 1886. Four years there, then one season with Buffalo in Players League, 1890. Joined Pittsburgh, 1891, remaining there through 1896. In this period Mack was good catcher, played some outfield and first base, with very rare fling in infield. Did not hit with power, but occasionally hit for pretty good average. Career totals, however, showed .251 lifetime mark for 695 major league games.

During fourth season with Pittsburgh was named playing manager. Celebrated by leading team to victory over Washington NL by 22–1 score 9/3/94. Won 12, lost 10, remainder of that season. His clubs then had seventh- and sixth-place finishes in 12-club league for 1895–96. Following season became manager of Milwaukee, Western League, played just 27 games, and bossed team from sidelines thereafter until end of 1900. This club never finished lower than fourth while Mack was there.

Through friendship with Ban Johnson and Charlie Comiskey, when Western League was reorganized and went for major status as AL, Mack took over Philadelphia franchise with 25% of stock. Mack recruited most of his better players from NL; since NL had $2400 salary limit, was no great trick for new circuit to raid older organization. Athletics finished fourth in 1901, then moved up to first place, 1902.

As Mack began operations with Athletics, John McGraw ridiculed efforts, saying club would become white elephant. Mack reacted by making white elephant team symbol and later used it on uniforms. McGraw's Giants had satisfaction of defeating Athletics in 1905 WS, four games to one, when Christy Mathewson pitched three shutouts and Joe McGinnity one for New Yorkers. But Mack came out best in two later WS, 1911 and 1913, Athletics defeating Giants 4–2 in first classic and 4–1 in other. These were only times two rivals met in WS—Mack winding up with nine victories to seven for McGraw.

Connie built many of his teams around collegians, among them Eddie Collins, Eddie Plank, Chief Bender, Jack Barry, Jack Coombs. Mack used no profanity, did not smoke, rarely tasted alcohol, seemed to get along not only with erudite players but those who came from rough-and-tumble neighborhoods. One most difficult star was Rube Waddell, eccentric problem child. But Connie seemed to get best from all his men, using quiet, gentle approach.

Once when Max Bishop foolishly tried to stretch hit and was tagged out easily at third base, Mack got point across by softly telling Max, "Next time you hit another triple, please stop at second base."

In 1914 his "$100,000 infield" of McInnis, Collins, Barry, and Baker was best in business. Wally Schang, fine catcher, was in his prime. Chief Bender, Eddie Plank, Joe Bush, Herb Pennock, and Bob Shawkey were on pitching staff. Athletics waltzed to pennant by 8-1/2 games, only to lose four straight to Miracle Boston Braves in WS. Various reasons were given why Mack broke up club and finished last in 1915. Facts were that Federal League was tempting several of stars to jump from AL and Connie didn't want to get caught holding bag. Eddie Collins was one of first to go—to Chicago White Sox. Bender jumped to Feds. Baker found it more attractive to play independent ball. Plank shifted to Federal League.

After defeat in 1914 WS, Athletics finished in cellar seven straight seasons, then began slow tedious climb upward again. Parade of collegians and inexperienced semipro tyros did not produce results Mack had obtained earlier. Finally he and partners began paying fairly fancy prices for stellar minor leaguers—Mickey Cochrane, Joe Boley, George Earnshaw, Max Bishop, Al Simmons, and others. Paid $100,600 for Lefty Grove—and Athletics finally returned to top of heap, winning AL flags 1929, 30, 31. Then came depression years. Once again Mack and partners needed money. Grove, Foxx, and Bishop found way to Boston; Simmons and Dykes sold to Chicago; Mickey Cochrane went to Detroit. And Mack's final days in AL were just about as dismal as those seven consecutive cellar finishes after he dismantled 1914 club. Finally, Philadelphia franchise itself went on block and was sold to syndicate that transferred it to Kansas City.

No other pilot will ever come close to Connie's record of managing major league club 50 years. Connie was stockholder and, in later years, majority owner of Athletics, which enabled him to retain job during all those lean years. Yet, given same financial conditions, same players to work with, no other manager or succession of managers could have done any better. Never was Mack expelled from ball game by umpire. Many will remember picture of him, thin, gaunt, dressed in civilian clothes, seated in dugout, waving scorecard, positioning outfielders while game was in progress.

True, many players were unhappy about size of salaries while toiling for Athletics. But Mack never had bankroll of New York Yankees, of Wrigley, or of Tom Yawkey to work with. Unforgettable character.

McGINNITY, JOSEPH JEROME (Iron Man)   P-BR-TR. B. 3/19/71,

Rock Island, Ill. D. 11/14/29, Brooklyn, N. Y. 5'11", 206. When Joe McGinnity, pitcher, joined Brooklyn Superbas, 1900, sports writers asked about his off-season occupation. Deadpan, he replied: "I'm an iron man. I work in my father-in-law's iron factory." Barrel-chested strong man proved he was not lying. Set major league record by pitching two games in one day on five separate occasions. Set modern NL record for most innings pitched in one season, 434, in 1903. Led NL twice in total innings pitched, and once in AL. Had seven 20-game seasons, twice reaching 30-victory mark.

Started career at Montgomery, Southern Association, 1893. Friend of manager recommended him, saying McGinnity had fanned 18 or 19 men in local game. Manager wired back, "If he fanned 19 women, he'd help me. Send him along!" Next season at Kansas City, Western League, then played independent ball until joined Peoria, Western Association, 1898. Next season was in majors with Baltimore Orioles, NL, winning 28, losing 17. Then came shift to Brooklyn and 29–9 record. Baltimore AL, 1901, with 26–21. Had 13–10 mark, 1902 before jumping to N. Y. Giants, same season. Before leaving AL, Iron Man became enraged at decision by umpire Tommy Connolly, stepped on his toes, spat in face, and punched him. Fined and suspended, later apologized publicly to Connolly.

In 1903 McGinnity had 31–20 season. Pitched and won doubleheaders August 1, 8, 31. In 1904 captured 35 decisions, lost only eight. At one point had winning streak of 14 straight. It took sterling performance by Bob Wicker of Cubs to end streak. Wicker pitched nine no-hit innings, allowed one hit in 10th, then Cubs won game in 12th.

Joe came up with 21–15 and 27–12 records next two seasons, then 18–18 and 11–7. Got chance to become owner-manager of Newark club, Eastern League, 1909. Also pitched; won 29, lost 16. Back to old tricks, had 30-victory season, 1910, losing 19. Continued in triple role with Newark through 1912. Manager-pitcher for Tacoma, Northwestern League, 1913–14, coming up with two 20-victory seasons. Joined Venice, Pacific Coast League, 1914, in time for eight games, but won one, lost four. Back to Tacoma as manager-pitcher, 1915 and had 21–15 record. Another 20-win season at Butte, Northwestern League, doubling as manager, 1916. Managed at Butte following year but only won seven. Vancouver, Pacific Coast-International League, 1918. Managed independent clubs next few years, then bossed Dubuque team, Mississippi Valley League, 1922–23. Stepped out for 1924, but came back to Dubuque as manager and part owner. Still pitching—won six, lost six, although was 54 at time.

Coach, Brooklyn Dodgers, 1926. Got job in laboratory of Brooklyn physician, 1927, but seldom missed ball game at Ebbets Field or Polo Grounds. Cut down by cancer in closing years of life.

McGinnity used off-beat underhand delivery. This is supposed to have enabled him to snap curve balls with minimum strain on arm. Hall of Fame 1946. Major league record: 247 victories, 145 defeats, 467 games pitched, 3455 innings, 32 shutouts. Since earned runs were not kept statistically through much of his career, impossible to give ERA accurately. In his only WS, 1905, pitched two games. Lost first start against Philadelphia Athletics, 3–0, but all three runs were results of Giant errors. In next start won 1–0, so ERA for 17 innings of classic was 0.00. Christy Mathewson pitched three shutouts for Giants, so New Yorkers won WS four games to one.

McGLOTHLIN, JAMES MILTON (Red) P-BR-TR. B. 10/6/43, Los Angeles, Calif. 6'1", 185. Jim McGlothlin reports that Bob Lemon, manager at Seattle, Pacific Coast League, 1965, taught him sidearm fast ball, slider, and change of pace. Jim belonged to California Angels at time, having signed for $5000 bonus, 1962. Used money for new car. Previously had tryout with Los Angeles Dodgers. Though felt he displayed sizzling fast ball, they did not offer contract. Won 13, lost 5 in first pro season at Quad Cities, Midwest League. Divided following season between Nashville and Hawaii; spent 1964 with Hawaii; then had 14–8 season at Seattle. With Angels part of 1965–66, but back to Seattle for portion of 1966. Three years with Angels, with 12–8, 10–15, and 8–16 marks. Traded to Cincinnati 11/25/69. Helped Reds to 1970 pennant with 14 victories, 10 defeats. Had 8–12 mark, 1971, and 9–8 record, 1972.

Jim's pitching hurt in 1971 by sore elbow. Very easily could have had more impressive won-lost total that year because during 12 defeats Reds scored only 17 runs, less than two per game. Best ERA came in 1967 with Angels, 2.97. Career ERA in majors 3.45 for 1219 innings in 227 games. Won 64, lost 73. Walked 382 men, fanned 677, with 36 complete games, 11 shutouts. (Figures to start of 1973.) AL All-Stars 1967: two innings, no runs. Not impressive in 1970 or 1972 WS. Had 8.31 ERA in first one, and 12.00 in second. No decisions. Eight earned runs in 7-1/3 innings.

McGOWAN, WILLIAM A. Umpire. B. 1/18/96, Wilmington, Del. D. 12/9/54, Silver Spring, Md. 5'9½", 178. Bill McGowan went through 16-1/2 seasons, 2541 AL games, without missing single inning of umpiring. Those 2541 games represented endurance record well beyond Lou Gehrig's 2130 consecutive games. Officiated in AL 1925–54. Eight WS, four All-Star Games. Operated umpire school at Coca, Fla., and Daytona Beach, Fla., during last dozen years of life. Rules then in effect entitled Bill to $3000 retirement annuity but AL voted $6000 pension in recognition of 30 consecutive years of "brilliant service to league." Two days later was dead.

Bill had rough moments but generally respected as good official. In July, 1948, Washington manager Kuhel accused McGowan of cursing and throwing baseball at Senator outfielder Ed Stewart; of cursing and throwing indicator at pitcher Scarborough. AL prexy Will Harridge suspended McGowan for 10 days. In 1952, again suspended, this time four days. After banishing players from Detroit bench during game in St. Louis, McGowan refused to tell sports writers whom he had expelled.

McGowan umpired baseball games while in high school. Later took job as office boy in Du Pont Company and officiated on side, then became manager of plant team. Took umpiring job at 19 in Virginia League, later went to New York State League, Blue Ridge League, then officiated four years in International League and two years in Southern before moving into AL.

McGRAW, FRANK EDWIN (Tug) P-BR-TL. B. 8/30/44, Martinez, Calif. 6', 185. Tug McGraw blossomed as fine relief pitcher, 1971, then improved on specialty in 1972. Ex-marine had 11 victories, four defeats in 1971; saved eight other ball games. Finished 34 games in all and had 1.70 ERA. In 1972 won-lost record was 8–6; however, saved 27 other games, finished 47, and again had 1.70 ERA. Compare this effectiveness record with that of Steve Carlton. Philadelphia ace was tops among those pitching 160 innings or more, with 1.98.

McGraw is ebullient type who on occasions has shown enthusiasm after final out in ball game. Would jump high off mound, flap arms around in apparent joy. Or could this have been for benefit of television cameras? Probably touch of both.

Tug attended Vallejo Junior College in California, signed with New York Mets' organization, and sent to Cocoa, Fla., in rookie league. In first appearance as pro 7/3/64, less than three weeks after graduation from college, threw seven-inning no-hitter and won game 4–0. Later moved to Auburn in N.Y.-Pa. League that same summer, and spent 1965, first full year in game, with Mets. Won two, lost seven. But next three seasons divided time between Mets and Jacksonville. Returned to Mets to stay, 1969, year they won pennant and WS. Tug's contribution was nine-victory season against three losses, with ERA of 2.25. Pitched three scoreless innings during playoffs that fall, but not called upon during WS.

In 1970 McGraw 4–6, 3.26 ERA. Got rolling in 1971. Going into 1973, with pretty fancy salary for reliever, Tug was 36–38 in majors; pitched in 260 games, starting 30 of them but finishing only four; 585 innings, walked 263, struck out 483, 2.88 ERA. Specialty is screwball, effective against both righthanders and lefthanders.

McGRAW, JOHN JOSEPH (Little Napoleon) Mgr.-3B-BL-TR. B.

4/7/73, Truxton, N. Y. D. 2/25/34, New Rochelle, N.Y. 5'7", 155. Brilliant, belligerent, brawling, intolerant, hated genius. Possibly greatest manager in baseball. But his methods, which got results in an earlier epoch, could not be used in second half of 20th century. Dominating personality in NL from 1902 until resignation as manager of N.Y. Giants 6/3/32. Winner of 10 pennants in first 21 years bossing this team; victor in three WS. Hall of Fame 1937.

McGraw, fiery bantam rooster, fought umpires, battled opposing players, tried to intimidate league presidents, needled, bullied, belittled anyone and everyone who stood in way of his winning. In ball game used every imaginable trick, everything rules allowed and whole lot they did not, to confuse opponents.

Rugged personality got start in unhappy boyhood. When was 12, mother, one step-sister, three brothers died of diphtheria. John ran away from home after inebriated father beat him for breaking windows and other transgressions. Came back, but situation wasn't ideal. Became candy salesman on trains at 16. Pitched baseball in spare moments, then landed job at Olean, N.Y.-Pa. League, 1890. Played shortstop, made nine errors in one game, and was released. Following year did somewhat better at Cedar Rapids, Iowa, although *Sporting News* says had fielding average of .875 and batting average of .275 for 85 games. Before 1891 season was over, McGraw had moved up to Baltimore, then in American Association, despite an .842 fielding average and .245 bat mark for 31 games. Then had eight seasons with old Baltimore Orioles of NL. Teammates included Hugh Jennings, Willie Keeler, Kid Gleason, Wilbert Robinson, and Jack Doyle. Orioles of old were noted for variety of tricks. They would trip opposing base runners; hide extra baseballs in outfield grass to substitute for ball in play; freely use their spikes to cut down infielders; do anything they could get away with when umpire wasn't looking. Keeler and McGraw invented hit-and-run play and used it to perfection. McGraw had no power for distance hitting, but stole bases freely. One year pilfered 77, another season 73, and eight times had at least 25 thefts to credit.

Shortstop early in career with Orioles but soon shifted to third base. Seven straight seasons hitting above .300 with Orioles, including .374 in 1895 and .390 in 1899. Playing manager of Orioles that year. Then traded to St. Louis NL for 1900. Fans felt was unhappy in Mound City and accused him of deliberately arguing with umpires in hopes would be ejected. Then he could go to horse races. In 1901 jumped to new major, AL, at Baltimore, as playing manager. Though Ban Johnson, president of AL, was instrumental in getting him this job, McGraw openly criticized Ban for alleged incompetence of umpires. Bossed Orioles until 7/16/02, when he jumped again, this time to N. Y. Giants. Became manager of New Yorkers, and brought along several good players who had also been in Baltimore. By this time was practically through as player, but appeared in occasional games with Giants as late as 1906.

In 1904 McGraw won first pennant with Giants; had another one in 1905, and additional winners 1911,12,13,17. Then had four straight first-place teams, 1921–24. Won WS 1905,21,22.

During tempestuous career McGraw once threw baseball at umpire Bob Emslie; slugged another umpire, Bill Byron; publicly called NL president "fathead." Accused Pittsburgh club owner Barney Dreyfuss of welching on bets, owing money to bookies; carried on feuds with several other league presidents and with old Oriole friend Wilbert Robinson; challenged Ty Cobb to fisticuffs; fought actor Bill Boyd in Lambs Club, New York.

Comparison of McGraw to Napoleon was apt, in views of close observers. Branch Rickey said Mac ran ball game like competent general planned strategy on battlefield. Oftentimes McGraw, on bench, called every pitch moundsmen threw, gave specific instructions to Giants' batsmen whether to hit or "take," and where to hit ball. In 1922 WS against N. Y. Yankees, McGraw's schemes were particularly effective against Babe Ruth. Bambino hit 35 homers that year, had .315 batting average in AL. But against Giants in WS, average was .118, just two hits in 17 trips. McGraw told his battery to advise Ruth what was coming when Art Nehf pitched, nothing but slow curves. And once, with Rosy Ryan on mound, Giant pitcher quickly got two strikes on Babe. McGraw then signaled for Ryan to throw next pitch into dirt, saying, "He'll swing at anything, he's so anxious." Ryan followed instructions, and Babe went down swinging at third strike.

McGraw demanded complete obedience on field, and enforced strict rules, including curfew, off field. Those who violated instructions were fined. And after lost ball games, on many occasions Giant players had to sit in soggy uniforms in clubhouse for hour or more while McGraw dressed them down with tongue lashings.

McGraw preferred not to experiment with promising young players. Wanted proven major leaguers, and usually was able to make trades or buy men like Nehf, Groh, Bancroft, Meusel, Herzog, and many others who helped win pennants. Sentiment played no part in trades. Even traded away brilliant pitcher and close friend Christy Mathewson when Christy's best days over. However McGraw often brought old pals back to Giants as coaches. Mathewson spent three years as coach for McGraw after playing days were over. McGraw also was "soft touch" for dozens of old ball players known when they were active.

In later years as manager, McGraw began to find iron fist wasn't working as well as earlier. Frank Frisch, a favorite, rebelled in 1926 after getting fed up with McGraw's diatribes, jumped club, and was traded to St. Louis Cardinals. Freddy Lindstrom and Bill Terry talked back to "old man" and got away with it. Though McGraw and Terry hardly spoke to one another for extended period, Mac did not let this affect judgment; when McGraw resigned in 1932, urged appointment of Terry as successor.

Besides his NL pennants, McGraw manager of NL entry in first All-Star game, 1933.

In 1901 McGraw had Negro on Baltimore Oriole club. Player was Charlie Grant, whom he saw play at Hot Springs, Ark. McGraw knew of unwritten law in baseball that black players could not be hired. Tried to palm him off as "full-blooded Cherokee" named Charlie Tokohoma. Mac wasn't trying to advance integration or anything of sort—simply felt Grant could help club. But this was one battle McGraw couldn't win—and baseball had to wait for Jackie Robinson and Branch Rickey to break color barrier 46 years later.

As player, McGraw took part in 1082 major league games; hit .334, with 1307 hits, 124 doubles, 71 triples, 12 homers. Scored 1019 runs, stole 444 bases. As manager at Baltimore, 1899, McGraw's Orioles finished fourth. Bossing Orioles in AL, 1901, finished fifth. Club wound up last in 1902, McGraw jumping to Giants in midseason. Giants also finished last that season. In 29 full seasons as boss of New Yorkers, had only two second-division teams.

McHALE, JOHN JOSEPH 1B-BL-TR. B. 9/21/21, Detroit, Mich. 6', 200. John McHale played only 64 major league games and hit .193 but was smart enough to turn to executive side of baseball while still young. Also married relative of Detroit Tigers' owner, Walter Briggs, which didn't hurt when he moved into front office, 1948, while just 26. President of Montreal Expos since Canadian metropolis entered NL, 1969. McHale, some months after accepting Expo job, was seriously considered for position as commissioner of baseball when General William Eckert was eased out. McHale, however, requested that name be withdrawn from consideration because of obligations to Montreal partners.

John played football at Notre Dame two years, then entered Detroit organization. Performed at Muskegon, Beaumont, Winston-Salem, and Buffalo, as well as with Tigers, for whom he played 1943–48, with stretch in navy, 1943–44. When couldn't win regular job on field, moved into office. Served under general managers Rolfe, Gehringer, Ruel, and Spike Briggs before becoming general manager himself 4/30/57. Moved to Milwaukee Braves as general manager early in 1959. Named president of Braves 9/23/61, also retaining title as general manager. Franchise moved to Atlanta before 1966 season. By end of 1966 coolness had developed between McHale and Paul Richards, vice president for baseball operations. In fact, Richards alone made trade that sent Eddie Mathews to

Houston Astros 12/31/66. Mathews was popular favorite, gate attraction in Atlanta. McHale didn't know about deal until announced by Richards in Dallas. There was no room in Braves' organization for both McHale and Richards. Shortly afterwards McHale left Atlanta club to serve in commissioner's office, which post he filled until moving into Montreal picture. Member of baseball's executive council; vice president of NL; chairman of Major League Baseball Promotion Corporation; also is member of board of directors of Perini Corporation that formerly owned Boston and Milwaukee Braves.

McINNIS, JOHN PHALEN (Stuffy) 1B-BR-TR. B. 9/19/90, Gloucester, Mass. D. 2/16/60, Ipswich, Mass. 5'9½", 170. Stuffy McInnis was first baseman in Connie Mack's famous $100,000 infield before World War I got into full steam. Eddie Collins was second baseman, Jack Barry shortstop, and Frank (Home Run) Baker third baseman. Connie didn't pay anything like $100,000 for these players; but could have sold them for this amount, which was astronomical sum in those days. Stuffy not big as first basemen go, but set various fielding records, including .999 mark in 1921. Made just one error that season; played 163 errorless games in succession, 5/31/21 to 6/2/22. Not a slugger; only 21 career homers. But compiled healthy .308 lifetime major league average for 2128 games.

McInnis played second base with Haverhill in New England League in 1908. Joined Philadelphia Athletics, 1909, and was used sparingly at shortstop only. Following season Connie Mack played him in several positions. In 38 games hit .301. Although still played 24 games at shortstop in 1911, Stuffy was used at first base 97 games, taking over job from veteran Harry Davis. Hit .321 and drove in 79 runs, helping Athletics win AL pennant. In WS that fall, however, Mack used veteran at first base. Athletics won series from Giants. McInnis only got into part of one WS game. But Davis was gone to Cleveland before 1912 rolled around and McInnis had job to self thereafter. This time hit .327 and drove in 103 runs. Though didn't quite make 100 RBI next two seasons, batted well over .300 and Athletics captured two more flags.

When Philadelphia lost 1914 WS to Miracle Boston Braves, Mack began to dismantle team. Did he fear war clouds? Boredom on part of fans at winning so often? Or did he think stars had become complacent? Whatever the reason, Eddie Collins was gone in 1915 to Chicago; Baker refused to report for whatever Connie Mack offered; $100,000 infield was thing of past, and Athletics tumbled into last place, 1915. McInnis still hit .314, but not many teammates were on base when he came to bat, so RBI total dropped to 48. Hit .295 for A's in 1916, and .303 in 1917. Then moved to Boston Red Sox for four seasons. Stuffy hit above .300 in two of them, missed .300 mark by three points one other year.

Continued above .300 in 1922, only season with Cleveland Indians. Then moved into NL with Boston two years, Pittsburgh two, and Philadelphia one. With Phillies, served as manager; played just one game.

Boston Braves had handed him unconditional release 4/13/25. Signed with Pirates in May, hit .368 in 59 games, helping Bill McKechnie win pennant for Pittsburgh, capped by world championship. Phillies were tail-end ball club, 1927, so Stuffy was out as manager at season's close. Following year managed Salem club of New England League, played 38 games, and still batted .339. Called it quits after that.

In major league career McInnis hit safely 2406 times; had 312 doubles, 100 triples, 21 homers; scored 872 runs, drove in 1064. As WS performer, 1911,13,14 with Athletics, 1918 with Red Sox, and 1925 with Pittsburgh, batted an even .200—13 for 65, 4 RBI.

McKECHNIE, WILLIAM BOYD (Deacon) Inf.-BLR-TR. 8/7/87, Wilkinsburg, Pa. D. 10/29/65, Bradenton, Fla. 5'10", 180. Bill McKechnie must have lost track of some of countless clubs was associated with as professional ball player, coach, and manager. Sober, circumspect individual, never accused of intemperance, once had amusing experience with airplanes. Bill, by this time veteran major league manager, boarded plane, took seat, and proceeded to read magazine. In due time plane landed and McKechnie followed crowd into airport, headed for taxi. Taxi driver asked, "Where to, sir?" "Schenley Hotel," said Bill. "Where? Never heard of it. What street is it on?" quizzed cab driver: McKechnie gave him name of intersecting streets. "Never heard of them either," said taxi driver. "Everybody knows the Schenley Hotel," said Bill. "How long have you been driving a cab?" "Twenty-five years," said cabbie, "and then some! But so help me, I never heard of the Schenley Hotel! Mister, you must be in the wrong town. Where in heck do you think you are?" "Pittsburgh, of course," replied McKechnie. "Pittsburgh, hell!" said the cab driver. "You're really lost. This is Detroit!"

McKechnie, however, found way to top spot in NL four times, with two world championships. *Sporting News* named him Major League Manager of Year, 1937 and 1940.

Bill had some rather rugged experiences as manager, however. Became manager of Pittsburgh Pirates, July 1922. Won pennant and world championship, 1925, defeating Washington Senators in seven-game Series. Following year Pirates didn't do so well, and owner Barney Dreyfuss brought Fred Clarke back as vice president and assistant manager. Clarke had managed team some years previously and presence in uniform had effect of undermining McKechnie's authority. Situation was not conducive to good morale and at end of season there was house cleaning—and both McKechnie and Clarke were gone. Bill caught on as coach for St. Louis Cardinals, 1927, became manager, 1928. Team won pennant, only to be flattened by Yankees in WS, four straight. Sam Breadon, Cardinal owner, so chagrined he fired McKechnie, but offered job at Rochester, N. Y. farm club for 1929. Bill needed job, swallowed pride, and accepted demotion. Breadon had reason to regret move. Billy Southworth, highly successful at Rochester, was not ready to manage 1929 Cardinals, most of whom had been his teammates in 1927. Players resented rules, and team dropped out of pennant contention. In July, Breadon shipped Southworth back to Rochester and brought McKechnie back to boss Redbirds.

Bill managed Boston Braves, 1930 through 1937. But had another nasty situation, 1935, when Babe Ruth, just about through as player, became vice president and assistant manager. Babe was law unto self as far as training rules concerned, and McKechnie's hands were tied. Morale of team was shot and club finished bad last.

Then Warren Giles, who had been president of Rochester Red Wings when McKechnie piloted team briefly, had become general manager for Cincinnati. Gave Bill fancy salary to take over management of Reds, 1938. Bill won pennant for Giles, 1939, repeated in 1940, following up with victory over Detroit Tigers in WS that fall.

After sixth-place finish, 1946, McKechnie stepped out of Cincinnati picture. Moved to Cleveland as coach, 1947, under Lou Boudreau, 1947–49; coach for Boston Red Sox, 1952–53. Hall of Fame 1962.

Bill's first managerial experience came in Federal League with Newark club, as playing pilot, from 6/19/15 until end of season. Bill won 54 games, lost 45 and team finished in fifth place. Was 27 years old when given this assignment.

McKechnie started in minors, 1906, at Washington, Pa. Played with Canton, Ohio; Wheeling, St. Paul, as well as Pittsburgh Pirates, Boston NL, New York AL, and Indianapolis, Federal League, before joining Newark. Afterwards was with New York, NL, Cincinnati, and Pittsburgh, finally at Minneapolis, 1921. As player was shifted frequently. Appeared in 546 games, mostly as third baseman, with .234 average. Not much for power: eight career homers. Stole 127 bases.

Bill's son, William Jr., president of Pacific Coast League.

McKEON, JOHN ALOYSIUS (Jack) Manager. B. 11/23/30, South Amboy, N.J. Jack McKeon, appointed manager Kansas City Royals, 1973, never got very high in minors as player. After attending Holy Cross College one year, signed with Pittsburgh organization, 1949, but played in such places as Greenville, Ala.; York, Pa.; Gloversville, N.Y.; Hutchinson, Kans.; Burlington, Iowa; Fayetteville, N.C.; Greensboro, N.C.; Missoula, Mont.; Fox Cities, Wis. Durable catcher, never hit much. At Burlington, 1953, caught all but one of team's 140-game schedule, but managed only .181 average. Two years later, became playing manager at Fayetteville, Carolina League, and brought club home in third place. Moved to Missoula, Pioneer League, as playing manager for next three seasons. Then to Fox Cities, III League, as pilot, appearing in just 11 games as player. After that, concentrated on managing. Wilson, Carolina League, 1960–61; Vancouver, Pacific Coast League, 1962; Dallas–Fort Worth, 1963; Atlanta, International League, 1964 until 6/21. Scout, Minnesota Twins, 1965–67. Joined Kansas City organization, 1968, managing High Point-Thomasville team in Carolina League. Promoted to Royals' Omaha team of American Association, 1969, remaining there until advancement to Kansas City at end of 1972 campaign. At Omaha, McKeon had second-place team, third-placer, and two first-placers. Had another pennant winner at Wilson in Carolina League.

When McKeon took over management of Fayetteville in 1955 was just 24, one of youngest men ever to pilot professional ball club. When Kansas City selected him as successor to Bob Lemon, was 41, making him one of younger managers in majors.

McKeon is college man, having attended Elon College, North Carolina. Also served 21 months in air force. Jack seems to get along with "new breed" of ball players. In minors, while managing in Minnesota Twins organization, had hand in development of Tony Oliva, Cesar Tovar, Rich Rollins, and others. After appointment to Kansas City job, said, "I speak softly—a lot—and I carry a big stick, which I may or may not hit you over the head with. But don't forget it's there." Frowns on card-playing in clubhouse. Likes few rules, but those rules must stick. Declares, "I'm not running babysitting service."

McLAIN, DENNIS DALE (Denny) P-BR-TR. B. 3/29/44, Chicago, Ill.

5'11", 186. *Sic transit gloria mundi.* Denny McLain might translate it, "Up today, down tomorrow." Too bad he never learned this Latin phrase, 1968. That year played organ, piloted plane, won 31 ball games for Detroit Tigers, disputed with newsmen, and still won AL's MVP designation and Cy Young Award, both unanimously.

Space prevents detailing all that happened since then. Traded to lowly Washington Senators. Two suspensions from Commissioner Kuhn. Brief spell with Oakland A's and demotion to minor leagues. Back to majors, at Atlanta, but without impressing anybody with pitching. Collected $75,000 salary, 1972; in return, McLain won one game for Oakland, three for Braves. Lost seven in process. ERA with A's was 6.14; with Atlanta 6.50. Unimpressive spring training 1973. Braves put on waivers—no takers. Given unconditional release. McLain then signed with Iowa club of AA. Major league record at time was impressive, but on cumulative basis. In 280 games had won 131, lost 91, with 3.39 ERA in 1885 innings. Strikeouts totaled 1282, contrasted with 548 walks allowed.

But where was fast ball? When Dick Williams, Oakland manager, sent him to Birmingham in May, 1972, Dick said, "I don't think he could help anybody right now. I don't think he has the velocity he had in the past." Apparently loss of fast ball was connected, at least partially, with trying to lose weight.

Texas Rangers and AL Red Book for 1972 listed McLain's weight at 185 pounds. Rangers traded him to A's in spring, and he reported to Oakland camp weighing 218 pounds. Reportedly pills he took to try to lose fat had adverse effect on system, causing muscle weakness. In any event, Denny didn't have it on pitching mound; failed to finish any of five starts for A's. And in first appearance for Birmingham, was blasted for nine hits, including three homers, in five innings.

McLain's approach to public relations has differed from that of Dale Carnegie. While still with Tigers, poured buckets of water over two Detroit sports writers. This approach also differed greatly from manners his father-in-law, Lou Boudreau, showed toward media representatives. Lou received great honors as ball player and manager but remained friendly and gracious with press.

McLain's feats on pitching mound started with first pro game. Pitched no-hitter for Harlan, Ky., Appalachian League, 1962, after getting reported $17,000 bonus to sign with Chicago White Sox organization. Lost next game with same team, even though allowed no earned runs. Shifted to Clinton, Iowa, Midwest League; won four, lost seven. Tigers got him on first-year waivers 4/8/63. Divided that year between Duluth and Knoxville, with brief stint at Detroit during which won two, lost one. Divided following season between Tigers and Syracuse. Won four, lost five with Detroit, then stayed in majors. Won 16, lost six, with 2.62 ERA in 1965, first full season in big time. Then had 20–14 and 17–16 marks before brilliant 31–6 season in 1968. Besides MVP and Cy Young awards that year, Denny took *Sporting News* honors as AL Pitcher of Year and Major League Player of Year. Led league in innings pitched, with 336; in victories; in percentage, with .838; struck out 280 men while walking 63; had 1.96 ERA. Helped Tigers win AL flag. Denny lost first two starts in WS against St. Louis Cardinals but won sixth game by 13–1 score. Had 3.24 ERA for 16-2.3 innings pitched.

McLain had another good season, 1969, 24–9. Pitched oftener than any other pitcher in AL, with 325 innings; had 2.80 ERA. In 1970 Denny ran afoul of Commissioner Kuhn. Suspended until July 1 for alleged bookmaking activities. When he came back, pitching was way off form— won three, lost five, with 4.65 ERA. Drenched two sports writers, and suspended by team management. Later, again suspended by Kuhn for carrying gun.Next move was Bob Short's fantastic trade. Detroit got Ed Brinkman, Aurelio Rodriguez, and Joe Coleman in deal, although other players were involved. Trade was made over objections of Ted Williams, manager of Washington Senators. Short got high-salaried pitcher who had lost stuff, problem man-child—and gave away two brilliant infielders and pitcher who won 49 games for Tigers in next two seasons. Few trades have ever been so one-sided. Denny proceeded to lose 22 games for hapless Senators, 1971, managing to win 10. Had ERA of 4.27. During one spell lost nine straight. But in justice it should be noted Senators got only 10 runs for him in those nine games.

McLain's 31 victories in 1968 marked first time any major leaguer had won as many as 30 since Dizzy Dean did it in 1934 with St. Louis Cardinals. Denny's other accomplishments include fact he hit home run and defeated Chicago White Sox 4–3 in first major league appearance, 1963. Co-winner of Cy Young Award for AL pitchers, 1969, with Mike Cuellar. Posted nine shutouts, 1969. Fanned seven consecutive Boston Red Sox hitters in relief 6/15/65, tying AL record. AL All-Star squads, 1966, 68, 69: six innings, one earned run, ERA 1.50.

McLISH, CALVIN COOLIDGE JULIUS CAESAR TUSKAHOMA (Bus)

P-BLR-TR. B. 12/1/25, Anadarko, Okla. 6'1", 204. When Cal McLish joined Brooklyn Dodgers in 1944, pitched batting practice to Dixie Walker. Cal threw first couple of pitches righthanded. While Dixie picked up some dust on hands, McLish switched glove to right hand and began pitching to Walker lefthanded. Dixie was flabbergasted. Mickey Owen and other Dodgers tried to convince Walker that McLish was lefthander, had been throwing lefthanded to Dixie from start. Almost got him believing Cal was natural southpaw, with plenty of stuff on ball throwing with either hand. Later, when McLish had arm trouble, wanted to become lefthanded first baseman.

Cal now is studious pitching coach for Montreal Expos. Manager Gene Mauch insists he is "best pitching coach in baseball."

McLish called "Bus" by father because weighed 12 pounds at birth. Also gave handful of names, one honoring Indian ancestry. Cal belonged to Dodgers three years but spent most of 1945–46 in military service. Pittsburgh 1947. Kansas City, American Association, 1947. Pittsburgh and Indianapolis 1948. Chicago NL 1949. Los Angeles, Pacific Coast League, 1949–55, with brief stint with Cubs, 1951. San Diego, PCL, 1955. Cleveland 1956–59. Cincinnati 1960. Chicago AL 1961. Philadelphia NL 1962–64. Coach, Phillies, 1965–66. Scout, Phillies, 1967–68. Coach, Montreal NL, 1969–73.

Best seasons were at Cleveland. Had 16–8 in 1958 and 19–8 in 1959. Pitched in 352 major league games, winning 92, losing same number. In 1609 innings had 4.01 ERA; 713 strikeouts, 532 walks. Tied major league record for most home runs allowed in one inning, four, 5/22/57. AL All-Star Game 1959, second game: no runs, two innings.

McMAHON, DONALD JOHN   P-BR-TR. B. 1/4/30, Brooklyn, N.Y. 6'2", 215. Don McMahon, pitching coach for San Francisco Giants, proved could still fool opposition as relief hurler during 1972 season. Appearing in 44 games, won three, lost three, struck out 45 while walking 21. This brought major league record to 843 appearances, 1270 innings pitched, with 2.99 ERA. Won 86 decisions, lost 68, walked 570, struck out 978.

Don started just two games during career; rest of trips to mound were as reliever, with fine fast ball, most effective when going just an inning or two. One of most effective seasons was 1971, when won 10, lost six, and had four saves.

McMahon, whose hobby is photography, started as third baseman. But when Milwaukee Braves signed him, 1950, they felt strong right arm could be more useful pitching. Minor league experience at Owensboro, Ky.; Denver, Evansville, Atlanta, Toledo, and Wichita. Spent 1952 in military service. Joined Milwaukee NL during 1957 season, had 1.53 ERA in 47 innings. Remained with Braves until 5/9/62, when Houston NL bought contract. Sold to Cleveland 9/30/63; traded to Boston Red Sox 6/2/66. One year later traded to Chicago AL. White Sox traded him to Detroit 7/26/68. Remained with Tigers until sale to San Francisco 8/9/69.

Don was in two WS with Milwaukee Braves, 1957,58, and one with Detroit, 1968. Pitched total of 10-1/3 innings in eight separate games, had no wins, no losses. ERA was 4.35. NL All-Star team 1958, no action.

McMANUS, MARTIN JOSEPH   2B-3B-BR-TR. B. 3/14/1900, Chicago, Ill. D. 2/18/66, St. Louis, Mo. 5'10", 160. Marty McManus played second base for old St. Louis Browns; fought with Ty Cobb; managed Boston Red Sox; urged minor league baseball players to unionize; wound up as house detective in Chicago hotel. Might have remained bookkeeper all his life but for World War I. Drafted into army, was sent to Panama Canal Zone. There played baseball for first time with any degree of regularity. After war, played semipro ball in Chicago, then landed with Tulsa club of Western League, 1920. Before year was out Browns had taken him on.

In 1921 nailed down second-base job, hit .260 with 64 RBI. Hit above .300 next three seasons. His 109 RBI and 11 homers helped greatly in Browns' 1922 drive for AL flag. They missed out, but only by one game. Traded to Detroit after 1926 season, remaining with Tigers through most of 1931. Then to Red Sox for 17 games. Appointed playing manager 6/19/32; team finished last. Rose to seventh place in 1933, but Marty dropped as pilot at end of year. Played with Boston Braves, 1934, last season in majors.

Marty played 1830 major league games, hit .289; had 401 doubles among 1925 hits; also 88 triples, 120 homers. Peak home run production came while with Tigers, 1929, with 18. Marty's 23 stolen bases gave AL leadership for 1930; stole 127 altogether.

McManus managed in minors off and on until 1947. Attempt to get minor leaguers to unionize consisted of appearing before executive council of American Federation of Labor in Chicago. Contended that if minor leaguers would organize first, then big league players would also unionize within few years. Died in veterans' hospital, St. Louis, of cancer after period as house detective in Chicago hotel.

McMILLAN, ROY DAVID SS-BR-TR. B. 7/17/30, Bonham, Tex. 5'11", 164. Brilliant-fielding shortstop with Cincinnati Reds, 1951–60. Set NL record for most double plays by shortstop, 129, during 1954 season. Also played more consecutive games at shortstop, 584, than any other NL infielder, 9/16/51 to 8/6/55. Led NL shortstops in fielding four times. Member of 1956,57 NL All-Star squads.

McMillan played with two Texas teams, Tyler, Ballinger, 1947–48; spent 1949 with Tulsa, Okla., and Columbia, S.C.; then Tulsa, 1950. Then began fine career with Reds. Three full seasons with Milwaukee NL, 1961–63, then traded to New York Mets 5/8/64, remaining until 1967, when became playing coach for Jacksonville, International League. Nonplaying manager, Visalia, California League, 1968, then managed Memphis, 1969, taking that team to Texas League's Eastern Division title and winning playoffs. Coach, Seattle AL, 1970, then continued as coach for team when it moved and became Milwaukee AL Brewers, 1971. Coach, N.Y. Mets, 1973.

Roy played 2093 major league games, hit .243. Although not a power hitter, slapped 68 homers, 253 doubles, 35 triples among his 1639 hits. Scored 739 times and drove in 594 runs. Led NL shortstops in double plays four seasons.

McMULLEN, KENNETH LEE 3B-BR-TR. B. 6/1/42, Oxnard, Calif. 6'3", 200. Ken McMullen got estimated $60,000 to sign with Los Angeles Dodgers, 1960. Played with them parts of three seasons, then traded away. Five seasons with Washington Senators; three with California Angels. Then, in 1973 found self back with Dodgers. During 1297 games in majors before returning to Los Angeles, Ken hit for average of .250, with 136 homers among 1154 hits. Also had 152 doubles, 22 triples, with 518 runs scored and 520 RBI. Considered one of best-fielding third sackers in AL. Great at coming in for slow rollers, with ability to scoop up bunts and get man at first base.

Ken spent first year in pro ball at Reno, 1961, hit .288, smacked 21 homers, drove in 96 runs. At Omaha, following year, did almost as well, even though in faster league. Dodgers looked at him in six games, then put him on their Spokane club for 1963, for 38 games. Played 79 contests with parent club, but hit only .236. Fielding, however, was spectacular in Dodgers' September stretch drive for NL pennant. However, pulled muscle running out two-bagger and missed playing in WS, which Los Angeles won from New York Yankees in four straight.

McMullen wasn't too successful in 24 games with Dodgers, 1964, nor did he hit much for Spokane in 93 games, although had 14 homers. Average was .234. Traded to Washington Senators with Frank Howard 12/4/64. Played regularly with Senators until end of 1969 season. Best year for average was 1969 when hit .272 with 19 homers, 87 RBI. Traded to California Angels 4/26/70 and had best season at plate for Anaheim club in 1972, with .269 average. Led AL third basemen in double plays, 1967, with 38. Tied major league record for most assists in nine-inning game by third baseman with 11, 9/26/66.

McNALLY, DAVID ARTHUR P-BR-TL. B. 10/31/42, Billings, Mont. 5'11", 191. Dave McNally cost Baltimore Orioles reported bonus of $80,000 to sign in 1960, after brilliant career in American Legion ball in Montana. But he put together some dazzling statistics even though able to win only 13 games in 1972 while losing 17. As 1973 season came up, Dave owned 148 victories in AL against 86 defeats. In 335 games pitched 2128 innings, with 739 earned runs allowed, giving ERA of 3.13. Had 1278 strikeouts against 628 walks; 25 shutouts and 90 complete games. Despite failure to win oftener in 1972, Dave had six shutouts. Three came in his first four starts. But as season progressed, defeats came oftener than victories. Salary, 1972, was $105,000. Finest seasons were 1968–71 when took at least 20 decisions each campaign. In 1970 had 24–9 record. Percentagewise, 1971 mark even better, 21–5 for .808, which topped AL.

Dave's first contract in Baltimore organization was with Ardmore, Okla., 1961, moving to Appleton, Wis., later same season. Won 15, lost 11 at Elmira, 1962, and has been with Orioles ever since. Pitched two-hitter against Kansas City A's, 9/26/62, but in first two seasons in majors after that, won 16, lost 19. Had 11–6 mark, 1965, and 13–6 following year. Broke even, 7–7, and then began four straight 20-victory seasons.

McNally had one victory each year in AL playoffs of 1969,70,71. One victory in 1966 WS; one loss in 1969 classic; one victory in 1970 WS; and two wins, one loss in 1971 Series. During third game of 1970 WS, helped own cause by belting grand slam homer against Cincinnati en route to 9–3 victory. Also homered in fifth game of 1969 Series against N.Y. Mets.

By winning 17 consecutive games between 9/22/68 and 7/30/69, shares AL mark for straight wins with Johnny Allen of Cleveland

Indians. WS record: 4–2 50 innings, ERA 2.34, 35 strikeouts, 19 walks. AL All-Star squads 1969, 70, 72.

McNAMARA, JOHN FRANCIS Coach-manager. B. 6/4/32, Sacramento, Calif. 5'10½", 175. John McNamara belongs to group of baseball men who have been fired by Charles O. Finley. Managed Oakland A's briefly at end of 1968 season and all of 1969. Although team came home second in Western Division of AL both times, was fired. Was 10th manager of A's in 10 years. McNamara credited with helping numerous major league players on way to stardom, notably Reggie Jackson. Coach for San Francisco Giants since 1971, and again many NL players attest he boosts their egos, convinces them they can do job, helps morale when breaks seem to go against them.

John also belongs to group of baseball men who made grade as manager or coach without ever playing in majors. Started in St. Louis Cardinal organization at Fresno, California League, 1951, and continued as player until took part in two games at Birmingham, Ala., 1967. Saw service as catcher also at Houston and Tulsa in Texas League; Lynchburg, Piedmont circuit; Lewiston, Northwest; Albuquerque and Amarillo, Western League; Sacramento, PCL. Managed at Lewiston four of five seasons there; bossed Binghamton in Eastern League; Dallas, PCL; Birmingham and Mobile in Southern.

As catcher, McNamara set various records for fine fielding in minor leagues; landed on various all-star teams. Never quite hit .300. Named Manager of Year in Northwest League three seasons, 1960, 61, 62, bossing Lewiston; also named Manager of Year, 1966, piloting Mobile in Southern Association. His Birmingham club won Dixie Series, 1967.

As youth played basketball, American Legion baseball. Attended Sacramento State College, majoring in accounting. Coach, Oakland, 1968–69, until appointed manager 9/19/69.

McNEELY, GEORGE EARL OF-BR-TR. B. 5/12/99, Sacramento, Calif. D. 7/16/71, Sacramento, Calif. 5'9", 155. Earl McNeely, then rookie outfielder, got one hit in six trips to plate in WS game 10/10/24. But that hit won ball game in 12th inning, 4–3, and won world championship for Washington Senators. Lady Luck was with McNeely and Senators that afternoon. In crucial seventh game, N.Y. Giants leading 3–1 in eighth inning. Mgr. Bucky Harris hit grounder to Lindstrom at third base. Ball took crazy bounce past New York third baseman, and Washington tied ball game 3–3. Then in 12th frame, Muddy Ruel should have been retired on foul fly. But Catcher Hank Gowdy's foot tangled in own mask, and Muddy got new life; promptly doubled. This was setting when McNeely came to plate. McNeely hit what seemed like ordinary grounder in direction of Lindstrom. As latter about to field ball, must have hit pebble. In any case it bounded over his head for single, Ruel scored, and Senators had first world championship.

McNeely had eight seasons in majors, half with Washington, rest with St. Louis Browns. Played 683 games and had lifetime average of .272. His 614 hits included 107 doubles, 33 triples, four homers. Scored 369 runs, drove in 213. Stole 68 bases.

Earl started with Sacramento club, Pacific Coast League, 1922. Next two seasons hit .333. In midsummer, 1924, Senators bought his contract for reported $35,000 and three players. Joined club immediately and hit .330 for Washington in remaining 43 games, helping club win first AL pennant. In WS that fall, besides lucky hit in crucial game, Earl had three doubles, two singles, and batted .222. In 1925 hit .286 in 122 games. Senators again won pennant, but lost WS to Pittsburgh. McNeely rode bench for most of WS, giving way to more powerful hitters. Did not have time at bat, so overall WS average was .222 in 11 games.

Had .303 mark in 1926 and .276 in 1927, after which was traded to Browns with pitcher Dick Coffman for hurler Milt Gaston. McNeely's average while with Browns next four seasons varied from .225 to .272, after which returned to West Coast as manager of Sacramento club. In 1928 bought farm and cattle business in Orangeville, Calif., suburb of Sacramento, pursuing this occupation until retirement in 1959.

McNERTNEY, GERALD EDWARD (Jerry) C-BR-TR. B. 8/7/36, Boone, Iowa. 6'1", 195. Jerry McNertney, who had previously played in AL, joined St. Louis Cardinals, 1971; promptly became known as "Super Sub" because of work as catcher when Ted Simmons was on army reserve duty. Hit .289, best mark of major league career, and did well as pinch hitter with men in scoring position.

McNertney is graduate of Iowa State. Originally first baseman, started in pro ball at Holdrege, Nebr., 1958; later with Duluth-Superior; Lincoln, Nebr.; and Idaho Falls, Idaho. In last-named city, Jerry hit .341, drove in 125 runs, scored 109, and had 13 homers. But following year was switched to catching in belief he did not have power generally expected of major league first sackers.

Did switch at Charleston, S.C., in Sally League, 1961. While learning, led league in passed balls with 23. Then two seasons at Indianapolis. With Chicago White Sox, 1964, then back at Indianapolis for 1965. Oddly enough, in three campaigns with Indianapolis was in three different leagues and consequently saw most parts of country. Indianapolis was in American Association, 1962; in International League, 1963; and when Jerry joined again in 1965 it was in Pacific Coast circuit. With White Sox 1966–68. Seattle Pilots AL 1969. Milwaukee AL 1970, before joining Cardinals. Released by Cards 1972, signed with Oakland for 1973 but soon landed with Tucson. Pittsburgh bought contract May 1973.

McNertney, returning to majors, brought with him .237 lifetime mark for 581 major league games; 27 homers, 51 doubles, 6 triples among 336 hits. Scored 129 runs, drove in 163.

MacPHAIL, LELAND STANFORD (Larry) Executive. B. 2/3/90, Cass City, Mich. Larry MacPhail belongs in Hall of Fame despite everything he did to discourage selection. MacPhail did not deliberately indicate he didn't want Cooperstown shrine honors. But so many things he did in 1930s and 1940s, capped by cyclonic departure from Yankee presidency, 1947, slowed down serious consideration of his case. MacPhail's exit from Yankee organization was unbelievable if there were not so many eyewitnesses to attest to what happened. His ball club had just won AL pennant and WS. What should have been happy occasion for all— $10,000 victory dinner celebration for Yankee organization and their friends—was turned into colossal shambles by man who contributed greatly to making world championship possible. Scene was Biltmore Hotel, New York. MacPhail apparently started celebrating Yankee victory over Brooklyn Dodgers long before game was over. Dodgers were behind from fourth inning on, with reliever Joe Page mowing down one batter after another. When game ended, MacPhail and George Weiss, vice president and farm director for Yanks, headed for clubhouse to congratulate manager Stanley Harris and ball players. Larry asked news photographers to take picture of them both together, saying, "Here's the guy who built up this winning club—I built up losers, Brooklyn club." Short time later, grabbing radio microphone, MacPhail declared: "This is it! I said I'd resign as soon as Yankees reached top. If we had lost this game I would go on. But we won, and I'm stepping out!"

Few hours later, in WS press headquarters, MacPhail belligerently fended off newsmen who wanted to question him about remarks on resignation. "Stay away," he told some of them, "or get punched!" Among those present was Sid Keener, St. Louis sports writer. Sid tried to calm down MacPhail, who was popping off about press criticism. Keener said something about Branch Rickey also having been unfairly criticized in press. Rickey, of course, was man who gave MacPhail first chance in baseball at Columbus, Ohio; Rickey later had recommended MacPhail for Brooklyn general managership. "There's only one honest guy in baseball worth talking about," shouted MacPhail, "and that's Sam Breadon." Breadon for many years was president of St. Louis Cardinals. Larry then moved into dining room of hotel, up to that point holding happy gathering. Soon got into argument with John McDonald who had been traveling secretary for Cincinnati Reds and Dodgers when MacPhail headed those teams. McDonald defended Rickey, at which point MacPhail slugged McDonald in eye, blackening it, causing huge welt. At another table sat George Weiss; Ed Barrow, former business manager of Yankees; Bob Cobb, president Hollywood Baseball Club; and several ladies, including Mrs. Weiss. MacPhail approached Weiss and bellowed at him, "Look, you _____ _____ _____, I'm going to give you 48 hours to make up your mind what you're going to do." "I don't want to make a decision tonight," replied Weiss. "You make up your mind now, or you're fired!" shouted MacPhail. "You're fired right now! Stop tomorrow morning at office and pick up your check. You're out of this organization!" Next target was Dan Topping, partner of MacPhail and Del Webb as owners of Yankees. "You're just guy who was born with silver spoon in your mouth," Larry told Dan. "You've never made a dollar in your life!" MacPhail's next insult was directed at wife of baseball player whom MacPhail characterized as "bum." Finally Topping told MacPhail, "I have taken enough. Come with me and we will settle this thing once and for all." Dan half-shoved MacPhail into nearby kitchen. Some time later MacPhail returned to dining room, somewhat freshened up, hair combed, and things quieted down. Next day Yankees announced Topping and Webb had bought out MacPhail's interest in club. Larry got $1 million check immediately, and another $500,000, 3/16/48. Topping took over presidency and Weiss became general manager. MacPhail retired to farm near Bel Air, Md., where he raised Black Angus cattle. Also became involved with race horses and race track.

Larry's earlier days were never dull. Restless, daring, imaginative. Dreamed up own ideas; improved on those of others. Loved turmoil, tumult, uproar. Thrived on controversy. Capable of being bully, violently insulting, parsimonious, domineering, to same people whom he also, at other times, praised and admired. Complex character whom Bill Terry once called "brilliant screwball."

MacPhail at 14 played organ at Episcopalian church. Attended various schools, including military academy at Staunton, Va. At 16 passed entrance exam for U.S. Naval Academy but parents persuaded him not to enter because of youth. At Beloit College, Wis., got reputation for being one of loudest debaters ever. Next stop Michigan Law School. Then got idea of going into consular service and transferred to George Washington U. in nation's capital. At 20 finished work toward bachelor of laws degree; offered consular job, but again changed mind. Joined Chicago law firm; wanted to become partner after six months. When couldn't make it, switched to another legal job as junior partner. This led to reorganizing tool company, later to management of Nashville department store.

When U.S. entered World War I, Larry enlisted as private. Soon became captain. Took part in St.-Mihiel and Argonne offensives. Wounded, gassed. When war ended he and several others tried to kidnap Kaiser Wilhelm, who had taken refuge in Holland. Plot didn't click, but

MacPhail claimed picked up Kaiser's ash tray as souvenir. Back in U.S., MacPhail moved from job to job. Tried to sell automobiles. As depression got worse, hooked on as football referee for Big Ten games. Finally got idea of going into baseball; managed it thus: Took option on Columbus franchise of American Association, then in dire straits—broken-down ball park, poor excuses for players on roster. Then decided to peddle option to major league team. Went to Branch Rickey, general manager of St. Louis Cardinals. Rickey was native of Ohio; had attended Ohio Wesleyan U. near Columbus; was receptive to idea of having another ball club where Cardinal prospects could gain experience in league one notch below majors. Cardinals already owned Rochester team in International League, but their farms were producing fine crop of young players good enough to be promoted, but not quite ready for majors.

Rickey, good businessman, recognized chance to buy Columbus franchise for "song." One proviso of deal, however, was that MacPhail would become president and general manager of Columbus club, at $10,000 salary. Though Larry had no experience whatever in running ball club, Rickey felt could be guided. He and MacPhail then sold Sam Breadon, hard-headed business man, on idea. Cardinals sent plenty of fine ball players to Columbus, took advantage of depression prices for material and labor, built new ball park. MacPhail furnished office in style: Oriental rugs and all that went with them. Sam Breadon, whose own office in St. Louis suffered by comparison, was shocked when saw expensive tastes of his underling. MacPhail persuaded Cardinals to introduce night baseball in new park. Crowds flocked to see team, now flirting with first place instead of wallowing in cellar.

Larry's free wheeling, however, soon irritated Breadon and Rickey. Spent lavishly; took Columbus team on plane for one jump. First time any club had ever flown as unit. Some maneuvering of player contracts ran afoul of rules and league president Tom Hickey fined him. Allegations of altercations with Columbus people whom MacPhail was said to have insulted. So Cardinals fired MacPhail, June 1933. MacPhail immediately began scheming bigger things. Cincinnati Reds were in miserable shape financially as well as on field. Larry contacted bank that had loaned team considerable money. Convinced bank he was man to lead Reds out of wilderness. Bank did not want to risk more cash, so MacPhail went to Powel Crosley, Jr., who owned radio stations and manufactured radio receivers and electrical appliances. Crosley knew nothing whatever about baseball, but salesman MacPhail convinced him ought to advance some money to team as public citizen. In turn, Crosley got option on club—and MacPhail got job as general manager, 1934. MacPhail immediately jazzed things up in Cincinnati, brought in Bob O'Farrell as manager, fired him after few months, and hired Chuck

Dressen. Persuaded NL to let him install lights in renamed Crosley Field. This was first night baseball in major leagues, and represented big break with tradition. Hired James B. (Scotty) Reston as club publicity man, and when he quit, hired Gene Karst, Cardinal publicity man, to help tell world about Reds. Pulled strings in Washington so that president Franklin Delano Roosevelt pushed button that inaugurated first night ball game in major league history, 1935. Gave fans mammoth fireworks display before or after each night game. Sponsored field meets, invited drum and bugle corps, school bands, and generally whooped things up. Installed microphone on desk, often broke into one radio station's programming to broadcast conversations with visitors talking baseball. Took Reds on plane trip between Cincinnati and Chicago—another first for big league ball club. Took team to Puerto Rico for spring training, another break with tradition. Flew ball club back to Florida. Reds didn't rise very high in league standings, but there was big increase in attendance and dull moments were rare. But not everything went smoothly. Altercation with cop in leading Cincinnati hotel lobby, MacPhail emerging with black eye. Argument with Crosley over whether MacPhail would get some club stock. Crosley exercised option on team 6/30/36 and, whether was fired or not, MacPhail left Reds at end of season.

One year in banking business in Michigan, then to Brooklyn, where Larry found another bank tired of lending money to floundering ball club. MacPhail became president, talked bank into advancing more money so could buy players like Dolph Camilli, Mickey Owen, Pee Wee Reese, Joe Medwick, and others. Hired Leo Durocher as manager. Introduced night baseball to New York area. Ended gentleman's agreement among Giants, Yankees, and Dodgers that they would not broadcast ball games. Brought Red Barber to Brooklyn to announce. First night game in Brooklyn Johnny Vander Meer pitched second consecutive no-hit game for Cincinnati—and got Dodgers nationwide publicity. Ebbets Field soon became rhubarb center, both on and off field. Dodgers got into contention, finished third in 1939, second in 1940, and won pennant 1941. Reportedly fired Durocher because Leo ordered special train to whiz past 125th Street, New York, while Dodgers were returning home after clinched pennant in Boston. It didn't stick, nor did other firings of Lippy Leo. MacPhail later said he never fired Leo. Durocher said Larry had fired him "so often I lost count."

MacPhail's personal finances were tangled when Dodgers finished second, 1942. This time MacPhail put on uniform as colonel and became special assistant to Undersecretary of War in Washington, for duration. At end of war tried to form syndicate of 15 who would put up $100,000 each to buy Yankees from heirs of late owner, Col. Ruppert. Saw Dan Topping, wealthy sportsman, and instead of syndicate that had been envisioned, worked up deal in which Topping, Del Webb, and MacPhail became partners, with Dan and Del putting up money. MacPhail brought baseball savvy and, besides getting one-third interest, got 10-year contract. Ruppert heirs got most of $2,811,835. Ed Barrow got $250,000 for stock.

One of MacPhail's first moves with Yankees was to initiate night baseball. Frequent clashes with Joe McCarthy, holdover manager, McCarthy finally resigning. Bill Dickey hired as successor, then Johnny Neun, and finally Stanley Harris. Allegedly steamrollered candidacy of Happy Chandler to become commissioner of baseball. Involved in big hassle with Rickey, who had become majordomo in Brooklyn, that finally resulted in Leo Durocher being suspended by Chandler for 1947 season.

Several books could be written about MacPhail. Tom Meany, sports writer, summed it up, declaring that with MacPhail, "bizarre is orthodox."

MacPHAIL, LELAND STANFORD, JR. (Lee) Executive. B. 10/25/17, Nashville, Tenn. Lee MacPhail holds job as executive vice president and general manager of N.Y. Yankees not because father presided over same organization 1945–47, but possibly in spite of it. Like several present-day executives in baseball, Lee got first baseball jobs because of father's connections. But, given opportunity, has made it on own abilities. Young MacPhail signed new three-year contract 9/3/72 at same time manager Ralph Houk was given similar contract. Lee's success in baseball has come in entirely different manner than that used by father, Larry. Where Larry was flamboyant, bombastic, loquacious, unpredictable, though admittedly brilliant, Lee has been quiet, generally soft-spoken, accomplishing things in an almost self-effacing manner.

Larry came into baseball with vast ignorance of game's inner workings. Learned quickly, brought dozens of innovations into game, became general manager of major league club after little more than two seasons bossing minor league team. Lee, on other hand, had several years of solid minor league executive experience before going on to important major league jobs.

Lee graduated from Swarthmore College. Business manager, Reading club, 1941. Later general manager, Toronto. Business manager and later general manager for Kansas City, American Association, then farm club of Yankees. Midwest farm director for Yankees. Co-farm director, then director of player personnel, also for Yanks. Joined Baltimore AL organization as general manager, 1959. President, Baltimore Orioles, 1960–65. With Oriole setup was instrumental in putting together most of team that won 1966 AL pennant and WS. When General William D. Eckert became baseball commissioner without any previous experience in game, Lee moved into his office as baseball administrator to assist general with details and technicalities of job.

Sporting News named him Executive of Year, 1966. Then in 1967 returned to Yankee organization, this time in job he currently holds. Yankees had finished in 10th place, 1966. MacPhail told media club would need about five years to get back into top contention, building with youth. Moved up notch to ninth in 1967; fifth in 1968, seventh in 1969; then third-place finish, 1970, and sixth in 1971. In 1972 Yankees really got into contention for top spot in AL East.

During World War II, Lee was lieutenant (j.g.) in navy. Brother, Bill, is top sports executive with Columbia Broadcasting System. Sister, Marian, for many years held important research position with *Time* magazine.

McQUINN, GEORGE HARTLEY 1B-BL-TL. B. 5/29/11, Ballston, Va. 5'11", 170. No wonder they called him "Patient Scot." New York Yankees signed George McQuinn for their organization in 1930—but was 17 years before joined parent team. When he did, helped them win pennant and WS, 1947. Lou Gehrig one of principal reasons why McQuinn was frustrated in desire to become Yankee. Lou, like McQuinn, was first baseman. During George's apprenticeship in minors nobody could pry Gehrig off job, even for day. So Yankees let McQuinn have trial with Cincinnati Reds; eventually let St. Louis Browns draft him from their Newark club. George made good with Browns, 1938. And it was May 1939 before Gehrig ended fantastic consecutive-game streak.

McQuinn, brilliant fielder. While no Gehrig at plate, was respectable hitter, three times averaging above .300 in major league career of 1550 games. Slapped 135 homers—reaching high mark of 20 while with Browns, 1939. Had 315 doubles, 64 triples among 1588 hits. Scored 832 times, drove in 794.

McQuinn's minor league experience, 1930–37, was with New Haven, Wheeling, Scranton, Albany, Binghamton, Toronto, and Newark. Played 38 games with Cincinnati first part of 1936 but hit only .201, so Reds sent him back to minors and put Les Scarsella, .313 hitter that year, on first base instead.

After McQuinn hit .330 for Newark, 1937, and with Gehrig looking like he'd go on forever, Yankees permitted Browns to draft George. Browns did not regret move—hit .324 for them in first full season in majors; batted safely 34 consecutive games. Came back with .316 in 1939. Had .277 season, 1945, then dropped down to .225 with Philadelphia Athletics, 1946.

Larry MacPhail, general manager in 1936 when McQuinn was with Reds, by now was president of Yankees. Always admirer of George's dazzling fielding, Larry picked up McQuinn for Yankees. George came back with .304 record in 144 games as Yanks captured pennant and WS. In 1948, last season in majors, hit .248 for Gothamites in 94 games.

McQuinn did all right with stick during St. Louis' city WS, 1944, with .438 average. In 1947 WS hit .130, so his WS tally shows .256 for 13 games. His home run in first game of 1944 WS enabled Browns to beat Mort Cooper 2–1, but Cardinals won Series.

After leaving Yankees, McQuinn was playing manager couple of years at Quebec, then continued piloting ball clubs from sidelines at Quebec, Atlanta, Boise. While still in majors George became interested in sporting goods store. Has done some scouting for Montreal Expos. Lives in Alexandria, Va.

McRAE, HAROLD ABRAHAM OF-Inf.-BR-TR. B. 7/10/46, Avon Park, Fla. 5'11", 180. Hal McRae didn't get to play regularly while with Cincinnati Reds, principally because Mgr. Sparky Anderson didn't seem satisfied with fielding. However, traded to Kansas City Royals for 1973, seemed destined to see more action, either in infield or outfield. Hal started as second baseman after attending Florida A. and M. U., 1965, at Tampa. Gained experience at Peninsula, Buffalo, Knoxville, and Indianapolis. Had 17 games with Reds, 1968, playing 16 at second base.

Suffered broken ankle winter of 1968 playing in Caribbean. Played only 17 games that year, at Indianapolis; spent most of season on disabled list. Had 70 games with Cincinnati, 1970, filling in at second, third, and in outfield. Then 99 games, mostly in outfield, 1971, hitting .264.

In 1972 McRae raised average to .278, including five homers among 27 hits, with 26 RBI—almost one RBI for every time hit safely. Followed this with .444 mark in WS against Oakland A's. Hal played right field at times, but came through nobly as pinch hitter. Had two singles and sacrifice fly in three chances as pinch hitter; had four hits in nine trips, with two RBI.

Hal's average in 1970 WS was even higher—.455, 5 for 11, 3 RBI. Overall WS record: 9 for 20, .450 average, 2 runs scored, 3 doubles, 5 RBI. Major league career record as started in AL, 1973: .257 average, 248 games; 167 hits good for 35 doubles, 3 triples, 22 homers; 67 runs, 85 RBI.

MADDOX, GARRY LEE (Buggy Whip) OF-BR-TR. B. 9/1/49, Cincinnati, Ohio. 6'3", 175. Was Willie Mays deal in works when San Francisco Giants suddenly called up Garry Maddox from Phoenix 4/25/72? Garry, brilliant youngster, had less than two years of professional experience in baseball. Fully expected to spend 1972 season in Pacific Coast League. Then came hurry-up call to join Giants. Couple of weeks later Mays sent to New York Mets, and Maddox soon had Bay

Area fans buzzing about great potential. During one week in June Garry slapped two homers each good for three runs; two triples, one double; scored seven runs himself and drove in total of nine markers. When season ended owned .266 average for 125 games, with 26 doubles, 7 triples, 12 homers among 122 hits. Scored 62 runs, drove in 58, stole 13 bases.

Got nickname from way swings bat. Fast, excellent outfielder with good arm; daring base runner.

Maddox had fine athletic record in high school in San Pedro, Calif., then entered Los Angeles Harbor Junior College. Signed with Giants' organization, 1968, and spent most of summer at Salt Lake City in Pioneer League. Hit .252 in 58 games. Also had five games with Fresno, California League, then entered military service. Two years in army uniform, one of them in Vietnam. Then back to Fresno for 1971 season. In 120 games put together .299 average with 30 homers, 25 doubles, five triples, and 106 RBI. Garry spent spring training, 1972, with Giants, but was ticketed for one more year of experience, this time in AAA ball. So went to Phoenix. But after 11 games owned .438 batting average with 21 hits in 48 trips; had hit 9 home runs, 3 doubles, 2 triples, and had scored 14 runs. Small wonder Horace Stoneham began to think he could trade aging Mays with his tremendous salary.

MAGERKURTH, GEORGE LEVI Umpire. B. 12/30/88, McPherson, Kans. D. 10/7/66, Rock Island, Ill. 6'3", 225. Pugnacious NL umpire fought about 70 professional boxing matches before becoming big league official. Fought several times afterward, but these altercations cost fines, suspensions, damage to ego. Still kept job in NL 1929–47. Most embarrassing moment came at Ebbets Field, 1940. After had called one against Brooklyn Dodgers, fan jumped from stands and sneaked up behind him. In surprise attack, managed to overturn big ump, who landed on back. Then fan proceeded to pummel him several times before Magerkurth could extricate self. Alert photographer captured scene, and one of New York's tabloids gave it full-page spread. Not only was ex-boxer humiliated before thousands in stands at time, but for weeks later Magerkurth's mail brought copies of newspaper photo, accompanied by gloating comments from irate Dodger fans. George didn't prosecute offender. But story goes that attacker really didn't care much about Dodgers. Was convict out on parole who jumped Magerkurth so that all in ball park would focus attention on field. Meanwhile, confederate, pickpocket, could ply trade among fans who were busily watching Magerkurth's downfall.

Magerkurth frustrated minor league catcher as well as pro boxer in youth. Played at Hannibal, Illinois-Missouri League, 1909; Kearny, Nebr., 1910–11; Duluth, 1912; then took factory job in Moline, Ill.

Started umpiring professionally in Mississippi Valley League, 1922; International League, 1923; later in American Association and Pacific Coast League before joining NL. While in American Association, 1926, got into argument with Ivy Griffin, Milwaukee first baseman. Later attacked him in hotel room, dislocated his shoulder, ending Griffin's career as player. Magerkurth fined $25, suspended 30 days, then fired.

Shortly after entry into NL Magerkurth banished John McGraw, manager of N.Y. Giants. Attracted widespread attention since not many officials dared to cross "Little Napoleon." Exchanged punches with Bill Jurges, 1939. Both suspended 10 days. Once Magerkurth chased 15 Brooklyn Dodgers off bench while Leo Durocher was managing there. Another time cleared Pittsburgh bench of 10 players while Frankie Frisch bossing Pirates. In 1945 in Cincinnati, fan was riding Magerkurth. After game ended, George went over and gave one of spectators haymaker. Found out later it was wrong man—had to give $100 to avoid lawsuit. After leaving NL Magerkurth umpired some college and semi-pro games and for while acted as baseball commentator for Moline TV station.

MAGLIE, SALVATORE ANTHONY (Barber) P-BR-TR. B. 4/26/17, Niagara Falls, N. Y. 6'2", 185. Mean money pitcher with baffling curve, pinpoint control. Some called him "Renaissance assassin." Got nickname "Barber" because threw ball dangerously close to batter's chin. Probably next pitch would fool intimidated batter, backing away from plate, with curve breaking over lower outside corner. Was called "Sinister Sal" and many other names seldom used in intellectual circles. "When I'm pitching I figure plate is mine," Sal once declared. "I don't like anybody getting too close to it."

Maglie had four outstanding seasons with New York Giants in 1950s, during which Brooklyn fans learned to hate him with violent passion. Mildest accusations were that he threw illegal spitballs and beanballs. Some years later Sal became Dodger, and Flatbush fans learned to applaud him, 1956, when helped them to NL flag with last fine performance.

Sal was good basketball player as young man, but when turned to pro baseball, 1938, at Buffalo, wasn't very successful. Won three, lost 15 in three seasons with Bisons. Another losing season at Jamestown, N.Y., in Pony League, 1940. Finally won 20, lost 15 at Elmira, Eastern League, 1941, and Giants drafted him; farmed out to their Jersey City club, 1942, where won nine, lost six. Worked in defense plant, 1943–44, then had 6–7 season at Jersey, 1945, and 5–4 mark with Giants same year. At this point Sal succumbed to temptations of Mexican baseball, then considered "outlaw." Disappointed with conditions found there, but couldn't come back to organized baseball for four years as penalty for ignoring reserve clause. During this period played in Caribbean, Canada, and semipro circuits. Returned to Giants, 1950, and immediately won 18, lost four, leading NL pitchers in winning percentage. Did even better in total wins for Leo Durocher's gang, 1951, taking 23 wins, losing six, landing on pennant winner for first time in major league career. It was 18–8 for Sal in 1952, then 8–9, 14–6, and 9–5.

Sal was drawing $35,000 salary, pretty fancy for those days. Was 38 and suffering from back problems, so Indians got him on waivers 7/31/55. Didn't impress much in Cleveland, 1955, nor in spring of 1956. Then Indians played exhibition game in May against Brooklyn Dodgers at Jersey City. Maglie pitched four innings, during which time Dodgers got just one single. Buzzie Bavasi, then with Dodgers, and Walter Alston agreed Sal might help. Were able to buy him from Cleveland for $1000— one of best investments they ever made. Won 13, lost five during rest of 1956. And from 7/28 until end of season won 10, lost two, with ERA of 1.88. Sal's two losses were by 2–1 and 3–2 scores. During last week of season pitched no-hit game against Philadelphia 9/25/56, winning 5–0. This was crucial contest since loss that day would have put Dodgers out of pennant race. But Dodgers won flag.

Sal's best days were behind after 1956. Had 6–6 mark with Dodgers, then sold to New York Yankees, 9/1/57, for $25,000 and two minor league players. Won two, lost none for Yanks in final month of season. After 1–1 record in first part of year, Yanks sold him to St. Louis Cardinals 6/14/58. Had 2–6 mark with Cards rest of season. Released 4/10/59. Since then Maglie coached Boston Red Sox 1960–62 and again 1966–67; had brief spells coaching at Buffalo and Newark, with periods when was out of baseball entirely. Coach, Seattle AL, 1969. General manager, Niagara Falls club, N.Y.-Pa. League, 1970–71, in Pittsburgh organization. Out of baseball after that, due to heart attack.

Maglie lost one WS decision, 1951, while with Giants; pitched seven innings, 1954 WS, without decision. While with Dodgers, 1956, got team off to 6–3 victory in opening game against Yankees. Then was his fate to pitch on day Don Larsen pitched only perfect game in history of WS. Maglie allowed five hits, one of them homer by Mickey Mantle, and Yanks won 2–0. Sal's complete WS record: 1–2, 3.41 ERA, 29 innings. Pitched three innings for NL in 1951 All-Star game and credited with victory.

Sal's career major league totals showed 303 games with 119 victories, 62 defeats with 3.15 ERA for 1721 innings. Walked 562, struck out 862.

MAHAFFEY, ARTHUR, JR. P-BR-TR. B. 6/4/38, Cincinnati, Ohio. 6'2", 200. Art Mahaffey lost more games than he won in majors, winning 59 and dropping 64. One good reason was fact he toiled for Philadelphia Phillies in six of seven seasons he was in NL. Phillies had 23-game losing streak, 1961. Mahaffey lost 10 straight decisions himself, but was charged with only six or seven of the 23 losses, which is three more than Philadelphia Athletics were able to drop in either 1916 or 1943. Phillies' record was worst of any major league team since 1900.

Mahaffey's best season was 1962 when he had 19 victories and lost 14. Phils weren't last that year—ended up seventh.

Art, however, has other claims to distinction. Reported to Phils, 1960 midseason. Used in relief against St. Louis Cardinals, allowed two hits in two innings pitched. Picked both men off base. Next time on mound started against N.Y. Giants. First man up got single; Art promptly picked him off base. Held Giants in check until eighth inning, and was ahead 4–0 when taken out. "That game broke my heart," he said later. "After I left, we lost it."

Although he won 11, lost 19 in 1961, it wasn't all bad. Struck out 17 members of Chicago Cubs in one game 4/23/61. Got Ernie Banks on strikes three times with overpowering fast ball. Another accomplishment of Mahaffey in 1961 was picking five men off second base during year. Art personally tagged out three of them.

Mahaffey started at Mattoon, Ill., in Midwest League, 1956, and pitched for High Point-Thomasville, Carolina League; Salt Lake City, Pioneer League; Williamsport, Eastern League; and Buffalo, International League; then Phillies. Spent final year in majors with St. Louis Cardinals, 1966.

MAILS, JOHN WALTER (Duster)   P-BL-TL. B. 10/1/95, San Quentin, Calif. 6'1", 195. One of those eccentric, boastful lefthanders who parlayed modest ability into lifetime occupation. Walter, self-styled "The Great," helped Cleveland Indians win 1920 pennant—and stayed in game until 1972 when retired as member of San Francisco Giants' speakers bureau.

Mails attended St. Mary's College in California, then joined Seattle, Northwestern League, 1914. Won two and lost two that year, but in 1915 chalked up 24 victories while dropping 18 decisions. Resulted in sale to Brooklyn Dodgers for $1750, 9/15/15. With Dodgers through 1916 without pitching much. Waived to Pittsburgh, May 1917, and Pirates sent him to Portland, Pacific Coast League. Won three, lost two that year, then entered army. Discharged early in 1919, joined Sacramento, PCL, winning 19, losing 17. Continued good pitching, 1920, and Indians bought him late in August for immediate delivery.

Cleveland was battling White Sox for pennant. This was before disclosure that 1919 WS had been fixed. In conversation with AL umpire Billy Evans, supremely confident rookie, Mails, told Billy his plans for pitching against Sox. "We're going to take them," said Duster. "They'll be lucky if they even score when I'm pitching against them." Evans said,

"That's the spirit, kid, but remember they've got some pretty fair hitters in their lineup—like Joe Jackson, Buck Weaver, and Eddie Collins." "Never heard of 'em," replied Mails. "Just see what I do to them." Evans told Cleveland owner Jim Dunn that Mails was either fresh busher or else had lot of confidence in ability. Cleveland had half-game lead 9/24/20 when Mails went to mound against Red Faber. Indians were in front by 2–0 score in fifth inning when Duster walked three men to load bases. Tris Speaker, playing manager of Indians, trotted in from center field to talk things over, ready to send in reliever. But Mails convinced Spoke he ought to have one more chance. "All I did was to strike out Buck Weaver and Eddie Collins," said Mails later. "Believe me, I felt like throwing out my chest when I walked to bench." Overflow crowd of 20,000 cheered brash southpaw.

Mails won seven straight for Indians down stretch, losing none, with 1.85 ERA. Cleveland won pennant by two games, so is apparent Mails made difference between first place and finish in either second or third place. In WS against Brooklyn that fall, Mails used in relief in one game, pitching 6-2/3 innings without allowing run. Indians lost, but defeat charged to starter Caldwell. Then Walter pitched seventh game of set, winning 1–0 shutout 10/11/20 over Sherry Smith. Indians wrapped it up next day, needing five victories to clinch WS that year.

Mails' glory days behind him now, even though won 14, lost eight in 1921. Sagged to 4–7 mark in 1922, then dropped back to PCL, with Oakland. St. Louis Cardinals brought him up in 1925 and he broke even in 14 decisions. After losing one game, winning none for Redbirds in 1926, dropped back into minors again, first with Syracuse, and then back home to California, with San Francisco. Pitched in PCL until 1937, then moved into Seals' front office as publicity and promotion man. When Giants moved to Golden Gate, Mails joined organization's speakers bureau.

Mails won 32, lost 25 in his brief major league career, but is remembered as one of game's more colorful off-beat characters. Had 4.10 ERA for 516 innings pitched, 5 shutouts, walked 220, struck out 232.

MALONE, FERGUSON G. C-BL-TL. B. 1842, Ireland. D. 1/18/05, Seattle, Wash. 5'8", 156. First lefthanded catcher on record in major leagues. Malone, whose exact birth place and birthday are lost in mists of Old Sod, caught for Philadelphia NL back in 1876, year senior circuit was organized. Got into just 22 games, but enough to title him pioneer among southpaw receivers in big league.

Malone had played for various teams in Philadelphia and Chicago from 1871 onward, when NL came into being. Hit just .299 in 1876, then dropped out of major league picture until 1884 when Union Association born. Malone managed Philadelphia club that year for 41 games. Team won 11, then Tom Pratt took over. Malone got into one game that year, had one hit in four trips. So his brief major league record shows .230 average for 23 games. Lefthanded catcher Jack Clements with longer, more impressive record played with Philadelphia and other clubs, but he wasn't first.

MALONE, PERCE LEIGH (Pat) P-BL-TR. B. 9/25/02, Altoona, Pa. D. 5/13/43, Altoona, Pa. 6', 200. Fun-loving pitcher divided major league career between Chicago Cubs and New York Yankees. Only player to take part in two WS in different leagues under same manager, Joe McCarthy. While Malone enjoyed pranks off field, was rough competitor as pitcher. With Cubs had 18–13 record as rookie, 1928. Then won 22, lost 10 following season; had 20–9 in 1930, and 16–9, 1931. Had two off-seasons when lost oftener than he won, but came back to 14–7 mark in 1934. With Yankees, it was 3–5 in 1935, then 12–4 mark in 1936. Broke even 1937, last year in majors. Wound up with 134 wins, 92 losses, and 3.74 ERA for 1915 innings. Walked 705, struck out 1024. Lost three decisions in WS play, two of them in 1929 with Cubs. Brief appearance on mound in 1932 WS, without win or loss. Charged with one defeat in 1936 WS while with Yankees. Overall WS ERA was 3.05 for 20-2/3 innings pitched.

Pat Malone used to amuse self in Manhattan by luring pigeons to window ledge with peanuts, then trying to capture them. Usually let them loose, but on one occasion tucked several into bed, under covers with sleeping roommate, Percy Lee Jones. Jones woke up forthwith while squawking birds scrambled around trying to escape sheets and Jones' thrashing limbs. Bill Veeck, Sr., then president of Cubs, often willingly paid expenses for Mrs. Malone to make road trips with team. Her presence usually kept Pat on straight and narrow—investment paid off in victories for Malone.

Pat was big for age as youth; got job as railroad fireman at 16, though minimum was 18. Likewise, lied to get into army while still 16. Parents got him out, but he later returned to uniform. After one season at Knoxville, Tenn., 1921, New York Giants bought him, but did not keep him. Pitched for Waterbury, Eastern League; Toledo, Shreveport, Des Moines, and Minneapolis before Cubs bought him after he won 20 games in American Association, 1927.

Malone left majors decade later, pitched briefly for Baltimore, then in International League, 1938; also for Minneapolis and Chattanooga. Operated cafe in Altoona for time, then retired to farm.

MALONEY, JAMES WILLIAM P-BL-TR. B. 6/2/40, Fresno, Calif. 6'2", 210. Jim Maloney, who pitched two NL no-hitters, gave up game in mid-June 1972, and decided to travel with family for while before settling down to more prosaic life than that of big league ball player. Jim, just 32, had been pitching for Phoenix, farm club of San Francisco Giants during early weeks of 1972 season. Won five games, lost one in Pacific Coast League, and truly believed could pitch and help some major league club. But when June 15 major league cut-down date arrived and no team called for services, he quit rather than continue in minors.

Jim won 23 games for Cincinnati Reds in 1963, his second full year in NL. Followed with six more highly effective seasons. Over seven-year span won almost twice as many decisions as lost. Had 117–60 mark.

Maloney tied NL record for most one-hitters with fifth such masterpiece in 1969. Almost had third no-hitter once against N. Y. Mets. Kept them hitless 10 innings, only to allow two hits in 11th, and lost game by 1–0 score. Also had 30 shutouts to credit in NL.

Maloney played Little League, Babe Ruth, and American Legion baseball. In high school was hard-hitting shortstop, but turned to pitching. Attended Fresno City College and U. of California. Pro debut at Topeka, 1959. Won 14, lost five at Nashville, 1960, and with Cincinnati same season had 2–6 mark. Spent all of 1961 with Reds, won six, lost seven, then divided 1962 season between Reds and San Diego, then in Pacific Coast League. Following year began fine mound work for Cincinnati with 23–7 mark. Went 15–10 in 1964 and had 20 wins, nine losses in 1965. That year had his lowest ERA in NL, 2.54. Sixteen victories, 1966, against eight losses; then 15–11, 16–10, and 12–5. After injury and being on disabled list most of 1970, Reds traded him to California Angels 12/15/70. Lost three decisions, won none, and spent much of year on sidelines because of pulled hamstring and groin injury. Angels gave him unconditional release 1/3/72 and he signed with St. Louis Cardinals. Redbirds released him after spring training and he caught on with Phoenix.

When at peak there were those who insisted he was faster than Sandy Koufax. Pitching against Braves 5/21/63 Maloney tied modern record by striking out eight consecutive batsmen. After seventh straight, up came Eddie Matthews, certainly no slouch, who went down to tie record. Hank Aaron was next at bat. Maloney quickly got two strikes on him. Then threw sidearm change-up curve. Hank tapped roller to infield, breaking strikeout string. Jim, at this point, had 15 strikeouts for game, with three innings to go. But was tiring, and got just one more strikeout rest of way—Hank Aaron. With two men out in ninth inning Maloney had to be relieved.

Maloney at times was wild—led NL in wild pitches, 1963. Overall major league record showed 302 games pitched, 134 victories, 84 defeats. In 1849 innings allowed 655 earned runs, walked 810, struck out 1605. Lifetime ERA was 3.19. Fireballer struck out 265 in 250 innings in 1963, and had four seasons with more than 200 strikeouts. Only one WS game,

1961: two-thirds of inning, four hits, two runs, one walk, ERA 27.00. Member 1965 NL All-Star squad: 1-2/3 innings, five hits, five runs, two walks, ERA 27.00.

MANCUSO, AUGUST RODNEY (Blackie) C-BR-TR. B. 12/5/05, Galveston, Tex. 5'10", 185. Gus Mancuso grew up in St. Louis Cardinal organization, but found his progress blocked by fact Redbirds were well supplied with stellar catchers in those days—Bob O'Farrell and Jimmy Wilson in particular. At one point Branch Rickey, GM of Cards, wanted to farm him out again, but Kenesaw Mountain Landis said, in effect, "No! If he goes back to the minors one more time, it must be to a club not controlled by the Cardinals." Rickey knew Mancuso's potential cash value, so Gus stayed with Cardinals, 1930—hit .366 in 76 games. Helped Cards win pennant that year and following season. But still remained second-stringer. Then Bill Terry, manager of New York Giants, made deal for Mancuso after 1932 season. As Terry's regular catcher, he helped Giants win pennant and WS, 1933. Remained with Giants through 1938, helped them to two more pennants, 1936, 37. Chicago NL 1939. Brooklyn 1940. Cardinals again, 1941—42. Giants 1942—44. Philadelphia NL 1945. While Gus never equaled .366 average he had with 1930 Cards, he played 1460 major league games, hit .265—1194 hits, 197 doubles, 16 triples, 53 homers, 386 runs, 418 RBI, 8 stolen bases.

Before Landis stepped in, Gus played at Mount Pleasant and Longview in Texas; Beaumont, Houston, Fort Smith (Ark.), Syracuse, Minneapolis and Rochester. Gus got into 18 WS games, hit .173, 9 hits in 52 times at bat; 3 doubles, 6 runs, 4 RBI. NL All-Star game squads 1935—37.

MANGUAL, ANGEL LUIS OF-BR-TR. B. 3/19/47, Juana Diaz, Puerto Rico. 5'10", 180. Roberto Clemente, when playing winter ball in Puerto Rico, used to go to Ponce on occasion. Got acquainted with Angel Mangual, used to give free tickets to ball games. Finally Angel got around to telling Clemente he was ball player with ambitions to play in majors. Roberto passed word to Pittsburgh officials and Mangual was signed. Worked way up to Pirates from 1966 to 1969. Clemente told him he would be fine player.

But when he put on Pittsburgh uniform it was friend Clemente who kept him out of lineup. Clemente hit at .345 clip, 1969, so Angel got into just six games with team. It was back to Columbus, Ohio, for 1970. Prospects of breaking into Pirate lineup still were dim with Stargell, Oliver, Davalillo, Clines, as well as Clemente on roster. So Mangual sold to Oakland 10/20/70. Hit .286 in 1971 in 94 games. Came back with .246 mark in 91 contests, 1972. But had .300 average in WS, 3 for 10. As he went into 1973, major league average to date was .266 for 191 games. Among 150 hits, 9 homers, 22 doubles, 3 triples.

Between time Mangual signed with Pirate system and sticking in majors, played at Clinton, Iowa; Raleigh; York, Pa.; and Columbus. At

York led league in hits (159), in total bases (271), in homers (26), and in RBI (102). Second in league in hitting with .320; named Player of Year as well as MVP. Angel's brother, Jose Mangual, is player in Montreal Expos' organization.

MANN, LESLIE OF-BR-TR. B. 11/18/93, Lincoln, Nebr. D. 1/15/62, Pasadena, Calif. 5'9", 172. Rogers Hornsby used to ridicule Leslie Mann, saying "You're not ball player, you're just a track man." Basis for needling was that Branch Rickey, as manager for St. Louis Cardinals when Hornsby and Mann were teammates, often used Les as pinch runner for lumbering guys like Tubby Clemons, Ainsmith, and other slow pokes. Mann, even in later years, was fast base runner and good outfielder.

Rickey rarely used Mann against righthanded pitching; could hit lefthanders well but found righthanders difficult. Helped Mann's batting average too—he hit .328 for Cardinals in 1921 and .347 in 1922. Had .371 average for Redbirds, 1923, when sent to Cincinnati.

Mann a good journeyman player without ever achieving stardom. Starting at Nebraska City, 1910, played for Seattle and Buffalo en route to Boston Braves, where he won regular job, 1913 and took part in 120 games. Member of famous miracle team that swept 1914 WS from Philadelphia Athletics in four straight. Jumped to Chicago Federal League club, 1915, then with Cubs 1916 until traded to Braves early in 1919 season. Cardinals got him on waivers 11/9/20. Moved to Cincinnati during 1923, then with Braves again, 1924 until midyear, 1927. With N.Y. Giants rest of that season and 1928.

Quit majors with .282 average for 1493 games. His 1332 hits included 203 doubles, 106 triples, 44 homers. Scored 677 times, drove in 503 markers and stole 129 bases. In his two WS, 1914 at Boston and 1918 with Cubs, had .241 average, 7 for 29.

After leaving majors Mann worked with YMCA; did some scouting for major league teams. Was involved with banishment of Phil Douglas from baseball, 1922. Cardinals were battling Giants for pennant. Douglas, ignorant fellow who had weakness for getting drunk, incurred wrath of John McGraw, manager of Giants. Late in August, Phil disappeared for several days. When was found, was taken to sanatorium to dry out for five days. Returning to uniform, McGraw plastered $100 fine, docked his pay for days was absent and charged $224.30 for sanatorium and other expenses. Then delivered one of his famous tongue lashings. Unhappy Douglas then wrote note offering to "go fishing" if Cardinal players would get together enough money to make it interesting. Phil sent note to Mann, who immediately turned it over to his manager, Rickey. Branch, in turn, sent it to Landis, who then barred Douglas from baseball.

MANTLE, MICKEY CHARLES OF-BLR-TR. B. 10/20/31, Spavinaw, Okla. 6', 201. Mickey Mantle greatest switch hitter baseball has ever seen. But more than this, probably no superstar ever achieved greatness with anything like as many physical handicaps. Plagued by osteomyelitis from youthful football injury, Mickey had to wear so much tape, so many bandages, he resembled Egyptian mummy before putting on uniform. Knee injuries, shoulder problems, abcessed hip—these are just some of ailments Mantle had to face in addition to chronic bone disease. Would he have hit more than 536 AL home runs if he had not been so physically handicapped? Would he have smashed balls 50 feet, 100 feet farther than his fabulous drives wherever he played? One can only speculate—and reflect on courage it took to remain relatively even-tempered when unfeeling fans booed him for occasional failures to hit or field like superman.

Mantle was, is, human. Born with fabulous baseball skills, but still basically shy, retiring country boy who likes hillbilly music. Perform-ances speak for themselves, although baseball records do not reveal spectacular mileage of numerous prodigious home runs. But N. Y. Yankees won 12 pennants with him in lineup during his first 14 seasons. In two seasons when Yanks missed flag, they came in second, 1954; third, 1959.

Mantle finished career of 2401 major league games with .298 average. In last four years as player, physical ills made further inroads. Until then lifetime average was .309. Wound up with 2415 hits in 8102 times at bat. Banged 344 doubles, 72 triples; scored 1677 runs, drove in 1509. Also stole 153 bases. Ten seasons batting .300 or better; one AL batting title, 1956, with .353; four home run titles, 1955, 56, 58, 60; led AL in runs scored five times and tied for lead in another season; RBI champ, 1956, with 130; led AL outfielders in fielding, 1959. Seemed to have additional injuries before or during most of his WS play. But took part in 65 games, hit .257, with 6 doubles, 2 triples, 18 homers, as well as 40 RBI. In 230 times at bat had 59 hits, scored 42 runs, stole three bases.

Despite those autumnal injuries, Mantle left mark on WS play by hitting homer with bases loaded 10/4/53; his homer total, runs scored, RBI, total bases, set WS records. Also drew more walks than any other WS player, 43, and struck out oftener. Set or tied several other marks.

Tom Greenwade, scout who signed Mickey for Yankee organization, 1949, said that Mutt Mantle, Mickey's father, knew more baseball than father of any player he ever signed. Mutt idolized Mickey Cochrane, named son after him. Mickey practically breathed baseball from cradle. When quite young, his father took sizable chunk of week's salary to buy him $22 Marty Marion professional glove. When Mickey reached high school, countryside began to hear about his exploits on diamond. Mutt took Mickey to St. Louis, but Browns were not interested in high school kids who claimed to play shortstop. Later Runt Marr, Cardinal scout who had seen Mickey play, asked Mutt and Mickey not to sign with anybody until Redbirds could make offer. But Greenwade got signatures for something in neighborhood of $1100 bonus plus $400 to play rest of summer in minors. Bonus used to pay off mortgage on family home.

At Independence, in Kansas-Oklahoma-Missouri League, Mickey hit .313 in 89 games; moved up to Joplin, Western Association, following year. This was first full season in pro ball. Proceeded to take batting title with .383 average; led league in hits and runs scored; drove in 136 runs and banged 26 homers. Joined Yankees late that season. Following spring began receiving great publicity because of power demonstrated from both sides of plate. Casey Stengel, however, watched his infield play and declared, "He's no shortstop." Shifted to outfield, farmed out to Kansas City, American Association farm club of Yankees, for 40 games. Hit .361, got 11 homers, drove in 50 runs. Back with Yankees, 96 games, .267 average with 13 homers. Still couple of weeks from 20th birthday, played right field and was leadoff man in first two games of WS that fall. In second game Willie Mays of Giants hit fly to center field. Joe DiMaggio caught it, but Mickey ran to back him up. Accidentally stepped on wooden top covering outfield drain. Spikes caught in it, and Mantle dropped as though had been shot. This time was his knee.

Landed in hospital in bed next to father, suffering from Hodgkin's disease. Mutt lived until following spring. During winter, though doctors advised Mickey not to strain knee, he did strain it playing basketball.

Although knee bothered in 1952, Mickey played 142 games, hit .311 with 23 homers, 87 RBI. Played all seven WS games that fall, hit .345, including two homers, one giving Yanks edge in crucial game against Brooklyn. Mickey later drove in another run with single, Yanks winning game by 4–2 score—and world championship.

Knee operation that winter. Played 127 games, hit .295 in 1953; in WS hit only .208 but two of five hits were homers—one of them grand slammer against Brooklyn in fifth game. Mickey's best year was 1956 when won triple crown. Took AL batting championship with .353; led in homers with 52; and in RBI with 130. Also led in runs scored, 132.

On opening day that season, performing in Washington before President Dwight Eisenhower, Mickey hit Camilo Pascual for two tremendous home runs over center field fence. For time was thought he had chance to exceed Babe Ruth's 60-homer total for one season; had 47 going into September, then slumped. However, led majors in batting, homers and RBI. Unanimous choice for MVP. That fall, three homers in WS.

Following season Mickey reached $60,000 salary, hit .365, but Ted Williams led in hitting with .388. Again won MVP honors. WS that fall saw Yanks opposing Milwaukee Braves. Another injury for Mantle. In third game Buhl tried to pick him off second base. Red Schoendienst, playing second base, dived to catch throw, accidentally fell on Mickey's shoulder. Next day it was stiff, and he missed parts of rest of Series as result.

Came 1961, year of M and M boys in home run derby. By 9/13 Roger Maris had slipped ahead, 56 to Mantle's 53. Maris went on to hit 61, while Mantle wound up with 54, highest homer total of career. That fall played part of WS with badly abscessed hip—one hit, .167 average for Series.

Such was story of courageous, quiet young man, injury succeeding injury, ailment after ailment. But fans can't forget he hit two home runs in one game, one righthanded, one lefthanded, 10 times during career; they remember "tape measure" homer in Washington, 1953—565 feet; his 1962 season, when won MVP honors for third time. His appearances on AL All-Star squads, 1952–65, 14 consecutive years, then making it twice more, 1967,68. Did not play in 1952 and 1963. Mickey hit .233 in All-Star games. Sure bet for Hall of Fame.

Mantle took job as coach with Yankees part of 1970 season; in 1973 spent fifth spring as special hitting instructor in Yankee training camp.

MANUSH, HENRY EMMETT (Heinie) OF-BL-TL. B. 7/20/01, Tuscumbia, Ala. D. 5/12/71, Sarasota, Fla. 6', 200. Heinie Manush was first ball player ejected from WS game. It occurred 10/5/33 before Franklin D. Roosevelt and 25,727 paying customers at old Griffith Stadium, Washington, D.C. Umpires in those days often wore bow ties. After close play, Heinie, base runner, argued he was safe. As discussion warmed up at close quarters, Heinie grabbed ump's bow tie, held in place by elastic band, then let go, snapping it back to arbiter's neck. Exit Manush. FDR threw out first ball as game started; in wild scramble resembling football scrimmage, Manush came up with ball. Heinie didn't do much else that day—0 for 4—but his team, Washington Senators, won ball game 4–0, their only victory over N. Y. Giants during 1933 WS.

Manush, however, did plenty of hitting on other occasions. Led AL in batting 1926 with .378. Compiled lifetime batting average of .330. Hit better than .300 11 times. Four times had over 200 hits, leading AL in this respect, 1928, with 241, and again in 1933 with 221. Hall of Fame 1964.

Heinie reported to Detroit Tigers in spring training 1923 after hitting .376 at Omaha, Western League, previous season. First day in camp tried to take turn in batting practice. Every time he did so, Ty Cobb, manager of Tigers, yelled at him, "Get out of there, busher!" Eventually Harry Heilmann told Manush to take his (Heilmann's) turn. After practice was finished, Cobb got pitcher to throw to Manush—and was properly impressed with way could hit—so much so he used Heinie in 109 games that year. Heinie responded with .334 batting average.

After five years with Tigers, Manush traded to St. Louis Browns.

Came up with another .378 average, 1928, first season there, but Goose Goslin beat him out with .379 in race for batting title. Hit .355 for Browns following season; hit .350 in 1930, but divided that season between St. Louis and Washington Senators. Remained with Senators through 1935. Boston AL, 1936; Brooklyn, 1937. Dodgers released him to Pittsburgh on waivers, May, 1938. Then to Toronto for 81 games that same season. Ten games with Pirates, 1939, and 66 with Toronto.

By this time Manush was tapering off as player; became minor league manager and got into games occasionally as late as 1945. In years 1940–45 bossed teams at Rocky Mount, Greensboro, N.C.; Scranton, Pa.; Martinsville, Va.; and Roanoke, Va. Scout, Boston NL, 1946. Scout, Pittsburgh, 1947–48. Coach, Washington, 1953–54. Scout, Washington, 1961–62.

Manush had Johnny Pesky as young ball player at Rocky Mount while managing there. Pesky credits Heinie with making him into .300 hitter by changing his stance and showing where to stand in batter's box.

Manush played 2009 major league games, got 2524 hits, scored 1287 runs and drove in 1173. His extra-base blows included 491 doubles, 160 triples, 110 homers. In solitary WS, 1933: 2 for 18, .111 average.

Manush's first pro season was 1921 with Edmonton club of Western Canada league.

MARANVILLE, WALTER JAMES VINCENT (Rabbit) SS-BR-TR. B. 11/11/91, Springfield, Mass. D. 1/5/54, New York, N.Y. 5′5″, 155. Carefree, frolicsome spirit who cavorted through 2670 major league games. Hall of Fame 1954. Served country in navy in two world wars, played shortstop for Miracle Boston Braves of 1914, tried hand at managing Chicago Cubs and lasted less than two months. Drank more than his share of alcohol, relegated to minors. Reformed 5/24/27, returned to majors with St. Louis Cardinals, 1928, helping them to another pennant. Had several more years as big league regular.

When Rabbit bid good-bye to hard liquor, said, "From now on my hobby is staying sober." In later years coached kids in half-dozen sports. Stories endless about clowning before his reformation. But infectuous good humor lasted as long as he lived.

On ball field was famous for basket catches of pop flies. Once got laugh by crawling through legs of umpire Hank O'Day—when arbiter wasn't looking. Sometimes sat on top of players sliding into second base—after had tagged them out. Off field, Maranville alleged to have swum Charles River in Boston—in preference to crossing over bridge because it was several blocks away. Once, telling baseball stories on stage, demonstrated slide into second base so realistically he slid over footlights into orchestra, leg puncturing big drum.

On dare, once dived into gold fish pool in St. Louis hotel, fully clad. Emerging, told teammates, "There's a tough fish in there. He bit me."

"What did you do?" someone asked. "Bit him back," replied Maranville.

Another time Rabbit fined $100 for violation of Volstead Act in Brookline, Mass. After paying fine, got in car and in matter of minutes Newton, Mass., police fined him $25 for failing to stop when ordered.

Rabbit had two seasons at New Bedford in New England League, 1911–12, before joining Boston Braves late in 1912. Won regular shortstop job, 1913, and in 1914, after Miracle team had won NL pennant and swept Philadelphia Athletics off feet in four straight WS games, George Stallings, manager of Braves, insisted Rabbit was "greatest player to come to majors since Ty Cobb." After 1920 season Braves traded Maranville to Pittsburgh. There, found plenty of drinking companions despite prohibition. Some of most mischevious stunts were concocted while with Pirates. Buccaneers thought they had NL pennant in bag, 1921, but rolled into New York in September, lost five straight to Giants, and McGraw's team captured flag.

Maranville remained with Pirates until 1925. Started as player in ranks with Cubs, but named manager 7/7/25. In club's first train trip afterward, Rabbit celebrated appointment by going through Pullman cars pouring ice water on every player found sleeping in berth. Wild antics continued—and 9/3/25 Maranville divested of job as manager.

One season enough for Chicago management, and Maranville went to Brooklyn Dodgers for waiver price that winter. Played 78 games for Flatbush club, then dropped into minors with Rochester, International League. Walter, 35 at time, decided had imbibed more than his share. Result was great comeback. Played 135 games, hit .298 and attracted attention of Branch Rickey, general manager of St. Louis Cardinals. Redbirds needed shortstop after Tommy Thevenow broke leg, so Rabbit went to St. Louis for nine games, 1927, then became regular shortstop, 1928.

Maranville, who had hit .308 in WS of 1914, came back with identical record in 1928 Series—four hits in 13 trips. Difference was that in 1914 his team won WS in four straight—in 1928 his club lost Series in four straight, to Yankees.

Cardinals had Charlie Gelbert for shortstop, 1929, so Maranville went to Boston Braves 12/8/28. Remained with Braves through 1935. For all practical purposes big league career ended in spring of 1934 when he broke leg sliding into home plate during exhibition game. Missed entire season, but did get into 23 games, 1935.

While at Boston second time Rabbit served as manager from July 1929 until end of season. Managed Elmira, N.Y.-Pa. League, 1936; Montreal, International League, 1937–38; Albany, Eastern League, 1939; Springfield, Eastern League, 1941. At Elmira, 1936, Rabbit played 123 games and hit .323 as playing pilot. Got into six games at Albany, 1939, then into no more box scores.

Maranville was one of few men to go to bat 10,000 times. Had 10,078 AB during major league career, 2605 hits; 380 doubles, 177 triples, 28 homers. Scored 1255 times, had 874 RBI. Stole 291 bases. Overall big league mark .258. Best years were at Pittsburgh where he had .294 one season, .295 another.

MARBERRY, FRED (Firpo) P-BR-TR. B. 11/30/98, Streetman, Tex. 6'2", 210. Probably most successful of early specialists in relief pitching. Bucky Harris, manager of Washington Senators, 1924, used Marberry both as starter and reliever that year when they won AL pennant and WS. Started 15 games but also saved 15 in relief. Wound up with 11 wins, 12 defeats, but still vital cog in Washington's victory. Lost decision in one game he started in WS that year but saved two others. In 1925 Bucky used Firpo exclusively in relief. Did not start game, but saved 15 again and had 8–6 mark. In 1926 saved 22; started five games, wound up with 12–7 record. Harris shifted to Detroit as manager, 1929. That year Marberry, still with Washington, won 19 games, lost 12, and saved 11 others. Came up with 15–5 record, 1930; 16–4 mark, 1931; and 8–4 in 1932. Then came chance for Harris to get Marberry in trade. Tigers gave up Earl Whitehill and Carl Fischer. Marberry won 16, lost 11 in Detroit, saved two other games in relief. Bucky was gone, 1934; Mickey Cochrane took over reins for Tigers. Marberry came through with another fine season, 15–5, with three saves, helping Detroit to AL pennant. Didn't fare so well in WS that autumn against St. Louis Cardinals. Redbirds roughed him up in only appearance in series, as reliever in first game. Marberry allowed five hits, one walk, and four earned runs in 1-2/3 innings. Tigers lost that game—and series.

Marberry got his nickname from Luis Firpo, Argentine giant who took on Jack Dempsey in boxing ring. Fred started out Mexia, Texas-Oklahoma League, 1922. Also pitched for Little Rock, Southern Association, and Jackson, Miss., Cotton State League same season. Little Rock and Washington, 1923. Fred 4–0 in first part-season with Senators.

After Marberry's great days, sagged in effectiveness, 1935. Detroit let him go, and he spent last season in majors with New York Giants and Washington. Major league totals showed 147 victories, 89 defeats, and 3.63 ERA. Pitched in 551 games, 86 of them complete. Saved 101 contests. In 2067-1/3 innings struck out 822, walked 686, had 7 shutouts. WS efforts: 0–1, 3 saves, 12 innings, ERA 3.75.

MARICHAL, JUAN ANTONIO P-BR-TR. B. 10/20/38, Laguna Verde, Dominican Republic. 6', 185. Juan Marichal, in first major league game 7/19/60, gave indication of what was in store for opposing teams in years ahead. Fanned first two Philadelphia NL hitters he faced, Bob Del Greco and Tony Taylor. Retired first 19 men to face him, then error and walk put men on base. In eighth inning Dalrymple hit single to center field with two men out. That was only hit allowed all evening; also first of 50 NL shutouts to his credit going into 1973 season.

Marichal has had some unusual experiences connected with baseball. Was in Dominican Air Force at 18 when dictator Trujillo was in power. Air Force team was best in country, but somehow lost doubleheader. Officers came to find out why. Decision was to put everybody in jail for five days and fine them $2 apiece—except manager, captain, and one player who could fly plane. They got $50 fines and 10 days in calaboose.

Juan came near landing in jail many years later in game against Los Angeles Dodgers. It was third inning of game 8/22/65 with Dodgers leading by 2–1 score; Marichal at bat for Giants. Second pitch was low, outside. Catcher Johnny Roseboro dropped ball, picked it up and fired to pitcher, right past Juan's right ear. Marichal claimed it ticked ear, and demanded of catcher, "Why did you do that?" Roseboro reportedly did not answer, but charged at Marichal. Juan, with bat already in his hands, used it as weapon, clubbing him three times on head, according to some witnesses. Marichal claimed he hit him only once. In any case, big rhubarb ensued. NL president fined Marichal $1,750 and suspended him eight playing days. No penalty given Roseboro.

Giants and Dodgers met in exhibition game following spring in Phoenix. Roseboro landed on one of Marichal's pitches, lined to right field. Jesus Alou, playing there for Giants, came in. Ball took high hop, bounded away, and Johnny had inside-park home run.

Juan claims threw good curve ball at age 10 and experimented with screwball at 15. After some dickering with N. Y. Yankees and Brooklyn Dodgers, signed with Giants 9/17/57. First stop, Michigan City, Midwest League, where won 21 games, lost eight. Got gift of free chicken for every victory. Following season spent at Springfield, Eastern League. There Manager Andy Gilbert taught him trade mark—unusually high kick while delivering ball. No free chickens, but still won 18, lost 13. In 1960, after 11 victories, five defeats at Tacoma, Pacific Coast League, called up to San Francisco team. Won six, lost two during rest of season. Juan then had 13–10 record, followed by 18–11. In 1963 greatly improved performance with 25 wins, eight losses, and ERA of 2.41. This was first of four straight years with 21 or more victories. In 1966 mark was 25–6, with 2.23 ERA. Leg injury handicapped him in 1967; had 14–10 record. Came back strong, 1968. Won 26, lost nine, pitched 326 innings, more than anyone else in league; fanned 218, walked 46, with 2.43 ERA. Following year won "only" 21 games, lost 11, but led NL hurlers in effectiveness with lowest ERA of big league career, 2.10. Had 12–10, 18–11, and 6–16 marks in subsequent seasons.

Marichal had back operation after losing 1972 season. To this point had pitched in 424 NL games, won 227, lost 125. In 3236 innings allowed 998 earned runs for 2.78 ERA. Six times threw over 200 strikeouts per season, for career total of 2194. Walked 653. Twice Marichal led NL in complete games—22 in 1964, 30 in 1968. As he entered 1973 season, had

235 complete games to credit in NL, an amazing total in modern times when managers are so prone to display alleged wisdom by switching pitchers every time runner gets in scoring position.

NL All-Star squads eight times. In only WS appearance, 1962, in fourth game of set Juan pitched four innings, allowed two hits, walked two, but no runs scored off him. Larsen got credit for San Francisco victory.

Marichal pitched no-hitter against Houston, 6/15/63, winning 1–0. Few pitchers have such varied pitches as Marichal. Originally threw sidearm, at times almost underhand. Uses two different speeds for fast ball, mixes them with sliders and slow, floating pitch. Now generally comes overhand with pitches, that high kick proving distracting to batters.

MARION, MARTIN WHITEFORD (Slats) SS-BR-TR. B. 12/1/17, Richburg, S.C. 6'2", 165. Burt Shotton gave Marty Marion his nickname "Slats" because was tall and thin when he joined Cardinal organization, 1936. Some years later Billy Southworth, managing St. Louis NL, gave another nickname, also appropriate, "Mr. Shortstop."

Marty Marion became brilliant short fielder despite physical handicap. When 12 years old was playing in woodlands outside Atlanta, Ga., with other kids. After while, somebody noticed Marty was missing. Two-hour search ensued. They found Marty at base of 20-foot embankment. Had accidentally fallen, shattering right thigh.

Spent seven months in cast from chest to toe; another year on crutches. Right leg permanently one inch shorter than left. But this did not stop him. His brother played outfield for Chattanooga, farm club of Washington Senators; persuaded team to give Marty contract. But Cal Griffith canceled deal, and that's how Marty ultimately landed with Redbird organization at Huntington, W. Va., 1936.

One year there in Middle Atlantic League, then three seasons with Rochester, International League, and was ready to take over shortstop job with Cardinals, 1940. Helped Cards to NL pennants, 1942, 43, 44, 46, and three world championships. Best season at plate was 1943 when hit .280. Led NL in doubles 1942 with 38. Led NL shortstops in fielding four times. MVP in NL for 1944. Played on NL All-Star squads 1943, 44, 46, 47, 50. Selected in 1948 but begged off because of bad back.

Marty got one of biggest kicks in final game of 1942 WS. Cards leading 4–2 in fifth game of Series; had won three games, Yankees winning one. Yanks threatened in last half of ninth when Joe Gordon singled and Bill Dickey safe on error by second baseman. Then dashed over to bag to take catcher Walter Cooper's throw—and Gordon picked off second. Marion said had used no signal, but play worked perfectly—and Yankee rally was ruined. Cards soon wrapped up game and Series.

Marty's career as "Mr. Shortstop" came to end with 1950 season.

Manager of Cardinals, 1951, club coming home third. After being released as manager of Redbirds that fall, became playing coach for St. Louis Browns, 1952, under Rogers Hornsby. When Rajah dropped as pilot, Marty bossed Browns from 6/10/52 until close of 1953 season. Browns were seventh in 1952; eighth, 1953. Marty played 67 games for Browns, 1952, and three in following year. Signed with Chicago White Sox, 1954; piloted club for nine games at end of season when Paul Richards was dropped. Managed White Sox to third-place finish, 1955, and again in 1956. Since then Marion has been active businessman, mostly in St. Louis. Served as one of owners and business manager for Houston club, American Association, 1959, on eve of Houston's entry into NL. More recently has been in restaurant business and manager of Stadium Club at Busch Memorial Stadium where St. Louis Cardinals play ball.

Marion was never power hitter but did slap 36 homers during major league career. Had 272 doubles, 37 triples, .263 average. Hit total came to 1448, with 602 runs scored, 624 RBI in 1572 games. In four WS with Cardinals played 23 games, hit .231; 18 hits in 78 AB, with 7 doubles, 1 triple, 1 homer, and 11 RBI. Solitary WS homer came off Tiny Bonham 10/6/43 when Cardinals won only game of that classic from Yankees by 4–3 score.

Before taking up pro baseball, Marion attended Georgia Tech, specializing in mechanical drawing. Marty one of instigators and played important role in setting up pension plan for players, 1946.

MARIS, ROGER EUGENE   OF-BL-TR. B. 9/10/34, Fargo, N. Dak. 6', 205. Roger Maris hit 61 home runs in 1961, more than Babe Ruth ever did in single season. Both were New York Yankee ball players, left-handed hitters and outfielders. But that's about as far as you can go in comparing the two. Poles apart in disposition, attitudes, physical appearance, appeal to public. Babe Ruth naturally of heroic proportions in almost every direction—stuff from which legends are made. Maris deficient in dramatics; routine, reticent by nature. And while Maris happy to break Babe Ruth's home run record, was very unhappy about almost everything connected with breaking the mark. Ruth lived in less hectic world. Pressures in press, radio, and television had intensified competition among members of media when Maris came along. Where most sports writers could do jobs and remain gentlemen for most part in Ruthian era, anxiety for different or exclusive "angle" on story assumed cut-throat proportions when it seemed Maris might hit 60 or more homers in single season.

So, in closing days of 1961 campaign, Roger had daily inquisition—meetings with media representatives became torture. Quoted and misquoted, words twisted out of context at times; made to appear mercenary, unfriendly, hostile; pressure mounted day after day. Finally Maris did hit 60th and 61st home runs, but only in 162-game season. Ford Frick, baseball commissioner, had added to controversy by indicating that record books should carry an asterisk after Maris' home run record to indicate it wasn't quite kosher, since Babe had made record during 154-game season.

But for all this rhubarb and hullabaloo, Maris might well have hit more than 60 home runs during first 154 games of 1961 season. Hit 56th round-tripper 9/9/61 and had 11 games in which to catch Ruth's record in 154-game span. No homers while club was in Chicago. Tension between Maris and overzealous newsmen became so great that for time he refused any interviews. Slapped two homers in Detroit, last one coming in club's game no. 152. Yankees moved to Baltimore. Had two games in which to equal Babe's mark—needed two to tie, three to break record. Playing under intense pressure, in Ruth's old hometown, before hostile fans and in ball park not favorable to home run hiters, Maris didn't make it. Homer no. 59 came off Milt Pappas in Yankees' 155th game, 9/20/61. It was six days later before Roger got no. 60, and record-breaking homer came 10/1/61 in Yankee Stadium in Yanks' 163d game.

Maris, himself, played just 162 games in 1961. The 163d game was played as result of tie contest 4/22/61. So, depending on interpretation, Maris did and did not break Ruth's record. Fact remains, however, that only Maris ever hit 61 homers in any major league season, even though that season's schedule was planned to be eight games longer than in Ruthian era—and actually went nine games over 1927 schedule.

While Maris never became "modern Babe Ruth," he could be proud of major league record. Was MVP in AL, 1960–61. AL All-Star squads 1959, 60, 61, 62. Hit seven homers in six consecutive games, 1961; named by *Sporting News* as Player of the Year, 1961; set AL record for most intentional walks in one game, getting four during 12-inning contest 5/22/62.

Maris was avid hockey player in youth in North Dakota; fine halfback in football in high school; good enough that several colleges offered athletic scholarships. Decided on baseball. Chicago Cubs gave brief tryout but thought he was too small. Cleveland gave $5,000 to sign, with promise of another $10,000 if and when he made grade with Indians. That was in 1953. Farmed out to Fargo-Moorehead, Keokuk, Tulsa, Reading, and Indianapolis before sticking with Cleveland, 1957.

Hit .235 in 116 games as rookie, and traded to Kansas City AL 6/15/58. Season's average wasn't much higher, just .240, but had 28 homers and 80 RBI. One more year at Kansas City, boosting average to .273, but homer production dropped off to 16 and RBI's to 72.

However, Yankees were interested and got him in trade involving Hank Bauer 12/11/59. Proceeded to hit .283, with 39 homers, 112 RBI, first season at Stadium. Had fine start by hitting two homers, double, and single in Yankee debut.

When 1961 season started, Maris got off poorly—it was game no. 11 before he got first round-tripper. About this time Dan Topping, president of Yankees, and Roy Hamey, general manager, took Maris to lunch. They explained they were paying him good money to hit homers, not to pile up high batting average. Evidently Maris got idea, as homers began to increase. Besides 61 homers, Roger drove in 142 markers, leading AL for second consecutive season. Strains of that season took toll; Maris never had another like it. Hit just 33 homers in 1962, with 100 RBI. After that his performance, while good, was nowhere near peak playing. And after 1966 season, was delighted to get away from metropolis; traded to St. Louis Cardinals 12/8/66. It was a much happier Maris who helped Cardinals to NL pennants 1967, 68. Hit .261 with nine homers, 55 RBI in 1967, and .255 with five homers, 45 RBI, in 100 games in 1968.

Years later, when invited to take part in old-timers' games, Maris refused to put on Yankee uniform and appear with DiMaggio, Dickey, Gomez, and other immortals from Yankee Stadium. But he gladly accepted offers to play in old-timers' games in Cardinal uniform.

Maris quit with record of 1463 major league games, 5101 times at bat, with 826 runs scored, 1325 hits, good for 195 doubles, 42 triples, and 275 homers. Drove in 851 runs, stole 21 bases. Lifetime average of .260.

In WS competition, Maris had spectacular debut 10/5/60. In first inning of first game against Pittsburgh, nicked home run off Vernon Law. Slapped another later in Series and hit .267 for that classic. Had one homer each in three of next four WS, but hit only .187 in all his Series with Yankees. In 1967 WS, as member of Cardinals: .385 average, 10 for 26 trips; 1 homer, 7 RBI. In final WS, 1968: 3 for 19, .158. Overall WS performance: 41 games, 152 AB, 26 R, 33 H, 5 doubles, 6 homers, 18 RBI, .217 average.

MARQUARD, RICHARD WILLIAM (Rube) P-BLR-TL. B. 10/9/89, Cleveland, Ohio. 6'3", 180. Rube Marquard was no square—handsome, dark-haired, tall, city-bred young man from Cleveland moved with swinging set of his day. One of best-dressed men in country; at home on stage; married Broadway actress; but is remembered for putting together longer winning streak than any other pitcher in modern times. Hall of Fame 1971.

Rube got nickname because was lefthanded hurler, and so was Rube Waddell. This is about only resemblance. Where Waddell imbibed freely, often far too much, Marquard neither drank nor smoked. Marquard won 201 games in major leagues—Waddell 191. Both, however, are enshrined in Cooperstown, Waddell making it in 1946.

Record books say Marquard won 19 consecutive victories, 1912, but Rube says should have been 20. Under rules of present time would have had 20. In one contest, entered game in eighth inning with his club, New

York Giants, behind 3–2. In ninth, Giants scored two runs, to win game 4–3. Official scorer, however, gave victory to Jeff Tesreau who pitched first seven rounds and part of eighth.

Marquard, as boy, loved baseball and at times acted as unofficial batboy for Cleveland AL in early 1900s. Hero worshiper of Nap Lajoie, then with club. At 16 rode freight trains to Waterloo, Iowa; pitched and won one game but returned home when manager failed to give contract. Attracted considerable attention around Cleveland but AL club wouldn't raise offer above $100 monthly, so he signed with Indianapolis, American Association, 1907, for $200 a month. Farmed out to Canton, Ohio, Central League, where he promptly won 23 games, lost 13. Then in 1908 captured 28 games for Indianapolis, losing 19.

Late in season, after attracting attention of major league people, Rube pitched rare game in Columbus. Time had come for Indianapolis team to sell his contract or else could be drafted. Rube pitched perfect game; no Columbus player reached base. N. Y. Giants outbid all others with $11,000 offer and Marquard reported to Mgr. John McGraw that same September. Price was highest paid for minor league player to that time. Rube was hit pretty hard in only start that season—touched for six hits, two walks, five runs in five innings, and lost decision. In 1909 was 5–13, acquired tag, "$11,000 lemon." Broke even in 1910, 4–4. Then began to pay off on investment. Came up with 24–7 following season, then 26–11 and 23–10. Giants won NL flag each of those three years. Marquard lost one game in 1911 WS to Eddie Plank of Philadelphia AL, but had ERA of 1.54. Lost his only decision in 1913 classic with 7.00 ERA.

But in 1912 won two of three games taken by Giants in WS against Boston Red Sox; had 0.50 ERA.

Marquard had couple of mediocre seasons 1914,15 then went to Brooklyn Dodgers September 1915. In 1916 helped Flatbush crew to pennant with 13–6, but lost two WS contests to Red Sox. Won 19 for Brooklyn, 1917, dropping 12. Traded to Cincinnati for Walter (Dutch) Reuther 12/15/20 and had 17–14 record in only year with Reds, 1921. Boston NL 1922–25. Years with Braves were not distinguished, and 1926 found him in minors with Providence, Eastern League, as manager. Baltimore, International League, appearing in only seven games; Birmingham, Southern Association, 1927.

Out of baseball, 1928. Pitched a little and managed Jacksonville, Southeastern League, 1929–30; umpire in Eastern League, 1931; pitched, coached, scouted for Atlanta team of Southern Association, 1932.

His major league statistics: 536 games, 3307 innings pitched, allowing 3233 hits, 1443 runs, 858 walks, struck out 1593. Since no records were kept differentiating runs from earned runs before 1912, only an estimate can be made about his ERA average. Observers figure somewhere between 3.08 and 3.18.

Marquard's WS records included two with Brooklyn (1916, 20) and showed 58-2/3 innings pitched in 11 games; 2–5, 19 earned runs, 35 strikeouts, 16 walks, 2.91 ERA.

While Rube was going great guns with Giants, did considerable work on stage after seasons. At one point flirted with Federal League, but decided to stick with Giants.

MARQUEZ, GONZALO (Hurricane) 1B-BL-TL. B. 3/31/46, Carupano, Sucre, Venezuela. 5′11″, 180. Gonzalo Marquez hit just .315 in American Association, 1972, but found AL pitching much more to his liking after joining Oakland 8/11/72. Hit .381 in 23 games. In playoffs, average was .667. And in WS it dropped to .600. Without Marquez and his phenomenal pinch hitting, Finley, Williams, Tenace, and company might never have won AL pennant and 1972 world championship. Besides eight hits and four RBI in latter stages of AL flag race, Gonzalo drove in Oakland's tying run in 11th inning of first playoff game against Detroit. Gene Tenace then scored A's winning marker when Kaline's throw to third base bounced away from Rodriguez. Marquez failed when he pinch hit in third game. But in fourth contest, pinch hit in 10th inning, singled, and later scored. It wasn't his fault that Tigers came back to win that game.

In WS Gonzalo pinch hit in opener, popped out. Batted for Green in seventh inning of third game, singled, but did not score. Helped A's win fourth contest. Batted for Hendrick in ninth inning and started rally with single. Allen Lewis ran for him and later scored tying run for Oakland. A's then won game when Mincher's single brought Gene Tenace home. Marquez again was used as emergency batsman in fifth game of WS: his single drove in one run in fourth inning. In sixth game, when pinch hitting again, best was an infield grounder. Did not get into seventh game of classic, but his three pinch hits in WS equaled existing record.

Marquez was stellar athlete in high school in baseball, track, and volley ball. Started at Leesburg, Florida State League, 1966. Later played with Peninsula club, Carolina League; Birmingham in Southern, and Iowa, American Association. Best season was 1970, at Iowa, when he hit .341 with six homers. But has hit very few homers in pro career—none in 1972. Played considerable winter ball in Venezuela.

MARSHALL, MICHAEL GRANT P-BR-TR. B. 1/15/43, Adrian, Mich. 5′10″, 178. By virtue of being named player of year for Montreal Expos, 1972, Mike Marshall received $10,000 El Dorado Cadillac, presented to him by O'Keefe's Brewery of Canada. Marshall had just won 14 games for team, saved 18, and carved earned run average of 1.78. Lost eight decisions. Gene Mauch, manager of Expos, claims Marshall is best relief pitcher he has ever seen. Mike, day after presentation, was in East Lansing, Mich., conducting class in physical education, continuing work toward doctorate at Michigan State.

Marshall began in baseball as shortstop. Played position in pro ball, starting 1961 at Dothan, Ala. Later at Bakersfield, Magic Valley, and Chattanooga. Switched to pitching, 1965, then bounced around to Eugene, Northwest League; Montgomery, Toledo, Oklahoma City, and Winnipeg. Had 3–10 record with Seattle Pilots in their solitary season in AL, 1969; had 1–3 record while briefly with Detroit Tigers, 1967. Joined Houston Astros, 1970; pitched in just four games and was sold to Expos. Had 3–7 mark for Montreal. Got rolling, 1971, with mixture of screwballs, sliders, and fast balls. Despite midseason slump, had 23 saves, being second to Dave Giusti of Pirates in this respect. Won three, lost seven. Then came fine year in 1972. Faced 1973 with major league record of 444 innings pitched in 216 games; won 26, lost 37; fanned 311 and walked 185. Career ERA: 3.43.

MARTIN, ALFRED MANUEL (Billy) Inf.-BR-TR. B. 5/16/28, Berkeley, Calif. 5'11", 170. Combative, bellicose, belligerent; pugnacious, aggressive needler whose first instincts in many situations seem to be to use fists. As brash rookie with New York Yankees, didn't hesitate to tell established, older players, some of them stars, what he thought they were doing wrong. As manager, isn't content to goose own players, but gets on other performers and managers as well. Once slugged one of own pitchers, Dave Boswell, while bossing Minnesota Twins.

Billy Martin played 1021 major league games, was in five WS. Career average as hitter wasn't distinguished, .257, with 64 homers, 24 triples, 139 doubles among 877 hits. Scored 425 runs, drove in 313. Did considerably better in WS play—hit .333 in 28 games, with five homers, five triples, two doubles among 33 hits. Fifteen runs scored, 19 RBI. Specially hot in 1953 series when he batted .500; 12 hits in 24 trips.

Though numerous second basemen better than Martin, none with more zest. Few players were more outspoken, regardless of occasion. Once was present at old-timers' dinner honoring Ty Cobb, by that time univerally held in awe as an immortal. Not by Martin, however. "I've got respect for old-timers," he said to Cobb. "But if I had been playing and you would have come into second base high on me only once, after that you wouldn't have any teeth."

Maybe Billy is still frustrated pugilist. At 19, fight promoter wanted him to become pro boxer as middleweight. But by then was determined to become major league ball player. At 16 smuggled into ball park to warm up with Oakland Acorns of Pacific Coast League. Signed first pro contract at 17; sent to Idaho Falls in Pioneer League, 1946. Played most of 1947 with Phoenix, Arizona-Texas League—hit .392 in 130 games; then spent couple of weeks with Oakland, playing 15 games. Two full seasons at Oakland. Was drawing $9000 salary in 1949. Late that year, playing night game, looked into sky and saw blimp with electric news sign reading, "Billy Martin sold to Yankees." If Billy thought promotion to majors would mean raise in pay, he was mistaken. Yankees offered

$6000 contract and refused to budge. Then Yanks ordered him to report to Kansas City farm club in American Association. Martin told George Weiss, then farm-system boss for Yankees, "I'll make you pay for abusing me like this! I'll get even!"

Term at Kansas City was brief—29 games. He was recalled and played 34 games that year with New York; hit .250. Following season got into 51 games—and got into one WS game as pinch runner. While Martin was still trying for regular job, tangled with Clint (Scrap Iron) Courtney, catcher for St. Louis Browns. Free-for-all followed after Martin put ball in Clint's teeth. League president dished out $850 in fines, Martin paying $150 as his penalty. Began to be called "Kayo" and "Agitator" after this melee and fights with Matt Batts and Jimmy Piersall. "Somebody has to take charge," Martin said. "Yankees haven't had captain since Lou Gehrig."

Billy played 109 games in 1952, and in WS that fall displayed leadership qualities even though hit just .217 in classic. Yankees were playing Dodgers. In fourth game, with Dodgers trailing by one run, Andy Pafko was on third base. Charley Dressen, Brooklyn manager, was coaching at third base, with Joe Black batter at plate. Martin had played for Dressen while at Oakland, 1949. Knew that in this situation Dressen had used squeeze play in PCL. Warned Yankee pitcher Allie Reynolds. As result, Yanks caught Pafko 15 feet off bag, spelling ruin to Brooklyn rally.

Martin played 149 games at second and short for Yanks, 1953. Then came his dazzling WS. His 12 hits set new record for six-game Series. Two singles and triple in first game against Dodgers. Single and homer in second contest. Carl Erskine held him to solitary single in third game and Dodgers were able to win after two losses. A single and triple in next contest, which also went to Dodgers. Homer and single in fifth game. Then single and double—and scored winning run for Yankees in sixth contest, which wrapped things up for another Yankee world championship.

Billy was in military service 1954, out of baseball all season and most of 1955, when he got into just 20 games. But he was there for WS, this time hitting .320 with eight hits in 25 at bats. One more full season with Yankees, and another WS, 1956, this time with .296 mark in classic. Traded to Kansas City, AL, 6/15/57. Detroit, 1958. Cleveland, 1959. Cincinnati, 1960. Milwaukee, NL, 1961 until June 1, when traded to Minnesota. Played 114 games that year, last as an active player.

No dull moments while Martin was with Yanks. In March 1952 Billy broke two bones in ankle while sliding. Not in ball game, however. He was making kinescope for spaghetti commercial.

When Casey Stengel put him eighth in batting order Billy told sports writers Casey was crazy. After Yanks won pennant, 1953, Martin and several teammates celebrated in nightclub. When time came to settle up, bill was colossal. Somebody, not Martin, suggested sending the bill to Dan Topping, president of Yanks. This was done—and Topping was hopping mad. Martin got most of publicity and blame for incident.

On another occasion Billy missed plane—and it cost him $250 fine. Another well-publicized nightclub happening involved Martin and Mickey Mantle, among others, at Copacabana.

While at Cincinnati, Martin got into fight with Pitcher Jim Brewer, then with Chicago Cubs. Billy accused Brewer of throwing at him, went to mound and hit him in eye. Brewer was in hospital 17 days and needed two operations as result of fight. Brewer sued Billy for $1 million. Court first awarded Brewer $100,000 damages, then Circuit Judge reduced amount to $35,000.

After active playing days ended, Billy scouted for Twins, 1962–64. Coach for Twins, 1965 until 5/26/68 when he became manager of their Denver farm club, PCL. Manager, Minnesota, 1969; brought team home first in AL Western Division but lost to Baltimore in playoffs. Then was fired "for ignoring Twin policies."

Billy came back as major league manager, 1971, as pilot of Detroit Tigers, with reported $60,000 salary. First thing he did was to visit many players on roster in their off-season homes. Tigers finished second in Eastern Division of AL. Then in 1972, Billy had club in thick of things and took top honors in AL East, finishing half-game ahead of Boston Red Sox, only to lose playoffs to Oakland in bitter struggle, which went full five games.

Did Billy order pitcher LaGrow to throw at Campy Campaneris' legs in second game of playoffs? Who knows? Then Campy threw bat at pitcher and only combined restraint by umpires John Rice and Larry Barnett kept Martin from more active participation in rhubarb that followed. Martin emerged without penalties from AL president Joe Cronin.

Billy's fisticuffs in 1972 seemingly were confined to slugging an annoying fan in parking lot outside Baltimore ball park.

Martin's real name is Alfred Manuel Pesano.

MARTIN, JOHN LEONARD (Pepper) OF-3B-BR-TR. B. 4/29/04, Temple, Okla. D. 3/5/65, McAlester, Okla. 5'8", 170. Pepper Martin, alias "Wild Horse of Osage," isn't Hall of Famer, but what he did in 1931 WS alone could justify consideration. Joe Tinker and Johnny Evers got elected largely because of legend engendered by famous poem "Tinker to Evers to Chance." Fact is, in four years they worked together this pair made total of just 54 double plays. And neither was much as hitter. Martin played baseball with spontaneity and joyous abandon rare in organized baseball today. In fall of 1931 he Martinized Mickey Cochrane and powerful Philadelphia Athletics with .500 batting average and brash blazing speed on bases, climaxed by spectacular head-first slides into base.

Pepper was outfielder then. Later became third baseman for NL All-Star team and was Cardinal third sacker during their 1934 dash for pennant and world championship. Even pitched for Redbirds—after Dizzy Dean and Brother Paul went on strike during 1934 season. Martin's willingness to do anything to help club win was tremendous morale booster for Cardinals during crisis when they lost two of their stellar pitchers.

When 1931 WS started Martin's name meant little to average fan. Attention was focused on such greats as Al Simmons, Mickey Cochrane, Lefty Grove, Frisch, Grimes, Bottomley, Hafey, Haines, Hallahan. Eight participants in that 1931 WS later were elected to Hall of Fame. When Series was over, Martin had become household word; had befuddled Athletics completely. Almost single-handedly provided ingredient that enabled Cardinals to snatch world championship from team that had won it in both 1929 and 1930.

Philadelphia, winner of 107 games during AL season, was heavy favorite to win 1931 WS. Lefty Grove, winner of 31 games against four losses, was on mound in opening game. Not at his best, but won by 6–2 score. Allowed 12 Cardinal hits. Martin got three of those hits and stole one base. Next day, against Earnshaw, Pepper got two of Cardinals' six hits. Walked once and scored both St. Louis runs. Converted routine "single" into double by daring base running. Stole second once and stole third once. Meanwhile Bill Hallahan was blanking A's, and Cards evened series, 2–0.

In third game, again facing Grove, Martin singled and doubled, helping Burleigh Grimes and his teammates to 5–2 victory. In next game George Earnshaw pitched Athletics to win, bringing game count to two apiece. Earnshaw allowed only two hits; Pepper singled in fifth inning for first hit off Philadelphia righthander. Promptly stole second base. Next time up, in eighth, Martin doubled to left field corner. Stranded both times and Athletics took game 3–0. In fifth game it was Hallahan against Hoyt. Pepper drove in first Cardinal run with long liner to left, enabling Andy High to score from third base after catch. Bunted safely in fourth inning. Then in sixth inning Martin slapped ball into upper deck of left field pavilion, with one man on base. And in eighth inning drove in another run with single. By this time Pepper owned .667 batting average, with 12 hits in 18 times at bat. Lefty Grove held Martin hitless in sixth game. But in seventh and crucial contest, while Pepper did not hit safely he was very much in ball game. In first inning Redbirds got men on second and third with Martin coming up to plate. Earnshaw uncorked wild pitch, enabling one Cardinal run to score. Then Pepper walked. Immediately stole second, after which Mickey Cochrane let a third strike get by, allowing second Cardinal run to come in. Was Martin's presence at plate cause of wild pitch? Or was Cochrane so jittery with Martin's base running that he allowed third strike to get past him? In any case, things always seemed to happen around Martin. With poetic justice, Martin figured in climax of Series. Cardinals had two-run lead in ninth inning. Athletics got two men on base, representing tying runs. Bill Hallahan came in to relieve Grimes. Max Bishop was hitter; slapped short but tricky fly ball to center field. Pepper dashed in, squeezed ball for third out—and Cardinals were world champions, due mostly to dazzling work of John Leonard Martin.

Martin by this time had captured imagination of American people. Young man whose baseball contract brought him just $4,500 for year, now got crack at going on stage at $1500 a week. Pepper took the relatively easy money for few weeks, then turned down chance for five additional weeks. Tossed away potential $7500, saying, "Hell, I ain't no actor."

Hurried back to Oklahoma, ignoring mash notes, invitations to dinners and luncheons, hunting trips, endorsements, and spent winter quail and duck hunting, enjoying great outdoors. Following season, 1932, fans expected impossible of Martin. Still untamed, Pepper slept in grass and was bitten by insect, leading to bothersome skin infection. Broke hand. Tried too hard, couldn't extricate himself from doldrums. Before season was over lost regular job; hit just .238 and rode bench. When 1933 came, looked like Martin might not even make ball club. But Cardinals had numerous infield problems, and Martin was given crack at third base job. Incredibly horrible at start—couldn't field cleanly, and when he did stop ball with barrel chest, oftentimes throws were miles above first baseman's head or into dirt. Couldn't hit. Then in miserable Sunday game in St. Louis, Martin made errors, struck out two or three times. After final whiff, disgustedly threw bat toward dugout. When he reached batrack, kicked collection of bats. One of them uncannily bounded into box seats and landed in lap of Mrs. Sam Breadon, wife of Cardinal owner. Roar of boos filled ball park. It was tragic moment for fallen hero. Never before had home player been booed so unmercifully. Fortunately Cardinals went on road that night. Gabby Street, then Cardinal manager, kept Martin in lineup and, away from St. Louis, Pepper pulled himself together. When club returned home couple of weeks later, Martin was doing quite well in field and at bat. When baseball fans around country voted for players to be on NL All-Star squad, they remembered his 1931 WS play, so was one of those selected. So was Pie Traynor, considered by many as greatest third baseman of all time, at least until Brooks Robinson. John McGraw managed NL team in game played at Comiskey Park, first of All-Star games. Little Napoleon, considered one of great managers of all times, used Pepper Martin as third baseman throughout game—and Traynor rode bench.

Martin started pro career at Greenville, East Texas League, 1924, later bounced around Cardinal farm system at Fort Smith, Syracuse, Houston, and Rochester before finally staying with Redbirds, 1931. Had been with Cardinals 1928, but used mostly as pinch runner. In 1930, at Rochester, had feasted on International League pitching with .363 average. Batted an even .300 with Cardinals, 1931. And after that miserable 1932 performance, had come back with .316 average in 1933, when he also led NL in runs scored (122) and in stolen bases (26). Led league in thefts again in 1934 and 1936 with 23 each time. After 1940 season Martin went to minors as manager, going from Sacramento to Des Moines, Portsmouth, Va., Macon, Miami, and Fort Lauderdale. In 1944 was back with Cardinals and hit wartime pitching at .279 rate in 40 games. Final appearance in big league uniform was with Chicago Cubs in 1965 as coach under manager Stan Hack.

Once, while managing at Miami, tried to choke an umpire. Suspended and brought before Commissioner Chandler, sympathetic Happy offered opinion that maybe Pepper didn't mean any harm. Martin blurted out truthfully, "I wanted to kill the buzzard!" Was softie at heart, however.

Served briefly as director of Oklahoma State Penitentiary at McAlester, near his prosperous cattle ranch. Heart attack wrote finis 3/5/65 shortly before was due to return to baseball as coach for Tulsa Oilers of Texas League. "One of nature's noblemen," Branch Rickey characterized this legendary figure.

Pepper's big league statistics showed 1189 games played; 1227 hits, with 270 doubles, 75 triples, 59 homers. Scored 756 runs, drove in 501. Lifetime average of .298. In three WS, 1928,31,34: .418 average, with 23 for 55; 15 games, 7 doubles, 1 triple, 1 homer, 7 stolen bases. Hit .500 in 1931 Series, and .355 in 1934 classic.

MARTIN, JOSEPH CLIFTON (J.C.)   C-1B-BL-TR. B. 12/13/36, Axton, Va. 6'2", 195.

J. C. Martin got into one WS game during career, had just one time at bat as pinch hitter. But Baltimore Oriole players and fans are still muttering, "We wuz robbed!" Martin was with "Miracle Mets" of 1969. Mets had taken two of first three games of WS, and score was tied in 10th inning of fourth game when Manager Gil Hodges called on J.C. to pinch hit with two men on base. With nobody out, Martin bunted. Ball was fielded by Oriole pitcher Pete Richert. Pete's throw to first baseman Boog Powell hit Martin on wrist, bounded away, and Mets scored winning run on error. Orioles claimed Martin had run illegally out of base path, thereby blocking Richert's throw. Movies later seemed to substantiate their claim, but umpires ruled there was no obstruction. So Mets won their third game and next day wrapped up Series, four games to one, winning world championship.

Martin came out of Nebraska State League, 1956, playing with Holdrege club. Later with Davenport and Dubuque in Iowa; Duluth-Superior, Minn.; Indianapolis; Savannah; and San Diego, then in Pacific Coast League. First games with Chicago White Sox, 1959–60; played 110 games for them in 1961, but farmed out for most of 1962.

Remained with Sox through 1967 season, then with Mets, 1968–69. Traded to Chicago Cubs 3/29/70. Cubs released unconditionally, March 1973. Later signed with Wichita as player-coach.

J. C. originally was first baseman, but Al Lopez, then manager of White Sox, converted him to catcher. At end of 1972 season Martin had appeared in 908 major league games, owned .222 batting average with 32 homers, 12 triples, 82 doubles among 487 hits. Scored 189 times and drove in 230 runs.

MATHEWS, EDWIN LEE, JR. 3B-BL-TR. B. 10/13/31, Texarkana, Tex. 6′1″, 195. Eddie Mathews hit 512 career home runs in majors, many of them tape measure variety. Named to NL All-Star squads nine times, 1953 and 1955–62. Poor fielder at third base when young; but learned skills, led NL third sackers in fielding, 1963. Named manager of Atlanta Braves 8/7/72, succeeding Luman Harris.

Mathews may have been only ball player to sign first pro contract in tux. Baseball rules prevented big league scouts from signing players until day after graduation from high school. Fifteen scouts, however, were on trail, ready with offers.

Johnny Moore, scout for Boston Braves, outwitted competition. Mathews went to senior prom night of graduation. Moore got head start by sending Eddie's date a corsage. And while other scouts waited in lobby for dance to end, Moore somehow spirited Eddie out back door at one minute after midnight, got his signature and that of father on contract calling for bonus of $5999. This enabled Braves to farm him out. Had bonus reached $6000 figure, Mathews would have had to stay on major league roster. Scouts who were outwitted reportedly would have raised offers as high as $30,000 bonus. However, Mathews family liked Moore. Moore also told Mathews that Billy Southworth, then manager of Braves, wanted to see Eddie. So first stop was Boston, then Evansville briefly, then to North Carolina State League. There Eddie, 1949, hit .363, with 17 home runs. Spent 1950 with Atlanta, Southern League; divided 1951 between Atlanta and Milwaukee, then in American Association. Made grade with Braves, 1952, starting off with 25 homers, 58 RBI, and .242 average in 145 games.

Mathews was just 20 when he took over Braves' hot corner regularly. Long-distance clouts amazed veteran baseball men. Then Braves moved to Milwaukee, 1953. Eddie proceeded to slap 47 homers to lead NL, boosted batting average to .302, and drove in 135 runs.

Fans showered him with adulation but he wasn't ready for it. Became cynical, suspicious, bored with requests for autographs. Once when he made an error late in first game of doubleheader, fans booed him. Eddie was supposed to appear on field between games to receive award for making All-Star team. Refused to go out until finally persuaded to do so by cooler heads on team. By then it was too late, so got more boos, more newspaper criticism.

Once Mathews was fined $50 for reckless driving and another $100 for missing curfew. Threatened photographers who tried to take picture at court—also blasted photographers at his wedding.

Continued slugging. Four times had at least 40 homers. Led NL for second time in 1959 with 46. Fourteen times had more than 20 round-trippers. By time Milwaukee franchise was moved to Atlanta, 1966, Mathews beginning to slow down: hit .250, with 16 homers, 53 RBI. Traded to Houston NL for 1967. Sent to Detroit 7/22/67. Back with Tigers, 1968, though hit just .212 in 31 games, missing several weeks because of back injury. That ended active career as player. Mathews rejoined Braves, 1971, as coach, continuing in that capacity until appointment as manager.

Eddie played in three WS, 1957,58 with Milwaukee, 1968 with Detroit. Hit just .200 in 16 games, with one homer, seven RBI. It wasn't slugging but his fielding that saved 1957 WS for Braves. Yankees were threatening in ninth inning of seventh, crucial game. Loaded bases. With two outs Skowron blasted drive down line, ticketed for double or triple. Eddie leaped at ball, backhanded it, dived to third base to get forceout, giving Braves world championship. Mathews' homer, however, had given Braves fourth game of classic. Blasted it out of park in 10th inning off Bob Grim.

Eddie was rookie when he hit three homers in one game 9/27/52. Facing Joe Black of Brooklyn Dodgers at Ebbets Field, got first one on fast curve in third inning; in sixth inning drove one of Ben Wade's pitches over scoreboard in left center. Up again in eighth, hit number three, also off Wade. It was first time in NL history that rookie hit three homers in one game.

Mathews held major league record for most games by third baseman, but Brooks Robinson since surpassed it; struck out 1487 times, putting him near top in this respect; had most consecutive years with 30 or more homers, nine. Hit eight grand slammers.

MATHEWSON, CHRISTOPHER (Big Six) P-BR-TR. B. 8/12/80, Factoryville, Pa. D. 10/7/25, Saranac Lake, N.Y. 6'1½", 195. Christy Mathewson once played 12 opponents simultaneously in chess matches at Pittsburgh Athletic Club and won all of them. But there wasn't any money in chess those days before Bobby Fischer, so Matty stuck to pitching. Great pitcher—greatest of his generation. Cy Young won more games, 511, but was tapering off when Mathewson came along. Christy won 373 games, NL record he shares with Grover Cleveland Alexander, who belonged to later generation.

During early years of 20th century Mathewson was model athlete. Handsome, conducted himself in manner to merit admiration of practically everybody. Drank only occasionly, never to excess. Could swear if situation got annoying. All of which merely proved he was human, despite all adulation poured on him.

Matty won 37 games in 1908, modern NL record. Pitched 83 shutouts in NL competition. In WS of 1905, pitched three shutouts. Did numerous other improbable things on mound with fine assortment of fast balls, curves—and famous fadeaway.

Christy attended Bucknell U. where he played football, baseball, and basketball. Collegiate rules were such that he was able to play semipro ball in summers. Was class president, member of Glee Club and literary society. In 1899 joined Taunton club of New England League, won five games, lost two. While there developed fadeaway, or reverse curve, copying it from another pitcher on same club. Did not perfect it, however, until some years later while member of New York Giants. Before joining Giants, however, Matty had record of 20 wins against just two losses pitching for Norfolk, Virginia League, 1900. With N. Y. that season, pitched in six games, lost three of them, and Giants sent him back to Norfolk.

Cincinnati club then proceeded to draft him, after which was traded to Giants who must have had second thoughts about youngster. Matty justified return to New York by pitching 20 victories in first full season in majors, losing 17. Giants were seventh that year. Following season team ended up in cellar, Matty experiencing 14–17 mark. That was season when John McGraw took over management of team in July.

Combination of McGraw and Mathewson worked transformation for Giants. Matty won 30 games, lost 13 in 1903 and team bounded to second place. In 1904 Matty won 33, lost 12, and McGraw won first pennant with New Yorkers.

Christy dropped back to 31 victories in 1905, lost nine. Then had couple of "off-seasons." Won 22, lost 12, and then had 24–12 mark in 1907. Then came 37-victory season, followed by six more years in which he had at least 23 victories every season.

Matty's last big year was 1914 when won 24, lost 13. That fadeaway must have taken toll of his arm, for at age 35, Christy could win only eight games while losing 14. And in 1916, final year as active player, won four, lost four for Giants and Reds. Giants traded him to Cincinnati 7/20/16 so could become playing manager. Matty took team that finished seventh that year and led it into fourth place, 1917. Then, U. S. having entered World War I, he enlisted with Chemical Warfare Service. When war ended, had been replaced as manager of Reds and spent 1919–21 as coach with Giants. President of Boston Braves, 1923 until his death.

In all, Matty pitched in 635 major league games, won 373, lost 188 for .665 winning percentage. In 4781 innings allowed 4203 hits, 1613 runs. During his earlier years no statistics were kept on whether runs were earned or not, but with all those shutouts, you may be sure he was stingy with earned runs. In 1912, first year for which reliable information is available, had an ERA of 2.12. Following year, 1913, was best in NL with 2.06.

Matty had good control. Eleven times pitched more than 300 innings. Consistently had far more strikeouts than walks allowed—*2505* to *837*. *Six* times led NL in strikeouts, greatest number being 267 in 1903. Pitched 68 consecutive innings during one stretch in 1913 without giving base on balls. Pitched two no-hit ball games.

Matty had great success against St. Louis Cardinals—beat them 23 consecutive times; and against Cincinnati Reds, from whom won 22 in row. Didn't waste much time when on mound. In one game against Philadelphia 4/23/13, made just 67 pitches; on another occasion used 69 pitches against Pittsburgh 8/13/16.

While Matty had great moments, also had off days. Jack Dalton, rookie outfielder with Brooklyn Dodgers, made debut against Big Six 6/21/10; slapped Matty's pitches for five straight hits. Dalton's average for whole season was .227.

And great control pitcher ran into weird situation 6/7/06. Matty walked six Chicago Cub batters in one inning—and that day Cubs won ball game by 19–0 score.

Mathewson's greatest moments probably were three shutouts pitched against Philadelphia Athletics in 1905 WS. Victories came on Monday, Thursday, and Saturday, all in same week. In those 27 innings, Matty allowed 14 hits, struck out 18 and walked just one man. No wonder Giants won Series, four games to one.

In 1911 Series, although Matty wasn't so effective, he still had ERA of 2.00 for classic. Won one game by 2–1 score, but lost others by 4–2 score and 3–2 in eleven innings. In 1912 Matty was charged with two defeats against no victories. His teammates, however, were largely responsible: Matty had ERA of 1.57 for 28-2/3 innings. But Giants' errors accounted for six unearned runs, victimizing Christy. And in Matty's final WS, his ERA was just 0.95—two earned runs in 19 innings. This time lost one game by 3–1 score, but had to go 10 innings to win 3–0 shutout.

Mathewson's WS performance added up to 11 games pitched, 101-2/3 innings, 5–5, ERA 1.15. Had four shutouts; allowed 22 runs, only 13 of which were earned; walked 10 and struck out 48.

Tuberculosis caught up with him; after spending many months at Saranac Lake, N.Y., death came at age 45. Posthumously elected to Hall of Fame 1936.

MATLACK, JONATHAN TRUMPBOUR P-BL-TL. B. 1/19/50, West Chester, Pa. 6'3", 205. When Jon Matlack in high school, pitched eight no-hitters. Won 22 games, lost one. Losing effort was one-hitter—fanned 16. But that was against high school opposition. In 1972 Jon proved could pitch against major leaguers. Not only won 15 games for New York Mets, losing 10, but finished fourth in NL in effectiveness among those pitching at least 160 innings. His 2.32 ERA bettered only by Steve Carlton, Gary Nolan, Don Sutton.

Matlack attended U. of Pittsburgh and West Chester State College. Signed to Mets' organization 8/9/67 by scout Ollie Vanek. Rough initiation into pro ball, giving up eight runs in five innings pitched for Williamsport in Eastern League that season. Did better at Raleigh-Durham, Carolina League, 1968, with 13–6 record, 2.76 ERA. With Tidewater club in International League next three seasons. Had 14–7, 12–11, 11–7 marks. Mets 1971—0–3, 4.14 ERA.

Jon started all of his 100 games while in minors. With Mets was used as starter in 38 of 41 games pitched, 1971–72. Faced 1973 with 2.56 ERA for 281 innings in NL, 15 wins, 13 losses; 193 strikeouts; 86 walks (14 intentional), 8 complete games.

MAUCH, GENE WILLIAM Mgr.-Inf.-BR-TR. B. 11/18/25, Salina, Kans. 5'10", 173. Perfectionist, nimble-minded tactician, intolerant of losing, but suffered through longest streak of defeats in majors during 20th century. Managing Philadelphia Phillies, 1961, club was loser for 23 consecutive games. Still Gene Mauch winningest of Phils' managers in modern times: from 1960 to 1968 teams won 646 games. Twice NL Manager of Year, 1962,64; piloted NL All-Stars to victory over AL squad, 1965.

Mauch might have managed Phillies considerably longer but for Richie (or Dick) Allen. Allen was with Phillies close to five years while Gene was boss there. Almost inevitable that intense man like Mauch would clash with player who seemingly made own rules.

Playing career from 1943 to 1959. Originally Gene in Brooklyn organization at Durham, Montreal, St. Paul. Also played with Indianapolis, Milwaukee, Atlanta, Los Angeles, and Minneapolis in minors. Major league batting average for 304 games was .239, with just five homers among 176 hits. Briefly with Brooklyn, Chicago, St. Louis Pittsburgh, Boston in NL and Boston AL.

First taste of managing at Atlanta, in Southern Association, 1953, bringing team home in third position. Resigned at end of season because felt he lacked maturity to handle job way he wanted to. Continued as player, and got second crack at field management, 1958—again third. In 1959 got into only eight games as pinch hitter, but managed Minneapolis into second place in Eastern Division of American Association. Managed Phillies following years. Led them into fourth place twice, and into second-place tie, 1964. Term in Philadelphia ended 6/16/68. Manager, Montreal Expos, starting in 1969.

In 1963, while bossing Phillies, team lost tough game in Houston. Caterers had set up beautiful smorgasbord in clubhouse after game. Mauch came in in roaring temper. Soon food flying in every direction, at lockers, against walls. Colossal mess. Dressed down players with choicest vocabulary. An occasion never forgotten by eyewitnesses.

Mauch decided he wanted to become manager when he was rookie and met Leo Durocher, then manager of Dodgers. "To Leo, managing was not going out to play a game; it was a crusade. You don't just go out to play, you go out to win."

Another story told about Mauch happened in Minneapolis. Came in from ball field, called to clubhouse boy to get hammer and nails. "What for?" asked young man. "Just get them," replied Gene. Mauch then proceeded to nail his spiked shoes to clubhouse wall—a way of announcing to everyone, including himself, that he had played his last game of ball, so disgusted was he with own play.

Mauch eats, sleeps, talks baseball constantly. Has fantastic grasp for detail, has practically total recall about any play, any situation in years gone by. Can tell you the count on hitter, where pitch was, and who hit it. Insists on drilling his players in fundamentals. Nothing subtle about him in dealing with press, which he regards as necessary evil. Detests questions that he thinks stupid.

MAY, CARLOS 1B-OF-BL-TR. B. 5/17/48, Birmingham, Ala. 6', 215. Carlos May has shown steady improvement in batting average with Chicago White Sox since accident in August 1969 cost most of right thumb. Brother of Lee May, now with Houston Astros, Carlos was on duty with marines at Camp Pendleton, Calif., when mortar misfire seriously endangered budding baseball career. At time, owned .281 batting average for 100 games that season, with 18 homers, 62 RBI. Named AL Rookie of Year by *Sporting News.* Long hospitalization followed, with repeated surgery and skin grafts. Nevertheless Carlos overcame handicap, played 150 games in 1970, hit .285; homer production dropped to 12. In 1971 spent most of season at first base, hit .294, with 70 RBI, 7 round-trippers. In 1972 boosted average to .308, with 68 RBI, 12 home runs. In outfield most of 1972, making way for Richie Allen to play first base.

May started at Sarasota, 1966. Later played with Winter Haven, Appleton, Lynchburg. In 17 games with White Sox, 1968, hit .179. Pinch hit in 1969 All-Star game; again with AL All-Stars 1972 but saw no action.

Carlos, going into 1973, had .289 major league average for 556 games; 581 hits, 94 doubles, 16 triples, 49 homers; 296 runs scored and 269 RBI.

MAY, FRANK SPURIELL (Jakie) P-BR-TL. B. 11/25/95, Wendell, N. C. D. 6/3/70, Wendell, N. C. Jakie May had two good seasons with Cincinnati Reds, 1926–27. Before that, Branch Rickey, managing St. Louis Cardinals, had given up on him, believing his chronic wildness on mound incurable. May was with Redbirds from 1917 into early 1921, missing part of 1918 season because of military service.

May came to Cardinals after 11–12 record at San Antonio, Texas League, 1917. Got into 15 games without victory or defeat. Could throw hard, which intrigued Rickey. But lack of control in pitcher can be judged by comparing bases on balls he allows, with strikeouts. Jakie, in his earlier years, consistently walked more men than he fanned. In 1919, for example, he led NL in giving walks, 87, while strikeouts totaled 58. Had 5–6, 3–12, and 1–4 records, 1918, 19, 20. Then in 1921 won one game, lost three.

It wasn't this record that distressed Rickey so much as fact he walked 12 in 21 innings. More than that, in final games with Cards several of his pitches never came near plate—hit backstop on fly. Rickey first sent him to Syracuse, Cardinal farm, where he had 3–4 record. Then cut him loose entirely. At Vernon, Pacific Coast League, 1922, May came through beautifully—Won 35 games. Walked 100, fanned 238 in 362 innings. Lost only nine games and had 1.84 ERA. Had 19–22 mark with Vernon, 1923; then went to Cincinnati where he remained through 1930 season, with unimpressive records except in 1926,27. Those years he won 13, lost nine, and had 15–12 mark. Jakie spent 1931–32 with Chicago Cubs. There he had 5–5 and 2–2 records.

Jakie had climax of sorts during 1932 WS. Used in relief in fourth and final game against New York Yankees, he was charged with defeat. Allowed eight hits, three walks, six runs in 3-1/3 innings. But he struck out Babe Ruth in sixth inning, giving frustrated Chicago crowd in stands something to cheer about. There were two men on base at time. Fans had been riding Ruth throughout game, and terrific roar welled up when May fanned Bambino. But Cubs went down to defeat, 13–6, and Yanks had swept another WS in four straight.

Following year Jakie toiled for Nashville, Southern Association, then went back to farm in North Carolina. Had 11.57 ERA for his only WS; pitched 4-2/3 innings in two games, four strikeouts, three walks. His major league totals showed 72 victories, 95 defeats, with an ERA of 3.88. In 1562-1/3 innings he walked 617, struck out 765.

MAY, JERRY LEE C-BR-TR. B. 12/14/43, Staunton, Va. 6'2", 200. Shares birthplace with Woodrow Wilson. Has been beset by more than share of injuries. Was in second season as regular catcher for Pittsburgh Pirates, 1969, when he crashed into dugout in Montreal. Ambulance taking him to hospital also was involved in accident; suffered injuries to right arm and shoulder. In 1971 was on disabled list twice and out of action for extended periods three other times.

Jerry started in minors, 1961, at Kingsport, Tenn., in Pittsburgh chain. Worked way upward at Batavia, N.Y.; Asheville, N.C.; Columbus, Ohio, into 1965, although he did have 11 games with Pirates, 1964. In 1965, was Pirate catcher when Bob Veale struck out 16.

Got into 42 games in 1966, then hit .271 in 110 games, 1967. Has caught less frequently since 1968. Pirates traded him to Kansas City AL 12/2/70 in same deal that gave Royals Fred Patek and Bruce Dal Canton. Made only one error with Royals, 1971; had .997 fielding average in 353 chances. In 1972 appeared in 53 games and hit .190. Going into 1973, lifetime average .236, 541 major league games.

MAY, LEE ANDREW 1B-BR-TR. B. 3/23/43, Birmingham, Ala. 6'3", 205. Lee May was one of key men in big deal between Houston Astros and Cincinnati Reds 11/29/71. With Astros, 1972, hit .284 with 29 homers, 98 RBI. Slugger, however, still strikes out too often: 144 times in 1972. But by end of that season had compiled major league record of 176 homers and batting average of .276 for 909 games. His 947 hits also included 180 doubles, 14 triples; scored 482 runs, drove in 547.

Although he is righthanded batsman, Lee hit far better against right-handed pitchers than against southpaws—.303 against .195, during 1972 season.

May was signed by Cincinnati scout Jimmy Bragan. Moved up through Reds' farm system, starting at Tampa in Florida State League, 1961. Later stops at Rocky Mount, N.C.; San Diego, while it was in Pacific Coast League; and Buffalo in International. Brief spells with Reds 1965–66, then came to majors to stay, 1967.

Played 127 games—12 homers, 57 RBI, and .265 average that year; then .290, with 22 homers, 80 RBI in 1968. Following year boosted home run production to 38, drove in 110 markers, and hit .278. Had 34 homers, 94 RBI, and .253 average in 1970 when Cincinnati won NL flag. In final season with Cincy, average was .278, homer total 39, and his RBI added up to 98. It wasn't May's fault Reds didn't do better in 1970 WS; he hit .389, 7 for 18. Also scored six runs, drove in eight. It was his homer, with two men on base in fourth game, that gave Cincinnati its only victory of classic, 6–5. Lee also had driven in one run earlier in contest and scored another.

May was named NL Rookie of Year 1967 by *Sporting News*. Led NL first basemen in double plays with 143 in 1970. NL All-Star game 1969–71. Brother Carlos is outfielder with Chicago White Sox.

MAY, RUDOLPH, JR. P-BL-TL. B. 7/18/44, Coffeyville, Kans. 6'2", 205. Rudy May on occasion is quite a strikeout pitcher. Fanned 16 during game 8/10/72 and his club, California Angels, took decision by 3–1 score. In 1971 had two games in which he struck out 13 men each. Has plenty of "stuff" on ball, but has had propensity for throwing "gopher" ball.

May attended San Francisco State. Started pro ball 1963, playing at Bismarck and Mandan, N. Dak.; Tidewater, Indianapolis, El Paso, San Jose, and Seattle while last-named club was in Pacific Coast League. Spent 1965 with Angels, had 4–9 record, and returned to minors. Back with California, 1969. Had 10–13, 7–13, and 11–12 marks, then finally had first winning season in majors, 12–11 in 1972. Also posted best effectiveness rating with ERA of 2.94. Ten complete games, one save as reliever.

Rudy thus faced 1973 with overall major league ERA of 3.43 for 926 innings; 44 victories, 58 defeats; 394 walks allowed, 698 strikeouts.

MAYBERRY, JOHN CLAIBORN 1B-BL-TL. B. 2/18/50, Detroit, Mich. 6′3″, 225. Kansas City Royals obtained John Mayberry from Houston Astros in trade 12/2/71. Year later Royals delighted with deal. Mayberry had fine season: played 149 games, batted .298, and drove in 100 runs, with 25 homers to credit. Just about all anyone could reasonably expect from guy spending first full year in majors.

Mayberry was Houston's No. 1 draft choice in June 1967; Got $30,000 bonus to sign. John turned down numerous offers from various universities to play basketball after leaving Detroit's Northwestern High School, same school that produced Willie Horton and Alex Johnson, as well as football's Ron Johnson. Attended U. of Michigan.

Houston farmed him out to Covington, Appalachian League; Cocoa, Florida State League; and Greensboro, Carolina League; then in 1968–71 shuttled him between their Oklahoma City team and Astros. John hit .303 at Oklahoma City, 1969, with 21 homers, 78 RBI in 123 games. But in 105 games with Astros over four-year period could hit only .191.

Mayberry wasn't exactly happy about coaching he received from Harry Walker, Houston manager. Said Harry "was constantly telling me to do this and do that. I couldn't do some of things he wanted me to. But he was manager. What was I going to do?" Royals' batting coach, Charley Lau, in contrast, left Mayberry pretty much alone—and John almost hit .300. Has power to all fields. Has been compared to Willie McCovey and Willie Stargell.

As Mayberry faced 1973, major league totals for 254 games were 207 hits, 27 doubles, six triples, 37 homers, 128 RBI, with 104 runs scored. Poor showing at Houston held overall average to .258.

MAYS, CARL WILLIAM P-BL-TR. B. 11/12/93, Liberty, Ky. D. 4/4/71, El Cajon, Calif. 6′, 215. Carl Mays had misfortune to throw pitch that resulted in only death of major leaguer directly from accident on field. Ray Chapman, shortstop for Cleveland Indians, died some hours after being hit by Mays' pitch during 1920 season. Mays with N. Y. Yankees. After accident, Carl told police, "It was fast ball, straight as string. It was not curve. It was not freak pitch of any kind." Mays threw with underhand delivery, his body bent over to right, his pitching hand seeming to brush ground or his shoetop. When Chapman was hit, Mays had been in AL well over five years. Players had batted against him countless times. Joining Boston Red Sox, 1915, Mays had 6–5 record. Then came up with 18–13, 22–9, and 21–13 seasons. Won 14, lost 14 in 1919 when was traded to Yankees during July. And in 1920 was on way to 26 victories, 11 defeats, when fatal pitch thrown. In later years Eldon

Auker used similar underhand pitch, and other pitchers have had deliveries reminding older observers of Mays.

After Chapman's death many hostile things were said against Mays. Members of Detroit Tigers and his ex-teammates, Boston Red Sox, swore they would never play against him again. St. Louis Browns almost did same. Mays went into seclusion several days. Carl, in rebuttal, later declared, "All of them have pitchers who have hit more batters than I did. Ehmke (then with Detroit) led league with 13 hit batsmen(in 1920). Joe Bush (Boston) hit 10." Mays was eighth on list in AL, hitting seven. Mays declared Chapman had been good friend, that he was deeply sorry for what happened; adding, "But I've never regretted anything I did. I was pitching honestly." Chapman reportedly seemed to freeze on pitch instead of avoiding it. Boycott by players did not stick. In next start, against Tigers, Mays shut them out 8–0.

Carl was dogged competitor; never would have been voted most popular man on ball club, either by teammates, opponents, fans, or club officials. Was involved in big controversy, 1919, leading to violent dissension among officials. Mays had rocky going early part of season; had won five games, lost 11. Blamed this showing on sloppy fielding of teammates. Had been in trouble also, for throwing baseball at spectator with whom he had an argument. In game in Chicago his catcher, throwing to second base to head off runner, hit Mays in back of head with ball 7/13/19. After two innings Mays walked off field and said to Mgr. Ed Barrow, "I'm through with this ball club; I'll never pitch another game for Red Sox." Carl took train to East. Barrow and club owner Harry Frazee both appealed to him to return, but Mays went on fishing trip instead. Several AL clubs sent feelers on possible deals for him. Ban Johnson, AL president, was annoyed that Red Sox had not suspended Mays. Then came news Sox had traded him to Yankees for two players and $40,000, 7/29/19. Johnson immediately announced league was suspending Mays indefinitely; told press, "Baseball cannot tolerate such a breach of discipline." Called him contract breaker; instructed umpires not to permit Carl to appear in game in Yankee uniform. Court order sought by Yankees resulted in temporary injunction, and Mays pitched and won second game of doubleheader against St. Louis Browns at Polo Grounds, 8–2, 8/7/19. Bitter row that followed almost led to breakup of AL, but when it was over, Johnson had lost ironclad power as league president and Mays was firmly established in Yankee uniform.

Despite his 26 victories in 1920, Yanks did not win pennant, but Carl's 27 wins to nine losses certainly were vital to their reaching top in 1921. Ran into mediocre season, 1922 with 13–14 record, but Yanks won their second flag. Used sparingly, 1923, Mays won five, lost two. By this time Yanks had Herb Pennock, Waite Hoyt, Bob Shawkey, Sam Jones, and

Joe Bush on staff and felt they could dispose of 30-year-old Mays. Sold him to Cincinnati 12/11/23. Carl immediately won 20, lost nine for Reds, 1924; had one more fine season, 1926, with 19 victories, 12 defeats. But otherwise did not pitch often. Reds handed him unconditional release late in 1928; spent final year in majors with N.Y. Giants, 7–2.

Mays' minor league experience before going to Red Sox, 1915, had been gained at Boise, 1912; Portland, 1913; and Providence, 1914. After leaving majors, pitched for Portland again, 1930; Toledo, 1930–31; Louisville, 1931.

Mays' major league record showed 490 games pitched; 208 victories, 126 defeats, with 2.92 ERA in 3022 innings. Walked 734, fanned 862; allowed 2912 hits and 979 earned runs. Once pitched first 15 innings of scoreless tie with Ernie Koob of St. Louis Browns 7/14/16. Game went 17 innings. Pitched and won both games against Philadelphia Athletics 8/30/18, clinching pennant for Red Sox. From 1918 to 1923 won 23 straight games from Athletics. Became first man to lead both AL and NL in complete games pitched in single season; and first one to be 20-game winner in both circuits.

Carl was on five pennant winners: Red Sox, 1916,18; Yankees, 1921,22,23. Pitched 57-1/3 innings in eight games; won three, lost four, and had 2.20 ERA. Allowed 47 hits, 14 earned runs, fanned 17, walked eight. In three games against Giants in fall of 1921, did not walk single man in 26 innings, but lost two games, 4–2 and 2–1 after blanking Giants in opener, 3–0. In 1918 WS Mays teamed with Babe Ruth to win it from Chicago Cubs. Babe, as pitcher, won two, lost none; Mays won two, lost none, allowing just two earned runs in 18 innings.

Mays rugged competitor at plate as well as on mound. In 502 games as hitter had .268 average, with 287 hits, 110 runs scored, 36 doubles, 20 triples, 5 homers and 99 RBI.

Carl scouted for Cleveland Indians, 1958–61; for Kansas City AL, 1962; and for Milwaukee NL, 1963.

MAYS, WILLIE HOWARD, JR. (Say-Hey)   OF-1B-BR-TR. B. 5/6/31, Westfield, Ala. 5'11", 187. So many superlatives have been used in describing Willie Mays it is unnecessary to sing praises here. Nor necessary to list all his record-breaking achievments on diamond. He is in class with such immortals as Ty Cobb, Walter Johnson, Rogers Hornsby, Babe Ruth, Christy Mathewson, Stan Musial, and Hans Wagner.

Willie spent most of playing career with New York Giants and with same team in San Francisco. However, in May 1972 joined N. Y. Mets. Giants received pitcher Charlie Williams and $50,000 cash. This represented only fraction of amount Giants could have received for Mays' contract had they marketed him 10 or 15 years before. At time of transfer to Mets it was explained that move would give Willie lifetime security, something Horace Stoneham, president of Giants, could not offer. Prosperous Met ownership picked up his $165,000 playing contract. Mays also signed three-year contract that takes effect when he is no longer playing. Indications were that Willie would either coach for Mets or would do public relations work for team. Mets also are reported to have guaranteed security of Mays' various real estate holdings.

Willie's debut with Mets was worthy of reputation. In fifth inning of game against old team, Giants, 5/14/72, slapped home run to break 4–4 tie. Mets kept this margin rest of way, and 35,505 cash customers in Shea Stadium, New York, roared thunderous ovation to veteran star. Continued to scintillate in next few games: reached base 14 times in first 27 trips; won three games with hits—two homers and one 14th inning single. However, as season wore on, Willie showed signs of age.

In 88 games for 1972, hit .250, with 11 doubles, one triple, and eight homers among 61 hits. This brought career major league average down one point, to .304 in 2924 games. At season's end had been to bat 10,672 times with 3239 hits. These included 513 doubles, 140 triples, 654 home runs. Had scored 2038 runs and driven in 1878.

Hank Aaron passed Mays in total career homers during 1972, but Willie was in third place with his 654. Babe Ruth's grand total was 714 and Hank's 673. It was apparent, however, that Mays had no real chance to reach Babe's mark. Mays very high in lists of players in total bases, slugging percentage, long hits, runs scored, and times at bat.

Willie was with Birmingham Black Barons when Giants sent scout Eddie Montague to inspect Alonzo Perry, first baseman. Montague, however, couldn't take eyes off 19-year old outfielder with great arm, quick hands—agile, speedy jackrabbit who also could hit. Deal soon was arranged. Giants gave Barons $14,000 for Mays and sent him to Trenton club of Inter-State League, 1950. All he did was hit .353 for 81 games. It was evident he belonged in higher classification than Class B loop.

So Mays went to Minneapolis in 1951 in American Association, just one notch below major leagues. That was too easy for him, also. In 35 games Willie hit .477. So, with 116 minor league games behind him, Willie was brought up to Giants. Reported to Leo Durocher, then manager of Giants. Leo put him in lineup but Willie went 22 times without hit. Finally Willie went to Leo and suggested he be taken out of lineup, saying, "I just can't hit them." Durocher, however, told him, "You're my center fielder if you don't get hit rest of season." Willie began hitting after that. Not like he would do later, but at season's end had very respectable .274 average with 20 homers, 68 RBI in 121 games. Helped Giants win NL pennant after being 13-1/2 games behind Brooklyn Dodgers at one point during August. Willie, however, didn't sparkle in WS against Yankees. Hit .182 with four singles in 22 trips. But he still won Rookie of Year honors for NL.

It was along about then when Durocher cracked, "If he could cook, I'd marry him." Bill Rigney later said Mays' only weakness was wild pitch.

Willie got off to slow start in 1952; hit .236 in 34 games, then went into military service. Came back, 1954, and began hitting in high gear. Captured NL batting title with .345 for 151 games. Showed power with 41 homers; led NL in triples with 13; hit 33 doubles, and drove in 110 runs. Giants won pennant. In WS, Mays made unbelievable catch in first game against Cleveland. With two men on base, Vic Wertz hit tremendous drive deep into center field at Polo Grounds. It seemed impossible that anyone could get near ball, let alone catch it. But Willie raced to spot 460 feet away from home plate, stuck up his glove and caught ball over his left shoulder. Instantly he fired ball back to infield to keep runners in check. In poll taken by *Sporting News,* majority of sports writers singled out this catch as most exciting play of 1954 in any sport, not just baseball. And there are plenty of people today who still say it was greatest catch ever made on any baseball diamond. Catch saved that game, and Giants went on to win Series in four straight.

Perhaps Mays never made another catch quite as good as that one, but through years he continued to astound all who saw him with brilliant plays, great hitting, fine base running. Hit better than .300 ten times. Led league in homers four times, high high mark being 52 in 1965. This was second time he had gone over 50-homer mark. Eleven times hit 30 or more homers in one season, and on two other occasions barely missed this mark by one. Twelve consecutive seasons scoring over 100 runs.

MVP in NL 1954, 65. Named by *Sporting News* as Baseball Player of Decade (1960–69). NL All-Star game every season, 1954 through 1973. Hit .315 in these games with 23 hits in 73 official trips. Hits included three homers, three triples, two doubles. Scored 20 runs and drove in nine.

Willie hit four home runs in one game 4/30/61, which tied major league record. Hit three homers in one game twice 6/29/61 and 6/2/63. Set NL record by slapping two or more homers in one game 63 times.

Mays hit .286 in 1954 WS and .250 in 1962 classic. So overall WS record shows 17 games played, 64 AB, 8 runs, 15 hits, 3 doubles, no triples, no homers, 5 RBI, for .234.

Besides hitting, Willie great base thief. As late as 1971 stole 23 bags. In 1956 pilfered 40, and in 1957, 38. His career total at end of 1972 was 337. At same time, had set NL marks for most putouts as an outfielder and most chances accepted (excluding errors).

San Francisco apparently never quite accorded Mays acclaim received in Gotham. Although Giants moved to West Coast 1958 and Willie played for San Francisco until early 1972, names like Joe

DiMaggio, Lefty O'Doul evoked warmer memories than Mays' ongoing teats. Mays accused of being aloof to fans and press; was whispered he wanted to be treated like prima donna; at least two Giants managers would have been happy to see him move.

However, in defense of Willie, it should be said he wants privacy off field. And signing autographs can rob player of patience and endurance if there is no limit to demands of fans. Regardless of those who would downgrade his personal relations with public, Mays remains one of greatest, if not greatest player of generation.

MAZEROSKI, WILLIAM STANLEY   2B-BR-TR. B. 9/5/36, Wheeling, W. Va. 5'11", 203. Mention Mazeroski and baseball fans think of his home run in ninth inning of seventh game, 1960 WS. That gave Pittsburgh 10–9 victory and clinched WS title over N. Y. Yankees, four games to three.

Mazeroski, however, had plenty of other diamond achievments to be proud of during big league career from 1956 to close of 1972. Then he became Pirate coach. Brilliant-fielding second baseman led NL in double plays eight successive seasons—record. Holds NL career record for second basemen in total chances accepted, putouts, games, and assists. Eight times *Sporting News* named him its selection as finest fielder at keystone. NL All-Star squads 1958,59,60,62,64,67. Named in 1963 but replaced because of injury.

Bill signed with Pirates 6/16/54 and spent rest of summer at Williamsport, Eastern League. Divided 1955 between Hollywood, Pacific Coast League, and Williamsport. Had 80 games and .306 average with Hollywood, 1956, then joined Pirates for 81 contests, and .243 mark. Played well over 100 games for next dozen seasons in row. Best hitting average was .283 in 1957; best home run production, 1958, with 19, and reached 16 in 1966.

Mazeroski played 2163 games, had 2016 hits, scored 769 times. Doubles, 294; triples, 62; 138 home runs; 27 stolen bases; 853 RBI for lifetime major league average of .260.

In 1960 WS hit .320 with eight hits in 25 times at bat, scored four runs, drove in five, and had two doubles. Pinch hit unsuccessfully once in 1971 WS, which lowered WS average to .308.

Maz played more games at second base during career than any other man; set NL fielding mark at position, 1966 with .992. Made more double plays at second base than any other player in majors, ever.

Owns nine-hole golf course at Rayland, Ohio. Served as team captain before becoming coach.

MEADOWS, HENRY LEE (Specs)   P-BLR-TR. B. 7/12/94, Oxford, N.C. D. 1/29/63, Daytona Beach, Fla. 6', 170. *Sporting News Baseball*

Record Book says first pitcher in majors to wear glasses was William H. White, Boston NL, 1877. White later played with Detroit and Cincinnati; won 222 games, lost 166. In this century Lee Meadows seems to have been first moundsman to wear spectacles while playing. Other players later were George Toporcer, St. Louis Cardinal infielder; Carmen Hill, pitcher for Pittsburgh; Chick Hafey, Redbird outfielder. Wearing glasses on diamond was so unusual that sports article rarely was written about Meadows without mentioning fact—how he had to stop game to wipe off perspiration; danger of being hit by line drive and lenses shattering; whether other players would follow in path and benefit from using glasses.

Meadows was fine pitcher when had decent ball club behind him. Twice led NL in defeats. First time was 1916: pitching for Cardinals, lost 23 decisions, won 12, with tailend ball club. Redbirds finished in tie for seventh (also eighth) place. Then in 1919 had unhappy experience of being traded from team that finished seventh to one that finished bad last—Philadelphia Phillies. That year he lost 20 while winning even dozen. Had 15–9 season with Cards, 1917; won 16 games for Phillies, 1920, even though team again finished last. Traded to Pittsburgh Pirates 5/22/23, came up with 17–13 mark. Won 19, lost 10 for pennant-winning Pittsburgh team of 1925, then had 20–9 mark, and 19–10, after which lost effectiveness.

Meadows had three years of minor league seasoning, starting with Morristown, Tenn., 1912. Won 40 games over two-year period with Durham, N. C., 1913–14, then went to Cardinals, starting with 13–11 mark and 2.99 ERA as rookie in majors.

When Meadows bowed out of majors in 1929, had pitched 3151 innings, allowed 1185 earned runs. Walked 956, struck out 1063, and had 3.38 ERA. Won 188, lost 180. Oddly enough, lowest ERA came during season he lost 23 games—1916. In two WS efforts Meadows was not at best, losing first start in opening game, 1925, against Washington, by 4–1 score to Walter Johnson and Washington Senators. Two years later started third game of classic against Yankees, and bowed to Herb Pennock by 8–1 score. ERA for 14-1/3 innings was 6.28. Dropped back into minors 1929. Pitched with decreasing effectiveness for Indianapolis, Newark, Atlanta, Dallas, and Durham through 1932 season. Managed Leesburg, Florida State League, 1937; De Land, same circuit, 1939.

MEDWICK, JOSEPH MICHAEL (Ducky) OF-BR-TR. B. 11/4/11, Carteret, N.J. 5'10", 178. Joe Medwick, wild-swinging member of old Gas House Gang St. Louis Cardinals, reached peak, 1937, when he was NL MVP. Just about led league in all hitting departments. Tops in average, with .374; in hits with 237; in runs scored, 111; in doubles, 56; in RBI, 154; tied for lead in homers, 31; but somehow had only 10 triples, compared with 17 by Arky Vaughan. Also played most games, 156; had most at-bats, 633. Rounded out fine season by leading NL outfielders in fielding.

Friction and controversy swirled about Medwick, some of it resulting from Joe's abrasive personality when he was star. Probably would have been named to Hall of Fame sooner or later, but Medwick campaigned hard to hurry selection, made in 1968.

Medwick seemed able to hit bad balls harder than just about any other player. He went to plate swinging. How successfully is seen from lifetime .324 major league average in 1984 games. Had 2471 hits good for 540 doubles, 113 triples, 205 homers. Scored 1198 runs and drove in 1383. Six straight seasons with more than 100 RBI, leading NL 1936–38; led NL in doubles three years.

Joe was discovered by Cardinal scout Charlie Kelchner. At 18 he hit .419 at Scottsdale, Pa., to lead Middle Atlantic League. Then two seasons at Houston, Texas League, with .305 and .354 averages. Promoted to parent club in St. Louis, Joe started off late in 1932 with .349 average in 26 games. Hit .300 or better next 10 consecutive years. Besides that .374 average in 1937, hit above .350 for Cardinals, 1935,36.

Larry MacPhail cooked up deal for Medwick 6/12/40, bringing Curt Davis to Dodgers with Joe. Brooklyn sweetened pot by giving St. Louis $125,000 cash plus four players. Not too long after trade, Pitcher Bob Bowman of Cardinals threw ball that hit Medwick in head, causing concussion. Charges and countercharges reached such intensity that both district attorney of New York and Ford Frick, then NL president, conducted investigations. While Joe continued to hit above .300 that year and four more times in NL, observers felt he was somewhat "gun-shy" at plate after beaning.

Another big rhubarb swirled around Medwick during 1934 WS. Sliding hard into third base after triple, he and Marvin Owen had words that led to Detroit fans pelting Medwick with fruit, vegetables, debris to such extent Judge Landis removed Medwick from game.

In 1943 Dodgers sold Medwick to N.Y. Giants during summer. Joe hit .337 for Giants in 128 games, 1944. Traded to Boston NL 6/14/45. Released that fall, signed with St. Louis Browns for 1946 but released during April. Later signed with Dodgers, for whom played 41 games and hit .312. Released 10/9/46, signed with Yankees, but released 4/29/47. Then had two part seasons with Cardinals, with .211 average in 20 games, 1948. Houston, Texas League, 1948. Playing manager, Miami Beach, 1949. Playing manager, Raleigh, Carolina League, 1951. Playing manager, Tampa, Florida International League, 1952. Since 1966, minor league hitting instructor for Cardinals.

One of Medwick's hitting accomplishments was streak of 10 hits in succession; stopped by Carl Hubbell in seventh inning of game in N. Y.,

7/21/36. His 64 doubles in 1936 set NL record. NL All-Star game 1934–40,42,44. Hit 40 or more doubles, seven consecutive years, 1933–39.

Medwick hit .379 in 1934 Series for Cardinals and .235 for Dodgers in 1941 classic. Overall WS statistics show 12 games, 46 times at bat, with 15 hits, including double, triple, and homer for .326 average; 5 RBI.

MELE, SABATH ANTHONY (Sam) OF-1B-BR-TR. B. 1/21/22, Astoria, N.Y. 6'1", 198. Cal Griffith, president of Minnesota Twins, was reasonably patient with Sam Mele as manager for more than four years and his club won its first AL pennant, 1965, after franchise was shifted from Washington. After that, Griffith wasn't so patient. Team finished second in 1966; and after club broke even in first 50 games of 1967, Mele went way of all managers sooner or later—fired 6/9. Dodgers won 1965 Series, four games to three. *Sporting News* named him Manager of Year, 1965. At time of dismissal Griffith indicated that Mele "had lost control" of players. Team went on to improved play and finished third. Sam, as Minnesota manager, won 518 games, lost 427.

Mele got his nickname from his initials. Related to Tony Cuccinello by marriage.

Mele never achieved stellar class as player but appeared in 1046 big league games and hit .267. His 916 hits included 168 doubles, 39 triples, 80 homers; scored 406 runs, drove in 544. Red-letter day 6/10/52: tied two modern records by slapping three-run homer, tripling with bases loaded, all in fourth inning. This tied record for RBI in single inning (6), and most long hits in same inning (2).

Sam attended New York U. Joined Louisville, 1946, and played 119 games with Scranton in Eastern League same season; hit .342. Boston Red Sox, 1947; 302 in 123 games, with 12 homers, 73 RBI. Traded to Washington 6/13/49. To Chicago AL 5/3/52; to Baltimore AL 2/5/54. Boston AL 7/29/54 on waivers. Sold to Cincinnati 6/23/55. Released 1/18/56, and signed with Cleveland. Indianapolis 1957–58; Buffalo 1958. Scout for Washington, 1959, until he became coach, 7/3; remained as coach with Senators and continued in same capacity with Twins after franchise was moved to Minnesota, 1961. Then moved into manager's spot, replacing Cookie Lavagetto 6/23/61.

MELTON, WILLIAM EDWIN 3B-BR-TR. B. 7/7/45, Gulfport, Miss. 6'1", 195. White Sox fans couldn't help wondering how far their team would have gone in 1972 but for Bill Melton's ruptured disc which sidelined him in June. Bill hit 33 homers in both 1970 and 1971. Then Sox acquired Dick Allen, who walked off with MVP honors in AL, 1972, with his all-round play. Melton, however, could play in just 57 games and hit only seven homers with .245 average. Seemed to be responding to treatment for ailment so painful that for while could remain on feet no longer than one hour. Went into 1973 with background of 539 major league games and .261 batting average. His 503 hits included 72 doubles, five triples, 98 homers. Had driven in 315 runs, scored 240.

Bill's back problem followed season when had shown great improvement as third baseman. Acceptability as major league third sacker wasn't easy; Melton had power at plate, but question was where to put him in field. Played considerable outfield, but was claimed they moved him to infield so wouldn't get killed by fly ball. Chicago manager Don Gutteridge put him at third 5/8/70 in game in Baltimore. Dave Johnson of Orioles lifted little foul fly outside third. Bill lost ball in lights; it landed squarely on nose. At one point Bill charged with 10 errors in first 24 games. Later, was piqued by statement in magazine that he was less than mediocre as fielder at third base.

Melton, 1971, requested extra practice before games. And eventually manager Chuck Tanner insisted he had become second-best fielder in AL at hot corner. Brooks Robinson, of course, was first in Tanner's book.

Another big Melton problem has been tendency to strike out. During 1970 struck out 11 consecutive official times at plate. String ended when was hit by pitched ball next time up.

Bill signed with Chicago after being scouted by Hollis Thurston, who pitched for Sox many years ago. In high school had been outstanding end and linebacker in football, but didn't play baseball until entering Covina Junior College in California. Played with Sarasota, 1964–65, then moved up to Fox Cities, Evansville, Hawaii, and Syracuse next three seasons. Played 34 games for Sox, 1968, then became regular, 1969. Came up with .255 average, 23 homers, 87 RBI that year; .263, with 33 homers, 96 RBI following season; and .269 mark, 1971, leading AL in homers with 33, and driving in 86 runs.

Bill hit three homers in one game 6/24/69. AL All-Star game 1971, didn't see action.

MENKE, DENIS JOHN Inf.-BR-TR. B. 7/21/40, Algona, Iowa. 6', 180. Denis Menke played steady, fine brand of third base for Cincinnati Reds, 1972, helped them win NL flag. Wasn't usually sensational, but very few complaints about infielding. Did not hit up to expectations, however, with .233 average. After 1972 flag race Denis owned .254 lifetime major league average for 1429 games. His 1221 safe hits included 214 doubles, 40 triples, 98 homers. Had 565 runs scored and 579 driven in.

Menke, in 1973, went into 11th season in NL. Milwaukee Braves signed him, 1958, for reported bonus of $125,000. Farmed out four full seasons and part of another, to Cedar Rapids; Midland, Tex.; Yakima, Vancouver, and Toronto. Had 50 games with Braves, 1962, but hit just .192. Following year got into 146 Milwaukee games, hit .234. Raised hitting mark to .283 in 1964, played various infield positions. Franchise shifted to Atlanta, 1966. Traded to Houston 10/8/67, remaining with

Astros until sent to Cincinnati in deal involving Joe Morgan, Tommy Helms, Lee May, and others 11/29/71.

Denis never really concentrated on one position until with Reds. Best season at bat was 1970 when he reached .304, with 13 homers, 92 RBI. However, hit 20 homers for Milwaukee, 1964; had 90 RBI with Astros, 1969.

Menke's WS record, 1972, showed .083 average for seven games. Got two hits, scored one run, walked twice, drove in two runs, fanned six times. Hit home run in fifth game. All-Star games 1969,70.

It was reunion for Menke to play for Reds' manager, Sparky Anderson. Sparky played second base, Menke first base on same club at Toronto, 1962.

MERKLE, FREDERICK CHARLES 1B-BR-TR. B. 12/20/88, Watertown, Wis. D. 3/2/56, Daytona Beach, Fla. 6'1", 190. Despite cruel, lifelong persecution by press and heartless fans, Fred Merkle had long major league career with N. Y. Giants, Chicago Cubs, Brooklyn Dodgers, and N. Y. Yankees. Labeled "bonehead" because of one play during 1908 season while Fred was 19-year-old rookie with Giants, who were battling Chicago Cubs for NL pennant. Cubs came to N. Y., and took first two games of series. Giants apparently had third game won when incident occurred. In last of ninth Moose McCormick was on third base, Merkle on first, when Al Bridwell, Giant shortstop, hit ball to center field for what looked like tie-breaking single, giving New Yorkers ball game. Merkle ran perhaps two-thirds of way to second base while McCormick crossed plate. Crowd meanwhile leaped on field. In confusion, Cub second baseman, Johnny Evers, yelled frantically for ball and center fielder Hofman threw it in. With people swarming around, there was confused story about what actually happened. Joe McGinnity of Giants apparently sensed what Evers had in mind, scuffled with Evers, grabbed ball and threw it into left field. One Cub player who had not been in game, ran to left field, recovered ball from spectator, and threw ball to Evers, who touched second base. Umpire Hank O'Day then called Merkle out for failing to touch second base, making it force play for third out, and ruled that run did not count. Therefore game ended in 1–1 tie, since it was impossible to clear field for further play. Cubs and Giants ended season in tie for first place and NL ordered one-game playoff for 1908 pennant. Cubs won 4–2 and Merkle forever afterward was blamed for losing flag for Giants. Derided, abused. Cartoons depicted him with thick, exaggerated skull. Nevertheless, Merkle had simply followed custom of starting to leave field when winning run crossed plate. But violent criticism caused him to lose 15 or 20 pounds in next few weeks, embittered him against newsmen. Manager John McGraw, however, never uttered word of criticism, encouraged him to bounce back, raised salary for following season.

Actually, had much higher I.Q. than most players of day, was fine chess player, good at bridge, and proficient in golf. Fred became regular, 1910, hit .292; then in 1911 helped Giants to pennant with .283 average. Following year boosted his hitting mark to .309. Another pennant for Giants—and another misfortune for Merkle. In WS against Boston Red Sox, Christy Mathewson was on mound in seventh and crucial contest. Looked like N. Y. victory in first half of 10th inning when Giants scored their second run of game. But in last half, Red Sox got men on first and second with Tris Speaker at bat. Speaker lifted easy foul fly between first base and plate. For some reason, Mathewson yelled for catcher Meyers to take foul, though Merkle could have caught it easily. In any case, foul fell to ground. Speaker, given new life, then singled home tying run, and Sox scored their second run of inning, winning game and Series, moments later. Again Merkle was blamed as stupid bonehead.

But though maligned unmercifully, Merkle continued with Giants into 1916 season when traded to Brooklyn. During 1917 season was sent to Chicago Cubs, remaining there through 1920. Four seasons at Rochester, 1921–24. Returned to majors, 1925, as coach and pinch hitter with Yankees. Hit .385 in seven games. Got into one game with Yanks, 1926, then was released to make room for Art Fletcher to become Yankee coach. Moved to Florida after that. Lost savings during depression; worked on WPA for while. Later fared somewhat better economically in small business making fishing equipment.

Merkle was with Newark briefly, 1906, then with Tecumseh, in Southern Michigan League, until sold to Giants 8/29/07 for reported $2500. This was goodly sum to pay for Class D player in those days.

Fred wound up major league career with .273 average for 1637 games. Took part in five WS, but none of them was winner. With Giants, 1911,12,13; Brooklyn, 1916; Chicago Cubs, 1918. Hit .239 in 27 games. Was eligible for 1926 WS with Yankees, but did not play.

MESSERSMITH, JOHN ALEXANDER (Andy) P-BR-TR. B. 8/6/45, Toms River, N.J. 6'1", 200.

When Andy Messersmith traded to Los Angeles Dodgers after 1972 season, owned record of 59 major league victories against 47 defeats. In 168 AL games pitched 973 innings and had 2.77 ERA with 768 strikeouts, 402 bases on balls. Billy Martin, manager of Detroit Tigers, has said that Andy was "about best pitcher in AL." "Give him three runs and you can forget about it. He's as deadly as Koufax and Drysdale were," chirped Billy.

Won 20 games for Angels, 1971, despite ups and downs. During May, after four-hit victory over Tigers, was driving home from Anaheim Stadium when another car suddenly made illegal left turn in front of him. Crash was unavoidable. Messersmith's car exploded into flames, jacket caught fire, hair was singed. Somehow managed to escape death.

On 8/13 Andy had 11–12 record. Then pitched two shutouts, lost one shutout, and put together six victories in row. In final 83-2/3 innings yielded only eight earned runs for ERA of 1.61. ERA for season, 2.99. In 1972, disabled six weeks with torn tendon sheath, middle finger of right hand.

Messersmith attended U. of California at Berkeley, where he attracted national fame in baseball. Started pro career at Seattle, Pacific Coast League, 1966, winning four, losing six. Had 9–7 record at El Paso, Texas League, 1967. Divided 1968 between Seattle, PCL, and Angels. In first full year in majors captured 16 victories against 11 defeats, then had 11–10 season in 1970. AL All-Star squad 1971.

MEUSEL, EMIL FREDERICK (Irish)   OF-BR-TR. B. 6/9/93, Oakland, Calif. D. 3/1/63, Long Beach, Calif. 6', 180. Various brother combinations played in major leagues, but Irish and Bob Meusel are only ones who competed with each other in three consecutive WS. Irish played left field for N.Y. Giants; Bob played right field for N.Y. Yankees in 1921 Series, played left field for 1922,23 Series. Irish outhit Bob in first classic .345 to .200, drove in seven runs compared to three for Robert. Following autumn, Yankee Meusel had .300 average with two RBI, compared to Emil's .250 mark. But Emil again had seven RBI. In final meeting, 1923, Bob hit just .269 but drove in eight runs, while Emil had .280 average, with two RBI. Emil hit one homer in each Series; Bob hit none, though had two triples and double in 1923 WS, helping Yankees to victory after they had lost 1921,22 Series to Giants.

Emil Meusel started in 1913 with Fresno. Played with Los Angeles, Pacific Coast League; Elmira, and Birmingham before making grade with Philadelphia NL, 1918. Had "cup of coffee" with Washington Senators, 1914, but played only one game and got no hits in two at bats. Meusel hit above .300 for Phillies, 1919,20, then was coveted by John McGraw, manager of Giants. Three players plus $30,000 turned trick 7/25/21, causing another charge that McGraw was "buying NL pennant" fairly late in season. Giants won with Meusel's help—he hit .343 for season with 14 homers, 87 RBI. Came up with .331 average, 16 homers, 132 RBI, 1922. In 1923 Irish's 19 homers and .297 average were accompanied by 125 RBI, which led NL in runs driven in. Emil hit above .300 again in 1924–25, had two more 100-RBI seasons, and in 1925 boosted homer total to 19. After .292 season, 1926, Giants handed Emil unconditional release. Started 1927 with Brooklyn; hit .243 in 42 games, then spent rest of year at Toledo; Oakland, Pacific Coast League, 1928; Sacramento, 1929; Coach, Giants, 1930; Omaha as player, seven games, 1931.

Irish had four straight cracks at WS play, 1921–24. Record added up to .276 average, 23 games; 3 doubles, 2 triples, 3 homers among 24 hits; scored 10 runs, drove in 17. Career major league record: 1289 games, .310 average, 1521 hits, 250 doubles, 93 triples, 106 homers, 701 runs, 815 RBI.

MEUSEL, ROBERT WILLIAM   OF-BR-TR. B. 7/19/98, San Jose, Calif. 6'3", 190. Bob Meusel, younger brother of Emil ("Irish") Meusel, was noted for throwing arm, one of finest of era. Solid batsman, too; led AL in home runs with 33 in 1925; same season led circuit in RBI with 138. Hit better than .300 seven times with N. Y. Yankees; helped them get into six WS.

Bob was with Vernon club, Pacific Coast League, 1917–19. Broke in with Yankees, 1920, starting with .328 batting average, 11 homers, 83 RBI. Following year had .318 mark, 24 homers, 135 RBI. Best year for average was 1927, with .337. Had better than 100 RBI four times. Meusel tailed off to .261 in 1929, then sold to Cincinnati. In one NL season, 1930, hit .289, with 10 homers, 62 RBI. Teammate that year was another fine ex-AL righthanded hitter, Harry Heilmann. Reds, however, couldn't rise above seventh. Meusel spent 1931 at Minneapolis and 1932 at Hollywood, then called it quits as active player. Hit .309 for 1407 major league games, one point less than Brother Emil's lifetime average. Exceeded Emil's totals in lifetime hits, with 1693; also in doubles, 368; triples, 95; homers, 156; scored 826 runs, drove in 1067. Hit .225 in 34 WS games with Yankees, getting 29 hits in 129 trips; 6 doubles, 3 triples, 1 homer, 15 runs, 17 RBI.

Incurred Judge Landis' wrath by defying rule against WS players barnstorming after 1921 Series. Suspended till May 20 following year.

MEYERS, JOHN TORTES (Chief)   C-BR-TR. B. 7/29/80, Cahuilla, Calif. D. 7/25/71, San Bernardino, Calif. 5'11", 194. Chief Meyers enjoyed fine career spanning nine seasons in NL and lived within few days of 91st birthday. Full-blooded Indian who maintained composure despite occasional epithets like "nigger" shouted by smart-aleck fans. Hit better than .300 for New York Giants three times, helping win three pennants those same seasons. Helped Brooklyn Superbas win 1916 flag.

Good-humored, cultured college man attended Dartmouth. Did not get chance in organized ball until almost 26. Did not advertise real age until reached 65 and began receiving social security benefits.

Meyers was member of tribe that, with other tribes, have generally been called Mission Indians; believed he was descendant of Shoshones. Moved to Riverside at early age, then began playing baseball as catcher, eventually going into semipros. When he discovered that Dartmouth had scholarship fund set up to help educate qualified Indians, he attended that institution in school year 1905–06. After one year in college and playing summer ball, illness in family prevented return to Dartmouth. Played at Harrisburg, Pa., Tri-State League; Butte, Mont., in Northwestern League; and finally St. Paul, American Association. Giants bought him toward end of 1908 season, not knowing real age. By time he reported to John McGraw was close to 29 years old. Played 90 games, 1909, hit .277; following year, doing most of catching, took part in 127 contests, raised batting average to .285. Then came three seasons above .300. In 1912 was at .358 level. In WS play with Giants, Chief hit .300 in six games, 1911; .357 in next WS, eight games; but went hitless in four trips in one game, 1913 Series.

Meyers, traded to Brooklyn before 1916 season, played 80 games, hit .247, and followed up with .200 average in WS, 2 for 10. Overall WS average .290 in 18 games, with two doubles, two triples among 18 hits. Scored four runs, drove in six. Age began to take toll, 1917, although took part in 72 games with Brooklyn and old Boston Braves. Bowed out of major league picture after that. Later worked for U.S. Bureau of Indian Affairs. In final years occasionally attended ball games as guest of Los Angeles Dodgers and California Angels. Overall major league average .291 for 951 games. No great slugger, but hit 14 homers; stole 44 bases.

MICHAEL, EUGENE RICHARD (Gene) SS-BLR-TR. B. 6/2/38, Kent, Ohio. 6'2", 183. Gene Michael, among other things, is master of that almost-forgotten art, hidden-ball trick. Has pulled stunt at least four times while with New York Yankees. Career with Yanks dates back to 1968. Considered utility man pretty much until 1971–72, when played shortstop regularly. Fine defensive player but hasn't hit much, usually bats in eighth place, or low in batting order. Owned .228 career average as entered 1973 season after 707 major league games. During those games hit safely 471 times, with 64 doubles, 11 triples, nine homers. Scored 185 runs, drove in 153.

Gene, called "Stick" because there isn't much meat on his bones, started pro ball, 1959, and got minor league experience at Grand Forks, Savannah, Hobbs, Kinston, and Columbus, Ohio, before coming up to majors with Pittsburgh for 30 games, 1966. Hit .152 in that brief period, then was traded to Los Angeles Dodgers with Bob Bailey for Maury Wills. Michael remained with Los Angeles one year, played 98 games, hit .202, and sold to Yanks 11/30/67.

Michael attended Kent State, received B.S. in education. During off-season considered one of best speakers in public relations work for Yankees.

MILAN, JESSE CLYDE (Deerfoot) OF-BL-TR. B. 3/25/87, Linden, Tenn. D. 3/3/53, Orlando, Fla. 5'8½", 170. Cliff Blankenship, Washington Senators catcher who had broken finger, was sent on scouting trip, 1907 and bought Clyde Milan from Wichita club of Western Association for $2,000. Told Milan afterward he had to go on to Idaho to look over some young punk out there. "Probably waste of train fare," he said, but he went—and signed Walter Johnson. Quite successful scouting trip. Milan had long fine playing career for Washington and stayed with club almost all rest of life. Johnson, of course, won 416 games for Senators.

Milan had started previous year with Wichita, and was hitting .304 when Senators bought him after 114 games. Joined Washington in time for 48 games, hitting .279. Continued as regular through 1921 season, going over .300 mark three times, but rarely falling much below that. Lifetime major league average .285 for 1981 games. Not power hitter, just 17 homers during career; 240 doubles and 105 triples among 2099 hits. Speed Milan's specialty. Stole 44 bases, 1910; 58 following year. Then broke through to take base-stealing crown from Ty Cobb—with 88 thefts. Did it again in 1913 with 74. Tapered off somewhat after that, but had 494 for his career. Stole five in one game 6/14/12. Played center field shallower than anyone else, including Tris Speaker. But with his great speed could go back for long flies.

Clark Griffith made him playing manager, 1922, but Milan was considered "too easygoing" by some. Team finished sixth. Following year was back in minors with Minneapolis, as player. Hit .296 in 101 games. Playing manager, New Haven, Eastern League, 1924, hitting .316 in 121 contests. Playing manager, Memphis, 1925–26, winding up active play with .324 in 84 games, 1925, and finally .219 in 27 sessions. Coach, Washington, 1928–29; manager, Birmingham, 1930–35; manager, Chattanooga, 1935–37; scout, Washington, 1937; coach, Washington, 1938–52.

Milan was on job in spring training, 1953, when he died. Had been hitting fungoes to outfielders two hours in 80-degree heat when suffered heart attack. Two hours later was dead.

MILETI, NICK Executive. B. 4/22/32, Cleveland, Ohio. Majority owner of Cleveland Indians since spring 1972. Took over from Vernon Stouffer. Sportsman, civic-minded attorney who brought major league franchises in basketball (Cavaliers) and in hockey (Barons) to Cleveland.

Mileti worked way through Bowling Green State U. in Ohio; later received law degree at Ohio State. Prosecuting attorney at Lakewood, Ohio; founder of a senior-housing consulting business, and regarded an expert in field of nonprofit housing for elderly. Director in various business and civic organizations, including Cleveland zoo. Owns Cleveland radio station WKYC and its FM affiliate; also owns Cleveland Arena. Shortly after taking over Indians, squelched hopes of New Orleans getting AL team to play part of season there and rest of schedule in Cleveland. Said, "My feeling is that it is hard enough to develop one area and do it right."

MILLAN, FELIX BERNARDO MARTINEZ 2B-BR-TR. B. 8/21/43, Yabucoa, Puerto Rico, 5'11", 172. NL managers and coaches, in 1972, voted second-base fielding honors to Felix Millan, whom Atlanta Braves traded to New York Mets after season closed. Mets management and fans hoping Felix would hit like he did in 1970 when had .310 average.

Went into 1973 with .281 lifetime major league average, which Shea Stadium habitues couldn't find much fault with. At same time, in 799 NL games had 118 doubles, 26 triples, 14 homers among 874 hits. Scored 391 runs, drove in 221, stole 56 bases. Yogi Berra, Mets' manager, calls him good line-drive hitter, good hit-and-run man. In 1970 once had five-for-five game, and went six-for-six 7/6/70. Grand slam 4/8/69 against San Francisco Giants. But Millan's greatest asset is fielding. Took part in six double plays in one game against Mets 7/5/71. Led NL second basemen in fielding, 1969. Made only eight errors in 121 games, 1972.

Felix signed originally with Kansas City AL organization, 1964. Played 95 games at Daytona Beach, Florida State League, and Milwaukee Braves drafted him 11/30/64. Divided 1965 between Yakima and Austin. In 1966 had 35 games at Austin, 37 games with Braves, by then in Atlanta; also had 41 games at Richmond, International League. With Richmond, 1967, 106 games; 41 with Braves. In 1968 spent first full season with Braves and hit .289 for 149 contests. Then had .267, .310 and .289 seasons in succession. In 1972 average dropped to .257.

In 1970 Millan underwent minor surgery in spring; suffered hairline fracture of hand and sprained ankle but still played 142 games. Hand injury kept him out of All-Star game that year. NL All-Star squads 1969,71. In 1969 game his double drove in two runs for National Leaguers.

MILLER, EDMUND JOHN (Bing) OF-BR-TR. B. 8/30/94, Vinton, Iowa. D. 5/7/66, Philadelphia, Pa. 5'11", 187. Bing Miller was good-hitting outfielder who stretched career by stretching leg muscles systematically during off-seasons. Played most of career with Philadelphia Athletics. When fatally injured, 1966, was wearing diamond tie clasp with inscription, "1930 World Champions." Bing was member of WS team last time Connie Mack won top baseball honors. Bing, however, helped Connie to two other flags, 1929 and 1931. Made contribution to 1929 world championship by getting single and being hit by pitched ball during famous 10-run inning that overcame Chicago Cubs' eight-run lead—and ruined Cubs' chances of ultimate victory in Series. Miller's average was .368 for that WS, seven hits in 19 trips, with four RBI; overall WS average was .258, with 17 hits in 66 trips to plate.

Miller started at Clinton, Iowa, Central Association, 1915, as pitcher; shifted to outfield next season. Sold to Detroit Tigers during 1917 season, for $600. Few weeks later Detroit optioned him to Peoria, later to Atlanta, San Antonio, and Little Rock. Dispute arose about handling of his contract, Pittsburgh Pirates being involved. But his sale to Washington 7/9/20 for two players and $4000 ultimately was upheld.

So Bing first made it into AL records with Senators, 1921. Hit .288 in 114 games. Athletics got him in trade before 1922 season. Remained with Philadelphia until 6/15/26 when traded to St. Louis AL for Baby Doll

Jacobson. Philadelphia regained him before 1928 season by sending Pitcher Sam Gray to Browns. Continued with Athletics through 1934; last two seasons, 1935–36, with Boston Red Sox. Coach, Red Sox, 1937; Detroit, 1938–41; Chicago AL, 1942–49; Philadelphia AL, 1950–53.

Bing's lifetime major league average was .312 for 1821 games. Hit safely 1937 times, with 389 doubles, 95 triples, 117 homers; scored 946 runs, had 990 RBI. Hit above .300 nine times and missed magic number once by one point. Best season 1924, .342.

MILLER, LAWRENCE (Hack)   OF-BR-TR. B. 1/1/94, Chicago, Ill. D. 9/17/71, Oakland, Calif. 5'9½", 195. Hack Miller, outfielder who once hit .352 for Chicago Cubs in 1920's, was one of strongest men ever to play baseball. Son of former wrestler and strong man, Hack was chip off old block. Old-timers claimed Hack could pull up fair-sized trees by roots. Occasionally demonstrated strength by hammering nails into wood with hand, protected only by baseball cap. Reportedly also lifted automobile off woman who had been knocked down crossing street. Generally used 47-ounce bat, but on occasion is said to have used 65-ounce bludgeon "because it didn't sting my fingers so much."

Miller started pro ball at Wausau, Wis., 1914; played with St. Boniface and Winnipeg in Northern League, and Oakland, Pacific Coast League. (Brief trials with Brooklyn, 1916, three games; Boston Red Sox, 1918, 12 games.) With Oakland 1919, hit .346; then had two .347 seasons before joining Cubs, 1922. That .352 average with Cubs came in rookie season—and he played in 122 games, hit 12 home runs, and drove in 78. Hack followed up with .301 mark in 1923, hit 20 homers, had 88 RBI in 135 contests. Hit .336 in 1924, but was in just 53 games; then dropped out of major league picture after 24 games in 1925 with .279 average.

Miller had lifetime average of .323 for 349 major league games, with total of 65 doubles, 11 triples, 38 homers among 387 hits. Drove in 205 runs, scored 164. One game in WS with 1918 Red Sox, 0 for 1.

After majors, Hack played for Oakland, Houston, Danville, Topeka, North Platte. Later worked on San Francisco wharves.

MILLER, ROBERT LANE   P-BR-TR. B. 2/18/39, St. Louis, Mo. 6'1", 197. Bob Miller may have reached peak of his effectiveness in 1971 while with Pittsburgh Pirates. Started that year with San Diego Padres and came up with no mean achievement by winning seven and losing three with tail-end team in NL's Western Division; had 1.41 ERA in 64 innings. Then went to Pirates during same season and lowered his ERA to 1.29 for 28 innings, helping Buccaneers to NL pennant; saved three games, won another.

Miller has been around. Pirates represented his ninth major league team. Attended St. Louis U. and reportedly collected $20,000 bonus to sign up with St. Louis Cardinals, 1957. Got into five games with Redbirds that season then spent 1958 and part of 1959 with Rochester and Houston (Houston then in Texas League). Rejoined Cardinals, 1959: 4–3. Had identical record in 1960, but also pitched three games that season for Memphis in Southern loop. Back with Cardinals for 1961, had 1–3 mark.

When New York Mets came into existence Miller was one of their major league draft choices 10/10/61—member of Casey Stengel's first Met organization, 1962; did about as well as rest of Casey's team—1–12. But better days in store. Los Angeles Dodgers acquired him 12/1/62 and he remained with Walter Alston's club 1963–67, enabling him to pitch in WS of 1965,66. Minnesota 1968–69. Cleveland 1970. Chicago AL and Chicago NL 1970. Chicago NL, 1970 until released 5/10/71. Signed with Padres next day and proceeded to do excellent relief work for them until his transfer to Pittsburgh in August.

Pirates gave Miller unconditional release just before opening day 1973. Bob needed just five more appearances to give him record of 600 major league games. Owned 3.34 ERA for 1400 innings with 63 victories, 77 defeats; 535 walks allowed, 821 strikeouts. Pitched nine innings in WS of 1965–66–71, had ERA of 2.00. One defeat in 1971 set against Baltimore Orioles.

MINCHER, DONALD RAY (Mule) 1B-BL-TR. B. 6/24/38, Huntsville, Ala. 6'3", 210. Don Mincher wasn't too happy in July 1972 when traded from hapless Texas Rangers to Oakland A's. He knew would not be playing regularly for Dick Williams while Mike Epstein was on club. But he received half share of winner's WS loot, amounting to something over $10,000 to soothe him. Don, however, contributed to Oakland's victory over Cincinnati. In fourth game of series his pinch single in ninth inning drove in tying run from second base and put Gene Tenace on third base. Tenace scored moment later on Mangual's single, and A's won 3–2. Don announced retirement after 1972 season, from his home in Meridianville, Ala.

Mincher was man-on-move throughout baseball career. Started at Duluth-Superior in Northern League, 1956. Also played with Davenport; Charleston, S. C.; and Buffalo in minors. Had 27 games with old Washington Senators, 1960, before franchise moved to Minnesota. Then 35 games with Twins, 1961, and after that five full seasons with them. Best average while with Minnesota was .258, but also hit 17 homers that season, 1963. Had 23 homers following year but average sagged to .237. Traded to California Angels for 1967–68. Reached .273 his first season there, with 25 homers. Selected by Seattle Pilots in AL expansion draft 10/15/68. Slapped 25 homers, drove in 78 runs, and hit .246. Next move to Oakland for 1970. Finished with .246 average, 27 homers, 74 RBI. Traded to Washington 5/8/71 and chalked up best average of career,

.280. Another move, Senators being transformed into Texas Rangers for 1972. Don's record with Rangers and A's added up to .216 for 108 games.

As Mincher retired, had overall major league average of .249 for 1400 games. Among 1003 hits were 176 doubles, 16 triples, 200 homers, with 530 runs scored, 643 RBI.

Mincher's 1.000 batting average for 1972 WS was offset by .130 mark in 1965 classic, so overall record shows four hits in 24 trips, for .167. However, had distinction in 1965 games. Facing Don Drysdale in first game, Don banged homer in first time at bat. Didn't hit much after that, but did tie WS record for most assists by first baseman in nine-inning game, four.

In 1971 Don had unusual experience of hitting .615 in five games pitched by roommate, Paul Lindblad. Helped him win all with his batting, including three homers, one of them grand slammer. Both were with Senators at time.

MITCHELL, CLARENCE ELMER P-BL-TL. B. 2/22/91, Franklin, Nebr. D. 11/6/63, Aurora, Nebr. 5'11½", 190. Clarence Mitchell was unique in couple of ways. Only man to hit into WS unassisted triple play. Only NL southpaw licensed to use spitball after it was outlawed for most pitchers, 1920. Mitchell claimed nobody ever heard of spitballer with sore arm. Career lasted from 1909 to 1932. Mitchell had relieved Bureigh Grimes for Brooklyn Dodgers in fifth game of 1920 WS, in Cleveland. Indians were ahead, 7–0, but Flatbushers hoped they had rally under way when first two hitters in fifth inning reached base. Up came Mitchell, good hitter who often was used as pinch batsman throughout career. Facing Jim Bagby, Clarence got hold of pitch and gave it solid smash. Sharp liner went to Bill Wambsganss, Cleveland second baseman. Bill, who had already been running in direction of second base, tagged bag to double up man who had been there. And Otto Miller, who had started with pitch, was so close to second base when Wamby caught ball, that he had no chance to retreat to first. Bill tagged him for historic unassisted triple play. No wonder Dodgers lost game and Series.

Clarence saw plenty of country before sticking in majors. Began at Franklin, Neb., 1909; later pitched for Red Cloud, Saginaw, Providence, Denver, with brief trials with Detroit Tigers, 1911–12. Twenty-two victories in final season with Denver, 1915, then to Cincinnati, 1916–17; Brooklyn, 1918–22; Philadelphia NL, 1923–28; St. Louis NL, 1928–30; New York NL, 1930–32. Won 125 games, lost 139 during big league career; took part in 390 games, of which 145 were completed; pitched 12 shutouts in 2217 innings, with an ERA of 4.12. Won 13 games, maximum number of victories in any one season, late in career, 1931, toiling for Giants.

Mitchell was good enough hitter that he occasionally filled in at first base. Had .252 lifetime batting average. Despite misfortune of hitting into that famous triple play, emerged from WS with good pitching record—one earned run in 10-1/3 innings during 1920 and 1928 WS, with ERA of 0.87.

Operated tavern in Aurora, Nebr., in later years. Bad health five years before death.

MITCHELL, FREDERICK FRANCIS P-C-BR-TR. B. 6/5/78, Cambridge, Mass. D. 10/13/70, Newton, Mass. 5′9½″, 185. Fred Mitchell is remembered nowadays more as baseball coach at Harvard than for his pitching, catching, and managing in major leagues. However, this gentleman, born Frederick Francis Yapp, soon discarded last name and was one of members of first AL club in Boston, Red Sox of 1901, as hurler. Won six, lost six, best he did in majors. Divided following season between Red Sox and Philadelphia Athletics, switched to Phillies in 1903, then to Brooklyn during 1904 season and in 1905.

Arm trouble ended pitching career with record of 30 wins, 48 defeats, and he went back to minors, became catcher. Five years later was back in AL, caught 68 games for New York Highlanders, 1910, hit .286. Out of major league picture after that until turned up with Boston Braves, 1913, catching on with team as coach under manager George Stallings. Got into four games that year, pinch hitting. Playing career ended with .210 batting average overall for 202 major league games.

Fred was with Braves as coach during their "miracle" season, 1914, when they drove on to NL pennant and four straight wins over favored Philadelphia Athletics. Managed Chicago Cubs, 1917–20, leading them to pennant in 1918. His old team, Red Sox, however, defeated Cubs in WS that year, four games to two. Managed Boston Braves, 1921–23. Coached Harvard nine after that until 1939, when retired.

MIZE, JOHN ROBERT (Big Cat) 1B-BL-TR. B. 1/7/13, Demorest, Ga. 6′2″, 215. When Dr. Robert Hyland, "Surgeon General of Baseball," operated on Johnny Mize in 1930s, there was fifty-fifty chance big left-handed slugger would never again play baseball. Had bone spur high in inside of leg that caused severe pain and greatly slowed down movement. One can't help wondering about consequences if surgery performed by less skillful hands—consequences to Mize himself and to fortunes of New York Yankees many years later. And one must wonder about what would have happened if Cincinnati Reds had gambled on Mize before operation in spring of 1935.

Yankees gambled on Joe DiMaggio's knee, bought him for bargain price of $25,000 plus five players—and look how investment paid off. But Cincinnati Reds, in 1935, couldn't afford to gamble $55,000 on Mize when it looked like he would never be able to play first base in majors. Johnny belonged to St. Louis Cardinals. Branch Rickey, then general manager at St. Louis, offered him to Larry MacPhail, then major domo at Cincinnati, on conditional basis. Mize spent spring training with Reds, hit several long drives, but couldn't move rapidly either in field or on base paths. So deal was never completed—and Cardinals sent Johnny back to minors. Leg continued to bother seriously, and finally he consented to go into operating room knowing future as player was at stake. After operation, Mize won regular first base job with Cardinals, 1936. Not most graceful fielder in world, but was big, with long reach, and lost no time showing power at plate. Hit .329 with 30 doubles, eight triples, 19 homers, and drove in 93 runs. Was on way. Next season boosted home run total to 25, RBIs to 113, and average to .364.

For five seasons with Cardinals Mize batted in 100 runs or more, climaxed by 137 RBI mark in 1940. Led NL in homers in 1939 with 28 and in 1940 with 43. Won NL batting title, 1939, with .349. Traded to N.Y. Giants 12/11/41. For sixth consecutive year bettered 100 in RBI, leading NL with 110 in 1942, batting .305. Then entered military service, rejoining Polo Grounders for 1946 season. In 1947 Johnny hit .302 but tied Ralph Kiner for home run leadership with 51. Again led league in RBI with 138. In 1948 race for home run laurels again a tie between Mize and Kiner, each with 40. John had 125 RBI, but did not lead league. Mize's batting average dropped to .263 in 1949 and he appeared in 106 games. Giants were in second division and Leo Durocher, then manager, wanted to revamp club. Yankees, smelling chance to win another AL pennant with pinch-hitting help, offered $40,000 for Mize after NL waivers had been secured. Deal was made 8/22/49. Johnny got into 13 games for Yanks, hit .261, smacked first AL home run. And in WS that fall began to pay off on investment.

Johnny pinch hit successfully in second game of WS but Brooklyn won 1-0. In third game Casey Stengel sent Mize in to bat for Mapes in ninth inning; score tied, bases loaded, with one out. Johnny's single drove in two vital runs, after which Coleman drove in another. Dodgers came up with two in their half of ninth, but Yanks won 4-3, with big assist from Mize. Was 2 for 2 in WS, for 1.000.

Mize played some first base, but did lot of pinch hitting for Yanks next four years. Did not hit for average, but in 1950, in 90 games, smacked 25 homers and drove in 72 runs. In 1952 his WS play was pretty nifty—hit three home runs, one of them as pinch batsman, drove in six runs, and had .400 average.

Johnny compiled plenty of worthy records. Thirty times hit at least two homers in league game. Seven times hit home runs in pinch, not counting that WS emergency swat. Six times had three homers in one game. Four times had three consecutive homers in one contest. And when he banged 51 home runs in 1947, was new NL record for lefthanded hitters. Furthermore, Johnny had distinction of hitting home runs in all 15 ball parks in use during his career.

Mize was product of Cardinal farm system, climbing through ranks from Greensboro, N.C., 1930, to Elmira and finally to Rochester, N. Y. While with Yankee organization, 1950, spent brief period at Kansas City farm team but got back to Gotham in time for WS eligibility.

Mize played 1884 major league games, hit .312 with 2011 hits, 367 doubles, 83 triples, 359 home runs. Scored 1118 times, drove in 1337. His five WS, all of them consecutive with Yankees, starting 1949: 12 for 42, .286 average, 18 games; 5 runs, 12 hits, 2 doubles, 3 homers, 9 RBI.

Scout, Giants, 1955. Coach, Kansas City AL, 1961. Owned orange groves in Florida.

MIZELL, WILMER DAVID (Vinegar Bend) P-BR-TL. B. 8/13/30, Leakesville, Miss. 6'3½", 205. Washed-up, sore-armed southpaw pitcher who became North Carolina Congressman, 1969. Got nickname from Alabama hamlet with population of 37 when Mizell left. Former Cardinal and member of Pittsburgh Pirates when they won 1960 world championship, settled in North Carolina when playing days were over. Got job as representative for Pepsi-Cola; liked kids and young people and never turned down invitation to appear before youth groups. Averaged 100 speaking engagements annually, so became personally acquainted with countless people. Republicans asked him to run for county commissioner, Davidson County, 1966. Two years later, with colorful name and friendly down-to-earth personality, seemed natural candidate for U.S. Congress and was elected from Fifth District.

Mizell explains origin of nickname. They were building railroad in that part of Alabama long time ago, some 50 miles from Mobile. Diet of railroad workers included sorghum molasses. Barrel of the stuff soured into vinegar and laborers poured it into Escatawpa river at place where it makes bend. Ever since, place has been called Vinegar Bend, and sports writers so dubbed Mizell at start of professional career. Mizell lived there in youth. Joe Garagiola, interviewing Wilmer on NBC's "Today Show," said that when telephone booth installed in village they had to move city limits out a few feet.

Mizell started at Albany, Ga., 1949; Winston-Salem, 1950; Houston, Texas League, 1951. Then stuck with Cardinals, 1952. Won ten, lost eight as rookie, with 3.65 ERA. Had 13–11 mark, 1953; military service, 1954–55; spent next four seasons with Cardinals, winning 45, losing 48. Then, after winning one and losing three for Redbirds at start of year, was traded to Pittsburgh 5/28/60. Won 13 and lost five for Pirates rest of way, helping Danny Murtaugh's team win flag. With ERA of 3.50 for entire season, won 14 and lost eight. Vinegar Bend lost third game of WS against Yankees that fall: pitched 2-1/3 innings, hammered for four hits, four earned runs, walked two, struck out one, and wound up with ERA of 15.43. But Pirates won seventh and final game of hectic Series on Bill Mazeroski's homer, so Congressman Mizell proudly wears world championship ring on finger today.

Mizell won seven, lost 10 for 1961 Pirates; divided 1962 between Pittsburgh and New York NL, with one victory, three defeats. Called it quits after that, because of arm trouble, with lifetime major league record of 90 wins, 88 defeats, ERA 3.85, 1528-2/3 innings; walked 680, fanned 918, 15 shutouts.

When U.S. senators and congressmen play annual baseball game, Mizell has been accused of professionalism—still in good physical shape and can outpitch most of colleagues.

MONDAY, ROBERT JAMES, JR. (Rick) OF-BL-TL. B. 11/20/45, Batesville, Ark. 6'3", 195. Rick Monday is another of collegians coached at Arizona State U. by Bob Winkles, who became manager of California Angels, 1973. Rick helped team to College WS championship and was named All-American, as well as College Player of Year. Then was very first player ever selected in free-agent draft conducted by major leagues. Kansas City Athletics gave him reported $104,000 to sign, 1965. Monday farmed out to Lewiston, Northwest League, 1965, and to Mobile, Southern Association, 1966. Hit .098 in 17 games with A's, then still in Kansas City, 1966, but became regular following year. After one full season in midwest, Monday went to Oakland with team, 1968. Best season at bat was 1970, with .290 average; but hit greatest number of homers, 18, in 1971, although average sagged to .245. Prone to strike out—whiffed 93 times.

Chicago Cubs were anxious to get good center fielder and A's wanted lefthanded pitching. So, Monday traded to Chicago for Ken Holtzman 11/29/71. Cubs plugged gap in center field all right, but probably were disappointed with Rick's hitting—.249, with 11 homers, 42 RBI, in 1972.

Monday approached 1973 season with .261 average for 777 major league games. Owned 650 hits in 2493 official trips to plate. Scored 353 runs, had 298 RBI. His safe hits were good for 106 doubles, 33 triples, 73 home runs. Not proud of some of his records: tied major league mark 4/29/70 by striking out five times in nine-inning game; tied AL record by striking out seven consecutive times at bat 4/28–29/70; set major league record by striking out eight times in two consecutive nine-inning games, 4/28–29/70.

But in field made six double plays, 1967, tying for AL lead that year among outfielders. AL All-Star game 1968.

MONEY, DONALD WAYNE Inf.-BR-TR. B. 6/7/47, Washington, D.C. 6'1", 190. Don Money, who broke NL record for fewest errors by third baseman playing at least 150 games, was key man in autumn 1972 trade that landed him with Milwaukee Brewers. Money, in 1972, made 10 errors, handled 163 consecutive chances without miscue. Fielding average of .978 set new NL record for third sackers in at least 150 games.

677

Don made these marks playing for Philadelphia Phillies.

Money has quick hands, strong arm, as well as youth on his side. At plate has fine, level swing, but has done well with bat in only one major league season, 1970. Hit .295 for Phils in 120 games, with 25 doubles, 4 triples, 14 homers, and 66 RBI. His hitting disappointed in both 1971–72: had .223 and .222 marks. Fifteen homers 1972. Phillies traded him to Brewers in deal involving Jim Lonborg and Ken Sanders. Money originally belonged to Pittsburgh Pirates. Signed with their organization, 1965, and started out Salem club of Appalachian League. Clinton, Iowa, 1966. Raleigh, 1967, where he hit .310 in 136 games. Recalled by Pirates and traded to Philadelphia 12/15/67. Four games with Phillies, 1968, and 127 with San Diego, then in Pacific Coast League, batting .303. Became regular with Phils, 1969; hit .229 in 127 games.

Money brought to Milwaukee lifetime average of .241 for 524 major league games. Had 455 safe hits, 87 doubles, 16 triples, 42 home runs. Scored 202 times with Phils and drove in even 200 markers.

MOON, WALLACE WADE (Wally) OF-BL-TR. B. 4/3/30, Bay, Ark. 6', 175. Wally Moon, after four good seasons with St. Louis Cardinals, had off-year, 1958. Dropped from .295 batting average, with 24 homers and 73 RBI, to .238, with seven homers, 38 RBI. So Cardinals traded him to Los Angeles Dodgers 12/4/58 in deal for Gino Cimoli. Moon immediately made good comeback: hit .302, with 19 homers, 74 RBI, and helped Walter Alston's club win first West Coast flag and world championship.

Moon studied education at Texas A. & M., received $6000 bonus to sign with Cardinal organization, 1950. Refused to let baseball interfere with studies, so played 82 games at Omaha, 1950, batting .315; sixteen games, 1951. Got master's degree and had one more season at Omaha before moving up to Rochester, where hit .307 in 131 games. Moved up to Cardinals, 1954, played in 151 contests, hit .304 with 76 RBI in rookie year. Hit homer in first time at bat. NL Rookie of Year. Then three more seasons hitting .295 or better before that aforementioned off year. Wally followed up first Los Angeles season with .299, then chalked up .328 with 17 homers, 88 RBI. Tapered off after that; finished major league career after 1965 season: 1457 games, lifetime average .289, 1399 hits, 212 doubles, 60 triples, 142 homers, 737 runs, 661 RBI, 89 steals.

Wally was in 1959 and 1965 WS with Dodgers; hit .240 in eight games, with one homer, two RBI, three runs scored.

MOORE, TERRY BLUFORD OF-BR-TR. B. 5/27/12, Memphis, Tenn. 6', 175. Terry Moore was stellar center fielder for St. Louis Cardinals 11 years, 1935–48, missing three years, 1943–45, for military service; coach for Cardinals, 1949–52 and 1956–58; manager, Philadelphia Phillies, part of 1954.

Moore worked for printer in St. Louis, had good-paying job during depression when minor league baseball salaries were pretty skimpy. When he did not make grade at Columbus, American Association, 1932, kept job through 1933 and played ball on side. Finally was persuaded to try his luck, 1934. In 24 games at Elmira, hit .316; and played 130 contests for Columbus, hitting .328, with 14 homers, 84 RBI. This was in league just one notch below majors. Made grade with Cardinals, 1935, and soon recognized as one of baseball's finest outfielders. Averaged .280 for major league career, going to .304 in 1940. Twice hit 17 homers in single season, though was usually leadoff man and not primarily power hitter.

Terry had six hits in six consecutive times at bat 9/5/35; equaled major league record. When he stopped playing, had 1298 major league games and 1318 hits, including 263 doubles, 28 triples, 80 homers. Scored 719 runs, drove in 513, and stole 82 bases.

NL All-Star squads 1939–42. Hit .294 in 1942 WS when Cardinals beat Yankees four games to one. Hit .148 in 1946 Series, which Cards took from Boston Red Sox. Overall WS mark .205; 9 for 44, 3 runs, 4 RBI.

MOORE, WILLIAM WILCY (Cy) P-BR-TR. B. 5/20/97, Bonita, Tex. D. 3/29/63, Hollis, Okla. 6'1", 200. Wilcy Moore was N.Y. Yankees' secret weapon in 1927. Plucked from Greenville club of South Atlantic League, Class B circuit, Moore won flock of games in AL and saved many more, mostly in relief. Though Yankees of those days had Babe Ruth, Lou Gehrig, Bob Meusel, and Tony Lazzeri in their "murderer's row," they still needed pitching. Moore supplied missing ingredient, while Pennock, Hoyt, and Shocker, who were holdovers, rounded out mainstays of staff. Moore, to whom nobody paid attention in spring training, was 19–9 with 13 saves. Then went into WS against Pittsburgh Pirates. That was one of classics Yankees swept over opposition in four straight. Moore relieved Waite Hoyt in opening game, pitched 1-2/3 innings, saved game for Yanks. Then, after George Pipgras and Herb Pennock won games, Cy was starting pitcher in fourth contest. Moore won game by 4–3 score, and once again Yankees were world champions.

After that fabulous 1927 season, Moore never approached same heights. Had 4–4 record in 1928, 6–4 performance in 1929. Then, following season Cy was back in minors, with St. Paul, American Association. Won 22, lost nine, resulting in return to AL, this time with Boston Red Sox. But best he could do was win 11, lose 13. Following year was with Sox for while, then back with Yankees. Had 6–10 record. Final fling with Yanks was 1933, 5–6.

Moore started pro ball 1922, Fort Worth, Texas; later with Paris, Texas; Ardmore, Okmulgee before going to Greenville. His 30 wins against four losses in 1926 brought about purchase by Yankees for $4500.

Poor hitter, but Cy hit one home run in majors; 1927, at Yankee Stadium. According to Moore, Babe Ruth so astonished he fell off bench laughing.

Wilcy won 51 AL games, lost 44, had ERA of 3.69. Pitched 692 innings, walked 232, fanned 204. In 1932 WS chalked up second autumn-classic victory, this one over Chicago Cubs. Pitched final 5-1/3 innings of fourth game, allowed no runs, and walked off mound with 13–6 victory. As in 1927, this Series also was four-game sweep for Bronx Bombers. Thus Moore had honor of being winning pitcher in final game of two Series swept by Yankees. WS record overall was 2–0, ERA 0.56.

MOOSE, ROBERT RALPH, JR. P-BR-TR. B. 10/9/47, Export, Pa. 5'11", 194. Back in 1927 John Miljus threw wild pitch in ninth inning of fourth WS game, allowing Earl Combs of N.Y. Yankees to score winning run from third base. Anticlimactic end to game and WS in which Pittsburgh Pirates succumbed to four-game defeat. In 1972 another Pittsburgh baseball season came to end with wild pitch, this one thrown by Bob Moose in fifth game of NL playoff series against Cincinnati Reds. George Foster was on third base with two men out in ninth inning, score tied. Bob's pitch to Hal McRae hit in front of plate and bounced past catcher Manny Sanguillen—and Cincinnati had pennant wrapped up. Moose, despite unfortunate wild pitch, has been known as good control pitcher. In 912 innings in majors to start of 1973 season had walked 253 men while whiffing 629. Had 58 victories to credit against 42 defeats. In 173 games had 28 complete contests, including first game he pitched in majors. That was in September 1967 against Houston Astros. Bob's overall effectiveness record at start of 1973 was 3.30 ERA.

Bob might have had many more complete games if he had not been used extensively in relief as well as starter. Minor league apprenticeship began, 1965, at Salem, Appalachian League; divided 1966 between Gastonia and Raleigh; and 1967 between Columbus, Ohio, and Macon. That fall made NL debut with Pirates—one game. Was 8–12 with Pirates 1968, then had best percentage of victories in NL, 1969, taking 14 wins, losing three for .824. Then had 11–10 and 11–7 records, followed by 13–10 in 1972. In 1969 and 1972 had best ERA marks, 2.91 each time.

Moose's WS record, 1971, showed ERA of 6.30 in 10 innings pitched. Hurled strong five innings in sixth game, allowing one run, although not involved in decision. Pitched no-hitter 9/20/69, winning 4–0 over N.Y. Mets.

MORAN, PATRICK JOSEPH C-BR-TR. B. 2/7/76, Fitchburg, Mass. D. 3/7/24, Orlando, Fla. Pat Moran never mentioned as outstanding catcher but compiled excellent record as manager. Took over Philadelphia Phillies as pilot, 1915, and immediately won NL pennant. Took over Cincinnati Reds, 1919, and again won pennant. Bossed major league clubs nine years and had only two teams in second division. Four other times led his club into runner-up position. Moran's 1915 Phillies lost WS to Boston Red Sox, four games to one, but 1919 Reds took autumn games from Chicago White Sox, five games to three. While that Series was tainted through skulduggery of "Black Sox," Moran always insisted team would have won even if Sox had all given their level best.

Pat started in pro ball with Lyons, New York State League, 1897, moved to Cortland, Hudson Valley League, 1898, and to Boston NL, 1901. After five seasons there, landed with Chicago Cubs in time for their NL pennants, 1906,07,08. Appeared in only three WS games as sub, got no hits in two trips to plate. Joined Philadelphia, 1910, but was through as active player, 1912, appearing in only two games thereafter. Johnny Kling had been Cubs' first-string catcher during Moran's days in Windy City, and Bill Killefer came along in Philadelphia, to grab regular backstop job there. Moran then moved into managing Phillies and had great deal to do with early development of Grover Cleveland Alexander, who won 31 games for him in 1915.

Pat ran clubs with loose rein and was popular with players, press, and fans. When management of Phils sold Alexander and Killefer, his stellar battery, to Chicago Cubs 11/11/17, Moran criticized deal. This hastened his departure from Phillies' after 1918 season. Deprived of stars, Phils landed in sixth place. Moran's death just before start of 1924 season believed hastened by consumption of poor liquor in circulation during Prohibition days. Pat compiled .236 average in 764 major league games.

MORGAN, JOE LEONARD 2B-BL-TR. B. 9/19/43, Bonham, Tex. 5'7", 150. Joe Morgan, who spent seven full seasons with Houston Astros, lost no time in becoming one of most popular and valuable players with Cincinnati Reds, 1972. Came to Reds in widely criticized deal, since trade of 11/29/71 meant departure of Lee May and Tommy Helms from Rhineland. But enjoyed finest season of career, hitting better than ever before, stealing more bases, and helping Cincinnati to NL pennant. At second base made just eight errors all year and had best fielding average ever—.990.

Morgan proved self good team player, drawing plenty of walks as well as hitting .292. Displayed unexpected power too, with 16 homers during regular season. Then in playoffs against Pittsburgh, slapped homers in each of first two games. Oakland pitchers kept Joe's batting average down in WS, just three hits in 24 official trips, for .125 mark. Still, Joe drew six walks and scored four runs.

Little Joe—seldom weighs above 150—has considerable value to team that doesn't show in statistics. Speed plus daring base-running often upsets opposing pitcher and catcher, benefiting teammate at plate. And Morgan has been able to score many more runs after stealing second base than would have by remaining at first.

During conversation with Maury Wills, Morgan came to conclusion that stealing third base, even with two out, can prove valuable to team. Wills convinced him that theft of third must have 99 chances in 100 of success to make it gamble worth taking. With man on third base, Maury and Joe figure man at plate will get better ball to hit. Pitcher's fear of throwing wild pitch on slider or on low-and-away pitch is increased.

Morgan had two years of minor league experience after graduating from same high school in Oakland, Calif., that produced Frank Robinson and Vada Pinson. Had 45 games at Modesto, Calif., and 95 at Durham, N.C., 1963; and 140 games with San Antonio, 1964. There he hit .323, stole 47 bases, led league in doubles, drew 105 bases on balls, drove in 90 runs, and scored 113 times. Brief spells with Houston, 1963 and 1964; by 1965 nailed down Astros' second base job and kept it until end of 1971, except for one year when knee injury kept him on bench for all but 10 games. *Sporting News* named him Rookie of Year for NL, 1965. NL All-Star game 1966 but replaced because of injury; also All-Star 1970, 72, 73. Went six-for-six consecutively 7/8/65; drew five bases on balls in one game 6/2/66, which tied modern NL record. Best season prior to 1972 was 1966, when hit .285 in 122 games, although missed several weeks of play because of fractured knee cap.

Base stealing resulted in 49 thefts, 1969; 42 following year, and 40 in 1971. Pilfered 58 in first season with Reds. Claims could steal much oftener if it would help team, but doesn't believe in trying when club is several runs ahead.

Morgan faced 1973 with 1040 major league games behind him; had 1021 hits, 159 doubles, 62 triples, 77 homers to credit; scored 653 runs, drove in 351, and had 253 stolen bases. Overall average: .267.

MORIARTY, GEORGE JOSEPH 3B-BR-TR. B. 7/7/84, Chicago, Ill. D. 4/8/64, Miami, Fla. 6', 185. Ball player. Umpire. Writer. Lecturer. Ever ready with opinion. Vaudeville performer. Inventor of improvements on typewriter. Manager, Detroit Tigers, two seasons. Song writer. Syndicated his baseball articles many years. Moriarty belonged to rough and ready era; used fists when language failed, both as player and as umpire. In 1932, while officiating in AL, challenged entire Chicago White Sox team. Milt Gaston stepped up; Moriarty flattened him, breaking own hand with blow. Other White Sox players stepped in, and soon Moriarty was on losing end of battle. Despite such experiences, *Sporting News* poll among AL players in 1935 indicated they thought George best umpire in league.

George averaged only .251 as major leaguer in 1072 games. Had five career homers. Tried to offset lack of power by stealing bases, running aggressively. Stole home many times. Claims have been made that he pilfered home 11 times in 1909, but *Sporting News Baseball Record Book* says that Rod Carew, with seven thefts of home in 1969, has AL record, while Pete Reiser of Brooklyn holds NL mark with seven in 1946. Nevertheless, William Cameron, wrote an editorial in *Detroit News* about George, which said in part:

"Moriarty is crouched like a tiger about to spring."

"Now! Now!"

"There is a white streak across the field. A cloud of dust at home plate. The umpire stands with his hands extended, palms downward."

"All the world's a baseball diamond. From third you either become a splendid success or a dismal failure."

"Don't die on third."

Editorial was quoted many times by chautauqua lecturers, clergymen, schoolteachers, luncheon speakers. Reportedly translated into many languages, with its lesson, don't stop until you've reached your goal.

Moriarty worked in typewriter factory, Woodstock, Ill., played semi-pro ball on side. Brief tryout with Chicago Cubs, 1903–04; Little Rock, 1904; then to Toledo. Joined N.Y. Yankees, alias Hilltoppers or Highlanders, 1906 and remained with them through 1908. Detroit, 1909–15; became captain of team. Chicago AL 1916; playing manager, Memphis, same season. Became AL umpire 1917–40, except for two years as manager of Tigers, 1927–28. Detroit finished fourth and sixth under his leadership.

Did motion-picture work and public relations work for AL. Scouted for Detroit Tigers. Among players he signed were Harvey Kuenn, Billy Hoeft, Bill Tuttle. Retired 1959.

MOSTIL, JOHN ANTHONY (Bananas) OF-BR-TR. B. 6/1/96, Chicago, Ill. D. 12/10/70, Midlothian, Ill. 5'8", 169. Johnny Mostil, as boy, tore first communion suit climbing fence into Wrigley Field, Chicago. On another occasion he and several other boys were grabbed sneaking into White Sox ball park. They were ushered into presence of old Charlie Comiskey, president of White Sox, who proceeded to give them stern lecture about virtues of paying your way into stadium and being good citizens. Not too many years later, Comiskey was paying Mostil to come into White Sox park to play center field. And how he played it! Eddie Collins, teammate for some years, called him "greatest." Added: "I never saw anyone with his ability to cover ground. He could go farther than Tris Speaker to get fly ball." Johnny may have been only center fielder ever to catch foul ball in left field area. Happened in exhibition game in Nashville, Tenn. Bibb Falk, playing left, evidently didn't figure he himself had chance to catch ball. But Mostil started running at crack of bat, whizzed past left fielder, and pulled down high lazy fly ball well into foul territory.

Mostil no slouch as hitter—finished major league career with .301 average. Never hit for power. Hit seven homers, 1922, but otherwise only reached four homers twice in AL career. Johnny said it was fielding kept him in majors for 972 games. In those days .300 hitters were plentiful. However, Mostil reached base often, stole often as well. Led AL in runs scored with 135 in 1925; led league in base thefts in 1925,26; pilfered 41 in 1923 when Eddie Collins led with 49. Had 176 stolen bases when went back to minors.

Johnny went right from Chicago sandlots to trial with White Sox, 1918. Played 10 games as second baseman, hit .273 with nine hits in 33 trips, two of blows being doubles, two others triples. Milwaukee, 1919, hitting .268 in 132 games. Then White Sox management must have realized Eddie Collins still pretty fine second baseman, not likely soon to be replaced. So Mostil shifted to outfield, 1920, played 155 games and hit .318 in final American Association season before returning to parent club. Played 100 games for Sox, 1921, hit .301, same figure that proved to be lifetime major league average. Mostil reached .325 in 1924, and .328 in 1926. Then encountered severe depression, tried to commit suicide by slashing wrists. Got into just 13 games, 1927, hit .125. Played 133 games in 1928. Broke ankle 5/19/29, played just 12 games that year. Back in minors, two seasons at Toledo and one at Little Rock. Then became playing manager at Eau Claire in Northern League, 1933–37; managed at Grand Forks in same circuit, 1938–39, getting into game occasionally as pinch hitter; piloted Jonesboro, Ark., team, 1940–41; manager, Waterloo, Iowa, 1941–47; manager, Superior, Northern League, 1948. After that Mostil served as scout for White Sox until retirement due to poor health about one year before death.

It was Mostil, playing left field, who caught last out when Charlie Robertson pitched perfect game against Detroit Tigers 4/30/22. Johnny caught pinch hitter Johnny Bassler's fly ball and started toward dugout. Fans scrambled onto field, grabbed ball from Mostil's glove. Reaching clubhouse, someone asked, "Where's that last ball?" Mostil hurriedly grabbed another baseball from ball bag. In excitement nobody noticed what he was doing. Ball then was autographed by all teammates, and for years Robertson prized it—never learning it was not actual ball used for last pitch.

Mostil wound up major league career with 1054 hits, 618 runs scored, 374 RBI, 209 doubles, 82 triples, 23 homers. Tied AL record for outfielders, making 11 putouts in one game and accepting 12 chances 5/22/28.

MOTA, MANUEL (Mickey) OF-BR-TR. B. 2/19/38, Santo Domingo, Dominican Republic. 5'11", 168. Somehow Manny Mota gets overlooked when All-Star teams are looked over, but this fellow from Caribbean belongs in very select group of major leaguers. Among those who were active spring of 1973, Manny owns .302 lifetime batting average for 1138 games. You hear great deal about Hank Aaron, Roberto Clemente, Willie Mays, Rico Carty and Pete Rose. Perhaps reason you don't hear so much about Mota is fact he doesn't hit long ball too often. Also, for various reasons, traded several times. Unlike many players who bounce from club to club, Mota has never been problem to his managers. Versatility may not have helped nail down job at one position. Besides outfield, often filled in at first, second, and third base and even caught one game in 1964 with Pittsburgh Pirates.

Mota started pro ball at Michigan City, Midwest League, 1957. En route to San Francisco Giants, also played at Danville, Carolina League; Phoenix; Springfield, Mass.; Harlingen, Tex.; Tacoma, El Paso. In 47 games with Giants, 1962, Manny hit only .176. That fall traded to Houston NL, and following spring traded to Pittsburgh. Divided 1963 between Columbus, where hit .293 in 75 games, and Pittsburgh, where average was .270 for 59 engagements. Took part in at least 110 games each of next five seasons with Pittsburgh, batting average moving between .277 and .332. When NL expanded before 1969 season, Montreal got Mota in draft, but he went to Los Angeles Dodgers in trade 6/11/69. Hit .321 that year in 116 games; then .305 in 124 contests, and .312 for 91 games in 1971. In 1972 had .323 mark for 118 games, including 48 RBI, five homers. Going into 1973 season, Manny's .302 average showed 970 hits; 106 doubles, 50 triples, 30 homers; scored 446 runs, drove in 361, and stole 48 bases.

Manny, as youngster, played barehanded. Picked lemon from tree, wrapped it in paper and string, called it baseball. Since becoming big leaguer, has promoted Manny Mota Little Leagues in Dominican Republic. At Christmas buys dozens of bats and balls, drives around area and gives them to kids. Boy is eligible if he goes to church and minds parents.

MUELLER, CLARENCE FRANKLIN (Heinie)   OF-BL-TL. B. 9/16/99, Creve Coeur, Mo. 5'8", 158. Heinie Mueller gave St. Louis sports writers something colorful to write about in days when Cardinals had never won pennant, early 1920s. Often hit well over .300 for Redbirds, but base running at times kept him from winning regular job. On first base one day when next batter lofted high foul fly near plate. With crack of bat Heinie put head down, set sail for second base, slid into third base running like mad. Catcher caught ball couple of steps from plate, casually threw to first base, doubling Mueller off bag. After that play, Branch Rickey, Cardinal manager, shipped him to Houston farm club that night. Mueller later recalled play: "That was first time player went from first base to Houston on pop foul."

When Rickey was talking to Mueller before he signed with Cardinal organization, Branch asked if he was as fast as Jack Smith, then a speedy outfielder with team. Mueller averred he was. "Judas Priest, he's fast!" said Rickey. "I don't know about Judas Priest," said Heinie. "I never saw him play."

Mueller played four games with Cards, 1920, then had experience at Fort Smith, Ark.; Milwaukee, American Association; Syracuse, and Houston, then in Texas League. Had spells with Cardinals during those years, remaining with club 1924–25. Traded to New York Giants for Billy Southworth during 1926 season. Remained with Giants until after 1927 campaign.

While Heinie was with Giants, playing left field, Southworth was base runner on first base, with one man out. Next hitter lofted fly ball to Mueller. Heinie forgot how many outs there were, so nonchalantly flipped ball to Eddie Roush in center. Southworth didn't budge off first base. When inning was over, Mueller went to bench expecting purple language and blistering bawling out from John McGraw. "How much will that cost me?" asked Mueller. "It won't cost you anything," replied McGraw. "Wasn't that a decoy play trying to get Southworth to run so you could double him up?"

But Heinie didn't always escape McGraw's wrath. On one occasion he was castigating Mueller in choicest profanity for making dumb play. "Mr. McGraw," interrupted Mueller, "I was trained by Mr. Rickey, and I'm not used to that kind of language!"

Mueller, Catholic, once slid into second base. Umpire, also Catholic and member of Knights of Columbus, called Heinie out. "Fine Knight of Columbus you are," roared Mueller. "Why, even a Shriner would have called me safe on that play."

Mueller spent 1928–29 with Boston NL; was with Buffalo, 1929–34; briefly with St. Louis Browns, 1935, but also managed Greensburg, Pa., team that year. Manager, Union City, Tenn., 1936, and Monett, Mo., club, 1938. Camp supervisor for minor league clubs in Cardinal organization, 1939–41.

Outside baseball Mueller was electrician, and later had flower shop in partnership with Phil Todt, who also played for various teams in majors. Was proud of fact once hit homer and triple in same inning while with Giants. Played total of 693 major league games and hit .282, with 22 homers, 37 triples, 87 doubles among 597 hits.

MUNGO, VAN LINGLE P-BR-TR. B. 6/8/11, Pageland, S.C. 6'2", 210. Van Mungo had tools to be great pitcher. Missed connections, however, possibly because he landed with free-wheeling, hard-drinking, fun-loving Brooklyn Dodgers as 21-year-old, 1931. Debut sensational. Pitched against Tom Zachary of Boston Braves 9/7/31, allowed three hits, struck out 12, and won game 2–0. Knocked in both Brooklyn runs with single and triple. Won two more games that fall, lost one, and had 2.32 ERA. Went up to Dodgers after 15–5 record earlier in 1931 at Hartford, Eastern League. Pitched for Fayetteville and Charlotte, 1929–30. Mungo was 13–11 in first full year with Brooklyn. Then had two 16-victory seasons and two with 18 wins.

Van had problems on and off field while with Dodgers. Once had victory in sight with two men out in ninth inning. With runners on base, hitter sent soft fly in direction of Tom Winsett in right field. Tom dropped ball, then kicked it, and everybody scored—losing pitcher, Mungo. Van went to clubhouse, broke furniture, and when calmed down enough sent telegram to wife that said: "Pack your bags and come to Brooklyn. If Winsett can play in big leagues, it's cinch you can too."

Van had some fine games too. In 1934, on next-to-last day of season, pitched for Dodgers against Giants, who were battling for NL pennant. That was year after Bill Terry, N.Y. manager, had offended all Dodger fans by asking whether Brooklyn was still in league. Casey Stengel, then Brooklyn boss, held brief meeting before game, read telegram, asked Dodgers to "avenge worst insult ever perpetrated." Mungo beat Giants 5–1—and St. Louis Cardinals won pennant.

All-Star squads 1934,37; Van hurt arm in 1937 game and work with Dodgers downhill after that. When Dodgers trained in Havana in spring of 1941, Van became involved with former bull fighter and his girl friend, and was hurriedly sent to U.S. mainland. Pitched two innings, and was sent to Montreal, Brooklyn farm club. Van won three games, lost one, pinch hit and played some outfield. Montreal team won International League playoffs but en route to Columbus, Ohio, in Junior World Series, Mungo was in fracas with top officials of Montreal club and was traded to Minneapolis.

In 1942 pitched well enough in American Association to merit another chance in majors—this time with Giants. While had indifferent success with Giants 1942–43, in 1945, after serving in army, returned to Giants and had 14 victories to credit, against seven defeats. By this time ulcers and an operation caused him to retire from game. Van later indicated that after hurting arm in 1937 All-Star game, had come up with "slippery" pitch. Said to have put slippery elm on inner sock; kept it wet between innings. When all eyes were on infielders or outfielders making plays, Van would stroke sock just enough to get slippery elm on fingers.

Mungo got into 364 major league games, pitched 2113 innings, won 120 games, lost 115. Had ERA of 3.47 with 1242 strikeouts, 868 bases on balls. His 238 strikeouts in 1936 was tops in NL. Was unusually fast runner and fair hitter for pitcher. Had .345 average in 1939, and lifetime batting average of .221.

After returning home to Pageland, S.C., Van coached American Legion ball players. Son Ernest, then 18, had brief tryout with Washington Senators, 1961.

MUNSON, THURMAN LEE (Squatty) C-BR-TR. B. 6/7/47, Akron, Ohio. 5'11", 188. One of quieter but effective members of New York Yankees is catcher Thurman Munson. Named by Baseball Writers Association of America as Rookie of Year for AL, 1970. Made good with less than 100 games of minor league experience; hit .302 in 132 contests. Work fell off somewhat in 1971—worried about wife's difficult pregnancy. Bounced back in 1972 to play 140 games, hit .280. Fast enough to bat second in Yankee lineup. Good at hitting behind runner.

Frank Robinson, when he saw Munson early in career, said Thurman some day would lead league in hitting. As he went into 1973, Munson had .276 lifetime average in majors for 423 games. his 415 hits included 57 doubles, 13 triples, 24 homers. Scored 190 times, drove in 150 markers.

Munson attended Kent State as did teammate Gene Michael. Was halfback and linebacker in football; won several handball titles; played basketball; All-American in baseball. Signed for Yankees by scout Gene Woodling. Had 71 games at Binghamton, Eastern League, 1968. Hit .301. Divided 1969 between Syracuse and Yankees. Hit .363 in 28 International League games and spent 26 games with parent club, not enough to disqualify him for consideration as rookie in 1970. Selected for 1971 All-Star team in AL when led major league catchers in fielding with .998 record, one error in 615 chances. Again All-Star 1973.

Munson carries nickname "Tug" among teammates. Excellent golfer, shooting in 70s.

MURCER, BOBBY RAY (Okie) OF-BL-TR. B. 5/20/46, Oklahoma City, Okla. 5'11", 180. They compare him with Mickey Mantle. Probably because, like Mickey, comes from Oklahoma; and, like Mickey, was signed to first contract by Scout Tom Greenwade; then too, they gave him Mantle's old locker in Yankee Stadium. Bobby doesn't consider self another Mantle. But is solid performer in same center field where Mantle, Joe DiMaggio, Combs, and other stars have sparkled.

Bobby's best year was 1971 when hit .331 in 146 games. But 1972 was even better in some respects. Hit 33 homers compared to 25 previous season. Drove in 96 runs, two more than in 1971. But average dropped to .292, still very respectable figure in era when pitchers seem to dominate game.

Murcer reportedly received $20,000 bonus to sign with Yankee system in midsummer 1964. Like his idol, Mickey Mantle, Bobby began as shortstop. Tried to become third baseman but did not satisfy. Finally shifted to outfield where seems much more at home.

Bobby, variously called "Lemon" by teammates, and "Okie" at times, played short for Johnson City, Greensboro, and Toledo in early years. spent two years in military service, 1967–68. Had played 33 games with Yanks before that, but got into 152 contests, 1969. Hit .259, with 26 homers, 82 RBI. Full-time outfielder starting 1970, with .251 average, 23 homers, 78 RBI. Then boosted average 80 points, 1971. That summer made All-Star squad, repeated 1972, 73.

Murcer tied major league mark 6/24/70 by hitting home runs in four consecutive appearances at plate during doubleheader.

Attended U. of Oklahoma. Lifetime average at start of 1973 was .279 for 642 games; 659 hits included 103 doubles, 22 triples, 108 homers; 378 runs, 359 RBI.

MURNANE, TIMOTHY HAYES 1B-OF-BL-TR. B. 6/4/52, Bridgeport, Conn. D. 2/13/17, Boston, Mass. 5′9½″, 172. Inventor of bunt. Otherwise omitted in this book since without other claims to fame. Tim was weak hitter in old National Association, NL and Union Association in early days of organized ball, 1870s and 1880s. Boston NL 1876–77.

One day during this period Murnane swung at pitch mightily—but ineffectively. Result was feeble tap that stopped rolling not far from plate. By time pitcher got to ball, Murnane had crossed first base. This set Tim to thinking. Went home, whittled side of bat to flatten it, then began practicing bunt. Soon developed considerable proficiency. Eventually other players followed suit until bunt became important part of team strategy, as it still is today.

Murnane allegedly was good fielder, especially at first base, but had no power as hitter. Hit somewhere around .280 in his two seasons at Boston. Rest of his records confused, unreliable, unimpressive. Remembered solely for his ingenious invention—bunt. Later became Boston sports writer.

MURPHY, JOHN JOSEPH (Grandma) P-BR-TR. B. 7/14/08, New York, N.Y. D. 1/14/70, New York, N.Y. 6′2″, 195. Lefty Gomez helped make Johnny Murphy famous as relief pitcher. Lefty, whose glibness never flagged, exaggerated number of times Murphy saved games for him in relief. When asked how he felt, Gomez often would reply, "It isn't important how I feel. What's important is how Murphy feels." Still, Johnny was terrific relief pitcher for N.Y. Yankees. Won 93 major league games for them, lost 53, saved another hatful. Helped them to seven pennants and six world championships.

Murphy spent one season with Boston Red Sox at end of career, 1947, then had nearly 15 years as director of Sox minor league operations. In winter of 1961 owner Tom Yawkey made wholesale changes in Boston front office and Murphy was one of those who lost out. Johnny soon signed with N.Y. Mets as chief scout in anticipation of their fielding an expansion club in 1962. Became vice president, 1964, and general manager for Mets 12/27/67 after Bing Devine left to return to St. Louis Cardinals. Johnny credited much with bringing Gil Hodges to Mets as manager.

Murphy got nickname because teammates regarded him orderly, fastidious. When Yankee starting pitcher got into jam and John was designated to head for mound, bench would chant, "Here comes Grandma!" Johnny didn't pitch like "Grandma." Cool in crises, with plenty of stuff plus good curve ball; wild enough to put some fear into opposing batsmen. Pitched in 415 games in AL, only 17 of them complete. Saved 107 games, with 3.50 ERA in 1045 innings.

John attended Fordham U.; signed by Paul Krichell for Yankee organization, 1929. Pitched at Albany, St. Paul, and Newark before sticking with parent team, 1934. Came up with 14–10, 10–5, 9–3, 13–4, 8–2 records before suffering losing season, 1939. In 1943 had another fine mark, 12–4.

Murphy felt one of best efforts as relief artist came in sixth game of 1936 WS against N.Y. Giants. Lefty Gomez went into seventh inning with 5–3 lead. Bartell doubled, Terry singled, and when DiMaggio let ball get away from him, Bartell scored, Terry reaching second. Hank Leiber sacrificed Giant manager to third base. Up came three pinch hitters in succession. Murphy walked one of them harmlessly, but got other two to retire side and preserve Yankee lead. That Yanks later scored flock of runs to win game and Series did not diminish fact that if Murphy had allowed Terry to score, it would have been tie ball game.

Johnny 2–0 for 16-1/3 innings of WS pitching; 4 saves, 1.10 ERA.

As player, Murphy one of organizers of Major League Players Association.

MURTAUGH, DANIEL EDWARD Mgr.-2B-BR-TR. B. 10/8/17, Chester, Pa. 5'9", 170. If Danny Murtaugh had not become baseball player and later highly successful manager of Pittsburgh Pirates, probably could have made good living as comedian, possibly on network TV. Rates as fine raconteur with Irish wit, usually on subtle side. Some of best stories come out with Danny himself as goat. Possibly would qualify as most popular major league manager in recent years.

Danny wasn't much of ball player, though did lead NL in stolen bases with 18 in 1941. Lifetime major league average came out .254 for 767 games, mostly with ball clubs headed nowhere, Philadelphia Phillies and Pirates of 1940s. His 661 hits in majors did not distinguish him, nor did 97 doubles, 21 triples, 8 home runs, 263 runs, 218 RBI, 49 stolen bases. By winning pennants for Pittsburgh, 1960 and 1971, gained widespread respect for sagacity and, above all, for patience. Followed up both flag victories by winning world championships. Had to do it the hard way both times.

In 1960, N.Y. Yankees beat Pirates unmercifully in three games by scores of 16–3, 10–0, 12–0. Yanks had team batting average of .338 to Pittsburgh's .256. Yankee pitchers allowed 3.54 ERA, Pirates' hurlers, 7.11. New Yorkers slapped 10 home runs, Buccaneers, four. But Pirates never gave up, and finally won crucial game and WS on Mazeroski's famous ninth-inning home run in seventh contest. Pirates faced powerful Baltimore Orioles in 1971 WS. It looked like walkaway at first, Orioles taking first two games. Pirates refused to quit, however, and won next three. Baltimore evened count in sixth game. Then Steve Blass held Orioles to four hits and one run in seventh game, while Roberto Clemente and Jose Pagan supplied punch for two Pirate markers. After 1971 world championship Murtaugh retired. Was second time Danny left Pirate job voluntarily. Retired to sidelines after 1964 season because of health. Doctors gave him permission to go back to managing as full-time job before 1970 season. In between, took over as interim pilot in 1967, replacing Harry Walker.

Danny started at Cambridge, Md., 1937; later played with St. Louis Cardinal farm clubs at Rochester, Columbus, and Houston before joining Phillies, 1941. Season was well under way, and Murtaugh appeared in just 85 games, but was enough for him to win NL base-stealing honors with 18. With Phillies into 1946 season, though missing all of 1944–45 for military service. Spent most of 1946 with Rochester, then drafted by Boston Braves. Three games for them in 1947, then farmed out to their Milwaukee, American Association, club for 119 games. Recalled and traded to Pirates for 1948. Danny had solid season as keystone guardian, with .290 average in 146 games. Remained with Pirates through 1951. Playing manager at New Orleans, 1952–53; bench manager there in 1954; manager, Charleston, American Association, 1955; coach for Pirates 1956–57; replaced Bobby Bragan as manager 8/3/57. Continued in same role through 1964.

In periods between managing club on field, Murtaugh served Pirate organization as superscout. As Pittsburgh manager, Danny had nine full seasons at helm; one eighth-placer; two sixth-placers; two fourth-placers, one second-placer. First in 1960; first in Eastern Division of NL in both 1970 and 1971; won NL playoffs, 1971. Coach for 1959 and 1971 NL All-Star squads, and managed NL entries, 1961 and 1972. In 1961 two games were played, NL taking one, other ending in tie. National Leaguers won 1972 game, so Murtaugh's last appearance in major league uniform was as winner, just as had been in WS play.

MUSIAL, STANLEY FRANK (The Man) OF-1B-BL-TL. B. 11/21/20, Donora, Pa. 6′, 180. When Stan Musial got 3000th hit, 1958, St. Louis Cardinal players presented plaque that read: "To Stanley Frank Musial, an emblem of esteem from his teammates. An outstanding artist in his profession; possessor of many baseball records; gentleman in every sense of word; adored and worshipped by countless thousands; perfect answer to a manager's prayer; to this, we, the Cardinals, attest with our signatures." Plaque reflected and continues to indicate high regard in which Musial has been held among fans and those more closely connected with baseball. No such plaque would be appropriate for most superstars, but "comparisons are odious."

Stan set or equaled so many baseball records it would be boring to list all. NL MVP 1943, 46, 48. *Sporting News*, 1956, named him Player of Decade. Compiled 3630 hits. Played 3026 big league games, not counting 23 WS contests and 24 All-Star games. Lifetime average of .331. Led NL in hitting seven times. Hit well above .300 in first 16 full seasons in majors. When playing career ended after 1963 season, Stan retained connection with St. Louis Cardinals and for 10 months, 1967, served as general manager. During this period Redbirds won pennant and world championship. This marked first time in major league history that flag and WS had been won in first year any general manager was in charge. Stan resigned because of other business interests and became senior vice president of club.

Experience as general manager just one more incident in charmed life. Son of Polish immigrant. In high school played basketball and pitched baseball. Also could hit. Struck out 17 in 7-inning game. Playing for Donora (Pa.) "Zincs," hit 450-foot grand slammer. Cleveland, Yankees interested, but Cardinals were more persistent, and signed Stan for their minor league organization. First stop, Williamson, West Va., in Mountain States League, 1938. Won six, lost six as southpaw pitcher. Following season, 9–2, but also pinch-hit and played in total of 23 games, hitting .352. Sore arm handicapped him. Spent 1940 season with Daytona Beach, Florida State League, where Dick Kerr, former Chicago White Sox star, managed team for Cardinals. Stan, by this time married, was making $100 monthly salary and wife was expecting. Kerr invited Musials to move into their home. When son born, named Richard, in honor of hospitable manager. Many years later when Stan was earning big money and was well established financially, realized that baseball had not been generous with Dick Kerr and his wife. Secretly bought house for them in Houston, presented it in gratitude for help and friendship through many years. Eventually secret disclosed by newsman—not by Musial.

Although 18–5, there were doubts about how far could go as pitcher. Played outfield when not pitching. Tried to make shoestring catch of fly ball, fell on left shoulder injuring throwing arm. That was 1940. In 1941, during spring training, still tried to pitch. Cardinals came to Columbus, Ga., for exhibition game. Clay Hopper, manager of Redbird farm team in Columbus, used Musial against big leaguers. Terry Moore and Johnny Mize both clobbered him for home runs. Few days later, used against Philadelphia Phillies, another disaster. End of pitching career.

Amazing rise as hard-hitting outfielder began. Before snow fell that same year, Musial was hitting .426 for major league club in 12 games. Graduate of Class D team in spring. Hit .379 in 87 games with Springfield, Western Association, Class C. Moved to Rochester for 54 games in International League, then Class AA, one notch below majors.

Hit .326 there, then reported to Cardinals for dozen games at end of season—all in 1941! Few, if any, have ever moved up so rapidly. Had $100 per month contract in springtime; boosted to $150 at Springfield; $350 at Rochester; $400 at St. Louis. Musial faced Jim Tobin of Boston Braves and popped out first time up. Next time at bat lined double to right center for first big league hit—and drove in two runs. Later singled in same game, and was on way to those 3630 hits and 1951 RBI. Few days later Stan hit first major league homer off Rip Sewell of Pittsburgh Pirates. Reminiscing, when Musial reminded Terry Moore and Johnny Mize he was same lefthanded pitcher they had victimized with long homers in Columbus, Ga., that spring, they found it hard to believe. In 1942, playing full season, Musial hit .315. Captured first batting title, 1943, with .357 average. Led NL in hits, doubles, and triples. Another batting championship, 1946, after spending previous season in navy. This time also led in hits, runs, doubles, and triples. But peak came in 1948. Hit .376 for best average of career for complete season. Led NL in hitting, hits, runs, doubles, triples, RBI, and came within one of tying for home run lead, with 39. Stan actually hit 40 homers in major league competition that year, but one was "washed out" because rain forced cancellation of game before legal number of innings were played.

Listing more exploits would be repetitious. Got five hits in five swings 9/22/48 despite playing with great pain in left wrist. On that occasion, did not hit single foul or swing at any strikes except the five he hit safely.

Hit five homers in doubleheader, 5/2/54; four homers in four consecutive times at bat, 7/7-8/62. In 1955 All-Star game in Milwaukee, Musial came to bat for NL squad in 12th inning. Yogi Berra was catching for AL. "My feet are killing me," said Yogi, who caught whole game. "Relax," replied Musial, "I'll get you out of here in hurry." Did exactly that. Hit first pitch for home run, giving NL victory by 6–5 score. Played more All-Star games than any other player: 24. When he hung up uniform, besides statistics mentioned, had been to bat 10,972 times. His 3630 hits included 725 major league doubles, 177 triples, 475 homers. In WS play, 1942,43,44,46: 23 games 22 hits in 86 trips, 7 doubles, 1 triple, 1 homer 8 RBI, .256 average.

Besides all his hitting, Stan led league in fielding as outfielder three times. But also recalls one embarrassing game 5/14/44. Misjudged fly ball by Jim Wasdell of Phillies; somehow hit him squarely on top of head, bounded high and away. Two men on base scored.

Musial operates St. Louis restaurant in addition to duties as senior vice president of Cardinals. Also involved in bank and other businesses. Hall of Fame 1969.

MYER, CHARLES SOLOMON (Buddy)   2B-BL-TR. B. 3/16/04, Ellis-ville, Miss. 5'10½", 165. Buddy Myer was bargain for Washington

Senators when they bought him for $25,000; and was bargain when they had to give five players to get him second time. Graduated from Mississippi A. & M., and agreed to go to spring training camp with Cleveland Indians, 1925. Indians figured he needed minor league experience, wanted to farm him out to Dallas. But remuneration wasn't attractive enough, so Myer left camp unsigned, free agent. Signed with New Orleans, proved ability as hitter with .336 average in 99 games as shortstop; attracted bevy of major league scouts. Joe Engel of Senators offered $25,000, and New Orleans club agreed. No sooner had deal been completed than other big league teams offered much more for Myer. But was too late; Washington owned contract. Senators ordered Myer to report promptly, and he was eligible for WS that fall. Bucky Harris, manager of Senators, did not expect to use rookie in series, but Vic Aldridge of Pittsburgh Pirates hit Ossie Bluege in head with pitch and Myer replaced him at third base in three games. Following year Senators made Myer their regular shortstop, replacing Roger Peckinpaugh. Harris, however, wasn't happy with Buddy's fielding; swapped him to Boston Red Sox 5/2/27 for older Emory Rigney. Red Sox used Myer at third base, 1928. Buddy hit .313, led AL in stolen bases. At this point Senators began to regret Harris' hasty trade. They wanted Myer back, but it cost them five players, Milt Gaston, Lisenbee, Reeves, Gillis, and Bigelow to induce Red Sox to let him go, 12/15/28. Senators used Myer at third base—and second base, 1929; after that was their regular keystone guardian for many years, remaining with Washington until he left majors after 1941 season.

Never was much question about Buddy's hitting—led AL with .349 average in 1935 and had lifetime AL average of .303 for 1923 games. Didn't hit for great distance—had 38 homers, six being maximum in any one season. His 2131 hits also included 353 doubles, 130 triples. Stole 156 bases, scored 1174 runs, drove in 850. In two WS, 1925,33: 8 games, .286, 8 for 28, 2 runs, 2 RBI.

MYERS, HENRY HARRISON (Hy) OF-BR-TR. B. 4/27/89, East Liverpool, Ohio. D. 5/1/65, Minerva, Ohio. 5'9½", 175. People who heard orator Branch Rickey may remember one of his favorite stories—about Hy Myers, who joined St. Louis Cardinals after long career with Brooklyn Dodgers. Myers was aging veteran when Cards gave up Jack Fournier to get him. But never-say-die spirit still fired Myers as long as he played, even in exhibition games.

Rickey often told Rotarians, Lions, Optimists, and other audiences about incident that took place in Bradenton, Fla., where Cardinals were training one spring. Myers was playing center field when batsman on visiting club walloped ball over Myers' head. No chance whatever to catch ball, but Hy started chasing as it bounded farther and farther from plate. Looked like certain home run, since there were no fences to stop ball. "You old fool!" Rickey claimed he yelled at Myers from Cardinal bench as he chased ball. But Myers didn't hear him—and continued pursuit. There was one solitary palmetto tree in center field, right in path of ball. Somehow, ball hit palmetto, bounced back into Myers' hands. Hy wheeled, fired ball to relay man who, in turn, came up with perfect throw to home plate, just in time for catcher to tag runner sliding in. Umpire yelled, "You're out!" Rickey repeatedly used story to illustrate thesis that man should never stop trying, regardless of odds against him; that if man always gives best, oftentimes will be rewarded with success even though goal seemed impossible.

Myers made grade with Dodgers, 1914, after experience at Connellsville, Pa.; Rochester, N.Y.; Sioux City, Newark, starting in 1909. Remained with Brooklyn until after 1922 season. With Redbirds into 1925 season, when also appeared briefly with Cincinnati Reds.

Hy, while still with Brooklyn, managed to wangle raise out of club president Ebbets. Story included in sketch on Charles Ebbets in this book. Ingenious.

Myers played 1310 NL games, hit for .281 career average, with 179 two-baggers, 100 triples, 32 homers among 1380 hits. Scored 555 times, drove in 559 runs, and stole 107 bases. In two WS, both with Brooklyn, 1916, 20, had .208 average; 10 hits in 48 trips.

NASH, JAMES EDWIN (Jumbo) P-BR-TR. B. 2/9/45, Hawthorne, Nev. 6'5", 220. Jim Nash broke into AL with 12–1 record with Kansas City A's, 1966; gained *Sporting News* designation as AL Rookie of Year. His .923 winning percentage was best in league that year. Since that time he has had problems, including sore right shoulder in 1972. Entered 1973 campaign with record of 68 major league victories against 64 defeats.

Nash collected his first pro pay from A's organization, 1963; Burlington, Iowa, 1964; Birmingham, 1964; Lewiston, Idaho, 1965; Mobile, 1966. Had 7–4 record with 2.67 ERA in Southern League that year, then moved into AL where he proceeded to improve on both his winning percentage and his ERA with that 12–1 mark and an ERA of 2.06. One more season with Kansas City, 1967, resulted in 12–17 mark; club moved to Oakland, and Nash broke even next two years, 13–13 and 8–8. At this point he was traded to Atlanta Braves for Felipe Alou. Came up with 13–9 and 9–7 records in Georgia metropolis. Then in 1972 Jim had 1–1 mark with Braves before shifting to Philadelphia Phillies. Lost all eight games he was responsible for with Phils. Unconditionally released spring 1973. Had overall ERA of 3.59 for his 1107 innings pitched in majors, 771 strikeouts, 401 walks.

Jim attended U. of Georgia; plans to continue, to get degree in business administration and real estate. Has Georgia real estate license, hopes to earn one in Philadelphia area. With wine and spirits company off-season, also winter 1972–73 worked for Phillies' speakers bureau.

NEHF, ARTHUR NEUKOM P-BL-TL. B. 7/31/92, Terre Haute, Ind.

D. 12/18/60, Phoenix, Ariz. 5'9", 170. Art Nehf would never be compared to Iron Man McGinnity, fellow who used to pitch all those doubleheaders. Yet this slight southpaw, not very tall, once pitched 21-inning game for Boston against Pittsburgh Pirates. Unfortunately lost 2–0, 8/1/18. While not ironman, was fine pitcher with Braves. John McGraw of N.Y. Giants usually coveted stars on other NL clubs, often able to tempt bosses of other clubs with cash and players to get those he wanted. True in case of Nehf, who was traded to Giants 8/17/19.

Nehf was 17–8 for Braves, 1917, then broke even with 15–15 mark in 1918. In season he was traded to Giants, Braves, Boston club, was headed for second-division finish and Nehf had won eight, lost nine, when deal was completed. But with Giants, Artie 9–2. Despite this late-season infusion of good pitching, Giants still unable to catch Cincinnati Reds, and finished second. Slender southpaw won 21 games, lost 12 for McGraw in 1920, but Giants again had to be content to finish second to rival Brooklyn. Nehf won 66 games over next four years, losing 37, and Giants won four consecutive pennants. Was 20–10 in 1921, then 19–13, 13–10, 14–4. Lost first two WS starts against Yankees in 1921, but hardly could be faulted—teammates made one run in 18 innings. In third start, found solution by shutting out Yankees. Giants got only one run in that contest, but it was enough, and it wrapped up world championship for Giants. In 1922 Series Nehf started in opening game, allowed just one earned run in seven innings. Giants won game after Nehf had retired for pinch batsman, so did not get credit for win. Came back fifth game to defeat Yankees, 5–3. Again was Nehf who wrapped up another world championship for Giants. Nehf pitched shutout victory over Yanks in third game of 1923 WS, 1–0, but in sixth and final game was driven to cover in eighth inning after holding Yankees to one run in first seven rounds. So Yankees wrapped up their first world championship, four games to two. Artie was matched against Walter Johnson in first game of 1924 WS in Washington. Nehf came out winner by 4–3 score in 12 innings. But lost sixth game of series to Tom Zachary by 2–1 score. Had one more WS experience, while with Chicago Cubs, 1929, but did not figure in any decision. Overall, Nehf took part in 12 WS games, pitched 79 innings, won four, lost four, including some heartbreakers, and had 2.16 ERA. Walked 32, fanned 28, allowing 19 earned runs and 50 hits.

Nehf 11–9 for 1925 Giants. Sold down river to Cincinnati early in 1926, was used infrequently, just 19 innings—0–1. Reds gave him release late in 1927 and he caught on with Chicago Cubs. Had 4–6 record for year. Won 13, lost 7 for Cubs in 1928, then went to Arizona after 1929 season when won eight, lost five.

By this time was suffering from arthritis, and went into real estate business. Overall major league record for 451 games showed 184 wins, 120 losses, with 3.20 ERA. Had exceptional effectiveness in his 17–8 season at Boston in 1917 with 2.16. With 2708 innings pitched, Nehf had 182 complete games, including 30 shutouts. Took part in 12 double plays in 1920, which is equal of best record for any NL pitcher.

Nehf started in 1913 at Kansas City, American Association, and pitched for Sioux City and Terre Haute before joining Braves, 1915.

NELSON, ROGER EUGENE (Spider) P-BR-TR. B. 6/7/44, Altadena, Calif. 6'3", 205. Cedric Tallis gambled at December 1972 baseball meetings when he traded away best pitcher on staff of Kansas City Royals. At least Roger Nelson was best performer in 1972—11 victories, six defeats, two saves and 2.08 ERA. Hard-throwing righthander went to Cincinnati Reds with Richie Scheinblum for Hal McRae and Wayne Simpson. Tallis, executive vice president of Kansas City, had helped build up team with major trades in three previous winters, obtaining fellows like Patek, Mayberry and Otis. Reds, however, also were gambling on Nelson's arm. Shoulder trouble, 1970, confined work with Royals to just four games, during which pitched total of nine innings and allowed 10 runs.

Nelson picked up nickname "Spider" from pass-stealing ability in basketball. Attended Mount San Antonio Junior College in California. Joined Chicago White Sox organization and saw service at Middlesboro, Ky.; Portsmouth, Va.; Sarasota, Tidewater, Evansville, Indianapolis, and Rochester in minors, from 1963 through 1968. Pitched seven innings for White Sox, 1967, then sent out again.

While working for Sarasota, 1964, retired 28 consecutive batters from second to 11th inning of game against Daytona Beach. Roger pitched first 14 innings, struck out 22. Game ultimately went to Daytona Beach by 2–1 score in 17 innings.

Nelson shifted to Baltimore Orioles, 1968; won four, lost three. Then selected by Kansas City Royals in expansion draft as first choice. Had 7–13 record, 1969, then shoulder problems, 1970. Sent to Omaha, 1971, and any major league club could have bought him for $25,000 draft price at end of year. But nobody took him, and he returned to Kansas City.

Overall major league record as 1973 began showed 22 wins, 26 losses, with 2.98 ERA. Fanned 308, walked 127 in 487 innings. Pitched six shutouts in 1972.

NETTLES, GRAIG 3B-BL-TR. B. 8/20/44, San Diego, Calif. 6', 180. When New York Yankees obtained Graig Nettles from Cleveland Indians during baseball winter meetings late in 1972, they were investing in power hitter and one of better-fielding third basemen in AL. Graig hit 23 homers for Indians, 1970, and 28 in 1971. Dropped off to 17 in 1972. Brought to Yankees record of 586 AL games, hitting .246, with 494 safeties including 71 doubles, five triples, 83 four-baggers.

Nettles attended San Diego State College on basketball scholarship. Won all sorts of honors as baseball player, however, in collegiate and semipro days. Helped Alaska Goldpanners in Fairbanks to state semipro titles, 1964,65 and to runner-up position in National Baseball Congress Tournament in Wichita. Cast lot with Minnesota Twins organization, 1966, at Wisconsin Rapids. Though hitting just .269, led Midwest League in homers with 28. Tied for homer leadership of Southern Association, 1967, with 19, but hit just .232 for Charlotte. Three games with Twins that same year. Played at Denver, Pacific Coast League, 1968; got average up to .297, hit 22 homers, drove in 83 runs, and tied for league leadership in triples with 12. Also 22 games with Twins that season. Spent all of 1969 with Twins—played 96 games, hit .222, with seven homers. Traded to Cleveland 12/12/69. Hit .235 and .261 in first two years with Indians, and .253 in 1972. During 1971 Nettles set two major league records for third basemen by making 412 assists and most double plays, 54. Also led circuit in putouts at hot corner with 159.

Graig something of streak hitter. His 19-game hitting streak in 1971 was best in AL; but also went 0-for-16 and 4-for-50 in earlier games. Elder brother of Jim Nettles, outfielder for Twins, 1971–72.

NEUN, JOHN HENRY 1B-BLR-TL. B. 10/28/1900, Baltimore, Md. 5'10½", 175. Johnny Neun, scout for California Angels in 1972, also managed New York Yankees briefly, as well as Cincinnati Reds little less than two seasons. But record books turn spotlight on his performance as part-time first baseman with Detroit Tigers in 1927, day after Memorial Day. Johnny pulled unassisted triple play—and it was more than 40 years before another major leaguer was able to do it again (Ron Hansen of Washington vs. Cleveland 7/30/68).

Oddly, Neun's unassisted triple play came *one* day after Jimmy Cooney, playing shortstop for Chicago Cubs, had pulled one against Pittsburgh Pirates. Tigers were playing in Detroit on eventful occasion; was ninth inning and they led by 1–0. Things didn't look too promising when first two Cleveland Indians reached base with nobody out. Rip Collins was pitching for Detroit. Glenn Myatt, Cleveland catcher, was base runner on second; Charlie Jamieson, outfielder, on first. Homer Summa, lefthanded hitter, was at plate with orders to bunt runners along to put them in scoring position. Summa bunted one and it rolled foul. Tried again. Another foul. Whaled away against next pitch. Result was line drive directly at Neun. Johnny didn't have to move. Both runners had been off with crack of bat. No trick to tag Jamieson before could get very far on return trip to first base. "I looked over toward second base but there was no sign of Myatt," said Neun later. "He had had good-sized lead and was just about rounding third base when I touched Jamieson. He knew it was hopeless to try to get back. I just trotted over to second base and tagged bag for third out—ending ball game and giving us our 1–0 victory."

Neun never made it big as major leaguer. Most games he ever played was 97 in 1926. Was with Detroit Tigers four seasons, 1925–28. Missed most of last season with appendix trouble, and spent 1929 in minors with Toledo and Baltimore, then in International League. Back in majors with Boston Braves, 1930–31. Besides famous triple play, Neun stole five bases in one game against N.Y. Yankees, 1927. Another occasion, stole home twice during double-header against Washington, once in each game. But was not power hitter; just two homers during big league career, both in 1930 while with Boston. Had .289 lifetime average with 273 hits in 432 games, including 42 doubles, 17 triples. Stole 41 bases, 22 in 1927.

In minors, Neun got start at Martinsburg in Blue Ridge League, 1920–21; Birmingham, 1922–23; St. Paul, 1924. In latter season, .353 average with 55 stolen bases helped gain promotion to Tigers. After leaving majors, Johnny played first base for Newark Bears, 1932–33, and following year became player-coach for same club.

Manager of Yankees' farm club, Akron, Ohio, 1935, doubling as own general manager. Piloted Norfolk club to two pennants, 1936–37, and Yankees promoted him to boss of Newark, 1938–41. Then switched to Yankees' team at Kansas City, 1942–43, and Joe McCarthy then selected him to become coach for parent team in New York, 1944, job he held until 9/13/46 when became interim manager of Yankees. Following winter Warren Giles, then president of Cincinnati Reds, named him manager for 1947. Team won 73, lost 81 and finished fifth. In 1948 was replaced by Bucky Walters after Reds had won 44, losing 56. Team wound up in seventh place.

Neun, besides baseball activities, for many years was soccer editor on staff of Baltimore Sun in winter months and worked as basketball official.

NEWCOMBE, DONALD (Newk) P-BL-TR. B. 6/14/26, Madison, N.J. 6'4", 220. When Branch Rickey, then president of Brooklyn Dodgers, offered contract to Don Newcombe, Don thought would be pitching for all-Negro team. That was before Jackie Robinson broke color line by playing for Brooklyn farm team, Montreal. Actually, Robinson joined Montreal, 1946, and Newcombe joined Dodger farm club at Nashua, N.H., in New England League. Battery mate there was Roy Campanella, another black.

Two highly successful seasons at Nashua, then fine season at Montreal. Five games with Montreal, 1949, then Don was member of parent Dodgers. Chalked up 17–8 mark in rookie year in majors. White players didn't make it any easier for Newcombe than they had for Jackie

Robinson, who reached NL two seasons ahead of Don. Phillies one day were giving Newcombe rugged time verbally. Finally, Del Ennis, Philly first baseman, batsman at time, went to own dugout and told teammates: "Shut up! I'm the guy who has to stand up there when he's throwing. If you have anything to say to him, do it from the batter's box!"

Newcombe's performance, 1949, won him rookie of year award for NL. Came back with 19–11 season, 1950, and 20–9 in 1951. Military service 1952–53. Then 9–8 in 1954. Another 20-game victory season, 1955, against five losses, then up to 27 wins in 1956, dropping seven. Downhill after that. Dodgers moved to Los Angeles 1958 and Newcombe lost six games, won none, before going to Cincinnati. Had 7–7 record with Reds. Came back with 13–8 record for Cincinnati, 1959. Final season in majors, 1960, won six, lost nine, dividing time between Reds and Cleveland.

Career major league totals: 149 wins, 90 defeats, with 3.56 ERA. Don unsuccessful in WS, losing two, 1949, one each in 1955 and 1956. Had ERA of 8.59 in WS, pitching 22 innings.

Newcombe good hitter for pitcher; often used as pinch hitter. Had 238 hits in majors, 33 doubles, 3 triples, 15 homers 7 in 1955, and wound up with .271 average in 452 games.

Before joining Brooklyn organization, Newcombe pitched for Newark Eagles, black team. While in majors, Don found it necessary to go to hypnotist to cure fear of flying. After retirement from baseball, ran liquor store in Newark.

NEWHOUSER, HAROLD (Hal)   P-BL-TL. B. 5/20/21, Detroit, Mich.

6'2", 180. Hal Newhouser came from poor family, so when Detroit Tiger scout Wish Egan, accompanied by Del Baker, club manager, offered him $500 in cash plus $150 monthly salary, Hal and father jumped at it. Egan doled out five $100-bills to father, who handed one to Hal, still 17 years old. Little later Cy Slapnicka and Bob Feller drove up in $4000 new car and held out certified check for $15,000 to Newhouser father and son. Slapnicka was general manager for Cleveland, Feller then young pitching star for Indians. Sadly, Newhousers said they had already signed with Tigers. Hal, however, eventually made big money for those days, reaching $65,000 salary, 1945, and is believed to have made close to half-million dollars during baseball career.

Tigers farmed Newhouser out, 1939, to Alexandria in Evangeline League, and Beaumont, Texas League. Before year was out was with parent club for one game, then stuck with Tigers for 14 full seasons. Won MVP award 1944, when won 29, lost nine, with 2.22 ERA; and won it again, 1945, with 25–9 record and 1.81 ERA. Newhouser came up with third 20-game season in 1946, taking 26 decisions, dropping nine. Then 17–17 and 21–12, 18–11, and 15–13. Broke even next two seasons. In

1953 appeared in just seven games, won none, lost one, and drew unconditional release. Signed by Cleveland for 1954, Newhouser won seven, lost two. Pitched just two innings in 1955 and drew release in May. Major league totals showed 207 victories, 150 defeats, with ERA of 3.05. In 2993 innings walked 1249 and fanned 1796.

Hal won two games in WS of 1945, losing one. His second victory came in crucial seventh contest against Chicago Cubs, giving Tigers world championship. Also worked part of an inning in 1954 WS with Cleveland. In 20-2/3 innings, 6.53 ERA, 2–1, 5 walks, 22 strikeouts.

After retirement from pitching, Newhouser became vice president of bank in Pontiac, Mich., and scouted for Baltimore (1956–61) and Cleveland (1961–64). Signed Dean Chance for Orioles for $30,000 bonus, but Orioles let him go to Los Angeles Angels in expansion draft.

NEWSOM, LOUIS NORMAN (Buck; Bobo) P-BLR-TR. B. 8/11/07, Hartsville, S.C. D. 12/7/62, Orlando, Fla. 6'2¾", 205. Colorful, loquacious gypsy pitcher had five different tours with Washington Senators, three with St. Louis Browns, and two each with Brooklyn Dodgers and Philadelphia Athletics. Raconteur whose stories sometimes resembled truth. When fact-minded listeners suggested there might be inaccuracies in tales, Newsom would ask, "Who are you going to believe, Bobo, me or the record book?" Facts about Newsom are colorful enough not to need embellishment. Pitched with at least 18 clubs in organized baseball in period 1928–53. Won 211 major league games, lost 222, and had 3.99 ERA in 3758 innings. Walked 1732, struck out 2082. Might easily have had better record if he hadn't landed with as many second-division clubs.

First major league club was Brooklyn, 1929. Bounced around, including brief spell with Chicago Cubs, 1932. Won 30 games for Los Angeles, Pacific Coast League, 1933. Next travels put him in Brownie, Senator, and Red Sox uniforms. In 1938 won 20 games for Browns, who finished seventh. Divided 1939 between Browns and Detroit, again winning 20, then had 21-game season for Tigers, 1940. Rest of major league records were not impressive but came up on rosters of Senators again and again, Philadelphia AL, N.Y. Giants, N.Y. Yankees.

While with Browns 9/18/34 Bobo pitched nine hitless innings against Boston, only to lose in 10th, when he permitted one safe blow. Four different seasons was biggest loser in AL.

Newsom wouldn't tie own shoestrings on day was pitching. Usually managed to get clubhouse boy or teammate to tie them. Battled various managers—Hornsby in St. Louis, Harris in Washington, Durocher in Brooklyn—words only, however. Got mad at Clark Griffith because Griff wouldn't give him money received when Yankees bought him on waivers, 1947.

Talkativeness worked with Connie Mack. Convinced old gentleman he ought to have unconditional release 6/3/46. Got away from cellar ball club headed nowhere. Two days later convinced Clark Griffith he could help Senators, to tune of $22,000 salary, big raise over what he was getting with Athletics. Newsom's peak came when Tigers won pennant, 1940, his best season. Won 21 games, lost five. Won first game of WS over Paul Derringer of Cincinnati Reds by 7–2 score. Bobo's father saw victory, but next morning died unexpectedly. Newsom blanked Cincinnati in next start, but went down to defeat in seventh and crucial game by 2–1 score. Following spring Newsom reportedly was highest-paid pitcher in majors. Arrived in training camp with horn on car that blared "Hold that Tiger!" Car also had neon sign on it: "Bobo." Once while pitching for Browns, Earl Averill of Indians drove terrific smash off Bobo's knee in third inning. Newsom hobbled to ball, threw out runner. Finished game, won it 5–4. X rays taken afterward showed kneecap shattered. Out of action, wearing cast for five weeks. One opening day while with Senators, pitched with Franklin Delano Roosevelt in stands. Opposing hitter bunted, and Bobo must have been smiling at President. In any case, paid no attention to play. Third baseman Ossie Bluege picked up ball, fired to first base. Ball hit Newsom in back of head. He staggered, but continued on mound, pitching shutout.

After 1953 spell with Athletics, Newsom turned to sports broadcasting in St. Louis and elsewhere. Besides 1940 WS experience, was used in 1947 classic while with Yankees. Overall WS figures: 2–2, 2.86 ERA.

NICHOLS, CHARLES AUGUSTUS (Kid) P-BR-TR. B. 9/14/69, Madison, Wis. D. 4/11/53, Kansas City, Mo. 5'10½", 145. You don't hear name of Kid Nichols when baseball people talk about great pitchers of all time. Instead, you listen to exploits of Cy Young, Christy Mathewson, Walter Johnson, Dizzy Dean et al. But Nichols had to be terrific. Any man who wins 30 games or more for seven consecutive seasons must have had pitching skills. No wonder elected to Hall of Fame 1949, somewhat belatedly.

Nichols won 360 ball games in majors. Who has done better? Only six others, Cy Young, Johnson, Mathewson, Grover Alexander, Warren Spahn, and James Galvin. Only four men have hurled more complete games, and nobody has ever won 30 games in seven consecutive seasons but Nichols.

Nichols played at Kansas City, Memphis, and Omaha, 1887–89, then moved into NL at Boston, 1890. Won only 27 that year as rookie, lost 19. Then began skein of 30-victory seasons, reaching 35 wins, 1892. In 1898, although his winning games led league, had to be content with only 29, while losing 12. Dropped down to 21–17 in 1899. After 18–15 record in 1901, Kid went to Western League as player manager for two seasons at Kansas City. Back in majors with St. Louis Cardinals, 1904 and chalked up 21 wins, against 13 losses. Also managed Cardinals that year, but club finished fifth. In 1905 again essayed role of player-manager but was removed during season, winding up as pitcher with Philadelphia NL. Had 11–11 mark for year. Then bowed out after pitching in four games with Phils, 1906, losing one, winning none.

Nichols took part in 582 big league contests, had 530 complete games. In 5067 innings fanned 1866, walked 1245 and had 48 shutouts. Against those 360 victories were 202 losses. ERA statistics were not kept in those days, but Kid must have been effective.

NIEKRO, JOSEPH FRANKLIN   P-BR-TR. B. 11/7/44, Martins Ferry, Ohio. 6'1", 190. Younger brother of Phil Niekro, Atlanta Braves. Joe, like Phil, was stellar baseball and basketball player during high school days. Attended West Liberty State College in W. Va. before signing with Chicago Cubs, 1966. Got less than one full season of experience in minors, with Treasure Valley, Idaho, in Pioneer League; Quincy, Ill., in Midwest circuit, and Dallas–Fort Worth in Texas League. Following spring Cubs took him to training camp, but was not on their roster. Showed enough promise to stick with parent team; won 10, lost seven. Following year upped victory total to 14, dropping 10 games. But Cubs traded him to San Diego NL 4/24/69. That year record was 8–18. Detroit then got him in deal 12/4/69, and Niekro had 12–13 record for Tigers in 1970. Following season was 6–7. Billy Martin, Detroit manager, seemed to lose confidence in Joe during 1972 season, and midsummer was optioned to Tigers' International League farm at Toledo. Niekro, on 7/16/72 drove to Toledo, signed contract, and less than one hour later was starting pitcher in nightcap of doubleheader. All he did was pitch seven-inning perfect game against Tidewater. Recalled by Tigers later, Joe wound up 1972 with three wins, two losses, one save. So was ready for 1973 with major league record of 53 wins, 57 losses, with 3.94 ERA for 950 innings.

Niekro throws pretty fair fast ball, slider, and now has knuckler, although doesn't throw it as often as brother Phil.

NIEKRO, PHILIP HENRY   P-BR-TR. B. 4/1/39, Blaine, Ohio. 6'1", 180. It was Niekro vs. Niekro when Atlanta Braves opposed Chicago Cubs 7/4/67—first time any brothers pitched against each other in NL game. Phil, with Braves, emerged victor over Joe, with Cubs. Phil went entire distance while younger brother was shelled from mound after three innings. Final score, Atlanta 8, Chicago 3. Papa Niekro, former coal miner and ex-pitcher for semipro clubs, sat in box seat behind home plate, equidistant from each dugout. In later meetings Joe won couple of decisions, Phil another one. So when Joe left NL to pitch for Detroit

Tigers after 1969 season, brothers stood 2–2.

Phil specializes in knuckle ball; has excellent control. His knuckler has quite an arch as it travels from mound to plate, rising 10 or 15 feet above ground. This, however, is not as high as Rip Sewell's famous blooper pitch, which rose as high as 25 feet en route to home plate.

Niekro was winner as high school pitcher. Suffered only loss when Bill Mazeroski, later with Pittsburgh Pirates, hit homer off his delivery. Also good enough in basketball that U. of Detroit and U. of West Virginia both offered athletic scholarships. But signed with Braves for $500 bonus.

From 1959 to 1966 Phil pitched in places like Wellsville, N. Y.; McCook, Nebr.; Louisville, Austin, Denver, and Richmond, with occasional spells with Braves, first in Milwaukee and then in Atlanta; also served time in military, 1963. In first full season with Atlanta, 1967, won 11, lost nine, but led majors in effectiveness with 1.87 ERA. Had 14–12 season in 1968; tied for major league lead that year by picking eight runners off base. Then had highly successful record, 1969, with 23 wins, 13 losses; beat Cincinnati Reds six times. With bit of luck might have won 25 that year, as lost 8–0 and 5–0 leads through rainouts.

Appendectomy prior to spring training, 1970, then had 12–18 record. Following year it was 15–14, then 16–12 in 1972. One of Phil's achievements was victory over Steve Carlton by 2–1 score in 11 innings 8/21/72. Steve had 15 consecutive victories and was hoping to extend winning streak. Crowd of 41,212 watched pitching duel. Niekro said 95% of pitches were knucklers. Best effort, no-hitter vs. San Diego, 8/6/73.

Phil's 1972 performances brought lifetime record to 97 wins, 84 losses, with 2.95 ERA. Had taken part in 316 major league games; pitched 1669 innings, allowed 404 walks, but struck out 1041.

For past several winters Phil has been active in helping raise funds for March of Dimes campaigns.

NOLAN, GARY LYNN P-BR-TR. B. 5/27/48, Herlong, Calif. 6'3", 190. Gary Nolan had fine season, 1972, helping Cincinnati Reds win pennant. Won 15 games, lost five, and 1.99 ERA was second to Steve Carlton's 1.98 among NL pitchers hurling at least 160 innings. But Gary couldn't cope with Gene Tenace in first game of WS. Oakland catcher hit two of Nolan's pitches over fence for home runs. Drives were good for three runs, enough to win ball game by 3–2 score. Gary pitched well in sixth game of Series after reporting shoulder ailment. However, was removed from game after 4-2/3 innings. Cincinnati won that one by 8–1 score but Ross Grimsley received credit for victory.

Nolan, just 25 in 1973, has been dean of Reds' pitching staff for quite some time. Received bonus estimated at $65,000 to sign with club, 1966. Made road trip with Reds, then pitched in 12 games for Sioux Falls,

Northern League. Won seven, lost three. Following spring, less than one year out of high school, Nolan made ball club. Not only made grade, but won 14 games, losing eight, with 2.58 ERA. Struck out 206 men in 227 innings with dazzling fast ball.

Night game in 1967 indelibly etched in Nolan's memory. Reds in seventh inning leading San Francisco Giants 3–0; two men on base, Willie Mays at plate. Gary fanned Mays for fourth consecutive time that evening. Another story with Willie McCovey. Giant first baseman got hold of youngster's offering, drove it over bleacher wall in right field, tying score. Nolan then struck out Jim Hart, 15th such victim. Nolan, 19, walked from mound after those seven innings, brokenhearted. It was enough to make strong man cry. And he did. But didn't quit. Not even when it looked like career was in danger because of sore arm. Following season Gary able to pitch less frequently. Arm troubles plus experience taught that he needed something more than fast ball, however sizzling. Developed fine change of pace and varying speeds on other deliveries. But only after pitching couple of games for Tampa in Florida State League, and having 9–4 mark for Reds, 1968. Still bothered by arm trouble, 1969, pitched seven games at Indianapolis, American Association. With Reds, broke even, 8–8. Came back strong, 1970, with 18–7 mark, helping team to NL flag. Then an off-season, 1971, winning 12, losing 15. Nolan, however, felt was better pitcher in 1971 than previous season. Lost six one-run decisions. In one five-game losing streak, Reds scored only three runs. Once was victim of no-hitter thrown by Ken Holtzman, then with Chicago Cubs. Another occasion, permitted just one hit, but that was home run that beat him 2–1.

Nolan went into 1973 season boasting 76 victories against 47 defeats in NL. Had 2.83 ERA for 1158 innings in majors. Fanned 817, walked 336. Among games were 33 complete ones, 12 shutouts.

In 1972, WS performance added up to 3.38 ERA in 10-2/3 innings; in 1970 WS lost opening game to Baltimore by 4–3 score. His ERA for that classic was 7.71 in 9-1/3 innings pitched, since he also relieved in fourth game, without success. No victory, one defeat.

NORMAN, FREDDIE HUBERT P-BLR-TL. B. 8/20/42, San Antonio, Tex. 5'8", 160. Fred Norman won nine games for San Diego Padres, 1972, but it was struggle. Had to pitch six shutouts for ball club that ended up last in Western Division of NL. But was even rougher struggle for Norman in 1971 when could negotiate just three wins against dozen losses. Five of losses that year were by one-run margin.

Norman has been around in pro baseball since 1961. His catalogue of stops include Shreveport, Birmingham, Binghamton, Salt Lake City, Fort Worth, Dallas, Tulsa, Spokane, Albuquerque; Lewiston, Idaho; and Wenatchee, Wash. With Kansas City AL, 1962–63 for brief periods;

Chicago NL, 1964, 66, 67 for parts of three seasons; divided 1970 between Los Angeles Dodgers and St. Louis Cardinals; St. Louis and San Diego, 1971. Then with Padres all of 1972.

By this time Fred's overall record was not statistically impressive—14 victories, 28 defeats with 4.03 ERA. But most of 453 innings pitched in majors were for rather hapless aggregations whose fielding and hitting did not help moundsmen very much.

Norman remembers day he won first 1971 victory. It was July 25—and was achieved against hard-hitting Pittsburgh Pirates by 2–1 score. That day, sent Willie Stargell down on strikes four consecutive trips to plate.

NORTHEY, RONALD JAMES OF-BL-TR. B. 4/26/20, Mahanoy City, Pa. D. 4/16/71, Pittsburgh, Pa. 5'10½", 195. Ron Northey played outfield for Philadelphia Phillies in his early years in majors, but later concentrated on pinch hitting, doing so quite successfully for several clubs. Ron hit .276 as emergency batsman; slapped nine home runs in pinch, three with bases loaded. In all, when career ended, could look back on eight grand slammers, five while playing regularly.

Northey started pro ball at Williamsport, Eastern League, 1939. Moved to Federalsburg in Eastern Shore League same year, then back to Williamsport for 1940–41. Joined Phillies, 1942, hit .251 with five homers in 127 games, 31 RBI. Following year boosted homer total to 16, with .278 average. Improved further, to 22 homers, 104 RBI, and .288 average in 1944. Spent 1945 in army, returning to Phils following year. Traded to St. Louis NL, 5/3/47, for Harry Walker, Fred Schmidt, and cash. Involved in another trade where Harry Walker, now Cardinal batting coach, figured. Walker went from Phils to Cincinnati, and Cardinals reacquired him 12/14/49. This time Northey sent to Cincinnati in deal. Reds then traded him to Chicago Cubs 6/7/50 for Bob Scheffing, now general manager of N.Y. Mets. Northey dropped out of majors, 1951, but was back with Cubs, 1952, for one game. Came back to majors, 1955–57, with Chicago White Sox; and closed big league career with Phillies, 1957, moving over from Chicago.

Ron had 15 hits in 39 trips as pinch hitter, 1956, and appeared in only four games as outfielder. In 1948, pinch batting was tops, 11 hits in 25 trips, but also played 67 games in field that year.

Overall major league record: .276 in 1084 games, 874 hits, 172 doubles, 28 triples, 108 homers, 385 runs, 513 RBI.

NORTHRUP, JAMES THOMAS OF-BL-TR. B. 11/24/39, Breckenridge, Mich. 6'2", 205. Jim Northrup cultivated habit of hitting grand slam home runs, 1968. Hit four during regular season, two in consecutive times at bat 6/24. This tied major league record. Had hit three grand slammers earlier in career. Then, during WS that fall, hit another grand slammer off Larry Jaster of St. Louis Cardinals in third inning of sixth game.

Going into 1973 Northrup had hit 122 homers for Tigers, including eight grand slammers besides that 1968 WS blow, and had .266 career average in majors, dating to 1964 when he played five games for Detroit. Prior to that had been with Duluth, Decatur, Knoxville, and Syracuse, starting in 1961.

Jim played various sports at Alma College in Michigan, including football, as quarterback. Chicago Bears and New York Titans offered pro contracts. But signed with Detroit organization for reported $20,000 bonus, 1960. Had problems during first full year with Tigers. Hit just .205 in 80 games, with two homers; struck out 50 times, almost every fourth time went to plate. Following year began to get range with .265 mark, 16 homers, 58 RBI. Had 21 homers, 90 RBI, and .264 average in 1968. Best hitting average came in 1969—.295, with 25 homers, one of them terrific clout over right field roof at Tiger Stadium. Also had six hits in 13-inning game 8/28/69.

Besides his homers, during AL career Northrup, at start of 1973, had 178 doubles, 34 triples among 971 hits, with 475 runs scored, 484 RBI. His solitary WS was 1968 when had .250 mark for seven games, 7 for 28, 2 homers, 8 RBI.

NOVIKOFF, LOUIS ALEXANDER (Mad Russian) OF-BR-TR. B. 10/12/15, Glendale, Ariz. D. 9/30/70, Los Angeles, Calif. 5'10'', 185. Lou Novikoff made Softball Hall of Fame but nobody ever suggested he be candidate for baseball Hall of Fame after he played with Chicago Cubs in early 1940s. Nevertheless, when Cubs brought him up from minors, was touted as "another Babe Ruth." Had led III League in batting, hits, triples, and RBI in 1938; had led Pacific Coast League in batting, runs, homers, and RBI in 1940; and had romped off with batting championship for American Association, 1941.

Mad Russian managed to stick in majors for total of 356 games, most with Cubs, 17 with Philadelphia Phillies. Hit .282, had 15 homers, 10 triples, 45 doubles among 305 hits. Might have stuck around longer but for his fielding. While playing for Charlie Grimm at Milwaukee, Charlie told him were two ways for him to field ball that came in his direction: fall down in front of ball or simply wait until it stops rolling. In either case, pick up ball and throw it to third base so batter can't stretch it to triple. Lou explained why had fielding problems in Chicago: "I can't play in Wrigley Field because left field foul line isn't straight like it is in other parks. It's crooked."

Grimm also claims this happened in Milwaukee: "From our dugout we couldn't see left field corner of ball park. Lou was playing left and ball was hit out there. He was gone so long that I got off bench and went out to see what happened. Finally I see Lou coming out from behind concession stand with hot dog in one hand, coke in other—but no ball."

Novikoff was softball pitcher—and hitter—before taking up pro baseball at Ponca City, Okla., 1937; played at Moline, Ill.; Tulsa; Los Angeles, then in PCL; Milwaukee, American Association.

With Cubs for 62 games, 1941, hit .241; in 1942 hit even .300 for 128 contests; it was .279 in 78 games, 1943; and .281 for 71 games following season. In 17 games with Phillies, 1946, hit .304. Served in military, 1945. With his later major league play, Novikoff had spells with Seattle, PCL 1946–48; Newark, 1948–49; Houston, Texas League, 1949; Yakima and Victoria, 1950, both in Western International League.

Once, while playing at Shreveport in Texas League, Lou did bit of showboating. Art Passarella was plate umpire. "Call first two pitches strikes," instructed Novikoff. Passarella did so, while crowd booed. Lou stepped from batter's box, dusted palms, pointed to left field fence. Stepped back to plate while crowd booed louder than ever. Lou swung— and ball disappeared over left field wall for tremendous home run.

Jimmie Dykes, then manager of Chicago White Sox, one day while his team was playing Cubs in exhibition game, yelled at Novikoff, "Say, you clumsy Russian, if I couldn't hit or field any better than you I'd be mad too."

NUXHALL, JOSEPH HENRY   P-BL-TL. B. 7/30/28, Hamilton, Ohio. 6'3", 235. Joe Nuxhall, now sportscaster for Cincinnati Reds, walked on mound and pitched two-thirds of inning for Reds 6/10/44. Thereby became youngest player ever to participate in major league ball game. Was 15 years old plus ten months and 11 days. Joe must have been nervous. At least he was wild—walked five batsmen, allowed two hits, and was responsible for five runs. Then went to minors and it was 1952 before he appeared in another big league game. Joe eventually won 135 games, lost 117 in majors, most of them with Cincinnati. Over 16-season period pitched 2302-2/3 innings and had 3.90 ERA. His strikeouts far exceeded walks—1372 to 776. Of his 526 games, started 287 and completed 83. Twenty were shutouts. Had unusual experience of striking out four batters in one inning 8/11/59.

Nuxhall bounced around from Birmingham to Syracuse; Lima, Ohio; Muncie; Tulsa; Columbia, S.C.; and Charleston, W. Va., before returning to Reds. In 1954 had 12–5 season, and then 17–12 following year. Effectiveness fell off after that until 1960 season when won just one game while losing eight. Shifted to Kansas City AL 1961, won five, lost eight. In 1962 Joe trained with Baltimore Orioles in spring, but did not stick; caught on with Los Angeles AL briefly, then signed with San Diego, Cincinnati farm then, 5/19/62. Excellent comeback, 9–2; again brought up to Reds, in July—5–0, saved another in relief, and had 2.45 ERA, best of major league career. Continued good work into 1963 with 15–8 season, 2.61 ERA, and saved two games in relief. His 1964 performance was so-so, but won eleven, lost four in 1965. Won six, lost eight in 1966, and, with arm trouble, hung up spikes as active competitor. NL All-Star squads 1955, 56.

O'CONNELL, DANIEL FRANCIS Inf.-BR-TR. B. 1/21/27, Paterson, N.J. D. 10-2-69, Clifton, N.J. 6′, 180. Danny O'Connell met death in automobile accident seven years after playing last major league games with Washington Senators. Got start with Pittsburgh Pirates, 1950 after apprenticeship at Bloomingdale, N.J.; Three Rivers, Quebec; Greenville, S.C.; St. Paul, and Indianapolis during period 1946–50. Played 79 games with Pirates, 1950, then spent couple of seasons in military service. Returned to Pirates, 1953; hit .294 in 149 games; used at second and third bases. Traded to Milwaukee NL 12/26/53, remaining with Braves until midseason, 1957, when landed with New York Giants. Following year they were San Francisco Giants and Danny remained with them until 1959. O'Connell was with Tacoma, Pacific Coast League, 1960, hit .312 in 143 games, and returned to majors for 1961–62, this time with Washington.

Danny's best season at bat was 1953, first full season with Pirates. Maximum home run production was eight, in 1950, and again in 1957 when he divided efforts between Braves and Giants. Wound up with .260 average for 1143 games in majors.

O'CONNELL, JAMES JOSEPH OF-1B-BL-TR. B. 2/11/01, Sacramento, Calif. 6′1″, 175. Jimmy O'Connell had makings of greatness as major league player but brief career ended tragically. Joined San Francisco Seals in Pacific Coast League, 1920; hit .262 as 19-year-old youngster in 102 games. Following year boosted hitting up to .337 in 170 contests, and New York Giants forked out $75,000 for his contract.

Figured he needed one more year of seasoning so was left with Seals through 1922. That time he hit .335 in 187 games, stole 39 bases. John McGraw used him in 87 games, 1923; he hit .250. Following season took part in 52 games, hit .317. Then, with Giants in thick of fight for another pennant, O'Connell approached Heinie Sand of Philadelphia Phillies before game of 9/27/24. Told him it would be worth $500 if he didn't bear down too hard that day. Sand was Phillie shortstop. Sand told his manager, Art Fletcher. Giants defeated Phils by 5–1 score. Sand handled his only three fielding chances without flaw. Giants won pennant, but even if had lost, still could have done no worse than tie for flag. Fletcher advised John Heydler about O'Connell's offer; he in turn advised Judge Landis, commissioner of baseball. Result was that O'Connell was forever barred from baseball. Coach Cozy Dolan of Giants also was barred in same case, while George Kelly, Frank Frisch, and Ross Youngs, also members of McGraw's team, were exonerated. Testimony had cast suspicion that they were somehow involved in deal.

After losing his share of WS money in addition to being barred, Jimmy worked for time as longshoreman in California. Then worked for Richfield Oil Co., 32 years. Retired from job as general storekeeper for Southern California area at age 65. Lives in Bakersfield, Calif.

O'CONNOR, JOHN JOSEPH (Jack)   C-OF-1B-BR-TR. B. 3/3/67, St. Louis, Mo. D. 11/14/37, St. Louis, Mo. 5'10", 170. Jack O'Connor, also known as "Peach Pie" and "Rowdy," was one of rugged old-timers who played for keeps. Starting in 1887, played for Cincinnati and Columbus in old American Association, then considered major league. Cleveland NL 1892–98. St. Louis NL 1899–1900. Pittsburgh 1900–02. Then led several Pirate teammates to AL, jumping to New York Highlanders for 1903 season. When he got thrown out of ball game as catcher, Branch Rickey replaced him, launching Rickey's brief playing career in majors. With Browns in St. Louis, 1904, again 1906–07. Was with Little Rock club later. Browns called him back to fold, 1910, as manager. Gave him two-year contract; but team finished last. Furthermore, was involved in controversial finish of AL batting race between Ty Cobb and Nap Lajoie. Winner of batting championship was to get Chalmers automobile from manufacturer. On last day of season, when Browns were playing double-header with Cleveland Indians, O'Connor stationed rookie third baseman back at grass. Lajoie collected six bunt singles. Cobb still won batting title, but only by fraction of point. Chalmers people, however, awarded both Cobb and Lajoie cars. O'Connor then was dropped by club owner Robert Lee Hedges—but still collected $5000 salary for 1911. Ban Johnson, AL president, exonerated O'Connor.

Jack was fiery competitor, suspended on several occasions. On one of them while with Browns; got into bitter argument with umpire Jack

McNulty. Broke arbiter's jaw. Later was forced to pay $1250 in damages. In later years O'Connor became tavern keeper.

Played 1454 big league games, hit .263, with 1417 hits that included 18 home runs. Stole 219 bases.

O'DAY, HENRY F. (Hank) P-BR-TR. B. 7/8/63, Chicago, Ill. D. 7/2/35, Chicago, Ill. Hank O'Day best remembered as NL umpire, though was major league pitcher before that; also managed Chicago Cubs, 1914, and Cincinnati Reds, 1912. It was O'Day who ruled that Fred Merkle had not touched second base, the "bonehead" play, in famous game between N. Y. Giants and Chicago Cubs, 1908. Merkle, who had been on first base, apparently thought game was over when teammate Al Bridwell drove ball cleanly to center field and McCormick scored from third base. When O'Day ruled it was a force-out, run did not count. Game ended in tie. In playoff later, Cubs won, taking pennant. Controversial play was probably most widely discussed aspect of rules for many years.

O'Day, as pitcher, worked for Toledo club of American Association, then considered major league, 1884; Pittsburgh AA 1885. Washington NL 1886–89. New York NL 1889–90. While there are discrepancies in some of old records, he won at least 70 games, possibly as many as 76. Lost somewhere between 110 and 114. Was at best, however, in last active year as pitcher with New York NL, 1890, when he won 22.

Previous autumn won two games in old WS, first of all–New York Series, between Giants of NL and Brooklyn, American Association. With Hank on mound, Giants won one game 2–1 and another 3–2. Giants were winners, six games to three.

After playing days were over, O'Day became strong umpire who ruled game with iron hand. Gruff, but considered excellent judge of balls and strikes. Except for two seasons as manager, umpired until close of 1927 season, after which served in advisory capacity.

Reds of 1912, whom he bossed, finished fourth in NL; two years later, as manager of Cubs, had another fourth-placer, but preferred umpiring to managing.

ODOM, JOHNNY LEE (Blue Moon) P-BR-TR. B. 5/29/45, Macon, Ga. 6', 185. Blue Moon Odom got shot twice trying to break up burglary 1/6/72. One shot hit neck, other hit right side. Neither proved to be serious. Odom commented, prophetically as it turned out, "Maybe this shooting is what I needed to turn my luck around. Maybe this means I'll have good season this year." Odom, like other members of Oakland A's, did have good season, 1972, climaxed by winning WS. In case of Odom, regained form he had when won 16 games, 1968, and 15 in 1969. Won 15, lost six in 1972, with 2.51 ERA. Was victor in payoff playoff game against Detroit Tigers that gave Oakland its first AL pennant, although Vida Blue finished for him. Continued stingy pitching in WS against Cincinnati. Although was charged with one defeat, his 1.59 ERA was better than any other Oakland pitcher's performance except Locker, who hurled just one-third of inning.

When Odom reported to manager Dick Williams in spring training, 1972, was told he'd have to show pilot he could throw hard. Otherwise there were too many good pitchers on staff for pilot to fuss around with Blue Moon. Odom had 9–8 season, 1970, handicapped by floating bone chip in right elbow. Operation followed that winter, but recovery was slow. In 1971, trying to get by without fast ball, was able to win ten but lost 12 with 4.28 ERA. Then came comeback, 1972.

Odom represented $75,000 investment for Kansas City A's when signed 1964. After getting that bonus, was farmed out to Birmingham; Lewiston, Idaho; Mobile, and Vancouver, spending parts of four seasons with parent club. By time was ready to stick in AL full season, 1968, Kansas City team had moved to Oakland. Problems with wildness, 1968, when led AL in wild pitches with 17. His walks vs. strikeouts record isn't good. As he went into 1973 season had given almost as many free passes, 602, as had struck out batters, 660. At same time, career totals were 74 wins, 57 defeats. In 198 games had pitched only 35 complete contests; worked 1165 innings, allowing 428 earned runs for lifetime ERA of 3.31.

WS record, 1972: 0–1, 11-1/3 innings, 2 earned runs, 6 walks, 13 strikeouts, 1.59 ERA. Loss was 1–0 affair in third game; Billingham of Reds was winner. Odom replaced by pinch hitter after hurling seven frames. AL All-Star squads 1968,69.

O'DOUL, FRANK JOSEPH (Lefty)   OF-BL-TL. B. 3/4/97, San Francisco, Calif. D. 12/7/69, San Francisco, Calif. 6', 180. "Man in the Green Suit." Sore-armed southpaw pitcher who converted self into NL batting champion. Baseball ambassador to Japan. For many years probably best-known San Franciscan. Long-time manager in Pacific Coast League who spurned chances to boss big league clubs. Loved baseball so much he took salary cut of $1000 after winning NL batting championship with .368 average. Set NL record for most hits in single season, 254, later equaled by Bill Terry. Missed tying George Sisler's major league mark of 257. Lefty finished major league career with .349 lifetime average. Darn close to that of Ty Cobb (.367) and Rogers Hornsby (.358). Browning, Orr, Brouthers, and Joe Jackson also finished with better lifetime marks. Among those known to present-day fans, Ted Williams' career mark came closest with .344.

O'Doul signed with San Francisco Seals in PCL, 1917, as pitcher. Farmed to Des Moines, Western League, had 8–6 record. Won 13, lost nine for Seals, 1918. Looked good enough for Yankees to buy him. Spent

1919–20 with Yanks but seldom used; total of 32 games in two seasons. Pitched only 8-2/3 innings and neither won nor lost decision. Rest of time pinch hit or filled in as reserve outfielder. Yanks optioned Lefty to San Francisco for 1921 season and he won 25, lost nine. Back to Yanks for 1922, but again saw little service—just 16 innings with no decisions. Managed three hits in nine trips to plate, giving some indication of ability with stick. Went to Boston AL on waivers 10/12/22. Pitched 53 innings for Red Sox, 1923; won one game, lost one, had 5.44 ERA. Hurt arm and never pitched much after that. Sox sold O'Doul to Salt Lake, PCL, for 1924. Lefty told manager he was now an outfielder, and proceeded to show could hit with best of them—.392 average in 140 games. Following year dropped down to .375, but had 24 homers, 63 doubles; led league in hits, with 309, and in triples, with 17. Played 198 games. Chicago Cubs took Lefty on "look-see" basis, with $40,000 tag on contract if they kept him. Joe McCarthy was then in first year as major league manager; apparently somewhat reluctant to risk gamble of that much Wrigley money, so sent him back to PCL. Cubs probably could have used him, but instead, when Salt Lake franchise was transferred, Lefty spent 1926 with Hollywood, PCL, hitting .338. After 1927 season with San Francisco, when he hit .378 in 189 games, with 33 homers, O'Doul finally went to majors to stick as hard-hitting outfielder. New York Giants 1928, with .319. Philadelphia NL 1929, with .398, gaining first NL batting title. Then .383 with Phillies, 1930. Shifted to Brooklyn for 1931, hit .336. Won second NL batting championship with .368 mark, with Dodgers, 1932. Divided 1933 between Dodgers and Giants. Spent final major league season with Giants, 1934, winding up with .316 average.

Although Lefty eligible to play in WS of 1922 with Yankees, only appearance in autumn classic occurred during 1933 set when Giants battled Washington Senators. Lefty made most of it. In sixth inning of second game, Giants trailed 1–0. O'Doul batted for George Davis and smacked clean single off Alvin Crowder with bases loaded, driving in two runs—tying run and marker that sent New Yorkers ahead. "I'll never forget that feeling as I was running down to first base," Lefty said later. "It was just like I was running on clouds." Later, fans jumped on field and carried O'Doul on shoulders to clubhouse. "I was really a hero that day," said Lefty. This was O'Doul's solitary appearance in WS game, so he went to his grave with 1.000 batting average in world championship play.

O'Doul had chance to manage San Francisco, PCL, 1935, and continued through 1951. Player manager for several years, gradually appearing in lineup less and less. Vice president as well as manager for Seals, 1948–51. Manager, San Diego, PCL, 1952–54. Manager, Oakland, PCL, 1955. Manager, Vancouver, PCL, 1956. Manager, Seattle, PCL, 1957.

For many years Lefty also operated smart cocktail lounge in San Francisco, near famed Union Square.

When Lefty broke Rogers Hornsby's NL mark of 250 hits for season, was done on last day of 1929 season. Playing for Phillies, had 247 safeties when day started. Needed three to tie record, four to beat it. Nicked Carl Hubbell for four hits in four trips in opening game, breaking old record. Then in second game of doubleheader got three more hits off Bill Walker, another lefthander. Wound up day with seven hits in eight chances, setting record of 254 hits, later equaled by Terry.

O'Doul played 970 major league games, hit safely 1140 times in 3264 trips. Scored 624 runs and drove in 542. Had 175 doubles, 41 triples, 113 homers, and that .349 batting average.

Lefty a keen student of hitting. Constantly studied movies of own batting stance to try to improve, even when batting well over .300. Practiced incessantly. Virtually every morning went to ball park, working out with other players or anybody he could get—practicing swing, timing, keeping eye on ball.

OESCHGER, JOSEPH CARL   P-BR-TR. B. 5/24/91, Chicago, Ill. 6', 190. Joe Oeschger is remembered today not because of overall pitching record but because he pitched 26-inning ball game for old Boston Braves against Brooklyn Dodgers 5/1/20. His opponent was Leon Cadore, who also went entire distance in game that ended in 1–1 tie. Lengthy games seemed to gravitate toward Oeschger. Some years earlier he pitched 19-inning game for Philadelphia NL, this one also against Dodgers. Also pitched 17-inning game vs. St. Louis Cardinals on another occasion. Oeschger, after retiring from game, said never had sore arm in life. Claimed wasn't tired after 26-inning stint, and would have taken regular turn next time around. However, was running in outfield day after marathon game, pulled leg muscle, and so didn't pitch until one week after long contest.

Joe started out to be engineer. Got degree in this field at St. Mary's College in California, but pursued professional baseball instead. Joined Phillies, 1914, won four, lost eight. Optioned to Providence, International League, 1915 and had 21–10 record. Back with Phils 1915–19. Traded to New York Giants 5/27/19 and to Braves 8/1/19. Remained with Boston until end of 1923. Divided 1924 between Phillies and Giants. Last major league engagement was with Brooklyn, 1925.

Had 16–14 mark with Phils in 1917; 15–13 in 1920 and 20–14 in 1921, while with Braves. Overall major league record was 83 wins, 116 defeats, with 3.81 ERA for 1818 innings. Spent 1926 with San Francisco and Oakland teams in Pacific Coast League, then retired after brief spell with Mobile, Southern Association, 1927.

At this point Oeschger went back to college, got degree in education at Stanford. Then spent 27 years at Portola Junior High School, San Francisco, as head of physical education department.

Years after 26-inning game Oeschger was still receiving dozen letters every week asking about it. Players must have moved fast that afternoon—game took three hours, 50 minutes. Joe didn't want umpires to call game. Cadore was curve ball pitcher; Oeschger depended on fast ball and figured Braves might get to Leon sooner than Dodgers could hit his fast one as shadows lengthened. Brooklyn got its run in fifth inning on broken-bat single by Ivy Olson. Braves tied it in sixth. Oeschger claims Braves would have won game in regulation time but for marvellous catch by Zack Wheat. "I hit terrific belt which should have gone for triple anyway," said Joe. "But Wheat, playing left field for Dodgers, somehow leaped up right at fence and caught ball. This would have given us another run."

O'FARRELL, ROBERT ARTHUR C-BR-TR. B. 10/19/96, Waukegan, Ill. 5'10", 180. Bob O'Farrell was fine, smart catcher but did not make grade as major league manager, despite two chances. Managed 1927 Cardinals in St. Louis, club loaded with talent. Also piloted Cincinnati Reds, 1934, team of youngsters and inept veterans. But did not satisfy on either occasion.

Bob got start in pro baseball through old-time catcher Roger Bresnahan, who saw him playing on sandlots and later coached him in art of backstopping. Signed with Chicago Cubs, 1915, but sent to Milwaukee and Peoria for seasoning; then came back to Cubs to stay, 1918. Remained with Chicago until 5/23/25 when traded to St. Louis NL for Mike Gonzalez and Howard Freigau. O'Farrell gradually took over more and more of Chicago catching duties from Bill Killefer, but when Gabby Hartnett began to develop into star, Cubs could afford to trade fine catcher. Bob's best years with Cubs were 1922–23. In 128 games first of those seasons, hit .324, then came up with .318 in 131 games following season.

Bob's best year in majors was 1926, when proved to be ironman behind plate; caught 146 games and pinch-hit successfully in one other contest. Slapped ball at .293 average, and was universally recognized as key factor in Cardinals' pennant-winning season. League recognized his performance by awarding him Most Valuable Player citation, which then brought with it $1000 cash. Bob received 79 of possible 80 votes.

When playing manager Rogers Hornsby, boss of 1926 Cardinals, came to parting of ways with owner Sam Breadon in December, popular Bob O'Farrell was named successor. Bob didn't use himself as often in 1927, just 61 games, and hitting went down to .264. In close NL race Cardinals lost out to Pittsburgh by 1-1/2 games. Critics claimed O'Farrell failed as manager principally because was reluctant to remove starting pitchers who had lost effectiveness. In any case, Breadon, an impatient man, returned O'Farrell to ranks, gave him $5000 raise in salary, and appointed Bill McKechnie as successor. Breadon grabbed first opportunity to unload high-salaried man, traded O'Farrell to N.Y. Giants 5/10/28 for George Harper, who helped Cardinals win another flag. O'Farrell remained with N.Y. through 1932 but never sparkled as in Chicago and St. Louis. Cardinals regained his contract 1933, using him as reserve receiver. In 1934 Larry MacPhail named him playing manager, Cincinnati Reds. Bob hit .244 in 44 games, but came to grief after Reds lost their 58th game, having won just 26. MacPhail encountered Bob in office, swinging golf club. Larry exploded at what he considered O'Farrell's nonchalance about another monotonous defeat, and Bob was through as big league pilot.

O'Farrell later played in 22 games that year for Cubs, then had final fling, 14 games with Cardinals, 1935. Had 1492 major league games and .273 average. Made 1120 hits, 201 doubles, 58 triples, 51 homers. Scored 517 runs, drove in 549. Stole 35 bases. In WS, 1918 with Cubs and 1926 with Cards, seven hits in 26 trips for .269 average.

In later years O'Farrell said his greatest thrill came in 1926 WS when Babe Ruth tried to steal second base in seventh and final game of classic. Ruth represented potential tying run in ninth inning. O'Farrell's peg cut down Babe for third out, and Cardinals won game 3–2, and WS as well.

O'Farrell as youth, took fling at pro football and basketball, but gave them up for baseball. Particularly good basketball player.

OLIVA, PEDRO, JR. (Tony) OF-BL-TR. B. 7/20/40, Pinar del Rio, Cuba. 6'2", 190. Could Tony Oliva come back after fourth operation on right knee? This was more than $64,000 question for Cuban outfielder who won three AL batting championships and went into 1973 season with higher career batting average than any other active AL player. Because of knee, Oliva, in 1972, played only 10 games for Minnesota Twins, but drew $105,000 salary. Oliva had operations after 1966 and 1967 seasons for torn ligaments in right knee. Then, 7/29/71, tried for diving catch while in Oakland. Fell on knees and limped from field. Was hitting .375 at time with 18 home runs. Though he played until September, hitting slumped. Was good enough, however, to win third batting title with .337. Home run total 22, with 81 RBI. Third operation took place 9/22/71. Exercised faithfully during off-season, including weight lifting. But in 1972 when he tried to play, limping and with leg heavily bandaged, it soon became evident that knee was not right. Pain all time. Couldn't pull ball. After 10 games was decided only course was fourth operation. Besides knee problems, Tony, during years, has overcome injured knuckles, shoulder separation, and sore arm.

Tony really isn't Tony Oliva. Tony is his brother. But Pedro used Tony's passport to get into U.S., and has been Tony ever since. Got start in Appalachian League at Wytheville, 1961. Gave an inkling of what to expect by winning league batting title with .410 in 64 games. Also led circuit in RBI with 81. Following year, at Charlotte, Southern Association, hit .350. And in nine games with Twins that same season, had .444 average—4 for 9. Twins farmed him out one more season, this time with Dallas-Fort Worth, Pacific Coast League. Hit .304 in 146 games, getting 23 homers, 74 RBI. Also had three hits in seven trips with Minnesota that year, so had .429 mark.

His .323 mark in 1964, first full season in AL, was good enough to lead league in batting, first time rookie ever won title. His 32 home runs, 94 RBI proved he was no flash in pan. Came back to reinforce respect from pitchers in 1965, again winning batting championship. This time average was .321 with 16 homers, 98 RBI. In next season hit .307, and while this did not gain batting championship, led AL in total base hits for third consecutive year. In 1969–70 Tony went over 100-mark in RBI both years. Led AL in doubles three seasons, tied for lead in another campaign.

Among honors Oliva has taken have been AL Rookie of Year designation by Baseball Writers Association of America and by *Sporting News*, 1964. Latter selection covered both majors. *Sporting News* also named him AL Player of Year for both 1965 and 1971. AL All-Star Game squads 1964 through 1971. Only WS, 1965: .192 average, 7 games, 5 for 26.

Oliva's background statistics as he faced 1973 were 1205 games, 4693 AB, 715 runs, 1471 hits, 46 doubles, 177 homers, 724 RBI, 84 stolen bases, with .313 average. Despite all his problems in 1972, Tony hit .321, 9 for 28.

OLIVER, ALBERT, JR. (Mr. Scoop) 1B-OF-BL-TL. B. 10/14/46, Portsmouth, Ohio. 6'1", 202. Al Oliver comes from same part of Ohio that gave baseball Branch Rickey, Gene Tenace, and several others. In 1972 began to come into own when hit .312 in 140 games, tying for fifth place among NL batsmen who took part in at least 125 games. Raised lifetime batting average to .287. So, entering 1973 season could look back on 567 major league games, with 607 hits good for 110 doubles, 18 triples, 55 homers. Scored 276 runs, drove in 306, and stole 15 bases.

Smiling Al may give impression of carefree attitude. But is dedicated, highly confident young man who is beginning to master center field play after having been primarily first baseman. Oliver, in 1972, proved could hit all types of pitching. In 1971, average against southpaws was .238; against righthanders .302. In 1972, although often hit second in batting order, had 89 RBI.

Oliver figures missed about $20,000 in bonus money by signing with Pirates instead of Philadelphia Phillies. Went to Salem, Va., camp for Pittsburgh organization and signed 6/13/64. Later scout for Phillies indicated they would have boosted bonus offer considerably. Knee injury kept him from playing that summer. Surgery on cartilage. Spent succeeding seasons at Gastonia, Raleigh, Macon, and Columbus, Ohio. Joined Pirates for four games, 1968; hit .285 in 129 games with Pittsburgh, 1969. It was .270 with 83 RBI, 1970.

While Oliver has power, his line drives to all fields do not produce great number of homers. Hit 17 in 1969, 14 in 1971, and had even dozen round-trippers in both 1970 and 1972.

Al had close call late in 1969. Someone sent large cake to Pirate clubhouse. Ate three or four pieces. After game started, began to itch and feel dizzy. Later passed out. Discovered that cake had pulverized nuts in it. Hospital rescue squad was called. Oliver knew was allergic to nuts, but didn't realize cake had them. Almost died.

Oliver picked up his nickname at Gastonia because of ability to dig throws out of dirt as first baseman. Made definite move to outfield, 1971, though available for first base duty. Teammate of his in high school was Larry Hisle. Attended Kent State.

Al's WS record was .211, 4 for 19, during 1971 classic.

OLSON, IVAN MASSIE SS-2B-BR-TR. B. 10/14/85, Kansas City, Mo. D. 9/1/65, Inglewood, Calif. 5'10½", 175. Rugged infielder who spent most of major league career with Brooklyn Dodgers when they were known as Robins because "Uncle" Wilbert Robinson was their colorful manager. Casey Stengel, talking about Olson's play around second base, told how Ivy treated runners sliding into bag. "Olson spiked his name and forwarding address on practically every infielder in league. Seemingly paid no attention to runner coming into second base. If somebody slid into him in rough manner, it didn't happen again. Olson would get them next time. He'd be waiting for them with ball in his hand and put it right between horns. Very corrective method, that."

Ivy played at Webb City, Mo., 1906–07; Hutchinson, Kans., 1908; then two years at Portland, Pacific Coast League. With Cleveland, 1911–14. Started 1915 with Cincinnati, then sent to Dodgers same season. Stayed with Flatbush crew until he had 10 games with them in 1924. Used mostly at shortstop, hit .258 for 1572 major league games. No power hitter, just 13 homers in big leagues. Hit .250 in 1916 WS with Brooklyn; had .320 mark in 1920 classic. Overall WS record: .293, 12 games.

Out of baseball 1925. Player-manager, Sarasota, Florida State League, 1926. Again played, managed at Pocatello, 1927, in Utah-Idaho League. Bopped umpire in this league. Out of game 1928–29. Returned to

Brooklyn as coach 1930–31. Coach, New York Giants, 1932, until July when released.

O'MALLEY, PETER Executive. B. 12/12/37, Brooklyn, N.Y. President of Los Angeles Dodgers since March, 1970. Son of Walter F. O'Malley, who headed Dodger organization in Brooklyn and moved club to Los Angeles before 1958 season. Majored in business law at Wharton School of Finance, U. of Pennsylvania, then began learning workings of Dodger organization firsthand. Director of Dodgertown, spring-training camp for Dodger organization, Vero Beach, 1962. Spent 1965–66 as president and general manager of Dodgers' farm team in Pacific Coast League at Spokane, Wash. Moved to Los Angeles Dodgers 1967, vice president in charge of stadium operations. Executive vice president of Dodgers 1969 until accession to presidency when father became chairman of board.

O'Malley has been especially interested in Japanese-American relations after visiting Japan with Brooklyn Dodgers, 1956, and Los Angeles Dodgers, 1966. Actively promoted visit of Tokyo Yomiuri baseball team to Dodgertown, Vero Beach, Fla., 1961 and 1966. Active in several civic organizations. Hobbies include outdoor sports. Made three African safaris, hunted polar bears in Spitsbergen; also hunted in India.

O'MALLEY, WALTER FRANCIS Executive. B. 10/9/03, New York, N.Y. Walter O'Malley gained nationwide attention as owner of old Brooklyn NL club, which he transformed into Los Angeles Dodgers. But has had fingers in many other lucrative enterprises. So much so that author Roger Kahn asked how much he was worth. Walter replied it must have been around $24 million. Buzzie Bavasi later commented to Kahn, "All he left out were 300 acres of downtown Los Angeles." It's anyone's guess how many millions downtown Los Angeles real estate is worth.

O'Malley has been power in baseball since 1940s. Some claim he picked General Eckert and Bowie Kuhn to be baseball's commissioners; and that he was responsible for Chub Feeney's election as NL president. Since 10/8/51 has been NL representative in baseball's executive council. It was he who instigated moves of Dodgers and N.Y. Giants to West Coast. "Carpetbagger" is only one of epithets hurled against him. Certainly would have hard time winning popularity contest in Brooklyn.

O'Malley attended Culver Military Academy, U. of Pennsylvania, and Fordham and Columbia Law Schools. Became attorney, 1930. In 1943 took over legal work for Brooklyn Dodgers. Within two years he, John L. Smith, and Branch Rickey purchased 75 percent of Dodgers' stock. Smith was tycoon with Pfizer Company. After Smith died, O'Malley took over his stock, and soon Rickey and he came to parting of ways. In 1950 Walter had 67 percent of ball club's stock and became president of Dodgers. After considerable talk about new stadium in Brooklyn, and much jockeying, O'Malley, 1956, bought Los Angeles franchise in Pacific Coast League, which somewhat eased problems connected with transfer of Dodgers to City of Angels. This was effected before start of 1958 season.

Besides holdings in Dodgers and their minor league organization, O'Malley has had other business interests—building materials, part ownership of Long Island Railroad, Brooklyn Borough Gas Co., N. Y. Subways Advertising Co. Served as director for other businesses, as well as for various civic and charitable organizations.

O'Malley, reviewing experience of Brooklyn management before he became connected with club, once declared Dodgers had paid more men not to manage team than any other club. Hence policy of offering Walter Alston only one-year contracts. "One-year contract is our policy here. And if it weren't, I'd make it our policy," he declared. Alston's 20th one-year contract was for 1973 season.

O'Malley keenly interested in development of baseball in Japan, and predicts Tokyo and Osaka should be ready for major league franchises within five years or so. Once favored interleague play for AL and NL, but now firmly opposed to it.

Jim Murray, *Los Angeles Times* columnist, once wrote about O'Malley, "His idea of a love story is an annual carloading report. His idea of a beautiful figure is $1 million."

O'NEILL, JAMES EDWARD (Tip) OF-BR-TR. B. 5/25/58, Woodstock, Ontario. D. 12/31/15, Montreal, Quebec. 6'1½", 187. Look in record books and you'll see that Tip O'Neill batted cool .492 for St. Louis Browns in old American Association, then recognized as major league. This fantastic batting average, however, needs explanation. They gave batter credit for base hit every time he walked. While O'Neill was good hitter, was not .492 batsman. Averaged .340 for career, including that one season when walks were as good as hits.

Tip started with old Metropolitans, 1882. New York NL, 1883, as outfielder and pitcher. Won six, lost 12 as moundsman. Then moved to St. Louis, AA. Won 10, lost four as pitcher, but played in outfield rest of time and compiled .272 average. Concentrated on outfield after that and never hit less than .324 for remaining years with Browns. During stay in St. Louis, Browns won flags, 1885,6,7,8.

O'Neill played in old WS of that era that pitted AA champions against NL flag winners. Hit .421 in 1886 Series, won by Browns, but had overall .240 mark.

O'Neill first player to hit two home runs in WS game, 10/19/86. Last year with Browns was 1889. With Chicago, Players League, 1890, then back to Browns for 1891. Cincinnati NL, 1892. Called it quits as active player then, with that .340 average for 1038 major league games. Turned to umpiring in several minor leagues after playing days were over.

O'NEILL, STEPHEN FRANCIS C-BR-TR. B. 7/6/91, Minooka, Pa. D. 1/26/62, Cleveland, Ohio. 5'10'', 165. Steve O'Neill played in 1586 AL games, later managed four major league teams and several in minors. Durable catcher, hit .263 for big league career, three times going well over .300 mark. Possibly one of best-liked men associated with baseball. Led Detroit Tigers to AL pennant and world championship, 1945.

O'Neill had three brothers who played in majors, Jim, Jack and Mike. Steve most successful. Started with Elmira, 1910, in New York State League. Philadelphia Athletics owned contract early in 1911, but did not get chance to play and was sold to Worcester, New England League. Took part in 101 games, hit .282, and moved up to Cleveland that same season for nine games. Remained with Cleveland until after 1923 season, when traded to Boston AL with Bill Wambsganss. Reached .321 as hitter, 1920, when Cleveland won first AL pennant and WS. That year caught 148 games and pinch hit in another.

While was more active that year than any other season, Steve had nine consecutive years in which caught well over 100 games each campaign, 1915–23. Hit .322 for Indians, 1921, and .311 in 1922. After one season with Red Sox, 1924, Steve went to Yankees on waivers, 1925, and after 35 games with New York, was in minors with Reading, International League. Toronto, 1926, then with St. Louis Browns, 1927–28. Manager, Toronto, 1929,30,31; coach and player for Toledo, 1932; player-manager, Toledo, 1933–34; coach, Cleveland, 1935 until named manager, succeeding Walter Johnson, 8/5/35. Continued as Cleveland manager through 1937. Back in minors as manager of Buffalo, 1938–40. Coach, Detroit Tigers, 1941. Manager, Beaumont, 1942. Then managed Detroit, 1943–48. Coach, Cleveland Indians, 1949. Coach, Boston Red Sox, 1950 until named manager, 6/23/50, succeeding Joe McCarthy. Piloted Red Sox until close of 1951. Manager, Philadelphia NL, 6/27/52 through 1954.

While Steve had several first-division finishes managing other teams, Detroit span was most successful. In six seasons in Motor City, had three runner-up teams and one pennant winner, capped by WS victory over Chicago Cubs, four games to three.

Steve's lifetime major league batting average of .263 covered 1586 games, with 1259 hits good for 248 doubles, 34 triples, 13 homers. Scored 448 runs, drove in 565. In only WS as player, 1920, with Cleveland, batted .333, 7 for 21. Had three doubles, drove in two runs and scored another himself.

ONSLOW, JOHN JAMES (Jack) C-BR-TR. B. 10/13/88, Scottdale,

Pa. D. 12/22/60, Concord, Mass. 5'11", 180. When Jack Onslow managed Chicago White Sox, 1949 and part of 1950, he and Frank Lane, general manager of Sox, were constantly at odds. It was claimed—and nobody denied it—they never agreed on anything. Onslow was hired ahead of Lane, so Frank inherited him. Team finished sixth in 1949 with 63–91 record. Following year, after club had won just eight games of its first 30, Lane persuaded Comiskey family to let Onslow go as manager. Red Corriden replaced him for rest of year. White Sox again finished sixth in AL standings.

Onslow spent most of playing days in minor leagues. Caught 31 games for Detroit Tigers in 1912, hit .159, and went back to bushes. Popped up again with New York Giants, 1917, when he caught nine games, hit .250, and returned to minors. Jack coached Pittsburgh Pirates, 1925–26; Washington, 1927; St. Louis Cardinals, 1928; Philadelphia NL, 1931–32. During early 1930s Jack managed at Richmond, Va., and Hartford, Conn. Had been out of baseball four years when White Sox hired him as scout, 1946. Left that job to manage Memphis Chicks in Southern League, then became field boss for Sox.

At time of death had been scout for Boston Red Sox since 1952. His major league totals showed 40 games with 13 hits in 77 trips for .169 batting average.

O'ROURKE, JAMES HENRY (Orator Jim) OF-BR-TR. B. 8/24/52, East Bridgeport, Conn. D. 1/8/19, Bridgeport, Conn. 5'8", 185. Orator Jim O'Rourke, graduate of Yale Law School, made *the* first base hit in NL 4/22/1876 for Boston in game against Philadelphia Athletics. Same man still holds record of having been oldest player ever to appear in NL box score. Was 52 years, 29 days old when caught complete game 9/22/04 for New York Giants.

O'Rourke played for Mansfield club of National Association, 1872, then had three seasons with Boston team in same circuit. With birth of NL, 1876, was with Boston for three more years. Providence NL 1879. Boston NL 1880. Buffalo NL 1881–84. New York NL 1885–92, except 1890 when was with N.Y. club of Players League. Washington NL 1893. N.Y. NL 1904, for that one last game in majors. Played and managed at Buffalo, 1881–84. Umpired in 1894. managed Victors of Bridgeport, 1895–96. Managed Bridgeport club, Connecticut League, 1897–1908. President, Connecticut League, 1909–13. President, Eastern Association, 1914.

O'Rourke and brother John, also with Boston NL 1879, objected to custom of club deducting $20 each from their salaries to pay for uniforms. When club would not give in, admiring fans raised enough money to take care of cost. *Chicago Tribune* called them couple of "fastidious young men."

Orator Jim was one of baseball's first "missionaries"; one of players who went to England, 1874, to try to promote baseball there.

In all, Jim appeared in 1750 major league games, got 2314 hits, 385 doubles, 139 triples, 49 homers, .314 average. His .350 average in 1884 with Buffalo led NL. While he played outfield more than any other position, O'Rourke appeared at all other positions, including few games on pitching mound. Hall of Fame 1945.

ORSATTI, ERNEST RALPH OF-BL-TL. B. 9/8/04, Los Angeles, Calif. D. 9/4/68, Canoga Park, Calif. 5'7¼", 154. In golden days of Hollywood, Orsatti Brothers were agents for some of greatest actors and actresses in movieland, with offices on Sunset Boulevard and in London. Ernie, one of brothers, had another occupation in summer time— colorful outfielder for St Louis Cardinals during period when they won four pennants and two world championships.

Ernie never considered for Hall of Fame, but did hit .306 for major league career consisting of 701 games. And though Dean brothers hogged limelight in 1934 WS, gaining all four victories as pitchers, Orsatti played center field six games in that Series, pinch hit in another game, and hit respectable .318.

Orsatti had something of ham in makeup. Often tried for shoestring catches, slid into bases and frequently came up limping. Yet when was running out base hit or chasing fly ball, did not favor injured leg. "It doesn't hurt any more to run full steam with gimpy leg than to run with limping gait," said Ernie. But when pressure was off, he'd limp to bench or to position in field.

Ernie tried to make Vernon club, Pacific Coast League, 1924–25, but was farmed out to Cedar Rapids, Mississippi Valley League. Hit .347 in 1925, 89 games, and was bought by St. Louis NL. Eight games at San Antonio, 1926, with .385 average—then 57 games at Omaha, with .386. Then hit .330 for Houston, Texas League, 1927, and .315 for Cardinals in 27 games. Burned up American Association with .381 average, 1928, and was brought into St. Louis again, this time to stay. Hit .304 in 27 games, got into all four WS games that fall, hitting .286. But Cardinals lost set to Yankees in four straight.

Called it quits as big leaguer after 1935 season and headed back to Hollywood and movies. Among his 663 major league hits were 129 doubles, 39 triples, 10 homers. Stole 46 bases. Hit .273 in four WS.

OSTEEN, CLAUDE WILSON (Gomer) P-BL-TL. B. 8/9/39, Caney Springs, Tenn. 5'11", 173. Claude Osteen proved he was good pitcher in 1964 by winning 15 games for old Washington Senators, who finished in ninth place in AL that year. Since then, with Los Angeles Dodgers, only once failed to win at least 14 games, and twice reached 20 victories. His

1972 performance was best yet, with 20 wins, 11 defeats, and ERA of 2.64. Osteen throws fast ball that seems to break in on lefthanded batsmen and away from righthanders. His curve, slider, and change-up have all become more effective since he developed screwball.

Started with Cincinnati Reds, 1957, spending part of that season with Nashville. Won 14, lost four for Wenatchee, Northwest League, 1958. Part of that same season and next with Seattle, PCL. Reds brought him up for two games, 1959. Optioned to Indianapolis during 1961 season, where won 15, lost 11; then traded to Washington 9/16/61. Had 1–1 record that fall, then 8–13 and 9–14 before 15–13 season in 1964. Senators sent Claude to Dodgers in deal for Frank Howard. Broke even, 15–15, first year with Los Angeles; then had 17–14 and 17–17 seasons. Won 12, lost 18, 1968; then 20–15, 16–14, 14–11 before returning to 20-victory class in 1972.

Claude, as 1973 began, had pitched in 440 major league games; 2857 innings, with 3.19 ERA. Won 164, lost 157; walked 729 and struck out 1412; owned 116 complete games. Took part in 1965,66 WS, pitching total of 21 innings with 0.86 ERA. Won one game, 1965, shutting out Minnesota Twins 5–0 in third game of series. Lost sixth game 5–1. In 1966 lost 1–0 decision to Wally Bunker and Baltimore Orioles although allowed only three hits. All-Star squads 1967, 70, 73.

OTIS, AMOS JOSEPH OF-BR-TR. B. 4/26/47, Mobile, Ala. 5'11½", 169. Amos Otis is young man with plan. Hopes to be $100,000 ball player no later than 1975. With Kansas City Royals, seemed to be heading in that direction. During 1972 succeeded in raising career batting average in majors from .279 to .283 for 516 games. Went into 1973 season with 528 hits, 95 doubles, 16 triples, 37 homers. Scored 258 runs to that point, had 196 RBI, and had stolen 114 bases.

Otis was genuine bargain for Royals. New York Mets wanted third baseman Joe Foy, and gave Kansas City Otis and pitcher Bob Johnson for him, 12/3/69. Foy was at end of string and did not solve Mets' third base problem. Johnson later traded for valuable players; and Otis became one of key men in Kansas City setup. Amos patrolled center field in brilliant fashion, 1970; hit .284 and drove in 58 runs. Stole 33 bases, without being thrown out at second or third. Only unsuccessful attempts at pilfering were one pickoff at first base and one attempted theft of home during double-steal try. In 1971 Otis blossomed still more. Raised average to .301, hit 15 homers, drove in 79 runs; stole 52 bases, more than anyone else in AL. In center field, went from 7/18/70 to 7/29/71, span of 165 consecutive games, without error. In 1971 tied Willie Davis of Dodgers for major league lead in putouts (404); paced majors in total chances. His base running, hooked up with that of Freddie Patek, gave Royals best 1–2 base-stealing record in AL since

1917, when Ray Chapman and Roth stole 103 bases for Cleveland. Otis-Patek combination resulted in 101 thefts.

As 1972 began, Otis was off to poor start. Had kidney ailment in Florida. As of 5/25 was batting only .227, with one home run, 11 RBI, and four stolen bases. Picked up by mid-July, then tapered off somewhat. Otis and Patek were benched 8/14/72, accused of not giving best. Manager Bob Lemon seemed to think Amos' fielding was suffering from fear of running into fence. Otis had crashed into fence during July. Game after benching, Lemon used Otis as pinch hitter. Singled to ignite three-run rally that defeated Yankees, 7–6. Otis finished season with .293 average, 11 homers, 28 steals.

Amos started in Boston Red Sox organization, 1965, at Harlan, Appalachian League. Hit .329 in 67 games, stole 10 bases. Oneonta, N.Y.-Pa. League, 1966; hit .270 that year and New York Mets drafted him. Spent 1967 and 1968 at Jacksonville, International League, with brief spells with Mets both seasons. Divided 1969 between Mets and Tidewater; then came trade to Kansas City. Mets used him at third base and outfield, but Royals planted him in outfield permanently. All-Star squads 1970, 71, 72, 73.

OTT, MELVIN THOMAS OF-BL-TR. B. 3/2/09, Gretna, La. D. 11/21/58, New Orleans, La. 5'9", 170. Love at first sight. That's what happened when grizzled, weather beaten, hard-nosed John McGraw saw apple-cheeked youngster of 16 take first cuts in special batting practice. Callow youth was Mel Ott, sent to New York by Harry P. Williams, Louisiana lumberman and friend of manager of Giants. McGraw astonished at youthfulness of Ott when Mel walked into office. But Williams had been so persuasive in extolling potentials of young man that Mac went down to field specially to see him bat. Before workout had finished, McGraw had made up mind. Not only signed Ott to contract then and there, but decided to keep him close by, so no minor league manager or coach could tamper with batting style. Within few weeks McGraw was quoted as saying Mel was "most natural hitter" he had ever seen; and that his style was perfect. Ott's attack on pitch was unique. Lefthanded batter, as ball neared plate he lifted right foot, almost as though starting to goose-step. Brought it down again and swung with good level stroke.

McGraw kept Ott on bench rest of that season, 1925. In 1926 put him into 35 games—and Mel hit .383. Used him sparingly again in 1927, Ott going to bat 163 times and hitting .282. That season got his first home run. It was something of fluke, as Hack Wilson, playing center field for Chicago Cubs, slipped and fell on muddy turf, allowing ball to skip past him. But this was only first of 511 Ottie hit during career, most over right field fences. By 1928, when Ott was 19, was playing regularly in outfield.

Had been catcher in Louisiana, but McGraw shifted him to outfield. Some years later, 1935–40, Mel played quite a number of games at third base, but did best work in right field. Mel came up with .322 in 1928, 18 homers, 77 RBI. Boosted homer production to 42 following season, drove in 151 markers, hit .328. Came up with another fine season, 1930, with highest average of career as regular, .349, with 25 homers, 119 RBI.

Consistently dangerous at plate and played regularly through 1945 season. Three times tied for lead in homers in NL and three times led circuit in this respect. Reached 30 homers or more eight times. Led NL in RBI, 1934, with 135.

In 1942 Ott became playing manager of Giants. Led NL in homers with 30, in runs scored with 118, hit .295. His team wound up in third place. But in 1943 Giants dropped down to cellar, and Ott's own average slumped to .234. Things were a bit better in 1944. Ott hit .288 and Giants got up to fifth. Then 1945 was last season as regular. Hit .308. Played 31 games in 1946 and just four in 1947.

After that, Giants managed to get as high as fourth just once under Ottie's leadership and had another last-place finish, 1946. By mid-July of following year, Horace Stoneham, owner of Giants, reluctantly decided had to make change. He and Branch Rickey, then top man at Brooklyn, engineered shocking maneuver that put fire-eating Leo Durocher in manager's job at Polo Grounds. Durocher was same guy who, referring specifically to Ott, had said, "Nice guys finish last." Mel certainly qualified as "nice guy," one of most popular players ever to grace Giant uniform. In this shuffle, Ott landed in front office as assistant to Carl Hubbell, director of Giants' farm system.

Ott finally left Giants' organization to take over management of Oakland Oaks in Pacific Coast League, 1951–52; for while was broadcaster for radio's "Game of the Day" program, then put in three seasons as sportscaster for Detroit Tigers' network. Then, on foggy night 11/14/58, he and wife were involved in head-on collision on highway. Both critically injured and Mel died several days later.

Though Ott did not sparkle as manager, left plenty of deeds on field for which he is remembered. Besides those 511 home runs, hit 488 doubles, 72 triples, and scored 1859 runs. Had over 100 RBI eight consecutive seasons, 1929–36, and added one more in 1938. His grand total came to 1860. Played 2730 NL games. Good eye at plate. Feared by most pitchers, so got plenty of intentional walks in critical situations. Once received five such intentional walks in one game. Received 100 or more walks 10 different seasons and, at this writing, his record of 1708 walks is an NL mark. On two separate occasions Ottie scored six runs in one game.

Mel was on three pennant-winners, 1933,36,37. In very first inning of 1933 WS against Washington, Ott slammed 400-foot homer with one man on base; later singled in another run. Carl Hubbell won game 4–2, Ottie being responsible for three of four runs. Hit .389 for Series and drove in crucial run for his team in final game of set when New Yorkers won by 4–3 score on Mel's 10th-inning homer. This gave Giants world championship. Had one homer each in two other WS, drove in three runs each time. Overall Series mark of .295 for 16 games; 18 hits in 61 trips, 8 runs, 10 RBI, 4 homers, 2 doubles. NL All-Star squads 1934,35,36,38. Hall of Fame 1951.

OWEN, ARNOLD MALCOLM (Mickey) C-BR-TR. B. 4/4/16, Nixa, Mo. 5′10″, 190. Mickey Owen caught 128 games for Brooklyn Dodgers in 1941 and helped Beloved Bums to NL pennant. Set NL record by accepting 476 chances without error over period from 4/15 to 8/29, 100 games in all. Set major league record by catching three foul flies in one inning 8/4. Set all-time Dodger record for catchers by compiling .995 fielding average. Baseball fans, however, gloss over all these 1941 achievments. Instead, Mickey has been labeled goat of 1941 WS because of unfortunate error with two men out in ninth inning of fourth game. Situation thus: Yankees had two victories, Dodgers one. But now Bums leading Yanks by 4–3 score, with one out to go. It looked like Series would be evened in matter of minutes. Nobody on base. Tommy Henrich, at plate, worked count against Hugh Casey to three balls, two strikes. Casey's next pitch fooled Henrich. Swung and missed. Strike three! Ball game wasn't over. Owen somehow missed ball, which rolled to stands, and Tommy reached first base. Given new lease on life, Joe DiMaggio singled, Keller doubled, and Gordon doubled after Dickey had walked—four runs, putting Bombers ahead 7–4. Disheartened, and facing an effective relief hurler, Johnny Murphy, Dodgers went down in order in their half of ninth. So, instead of having Series tied at two games apiece, it was now Yankees, three games, Brooklyn one. Yanks wrapped it up next day and once again were world champs.

Mickey freely admits he made another mistake, of another sort. After serving in navy during World War II, Owen succumbed to lure of Pasquel brothers' promises in Mexico, as did Sal Maglie, Hal Lanier, Luis Olmo, Ace Adams, several others. Organized baseball considered Mexican venture outlaw; suspended those who ignored their contracts containing reserve clause. Owen, given five-year player-manager contract by Veracruz club, was fired after one year, but it was 1949 before his supension was lifted.

Owen started in St. Louis Cardinal chain at Springfield, in 1935. Next season was regular catcher at Columbus in American Association, hitting .336 in 125 games. Moved up to Cardinals in third year in pro ball, played 80 games, hit .231. Though wasn't able to hit higher than .267 in four years at St. Louis, became recognized as fine catcher. Brooklyn gave $60,000 plus two players to get him 12/4/40.

After unfortunate experience in 1941 WS, Owen remained regular Dodger catcher through 1944 season. Caught 24 games for Bums in 1945. In this period, best hitting season was .273 in 1944, although he raised mark to .286 in following year for those 24 games.

Following suspension, Owen was reserve receiver with Cubs three years, then player-coach for Kansas City, American Association, 1952; player-manager, Norfolk, Piedmont League, 1953; utility catcher, Boston Red Sox, 1954. Manager, Jacksonville club of South Atlantic League, 1956. Scout, Baltimore Orioles, 1958–59. In 1960 set up Mickey Owen Baseball School for Boys, Miller, Mo. When elected sheriff of Greene County, Mo., 1964, sold interest in school. Reelected 1968, again 1972.

Owen, now gray-haired lawman, says job of being sheriff is far tougher than playing baseball. Friends in southwest Missouri wanted Mickey to run for U.S. Congress, but he declined, saying had done enough traveling as ball player and wanted to stay close to home.

OWEN, MARVIN JAMES 3B-BR-TR. B. 3/22/08, San Jose, Calif. 6'1", 175. Many years after Detroit fans showered Joe Medwick with fruits and vegetables during seventh game of 1934 WS, resulting in Judge Landis ejecting Medwick from game, Marvin Owen confessed it probably was largely his fault. Here was situation: Cardinals, with Dizzy Dean pitching shutout ball, had piled up seven-run lead when Joe Medwick tripled in two more runs in sixth inning. "I was straddling bag," said Owen. "Medwick slipped into base, between my legs, bumping me. I started to fall, and in so doing, accidentally stepped on Joe's foot as I was going down. He got mad, started kicking at me with his spikes, but did not cut me. We tangled a bit in the dust, then things quieted down. Joe got up, said he was sorry and wanted to shake hands. I was mad, so I just glared at him, told him to go to blazes and gestured with both hands for him to go away from me. That was about it. If I had stuck out my hand and shook his, fans in left field wouldn't have thrown all that stuff."

It was bitter pill for Tigers to lose that seventh game of WS. Owen, with 96 RBI that season, was low man in infield in that respect, 1934. Fellow infielders Hank Greenberg, Charley Gehringer, Bill Rogell *each* drove in 100 or more runs. Probably hardest-hitting infield in history, with grand total of 462 RBI for season.

Owen was in majors nine years, played 1011 games and hit .275. Graduated from Santa Clara with B.S. in physical education. Played 138 games for Seattle, Pacific Coast League, 1930, hitting .300. Then 37 games for Toronto, 1931—and 105 for Tigers, with little over one season's experience in minors. Hit .223, so Detroit farmed him out to

Toronto first, then to Newark, 1932. Gained MVP honors for International League with .317 average and 92 RBI. For next five years was Detroit's regular third baseman. Hit .317 in 1934, and in 1936 had 105 RBI with .295 average. That year hit nine homers, highest number reached in any major league season. Chicago AL 1938–39. Boston AL 1940. Portland PCL 1941. Manager, Portland, 1944–46, winning PCL pennant, 1945. Later managed San Jose club, California League. For many years has served as Detroit scout in San Jose area.

Owen didn't fare too well at plate in his WS games, 1934,35, with just three hits in 49 trips for .061 average.

Made unassisted double plays as third baseman in two successive games, 4/28,29/34. Equaled major league record by getting four doubles in one game 4/23/39.

OWENS, PAUL FRANCIS 1B-BR-TR. B. 2/7/24, Salamanca, N.Y. 6'3", 185. Paul Owens managed Philadelphia Phillies through their last 80 games, 1972. Team that had .338 winning percentage earlier in year under Frank Lucchesi did somewhat better under Owens, moving at .413 pace. Owens, before becoming field manager, had been appointed general manager of Phillies just 37 days previously. After close of 1972 season, Owens returned to single role of being general manager, turning reins over to Danny Ozark. Then, short time later, was named vice president and director of player personnel.

Owens' background includes such varied experiences as playing in Pony League, teaching physical education, coaching football, basketball, and baseball, and operating filling station. Also managed baseball clubs five seasons in minors.

Paul joined army after leaving high school, becoming sergeant of engineering company. After three years in service, returned to U. S., enrolled at St. Bonaventure. Received B. S. degree in physical education, 1951. Played baseball at college, also basketball. Signed with Olean, N.Y., club, then farm of St. Louis Cardinals. Promptly won league batting title with .407 average for 111 games, with 17 homers, 101 RBI. Moved up to Winston-Salem, Piedmont League, 1952, hit .338 in 136 games. Although moved up still more in 1953, to Houston, Texas League, Owens failed to see much action and returned to Salamanca to become director of City's youth activities. In 1955 returned to pro baseball as player-manager of Olean club. Came up with .387, .368, and .407 marks, playing regularly over three-year period. Topped league in hitting in both 1956,57. Started his connection with Phillies organization, 1956, when Olean and Phils had working agreement. Owens shifted to Bakersfield, Phillies' farm team in California League, 1958. Played 31 games, hit .255; bowed out as player with brief appearance, 1959; managed both years. Became scout for Phillies after 1959 season, roaming Southwest. Became director of Phillies' farm system 5/22/65, remaining in that capacity until designated general manager 6/3/72. Succeeded John Quinn. Assumed both roles as field manager and general manager 7/10/72.

OZARK, DANIEL LEONARD (Ike) Coach-manager. B. 11/26/23, Buffalo, N.Y. 6'3", 210. Danny Ozark got chance to manage major league club 1973 after spending all baseball career to that time with Brooklyn–Los Angeles Dodger organization. Never reached majors as player, but coached Dodgers, 1965–72. Appointed pilot, Philadelphia NL, November 1972, with two-year contract.

Ozark started with Dodger farm club, Olean, N.Y., 1942, as second baseman. Spent next three years in army; served at Omaha Beach, in Battle of Bulge, and in Germany; wounded in knee, received Purple Heart and five battle stars. Became first baseman, 1946 and played for Abilene, Fort Worth, Newport News, Elmira, St. Paul. Playing manager, Wichita Falls, 1956; also at Cedar Rapids, 1957, and Macon, 1958–59. Manager, St. Paul, 1960. Manager, Omaha, 1961–62. Manager, Spokane, 1963–64. In 1963 was named PCL Manager of Year after bringing Spokane club home first in Northern Division. As player, 1949, on last day of season, went 7 for 9, helping St. Paul win doubleheader and take American Association pennant by half game.

PADGETT, ERNEST KITCHEN (Red) Inf.-BR-TR. B. 3/1/99, Philadelphia, Pa. D. 4/15/57, East Orange, N.J. 5'8", 155. Ernie Padgett got
name in record books in only his second game in major leagues. Pulled
that rare trick, unassisted triple play. Ernie was at shortstop for Boston
Braves 10/6/23, playing against Philadelphia, at Boston. In fourth
inning, with men on first and second and nobody out, Walter Holke hit
line drive to Padgett. Ernie ran to second to retire Cotton Tierney, some
distance off bag en route to third; and before Cliff Lee, man who had
been on first, could reverse self, Padgett tagged him for third out.
Padgett didn't do much else in majors to gain fame. Hit .266 over five
seasons, three with Braves and two with Cleveland Indians. Ernie started
at Charlotte in South Atlantic League, 1920, later playing with Winston-
Salem and Memphis. Had two seasons batting above .300, gaining
promotion to Braves at end of 1923 season. Played just four games for
Boston that fall, but had 138 games with them in 1924, mostly at third
base. Hit .255. In 86 games with Braves, 1926, with .305 mark, then
moved to Cleveland Indians for 1927–28, playing just 43 games in AL.
Then Padgett dropped from major league scene after 271 games. His 223
hits included 34 doubles, 17 triples, 1 homer.

PAFKO, ANDREW OF-BR-TR. B. 2/25/21, Boyceville, Wis. 6', 190.
Andy Pafko, who hit .285 and banged 213 home runs during major
league career with Chicago Cubs, Brooklyn Dodgers and Milwaukee
Braves, is enjoying baseball pension, taking things easy in Windy City.
Checks for $780 started coming in during early 1971 on monthly basis.

After playing days were over in 1959, Andy coached Braves three years, managed minor league teams at Binghamton, N.Y.; West Palm Beach; Kinston, N.C., and scouted for Montreal Expos.

Pafko was solid hitter for Cubs, going over .300 mark three separate seasons as regular; twice had more than 100 RBI. In 1950 hit 36 homers; 30 round-trippers in 1951, which he divided between Cubs and Dodgers. Had couple of strong seasons with Braves while still in Wisconsin, then began to taper off. Andy led NL outfielders in fielding, 1945; then in 1948, playing third base, led NL competitors in double plays at hot corner. Also led them in assists and in errors. Hit three homers in one game 8/2/50.

Pafko, farm boy, got minor league schooling at Eau Claire, Green Bay, Macon, Los Angeles (PCL) during 1940–43. Cubs brought him to majors, 1943 and kept him until traded to Brooklyn 6/15/51. Finished that year with Dodgers, remained through 1952, then landed with Milwaukee Braves where stayed for rest of playing days. Overall record: 1852 big league games, 1796 hits, 844 runs, 264 doubles, 62 triples, 213 homers, 976 RBI.

During career one of saddest moments came in NL playoff game, 1951. Dodgers were leading 4–1, entering ninth inning. If they could get three outs, NL flag theirs. Got only one. Giants scored once and had runners on second and third when Bobby Thomson came to bat. Dressen, bossing Flatbush crew, switched pitchers, Ralph Branca replacing Don Newcombe. After Branca threw one strike, Thomson lined toward left field. Pafko, playing left, thought he had chance to catch ball. Backed against wall but drive continued over fence for home run and Giant pennant.

Pafko's WS performances in 1945 with Cubs, 1952 with Brooklyn, and 1957,58 with Braves, showed .222 average—24 games, 72 trips, 16 hits, 3 doubles, 1 triple, 5 RBI. All-Star games 1947–50, 4 for 10.

PAGAN, JOSE ANTONIO   Inf.-BR-TR. B. 5/5/35, Barceloneta, Puerto Rico. 5'9", 170. Jose Pagan joined Philadelphia Phillies, 1973, after dividing earlier years in NL between San Francisco Giants and Pittsburgh Pirates. Helped Giants to pennant, 1962, and Pirates to world championship, 1971. Key man for Giants, 1962. Played 164 games, led NL shortstops in fielding, hit .259, drove in 57 runs. Followed it with .368 average in WS against New York Yankees, including home run off Ralph Terry in Yankee Stadium 10/10/62. Proving he is strong under fire, Pagan was one who drove in run in seventh game of 1971 WS that gave Pittsburgh world championship. Score was tied in eighth inning; with Stargell on first base, Pagan doubled. Pittsburgh won 2–1.

Jose started at El Dorado, Ark., 1955; played with Danville, Carolina League; Springfield, Eastern League; Phoenix and Tacoma, Pacific

Coast League, en route to Giants. Had 31 games with San Francisco, 1959; came back for 18 in 1960. Remained with them until 5/22/65 when traded to Pittsburgh. Filled in at all infield positions, outfield, and even caught while with Pirates. Pittsburgh gave him unconditional release after 1972 season, offered chance to manage one of their minor league teams. But Jose preferred to stay in majors as player.

Pagan, although good fielder, and versatile, had one really rough experience. Tied NL record for most errors in one inning by third baseman—three—in fourth round 8/18/66, while with Pirates. Jose, as he started new career with Phillies, had .251 lifetime major league average. His 906 hits were good for 133 doubles, 26 triples, 52 homers. Scored 383 runs, drove in 367. In his two WS, played 11 games, hit .324 with 11 hits in 34 trips.

Plays winter ball in Caribbean. In 1972–73 off-season was with San Juan club in Puerto Rican League.

PAGE, JOSEPH FRANCIS (Fireman) P-BL-TL. B. 10/28/17, Cherry Valley, Pa. 6'2", 205. One of best relief pitchers of all time. Pretty much of playboy until Stanley Harris, then managing N.Y. Yankees, gave chance to save important game 5/26/47 against Boston Red Sox. Sox had won AL flag in 1946 and Yankees needed strong reliever if they were to win pennant. Page entered game with two men on base, score 3–1 in favor of Sox, with none out. An error loaded bags. Page struck out next two batsmen, got third on fly ball. Allowed two hits rest of way; Yankees got some runs and won ball game 9–3. Without Page, Harris could not have won pennant. Joe got into 56 games, won 14, lost eight and saved 17 others. Started two games, and one of his losses was as starter. Had ERA of 2.15 as reliever, 2.48 ERA overall. Relieved in four games in WS against Brooklyn that fall. Charged with one defeat, but won game that made Yankees world champions. Allowed one hit, no runs in last five innings and Yanks won 5–2.

Joe's father was coal miner; Joe first of seven children. After high school, worked in mines off and on for two years. Got $50 pitching one exhibition game, then, encouraged by father to get away from mines, started playing semipro ball. Career interrupted when was run over by truck; spent 11 months in hospital. For time, strong possibility left leg would have to be amputated. And after recovery had to wear special shin guard until 1947.

Page had brief but unsuccessful tryout with Pittsburgh farm club, in Pennsylvania State Association, 1939, and played semipro rest of year. Following season joined Butler team in same league. Butler was in Yankee organization. Joe had appendectomy but won 11 games. With Augusta, 1941, broke even, 12–12, but pitched no hitter. Made good with Yankee farm team at Newark, 1943, with 14–5 record. Then, with

Yankees in 1944, won five of his first six games. Suffered shoulder injury, which he did not report. Selected for AL All-Star squad but not used. His record ultimately showed five wins, seven losses, and Joe wound up at Newark again. Back with Yankees, 1945, won six, lost three; in 1946, 9–8, with just six complete games, though started 17. Then came transformation into topflight reliever, 1947. After that banner year, Page 7–8, with 16 saves. Came back strong in 1949—13–8, all in relief. Saved 27 other ball games and had 2.59 ERA. This was Casey Stengel's first year at helm. Yanks captured flag by one game. Joe pitched one inning in relief in second game of WS. Next day, replaced Tommy Byrne in fourth inning with score tied 1–1. Went rest of distance against Brooklyn Dodgers and won by 4–3 score, although Flatbush crew scored two runs off him in ninth. Relieved again in final game of set, pitching last 2-2/3 innings and holding Dodgers scoreless. That WS he had 2.00 ERA for nine innings, one victory, no defeat. In 1950 Page had 3–7 record with 13 saves. ERA of 5.04, all in relief. Not used in 1950 WS. Dropped out of majors after that, returning briefly with Pittsburgh in 1954. Comeback not successful: pitched 9-2/3 innings, ERA 11.17.

Joe's major league totals: 285 games, 790 innings over eight seasons, 57–49, 3.53 ERA, walked 421, struck out 519, saved 76 games.

PAIGE, LEROY ROBERT (Satchel) P-BR-TR. B. 7/7/06, Mobile, Ala. 6'4", 190. Satchel Paige, in younger days, threw fast ball described as "just a blur, or a noise in catcher's glove." All evidence indicates was one of greatest pitchers of all time, certainly rivaling Walter Johnson; and that he belongs in Hall of Fame, where he was enshrined in 1971.

Paige did not get chance to show skills in major leagues until well past his prime. Still, when he was 42, made debut in AL, won six important victories for Cleveland Indians, losing one. Without those six victories, Indians could not have won pennant that year, 1948. Took one-game playoff to decide flag, since Cleveland and Boston finished regular race in tie. Satchel not only helped Indians win pennant. More than earned salary in first three starts when more than 200,000 fans jammed stands to see legendary black man pitch in big league. Despite late start in majors, Paige was member of AL All-Star squads 1952,53, while with St. Louis Browns. Did not get into 1952 game because was cut short by rain after five innings; Satchel due to pitch eighth inning. In 1953 game, at Crosley Field, Cincinnati, pitched one inning at end of game, allowed two runs as NL team won game 5–1. In 1948 WS pitched two-thirds of an inning. Allowed no hits, no runs, no walks, but charged with balk.

Paige's overall big league record: 28–31. After 6–1 season with Indians, 1948, had 4–7 mark in 1949. Won three, lost four with Browns, 1951; then had 12–10 and 3–9 records, also with St. Louis. Made final official appearance in majors with Kansas City AL 9/25/65. On that occasion pitched three innings. Assuming Paige born in 1906, was 59 years, two months, and 18 days old at time. This made him oldest man to appear in major league lineup. Previous record held by Nick Altrock. Satch made one more appearance for big league team, in 1968. Atlanta Braves signed him as coach; needed few more months to round out eligibility for baseball pension. In exhibition game against Richmond club, pitched one inning. Got two strikeouts and retired other batter on infield grounder.

Paige's complete major league record showed he pitched in 179 games. In 476 innings, walked 183, struck out 290, had ERA of 3.29.

Claims have been made Paige born in 1904; was sixth of eight children. As boy, tossed stones at cans, which helped him later with accurate control. Played baseball when wasn't busy delivering ice or working as porter in Mobile's Union Station. About 1925, was good enough to join Chattanooga Lookouts; later pitched for Birmingham Black Barons, New Orleans Pelicans, Baltimore Black Sox, Chicago American Giants. Spent seven years with Pittsburgh Crawfords. These all were teams in Negro leagues. Pay was not fancy, nor were playing conditions on field. Off field, it was rugged life, whether in hotels or boardinghouses; oftentimes was necessary to ride railroad coaches, buses, or crowded private automobiles all night to get from one city to another. Paige reportedly won 31 games, lost four in 1933; had 21 consecutive victories, 62 straight scoreless innings. In 1934 Satch was with team from Bismarck, N. Dak. "We won 104 games out of 105. I pitched every game, I guess. I know I started 29 games one month."

When major league season ended, Bill Veeck saw him pitch 1–0 victory over Dizzy Dean in exhibition game. Veeck, later, played important role in Paige's life. Bill, president of Cleveland Indians in 1948, signed him to first big league contract. Veeck also his employer at St. Louis, 1951–53. And was Bill who insisted, when Paige admitted to Hall of Fame, he be given equal status with other immortals and not have plaque hung in "special" wing.

Before Satchel got chance in AL, frequently spent summers in United States, winters in Caribbean. Pitched for Homestead Grays and Kansas City Monarchs. In fall of 1946, Veeck saw Paige beat Bob Feller in exhibition game, shutting out Feller's team. This revived interest. Jackie Robinson broke color line with Brooklyn Dodgers, 1947. Indians signed Satch July 1948. His first game, against Chicago White Sox, Paige won 5–0, allowing nine hits. One week later threw another shutout against White Sox. After Veeck sold out at Cleveland, 1949, Paige was released. Returned to Kansas City Monarchs for 1950. Then Veeck, having taken over St. Louis Browns, signed Satchel for that club, 1951. Between time with Browns and final big league appearance with Kansas City, Paige pitched for Miami in International League and Portland, Pacific Coast

League.

It has been estimated that during career covering approximately 40 years, Paige appeared in 2600 games; believed to have thrown perhaps 300 shutouts, 55 of them no-hitters. Of course he pitched against all kinds of hitters, good, bad, indifferent. True story of skills can never be translated into statistical record. As years wore on, Paige made good money, sometimes as much as $50,000 in single year. But had to work for it, day in, day out.

Paige had sizzling fast ball, but also famous for "hesitation pitch." Threw curves, sliders, whatnot. Delivered ball with unique contortions somewhat resembling hyperactive windmill. This helped deceive batter, especially in later years when some of zing had departed from fast ball.

Satchel got nickname from "satchelfoot," referring to his oversized feet. Happy fellow, took guitar on most of trips; loves to sing and dance. Great believer in steaming hot baths. Connoisseur of antique silverware and fine china. When inducted into Hall of Fame, Paige told crowd at Cooperstown, "I am the proudest man on the face of the earth today." Later commented about current crop of baseball players, "Baseball is too much a business to them now. I loved baseball. I ate and slept it. But now, players, instead of picking up sports page, pick up *Wall Street Journal*. It's different."

PALMER, JAMES ALVIN P-BR-TR. B. 10/15/45, New York, N.Y. 6'3", 196. Jim Palmer's 21st victory of 1972 season was 100th of his AL career. Helped own cause by hitting safely once, scoring two of four Oriole runs needed for 4–3 win over Milwaukee Brewers. Earl Weaver, Baltimore manager, remarked earlier in season, "Palmer is darn near perfect pitcher right now. He's going to keep getting better too until natural erosion of time eventually catches up with him. But that shouldn't happen for long while, because Jim keeps himself in such excellent physical condition." Palmer may get better but will be hard to improve on his winning percentage. Against those 100 wins as he went into 1973 were only 48 defeats, many of them heart-breaking variety. Working in 204 career games, had 74 complete contests to credit despite arm trouble some years ago that resulted in return to minors. Pitched 1391 innings and compiled 2.72 ERA, with 935 strikeouts, 507 walks. Had 18 shutouts to credit.

Jim, who received bonus reported to be $60,000 when he signed 6/12/64, easily could have been lost to Orioles after tendinitis of arm and shoulder. While in minors was exposed to draft, but no other major league club took him. Spent first pro season with Baltimore farm club, Aberdeen, S. Dak., where won 11, lost three. Won five, lost four for Orioles, 1965, then came up with 15–10 season as sophomore. Followed that with WS victory over Los Angeles Dodgers. Blanked them 6–0 in second game of set, becoming youngest pitcher in WS history to hurl shutout. Lacked nine days of being 21 at time. Palmer's arm and shoulder problems began in 1967. Sent to Rochester, Miami, and Elmira, returned to Orioles, 1969, with brilliant comeback. Won 16 games, lost only four, and had 2.34 ERA. Next three seasons came up with 20-game victories. Pitched 8—0 no-hitter against Oakland, 8/13/69.

Despite Palmer's history of arm, shoulder, and back problems, fast ball was sizzling in 1973. Often helps own cause by good hitting.

Jim lost one game in 1969 WS against N.Y. Mets; won one game in each of 1970 and 1971 WS. Overall record for four Series came to 3–1, ERA 3.21, 25 walks, 35 strikeouts 47-2/3 innings. All-Star games 1970,71,72.

Pressure doesn't bother Palmer. Pitcher when Orioles clinched pennant, 1966—and pitched crucial game that gave Baltimore flag in each of three playoff series—1969,70,71.

Excellent golfer. Fine speaker.

PAPPAS, MILTON STEVEN (Gimpy)   P-BR-TR. B. 5/11/39, Detroit, Mich. 6'3", 204. Milt Pappas, alias "Golden Greek," came within shade of joining select few pitchers who have hurled perfect game in majors. Retired first 26 San Diego batters to face him at Wrigley Field, 9/2/72. Then walked one man and got next hitter on routine pop fly.

Pappas, like so many pitchers, seemed to improve with age. In early games, 1972, pitching for Cubs, had arm problems; at one point had 6–7 record, then got going—won 11 straight to finish with 17–7 for season. Pappas, in 1971, won 17 for Cubs, more than had ever won for any club before, but dropped 14 decisions. Milt's 1972 performance raised career victory total to 202 against 152 defeats. His 2.77 ERA almost as good as 2.61 mark while pitching for Baltimore Orioles, 1965. That year, won 13, lost 9. As 1973 dawned, Pappas had pitched 3024 innings in 490 games. Good control—818 walks against 1680 strikeouts, although led AL in wild pitches in 1959 with 14, and in 1960 with ten.

Pappas signed with Baltimore Orioles, 1957, and farmed out briefly to Knoxville. After three games, returned, pitched nine innings in AL with one run scored off him, but had no decisions. Following year chalked up 10–10 record, then 15–9, 15–11. Posted 16–9 and 16–7 marks for Orioles, 1963,64. Traded to Cincinnati 12/9 /65 in Frank Robinson deal. Reds disappointed with exchange since Robinson immediately won AL bat title; also led league in homers, RBI, and runs scored. Same season, 1966, Milt won 12, lost 11, had mediocre 4.29 ERA. Improved performance, 1967, with 16 wins, 13 losses. Cincinnati disposed of him 6/11/68, sending him to Atlanta. Did not distinguish himself there, and was considered question mark when acquired by Chicago NL 6/25/70. However, went on to win 17 games for season. Two All-Star Games for

AL, 1962,65; three innings, allowing four earned runs, but had no decisions.

PARENT, FREDERICK ALFRED SS-OF-BR-TR. B. 11/25/75, Bidde-ford, Maine. D. 11/2/72, Sanford, Maine. 5'5½'', 148. Fred Parent, who played in first modern WS as member of Boston AL team, then known as Puritans, outlasted all other participants in that Series, living until almost 97. Also believed to be last man who played in major leagues during 1890s when death came 11/2/72. Parent, in that first WS, contributed three triples among nine hits, scored eight runs, and drove in four with .281 average. Boston defeated Pittsburgh, five games to three.

Fred had brief spell with St. Louis NL, 1899, just two games. Spent 1900 with Providence and joined Boston, 1901, remaining until end of 1907. Chicago AL 1908–11. Then to minors.

Parent played 1328 major league games, hit .265. Best year for average was rookie year with Boston, 1901, with .318; hit .304 in pennant-winning season, 1903. Stole 184 bases in majors, pilfering 20 or more four times.

PARKER, FRANCIS JAMES (Salty) SS-BR-TR. B. 7/8/13, East St. Louis, Ill. 6', 185. Salty Parker has been in baseball much longer than most ball players have been on earth. Began at age 17 under assumed name. Though he only played 11 games with Detroit Tigers, was only man on team rewarded with free automobile—because was only one who accepted dinner invitation by big car manufacturer. Managed New York Mets briefly—they won four games, lost seven while he was interim boss, 1967, after Wes Westrum dropped. Coach for California Angels, 1973.

Parker's first ball club was Moline, Mississippi Valley League, 1930, using name Charles Francis. Specialized in shortstop those days. Later played with Beaumont and Toledo en route to Detroit. In those 11 games with Tigers, 1936, had .280 average with seven hits in 25 trips—and this proved to be his lifetime major league average. Never again got into big league box score.

Back in minors, played at Indianapolis, Tulsa, Shreveport, Dallas, Montreal, St. Paul. In 1939 got first crack at managing while still player, at Lubbock. Won first-place honors in both halves of season in West Texas–New Mexico League. Later player manager at Marshall, Tex.; Shreveport; Temple and Tyler, Tex. Continued managing from sidelines at El Dorado, Ark.; Danville, Va.; Dallas. Coach, San Francisco Giants, 1958–61; Cleveland, 1962; Scout, Pittsburgh, 1963. Coach, Los Angeles Angels, 1964–65. Coach and interim manager, N.Y. Mets, 1967. Coach, Houston Astros, 1969–72. Coach, California Angels, 1973.

PARKER, MAURICE WESLEY (Wes) 1B-BLR-TL. B. 11/13/39, Chicago, Ill. 6'1", 190. Wes Parker, most unusual young man, smooth-fielding first baseman for Los Angeles Dodgers since 1964, announced retirement from game after close of 1972 season. Turned back on $70,000 salary so could "enjoy whole spectrum" of life now. Then agreed to join 1973 telecasting team for Cincinnati Reds. While Parker enjoys baseball, believes it is game to be played by single men in their 20s. Wes was still single when he retired, said had no immediate plans for matrimony. Wanted to enjoy many other things while still young, such as reading, writing, bridge, music, travel, golf, going to beach. No job when he quit—but felt human values were more important than continuing demanding rigors of major league schedule. "If you're in baseball too long, you're trapped," he declared.

Besides playing brilliant first base, Parker dedicated to fighting drug abuse among young people. Sincerely believes credo of "Athletes for Youth," saying, "If we succeed in getting just one youngster to kick drug habit, it will have been worth it."

Wes, in 1972, for sixth consecutive year, voted finest first baseman in NL by managers and coaches. In nine years made only 45 errors. Career fielding average .996, one point better than average of Frank McCormick, whose fielding average was highest for any first basemen playing at least 1000 games.

Parker, called "Tiger" by teammates despite his genuine philosophy of sportsmanship, attended Claremont Men's College and received A.B. from Southern Cal before signing with Dodger organization, 1963. Hit .305 in first pro season that summer at Santa Barbara, and .350 in 26 games at Albuquerque same year. Joined Dodgers, 1964 and remained with them until announced retirement. Led first basemen in fielding five times. Peak season at plate was 1970 when was only player in NL to play every game; first NL switch hitter in 35 years to drive in 100 runs—had 111; first major leaguer in 20 years to drive in 100 with 10 or fewer homers. Hit .319 with 196 hits; led NL in doubles with 47; scored 84 runs.

His .997 fielding average in 1965 tied NL record; also had .997 mark in 1972. Parker's overall major league hitting was .267 for 1288 games. His 1110 hits included 194 doubles, 32 triples, 64 homers. Scored 548 runs, drove in 470; stole 60 bases.

When Parker quit, was writing book on how to play first base.

PASCUAL, CAMILO ALBERTO, JR. P-BR-TR. B. 1/20/34, Havana, Cuba. 5'11", 190. Camilo Pascual, during first five years in majors, won 28 and lost 66. But in next 10 seasons won 142, losing 97. It should be noted, however, that in first five seasons was with Washington Senators and they finished eighth three times, seventh once, and sixth once. Still,

Camilo won 17 games, lost 10 for Senators in 1959 when they again had cellar ball club. Pascual had 12–8 record in 1960, then moved to Minnesota with franchise, and things began to look up. In six seasons with Twins, club finished in runner-up position twice; had one third-place finish and one pennant winner.

Pascual led AL in strikeouts three seasons, 1961–63. Anytime pitcher strikes out twice as many men as he walks, it shows good control of fine "stuff." Camilo, during major league career, struck out total of 2167 while walking just 1069 batsmen.

Pascual's best years with Twins were 1962–63 when he won 20 and lost 11 and came back with 21–9. In latter season chalked up best ERA mark with 2.47. Tapered off after that; encountered arm trouble in 1966 and traded to Washington 12/3/66. In 2-1/2 years in nation's capital won 27 and lost 27, then sold to Cincinnati Reds 7/7/69. No wins or losses in five games with Reds that season. In 1970 with Los Angeles Dodgers, but spent part of season on disabled list and pitched in just 10 games without decision. Final fling came in 1971 with Cleveland Indians, 2–1. Retired.

Pascual could look back with satisfaction on 1960 opening day performance. Pitching for Senators against Boston Red Sox, struck out 15 men. And 7/19/61 struck out 15 members of Los Angeles Angels while on mound for Twins. Led AL in shutouts, 1959 and tied for lead two other seasons. AL All-Star squads 1959–62,64. Took part in just three of these games; charged with loss of first game of 1962 pair. In 1965 WS, only appearance in fall classic, Pascual started third game against Dodgers, but left after five innings, trailing by three runs. Los Angeles won contest 4–0. His ERA 5.40.

Before coming to major leagues, Pascual pitched for Geneva, N.Y., in Border League; Big Spring, Tex.; Chickasha, Okla.; Havana, and Tampa in three-year period 1951–53.

PASKERT, GEORGE HENRY (Dode) OF-BR-TR. B. 8/28/81, Cleveland, Ohio. D. 2/12/59, Cleveland, Ohio. 5'11", 167. Dode Paskert risked baseball career as well as own life, 1920, when he rescued 15 children from burning apartment building in Cleveland. Wrapped each one in overcoat and carried them individually to safety. Was severely burned but recovered in time to play with Chicago Cubs that year.

Dode came off Cleveland sandlots, like many other greats including Tommy Leach, Bill Bradley, Jimmy Austin, and George Uhle. Signed first pro contract with Dayton, Central League, 1904. Moved up to Atlanta, Southern Association, 1907, and later same season with Cincinnati Reds for 16 games. Then three full seasons with Reds, reaching .300 mark in 1910. Trade took him to Philadelphia NL for 1911. Hit .273 that year but boosted average to .315 in 1912. Helped Phils win first NL pennant, 1915, but was able to hit only .158 in WS, taken by Boston Red Sox. After 1917 season another deal put him in uniform of Chicago Cubs. Three seasons in Windy City. Then Cincinnati bought contract, intending to send him to Seattle, Pacific Coast League. Rule said 10-year man could not be sent to minors without consent, so Dode remained with Reds through 1921 season. After release by Cincinnati, Paskert played in American Association and Southern Association briefly. Retired 1924. Spent rest of life in Cleveland as machine operator.

Dode was speedy outfielder who stole 293 bases in majors. Had 51 steals, 1910, and 36 in 1912. Wound up big league career with .268 average for 1715 games. Hit 280 doubles, 78 triples, 40 homers, with 1613 safeties in all. Scored 868 runs; 715 RBI. In two WS, 1915 with Phils, 1918 with Cubs, hit .175 in 11 games.

PATEK, FREDDIE JOE (Midge) SS-BR-TR. B. 10/9/44, Oklahoma City, Okla. 5'4", 140. Smallest man in majors. Intense competitor; speedy base runner; rifle arm. Second season in Kansas City, 1972, not so successful as 1971, when hit .267, stole 49 bases. Led majors in putouts and double plays at shortstop; led AL in total chances at position. Also led league in triples, with 11.

Patek's 1972 season started wrong. Had groin injury, then stomach ailment that kept him from eating. Grew tense with nervous exhaustion. On return to lineup delivered some timely hits, but had .212 average for season. Stole 33 bases instead of 49. And in August, manager Bob Lemon benched him and Amos Otis for lack of hustle. Freddie made peace with Lemon in short order, saying, "If I ever dog it again I hope he tells me about it. I want him to get on me. I needed a kick in the rear and he gave it to me. One of his pet peeves is guys not running full speed to first base. And he's right."

Patek started in Pittsburgh organization, 1966. Most of 1966 with Gastonia, Western Carolina League, where hit .310, stole 38 bases. Also with Columbus and Asheville, 1966; then put in full season with Columbus, leading International League in steals with 42. Hit .248 that year. In 1968 hit .304 for Columbus in 33 games. Joined Pirates 6/3/68. Was breezing along at .281 clip first couple of weeks, then stopped pitch thrown by Don Drysdale of Dodgers. X rays of left wrist did not reveal fracture. Played nine more games, but hitting fell off. Another X ray revealed hairline fracture and he was out for three weeks. Needed surgery after season to correct wrist condition. Played 147 games as regular Pirate shortstop, 1969. Hit .239, stole 15 bases. Somewhat unhappy when had to share job with Gene Alley and Jose Pagan, 1970. Then traded to Kansas City 12/2/70.

Freddie looked forward to 1973 season in hopes of improving .243 lifetime major league average for 575 games. Owned 489 hits, with 69 doubles, 23 triples, 14 homers. Scored 266 runs; had 137 RBI and 123 stolen bases. Off-season works in sporting goods store.

PAUL, GABRIEL Executive. B. 1/4/10, Rochester, N. Y. Gabe Paul, for many years with Cincinnati and Cleveland clubs, shifted to New York Yankees' front office early in 1973. Paul became one of 15 new owners of franchise, bought from Columbia Broadcasting System. No title was announced for him, but it was expressly stated by Mike Burke, then president of Yankees, another of new owners, that Paul would not replace general manager Lee MacPhail.

Gabe started his connection with baseball in St. Louis Cardinal organization while in early teens. Cardinals owned Rochester franchise in International League. Warren Giles, who eventually became NL president, then was president of Rochester Red Wings. Gabe loved baseball, impressed Giles, and soon became general handy man. Began writing publicity releases about Red Wings. Learned front office detail, concessions, and was ready for bigger things when opportunity knocked for Giles. Larry MacPhail left Cincinnati club as general manager at close of 1936 season. Giles was successor, and Gabe moved into spot vacated by Gene Karst, Reds' publicity chief, who resigned to go to China. Paul became Giles' first assistant; remained with Cincinnati after Giles became NL president, 1951. Vice president and general manager until 1960 when he went to Houston NL expansion club as general manager. Houston did not field team until 1962. After few months with Houston organization Gabe shifted to Cleveland, 1961, as general manager. Added titles of president and treasurer two years later when he and others bought Indians. In August 1966, sold most of stock to Vernon Stouffer. For time during late 1960s, Alvin Dark, field manager of Indians, took over many front office responsibilities that had been Paul's. But Dark released 7/29/71, and Paul returned to power under Stouffer. Continued as general manager after Nick Mileti bought ball club, 1972, Mileti becoming president. Then came shift to Yankees.

Paul and wife have five children. Gabe, Jr., director of stadium operations for Milwaukee Brewers.

PAYSON, JOAN WHITNEY Executive. B. 2/5/93, New York, N. Y. President of New York Mets is multimillionaire who enjoys life. One of favorite pastimes is baseball. N. Y. Giants used to be her favorites but they deserted Gotham for West Coast, so she later put up some $4 million to get Mets into major league picture. Leaves most detail work of running Mets to M. Donald Grant, chairman of board of directors; Bob Scheffing, vice president and general manager; and Yogi Berra, field manager. She concentrates on rooting for team, eating popcorn and candy, trying to court good luck for Mets with pet superstitions.

Joan Whitney was born into family of great wealth; learned to ride horses while learning to talk; attended Miss Chapin's School, then Barnard College. Married Charles Shipman Payson 7/5/24. She and brother Jock Whitney own Greentree Stables with plenty of blooded race horses; together they have backed motion pictures and Broadway plays, including hits *Rebecca, A Streetcar Named Desire, Gone with the Wind.*

Patron of art and civic institutions; donor to medical causes and hospitals. Bought into N. Y. Giants as minority stockholder. When Horace Stoneham decided to move Giants to San Francisco, Joan tried to persuade him to stay in New York; failing this, tried to buy controlling interest in team. Later put up money to help get Mets started.

Mrs. Payson's greatest thrill probably came in 1969 when "Amazing Mets" won NL flag and world championship. Besides dedicated interest in baseball, has financially aided art galleries, bookstore, and Payne Whitney Gymnasium at Yale, one of best equipped in world.

PECKINPAUGH, ROGER THORPE SS-BR-TR. B. 2/5/91, Wooster, Ohio. 5'10½", 160. Fine shortstop for many years in AL. Respected manager and club official in later years. Yet also remembered by many fans for horrible WS, 1925, when he made eight errors after announcement that had been named MVP in AL. His miscues directly responsible for Washington Senators losing second and seventh games of classic. Other errors simply added to chagrin. In second game Roger had two misplays; Pirates got unearned run and walked off field with 3–2 victory. Then in crucial seventh contest, Peck's errors were responsible for four Pittsburgh runs. Pirates took game, 9–7, and won WS, four games to three. As result of Peck's disastrous Series, was decided not to announce MVP in later years until after WS, although votes were in and based solely on season's play.

Peckinpaugh impressed baseball people at early age, not only as player but as leader. In 1914, when Roger 23 years old, New York AL club, then known as Highlanders, named him interim manager when Frank Chance was dropped as manager 9/16/14. Won nine, lost eight, rest of that season.

Peck, like Delahantys—Ed, Jim, Frank—George Uhle, Joe Vosmik, and Joe Kuhel, got start on sandlots of Cleveland. Signed with Indians, 1910, played 15 games, but farmed out to New Haven that year and Portland, Oreg., next season. Back with Indians, 1912. Traded to N.Y. AL 5/20/13, remaining until close of 1921. Involved in two deals that transferred contract to Boston AL, but before 1922 rolled around was sent to Washington. With Senators until after 1926 season. Chicago AL 1927. Then manager, Cleveland, 1928 until 6/9/33. Manager, Kansas City, American Association, 1934. AL promotional bureau 1935–38.

Vice president–manager, New Orleans, Southern Association, 1939. AL promotional bureau, 1940. Manager, Cleveland, 1941. Vice president–general manager, Cleveland, 1942–46. General manager, Buffalo, 1947.

Roger won no pennants as manager, but was good, sound baseball man and earned keep. As player, took part in 2008 major league games, hit for .259 average. His 1873 hits included 256 doubles, 75 triples, 48 homers. Scored 1005 runs, drove in 749, stole 207 bases. In WS 1921,24,25, hit .250, with 16 hits in 64 trips. In 1924 Series against Giants, hit .417.

Peck once went through 10-inning game 9/17/23 without having fielding chance. His record of nine assists in WS game of 10/5/21 has not been equaled since then. In 1919 had 29-game hitting streak.

PELEKOUDAS, CHRIS G. Umpire. B. 1/22/18, Chicago, Ill. 5'10", 185. Spitball was outlawed more than 50 years ago but most ball players will testify thousands of spitballs have been thrown since then. Plenty of other illegal pitches also have been thrown in major leagues. Chris Pelekoudas, who became NL umpire, 1960, stirred up storm few years ago by trying to enforce rule against illegal pitches. Phil Regan, then pitching for Chicago Cubs, was victim of his ruling. Umpire declared three of his pitches illegal during game 8/18/68. Once ruled foul ball was simply ball; twice allowed Cincinnati batters to hit over again after they had made outs. In one case Pete Rose singled after apparently striking out. Pelekoudas based his ruling on flight and break of ball, not on evidence of saliva or Vaseline on ball. Chicago fans booed and threw debris on field. Leo Durocher, then managing Cubs, led violent protest. Said Pelekoudas: "I've been umpiring long enough to know an illegal pitch when I see one. We're not stupid. We can spot an illegal pitch. Anybody can spot one. Even the spectators can tell." Warren C. Giles, then president of NL, did not support his umpire's approach to problem. Though he did not so state in specific terms, apparently Giles told umpires not to penalize pitchers unless they had concrete evidence of use of foreign substance on ball.

Pelekoudas umpired in Eastern Shore League, 1948; Inter-State League, 1949; Western League, 1950–52; Pacific Coast League, 1953–59; NL, since 1960. Umpired in WS of 1966 and 1972. Worked in two All-Star games. Spent five years in army and air force.

PENNOCK, HERBERT JEFFERIES P-BLR-TL. B. 2/10/94, Kennett Square, Pa. D. 1/30/48, New York, N.Y. 6', 165. Miller Huggins, manager of N.Y. Yankees in 1920s, called Herb Pennock "greatest lefthander of all time." Many would dispute this opinion, of course, but Herb certainly was classy southpaw who got into Hall of Fame, 1948, on unquestioned merit. Credentials included such things as 22 major league seasons; 240 victories against 162 defeats; five WS wins—and no losses, with ERA of 1.95.

Pennock started pitching before World War I. Left Wenonah Military Academy to pitch in Atlantic City at age 17. When Connie Mack heard about his no-hitter against black team from St. Louis, offered him spot on Athletics' roster. And at 18, got into 17 games in AL, winning one, losing two. That was in 1912, while William Howard Taft was still President of U.S. Didn't get much work, 1913, but won 11, lost four for Athletics when they won flag in 1914. Mack then broke up team after losing WS to Miracle Boston Braves in four straight games. Pennock departed for Boston Red Sox, June 1915. Slender southpaw didn't do anything spectacular next few years, missing 1918 season because of military service. But won 16 games in 1919 and again in 1920, for second-division clubs. Lost more than he won in 1921–22, but was obvious his work would improve if he had good team behind him. Chance came when Yankees again raided Red Sox. Traded to New York 1/30/23, Pennock paid off immediately. His 19–6 record for winning percentage of .760 topped AL pitchers, helped Yankees to another pennant and their first WS. Stylish lefthander won both starts against Giants and relieved in another game Bombers captured.

Pennock was even better in total victories, 1924, with 21, dropping nine decisions, but had 16–17 record in 1925 when Yanks dropped to seventh place. But Pennock and teammates came back strong, 1926, to win another AL flag. Herb did his share with 23 victories, 11 defeats. Not his fault Yanks defeated by Rogers Hornsby's St. Louis Cardinals. Pennock won opening game of WS 2–1 and fifth contest 3–2, and pitched three scoreless innings in final, seventh, game. But Redbirds already had enough runs off Waite Hoyt, even though none was earned, to win by 3–2 score. Herb had 1.22 ERA for that Series. Came up with 19–8 in 1927, another Yankee flag year. And took his 1927 WS start by 8–1 score, getting ERA down to an even 1.00. With Yankees through 1933, but age was catching up with arm. Did not pitch in 1928 WS, and hurled four innings in 1932 classic, but his five WS wins and no defeats stood. Overall WS effectiveness 1.95 for 55-1/3 innings; 8 walks, 24 strikeouts.

Pennock added two more AL victories, no losses, for his bag in 1934 while member of Boston Red Sox. Quit active pitching with record of 3558 innings in majors, 1403 earned runs allowed, 1227 strikeouts, and 916 walks.

Herb coached Red Sox 1936–40; supervisor of Red Sox farm system 1941–43. General manager, Philadelphia NL, 1944 until death.

PEPITONE, JOSEPH ANTHONY   1B-OF-BL-TL. B. 10/9/40, Brooklyn, N.Y. 6'2", 199. "You're dumbest manager I ever played for," Joe Pepitone reportedly told Leo Durocher during clubhouse meeting 8/23/71. Leo was still bossing Chicago Cubs. In May 1972, Pepitone announced voluntary retirement from baseball. Few weeks later changed mind—after dropout had cost him estimated $15,000 to $20,000. Joe's desertion of Cubs was not first time he left major league ball club. Jumped N.Y. Yankees, also Houston Astros. During absence from Cubs, 1972, Pepi devoted time to his cocktail bar named "Joe Pepitone's Thing."

Prodigal first baseman-outfielder got start with Yankee organization, 1958, before he developed yen for great quantities of hair on head. Bonus estimated at $20,000. Played for Auburn, Fargo-Moorehead, Binghamton, Amarillo, Richmond clubs. First session with Yanks, 1962—63 games. Following year showed great promise by hitting .271, getting 27 homers and driving in 89 runs, helping club to AL pennant. Average dropped to .251 in 1964, but still sent 100 runs across plate and slapped 28 homers, again assisting Yanks to flag. Yankees disappointed with his play after that though he hit 31 homers in 1966 and drove in 83 runs. Accused of indifference on field. Finally Yanks gave up on him and traded him to Houston Astros 12/4/69 for Curt Blefary. Wasn't happy at Houston, 1970, jumped club, and after spell on disqualified list, sold to Cubs 7/27/70. Still managed 26 homers in first NL season, hit .258, with 79 RBI. In 1971, though handicapped by bone chip in elbow of left arm, Pepi had highest batting average of big league career, .307. Played 115 games, hit 16 homers, had 61 RBI, but before season's end was manifestly unhappy. Traded by Cubs to Atlanta 5/19/73. Retired after few games. Signed up to play in Japan.

Pepi set couple of marks in AL that helped raise expectation of Yankee management he might become superstar. Two home runs in one inning 5/23/62; led AL first basemen in double plays, 128, in 1964. Led AL first sackers in fielding, 1965,66. AL All-Star squads 1963,64,65. In WS didn't hit much for average—.154 in 11 games, but did slap grand slammer 10/14/64 off Gordon Richardson of St. Louis Cardinals. Yanks won game, 8–3, but Pepitone went hitless next day when Redbirds captured crucial seventh contest, 7–5.

Pepitone's lifetime major league average hovered near .260 as 1973 season dawned. In 1363 games to then, had 1281 hits, 155 doubles, 35 triples, 216 homers, 702 RBI, 590 runs.

PEREZ, ATANASIO RIGAL (Tony)   3B-1B-BR-TR. B. 5/14/42, Ciego de Avila, Camaguey, Cuba. 6'2", 200. Sparky Anderson, manager of Cincinnati Reds, declares that Tony Perez has perfect temperament for baseball player: "Never complains, never asks favors, just plays." Most players prefer to play one position, but Tony has played first base, then third base, then shifted back to first at Cincinnati, depending on club's personnel. 1972 marked sixth consecutive season he batted in at least 90 runs.

Perez started playing ball in Cuba, where father was sugar cane worker. At age 15 was on local team. At 18 was getting start in pro ball at Cincinnati farm club at Geneva, N.Y.-Pa. League. In second season there, 1961, racked up league batting championship with .348; also led circuit in RBI with 132 and in total hits, 160. Spent 1962 at Rocky Mount, Carolina League, and most of 1963 at Macon, Sally League. Briefly with San Diego, Pacific Coast League, 1963, and most of 1964. MVP in PCL that year with .309 average and 107 RBI. Joined Cincinnati for 12 games that year, then took over regular first base job for Reds, 1965. In 1967 made shift to third base and played there most of time until Lee May traded to Houston after 1971 season. Then back to first base.

Perez' power may be judged from his homer totals. In 1967 hit 26, then 18, 37, 40, and 25 in successive seasons. In 1972 had to be content with 21. His 1972 average of .283 was just one point below lifetime major league record, .284 at season's end. At same time he had made 1174 hits, 192 doubles, 40 triples, 183 homers; scored 583 runs, drove in 713. Base-stealing total stood at 24.

Tony is something of streak hitter. Unfortunately for Reds, wasn't hot during his first WS. In 1970 classic his average was .056. In 1972 games, another story: batted .435, with 10 hits in 23 trips. All-Star games 1967–70.

Tony and family became citizens of U.S. in 1971.

PERINI, LOUIS ROBERT   Executive. B. 11/29/03, Ashland, Mass. D. 4/16/72, West Palm Beach, Fla. Former owner of Boston and Milwaukee Braves. One of "Three Steam Shovels," with Guido Rugo and Joe Maney, who bought Braves in 1942. Trio were in construction business. Perini, who started as water boy for father's small construction company, became top man for worldwide company. Built office buildings, dams, factories, gas and oil lines, almost anything sufficiently big enough to bring sizable profit. Widely criticized as "carpetbagger," since Boston NL franchise was shifted unexpectedly 3/18/53. While Milwaukee welcomed major league team at first, disenchantment later set in, with plenty of criticism about absentee ownership.

Perini was first major league club owner in modern times to move franchise. Proved highly profitable for Perini and associates. Team drew 302,667 in first 13 home dates in Wisconsin metropolis—more than Braves attracted all year in Boston, 1952. Set record of 1,826,397 in 1953 in Milwaukee, and then drew 2,131,388 in 1954.

Perini and his brothers, Charles and Joseph, became practically full owners of old Boston Braves in 1951 for about $500,000. Sold out to Chicago group in 1962 for $5,500,000, but Lou kept 10 percent interest and remained member of board of directors. Move to Milwaukee prompted by efforts of Bill Veeck, then president of St. Louis Browns, to take his franchise to Wisconsin city. Veeck had owned American Association club in Milwaukee, and had great faith in city. After Veeck's departure from Milwaukee, team had become farm club for Braves. So Perini decided to take Braves there, and reaped handsome profits in short order. *Sporting News* named him Major League Executive of Year, 1953, citing his "courage and foresightedness" in moving Braves' Franchise.

After Perini interests were sold, Braves moved to Atlanta, 1966.

PERKINS, RALPH FOSTER (Cy) C-BR-TR. B. 2/27/96, Gloucester, Mass. D. 10/2/63, Philadelphia, Pa. 5'10", 185. Cy Perkins caught six games for Philadelphia Athletics in 1915, season after Connie Mack broke up his great ball club which lost four straight to Boston Braves in WS. Cy, during next decade, was regarded by many as best catcher in AL. Then came Mickey Cochrane. Mickey had started out as anything but catcher—pitcher, infielder or outfielder. When he reported to Athletics, Connie Mack, A's mentor, recognized Cochrane's great potential—fine arm, speed, hitting power. During spring training asked Perkins to coach youngster in fine art of being major league backstop. Perkins worked tirelessly with Mickey. Opening day 1925, Cy was Philadelphia catcher—until about eighth inning. Mickey pinch hit for Perkins, doubled off scoreboard in right center. "I knew right then I had lost my job as regular," said Perkins later. During five previous seasons, Cy had caught average of nearly 140 games every year. But after helping Cochrane, he was second-stringer rest of his active career. Behind this was fact that Perkins never was hitter in class with Cochrane. His major league average for 1171 games was .259. Had total of 30 homers, 12 of them in 1921.

Perkins started pro ball at Raleigh, 1914–15. Brief trial with A's, 1915. Spent 1916, most of 1917 at Atlanta. Back with A's for seven games, 1917. Then remained with them through 1930. New York AL 1931. Coached for Yankees, 1932–33; then when Cochrane became manager at Detroit, he fondly remembered help Perkins had given him when he broke in. Perkins coached for Tigers, 1934–39, later for Philadelphia NL, 1946–54. In 1940 Perkins managed Hazleton and Lancaster in Inter-State League, and in 1945 bossed Burlington club of Carolina League.

PERRANOSKI, RONALD PETER P-BL-TL. 4/1/37, Paterson, N.J. 6', 190. Ron Perranoski, by end of 1972 season, had pitched in 729 major league games. Started one, back in 1961. Never again did name ever grace starting lineup. Specialized in relief. Reportedly had $65,000 contract when Los Angeles Dodgers handed him release. Pretty fair for man on relief. Hoped to make grade with California Angels, 1973. Chicago Cubs were his first admirers. Paid estimated $21,000 to sign him, 1958, after attendance at Michigan State. Cubs farmed him to Fort Worth and Burlington that season and to San Antonio following year. Won-and-lost records not impressive but Los Angeles Dodgers traded for him, sent him to their Montreal farm club, then to St. Paul in 1960. Broke even with St. Paul, 3–3, with 1.58 ERA. Following year began Dodger career.

With exception of 16–3 season in 1963, W-L records have never been impressive. That year had 1.67 ERA and worked in 69 games. Helped Walter Alston's crew to NL pennant. Tied NL record for most consecutive strikeouts by relief pitcher 9/12/66, with six. Named Fireman of Year 1969 with nine wins, 31 saves, while with Minnesota Twins; shared 1970 honors for same distinction, with 34 saves.

Led NL in mound appearances twice, 70 in 1962, 69 in 1963; tied for lead 1967 with 70. Traded to Minnesota 11/28/67; went to Detroit Tigers on waivers 7/30/71. Unconditionally released during 1972 season after allowing 16 runs in 19 innings. Caught on with Dodgers after that; won two games, lost none, working in total of nine contests. Released at end of season. Ron explained were nine reasons for his release by Los Angeles—Dodgers had eight lefthanders and he was almost 36 years old, ninth reason.

Perranoski's lifetime ERA in majors at time was 2.77 for 1165 innings; 79 wins, 72 losses; 682 strikeouts, 461 walks allowed. One solitary game started; no complete game ever, in majors.

PERRY, GAYLORD JACKSON P-BR-TR. B. 9/15/38, Williamston, N.C. 6'4½", 205. Does Gaylord Perry throw spitter? Plenty of major league players and managers say he does. Ask Chuck Tanner, Mike Epstein, Billy Martin, Hank Aaron et al. Ask Perry himself, and he, in effect, says he neither affirms nor denies allegation. So far, though NL and AL umpires have inspected him, his uniform, glove, body, and have watched his delivery constantly, they have not ruled he has thrown illegal pitch. With or without spitter, Perry, 1972, won Cy Young Award in AL, pitching for Cleveland. Captured 24 games, lost 16, for team that finished fifth in Eastern Division. Won exactly one third of team's total victories.

Gaylord came to Indians from San Francisco Giants 11/30/71. With him came infielder Frank Duffy, Cleveland giving up Sam McDowell in exchange. After one year, Cleveland certainly seemed to have all best of deal. Gaylord's victory total with relatively weak Cleveland club in 1972 was greater than ever before. In 1970, when Giants finished third in NL West, he won 23, lost 13.

Perry deliberately uses psychology against opposing hitters. On mound seems to be extremely nervous. Fidgets, touches face, glove, cap, goes through numerous motions before actually throwing ball. But though umpires have practically undressed him, have not found him to be using saliva, grease, or any other foreign substance on ball.

Gaylord is brother of Jim Perry, pitcher for Minnesota Twins. Was fine athlete in high school, starring in football and basketball as well as baseball. Started at St. Cloud in Northern League after receiving reported $90,000 bonus to sign with San Francisco organization, 1958. Later pitched for Corpus Christi, Tacoma, Harlingen, Tacoma. Joined Giants during 1962, won three, lost one. Back to Tacoma in 1963 for one game, then with San Francisco until trade to Cleveland. Came up with 12–11, 8–12 records in first two full seasons in majors, then had 21–8 mark in 1966. Gaylord then had two years when he lost about as many as he won; then took 19 games in 1969, losing 14. That same season put together his lowest ERA in NL, 2.44. Improved on that with Cleveland, 1972, with 1.92. And with Indians, pitched more innings than ever before, 343; more complete games than ever with Giants, 29; and struck out more men, 234, than in any previous season.

Perry's lifetime record in majors at start of 1973 was 408 games, 2638 innings pitched, 154 complete games, 158 victories, 125 defeats; allowed 828 earned runs, walked 663, struck out 1840, and had ERA of 2.82.

Pitched no-hitter against St. Louis NL 9/17/68. NL All-Stars 1966,67, AL squad 1972. Attended Campbell College in North Carolina. Off-season, farms and works as insurance agent.

PERRY, JAMES EVAN, JR. P-BLR-TR. B. 10/30/36, Williamston, N.C. 6'4", 205. Two Cy Young Awards in same family. Jim Perry took this honor, 1970, pitching for Minnesota Twins. Then younger brother, Gaylord, won same honor, 1972, pitching for Cleveland Indians. Going into 1973 season Jim had edge in winning percentage with .564 mark for 180 victories, 139 defeats; Gaylord's statistics at same time were 158 wins, 125 defeats, for .558 mark. However, Gaylord more effective as far as earned runs with 2.82 ERA; Jim had 3.37.

Jim Perry attended Campbell College in North Carolina. Had three years in minors: 1956 at North Platte, Nebr.; following year at Fargo-Moorhead; then 1958 at Reading, Pa. By this time was ready for AL. Won 12, lost 10 in his first season with Cleveland Indians, 1959. Following year had 18–10 record, then had several not particularly distinguished seasons. Indians traded him to Minnesota Twins for pitcher Jack Kralick 5/2/63. But it was 1969 before became 20-game winner. Lost six decisions that year. Then came big 24–12 year, 1970, when won Cy Young Award for AL; had 3.03 ERA that season. He was 17–17 in 1971, 13–16 in 1972.

Member of AL All-Star Game squads in 1961 and 1971 without

getting into fray. Pitched two innings in 1970 game. His WS experience came in 1965 when he got into two games, pitched four innings, and had 4.50 ERA without any decisions.

Traded to Detroit shortly before 1973 season began, Jim had 536 major league games behind him. His figures also include 835 walks, 1395 strikeouts, 2727 innings.

PESKY, JOHN MICHAEL Inf.-BL-TR. B. 9/27/19, Portland, Oreg. 5'9", 168. Greater-Boston fans recognize him as sportscaster for Red Sox since 1969. Fans of earlier vintage remember him as fine shortstop, manager of Sox two years; and back in Pacific Northwest there are some who remember him as John Michael Paveskovich, clubhouse boy for Portland team of Pacific Coast League who shined players' shoes, ran errands, and dreamed of becoming big leaguer.

Johnny signed with Red Sox organization, 1939 and sent to Rocky Mount, Piedmont League, 1940. As leadoff man, wasted no time in amassing 187 hits to lead league in this respect; his 16 triples also led circuit in three-baggers; batted .325, which gave him third place among those who played in 100 games. One year later Pesky's record was almost identical—except was playing in American Association, just one step below majors. His .325 average with Louisville, however, only gained him fifth place in league among batsmen appearing in 100 games. Again led circuit in hits—this time with 195. MVP in AA. Moved up to Red Sox, 1942, Pesky actually improved on minor league batting average and hits total. Came up with .331 and 205 safeties, more hits than anybody else in majors. Entered armed services after rookie season, but after three years came right back and again led AL in hits with 208, boosting batting average to .335. Only Mickey Vernon and Ted Williams did better than that among regulars. And following season hit safely 207 times, tops in majors. Averaged dropped slightly to .324.

Batted above .300 three more times for Red Sox. Traded to Detroit, 6/3/52. Tigers sent him to Washington 6/13/54. Served as player-coach under Mgr. Ralph Houk at Denver, 1955. Player-manager, Durham, 1956. Manager, Birmingham, 1957; Lancaster, Pa., 1958; Knoxville, 1959; Victoria, Texas, 1960; Seattle, Pacific Coast League, 1961–62; Boston Red Sox, 1963–64. Coach, Pittsburgh, 1965–67. Manager, Columbus, International League, 1968.

As pilot, Johnny led Lancaster and Knoxville teams to league flags. Under his direction, Red Sox finished in seventh place, 1963, and eighth in 1964. Both of those years AL fielded 10 teams.

Pesky one of most popular players ever to wear Red Sox uniform. Some of this popularity originated in 1946. Returning from service as flying lieutenant, junior grade, in air arm of navy, Johnny teamed with Dom DiMaggio as "table setters" for slugging Ted Williams. Dom hit

.316; Pesky .335, Williams .342. Result was hatful of runs—and pennant for Red Sox. That fall Pesky, playing third base, hit .233 in WS but did not do so well in field—made four errors. Sox lost to St. Louis Cardinals in seven games.

Johnny's major league figures show 1270 games with .307 average; 1455 hits, 226 doubles, 50 triples, 17 homers; 867 runs scored and 404 RBI. His six runs scored in one game, 5/8/46, AL record.

Johnny turned to microphone and TV cameras as profession, 1969.

PETERS, GARY CHARLES (Pete)   P-BL-TL. B. 4/21/37, Grove City, Pa. 6'2", 202. Lefthanders usually have problems in Fenway Park, but Gary Peters had two winning seasons with Boston Red Sox, 1970–71: 16–11 record first season in Beantown after being traded by Chicago White Sox 12/13/69; then 14–11. Pitched only 85 innings, 1972, won three, lost three, had one save. Then Red Sox handed him release. Peters then signed contract with Omaha farm club of Kansas City Royals, hoping he could make midwest AL club for 1973. Peters, when he lined up with Kansas City organization as he was approaching 36th birthday, had 124 major league victories against 103 defeats. In 2081 innings, over span of 357 games, had ERA of 3.25 with 1420 strikeouts, 706 walks. Twice led AL in effectiveness: 1963, with 2.33 ERA; 1966, with 1.98.

With White Sox, Gary had some notable winning seasons, 19–8 in 1963; 20–8 in 1964. Had 16–11 mark in 1967. Ran into plenty of problems, 1968, when Chicago finished ninth in 10-club circuit. Pete won four, lost 13.

When White Sox originally looked at Peters, was sandlot first baseman. High school team didn't have baseball squad but Gary starred in basketball. After signing with White Sox organization, attended Grove City College in Pennsylvania where specialized in math. Started pro career in Nebraska State League, 1956, at Holdrege; worked way up with stops at Dubuque, Iowa; Colorado Springs; Davenport, Iowa; Indianapolis, and San Diego then in Pacific Coast League. During this period had "cup of coffee" with White Sox three different seasons, but first full year in majors was 1963 when he copped AL Rookie of Year honors from Baseball Writers Association of America, and AL Rookie Pitcher of Year from *Sporting News*. AL All-Star Game squads in 1964,67. Pitched 5–0 no-hit victory over Minneapolis 7/24/59. Led AL in wild pitches, 1964, with 15.

PETERSON, FRED INGELS (Fritz)   P-BLR-TL. B. 2/8/42, Chicago, Ill. 6',207. Fritz Peterson, one of worst worriers in majors, seems to have trouble winning ball games early in year. In 1967 lost his first eight decisions for New York Yankees. In 1972 lost six straight before he notched first win. After those six losses, record was very respectable 17–9.

Peterson lefthanded control pitcher with five or six specialties for fooling batsman. Additionally, has one of most deceptive moves toward first base, helping to keep runners honest.

Peterson is thinking man with master's degree from Northern Illinois U., where he teaches in off-season. Before taking up baseball seriously was semipro hockey player.

Fritz, entering 1973, already owned 101 career victories with Yanks. Against these wins were 91 defeats. Pitched in 254 games, walked 281, struck out 829. Amassed 76 complete games and 18 shutouts. His ERA, which was 2.96 entering 1972, slipped slightly. It was 3.24 in 250 innings worked in 1972.

Signed with Yankee organization, 1963. Got minor league experience at Harlan, Appalachian League; Shelby, Western Carolina circuit; Greensboro, Carolina League; and Columbus, Ga., Southern Association. In first year with Yanks, 1966, won 12, lost 11. Then came up with 8–14, 12–11 and 17–16 seasons. Reached 20 victories, 1970, with 11 defeats and ERA of 2.91. Then 15–13 in 1971, 17–15 in 1972.

PETROCELLI, AMERICO P. (Rico) SS-3B-BR-TR. B. 6/27/43, Brooklyn, N.Y. 6′, 182. Rico Petrocelli got estimated $40,000 bonus for signing with Boston Red Sox, 1961. Hit numerous home runs, but several times has threatened to retire from baseball when things didn't suit him. While Billy Herman was manager of Sox, Petrocelli fined $1000 for walking off field during ball game and going home; threatened to become carpenter instead of ball player; also talked about becoming professional jazz drummer. Didn't like Dick Williams when Dick managed Red Sox; unhappy with Eddie Kasko, who had been roommate and friend as player; did not want to shift from shortstop to third base when Luis Aparicio was obtained, but made change successfully.

Rico's best season was 1969 when .297 average and 40 home runs helped Red Sox to AL pennant. Drove in 97 runs that year. In 1970, average dropped to .261 and homer total was lower, 29, but he drove in 103 runs. As 1973 got under way, Petrocelli owned .253 major league average in 1124 games; needed three more hits to have even 1000; had 179 doubles, 18 triples, 172 homers, with 508 runs scored, 569 RBI.

Petrocelli began as pitcher. While hurling, heard cracking sound as though arm was breaking; pain persisted and he shifted to infield. Later had disc problem and operation. Calcium removed from elbow. Took up drumming to strengthen wrists.

Rico has quick hands and good wrists as hitter. Those 40 homers in 1969 set AL record for most round-trippers by shortstop.

Petrocelli got minor league experience at Winston-Salem, 1962; Reading, 1963; and Seattle, 1964. One game with Red Sox, 1963, but grabbed regular shortstop job, 1965. Permanent shift to third base came in 1971 with arrival of Aparicio on team. Set major league record for third baseman, 1971, by going 77 consecutive games without error. In WS, 1967, had .200 average with four hits in 20 trips, two of them homers. AL All-Star squads 1967,69.

PHELPS, ERNEST GORDON (Babe) C-BL-TR. B. 4/19/08, Odenton, Md. 6'2", 225. Babe Phelps didn't like Charlie Dressen, then coach for Brooklyn Dodgers; didn't like Larry MacPhail, then president of Dodgers; didn't like flying—and Dodgers wanted him to fly to Cuba during spring training. There were other irritations, and finally Babe went home to Maryland and turned back on baseball for most of 1941 season. Cost him some $10,000 in salary, plus WS share that gave each of teammates $4,829.40. Phelps said he learned to like Durocher, then manager at Brooklyn. Added: "But I always felt Dressen was stooge for Larry MacPhail. I almost belted Dressen when I suspected him of telling lie—that I didn't like to hit against lefthander, Max Lanier." When MacPhail started using planes for ball club, Phelps said, "Train is fast enough for me."

Babe good-hitting catcher who wound up major league career with .310 average for 726 games. His 657 hits included 143 doubles, 19 triples, and 54 home runs. Scored 239 runs and drove in 345. NL All-Star squads 1938,39,40.

Babe started in Blue Ridge League, 1930, at Hagerstown. Hit .376 that year; then hit .408 in Middle Atlantic League at Youngstown, 115 games. Washington Senators had him for three games that year, but was back at Youngstown, 1932. That season he batted only .372 in 135 contests. Next stop, Albany, International League, with .293 average. Chicago Cubs bought him, but didn't have much chance to play with Gabby Hartnett on same team—just 47 games, part of 1933 and all of 1934. Moved to Dodgers on waivers 12/31/34. In 47 games, 1935, hit .364; in 1935 boosted it to .367 in 115 games, losing bat title to Paul Waner in last two days of season. Waner hit .373 that year. Continued above .300 for Dodgers next two seasons. Best season for homers, 1940, when had 13. After Phelps' suspension for leaving club, Dodgers traded him to Pittsburgh 12/12/41 and he spent last season in majors with Pirates, catching or hitting in 95 games. Hit .284.

Babe and Brooklyn teammates ended Carl Hubbell's 24-game NL winning streak on Memorial Day 1937. Carl won 16 straight in 1936, then took first eight decisions, 1937, before Babe and colleagues went wild at bat. Phelps got 5 for 6 that game, Giants going down to defeat 10–3.

PHILLIPPE, CHARLES LOUIS (Deacon) P-BR-TR. B. 5/23/72, Rural Retreat, Va. D. 3/30/52, Avalon, Pa. 6'1", 180. Was 20-game winner in

NL five times. Winner of first WS game between NL and AL, 1903. That Series pitched five complete games, record that may stand forever. First WS was decided on best five-out-of-nine basis. Eight games were played, Boston Red Sox winning, five games to three, over Deacon's club, Pittsburgh Pirates. Phillippe won three, lost two decisions.

Phillippe had two years, 1897–98, with Minneapolis club in Western League. After 21–19 record in second season, moved into NL with Louisville, 1899. That club was combined with Pittsburgh team, 1900 and he spent rest of career, into 1911, with Pirates. Averaged better than 18 victories per season in first nine years in NL. Then pitched only 12 innings, 1908; came back with 8–3 in 1909, and fancy 14–2 record in 1910. No decisions in three games, 1911, and disappeared from major league stage.

Deacon won 186 games in big time, lost 110. Took part in 372 games, 2610 innings, allowed 1059 runs (earned and unearned), struck out 926, walked 357. Had 244 complete games and 28 shutouts.

Phillippe also pitched in 1909 Series with Pirates but had neither win nor loss in six innings he threw. His WS figures: 50 innings, 3–2, ERA 2.88.

PHILLIPS, HAROLD ROSS (Lefty) Coach-manager. B. 6/16/19, Los Angeles, Calif. D. 6/12/72, Fullerton, Calif. 5'11", 192. Lefty Phillips, who coached Los Angeles Dodgers and managed California Angels, was called by Buzzie Bavasi, "man most dedicated to baseball since Branch Rickey." Phillips bossed Angels from May 1969 until end of 1971 season. Club finished third in AL West both 1969, 70, and fourth in 1971. Phillips lost managerial job after miserable summer trying to solve problems that might have stumped Solomon. One was Tony Conigliaro. But worse were attitude and actions of Alex Johnson, who was repeatedly suspended and fined, for loafing, missing practice, or being late. Johnson and Chico Ruiz also were involved in dispute in clubhouse involving gun. Nasty situation ultimately resulted in Johnson being traded, with Phillips and Angels' general manager, Dick Walsh, being fired.

Phillips career as professional player was extremely brief. Spent less than two months as pitcher with Bisbee club of Arizona-Texas League in 1939. Gave up after arm trouble, but became "bird-dog," passing on tips about promising young players to regularly employed scouts. This led to his becoming scout for Cincinnati Reds, 1948 through 1950; scouted for Brooklyn Dodgers, 1952–57; Los Angeles Dodgers, 1958–64. Walter Alston then put Phillips on coaching staff, 1965 until chance came to manage Angels, 1969.

Lefty bossed Dodgers some weeks in 1967 when Alston was ill.

Among players he signed were Don Drysdale, Larry Sherry, Ron Fairly. Credited with being instrumental in Dodgers' acquisition of Bill Singer, Jim Lefebvre, Ken McMullen.

PHOEBUS, THOMAS HAROLD P-BR-TR. B. 4/7/42, Baltimore, Md. 5'8", 191. Atlanta Braves hoped Tom Phoebus would return to early form with Baltimore Orioles when they bought his contract from Chicago Cubs at WS time, 1972. He didn't. Signed with Richmond in 1973. Phoebus broke into majors in spectacular fashion in September 1966. Pitched two consecutive shutouts for Orioles, which tied major league record. His ERA for 22 innings with Birds that fall was 1.23, including 17 strikeouts. Had 14–9 record following year and 14–7 mark in 1969. *Sporting News* named him Rookie Pitcher of Year, 1967. Also had three straight shutouts. Pitched no-hitter against Boston Red Sox 4/27/68, winning by 6–0 score.

Harry Dalton, now general manager of California Angels, signed Phoebus to first pro contract in 1960. Dalton then with Baltimore organization. Phoebus pitched at Bluefield, W. Va.; Leesburg, Fla.; Aberdeen, S.Dak.; Elmira and Rochester, N.Y., before joining Orioles late in 1966. Remained with hometown team until trade to San Diego 12/1/70. That deal brought Pat Dobson and Tom Dukes to Maryland metropolis. Not much luck with Padres: won three, lost 11 in 1971, then in 1972 had 3–4 record. Pitched in one game for Padres, 1972, before being sent to Chicago Cubs. Started Atlanta connection with record of 56 victories, 52 defeats in 201 major league games; 1030 innings, with overall ERA of 3.30. Control problems beset him while with Padres and Cubs.

Phoebus not used during 1969 WS while with Orioles. In 1970 series pitched 1-2/3 innings against Cincinnati Reds in second game and credited with victory. Allowed one hit but no runs.

PICINICH, VALENTINE JOHN C-BR-TR. B. 9/8/96, New York, N.Y. D. 12/5/42, Nobleboro, Me. 5'9", 165. Val Picinich wasn't big as catchers go, but major league career lasted over 18-year span. Played 1048 games in all, hit .258, and once got as high as .302 while with Cincinnati Reds, 1928. Smart receiver. Said to have been Walter Johnson's favorite backstop during Val's five years with Washington Senators. Reportedly caught all but two of Johnson's starts in this period. One of these was no-hitter Big Train pitched against Boston Red Sox 7/1/20.

Val was with Red Sox 9/7/23 when he caught Howard Ehmke's no-hitter against Philadelphia Athletics. That was his third no-hitter because Picinich was behind plate 8/26/16 when Bullet Joe Bush fired a no-hitter for Athletics against Cleveland Indians.

Picinich attended Princeton for one year. One day in 1916 took train to nearby Philadelphia and asked Philadelphia Athletics for tryout. Connie Mack, then manager, duly impressed, put him in lineup immediately. Athletics were headed for second straight cellar finish anyway, so Connie didn't mind using totally inexperienced catcher. Val got into 40 games but didn't hit much—just .195. Optioned to Atlanta, 1917, hit .263 in 96 games; and two games with Athletics. Divided 1918 between Atlanta and Washington Senators, then stayed with Senators through 1922. Boston AL 1923–25. Cincinnati 1926–28. Brooklyn 1929–33. Pittsburgh 1933.

Val managed Charleston, W. Va., 1938–39; Allentown, Pa., 1940. Bought chicken farm at Nobleboro, Me. After Pearl Harbor went to work at Bath Iron Works in Maine. Became company's morale director after earlier stint as electrical worker. Before he could finish preparations for company's baseball team, contracted bronchial influenza and died.

PIERSALL, JAMES ANTHONY OF-BR-TR. B. 11/14/29, Waterbury, Conn. 6', 189. High-strung, fine-fielding, colorful outfielder spent most of good years in majors with Boston Red Sox. Suffered mental breakdown, 1952, but came back and continued playing until 1965. After hospitalization, his experiences resulted in book, *Fear Strikes Out*, also made into movie still occasionally seen on TV.

Jimmy started at Scranton, 1948; Louisville, 1949–51; brief stay with Red Sox, 1950; hit .346 for Birmingham in 121 games, 1951; then to Red Sox, 1952. To this point Jimmy had been outfielder. Sox used him at shortstop about 30 games. This may have been breaking point: fear on Piersall's part he could not make switch successfully.

So many tales have been told about Piersall's antics it is hard to determine which took place before, during, or after his worst period. Many of those that occurred afterward were deliberate, to annoy or distract opposing pitchers, or to amuse fans, court publicity. Once squirted water pistol in face of umpire. On one occasion hit home run— and next time came to bat, hit lefthanded, although was not switch hitter. Another time, when he came to plate, squatted on heels as pitcher was about to throw. Fought Billy Martin, then with Yankees. Kicked at spectator who had come on field to attack him. Once when name wasn't in lineup posted on dugout wall, spat at lineup card. And when one pitch came dangerously close to head, got down on knees and prayed. Took part in hassles with managers, umpires, players, members of press. Playing golf with Jack Kennedy, then U.S. senator, threw club at tree after bad shot.

During 1952 season, when Piersall's illness getting worse, Red Sox sent him to Birmingham, where had enjoyed fine season previous year.

But soon was apparent hospitalization was necessary. Recovered quickly, and in 1953 was able to return to Boston and play 151 games. Remained with Red Sox through 1958, then traded to Cleveland for 1959–61; Washington, 1962. Senators sent him to N.Y. Mets 5/22/63 in deal for Gil Hodges, who became Washington manager. Mets handed Piersall unconditional release 7/27/63 and he joined Los Angeles Angels, remaining with them in 1964 when they became known as California Angels. Released 1967. After playing career ended, Angels gave him job in public relations department and speakers bureau. Assigned to talk to high school students on subject of mental health. Honored with special night 5/27/67, when Angel management presented gifts in form of $1000 bond for each of Jimmy's nine children. Wife and children were on field with him.

Piersall said it took about seven years after breakdown to be fully accepted, to get speaking engagements and to be interviewed on radio and television.

Jimmy later moved activities to Oakland, working for A's. Handled group sales, sat in as color man during home-game telecasts, and made speeches in Bay Area. Resigned, however, before 1973 season. Became manager of Orangeburg Cardinals in Western Carolinas League.

Piersall had .272 lifetime average in 1734 major league games. Made 1604 hits good for 256 doubles, 52 triples, 104 homers. Scored 811 runs, drove in 591, stole 115 times. AL All-Star squads 1954,56. Three times led AL outfielders in fielding. Made six hits in six trips 6/10/53.

PINA, HORACIO GARCIA P-BR-TR. B. 3/12/45, Matamoros, Coahuila, Mexico. 6'3", 177. Horacio Pina, in 1973, found himself member of Oakland A's, world champions, after three seasons with Washington and Texas. In final year working for Bob Short and Ted Williams, Pina began to get recognition as relief man, since was credited with saving 15 games for Rangers and won two others. Texas had only 37 other victories all year. Pina is short-relief specialist. In 220 AL games pitched before start of 1973 season, had worked 283 innings, an average of less than 1-1/3 innings each appearance. In that time had won 13, lost 14, and had ERA of 3.34. Strikeouts outnumbered walks, 195 to 151.

Horacio pitched for Zacatecas and Puebla in Mexican leagues 1965–67; joined Reno, California League, briefly, 1967. Portland and Puebla 1968, then to Cleveland Indians 1968–69. Five victories and three defeats in stint there, lasting less than two seasons. With Washington, 1970, won five, lost three; following year, mark was 1–1 with two saves. Moved with franchise to Texas, 1972; record 2–7, plus those 15 saves. Then came trade for Mike Epstein.

Horacio's English is limited. Is master at sleight of hand.

762

PINIELLA, LOUIS VICTOR (Piney) OF-BR-TR. B. 8/28/43, Tampa, Fla. 6'2", 197. Has been angry young man who threw tantrums, kicked walls, smashed helmets in frustration, especially after striking out or disliking umpire's call. Still most major leaguers would happily trade their batting average for his. Piniella, in 1972, hit .312, runner-up position in AL batting race. Also raised career average to .294 for 566 games during which he hit safely 606 times, scored 206 runs; had 99 doubles, 20 triples, 36 homers, and 280 RBI; 17 stolen bases.

Marriage and experience seem to have made Lou's temper tantrums less frequent. Now, besides solid hitting for Kansas City Royals, Piniella has reputation of being affable fellow, modest, ready to cooperate to further public relations interests of baseball. If player is needed for speech or other public appearance, Lou is usually available. "I'm getting paid to perform public service," he says. "Baseball is my job. If public relations work is part of it, okay. Some major league players may think they have world by tail, but I don't think so."

Spud Chandler signed Piniella to first baseball contract, for Cleveland organization, 1962. Had been outstanding basketball player in high school, and stellar baseball player at U. of Tampa. Played 70 games for Selma, Alabama-Florida League, then moved to Peninsula club of Carolina League, 1963. By this time Cleveland lost title to him, Washington Senators taking over his destiny; Senators traded him to Baltimore 8/4/64. Spent early part of that year in military service, then optioned to Aberdeen, Northern League. Four games with Orioles that same season.

Piniella spent 1965 at Elmira; traded again to Cleveland 3/10/66. Indians sent him to Portland, Pacific Coast League, 1966–68. Seattle AL club picked him up in expansion draft after 1968 season but soon traded him to Kansas City. Grabbed regular spot in Royals' outfield, 1969. Hit .282 in 135 games, with 11 homers, 68 RBI. This earned Rookie of Year Award from Baseball Writers Association of America. Boosted hitting to .301 in sophomore season in AL, with 11 homers, 88 RBI. Then dropped off bit to .279 in 1971, with three homers, 51 RBI in 126 games. In 1972, with .312 average, Lou got home run total back to 11; hit 33 doubles and drove in 72 markers. Member 1972 AL All-Star Game squad. In off-season has worked as investment banker.

PINSON, VADA EDWARD, JR. OF-BL-TL. B. 8/11/38, Memphis, Tenn. 5'11", 184. Vada Pinson went to school with Frank Robinson in Oakland, Calif., roomed with him seven years while both were with Cincinnati Reds. In 1973 they became teammates again, with California Angels, when Frank landed in Anaheim after year with Dodgers. Pinson has never achieved Robinson's superstar status, but if he and Robby were to compare notes when 1973 began, Vada could be proud of record for 2127 major league games. Owned .290 lifetime average; 2453 hits, 439 good for two bases; 114 triples, 238 homers; 1226 runs scored, 1050 RBI, and 274 stolen bases.

Vada is articulate fellow, leader on field and off. During winters works as labor negotiator for aerospace firm. Speed and durability characterized Pinson's career. As young man, clocked at 3.3 seconds going from plate to first base. Excellent drag bunter. Once played 508 consecutive games for Reds. Since 1959, first full season with Cincinnati, never played less than 130 games in 14 seasons; took part in 145 or more games 11 of those years.

Vada was pitcher and first baseman in high school. First pro engagement at Wausau, Northern League, 1956. Following year burned up California League at Visalia. Led in hits, runs scored, doubles, and triples. Had .367 average with 20 homers, 97 RBI. In outfield, led circuit with 30 assists. Following spring his work with Reds was sensational. Despite making jump from Class C to majors, was given opening-day spot in lineup, 1958. However, was farmed out to Seattle, Pacific Coast League, 5/12/58. Again performed in brilliant fashion; hit .343. Then came first full year in NL. Tied major league record by making at least 200 hits in first full season. Led league in runs scored with 131, in doubles with 47. Slapped 20 homers and hit .316. Also made more putouts in outfield than any other player in NL, 423. While with Cincinnati, Pinson's best year for average was 1961, when hit .343. Had six seasons with at least 20 homers each, but reached peak in this respect playing for Cleveland, 1970, when had 24. Cincinnati years came to end 10/11/68 when he went to St. Louis Cardinals in deal involving Bobby Tolan. One year with Redbirds, then traded to Cleveland for Jose Cardenal 11/20/69. After two seasons with Indians, traded to California Angels 10/5/71 when Alex Johnson went to Indians.

Vada didn't do so well in WS after fine 1961 season with Reds. Had .091 average, two hits in 22 trips. NL All-Star squads 1959,60.

Vada received $4000 bonus when he signed with Cincinnati organization, 1956.

PIPGRAS, GEORGE WILLIAM P-BR-TR. B. 12/20/99, Denison, Iowa. 6'1½", 185. George Pipgras started three WS games for N.Y. Yankees. Finished each of them. Won them all—undefeated in WS play. George won his games in 1927, 28, 32, allowing total of nine runs. Didn't have to worry, Yanks on scoreboard often enough and won by scores of 6–2, 9–3, and 7–5. Beat St. Louis, Pittsburgh, and Chicago in that order. ERA of 2.77 overall in 26 innings pitched.

Pipgras didn't always have such easy time of it. In 1920 used to work on farm. Out of bed at 4:30 A. M. to feed 150 hogs, 200 sheep, take care of horses. Ploughed and planted, and occasionally took time out to play catch with his boss. One Sunday George pitched against one of better sandlot teams of area and, though he lost in ninth inning, 2–1, received offer of $350 monthly salary to pitch semipro. This was fabulous offer for farm boy. Said he'd think it over. Next came offer of $400 plus expenses. George was on way. Following year lined up with Madison in Dakota League; won 12, lost six, and sold to Boston Red Sox. Optioned to Charleston, South Atlantic League, George 19–9. Attracted attention of Yankee scouts. Deal worked out and promising youngster found self property of N.Y. club for 1923–24, but wasn't used often. Farmed out again, 1925, to Atlanta and Nashville, with 19–15 record; and to St. Paul, 1926, taking 22 decisions against 19 defeats. In 1927 stuck with Yanks, 10–3. best season next, 24–13 with 3.38 ERA. Won 56, lost 42 in following four campaigns. In 1933 after winning two, losing two for Yanks, traded back to Red Sox. By this time, however, George was suffering from elbow injury, and called it finish in 1935 with 102 major league victories 15 shutouts, 73 defeats. His ERA was 4.09 for 1488-1/3 innings. Later umpire several years in AL.

PIPP, WALTER CLEMENT 1B-BL-TL. B. 2/17/93, Chicago, Ill. D. 1/11/65, Grand Rapids, Mich. 6'1", 180. Wally Pipp was regular first baseman for N.Y. Yankees more than 10 years. Early in 11th season, when had not been hitting up to par, that is, in neighborhood of .300, complained about not feeling well and took day off. That was 6/1/25. Lou Gehrig subbed for him—and Pipp never got job back. That was when Gehrig started fabulous streak of 2130 consecutive games. Wally stayed with Yankees rest of year, did some pinch hitting, but following year, 1926, went to Cincinnati Reds where played three seasons. Pipp was excellent first baseman; hit .281 for major league career, but of course never had anything like power Gehrig had. Wally led AL in homers twice: had 12 in 1916, 9 in 1917. Gehrig, his successor, also led AL in homers twice, and tied for lead on another occasion. Lively ball had come in, however, when Gehrig was in prime. "Iron Horse" had 49 round-trippers both years he led AL. When tied Ruth for lead, 1931, each had 46 homers.

Pipp was with Grand Rapids and Kalamazoo teams, 1910–12 before joining Detroit Tigers, 1913. Farmed out to Providence and Scranton, 1913; Rochester, 1914; recalled by Tigers after hitting .312 in 154 International League games, Wally was sold to Yankees 1/7/15, and took charge at first base for next decade. Pipp batted above .300 three times with Yanks, had 90 or more RBI five times; in first season with Reds Wally drove 99 markers across plate.

When Pipp left majors after 1928 season, had played 1871 games; his 1941 hits included 311 doubles, 148 triples, 90 homers; scored 974 runs, drove in 996; stole 125 bases.

In WS three autumns with Yanks, 1921,22,23: .224, 15 for 67, 3 runs, 7 RBI.

PIZARRO, JUAN P-BL-TL. B. 2/7/37, Santurce, Puerto Rico. 5'11", 190. Could ageless Latino, Juan Pizarro, still help major league club? Some were asking this question as veteran southpaw pitched three consecutive shutouts in closing days of Puerto Rican League season 1972–73 and playoffs. Pitching in 18th consecutive winter in island commonwealth, had 10–2 record. Chicago Cubs apparently thought so; Juan on roster going into 1973 season, despite fact he had spent parts of 1970, 71 in minors. Cubs, however, optioned him to Wichita midseason 1973. Sold to Houston Astros soon after. Pizarro owned 3.40 ERA for 464 major league appearances as 1973 started, with 129 victories, 103 defeats, 1502 strikeouts, 865 walks. Four victories posted in 1972 for Cubs, against five defeats. Saved one other game.

Pizarro signed first pro contract with Milwaukee Braves, 1956; pitched 23 victories that year for Jacksonville in Sally League, going down in defeat six times. Struck out 318 to lead loop in this respect. Divided following year between Wichita and Braves, and again in 1958. In 1959 spent part of year with Louisville, but also won six, lost two for Braves. After 6–7 mark for Milwaukee NL in 1960 was traded to Chicago AL; was 14–7 first big year in majors. Had 12–14 mark following season. Bounced back with two fine performances, 16–8 and 19–9 for White Sox; ERA those seasons 2.39 and 2.56.

Juan's work slumped after that. Sox sent him to Pittsburgh for 1967–68; Pirates sold him to Boston Red Sox 6/27/68; Red Sox traded him to Cleveland in Ken Harrelson deal 4/19/69; sold to Oakland AL 9/21/69. Back in minors, first with Iowa, then, 1970, with Hawaii, Pacific Coast League. Proceeded to come back in spectacular fashion; won nine games without loss, struck out 67 PCL batters in 89 innings. Cubs bought contract but he had no decisions in 16 innings with them that year. In 1971 was at Tacoma, PCL, fanned 116 men in 127 innings, and was brought back to Chicago NL. Used as spot starter, won seven games in second half of season. Defeated Tom Seaver twice, once by pitching six-hit shutout against Mets; added insult to injury by slamming home run off Tom Terrific to win own game 1–0. Lost six games, however.

Juan pitched total of 3–1/3 innings in WS of 1957,58 with Milwaukee Braves; his ERA worked out to 8.10. AL All-Star squads 1963,64.

PLANK, EDWARD STEWART P-BL-TL. B. 8/31/75, Gettysburg, Pa. D. 2/24/26, Gettysburg, Pa. 5'11½", 175. Eddie Plank won more than 300 games in AL and undoubtedly earned place in Hall of Fame, gained 1946. *Sporting News* publication *Daguerrotypes* says he won 305 major league games, not counting 21 games won for St. Louis Federal League team, 1915. Some records give him only 304 AL victories; and number of defeats varies between 179 and 181, apart from 11 losses while in Federal League. Since earned-run records were not kept in old days, to quote overall career figure might be misleading. In any case, Plank one of greatest southpaws ever. One of early collegians, went direct to Philadelphia Athletics, 1901, from Gettysburg College, and immediately won 16 or 17 games. Had deceptive crossfire delivery. But used to agitate batters by fidgeting on mound. Pulled on belt, adjusted cap, kicked at dirt, and fiddled around until batter was overanxious. Umpires tried to speed up delivery, but usually in vain.

Eddie got into 20-victory class in second season in majors; stayed there four years. In 1906, when he just missed 20 wins, his 19–6 record was best winning percentage in AL. Then came back with 24–16. Plank was consistently good, rarely breaking even or losing more games than he won. In 1910, he was 16–10, but Connie Mack did not use him in WS because of lame arm. Pitching just two men, Jack Coombs and Chief Bender, Athletics took WS from Chicago Cubs, four games to one.

Then after 1914 WS when Athletics went down before Boston Braves in four games, Mack broke up team. Connie feared many of stars would jump to Federal League. Plank was one who was ready to make move and Mack wanted to sell him to Yankees first. However, recognizing inevitable, instead gave Plank unconditional release although he was 15–7. Eddie signed with St. Louis Feds for 1915. Won 21 games, lost 11. With settlement of Federal League war, Plank landed with St. Louis Browns. Had 16–15 record, 1916, then called it quits after 5–6 mark in 1917. Traded to Yankees early in 1918 but never reported.

In seven WS games with Philadelphia, 1905,11,13,14, Plank pitched 54-2/3 innings, was 2–5, but had 1.15 ERA; 32 strikeouts, 11 bases on balls. In AL, Plank won 20 games or more seven times. Reached 26 victories twice, 1904 and 1912. Had 64 AL shutouts and six more in Federal League. In AL struck out 2112 and walked 984.

PODGAJNY, JOHN SIGMUND (Specs) P-BR-TR. B. 6/10/20, Chester, Pa. 6'2", 170. Johnny Podgajny never quite lived up to early promise. But in five seasons in majors was always with second-division clubs, three of them cellar dwellers. Won 20, lost 37 major league games, with 4.20 ERA. It wasn't his pitching that puts him in this book—it was his explosive nature. Low boiling point caused frequent ejection from ball game. Ready to do battle against foe or friend.

With Philadelphia NL 1940–43. Had 1–3 season, then 9–12 and 6–14, which weren't bad considering Phils were chronic eighth-placers at time. Merrill May, third baseman for Phils, on one occasion moved over to mound while Johnny was pitching. Men on base, looked like real jam.

All May wanted to do was bolster Podgajny's morale. Said something about not giving up, "We'll get 'em, boy!" Pitcher misunderstood, grabbed May by neck, started to throttle him right there on diamond. May was astonished. Fortunately shortstop, catcher, other teammates rushed to Merrill's side and saved him from being choked. "I felt pretty silly later," said Johnny. Always had rough time controlling reactions.

Podgajny won 15, lost 10 for Moultrie in Georgia-Florida League, 1939; then after 18–7 mark with Ottawa-Ogdensburg in Canadian-American League, went up to Phils, 1940. During 1943 season shifted to Pittsburgh Pirates; had four wins, eight defeats that year. Dropped out of majors after that, except pitched nine innings with Cleveland Indians, 1946.

Johnny was frank about shortcomings. "I wouldn't have made much of scout," he said after career was over. "I said Stan Musial would never hit and Bob Lemon would never make it as pitcher."

In contrast to salaries and bonuses paid now, when Podgajny was youth playing semipro ball around Chester, Pa., St. Louis Browns offered him $60 monthly salary. Turned them down—was making $100 a month.

PODRES, JOHN JOSEPH P-BL-TL. B. 9/30/32, Witherbee, N. Y. 5'11", 185. Johnny Podres, whose pitching career was spent mostly with Brooklyn and Los Angeles Dodgers, returned to majors 1973 as pitching coach for San Diego Padres. Had been serving as their minor league pitching coach.

Johnny won 148 games in majors, lost 116. Compiled 3.67 ERA for 2266 innings. In 440 major league games, struck out 1435 and walked 743. Also won four out of five decisions in WS play and had 2.11 ERA.

Podres had two years of minor league experience before joining Brooklyn club, 1953. Briefly with Newport News in Piedmont League, 1951; then captured 21 decisions against three defeats with Hazard, Ky., in Mountain State League. Led that circuit in pitching percentage (.875), in strikeouts (228) and in effectiveness with 1.67 ERA. Broke even at Montreal, International League (5–5) in second pro season, but with Dodgers, as rookie, won nine, lost four. Had 11–7 and 9–10 records next two seasons, then went into military service, 1956. When he returned, following season, his 2.66 ERA was best in NL; won 12, lost nine. Best years after that were 1959 when had 14–9 record, and 1961, when winning percentage of .783 (18–5), was tops in NL.

Johnny tied major league record in first game of twi-night twin bill 7/2/62 by striking out eight consecutive batsmen who faced him. Victims were members of Philadelphia Phillies. Led NL in shutouts, 1957, with six.

Podres was shelled from mound in only start against New York

Yankees in WS of 1953, being charged with defeat. Had revenge two years later. Won first start against Yanks by 8–3 score in third game. Then, in seventh and crucial contest, blanked Yanks, 2–0. Thus, had honor of pitching Dodgers to victory in game that gave them their first world championship in history. Podres, however, could thank Sandy Amoros for saving game with spectacular catch of Yogi Berra's threatening drive to left field in sixth inning.

Podres posted one win in each of 1959 and 1963 WS with Dodgers after they moved to Los Angeles. In All-Star games, Johnny pitched four innings for NL squad, 1960,62; not scored upon.

Johnny with Detroit Tigers part of 1966 and in 1967, posting 7–6 mark in AL. Out of baseball 1968. San Diego Padres 1969—5–6. Voluntary retired list 6/27/69.

POFFENBERGER, CLETUS ELWOOD (Boots)   P-BR-TR. B. 7/1/15, Williamsport, Md. 5'10", 178.

Had short major league career, but merry one. Drew almost as many fines as paychecks. Jumped Detroit Tigers; jumped Brooklyn Dodgers. Sports writers wrote reams of copy about him, far more than importance as pitcher warranted. In fact, won 10 games for Tigers, 1937, lost five, saved three others in relief. Following year won six, lost seven, with one save. With Dodgers briefly, 1939, got into only three games, pitched five innings and had no decisions. That was it.

Writers made much of alleged request for room service one morning after rugged night. Poffenberger requested "breakfast of champions." "Cereal?" asked dining room. "Hell no," replied Boots, "Two fried eggs and a bottle of beer!"

When Boots first saw Joe Cronin, then stellar shortstop and manager of Boston Red Sox, Poffenberger, fresh rookie, greeted him, "Hiyah, showboat!"

In recent years Boots has been working in truck factory; was asked about one of stories circulated about him. "I never bought a dog a beer and he never bought me one. That story was told so many different ways I even enjoyed hearing it myself. As far as I know, it wasn't true."

One time Mickey Cochrane, his manager at Detroit, asked Poffenberger where he had been on previous night. "I refuse to reveal my identity," said Boots.

Poffenberger started in Bi-State League, 1935, with Fieldale, Va.; Charleston, W. Va., 1936; Beaumont, 1937, moving up to Tigers same season. During 1938 season Boots hit leadoff man in game he started in Washington. Pitched carelessly to next man, walking him. Next batsman hit grounder to first baseman and Boots failed to cover bag. Cochrane told him to go to clubhouse, and afterward told him to go back to Detroit. Instead, went home to Maryland. Later joined Toledo, American Association, won eight, lost three. That winter was sold to Dodgers. After being used in just five innings over two-month period, Boots went home again, and never returned to majors. With Nashville, 1940–41, winning 26, losing nine, his first year, and having 7–3 record following season. With San Diego, Pacific Coast League, 1942, and then joined marines.

Boots had 4.75 ERA for those 267-1/3 innings pitched in majors.

POLLET, HOWARD JOSEPH P-BL-TL. B. 6/26/21, New Orleans, La. 6′, 175. Howie Pollet's career as pitcher interrupted twice. In 1943, pitching for St. Louis Cardinals, won eight, lost four, and was breezing along in sensational fashion when he entered air force. Before joining up, pitched three straight shutouts and had mark of 28 consecutive scoreless innings. Back from war, 1946, Howie was 21–10, with 2.10 ERA, leading NL in effectiveness. Late that season hurt arm, and following year was 9–11. That fall, Dr. Robert Hyland, "surgeon-general of baseball," operated. Came back with 13–8 mark in 1948, and improved greatly following season, 20–9, 2.77 ERA. Cardinals traded him to Pittsburgh 6/15/51; Pirates sent him to Chicago Cubs 6/4/53. Moved to Chicago White Sox 4/16/56. Released in July, and finished 1956 season with Pittsburgh. After Pollet's 20-game season with Cardinals, 1949, pitched less effectively and less often. Finished major league career with 3.51 ERA in 2105 innings, with 131 victories, 116 defeats. Walked 745, fanned 934.

Pollet serious-minded, studious fellow. Signed for Cardinal organization originally by Eddie Dyer, then scouting for St. Louis, 1938. Howie got $3500 bonus. Pitched for Houston, Texas League, 1939–41, with part of 1939 at New Iberia. Won 20 games for Houston in each 1940,41, losing seven, then in 1941 dropping just three. Cardinals needed pitching help as 1941 drew toward end of season. Branch Rickey, then general manager of Redbirds, insisted Pollet sign 1942 contract for $600 per month or else would not put him on Cardinal roster for remainder of 1941. Howie objected strenuously but finally agreed. Then proceeded to win five games for Cardinals, lose two, with 1.93 ERA. Two of games were shutouts, and one of two losses was 2–1 pitching duel with Whit Wyatt of Dodgers.

Howie pitched one-third of an inning in 1942 WS. In 1946 classic, after fine 21-victory season, was starting pitcher against Boston Red Sox in opening game. Cardinals led by 2–1 score into ninth inning. Then Pinky Higgins hit grounder that took freak hop, enabling Sox to tie score. Rudy York's homer in 10th gave Boston 3–2 win. Cards, however, took WS in seven games. Pitched in 1949 All-Star game.

Pollet coached Cardinals, 1959–60. In off-seasons entered insurance business with late Eddie Dyer, and has continued in insurance in

Houston after Dyer's death. When Houston got NL franchise, Pollet served as pitching coach for while.

POPOVICH, PAUL EDWARD Inf.-BLR-TR. B. 8/18/40, Flemington, W. Va. 6′, 175. Paul Popovich has been valuable utility infielder for Chicago Cubs in recent years, but has found presence of Glenn Beckert obstacle to playing more often at second base. Good fielder but light hitter.

Cubs paid estimated $40,000 bonus to sign with them, 1960. Farmed out to San Antonio; Wenatchee, Wash.; Amarillo; Salt Lake City, and Tacoma, 1960–66. Brief stays with Cubs, 1964–66. Up to this time had been righthanded hitter, but management felt would profit by becoming switch hitter. Sent to Cubs' instructional camp in winter of 1966 to learn hitting lefthanded against righthanded pitchers. This move enabled him to stick with major league club, 1967, though he broke down no fences with .214 average for 49 games. Only extra-base hits among 34 safeties were four doubles. Then Cubs traded him to Los Angeles Dodgers 11/30/67. Played 134 games for Dodgers, 1968; got first major league triple, popped two homers, and hit for .232 average. Started following season with Los Angeles, but on 6/11/69 was traded twice in same day: first to Montreal, then to Cubs. That year put together .284 batting average, with one homer to credit. In 1970, average was .253, with four homers; in 1971, .217 in 89 games, with another four round-trippers. One of them was his first major league grand slammer.

Popovich got into 58 games in 1972, hit .194. Lifetime average going into 1973 season stood at .234 for 499 games in majors, with 12 homers, 5 triples, 33 doubles among 311 hits; scored 138 runs, drove in 104.

POSEDEL, WILLIAM JOHN (Barnacle Bill) P-BR-TR. B. 8/2/06, San Francisco, Calif. 6′, 195. "Sailor Bill," "Porthole," "Chief" are some of nicknames given Bill Posedel, who climaxed his baseball career in 1972 AL pennant race, playoffs, and WS. It was not accidental that Oakland A's displayed the brilliant pitching that led them to world championship. Bill served as pitching coach for A's 1968–72. Retiring from this job after WS, Posedel took on somewhat less demanding work as coach and advisor for Oakland minor league teams.

Posedel acquired acquatic nicknames because he twice served in navy: four years, 1925–29, and again for 46 months during World War II, 1941–45. But for these hitches probably would have had much longer major league career. Won 41, lost 43 and had 4.56 ERA.

Posedel joined Portland, Pacific Coast League, 1929. Moved to Pueblo for part of 1930 season, then back to Portland, 1931. Tulsa, Texas League, 1932–35. Portland 1935–37. Brooklyn 1938. Boston NL 1939–46, except for time in navy. Seattle, Pacific Coast League, 1947. Scout,

Pittsburgh, 1948. Coach, Pittsburgh, 1949–53; St. Louis NL, 1953–57. Manager, Portland, 1957. Coach, Philadelphia NL, 1958; San Francisco NL, 1959–60. Scout, Cleveland, 1961; Kansas City AL, 1962–67. Coach, Oakland AL, after that until retirement.

Bill's best seasons included 1936, when he won 17 of last 20 starts, helping to Portland's winning PCL flag, and 1939 at Boston, when he won 15 games for Braves, losing 13, with 3.91 ERA.

POWELL, ALVIN JACOB (Jake) OF-BR-TR. B. 7/15/08, Silver Spring, Md. D. 11/4/48, Washington, D.C. 5'11¾", 187. Jake Powell had considerable ability as outfielder and hitter but never lived up to full potential. Explosive, hot-tempered, erratic, battled several other players, fractured training rules, and came to tragic end. Committed suicide in police station after being booked on charge of passing $25 rubber check. Was being questioned about other worthless checks. Pulled .25-caliber pearl-handled revolver from pocket and shouted, "To hell with all this. I'm going to end it all." Shot himself first in chest, then in temple.

Powell played baseball in and around Washington as youth and cast fortunes with Senators, 1930. Three AL games that season, spending most of summer at Chattanooga and New Haven. Springfield, Eastern League, 1931. Youngstown, Central League, 1932. Dayton, Middle Atlantic League, 1933. Albany, Eastern League, 1933–34. Washington 1934 until 6/14/36, when swapped to Yankees for Ben Chapman. Remained with Yanks into 1940 season, then sold to San Francisco, Pacific Coast League, for $10,000. Divided 1941 season between San Francisco and Montreal Royals, then International League farm club for Brooklyn. St. Paul 1942. Returned to Washington 1943–45. Philadelphia NL 1945. Back to minors, drawing release from Gainesville, Florida State League, after 1948 season, few weeks before death.

Powell starred in 1936 WS while still with Yankees. Before Series against N. Y. Giants started, declared, "Carl Hubbell is just an ordinary pitcher. He won't bother me." Got two singles and double off Carl in opener. Hit .455 for WS with 10 hits in 22 trips, including home run; scored eight runs, drove in five. Got into 1937,38 WS briefly. Had overall WS record of .434 for eight games.

Jake was fast; beat out many bunts, especially early in big league career. However, was repeatedly fined for breaking training rules. Once during spring training, missed club's train. Chartered plane to next stop—but charged it to club's expense. Battled Joe Kuhel, then with Senators. Several of Joe's teammates rushed to defense, and Powell got worst of it. Crashed into Hank Greenberg at first base early in 1936, breaking Hank's wrist, but there was no apology from Jake. Exchanged punches with Joe Cronin 5/30/38. And in American Association, 1943, got into fight with Eric McNair—and reported to Washington with black eye.

During 1940 Powell ran headlong into outfield wall trying to make play. Suffered fractured skull; for weeks it was touch and go if would recover. Reached .300 mark just once in big league career, 1935, with Washington. Missed it by one point, 1936. Wound up with .271 average for 688 major league games.

POWELL, JOHN WESLEY (Boog) 1B-BL-TR. B. 8/17/41, Lakeland, Fla. 6'4", 250. Boog Powell is fearsome slugger apt to hit ball country mile. As 1973 season dawned, had 280 homers to credit, many of them prodigious clouts worthy of Babe Ruth. For example, they still talk about one hit in Detroit 7/5/69 over right field roof of Tiger Stadium; and his 469-foot drive over center field hedge in Baltimore 6/22/62. But they also talk about his .111 batting average in WS of 1971 when Pittsburgh pitchers held him to three singles in seven games. Boog is at loss to explain inconsistency at plate. Many examples could be cited. Hit 34 homers, drove in 109 runs, 1966. Following year could get only 13 round-trippers; RBI total was cut in half—and batting average dropped 53 points. At one point in June 1972 was batting .152, but wound up with .252 for season. There have been some excuses for inconsistency. During 1971 suffered hairline fracture of right wrist. During 1972 discovered that sight in left eye slightly inferior to right eye. Wore glasses for while; but that didn't help so discarded them. Improved hitting late in season, among other things belting sixth grand slammer of career.

Powell reportedly received $25,000 bonus to sign, 1959. Hit .351 for Bluefield, Appalachian League, that summer and .312 following year with Fox Cities, III League. His 32 homers with Rochester, 1961, led International League; batted .321. Joined Baltimore for four games. In 1962 became regular with Orioles, hitting .243 and garnering 15 homers.

Boog's batting average reached .290 in 1964; .304 in 1969 and .297 in 1970. Had 39 homers, 1964, 34 in 1966, 37 in 1969, and 35 in 1970. Prior to 1973 batted in as many as 100 runs just three times. Lifetime figures showed 1539 major league games, 1385 hits, 217 doubles, 9 triples, 280 homers; scored 707 runs, drove in 964, and had .266 average. Base steals stood at 18.

Boog hit .357 in first WS, 1966; .263 in 1969 games; had two homers, five RBI, and .294 average in set against Cincinnati, 1970; his .111 mark against Pirate pitching, 1971, lowered overall WS average to .234 in 21 games. All-Star games 1968,69,70; named to 1971 squad but replaced because of wrist injury.

Powell drove in 11 runs during twin bill 7/6/66, which tied AL record. On three occasions hit three homers in one game; Once they were in consecutive times at bat, 8/10/63. MVP 1970. Signed $90,000 contract for 1971.

POWER, VICTOR FELIPE 1B-BR-TR. B. 11/1/31, Arecibo, Puerto

Rico. 6', 199. When Vic Power started professional ball, 1950, he used correct name, Victor Pellot, in Drummondville, Quebec, in French Canada. Name evoked repeated peals of ribald laughter because last name sounded like off-color slang word in French. Vic then thought he'd use mother's last name, Pove. But this soon was pronounced "Power," so that's way he has been known since. Also was called many other names, among them "showboat" because of actions on field. Played 1627 major league games, most in AL, 1954–65. Led AL first sackers in fielding three times, but also played 139 games at second base, 115 in outfield, 89 at third, and eight at shortstop in majors. Hit .284 with 1716 hits; 290 doubles, 49 triples, 126 homers. Scored 765 runs, drove in 658. Stole 45 bases, many of them thefts of home.

Power hit .334 at Drummondville, Provincial League, and impressed New York Yankees enough that they paid $7,000 for him. Vic insists he refused to report until Yanks gave him $3,000 of purchase price. Never played for Yankees, although had excellent record in minors. Hit .294 for Syracuse, 1951, then came up with .331 and .349 marks next two seasons playing regularly for Yankee farm club at Kansas City, American Association. In 1953 led AA in batting and total hits. Previous year had led in doubles and triples, and had driven in 109 runs.

Yankees did not have black player on their major league roster. In August, 1953, when Yanks' first basemen Joe Collins and Don Bollweg were injured, Power remained in Kansas City. Negro groups picketed Yankee Stadium, but club steadfastly kept white roster until 1955 when Elston Howard was brought up.

In 1954 Power reached majors, but Yankees had traded him to Philadelphia Athletics. Hit .255 that year in 127 games. Remained with A's when franchise shifted to Kansas City, 1955. Hit .319 that year and .309 next. In 1958 traded to Cleveland 6/15 and had .312 average that season. Minnesota, 1962–63 and part of 1964. Also with Philadelphia NL and Los Angeles AL, 1964, then bowed out of majors after spending 1965 with Angels. Started 1973 as manager of Veracruz club in Mexican League.

Vic stole home twice in one game 8/14/58 while playing for Cleveland against Detroit. Second steal came in 10th inning and won ball game. Stole home one other time that year, so all stolen bases that year were thefts of home!

Power unorthodox hitter. Held bat straight down, as though were going to hit hockey puck with it—until ball was pitched. Something of bucket hitter, but had power.

PROTHRO, JAMES THOMPSON (Doc) 3B-BR-TR. B. 7/16/93, Memphis, Tenn. D. 10/14/71, Memphis, Tenn. 5'10½", 170. Name Prothro probably means much more to football fans of current era than it does to baseball fans. Tommy Prothro attracted attention as coach for Los Angeles Rams. But Doc Prothro, his father, was .318 hitter in major leagues and managed Philadelphia Phillies. Prothro's big league experience both as player and pilot was not long one. But in Memphis, where lived most of life, was one of that city's most beloved and respected citizens.

Got nickname "Doc" honestly. Graduated from U. of Tennessee's Dental School and practiced several years before concentrating on professional baseball. Had brief tryout with Washington Senators, 1920, played six games, got five hits in 13 times at bat for .385. However, was more interesting to play ball nearer home for next couple of years. Joined Memphis club, Southern Association, 1923, played 111 games and hit .296. Then back to Washington for parts of that year and next. In 1924 played 46 games with Senators and hit .333, but spent most of season with Memphis, hitting .326 in 119 contests. Boston Red Sox took him on in 1925; had .313 average for 119 AL games. Hit .326 for Portland, Pacific Coast League, 1926, and took part in three games with Cincinnati that same year. Back to Portland for 1927, with .330 average. From 1928 through 1934 Doc played and managed at Memphis, hitting above .300 three of seven seasons. Manager, Little Rock, 1935–38. Manager, Phillies, 1939–41. Then Prothro returned to Memphis as manager and part owner. Pulled out of baseball after 1947, selling interest in Memphis team to Chicago White Sox.

Doc used to say experience with Phillies was high point and low point of career. Each of three seasons Phillies finished last. "Every time we came up with good player, we had to sell him, in order to stay in business," said Prothro. "It was nightmare."

In 1951 Prothro had chance to return to majors as manager but refused, saying that at age 58 was too old to start building team, which would have taken five years.

Doc played 180 games in majors and hit .318. While good hitter for average, did not go for long ball and had no homers among 191 hits in big leagues.

PRUETT, HUBERT SHELBY (Shucks) P-BR-TL. B. 9/19/1900, Malden, Mo. 5'10½", 165. Hub Pruett's claim to fame rests solely on what he used to do to Babe Ruth. For one shining season, 1922, when St. Louis Browns challenged supremacy of mighty New York Yankees, Pruett was Ruth's nemesis. Young medical student, playing baseball until could become an M.D., donned Brownie uniform that year and proceeded to strike out mighty Babe no fewer than 13 times in 16 official at bats.

No pitcher ever came near equaling Pruett's feat. His secret was an overhand screwball that broke over inside of plate to lefty slugger. It took brave man to pitch Ruth inside for fear he would break down right field fence or decapitate first baseman. Pruett defied strategy and confounded Ruth.

Browns in 1922 came within one game of tying Yankees for AL flag. That was year George Sisler hit .420; when five more of their regulars hit well above .300; when Urban Shocker was victorious in 24 games. Battle for pennant reached peak in crucial three-game series in St. Louis in September. Yankees took first game on Saturday. Although Pruett was far from husky and had been used mostly in relief, he was St. Louis pitcher for Sunday contest. Hub had Yankees eating out of his hands, struck Ruth out once, but did allow him to hit one out of park. Browns and Pruett walked off field with 5–1 victory. Yankees, however, beat Browns following day, and were able to maintain narrow margin for rest of flag race.

Pruett only so-so against ordinary hitters. Had 7–7 record in 1922, although he saved seven games and had overall 2.33 ERA for 119-2/3 innings. Had 4–7 mark in 1923 and 3–4 in 1924. Was generally believed screwball had ruined arm. However, after dropping out of majors two seasons, Pruett was back in big time, 1927, pitching for Philadelphia NL. Was 7–17, 6.05 ERA, with hopelessly last-place club. Won two, lost four for Phils in 1928. Once again Hub returned to majors, 1930, this time with New York Giants. Won five, lost four—only season in which won more decisions than lost. Skipped 1931, but was with Boston Braves, 1932, winning one, losing five.

Career record: 29–48 in majors, 4.63 ERA, 745 innings, 396 walks, 357 strikeouts.

QUILICI, FRANK R. Inf.-BR-TR. B. 5/11/39, Chicago, Ill. 6', 175. Minnesota Twins 1965, 1967–70. Hit .214 in 405 games as utility man. Named coach with Twins in 1971 and replaced Bill Rigney as manager of club during 1972 season (41–43). Currently youngest manager in major leagues.

QUINN, JOHN P. (Jack) P-BR-TR. B. 7/5/84, Hazleton, Pa. D. 4/17/46, Pottsville, Pa. 6', 200. New York Yankees 1909–12, 1919–21; Boston Braves 1913; Baltimore (Federal League) 1914–15; Chicago White Sox 1918; Boston Red Sox 1922–25; Philadelphia A's 1925–30; Brooklyn Dodgers 1931–32; Cincinnati Reds 1933. Won 212, lost 180 in 662 games with 1046 strikeouts and 731 walks in 3318 innings. Won 10 or more games 12 times, including 26 in 1914 in Federal League. World Series 1921,29–30: 0–1.

Spitballer Quinn is oldest player to win game in major leagues. Hung on in major leagues until 6/28/33 at the age of 48 years, six weeks. As regular pitcher, longevity record surpassed only by reliefer Hoyt Wilhelm in 1972. Managed in minor leagues in 1935.

RADATZ, RICHARD R. (Dick; The Monster) P-BR-TR. B. 4/2/37, Detroit, Mich. 6'5", 260. Boston Red Sox 1962–66; Cleveland Indians 1966–67; Chicago Cubs 1967; Detroit Tigers 1969; Montreal Expos 1969. Won 62, lost 43 in 381 games with 745 strikeouts and 296 walks in 694 innings. Best years: 15–6 in 1963 and 16–9 in 1964. Won *Sporting News*' Fireman of the Year Trophy in 1962 and 1964. Led AL in games 1962 (62). All-Star game, 1963–64: 0–1 with 10 strikeouts in 4-2/3 innings.

Racked up over 100 saves in fairly short career, and averaged better than one strikeout per inning. Struck out 181 in 157 innings of relief in 1964. Developed control problems and lost effectiveness in 1966. Imposing figure on mound, captivated Boston fans with late-inning heroics, thrusting fist in air after win or save. Most recently was insurance salesman in Farmingham, Mich.

RADBOURN, CHARLES (Old Hoss) P-OF-BR-TR. B. 12/9/53, Rochester, N.Y. D. 2/5/97, Bloomington, Ill. 5'9", 168. Buffalo (NL) 1880; Providence Grays (NL) 1881–85; Boston (NL) 1886–89; Boston (Players League) 1890; Cincinnati Reds 1891. Won 308, lost 191 in 517 games with 1746 strikeouts and 856 walks in 4543 innings. Won 20 or more games nine times, including 31 in 1881, 49 in 1883 and incredible 60 in 1884. Led NL innings pitched 1884 (679), wins, percentage (.833) and strikeouts (411). Also led NL wins (49) 1883 and strikeouts (194) 1882. Led percentage (.694) 1881. Pitched 35 shutouts, leading league in 1882 (6). "World Series" 1884: 3–0. No-hitter against Cleveland, 7/25/83.

Won two complete games in one day, 5/30/84. Hall of Fame 1939.

Iron man, pitched almost every day in last few months of season in 1884 and completed almost every game he pitched in majors. During 1884 season, won 18 consecutive games, 8/7 through 9/6, including 14 in month of August. After season ended, won all three games in "World Series" against New York Metropolitans of American Association. Later operated poolroom. Lost an eye in hunting accident and died of paresis.

RADCLIFF, RAYMOND A. (Rip) OF-1B-BL-TL. B. 1/19/06, Kiowa, Okla. D. 5/23/62, Enid, Okla. 5'10½", 175. Chicago White Sox 1934–39; St. Louis Browns 1940–41; Detroit Tigers 1941–43. Hit .311 in 1,081 games with 1267 hits, 598 runs, 205 doubles, 50 triples, 42 home runs and 533 RBI. Hit .300 or better five times. Best year: .342 in 1940. Hit 20 or more doubles six times; made 6 hits in game, 7/8/36. Led AL in hits 1940 (200). All-Star game: 1936 (.500). Managed in minor leagues, 1948.

RADER, DAVID M. (Rooster) C-BL-TR. B. 12/26/48, Claremore, Okla. 5'11½", 165. San Francisco Giants 1971–72. Hit .259 in first full season in 1972 with 14 doubles, 1 triple, 6 home runs, 44 runs and 41 RBI. Could be fixture behind plate for Giants for many seasons. Named Rookie of the Year in 1972 by *Sporting News*.

RADER, DOUGLAS L. (Rooster) Inf.-BR-TR. B. 7/30/44, Chicago, Ill. 6'2", 210. Houston Astros 1967–72. Hit .253 in 743 games with 677 hits, 339 runs, 121 doubles, 25 triples, 78 home runs and 385 RBI. Best year: .252 in 1970 with 25 HR and 87 RBI. 1972 record: .237 in 152 games with 22 HR and 90 RBI. Hit 20 or more doubles, 1969–72. Led NL third basemen in putouts, assists and fielding average, and tied for most double plays in 1972.

RAFFENSBERGER, KENNETH D. (Ken) P-BR-TL. B. 8/8/17, York, Pa. 6'2", 185. St. Louis Cardinals 1939; Chicago Cubs 1940–41; Philadelphia Phillies 1943–47; Cincinnati Reds 1947–54. Won 119, lost 154 in 397 games with 806 strikeouts and 449 walks in 2151 innings. Won 13 or more games five times. Best year: 18–17 in 1949. Pitched 31 shutouts. Led NL in losses 1944 (20) and 1951 (17). Pitched two innings of 1944 All-Star game, receiving credit for victory.

RAMOS, PEDRO (Pete) P-BLR-TR. B. 3/28/35, Pinar Del Rio, Cuba. 6', 190. Washington Senators 1955–60, 1970; Minnesota Twins 1961; Cleveland Indians 1962–64; New York Yankees 1964–66; Philadelphia Phillies 1967; Pittsburgh Pirates 1969; Cincinnati Reds 1969. Won 117, lost 160 in 582 games with 1305 strikeouts and 720 walks in

2347 innings. Won 10 or more games seven straight years. Best season: 14–18 in 1958. Tied for lead in innings pitched 1960 (274). Tied major league mark for most years leading league in losses (4): 1958 (18), 1959 (19), 1960 (18), and 1961 (20). Holds AL record for most homers allowed in season (43) in 1957.

Good hitter, he whacked 15 home runs and drove in 56 runs. Pitched alongside Camilo Pascual on futile Senator teams in mid-50s.

RAMSEY, THOMAS A. (Toad) P-BR-TL. B. 8/8/64, Indianapolis, Ind. D. 3/27/06, Indianapolis, Ind. Louisville (American Association) 1885–89; St. Louis (NL) 1889–90. Won 115, lost 122 in 252 games with 1515 strikeouts and 671 walks. Won 37 games in 1886 and followed with 39 wins in 1887. No-hitter against Baltimore, 7/29/86. Led league in strikeouts, 1887 (355).

Baseball's first knuckleball pitcher, at one time considered the best lefthander in game. Unfortunately, drank himself out of big leagues. Umpired in minor leagues and helped organize league in Indiana before returning to bricklaying trade in same state. Died of pneumonia.

RASCHI, VICTOR A. (Vic) P-BR-TR. B. 3/28/19, West Springfield, Mass. 6'1", 205. New York Yankees 1946–53; St. Louis Cardinals 1954–55; Kansas City A's 1955. Won 132, lost 66 in 269 games with 944 strikeouts and 727 walks in 1819 innings. Lifetime percentage of .667 one of best in baseball. Won 21 games three straight years, 1949–51. Led AL in percentage 1950 (.724) and in strikeouts 1951 (164). Pitched 27 shutouts in majors. All-Star game: 1948–50, 52 (1–0). World Series: 1947, 49–53. Won 5, lost 3 in 11 Series games, including two wins in 1952 classic. Holds AL record most RBI by pitcher in game (7) on 8/4/53.

Later owned liquor store in Geneseo, N.Y. Baseball coach at Geneseo State College 1960–61. Now teaches high school in Geneseo.

RAWLINGS, JOHN W. (Red) Inf.-OF-BR-TR. B. 8/17/92, Bloomfield, Iowa. D. 10/16/72, Los Angeles, Calif. 5'8", 158. Cincinnati Reds 1914; Kansas City (Federal League) 1914–15; Boston Braves 1917–20; Philadelphia Phillies 1920–21; New York Giants 1921–22; Pittsburgh Pirates 1923–26. Hit .249 in 1080 games with 928 hits, 409 runs, 122 doubles, 28 triples, 14 home runs and 303 RBI. Best season: .284 in 1923. World Series: 1921 (.333).

Helped Giants win 1921 Series with 10 hits and sensational stop of smash by Frank Baker with one out and man on base in ninth inning of final game. Catch led to inning-ending double play to preserve New York's 1–0 victory and championship. Later sold admission tickets to Los Angeles Sports Arena and local race track.

RAY, JAMES F. (Sting) P-BR-TR. B. 12/1/44, Rock Hill, S.C. 6'1", 194. Houston Astros 1965–66, 1968–72. Won 36, lost 23 in 238 games with 365 strikeouts and 204 walks in 497 innings. Best year: 10–4 in 1971 with 8 saves and 2.11 ERA. 1972 record: 10–9 in 54 games with 3 saves and 4.30 ERA. Won 8, lost 2 in 40 games in 1969 with 3.91 ERA.

One of best relievers in Houston club's history, has penchant for picking up wins instead of saves in relief.

RAYMOND, ARTHUR L. (Bugs) P-BR-TR. B. 2/24/82, Chicago, Ill. D. 9/7/12, Chicago, Ill. 6', 190. Detroit Tigers 1904; St. Louis Cardinals 1907–08; New York Giants 1909–11. Won 46, lost 57 in 138 games with 401 strikeouts and 282 walks in 854 innings. Best year: 18–12 in 1909. Led NL in losses 1908 (25).

Talented fastball pitcher but problem child of Giant manager John McGraw. Despite McGraw's concern, couldn't stay off sauce. Quit baseball; died in 1912 in Chicago hotel room, despondent over recent death of two children.

RAYMOND, JOSEPH C. (Claude) P-BR-TR. B. 5/7/37, St. Jean, Que. 5'10", 180. Chicago White Sox 1959; Milwaukee Braves 1961–63; Houston Astros 1964–67; Atlanta Braves 1967–69; Montreal Expos 1969–71. Won 46, lost 53 in 449 games with 497 strikeouts and 225 walks in 720 innings. Overall best year 1970: 6–7 with 23 saves and 4.45 ERA in 59 games. Accumulated 52 saves and won 23 games from 1966 through 1970. All-Star game: 1966 (0–0).

One of 123 Canadians to play major league ball, French-speaking hurler found home as relief specialist with Montreal.

REACH, ALFRED J. (Al) Inf.-OF-TL B. 5/25/40, London, England. D. 1/14/28. Played five years with Athletics of National Association. Batted .371 in 1871. Considered baseball's first professional player for receiving $1000 salary to play for Philadelphia in 1864. Later founded the A. J. Reach Sporting Goods Co. Patented baseball with cork center which was invented by Ben Shibe, Reach's business partner and later owner of the Philadelphia A's.

REED, RONALD, L. (Ron) P-BR-TR. B. 11/2/42, La Porte, Ind. 6'6", 215. Atlanta Braves 1966–72. Won 62, lost 61 in 160 games with 596 strikeouts and 265 walks in 1042 innings. Best year 1969: 18–10 with 160 strikeouts and 3.47 ERA. 1972 record: 11–15 in 31 games with 111 strikeouts and 3.93 ERA. All-Star game: 1968 (0–0). Playoff series against Mets, 1969 (0–1).

Played both professional baseball and basketball in 1965 and 1967. Played both years with Detroit Pistons of NBA, scoring 951 points and grabbing 762 rebounds in 119 games. Last player to play two sports since Gene Conley, who also played in off-season with Boston Celtics.

REESE, HAROLD H. (Pee Wee) SS-3B-BR-TR. B. 7/23/19, Ekron, Ky. 5'9½", 178. Brooklyn Dodgers 1940–42, 1946–57; Los Angeles Dodgers 1958. Hit .269 in 2166 games with 2170 hits, 1338 runs, 330 doubles, 80 triples, 126 home runs and 885 RBI. Led NL runs 1949 (132). Tied for most walks NL 1947 (104). Stolen base leader 1952 (30). Hit 20 or more doubles 10 seasons. Led NL shortstops in putouts 1941–42, 48–49; assists 1942; double plays 1942, 48; fielding average 1949. All-Star game 1942: 46–54 (.118). World Series 1941,47,49,52–53, 55–56: .272 in 44 games. Best year: .309 in 141 games, 1954.

Purchased by Dodgers from Boston Red Sox, where development was stymied by presence of Joe Cronin, Reese named all-time Dodger shortstop by fans in 1969 poll. Reese and Jackie Robinson gave old Dodgers—and baseball—one of most memorable keystone combinations in game. Later Reese gained fame broadcasting baseball games on national television with Dizzy Dean. Coach, Dodgers, 1959. Now businessman in Louisville, Ky.

REESE, RICHARD B. (Rich) OF-1B-BL-TL. B. 9/29/41, Leipsic, Ohio. 6'3", 180. Minnesota Twins 1964–72. Sold to Detroit after 1972. Hit .261 in 785 games with 494 hits, 231 runs, 71 doubles, 16 triples, 49 home runs and 238 RBI. Best year: .322 in 1969 with 16 HR and 69 RBI. 1972 record: .218 in 132 games with 5 HR and 26 RBI. Championship Series: 1969–70 (.158).

Tied AL record for most pinch-hit, grand slam home runs (2), 8/3/69 and 7/7/70.

REGAN, PHILLIP R. (Phil; Vulture) P-BR-TR. B. 4/6/37, Ostego, Mich. 6'3", 200. Detroit Tigers 1960–65; Los Angeles Dodgers 1966–68; Chicago Cubs 1968–72; Chicago White Sox 1972. Won 96, lost 81 in 551 games with 743 strikeouts and 447 walks in 1373 innings. Best year: 14–1 in 1966 with 17 saves. Winner of Fireman of the Year Award for best relief pitcher in '66 and in 1968 with 12–5 and 21 saves. Finished 62 games in relief in 1968, an NL record. All-Star game: 1966 (0–0). World Series: 1966 (0–0).

Once a starting pitcher who racked up 15 wins in 1963, fell off in next two years before regaining touch as relief specialist. Won Comeback of Year Award in 1966.

REICHARDT, FREDERIC C. (Rick) OF-BR-TR. B. 3/16/43, Madison, Wis. 6'3", 215. Los Angeles Angels 1964; California Angels 1965–70; Washington Senators 1970; Chicago White Sox 1971–72. Hit

.262 in 909 games through 1972 with 793 hits, 361 runs, 96 doubles, 21 triples, 110 home runs and 412 RBI. Best year: .278 in 1971 with 19 HR and 62 RBI. 1972 record: .251 in 101 games with 8 HR and 43 RBI.

Received $175,000 bonus to sign with Angels from the U. of Wisconsin campus. Sidelined much of 1966 with kidney disorder.

REILLY, JOHN G. (Long John) 1B-BR-TR. B. 10/5/58, Tusculum, Ohio. D. 5/31/37, Tusculum, Ohio. 6'3", 178. Cincinnati (NL) 1880, 1890–91; Cincinnati (American Association) 1883–89. Hit .284 in 1133 games with 1352 hits, 898 runs, 215 doubles, 139 triples, 67 home runs. Hit .300 or better five times. Best season: .339 in 1884. Hit 20 or more doubles seven years and 11 or more triples nine consecutive years. Six hits in game, 9/12/83. Led AA in home runs, 1884 (11) and 1888 (13).

Fine defensive first baseman who played in era of barehanded fielders.

REISER, HAROLD P. (Pistol Pete) OF-3B-BLR-TR. B. 3/17/19, St. Louis, Mo. 5'11", 185. Brooklyn Dodgers 1940–42, 1946–48; Boston Braves 1949–50; Pittsburgh Pirates 1951; Cleveland Indians 1952. Hit .295 in 861 games with 786 hits, 473 runs, 155 doubles, 41 triples, 58 home runs and 368 RBI. Hit .300 or better three times. Best year: league-leading .343 in 1941. In 1941 also led NL in total bases (299), slugging percentage (.558), triples (17) and runs (117). Led league in stolen bases 1942 (20) and 1946 (34). All-Star game: 1941–42, 46 (.143). World Series: 1941,47 (.214).

Premier defensive outfielder. Fearless pursuit of flyballs shortened career. Suffered debilitating injuries from crashing into fences in 1947 and '48. Managed in minor leagues, 1955–59, 65–66. Coach with Los Angeles Dodgers, 1960–64, California Angels, 1970–71; scout, Chicago Cubs, 1966; coach with Cubs, 1966–69, 1972–73.

RENKO, STEVEN (Steve) P-BR-TR. B. 12/10/44, Kansas City, Kans. 6'5", 230. Montreal Expos 1969–72. Won 35, lost 42 in 129 games with 405 strikeouts and 456 walks in 699 innings. Best year: 15–14 in 1971 with 129 strikeouts and 3.75 ERA. 1972 record: 1–10 in 30 games with 66 strikeouts and 5.20 ERA. Pitched one-hitters against San Francisco, 6/9/71, and Philadelphia, 7/9/71.

Quarterbacked U. of Kansas football team which included former Chicago Bear Gale Sayers. Renko drafted by Oakland Raiders in 1966.

RETTENMUND, MERVIN W. (Merv) OF-BR-TR. B. 6/6/43, Flint, Mich. 5'11", 190. Baltimore Orioles 1968–72. Hit .290 in 475 games with 401 hits, 218 runs, 65 doubles, 11 triples, 41 home runs and 186 RBI. Hit .300 or better twice. Best year: .322 in 1970 with 18 HR and 58 RBI. 1972 record: .233 in 102 games with 6 HR and 21 RBI. Championship Series: 1969–71 (.273). World Series: 1969–71 (.219). Named to *Sporting News'* All-Star team in 1971 and Minor League Player of the Year in 1968.

Played football at Ball State (Ind.) U. Drafted by Dallas Cowboys in 1964.

REULBACH, EDWARD M. (Big Ed) P-BR-TR. B. 12/1/82, Detroit, Mich. D. 7/17/61, Glens Falls, N.Y. 6'1", 190. Chicago Cubs 1905–13; Brooklyn Dodgers 1913–14; Newark (Federal League) 1915; Boston Braves 1916–17. Won 181, lost 105 in 400 games with 1137 strikeouts and 892 walks in 2632 innings. Won 15 or more games seven times, including 24 in 1908 and 21 in 1915. Led NL in percentage 1906 (.826), 1907 (.810) and 1908 (.774). Won 14 consecutive games in 1909. Pitched 39 shutouts, including two in one day against Brooklyn, 9/26/08. World Series: 1906–08, 1910 (2–0).

Won 60 games, lost only 15 for pennant-winning Cubs of 1906–08.

REUSS, JERRY P-BL-TL. B. 6/19/49, St. Louis, Mo. 6'5", 200. St. Louis Cardinals 1969–71; Houston Astros 1972. Won 31, lost 35 in 90 games, with 382 strikeouts and 244 walks in 537 innings. Best year: 14–14 in 1971 with 131 strikeouts and 4.78 ERA. 1972 record: 9–13 in 33 games with 174 strikeouts and 4.17 ERA.

REYNOLDS, ALLIE P. (Chief) P-BR-TR. B. 2/10/15, Bethany, Okla. 6', 195. Cleveland Indians 1942–46; New York Yankees 1947–54. Won 182, lost 107 in 475 games with 1423 strikeouts and 1261 walks in 2492 innings. Won 10 or more games 12 seasons. Best Year: 20–8 in 1952. Had lifetime percentage of .630, led AL percentage 1947 (.704). Pitched 37 shutouts. Led AL strikeouts 1943 (151) and 1952 (160); ERA 1952 (2.06). No-hitters against Cleveland, 7/12/51, and Boston, 9/28/51 (after Yogi Berra caught second pop foul by Ted Williams). All-Star game: 1949–50; 52–54 (0–1). World Series: 1947, 49, 50–53. Won 7, lost 2 in 15 games with 2.79 ERA.

One of Yankees' greatest hurlers. President of the American Association 1969–71. President of oil well engineering firm, Oklahoma City, since 1957. Named to Oklahoma Sports Hall of Fame 1969.

REYNOLDS, CARL N. OF-BR-TR. B. 2/1/03, LaRue, Tex. 6', 195. Chicago White Sox 1927–31; Washington Senators 1932,36; St. Louis Browns 1933; Boston Red Sox 1934–35; Chicago Cubs 1937–39. Hit .302 in 1222 games with 1357 hits, 672 runs, 247 doubles, 107 triples, 80 home runs and 699 RBI. Hit .300 or better six years. Best season: .359 in 1930. Hit 20 or more doubles eight times, and 10 or more triples six times. Hit three homers in game 7/2/30. World Series: 1938 (0–0).

RHEM, CHARLES F. (Flint; Shad) P-BR-TR. B. 1/24/03, Rhems, S.C. D. 7/30/69, Columbia, S.C. 6'2", 180. St. Louis Cardinals 1924–32, 1934, 36; Philadelphia Phillies 1932–33; Boston Braves 1934–35. Won 105, lost 97 in 294 games with 536 strikeouts and 569 walks in 1726 innings. Won 10 or more games six times. Best year: 20–7 in 1926. World Series: 1926, 28, 30–31 (0–1).

Drinking companion of immortal Grover Cleveland Alexander, came from wealthy family. Once missed game as Cardinal by claiming he was kidnaped and forced to consume whisky by abductors.

RHINES, WILLIAM P. (Billy; Bunker) P-BR-TR. B. 3/14/69, Ridgway, Pa. D. 1/30/22, Ridgway, Pa. 5'11", 170. Cincinnati NL 1890–92, 1895–97; Louisville NL 1893; Pittsburgh Pirates 1898–99. Won 113, lost 103 in 231 games with 555 strikeouts and 576 walks. Won 20 or more games twice, including 28 in rookie season.

A submarine pitcher, Bunker gained immediate fame with Cincinnati by winning 13 of first 14 games in first year.

RHOADES, ROBERT B. (Dusty) P-BR-TR. B. 10/4/79, Wooster, Ohio. D. 2/12/67, San Bernardino, Calif. 6'1", 215. Chicago Cubs 1902; St. Louis Cardinals 1903; Cleveland Indians 1903–09. Won 99, lost 85 in 231 games. Best season: 22–10 in 1906. Pitched no-hitter against Boston, 9/18/08.

RHODES, JAMES L. (Dusty) OF-BL-TR. B. 5/13/27, Mathews, Ala. 6', 178. New York Giants 1952–57; San Francisco Giants 1959. Hit .253 in 576 games with 296 hits, 146 runs, 44 doubles, 10 triples, 54 home runs and 207 RBI. Best year: .341 in 82 games with 15 homers in 1954. Hit three homers in game, 8/26/53 and 7/28/54.

Captivated fans across country during 1954 World Series with four hits, including two "Chinese" home runs. Three of four blows were pinch hits.

RICE, DELBERT (Del) C-BR-TR. B. 10/27/22, Portsmouth, Ohio. 6'3", 205. St. Louis Cardinals 1945–55, 1960; Milwaukee Braves 1955–59; Chicago Cubs 1960; Baltimore Orioles 1960; Los Angeles Angels 1961. Hit .237 in 1309 games with 908 hits, 342 runs, 177 doubles, 20 triples, 79 home runs and 441 RBI. Best season: .259 in 1952 with 11 HR and 65 RBI. Led NL catchers in putouts and assists, 1952; tied for lead in double plays, 1951. World Series: 1946,57 (.333).

Coach with Los Angeles Angels, 1962–65; California Angels 1965–66; Cleveland Indians 1967. Managed in minor leagues, 1968–71; appointed manager of California Angels in 1972. Led team to 75 wins and 80 losses in 1972 and was replaced by Angel coach Bobby Winkles at season's end. Scout, Angels, 1973. Named Manager of the Year in minor leagues by *Sporting News* in 1971.

RICE, EDGAR C. (Sam) OF-P-BL-TR. B. 2/20/92, Morocco, Ind. 5'10", 155. Washington Senators 1915–33; Cleveland Indians 1934. Hit .322 in 2404 games with 2987 hits, 1515 runs, 2987 hits, 497 doubles, 184 triples, 34 home runs and 1077 RBI. Hit .300 or better 13 times. Best year: .350 in 1925. Hit 30 or more doubles 10 straight years and 10 or more triples 10 consecutive seasons. Tied for AL lead triples 1923 (18). Had 200 or more hits in season six times, leading AL hits 1924 (216) and tying for most hits 1926 (216). 31-game hitting streak in 1924. Holds AL record most singles season (182) in 1925. Led AL stolen bases 1920 (63) and had 351 stolen bases during career. Pitched nine games for Senators, compiling 1–1 mark. World Series: 1924–25, 33 (.302 in 15 games). Hall of Fame 1963.

Missed out on greater fame by falling 13 hits shy of 3000 mark. Had 12 hits in 1925 World Series and made brilliant catch of fly ball off bat of Earl Smith, diving into temporary bleachers to rob Pirate catcher of home run. Later raised chickens near Washington, D.C.

RICE, HARRY F. OF-3B-BL-TR. B. 11/22/01, Anna, Ill. D. 1/1/71, Portland, Oreg. 5'9", 185. St. Louis Browns 1923–27; Detroit Tigers 1928–30; New York Yankees 1930; Washington Senators 1931; Cincinnati Reds 1933. Hit .299 in 1024 games with 1118 hits, 620 runs, 186 doubles, 63 triples, 48 home runs and 506 RBI. Hit. 300 or better five times. Best season: .359 in 1925. Hit 20 or more doubles six seasons.

Noted for fine fielding, made 11 putouts in one game, 6/12/30. Rifle arm compared with that of Bob Meusel of New York Yankees. Managed several minor league clubs after playing days.

RICHARD, JAMES R. P-BR-TR. B. 3/7/50, Vienna, La. 6'8", 222. Houston Astros 1971–72. Won 3, lost 1 in eight games with 37 strikeouts and 24 walks in 27 innings. 1972 record: 1–0.

Overpowering fastball helped him tie record of former Brooklyn Dodger Karl Spooner for most strikeouts (15) in first major league start, 9/5/71, against San Francisco.

RICHARDS, PAUL R. C-BR-TR. B. 11/21/08, Waxahachie, Tex. 6'1½", 180. Brooklyn Dodgers 1932; New York Giants 1933–35; Philadelphia A's 1935; Detroit Tigers 1943–46. Hit .227 in 523 games with 321 hits, 140 runs, 51 doubles, 5 triples, 15 home runs and 155 RBI. World Series: 1945 (.211). Hit two doubles and drove in four runs in seventh game of '45 Series to lead Tigers to championship over Chicago Cubs.

Despite light hitting and limited playing experience, gained reputation later as shrewd developer and handler of pitching talent. Managed in minor leagues, 1947–50; manager Chicago White Sox, 1951–54, and Baltimore Orioles, 1955–61. Record as manager in majors: 865–794 with six first division teams. General manager Houston Astros, 1962–65; vice president for baseball operations Atlanta Braves, 1966–72. Member of Texas Sports hall of Fame.

RICHARDSON, ARTHUR H. (Hardy) Inf.-OF-BR-TR. B. 4/21/55, Paulsboro, N.J. D. 1/14/31, Utica, N.Y. 5'9½", 170. Buffalo (NL) 1879–85; Detroit (NL) 1886–88; Boston (NL) 1889; Boston (Players League) 1890; Boston (American Association) 1891; Washington (NL) 1892; New York (NL) 1892. Hit .302 in 1,316 games with 1705 hits, 1112 runs, 305 doubles, 125 triples, 70 home runs. Hit .300 or better seven times. Best year: .363 in 1887. Hit 17 or more doubles 12 times, 10 or more triples five years. Led NL homers 1886 (11), and tied for most home runs in Players League 1890 (13).

Played second and third as well as outfield. One of top players of his day, member famed "Big Four" on Buffalo team which included James (Deacon) White, Dan Brouthers and Jack Rowe. Buffalo astounded baseball world by selling foursome to Detroit after 1885 season for $7000.

RICHARDSON, ROBERT C. (Bobby) 2B-BR-TR. B. 8/19/35, Sumter, S.C. 5'9", 170. New York Yankees 1955–66. Hit .266 in 1412 games with 1432 hits, 643 runs, 196 doubles, 37 triples, 34 home runs and 390 RBI. Hit .300 or better twice. Best year: .302 in 1962. Hit 20 or more doubles five times. Led AL in hits 1962 (209). All-Star game: 1957, 59, 62–66 (.091). World Series: 1957–58, 1960–64, hit .305 in 36 Series games and batted in six runs in game, 10/8/60. Collected 13 hits in seven-game Series in 1964 and 11 in 1960 classic. Led AL second basemen in putouts, 1961, and double plays, 1961, 62, 65. Played shortstop on occasion.

Now baseball coach at U. of South Carolina and active in Fellowship of Christian Athletes. Delivered closing benediction at session of 1972 Republican National Convention in Miami Beach.

RICHERT, PETER G. (Pete) P-BL-TL. B. 10/29/39, Mineola, N.Y. 6', 195. Los Angeles Dodgers 1962–64, 1972; Washington Senators 1965–67; Baltimore Orioles 1967–71. Won 75, lost 69 in 356 games with 881 strikeouts and 390 walks in 1083 innings. Best year: 15–12 in 1965 with 161 strikeouts and 2.60 ERA. 1972 record: 2–3 in 37 games with 38 strikeouts and 2.25 ERA. All-Star game: 1965–66 (0–1). Championship Series: 1969 (0–0). World Series: 1969–71 (0–0).

Struck out six consecutive batters in relief in first big league game, 4/12/62. Fanned seven straight batters in game, 4/24/66.

RICHMOND, JOHN L. P-OF-BL-TL. B. 5/5/57, Sheffield, Ohio. D. 9/30/29, Toledo, Ohio. 5'10", 142. Boston (NL) 1879; Worcester (NL) 1880–82; Providence (NL) 1883; Cincinnati (American Association) 1886. Won 74, lost 102 in 247 games with 552 strikeouts and 269 walks in 1583 innings. Won 31 games in 1880 and 25 in 1881 at peak of career.

Holds distinction of being first major league pitcher to hurl perfect game, 1–0 victory over Cleveland, 6/12/80. Later became high school principal in Worcester, Mass.

RICKEY, W. BRANCH (Mahatma) C-BL-TR. B. 12/20/81, Lucasville, Ohio. D. 12/9/65, Columbia, Mo. 5'9", 175. St. Louis Browns 1905–06, 1914; New York Yankees 1907. Hit .239 in 119 games. Holds modern record for allowing 13 runners to steal base in game, 6/28/07. Manager St. Louis Browns 1913–15 (139–179) and St. Louis Cardinals 1919–25 (458–485). Coached at U. of Michigan 1909–11. Vice president, St. Louis Browns, 1916. Vice president, St. Louis Cardinals, 1917–20, 1925–42. Vice president, Brooklyn Dodgers, 1942–50. General manager, Pittsburgh Pirates, 1951–55. Member of Pirates' board of directors 1956–59. Advisor, St. Louis Cardinals, 1963–65.

Great innovator in baseball, Rickey created minor league farm system while with Cardinal organization, paved the way for blacks to play major league ball by bringing Jackie Robinson to Brooklyn Dodgers in 1947, even conceived idea of Knothole Gang to attract youth to game. Also organized Continental League in 1960, which spurred majors to set off era of expansion in 1960s.

Deeply religious—he was named "Wesley Branch Rickey" after founder of Methodist Church, John Wesley—refused to play games on Sunday because of promise made to his mother when he first launched pro career. Kept promise even when field manager of St. Louis Browns and St. Louis Cardinals. Hall of Fame 1967.

RIDDLE, ELMER R. P-BR-TR. B. 7/31/14, Columbus, Ga. 5'11½", 170. Cincinnati Reds 1939–45, 1947; Pittsburgh Pirates 1948–49. Won 65, lost 52 in 191 games with 342 strikeouts and 458 walks in 1023 innings. Best year: 21–11 in 1943, tying for NL lead in victories. Led NL in percentage in 1941 (.826) on 19–4 mark. Also led in ERA, 1941 (2.24). All-Star game: 1948 (0–0). World Series: 1940 (0–0).

RIGNEY, JOHN D. (Johnny) P-BR-TR. B. 10/28/14, Oak Park, Ill. 6'2", 190. Chicago White Sox 1937–42, 46–47. Won 64, lost 64 in 198 games with 605 strikeouts and 450 walks in 1186 innings. Best year: 15–8 in 1939.

Married Dorothy Comiskey, granddaughter of Charles A. (Roman) Comiskey, founder of the White Sox, and daughter of then owner J. Louis Comiskey. Joined the White Sox front office after playing days and later became club's farm director. Appointed vice president of White Sox in 1955. Now operates racing stable he owned with late wife.

RIGNEY, WILLIAM J. (Bill)   3B-2B-SS-BR-TR. B. 1/29/18, Alameda, Calif. 6'1'', 183. New York Giants 1946–53. Hit .259 in 654 games with 510 hits, 281 runs, 78 doubles, 14 triples, 41 home runs and 212 RBI. Best year: .267 in 1947 with 17 HR and and 59 RBI. All-Star game: 1948 (.000). World Series: 1951 (.250).

Player-manager in minor leagues, 1954–55. Manager, New York Giants, 1956–57; San Francisco Giants, 1958–60; Los Angeles Angels, 1961–64; California Angels, 1965–69; Minnesota Twins, 1970–72. Managerial record: 1255–1223. Led Minnesota to division title in 1970 before losing playoffs to Baltimore. Named Manager of the Year by *Sporting News* in 1962. Administrative assistant and member of broadcasting team for Oakland A's 1973.

RING, JAMES J. (Jimmy)   P-BR-TR. B. 2/15/95, Brooklyn, N.Y. D. 7/2/65, New York, N.Y. 6'1'', 170. Cincinnati Reds 1917–20; Philadelphia Phillies 1921–25, 1928; New York Giants 1926; St. Louis Cardinals 1927. Won 118, lost 149 in 391 games with 835 strikeouts and 953 walks in 2389 innings. Won 10 or more games eight consecutive years. Best season: 18–16 in 1923. Tied NL record for most years leading league in walks (4) 1922–25. World Series: 1919 (1–1).

RIPPLEMEYER, RAYMOND R. (Ray)   P-BR-TR. B. 7/9/33, Valmeyer, Ill. 6'3'', 200. Washington Senators 1962. Only 1–2 in 18 games but is knowledgeable pitching instructor. Managed in minor leagues, 1965; coach in minors, 1965–67; pitching instructor in Phillies' chain, 1968–69; Philadelphia pitching coach since 1970. In off-season operates farm in Valmeyer and officiates college basketball games in the Big Ten and Missouri Valley conferences.

RISBERG, CHARLES A. (Swede)   SS-BR-TR. B. 10/13/94, San Francisco, Calif. 6', 175. Chicago White Sox 1917–20. Hit .243 in 476 games. One of eight players on Chicago team barred from baseball for life following 1919 "Black Sox" scandal. World Series: 1917,19 (.111). Later became dairy farmer. Shortly after expulsion from baseball, charged Detroit Tigers threw baseball games to White Sox in 1917, and claimed knowledge of other irregularities. Implicated Ty Cobb and Tris Speaker, among other stars.

RIVERA, MANUEL J. (Jungle Jim) OF-BL-TL. B. 7/22/22, Brooklyn, N.Y. 6', 196. St. Louis Browns 1952; Chicago White Sox 1952–61; Kansas City A's 1961. Hit .256 in 1171 games with 911 hits, 503 runs, 155 doubles, 56 triples, 83 home runs and 422 RBI. Best season: .286 in 1954. Hit 20 or more doubles five times. Led AL in triples 1953 (16). World Series: 1959 (.000). Led AL outfielders in assists and double plays in 1955. Stole 160 bases, leading AL in 1955 (25).

Fleetfooted flyhawk helped propel the Go-Go White Sox, along with Nellie Fox, Luis Aparicio and Minnie Minoso.

RIXEY, EPPA P. (Jeptha) P-BR-TL. B. 5/3/91, Culpeper, Va. D. 2/28/63, Cincinnati, Ohio. 6'5", 210. Philadelphia Phillies 1912–20; Cincinnati Reds 1921–33. Won 266, lost 251 in 694 games with 1350 strikeouts and 1082 walks in 4494 innings. Won 10 or more games 14 seasons, including 20 or more four years. Led NL wins 1922 (25). Shares record with Warren Spahn for most years pitched in NL (21). Pitched 29 shutouts during long career. World Series: 1915 (0–1). Hall of Fame 1963.

Scouted and signed by umpire Cy Rigler, Eppa named all-time lefthanded pitcher in Cincinnati history by fans in 1969. Later owned prosperous insurance firm in Cincinnati.

RIZZUTO, PHILLIP F. (Phil; Scooter) SS-BR-TR. B. 9/25/18, Glendale, N.Y. 5'6", 150. New York Yankees 1941–42, 1946–56. Hit .273 in 1661 games with 1588 hits, 877 runs, 239 doubles, 62 triples, 38 home runs and 563 RBI. Best year: .324 in 1950. Hit 20 or more doubles eight times. Named AL's Most Valuable Player in 1950. All-Star game: 1942, 1950–53 (.222). World Series: 1941–42, 47, 1949–53, 1955 (.246 in 52 games). Led AL shortstops in putouts, 1942,50; assists, 1952; fielding average, 1949–50, and double plays, 1941–42, 1952.

Little pepper pot considered one of finest shortstops to play the game. Now does telecasts of Yankee games.

ROBERTS, DAVID A. (Dave) P-BL-TL. B. 9/11/44, Gallipolis, Ohio. 6'3", 172. San Diego Padres 1969–71; Houston Astros 1972. Won 34, lost 41 in 137 games with 367 strikeouts and 180 walks in 693 innings. Best year: 14–17 in 1971 with 135 strikeouts and 2.10 ERA, second lowest in NL. 1972 record: 12–7 in 35 games with 111 strikeouts and 4.50 ERA.

ROBERTS, ROBIN E. P-BLR-TR. B. 9/30/26, Springfield, Ill. 6'1", 190. Philadelphia Phillies 1948–61; New York Yankees 1961; Baltimore

Orioles 1962–65; Houston Astros 1965–66; Chicago Cubs 1966. Won 286, lost 245 in 676 games with 2357 strikeouts and 902 walks in 4689 innings. Won 20 or more games 1950–55, leading NL in wins 1952 (28), 1954 (23) and 1955 (23). Tied for most wins 1953 (23). Pitched in 250 or more innings 11 times, leading NL innings pitched 1951 (315), 1952 (330), 1953 (347), 1954 (337) and 1955 (305). Led NL strikeouts 1953 (198) and 1954 (185). Led NL complete games 1952 (30), 1953 (33), 1954 (29), 1955 (26) and 1956 (22). Holds major league record for most homers allowed in season (46) in 1956 and lifetime (502). Named Pitcher of the Year by *Sporting News* 1952, 55. Threw 45 shutouts during career. All-Star game: 1950–56 (0–0 in 14 innings). World Series: 1950 (0–1).

Famous for pinpoint control, started 13 opening day games in NL. Missed coveted 300-victory mark by 14. Clinched pennant for Philadelphia Whiz Kids of 1950 and won 20th game, 10/1, by defeating Brooklyn's Don Newcombe 4–1 with aid of Dick Sisler's three-run home run. Now employed by brokerage firm in Pennsylvania.

ROBERTSON, CHARLES C. (Charlie) P-BL-TR. B. 1/31/97, Sherman, Tex. 6', 175. Chicago White Sox 1919, 1922–25; St. Louis Browns 1926; Boston Braves 1927–28. Won 49, lost 80 in 166 games. Best year: 14–15 in 1922. Highlight of brief career was pitching the fifth perfect game in the history of baseball against Detroit Tigers, 4/30/22. Later coached college baseball before retiring.

ROBERTSON, DAVIS A. (Dave) OF-BL-TL. B. 6/10/89, Norfolk Va. D. 11/5/70, Virginia Beach, Va. 6', 186. New York Giants 1912, 1914–17, 1919, 22; Chicago Cubs 1919–21; Pittsburgh Pirates 1921. Hit .287 in 801 games with 812 hits, 366 runs, 117 doubles, 44 triples, 47 home runs and 345 RBI. Hit .300 or better three times. Best year: .307 in 1916. Tied for NL lead in home runs 1916 (12) and 1917 (12)

Led Giants' hitters in 1917 World Series with .500 batting average on 11 hits.

ROBERTSON, ROBERT E. (Bob) 1B-3B-OF-BR-TR. B. 10/2/46, Frostburg, Md. 6'1", 195. Pittsburgh Pirates 1967–72. Hit .250 in 404 games with 324 hits, 170 runs, 52 doubles, 7 triples, 68 home runs and 208 RBI. Best year: .287 in 1970 with 27 HR and 82 RBI. 1972 record: .193 in 115 games with 12 HR and 41 RBI. Fell into slump in '72 after .271 average in 1971 with 26 HR and 72 RBI. Championship Series: 1970–72 : (.381). World Series: 1971 (.240). Led NL first basemen in assists in 1971. Credited with eight assists in game at first base, 6/21/71, a major league record.

Missed all of 1968 with kidney ailment. Led Pirates to World Series in 1971 with four homers in playoffs against San Francisco. Won third game of 1971 Series for Bucs by hitting home run after missing bunt sign.

ROBERTSON, SHERRARD A. (Sherry) OF-Inf.-BL-TR. B. 1/19/19, Montreal, Que. D. 10/23/70, Houghton, S.Dak. 6', 180. Washington Senators 1940–43, 1946–52; Philadelphia A's 1952. Hit .230 in 597 games. Often booed by Washington fans, who took out frustrations at owner Clark Griffith on Sherry, Griffith's nephew. Later coach, farm director and vice president of Minnesota Twins. Killed in automobile crash while on hunting trip in South Dakota.

ROBINSON, BROOKS C., JR. 3B-BR-TR. B. 5/18/37, Little Rock, Ark. 6'1", 190. Baltimore Orioles 1955–72. Hit .272 in 2349 games with 2398 hits, 1064 runs, 413 doubles, 63 triples, 242 home runs and 1158 RBI. Best year: .317 in 1964 with 28 HR and 118 RBI. 1972 record: .250 in 153 games with 8 HR and 64 RBI. Hit 25 or more doubles 10 years, and 20 or more HR in six seasons. Led AL RBI 1964 (118). Named AL's Most Valuable Player in 1964. All-Star game: 1960–72 (.325 in 16 games). Championship Series: 1969–71 (.486 in nine games). World Series: 1966, 69–71 (.263 in 21 games). Named MVP of 1970 Series. Led AL third basemen in putouts, 1958, 60, 64; assists, 1960, 63–64, 66–69; double plays, 1963–64, and fielding average, 1960–64, 66–68, 72. Tied for best fielding average, 1969.

Holds major league record for most games played by third baseman, assists, total chances, double plays and years leading in fielding average. Made several defensive gems in the 1969 and '70 World Series. The human vacuum cleaner has won the Gold Glove Award every year since 1960. A future Hall of Famer, named Baltimore's Man of the Decade in 1972.

ROBINSON, FRANK OF-1B-BR-TR. B. 8/31/35, Beaumont, Tex. 6'1", 195. Cincinnati Reds 1956–65; Baltimore Orioles 1966–71; Los Angeles Dodgers 1972; California Angels 1973. Hit .297 in 2432 games with 2614 hits, 1639 runs, 467 doubles, 69 triples, 522 home runs and 1613 RBI. Hit .300 or better nine times. Best year: .342 in 1962 with 39 HR and 136 RBI. 1972 record: .251 in 103 games with 19 HR and 59 RBI. Hit 25 or more doubles 11 times, leading NL 1962 (51). Hit 30 or more homers 10 times, including record-tying 38 in rookie season. Won Triple Crown in 1966, leading AL in batting (.316), HR (49) and RBI (122). Drove in 100 or more runs six times. Led NL runs 1962 (134) and AL runs 1966 (122). Led NL slugging percentage 1960 (.595), 1961 (.611) and 1962 (.624). Led AL in slugging percentage 1966 (.637). Hit three homers in game, 8/22/59. Topped NL first basemen in double plays, 1959. All-Star game: 1956–57, 59, 61–62, 65–67, 69–71 (.261 in 11 games). Championship Series: 1969–71 (.206 in nine games). World

Series: 1961, 66, 69–71 (.250 in 26 games with 8 HR). Named Rookie of the Year in 1956 by *Sporting News* and baseball writers.

Robinson's 522 home runs rank sixth on all-time list. Became inspirational as well as slugging leader of the Baltimore Orioles during his six years with team. First player to win Most Valuable Player Award in both leagues, taking the honor in NL in 1961, and in 1966 while playing in AL.

ROBINSON, JACK R. (Jackie) 2B-3B-1B-OF-BR-TR. B. 1/31/19, Cairo, Ga. D. 10/24/72, Stamford, Conn. 5'11½", 225. Brooklyn Dodgers 1947–56. Hit .311 in 1382 games with 1518 hits, 947 runs, 273 doubles, 54 triples, 137 home runs and 734 RBI. Hit .300 or better six times. Best season: .342 in 1949 to lead all NL hitters. Scored 100 or more runs five times. Hit 30 or more doubles six seasons. NL's Most Valuable Player 1949. *Sporting News'* Rookie of the Year in 1947. Led NL stolen bases 1947 (39) and 1949 (37). Hit for cycle, 8/29/48. Hall of Fame 1962. All-Star game: 1949–54 (.333). World Series: 1947, 49, 52–53, 55–56 (.234). Led NL second basemen putouts, 1951; assists, 1951; fielding average, 1948, 50–51; double plays, 1949–52. Stole home 19 times and once in World Series play, 9/28/55.

Talented, outspoken Robinson broke color barrier for blacks in major leagues with aid of Branch Rickey. Before joining Dodgers, played with Montreal in International League and the Kansas City Monarchs. Athletic ability also extended to football, where he was standout back for UCLA. Later became executive with New York restaurant firm as well as bank official and president of land development company. Also worked for programs combating drug addiction before his death.

ROBINSON, WILBERT (Uncle Robby) C-1B-OF-BR-TR. B. 6/2/64, Hudson, Mass. D. 8/8/34, Atlanta, Ga. 5'8½", 215. Philadelphia A's (American Association) 1886–90; Baltimore AA 1890–91; Baltimore NL 1891–99; St. Louis NL 1900; Baltimore Orioles 1901–02. Hit .280 in 1316 games with 1386 hits, 632 runs, 210 doubles, 54 triples, 18 home runs and 219 stolen bases. Hit .300 or better four times. Best year: .348 in 106 games in 1894. Made seven hits in one game, 6/10/1892. Only player to accomplish feat in nine innings. Hall of Fame 1945. Manager, Baltimore, 1902. Coach, New York Giants, 1911–13. Manager, Brooklyn Dodgers, 1914–31; president, Brooklyn, 1926–29. President and manager, Atlanta (Southern Association), 1933. President, Southern Association, 1934. Managerial record: 1397–1395.

Beloved manager of Brooklyn, won pennants in 1916 and 1920. Brooklyn team often termed Robins during his reign. Noted for running feud with New York Giants manager John J. McGraw. Once caught grapefruit from plane flying at 400 feet as stunt. Aviatrix Ruth Law took part in celebrated catch.

ROBINSON, WILLIAM E. (Eddie) 1B-BL-TR. B. 12/15/20, Paris, Tex. 6'2½", 210. Cleveland Indians 1942, 1946–48, 1957; Washington Senators 1949–50; Chicago White Sox 1950–52; Philadelphia A's 1953; New York Yankees 1954–56; Kansas City A's 1956; Detroit Tigers 1957; Baltimore Orioles 1957. Hit .268 in 1314 games with 1145 hits, 545 runs, 171 doubles, 24 triples, 172 home runs and 723 RBI. Best year: .311 in 1950. Hit 20 or more doubles four times and 15 or more homers seven years. All-Star game: 1949, 51–53 (.222). World Series: 1948, 55 (.348 in 23 at bats). Led AL first basemen in putouts, 1951; double plays, 1951–52, and fielding average, 1948.

Later became front office executive with Baltimore Orioles, Houston Astros, Kansas City A's and Atlanta Braves. Currently serves as Braves' director of minor league operations.

RODGERS, ROBERT L. (Bob; Buck) C-BLR-TR. B. 8/16/38, Delaware, Ohio, 6'2", 190. Los Angeles Angels 1961–64; California Angels 1965–69. Hit .232 in 932 games with 704 hits, 259 runs, 114 doubles, 18 triples, 31 home runs and 288 RBI. Best season: .258 in 1962. Led AL catchers in assists, 1964, 66–67, and double plays, 1962, 64. Holds AL record for most games caught in rookie season (150). Coach with Minnesota Twins since 1970.

RODRIGUEZ, AURELIO Inf.-BR-TR. B. 12 /28/47, Cananea, Mexico. 5'10", 180. California Angels 1967–70; Washington Senators 1970; Detroit Tigers 1971–72. Hit .243 in 730 games with 662 hits, 278 runs, 116 doubles, 23 triples, 56 home runs and 251 RBI. Best year: .249 in 1970 with 19 HR and 83 RBI. 1972 record: .236 in 153 games with 13 HR and 56 RBI. Hit 30 or more doubles in 1970 and '71.

Tagged for greatness, but hasn't realized full potential at bat. In the field, an accomplished artist. Led AL third basemen in doubles plays, 1969–70; putouts, 1972, and assists, 1970.

RODRIGUEZ, ELISEO C. (Ellie) C-BR-TR. B. 5/24/46, Farjardo, Puerto Rico. 5'11", 185. New York Yankees 1968; Kansas City Royals 1969–70; Milwaukee Brewers 1971–72. Hit .241 in 415 games with 288 hits, 112 runs, 42 doubles, 5 triples, 6 HR and 101 RBI. Best Year: .285 in 116 games in 1972 with 2 HR and 35 RBI. All-Star game: 1969, 72 (.000).

ROE, ELWIN C. (Preacher) P-BR-TL. B. 2/26/15, Ash Flat, Ark. 6'2", 170. St. Louis Cardinals 1938; Pittsburgh Pirates 1944–47; Brooklyn Dodgers 1948–54. Won 127, lost 84 in 333 games with 956 strikeouts and 504 walks in 1914 innings. Won 10 or more games eight times. Best year: 22–3 in 1951. Led NL percentage 1951 (.880) and in 1949 (.714). Led league in strikeouts 1945 (148). All-Star game: 1949–52 (0–0). World Series: 1949, 52–53 (2–1).

Colorful member of brilliant Dodger teams of 1950s, Roe shocked baseball world after retirement by admitting in article that he threw spitter. Now grocer in West Plains, Mo.

ROEBUCK, EDWARD J. (Ed) P-BR-TR. B. 7/3/31, East Millsboro, Pa. 6'1", 185. Brooklyn Dodgers 1955–57; Los Angeles Dodgers 1958, 1960–63; Washington Senators 1963–64; Philadelphia Phillies 1964–66. Won 52, lost 31 in 460 games with 477 strikeouts and 302 walks in 791 innings. Best season: 10–2 in 1962. World Series: 1955–56 (0–0).

A highly effective reliever despite history of arm problems, once pitched 83 consecutive games for Dodgers over two-year period in 1961–62 without suffering defeat. Streak began after Roebuck was told by doctors that his career was over. Also poor hitter but star fungo artist; caused some concern in Houston after hitting roof of Astrodome with ball hit by fungo bat. Scout for Atlanta Braves in California since 1967.

ROGELL, WILLIAM G. (Billy) Inf.-BLR-TR. B. 11/24/04, Springfield, Ill. 5'10½", 163. Boston Red Sox 1925, 1927–28; Detroit Tigers 1930–39; Cincinnati Reds 1940. Hit .267 in 1481 games with 1375 hits, 755 runs, 256 doubles, 75 triples, 42 home runs and 609 RBI. Best year: .296 in 1934 with 100 RBI and 3 homers. Also hit .295 in 1933 with 42 doubles and 11 triples. Hit 20 or more doubles seven times. World Series: 1934–35 (.283). Led AL shortstops in putouts, 1933; assists, 1934; fielding average, 1936–37, and double plays, 1933, 35.

Contributed vitally to Tiger pennants in 1934 and '35. Took up politics after retirement and has served as Detroit alderman since 1942.

ROHE, GEORGE A. Inf.-BR-TR. B. 9/15/75, Cincinnati, Ohio. D. 6/10/57, Cincinnati, Ohio. Baltimore Orioles 1901; Chicago White Sox 1905–07. Hit only .227 in 226 games as substitute but almost singlehandedly defeated Chicago Cubs in 1906 World Series.

Collected seven hits in 21 at bats for Hitless Wonders to help White Sox knock off team which won 116 regular season games. Rohe hit two triples to win first and third games after replacing regular third baseman George Davis, who was injured before start of Series. Also played second base.

ROJAS, ALEJANDRO M. (Minnie) P-BR-TR. B. 11/23/38, Las Villas,

Cuba. 6'1", 185. California Angels 1966–68. Won 23, lost 16 in 157 games, all but two in relief. Struck out 153 and walked 68 in 261 innings and had ERA of 3.00. Won *Sporting News'* Fireman of the Year Trophy in 1967 after winning 12 and saving 22 games in 72 appearances.

Career ended suddenly by automobile crash prior to opening of 1969 baseball season in which Rojas was paralyzed. Now resides in Miami.

ROJAS, OCTAVIO (Cookie) Inf.-OF-BR-TR. B. 3/16/39, Havana, Cuba. 5'10", 170. Cincinnati Reds 1962; Philadelphia Phillies 1963–69; St. Louis Cardinals 1970; Kansas City Royals 1970–72. Hit .262 in 1292 games with 1187 hits, 531 runs, 175 doubles, 18 triples, 40 home runs and 401 RBI. Hit .300 or better twice. Best year: .303 in 1965 with 3 HR and 42 RBI. 1972 record: .261 in 137 games with 3 HR and 53 RBI. Led NL second basemen in double plays and putouts in 1968. Led AL second basemen in fielding average, 1971. Played in 52 consecutive games without error in 1971. All-Star game: 1965, 71–72 (.333). Smacked two-run homer in 1972 All-Star contest to tie score in eighth inning for AL. Played eight positions, including pitcher, in game for Philadelphia in 1967, but has played all nine positions.

ROJEK, STANLEY A. (Stan) Inf.-BR-TR. B. 4/21/19, North Tona-wanda, N.Y. 5'10", 170. Brooklyn Dodgers 1942, 46–47; Pittsburgh Pirates 1948–51; St. Louis Cardinals 1951; St. Louis Browns 1952. Hit .266 in 522 games. Best season: .290 in 1948. Made eight hits in 1948 doubleheader. Led NL shortstops in assists 1948. Teamed with Danny Murtaugh to give Pirates classy double-play combination. Now owns bowling establishment in North Tonawanda.

ROLFE, ROBERT A. (Red) 3B-SS-BL-TR. B. 10/17/08, Penacook, N.H. D. 7/8/69, Gilford, N.H. 5'11½", 170. New York Yankees 1931, 1934–42. Hit .289 in 1175 games with 1394 hits, 942 runs, 257 doubles, 67 triples, 69 home runs and 497 RBI. Hit .300 or better four times, with high of .329 in 1939. Led AL in hits 1939 (213), doubles 1939 (46), triples 1936 (15). Scored over 100 runs seven consecutive seasons, leading AL in runs in 1939 (139). All-Star team: 1937, 39: (.375). World Series: 1936–39, 1941–42: (.284 in 28 games). Named to all-time Yankee team by fans in 1969. Career cut short by chronic kidney ailment.

Baseball and basketball coach at Dartmouth College, 1943–45; athletic director Dartmouth, 1954–67. Coach, New York Yankees, 1946. Director of Detroit Tiger farm system; manager, Tigers, 1949–52 (278–256). Manager of the Year in 1950. Also onetime basketball coach of professional team in Toronto. Led AL third basemen in fielding average, 1935–36.

ROMMEL, EDWIN A. (Eddie) P-BR-TR. B. 9/13/97, Baltimore, Md. D. 8/26/70, Baltimore, Md. Philadelphia A's 1920–32. Won 171, lost 119 in 507 games with 599 strikeouts and 724 walks in 2556 innings. Won 10 or more games nine times, leading AL in wins 1922 (27) and tying for most wins 1925 (21). Victory total of 27 in '22 was compiled with team which won only 65 games. World Series: 1929, 31 (1–0).

Due to a shortage of pitchers, pitched 17 innings of 18-inning game won 18–17 by Philadelphia, 7/10/32. Set record for most hits allowed in extra inning game (29). Also walked nine batters during marathon. Coach for Philadelphia, 1933–34; managed in minors before becoming popular AL umpire, 1938–59. After '59 season became aide to then governor of Maryland, Millard Tawes.

ROMO, VICENTE P-BR-TR. B. 5/21/43, Santa Rosalia, Mexico. 6'1", 190. Los Angeles Dodgers 1968; Cleveland Indians 1968–69; Boston Red Sox 1969–70; Chicago White Sox 1971–72; San Diego Padres 1973. Won 24, lost 23 in 217 games with 315 strikeouts and 184 walks in 451 innings. Best year: 7–3 in 48 games in 1970 with 9 saves and 4.08 ERA. 1972 record: 3–0 in 28 games with one save and 3.29 ERA.

Made headlines in Boston once by disappearing mysteriously for two days during road trip in Chicago.

ROOKER, JAMES P. P-BR-TL. B. 9/23/42, Lakeview, Oreg. 6', 195. Detroit Tigers 1968; Kansas City Royals 1969–72; Pittsburgh Pirates 1973. Won 21, lost 44 in 106 games with 304 strikeouts and 224 walks in 493 innings. Best year: 10–15 in 1970 with 117 strikeouts and 3.53 ERA. 1972 record: 5–6 in 18 games with 44 strikeouts and 4.38 ERA.

Not the league's worst hitting pitcher, he hit two homers in game, 7/7/69, and collected five RBI in game, 5/17/70.

ROOT, CHARLES H. (Chinski) P-BR-TR. B. 3/17/99, Middletown, Ohio. D. 11/7/70, Hollister, Calif. 5'10½", 189. St. Louis Browns 1923; Chicago Cubs 1926–41. Won 201, lost 160 in 632 games with 1459 strikeouts and 889 walks 3197 innings. Won 10 or more games 10 times. Best year 26–15 in 1927. Led NL wins, 1927, and percentage, 1929 (.760). World Series: 1929, 32, 35, 38 (0–3). Named Cubs' all-time righthander in 1969.

Gained fame as victim of Babe Ruth's "called shot" home run in fifth game of 1932 World Series which was won by Yankees. On two-strike count, Ruth supposedly signaled to Root and razzing Cub dugout that homer was forthcoming and delivered shot into center field stands on next pitch. Root later coached and managed in minors, 1943–50; coach with Chicago Cubs, 1951–53, and later coach with Milwaukee Braves. Retired to ranch in California.

ROSAR, WARREN V. (Buddy) C-BR-TR. B. 7/3/14, Buffalo, N.Y. 5'9", 190. New York Yankees 1939–42; Cleveland Indians 1943–44; Philadelphia A's 1945–49; Boston Red Sox 1950–51. Hit .261 in 988 games with 836 hits, 335 runs, 147 doubles, 15 triples, 18 home runs and 367 RBI. All-Star game: 1942–43, 1946–48 (.143). World Series: 1941–42 (1.000).

Not great hitter but named to five All-Star squads due to outstanding defensive ability. Led AL catchers in assists, 1943, 46–47; double plays, 1944, and fielding average, 1946–47. Holds major league record for fielding percentage for catcher with 1.000 on 605 chances in 117 games in 1946.

ROSE, PETER E. (Pete; Charlie Hustle) OF-2B-BLR-TR. B. 4/14/41, Cincinnati, Ohio. 5'10½", 189. Cincinnati Reds 1963–72. Hit .309 in 1537 games with 1922 hits, 992 runs, 313 doubles, 76 triples, 109 home runs and 586 RBI. Hit .300 or better eight consecutive years, 1965–72. Best season: .348 in 1969 with 16 HR and 82 RBI. 1972 record: .307 in 154 games with 6 HR and 57 RBI. Banged out 200 or more hits five times, leading NL 1965 (209) and 1972 (198). Tied for most hits 1968 (210) and 1970 (205). Led NL batting 1968 (.335) and 1969 (.348). Hit 30 or more doubles seven times. Tied for league lead in runs 1969 (120). Championship Series: 1970, 72 (.360). World Series: 1970, 72 (.229). Led NL second basemen putouts, 1965. Led outfielders in fielding average, 1970, and tied for most assists by outfielder, 1968. All-Star game: 1965, 67–71 (.143).

Aggressive, earned nickname by running to first base even when walked. Named Rookie of the Year in 1963 by baseball writers and rookie player of year by *Sporting News*.

ROSEBORO, JOHN H. (Gabby) C-BL-TR. B. 5/13/33, Ashland, Ohio. 5'11½", 200. Brooklyn Dodgers 1957; Los Angeles Dodgers 1958–67; Minnesota Twins 1968–69; Washington Senators 1970. Hit .249 in 1585 games with 1206 hits, 512 runs, 190 doubles, 44 triples, 104 home runs and 548 RBI. Best season, .287 in 1964. All-Star game: 1958, 61–62, 1969 (.141). World Series: 1959, 63, 65–66 (.157). Led NL catchers putouts, 1959, 61–62, 66. Holds major league record for most putouts for catcher (9291) and chances accepted in career (9966). Led catchers in double plays, 1960–61.

Took over for Hall of Famer Roy Campanella and caught Sandy Koufax and Don Drysdale in their prime. Coach with Washington Senators, 1971, California Angels, 1972.

ROSEN, ALBERT L. (Flip) 3B-1B-BR-TR. B. 2/29/24, Spartanburg,

S.C. 5'10½", 180. Cleveland Indians 1947–56. Hit .285 in 1044 games with 1063 hits, 603 runs, 165 doubles, 20 triples, 192 home runs and 717 RBI. Hit .300 or better three times, including high of .336 in 1953. Hit 20 or more homers six times, leading AL HR 1950 (37) and 1953 (43). Led in runs scored 1953 (115). Drove in 100 or more runs five times, leading AL in RBI 1952 (105) and 1953 (145). Led in slugging percentage 1953 (.613). Hit 20 or more doubles five times. All-Star game: 1952–55 (.273). Hit two HR and single in 1954 All-Star contest to drive in five runs in 11–9 AL victory. Led AL third basemen assists, 1950,53, and double plays, 1953. Named AL's Most Valuable Player, 1953. World Series: 1948, 54 (.231). Hit three HR in one game, 4/29/52.

Despite hitting credentials, often criticized by fans in Cleveland. Retired over salary squabble and now is vice president of brokerage firm in Cleveland.

ROUSH, EDD J. OF-BL-TL. B. 5/8/93, Oakland City, Ind. 5'11", 175. Chicago White Sox 1913; New York Giants 1916, 1927–29, 1930; Cincinnati Reds 1916–26, 1931. Hit. .325 in 1748 games with 2,158 hits, 1001 runs, 331 doubles, 168 triples, 63 home runs, and 882 RBI. Hit. 300 or better 12 times. Led NL in batting 1917 (.341) and 1919 (.321). Hit 20 or more doubles seven times, leading NL doubles 1923 (41). Hit 10 or more triples 10 seasons, leading NL triples 1924 (21). Eight hits in doubleheader, 6/19/27. Hit safely in 27 consecutive games in 1924 and 1927 seasons. World Series: 1919 (.214). Hall of Fame 1962. Named to all-time Cincinnati team, 1969.

Best player to come out of Federal League, Roush was forerunner of modern ball player. Balked at salary offers all during long career, missing much of 1922 and all of 1930 because of pay squabbles. Coach, Cincinnati, 1938.

ROWE, JOHN C. (Jack) SS-C-OF-BL-TR. B. 12/8/57, Harrisburg, Pa. D. 4/26/11, St. Louis, Mo. 5'8", 170. Buffalo (NL) 1879–85; Detroit (NL) 1886–88; Pittsburgh (NL) 1889; Buffalo (Players League) 1890. Hit .292 in 1034 games with 1256 hits, 764 runs, 202 doubles, 88 triples, 28 home runs and 503 RBI. Hit .300 or better four times. Brother of major league outfielder and shortstop Dave Rowe, who played from 1877–88. Led NL triples 1881 (11). Member of baseball's Big Four, including Dan Brouthers, James (Deacon) White and Hardie Richardson, all of whom were traded to Detroit after 1885 season. Managed Buffalo, 1890 (36–96).

ROWE, LYNWOOD T. (Schoolboy) P-BR-TR. B. 1/11/12, Waco, Tex. D. 1/8/61, El Dorado, Ark. 6'4½", 210. Detroit Tigers 1933–42; Brooklyn Dodgers 1942; Philadelphia Phillies 1943, 1946–49. Won 158, lost 101 in 491 games with 913 strikeouts and 558 walks in 2219 innings.

Won 10 or more games nine times, Best year: 24–8 in 1934. AL percentage leader 1940 with .842. All-Star game: 1935–36, 1947 (0–0). World Series: 1934–35, 1940 (2–5). Tied AL record most consecutive wins in season (16) in 1934.

ROWLAND, CLARENCE H. (Pants) B. 2/12/79, Platteville, Wis. D. 5/17/69, Chicago, Ill. Rose from minor league catcher to respected baseball executive. Managed Chicago White Sox 1915–18, winning pennant and World Series in 1917. Record: 339–247. Part owner and manager of minor league team, 1919. Umpire in American League, 1923–27. Scout for Cincinnati Reds, 1929–30, and for Chicago Cubs, 1933–41. Named general manager of Cubs' Los Angeles farm club in 1942 and later elected president of Pacific Coast League. Vice president, Chicago Cubs, 1954–55, 59. Died in Chicago nursing home.

RUCKER, GEORGE N. (Nap) P-BR-TL. B. 9/30/84, Crabapple, Ga. D. 12/19/70, Alpharetta, Ga. 5'11'', 190. Brooklyn Dodgers 1907–16. Won 134, lost 134 in 336 games with 1217 strikeouts and 701 walks in 2375 innings. Won 10 or more games seven seasons, winning 22 in 1911. Pitched 38 shutouts, leading NL in shutouts in 1912 (6). Pitched first game in Ebbets Field, 4/13/13, beating New York Giants 3–2. Struck out 16 batters in game against Pittsburgh, 7/24/09. Pitched no-hitter against Boston, 9/5/08. World Series: 1916 (0–0).

Later scout for Dodgers. Gained nickname from sports writer Grantland Rice. Also served as mayor of Roswell, Ga., for several years.

RUDI, JOSEPH O. (Joe) OF-1B-BR-TR. B. 7/7/46, Modesto, Calif. 6'2'', 200. Kansas City A's 1967; Oakland A's 1968–72. Hit .271 in 502 games with 489 hits, 220 runs, 88 doubles, 17 triples, 43 home runs and 188 RBI. Hit .300 or better twice. Best year: .305 in 1972 with 19 HR and 75 RBI. Led AL in hits in '72 (181) and finished second in runs, doubles, triples, and fifth in batting. All-Star game: 1972 (1.000). Championship Series: 1971–72 (.200). World Series: 1972 (.240).

Won second game of 1972 Series for Oakland with homer and tremendous catch of drive by Denis Menke in ninth inning of contest in Cincinnati.

RUDOLPH, FREDERICK D. (Don) P-BL-TL. B. 8/16/31, Baltimore, Md. D. 9/12/68, Granada Hills, Calif. 5'11'', 195. Chicago White Sox 1957–58; Chicago Cubs 1959; Cincinnati Reds 1959; Cleveland Indians 1962; Washington Senators 1963–64. Won 18, lost 32 in 124 games.

Probably only pitcher married to striptease artist; husband of Patti Waggon. Noted as fast-working hurler. Died of injuries in automobile accident.

RUDOLPH, RICHARD (Baldy) P-BLR-TR. B. 8/25/87, New York, N.Y. D. 10/20/49, Bronx, N.Y. 5'9½", 160. New York Yankees 1910–11; Boston Braves 1913–20, 1922–23, 1927. Won 122, lost 108 in 284 games with 786 strikeouts and 402 walks in 2049 innings. Won 20 or more games twice. Best year: league-leading 27 wins in 1914. Led NL in losses 1915 (19) while winning 22. Pitched over 300 innings three years and threw 30 shutouts.

Teamed with Bill James to pitch Miracle Braves of 1914 into first place finish. Spitballer won two games in Series to match two by James as Braves scalped Connie Mack's A's.

RUEL, HEROLD D. (Muddy) C-BR-TR. B. 2/20/96, St. Louis, Mo. D. 11/13/63, Palo Alto, Calif. 5'9", 150. St. Louis Browns 1915, 33; New York Yankees 1917–20; Boston Red Sox 1921–22, 1931; Washington Senators 1923–30; Detroit Tigers 1931–32; Chicago White Sox 1934. Hit .276 in 1469 games with 1242 hits, 494 runs, 187 doubles, 29 triples, 4 home runs and 528 RBI. Hit .300 or better three times. Best year: .316 in 1923. World Series: 1924–25 (.200). Led AL catchers in putouts, 1923–25; assists, 1923–25; double plays, 1922–25, and fielding average, 1926–28.

Scored winning run in final game of 1924 World Series after getting on base on second chance after his foul pop fell untouched when New York Giant catcher caught his foot in discarded mask. Later coached with Cleveland Indians, 1948, after managing St. Louis Browns in 1947 (59–95). An attorney, Ruel later worked as aide to baseball commissioner Happy Chandler and finished baseball career as director of Detroit Tigers' farm system.

RUETHER, WALTER H. (Dutch) P-BL-TL. B. 9/13/93, Alameda, Calif. D. 5/16/70, Phoenix, Ariz. 6'1½", 180. Chicago Cubs 1917; Cincinnati Reds 1917–20; Brooklyn Dodgers 1921–24; Washington Senators 1925–26; New York Yankees 1926–27. Won 138, lost 95 in 487 games, with 710 strikeouts and 739 walks in 2123 innings. Won 14 or more games six times. Best year: 21–12 in 1922. Led NL percentage 1919 (.760). World Series: 1919, 26 (1–1).

Managed in minor leagues in 1930s. Later scouted for the Cubs for seven years and 24 years for the New York and San Francisco Giants until his death. Good hitter, Dutch frequently used as pinch hitter.

RUFFING, CHARLES H. (Red) P-BR-TR. B. 5/3/04, Granville, Ill. 6'1½", 210. Boston Red Sox 1924–30; New York Yankees 1930–46; Chicago White Sox 1947. Won 273, lost 225 in 624 games with 1987 strikeouts and 1541 walks in 4342 innings. Won 10 or more games 13 times, including 20 or more four consecutive years, 1936–39. Led AL wins 1938 (21); percentage 1938 (.750); losses 1928 (25) and 1929 (22); strikeouts 1932 (190). All-Star game: 1934, 38–42: (0–1). World Series, 1932, 36–39, 41–42: won 7, lost 2 with 2.63 ERA in 10 games. Pitched 52 shutouts during career. Hall of Fame 1967.

Blossomed into star with Yankees after pitching for lowly Red Sox teams. Gave up Ted Williams' first hit in majors—double. Feared hitter, compiled .269 average with 521 hits, 98 doubles, 13 triples and 36 home runs. Later employed by Mets' organization and served as pitching coach for Minnesota Twins' farm team.

RUIZ, HIRALDO S. (Chico)   Inf.-BLR-TR. B. 12/12/38, Santo Domingo, Cuba. D. 2/9/72, San Diego, Calif. 6', 169. Cincinnati Reds 1964–69; California Angels 1970–71. Hit .240 in 565 games with 276 hits, 133 runs, 37 doubles, 10 triples, 2 home runs and 69 RBI. Best year: .259 in 85 games in 1968.

Enthusiastic substitute relished utility role. Involved in celebrated feud with Alex Johnson while with Angels. Killed in automobile accident in San Diego.

RUNNELS, JAMES E. (Pete)   Inf.-BL-TR. B. 1/28/28, Lufkin, Tex. 6', 170. Washington Senators 1951–57; Boston Red Sox 1958–62; Houston Astros 1963–64. Hit .291 in 1799 games with 1854 hits, 876 runs, 283 doubles, 64 triples, 49 home runs and 630 RBI. Hit .300 or better six times, five of those with the Red Sox. Won AL batting crown twice with .320 in 1960 and .326 in 1962. Missed third batting title by six points in 1958, hitting .322 to teammate Ted Williams' .328. Hit 20 or more doubles six times. Tied major league record with nine hits in doubleheader, 8/30/60. All-Star game: 1959–60, 62 (.143).

Line drive hitter, he managed Red Sox briefly in 1966. Now co-director of children's camp in Pasadena, Tex., and co-owner of sporting goods store.

RUSH, ROBERT R. (Bob)   P-BR-TR. B. 12/21/25, Battle Creek, Mich. 6'4", 205. Chicago Cubs 1948–57, 1960; Milwaukee Braves 1958–60. Won 127, lost 152 in 420 games with 1244 strikeouts and 789 walks in 2410 innings. Won 10 or more games eight times. Best season: 17–13 in 1952. Led NL in losses 1950 (20). All-Star game 1950, 52 (1–0). World Series: 1958 (0–1). Received credit for victory in rain-shortened 1952 All-Star game.

RUSIE, AMOS W. (Hoosier Thunderbolt)   P-BR-TR. B. 5/30/71, Mooresville, Ind. D. 12/6/42, Seattle, Wash. 6'1", 210. Indianapolis (NL) 1889; New York Giants 1890–98; Cincinnati Reds 1901. Won 241, lost 158 in 412 games with 1953 strikeouts and 1637 walks in over 3700 innings. Won 20 or more games eight consecutive years. Won 30 or more three times, leading NL wins 1894 (36). Led NL percentage 1897 (.784). Led league strikeouts 1890 (345), 1891 (321), 1892 (303), 1893 (208), 1894 (204) and 1895 (199). Also led league in walks five years. Pitched 31 shutouts, leading league 1892 (6), and tying for lead in shutouts 1893 (4), 1894 (3), 1895 (4) and 1897 (3). Won two complete games in one day, 9/28/91 and 10/4/92. No-hitter against Brooklyn, 7/31/91. Won two games in 1894 Temple Cup Series to help Giants defeat Baltimore Orioles. Traded to Cincinnati from Giants for Christy Mathewson.

Another of baseball's fireballing righthanders, compared with greatest strikeout artists in game. In later years became attendant at New York's Polo Grounds.

RUSSELL, EWELL A. (Reb) P-OF-BL-TL. B. 4/12/89, Jackson, Miss. 5'11", 185. Chicago White Sox 1913–19; Pittsburgh Pirates 1922–23. Won 80, lost 61 in 251 games with 495 strikeouts and 267 walks in 1291 innings. Best season: 22–16 in rookie season. Holds modern major league mark for most shutouts by rookie (8). World Series: 1917 (0–0).

Left majors after '19 season and returned as outfielder with Pirates, hitting .368 in 60 games in 1922.

RUSSELL, WILLIAM E. (Bill; Ropes) SS-OF-BR-TR. B. 10/21/48, Pittsburg, Kans. 6', 180. Los Angeles Dodgers 1969–72. Hit .252 in 399 games with 286 hits, 141 runs, 43 doubles, 20 triples, 11 home runs and 92 RBI. Best year: .272 in 129 games in 1972 with four HR and 34 RBI. One of many promising youngsters on Dodger team along with Yeager, Lacy, Garvey and Buckner.

RUTH, GEORGE H. (Babe) OF-P-BL-TL. B. 2/6/95, Baltimore, Md. D. 8/16/48, New York, N.Y. 6'2", 215. Son of Baltimore saloonkeeper; mother died when Babe very young. Possibly saved from life of crime when placed in industrial home managed by Catholic order. Bought by the Red Sox in 1914 from Baltimore in International League for less than $3,000. Sold to Yankees after 1919 season by financially troubled Red Sox owner Harry Frazee, a theatrical producer who made and lost a fortune. Producer of *No, No, Nanette* gained greater fame by peddling superstar for $100,000 and $350,000 in attempt to keep franchise afloat. Ruth immediately made baseball world forget "Black Sox" scandal by crashing home runs at record pace. His 59 round-trippers in 1921 were matched only by himself until 1961 when Roger Maris whacked 61.

Boston Red Sox 1914–19; New York Yankees 1920–34; Boston Braves 1935. Hit .342 in 2502 games with 2873 hits, 2174 runs, 506 doubles, 134 triples, 714 home runs and 2209 RBI. Hit .300 or better 17 times. Best year. .393 in 1923. Led AL batting 1924 (.378). Hit 25 or more doubles 12 times and 10 or more triples four times. Scored 100 or more runs 12 times, leading AL 1919 (103), 1920 (158); 1921 (177—a major league mark); 1923 (151); 1924 (143); 1926 (139); 1927 (158) and 1928 (163). Drove in 100 or more runs 13 times, topping AL in 1919 (112); 1920 (137); 1921 (170); 1926 (155). Tied for most RBI 1923 (130) and 1928 (163). Drove in 100 or more runs 13 times, topping AL in 1919 (112); (11) and 1931 (46). Led league in homers 1919 (29), 1920 (54); 1921 (59); 1923 (41); 1924 (46); 1926 (47); 1927 (60); 1928 (54); 1929 (46) and 1930 (49). Hit 3 homers in game, 6/21/30 and 6/25/35, 7 homers in five games in 1921. AL's MVP 1923. Led outfielders in fielding average 1919. All-Star game: 1933–34 (.333). Hero of first All-Star game with two-run homer to help beat NL 4–2. World Series: 1915–16, 18, 21–23, 26–28, 32. Hit .326 in 41 games with 42 hits, and 15 HR and 33 RBI. Holds record for hitting four-games Series with .625 with 10 hits.

Suffered legendary "bellyache" in 1925, hitting "only" 25 homers in 98 games. Later that season fined $5000 for extracurricular escapades by Yankee manager and adversary, Miller Huggins.

In 1932 World Series hit famous "called shot" home run in 5th inning of third game against Cubs in Wrigley Field with score knotted at 4–4. Pointed at stands, delivered blast off Charlie Root which helped Yanks win 7–5, sweep Series.

Pitching record: Won 94, lost 46 in 163 games with 488 strikeouts and 441 walks in 163 games. Has lifetime ERA of 2.28 and led AL in ERA 1916 (1.75). Won 23 games in 1916 and 24 in 1917. Led AL percentage 1916 (.657). World Series: won 3, lost 0 in three games in 1916, 18 classics. Held Series record for most consecutive scoreless innings pitched (29 2/3) until broken by Whitey Ford in 1961.

Drew record 2056 walks, leading AL 11 times. Received record 170 free passes in 1923. Led AL in slugging percentage 13 times, including major league high of .847 in 1920. Led AL in total bases six times, including record 457 in 1921. Had lifetime slugging percentage of .690, highest of any player.

Rank on all-time list: games (14th); runs (2nd); home runs (1st); RBI (1st); total bases (5th); walks (1st); slugging percentage (1st); batting average (14th—tie).

Left Yankee organization after 1934 season when bid to manage club was rejected by business manager Ed Barrow. Joined Boston Braves under Judge Emil Fuchs to stimulate gate but played only 28 games. In one of last games on May 25, hammered three homers off Pirate pitching in Forbes Field. Left club in June, two months before bankrupt Fuchs forced to part with Braves.

Coached briefly for Brooklyn in 1938 and lived out retirement years in New York apartment. Subject of one of sport's most poignant photos at Yankee Stadium shortly before death. During ceremonies marking retirement of uniform number and 25th anniversary of stadium, once mighty Babe was photographed as he was forced to lean on his bat for support.

Undoubtedly greatest of all players when versatility is considered, Ruth became household word in almost every language around globe. The lusty legend was subject of movies and books and is as popular today as he was in his prime. Took baseball out of dead-ball era and manhandled the sport into nation's number one pastime. His gate appeal helped finance construction in 1923 of Yankee Stadium, appropriately tabbed "House That Ruth Built." Elected to Hall of Fame in 1936 but no doubt also would have gained entry if he had remained a pitcher. The Sultan of Swat in Golden Age of Sports, Ruth's name may well outlive the game itself.

RYAN, JAMES E. (Jimmy) OF-SS-P-BR-TL. B. 2/11/63, Clinton, Mass. D. 10/28/23, Chicago, Ill. 5'10", 175. Chicago Cubs 1885–89, 1891–1900; Chicago (Players League) 1890; Washington Senators 1902–03. Hit .314 in 2008 games with 2577 hits, 1640 runs, 439 doubles, 153 triples, 118 home runs, 1093 RBI. Scored 100 or more runs nine times. Hit 20 or more doubles 14 seasons. Led NL doubles 1888 (37). Led NL hits 1888 (182). Hit .300 or better 13 times. Best year: .359 in 1894. Stole 434 bases, including season high of 60 in 1888. Scored six runs in one game, 7/25/1894. World Series: 1886 (.250). As pitcher, won 5, lost 1 in 24 games. Later managed in minor leagues, 1901 and 1904.

RYAN, LYNN N. (Nolan) P-BR-TR. B. 1/31/47, Refugio, Tex. 6'2", 190. New York Mets 1966, 68–71; California Angels 1972. Won 48, lost 54 in 144 games with 822 strikeouts and 501 walks in 794 innings. Best year: 19–16 in 39 games in 1972 with 329 strikeouts and 157 walks in 284 innings. Had ERA of 2.28 in '72. Led AL in strikeouts in 1972, becoming only the sixth pitcher in AL history to fan more than 300 batters. Also led in shutouts (9) and struck out 16 in game twice and 17 once. Championship Series: 1969 (1–0). World Series: 1969 (0–0).

With Mets plagued by blisters from delivering blistering fast ball. Soaked hands in pickle juice to toughen skin. Now averaging better than one strikeout per inning.

RYBA, DOMINIC J. (Mike) P-C-BR-TR. B. 7/9/03, DeLancey, Pa. D. 12/13/70, Springfield, Mo. 5'11½", 180. St. Louis Cardinals 1935–38; Boston Red Sox 1941−46. Won 52, lost 34 in 250 games with 307 strikeouts and 247 walks in 783 innings. Best year: 12–7 in 42 games in 1944. Substitute catcher with both the Cardinals and Red Sox, he hit .235 in 247 at bats. Believed to be first player in major leagues to play both positions. World Series: 1946 (0–0).

Later managed in minor leagues and scouted for St. Louis Cardinals. Was killed after falling from ladder while trimming tree at his home.

SADECKI, RAYMOND M. (Ray) P-BL-TL. B. 12/26/40, Kansas City, Kans. 5'11", 195. St. Louis Cardinals 1960–66; San Francisco Giants 1966–69; New York Mets 1970–72. Won 116, lost 115 in 417 games with 1421 strikeouts and 789 walks in 2155 innings. Won 10 or more games five times. Best year: 20–11 in 1964 with 119 strikeouts and 3.63 ERA. 1972 record: 2–1 in 34 games with 3.08 ERA. World Series: 1964 (1–0). Received $50,000 bonus in signing with the St. Louis Cardinals in 1958.

SAIN, JOHN F. (Johnny) P-BR-TR. B. 9/25/17, Havana, Ark. 6'2", 194. Boston Braves 1942, 46–51; New York Yankees 1951–55; Kansas City A's 1955. Won 139, lost 116 in 412 games with 910 strikeouts and 619 walks in 2125 innings. Won 20 or more games four times. Best season: 24–15 in 1948 with 137 strikeouts and 2.60 ERA. Led NL wins, innings pitched (315) and complete games (28) in 1948. Also led complete games 1946 (24). All-Star game: 1947–48, 1953 (0–1). World Series: 1948, 51–53 (2–2 in 6 games). Coach with Kansas City A's, 1959; New York Yankees, 1961–63; Minnesota Twins, 1965–66; Detroit Tigers, 1967–69. Pitching instructor California Angels 1970. Coach, Chicago White Sox, 1971–73.

Half of jingle "Spahn and Sain and Pray for Rain" chanted by Brave fans in 1940s. Later became controversial pitching coach whose method of instruction resulted in numerous clashes with managers. Brilliant but different methods have made 20-game winners of Whitey Ford, Ralph Terry, Jim Bouton, Jim Grant, Jim Kaat, Earl Wilson, Denny McLain,

Wilbur Wood and Stan Bahnsen.

SALLEE, HARRY F. (Slim) P-BL-TL. B. 2/3/85, Higginsport, Ohio. D. 3/22/50, Higginsport, Ohio. 6′3″, 180. St. Louis Cardinals 1908–16; New York Giants 1916–18, 1920–21; Cincinnati Reds 1919–20. Won 174, lost 143 in 476 games with 835 strikeouts and 572 walks in 2818 innings. Won 10 or more games nine times. Best season: 21–7 to help Cincinnati win 1919 pennant. Pitched 25 shutouts and had career ERA under 2.60. World Series: 1917, 19 (1–3).

SANDERS, KENNETH G. (Ken) P-BR-TR. B. 7/8/41, St. Louis, Mo. 5′11″, 180. Kansas City A's 1964, 66; Boston Red Sox 1966; Oakland A's 1968; Milwaukee Brewers 1970–72. Won 20, lost 36 in 285 games with 293 strikeouts and 191 walks in 471 innings. Best year: 7–12 in 1971 league-leading 83 games. Won Fireman of Year Trophy in '71 with 31 saves and 1.92 ERA. 1972 record: 2–9 in 62 games with 17 saves and 3.13 ERA. Set major league record in 1971 by finishing 77 games. Traded to Philadelphia Phillies after 1972 season, then to Minnesota.

SANFORD, JOHN S. (Jack) P-BR-TR. B. 5/18/29, Wellesley Hills, Mass. 6′, 190. Philadelphia Phillies 1956–58; San Francisco Giants 1959–65; California Angels 1965–67; Kansas City A's 1967. Won 137, lost 101 with 1182 strikeouts and 737 walks in 388 games. Won 10 or more games eight times. Best season: 24–7 in 1962. Led NL in strikeouts 1957 (188). All-Star game: 1957 (0–0). World Series: 1962 (1–2).

Won 16 consecutive games during 1962 season. Selected Rookie of the Year in 1957 by *Sporting News* and Baseball Writers Association. Golf director for country club in West Palm Beach, Fla.

SANGUILLEN, MANUEL D. (Manny) C-BR-TR. B. 3/21/44, Colon, Panama. 6′, 195. Pittsburgh Pirates 1967, 69–72. Hit .309 in 561 games with 648 hits, 246 runs, 88 doubles, 28 triples, 26 home runs and 278 RBI. Hit .300 or better 1969–71. Best year: .325 in 1970 with 7 homers and 61 RBI. 1972 record: .298 in 136 games with 7 home runs and 71 RBI. All-Star game: 1971–72 (.500). Championship Series: 1970–72 (.263). World Series: 1971 (.379 with 11 hits). Led NL catchers in assists in 1971 and tied for most double plays in '71.

Great clutch hitter and free swinger, he rarely strikes out. Possesses great throwing arm, has surprising speed for catcher. Rated just shade less spectacular than Cincinnati's Johnny Bench.

SANTO, RONALD E. (Ron) 3B-OF-BR-TR. B. 2/25/40, Seattle, Wash. 6′, 194. Chicago Cubs 1960–72. Hit .280 in 1977 games with 2028 hits, 1044 runs, 324 doubles, 64 triples, 317 home runs and 1213 RBI. Hit

.300 or better four times. Best year: .313 in 1964 with 30 HR and 114 RBI. 1972 record: .302 in 133 games with 17 HR and 74 RBI. Hit 25 or more doubles six years, 25 or more homers eight times. Drove in 100 or more runs four times. Tied for NL lead in triples 1964 (13). Led NL walks 1964 (86); 1966 (95); 1967 (96) and 1968 (96). All-Star game: 1963–66, 68–69, 1971–72 (.286) Led NL third basemen in putouts, 1962–67; assists, 1962–68; fielding average, 1968, and double plays 1961, 64, 66, 67, and tied for lead in 1968. Holds many other NL records for fielding at hot corner.

Counterpart of Brooks Robinson in NL. Teamed with Ernie Banks to produce potent one-two home run punch for more than a decade.

SAUER, HENRY J. (Hank) OF-1B-BR-TR. B. 3/17/19, Pittsburgh, Pa. 6′4″, 200. Cincinnati Reds 1941–42, 1945, 1948–49; Chicago Cubs 1949–55; St. Louis Cardinals 1956; New York Giants 1957; San Francisco Giants 1958–59. Hit .267 in 1399 games with 1278 hits, 709 runs, 200 doubles, 19 triples, 288 home runs and 876 RBI. Hit 30 or more homers six times, including 41 in 1954. Tied for NL lead HR 1952 (37). Led NL RBI 1952 (121). Most Valuable Player NL 1952. Hit three homers in game, 8/28/50 and 6/11/52. Tied for NL lead for most assists by outfielder 1949 (16). Brother Edward played in NL 1943–45, 1949. All-Star game: 1950–52 (.250).

Slugger's home run in fourth inning of rain-shortened 1952 All-Star game provided NL with winning margin. Later coached S.F. Giants, 1959, and has scouted for Giants since 1960.

SAWATSKI, CARL E. (Swats) C-BL-TR. B. 11/4/27, Shickshinny, Pa. 5′10″, 210. Chicago Cubs 1948–50, 1953–54; Milwaukee Braves 1957–58; Philadelphia Phillies 1958–59; St. Louis Cardinals 1960–63. Hit .242 in 633 games with 351 hits, 133 runs, 46 doubles, 5 triples, 58 home runs and 213 RBI. World Series: 1957 (.000).

Former utility catcher and pinch hitter appointed general manager of Arkansas Travelers in Texas League 1968 to present. Named outstanding minor league executive in Double A baseball in 1970 by *Sporting News*.

SAWYER, EDWIN M. (Eddie) Manager. B. 9/10/10, Westerly, R.I. Minor league outfielder 1934–43, managed in minors 1939–48. Manager of Philadelphia Phillies 1948–52, 1958–60. (390–425). Directed 1950 Whiz Kids to pennant but dropped World Series to Yankees in four.

During off-season taught biology at alma mater, Ithaca College, in Ithaca, N.Y. Currently special scout for Kansas City Royals.

SCHAAL, PAUL Inf.-BR-TR. B. 3/3/43, Pittsburgh, Pa. 5′11″, 180.

Los Angeles Angels 1964; California Angels 1965–68; Kansas City Royals 1969–72. Hit .239 in 942 games with 708 hits, 362 runs, 111 doubles, 23 triples, 46 home runs and 257 RBI. Best year: .274 in 1971 with 11 HR and 63 RBI. 1972 record: .228 in 127 games with 6 HR and 41 RBI. Drew 103 walks in 1971, third best in AL.

Career nearly came to abrupt end on June 13, 1968, when Schaal was skulled by pitch thrown by Boston Red Sox pitcher Jose Santiago.

SCHACHT, ALEXANDER (Al) P-BR-TR. B. 11/11/92, New York, N.Y. 5'11", 142. Washington Senators 1919–21. Appeared only briefly in majors, winning 14 and losing 10 in 54 games. Coached for Senators 1921–24 and Boston Red Sox 1935–36. While coach earned the nickname of "Clown Prince of Baseball" as result of entertaining fans before games. Entertained at World Series in 1921–25 and later teamed with former Washington Senators pitcher Nick Altrock. Took entertainment show on road and appeared in many major and minor league parks. Also entertained U.S. and NATO troops on tours to North Africa, Sicily, Pacific Islands and later Korea. Opened restaurant in New York City and performed final show before retirement in Baltimore in 1968.

SCHAEFER, HERMAN A. (Germany) Inf.-OF-BR-TR. B. 2/4/78, Chicago, Ill. D. 5/16/19, Saranac Lake, N.Y. Chicago Cubs 1901–02; Detroit Tigers 1905–09; Washington Senators 1909–14; Newark (Federal League) 1915; New York Yankees 1916; Cleveland Indians 1918. Hit .256 in 1141 games with 972 hits, 497 runs, 117 doubles, 48 triples, 8 home runs and 308 RBI. Best season: .334 in 1911. World Series: 1907–08 (.135).

Zany, happy-go-lucky ball player stole 201 bases during career. Often rattled opposing pitchers by stealing second base and running back to first base.

SCHALK, RAYMOND W. (Cracker) C-BR-TR. B. 8/12/92, Harvey, Ill. D. 5/19/70, Chicago, Ill. 5'7", 155. Chicago White Sox 1912–28; New York Giants 1929. Hit .253 in 1760 games with 1345 hits, 579 runs, 199 doubles, 48 triples, 12 home runs and 580 RBI. Best year: .281 in 1922 with 4 HR and 60 RBI in 142 games. Hall of Fame 1955. World Series: 1917,19 (.286).

Catching wizard despite size, led AL catchers in putouts nine years, 1913–20, 22. Led in assists, 1916, 22, and putouts, 1914–17, 1920–22. Tied for league lead fielding average, 1913. Holds major league records most years leading catchers in fielding and putouts. Caught four no-hitters and made three assists in inning, 9/30/21.

Managed Chicago White Sox, 1927–28 (102–125). Also managed minor league teams, 1932–40, 1950. Also scouted for Chicago Cubs and later operated bowling establishment and served as assistant baseball coach at Purdue U.

SCHANG, WALTER H. (Wally) C-BLR-TR. B. 8/22/89, South Wales, N.Y. D. 3/6/65, St. Louis, Mo. 5'10", 180. Philadelphia A's 1913–17, 1930; Boston Red Sox 1918–20; New York Yankees 1921–25; St. Louis Browns 1926–29; Detroit Tigers 1931. Hit .284 in 1840 games with 1506 hits, 769 runs, 264 doubles, 90 triples, 60 home runs and 718 RBI. Hit .300 or better six times. Best year: .330 in 1926 with 50 RBI. Hit 15 or more doubles nine years. Holds AL record for most errors by catcher since 1900 (218). Also holds AL record for most assists in game (8) in 1920 and throwing out most men trying to steal in game (6). World Series: 1913–14, 18, 21–23 (.287 in 32 games).

SCHEFFING, ROBERT B. (Bob) C-BR-TR. B. 8/11/15, Overland, Mo. 6'2", 180. Chicago Cubs 1941–42, 46–50; Cincinnati Reds 1950–51; St. Louis Cardinals 1951. Hit .263 in 517 games. Best year: .300 in 102 games in 1948. Led Tigers to 101 wins in 1961 but finished second to Yankees.

Manager in minor leagues, 1939, 55–56. Coach, St. Louis Browns, 1952–53; Cubs, 1954–55; Milwaukee Braves, 1960. Manager, Cubs, 1957–59, and Detroit, 1961–63 (418–427). Scouted for New York Mets, 1963, and Detroit, 1965. Director of player development for Mets, 1965–66; general manager, Mets since 1969. Named vice president of Mets in 1971.

SCHEIB, CARL A. P-BR-TR. B. 1/1/27, Gratz, Pa. 6'1", 192. Philadelphia A's 1943–54; St. Louis Cardinals 1954. Won 45, lost 65 in 267 games with 290 strikeouts and 493 walks in 1071 innings. Best season: 14–8 in 1948.

A pitching phenom, set record as youngest player to perform in AL at 16 years, 8 months and 5 days. Developed sore arm in 1953 and concluded 11-year career at age of 27.

SCHEINBLUM, RICHARD A. (Richie) OF-BLR-TR. B. 11/5/42, New York, N.Y. 6', 175. Cleveland Indians 1965, 67–69; Washington Senators 1971; Kansas City Royals 1972. Hit .259 in 304 games with 212 hits, 90 runs, 38 doubles, 7 triples, 9 home runs, 94 RBI. Best year 1972: .300 with 8 HR and 66 RBI in 134 games. Batting average sixth best in AL. All-Star game: 1972 (.000). MVP in American Association, with Denver, in 1971.

Originally signed by Indians, finally produced in 1972, after failing trials with Cleveland and Senators. Named to *Sporting News* 1972 AL All-Star team. Traded to Cincinnati after 1972 season.

SCHERMAN, FREDERICK J. (Fred) P-BL-TL. B. 7/25/44, Dayton, Ohio. 6'1", 195. Detroit Tigers 1969–72. Won 23, lost 13 in 178 games with 160 strikeouts and 130 walks in 281 innings. Best year: 11–6 in 1971 with 20 saves and 2.71 ERA. 1972 record: 7–3 in 57 games with 12 saves and 3.64 ERA.

Headed bullpen with Chuck Seelbach to lift Detroit to top of its division in 1972 and into playoffs with Oakland.

SCHMITZ, JOHN A. (Bear Tracks) P-BR-TL. B. 11/27/20, Wausau, Wis. 6', 170. Chicago Cubs 1941–42, 1946–51; Brooklyn Dodgers 1951–52; New York Yankees 1952–53; Cincinnati Reds 1952; Washington Senators 1953–55; Boston Red Sox 1956; Baltimore Orioles 1956. Won 93, lost 114 in 368 games with 746 strikeouts and 757 walks in 1812 innings. Won 10 or more games six times. Best season: 18–13 in 1948. Led NL in strikeouts 1946 (135). All-Star game: 1946,48 (0–1).

Defeated St. Louis Cardinals on last day of 1946 season to force historic playoff between St. Louis and Brooklyn Dodgers. Now greenskeeper at Wausau golf course.

SCHOENDIENST, ALBERT F. (Red) 2B-SS-3B-OF-BLR-TR. B. 2/2/23, Germantown, Ill. 6'1", 192. St. Louis Cardinals 1945–56, 1961–63; New York Giants 1956–57; Milwaukee Braves 1957–60. Hit .289 in 2216 games with 2449 hits, 1223 runs, 427 doubles, 78 triples, 84 home runs and 773 RBI. Hit .300 or better seven times. Best season: .342 in 1953. Hit 20 or more doubles 14 times, leading NL doubles 1950 (43). Led NL hits 1957 (200). Hit eight doubles in three consecutive games in 1948. Led NL stolen bases 1945 (26). All-Star game: 1946,1948–51, 52–55,57 (.190). Hit homer off Ted Gray in 14th inning of 1950 All-Star contest to give NL 4–3 win. World Series: 1946, 1957–58 (.269). Led NL second basemen in putouts, 1949, 52–53; assists, 1949, 53–54; fielding average, 1946, 49, 53, 55–56, 58; tied for top fielding average in 1957. Holds NL record for most years leading in fielding for second basemen and for highest fielding average lifetime (.983).

Player-coach St. Louis Cardinals, 1962–64; manager of Cardinals since 1965 (689–596). Missed most of 1959 season after being stricken by tuberculosis after 1958 World Series. Recovered fully from disease and played until 1963. As manager, won pennants in 1967 and '68 and won Series against Boston Red Sox in '67.

SCHRIVER, WILLIAM F. (Pop) C-1B-BR-TR. B. 6/11/66, Brooklyn, N.Y. D. 12/27/32, Brooklyn, N.Y. 5'9½", 172. Brooklyn (American Association) 1886; Philadelphia NL 1888–90; Chicago NL 1891–94; New York NL 1895; Cincinnati NL 1897; Pittsburgh Pirates 1898–1900;

St. Louis Cardinals 1901. Hit .263 in 747 games with 720 hits, 367 runs, 117 doubles, 40 triples, 16 home runs and 375 RBI.

His best catch probably was made outside ball park. Thought to be first player to catch baseball thrown from top of Washington Monument. Schriver caught baseball lobbed from shrine by Clark Griffith, 8/25/84. Umpired in NL 1901.

SCHULTE, FRANK (Wildfire) OF-BL-TR. B. 9/17/82, Cohocton, N.Y. D. 10/2/49, Oakland, Calif. 5'11", 170. Chicago Cubs 1904–16; Pittsburgh Pirates 1916–17; Philadelphia Phillies 1917; Washington Senators 1918. Hit .270 in 1800 games with 1766 hits, 906 runs, 288 doubles, 124 triples, 92 home runs and 817 RBI. Hit .300 or better twice. Best season: .301 in 1910. Hit 20 or more doubles seven times and 10 or more triples six times. Tied for most triples 1906 (13). Led NL in homers 1911 (21) and tied for league lead 1910 (10). Led in RBI 1911 (121) and slugging percentage 1911 (.534). World Series: 1906–08, 1910 (Hit .309 in 21 games).

SCHULTE, FRED W. (Fritz) OF-BR-TR. B. 1/13/04, Belvidere, Ill. 6'1", 183. St. Louis Browns 1927–32; Washington Senators 1933–35; Pittsburgh Pirates 1936–37. Hit .292 in 1178 games with 1241 hits, 686 runs, 249 doubles, 54 triples, 47 home runs and 593 RBI. Hit .300 or better three times. Best year: .307 in 1929. Hit 30 or more doubles five times. World Series: 1933 (.333). Leading hitter for Senators in '33 Series.

SCHULTZ, GEORGE W. (Barney) P-BR-TR. B. 8/15/26, Beverly, N.J. 6'2", 190. St. Louis Cardinals 1955, 63–65; Detroit Tigers 1959; Chicago Cubs 1961–63. Won 20, lost 20 in 233 games. Helped Cardinals win pennant in 1964 after being recalled from minors late in season. World Series: 1964 (0–1). Shares major league record for most consecutive relief appearances, nine, with Cubs, 5/4 through 5/15/62. Minor league pitching instructor with St. Louis, 1967–70; Cardinal pitching coach since 1970.

SCHUMACHER, HAROLD H. (Prince Hal) P-BR-TR. B. 11/23/10, Hinckley, N.Y. 6', 190. New York Giants 1931–42, 1946. Won 158, lost 121 in 450 games with 906 strikeouts and 902 walks in 2481 innings. Won 10 or more games 10 times. Best year: 23–10 in 1934. Pitched 29 shutouts. All-Star game: 1933, 35 (0–0). World Series: 1933, 36–37 (2–2).

Member of mound corps on Giants team which also featured Carl Hubbell and Freddie Fitzsimmons. Later employed by bat manufacturer and retired after 21 years as executive vice president.

SCHUPP, FERDINAND M. (Ferdie) P-BLR-TL. B. 1/16/91, Louisville, Ky. D. 12/16/70, Los Angeles, Calif. 5'10", 150. New York Giants 1913–19; St. Louis Cardinals 1919–21; Brooklyn Dodgers 1921; Chicago White Sox 1922. Won 61, lost 39 in 217 games with 553 strikeouts and 464 walks in 1054 innings. Best year: 21–7 in 1917, leading NL in percentage (.750). World Series: 1917 (1–0). Beset by sore arm throughout career, nevertheless set major league record for lowest earned run average in 1916: 0.90 in 140 innings with 9–3 mark.

SCORE, HERBERT J. (Herb) P-BL-TL. B. 6/7/33, Rosedale, N.Y. 6'2", 185. Cleveland Indians 1955–59; Chicago White Sox 1960–62. Won 55, lost 46 in 150 games with 837 strikeouts and 573 walks in 858 innings. Won 20 games in 1956 and led AL in strikeouts in rookie season (245) and in 1956 (263). Struck out 10 or more batters in game 24 times, including high of 16. Named Rookie of the Year by *Sporting News* and Baseball Writers Association in 1955. All-Star game: 1955–56 (0–0).

Billed as lefthanded Bob Feller, lost wicked fastball, along with bright career, when hit in eye by line drive off bat Yankees' Gil McDougald in 1957. Never fully recovered and quit game. Now play-by-play announcer of Cleveland Indians' games.

SCOTT, GEORGE (Boomer) 1B-3B-BR-TR. B. 3/23/44, Greenville, Miss. 6'2", 220. Boston Red Sox 1966–71; Milwaukee Brewers 1972. Hit .261 in 1022 games with 954 hits, 426 runs, 131 doubles, 32 triples, 125 home runs and 478 RBI. Best year: .303 in 1967 with 19 HR and 82 RBI. 1972 record: .266 in 152 games with 20 HR and 88 RBI. Led Brewers in '72 in runs, hits, doubles, triples and RBI and finished one homer behind Johnny Briggs for team home run lead. Hit 27 homers in rookie year. All-Star game: 1966 (.000). World Series: 1967 (.231).

Dazzling glove man, led first basemen in putouts and double plays, 1966 and '67. Also adept at third base.

SCOTT, JAMES (Death Valley) P-BR-TR. B. 4/23/88, Deadwood, S.Dak. D. 7/7/57, Palm Springs, Calif. 6'1", 235. Chicago White Sox 1909–17. Won 107, lost 113 in 309 games with 945 strikeouts and 609 walks in 1872 innings. Won 20 or more games twice. Best season: 24–11 in 1915. Led AL in losses 1913 (20). Threw 28 shutouts and had sparkling career ERA of 2.32. Pitched no-hitter for nine innings against Washington, 4/14/14, but lost in 10th frame.

Member of great White Sox mound staff that included Eddie Cicotte and Red Faber.

SCOTT, JOHN W. (Jack) P-BL-TR. B. 4/18/92, Ridgeway, N.C. D. 11/30/59, Durham, N.C. Pittsburgh Pirates 1916; Boston Braves 1917, 1919–21; Cincinnati Reds 1922; New York Giants 1922–23, 1925–26,

1928–29; Philadelphia Phillies 1927. Won 103, lost 109 in 408 games with 657 strikeouts and 493 walks in 1814 innings. Won 10 or more games five times. Best season: 16–7 in 1923. Led NL in losses 1927 (21). World Series: 1922–23 (1–1).

Picked up as free agent by Giants in 1922, won eight games and contributed shutout over Yankees in World Series to help team win championship.

SCOTT, LEWIS E. (Deacon) SS-BR-TR. B. 11/19/92, Bluffton, Ind. D. 11/2/60, Fort Wayne, Ind. 5'8", 148. Boston Red Sox 1914–21; New York Yankees 1922–25; Washington Senators 1925; Chicago White Sox 1926; Cincinnati Reds 1926. Hit .249 in 1654 games with 1455 hits, 552 runs, 208 doubles, 58 triples, 20 home runs and 544 RBI. Hit 15 or more doubles eight times. World Series: 1915–16, 18, 22–23 (.154 in 27 games). Holds major league record for most years leading shortstops in fielding average, eight consecutive seasons, 1916–23. Also led shortstops in putouts, 1920–21; assists, 1921–22, and double plays, 1920–21.

Played in 1307 consecutive games, 6/20/16 through 5/5/25, second only to Lou Gehrig's streak of 2130. Scott's streak ended less than month before Gehrig's record total began.

SEATON, THOMAS G. (Tom) P-BLR-TR. B. 8/30/89, Blair, Nebr. D. 4/10/40, El Paso, Tex. 6', 175. Philadelphia Phillies 1912–13; Brooklyn (Federal League) 1914–15; Newark (F) 1915; Chicago Cubs 1916–17. Won 93, lost 65 in 231 games with 644 strikeouts and 530 walks in 1340 innings. Led NL wins 1913 (27), innings pitched (322), strikeouts (168) and walks (136).

One of genuine stars of short-lived Federal League. Jumped to that league in 1914, won 25 games same year for Brooklyn entry.

SEAVER, GEORGE T. (Tom) P-BR-TR. B. 11/17/44, Fresno, Calif. 6', 200. New York Mets 1967–72. Won 116, lost 66 in 215 games with 1404 strikeouts, 429 walks in 1651 innings. Best year: 25–7 in 1969 with 208 strikeouts and 2.21 ERA. Won 20 or more games three times, including 21–12 in 35 games in 1972 with 249 strikeouts and 2.92 ERA. Struck out 200 or more batters five straight years, 1968–72, leading league in 1970 (283) and 1971 (289). Led NL in ERA 1970 (2.81) and 1971 (1.76). Fanned 19 Padres, 4/22/70, tying one-game record. Rookie of Year 1967, Cy Young Award 1969. All-Star game: 1967–72 (0–0). Fanned five in two innings in 1968 All-Star contest. World Series, 1969, 1–1.

Turned hapless Mets into champions by winning 25 in year of improbable pennant and World Series championship in 1969.

SEELBACH, CHARLES F. (Chuck) P-BR-TR. B. 3/20/48, Lakewood, Ohio. 6′, 175. Detroit Tigers 1971–72. Won 9, lost 8 in 1972, considered his rookie year, with 77 strikeouts and 46 walks in 116 innings. Picked up 14 saves in 66 games with ERA of 2.89. Finished fourth in total points for Fireman of Year Trophy. Championship Series: 1972 (0–0). Pitched Dartmouth to championship in 1970 NCAA World Series.

SEEREY, JAMES P. (Pat) OF-BR-TR. B. 3/17/23, Wilburton, Okla. 5′10″, 200. Cleveland Indians 1943–48; Chicago White Sox 1948–49. Hit .224 in 561 games with 406 hits, 236 runs, 73 doubles, 5 triples, 86 home runs and 261 RBI. Led AL strikeouts, 1944–45, 48. Tied for league lead in strikeouts, 1947.

Hit only 86 career homers and never more than 26 in season, but whacked four in one game, 7/18/48, and three in another contest, 7/13/45. One of nine major leaguers to hit four in one game.

SEGUI, DIEGO P. P-BR-TR. B. 8/17/38, Holguin, Cuba. 6′, 190. Kansas City A's 1962–65, 67; Washington Senators 1966; Oakland A's 1968, 70–72; Seattle Pilots 1969; St. Louis Cardinals 1972. Won 77, lost 85 in 443 games with 993 strikeouts and 598 walks in 1418 innings. Best year: 12–6 in 1969 with 12 saves and 3.36 ERA. 1972 record: 3–2 in 40 games with 9 saves. Led AL in ERA 1970 (2.56).

SELBACH, ALBERT C. (Kip) OF-BR-TR. B. 3/24/72, Columbus, Ohio. D. 2/27/56, Columbus, Ohio. 5′7″, 190. Washington (NL) 1894–98; Cincinnati Reds 1899; New York Giants 1900–01; Baltimore Orioles 1902; Washington Senators 1903–04; Boston Red Sox 1904–06. Hit .296 in 1598 games with 1803 hits, 1064 runs, 299 doubles, 149 triples, 43 home runs and 779 RBI. Hit .300 or better eight times and led NL triples 1895 (22). Hit 11 or more triples nine times and 20 or more doubles 10 years. Six hits in one game, 6/9/01. Stole 334 bases during career, including high of 49 in 1896.

SELEE, FRANK G. Manager. B. 10/26/59, Amherst, N.H. D. 7/5/09, Denver, Colo. Managed Boston Braves, 1890–1901, and Chicago Cubs, 1902–05. Won pennants 1891–93 and 1897–98. Managerial record: 1299–872.

In lists of baseball's greatest managers, Selee's name usually is omitted. In 16 years of managing, Selee's teams finished in first division 12 times. His won-lost percentage of .598 ranks fourth highest among all managers.

SELKIRK, GEORGE A. (Twinkletoes) OF-BL-TR. B. 1/4/08, Hunts-ville, Ont. 6′1″, 182. New York Yankees 1934–42. Hit .293 in 846 games with 810 hits, 503 runs, 131 doubles, 41 triples, 108 home runs and 576 RBI. Hit .300 or better three times. Best season: .312 in 1935. Drove in 100 or more runs twice and received 103 walks in 1939. All-Star game: 1936, 39 (.500).World Series: 1936–39, 41–42 (.235 in 21 games).

Managed in minor leagues after active career and served as director of player personnel for Kansas City A's. General manager of Washington Senators, 1964–69, and vice president of Senators, 1967–69. Scout with New York Yankees since 1970. Inherited Babe Ruth's No. 3 before New York management retired number along with several others.

SELMA, RICHARD J. (Dick) P-BR-TR. B. 11/4/43, Santa Ana, Calif. 5'11", 170. New York Mets 1965–68; San Diego Padres 1969; Chicago Cubs 1969; Philadelphia Phillies 1970–72. Won 39, lost 51 in 282 games with 660 strikeouts and 359 walks in 808 innings. Best year: 12–10 in 1969 with 181 strikeouts and 3.68 ERA. Appeared in 73 games in relief with Phillies in 1970, winning 8 and picking up 22 saves. 1972 record: 2–9 in 46 games with 3 saves and 5.55 ERA.

Acted as cheerleader from bullpen for vocal Wrigley Field Bleacher Bums in 1969 during Cubs' ill-fated drive for pennant.

SEMINICK, ANDREW W. (Andy) C-BR-TR. B. 9/12/20, Pierce, W. Va. 5'11", 187. Philadelphia Phillies 1943–51, 1955–57; Cincinnati Reds 1952–55. Hit 243 in 1304 games with 953 hits, 495 runs, 139 doubles, 26 triples, 164 home runs and 556 RBI. Hit 24 homers in 1949 and 1950, including three in one game, 6/2/49. All-Star game: 1949 (.000). World Series: 1950 (.182). Led NL catchers putouts, 1948; assists, 1948, and double plays, 1946.

In last game of 1950 season, made tag at plate on Cal Abrams of Brooklyn Dodgers to set stage for tenth inning homer by Dick Sisler to clinch pennant for Philadelphia Whiz Kids. Retired after managing in Phillies' chain (Eastern League) in 1972.

SEVEREID, HENRY L. (Hank) C-BR-TR. B. 6/1/91, Story City, Iowa. D. 12/17/68, San Antonio, Tex. 6', 175. Cincinnati Reds 1911–13; St. Louis Browns 1915–25; Washington Senators 1925–26; New York Yankees 1926. Hit .289 in 1371 games with 1244 hits, 408 runs, 204 doubles, 42 triples, 17 home runs and 530 RBI. Hit .300 or better in four full seasons with Browns. Best year: .324 in 1921. Hit 20 or more doubles five times. World Series: 1925–26 (.280). Holds record for most chances accepted by catcher in doubleheader (27). Swung 48-ounce bat and in 1921 threw out 51 of 53 runners trying to steal on him.

Played in organized baseball for 29 years, catching 2357 games. Managed in minors, 1932; coached in minor leagues, 1938; connected with Cincinnati Reds' farm system, 1938–40. Also scouted for Chicago

Cubs, 1943, and for Boston Red Sox from 1944 until his death.

SEWELL, JAMES L. (Luke) C-BR-TR. B. 1/15/01, Titus, Ala. 5'9", 160. Cleveland Indians 1921–32, 1939; Washington Senators 1933–34; Chicago White Sox 1935–38; St. Louis Browns 1942. Hit .259 in 1630 games with 1393 hits, 653 runs, 273 doubles, 56 triples, 20 home runs and 696 RBI. Best season: .294 in 1927. Hit 20 or more doubles seven times. Brother of former major leaguers Joe and Tommy Sewell. World Series: 1933 (.176).

Managed St. Louis Browns, 1941–46, and Cincinnati Reds, 1949–52 (606–644). Won pennant in 1944. Later part owner of factory and machine shop in Akron, Ohio.

SEWELL, JOSEPH W. (Joe) SS-3B-2B-BL-TR. B. 10/9/98, Titus, Ala. 5'7", 155. Cleveland Indians 1920–30; New York Yankees 1931–33. Hit .312 in 1902 games with 2226 hits, 1141 runs, 436 doubles, 68 triples, 49 home runs and 1051 RBI. Hit .300 or better nine full seasons. Best year: .353 in 1923. Hit 30 or more doubles eight times, tying for AL lead in doubles 1924 (45). Drove in 100 or more runs 1923–24. World Series: 1920, 32 (.237). Led AL shortstops putouts, 1924–27; assists, 1924–25, 1927–29, and fielding average, 1927–28. Holds major league record for fewest strikeouts in season (4) in 155 games in 1925 and in 152 games in 1929. Struck out only 114 times in 7132 at bats in majors.

Brother of Luke Sewell, catcher and manager from 1921–52, and Thomas Sewell, infielder with Chicago Cubs in 1927. Flashy shortstop played in 1103 consecutive games, ranking behind Billy Williams, Everett Scott and Lou Gehrig in that category. Made debut in big leagues as replacement for Ray Chapman, killed during 1920 season by pitched ball thrown by Carl Mays. Jittery rookie made six errors in 1920 World Series at shortstop.

Became coach with New York Yankees, 1934–35; scouted with Cleveland Indians for 11 years and New York Mets for one season. Later baseball coach at U. of Alabama for six years, winning Southeastern Conference crown and Coach of Year Award in 1968. Named to Alabama Sports Hall of Fame and now representative for dairy in Tuscaloosa, Ala.

SEWELL, TRUETT B. (Rip) P-BL-TR. B. 5/11/08, Decatur, Ala. 6'1", 180. Detroit Tigers 1932; Pittsburgh Pirates 1938–49. Won 143, lost 97 in 423 games with 636 strikeouts and 748 walks in 2119 innings. Won 21 games twice, tied for most wins in NL 1943 (21). Won 10 or more games eight times. All-Star game: 1943–44, 46. (0–0).

Noted for throwing high, arching change of pace, or eephus, pitch which baffled batters. Threw "Blooper" in 1946 All-Star game which

Ted Williams timed perfectly and hit for home run. Involved in near players' strike by members of Pittsburgh Pirates squad in 1946.

SEYBOLD, RALPH O. (Socks) OF-1B-BR-TR. B. 11/23/70, Washingtonville, Ohio. D. 12/22/21, Greensburg, Pa. 5'11", 178. Cincinnati Reds 1899; Philadelphia A's 1901–08 Hit .293 in 996 games with 1082 hits, 478 runs, 215 doubles, 54 triples, 51 home runs and 556 RBI. Had three seasons of .300 or better. Hit 20 or more doubles seven times, leading AL in doubles in 1903 (43). Led AL home runs 1902 (16). World Series: 1905 (.125).

SEYMOUR, JOHN B. (Cy) OF-P-BL-TL. B. 12/9/72, Albany, N.Y. D. 9/20/19, New York, N.Y. 6', 200. New York Giants 1896–1900, 1906–10; Baltimore Orioles 1901–02; Cincinnati Reds 1902–06; Boston Braves 1913. Hit .304 in 1500 games with 1720 hits, 737 runs, 232 doubles, 97 triples, 52 home runs and 800 RBI. Hit .300 or better five full seasons. Best year: league-leading .377 in 1905. In 1905 also led NL in hits (219), doubles (40), triples (21), total bases (325) and slugging percentage (.559). Hit 20 or more doubles seven times. Tied for most putouts by NL outfielder, 1903.

Converted pitcher, won 63, lost 54 in 154 games before switching to outfield. Won 20 games for New York in 1897 and followed with 25 victories a year later. Led NL strikeouts 1898 (249). Also won two complete games in one day, 6/3/97.

SHAMSKY, ARTHUR L. (Art) OF-1B-BL-TL. B. 10/14/41, St. Louis, Mo. 6'1", 180. Cincinnati Reds 1965–67; New York Mets 1968–71; St. Louis Cardinals 1972; Chicago Cubs 1972; Oakland A's 1972. Hit .253 in 665 games with 426 hits, 194 runs, 60 doubles, 15 triples, 68 home runs and 233 RBI. Best year: .300 in 1969 with 14 HR and 47 RBI. 1972 record: .087 in 23 games. World Series: 1969 (.000).

Hit three homers in game, 8/12/66, and four in four consecutive trips to the plate, 8/12/66 and 8/14/66. Hit torrid .538 in 1969 Championship Series to help steer Mets into World Series against Baltimore.

SHANKS, HOWARD S. (Hank) Inf.-OF-BR-TR. B. 7/21/90 Chicago, Ill. D. 7/30/41, Monaca, Pa. Washington Senators 1912–22; Boston Red Sox 1923–24; New York Yankees 1925. Hit .253 in 1664 games with 1438 hits, 602 runs, 212 doubles, 96 triples, 23 home runs and 613 RBI. Hit 15 or more doubles in nine seasons and stole 185 bases during career. Best year: .302 in 1921 with 25 doubles and league-leading 19 triples.

SHANNON, THOMAS M. (Mike; Moonman) 3B-OF-C-BR-TR. B. 7/5/39, St. Louis, Mo. 6'3", 200. St. Louis Cardinals 1962–70. Hit .255

in 882 games with 730 hits, 313 runs, 116 doubles, 23 triples, 68 home runs and 367 RBI. Best year: .266 with 15 homers and 79 RBI in 1968. World Series: 1964, 67–68 (.235 in 21 games).

Developed into fine clutch hitter and defensive third baseman when felled by kidney disease and forced to retire from game. Currently broadcasts Cardinal games.

SHANTZ, ROBERT C. (Bobby) P-BR-TL. B. 9/26/25, Pottstown, Pa. 5'6", 154. Philadelphia A's 1949–54; Kansas City A's 1955–56; New York Yankees 1957–60; Pittsburgh Pirates 1961; Houston Colts 1962; St. Louis Cardinals 1962–64; Chicago Cubs 1964; Philadelphia Phillies 1964. Won 119, lost 99 in 537 games with 1072 strikeouts and 643 walks in 1935 innings. Best season: 24–7 in 1952 to lead AL in wins and percentage (.774) and Earn league's Most Valuable Player Award. Led AL in ERA 1957 (2.45). All-Star game: 1951–52, 57 (0–0). World Series: 1957, 60 (0–1). Drafted by two expansion clubs, Washington Senators and Houston Colts.

Great fielding pitcher, won eight Golden Glove Awards. Teamed with Billy Shantz as brotherly battery mates in 1954–55. In 1952 All-Star game, struck out Whitey Lockman, Jackie Robinson and Stan Musial in succession.

SHAUTE, JOSEPH B. (Lefty) P-BL-TL. B. 8/1/1900, Peckville, Pa. D. 2/21/70, Scranton, Pa. 6', 190. Cleveland Indians 1922–30; Brooklyn Dodgers 1931–33; Cincinnati Reds 1934. Won 99, lost 109 in 368 games with 512 strikeouts and 534 walks in 1818 innings. Won 10 or more games five times. Best year: 20–17 in 1924 with 68 strikeouts and 3.75 ERA. Led NL in losses 1924.

Noted for enviable ability to strike out Babe Ruth. Fanned Bambino more than 30 times during career. Later managed in minor leagues in 1938 and served as treasurer and sheriff of Lackawanna County, Pa.

SHAW, FREDERICK L. (Dupee) P-OF-TL. B. 5/31/59, Charlestown, Mass. D. 6/11/38, Everett, Mass. Detroit (NL) 1883–84; Boston (Union Association) 1884; Providence (NL) 1885; Washington (NL) 1886–88. Won 85, lost 125 in 236 games with 950 strikeouts and 396 walks in 1762 innings. Won 30, lost 33 in 1884, striking out 451 in 543 innings. Pitched no-hitter against Buffalo, 10/7/85, and pitched two complete games in one day, 10/7/85 and 10/10/85. Fanned 18 in game, 7/19/84, and followed with 16-strikeout performance two days later.

SHAW, ROBERT J. (Bob) P-BR-TR. B. 6/29/33, Bronx, N.Y. 6'2", 195. Detroit Tigers 1957–58; Chicago White Sox 1958–61; Kansas City A's 1961; Milwaukee Braves 1962–63; San Francisco Giants 1964–66;

New York Mets 1966–67; Chicago Cubs 1967. Won 108, lost 98 in 430 games with 880 strikeouts and 511 walks in 1778 innings. Won 10 or more games six times. Best year: 18–6 in 1959 to lead AL in percentage (.750). All-Star game: 1962 (0–0). World Series: 1959 (1–1).

Teamed with Early Wynn to pitch White Sox to pennant in 1959. Due to strict interpretation of balk rules by major league umpires in 1963, holds marks for most balks in season (8), game (5) and inning (3). Worked as pitching instructor in Los Angeles Dodgers' farm system in recent years. Named pitching coach for Milwaukee Brewers for 1973.

SHAWKEY, JAMES R. (Bob) P-BR-TR. B. 12/4/90, Brookville, Pa. 5'11", 168. Philadelphia A's 1913–15; New York Yankees 1915–27. Won 197, lost 150 in 482 games with 1355 strikeouts and 1025 walks in 2938 innings. Won 10 or more games 10 times. Best year: 24–14 in 1916. Also won 20 games in 1919–20 and 1922. Led AL in ERA 1920 (2.46). Struck out 15 in one game, 9/27/19. World Series: 1914, 21–23, 26 (1–3).

Coach, Yankees, 1929. Replaced Miller Huggins as manager of Yankees, 1930 (86–68). Managed in minor leagues, 1931–35, 47–49. Pitching instructor for several big league clubs. Later became baseball coach at Dartmouth College. Named to Pennsylvania Sports Hall of Fame.

SHECKARD, SAMUEL J. (Jimmy) OF-Inf.-BL-TR. B. 11/23/78, Upper Chanceford, Pa. D. 1/15/47, Lancaster, Pa. 5'9", 175. Brooklyn (NL) 1897–98, 1900–05; Baltimore (NL) 1899; Baltimore (AL) 1902; Chicago Cubs 1906–12; St. Louis Cardinals 1913; Cincinnati Reds 1913. Hit .276 in 2108 games with 2097 hits, 1296 runs, 355 doubles, 140 triples, 55 home runs and 813 RBI. Stole 475 bases during career. Led NL stolen bases 1899 (78) and tied for lead 1903 (67). Led NL runs 1911 (121) and home runs 1903 (9). Hit 20 or more doubles 11 times and 10 or more triples nine seasons. Led NL triples 1901 (21). Holds NL record for most sacrifices in season (46) in 1909. Led NL slugging percentage 1901 (.536) and walks 1911 (147) and 1912 (122). Sheckard's 147 walks was NL record until broken by Eddie Stanky (148) in 1945. World Series: 1906–08, 1910 (.182).

SHEEHAN, THOMAS C. (Tom) P-BR-TR. B. 3/31/94 Ottawa, Ill. 6'2½", 190. Philadelphia A's 1915–16; New York Yankees 1921; Cincinnati Reds 1924–25; Pittsburgh Pirates 1925 26. Won 17, lost 37 in 149 games. Later became superscout with New York and San Francisco Giants and is still scouting for that team. Managed S.F. on interim basis in 1960. Appointment on 6/18 made him the oldest manager to make debut at 66 years and 2 months. Record, 46–50.

SHEELY, EARL H. (Whitey) 1B-BR-TR. B. 2/12/93, Bushnell, Ill. D. 9/16/52, Seattle, Wash. 6'3½", 195. Chicago White Sox 1921–27; Pittsburgh Pirates 1929; Boston Braves 1931. Hit an even .300 in 1234 games with 1340 hits, 572 runs, 244 doubles, 27 triples, 58 home runs and 747 RBI. Hit .300 or better four times. Best season: .320 in 1924. Hit 20 or more doubles seven times. Drove in 100 or more runs twice.

Later scouted and became general manager of Seattle club in Pacific Coast League. Father of Hollis (Bud) Sheely, who caught for the White Sox in early 1950s.

SHEPARD, BERT R. P-BL-TL. B. 6/28/20, Dana, Ind. 5'11", 185. Washington Senators 1945. Appeared in only one game in major leagues with no decision but gained popularity with fans in couragous attempt to make comeback after losing leg in plane crash over France during World War II. Shepard was fitted with wooden leg and later pitched five innings of game during '45 season, but was forced to give up professional sports.

SHERDEL, WILLIAM H. (Wee Willie) P-BL-TL. B. 8/15/96, Hanover, Pa. D. 11/14/68, McSherrystown, Pa. 5'10", 160. St. Louis Cardinals 1918–30, 1932; Boston Braves 1930–32. Won 165, lost 146 in 549 games with 839 strikeouts and 661 walks in 2708 innings. Won 15 or more games six times. Best year: 21–10 in 1928. Led NL in percentage 1925 (.714). World Series: 1926, 28 (0–4). Possessed tantalizing slow ball which baffled batters.

SHERRY, LAWRENCE (Larry) P-BR-TR. B. 7/25/35, Los Angeles, Calif. 6'2", 205. Los Angeles Dodgers 1958–63; Detroit Tigers 1964–67; Houston Astros 1967; California Angels 1968. Won 53, lost 44 in 416 games with 606 strikeouts and 374 walks in 799 innings. Best year: 14–10 in 1960 with 5 saves. Finished third in Fireman of the Year derby in 1966 with 8 wins and 17 saves.

Contributed greatly to successful Dodger pennant drive in 1959 and won two games in relief as Los Angeles defeated White Sox in six games. Brother of Norm Sherry, who also played for the Dodgers. Managed in minor leagues, 1972.

SHIRES, CHARLES A. (Art the Great; Whattaman) 1B-BL-TR. B. 8/13/07, Italy, Tex. D. 7/13/67, Italy, Tex. 6'1", 195. Chicago White Sox 1928–30; Washington Senators 1930; Boston Braves 1932. Hit .291 in 290 games with 287 hits, 118 runs, 45 doubles, 12 triples, 11 home runs and 119 RBI. Best year: .312 in 100 games in 1929.

Fancied himself great ball player but an even greater fighter. Boxed teammate Al Spohrer, Chicago Bear center George Trafton until pugilistic career ended by Commissioner Kenesaw Landis. Perhaps got swelled head from collecting four hits in first major league game.

SHOCKER, URBAN J. P-BR-TR. B. 8/22/90, Cleveland, Ohio. D. 9/9/28, Denver, Colo. 5'10", 170. New York Yankees 1916–17, 1925–28; St. Louis Browns 1918–24. Won 187, lost 117 in 412 games with 979 strikeouts and 654 walks in 2674 innings. Won 20 or more games four consecutive years, 1920–23. Tied for AL lead in wins 1921 (27). Led AL strikeouts 1922 (149). Pitched 23 shutouts, won two complete games in one day, 9/6/24.

Spitballer who compiled lifetime percentage of .615, Shocker developed heart disease during 1928 season and died in Denver while on trip to recuperate from illness.

SHORE, ERNEST G. (Ernie) P-BR-TR. B. 3/24/91, East Bend, N.C. 6'4", 220. New York Giants 1912; Boston Red Sox 1914–17; New York Yankees 1919–20. Won 65, lost 41 in 159 games with 311 strikeouts and 274 walks in 987 innings. Won 10 or more games four times. Best year: 19–7 in 1915. Best known for pitching perfect game against Washington Senators, 6/23/17. Relieved Babe Ruth, who had been tossed out of the game after walking batter, and set down 26 men in row after runner at first was caught stealing.

After playing days, was elected sheriff of Forsyth County in North Carolina and served for 34 years.

SHORT, CHRISTOPHER J. (Chris) P-BR-TL. B. 9/19/37, Milford, Del. 6'3½", 215. Philadelphia Phillies 1959–72; Milwaukee Brewers 1973. Won 132 lost 127 in 459 games with 1585 strikeouts and 762 walks in 2252 innings. Best year: 20–10 in 1966 with 177 strikeouts and 3.54 ERA. 1972 record: 1–1 in 19 games. Won 17 or more games four times. Struck out high of 237 in 1965. All-Star game: 1964, 67 (0–0).

Formed formidable mound duo with Jim Bunning in mid-60s for Phillies. Greatest lefthander in Phillies' history. Strikeout total second only to Robin Roberts on Philadelphia team.

SHOTTON, BURTON E. (Barney) OF-BL-TR. B. 10/18/84, Brownhelm, Ohio. D. 7/29/62, Lake Wales, Fla. 5'11", 175. St. Louis Browns 1909–17; Washington Senators 1918; St. Louis Cardinals 1919–23. Hit .270 in 1390 games with 1338 hits, 747 runs, 154 doubles, 65 triples, 9 home runs and 275 RBI. Stole 294 bases, including 40 or more four straight years, 1913–16. Led NL walks 1913 (102) and 1916 (111).

Managed Philadelphia Phillies, 1928–33; Cincinnati Reds, 1934; Brooklyn Dodgers, 1947–50 (698–764). Led Dodgers to pennants in 1947 and 1949. Brought out of retirement to replace Leo Durocher as

Brooklyn pilot after former was suspended for year by Commissioner Happy Chandler. The former Dodger scout then established trademark by managing in street clothes.

SIEBERN, NORMAN L. (Norm) 1B-OF-BL-TR. B. 7/26/33, St. Louis, Mo. 6'3'', 195. New York Yankees 1956, 58–59; Kansas City A's 1960–63; Baltimore Orioles 1964–65; California Angels 1966; San Francisco Giants 1967; Boston Red Sox 1967–68. Hit .272 in 1408 games with 1217 hits, 662 runs, 206 doubles, 38 triples, 132 home runs and 636 RBI. Led AL in walks 1964 (106). Best season: .308 in 1962 with 25 HR, 114 runs and 117 RBI. All-Star game: 1962–64 (.000). World Series: 1956, 58, 1967 (.167). Led AL first basemen in putouts in 1962. Now serves as scouting supervisor for Kansas City Royals.

SIEBERT, RICHARD W. (Dick) 1B-OF-BL-TL. B. 2/19/12, Fall River, Mass. 6', 170. Brooklyn Dodgers 1932, 36; St. Louis Cardinals 1937–38; Philadelphia A's 1938–45. Hit .282 in 1035 games with 1104 hits, 439 runs, 204 doubles, 40 triples, 32 home runs and 482 RBI. Hit .300 or better twice. Best year: .334 in 1941. Hit 25 or more doubles seven consecutive years. All-Star game: 1943 (.000). Led AL first basemen in assists, 1945.

Baseball coach at U. of Minnesota for past 25 years, led teams to victory in college world series in 1956, 60, 64. Also sportscaster in Minnesota.

SIEBERT, WILFRED C. (Sonny) P-BR-TR. B. 1/14/37, St. Mary's, Mo. 6'3'', 205. Cleveland Indians 1964–69; Boston Red Sox 1969–72. Won 118, lost 88 in 321 games with 1309 strikeouts and 562 walks in 1808 innings. Best year: 16–8 in 1965 and 191 strikeouts and ERA of 2.43, and 16–8 in 1966 with 163 strikeouts and 2.80 ERA. 1972 record: 12–12 in 32 games with 123 strikeouts and 3.81 ERA. Won 10 or more games eight straight years. Struck out 15 batters in game against Washington, 1965. All-Star game: 1966, 71 (0–0). Pitched no-hitter against Washington, 6/10/66, winning 2–0.

SIEVERS, ROY E. (Squirrel) OF-1B-3B-BR-TR. B. 11/18/26, St. Louis, Mo. 6'1½'', 204. St. Louis Browns 1949–53; Washington Senators 1954–59, 1964–65; Chicago White Sox 1960–61; Philadelphia Phillies 1962–64. Hit .267 in 1887 games with 1703 hits, 945 runs, 292 doubles, 42 triples, 318 home runs and 1147 RBI. Hit 20 or more doubles eight times and 20 or more homers nine straight years. Led AL home runs 1957 (42). Drove in 100 or more runs four seasons, leading AL in RBI 1957 (114). Hit six home runs in six consecutive games in 1957. All-Star game: 1956–57, 59, 61 (.000).

Compiled best average, 306, in first year in major leagues. Named Rookie of Year in 1949 by baseball writers and *Sporting News*. During years with Senators, was then Vice President Richard Nixon's favorite ball player. Coach, Cincinnati Reds, 1966. Manager in minor leagues, 1967–68.

SILVERA, CHARLES R. (Charlie)   C-BR-TR. B. 10/13/24, San Francisco, Calif. 5'10", 178. New York Yankees 1948–56; Chicago Cubs 1957. Hit .282 in 227 games with 136 hits, 34 runs, 15 doubles, 2 triples, 1 home run and 52 RBI. World Series: 1949 (.000). Best year: .315 in 58 games in 1949.

Manager and coach in minor leagues, 1958–60, 1970; scout with Washington Senators, 1961–68; coach with Minnesota Twins, 1969; and Detroit Tigers, 1971–72. Played on five pennant-winning clubs in first five full seasons, but had to be content to live in shadow of Yogi Berra and collect World Series checks.

SIMMONS, ALOYSIUS, H. (Bucketfoot)   OF-BR-TR. B. 5/22/03, Milwaukee, Wis. D. 5/26/56, Milwaukee, Wis. 6', 210. Philadelphia A's 1924–32, 1940–42, 1944; Chicago White Sox 1933–35; Detroit Tigers 1936; Washington Senators 1937–38; Boston Braves 1939; Cincinnati Reds 1939; Boston Red Sox 1943. Hit .334 in 2215 games with 2927 hits, 1507 runs, 539 doubles, 149 triples, 307 home runs and 1827 RBI. Hit .300 or better 13 times, topped by .392 in 1927. Led AL in batting 1930 (.381) and 1931 (.390); scored 100 or more runs six times, leading in 1930 (152). Drove in 100 or more runs 12 times, leading AL 1929 (157). Hit 30 or more doubles 10 times and 10 or more triples seven years. Had 200 or more hits six times, leading AL 1925 (253) and 1932 (216). Hit three home runs in game, 7/15/32. AL's Most Valuable Player, 1929. All-Star game: 1933–35 (.462 in 13 at bats). World Series: 1929–31, 39 (.329 in 19 games). Hall of Fame 1953.

One of brilliant stars on great Connie Mack teams, along with Jimmie Foxx, Mickey Cochrane and Lefty Grove, ranks 10th on all-time list in RBI, 12th in doubles and 14th in total bases. Player-coach with Philadelphia A's 1940–42; coach only with A's, 1945–49; coach with Cleveland Indians, 1950. Resided at Milwaukee Athletic Club after retirement. Died of heart attack while walking on Milwaukee street.

SIMMONS, CURTIS T. (Curt)   P-BL-TL. 5/19/29, Egypt, Pa. 6', 195. Philadelphia Phillies 1947–50, 51–60; St. Louis Cardinals 1960–66; Chicago Cubs 1966–67; California Angels 1967. Won 193, lost 183 in 569 games with 1697 strikeouts and 1054 walks in 3349 innings. Won 10 or more games nine times: Best years: 17–8 in 1950 and 18–9 in 1964. Pitched 36 shutouts, tying for league lead in 1952 (6). All-Star game:

1952–53, 57. (0–1). World Series: 1964 (0–1).

Signed with Phillies for $65,000 bonus. Teamed with Robin Roberts on 1950 Whiz Kids club. Released by Phillies in 1960 as over the hill but hung on to win 78 more games before retiring. Owner-manager of golf course near Ambler, Pa.

SIMMONS, TED L. C-BLR-TR. B. 8/9/49, Highland Park, Mich. 5'11", 195. St. Louis Cardinals 1968–72. Hit .290 in 374 games with 408 hits, 163 runs, 76 doubles, 13 triples, 26 home runs and 200 RBI. Best year: .303 in 152 games in 1972 with 16 HR and 96 RBI. In 1971 hit .304 with 7 HR and 77 RBI in 133 games. Hit 30 or more doubles in 1970 and '71. Led catchers in putouts (842) and assists (78) in 1972.

One of fine young stars of NL, played much of 1972 season without signed contract before coming to terms. Broadcasts St. Louis Blues' hockey games in off-season.

SIMON, SYLVESTER A. (Syl) Inf.-BR-TR. B. 12/14/98, Evansville, Ind. D. 3/73 Evansville, Ind. 5'10½, 170. St. Louis Browns 1923–24. Plucky infielder's bat and glove enshrined in Hall of Fame despite brief trial with Browns in which Simon hit .242 in only 24 games. Lost four fingers on left hand in industrial accident after 1926 season in minors. Returned to organized baseball the following summer, used specially built glove and metal device on bat handle to aid grip. Saw action with four minor league teams after comeback until his retirement in 1932.

SIMPSON, WAYNE K. P-BR-TR. B. 12/2/48, Los Angeles, Calif. 6'3", 210. Cincinnati Reds 1970–72. Won 26, lost 15 in 72 games with 250 strikeouts and 207 walks in 423 innings. Best year: 14–3 in rookie season with 119 strikeouts and 3.02 ERA. 1972 record: 8–5 in 24 games with 70 strikeouts and 4.15 ERA. Led NL in percentage, 1970 (.824). All-Star game: 1970 (0–0).

Hampered by sore arm much of 1971 and '72, missed 1970 and '72 World Series. Traded to Kansas City Royals after 1972 season.

SIMS, DUANE B. (Duke) C-1B-BL-TR. B. 6/5/41, Salt Lake City, Utah. 6'2", 210. Cleveland Indians 1964–70; Los Angeles Dodgers 1971–72; Detroit Tigers 1972. Hit .241 in 715 games with 492 hits, 221 runs, 69 doubles, 6 triples, 88 home runs and 271 RBI. Best year: .264 in 1970 with 23 HR and 56 RBI. 1972 record: .241 in 89 games with 6 HR and 30 RBI. Championship Series: 1972 (.167).

Along with Woody Fryman, patched leaks in Detroit's lineup to help club reach playoffs. Bolstered catching staff when Bill Freehan was injured.

SINGER, WILLIAM R. (Bill)   P-BR-TR. B. 4/24/44, Los Angeles, Calif. 6'4", 200. Los Angeles Dodgers 1964–72; Won 69, lost 76 in 190 games with 989 strikeouts and 392 walks in 1273 innings. Won 10 or more games four times. Best year: 20–12 in 1969 with 247 strikeouts and 2.34 ERA. 1972 record: 6–16 in 26 games with 101 strikeouts and 3.67 ERA. Struck out 200 or more batters twice. Fired no-hitter against Philadelphia, 7/20/70. All-Star game: 1969 (0–0).

Pitched no-hit game in 1970 despite being sidelined by hepatitis earlier in season. Received $50,000 bonus from Dodgers. Traded to California Angels after 1972 season.

SINGLETON, KENNETH W. (Ken)   OF-BLR-TR. B. 6/10/47, New York, N.Y. 6'4", 210. New York Mets 1970–71; Montreal Expos 1972. Hit .263 in 326 games with 264 hits, 133 runs, 36 doubles, 2 triples, 32 home runs and 122 RBI. Best year: .274 in 1972 with 14 HR and 50 RBI in 142 games.

Traded to Montreal in deal for Rusty Staub. Led Expos in runs, hits and doubles in 1972.

SISLER, GEORGE H. (Gorgeous George)   1B-P-BL-TL. B. 3/24/93, Manchester, Ohio. D. 3/26/73, Richmond Heights, Mo. 5'10½", 170. St. Louis Browns 1915–22, 24–27; Washington Senators 1928; Boston Braves 1928–30. Hit .340 in 2055 games with 1284 runs, 2812 hits, 425 doubles, 165 triples, 100 home runs and 1180 RBI. Hit .300 or better 13 times, leading AL in hitting with .407 in 1920 and .420 in 1922. Hit 20 or more doubles 13 times and 10 or more triples eight times, leading AL in triples 1922 (18). Collected 200 or more hits in season six times, leading league 1920 and 1922 (246). His 257 hits in 1920 still stand as major league record for most hits in one season. Six hits in game 8/9/21. Had 41-game hitting streak in 1922. Scored 100 or more runs four times, leading league 1922 (134). Stole 375 bases, topping league 1918 (45), 1921 (35), 1922 (51) and 1927 (27). Al's Most Valuable Player, 1922. Led AL first basemen in assists, 1919–20, 22, 24–25, 27. Topped NL first sackers in assists in 1928. Holds major league mark for most lifetime assists, 1554. Hall of Fame 1939.

Won 5, lost 8 as pitcher in 22 games and chalked up victory over no less than Walter Johnson. One of game's immortals whose Achilles heel was sinus condition which plagued Sisler all through career. Forced to miss entire 1923 season when condition caused eye problems. Managed St. Louis Browns, 1924–26 (218–241), and managed in minors, 1932. Scout for Brooklyn Dodgers, 1946–50, and Pittsburgh Pirates, 1951–56, 62–72. Batting instructor with Pirates, 1956–61. Sisler and Hal chase considered two best defensive first sackers ever to play game.

SISLER, RICHARD A. (Dick) 1B-OF-BL-TR. B. 11/2/20, St. Louis, Mo. 6'2", 205. St. Louis Cardinals 1946–47, 52–53; Philadelphia Phillies 1948–51; Cincinnati Reds 1952. Hit .276 in 799 games with 620 hits, 302 runs, 118 doubles, 28 triples, 55 home runs and 360 RBI. Best season: .296 in 1950 with 29 doubles and 83 RBI. All-Star game: 1950 (1.000). World Series: 1946, 50 (.053).

Clinched pennant for 1950 Philadelphia Whiz Kids with three-run homer off Brooklyn's Don Newcombe on last day of season. Son of Hall of Famer George Sisler and brother of Dave Sisler, former major league pitcher, and George H. Sisler, Jr., current president of International League. Dick Sisler immortalized in Ernest Hemmingway's "Old Man and the Sea." Coached for Cincinnati Reds, 1961–64. Replaced late Fred Hutchinson as manager in 1964 and managed through 1965 (121–94). Coach with St. Louis Cardinals, 1966–70. Now staff director of recreation for Tennessee Department of Corrections in Nashville.

SIZEMORE, TED C. Inf.-OF-BR-TR. B. 4/15/45, Gadsden, Ala. 5'10", 170. Los Angeles Dodgers 1969–70; St. Louis Cardinals 1971–72. Hit .274 in 510 games with 506 hits, 215 runs, 61 doubles, 15 triples, 10 home runs and 160 RBI. Hit .306 in 96 games in 1970. Best year: .271 in 1969 with 4 HR and 46 RBI. 1972 record: .264 in 120 games with 2 HR and 38 RBI. Named NL Rookie of the Year in 1969 by Baseball Writers Association.

SKINNER, ROBERT R. (Dog) OF-1B-BL-TR. B. 10/3/31, La Jolla, Calif. 6'4", 190. Pittsburgh Pirates 1954, 1956–63; Cincinnati Reds 1963–64; St. Louis Cardinals 1964–66. Hit .277 in 1381 games with 1198 hits, 642 runs, 197 doubles, 58 triples, 103 home runs and 531 RBI. Hit .300 or better four times. Best year: .321 in 1958. All-Star game: 1958, 60 (.300). World Series: 1960, 64 (.375).

Managed San Diego in Pacific Coast League, 1967–68; named Sporting News' minor league manager of year, 1967. Manager of Philadelphia Phillies, 1968–69 (92–123). Line-drive hitter has been coach of San Diego Padres since 1970.

SKOWRON, WILLIAM J. (Moose) 1B-3B-BR-TR. B. 12/18/30, Chicago, Ill. 6', 200. New York Yankees 1954–62; Los Angeles Dodgers 1963; Washington Senators 1964; Chicago White Sox 1964–67; California Angels 1967. Hit .282 in 1658 games with 1566 hits, 681 runs, 243 doubles, 53 triples, 211 home runs and 888 RBI. Hit .300 or better five times. Best year: .309 with 26 HR and 91 RBI in 1960. Hit 20 or more doubles six times, and 15 or more HR in eight seasons. All-Star game: 1957–61, 65 (.426 in five games). World Series: 1955–58, 60–63 (.293). Led AL first basemen in putouts, 1960, 65; assists, 1956, and fielding average, 1958. Led in double plays, 1956, 61, 65.

Hampered by back problems throughout career, still was feared slugger in Yankee lineup. Hit eight home runs and drove in 29 runs in 39 World Series games. Hit grand slammer in 1956 Series. Now sales manager for real estate firm in Dunnellon, Fla.

SLAGLE, JAMES F. (Shorty) OF-BL-TR. B. 7/11/73, Worthville, Pa. D. 5/10/56, Chicago, Ill. Washington (NL) 1899; Philadelphia (NL) 1900–01; Boston Braves 1901; Chicago Cubs 1902–08. Hit .269 in 1292 games with 1339 hits, 779 runs, 124 doubles, 56 triples, 2 home runs and 344 RBI. Best year: .313 in 1902. World Series: 1907 (.273).

Fleet of foot, stole 273 bases, including 40 in 1902. Stole six bases in 1907 World Series as Cubs ran over Detroit Tigers in five games.

SLAUGHTER, ENOS B. (Country) OF-BL-TR. B. 4/27/16, Roxboro, N.C. 5'9", 190. St. Louis Cardinals 1938–42, 46–53; New York Yankees 1954–59; Kansas City A's 1955–56; Milwaukee Braves 1959. Hit .300 in 2380 games with 2383 hits, 1247 runs, 413 doubles, 148 triples, 169 home runs and 1304 RBI. Hit .300 or better eight full seasons. Best year: .336 in 1949. Hit 30 or more doubles nine times, leading NL 1939 (52). Hit 10 or more triples seven times, leading NL 1942 (17) and tying for most triples 1949 (13). Led NL in hits 1942 (188) and in RBI 1946 (130). Drove in 10 runs in doubleheader, 6/29/47. Led outfielders in putouts, 1939; assists, 1939 and 1946; and fielding average, 1953. All-Star game: 1941–42, 1946–53 (.381 in 21 at bats). Helped NL win 1953 game with diving catch of drive by Harvey Kuenn and collecting two hits and stolen base. World Series: 1942, 46, 1956–58 (Hit .291 in 27 games).

Electrifying Slaughter scored winning run in seventh game of 1946 World Series against Boston Red Sox by scoring from first base on hit and catching Johnny Pesky flatfooted. Sprint home considered one of most memorable highlights in Series history. Managed in minor leagues, 1960–61. Owns farm in North Carolina, coaches Duke baseball team.

SMITH, ALFRED J. (Al) P-BL-TL. B. 10/12/08, Belleville, Ill. 5'11", 180. New York Giants 1934–37; Philadelphia Phillies 1938–39; Cleveland Indians 1940–45. Won 99, lost 101 in 359 games with 587 strikeouts and 587 walks in 1662 innings. Won 10 or more games six times. Best year: 17–7 in 1943. All-Star game: 1943 (0–0). World Series: 1936–37 (0–0).

Along with Jim Bagby, Jr., stopped Joe DiMaggio's hitting streak after 56 games, 7/17/41. Both pitchers were aided by two great catches by Cleveland third baseman Ken Keltner.

SMITH, ALPHONSE E. (Al; Fuzzy) 3B-OF-BR-TR. B. 2/7/28, Kirkwood, Mo. 6'½", 195. Cleveland Indians 1953–57, 1964; Chicago White Sox 1958–62; Baltimore Orioles 1963; Boston Red Sox 1964. Hit .272 in 1517 games with 1458 hits, 843 runs, 258 doubles, 46 triples, 164 home runs and 676 RBI. Hit .300 or better twice. Best season: .315 in 1960. Hit 20 or more doubles eight times. Led AL runs 1955 (123). All-Star game: 1955, 60 (.000). World Series: 1954, 59 (.235).

Starred in famous World Series photo in 1959 when camera caught Smith being hit in the face by cup of beer while outfielder sped back to wall on home run ball.

SMITH, CARL R. (Reggie) OF-BLR-TR. B. 4/2/45, Shreveport, La. 6', 190. Boston Red Sox 1966–72. Hit .279 in 899 games with 936 hits, 513 runs, 181 doubles, 31 triples, 128 home runs and 466 RBI. Hit .300 or better twice. Best year: .309 in 1969 with 25 HR and 93 RBI. 1972 record: .270 in 131 games with 21 HR and 74 RBI. Hit 20 or more homers four times, with high of 30 in 1971. Hit 24 or more doubles six years, leading league 1968 (37) and 1971 (33). All-Star game: 1969, 71–72 (.000). World Series: 1967 (.250).

Fine fielder with rifle arm, he made three assists in game in 1972 and led outfielders in assists, 1970. Considered one of top outfielders in game today.

SMITH, EARL S. (Oil) C-BL-TR. B. 2/14/97, Hot Springs, Ark. 5'10½", 170. New York Giants 1919–23; Boston Braves 1923–24; Pittsburgh Pirates 1924–28; St. Louis Cardinals 1928–30. Hit .303 in 860 games with 686 hits, 225 runs, 115 doubles, 19 triples, 46 home runs and 352 RBI. Hit .300 or better five times. Best season: .346 in 1926. World Series: 1921–22, 25, 27–28 (.239 in 17 games). Robbed of home run in 1925 World Series as result of brilliant catch by Sam Rice of Washington Senators.

Temperamental ball player, Smith was benched during 1927 pennant drive after breaking jaw of Boston Braves manager Dave Bancroft. Later managed in minor leagues, 1935, 1938–40.

SMITH, ELMER E. (Mike) OF-P-BL-TL. B. 3/28/68, Allegheny, Pa. D. 11/5/45, Pittsburgh, Pa. 5'11", 178. Cincinnati (American Association) 1886–89; Pittsburgh Pirates 1892–97, 1901; Cincinnati (NL) 1898–1900; New York (NL) 1900; Boston (NL) 1901. Hit .314 in 1231 games with 1473 hits, 931 runs, 202 doubles, 131 triples and 38 home runs. Hit .300 or better five times. Best year: .366 in 1893.

Also fine pitcher, won 76, lost 58 in 142 games, including 22 victories in 1888 and 33 in 1887.

SMITH, ELMER J. OF-BL-TR. B. 9/21/92, Sandusky, Ohio. 5'10",

165. Cleveland Indians 1914–16, 1917–19, 1920–21; Washington Senators 1916–17; Boston Red Sox 1922; New York Yankees 1922–23; Cincinnati Reds 1925. Hit .277 in 1012 games with 881 hits, 469 runs, 181 doubles, 62 triples, 70 home runs and 556 RBI. Hit 20 or more doubles five times. Best year: .316 in 1920, helping Cleveland win pennant and World Series over Brooklyn Dodgers. World Series: 1920, 22: (.267). Hit first grand slam home run in World Series play with blast off Burleigh Grimes in first inning of fiveth game in 1920.

SMITH, FRANK E. (Nig) P-BR-TR. B. 10/28/79, Pittsburgh, Pa. D. 11/3/52, Pittsburgh, Pa. 5'10½", 194. Chicago White Sox 1904–10; Boston Red Sox 1910–11; Cincinnati Reds 1911–12; Baltimore (Federal League) 1914–15; Brooklyn (F) 1915. Won 138, lost 112 in 353 games with 1051 strikeouts and 676 walks in 2273 innings. Pitched 26 shutouts and won 25 games in 1909 and 22 in 1907. Led AL in strikeouts 1909 (177).

Pitched no-hitters against Detroit, 9/6/05, and Philadelphia, 9/20/08.

SMITH, HAROLD R. (Hal) C-BR-TR. B. 6/1/31, Barling, Ark. 5'10½", 186. St. Louis Cardinals 1956–61; Pittsburgh Pirates 1965. Hit .258 in 570 games with 437 hits, 126 runs, 63 doubles, 8 triples, 23 home runs and 172 RBI. Best year: .270 in 1959 with 13 HR and 50 RBI. Led NL catchers in fielding average, 1960. All-Star game: 1957, 59 (.000).

Forced to quit baseball after suffering heart attack. Came back to play four games in 1965 with Pirates while coaching with Pittsburgh. Also coached with Pirates in 1966. Now scout and special instructor with St. Louis Cardinals.

SMITH, HAROLD W. (Hal) C-3B-BR-TR. B. 12/7/30, West Frankfort, Ill. 6', 195. Baltimore Orioles 1955–56; Kansas City A's 1956–59; Pittsburgh Pirates 1960–61; Houston Astros 1962–63; Cincinnati Reds 1964. Hit .267 in 879 games with 715 hits, 269 runs, 148 doubles, 10 triples, 58 home runs and 323 RBI. Best year: .303 in 1957. World Series: 1960 (.375).

Hit least-remembered important homer in Series history. His three-run blast in eighth inning of seventh game of 1960 classic kept Pittsburgh in game and set stage for Bill Mazeroski's winning blow in ninth frame. Now employed by steel firm in Houston.

SMITH, JAMES C. (Red) 3B-BR-TR. B. 4/6/90, Atlanta, Ga. D. 10/11/66, Atlanta, Ga. 5'11", 165. Brooklyn Dodgers 1911–14; Boston Braves 1914–19; Hit .278 in 1117 games with 1087 hits, 477 runs, 208 doubles, 49 triples, 27 home runs and 514 RBI. Hit 20 or more doubles six times, leading NL in 1913 (40).

Joined Boston in midseason in 1914, sparking Miracle Braves' fantastic pennant drive by hitting .314.

SMITH, JOHN W. (Jack) OF-BL-TL. B. 6/23/95, Chicago, Ill. 5'8", 165. St. Louis Cardinals 1915–26; Boston Braves 1926–29. Hit .287 in 1406 games with 1301 hits, 783 runs, 182 doubles, 71 triples, 41 home runs and 377 RBI. Hit .300 or better four consecutive seasons. Best season: .310 in 143 games in 1922. Stole 228 bases during career.

SMITH, ROBERT E. (Bob) SS-P-BR-TR. B. 4/22/98, Rogersville, Tenn. 5'10", 175. Boston Braves 1923–30, 1933–37; Chicago Cubs 1931–32; Cincinnati Reds 1933. Won 106, lost 139 in 742 games, 435 as pitcher. Struck out 618 and walked 670 in 2238 innings. Won 10 or more games six straight years. Best season: 15–12 in 1931. World Series: 1932: (0–0).

Originally an infielder before switching to mound, hit .242 in 1689 at bats with 166 RBI.

SMITH, SHERROD M. (Sherry) P-BR-TL. B. 2/18/91, Mansfield, Ga. D. 9/12/49, Reidsville, Ga. 6'1", 170. Pittsburgh Pirates 1911–12; Brooklyn Dodgers 1915–17; 1919–22; Cleveland Indians 1922–27. Won 114, lost 118 in 381 games with 428 strikeouts and 440 walks in 2052 innings. Won 10 or more games seven times. Best season: 14–8 in 1915. World Series: 1916, 20 (1–2).

SNIDER, EDWIN D. (Duke) OF-BL-TR. B. 9/19/26, Los Angeles, Calif. 6', 200. Brooklyn Dodgers 1947–57; Los Angeles Dodgers 1958–62; New York Mets 1963; San Francisco Giants 1964. Hit .295 in 2143 games with 2116 hits, 1259 runs, 358 doubles, 85 triples, 407 home runs and 1333 RBI. Hit .300 or better seven times. Best year: .341 in 1954 with 40 homers and 130 RBI. Hit 40 or more HR five straight years, an NL record, leading league in 1956 (43). Hit 25 or more doubles nine times and drove in 100 or more runs six times. Led NL in RBI 1955 (136). Led league in hits 1950 (199), runs 1953 (132) and 1955 (126) and tied for most runs 1954 (120). Hit three home runs in game, 5/30/50 and 6/1/55. All-Star game: 1950, 52–56, 1963 (2.73). World Series: 1949, 52–53, 55–56, 59 (.286).

Just one more superstar on fabulous Brooklyn Dodgers teams of late 40s and 50s, cracked 11 homers and drove in 26 runs in 36 World Series games. Scouted for L.A. Dodgers, 1965, 67–68; manager in minor leagues, 1965–68, 72; batting instructor and broadcaster for San Diego Padres, 1969–71. Joined Montreal Expos' broadcasting team in 1973.

SNODGRASS, FRED C. OF-BR-TR. B. 10/19/87, Ventura, Calif.

5'11½", 175. New York Giants 1908–15; Boston Braves 1915–16. Hit .275 in 905 games with 852 hits, 453 runs, 143 doubles, 42 triples, 12 home runs and 339 RBI. Best year: .321 in 1910. Hit 20 or more doubles five times. Stole 215 bases with season high of 51 in 1911. World Series: 1911–13 (.182).

Committed famed "$30,000 Muff" with two-base error on fly ball hit by Boston Red Sox' Clyde Engel in tenth inning of eighth game of 1912 World Series to pave way for Giants' defeat. Later farmed in Ventura, Calif., was in banking business and served as mayor of Oxnard, Calif.

SNYDER, FRANK J. (Pancho) C-BR-TR. B. 5/27/93, San Antonio, Tex. D. 1/5/62, San Antonio, Tex. 6'2", 185. St. Louis Cardinals 1912–19, 1927; New York Giants 1919–26. Hit .265 in 1392 games with 1122 hits, 331 runs, 170 doubles, 44 triples, 47 home runs and 517 RBI. Hit .300 or better three times. Best year: .343 in 1922. World Series: 1921–24 (.273).

Giants' regular catcher during four straight pennant years. Led NL catchers in putouts, 1915, 23; assists, 1915; fielding average, 1914, 1923–24, and double plays, 1923.

SNYDER, RUSSELL H. OF-BL-TR. B. 6/22/34, Nelson, Nebr. 6'1", 195. Kansas City A's 1959–60; Baltimore Orioles 1961–67; Chicago White Sox 1968; Cleveland Indians 1968–69; Milwaukee Brewers 1970. Hit .271 in 1365 games with 984 hits, 488 runs, 150 doubles, 29 triples, 42 home runs and 319 RBI. Hit .300 or better twice. Best season: .306 in 1966. World Series: 1966 (.167).

SOCKALEXIS, LOUIS F. (Chief) OF-BL-TR. B. 10/24/73, Old Town, Me. D. 12/24/13, Burlington, Me. Cleveland (NL) 1897–99. Hit .307 in 93 games with Spiders following graduation from Holy Cross College. Full-blooded Indian (Penobscot) and first to play in the major leagues, traded his bat for the bottle and quickly faded from big leagues. Sockalexis returned to Maine, where he became beggar and died penniless.

SOLTERS, JULIUS J. (Moose) OF-BR-TR. B. 3/22/08, Pittsburgh, Pa. 6', 190. Boston Red Sox 1934–35; St. Louis Browns 1935–36, 39; Cleveland Indians 1937–39; Chicago White Sox 1940–41, 43. Hit .289 in 938 games with 990 hits, 503 runs, 213 doubles, 42 triples, 83 home runs and 599 RBI. Hit .300 or better three seasons. Best year, .323 in 1937. Hit 40 or more doubles three times and drove in 100 or more runs three years with high of 134 in 1936. Hit three homers in game, 7/7/35.

Slugger later developed eye trouble and eventually lost his sight.

SORREL, VICTOR G. P-BR-TR. B. 4/9/02, Morrisville, N.C. D. 4/4/72, Raleigh, N.C. 5'10", 180. Detroit Tigers 1928–37. Won 92, lost 101 in 281 games with 619 strikeouts and 706 walks in 1673 innings. Bespectacled pitcher won 10 or more games five times. Best season: 16–11 in 1930.

Managed in minor leagues and scouted for Detroit after playing days. Became baseball coach at N.C. State U., 1945–66.

SOUTHWORTH, WILLIAM H. (Billy) OF-2B-BL-TR. B. 3/9/93, Harvard, Nebr. D. 11/15/69, Cleveland, Ohio. 5'9", 170. Cleveland Indians 1913,15; Pittsburgh Pirates 1918–20; Boston Braves 1921–23; New York Giants 1924–26; St. Louis Cardinals 1926–29. Hit .298 in 1192 games with 1296 hits, 661 runs, 173 doubles, 91 triples, 52 HR and 540 RBI. Hit .300 or better six times. Best season: .320 in 1926 to help Cardinals win pennant. World Series: 1924, 26 (.333). Tied for NL lead in triples 1919 (14).

One of game's greatest managers, had lifetime managerial record of 1064–729. Led St. Louis to three straight pennants and two World Series championships, 1942–44, and won NL flag with Boston in 1948. Cardinal teams won 105 or more games, 1942–44. Also managed many teams in minor leagues and scouted for Boston and Milwaukee Braves, 1951–56.

SPAHN, WARREN E. P-BL-TL. B. 4/23/21, Buffalo, N.Y. 6', 175. Boston Braves 1942, 46–52; Milwaukee Braves 1953–64; New York Mets 1965; San Francisco Giants 1965. All-time leader in victories for lefthanded pitcher with 363–245 in 750 games with 2583 strikeouts and 1434 walks in 5246 innings. Tied with Christy Mathewson for most years winning 20 or more games in NL (13). Led or tied for most wins in NL 1949 (21), 1950 (21), 1953 (23), 1957 (21), 1958 (22), 1959 (21), 1960 (21) and 1961 (21). Tied for NL lead in percentage 1958 (.667). Led in innings pitched 1947 (290), 1949 (302), 1958 (290) and 1959 (292). Led NL strikeouts 1949 (151), 1950 (191) and 1952 (183) and tied for most strikeouts 1951 (164). Struck out 100 or more batters 17 straight years. Led NL in ERA 1947 (2.33), 1953 (2.10) and 1961 (3.01). Led NL in complete games 1949 (25), 1951 (26), 1957 (18), 1958 (23), 1959 (21), 1960 (18), 1961 (21), 1962 (22) and 1963 (22). Threw 63 shutouts, leading NL in 1947 (7) and 1951 (7) and tied for most shutouts 1959 (4) and 1961 (4). No-hitters against Philadelphia, 9/16/60, and San Francisco, 4/28/61. Winner of Cy Young Award, 1957. Struck out 18 batters in 15-inning game, 6/14/52. All-Star game: 1947, 49–54 56–63 (1–0 in 8 games). World Series: 1948, 57–58 (4–3 in 8 games).

Rank on all-time list: Wins, 5th; losses, tie for 6th; games, 7th; innings, 4th; walks, 8th, strikeouts, 5th; shutouts, 6th.

Good-hitting pitcher, Spahn cracked 35 homers, 57 doubles. Combined with Johnny Sain to give Braves one of NL's most feared mound duos in late 40s. Managed in minor leagues, 1967–71. Coach, Cleveland Indians since 1972. Hall of Fame 1973.

SPALDING, ALBERT G. P-BR-TR. B. 9/2/50, Byron, Ill. D. 9/9/15, Point Loma, Calif. 6'1", 170. Boston (National Association) 1871–75; Chicago (NL) 1876–78. Won 46 lost 14 in majors, entire total achieved in 1876. With Boston had yearly win totals of 21, 36, 41, 52 and 56 to become baseball's first 200-game winner. Lost only five games while winning 56 in 1875, including 24 consecutive victories. Pitched game's first one-hitter 6/27/71. Manager of Chicago (NL), 1876–77. Became part owner and president of Chicago club, 1882–91. Hall of Fame 1939.

Organized first worldwide baseball tour and helped draft NL constitution in 1876. Founded A. G. Spalding & Bros. sporting goods concern in 1876 and wrote, or ghosted, classic history of baseball in 1911. Later ran unsuccessfully for U.S. Senate.

SPARKS, TULLY F. P-BR-TR. B. 4/18/77, Monroe, La. D. 7/15/37. Philadelphia NL 1897, 1903–10; Pittsburgh Pirates 1899; Milwaukee AL 1901; New York Giants 1902; Boston Red Sox 1902. Won 122, lost 138 in 311 games with 778 strikeouts and 629 walks in 2236 innings. Won 10 or more games six times. Best season: 22–8 in 1907.

SPEAKER, TRISTRAM E. (Spoke; Grey Eagle; Tris) OF-BL-TL. B. 4/4/88, Hubbard City, Tex. D. 12/8/58, Lake Whitney, Tex. 5'11½", 193. Boston Red Sox 1907–15; Cleveland Indians 1916–26; Washington Senators 1927; Philadelphia A's 1928. Hit .344 in 2789 games with 3515 hits, 1881 runs, 793 doubles, 224 triples, 115 home runs and 1559 RBI. Hit .300 or better 18 times. Best year: .389 in 1925. Led AL in batting 1916 (.386). Hit 35 or more doubles 14 times, topping league in 1912 (53), 1914 (46), 1918 (33), 1920 (50), 1921 (52), 1922 (48) and 1923 (59). Tied for most doubles 1916 (41). Had 200 or more hits four times, leading league in 1914 (193) and 1916 (211). Hit 11 or more triples 13 times. Tied for most RBI in 1923 (130). AL's Most Valuable Player, 1912. World Series: 1912, 15, 20 (.306 in 20 games). Led AL outfielders in putouts, 1909–10, 13–15, 18–19, and assists, 1909, 12–13, and tied for most assists, 1914. Had best fielding average, 1921–22. Hall of Fame 1937. Led in total bases 1914 (287) and slugging 1916 (.502).

Rank on all-time list: games, 6th; hits, 3rd; runs, 7th; doubles, 1st; triples, 6th; RBI, 15th; total bases, 6th; batting average, 10th tie.

Unusually gifted outfielder, played shallow center field to trap unsuspecting runners but could easily go back on fly ball with speed that helped him steal 433 bases. Holds major league record for assists; incredibly made two unassisted double plays from centerfield position in

1918. Ranks second in putouts and total chances. Teamed with Harry Hooper and Duffy Lewis to give Red Sox one of finest outfields in baseball history. Managed Cleveland, 1919–26 (616–520), winning pennant and World Series in 1920 over Brooklyn. Managed in minor leagues, 1929–30. Later became sportscaster.

SPEIER, CHRIS E. SS-BR-TR. B. 6/28/50, Alameda, Calif. 6'1", 175. San Francisco Giants 1971–72. Hit .251 in 307 games with 292 hits, 148 runs, 42 doubles, 8 triples, 23 home runs and 117 RBI. Best year: .269 in 150 games with 15 home runs and 71 RBI, in 1972. Led NL shortstops in assists (517), 1972. All-Star game: 1972 (.000).

Hit .357 in 1971 Championship Series against Pittsburgh. Valuable asset to San Francisco defense, invites comparisons to Marty Marion because of his size and ability with glove.

SPENCE, STANLEY O. (Stan) OF-1B-BL-TL. B. 3/20/15, South Portsmouth, Ky. 5'10½", 180. Boston Red Sox 1940–41, 1948–49; Washington Senators 1942–44, 1946–47; St. Louis Browns 1949. Hit .282 in 1112 games with 1090 hits, 541 runs, 196 doubles, 60 triples, 95 home runs and 575 RBI. Hit .300 or better twice. Best year: .323 in 1942. Hit 20 or more doubles five times, including 50 in 1946. Led AL in triples 1942 (15). Made six hits in one game, 6/1/44. All-Star game: 1942,44,46–47 (.600). Led AL outfielders putouts 1946, assists 1944 and double plays 1944. Swatted pinch-hit single to drive in winning run for AL in 1947 All-Star game.

SPENCER, JAMES L. (Jim) 1B-BL-TL. B. 7/30/47, Hanover, Pa. 6'2", 195. California Angels 1968–72. Hit .248 in 508 games with 419 hits, 165 runs, 61 doubles, 9 triples, 41 home runs and 177 RBI. Best year: .274 in 146 games in 1970 with 12 HR and 68 RBI. 1972 record: .222 in 82 games with 1 homer and 14 RBI.

Fancy fielding first baseman, led AL in putouts and fielding average 1970–71, assists 1971 and double plays 1970.

SPIEZIO, EDWARD W. (Ed) 3B-OF-BR-TR. B. 10/31/41, Joliet, Ill. 5'11", 180. St. Louis Cardinals 1964–68; San Diego Padres 1969–72; Chicago White Sox 1972. Hit .238 in 554 games with 367 hits, 126 runs, 56 doubles, 4 triples, 39 home runs and 174 RBI. Best year: .285 in 110 games in 1970 with 12 HR and 42 RBI. 1972 record: .229 in 94 games with 2 HR and 26 RBI.

Helped keep White Sox in '72 pennant race until final week after being acquired from San Diego to replace injured slugger Bill Melton.

SPINKS, SCIPIO R. P-BR-TR. B. 7/12/47, Chicago, Ill. 6'3", 185.

Houston Astros 1969–71; St. Louis Cardinals 1972. Won 6, lost 6 in 27 games with 129 strikeouts and 82 walks in 163 innings. 1972 record: 5–5 in 16 games with 93 strikeouts and 2.67 ERA before being sidelined with injury. Throws blazing fast ball. Cousin of Kansas City Royals' pitcher Wayne Simpson.

SPLITTORFF, PAUL W. P-BL-TL. B. 10/8/46, Evansville, Ind. 6'3", 205. Kansas City Royals 1969–72. Won 20, lost 22 in 59 games with 230 strikeouts and 107 walks in 369 innings. Best year: 12–12 in 35 games in 1972 with 140 strikeouts and 3.13 ERA to pace Royals' staff along with Dick Drago.

Finished second in *Sporting News* Rookie of the Year poll in 1971. Helped pitch U.S. to baseball championship in 1967 Pan American Games.

SPOONER, KARL B. P-BR-TL. B. 6/23/31, Oriskany Falls, N.Y. 6', 185. Brooklyn Dodgers 1954–55. Won 10, lost 6 in 31 games during brief career but shares several major league records. Pitched two shutouts and struck out 27 batters in first two major league starts, 15 in first game. Shares record for most strikeouts in first game and most consecutive strikeouts in premier performance (6). Developed arm trouble in 1955 and faded from big time.

STAHL, CHARLES S. (Chick) OF-BL-TL. B. 1/10/73, Fort Wayne, Ind. D. 3/28/07, West Baden Springs, Ind. Boston Braves 1897–1900; Boston Red Sox 1901–06. Hit .306 in 1299 games with 1552 hits, 856 runs, 218 doubles, 116 triples, 35 home runs and 624 RBI. Hit .300 or better five times. Best season: .359 in rookie year. Hit 20 or more doubles seven times and 10 or more triples six times. Led AL in triples 1904 (22). Six hits in one game, 5/31/99. In 1906 led AL outfielders putouts and tied for most assists. World Series: 1903 (.303).

Managed Red Sox briefly in 1906 after Jimmy Collins resigned. During spring training in 1907, mysteriously committed suicide in hotel room. Brother of Jake Stahl, first baseman with Red Sox and Senators.

STAHL, GARLAND (Jake) 1B-OF-BR-TR. B. 4/13/79, Elkhart, Ill. D. 9/18/22, Los Angeles, Calif. Boston Red Sox 1903, 1908–10, 12–13; Washington Senators 1904–06; New York Yankees 1908. Hit .260 in 976 games with 981 hits, 149 doubles, 87 triples, 30 home runs and 437 RBI. Best year: .294 in 1909. Led AL in homers 1910 (10). Stole 178 bases. World Series: 1912 (.281).

Playing manager Washington Senators, 1905–06 (109–182), and playing manager Boston Red Sox, 1912–13 (144–88). Earned nickname "Giant Killer" for leading Red Sox to pennant and World Series win over New York in 1912. Brother of major league outfielder and manager Chick Stahl.

STAINBACK, GEORGE T. (Tuck) OF-BR-TR. B. 8/4/10, Los Angeles, Calif. 5'11½", 175. Chicago Cubs 1934–37; St. Louis Cardinals 1938; Philadelphia Phillies 1938; Brooklyn Dodgers 1938–39; Detroit Tigers 1940–41; New York Yankees 1942–45; Philadelphia A's 1946. Hit .258 in 817 games with 585 hits, 284 runs, 90 doubles, 14 triples, 17 home runs and 204 RBI. Best year: .306 in rookie season with Cubs. World Series: 1942–43 (.176).

Fashioned role as supersub, replacing Joe DiMaggio in Yankee outfield during war years. Now employed in public relations capacity for L.A. Dodgers.

STALEY, GERALD L. (Gerry) P-BR-TR. B. 8/21/20, Brush Prairie, Wash. 6', 190. St. Louis Cardinals 1947–54; Cincinnati Reds 1955; New York Yankees 1955–56; Chicago White Sox 1956–61; Kansas City A's 1961; Detroit Tigers 1961. Won 134, lost 111 in 640 games with 727 strikeouts and 529 walks in 1981 innings. Won 10 or more games six times. Best season: 19–13 in 1951 as starting pitcher. Also had 18–9 record in 1953. Later became outstanding relief hurler, helping White Sox win 1959 pennant. All-Star game: 1952–53, 1960 (0–0). World Series: 1959 (0–1 in 4 games).

Teamed with Turk Lown to form graybeard bullpen for White Sox in late 50s. Coached in minors, now is superintendent of parks and recreation for Clark County in state of Washington.

STALEY, HENRY E. P-BR-TR. B. 11/3/66, Jacksonville, Ill. D. 1/12/10, Battle Creek, Mich. Pittsburgh Pirates 1888–89, 1891; Pittsburgh (Players League) 1890; Boston (NL) 1891–94; St. Louis (NL) 1895. Won 136, lost 121 in 268 games with remarkable 231 complete games. Struck out 746 and walked 601 in 2269 innings and won 20 or more games four straight years, 1889–92. Umpired in NL in 1895.

STALLARD, EVAN T. (Tracy) P-BR-TR. B. 8/3/37, Herald, Va. 6'5", 204. Boston Red Sox 1960–62; New York Mets 1963–64; St. Louis Cardinals 1965–66. Won 30, lost 57 in 183 games with 477 strikeouts and 343 walks in 764 innings. Best season: 11–8 in 1965. Led NL in losses 1964 (20)

Earned niche in baseball history by giving up Roger Maris' 61st home run on last day of 1961 season in Yankee Stadium. Record smash was caught by Sal Durante of Brooklyn, who received $5000 for historic horsehide.

STALLINGS, GEORGE T. Manager. B. 11/17/67, Augusta, Ga. D. 5/13/29, Haddock, Ga. Brooklyn (NL) 1890 and Philadelphia (NL) 1897–98, playing only seven major league games. Gained fame as tyrannical, superstitious manager who led Miracle Braves of 1914 to NL pennant by 10-1/2 games after spending season in cellar until July 19. Braves went on to beat Philadelphia A's in World Series in four games. Son of Confederate general, Stallings managed Philadelphia, 1897–98; Detroit Tigers, 1901; New York Yankees, 1909–10; and Boston Braves, 1913–20. Managerial record: 880–900.

STANAGE, OSCAR H. C-BR-TR. B. 3/17/83, Tulare, Calif. D. 11/11/64, Detroit, Mich. 5'11", 190. Cincinnati Reds 1906; Detroit Tigers 1909–20, 1925. Hit .234 in 1094 games with 819 hits, 248 runs, 123 doubles, 34 triples, 8 home runs and 321 RBI. World Series: 1909 (.200).

Terrific receiver, he led AL catchers in putouts, 1911; assists, 1911–12, 14, and double plays, 1912. Holds AL record for most assists in season (212).

STANKY, EDWARD R. (The Brat) 2B-SS-BR-TR. B. 9/3/16, Philadelphia, Pa. 5'8", 170. Chicago Cubs 1943–44; Brooklyn Dodgers 1944–47; Boston Braves 1948–49; New York Giants 1950–51; St. Louis Cardinals 1952–53. Hit .268 in 1259 games with 1154 hits, 811 runs, 185 doubles, 35 triples, 29 home runs and 364 RBI. Best year: .300 in 1950. Hit 24 or more doubles five times. Led NL in runs 1945 (128). Drew 996 walks during career, leading NL 1945 (148), 1946 (137) and 1950 (144). Shares NL record with Jim Wynn for most walks in season (148). All-Star game: 1947–48, 50 (.000). World Series: 1947, 48, 51 (.213). Led NL second basemen in putouts, 1945–46, 50; assists, 1950, and double plays, 1945–47.

Manager St. Louis Cardinals, 1952–55, and Chicago White Sox, 1966–68 (466–435). Influenced by mentor Leo Durocher at Brooklyn and New York, brash, pesky hitter teamed with Pee Wee Reese and Al Dark to help win three pennants on three different clubs. Also served as director of player personnel for New York Mets. Baseball coach at U. of South Alabama since 1969.

STANLEY, MITCHELL J. (Mickey) OF-SS-BR-TR. B. 7/20/42, Grand Rapids, Mich. 6'1", 190. Detroit Tigers 1964–72. Hit .251 in 996 games with 821 hits, 415 runs, 123 doubles, 36 triples, 74 home runs and 330 RBI. Best year: .292 in 1971 with 7 HR and 41 RBI. 1972 record: .234 in 142 games with 14 HR and 55 RBI. Tied for best fielding average among outfielders in 1972, fielded 1.000 in 1968 and '70, tying major league record. Ran up errorless streaks in outfield of 164 and 220 games. Led outfielders in double plays in 1968.

Switched to shortstop in 1968 World Series when Al Kaline returned to lineup and stole show with brilliant glove work. Championship Series: 1972 (.400). World Series: 1968: (.214).

STANTON, LEROY B. (Baby Bull) OF-BR-TR. B. 4/10/46, Latta, S.C. 6'1", 200. New York Mets 1970–71; California Angels 1972. Hit .248 in 136 games with 106 hits, 46 runs, 16 doubles, 4 triples, 12 home runs and 41 RBI. Played all but nine career games with Angels and batted .251 in 1972. Considered one of brightest prospects for stardom in AL.

STARGELL, WILVER D. (Willie) OF-1B-BL-TL. B. 3/6/41, Earls-boro, Okla. 6'3", 215. Pittsburgh Pirates 1962–72. Hit .279 in 1341 games with 1305 hits, 689 runs, 224 doubles, 40 triples, 277 home runs and 892 RBI. Hit .300 or better twice. Best year: .315 in 1966 with 33 HR and 102 RBI. 1972 record: .293 in 138 games with 33 HR and 112 RBI. Hit 25 or more doubles five times and 30 or more home runs four years. Led NL in homers 1971 (48). Hit three HR in game, 6/24/65; 5/22/68; 4/10/71, and 4/21/71. Drove in 100 or more runs four years, including 125 in 1971. Led outfielders in assists, 1970. All-Star game: 1964–66, 1971–72 (.250). World Series: 1971 (.208).

Only player to reach upper deck in Three Rivers Stadium in Pittsburgh, blasting several balls into the right field section. Hit 7 of 18 homers hit over right field roof in Forbes Field. President of Black Athletes Foundation and active in fight against sickle cell disease. Championship Series: 1970–72 (.167).

START, JOSEPH (Old Reliable; Rocks) 1B-BL-TL. B. 10/14/43, New York, N.Y. D. 3/27/27, Providence, R.I. 5'9", 165. New York NL 1876; Brooklyn NL 1877; Chicago NL 1878; Providence NL 1879–85; Washington NL 1886. Hit .300 in 798 games with 1031 hits, 590 runs, 107 doubles, 55 triples, 7 home runs. Hit .300 or better five times. Best year: .351 in 1878.

Premier first sacker, earned nickname because he supposedly never dropped throw. First first baseman to play off sack towards second base.

STAUB, DANIEL J. (Rusty) OF-1B-BL-TR. B. 4/1/44, New Orleans, La. 6'2", 200. Houston Astros 1963–67; Montreal Expos 1969–71; New York Mets 1972. Hit .282 in 1379 games with 1370 hits, 610 runs, 250 doubles, 30 triples, 144 home runs and 678 RBI. Hit .300 or better three times. Best season: .333 in 1967 with 10 HR and 74 RBI. 1972 record: .293 in 66 games with 9 HR and 38 RBI. Hit 20 or more doubles seven times, leading NL in doubles 1967 (44). Led NL outfielders in assists in 1969 and 1971. All-Star game: 1967–71 (.333).

A $100,000 bonus baby, traded from Houston to Montreal, where he immediately made hit with Expos' fans. Red-haired slugger earned nickname "Le Grande Orange" and set most of Montreal's offensive records.

STEINFELDT, HARRY M. 3B-2B-BR-TR. B. 9/29/76, St. Louis, Mo. D. 8/17/14, Bellevue, Ky. 5′9½″. 180. Cincinnati Reds 1898–05; Chicago Cubs 1906–10; Boston Braves 1911. Hit .267 in 1631 games with 1576 hits, 758 runs, 284 doubles, 90 triples, 27 home runs and 762 RBI. Hit .300 or better twice. Best season: .327 in 1906. Hit 20 or more doubles eight times, tied for NL lead in doubles 1903 (32). Led NL in hits 1906 (176) and RBI 1906 (83).

Missed out on personal publicity by playing third base for Cub infield which had Tinker to Evers to Chance combination. Possessed fine throwing arm. Was professional actor before switching to baseball role.

STENGEL, CHARLES D. (Casey) OF-BL-TL. B. 7/30/89, Kansas City, Mo. 5′10″, 175. Brooklyn Dodgers 1912–17; Pittsburgh Pirates 1918–19; Philadelphia Phillies 1920–21; New York Giants 1921–23; Boston Braves 1924–25. Hit .284 in 1277 games with 1219 hits, 575 runs, 182 doubles, 89 triples, 60 home runs and 518 RBI. Best year: .316 in 1914. Hit 20 or more doubles five times and stole 131 bases. Made four hits in first major league game, 9/17/12. Led NL outfielders in assists, 1917. World Series: 1916, 22–23 (hit .393 in 12 games, including game-winning homers in first and third games of 1923 Series). Hall of Fame 1966.

Manager in minor leagues, 1925–31, 1944–48, and coach with Brooklyn Dodgers 1932–33. Manager of Brooklyn, 1934–36; Boston Braves, 1938–43; New York Yankees, 1949–60, and New York Mets, 1962–65. Won 1926, lost 1867 as manager. Guided Yankees to pennants in 1949–53, 55–58 and 1960, and won World Series championships in 1949–53, 56 and 58. Named Manager of the Year in 1949, 53 and 58.

Madcap player and later cagey manager, once doffed cap to fans in outfield and watched as bird flew off his head. As skipper, the "Old Perfesser" delighted and frustrated reporters and fans with confusing Stengelese, but made sense in winning 10 pennants. Executive scout with New York Mets since 1966. Also banker in Glendale, Calif.

STENNETT, RENALDO A. (Rennie) 2B-OF-BR-TR. B. 4/5/51, Colon, Panama. 5′11″, 160. Pittsburgh Pirates 1971–72. Hit .306 in 159 games with 160 hits, 67 runs, 19 doubles, 9 triples, 4 home runs and 45 RBI. Hit .353 in 1971 in 50 games. 1972 record: .286 in 109 games with 3 HR and 30 RBI. Championship Series: 1972 (.231).

A line-drive hitter who scatters shots to all fields, helped Pirates win division title in 1970 by ripping off 18-game hitting streak upon recall from Charleston in International League. Probably would be regular on any other club, but couldn't crack Bucs' formidable starting lineup.

STENZEL, JACOB C. OF-BR-TR. B. 6/24/67, Cincinnati, Ohio. D. 1/6/19, Cincinnati, Ohio. 5'10'', 168. Chicago Cubs 1890; Pittsburgh Pirates 1892–96; Baltimore NL 1897–98; St. Louis Cardinals 1898–99; Cincinnati Reds 1899. Hit .344 in 750 games with 1024 hits, 662 runs, 187 doubles, 71 triples, 33 home runs and 553 RBI. Stole 292 bases. Hit .300 or better five times, including .384 in 1895. Led NL in doubles 1897 (40). Six hits in game, 5/14/96.

STEPHENS, GLEN E. (Gene) OF-BL-TR. B. 1/20/33, Gravette, Ark. 6'3½'', 175. Boston Red Sox 1952–53, 1955–60; Baltimore Orioles 1960–61; Kansas City A's 1961–62; Chicago White Sox 1963–64. Hit .240 in 964 games with 460 hits, 283 runs, 78 doubles, 15 triples, 37 home runs and 207 RBI. Used as utility man by every team, often late-inning replacement in left field for Ted Williams while with Boston. Known by Boston fans as "Ted Williams' caddy." Despite little playing time, holds major league record for most hits in inning (3) on 6/18/53.

STEPHENS, VERNON D. (Junior) SS-3B-BR-TR. B. 10/23/20, McAlister, N.Mex. D. 11/4/68, Long Beach, Calif. 5'10'', 190. St. Louis Browns 1941–47, 53; Boston Red Sox 1948–52; Chicago White Sox 1953, 55; Baltimore Orioles 1954–55. Hit .286 in 1720 games with 1859 hits, 1001 runs, 307 doubles, 42 triples, 247 home runs and 1174 RBI. Best year: .307 in 1946. Hit 25 or more doubles seven times, 20 or more home runs six years. Led AL in homers 1945 (24). Led AL in RBI 1944 (109) and tied for most RBI 1949 (159) and 1950 (144). All-Star game: 1943–44, 46, 48–51 (.333 in 15 at bats). World Series: 1944 (.227).

A fine fielding shortstop as well as slugger, led AL in assists, 1947–49; fielding average, 1945; topped shortstops in double plays, 1949.

STEPHENSON, JACKSON R. (Riggs; Old Hoss) OF-2B-BR-TR. B. 1/5/98, Akron, Ala. 5'10'', 185. Cleveland Indians 1921–25; Chicago Cubs 1926–34. Hit .336 in 1310 games with 1515 hits, 714 runs, 321 doubles, 54 triples, 63 home runs and 773 RBI. Hit .300 or better 12 times. Best year: .362 in 1929 with 17 homers and 110 RBI in 136 games. Hit 20 or more doubles eight times, including high of 49 in 1932. Led NL in doubles 1927 (46). World Series: 1929, 32 (.378 in 9 games).

While with Chicago, formed great outfield along with Kiki Cuyler and Hack Wilson. Managed minor leagues, 1936–39. Later involved in number of business ventures in Tuscaloosa, Ala. Named to Alabama Sports Hall of Fame.

STEVENS, HAROLD (Harry) Sports concessionaire who built multi-million-dollar business from scorecard concession gained in 1900 in most major league parks. Concept proved so popular that Stevens branched out into sales of hot dogs and soft drinks. Firm later operated by four sons and based in New York City. "Scorecard Harry's" idea eventually led to owners placing numbers on backs of players' uniforms.

STEWART, WALTER C. (Lefty) P-BR-TL. B. 9/23/1900, Sparta, Tenn. 5'10", 160. Detroit Tigers 1921; St. Louis Browns 1927–32; Washington Senators 1933–35; Cleveland Indians 1935. Won 101, lost 98 in 282 games with 503 strikeouts and 498 walks in 1721 innings. Won 14 or more games four straight years. Best season: 20–12 in 1930. World Series: 1933 (0–1). Ace of fairly poor Browns' pitching staffs in 1930s.

STIRNWEISS, GEORGE H. (Snuffy) Inf.-BR-TR. B. 10/26/19, New York, N.Y. D. 9/15/58, Newark Bay, N.J. 5'8½", 175. New York Yankees 1943–50; St. Louis Browns 1950; Cleveland Indians 1951–52. Hit .268 in 1028 games with 989 hits, 604 runs, 157 doubles, 68 triples, 29 home runs and 281 RBI. Hit .300 or better twice. Led AL batting 1945 (.309). Led AL hits 1944 (205) and 1945 (195). Led AL triples 1945 (22) and tied for most triples 1944 (16). Also led in runs scored 1944 (125) and 1945 (107), stolen bases 1944 (55) and 1945 (33), slugging percentage 1945 (.476) and total bases 1945 (301). Led second basemen in putouts 1944–45, assists 1944, double plays 1945 and fielding average 1944, 48. Played third and short also.

Kept Yankee "star" tradition alive during war years by taking over while more famous teammates served in armed forces. World Series: 1943, 47, 49 (.250).

STIVETTS, JOHN C. (Jack) P-BR-TR. B. 3/31/68, Ashland, Pa. D. 4/19/30, Ashland, Pa. 5'11½", 204. St. Louis (American Association) 1889–91; Boston (NL) 1892–98; Cleveland (NL) 1899. Won 205, lost 128 in 357 games, with 1049 strikeouts and 1061 walks in 3911 innings. Won 20 or more games five times, including 33 in both 1891 and 1892. Led league in strikeouts 1891 (232). Pitched 281 complete games. Hurled no-hitter against Brooklyn, 8/6/92, and five-inning no-hitter against Washington, 10/15/92.

A part-time infielder and outfielder as well, Stivetts hit .303 in 523 games, including those as pitcher.

STOBBS, CHARLES K. (Chuck) P-BL-TL. B. 7/2/29, Wheeling, W. Va. 6'1", 200. Boston Red Sox 1947–51; Chicago White Sox 1952; Washington Senators 1953–58, 1959–60; St. Louis Cardinals 1958; Minnesota Twins 1961. Won 107, lost 130 in 460 games with 897 strikeouts and 735 walks in 1920 innings. Won 10 or more games seven seasons. Best year: 15–15 in 1956.

Gave up 565-foot home run blast to Mickey Mantle in Griffith Stadium in 1956. Now pitching instructor at Kansas City Royals Baseball Academy.

STOCK, MILTON J. 3B-2B-BR-TR. B. 7/11/93, Chicago, Ill. 5'8", 154. New York Giants 1913–14; Philadelphia Phillies 1915–18; St. Louis Cardinals 1919–23; Brooklyn Dodgers 1924–26. Hit .289 in 1628 games with 1806 hits, 839 runs, 270 doubles, 58 triples, 22 home runs and 702 RBI. Hit .300 or better four consecutive years. Best season: .328 in 1925. Hit 25 or more doubles seven times. World Series: 1915 (.118).

STOCK, WESLEY G. P-BR-TR. B. 4/10/34, Longview, Wash. 6'2", 182. Baltimore Orioles 1959–64; Kansas City A's 1964–67. Won 27, lost 13 in 321 games with 365 strikeouts and 215 walks in 518 innings. Won 5, lost none in 35 games in 1961 and won seven without defeat in 47 games in 1964.

Coach with Kansas City, 1967; minor league pitching instructor for New York Mets, 1968–69; coach with Milwaukee Brewers, 1970–72; appointed coach with Oakland A's, 1973.

STONE, GEORGE H. (Stoney) P-BL-TL. B. 7/9/46, Ruston, La. 6'3", 200. Atlanta Braves 1967–72. Won 42, lost 45 in 145 games with 416 strikeouts and 217 walks in 676 innings. Best year: 13–10 in 1969 with 102 strikeouts and 3.65 ERA. 1972 record: 6–11 in 31 games with 63 strikeouts and 5.51 ERA. Traded to N.Y. Mets after 1972 season. Cousin of Houston relief pitcher Cecil Upshaw.

STONE, GEORGE R. OF-BL-TL. B. 9/3/76, Clinton, Iowa. D. 1/5/45, Clinton, Iowa. Boston Red Sox 1903; St. Louis Browns 1905–10. Hit .301 in 848 games with 984 hits, 426 runs, 106 doubles, 68 triples, 23 home runs and 301 RBI. Played only five full seasons, but twice hit .300 or better, leading AL in batting 1906 (.358). Also led AL in hits 1905 (187), total bases 1905 (260) and 1906 (288) and slugging percentage 1906 (.496). Silent slugger later forced to quit baseball at peak of career because of illness.

STONE, JONATHAN T. (Rocky) OF-BL-TR. B. 10/10/05, Mulberry, Tenn. D. 11/30/55, Shelbyville, Tenn. 6', 180. Detroit Tigers 1928–33; Washington Senators 1934–38. Hit .310 in 1198 games with 1391 hits, 738 runs, 268 doubles, 105 triples, 77 home runs and 707 RBI. Hit .300 or better seven times. Best year: .341 in 1936. Hit 25 or more doubles seven times and hit safely in 34 consecutive games in 1930. Made eight hits in doubleheader, 6/16/35.

Fine hitter whose career was cut short by tuberculosis, he later served as scout for Detroit Tigers.

STONEMAN, WILLIAM A. (Stoney) P-BR-TR. B. 4/7/44, Oak Park, Ill. 5'10", 170. Chicago Cubs 1967–68; Montreal Expos 1969–72. Won 49, lost 69 in 203 games with 853 strikeouts and 516 walks in 1082 innings. Best year: 17–16 in 1971 with 251 strikeouts and 3.14 ERA. 1972 record: 12–14 in 36 games with 171 strikeouts and 2.98 ERA. Led NL in walks 1969 (123) and 1971 (146).

Mainstay of Expo hill staff; fired no-hitters against Philadelphia, 4/17/69, and New York, 10/2/72.

STOTTLEMYRE, MELVIN L. (Mel) P-BR-TR. B. 11/13/41, Hazelton, Mo. 6'2", 192. New York Yankees 1964–72. Won 142, lost 116 in 306 games with 1122 strikeouts and 693 walks in 2276 innings. Won 20 or more games three times. Best season: 21–12 in 1968 with 140 strikeouts and 2.45 ERA. 1972 record: 14–18 in 36 games with 110 strikeouts and 3.22 ERA. Threw seven shutouts in 1972, hiking career total to 36. Led AL complete games 1965 (18) and 1969 (24). Led league in innings pitched 1965 (291). All-Star game: 1965–66, 68–70 (0–1). World Series: 1964 (1–1).

One of best pitchers in Yankees' illustrious history, had misfortune to pitch on several poor New York teams.

STOVALL, GEORGE T. (Firebrand) 1B-2B-3B-BR-TR. B. 11/23/78, Independence, Mo. D. 11/5/51, Burlington, Iowa. 6'2", 180. Cleveland Indians 1904–11; St. Louis Browns 1912–13; Kansas City (Federal League) 1914–15. Hit .264 in 1409 games, mostly at first base, with 1381 hits, 545 runs, 231 doubles, 56 triples, 15 home runs and 564 RBI. Best year: .292 in 138 games in 1908. Acquired nickname from antics on and off field. Displayed celebrated temper in hotel lobby by smashing chair over head of Cleveland manager Napoleon Lajoie. Throwback to rowdy 1890s ball player. Managed Cleveland, 1911; St. Louis, 1912–13; Kansas City, 1914–15. Record: 313–376. Dropped by St. Louis Browns after series of incidents, including Stovall's refusal to give tryouts to college students and spitting tobacco juice in the eyes of umpires.

STOVEY, HARRY D. 1B-OF-BR-TR. B. 12/26/56, Philadelphia, Pa. D. 9/20/37, New Bedford, Mass. 5'11½", 180. Worcester NL 1880–82; Athletics (American Association) 1883–89; Boston (Players) 1890; Boston NL 1891–92; Baltimore NL 1892–93; Brooklyn NL 1893. Hit .320 in 1481 games with 1925 hits, 1467 runs, 348 doubles, 185 triples, 120 home runs and 744 stolen bases. Hit .300 or better seven times, including .404

in 1884 and .402 in 1887. Scored 100 or more runs nine times, leading league on four occasions. Hit 25 or more doubles 10 times and 10 or more triples in 11 seasons. Led or tied for most homers in a season six times. Hit three triples in game, 8/18/84 and 7/21/92.

Terror on the base paths, Stovey stole 100 or more bases four straight years, including major league high of 156 in 1888. Base stealing no doubt aided by fact he was first ball player to wear sliding pads.

STRANG, SAMUEL N. (Sammy) 3B-2B-OF-BLR-TR. B. 12/16/76, Chattanooga, Tenn. D. 3/13/32, Chattanooga, Tenn. Louisville NL 1896; Chicago NL 1900, 02; New York Giants 1901, 1905–08; Chicago White Sox 1902; Brooklyn Dodgers 1903–04. Hit .266 in 842 games. Best year: .319 in 1906. World Series: 1905 (.000).

Involved in unsuccessful attempt to pinch hit for umpire, who was forced by fans to stay out of ball park before game, 8/7/06. Instigator, John McGraw, was overruled and Strang remained in game.

STRATTON, MONTY F. P-BR-TR. B. 5/21/12, Celeste, Tex. 6'5", 180. Chicago White Sox 1934–38. Won 36, lost 23 in 71 games, including 15 in both 1937 and 1938. All-Star game: 1938 (0–0).

Career came to tragic end after 1938 season when Stratton lost leg in hunting accident near his home. Life story was later filmed by Hollywood—*The Monty Stratton Story,* starring Jimmy Stewart in title role, and June Allyson his faithful spouse.

STREET, CHARLES E. (Old Sarge; Gabby) C-BR-TR. B. 9/30/82, Huntsville, Ala. D. 2/6/51, Joplin, Mo. 5'11", 180. Cincinnati Reds 1904–05; Boston Braves 1905; Washington Senators 1908–11; New York Yankees 1912; St. Louis Cardinals 1931. Hit .208 in 501 games but later became noted manager of Cardinals, 1930, 32–33. Also managed St. Louis Browns, 1938. Managerial record: 368–339. Led Cardinals to pennants in 1930–31 and World Series championship in '31.

Fun-loving catcher believed to be second player to catch baseball thrown off top of Washington Monument. Later became popular broadcaster of St. Louis games.

STRICKLAND, GEORGE B. (Bo) Inf.-BR-TR. B. 1/10/26, New Orleans, La. 6'1", 190. Pittsburgh Pirates 1950–52; Cleveland Indians 1952–60. Hit .224 in 971 games with 633 hits, 305 runs, 84 doubles, 27 triples, 36 home runs and 284 RBI. Best year: .284 in 1953 with 5 HR and 47 RBI. Led AL shortstops in double plays in 1953 and fielding average, 1955. Shares major league record by making five double plays at short in game, 9/27/52. World Series: 1954 (.000).

Temporary manager of Cleveland Indians, 1964 (40–37), and scout with Cleveland, 1961. Coached for Minnesota Twins, 1962; Cleveland, 1963–69; Kansas City Royals, 1970–72.

STRIEF, GEORGE A. 2B-OF-BR-TR. B. 10/16/56, Cincinnati, Ohio. D. 4/1/46, Cleveland, Ohio. 5'7", 140. Cleveland (NL) 1879, 1884; Pittsburgh (American Association) 1882; St. Louis (AA) 1883–84; Kansas City (Union Association) 1884; Pittsburgh (UA) 1884; Philadelphia (AA) 1885. Hit .197 in 350 games and only 14 triples during career, but got four three-baggers in one game out of season total of five in 1885. Later umpire in NL, 1889–90.

STRIPP, JOSEPH V. (Jersey Joe) 3B-1B-BR-TR. B. 2/3/03, Harrison, N.J. 5'11½", 175. Cincinnati Reds 1928–31; Brooklyn Dodgers 1932–37; St. Louis Cardinals 1938; Boston Braves 1938. Hit .294 in 1146 games with 1238 hits, 575 runs, 219 doubles, 45 triples, 24 home runs and 464 RBI. Hit .300 or better six times. Best season: .324 in 1931. Hit 20 or more doubles five times.

STRUNK, AMOS A. OF-BL-TL. B. 11/22/89, Philadelphia, Pa. 5'11½", 175. Philadelphia A's 1908–17, 1919–20, 24; Boston Red Sox 1918–19; Chicago White Sox 1920–24. Hit .283 in 1507 games with 1415 hits, 695 runs, 212 doubles, 96 triples, 15 home runs and 539 RBI. Hit .300 or better three times. Best season: .332 in 1921. World Series: 1910–11, 13–14, 18 (.200 in 18 games). Led AL outfielders in fielding average, 1912, 14, 18, 20 and tied for best average in 1917.

Played on star-studded Connie Mack teams and traded to Boston with other stars in Mack's housecleaning to raise money. Later employed as insurance broker in Pennsylvania.

STUART, RICHARD L. (Dr. Strangeglove; Stonefingers) 1B-BR-TR. B. 11/7/32, San Francisco, Calif. 6'4", 210. Pittsburgh Pirates 1958–62; Boston Red Sox 1963–64; Philadelphia Phillies 1965; New York Mets 1966; Los Angeles Dodgers 1966; California Angels 1969. Hit .264 in 1112 games with 1055 hits, 506 runs, 157 doubles, 30 triples, 228 home runs and 743 RBI. Best season: .301 in 1961 with 35 homers. Hit 20 or more home runs six times, including 42 in 1963. Led AL in RBI 1963 (118) and total bases 1963 (319). Hit three HR in game, 6/30/60. Led AL first basemen in putouts and assists in 1963. All-Star game: 1961 (.500). World Series: 1960, 66 (.136).

Great slugger, who once hit 66 homers for Lincoln in Western League in 1956, he was less than perfect afield. Set major league mark for most times leading or tying for lead in errors at first base (7), 1958–64. Struck out 100 or more times five times, leading NL in 1961. Played ball in

Japan in 1967–68. Brash, swaggering Stuart never known for modesty. Feuded with Yankee manager Ralph Houk, who left Stuart off 1963 All-Star squad. Had television shows in Boston and New York during playing days.

STURDIVANT, THOMAS V. (Snake) P-BL-TR. B. 4/28/30, Gordon, Kans. 6'1", 185. New York Yankees 1955–59; Kansas City A's 1959, 63–64; Boston Red Sox 1960; Washington Senators 1961; Pittsburgh Pirates 1961–63; New York Mets 1964. Won 59, lost 51 in 335 games with 704 strikeouts and 449 walks in 1137 innings. Won 16 games in both 1956 and 1957. Led AL in percentage 1957 (.727). World Series: 1955–57 (1–0 in 6 games). Career took turn for worse after Sturdivant developed sore arm in 1958.

SUDER, PETER (Pete; Pecky) 2B-SS-3B-BR-TR. B. 4/16/16, Aliquippa, Pa. 6', 175. Philadelphia A's 1941–43, 46–54; Kansas City A's 1955. Hit .249 in 1421 games with 1268 hits, 469 runs, 210 doubles, 44 triples, 49 home runs and 541 RBI. Best season: .286 in 1953. Hit 20 or more doubles six times. Led AL second basemen in fielding average 1947, 1951.

Flashy fielder, he managed in minor leagues after playing days, later served as jail warden.

SUHR, AUGUST R. (Gus) 1B-BL-TR. B. 1/3/07, San Francisco, Calif. 6', 180. Pittsburgh Pirates 1930–39; Philadelphia Phillies 1939–40 Hit .281 in 1435 games with 1295 hits, 645 runs, 261 doubles, 100 triples, 84 home runs and 819 RBI. Hit .300 or better twice. Best season: .312 in 1936 with 111 runs and 118 RBI. Hit 30 or more doubles six times and 11 or more triples seven seasons. All-Star game: 1936 (.000).

Fine fielder, he led NL first basemen in putouts 1938, fielding average 1936 and double plays 1931, 33, 38. At one time held record most consecutive games played in National League (822).

SULLIVAN, FRANKLIN L. (Frank) P-BR-TR. B. 1/23/30, Hollywood, Calif. 6'6½", 230. Boston Red Sox 1953–60; Philadelphia Phillies 1961–62; Minnesota Twins 1962–63. Won 97, lost 100 in 351 games with 959 strikeouts and 559 walks in 1732 innings. Won 13 or more games five times. Best season: 18–13 in 1955 to lead league in wins. Led AL in innings pitched 1955 (260). All-Star game: 1955–56 (0–1). Nearly 6-foot, 7-inch tall pitcher served up winning home run to Stan Musial in 12th inning of 1955 All-Star game, losing contest to 6'8" hurler Gene Conley. Later quoted as saying while member of dismal Philadelphia club, "I'm in the twilight of a mediocre career." Assistant golf pro at Kauai, Hawaii.

SULLIVAN, THEODORE P. (Ted) Manager. B. 1852, County Clare, Ireland. D. 7/5/29, Washington, D.C. Kansas City (Union Association) 1884. Managed St. Louis (AA) 1882–83, St. Louis (UA) 1884 and Washington (NL) 1888. Record: 105–147. Generally credited as first person to refer to paying customers at baseball games as "fans."

SULLIVAN, WILLIAM J., SR. (Billy) C-BR-TR. B. 2/1/75, Oakland, Wis. D. 1/28/65, Newberg, Oreg. 5'9", 155. Boston Braves 1899–1900; Chicago White Sox 1901–14; Detroit Tigers 1916. Hit .213 in 1141 games, including first games ever played in American League, 4/24/01. World Series: 1906: (.000).

Father of Billy Sullivan, Jr., who hit .289 in 962 games in majors, 1931–47. Manager of Chicago White Sox, 1909 (78–74).

SUMMA, HOMER W. OF-BL-TR. B. 11/3/99, Gentry, Mo. D. 1/29/66, Los Angeles, Calif. 5'10", 165. Pittsburgh Pirates 1920; Cleveland Indians 1922–28; Philadelphia A's 1929–30. Hit .301 in 840 games with 905 hits, 413 runs, 166 doubles, 34 triples, 18 home runs and 361 RBI. Hit .300 or better three times. Best season: .328 in 1923. Hit 20 or more doubles five times with season high of 41 in 1927. World Series: 1929 (.000).

SUNDAY, WILLIAM A. (Billy; The Evangelist; Parson) OF-BL-TR. B. 11/19/62, Ames, Iowa. D. 11/6/35, Chicago, Ill. 5'10", 160. Chicago (NL) 1883–87; Pittsburgh (NL) 1888–90; Philadelphia (NL) 1890. Hit .258 in 488 games. Good fielder whose quickness helped him steal 236 bases, including 84 with two teams in 1890.

Used sliding techniques on stage later when he became world-famous evangelist in the tradition of fire-and-brimstone preachers. As popular in his time as Billy Graham and Oral Roberts are today. One of first to back and help implement the Prohibition era. Also fought against baseball being played on Sunday. Immortalized in song that boasts of Chicago as "the town that Billy Sunday could not shut down."

SUTTON, DONALD H. (Don) P-BR-TR. B. 4/2/45, Clio, Ala. 6'1", 185. Los Angeles Dodgers 1966–72. Won 102, lost 94 in 259 games with 1359 strikeouts and 455 walks in 1758 innings. Won 15 or more games four times. Best year: 19–9 in 1972 with 208 strikeouts and ERA of 2.08, third best in the NL. Led league in shutouts 1972 (9). Struck out 200 or more batters four times. All-Star game: 1972 (0–0).

Named *Sporting News* Rookie Pitcher of Year in 1966. Works as disc jockey at California radio station during off-season.

SWANSON, ERNEST E. (Evar) OF-BR-TR. B. 10/15/02, DeKalb, Ill. D. 7/17/73, Galesburg, Ill. 5'9", 170. Cincinnati Reds 1929–30; Chicago White Sox 1932–34. Hit .303 in 518 games with 573 hits, 325 runs, 87 doubles, 28 triples, 7 home runs and 166 RBI. Hit .300 or better four of five years in majors. Stole 33 bases in rookie year and still holds the record for fastest time in circling bases,: 13.3 seconds. Pro football mid-20s. Postmaster of Galesburg from 1958 till retirement in 1972.

SWEAZY, CHARLES J. (Charlie) 2B-OF-BR-TR. B. 9/3/47, Haverhill, N.H. D. 3/30/08, Newark, N.J. 5'9", 172. Olympics (National Association) 1871; Cleveland (NA) 1872; Boston (NA) 1873; Baltimore (NA) 1874; Atlanta (NA) 1874; Cincinnati Red Stockings (NA) 1875; Cincinnati (NL) 1876; Providence (NL) 1878. Played only 164 games with all teams. While with Cincinnati, became baseball's first holdout, demanding and receiving $200 raise from $800 salary in 1869.
    Managed the Red Stockings in 1875 and served as NL umpire in 1879.

SWEENEY, CHARLES J. (Charlie) P-OF-1B-TR. B. 4/13/63, San Francisco, Calif. D. 4/4/02, San Francisco, Calif. Philadelphia A's (American Association) 1882; Providence (NL) 1882–84; St. Louis (Union Association) 1884; St. Louis (NL) 1885–86; Cleveland (AA) 1887. Primarily a pitcher, won 77, lost 64 in 258 games. Struck out 19 batters in game, 6/7/84, a record which stood until 1969 when Steve Carlton struck out 19 with St. Louis Cardinals.
    Won 41 games in 1884, 24 with St. Louis club and 17 with Providence. Left Providence after feuding with Old Hoss Radbourn, forcing ironman to live up to nickname by pitching almost every day.

SWEENEY, WILLIAM J. (Bill) Inf.-BR-TR. B. 3/6/86, Covington, Ky. D. 5/26/48, Cambridge, Mass. 5'11", 175. Chicago Cubs 1907, 14; Boston Braves 1907–13. Hit .272 in 1034 games with 1004 hits, 442 runs, 153 doubles, 40 triples, 13 home runs and 377 RBI. Hit .300 or better two seasons. Best year: .344 in 1912. Played short, third and second.

SWIFT, ROBERT V. (Bob) C-BR-TR. B. 3/6/15, Salina, Kans. D. 10/17/66, Detroit, Mich. 5'11½", 180. St. Louis Browns 1940–42; Philadelphia A's 1942–43; Detroit Tigers 1944–53. Hit .231 in 1001 games with 635 hits, 212 runs, 86 doubles, 3 triples, 14 home runs and 238 RBI. World Series: 1945 (.250). Led AL catchers in fielding average 1948.
    Coach, Detroit Tigers, 1953–54, 1963–66. Coach, Kansas City A's, 1957–59. Coach, Washington Senators, 1960. Interim manager, Detroit Tigers, 1965–66 (32–25). Appointed temporary pilot of Tigers during illness of Charlie Dressen, who died 8/10/66. Bob died two months later.

SWOBODA, RONALD A. (Ron; Rocky) OF-BR-TR. B. 6/30/44, Baltimore, Md. 6'2", 210. New York Mets 1965–70; Montreal Expos 1971; New York Yankees 1971–72. Hit .244 in 893 games with 619 hits, 279 runs, 87 doubles, 24 triples, 72 home runs and 342 RBI. Best year: .281 in 1967 with 13 HR and 53 RBI. 1972 record: .248 in 63 games with one HR and 12 RBI. World Series: 1969 (.400).

Mediocre flyhawk, Swoboda made famous sliding catch of liner to rob Brooks Robinson of extra base hit in ninth inning of final game of 1969 World Series. Score remained tied until broken in tenth by Mets.

TABOR, JAMES R. (Rawhide)   3B-BR-TR. B. 11/5/16, Owens Cross-roads, Ala. D. 8/22/53, Sacramento, Calif. 6'2", 175. Boston Red Sox 1938–44; Philadelphia Phillies 1946–47. Hit .270 in 1005 games with 1021 hits, 473 runs, 191 doubles, 29 triples, 104 home runs and 598 RBI. Best year: .289 in 1939 with 14 HR and 95 RBI. Hit 25 or more doubles five times. Hit three homers in game, 7/4/39, and drove in 11 runs in doubleheader, 7/4/39. Led AL third basemen in putouts, 1942; assists, 1939, and double plays, 1943. Led NL in double plays, 1946.

TANNEHILL, JESSE N. (Jess)   P-BL-TL. B. 7/14/74, Dayton, Ky. D. 9/22/56, Dayton, Ky. 5'11", 170. Cincinnati Reds 1894, 1911; Pittsburgh Pirates 1897–1902; New York Yankees 1903; Boston Red Sox 1904–08; Washington Senators 1908–09. Won 194, lost 118 in 473 games with 917 strikeouts and 471 walks in 2768 innings. Won 20 or more games six times. Best year: 24–14 in 1898. Pitched 266 complete games and 36 shutouts. Led AL percentage in 1905 (.710). No-hitter against Chicago (AL), 8/17/04.
   One of many NL stars to jump to AL in 1903. Formed potent hill staff with Deacon Phillippe and Jack Chesbro on championship Pirate teams of 1901–02. Later managed in minor leagues 1914, 1923.

TANNER, CHARLES W. (Chuck)   OF-BL-TL. B. 7/4/29, New Castle, Pa. 6', 185. Milwaukee Braves 1955–57; Chicago Cubs 1957–58; Cleveland Indians 1959–60; Los Angeles Angels 1961–62. Hit .261 in 396 games with 231 hits, 98 runs, 39 doubles, 5 triples, 21 home runs and 105

RBI. Best season: .279 in 1957 with 9 HR and 48 RBI. Hit homer on first pitch in first major league at bat, 4/12/55. Manager minor leagues, 1963–70. Manager, Chicago White Sox, 1970–72 (169–163). Took White Sox from last place to second in two years with help of Dick Allen, Wilbur Wood and Stan Bahnsen. AL Manager of Year Award 1972.

TATUM, KENNETH R. (Ken) P-BR-TR. B. 4/25/44, Alexandria, La. 6'2", 205. California Angels 1969–70; Boston Red Sox 1971–72. Won 16, lost 12 in 165 games with 153 strikeouts and 105 walks in 258 innings. Best year: 7–2 in 1969 with 22 saves and 1.36 ERA in 45 games. Also won seven games in 1970 with 17 saves. Plagued by injuries since dealt to Red Sox. 1972 record: 0–2 in 22 games.

TAYLOR, ANTONIO (Tony) Inf.-BR-TR. B. 12/19/35, Central Alava, Cuba. 5'9½", 169. Chicago Cubs 1958–60; Philadelphia Phillies 1960–71; Detroit Tigers 1971–72. Hit .262 in 1944 games with 1892 hits, 950 runs, 279 doubles, 82 triples, 67 home runs and 541 RBI. Best year: .301 in 1970 with 9 HR and 55 RBI. 1972 record: .303 in 78 games with one home run and 20 RBI. Hit 20 or more doubles seven times. All-Star game: 1960 (1.000). Led NL second basemen in assists in 1959 and fielding average in 1963. Also competent at hot corner and first base.

TAYLOR, CARL M. OF-1B-BR-TR. B. 1/20/44, Sarasota, Fla. 6'2", 200. Pittsburgh Pirates 1968–69, 1971; St. Louis Cardinals 1970; Kansas City Royals 1971–72. Hit .274 in 342 games with 192 hits, 95 runs, 25 doubles, 5 triples, 10 home runs and 99 RBI. Best season: .348 in 1969 with four home runs and 33 RBI in 104 games. 1972 record: .265 in 63 games with no homers and 11 RBI.

Versatile ball player is stepbrother of Baltimore Orioles first baseman Boog Powell.

TAYLOR, DANIEL T. (Danny) OF-BR-TR. B. 12/23/01, Lash, Pa. D. 11/72, Latrobe, Pa. 5'10", 190. Washington Senators 1926; Chicago Cubs 1929–32; Brooklyn Dodgers 1932–36. Hit .297 in 674 games with 650 hits, 388 runs, 121 doubles, 37 triples, 44 home runs and 304 RBI. Best year: .319 in 111 games in 1932.

Became interested in baseball as means of escaping life in Pennsylvania coal mines, where he worked as boy. After playing days, managed in minor leagues in 1941.

TAYLOR, HARRY L. 1B-BR-TR. B. 4/14/66, Halsey Valley, N.Y. D. 7/12/55, Buffalo, N.Y. Louisville (American Association) 1890–91; Louisville (NL) 1892; Baltimore (NL) 1893. Hit .283 in 436 games but contribution to game was more important off the field.

A ball player turned attorney, he drew up articles for Protective Association of Professional Ball Players. Formed around the birth of the AL, organization won some important rights for ball players.

TAYLOR, JAMES W. (Zack) C-BR-TR. B. 7/27/98, Yulee, Fla. 5'11½", 180. Brooklyn Dodgers 1920–25, 1935; Boston Braves 1926–27, 1928–29; New York Giants 1927; Chicago Cubs 1929–33; New York Yankees 1934. Hit .261 in 914 games with 748 hits, 258 runs, 113 doubles, 28 triples, 9 home runs and 311 RBI. Best season: .310 in 1925. Led NL catchers in putouts and double plays in 1926 and assists in 1923. World Series: 1929 (.176).

Coach with Brooklyn Dodgers, 1936, St. Louis Browns, 1941–46, and Pittsburgh Pirates, 1947. Played and managed in minor leagues, 1937–40, 52–53. Manager of St. Louis Browns, 1946, 48–51 (235–410). Scouted with White Sox, 1954–60; Milwaukee Braves, 1961–65, Atlanta Braves, 1966–70, and Montreal Expos since 1971. Veteran of 58 consecutive years in organized baseball, he managed poor Browns teams under Bill Veeck, who once allowed fans to determine game strategy from stands and relay information to Taylor.

TAYLOR, JOHN B. (Brewery Jack) P-BR-TR. B. 5/27/73, West New Brighton, N.Y. D. 2/7/1900, Staten Island, N.Y. 6'1", 190. New York Giants 1891; Philadelphia Phillies 1892–97; St. Louis Cardinals 1898; Cincinnati Reds 1899. Won 123, lost 111 in 251 games with 528 strikeouts and 581 walks in 2079 innings. Won 20 or more games three times. Lost 31 games in 1898. Umpire in NL, 1899.

TAYLOR, JOHN W. P-BR-TR. B. 9/13/73, Straightsville, Ohio. D. 3/4/38, Columbus, Ohio. 5'10", 170. Chicago Cubs 1898–1903, 1906–07; St. Louis Cardinals 1904–06. Won 152, lost 139 in 310 games with 657 strikeouts and 582 walks in 2617 innings. Won 20 or more games four times. Assumed ironman role for Cubs and Cardinals, completing 278 games in 310 starts. Holds major league record for most consecutive games in season (39) in 1904. Record covered 352 innings without relief.

TAYLOR, LUTHER H. (Dummy) P-BR-TR. B. 2/21/76, Olathe, Kans. D. 8/22/58, Jacksonville, Ill. 6'1", 160. New York Giants 1900–01, 1902–08; Cleveland Indians 1902. Won 117, lost 106 in 272 games with 767 strikeouts and 551 walks in 1916 innings. Best season: 21–15 in 1904. Led NL in losses 1901 (27). Helped Giants win World Series in 1905 with 16–9 mark.

Fine pitcher who wasn't hampered by being deaf mute, he helped others with similar affliction after retirement.

TAYLOR, RONALD W. (Ron) P-BR-TR. B. 12/13/37, Toronto, Ont. 6'1", 201. Cleveland Indians 1962; St. Louis Cardinals 1963–65; Houston Astros 1965–66; New York Mets 1967–71; Montreal Expos 1972; San Diego Padres 1972. Won 45, lost 43 in 491 games with 464 strikeouts and 209 walks in 799 innings. Appeared in 50 or more games as relief pitcher seven times. Best season: 9–4 in 1969 with 13 saves and 2.72 ERA. Earned over 60 saves during career. 1972 record: 0–0 in four games. Championship Series: 1969 (1–0). World Series: 1964,69 (0–0). Allowed no runs in 3-1/3 innings of playoffs and shut out opposition in seven innings in four World Series games.

A brainy athlete, also working on postgraduate studies in electrical engineering.

TEBBETTS, GEORGE R. (Birdie) C-BR-TR. B. 11/10/09, Burlington, Vt. 5'11½", 170. Detroit Tigers 1936–42, 46–47; Boston Red Sox 1947–50; Cleveland Indians 1951–52. Hit .270 in 1162 games with 1000 hits, 357 runs, 169 doubles, 22 triples, 38 home runs and 469 RBI. All-Star game: 1941–42, 48–49 (.286). World Series: 1940 (.000). Fine defensive backstop, led AL catchers in putouts, 1942, assists, 1939–41, and double plays, 1940.

Managed Cincinnati Reds, 1954–58; Milwaukee Braves, 1961–62, and Cleveland Indians, 1963–66 (781–744). Now scouting for New York Mets.

TEBEAU, OLIVER W. (Patsy) 1B-3B-BR-TR. B. 12/5/64, St. Louis, Mo. D. 5/15/18, St. Louis, Mo. Chicago (NL) 1887; Cleveland (NL) 1889, 1891–98; Cleveland (Players League) 1890; St. Louis (NL) 1899–1900. Hit .284 in 1150 games with 1291 hits, 671 runs, 196 doubles, 57 triples, 25 home runs and 735 RBI. Hit .300 or better three times. Best year: .359 in 1893. Playing manager with Cleveland 1890 in Players League and with Cleveland in NL 1891–98. Also managed St. Louis 1899–1900 (732–575).

Fiery manager, well known for abrasive techniques in harassing umpires, opponents and own players. Brother of former major leaguer George Tebeau.

TEMPLE, JOHN E. (Johnny) 2B-BR-TR. B. 8/8/29, Lexington, N.C. 5'11", 175. Cincinnati Reds 1952–59, 1964; Cleveland Indians 1960–61; Baltimore Orioles 1962; Houston Astros 1962–63. Hit .284 in 1420 games with 1484 hits, 720 runs, 208 doubles, 36 triples, 22 home runs and 395 RBI. Hit .300 or better three times. Best year: .311 in 1959. Hit 20 or more doubles five times. Tied for NL lead in walks in 1957 (94) and coaxed 648 during career. All-Star game: 1956–57, 1959, 61 (.200). Led NL second basemen in putouts, 1954, 56, 58; assists, 1956, and double plays, 1955.

Composed slick double-play combination at Cincinnati with Roy McMillan and Ted Kluszewski.

TENACE, FURY G. (Gene) C-OF-1B-BR-TR. B. 10/10/46, Russellton, Pa. 6', 195. Oakland A's 1969–72. Hit .251 in 201 games with 138 hits, 68 runs, 18 doubles, 3 triples, 20 home runs and 79 RBI. Best year: .274 in 1971 with 7 HR and 25 RBI. 1972 record: .225 in 82 games with 5 HR and 32 RBI. Championship Series: 1971–72: (.083). Drove in key run in third playoff game with Detroit Tigers in Oakland's 2–1 victory.

Hit only five homers in 1972, but joined Babe Ruth, Lou Gehrig, Hank Bauer and Duke Snider as fifth player to hit four home runs in a World Series. Hit .348 in seven-game affair and drove in nine of Athletics' 16 runs. Set Series mark with .913 slugging percentage.

TENER, JOHN K. P-BR-TR. B. 7/25/63, County Tyrone, Ireland. D. 5/19/46, Pittsburgh, Pa. 6'4", 180. Baltimore (American Association) 1885; Chicago (NL) 1888–89; Pittsburgh (Players) 1890. Won 24, lost 33 in 72 games. Best year: 14–15 in 1889.

Rose quickly from obscurity to powerful force in baseball. Umpired briefly and later became president of NL from 1913 to 1918. Went on from there to be elected to Congress and capped political career by being elected governor of Pennsylvania.

TENNEY, FREDERICK 1B-BL-TL. B. 11/26/71, Georgetown, Mass. D. 7/3/52, Boston, Mass. 5'10½", 178. Boston (NL) 1894–1907, 1911; New York Giants 1908–09. Hit .295 in 1969 games with 2239 hits, 1271 runs, 264 doubles, 80 triples, 23 home runs and 281 RBI. Hit .300 or better in six full seasons. Best year: .350 in 1899. Six hits in game, 5/31/97. Led NL in runs 1908 (101). Led NL in putouts at first base 1905, 1907–08; assists 1899, 1901–07; fielding average 1897; tied for best average in 1908. Holds NL record for most assists (1365) at first base and major league mark for most years leading league in assists (8).

Manager of Boston Braves 1905–07, 1911 (202–402). Also managed in minor leagues, 1916, and wrote articles for newspaper syndicate. A flashy fielder and at one time lefthanded catcher, perfected 3–6–3 double play.

TERRY, RALPH W. P-BR-TR. B. 1/9/36, Big Cabin, Okla. 6'3", 190. New York Yankees 1956–57, 59–64; Kansas City A's 1957–59, 1966; Cleveland Indians 1965; New York Mets 1966–67. Won 107, lost 99 in 338 games with 1000 strikeouts and 446 walks in 1849 innings. Won 10 or more games six times, including league-leading 23 victories in 1962. Led AL in complete games 1963 (18) and innings pitched in 1962 (299).

All-Star game: 1962 (0–0). World Series: 1960–64 (2–4 in 9 games).

Gave up Bill Mazeroski's historic ninth inning home run in seventh game of 1960 World Series in Pittsburgh to give Pirates championship.

TERRY, WILLIAM H. (Bill) 1B-BL-TL. B. 10/30/98, Atlanta, Ga. 6'1½", 200. New York Giants 1923–36. Hit .341 in 1721 games with 2193 hits, 1120 runs, 373 doubles, 112 triples, 154 home runs and 1078 RBI. Hit .300 or better 11 times. Last National Leaguer to hit .400 mark with .401 in 1930. Hit 30 or more doubles nine years and drove in 100 or more runs six straight years. Led NL in triples 1931 (20), led in hits in 1930 with 254, a record for most NL hits in season shared with Lefty O'Doul. Scored 100 or more runs seven times, tying for lead in runs in 1931 (121). Hit three successive HR in game, 8/13/32. Nine hits in doubleheader, 6/18/29. All-Star game: 1933–35 (.400). World Series: 1924, 33, 36 (.295). Named *Sporting News'* Most Valuable Player in NL in 1930. Hall of Fame 1954.

Manager of New York Giants 1932–41 (823–661). Won three pennants and Series championship in 1933 as playing manager. Author of famed controversial quote, "Is Brooklyn still in the league?" Later ran auto agency in Jacksonville, Fla. Reformed pitcher finished with one of top lifetime batting averages in game. Also excellent fielder who led in putouts at first base 1928–30, 32, 34; assists 1927, 30–32, and led or tied for best fielding average 1925, 28, 34–35.

TERRY, WILLIAM J. (Adonis) P-BR-TR. B. 8/7/64, Westfield, Mass. D. 2/25/14, Milwaukee, Wis. Brooklyn (American Association) 1884–89; Brooklyn (NL) 1890–91; Baltimore (NL) 1892; Pittsburgh (NL) 1892–94; Chicago (NL) 1894–97. Won 205, lost 197 in 424 games with 1284 strikeouts and 1244 walks. Pitched 16 shutouts and won 20 or more games five times. Best season: 26 victories in 1890.

Pitched no-hitters against St. Louis, 7/24/86, and against Louisville, 5/27/88. Umpired in NL in 1900.

TESREAU, CHARLES M. (Jeff) P-BR-TR. B. 3/5/89 Ironton, Mich. D. 9/24/46, Hanover, N.H. New York Giants 1912–18. Won 115, lost 72 in 248 games with 880 strikeouts and 572 walks in 1679 innings. Won 22 games in 1913 and 26 in 1914. Led NL in ERA 1912 (1.96). Pitched 28 shutouts, including no-hitter against Philadelphia, 9/6/12. World Series: 1912–13,17 (1–3).

After compiling lifetime percentage of .621, retired to become baseball coach at Dartmouth College.

THEOBALD, RONALD M. (Ron; Little General) Inf.-BR-TR. B. 7/28/43, Oakland, Calif. 5'8", 165. Milwaukee Brewers 1971–72. Hit .248

in 251 games with 193 hits, 95 runs, 23 doubles, 2 triples, 2 HR and 42 RBI. Hit .276 in rookie season. 1972 record: .220 in 125 games with one homer and 19 RBI. Led AL in sacrifice hits in 1971 (19).

Missed chance for possible Rookie of Year honors when name was inadvertently left off ballots.

THEVENOW, THOMAS J. (Tommy) Inf.-BR-TR. B. 9/6/03, Madison, Ind. D. 7/28/57, Madison, Ind. 5'10", 155. St. Louis Cardinals 1924–28; Philadelphia Phillies 1929–30; Pittsburgh Pirates 1931–35, 38; Cincinnati Reds 1936; Boston Braves 1937. Hit .248 in 1229 games with 1030 hits, 380 runs, 124 doubles, 32 triples, 2 home runs and 454 RBI. Best year: .286 in 1930. World Series: 1926, 28 (.417). Exploded for 10 hits in 1926 Series against New York Yankees despite .256 average during season.

Protege of Cardinal manager Rogers Hornsby, was brought up from International League by Rajah to learn game in big leagues. Hampered by injuries during playing days.

THOMAS, ALPHONSE (Tommy) P-BR-TR. B. 12/23/99, Baltimore, Md. 5'10", 175. Chicago White Sox 1926–32; Washington Senators 1932–35; Philadelphia Phillies 1935; St. Louis Browns 1936–37; Boston Red Sox 1937. Won 117, lost 128 in 399 games with 735 strikeouts and 712 walks in 2173 innings. Won 10 or more games seven times. Best season: 19–16 in 1927.

Bellwether of White Sox pitching staff during club's lean years, pitched 72 complete games over three-year period, and in one stretch hurled 25 consecutive route jobs. Minor league coach, 1940–44; scout for Boston Red Sox, 1950, 57 and 1959 to present; general manager Minneapolis Millers of International League, 1958. Named to Maryland Hall of Fame and Maryland Shrine of Immortals, and International League Hall of Fame.

THOMAS, FRANK J. OF-3B-1B-BR-TR B. 6/11/29, Pittsburgh, Pa. 6'3", 205 Pittsburgh Pirates 1951–58; Cincinnati Reds 1959; Chicago Cubs 1960–61, 1966; Milwaukee Braves 1961, 65; New York Mets 1962–64; Philadelphia Phillies 1964–65; Houston Astros 1965. Hit .266 in 1766 games with 1671 hits, 792 runs, 262 doubles, 31 triples, 286 home runs and 962 RBI. Hit 20 or more doubles six times and 20 or more homers nine years. Hit six home runs in three consecutive games in 1962. Hit three home runs in one game, 8/16/58. All-Star game: 1954 55, 58 (.200).

Successor to Ralph Kiner as Pirates' slugger. Now high school representative for business school in Pittsburgh.

THOMAS, JAMES L. (Lee) 1B-OF-BL-TR. B. 2/5/36, St. Louis, Mo. 6'2", 195. New York Yankees 1961; Los Angeles Angels 1961–64; Boston Red Sox 1964–65; Atlanta Braves 1966; Chicago Cubs 1966–67; Houston Astros 1968. Hit .255 in 1027 games with 847 hits, 405 runs, 111 doubles, 22 triples, 106 home runs and 428 RBI. Best year: .290 in 1962 with 26 homers and 104 RBI. Tied major league record with nine hits in doubleheader, 9/5/61. Hit three homers in game, 9/5/61. All-Star game: 1962 (.000). Played with Nankai Hawks in Japan in 1969.

Along with Leon Wagner, Billy Moran, Albie Pearson and Jim Fregosi, made expansionist Angels respectable team from start. Coach with Cardinals 1971–72, but assigned to manage Cards' farm in Gulf Coast League, 1973.

THOMAS, ROY A. OF-BL-TL. B. 3/24/74, Norristown, Pa. D. 11/20/59, Norristown, Pa. 5'11", 150. Philadelphia Phillies 1899–1908, 1910–11; Pittsburgh Pirates 1908; Boston Braves 1909. Hit .291 in 1457 games with 1537 hits, 1011 runs, 100 doubles, 53 triples, 10 home runs and 299 RBI. Stole 244 bases and hit .300 or better five times. Scored 100 or more runs four times, setting NL record for most runs scored in rookie season (135).

Hard to keep off base paths, drew 100 or more walks in seven seasons.

THOMPSON, DANNY L. 2B-3B-SS-BR-TR. B. 2/1/48, Wichita, Kans. 6', 180. Minnesota Twins 1970–72. Hit .256 in 288 games with 239 hits, 89 runs, 33 doubles, 6 triples, 4 home runs and 77 RBI. Best year: .276 in 144 games in 1972 with 4 HR and 48 RBI. Championship Series: 1970 (.125). Flashy versatile infielder figures greatly in Minnesota plans, despite playing with blood disorder.

THOMPSON, HENRY C. (Hank) 3B-2B-OF-BL-TL. B. 12/8/25, Oklahoma City, Okla. D. 9/30/69, Fresno, Calif. 5'9", 174. St. Louis Browns 1947; New York Giants 1949–56. Hit .267 in 933 games with 801 hits, 492 runs, 104 doubles, 34 triples, 129 home runs and 482 RBI. Best year: .302 in 1953 with 24 HR and 74 RBI. Holds NL record for most double plays by third baseman in 154 games (43), in 1950. World Series: 1951, 54 (.240). Holds record for most walks in four-game series (7) in 1954. Hit three home runs in one game, 6/3/54.

One of first blacks in major league baseball, came to Browns from Kansas City Monarchs. Later served prison term in Texas for robbery conviction, then worked with youth groups in Fresno, Calif., after parole.

THOMPSON, LAFAYETTE F. (Fresco) 2B-BR-TR. B. 6/6/02, Centreville, Ala. D. 11/20/68, Fullerton, Calif. 5'8", 150. Pittsburgh Pirates 1925; New York Giants 1926, 34; Philadelphia Phillies 1927–30; Brooklyn Dodgers 1931–32. Hit .298 in 669 games with 762 hits, 400 runs, 149 doubles, 34 triples, 13 home runs and 245 RBI. Hit .300 or better twice. Best year: .324 in 1929. Hit 30 or more doubles four consecutive years.

Scrappy infielder scouted for Brooklyn Dodgers 1942, 46–47. Appointed Dodger farm director 1949–68. Elevated to vice president and general manager of Dodgers. Authored book *Every Diamond Doesn't Sparkle.*

THOMPSON, SAMUEL L. (Big Sam) OF-BL. B. 3/5/60, Danville, Ind. D. 11/7/22, Detroit, Mich. 6'2", 207. Detroit (NL) 1885–88; Philadelphia Phillies 1889–98; Detroit Tigers 1906. Hit .336 in 1405 games with 2016 hits, 1259 runs, 326 doubles, 146 triples, 129 home runs and 235 stolen bases. Hit .300 or better nine times, including .406 in 1887 and .404 in 1894. Led NL in hits 1893 (200) and tied for most hits 1890 (172). Led in doubles 1890 (38); triples 1887 (23) and tied for most triples 1895 (22). Led in home runs 1889 (20) and tied for most homers 1896 (13). Got six hits in game, 8/17/94. World Series: 1887 (.377).

In 1894 made up awesome outfield with his .406 season complimenting Ed Delhanty's .400 average and Billy Hamilton's .399 mark. Utility outfielder George Turner added to attack with .423 average. Thompson's 126 homers stood as major league record until broken by Babe Ruth in 1922.

THOMSON, ROBERT B. (Bobby; The Scot) OF-3B-BR-TR. B. 10/25/23, Glasgow, Scotland. 6'2", 180. New York Giants 1946–53, 1957; Milwaukee Braves 1954–57; Chicago Cubs 1958–59; Boston Red Sox 1960; Baltimore Orioles 1960. Hit .270 in 1779 games with 1705 hits, 903 runs, 267 doubles, 74 triples, 264 home runs and 1026 RBI. Hit 20 or more doubles eight times and 20 or more homers during eight seasons. Drove in 100 or more runs four years. Led NL in triples 1952 (14). All-Star game: 1948–49, 52 (.000). World Series: 1951 (.238).

Now residing in New Jersey and employed by paper firm, Thomson hit one of baseball's most dramatic home runs ("the shot heard round the world"), capping Giants' drive to pennant in 1951 after falling 13-1/2 games behind rival Brooklyn in mid-August. Thomson won flag for Giants with three-run shot off Dodgers' Ralph Branca in ninth inning of third and final playoff game. New York was trailing 4–1 going into that frame. One run scored, making it 4–2. Then with two men on, one out, Thomson lined Branca fast ball into baseball history.

THORPE, JAMES F. (Jim) OF-BLR-TR. B. 5/28/86, Prague, Okla. D. 3/28/53, Lomita, Calif. 6'1", 185. New York Giants 1913–15, 1917–19; Cincinnati Reds 1917; Boston Braves 1919. Hit .252 in 289 games with 176 hits, 91 runs, 20 doubles, 18 triples, 10 home runs and 91 RBI. World Series: 1917 (.000).

Possibly greatest of all athletes, failed to stick in major leagues after long trials with three clubs. All-American football star at Carlisle College, became worldwide legend as result of heroics in 1912 Olympic Games in Stockholm. Attempted to launch career as night club entertainer shortly before death.

THRONEBERRY, MARVIN E. (Marvelous Marv) 1B-OF-BL-TL. B. 9/2/33, Memphis, Tenn. 6'1", 190. New York Yankees 1955, 58–59; Kansas City A's 1960–61; Baltimore Orioles 1961–62; New York Mets 1962–63. Hit .237 in 480 games with 281 hits, 143 runs, 37 doubles, 8 triples, 53 home runs and 170 RBI. Best year: .250 in 1960. World Series: 1958 (.000).

Symbolized inept play of Mets in club's early years and was idolized in reverse by thousands of Mets' fans across country. Now sportscaster in Memphis. Brother of former major league outfielder Faye Throneberry.

THURSTON, HOLLIS J. (Sloppy) P-BR-TR. B. 6/2/99, Fremont, Nebr. 5'11", 165. St. Louis Browns 1923; Chicago White Sox 1923–26; Washington Senators 1927; Brooklyn Dodgers 1930–33. Won 89, lost 86 in 288 games with 306 strikeouts and 369 walks in 1534 innings. Best season: 20–14 in 38 games with league-leading 28 complete games.

One of baseball's more colorful performers, was on mound for White Sox when Babe Ruth was lifted for pinch hitter, Bobby Veach. Later played first base for San Francisco Seals and scouted for Pittsburgh Pirates, Cleveland Indians and White Sox for past 25 years.

TIANT, LUIS C. P-BR-TR. B. 11/23/40, Havana, Cuba. 5'11", 187. Cleveland Indians 1964–69; Minnesota Twins 1970; Boston Red Sox 1971–72. Won 98, lost 80 in 293 games with 1273 strikeouts and 570 walks in 1544 innings. Won 10 or more games six times, including 21–9 in 1968 with 264 strikeouts and league-leading 1.60 ERA. 1972 record: 15–6 in 43 games with 123 strikeouts and 1.91 ERA, best in AL. Lifetime ERA under three runs. Pitched six shutouts in 1972, hiking total to 28. Led AL in shutouts 1968 (9), and tied for most shutouts in 1966 (5). League-leading ERA in 1972 lowest in AL since 1919. Struck out 19 batters in 10-inning game, 7/3/68. All-Star game: 1968 (0–1). Championship Series: 1970 (0–0).

Won 11 of 12 games during Boston's run for division title in '72, making great comeback from lone victory in 1971. Holds unique record of fewest hits allowed per nine innings in season as starting pitcher: 5.29 in 258 innings in 1968. Winner of *Sporting News'* Comeback of the Year Award in 1972.

TIDROW, RICHARD W. (Dick) P-BR-TR. B. 5/14/47, San Francisco, Calif. 6'4", 215. Cleveland Indians 1972. Won 14, lost 15 in 39 games with 123 strikeouts and 70 walks in 237 innings. Pitched three shutouts and had ERA of 2.77.

Named Rookie Pitcher of the Year in 1972 by the *Sporting News*. An Indian with a future.

TIERNAN, MICHAEL J. (Silent Mike) OF-BL-TL. B. 1/21/67, Trenton, N.J. D. 11/9/18, New York, N.Y. 5'11", 165. New York Giants 1887–99. Hit .317 in 1474 games with 1875 hits, 1312 runs, 248 doubles, 159 triples, 108 home runs. Hit .300 or better eight times. Best season: .361 in 1896. Led NL in runs scored 1889 (146). Scored six runs in game, 6/15/87. Hit 10 or more triples 11 times, scored 100 or more runs seven years. Tied for league lead in homers 1890 (13) and 1891 (16). Stole 449 bases during career, including high of 56 in 1890. Led outfielders in fielding average, 1888 and 1898.

TILLMAN, JOHN R. (Bob) C-BR-TR. B. 3/24/37, Nashville, Tenn. 6'4", 205. Boston Red Sox 1962–67; New York Yankees 1967; Atlanta Braves 1968–70. Hit .232 in 775 games with 540 hits, 189 runs, 68 doubles, 10 triples, 79 home runs and 282 RBI. Best season: .278 in 1964. Hit three home runs in game, 7/30/69. Held Boston team record for most homers in season by catcher (17) until broken in 1972 by Carlton Fisk.

TIMMERMAN, THOMAS H. (Tom) P-BR-TR. B. 5/12/40, Breese, Ill. 6'4", 210. Detroit Tigers 1969–72. Won 25, lost 26 in 178 games with 230 strikeouts and 138 walks in 375 innings. Best year: 6–7 in 1970 with 27 saves and 4.13 ERA. 1972 record: 8–10 in 34 games with 88 strikeouts and 2.88 ERA. Sinker ball specialist turned into starting pitcher in 1972 after relieving in 1970 and '71.

TINKER, JOSEPH B. (Joe) SS-3B-BR-TR. B. 7/27/80, Muscotah, Kans. D. 7/27/48, Orlando, Fla. 5'9", 175. Chicago Cubs 1902–13, 1916; Cincinnati Reds 1913; Chicago (Federal) 1914–15. Hit .264 in 1642 games with 1565 hits, 716 runs, 238 doubles, 106 triples, 29 home runs and 783 RBI. Hit 20 or more doubles eight seasons and 10 or more triples five times. Led NL shortstops in putouts, 1911–12; assists, 1908, 11; fielding average, 1906, 08, 11, 13, and tied for best fielding average, 1909. Hall of Fame 1946. World Series: 1906–08, 1910 (.235). Manager Cincinnati Reds, 1913; Chicago Federals, 1914–15; Chicago Cubs, 1916. Record: 457–406. Also president and manager of team in American Association, 1917–20. Manager and owner of team in Florida State League, 1921–23.

Famed member of Tinker to Evers to Chance double-play combination. Feuded continually with Evers and didn't speak to him for three-year period. Later operated billiard parlor and bar and lost leg in bout with diabetes.

TITUS, JOHN F. (Silent John) OF-BL-TL. B. 2/21/76, St. Clair, Pa. D. 1/8/43, St. Clair, Pa. Philadelphia Phillies 1903–12; Boston Braves 1912–13. Hit .282 in 1371 games with 1400 hits, 738 runs, 252 doubles, 72 triples, 38 home runs and 561 RBI. Hit .300 or better twice. Best season: .309 in 1912. Hit 20 or more doubles eight times.

Until Oakland A's of 1972 came along, was the last player in big leagues to wear handlebar mustache. Also picked up trademark of munching on toothpick while batting.

TOBIN, JAMES A. (Abba Dabba) P-BR-TR. B. 12/27/12, Oakland, Calif. D. 5/19/69, Oakland, Calif. 6′, 185. Pittsburgh Pirates 1937–39; Boston Braves 1940–45; Detroit Tigers 1945. Won 105, lost 112 in 287 games with 498 strikeouts and 557 walks in 1900 innings. Won 12 or more ganes six times. Best year: 18–19 in 1944. Pitched no-hitter against Brooklyn, 4/27/44. Led NL in complete games 1942 (28) and 1944 (28), and innings pitched 1942 (287). All-Star game: 1944 (0–0). World Series: 1945 (0–0).

Durable knuckleball pitcher also fine batter, hit three home runs in one game, 5/13/42. Hit 17 home runs lifetime, including six in one season. Pinch hitter and played several games at first base for Boston in 1943. Brother of John P. Tobin, who played 84 games with Boston Red Sox in 1945. Later became bartender in Oakland.

TOBIN, JOHN T. (Johnny) OF-1B-BL-TL. B. 5/4/92, St. Louis, Mo. D. 12/10/69, St. Louis, Mo. 5′8″, 148. St. Louis (Federal League) 1913–15; St. Louis Browns 1916, 1918–25; Washington Senators 1926; Boston Red Sox 1926–27. Hit .315 in 1322 games with 1579 hits, 763 runs, 244 doubles, 76 triples, 51 home runs and 498 RBI. Hit .300 or better six times. Best year: .352 in 1921. Made 200 or more hits, 1920–23. Hit 30 or more doubles five seasons, 1920–24.

One of baseball's finest bunters, formed great outfield with Ken Williams and Bill (Baby Doll) Jacobson. Trio hit .300 or better from 1919 through 1923. Later managed in minors and coached for Browns, 1944–48. Also served as scout for Browns, 1949–51.

TOLAN, ROBERT (Bob) OF-1B-BL-TL. B. 11/19/45, Los Angeles, Calif. 5′11″, 175. St. Louis Cardinals 1965–68; Cincinnati Reds 1969–72. Hit .280 in 715 games with 711 hits, 385 runs, 113 doubles, 26 triples, 57 home runs and 316 RBI. Hit .300 or better twice. Best year: .316 in 1970 with 16 HR and 80 RBI. 1972 record: .283 in 149 games with 8 HR and 82 RBI. Hit 25 or more doubles three times. Led NL in stolen bases 1970 (57). Championship Series: 1970,72 (.292). World Series: 1967–68, 1970,72 (.229).

Came back from torn Achilles tendon in 1971 which caused him to miss entire season. Incredibly, stole 42 bases in 1972 and led outfielders in putouts, showing no signs of previous injury. Winner of *Sporting News'* Comeback of the Year Award in 1972.

TONEY, FREDERICK A. (Fred) P-BR-TR. B. 12/11/87, Nashville, Tenn. D. 3/11/53, Nashville, Tenn. 6'1", 195. Chicago Cubs 1911–13; Cincinnati Reds 1915–18; New York Giants 1919–22; St. Louis Cardinals 1923. Won 139, lost 102 in 337 games with 718 strikeouts and 583 walks in 2206 innings. Won 10 or more games seven times, including 24 in 1917 and 21 in 1920. Won two complete games in one day, 7/1/17. Tossed 29 shutouts, most memorable being 10-inning no-hitter against Chicago, 5/2/17. Toney's opponent, James (Hippo) Vaughn, hurled 9-1/3 innings of hitless ball before losing 1–0. Toney also threw no-hitter for 17 innings in Blue Grass League. World Series: 1921 (0–0).

TOPORCER, GEORGE (Specs) Inf.-BL-TL. B. 2/9/99, New York, N.Y. 5'10½", 165. St. Louis Cardinals 1921–28. Hit .279 in 546 games with 437 hits, 223 runs, 76 doubles, 22 triples, 9 home runs and 151 RBI. Best season: .323 in 1922. World Series: 1926 (.000).

First player in modern times to wear eyeglasses, proving infielders could play in majors wearing spectacles. Later lost his sight, but became fine front office executive.

TORGESON, CLIFFORD E. (Earl; Torgie) 1B-BL-TL. B. 1/1/24, Snohomish, Wash. 6'3", 190. Boston Braves 1947–52; Philadelphia Phillies 1953–55; Detroit Tigers 1955–57; Chicago White Sox 1957–61; New York Yankees 1961. Hit .265 in 1668 games with 1318 hits, 848 runs, 215 doubles, 46 triples, 149 home runs and 740 RBI. Best season: .290 in 1950 with league-leading number of runs (120). Hit 20 or more doubles six times. Had seven RBI in two consecutive innings, 6/30/51. World Series:1948, 59 (.368). Led Braves in hitting in 1948 Series with .389. Led NL first basemen assists, 1950. Hampered by shoulder injuries throughout career.

TORRE, FRANK J. 1B-BL-TL. B. 12/30/31, Brooklyn, N.Y. 6'1", 210. Milwaukee Braves 1956–60; Philadelphia Phillies 1962–63. Hit .273 in 714 games with 404 hits, 150 runs, 78 doubles, 15 triples, 13 home runs and 179 RBI. Best year: .309 in 1958. Led NL first basemen in fielding average, 1957–58.

Brother of St. Louis Cardinals star Joe Torre. Now executive with firm which manufacturers baseball bats.

TORRE, JOSEPH P. C-1B-3B-BR-TR. B. 7/18/40, Brooklyn, N.Y. 6'1", 210. Milwaukee Braves 1960–65; Atlanta Braves 1966–68; St. Louis Cardinals 1969–72. Hit .303 in 1667 games with 1851 hits, 799 runs, 270 doubles, 50 triples, 216 home runs and 971 RBI. Hit .300 or better four times. Best year: League-leading .363 in in 1971 with 24 HR and 137 RBI. 1972 record: .289 in 149 games with 11 HR and 81 RBI. Led NL in 1971 in hits (230) and total bases (352) as well as RBI. Named league's Most Valuable Player in 1971. Led NL catchers in fielding average, 1964, 68, and double plays, 1967. Hit 20 or more doubles eight times, 20 or more homers six times and drove in 100 or more runs five years. All-Star game: 1963–67, 70–72 (.111).

Brother of former major leaguer Frank Torre. Shed excess weight and moved to third base in 1971 and had field day on NL pitching. Led third basemen in putouts, 1971.

TORRES, HECTOR E. SS-2B-BR-TR. B. 9/16/45, Monterrey, Mexico. 6', 175. Houston Astros 1968–70; Chicago Cubs 1971; Montreal Expos 1972. Hit .205 in 307 games with 172 hits, 73 runs, 20 doubles, 4 triples, 4 home runs and 46 RBI. Best year: .223 in 1968 with one home run and 24 RBI. 1972 record: .155 in 83 games with two homers and seven RBI.

As teenager, led Monterrey team to Little League championship in Junior World Series played in Williamsport, Pa. Father was former minor league manager.

TORREZ, MICHAEL A. (Mike) P-BR-TR. B. 8/28/46, Topeka, Kans. 6'5", 220. St. Louis Cardinals 1967–71; Montreal Expos 1971–72. Won 37, lost 30 in 106 games with 294 strikeouts and 312 walks in 594 innings. Best year: 16–12 in 1972 with 112 strikeouts and ERA of 3.33. Led Expos in wins in first season with Montreal and tied for most complete games (13). Won 10, lost 4 in 1969 with 62 strikeouts and 3.58 ERA.

TOVAR, CESAR L. Inf.-OF-BR-TR. B. 7/3/40, Caracas, Venezuela. 5'9", 155. Minnesota Twins 1965–72. Philadelphia (NL) 1973. Hit .281 in 1090 games with 1164 hits, 646 runs, 193 doubles, 45 triples, 38 home runs and 319 RBI. Hit .300 or better twice. Best year: .311 in 1971 with one home run and 45 RBI. 1972 record: .265 in 141 games with two home runs and 31 RBI. Hit 25 or more doubles five years, tying for lead in 1970 (36). Led AL in triples 1970 (13). Championship Series: 1969–70 (.231).

Played every position, including pitcher, during nine-inning game,

9/22/68. Caused slight uproar after 1967 season by collecting lone dissenting first-place vote for Most Valuable Player, preventing clean sweep by Boston Red Sox slugger Carl Yastrzemski for honor. Traded to Philadelphia Phillies for Joe Lis and Ken Reynolds after 1972 season.

TRAVERS, ALOYSIUS J. P-BR-TR. B. 5/7/92, Philadelphia, Pa. D. 4/19/68, Philadelphia, Pa. 6'1", 180. Pitched and lost only major league game—setting a record in process for most runs allowed in nine-inning contest, 24, on 5/18/12. Member of St. Joseph College baseball team and along with teammates played as Detroit Tigers for one game when regular Detroit players refused to play Philadelphia A's in support of Ty Cobb. Tiger superstar suspended by AL president Ban Johnson for going into stands in game at New York and brawling with heckling fan. Travers later became Jesuit priest.

TRAVIS, CECIL H. 3B-SS-OF-BL-TR. B. 8/8/13, Riverdale, Ga. 6'1½", 195. Washington Senators 1933–47. Hit .313 in 1328 games with 1544 hits, 665 runs, 265 doubles, 78 triples, 27 home runs and 657 RBI. Hit .300 or better seven times. Best year: .359 in 1941. Hit 20 or more doubles nine times. Led AL in hits, 1941 (218). All-Star game: 1938, 40–41 (.143). Made five hits in first major league game, 5/16/33. Scouted for Washington, 1948–55. Now operates cattle farm in Georgia.

TRAYNOR, HAROLD J. (Pie) 3B-SS-BR-TR. B. 11/11/99, Framingham, Mass. D. 3/16/72, Pittsburgh, Pa. 6'½", 175. Pittsburgh Pirates 1920–37. Hit .320 in 1941 games with 2416 hits, 1183 runs, 371 doubles, 164 triples, 58 home runs and 1273 RBI. Hit .300 or better 10 times. Best season: .366 in 1930. Hit 22 or more doubles 11 times, 10 or more triples 11 times. Tied for NL lead in triples 1923 (19). All-Star game: 1933–34 (.500). World Series: 1925, 27 (.293). Hall of Fame 1948. Had 100 or more RBI seven times.

Considered game's greatest third baseman along with Brooks Robinson, Pie led NL third basemen in putouts, 1923, 25–27, 31, 33–34; assists, 1923, 25, 33, and fielding average, 1925. Holds NL mark (2288) for most putouts by third baseman. Managed Pittsburgh Pirates, 1934–39 (457–406). Scouted for Pirates, 1940–72. After managerial reign, became popular television announcer in Pittsburgh for more than two decades.

TRESH, MICHAEL (Mike) C-BR-TR. B. 2/23/14, Hazleton, Pa. D. 10/4/66, Detroit, Mich. 5'11", 170. Chicago White Sox 1938–48; Cleveland Indians 1949. Hit .249 in 1027 games with 788 hits, 326 runs, 74 doubles, 14 triples, two home runs and 297 RBI. Best year: .281 in 1940 with one home run and 64 RBI. Led AL catchers in putouts, 1940–41; assists, 1945, and double plays, 1946.

Father of Tom Tresh, outfielder and shortstop with New York Yankees and Detroit Tigers.

TRESH, THOMAS M. (Tom) OF-Inf.-BLR-TR. B. 9/20/38, Detroit, Mich. 6'1", 190. New York Yankees 1961–69; Detroit Tigers 1969. Hit .245 in 1192 games with 1041 hits, 595 runs, 179 doubles, 34 triples, 154 home runs and 530 RBI. Best season: .286 in 1962. Hit 20 or more doubles five times and 20 or more homers four years. Hit three successive homers in game, 6/6/65. All-Star game: 1962−63 (.500). World Series, 1962–64, .277. Led AL outfielders in fielding average, 1964.

Son of Mike Tresh, catcher with White Sox and Indians for more than decade. Named Rookie of the Year by *Sporting News* and baseball writers in 1962.

TRIANDOS, GUS C-BR-TR. B. 7/30/30, San Francisco, Calif. 6'3", 225. New York Yankees 1953–54; Baltimore Orioles 1955–62; Detroit Tigers 1963; Philadelphia Phillies 1964–65; Houston Astros 1965. Hit .244 in 1206 games with 954 hits, 389 runs, 147 doubles, 6 triples, 167 home runs and 608 RBI. Best year: .279 in 1956. Hit 20 or more home runs three times, including 30 in 1958. All-Star game: 1957–59 (.333). Led AL catchers in putouts, 1958; assists, 1957, 59, and double plays, 1957, 61.

TROSKY, HAROLD A. (Hal) 1B-BL-TR. B. 11/11/12, Norway, Iowa. 6'2½", 198. Cleveland Indians 1933–41; Chicago White Sox 1944, 46. Hit .302 in 1347 games with 1561 hits, 835 runs, 331 doubles, 58 triples, 228 home runs and 1013 RBI. Hit .300 or better four times. Best year: .343 in 1936. Hit 30 or more doubles eight times, 25 or more homers six years, and drove in 100 or more runs six straight seasons. Led AL in RBI 1936 (162). Hit three home runs in game, 5/30/34 and 7/5/37. Led AL first basemen in putouts, 1934–35, and assists, 1934.

Beset by migraine headaches which shortened his career. Missed all of 1942, 1943 and 1945 seasons because of illness. Incredibly, was never named to an All-Star squad in AL. Scouted for Chicago White Sox, 1947–48.

TROUT, PAUL H. (Dizzy) P-BR-TR. B. 6/29/15, Sandcut, Ind. D. 2/28/72, Chicago, Ill. 6'2½", 195. Detroit Tigers 1939–52; Boston Red Sox 1952; Baltimore Orioles 1957. Won 170, lost 161 in 535 games with 1256 strikeouts and 1046 walks in 2725 innings. Won 10 or more games nine times. Best year: 27–14 in 1944. Led AL in wins 1943 (20). Led in ERA, 1944 (2.12); shutouts, 1944 (7); complete games, 1944 (33), and innings pitched, 1944 (352). Pitched 27 shutouts lifetime. All-Star game:

1944, 47 (0–0). World Series: 1940, 45 (1–2).

Colorful pitcher teamed with Hal Newhouser to win combined 56 games for Detroit in 1944. Hurled six games in nine days—winning four—during Tigers' stretch drive for pennant in 1945. Later worked as Tiger broadcaster, then as director of Chicago White Sox speakers' bureau, 1959–72.

TRUCKS, VIRGIL O. (Fire) P-BR-TR. B. 4/26/19, Birmingham, Ala. 6', 210. Detroit Tigers 1941–52, 1956; St. Louis Browns 1953; Chicago White Sox 1953–55; Kansas City A's 1957–58; New York Yankees 1958. Won 177, lost 135 in 517 games with 1534 strikeouts and 1088 walks in 2684 innings. Won 10 or more games 10 times, including 20 in 1953 and 19 in 1949 and 1954. Threw 34 shutouts, three of them in 1952. Although win total was only five in '52, one shutout was one-hitter and other two were no-hitters against Washington, 5/15, and New York, 8/25. Led AL in strikeouts, 1949 (153). All-Star game: 1949, 54 (1–0). World Series: 1945 (1–0).

Counting two no-hitters in majors, pitched six in organized baseball. Later coach for Pittsburgh Pirates, 1963. Also worked as stockbroker in Pittsburgh. Scout for Atlanta Braves since 1969.

TUCKER, THOMAS J. (Foghorn) 1B-BLR-TR. B. 10/28/63, Holyoke, Mass. D. 10/22/35, Montague, Mass. 5'11", 165. Baltimore (American Association) 1887–89; Boston (NL) 1890–97; Washington (NL) 1897; Brooklyn (NL) 1898; St. Louis (NL) 1898; Cleveland (NL) 1899. Hit .295 in 1686 games with 1882 hits, 1084 runs, 240 doubles, 85 triples, 45 home runs and 848 RBI. Batted over .300 four seasons, including .375 in 1889. Led NL in hits, 1889 (196). Six hits in game, 7/15/97. Hit 15 or more doubles 12 times. Scored 100 or more runs five years. Stole 352 bases with season high of 85 in 1887.

TUCKER, THURMAN L. (Joe E.) OF-BL-TR. B. 9/26/17, Gordon, Tex. 5'10½". 165. Chicago White Sox 1942–44, 46–47; Cleveland Indians 1948–51. Hit .255 in 701 games with 570 hits, 325 runs, 79 doubles, 24 triples, 9 home runs and 179 RBI. Best year: .288 in 1946. World Series: 1948: (.333). Gained nickname from the late comedian Joe E. Brown, whom Tucker resembled.

TURLEY, ROBERT L. (Bullet Bob) P-BR-TR. B. 9/19/30, Troy, Ill. 6'2", 215. St. Louis Browns 1951,53; Baltimore Orioles 1954; New York Yankees 1955–62; Los Angeles Dodgers 1963; Boston Red Sox 1963. Won 101, lost 85 in 310 games with 1265 strikeouts and 1068 walks in 1712 innings. Best year: League-leading 21 wins in 1958. Led AL in strikeouts in 1954 (185), fanning 10 or more in game 17 times. Led in walks 1954 (181), 1955 (177) and 1958 (128). Hurled 24 shutouts. All-Star game: 1954, 55, 58 (0–0). World Series: 1955–58, 60 (4–3 in 15 games, including two wins in 1958 Series). Cy Young Award, 1958.

Had humming fast ball but plagued by control problems. Pitching coach with Boston Red Sox, 1964. Now sells securities in Atlanta, Ga.

TURNER, JAMES R. (Milkman) P-BL-TR. B. 8/6/04, Antioch, Tenn. 6′, 185. Boston Braves 1937–39; Cincinnati Reds 1940–42; New York Yankees 1942–45. Won 69, lost 60 in 238 games with 329 strikeouts and 283 walks in 1132 innings. Best year: 20–11 in rookie season at age of 33. In 1937 led NL in ERA (2.38), complete games (24) and tied for most shutouts (6). All-Star game: 1938 (0–0). World Series: 1940, 42 (0–1).

Celebrated 50th year in organized baseball in 1972, having played first minor league game for Paris club in Kitty League in 1923. Managed in minors, 1946–48, 1960. Coach with New York Yankees, 1949–59, 66–72, and Cincinnati Reds, 1961–65. One of game's more knowledgeable pitching instructors, helped develop host of fine Yankee hurlers, including Whitey Ford, Allie Reynolds, Vic Raschi, Ed Lopat, Mel Stottlemyre and Fritz Peterson.

TUTTLE, WILLIAM R. (Bill) OF-BR-TR. B. 7/4/29, Elmwood, Ill. 6′, 185. Detroit Tigers 1952, 54–57; Kansas City A's 1958–61; Minnesota Twins 1961–63. Hit .259 in 1270 games with 1105 hits, 578 runs, 149 doubles, 47 triples, 67 home runs and 443 RBI. Best season: .300 in 1959. Hit 20 or more doubles four times. Led AL outfielders in putouts, 1955, 60, and assists, 1959–60.

TYLER, GEORGE A. (Lefty) P-BL-TL. B. 12/14/89, Derry, N.H. D. 9/29/53, Lowell, Mass. Boston Braves 1910–17; Chicago Cubs 1918–21. Won 127, lost 118 in 392 games with 1003 strikeouts and 829 walks in 2230 innings. Won 10 or more games eight times. Best year: 19–8 in 1918. Durable hurler pitched 34 shutouts and completed 182 starting assignments. World Series: 1914, 18 (1–1).

Probably only player in organized sports to be prohibited from using toothpicks during game due to Tyler's proclivity for using sticks as catapult for BBs which he shot from his mouth at opposing players and umpires.

UECKER, ROBERT G. (Bob) C-BR-TR. B. 1/26/35, Milwaukee, Wis. 6'1", 190. Milwaukee Braves 1962–63; St. Louis Cardinals 1964–65; Philadelphia Phillies 1966–67; Atlanta Braves 1967. Hit .200 in 297 games but parlayed weak hitting into vehicle for humor on national television shows and banquet circuit. Claims to have gone "0 for June and July." Also broadcasts Milwaukee Brewer baseball games.

UHLAENDER, THEODORE O. (Ted) OF-BL-TR. B. 10/21/39, McAllen, Tex. 6'2", 188. Minnesota Twins 1965–69; Cleveland Indians 1970–71; Cincinnati Reds 1972. Hit .263 in 898 games with 772 hits, 343 runs, 114 doubles, 21 triples, 36 home runs, and 285 RBI. Best year: .288 in 1971 with 2 HR and 47 RBI. 1972 record: .159 in 73 games with no home runs and 6 RBI. Hit 18 or more doubles five times. Championship Series: 1969, 72 (.143). World Series: 1972 (.250).

UHLE, GEORGE E. (Bull) P-BR-TR. B. 9/18/98, Cleveland, Ohio. 6', 190. Cleveland Indians 1919–28, 1936; Detroit Tigers 1929–33; New York Giants 1933; New York Yankees 1933–34. Won 200, lost 166 in 513 games with 1135 strikeouts and 966 walks in 3120 innings. Won 10 or more games 10 times, including 20 or more three years. Led AL wins 1923 (26) and 1926 (27); led in innings pitched 1923 (358) and 1926 (318); led in percentage 1926 (.711) and walks 1926 (118). World Series: 1920 (0–0).

One of first pitchers to throw slider, exhibited durability in pitching 20 innings of 21-inning game, 5/24/29. Good hitter, hit three doubles in game, 6/1/23; drove in six runs in game, 4/28/21/. Coach with Cleveland Indians 1937, Chicago Cubs 1940, Washington Senators 1944; scout Brooklyn Dodgers 1941–42. Also coached in minor leagues 1938–39. Later employed as manufacturer's representative in Bay Village, Ohio.

UNSER, DELBERT B. (Del) OF-BL-TL. B. 12/9/44, Decatur, Ill. 6', 180. Washington Senators 1968–71; Cleveland Indians 1972. Hit .253 in 713 games with 634 hits, 264 runs, 68 doubles, 22 triples, 23 home runs and 175 RBI. Best year: .286 in 1969 with 7 HR and 57 RBI. 1972 record: .238 in 132 games with 1 HR and 17 RBI. Led AL outfielders in double plays 1968 (10).

Son of Al Unser, former major league catcher and currently scout with Cleveland Indians. Named Rookie Player of the Year by *Sporting News* in 1968. Traded to Philadelphia Phillies after 1972 season.

UPSHAW, CECIL L. P-BR-TR. B. 10/22/42, Spearsville, La. 6'6", 205. Atlanta Braves 1966–72. Won 30, lost 25 in 236 games with 243 strikeouts and 111 walks in 406 innings. Best year: 6–4 in 1969 with 27 saves and 2.91 ERA in 62 games. 1972 record: 3–5 in 42 games with 13 saves and 3.67 ERA. Championship Series: 1969 (0–0).

Never started game in entire career and earned 70 saves through 1972. One of NL's best relievers, missed all of 1970 season due to freak injury to pitching hand. Traded to Houston 1973.

VALO, ELMER W. OF-BL-TR. B. 3/5/21, Ribnik, Czechoslovakia. 5'11", 190. Philadelphia A's 1940–43, 46–54; Kansas City A's 1955–56; Philadelphia Phillies 1956, 61; Brooklyn Dodgers 1957; Los Angeles Dodgers 1958; Cleveland Indians 1959; New York Yankees 1960; Washington Senators 1960; Minnesota Twins 1961. Hit .282 in 1806 games with 1420 hits, 768 runs, 228 doubles, 73 triples, 58 home runs and 601 RBI. Hit .300 or better five times. Best year: .364 in 112 games in 1955. Hit 15 or more doubles seven times.

Fine utility man later in career, had 90 pinch hits in 386 at bats. Currently scout for Phillies.

VANCE, ARTHUR C. (Dazzy) P-BR-TR. B. 3/4/91, Orient, Iowa. D. 2/16/61, Homosassa Springs, Fla. 6'1", 200. Pittsburgh Pirates 1915; New York Yankees 1915, 18; Brooklyn Dodgers 1922–32, 35, St. Louis Cardinals 1933–34; Cincinnati Reds 1934. Won 197, lost 140 in 442 games with 2045 strikeouts and 840 walks in 2967 innings. Won 20 or more games three times, leading NL wins 1924 (28) and 1925 (22). Led NL in ERA 1924 (2.16); 1928 (2.09), and 1930 (2.61), the latter achieved in baseball's most offensive year ever. Led league in strikeouts an NL record of seven consecutive years: 1922 (134), 1923 (197), 1924 (262), 1925 (221), 1926 (140), 1927 (184) and 1928 (200). Struck out 100 or more batters 11 straight years. Threw 32 shutouts. Pitched no-hitter against Philadelphia, 9/13/25. NL's Most Valuable Player 1924. World Series: 1934 (0–0). Hall of Fame 1955.

Despite tremendous fast ball and trials with Pirates and Yankees, didn't win first major league game until reaching age of 31. Later operated fishing camp in Florida.

VANDER MEER, JOHN S. (Johnny) P-BR-TL. B. 11/2/14, Prospect Park, N.J. 6'1", 190. Cincinnati Reds 1937–49; Chicago Cubs 1950; Cleveland Indians 1951. Won 119, lost 121 in 382 games with 1294 strikeouts and 1132 walks in 2104 innings. Won 10 or more games six times. Best year: 18–12 in 1942. Led NL strikeouts 1941 (202), 1942 (186) and 1943 (174). Pitched 31 shutouts, including two no-hitters, 6/11/38 against Boston and 6/15/38 against Brooklyn. Loaded bases in ninth during second no-hitter. With one out, Ernie Koy hit into forceout at home for second out. Leo Durocher flied to Harry Craft to end game. Also pitched 15 innings of longest scoreless tie in baseball history, 19 innings against Brooklyn, 9/11/46. World Series: 1940 (0–0). All-Star game: 1938, 42–43 (1–0).

Hard-throwing southpaw developed sore arm in 1949. Later managed Class D to AAA in minor leagues and now is area sales manager for brewery in Tampa, Fla.

VANGILDER, ELAM R. (Russ) P-BR-TR. B. 4/23/96, Cape Girardeau, Mo. 6'1", 192. St. Louis Browns 1919–27; Detroit Tigers 1928–29. Won 99, lost 102 in 367 games with 474 strikeouts and 700 walks in 1715 innings. Won 10 or more games six times. Best year: 19–13 in 1922. Holds record for most games pitched in Browns uniform (323). Won three games in three days in relief against Philadelphia A's in 1925. Now farms in Cape Girardeau.

VAN HALTREN, GEORGE E. (Rip) OF-P-BL-TL. B. 3/30/66, St. Louis, Mo. D. 10/1/45, Oakland, Calif. Chicago (NL) 1887–89; Brooklyn (Players League) 1890; Baltimore (American Association) 1891–92; Pittsburgh (NL) 1892–93; New York Giants 1894–1903. Hit .322 in 1975 games with 2527 hits, 1606 runs, 293 doubles, 159 triples, 69 home runs and 537 RBI. Hit .300 or better 12 times. Best year: .353 in 1896. Hit 20 or more doubles nine times, 10 or more triples in nine seasons. Tied for NL lead in triples 1896 (21). Scored 100 or more runs 10 times and stole 537 bases with high of 57 in 1892. Pitching record: 41–30 in 87 games.

Much better hitter than hurler, he tied major league record for most walks issued by pitcher in game (16), 6/27/87. Umpired in minor leagues 1909, 12. Scouted for Pittsburgh Pirates 1910–11.

VAUGHN, HARRY F. (Farmer) C-1B-OF-BR-TR. B. 3/1/64, Rural Dale, Ohio. D. 2/21/14, Cincinnati, Ohio. 6'3", 177. Cincinnati (American Association) 1886, 91; Louisville (AA) 1888–89; New York (Players League) 1890; Milwaukee (AA) 1891; Cincinnati Reds 1892–99. Hit .276

in 877 games with 946 hits, 474 runs, 147 doubles, 54 triples, 19 home runs and 525 RBI. Had several seasons of .300 or above. Umpired in the NL in 1899.

VAUGHN, JAMES L. (Hippo) P-BL-TL. B. 4/9/88, Weatherford, Tex. D. 5/29/66, Chicago, Ill. 6'4", 215. New York Yankees 1908, 1910–12; Washington Senators 1912; Chicago Cubs 1913–21. Won 178, lost 137 in 386 games with 1416 strikeouts and 808 walks in 2729 innings. Won 20 or more games five times. Led NL in wins 1918 (22). Led in innings pitched 1918 (290) and 1919 (307); strikeouts 1918 (148) and 1919 (141); ERA 1918 (1.74). World Series: 1918 (1–2).

Pitched 41 shutouts. Included was 9-1/3 innings of hitless ball against Cincinnati Reds, 5/2/17. Unfortunately was on receiving end of 10-inning no-hitter by opponent Fred Toney, who won the game.

VAUGHN, JOSEPH F. (Arky) SS-3B-OF-BL-TL. B. 3/9/12, Clifty, Ark. D. 8/30/52, Eagleville, Calif. 5'11", 185. Pittsburgh Pirates 1932–41; Brooklyn Dodgers 1942–43, 1947–48. Hit .318 in 1817 games with 2103 hits, 1173 runs, 356 doubles, 128 triples, 96 home runs and 926 RBI. Hit .300 or better 12 times, including league-leading .385 in 1935. Hit 10 or more triples eight times, leading NL 1933 (19), 1937 (17), and 1940 (15). Hit 30 or more doubles seven times. Led NL runs 1936 (122), 1940 (113) and 1943 (112). Led NL stolen bases 1943 (20) and slugging percentage 1935 (.607). Named MVP by *Sporting News* 1935. Led NL walks 1934 (94), 1935 (97) and 1936 (118). World Series: 1947 (.500). All-Star game: 1934–42 (.364 in 22 at bats.) Hit two homers in 1941 All-Star game. Led NL shortstops in putouts 1936, 38–39, and assists 1938–40.

Truly complete, all-round player. Died in swimming accident in 1952.

VEACH, ROBERT H. (Bobby) OF-BL-TR. B. 6/29/88, St. Charles, Ky. D. 8/7/45, Detroit, Mich. 5'10", 160. Detroit Tigers 1912–23; Boston Red Sox 1924–25; New York Yankees 1925; Washington Senators 1925. Hit .310 in 1822 games with 2064 hits, 954 runs, 393 doubles, 147 triples, 64 home runs and 1170 RBI. Hit .300 or better eight full seasons. Best year: .355 in 1919. Hit 30 or more doubles eight times, leading AL in 1915 (40) and 1919 (45). Hit 10 or more triples 10 consecutive years, leading league 1919 (17). Six hits in game, 9/17/20. Led AL RBI 1917 (115) and tied for most RBI 1918 (74). Tied for lead in hits 1919 (191). Led outfielders in putouts 1921, tied for most assists 1920.

Master hitter in dead-ball era, became a great hitter after receiving batting instruction from the master, Ty Cobb.

VEALE, ROBERT A. (Bob) P-BLR-TR. B. 10/28/35, Birmingham, Ala. 6'5½", 209. Pittsburgh Pirates 1962–72; Boston Red Sox 1972. Won 118, lost 91 in 347 games with 1662 strikeouts and 842 walks in 1877 innings. Won 13 or more games six consecutive years. Best season: 18–12 in 1964 with 250 strikeouts and 2.73 ERA. 1972 record: 2–0 in 11 games. Struck out 200 or more batters four times, leading NL 1964 (250). Fanned season high of 276 in 1965. Led NL walks 1964 (124), 1967 (119) and 1968 (94). Tied for most walks in 1965 (119). Struck out 16 in game against Phillies, 6/1/65, and recorded personal high of seven shutouts in 1965. All-Star game: 1965–66 (0–0). World Series: 1971 (0–0).

A very competent pitcher but said to be unnerved by slightest movements of batter standing in box.

VEECK, WILLIAM, JR. Executive. B. 1914. Colorful owner of several major league teams, brought fun and excitement into game with innovative thinking. Son of former president of Chicago Cubs, operated highly successful Milwaukee franchise in American Association in early 1940s. Purchased Cleveland Indians and sent attendance soaring to unbelievable 2,620,627 in 1948 as Tribe took pennant. Later bought St. Louis Browns and in finest promotion, sent midget Eddie Gaedel to the plate in game against Detroit Tigers 8/19/51. Left baseball and returned as owner of the Chicago White Sox, winning pennant in 1959 and setting another attendance mark. Promotions included placing players' names on backs of uniforms and exploding scoreboards which were touched off by homers hit by home team. Later sold interest in team and most recently switched sports, serving as president of Boston's Suffolk Downs race track, 1969–71.

VERBAN, EMIL M. (Antelope) 2B-BR-TR. B. 8/27/15, Lincoln, Ill. 5'11", 165. St. Louis Cardinals 1944–46; Philadelphia Phillies 1946–48; Chicago Cubs 1948–50; Boston Braves 1950. Hit .272 in 853 games with 793 hits, 301 runs, 99 doubles, 26 triples, one home run and 241 RBI. Best year: .289 in 1949. All-Star game: 1946–47 (.000).

Led Cardinal hitters in 1944 World Series against St. Louis Browns with .412 average.

VERNON, JAMES B. (Mickey) 1B-BL-TL. B. 4/22/18, Marcus Hook, Pa. 6'2", 188. Washington Senators 1939–48, 1950–55; Cleveland Indians 1949–50, 1958; Boston Red Sox 1956–57; Milwaukee Braves 1959; Pittsburgh Pirates 1960. Hit .286 in 2409 games with 2495 hits, 1196 runs, 490 doubles, 120 triples, 172 home runs and 1311 RBI. Hit .300 or better four times, leading AL in batting average 1946 (.353) and 1953 (.337). Hit 27 or more doubles 12 times, leading AL in doubles 1946 (51), 1953 (43) and 1954 (33). Established AL record for most games played at first base

(2227), most putouts (19,754) and assists (1444). Set major league record for most assists by first baseman 1949 (155). Led AL first basemen in putouts 1949, 53, 54; fielding average 1950–52, 1954.

Coach with Pittsburgh Pirates 1960, 1964 and St. Louis Cardinals 1965. Manager, Washington Senators 1961–63 (135–227). Also managed minor leagues 1969–71. Currently minor league batting instructor for Kansas City Royals. Favorite player of former President Eisenhower, escorted from home plate by Secret Service men to presidential box to be congratulated after hitting game-winning homer in Washington in 1954.

VERSALLES, ZOILO (Zorro) SS-2B-BR-TR. B. 12/18/40, Marianao, Cuba. 5'10", 162. Washington Senators 1959–60, 69; Minnesota Twins 1961–67; Los Angeles Dodgers 1968; Cleveland Indians 1969; Atlanta Braves 1971. Hit .242 in 1400 games with 1246 hits, 650 runs, 230 doubles, 63 triples, 95 home runs and 471 RBI. Best year: .273 in 1965 with 19 HR and 77 RBI. Led AL runs 1965 (126). Tied for lead in doubles 1965 (45), tied for triples in same year (12) and led in total bases 1965 (308). Named AL's Most Valuable Player in 1965. Led AL in triples 1963 (13) and tied for most triples 1964 (10). Led AL shortstops in putouts 1962–63, assists 1962 and double plays 1962, 1966. All-Star game: 1963, 65 (.500). World Series: 1965 (.286).

Put it all together for one great year, 1965, then fell off and wound up in Mexican League before joining Atlanta for 66 games in 1971.

VIRDON, WILLIAM C. (Bill; Quail) OF-BL-TR. B. 6/9/31, Royal Oak Township, Mich. 6', 175. St. Louis Cardinals 1955–56; Pittsburgh Pirates 1956–65, 1968. Hit .267 in 1583 games with 1596 hits, 735 runs, 237 doubles, 81 triples, 91 home runs and 502 RBI. Best season: .319 in 1956. Hit 20 or more doubles eight times and 10 or more triples four times. Tied for NL lead in triples 1962 (10). World Series: 1960 (.241). Led NL outfielders in double plays (5) 1959.

A brilliant center fielder, named Rookie of the Year in 1955 by *Sporting News*, baseball writers. Managed in minor leagues, 1966–67; coach with Pittsburgh Pirates 1968–71. Replaced retiring Danny Murtaugh as manager of Bucs in 1972 and won division championship with record of 96–59.

VITT, OSCAR J. 3B-OF-BR-TR. B. 1/4/90, San Francisco, Calif. D. 1/31/63, Oakland, Calif. 5'10", 150. Detroit Tigers 1912–18; Boston Red Sox 1919–21. Hit .240 in 1062 games with 894 hits, 560 runs, 106 doubles, 48 triples, 4 home runs and 297 RBI. Manager of Cleveland Indians 1938–40 after directing New York Yankees' superb Newark farm team to International League pennant in 1937 by 25-1/2 games.

Fiery manager drove Cleveland players to near revolt in 1940, earning themselves nickname of "Crybaby Indians." 1940 team lost pennant in final series of season when Bob Feller lost to Detroit Tigers and Floyd Giebell, who won only two more games in big leagues. Vitt's managerial record with Indians: 282–198.

VOISELLE, WILLIAM S. (Big Bill; Ninety-Six) P-BR-TR. B. 1/29/19, Greenwood, S.C. 6'4", 200. New York Giants 1942–47; Boston Braves 1947–49; Chicago Cubs 1950. Won 74, lost 84 in 246 games with 637 strikeouts and 588 walks in 1373 innings. Best season: 21–16 in 1944. Led NL innings pitched 1944 (312), and strikeouts (161). All-Star game 1944 (0–0). World Series: 1948 (0–1).

VOSMIK, JOSEPH F. (Joe) OF-BR-TR. B. 4/4/10, Cleveland, Ohio. D. 1/27/62, Cleveland, Ohio. 6', 185. Cleveland Indians 1930–36; St. Louis Browns 1937; Boston Red Sox 1938–39; Brooklyn Dodgers 1940–41; Washington Senators 1944. Hit .307 in 1414 games with 1682 hits, 818 runs, 335 doubles, 92 triples, 65 home runs and 874 RBI. Hit .300 or better six times. Best year: .348 in 1935. Hit 30 or more doubles six times, leading league 1935 (47). Led AL in triples 1935 (20), hits 1935 (216) and 1938 (201). All-Star game: 1935 (.250). Led outfielders in fielding average 1932. Managed in minor leagues, 1947–51, and scouted for Cleveland Indians, 1951–52.

WADDELL, GEORGE E. (Rube)   P-BL-TL. B. 10/13/76, Bradford, Pa. D. 4/1/14, San Antonio, Tex. 6'1½", 196. Louisville (NL) 1897, 99; Pittsburgh (NL) 1900–01; Milwaukee (AL) 1900; Chicago Cubs 1901; Philadelphia A's 1902–07; St. Louis Browns 1908–10. Won 191, lost 142 in 407 games with 2310 strikeouts and 771 walks in 2958 innings. Won 19 or more games six times. Best year: 26–11 in 1905. Led AL in wins 1905, also won 26 games in 1904. Pitched 50 shutouts and led NL in strikeouts 1900 (133), and AL in whiffs six straight years: 1902 (210), 1903 (301), 1904 (349), 1905 (286), 1906 (203) and 1907 (226). Strikeout total of 349 in 1904 ranks as all-time high for AL pitcher, topping Bob Feller's best figure by one. Struck out 16 batters in game, 7/29/08. Hall of Fame 1946.

As eccentric as he was brilliant, Waddell withstood all attempts by manager Connie Mack to keep his mind on baseball. Offtimes would go fishing—even on pitching days. Boisterous pitcher's high living finally caught up with him in 1914 when he died on April Fool's day of tuberculosis in a sanatorium. During and after the baseball season, performed almost every task from tending bar to touring the country as actor.

WAGNER, JOHN P. (Honus)   SS-1B-BR-TR. B. 2/24/74, Carnegie, Pa. D. 12/6/55, Carnegie, Pa. 5'11", 200. Louisville (NL) 1897–99; Pittsburgh Pirates 1900–17. Hit .329 in 2785 games with 3430 hits, 1740 runs, 651 doubles, 252 triples, 101 home runs and more than 1700 RBI. Hit .300 or better 17 consecutive years, 10 or more triples 13 times, and

30 or more doubles 14 years. Led NL batting 1900 (.381), 1903 (.355), 1904 (.349), 1906 (.339), 1907 (.350), 1908 (.354), 1909 (.339), 1911 (.334). Led in RBI 1907 (91), 1908 (106), 1909 (102); most triples 1900 (22), 1903 (19), 1908 (19). Led or tied for most doubles 1900 (45), 1901 (39), 1902 (33), 1904 (44), 1906 (38), 1907 (38), 1908 (39), 1909 (39); leader in hits 1908 (201) and tied for lead in 1910 (178); most runs 1902 (105) and tied for most runs 1906 (103). Led NL slugging percentage 1900, 02, 04, 1907–09, and total bases 1904, 1906–09 and tied in 1900. Stole 720 bases, leading NL 1901 (48), 1902 (43), 1904 (58), 1907 (61) and 1908 (53). Led shortstops in putouts 1908–10; led or tied for best fielding average 1909, 12, 1914–15. Committed most errors at shortstop since 1900 (676). Holds NL record for most singles (2426) and triples (252). World Series: 1903, 09 (.275). Hall of Fame 1936.

Ranking on all-time list: Games (11th); hits (4th); runs (13th); doubles (4th); triples (3rd); total bases (10th); stolen bases (10th).

Unquestionably baseball's greatest shortstop and one of game's finest players. Mild-mannered, gangling superstar remained in Pirate uniform until 1951, signing on as coach in 1933. In interim after playing days, operated sporting goods store in Pittsburgh.

WAGNER, LEON L. (Daddy Wags; Cheeks) OF-BL-TR. B. 5/13/34, Chattanooga, Tenn. 6'1", 205. San Francisco Giants 1958–59, 1969; St. Louis Cardinals 1960; Los Angeles 1961–63; Cleveland Indians 1964–68; Chicago White Sox 1968. Hit .272 in 1352 games with 1202 hits, 636 runs, 150 doubles, 15 triples, 211 home runs and 669 RBI. Best season: .294 in 1965 with 28 homers. Hit 20 or more HR six consecutive years and drove in 100 or more runs twice. All-Star game, 1962–63: .455 in 11 at bats. Collected three hits, including homer, to help AL win 1962 All-Star tilt by 9–4 score after dropping first of two-game series to NL. Colorful outfielder gripped bat with hands apart, unusual for today. Noted for flashy clothes; was owner of clothing store.

WAITKUS, EDWARD S. (Eddie) 1B-BL-TL. B. 9/4/19, Cambridge, Mass. D. 9/15/72, Boston, Mass. 6', 170. Chicago Cubs 1941, 1946–48; Philadelphia Phillies 1949–53, 1955; Baltimore Orioles 1954–55. Hit .285 in 1140 games with 1214 hits, 528 runs, 215 doubles, 44 triples, 24 home runs and 373 RBI. Hit .300 or better twice and 25 or more doubles five times. All-Star game: 1948 (.000). World Series: 1950 (.267).

Victim of shooting by disturbed 19-year-old female fan in Chicago hotel, 6/15/49. Missed rest of '49 season while undergoing four operations, but went on to play in six more seasons. Later floor manager at department store in Waltham, Mass.

WAKEFIELD, RICHARD C. (Dick) OF-BL-TR. B. 5/6/21, Chicago,

Ill. 6'4", 210. Detroit Tigers 1941, 43–44, 1946–49; New York Yankees 1950; New York Giants 1952. Hit .293 in 638 games with 625 hits, 334 runs, 102 doubles, 29 triples, 48 home runs and 310 RBI. Best year: .316 in 1943, leading AL in hits (200) and doubles (38). All-Star game: 1943 (.500).

One of first high-priced bonus babies, signed for $52,000. Considered bust by 1940 standards, but lifetime average would be money well spent in expansionist era. Son of Howard Wakefield, former catcher for Cleveland Indians and Washington Senators.

WALBERG, GEORGE E. (Rube) P-BL-TL. B. 7/27/99, Seattle, Wash. 6'1½", 190. New York Giants 1923; Philadelphia A's 1923–33; Boston Red Sox 1934–37. Won 155, lost 141 in 547 games with 1085 strikeouts and 1031 walks in 2644 innings. Won 10 or more games seven times. Best year: 20–12 in 1931. Led AL innings pitched 1931 (291). Won 51 games on three straight pennant-winning teams 1929–31. World Series: 1929–31 (1–1).

A sturdy pitcher, once felled by heat stroke in seventh inning of game in 1932. Walberg was revived and went on to defeat opponents. Engaged in real estate, restaurant and gold course ownership after playing days.

WALKER, ALBERT B. (Rube) C-BL-TR. B. 5/16/26, Lenoir, N.C. 6'1", 180. Chicago Cubs 1948–51; Brooklyn Dodgers 1951–57; Los Angeles Dodgers 1958. Hit .230 in 608 games with 360 hits, 114 runs, 69 doubles, 3 triples, 35 home runs and 192 RBI. Best year: .275 in 79 games in 1948. World Series: 1956 (.000).

Managed in minor leagues, 1959–64; coach with Los Angeles Dodgers, 1958; Washington Senators, 1965–67, and New York Mets, 1968–72. Counterpart of Charlie Silvera of New York Yankees, played on four pennant winners with Dodgers but spent most days on bench watching Hall of Famer Roy Campanella behind plate.

WALKER, CLARENCE W. (Tilly) OF-BR-TR. B. 9/4/89, Telford, Tenn. D. 9/20/59, Erwin, Tenn. 5'11", 165. Washington Senators 1911–12; St. Louis Browns 1913–15; Boston Red Sox 1916–17; Philadelphia A's 1918–23. Hit .281 in 1421 games with 1423 hits, 696 runs, 244 doubles, 71 triples, 122 home runs and 686 RBI. Best year: .304 in 1921 with 23 homers and 101 RBI. Hit 20 or more doubles eight times, 10 or more homers five seasons. Tied for AL home run lead 1918 (11). Hit 37 homers in 1922. World Series: 1916 (.273).

One of earliest long-ball hitters, one of game's best centerfielders. Arm considered finest in major leagues until arrival of Bob Meusel with Yankees. Led AL outfielders in assists 1914–15, 1920.

WALKER, FREDERICK E. (Dixie) OF-BL-TR. B. 9/24/10, Villa Rica, Ga. 6'1", 175. New York Yankees 1931, 1933–36; Chicago White Sox 1936–37; Detroit Tigers 1938–39; Brooklyn Dodgers 1939–47; Pittsburgh Pirates 1948–49. Hit .306 in 1905 games with 2064 hits, 1037 runs, 376 doubles, 96 triples, 105 home runs and 1023 RBI. Hit .300 or better 10 full seasons, leading NL in batting 1944 (.357). Hit 20 or more doubles 10 times. Tied for most triples in AL 1937 (16). Led NL RBI 1945 (124). All-Star game: 1943–44, 46–47 (.200). World Series:1941, 47 (.222). Tied for most assists by NL outfielder in 1941.

Brother of NL batting star Harry Walker, son of Ewart Walker and nephew of Ernie Walker, also former major leaguers. Idolized by Brooklyn fans, gained nickname "The Peepul's Cherce," making Dodger front office reluctant to trade him. Managed in minor leagues, 1950–59; coach with St. Louis Cardinals, 1953, 55; scout Milwaukee Braves, 1960–62, and Atlanta Braves, 1966–68; coach Milwaukee Braves, 1963–65. Now batting instructor for L.A. Dodgers.

WALKER, GERALD H. (Gee) OF-BR-TR. B. 3/19/08, Gulfport, Miss. 5'11", 188. Detroit Tigers 1931–37; Chicago White Sox 1938–39; Washington Senators 1940; Cleveland Indians 1941; Cincinnati Reds 1942–45. Hit .294 in 1783 games with 1991 hits, 954 runs, 399 doubles, 76 triples, 124 home runs and 997 RBI. Hit .300 or better six times. Best year: .353 in 1936. Hit 20 or more doubles 12 times, including 55 in 1936. Scored 100 or more runs and drove in 100 or more runs twice and stole 223 bases. All-Star game: 1937 (.000). World Series: 1934–35 (.286). Plagued by arthritis late in career.

Tremendously popular with Detroit fans, who eagerly watched Walker battle fly balls in outfield. Hitting ability more than made up for shortcomings on defense. Named to Mississippi Sports Hall of Fame. Later engaged in real estate in Florida and Mississippi.

WALKER, HARRY W. (The Hat) OF-BL-TL. B. 10/22/18, Pascagoula, Miss. 6'2", 198. St. Louis Cardinals 1940–43, 46–47, 50–51, 1955; Philadelphia Phillies 1947–48; Chicago Cubs 1949; Cincinnati Reds 1949. Hit .296 in 807 games with 786 hits, 385 runs, 126 doubles, 37 triples, 10 home runs and 214 RBI. Had only two .300 plus seasons, but led NL in batting 1947 (.363). All-Star game: 1943, 47 (.000). World Series: 1942–43, 46 (.278). Led Cardinal hitters in 1946 Series against Boston Red Sox with .412 average. Brother of Fred (Dixie) Walker, former Brooklyn hitting star.

The Hat managed in minor leagues 1951–55, 56–58, 63–64. Coach with St. Louis Cardinals, 1959–62; hitting instructor Houston Astros, 1967–68; manager St. Louis Cardinals, 1955; Pittsburgh Pirates,

1966–67; Houston Astros, 1968–72 (631–604). Special hitting instructor St. Louis Cardinals, 1973. Loquacious authority on hitting helped several players become batting stars, including Matty Alou, Cesar Cedeno and Bob Watson.

WALKER, JAMES L. (Luke) P-BR-TR. B. 9/2/43, DeKalb, Tex. 6'2", 190. Pittsburgh Pirates 1965–66, 1968–72. Won 33, lost 30 in 178 games with 432 strikeouts and 288 walks in 612 innings. Best year: 15–6 in 1970 with 124 strikeouts and 3.04 ERA. 1972 record: 4–6 in 26 games. Championship Series: 1970, 72 (0–1). World Series: 1971 (0–0).

WALKER, JERRY A. P-BLR-TR. B. 2/12/39, Byng, Okla. 6'1", 195. Baltimore Orioles 1957–60; Kansas City A's 1961–62; Cleveland Indians 1963–64. Won 37, lost 44 in 190 games with 326 strikeouts and 341 walks in 747 innings. Best year: 11–10 in 1959, including 16-inning 1–0 shutout against Chicago White Sox. Saved Early Wynn's 300th victory while with Cleveland.

Member of Baltimore's Kiddie Korps, along with Milt Pappas, Steve Barber, Chuck Estrada and Jack Fisher. Manager in New York Yankees' farm system since 1968.

WALKER, MOSES F. C-BR-TR. B. 10/7/57, Mount Pleasant, Ohio. D. 5/11/24, Steubenville, Ohio. Toledo (American Association) 1884. Hit .251 in 41 games. Went from Oberlin College to major leagues; was first black man in baseball. Brother of Welday Walker, who played in six games with Toledo in 1884. Moses' career came to end, in part because of Adrian (Cap) Anson, whose vocalism against blacks forced unwritten rule expelling Negroes from game. Rule shattered by Branch Rickey and Jackie Robinson in 1947. Caught pitcher Tony Mullane while with Toledo.

WALKER, WILLIAM C. (Curt) OF-1B-BL-TR. B. 7/3/96, Beeville, Tex. D. 12/9/55, Beeville, Tex. 5'9½", 165. New York Yankees 1919; New York Giants 1920–21; Philadelphia Phillies 1921–24; Cincinnati Reds 1924–30. Hit .304 in 1359 games with 1475 hits, 718 runs, 235 doubles, 117 triples, 64 home runs and 688 RBI. Hit .300 or better six times. Best season: .337 in 1922. Hit 22 or more doubles seven times and 10 or more triples in eight seasons. Led NL outfielders in fielding average 1925.

The darling of bleacherites in Philadelphia and Cincinnati, suffered fractured skull in 1928 when struck in head by ball thrown by Woody English of Chicago Cubs during mishap on basepaths.

WALKER, WILLIAM H. (Bill) P-BR-TL. B. 10/7/03, East St. Louis, Ill.

D. 6/14/66, East St. Louis, Ill. 6', 175. New York Giants 1927–32; St. Louis Cardinals 1933–36. Won 97, lost 77 in 275 games, with 626 strikeouts and 538 walks in 1489 innings. Won 12 or more games five times. Best year: 16–9 in 1931. All-Star game: 1935 (0–1). World Series: 1934 (0–2). Led NL in ERA 1929 (.3.08) and in 1931 (2.26).

WALLACE, RODERICK J. (Bobby) SS-3B-P-BR-TR. B. 11/4/73, Pittsburgh, Pa. D. 11/3/60, Torrance, Calif. 5'8", 170. Cleveland (NL) 1894–98; St. Louis Cardinals 1899–1901, 1917–18; St. Louis Browns 1902–16. Hit .268 in 2369 games with 2308 hits, 1056 runs, 395 doubles, 149 triples, 37 home runs and 209 stolen bases. Hit 20 or more doubles 11 times. Pitching record: 25–18 in 57 games. Temple Cup: 1896 (.200 with 1 pitching loss). Led or tied for most putouts by AL shortstop, 1903–05; assists, 1901–03, 1907, and fielding average, 1902, 04, 08. Hall of Fame 1953.

Tied record for most years at shortstop (20). Managed St. Louis Browns, 1911–12, and Cincinnati Reds, 1937 (62–154). Managed in minor leagues,1917, 21. Umpire in AL, 1915–16. Scout, Chicago Cubs, 1924; Cincinnati, 1927–37, 1938–60. Coach, Cincinnati, 1926. Bona fide star in his day, at one time commanded highest salary in baseball with $6500 in 1906.

WALLS, RAY L. (Lee) OF-3B-1B-BR-TR. B. 1/6/33, San Diego, Calif. 6'3", 190. Pittsburgh Pirates 1952, 56–57; Chicago Cubs 1957–59; Cincinnati Reds 1960; Philadelphia Phillies 1960–61; Los Angeles Dodgers 1962–64. Hit .262 in 902 games with 670 hits, 331 runs, 88 doubles, 31 triples, 66 home runs and 284 RBI. All-Star game: 1958 (.000).

Had best year in 1958, hitting .304 and slamming 24 home runs. One of five members of '58 Chicago team to hit 20 or more home runs, the others being Ernie Banks, Bobby Thomson, Walt Moryn and Dale Long. Hit three home runs in game, 6/24/58.

WALSH, EDWARD A. (Big Ed) P-BR-TR. B. 5/14/81, Plains, Pa. D. 5/26/59, Pompano Beach, Fla. 6'1", 193. Chicago White Sox 1904–16; Boston Braves 1917. Won 195, lost 126 in 431 games with 1731 strikeouts and 620 walks in 2968 innings. Won 20 or more games four times, including league-leading 40 in 1908. In 1908 also led AL innings pitched (464), percentage (.727), games (66), strikeouts (269). Led league in losses 1910 (20), strikeouts 1911 (255), innings pitched 1911 (369) and 1912 (393). Hurled 58 shutouts, leading league 1906 (10), 1908 (12) and 1909 (8). Won two games in day twice, 9/26/05 and 9/29/08. No-hitter against Boston, 8/27/11. World Series: 1906 (2–0). Holds AL record most innings season (464). Hall of Fame 1946.

A spitball pitcher, learned wet one from teammate Elmer Stricklett. Managed in minors, 1920, and umpire in AL, 1922. Coach with Chicago White Sox, 1923–25, 1928–30. Also coached Notre Dame nine in 1926.

WALTERS, WILLIAM H. (Bucky) P-3B-BR-TR. B. 4/19/09, Philadelphia, Pa. 6'1/2'', 185. Boston Braves 1931–32, 1950; Boston Red Sox 1933–34; Philadelphia Phillies 1934–38; Cincinnati Reds 1938–48. Won 198, lost 160 in 428 games with 1107 strikeouts and 1121 walks in 3104 innings. Won 15 or more games seven consecutive years. Led NL wins 1939 (27), 1940 (22) and 1944 (23); innings pitched 1939 (319), 1940 (305) and 1941 (302); ERA 1939 (2.29) and 1940 (2.48); tied for most strikeouts in NL 1939 (137). Led NL pitchers in complete games 1939 (31), 1949 (29) and 1941 (27). All-Star game: 1937, 39–42, 1944 (0–0). World Series: 1939–40 (2–2). NL's Most Valuable Player 1939.

Converted third baseman hit .243 in 715 games as infielder and pitcher with 477 hits, 227 runs, 99 doubles, 16 triples, 23 home runs and 234 RBI. Teamed with Paul Derringer and Johnny Vander Meer to lead Cincinnati hill staff. Managed Cincinnati, 1948–49 (81–123). Also managed in minor leagues, 1952. Coach with Boston Braves, 1950–52; Milwaukee Braves, 1953–55; New York Giants, 1956.

WAMBSGANSS, WILLIAM A. (Bill) 2B-SS-BR-TR. B. 3/19/94, Garfield Heights, Ohio. 5'11'', 175. Cleveland Indians 1914–23; Boston Red Sox 1924–25; Philadelphia A's 1926. Hit .259 in 1491 games with 1358 hits, 710 runs, 215 doubles, 59 triples, 7 home runs and 519 RBI. Best year: .275 in 1924 with 41 doubles. World Series: 1920 (.154). Led AL second basemen in putouts and assists, 1924, and double plays, 1917.

Made World Series history in 1920 by making first and only unassisted triple play in fall competition in fifth game against Brooklyn Dodgers.

WANER, LLOYD J. (Little Poison) OF-BL-TR. B. 3/16/06, Harrah, Okla. 5'8½'', 150. Pittsburgh Pirates 1927–41; Boston Braves 1941; Cincinnati Reds 1941; Philadelphia Phillies 1942; Brooklyn Dodgers 1944. Hit .316 in 1993 games with 2459 hits, 1201 runs, 381 doubles, 118 triples, 28 home runs and 598 RBI. Hit .300 or better nine full seasons, including .355 in rookie year with a record 223 hits for a freshman. Tied for NL lead in runs 1927 (133), also a record for rookies. Hit 20 or more doubles eight times. Led league in triples 1929 (20). Led in hits 1931 (214). Holds NL record for most singles in season (198). Six hits in game, 6/15/29. All-Star game: 1938 (.000). World Series: 1927 (.400). Led NL outfielders in putouts 1929, 31–32, 1934. Hall of Fame 1967.

Brother of Paul Waner, another Hall of Famer who roamed Pirate outfield with Lloyd from 1927 to 1940. Scouted for Pittsburgh, 1946–49, and Baltimore Orioles, 1955.

WANER, PAUL G. (Big Poison) OF-1B-BL-TL. B. 4/16/03, Harrah, Okla. D. 8/29/65, Sarasota, Fla. 5'8½", 153. Pittsburgh Pirates 1926–40; Brooklyn Dodgers 1941, 43–44; Boston Braves 1941–42; New York Yankees 1944–45. Hit .333 in 2549 games with 3152 hits, 1626 runs, 603 doubles, 190 triples, 112 home runs and 1309 RBI. Hit .300 or better 14 years. Led NL hitting 1927 (.380), 1934 (.362) and 1936 (.373). Hit 10 or more triples 10 consecutive years, leading league 1926 (22) and 1927 (17). Hit 30 or more doubles 13 times, leading NL 1928 (50) and 1932 (62). Had 200 or more hits eight times, topping league 1927 (237) and 1934 (217), eight 200-hit seasons being an NL record. Led in runs 1928 (142) and 1934 (122) and RBI 1927 (131). Six hits in game, 8/26/26. Four doubles in game, 5/20/32. All-Star game: 1933–35, 37 (.000). World Series: 1927 (.333). NL's Most Valuable Player 1927. Led outfielders in assists 1931. Hall of Fame 1952. Became superstar despite well-known fondness for alcohol.

Brother and teammate of Lloyd Waner, himself in Hall of Fame, Paul is one of 11 players to reach 3000-hit plateau. Like Lloyd, a spray hitter who hit line drives in every direction. Minor league manager, 1946. Batting instructor for Milwaukee Braves, 1957, and St. Louis Cardinals, 1958–59. Batting coach, Philadelphia Phillies, 1960, 65.

Rank on all-time list: Games (11th); hits (9th); doubles (6th); triples (9th).

WARD, JOHN M. SS-2B-P-OF-BL-TL. B. 3/3/60, Bellefonte, Pa. D. 3/4/25, Augusta, Ga. 5'9", 165. Providence (NL) 1878–82; New York Giants 1883–89, 1893–94; Brooklyn (Players League) 1890; Brooklyn (NL) 1891–92. Hit .283 in 1810 games with 2151 hits, 1403 runs, 232 doubles, 95 triples, 29 home runs. Hit .300 or better three times. Best: .371 in 1887 and 1890. Led PL hits 1890 (207). Stole total of 605 bases, leading NL stolen bases 1887 (111), 1892 (94) and 1893 (72). Led shortstops in putouts 1885, 87, 90, and fielding average 1887. Led second basemen in assists 1893. Pitching record: 158–102 in 273 games with 25 shutouts. Led NL wins 1879 (44); also won 40 in 1880. Led in shutouts 1880 (9). Won two complete games in one day, 8/9/78. Perfect game against Buffalo, 6/17/80. Pitched 18-inning shutout, 8/17/82. Shares major league record for most assists by second baseman in nine-inning game (12). Hall of Fame 1964.

Managed Brooklyn (PL) 1890, Brooklyn (NL) 1891–92, New York (NL) 1893–94 (388–299). President of Boston Braves, 1911–12. Later attorney for NL, organized Brotherhood War, which turned into ill-fated Players League. Married to popular actress Helen Deuvray. Died of penumonia while on hunting trip in Georgia.

WARD, PETER T. (Pete) 3B-1B-OF-BL-TL. B. 7/26/39, Montreal, Que. 6'1", 185. Baltimore Orioles 1962; Chicago White Sox 1963 69; New York Yankees 1970. Hit .254 in 973 games with 776 hits, 345 runs, 136 doubles, 17 triples, 98 home runs and 427 RBI. Best season: .295 in 1963 with 34 doubles and 22 homers. Named Rookie Player of Year by *Sporting News* in 1963.

Managed Fort Lauderdale entry in Floria State League for Yankees in 1972.

WARHOP, JOHN M. (Crab; Chief) P-BR-TR. B. 7/4/84, Hinton, W. Va. D. 10/4/60, Freeport, Ill. 5'9½", 168. New York Yankees 1908–15. Won 69, lost 92 in 217 games, with 463 strikeouts and 400 walks in 1423 innings. Won 11 or more games four times. Hit 26 batters in 1909, an AL record. Claim to fame is serving up first of 714 home run balls to Babe Ruth, 6/6/15. Later worked as caretaker for estate on Long Island, N.Y.

WARNEKE, LONNIE (Lon) P-BR-TR. B. 3/28/09, Mount Ida, Ark. 6'2", 180. Chicago Cubs 1930–36, 1942–45; St. Louis Cardinals 1937–42. Won 192, lost 121 in 445 games, with 1140 strikeouts and 739 walks in 2781 innings. Won 20 or more games three times. Best year: League-leading 22 victories in 1932. Led NL percentage 1932 (.786) and in ERA (2.37). Threw 30 shutouts, tossed no-hitter against Cincinnati, 8/30/41. All-Star game: 1933–34; 1936, 39, 41 (0–0). World Series, 1932, 35: 2–1.

Umpired in minor leagues, 1946–48, and NL, 1949–55. Arbitration carried over to present; now a judge in Mount Ida, Ark.

WASHBURN, RAY C. P-BR-TR. B. 5/31/38, Pasco, Wash. 6'1", 200. St. Louis Cardinals 1961–69; Cincinnati Reds 1970. Won 72, lost 64 in 239 games with 700 strikeouts and 354 walks in 1143 innings. Best year: 14–8 in 1968, including no-hitter against San Francisco, 9/18. World Series: 1967, 68, 70 (1–1). Manager in minor leagues, 1972.

WATKINS, GEORGE A. OF-BL-TR. B. 6/4/02, Palestine, Tex. D. 6/1/70, 6', 175. St. Louis Cardinals 1930–33; New York Giants 1934; Philadelphia Phillies 1935–36; Brooklyn Dodgers 1936. Hit .288 in 894 games with 925 hits, 490 runs, 192 doubles, 42 triples, 73 home runs and 418 RBI. Hit .300 or better twice. Best year: .373 in rookie season. Hit 24 or more doubles six times. Hit three home runs game, 6/24/31. World Series: 1930–31: (.231).

Hit two-run homer in seventh game of 1931 World Series to lead Cardinals to victory over Athletics.

WATSON, ROBERT J. (Bull) OF-1B-BR-TR. B. 4/10/46, Los Angeles, Calif. 6'1½", 201. Houston Astros 1966–72. Hit .284 in 445 games with 441 hits, 188 runs, 73 doubles, 9 triples, 39 home runs and 227 RBI. Best year: .312 in 1972 with 16 HR and 86 RBI in 147 games. His '72 average fifth best in league. Along with Jim Wynn and Cesar Cedeno, formed one of National League's best outfields.

WATT, EDDIE D. P-BR-TR. B. 4/4/42, Lamoni, Iowa. 5'9½", 185. Baltimore Orioles 1966–72. Won 34, lost 30 in 333 games with 395 strikeouts and 199 walks in 545 innings. Best year: 5–2 in 1969 with 16 saves and 1.65 ERA. 1972 record: 2–3 in 38 games with 7 saves and 2.15 ERA. Championship Series: 1969, 71 (0–0). World Series: 1969–71 (0–3). Has racked up 67 saves since rookie season.

WEATHERLY, CYRIL R. (Roy; Stormy) OF-BL-TL. B. 2/25/15, Warren, Tex. 5'6½", 170. Cleveland Indians 1936–42; New York Yankees 1943,46; New York Giants 1950. Hit .286 in 811 games with 794 hits, 415 runs, 152 doubles, 44 triples, 43 home runs and 290 RBI. Hit .300 or better three times, including high of .335 in rookie year. World Series: 1943 (.000).

Got four hits in first game with Cleveland—including two triples—off pitching great Wes Ferrell. Now employed by steel firm in Beaumont, Tex.

WEAVER, EARL S. Manager. B. 8/14/30, St. Louis, Mo. Minor league player for 14 years, 1948–60, 65. Managed in minors, 1965–67. Managed Baltimore Orioles, 1968–72 (546–282). Piloted Orioles to three straight pennants, 1969–71, and won more than 100 games each season. Defeated Cincinnati Reds in 1970 World Series. Despite great success as big league skipper, has never won Manager of the Year honors.

WEAVER, GEORGE D. (Buck) SS-3B-BLR-TR. B. 8/18/90, Stowe, Pa. D. 1/31/56, Chicago, Ill. 5'11", 170. Chicago White Sox 1912–20. Hit .272 in 1254 games with 1310 hits, 625 runs, 199 doubles, 69 triples, 17 home runs and 379 RBI. Hit .300 or better twice. Best year: .333 in 1920. Hit 20 or more doubles five times. World Series: 1917,19 (.327).

One of eight members of infamous Chicago "Black Sox" to be barred from baseball for life for alleged participation in plot to throw 1919 World Series to Cincinnati Reds. Ironically, Weaver got 11 hits in '19 Series. Later became pari-mutuel clerk at race track in Chicago.

WEAVER, MONTGOMERY M. (Prof; Monte) P-BL-TR. B. 6/15/06, Helton, N.C. 6', 170. Washington Senators 1931–38; Boston Red Sox 1939. Won 71, lost 50 in 202 games with 297 strikeouts and 435 walks in 1052 innings. Best year: 22–10 in 1932. Helped Senators win flag in 1933 with 10–5 record. World Series: 1933 (0–0).

Now operates citrus groves and other property in Orlando, Fla.

WEBB, EARL W. OF-BL-TR. B. 9/17/99, Ravenscroft, Tenn. D. 5/23/65, Jamestown, Tenn. 6'1'', 185. New York Giants 1925; Chicago Cubs 1927–28; Boston Red Sox 1930–32; Detroit Tigers 1932–33; Chicago White Sox 1933. Hit .306 in 649 games with 661 hits, 326 runs, 155 doubles, 25 triples, 56 home runs and 333 RBI. Hit .300 or better three seasons. Best year: .333 in 1931.

Despite fairly short career, holds major league record for most doubles in season (67) in 1931.

WEHMEIER, HERMAN R. (Hermie) P-BR-TR. B. 2/18/27, Cincinnati, Ohio. D. 5/21/73, Dallas, Tex. 6'3'', 185. Cincinnati Reds 1945, 47–54; Philadelphia Phillies 1954–56; St. Louis Cardinals 1956–58; Detroit Tigers 1958. Won 92, lost 108 in 413 games with 794 strikeouts and 852 walks in 1803 innings. Won 10 or more games in season seven times, including 12 in 1956. Led NL in walks 1949 (117), 1950 (135), and 1952 (103). Sent to Philadelphia in 1954 partly because of unappreciative fellow townsmen who jeered him constantly for not becoming big winner. Scouted for Cincinnati 1959–61 and later became executive with shipping company. Died of apparent heart attack while testifying as government witness during trial involving theft from his firm.

WEIMER, JOHN W. (Tornado Jake) P-BR-TR. B. 11/13/83, Reading, Pa. D. 11/30/44. Chicago Cubs 1903–05; Cincinnati Reds 1906–08; New York Giants 1909. Won 97, lost 69 in 191 games with 657 strikeouts and 493 walks in 1472 innings. Won 20 or more games three times, including 20 in rookie season.

WEIS, ALBERT J. (Al) 2B-SS-BR-TR. B. 4/2/38, Franklin Square, N.Y. 6', 160. Chicago White Sox 1962–67; New York Mets 1968–71. Hit .219 in 800 major league games but stayed in big leagues because of fine defensive ability. Utility infielder hit only seven home runs in entire career but blasted homer to tie final game of 1969 World Series. Improbable hitter also led improbable Mets in hitting during their 1969 Series win over Baltimore, with .455 average.

WEISS, GEORGE M. Executive. B. 6/23/95, New Haven, Conn. D. 8/13/72, Greenwich, Conn. One of game's greatest and most knowledgeable executives, helped create New York Yankees' legend and sustain it. Hired by owner Jake Ruppert in 1932 to build Yankees' farm system, which produced such stars as Yogi Berra, Phil Rizzuto, Mickey Mantle and Whitey Ford. Took over Yankees' organization in 1948 as general manager after producing talents for nine Yankee pennants and eight World Series titles. Led New York to 10 more pennants and seven World Series titles in following 13 years. Brought Casey Stengel to New York to manage Yankees in 1949 and joined Stengel in move to Mets after both were eased out of Yankee organization. From beginning as operator of Yankees' Kansas City farm club, ended career as president of Mets in 1967. After death received tribute from "Trader" Frank Lane: "I never made a single deal with him. He was too smart." Hall of Fame 1971.

WELCH, CURTIS B. OF-BR-TR. B. 2/11/62, East Liverpool, Ohio. D. 8/29/96, East Liverpool, Ohio. 5'10", 175. Toledo (American Association) 1884; St. Louis (AA) 1885–87; Philadelphia (AA) 1888–90; Baltimore (AA) 1890–91; Baltimore (NL) 1892; Cincinnati (NL) 1892; Louisville (NL) 1893. Hit .269 in 1107 games with 1152 hits, 915 runs, 215 doubles, 66 triples and 15 home runs. Hit 20 or more doubles seven times and stole 394 bases, including high of 95 in 1888.

While playing in St. Louis, kept steady supply of beer behind billboards in Sportsman Park. In 1886 "World Series" he gained notoriety by scoring winning run in final game, coming home from third base despite pitchout by Mike Kelly of White Sox. Scoring play became known as Welch's $15,000 slide for amount of cash winning team picked up for winning Series.

WELCH, MICHAEL F. (Smiling Mickey) P-BR-TR. B. 7/4/59, Brooklyn, N.Y. D. 3/30/41, Nashua, N.H. Troy (NL) 1880–82; New York (NL) 1883–92. Won 315, lost 211 in 591 games with 1837 strikeouts and 1305 walks in 4775 innings. Won 30 or more games three times and 47 games in 1885. Pitched 524 complete games and 41 shutouts. Won 17 consecutive games in 1883 and two complete games in one day, 7/4/81. Struck out first nine batters to face him in game, 8/28/94. World Series: 1888–89 (1–2).

One of 13 pitchers to win 300 or more games, teamed with Tim Keefe, who also won more than 300 games. Duo won 76 games between them in 1885, upholding Welch's theory that beer helped him pitch better. Hall of Fame 1973.

WERBER, WILLIAM M. (Billy) 3B-SS-OF-BR-TR. B. 6/20/08, Berwyn, Md. 5'10", 170. New York Yankees 1930, 33; Boston Red Sox 1933–36; Philadelphia A's 1937–38; Cincinnati Reds 1939–41; New York Giants 1942. Hit .271 in 1295 games with 1363 hits, 875 runs, 271 doubles, 50 triples, 78 home runs and 539 RBI. Best season: .321 in 1934. Hit 30 or more doubles six seasons; hit 4 doubles in one game, 7/17/35. Stole 251 bases, leading NL stolen bases 1934 (40), 1935 (29), tied for league lead in 1937 (35).

Sold to Cincinnati Reds for $25,000, promptly led Reds to two pennants. World Series: 1939–40 (.326). Led all Reds hitters with 10 hits and .370 average in 1940 Series. Slick-fielding infielder now millionaire insurance executive in Hyattsville, Md.

WERTZ, VICTOR W. OF-1B-BL-TR. B. 2/9/25, York, Pa. 6′, 205. Detroit Tigers 1947–52, 61–63; St. Louis Browns 1952–53; Baltimore Orioles 1954; Cleveland Indians 1954–58; Boston Red Sox 1959–61; Minnesota Twins 1963. Hit .277 in 1860 games with 1692 hits, 867 runs, 289 doubles, 42 triples, 266 home runs and 1178 RBI. Hit .300 or better twice. Best year: .308 in 1950. Hit 20 or more homers six times, 20 or more doubles eight times and drove in 100 or more runs five years. Hit 4 doubles in game, 9/26/56, and 7 home runs in five straight games in 1950. All-Star game: 1949, 51–52, 57 (.286) World Series 1954 (.500). Led AL first basemen in putouts, 1956, and double plays, 1957.

Collected eight hits in 1954 World Series; was robbed of extra-base hit on back-to-the-wall catch by Willie Mays in center field. Stricken by nonparalytic form of polio in 1955 and missed half of season. Bounced back to hit 32 home runs in 1956. Now scouts for Tigers.

WEST, MAX E. OF-1B-BL-TR. B. 11/28/16, Dexter, Mo. 6′1½″, 182. Boston Braves 1938–42, 46; Cincinnati Reds 1946; Pittsburgh Pirates 1948. Hit .254 in 824 games with 681 hits, 338 runs, 136 doubles, 20 triples, 77 home runs and 394 RBI. Hit 20 or more doubles four times. All-Star game: 1940 (1.000). Hit three-run homer in 1940 All-Star game to give NL margin of victory but was injured in following inning while attempting to make catch in outfield.

Noted for hustle and one of few bright spots on futile Braves teams of late 30s and early 40s. Now operates sporting goods store in Sierra Madre, Calif.

WEST, SAMUEL F. OF-BL-TL. B. 10/5/04, Longview, Tex. 5′11″, 165. Washington Senators 1927–32, 1938–41; St. Louis Browns 1933–38; Chicago White Sox 1942. Hit .283 in 1753 games with 1838 hits, 934 runs, 347 doubles, 101 triples, 75 home runs and 838 RBI. Hit .300 or better eight times. Best year: .333 in 1931. Hit 25 or more doubles eight times and 10 or more triples in five seasons. Six hits in game, 4/13/33. All-Star game: 1933–35, 1937 (.250).

WESTRUM, WESLEY N. (Wes) C-BR-TR. B. 11/28/22, Clearbrook, Minn. 5′11″, 185. New York Giants 1947–57. Hit .217 in 919 games with 503 hits, 302 runs, 59 doubles, 8 triples, 96 home runs and 315 RBI. Best season: .236 in 1950 with 23 homers. Hit three home runs in game, 6/24/50. All-Star game: 1952 (.000). World Series: 1951, 54 (.250). Led NL catchers in assists, 1950, and double plays, 1950, 52.

Coach with San Francisco Giants, 1958–63, 68–71; New York Mets, 1964–65. Manager, Mets, 1965–67 (142–227).

WEYHING, AUGUST (Gus; Cannonball) P-BR-TR. B. 9/29/66, Louisville, Ky. D. 9/3/55, Louisville, Ky. 5'9", 145. Philadelphia (American Association) 1887–89, 1891; Brooklyn (Players) 1890; Philadelphia (NL) 1892–95; Pittsburgh Pirates 1895; Louisville (NL) 1895–96; Washington (NL) 1898–99; St. Louis Cardinals (NL) 1900; Brooklyn Dodgers (NL) 1900; Cleveland Indians (AL) 1901; Cincinnati Reds (NL) 1901. Won 269, lost 239 in 530 games, with 1571 strikeouts and 1569 walks in 4335 innings. Won 24 or more games seven straight years, including 31 wins in 1890 and 31 in 1891. Pitched 448 complete games and 29 shutouts. No-hitter against Kansas City, 7/31/88.

Small in stature but his strong right arm pitched 300 or more innings nine years and 400 or more in five seasons. Managed and umpired in Texas League, 1910. Later operated tavern in Louisville.

WHEAT, ZACHARIAH D. (Zack) OF-BL-TR. B. 5/23/88, Hamilton, Mo. D. 3/11/72, Sedalia, Mo. 5'10", 170. Brooklyn Dodgers 1909–26; Philadelphia A's 1927. Hit .317 in 2406 games with 2884 hits, 1289 runs, 476 doubles, 172 triples, 132 home runs and 1265 RBI. Hit .300 or better 14 times, leading NL in batting 1918 (.335). Best year: .375 in 1924. Hit 25 or more doubles 12 times, 10 or more triples 11 seasons. Hit safely in 26 consecutive games, 1918. World Series: 1916, 20 (.283). Hall of Fame 1959.

Brilliant outfielder led in putouts in 1914, fielding average, 1922, and tied for best average, 1912. Holds many Dodger records and was as popular as Ruth or Gehrig in his heyday. Mild-mannered superstar later operated bowling establishment in Kansas City, Mo., and fishing resort in Sunrise Beach, Fla.

WHITE, GUY H. (Doc) P-OF-BL-TL. B. 4/9/79, Washington, D.C. D. 2/17/69, Silver Spring, Md. 6'1½", 150. Philadelphia Phillies 1901–02; Chicago White Sox 1903–13. Won 190, lost 155 in 428 games with 1384 strikeouts and 670 walks in 3050 innings. Won 10 or more games 11 times. Best year: 27 wins in 1907. Pitched 46 shutouts, including 15 decisions by 1–0 scores. Pitched five shutouts in 19-day period, 9/12 to 9/30/04, and 65 consecutive innings without issuing walk. World Series: 1906 (1–1).

Later became part owner of team in Texas League and taught physical education at Washington, D.C., high school. Also coached baseball and basketball at Wilson Teachers College in Washington.

WHITE, JAMES L. (Deacon) 3B-C-BL-TR. B. 12/2/47, Caton, N.Y. D. 7/7/39, Aurora, Ill. Chicago NL 1876; Boston NL 1877; Cincinnati NL 1878–80; Buffalo NL 1881–85; Detroit NL 1886–88; Pittsburgh NL 1889; Buffalo (Players League) 1890. Hit .311 in 1291 games with 1612 hits, 828 runs, 205 doubles, 73 triples, 16 home runs. Hit .300 or better eight times. Led NL in batting 1877 (.385) Led NL in hits 1877 (82) and tied for lead in triples (9).

Playing manager of Cincinnati part of 1879 season (8–8). One of game's Big Four along with Dan Brouthers, Jack Rowe and Hardie Richardson. An innovative ball player, White was first catcher to play directly behind batter.

WHITE, ROY H. OF-2B-BLR-TR. B. 12/27/43, Los Angeles, Calif. 5'11", 160. New York Yankees 1965–72. Hit .273 in 952 games with 900 hits, 483 runs, 154 doubles, 27 triples, 84 home runs and 409 RBI. Hit .290 or better three times. Best year: .296 in 1970 with 22 HR and 94 RBI. 1972 record: .270 in 155 games with 10 HR and 54 RBI. Hit 20 or more doubles five times. All-Star game: 1969 (.000).

One of top three outfielders defensively in 1972. Led outfielders in fielding average in 1971 with 1.000 in 147 games. First Yankee in history to play full season without error.

WHITE, SAMUEL C. (Sammy) C-BR-TR. B. 7/7/28, Wenatchee, Wash. 6'3", 195. Boston Red Sox 1951–59; Milwaukee Braves 1961; Philadelphia Phillies 1962. Hit .262 in 1043 games with 916 hits, 324 runs, 167 doubles, 20 triples, 66 home runs and 421 RBI. All-Star game: 1953 (.000). Led AL catchers in putouts 1953, assists 1953–56 and double plays 1954, 57.

A tough, hard-nosed receiver, considered Boston's best catcher since departure of Birdie Tebbets and until arrival of Carlton Fisk. Businessman in Kauai, Hawaii.

WHITE, WILLIAM D. (Bill) 1B-OF-BL-TL. B. 1/28/34, Lakewood, Ohio. 6', 200. New York Giants 1956; San Francisco Giants 1958; St. Louis Cardinals 1959–65, 69; Philadelphia Phillies 1966–68. Hit .286 in 1673 games with 1706 hits, 843 runs, 278 doubles, 65 triples, 202 home runs and 870 RBI. Hit .300 or better four times. Best year: .324 in 1962. Hit 23 or more doubles nine times and drove in 100 or more runs four years. Belted 20 or more home runs seven years and hit HR in first trip to plate, 5/7/56. Three HR in game, 7/5/61. Tied major league mark with 14 hits in successive doubleheaders, 7/17 and 7/18/61. All-Star game: 1959–61, 63–64 (.286). World Series: 1964 (.111). Led NL first basemen in assists, 1966, and fielding average, 1964, 66. Won 'Golden Glove Award', 1960, 66.

Now broadcasts Yankee games with Phil Rizzuto.

WHITE, WILLIAM H. (Will) P-BLR-TR. B. 10/11/54, Caton, N.Y. D. 8/31/11, Fort Collier, Ont. Boston (NL) 1877; Cincinnati (NL) 1878–80; Detroit (NL) 1881; Cincinnati (American Association) 1882–86. Won 222, lost 166 in 403 games. Pitched 35 shutouts and won 40 or more games in 82–83. Brother of James (Deacon) White, noted catcher and infielder in 1880s.

The first ball player to wear eyeglasses in majors, White's brushback pitch resulted in initiation of modern-day rule which allows batter to take first base when hit by pitched ball. Manager, Cincinnati, 1884 (34–25). Later became somewhat of a song writer, publishing ditty entitled "Little Puff of Smoke Good Night" with lyrics by writer Ring Lardner.

WHITEHEAD, BURGESS U. Inf.-BR-TR. B. 6/29/10, Tarboro, N.C. 5'10½", 160. St. Louis Cardinals 1933–35; New York Giants 1936–37, 1939–41; Pittsburgh Pirates 1946. Hit .263 in 924 games with 883 hits, 415 runs, 100 doubles, 31 triples, 17 HR and 245 RBI. All-Star game: 1935, 37 (.000). World Series: 1934, 36–37 (1.35). Cracked eight hits in nine at bats during doubleheader.

Now in feed mill and livestock auction business in Windsor, N.C. Was favorite ball player of actress Ethel Barrymore during playing days with Giants.

WHITEHILL, EARL O. P-BL-TL. B. 2/7/99, Cedar Rapids, Iowa. D. 10/22/54, Omaha, Nebr. 5'10", 185. Detroit Tigers 1923–32; Washington Senators 1933–36; Cleveland Indians 1937–38; Chicago Cubs 1939. Won 218, lost 186 in 541 games with 1350 strikeouts and 1431 walks in 3563 innings. Won 14 or more games 10 times. Best season: 22–8 in 1933. World Series: 1933 (1–0).

Coach with Cleveland Indians, 1941, and Philadelphia Phillies, 1943. Player-coach in minor leagues, 1944.

WHITNEY, ARTHUR C. (Pinky) 3B-2B-BR-TR. B. 2/2/06, San Antonio, Tex. 5'10", 165. Philadelphia Phillies 1928–33, 1936–39; Boston Braves 1933–36. Hit .295 in 1539 games with 1701 hits, 696 runs, 303 doubles, 56 triples, 93 home runs and 927 RBI. Hit .300 or better four times. Best year: .342 in 1930. Hit 26 or more doubles six times. Drove in 100 or more runs four seasons. All-Star game: 1936 (.333). Led NL third basemen in putouts, 1929, 30, 32; assists, 1929, 30, 32, 34; double plays, 1929, 30, 32, and fielding average, 1932, 34, 37.

Later employed in San Antonio brewery and operated bowling establishment. Named to South Texas Sports Hall of Fame.

WHITNEY, JAMES E. (Grasshopper Jim) P-BL-TR. B. 1856, Binghamton, N.Y. D. 5/21/91, Binghamton, N.Y. Boston (NL) 1881–85; Kansas City (NL) 1886; Washington (NL) 1887–88; Indianapolis (NL) 1889; Philadelphia (American Association) 1890. Won 200, lost 210 in 542 games with 1571 strikeouts and 411 walks in 3496 innings. Won 20 or more games five times, including 31 in 1881 and 1884 and 38 in 1883. Won two complete games in day, 8/20/87. Led NL strikeouts 1883 (345). Scored six runs in game, 6/9/83.

Blazing fast-ball pitcher, he threw 26 shutouts and completed 373 of the 396 games he started.

WICKERSHAM, DAVID C. (Dave) P-BR-TR. B. 9/27/35, Erie, Pa. 6'3", 188. Kansas City A's 1960–63; Detroit Tigers 1964–67; Pittsburgh Pirates 1968; Kansas City Royals 1969. Won 68, lost 57 in 283 games with 638 strikeouts and 384 walks in 1123 innings. Best season: 19–12 in 1964. Missed chance for 20th victory when tossed out of last start of season in seventh inning.

Currently district manager for insurance firm in Leawood, Kans.

WILCOX, MILTON E. (Milt) P-BR-TR. B. 4/20/50, Honolulu, Hawaii. 6'2", 185. Cincinnati Reds 1970–71; Cleveland Indians 1972. Won 12, lost 17 in 55 games with 124 strikeouts and 96 walks in 221 innings. 1972 record: 7–14 in 32 games with 90 strikeouts and 3.40 ERA. Standout as 20-year-old with Cincinnati in 1970 Championship Series, winning final game of three-game playoff in relief for 1–0 record. World Series: 1970 (0–1).

WILHELM, JAMES H. (Hoyt) P-BR-TR. B. 7/26/23, Huntersville, N.C. 6', 190. New York Giants 1952–56; St. Louis Cardinals 1957; Cleveland Indians 1957–58; Baltimore Orioles 1958–62; Chicago White Sox 1963–68; California Angels 1969; Atlanta Braves 1969–71. Chicago Cubs 1970; Los Angeles Dodgers 1971–72. Won 143, lost 122 in 1070 games with 1610 strikeouts and 778 walks in 2253 innings. Lifetime ERA of 2.50. Won 10 or more games five times. Best year: 15–3 in 1952 with 108 strikeouts and 2.43 ERA. 1972 record: 0–1 in 16 games. Led NL games with 1610 strikeouts and 778 walks in 2253 innings. Lifetime Led NL percentage 1952 (.833) and tied for best percentage 1954 (.750). Led NL ERA 1952 (2.43) and led AL in ERA 1959 (.2.19). Pitched 1–0 no-hitter against New York Yankees, 9/20/58. All-Star game: 1953,59, 61–62, 70 (0–1). World Series: 1954 (0–0).

Greatest relief pitcher in history, used tantalizing knuckle ball to get hitters out for 21 seasons. Released by Dodgers just short of 49th birthday to make him oldest pitcher to play regularly in majors. Holds major league record for most wins in relief (124), most games finished (642), most games pitched (1070) and most innings hurled in relief (1845). Hit first and only home run in major leagues in first at bat with Giants. Staff sergeant in army, awarded Purple Heart for wounds in Battle of the Bulge.

WILKS, THEODORE (Cork; Ted) P-BR-TR. B. 11/13/15, Fulton, N.Y. 5'9", 178. St. Louis Cardinals 1944–51; Pittsburgh Pirates 1951–52; Cleveland Indians 1952–53. Won 59, lost 30 in 385 games with 403 strikeouts and 283 walks in 912 innings. Best year: 17–4 in rookie season, one of two years he worked as starting pitcher. Led NL percentage 1944

(.810). Later became outstanding relief pitcher. Led NL games pitched 1949 (59) and 1951 (65). World Series: 1944, 46 (0–1).

Along with Al Brazle, gave Cardinals all bullpen help they needed in '40s. Won 12 games without defeat over two-year period spanning 77 games, 1946–47.

WILLIAMS, BILLY L. OF-BL-TR. B. 6/15/38, Whistler, Ala. 6'1½", 170. Chicago Cubs 1959–72. Hit .298 in 1940 games with 2231 hits, 1179 runs, 358 doubles, 85 triples, 356 home runs and 1200 RBI. Hit .300 or better five times. Best season: .333 in 1972 with 37 HR and 122 RBI in 150 games. Led NL batting 1972 and finished third in hits and doubles and second in RBI. Had 200 or more hits three times, tying for NL lead 1970 (205). Hit 30 or more doubles seven times; best, 39, twice. Hit 25 or more home runs 10 times with high of 42 in 1970. Drove in 90 or more runs 10 years. Scored 100 or more tallies five times. Led NL runs 1970 (137). Hit four doubles game, 4/9/69, and three home runs in game, 9/10/68. Led NL total bases 1968 (321) and 1970 (373). All-Star game: 1962, 64–65, 1968, 1972 (.222). Named Player of Year by *Sporting News* in 1972. Named Rookie of the Year in 1961 by baseball writers and Rookie Player of the Year by *Sporting News*.

Baseball's unsung superstar, holds the ironman record in the NL with mark of 1117 consecutive games from 1963 to 1970. Member of Chicago's fearsome threesome, along with Ernie Banks and Ron Santo.

WILLIAMS, CLAUDE P. (Lefty) P-BR-TL. B. 3/9/93, Aurora, Mo. D. 11/4/59, Laguna Beach, Calif. 5'9", 160. Detroit Tigers 1913–14; Chicago White Sox 1916–20. Won 81, lost 45 in 190 games with 515 strikeouts and 347 walks in 1186 innings. Won 10 or more games four times, including 23 in 1919 and 22 in 1920. World Series: 1917, 19 (0–3).

Just realizing potential when banned from organized baseball by Commissioner Kenesaw Mountain Landis for alleged part in throwing 1919 World Series to Cincinnati along with seven other "Black Sox." Later operated garden nursery and went to his death denying involvement in conspiracy.

WILLIAMS, EARL C. C-1B-BR-TR. B. 7/14/48, Newark, N.J. 6'3", 219. Atlanta Braves 1970–72; Baltimore Orioles 1973. Hit .261 in 306 games with 282 hits, 140 runs, 42 doubles, 3 triples, 61 home runs and 179 RBI through 1972. Best year: .260 in 1971 with 33 HR and 87 RBI. 1972 record: .258 in 151 games with 28 HR and 87 RBI.

A powerful slugger, only Brave besides Hank Aaron to hit ball into upper deck at Atlanta Stadium. Named Rookie of the Year in 1971 by *Sporting News* and by baseball writers. Traded to Baltimore Orioles after 1972 season.

WILLIAMS, FRED (Cy) OF-BL-TL. B. 12/21/88, Wadena, Ind. 6'2",
180. Chicago Cubs 1912–17; Philadelphia Phillies 1918–30. Hit .292 in
2002 games with 1981 hits, 1024 runs, 306 doubles, 74 triples, 251 home
runs and 1013 RBI. Hit .300 or better six times. Best year: .345 in 1926.
Hit 20 or more doubles eight times, 20 or more homers four seasons.
First National Leaguer to hit 200 home runs, led league in homers 1920
(15) and 1923 (41). Tied for most homers 1916 (12) and 1927 (30). Hit
three homers in one game, 5/11/23.

One of baseball's first power hitters, aided by short right field wall in
Philadelphia's Baker Bowl. Now successful architect, he has won awards
for designs of hotel, theater and retirement areas. Designed famous
resort in Three Lakes, Wis.

WILLIAMS, JAMES T. (Buttons) 2B-3B-BR-TR. B. 12/20/76, St.
Louis, Mo. D. 1/16/65, St. Petersburg, Fla. 5'9", 175. Pittsburgh Pirates
1899–1900; Baltimore Orioles 1901–02; New York Yankees 1903–07; St.
Louis Browns 1908–09. Hit .276 in 1458 games with more than 1500 hits.
Hit .300 or better three times. Best season: .352 in rookie year. Hit 20 or
more doubles eight and 10 or more triples six years. Led NL triples 1899
(27). Led AL in triples 1901 (22) and 1902 (23). Six hits in one game,
8/25/02.

WILLIAMS, KENNETH R. (Ken) OF-BL-TR. B. 6/28/90, Grant's
Pass, Oreg. D. 1/22/59, Grant's Pass, Oreg. 6', 186. Cincinnati Reds
1915–16; St. Louis Browns 1918–27; Boston Red Sox 1928–29. Hit .319
in 1397 games with 1552 hits, 860 runs, 285 doubles, 77 triples, 196 home
runs and 914 RBI. Hit .300 or better 10 times. Best year: .357 in 1923.
Hit 30 or more doubles five times. Led AL homers 1922 (39) and RBI
(155). Led in slugging percentage 1925 (.613). Hit three homers in game,
4/22/22, and six homers in six straight games, 7/28 through 8/2/22.

One of first modern long-ball hitters, feats were overshadowed by
heroics of Babe Ruth and his own teammate, George Sisler.

WILLIAMS, RICHARD H. (Dick) 1B-3B-OF-BR-TR. B. 5/7/29, St.
Louis, Mo. 6', 190. Brooklyn Dodgers 1951–54, 56; Baltimore Orioles
1956–58, 1961–62; Cleveland Indians 1957; Kansas City A's 1959–60;
Boston Red Sox 1963–64. Hit .260 in 1023 games with 768 hits, 358 runs,
157 doubles, 12 triples, 70 home runs and 331 RBI. Best season: .288 in
1960. Also hit .266 in 1959 with 33 doubles and 16 homers. World
Series: 1953 (.500).

A fiery competitor and superb bench jockey, continued winning ways
as manager after playing days. Managed in minor leagues, 1965–66;
Boston Red Sox, 1967–69 (265–221); coach with Montreal Expos, 1970;

manager of Oakland A's since 1971 (194–122). Led Red Sox to pennant in 1967 and A's to division championship in 1971 and pennant and World Series victory in '72. Manager of the Year, as rookie pilot, in 1967; again in 1971.

WILLIAMS, STANLEY W. (Stan) P-BR-TR. B. 9/15/36, Enfield, N.H. 6'4", 225. Los Angeles Dodgers 1958–62; New York Yankees 1963–64; Cleveland Indians 1965, 67–69; Minnesota Twins 1970–71; St. Louis Cardinals 1971; Boston Red Sox 1972. Won 109, lost 94 in 482 games with 1305 strikeouts and 748 walks in 1763 innings. Best year: 15–12 in 1961 with 205 strikeouts and 3.91 ERA. 1972 record: 0–0 in three games. Won 10 or more games five times. Turned relief pitcher in 1970 and compiled 10–1 record with 15 saves Championship Series: 1970 (0–0). All-Star game 1960 (0–0). World Series: 1959, 63 (0–0). Beat Milwaukee Braves in last game of 1959 playoffs to put Dodgers in World Series.

WILLIAMS, THEODORE S. (Ted; The Kid; Splendid Splinter) OF-BL-TR. B. 8/30/18, San Diego, Calif. 6'4", 198. Brought to major leagues in 1939 by Eddie Collins, then general manager of the Boston Red Sox. Sent down to Minneapolis for more seasoning in 1938, but presumably later made good on prediction that year to return to big leagues and draw higher salary in single season than '38 Red Sox outfield composed of Ben Chapman, Joe Vosmik and Roger (Doc) Cramer.

  Boston Red Sox 1939–42, 1946–60. Hit .344 in 2292 games with 2654 hits, 1798 runs, 525 doubles, 71 triples, 521 home runs and 1839 RBI. Had 16 .300-plus seasons. Last player to hit .400 in majors. Led AL batting 1941 (.406), 1942 (.356), 1947 (.343), 1948 (.369), 1957 (.388) and 1958 (.328). Led league in RBI 1939 (145), 1942 (137) and 1947 (114) and tied for lead 1949 (159). Hit 30 or more doubles eight times, leading league 1948 (44) and 1949 (39). Led in HR 1941 (37), 1942 (36), 1947 (32) and 1949 (43). Most runs 1940 (134), 1941 (135), 1942 (141), 1946 (142), 1947 (125) and 1949 (150). Drew 2018 walks, leading league 1941–42, 1946–49, 1951, 54. Hit season high with 162 in 1947 and 1949. Lifetime slugging percentage of .645, topping AL 1941–42, 46–49, 51, 54, 57. Holds record in AL for most intentional walks in season (33) in 1957. Three home runs in game, 5/8/57, 6/13/57 and 7/14/46. MVP 1946, 1949. All-Star game: 1940–42, 1946–51, 1954–60. Hit .304 in 18 All-Star games with four home runs and 12 RBI. Won 1946 games with 2 home runs (one off Rip Sewell's eephus pitch), 2 singles and 5 RBI in 12–0 AL victory. Fractured elbow in 1950 All-Star game crashing into left field wall to rob Ralph Kiner of extra-base hit. Injury affected batting in 1951 but still managed to hit .318. World Series: 1946 (.200). Hall of Fame 1966.

  Rank on all-time list: runs (10th), doubles (15th), home runs (8th),

RBI (9th), total bases (11th), batting average (10th tie) and walks (2nd).

In 1941 became last of game's .400 hitters by refusing to sit out last two games on final day of season. Despite reaching mark with average of .3995, collected 6 for 8 in doubleheader against Philadelphia A's for .406.

Lost MVP title in 1941 to Joe DiMaggio's 56-game hitting streak and poor relations with the press. Also lost most valuable player crown in 1942 to Yank's Joe Gordon despite winning Triple Crown. Won Triple Crown again in 1947 but again lost MVP honors to DiMaggio by one point in balloting.

One of major disappointments was dismal showing in 1946 World Series, hitting only .200 with five singles as Boston lost to St. Louis Cardinals in seven games.

Joined Babe Ruth in becoming second player to be fined $5000 following spitting attack aimed at Boston fans and pressbox during game against Yankees in 1957. Also fined $250 for spraying booing fans in Kansas City in 1958, the same year he won his sixth and last batting title at the age of 40.

Hit dramatic home run in last at bat in majors off Jack Fisher of Baltimore, 9/28/60. Lost 4.8 years in baseball due to military service in both World War II and Korean War. A marine pilot, he logged 40 missions in Korea. Manager, Washington Senators, 1969–71; Texas Rangers, 1972 (273–364). Noted for outspoken look at world on and off field. Tempestuous Ted during career had running feuds with Boston press and fans, Selective Service System, Harry S. Truman and others.

Son of woman devoted to Ted and the Salvation Army, raised several million dollars for Children's Cancer Hospital in Boston during career through his affiliation with the Jimmy Fund. Now involved with all aspects of conservation.

WILLIAMS, WALTER A. (No Neck) OF-BR-TR. B. 12/19/43, Brownwood, Tex. 5'6", 185. Houston Astros 1964; Chicago White Sox 1967–72; Cleveland Indians 1973. Hit .269 in 613 games with 481 hits, 209 runs, 86 doubles, 9 triples, 20 home runs and 116 RBI. Best year: .304 in 1969 with 3 HR and 32 RBI. 1972 record: .249 in 77 games with 2 HR and 11 RBI.

Built like fireplug, generates enthusiasm in stands with hustle and free-swinging style.

WILLIAMSON, EDWARD N. (Ned) 3B-SS-C-BR-TR. B. 10/24/57, Philadelphia, Pa. D. 3/3/94, Hot Springs, Ark. 5'11", 170. Indianapolis (NL) 1878; Chicago (NL) 1879–89; Chicago (Players) 1890. Hit .267 in 1191 games with 1159 hits and 523 RBI. Hit 20 or more doubles five times, leading NL doubles 1883 (50). Hit only 73 home runs in majors but topped league in 1884 with 27, figure which stood until surpassed by Babe Ruth in 1919. First player to hit three homers in one game. 5/30/84.

A fine fielding third baseman, forced to quit game after gaining excess weight. Developed dropsy while taking treatment for condition in Hot Springs, Ark.

WILLIS, VICTOR G. (Vic) P-BR-TR. B. 4/12/76, Wilmington, Del. D. 8/3/47, Elkton, Md. 6'2", 205. Boston (NL) 1898–1905; Pittsburgh Pirates 1906–09; St. Louis Cardinals 1910. Won 242, lost 204 in 510 games with 1660 strikeouts and 1171 walks in 3994 innings. Won 20 or more games seven seasons, including 27 in 1899 and 1902. Won 23 games in rookie season. Pitched 300 or more innings eight times and hurled 387 complete games. Holds modern NL record for most complete games in season (45) in 1902. Had 50 shutouts, leading league in 1899 (5) and tied for lead in 1901 (6). Led in innings pitched in 1902 (411). Led in strikeouts 1902 (226) and losses 1902 (19) and 1905 (29). Tied for most losses 1904 (25). No-hitter against Washington, 8/7/99. World Series: 1909 (0–1). Holds modern NL record for most losses in season (29).

A great curve-ball artist, played on dreadful Boston Braves teams in early part of century and then helped Pittsburgh cop pennant in 1909.

WILLS, MAURICE M. (Maury) SS-3B-BLR-TR. B. 10/2/32, Washington, D.C. 5'10", 165. Los Angeles Dodgers 1959–66, 69–72; Pittsburgh Pirates 1967–68; Montreal Expos 1969. Hit .281 in 1942 games with 2134 hits, 1067 runs, 177 doubles, 71 triples, 20 home runs and 458 RBI. Hit .300 or better twice. Best year: .302 in 1967 with 3 HR and 45 RBI, and .302 in 1963 with no home runs and 34 RBI. 1972 record: .129 in 71 games with no home runs and four RBI. Led NL in singles four times; tied for lead in triples 1962 (10). Made 170 or more hits in season seven times. Fifteenth on all-time list for stolen bases with 587. Led NL stolen bases 1960 (50), 1961 (35), 1962 (104), 1963 (40), 1964 (53) and 1965 (94). Total of 104 in '62 is major league mark, topping old record of 96 by Ty Cobb. Led NL shortstops in assists, 1965. Named NL's Most Valuable Player in 1962. All-Star game: 1961–63, 65–66 (.357 in 14 at bats). World Series: 1959, 63, 65–66 (.244 in 21 games).

Spent more than eight years in minors before getting crack at big leagues. Caused as much excitement in baseball during 1960s as any other performer. Managed in Mexican Winter League in 1970. Signed as player-coach with team in Japanese league for 1973 after release from Los Angeles, but passed it up to replace Sandy Koufax on NBC television team.

WILMOT, WALTER R. OF-BLR-TL. B. 10/18/63, Stevens Point, Wis.

D. 2/1/29, Stevens Point, Wis. Washington (NL) 1888–89; Chicago Cubs 1890–95; New York Giants 1897–98. Hit .282 in 960 games with 1100 hits, 725 runs, 152 doubles, 91 triples, 58 home runs and 594 RBI. Hit .300 or better three times. Best year: .331 in 1894. Hit 10 or more triples five times, tying for league lead in 1889 (17). Stole 381 bases, including 76 in 1890 and 74 in 1894. Drew six walks in one game, 8/22/91.

WILSON, DONALD E. (Don) P-BR-TR. B. 2/12/45, Monroe, La. 6′3″, 205. Houston Astros 1966–72. Won 82, lost 63 in 196 games with 1022 strikeouts and 448 walks in 1304 innings. Won 10 or more games six straight years. Best season: 16–10 in 1971 with 180 strikeouts and 2.45 ERA. Also won 16 games in 1969. 1972 record: 15–10 in 33 games with 172 strikeouts and 2.68 ERA. All-Star game: 1971 (0–0).

Last two seasons has led Astros in wins, complete games, innings pitched and ERA. Pitched no-hitters against Atlanta, 6/18/67, and Cincinnati, 5/1/69.

WILSON, JAMES (Ace; Jimmy) C-BR-TR. B. 7/23/1900, Philadelphia, Pa. D. 6/1/47, Bradenton, Fla. 6′1½″, 200. Philadelphia Phillies 1923–28, 1934–38; St. Louis Cardinals 1928–33; Cincinnati Reds 1939–40. Hit .284 in 1525 games with 1358 hits, 580 runs, 252 doubles, 32 triples, 32 home runs and 621 RBI. Hit .300 or better four times. Best year: .328 in 1925. Hit 20 or more doubles five times. All-Star game: 1933, 35 (.250). World Series: 1928, 30–31, 1940 (.242). Led NL catchers putouts 1929, 31; assists, 1929, and double plays 1929–30.

Playing manager Philadelphia Phillies, 1934–38; manager Chicago Cubs, 1941–44. (493–735). As coach at Cincinnati in 1940, caught 15 regular season games when star catcher Ernie Lombardi was injured. Played in six games of 1940 Series and hit .353 to become hero in defeat of Tigers.

WILSON, JAMES A. P-BR-TR. B. 2/20/22, San Diego, Calif. 6′1½″, 200. Boston Red Sox 1945–46; St. Louis Browns 1948; Philadelphia A's 1949; Boston Braves 1951–52; Milwaukee Braves 1953–54; Baltimore Orioles 1955–56; Chicago White Sox 1956–58. Won 86, lost 89 in 260 games with 692 strikeouts and 608 walks in 1539 innings. Best year: 15–8 in 1957. No-hitter against Philadelphia, 6/12/54. All-Star game: 1955–56 (0–0).

Scouted for Houston Astros for eight years. Named director of scouting and player development for Milwaukee Brewers in 1971. Appointed vice president and director of Brewers' baseball operations in 1972, replacing Frank Lane.

WILSON, JOHN O. (Owen; Chief) OF-BL-TR. B. 8/21/83, Austin, Tex. D. 2/22/54, Bertram, Tex. 6'2", 185. Pittsburgh Pirates 1908–13; St. Louis Cardinals 1914–16. Hit .268 in 1278 games with 1246 hits, 520 runs, 157 doubles, 114 triples, 59 home runs and 568 RBI. Hit even .300 in 1911–12. Hit 10 or more triples six consecutive years. World Series: 1909 (.154). Holds major league record for most triples in one season, (36) in 1912.

WILSON, LEWIS R. (Hack) OF-BR-TR. B. 4/26/1900, Ellwood City, Pa. D. 11/23/48, Baltimore, Md. 5'6", 195. New York Giants 1923–25; Chicago Cubs 1926–31; Brooklyn Dodgers 1932–34; Philadelphia Phillies 1934. Hit .307 in 1348 games with 1461 hits, 884 runs, 266 doubles, 57 triples, 244 home runs and 1063 RBI. Had five consecutive .300-plus years. Best season: .356 in 1930. Hit 30 or more doubles six times. Led NL in homers 1926 (21), and 1930 (56) and tied for lead 1927 (30) and 1928 (31). Hit three home runs in game, 7/26/30. Drove in 100 or more runs six years, leading league 1929 (159) and 1930 (190). Led outfielders in putouts, 1927. World Series: 1924, 29 (.319).

Built like fireplug, slugger lost effectiveness due to bouts with liquor. Forced his retirement at 34 and he ended as tragic figure. His 56 home runs are still NL record and 190 RBI probably will stand as major league mark for many years.

WILSON, ROBERT E. (Earl) P-BR-TR. B. 10/2/34, Ponchatoula, La. 6'3", 216. Boston Red Sox 1959–60, 62–66; Detroit Tigers 1966–70; San Diego Padres, 1970. Won 121, lost 109 in 338 games with 1452 strikeouts and 796 walks in 2052 innings. Won 10 or more games eight times. Best season: league-leading 22 wins in 1967. World Series: 1967 (0–1). No-hitter against Los Angeles Angels 6/26/62.

Possessed live fast ball and lively bat, crashing 34 career home runs including seven in 1966 and seven in 1968.

WILTSE, GEORGE L. (Hooks) P-BR-TL. B. 9/8/80, Hamilton, N.Y. D. 1/21/59, Long Beach, N.Y. 6', 185. New York Giants 1904–15; Brooklyn (Federal League) 1915. Won 138, lost 91 in 367 games with 965 strikeouts and 498 walks in 2112 innings. Won 12 or more games eight consecutive years, including 23 in 1908 and 20 in 1909. Threw 29 shutouts, pitched 10-inning no-hitter against Philadelphia, 7/4/08. World Series: 1911 (0–0). Rounded out great Giants pitching staff which included Christy Mathewson, Rube Marquard and Joe McGinnity in different seasons.

WINE, ROBERT P. (Bobby; Wino) SS-3B-BR-TR. B. 9/17/38, Bronx, N.Y. 6'1", 185. Philadelphia Phillies 1960, 62–68; Montreal Expos

1969–72. Hit .215 in 1164 games with 682 hits, 249 runs, 104 doubles, 16 triples, 30 home runs and 268 RBI. Best year: .232 in 1970 with 3 HR, 21 doubles and 51 RBI. 1972 record: .222 in 34 games. Led NL shortstops in fielding average, 1967, and in total chances, 1970.

Superb glove man, established major league record for double plays by shortstop in season in 1970 (137). Returned to Philadelphia in 1972 as first base coach.

WINGO, IVEY B. (Ivy) C-BL-TR. B. 7/8/80, Norcross, Ga. D. 3/1/41, Norcross, Ga. 5'10", 160. St. Louis Cardinals 1911–14; Cincinnati Reds 1915–26, 29. Hit .260 in 1320 games with 1039 hits, 363 runs, 147 doubles, 81 triples, 25 home runs and 457 RBI. Best year: .300 in 1914. World Series: 1919 (.571). Led NL catchers in assists, 1916–17, and double plays, 1920. Led in errors, 1913, 16–18, 1920–21, and tied for most errors, 1912—a major league record. Also holds major league record for most errors by catcher since 1900 (234). Managed Cincinnati for two games in 1916.

WINKLES, BOBBY B. (Winks) Manager. B. 3/11/32, Swifton, Ark. Played minor league baseball, 1951–52, 1954–58. Coached Arizona State U. baseball team, 1959–71, winning NCAA championships in 1965, 67, 69. Managerial record: 524–173. Coach, California Angels, 1972; Manager of Angels, 1973.

Although never played in big leagues, Winkles developed such top-flight major leaguers as Reggie Jackson, Sal Bando, Rick Monday and Gary Gentry.

WISE, RICHARD C. (Rick) P-BR-TR. B. 9/13/45, Jackson, Mich. 6'2", 195. Philadelphia Phillies 1964, 66–71; St. Louis Cardinals 1972. Won 91, lost 92 in 254 games with 859 strikeouts and 398 walks in 1512 innings. Won 10 or more games five times. Best season: 17–14 in 1971 with 155 strikeouts and 2.88 ERA. 1972 record: 16–16 in 35 games with 142 strikeouts and 3.11 ERA. Led NL pitchers in fielding average, 1971. All-Star game: 1971 (0–0). Pitched no-hitter against Cincinnati, 6/23/71, and also hit two home runs in that game. Retired 32 consecutive batters in 12-inning game, 9/18/71, against Chicago.

A fine hitting pitcher, also hit two round-trippers, 8/28/71. Has 12 career homers going into 1973.

WISE, SAMUEL W. (Modoc) SS-2B-BL-TR. B. 8/18/57, Akron, Ohio. D. 1/23/10, Akron, Ohio. 5'10½", 170. Detroit (NL) 1881; Boston (NL) 1882–88; Washington (NL) 1889, 1893; Buffalo (Players League) 1890; Baltimore (American Association) 1891. Hit .285 and 48 homers in 1162 games. Had 20 or more doubles five times and hit 10 or more triples in six seasons. Hit .300 or better two years. Six hits in game, 6/20/83. Umpired in NL, 1893.

WITT, LAWTON W. (Whitey) OF-SS-BL-TR. B. 9/28/95, Orange, Mass. 5'7", 150. Philadelphia A's 1916–21; New York Yankees 1922–25; Brooklyn Dodgers 1926. Hit .287 in 1139 games with 1195 hits, 632 runs, 144 doubles, 62 triples, 18 home runs and 294 RBI. Hit .300 or better three times. Best year: .315 in 1921. Led AL in walks 1922 (89). Led AL shortstops in putouts and double plays in 1916 and topped outfielders in fielding average in 1923.

Helped Yankees defeat St. Louis Browns for pennant in 1923 by snapping back after being beaned by bottle thrown from stands into centerfield at beginning of crucial series with Browns. Witt came back with several timely blows after being knocked unconscious. League president offered reward for information leading to bottle thrower, but culprit never surfaced.

WOLF, WILLIAM V. (Chicken) OF-Inf.-BR-TR. B. 5/12/62, Louisville, Ky. D. 5/16/03, Louisville, Ky. Louisville (American Association) 1882–91; St. Louis (NL) 1892. Hit .296 in 1188 games with 1440 hits, 779 runs, 214 doubles, 109 triples, 17 home runs. Hit .300 or better three times, leading AA in batting 1890 (.366). Led league in hits 1890 (197). Hit 20 or more doubles six times and 11 or more triples six years. Stole 163 bases. Umpire in NL, 1895–97.

WOOD, GEORGE A. (Dandy) OF-BL-TR. B. 11/9/58, Boston, Mass. D. 4/4/24, Harrisburg, Pa. Worcester (NL) 1880; Detroit (NL) 1881–85; Philadelphia (NL) 1886–89; Baltimore (American Association) 1889; Philadelphia (Players) 1890; Athletics (AA) 1891; Baltimore (NL) 1892; Cincinnati (NL) 1892. Hit .278 in 1267 games with 1467 hits, 966 runs, 227 doubles, 132 triples, 70 home runs. Hit .300 or better three times. Best season: .342 in 1887. Hit 16 or more doubles 11 times and 10 or more triples seven times. Led NL in home runs 1882 (7). Umpired in NL in 1898.

WOOD, JOSEPH (Smokey Joe) P-OF-BR-TR. B. 10/25/89, Kansas City, Mo. 5'11", 180. Boston Red Sox 1908–15; Cleveland Indians 1917–22. Won 115, lost 57 in 225 games with 989 strikeouts and 421 walks in 1434 innings. Twice won 20 or more games, including league-leading 34 in 1912. Led AL ERA 1912 (1.49), percentage (.872) and shutouts (10). Won 16 consecutive games, 1912. Pitched 30 shutouts in career, including no-hitter against St. Louis 7/29/11. World Series: 1912, 20 (3–1).

Plagued by sore arm and injuries, lost blazing speed and switched to outfield with Cleveland. Hit .284 in 692 games with 553 hits and 325 RBI. Hit .366 in 66 games in 1921 and .297 in 142 games in 1922. Later baseball coach at Yale University, 1923–42. Father of Joe P. Wood, Boston Red Sox pitcher, 1944. Fast ball considered on par with that of Walter Johnson, Bob Feller, Sandy Koufax.

WOOD, WILBUR F.   P-BR-TL. B. 10/22/41, Cambridge, Mass. 6', 185. Boston Red Sox 1962–64; Pittsburgh Pirates 1964–65; Chicago White Sox 1967–72. Won 83, lost 76 in 458 games with 761 strikeouts and 326 walks in 1367 innings. Won 20 or more games twice. Best season: 24–17 in 1972 with 193 strikeouts and 2.51 ERA in 49 games. Pitched 15 shutouts in 1971–72. Led AL innings pitched 1972 (377), the most since Mickey Lolich's 376 in 1971 and 10th highest total in AL history. Led AL in games pitched 1968 with 88, a major league record; 1969 (76), and 1970 (77). Won *Sporting News'* Fireman of the Year Trophy in 1968 with 13 wins and 13 saves. Racked up 15 saves in 1969 and 21 in 1970. All-Star game: 1971–72 (0–0).

Became outstanding pitcher in starting role after coming out of bullpen to throw baffling knuckle ball more frequently. Finished second in voting for AL Cy Young Award in 1972.

WOODESHICK, HAROLD J. (Hal)   P-BR-TL. B. 8/24/32, Monaca, Pa. 6'3", 200. Detroit Tigers 1956, 61; Cleveland Indians 1958; Washington Senators 1959–61; Houston Colts 1962–64; Houston Astros 1965; St. Louis Cardinals 1965–67. Won 44, lost 62 in 427 games, most in relief, with 484 strikeouts and 389 walks in 847 innings. Best year: 11–9 in 1963. Led NL in saves 1964 (22) and finished second in Fireman of Year point total. All-Star game: 1963 (0–0). World Series: 1967 (0–0). Now salesman for manufacturing firm in Houston.

WOODLING, EUGENE R. (Gene)   OF-BL-TR. B. 8/16/22, Akron, Ohio. 5'9½", 195. Cleveland Indians 1943, 46, 55–57; Pittsburgh Pirates 1947; New York Yankees 1949–54; Baltimore Orioles 1955,58–60; Washington Senators 1961–62; New York Mets 1962. Hit .284 in 1796 games with 1585 hits, 830 runs, 257 doubles, 63 triples, 137 home runs and 790 RBI. Hit .300 or better five times. Best season: .321 in 1957. Hit 15 or more doubles 11 times. All-Star game: 1959 (.000). World Series: 1949–53 (.318 in 26 games.) Led AL outfielders in fielding average, 1952–53.

Named to all-time Oriole team by Baltimore fans. Now scouts for Yankees. Also raises horses on farm in Ohio and involved with firm which makes grips for golf clubs and baseball bats.

WOODSON, RICHARD L. (Dick; Woody)   P-BR-TR. B. 3/30/45,

Oelwein, Iowa. 6'5", 205. Minnesota Twins 1969–70, 1972. Won 22, lost 21 in 101 games with 238 strikeouts and 169 walks in 393 innings. Best year: 14–14 in 36 games in 1972 with 150 strikeouts and 2.71 ERA in 252 innings. Championship Series: 1969–70 (0–0).

WOODWARD, WILLIAM F. (Woody) 2B-SS-BR-TR. B. 9/23/42, Miami, Fla. 6'2", 185. Milwaukee Braves 1963–65; Atlanta Braves 1966–68; Cincinnati Reds 1968–71. Hit .236 in 880 games with 517 hits, 208 runs, 79 doubles, 14 triples, one home run and 148 RBI. Best season: .264 in 1966. Led NL second basemen in fielding average (.984) in 1967. Championship Series: 1970 (.100). World Series: 1970 (.200).

Strongest asset was good glove. Now employed by land development firm in Florida. Cousin to actress Joanne Woodward.

WORTHINGTON, ALLAN F. (Al) P-BR-TR. B. 2/5/30, Birmingham, Ala. 6'2", 200. New York Giants 1953–54, 56–57; San Francisco Giants 1958–59; Boston Red Sox 1960; Chicago White Sox 1960; Cincinnati Reds 1963–64; Minnesota Twins 1964–69. Won 75, lost 82 in 602 games with 834 strikeouts and 527 walks in 1245 innings. Best season: 10–7 in 1965 with 14 saves. Talented relief pitcher, led AL in saves in 1968 (17) and amassed 69 saves and 33 wins over five-year period. World Series: 1965 (0–0). Championship Series: 1969 (0–0). Coach with Twins.

WRIGHT, CLYDE (Skeeter) P-BR-TL. B. 2/20/43, Jefferson City, Tenn. 6'1", 190. California Angels 1966–72. Won 76, lost 66 in 229 games with 506 strikeouts and 373 walks in 1147 innings. Won 10 or more games four times. Best season: 22–12 in 1970 with 110 strikeouts and 2.83 ERA. 1972 record: 18–11 in 35 games with 87 strikeouts and 2.98 ERA. All-Star game: 1970 (0–1). Pitched 4–0 no-hitter against Oakland, 7/3/70.

Slumped badly in 1969, winning only one game. Came back with 22 victories in 1970 to win appropriate Comeback of the Year Award issued by *Sporting News*.

WRIGHT, FOREST G. (Buckshot) SS-BR-TR. B. 2/6/01, Archie, Mo. 5'11", 170. Pittsburgh Pirates 1924–28; Brooklyn Dodgers 1929–33; Chicago White Sox 1935. Hit .294 in 1119 games with 1219 hits, 584 runs, 203 doubles, 76 triples, 93 home runs and 720 RBI. Hit .300 or better four times. Best year: .321 in 1930. Hit 20 or more doubles six times and drove in 100 or more runs in four years. Set major league record in rookie season for most assists by a shortstop in one year (601). Also led NL shortstops in assists, 1925; double plays, 1924–25, and putouts, 1927. World Series: 1925, 27 (.175).

Topped all defensive achievements by becoming one of eight players to make unassisted triple play; turned trick against St. Louis Cardinals, 5/7/25. Named to American Association Hall of Fame. Managed in Boston Red Sox farm chain and has been scouting for Red Sox in Fresno, Calif., area for past 25 years.

WRIGHT, GEORGE SS-BR-TR. B. 1/28/47, New York, N.Y. D. 8/21/37, Boston, Mass. 5'9½", 150. Boston (National Association) 1871–75; Boston (NL) 1876–78, 1880–81; Providence (NL) 1879, 82. Hit .251 in 315 games. Played shortstop on famed Cincinnati Red Stockings of 1869–70. Brother of Harry Wright, one of game's founders and organizer of Cincinnati club.

Popular George said to have sparked phrase, "I'd rather be Wright than President." Managed Providence 1879 (59–25). Hall of Fame 1937. Later organized Wright and Ditson Sporting Goods Co. Athletic ability extended to son who later starred in Davis Cup tennis competition.

WRIGHT, TAFT S. (Taffy) OF-BL-TR. B. 8/10/13, Tabor City, N.C. 5'10", 180. Washington Senators 1938–39; Chicago White Sox 1940–42, 1946–48; Philadelphia A's 1949. Hit .311 in 1029 games with 1115 hits, 465 runs, 175 doubles, 55 triples, 36 home runs and 553 RBI. Hit .300 or better six times. Best year: .337 in 1940. Led AL outfielders in double plays in 1939. A fine pinch hitter, lost four years to military service.

WRIGHT, WILLIAM H. (Harry) Manager. B. 1/10/35, Sheffield, England. D. 10/3/95, Atlantic City, N.J. One of true founders of baseball, organized and managed Cincinnati Red Stockings in 1866. Formerly professional cricket player, switched to baseball in joining New York Knickerbockers in 1858. Batted .278 in 184 games. In 1871 took over as manager of Boston team in National Association, and in 1876, managed Boston club in newly formed National League. Also managed Providence in NL, 1882–83, and Philadelphia, 1884–93. Managerial record: 1042–848. Later became supervisor of umpires in NL. Elected to Hall of Fame 1953. Brother of George Wright, star shortstop for Boston in 1870s.

WRIGHTSTONE, RUSSELL G. (Russ) 3B-1B-OF-BL-TR. B. 3/18/93, Bowmansdale, Pa. D. 3/1/69, Harrisburg, Pa. 5'10½", 176. Philadelphia Phillies 1920–28; New York Giants 1928. Hit .297 in 929 games with 889 hits, 427 runs, 152 doubles, 34 triples, 60 home runs and 428 RBI. Hit 20 or more doubles four times and .300 or better five seasons. Best year: .346 in 1925.

Fine hitter but constantly shifted from infield to outfield and back because of inadequate defensive ability.

WYATT, JOHN T. P-BR-TR. B. 4/19/35, Chicago, Ill. 5'11½", 200. Kansas City A's 1961–66; Boston Red Sox 1966–68; New York Yankees 1968; Detroit Tigers 1968; Oakland A's 1969. Won 42, lost 44 in 435 games with 540 strikeouts and 346 walks in 687 innings. Best year: 1967 with 10 wins and 17 saves to lead Red Sox to pennant. Recorded 20 saves in 1964 and nearly 100 in career as relief specialist. All-Star game: 1964 (0–0). World Series: 1967 (1–0). Led AL in pitching appearances in 1964 with 81.

WYATT, JOHN W. (Whit) P-BR-TR. B. 9/27/07, Kensington, Ga. 6'1", 185. Detroit Tigers 1929–33; Chicago White Sox 1933–36; Cleveland Indians 1937; Brooklyn Dodgers 1939–44; Philadelphia Phillies 1945. Won 106, lost 95 in 364 games with 872 strikeouts and 642 walks in 1762 innings. Best year: 22–10 in 1941 to lead NL in victories and Dodgers to World Series. All-Star game: 1939–42 (0–0). World Series: 1941 (1–1). Later coached in minor leagues, 1951–53; for Philadelphia Phillies, 1955–57; Milwaukee Braves, 1958–64.

WYNN, EARLY (Gus) P-BLR-TR. B. 1/6/20, Hartford, Ala. 6', 200. Washington Senators 1939, 1941–44, 46–48; Cleveland Indians 1949–57, 63; Chicago White Sox 1958–62. Won 300, lost 244 in 691 games with 2334 strikeouts and 1775 walks in 4566 innings. Won 20 or more games five times. Best year: 23–11 in 1954. Led AL in wins 1959 (22) and tied for most wins in 1954 (23). Led in innings pitched 1951 (274), 1954 (270) and 1959 (255); ERA in 1950 (3.20) and strikeouts 1957 (184) and 1958 (179). Pitched 49 shutouts. All-Star game: 1955–60 (1–0). World Series: 1954, 59 (1–2). Cy Young Award winner in 1959. Hall of Fame 1972.

Coach with Cleveland Indians, 1964–66, and Minnesota Twins, 1967–69. Manager in Minnesota farm chain since 1970.

Rank on all-time list: Games (14th), innings (11th), wins (12th tie), strikeouts (12th), walks (1st), shutouts (14th).

Burly, grizzled righthander holds major league record for most years pitched in big leagues (23). One of few players to participate in majors in parts of four decades. Brushback pitch was feared by AL hitters even near his retirement.

WYNN, JAMES S. (Jim; Toy Cannon) OF-BR-TR. B. 3/12/42, Cincinnati, Ohio. 5'9", 165. Houston Astros 1963–72. Hit .259 in 1287 games with 1185 hits, 739 runs, 214 doubles, 27 triples, 203 home runs and 664 RBI. Best year: .249 in 1967 with 37 HR and 107 RBI. 1972 record: .273 in 145 games with 24 HR and 90 RBI. Hit 20 or more homers six times and 20 or more doubles six years. Hit three HR in game, 6/15/67. All-Star game: 1967 (1.000). Led NL outfielders in putouts, 1965, 67; double plays, 1968, and tied for most assists, 1968.

Tied Eddie Stanky's NL record of most walks received in season (148) in 1969. Received three intentional passes in game, 7/11/70.

WYROSTEK, JOHN B. OF-BL-TR. B. 7/12/19, Fairmont City, Ill. 6'2", 180. Pittsburgh Pirates 1942–43; Philadelphia Phillies 1946–47; 1952–54; Cincinnati Reds 1948–52. Hit .271 in 1221 games with 1149 hits, 525 runs, 209 doubles, 45 triples, 58 home runs and 481 RBI. Best year: .311 in 1951. Hit 20 or more doubles six times. All-Star game: 1950–51 (.000).

WYSE, HENRY W. (Hooks) P-BR-TR. B. 3/1/18, Lunsford, Ark. 5'11½", 185. Chicago Cubs 1942–47; Philadelphia A's 1950–51; Washington Senators 1951. Won 79, lost 70 in 253 games with 362 strikeouts and 373 walks in 1257 innings. Won 22 games in 1945 to help Cubs win pennant. World Series: 1945 (0–1).

Made up great mound foursome for Chicago, along with Hank Borowy, Claude Passeau and Paul Derringer.

YASTRZEMSKI, CARL M. (Yaz)   OF-1B-BL-TR. B. 8/22/39, South-ampton, N.Y. 6′, 180. Boston Red Sox 1961−72. Hit .291 in 1817 games with 1952 hits, 1065 runs, 386 doubles, 41 triples, 269 home runs, and 1007 RBI. Hit .300 or better five years. Best season: .329 in 1970 with 40 HR and 102 RBI. 1972 record: .264 in 125 games with 12 HR and 68 RBI. Won AL batting title 1963 (.321); 1968 (.301), and captured Triple Crown in 1967, leading the league in batting (.326), RBI (121) and tying for most homers (44). Led AL runs 1967 (112) and 1970 (125); doubles 1963 (40) and 1966 (39), and tied for most doubles 1965 (45). Hit 40 homers in 1969 and '70. Drove in 100 or more runs three times. Led AL in walks 1963 (95) and 1968 (119); slugging percentage 1965 (.536), 1967 (.622), and 1970 (.592), and total bases 1967 (360) and 1970 (335). Led outfielders in assists an unprecedented six times, 1962−64, 66, 69, 71. All-Star game: 1963, 65−72 (.304 in 23 at bats). World Series: 1967 (.400).

Worth every penny of $100,000 bonus he received to sign with Boston. Led Red Sox to pennant in 1967 almost solely on strength of his bat and nearly carried them to World Series victory with 10 hits against St. Louis Cardinals.

YELLOWHORSE, MOSES J. (Chief)   P-BR-TR. B. 3/28/1900, Pawnee, Okla. D. 4/10/64, Pawnee, Okla. 5′10″, 180. Pittsburgh Pirates 1921−22. Won 8, lost 4 in only 38 games in majors, but became extremely popular figure among Pittsburgh fans. Until recently, yells of "Bring in Yellow-horse" signaled fans' desire to see ineffective pitcher replaced. One of few full-blooded Pawnee Indians to play in big leagues, Chief even had name proposed as appellation for Pirates' new Three Rivers Stadium.

YERKES, STEPHEN D. SS-2B-BR-TR. B. 2/19/88, Hatboro, Pa. D. 1/31/71, Lansdale, Pa. 5'9", 165. Boston Red Sox 1909, 1911–14; Pittsburgh (Federal League) 1914–15; Chicago Cubs 1916. Hit .267 in 711 games with 675 hits, 307 runs, 124 doubles, 32 triples, 6 home runs and 219 RBI. Best year: .286 in 1915. Hit 20 or more doubles four times. World Series: 1912 (.250).

Scored winning run in eighth game of 1912 Series to give Red Sox championship over New York Giants. Winning run was set up by Fred Snodgrass' famed "$30,000 Muff". Later coached baseball at Yale.

YORK, RUDOLPH P. (Rudy) 1B-C-BR-TR. B. 8/17/13, Ragland, Ala. D. 2/5/70, Rome, Ga. 6'1½", 230. Detroit Tigers 1934, 37–45; Boston Red Sox 1946–47; Chicago White Sox 1947; Philadelphia A's 1948. Hit .275 in 1603 games with 1621 hits, 876 runs, 291 doubles, 52 triples, 278 home runs and 1152 RBI. Hit .300 or more three times. Best year: .316 in 1940. Drove in 100 or more runs six times, led AL in 1943 (118). Hit 20 or more doubles nine years. Slammed 20 or more home runs eight times, topping AL 1943 (34). Hit three home runs in game, 9/1/41, and belted 18 in month of August, 1937, a major league record. All-Star game: 1938, 41–44, 46–47 (.308 in 13 at bats). World Series: 1940, 45–46 (.221). Led AL first basemen in putouts 1945–46; assists 1942–43, 46, and fielding average 1947.

Managed and coached in minor leagues, 1957–58; coach with Boston Red Sox, 1959–62, and managed team for one game. After playing days worked as firefighter. Part Cherokee Indian, York had some of best years in Detroit despite booing and criticism of Tiger fans.

YOST, EDWARD F. (Eddie) 3B-BR-TR. B. 10/13/26, Brooklyn, N.Y. 5'10", 182. Washington Senators 1944, 46–58; Detroit Tigers 1959–60; Los Angeles Angels 1961–62. Hit .254 in 2109 games with 1863 hits, 1215 runs, 337 doubles, 56 triples, 139 home runs and 683 RBI. Best season: .295 in 1950. Hit 20 or more doubles seven times, tied for league lead in 1951 (36). Led AL in runs 1959 (115). Drew 1614 walks in career and 100 or more eight times, leading league 1950 (141), 1952 (129), 1953 (123), 1956 (151), 1959 (135) and 1960 (125). All-Star game: 1952 (.000). Led AL third basemen in putouts 1948, 50–53, 56, 59, tied for most putouts 1954; led in assists 1954, 56, and fielding average 1957–58. Holds AL record for most putouts lifetime by third baseman (2356), and major league mark for most years leading or tying for most putouts (8).

Ranks only behind Babe Ruth and Ted Williams for most walks received in a season. Coach with Washington Senators, 1963–67, and New York Mets since 1968.

YOUNG, DENTON T. (Cy) P BR-TR B. 3/29/67 Gilmore, Ohio. D. 11/4/55, Peoli, Ohio. 6'2", 210. Cleveland (NL) 1890–98; St. Louis (NL) 1899–1900; Boston Red Sox 1901–08, 1911; Cleveland Indians 1909–11. Won 511, lost 313 in 906 games with 2819 strikeouts and 1209 walks in 7277 innings. Won 20 or more games 16 years, including 30 or more five times. Led NL wins 1895 (35), and AL in wins 1901 (33), 1902 (32) and 1903 (28). Pitched 300 or more innings 16 times and had five years of 400 or more frames. Led NL strikeouts 1896 (137) and AL in strikeouts 1901 (159). Led or tied for most shutouts seven times, hurling 77. Struck out 100 or more batters 18 times. Led AL innings pitched 1902 (386) and 1903 (342). Won two complete games in day, 10/4/90. Pitched no-hitters against Cincinnati, 9/18/97, and New York Yankees, 6/30/08, and threw perfect game against Philadelphia A's, 5/5/04. Pitched 23 consecutive hitless innings in 1904. World Series: 1903 (2–1). Temple Cup: 1892 (3–1). Hall of Fame 1937. Manager Boston Red Sox 1907 (3–4).

Rank on all-time list: games (2nd), complete games (1st), innings (1st), wins (1st), losses (1st), strikeouts (3rd), shutouts (4th).

Baseball's all-time pitcher, Cy fashioned some records probably never will be broken. Pitched 22 years in majors, winning 28 games in 1891 and 21 games 18 years later in 1908. By his own admission the greatest pitcher ever to play game, he returned to farming in Ohio after playing days.

YOUNGS, ROYCE (Ross) OF-BLR-TR. B. 4/10/97, Shiner, Tex. D. 10/22/27, San Antonio, Tex. 5'8", 162. New York Giants 1917–26. Hit .322 in 1211 games with 1491 hits, 812 runs, 236 doubles, 93 triples, 42 home runs and 596 RBI. Hit .300 or better nine of 10 years in majors. Best season: .355 in 1924. Hit 24 or more doubles seven straight years. Led NL doubles 1919 (31). Hit 10 or more doubles five times. Led NL runs 1923 (121). World Series: 1921–24 (.285 in 26 games). Stole 153 bases.

A fine outfielder, led NL outfielders in assists, 1919 and 1922, and tied for most assists, 1920. Called "my greatest outfielder" by manager John McGraw. Career cut down after 1926 by Bright's disease. Hall of Fame 1972.

ZACHARY, JONATHAN T. (Tom) P-BL-TL. B. 5/7/97, Graham, N. C. D. 1/24/69, Graham, N. C. 6'1", 185. Philadelphia A's 1918; Washington Senators 1919–25, 1927–28; St. Louis Browns 1926–27; New York Yankees 1928–30; Boston Braves 1930–34; Brooklyn Dodgers 1934–36; Philadelphia Phillies 1936. Won 186, lost 191 in 534 games with 720 strikeouts and 915 walks in 3136 innings. Won 10 or more games 11 times. Best year: 18–16 in 1921. Also fashioned 12–0 record in 26 games in 1929. World Series: 1924–25, 1928 (3–0).

Played under name of Zack Walton in 1918. Later became a tobacco farmer. Holds distinction of giving up Babe Ruth's 60th home run, 9/30/27.

ZARILLA, ALLEN L. (Zeke) OF-BL-TR. B. 5/1/19, Los Angeles, Calif. 5'11", 180. St. Louis Browns 1943–44, 46–49, 52; Boston Red Sox 1949–50, 52–53; Chicago White Sox 1951–52. Hit .277 in 1120 games with 975 hits, 507 runs, 186 doubles, 43 triples, 61 home runs and 456 RBI. Best year: .329 in 1948 with 39 doubles. Hit four doubles in game, 6/8/50, and two triples in inning, 7/13/46. All-Star game: 1948 (.000). World Series: 1944 (.100). Led AL outfielders in double plays, 1946.

Scouted for several teams; now scout with Texas Rangers. Coached Rangers, 1971.

ZEIDER, ROLLIE H. (Bunions) Inf.-BR-TR. B. 11/16/83, Auburn, Ind. D. 9/12/67, Garrett, Ind. Chicago White Sox 1910–13; New York Yankees 1913; Chicago (Federal League) 1914–15; Chicago Cubs

1916–18. Hit .239 in 937 games with 769 hits, 393 runs, 89 doubles, 22 triples, 6 home runs and 256 RBI. World Series: 1918 (.000). Stole 223 bases, including 47 in 1912 and 49 in 1910, an AL record for player in rookie season. Could play any infield position.

ZERNIAL, GUS E. (Ozark Ike) OF-1B-BR-TR. B. 6/27/23, Beaumont, Tex. 6'2½", 210. Chicago White Sox 1949–51; Philadelphia A's 1951–54; Kansas City A's 1955–57; Detroit Tigers 1958–59. Hit .265 in 1234 games with 1093 hits, 572 runs, 159 doubles, 22 triples, 237 home runs and 776 RBI. Best year: .284 with 42 HR in 147 games, 1953. Hit 25 or more homers six times, leading AL in HR 1951 (33). Drove in 100 or more runs three straight years, leading AL in RBI 1951 (129). Hit three homers in one game, 10/1/50, and seven in four consecutive games, 1951. Hit 10 pinch-hit home runs during career. All-Star game: 1953 (.500).

A radio and television sportscaster since retirement, now sports director for TV station in Fresno, Calif.

ZIMMER, CHARLES L. (Chief) C-BR-TR. B. 11/23/60, Marietta, Ohio. D. 8/22/49, Cleveland, Ohio. 6', 190. Detroit (NL) 1884; New York (American Association) 1886; Cleveland (AA) 1887–88; Cleveland (NL) 1889–99; Louisville (NL) 1899; Pittsburgh (NL) 1900–02; Philadelphia Phillies 1903. Hit .272 in 1252 games with 1224 hits, 617 runs, 222 doubles, 76 triples, 20 home runs and 620 RBI. Six hits in game, 6/11/94.

Revived Players' Brotherhood in 1900, along with Hugh Jennings and Bill Clarke, and won important concessions for ball players. Group dissolved before Players League could be reestablished. Umpired in NL, 1904–05.

ZIMMER, DONALD W. (Don; Zim) 3B-2B-SS-BR-TR. B. 1/17/31, Cincinnati, Ohio. 5'9", 188. Brooklyn Dodgers 1954–57; Los Angeles Dodgers 1958–59, 63; Chicago Cubs 1960–61; New York Mets 1962; Cincinnati Reds 1962; Washington Senators 1963–65. Hit .235 in 1095 games with 773 hits, 353 runs, 130 doubles, 22 triples, 91 home runs and 352 RBI. Best year: .262 in 1958 with 17 homers. All-Star game: 1961 (.000). World Series: 1955, 59 (.200).

Managed in minor leagues, 1967–70; coach with Montreal Expos, 1971, and San Diego Padres, 1972. Named manager of Padres during 1972 season (54–88). Scrappy infielder came back twice from injuries sustained in batter's box. Nearly killed when beaned by pitch while in minors in 1953 and suffered fractured cheek in 1956 when hit by pitch thrown by Hal Jeffcoat of Cincinnati.

ZIMMERMAN, HENRY (Heinie) 3B-2B-SS-BR-TR. B. 2/9/87, New

York, N.Y. 5'11½", 176. Chicago Cubs 1907–16; New York Giants 1916–19. Hit .295 in 1403 games with 1556 hits, 695 runs, 275 doubles, 105 triples, 58 home runs and 793 RBI. Hit .300 or better three seasons. Best year: Triple Crown title in 1912 with .372 average and most HR (14) and RBI (98). In 1912 also led NL hits (207), doubles (41), total bases (318) and slugging percentage (.571). Led NL RBI 1917 (100). Hit 20 or more doubles eight seasons and had 10 or more triples six times. World Series: 1907, 10, 17 (.163).

Considered goat of 1917 World Series for chasing Eddie Collins across plate after two-base error moved Collins to third. Led to three-run inning climaxed by Collins winning foot race across unguarded home plate. Later dropped by Giants after being accused in alleged fixing of games during pennant race with Cincinnati in 1919. Became steamfitter after baseball career.